Neural Fuzzy Systems

A Neuro-Fuzzy Synergism to Intelligent Systems

Chin-Teng Lin

Department of Control Engineering
National Chiao-Tung University
Hsinchu, Taiwan

C. S. George Lee

School of Electrical and Computer Engineering
Purdue University
West Lafayette, Indiana

For book and bookstore information

http://www.prenhall.com

Prentice Hall P T R, Upper Saddle River, NJ 07458

Library of Congress Cataloging-in-Publication Data

Lin, C. T. (Chin Teng).
  Neural fuzzy systems : a neuro-fuzzy synergism to intelligent
systems / Chin-Teng Lin, C. S. George Lee.
      p.   cm.
  Includes bibliographical references and index.
  ISBN 0-13-235169-2
  1. Intelligent control systems.   2. Fuzzy systems.   3. Neural
networks (Computer science)   I. Lee, C. S. G. (C. S. George)
II. Title.
TJ217.25.L57   1995
629.8′9—dc20
                                              96-170
                                              CIP

Editorial/production supervision: *bookworks / Karen Fortgang*
Cover design director: *Jerry Votta*
Cover design: *Armine Altiparmakian*
Manufacturing manager: *Alexis R. Heydt*
Acquisitions editor: *Bernard Goodwin*

© 1996 by Prentice Hall P T R
Prentice-Hall, Inc.
A Simon & Schuster Company
Upper Saddle River, NJ 07458

MATLAB is a registered trademark of the Math Works, Inc.

The publisher offers discounts on this book when ordered in bulk quantities.
For more information, contact

  Corporate Sales Department
  Prentice Hall P T R
  One Lake Street
  Upper Saddle River, New Jersey 07458

  Phone: 800-383-3419
  FAX: 201-236-7141
  E-mail: corpsales@prenhall.com

Printed in the United States of America

10 9 8 7 6 5 4 3 2

ISBN 0-13-235169-2

Prentice-Hall International (UK) Limited, *London*
Prentice-Hall of Australia Pty. Limited, *Sydney*
Prentice-Hall Canada Inc., *Toronto*
Prentice-Hall Hispanoamericana S.A., *Mexico*
Prentice-Hall of India Private Limited, *New Delhi*
Prentice-Hall of Japan, Inc., *Tokyo*
Simon & Schuster Asia Pte. Ltd., *Singapore*
Editora Prentice-Hall do Brasil, Ltda., *Rio de Janeiro*

This book is dedicated to the Chiao-Tung University Centennial
(1896–1996)

Contents

Contents   **vii**

Contents

PART III   FUZZY NEURAL INTEGRATED SYSTEMS

17   INTEGRATING FUZZY SYSTEMS AND NEURAL NETWORKS 478

18   NEURAL NETWORK–BASED FUZZY SYSTEMS 496

19   NEURAL FUZZY CONTROLLERS 533

Contents   **xi**

Preface

Fuzzy systems and neural networks have attracted the growing interest of researchers, scientists, engineers, practitioners, and students in various scientific and engineering areas. Fuzzy sets and fuzzy logic are based on the way the brain deals with inexact information, while neural networks (or artificial neural networks) are modeled after the physical architecture of the brain. Although the fundamental inspirations for these two fields are quite different, there are a number of parallels that point out their similarities. The intriguing differences and similarities between these two fields have prompted the writing of this book to examine the basic concepts of fuzzy set theory, fuzzy logic, fuzzy logic control systems, and neural networks; to explore their applications separately and in combination; and to explore the synergism of integrating these two techniques for the realization of intelligent systems for various applications.

Since the publication of Lotfi Zadeh's seminal work, "Fuzzy Sets," in 1965, the number and variety of applications of fuzzy logic have been growing. The performance of fuzzy logic control and decision systems critically depends on the input and output membership functions, the fuzzy logic control rules, and the fuzzy inference mechanism. Although a great amount of literature has been published dealing with the applications and the theoretical issues of fuzzy logic control and decision systems, a unified and systematic design methodology has yet to be developed. The use of neural networks to automate and synthesize the design of a general fuzzy logic control or decision system presents a novel and innovative approach and a viable design solution to this difficult design and realization problem.

The publication of J. J. Hopfield's seminal work on a single-layer feedback neural network with symmetric weights in 1982 revived neural network research activity from its doldrums in the 1960s and 1970s because of the ability of neural networks to classify, store, recall, and associate information or patterns. The performance of neural networks depends on the computational function of the neurons in the network, the structure and topology of the network, and the learning rule or the update rule of the connecting weights. Publication of the article "Learning Representations by Backpropagation Errors," by Rumelhart, Hinton, and Williams in 1986 has further extended and improved the learning ability of neural networks. This concept of trainable neural networks further strengthens the idea of utilizing the learning ability of neural networks to learn the fuzzy control rules, the membership functions, and other parameters of a fuzzy logic control or decision system.

Fuzzy sets and fuzzy logic were developed as a means for representing, manipulating, and utilizing uncertain information and to provide a framework for handling uncertainties and imprecision in real-world applications, while neural networks were developed to provide computational power, fault tolerance, and learning capability to the systems. This happy marriage of techniques from fuzzy logic systems and neural networks reaps the benefits of both neural networks and fuzzy logic systems. That is, the neural networks provide the connectionist structure (fault tolerance and distributed representation properties) and learning abilities to the fuzzy logic systems, and the fuzzy logic systems provide a structural framework with high-level fuzzy IF-THEN rule thinking and reasoning to the neural networks. It is this synergistic integration of neural networks and fuzzy logic systems into functional systems with low-level learning capability and high-level thinking and reasoning that separates our book from other books on fuzzy set theory, neural networks, neural fuzzy systems, and fuzzy neural networks.

This textbook was written to provide engineers, scientists, researchers, and students involved in fuzzy systems, neural networks, and fuzzy neural integrated systems with a comprehensive, well-organized, and up-to-date account of basic principles underlying the design, analysis, and synthesis of fuzzy neural integrated systems.

This book is the outgrowth of lecture notes for courses taught by the authors at Purdue University and the National Chiao-Tung University. The material has been tested extensively in the classroom as well as through numerous tutorial short courses and several intensive summer courses taught by both authors for the past several years. The suggestions and criticisms of students in these courses have had a significant influence on the way the material is presented in this book.

The mathematical level in all chapters is well within the grasp of first-year graduate students in a technical discipline such as engineering, computer science, or technology requiring introductory preparation in classical set theory, discrete mathematics, matrix computations, probability, and computer programming. In presenting the material, emphasis is placed on the utilization of developed results from basic concepts. In addition to the MATLAB$^{®}$ examples in the appendices, numerous examples are worked out in the text to illustrate the discussion, and exercises of various types and complexity are included at the end of each chapter. Some of these problems allow the reader to gain further insight into the points discussed in the text through practice in problem solution. Others serve as supplements and extensions of the material in the book. A complete solutions manual is also available to the instructor from the publisher.

This textbook consists of three major parts and two appendices:

Part I (Chapters 2 to 8) covers fundamental concepts and operations of fuzzy sets, fuzzy relations, fuzzy measures, possibility theory, fuzzy logic and approximate reasoning, and their application to fuzzy logic control systems and other systems such as pattern recognition systems and fuzzy expert systems.

Part II (Chapters 9 to 16) covers important concepts and topics in neural networks, including single-layer and multilayer feedforward networks, recurrent networks, and unsupervised learning, supervised learning, and reinforcement learning for training neural networks. Genetic algorithms and their use for the structure and parameter learning of neural networks are also explored.

Part III (Chapters 17 to 21) covers three major integrated systems and their rationale for integration. Neural fuzzy (control) systems, fuzzy neural networks (for pattern recognition), and fuzzy neural hybrid systems are discussed and explored.

Finally, Appendices A and B illustrate the computer simulations of fuzzy logic systems and neural networks using the MATLAB Fuzzy Logic Toolbox and the Neural Network Toolbox. These toolboxes are useful for student projects and independent studies.

The authors have used the materials from this book to teach three different graduate courses (15-week semester courses):

- Fuzzy Control Systems: Chapters 1–8 and Appendix A
- Introduction to Neural Networks: Chapter 1, Chapters 9–16, and Appendix B
- Neuro-Fuzzy Control Systems: Chapters 1 and 2, Sections 3.1, 3.2, 3.4, and 6.1–6.3, Chapter 7, Chapters 9–10, Sections 12.1–12.4 and 12.6, Chapter 17, and Sections 19.1–19.3, and 19.5–19.6

Other combinations of the material in this book for teaching are also possible. For instance, for a neural network graduate course with an emphasis on (fuzzy) pattern recognition, Chapters 2–3 and 9–13 plus selected sections in Chapters 20 and 21 can be covered in one semester; Chapters 17–21 can be taught in a second-year graduate course on neural fuzzy systems with a prerequisite of courses in fuzzy logic and neural networks.

ACKNOWLEDGMENTS

We are indebted to a number of individuals who, directly or indirectly, assisted in the preparation of the text. In particular, we wish to extend our appreciation to Professors L. A. Zadeh, G. N. Saridis, T. T. Lee, J. Yen, W. H. Tsai, C. C. Teng, M. J. Syu, W. P. Yang, C. C. Jou, M. J. Chung, C. L. Chen, S. F. Su, and Dr. Harold Su. As is true with most projects carried out in a university environment, our students over the past few years have influenced not only our thinking but also the topics covered in this book. The following individuals have worked with us in the course of their graduate programs: C. J. Lin, C. F. Juang, I. F. Chung, Y. C. Lu, Dr. W. Hsu, Dr. S. Park, G. H. Kim, T. K. Yin, Y. J. Wang, L. K. Sheu, M. C. Kan, W. F. Lin, S. C. Hsiao, W. C. Lin, C. P. Lee, and C. Y. Hu. Thanks is also due to I. F. Chung, Linda Stovall, Kitty Cooper, C. F. Juang, W. F. Lin, S. C. Hsiao, and Dee Dee Dexter for typing numerous versions of the manuscript.

We would also like to express our appreciation to Purdue University's National Science Foundation Engineering Research Center for Intelligent Manufacturing Systems, the

National Science Council of Taiwan, R.O.C., the Ford Foundation, and the Spring Foundation of National Chiao-Tung University for their sponsorship of our research activities in neuro-fuzzy systems, robotic assembly and manufacturing, and related areas. Finally, we thank Bernard M. Goodwin, editor and publisher at Prentice Hall, for his strong support throughout this project, Karen Fortgang; production editor at bookworks; for her skillful coordination of the production of the book, and Cristina Palumbo of the MathWorks, Inc. for her continued support of our use of MATLAB and the Fuzzy Logic Toolbox and the Neural Network Toolbox.

Last but not the least, we would like to thank our parents, M. T. Lin and Y. L. Kuo, and M. K. Lee and K. H. Tin, for their constant encouragement. Without their constant encouragement, this book would not have been possible. C. T. Lin would also like to thank his brother C. I. Lin for providing an excellent environment for him to finish the manuscript; C. S. G. Lee would like to thank his wife, Pei-Ling, and his children, Lawrence, Steven, and Anthony, for understanding why their daddy could not spend more time with them at their ballgames.

C. T. Lin
Hsinchu, Taiwan
C. S. G. Lee
West Lafayette, Indiana

1

Introduction

1.1 MOTIVATION

Fuzzy systems (FSs) and neural networks (NNs) have attracted the growing interest of researchers in various scientific and engineering areas. The number and variety of applications of fuzzy logic and neural networks have been increasing, ranging from consumer products and industrial process control to medical instrumentation, information systems, and decision analysis.

Fuzzy logic (FL) is based on the way the brain deals with inexact information, while neural networks are modeled after the physical architecture of the brain. Although the fundamental inspirations for these two fields are quite different, there are a number of parallels that point out their similarities. Fuzzy systems and neural networks are both numerical model–free estimators and dynamical systems. They share the common ability to improve the intelligence of systems working in an uncertain, imprecise, and noisy environment. To a certain extent, both systems and their techniques have been successfully applied to a variety of control systems and devices to improve their intelligence. Both fuzzy systems and neural networks have been shown to have the capability of modeling complex nonlinear processes to arbitrary degrees of accuracy.

Although fuzzy systems and neural networks are formally similar, there are also significant differences between them. Fuzzy systems are *structured numerical estimators*. They start from highly formalized insights about the structure of categories found in the real world and then articulate fuzzy IF-THEN rules as a kind of expert knowledge. Fuzzy systems combine fuzzy sets with fuzzy rules to produce overall complex nonlinear behavior. Neural networks, on the other hand, are *trainable dynamical systems* whose learning, noise-tolerance, and generalization abilities grow out of their connectionist structures, their dynamics, and their distributed data representation. Neural networks have a large number of highly interconnected processing elements (nodes) which demonstrate the ability to learn and generalize from training patterns or data; these simple processing elements also collectively produce complex nonlinear behavior.

In light of their similarities and differences, fuzzy systems and neural networks are suitable for solving many of the same problems and achieving some degree of machine intelligence. Their differences have prompted a recent surge of interest in merging or combining them into a functional system to overcome their individual weaknesses. This innovative idea of integration reaps the benefits of both fuzzy systems and neural networks. That is, neural networks provide fuzzy systems with learning abilities, and fuzzy systems provide neural networks with a structural framework with high-level fuzzy IF-THEN rule thinking and reasoning. Consequently, the two technologies can complement each other, with neural networks supplying the brute force necessary to accommodate and interpret large amounts of sensory data, and fuzzy logic providing a structural framework that utilizes and exploits these low-level results. The incorporation of fuzzy logic and neural network techniques has been used in the conception and design of complex systems in which analytical and expert system techniques are used in combination. Moreover, the synergism of fuzzy logic and neural network techniques has been employed in a wide variety of consumer products, endowing these products with the capability to adapt and learn from experience. Most neuro-fuzzy products are fuzzy rule–based systems in which neural network techniques are used for learning and/or adaptation.

Viewed from a much broader perspective, fuzzy logic and neural networks are constituents of an emerging research area, called *soft computing,* a term coined by Lotfi Zadeh (the father of fuzzy logic). It is believed that the most important factor that underlies the marked increase in machine intelligence nowadays is the use of soft computing to mimic the ability of the human mind to effectively employ modes of reasoning that are approximate rather than exact. Unlike traditional hard computing whose prime desiderata are precision, certainty, and rigor, soft computing is tolerant of imprecision, uncertainty, and partial truth. The primary aim of soft computing is to exploit such tolerance to achieve tractability, robustness, a high level of machine intelligence, and a low cost in practical applications. In addition to fuzzy logic and neural networks, another principal constituent of soft computing is probabilistic reasoning, which subsumes genetic algorithms, evolutionary programming, belief networks, chaotic systems, and parts of learning theory. Among these, genetic algorithms and evolutionary programming are similar to neural networks in that they are based on low-level microscopic biological models. They evolve toward finding better solutions to problems, just as species evolve toward better adaptation to their environments. Coincidentally, fuzzy logic, neural networks, genetic algorithms, and evolutionary programming are also considered the building blocks of *computational intelligence* as conceived by James Bezdek. Computational intelligence is low-level cognition in the style of the human mind and is in contrast to conventional (symbolic) artificial intelligence. In the partnership of fuzzy logic, neural networks, and probabilistic reasoning, fuzzy logic is concerned in the main with imprecision and approximate reasoning, neural networks with learning, and probabilistic reasoning with uncertainty. Since fuzzy logic, neural networks, and probabilistic reasoning are complementary rather than competitive, it is frequently advantageous to employ them in combination rather than exclusively. Various important topics, both in theories and applications, of fuzzy systems and neural networks (with genetic algorithms) and their synergism are covered in this book.

1.2 FUZZY SYSTEMS

In the past decade, fuzzy systems have supplanted conventional technologies in many scientific applications and engineering systems, especially in control systems and pattern recognition. We have also witnessed a rapid growth in the use of fuzzy logic in a wide variety of consumer products and industrial systems. Prominent examples include washing machines, camcorders, autofocus cameras, air conditioners, palmtop computers, vacuum cleaners, automobile transmissions, ship navigators, subway trains, combustion control regulators, and cement kilns. The same fuzzy technology, in the form of approximate reasoning, is also resurfacing in information technology, where it provides decision-support and expert systems with powerful reasoning capabilities bound by a minimum of rules. It is this wealth of deployed, successful applications of fuzzy technology that is, in the main, responsible for current interest in fuzzy systems.

Fuzzy sets, introduced by Zadeh in 1965 as a mathematical way to represent vagueness in linguistics, can be considered a generalization of classical set theory. The basic idea of fuzzy sets is quite easy to grasp. In a classical (nonfuzzy) set, an element of the universe either belongs to or does not belong to the set. That is, the membership of an element is crisp—it is either yes (in the set) or no (not in the set). A fuzzy set is a generalization of an ordinary set in that it allows the degree of membership for each element to range over the unit interval $[0, 1]$. Thus, the *membership function* of a fuzzy set maps each element of the universe of discourse to its range space which, in most cases, is set to the unit interval. One of the biggest differences between crisp and fuzzy sets is that the former always have unique membership functions, whereas every fuzzy set has an infinite number of membership functions that may represent it. This enables fuzzy systems to be adjusted for maximum utility in a given situation. In a broad sense, as pointed out by Lotfi Zadeh, any field can be fuzzified and hence generalized by replacing the concept of a crisp set in the target field by the concept of a fuzzy set. For example, we can fuzzify some basic fields such as arithmetic, graph theory, and probability theory to develop fuzzy arithmetic, fuzzy graph theory, and fuzzy probability theory, respectively; we can also fuzzify some applied fields such as neural networks, genetic algorithms, stability theory, pattern recognition, and mathematical programming to obtain fuzzy neural networks, fuzzy genetic algorithms, fuzzy stability theory, fuzzy pattern recognition, and fuzzy mathematical programming, respectively. The benefits of such fuzzification include greater generality, higher expressive power, an enhanced ability to model real-world problems, and a methodology for exploiting the tolerance for imprecision. Hence, fuzzy logic can help to achieve tractability, robustness, and lower solution cost.

Fuzziness is often confused with probability. The fundamental difference between them is that fuzziness deals with deterministic plausibility, while probability concerns the likelihood of nondeterministic, stochastic events. Fuzziness is one aspect of uncertainty. It is the ambiguity (vagueness) found in the definition of a concept or the meaning of a term such as "young person" or "large room." However, the uncertainty of probability generally relates to the occurrence of phenomena, as symbolized by the concept of randomness. In other words, a statement is probabilistic if it expresses some kind of likelihood or degree of certainty or if it is the outcome of clearly defined but randomly occurring events. For example, the statements "There is a 50-50 chance that he will be there," "It will rain tomorrow," "Roll the dice and get a four" have the uncertainty of randomness. Hence, fuzziness and randomness differ in nature; that is, they are different aspects of uncertainty. The former conveys "subjective" human thinking, feelings, or language, and the latter indicates an "objective" statistic in the natural sciences. From the modeling point of view, fuzzy models and statistical models also possess philosophically different kinds of information: fuzzy memberships represent similarities of objects to imprecisely defined properties, while probabilities convey information about relative frequencies.

One major feature of fuzzy logic is its ability to express the amount of ambiguity in human thinking and subjectivity (including natural language) in a comparatively undistorted manner. Thus, when is it appropriate to use fuzzy logic? When the process is concerned with continuous phenomena (e.g., one or more of the control variables are continuous) that are not easily broken down into discrete segments; when a mathematical model of the process does not exist, or exists but is too difficult to encode, or is too complex to be evaluated fast enough for real-time operation, or involves too much memory on the designated chip architecture; when high ambient noise levels must be dealt with or it is important to use inexpensive sensors and/or low-precision microcontrollers; when the process involves human interaction (e.g., human descriptive or intuitive thinking); and when an expert is available who can specify the rules underlying the system behavior and the fuzzy sets that represent the characteristics of each variable.

With these properties, fuzzy logic techniques find their applications in such areas as [Munakata and Jani, 1994] (1) control (the most widely applied area), (2) pattern recognition (e.g., image, audio, signal processing), (3) quantitative analysis (e.g., operations research, management), (4) inference (e.g., expert systems for diagnosis, planning, and prediction; natural language processing; intelligent interface; intelligent robots; software engineering), and (5) information retrieval (e.g., databases).

1.3 NEURAL NETWORKS

Fundamentally, there are two major different approaches in the field of artificial intelligence (AI) for realizing human intelligence in machines [Munakata, 1994]. One is symbolic AI, which is characterized by a high level of abstraction and a macroscopic view. Classical psychology operates at a similar level, and knowledge engineering systems and logic programming fall in this category. The second approach is based on low-level microscopic biological models. It is similar to the emphasis of physiology or genetics. Artificial neural networks and genetic algorithms are the prime examples of this latter approach. They originated from modeling of the brain and evolution. However, these biological models do not necessarily resemble their original biological counterparts. Neural networks are a new generation of information processing systems that are deliberately constructed to make use of some of the organizational principles that characterize the human brain. The main theme of neural network research focuses on modeling of the brain as a parallel computational device for various computational tasks that were performed poorly by traditional serial computers. Neural networks have a large number of highly interconnected *processing elements* (*nodes*) that usually operate in parallel and are configured in regular architectures. The *collective* behavior of an NN, like a human brain, demonstrates the ability to learn, recall, and generalize from training patterns or data. Since the first application of NNs to consumer products appeared at the end of 1990, scores of industrial and commercial applications have come into use. Like fuzzy systems, the applications where neural networks have the most promise are also those with a real-world flavor, such as speech recognition, speech-to-text conversion, image processing and visual perception, medical applications, loan applications and counterfeit checks, and investing and trading.

Models of neural networks are specified by three basic entities: models of the processing element themselves, models of interconnections and structures (network topology), and the learning rules (the ways information is stored in the network).

Each node in a neural network collects the values from all its input connections, performs a predefined mathematical operation, and produces a single output value. The information processing of a node can be viewed as consisting of two parts: input and output. Associated with the input of a node is an integration function (typically a dot product) which serves to combine information or activation from an external source or other nodes into a *net input* to the node. A second action of each node is to output an activation value as a function of its net input through an *activation function* which is usually nonlinear. Each connection has an associated weight that determines the effect of the incoming input on the activation level of the node. The weights may be positive (excitatory) or negative (inhibitory). The connection weights store the information, and the value of the connection weights is often determined by a neural network learning procedure. It is through adjustment of the connection weights that the neural network is able to learn.

In a neural network, each node output is connected, through weights, to other nodes or to itself. Hence, the structure that organizes these nodes and the connection geometry among them should be specified for a neural network. We can first take a node and combine it with other nodes to make a *layer* of nodes. Inputs can be connected to many nodes with various weights, resulting in a series of outputs, one per node. This results in a *single-layer feedforward network*. We can further interconnect several layers to form a *multilayer feedforward network*. The layer that receives inputs is called the *input layer* and typically performs no computation other than buffering of the input signal. The outputs of the network are generated from the *output layer*. Any layer between the input and the output layers is called a *hidden layer* because it is internal to the network and has no direct contact with the external environment. There may be from zero to several hidden layers in a neural network. The two types of networks mentioned above are *feedforward networks* since no node output is an input to a node in the same layer or preceding layer. When outputs are directed back as inputs to same- or preceding-layer nodes, the network is a *feedback network*. Feedback networks that have closed loops are called *recurrent networks*.

The third important element in specifying a neural network is the learning scheme. Broadly speaking, there are two kinds of learning in neural networks: *parameter learning*, which concerns the updating of the connection weights in a neural network, and *structure learning*, which focuses on the change in the network structure, including the number of nodes and their connection types. These two kinds of learning can be performed simultaneously or separately. Each kind of learning can be further classified into three categories: *supervised learning, reinforcement learning,* and *unsupervised learning.* These three categories of learning will be covered in detail in Part II of this book.

Among the existing neural network models, two of the important ones that started the modern era of neural networks are the *Hopfield network* and the *back-propagation network*. The Hopfield network is a single-layer feedback network with symmetric weights proposed by John Hopfield in 1982. The network has a point attractor dynamics, making its behavior relatively simple to understand and analyze. This result provides the mathematical foundation for understanding the dynamics of an important class of networks. The back-propagation network is a multilayer feedforward network combined with a gradient-descent-type learning algorithm called the *back-propagation learning rule* by Rumelhart, Hinton, and Williams [1986b]. In this learning scheme, the error at the output layer is propagated backward to adjust the connection weights of preceding layers and to minimize output errors. The back-propagation learning rule is an extension of the work of Rosenblatt, Widrow, and Hoff to deal with learning in complex multilayer networks and thereby provide an answer to one of the most severe criticisms of the neural network field. With this learning algorithm, multilayer networks can be reliably trained. The back-propagation network has had a major impact on the field of neural networks and is the primary method employed in most of the applications.

Another important tool for the structure and parameter learning of neural networks is *genetic algorithms* (GAs). Genetic algorithms are search algorithms based on the mechanics of natural selection and natural genetics. The mathematical framework of GAs was developed in the 1960s and is presented in Holland's pioneering book [Holland, 1975]. Genetic algorithms have been used primarily in optimization and machine learning problems. A simple GA processes a finite population of fixed-length binary strings called *genes*. Genetic algorithms have three basic operators: *reproduction* of solutions based on their fitness, *crossover* of genes, and *mutation* for random change of genes. Another operator associated with each of these three operators is the *selection* operator, which produces survival of the fittest in the GA. Reproduction directs the search toward the best existing strings but does not create any new strings, the crossover operator explores different structures by exchanging genes between two strings at a crossover position, and mutation introduces diversity into the population by altering a bit position of the selected string. The mutation operation is used to escape the local minima in the search space. The combined action of reproduction and crossover is responsible for much of the effectiveness of a GA's search, while reproduction and mutation combine to form a parallel, noise-tolerant hill-climbing algorithm. The structure and parameter learning problems of neural networks are coded as genes (or chromosomes), and GAs are used to search for better solutions (optimal structure and parameters) for NNs. Furthermore, GAs can be used to find the membership functions and fuzzy rules of a fuzzy logic system.

Neural networks offer the following salient characteristics and properties:

1. Nonlinear input-output mapping: Neural networks are able to learn arbitrary nonlinear input-output mapping directly from training data.

2. Generalization: Neural networks can sensibly interpolate input patterns that are new to the network. From a statistical point of view, neural networks can fit the desired function in such a way that they have the ability to generalize to situations that are different from the collected training data.

3. Adaptivity: Neural networks can automatically adjust their connection weights, or even network structures (number of nodes or connection types), to optimize their behavior as controllers, predictors, pattern recognizers, decision makers, and so on.

4. Fault tolerance: The performance of a neural network is degraded gracefully under faulty conditions such as damaged nodes or connections. The inherent fault-tolerance capability of neural networks stems from the fact that the large number of connections provides much redundancy, each node acts independently of all the others, and each node relies only on local information.

With these properties, when is it appropriate to use neural networks? When nonlinear mappings must be automatically acquired (e.g., robot control and noise removal); when only a few decisions are required from a massive amount of data (e.g., speech recognition and fault prediction); when a near-optimal solution to a combinatorial optimization problem is required in a short time (e.g., airline scheduling and network routing); and when there are more input variables than can be feasibly utilized by other approaches [Simpson, 1992a]. Moreover, despite the possibility of equally comparable solutions to a given problem, several additional aspects of a neural network solution are appealing, including (VLSI) parallel implementations that allow fast processing; less hardware which allows faster response time, lower cost, and quicker design cycles; and on-line adaptation that allows the networks to change constantly according to the needs of the environment.

1.4 FUZZY NEURAL INTEGRATED SYSTEMS

Fuzzy logic and neural networks (with genetic algorithms) are complementary technologies in the design of intelligent systems. Each method has merits and demerits. A comparison of these techniques with symbolic AI and conventional control theory is presented in Table 1.1 [Fukuda and Shibata, 1994]. To combine their merits and overcome their demerits, some integration and synthesis techniques have been proposed. In this book, we shall mainly discuss the synergism of fusing fuzzy logic techniques and neural networks techniques into an integrated system.

Neural networks are essentially low-level computational structures and algorithms that offer good performance in dealing with sensory data, while fuzzy logic techniques often deal with issues such as reasoning on a higher level than neural networks. However, since fuzzy systems do not have much learning capability, it is difficult for a human opera-

TABLE 1.1 Comparisons of Fuzzy Systems (FS), Neural Networks (NN), Genetic Algorithms (GA), Conventional Control Theory, and Symbolic AI*

	FS	NN	GA	Control Theory	Symbolic AI
Mathematical model	SG	B	B	G	SB
Learning ability	B	G	SG	B	B
Knowledge representation	G	B	SB	SB	G
Expert knowledge	G	B	B	SB	G
Nonlinearity	G	G	G	B	SB
Optimization ability	B	SG	G	SB	B
Fault tolerance	G	G	G	B	B
Uncertainty tolerance	G	G	G	B	B
Real-time operation	G	SG	SB	G	B

*The fuzzy terms used for grading are good (G), slightly good (SG), slightly bad (SB), and bad (B).

tor to tune the fuzzy rules and membership functions from the training data set. Also, because the internal layers of neural networks are always opaque to the user, the mapping rules in the network are not visible and are difficult to understand; furthermore, the convergence of learning is usually very slow and not guaranteed. Thus, a promising approach for reaping the benefits of both fuzzy systems and neural networks (and solving their respective problems) is to merge or fuse them into an integrated system. This fusion of two different technologies can be realized in three directions, resulting in systems with different characteristics:

1. *Neural fuzzy systems:* use of neural networks as tools in fuzzy models
2. *Fuzzy neural networks:* fuzzification of conventional neural network models
3. *Fuzzy-neural hybrid systems:* incorporation of fuzzy logic technology and neural networks into hybrid systems.

The first two systems represent *supportive* combinations, where one technology assists the other, and the third system exhibits *collaborative* combination, where two technologies are incorporated intimately to perform a common task.

Neural fuzzy systems, or *neuro-fuzzy systems,* aim at providing fuzzy systems with automatic tuning abilities. With this approach, we witness the use of neural networks in learning or tuning membership functions and fuzzy rules of fuzzy systems. Neural network learning techniques can thus substantially reduce development time and cost while improving the performance of fuzzy systems. After learning, the user can understand the acquired rules in the network. With respect to learning speed, neural fuzzy systems are usually faster than conventional neural networks.

Fuzzy neural networks retain the basic properties and functions of neural networks with some of their elements being fuzzified. In this approach, a network's domain knowledge becomes formalized in terms of fuzzy sets, later being applied to enhance the learning of the network and augment its interpretation capabilities. For instance, a neural network can be fuzzified in such a way that it learns the mapping between input-output fuzzy sets. Furthermore, fuzzy logic can be used to determine the learning step of neural networks according to the state of convergence. By incorporating fuzzy principles into a neural network, more user flexibility is attained and the resultant network or system becomes more robust.

In a fuzzy-neural hybrid system, both fuzzy logic techniques and neural networks are utilized separately to establish two decoupled subsystems which perform their own tasks in serving different functions in the combined system. The architecture of fuzzy-neural hybrid systems is usually application-oriented. Making use of their individual strengths, fuzzy logic and neural network subsystems complement each other efficiently and effectively to achieve a common goal.

1.5 ORGANIZATION OF THE BOOK

This book covers basic concepts and applications of fuzzy sets, fuzzy logic, and neural networks and their integration synergism. Thus, it is logically divided into three major parts.

Part I (Chaps. 2–8) covers fuzzy set theory and its applications. In these seven chapters, we cover fundamental concepts and operations of fuzzy sets, fuzzy relations, fuzzy measures, possibility theory, fuzzy logic and approximate reasoning, and their application to fuzzy logic control systems and other systems such as pattern recognition systems and fuzzy expert systems.

Part II (Chaps. 9–16) covers important concepts and topics involving neural networks. Single-layer and multilayer feedforward networks as well as recurrent networks are covered. Unsupervised learning, supervised learning, and reinforcement learning for training neural networks are also discussed. Genetic algorithms along with their applications (Chap. 14) are briefly introduced, and the use of GAs and other techniques for the structure learning of neural networks are explored in Chap. 15. Various applications of neural networks are then discussed in Chap. 16.

Part III (Chaps. 17–21) covers the basic concepts of integrating fuzzy logic and neural networks into a working functional system. Three major integrated systems are discussed and explored: neural fuzzy (control) systems in Chaps. 18 and 19, fuzzy neural networks (for pattern recognition) in Chaps. 20 and 21, and neural fuzzy hybrid systems in Chap. 21. The rationale for their integration is discussed, and methods for realizing their integration are also explored with examples. Various applications of such integration are also considered.

Finally, Apps. A and B are included to illustrate computer simulations of fuzzy logic systems and neural networks using MATLAB neural network and fuzzy logic toolboxes. Some typical and interesting examples are worked out to illustrate the characteristics of these toolboxes which will be useful for student projects and independent study.

1.6 REFERENCES

A complete bibliography consisting of more than 1100 references is included at the end of the book for the reader to further pursue the subject area of interest to him or her. The bibliography is organized in alphabetical order by author and contains all the pertinent information for each reference cited in the text. In addition, the concluding remarks at the end of each chapter discuss references that are keyed to specific topics discussed in the chapter.

In addition to those, the general references cited below are representative of publications dealing with topics of interest regarding fuzzy neural (integrated) systems (including fuzzy systems, neural networks, genetic algorithms, and their synergism) and related fields. They include major journals and conference proceedings.

IEEE Transactions on Fuzzy Systems; Fuzzy Sets and Systems; IEEE Transactions on Neural Networks; International Neural Network Society Journal, Neural Networks; Evolutionary Computation; IEEE Transactions on Systems, Man, and Cybernetics; International Journal of Approximate Reasoning; Adaptive Behavior; Evolutionary Computation; Complex Systems; Proceedings of IEEE International Conference on Fuzzy Systems; Proceedings of IEEE International Conference on Neural Networks; Proceedings of IEEE Conference on Evolutionary Computation; Proceedings of International Conference on Genetic Algorithms; Proceedings of International Fuzzy Systems Association (IFSA) World Congress; Proceedings of International Conference on Fuzzy Logic, Neural Nets, and Soft Computing; Proceedings of the North American Fuzzy Information Processing Society (NAFIPS) Biannual Conference; Proceedings of the NASA Joint Technology Workshop on Neural Networks and Fuzzy Logic; Proceedings of the Conference of Parallel Problem Solving from Nature; Proceedings of the Workshop on the Foundations of Genetic Algorithms.

2

Basics of Fuzzy Sets

In this chapter, we introduce the principal concepts and mathematical notions of fuzzy set theory—a theory of classes of objects with unsharp boundaries. We first view fuzzy sets as a generalization of classical crisp sets by generalizing the range of the membership function (or characteristic function) from $\{0, 1\}$ to a real number in the unit interval $[0, 1]$. Various basic concepts of fuzzy sets such as representation, support, α-cuts, convexity, and fuzzy numbers are then introduced. The resolution principle, which can be used to expand a fuzzy set in terms of its α-cuts, is discussed and proved. Various set-theoretic operations and properties involving crisp sets and fuzzy sets are discussed; further fuzzy set operations such as t-norms, t-conorms, and other aggregation operations are also considered. Finally, the extension principle, which allows the generalization of crisp mathematical concepts to the fuzzy set framework, is presented with several examples. The material covered in this chapter will be used extensively in later chapters.

2.1 FUZZY SETS AND OPERATION ON FUZZY SETS

A classical *(crisp)* set is a collection of distinct objects. It is defined in such a way as to dichotomize the elements of a given universe of discourse into two groups: members and nonmembers. Finally, a crisp set can be defined by the so-called *characteristic function*. Let U be a universe of discourse. The *characteristic function* $\mu_A(x)$ of a crisp set A in U takes its values in $\{0, 1\}$ and is defined such that $\mu_A(x) = 1$ if x is a member of A (i.e., $x \in A$) and 0 otherwise. That is,

$$\mu_A(x) = \begin{cases} 1 & \text{if and only if } x \in A \\ 0 & \text{if and only if } x \notin A. \end{cases} \tag{2.1}$$

Note that (i) the boundary of set A is rigid and sharp and performs a two-class dicho-tomization (i.e., $x \in A$ or $x \notin A$), and (ii) the universe of discourse U is a crisp set.

A fuzzy set, on the other hand, introduces vagueness by eliminating the sharp boundary that divides members from nonmembers in the group. Thus, the transition between full membership and nonmembership is *gradual* rather than abrupt. Hence, fuzzy sets may be viewed as an extension and generalization of the basic concepts of crisp sets; however, some theories are unique to the fuzzy set framework.

A fuzzy set $\bar{A}$ in the universe of discourse U can be defined as a set of ordered pairs,

$$\bar{A} = \{(x, \mu_{\bar{A}}(x)) \mid x \in U\}, \tag{2.2}$$

where $\mu_{\bar{A}}(\cdot)$ is called the *membership function* (or characteristic function) of $\bar{A}$ and $\mu_{\bar{A}}(x)$ is the *grade* (or degree) of membership of x in $\bar{A}$, which indicates the degree that x belongs to $\bar{A}$. The membership function $\mu_{\bar{A}}(\cdot)$ maps U to the membership space M, that is, $\mu_{\bar{A}}: U \rightarrow M$. When $M = \{0, 1\}$, set A is nonfuzzy and $\mu_A(\cdot)$ is the characteristic function of the crisp set A. For fuzzy sets, the *range* of the membership function (i.e., M) is a subset of the nonnegative real numbers whose supremum is finite. In most general cases, M is set to the unit interval $[0, 1]$.

Example 2.1

Let U be the real line $\Re$ and let crisp set A represent "real numbers greater than or equal to 5"; then we have

$$A = \{(x, \mu_A(x)) \mid x \in U\},$$

where the characteristic function is

$$\mu_A(x) = \begin{cases} 0, & x < 5 \\ 1, & x \geq 5, \end{cases}$$

which is shown in Fig. 2.1(a). Now let fuzzy set[1] $\bar{A}$ represent "real numbers close to 5." Then we have

$$\bar{A} = \{(x, \mu_{\bar{A}}(x)) \mid x \in U\},$$

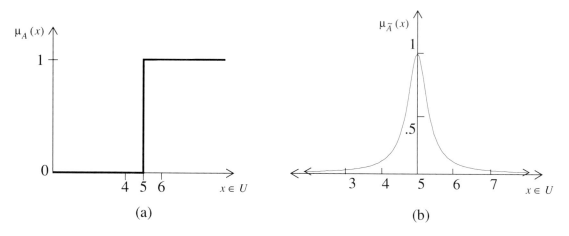

Figure 2.1 Characteristic functions of crisp set A and fuzzy set $\bar{A}$ in Example 2.1.

[1]If there is no confusion between a fuzzy set $\bar{A}$ and a crisp set A, the tilde above the fuzzy set A will be eliminated to simplify the notation.

where the membership function is

$$\mu_{\tilde{A}}(x) = \frac{1}{1 + 10(x-5)^2},$$

which is shown in Fig. 2.1(b).

The fuzzy set $\tilde{A}$ in the above example can also be represented as

$$\tilde{A} = \{ (x, \mu_{\tilde{A}}(x)) \mid \mu_{\tilde{A}}(x) = [1 + 10(x-5)^2]^{-1} \}. \tag{2.3}$$

It is noted that we can use another membership function for fuzzy set $\tilde{A}$ in Example 2.1; for example,

$$\mu_{\tilde{A}}(x) = \frac{1}{1 + (x-5)^2}. \tag{2.4}$$

These two different membership functions show that assignment of the membership function of a fuzzy set is *subjective* in nature; however, it cannot be assigned arbitrarily. A qualitative estimation reflecting a given ordering of the elements in $\tilde{A}$ may be sufficient. Furthermore, estimating membership functions is complicated, and a better approach is to utilize the learning power of neural networks to approximate them.

The above example shows that fuzziness is a type of imprecision that stems from a grouping of elements into classes that do not have sharply defined boundaries; it is not a lack of knowledge about the elements in the classes (e.g., a particular parametric value). It is worth pointing out that $\mu_A(x) \in [0, 1]$ indicates the membership grade of an element $x \in U$ in fuzzy set A and that it is not a probability because $\sum \mu_A(x) \neq 1$. The grades of membership basically reflect an ordering of the objects in fuzzy set A.

Another way of representing a fuzzy set is through use of the *support* of a fuzzy set. The support of a fuzzy set A is the *crisp* set of all $x \in U$ such that $\mu_A(x) > 0$. That is,

$$\text{Supp}(A) = \{ x \in U \mid \mu_A(x) > 0 \}. \tag{2.5}$$

Example 2.2

Assume that in an examination, all the possible scores are $U = \{ 10, 20, \ldots, 100 \}$. Consider three fuzzy sets, $A \equiv$ "High Score," $B \equiv$ "Medium Score," and $C \equiv$ "Low Score," whose membership functions are defined in Table 2.1.

TABLE 2.1 Fuzzy Sets in Example 2.2

Numerical Score	High Score (A)	Medium Score (B)	Low Score (C)
10	0	0	1
20	0	0	1
30	0	0.1	0.9
40	0	0.5	0.7
50	0.1	0.8	0.5
60	0.3	1	0.3
70	0.5	0.8	0.1
80	0.8	0.5	0
90	1	0	0
100	1	0	0

Then we have

Supp(A) = Supp ("High Score") = {50, 60, 70, 80, 90, 100},
Supp(B) = Supp ("Medium Score") = {30, 40, 50, 60, 70, 80},
Supp(C) = Supp ("Low Score") = {10, 20, 30, 40, 50, 60, 70}.

Instead, if $U = [0, 100]$ and $\mu_A(\cdot)$ is defined by the following continuous membership function,

$$\mu_A(x) = \mu_{\text{High\_Score}}(x) = \begin{cases} 0 & \text{for } 0 \le x \le 40 \\ \{1 + [(x-40)/5]^{-2}\}^{-1} & \text{for } 40 < x \le 120, \end{cases} \tag{2.6}$$

then Supp(A) = Supp(High_Score) = interval $(40, 120]$. Note that the summation of membership degrees of a fuzzy set $[\sum_{i=1}^{n} \mu_A(x_i)]$ is not necessarily equal to 1. An empty fuzzy set has empty support; that is, the membership function assigns 0 to all elements of the universal set U.

A fuzzy set A whose support is a single point in U with $\mu_A(x) = 1$ is referred to as a *fuzzy singleton*. Moreover, the element $x \in U$ at which $\mu_A(x) = 0.5$ is called the *crossover* point. The *kernel* of a fuzzy set A consists of the element x whose membership grade is 1; that is, ker $(A) = \{x \mid \mu_A(x) = 1\}$. The *height* of a fuzzy set A is the supremum of $\mu_A(x)$ over U. That is,

$$\text{Height of } A = \text{Height}(A) \equiv \sup_x \mu_A(x). \tag{2.7}$$

A fuzzy set is *normalized* when the height of the fuzzy set is unity [i.e., Height(A) = 1]; otherwise it is *subnormal*. The three fuzzy sets in Example 2.2 are all normalized. A nonempty fuzzy set A can always be normalized by dividing $\mu_A(x)$ by the height of A.

The representation of a fuzzy set can be expressed in terms of the support of the fuzzy set. For a discrete universe of discourse $U = \{x_1, x_2, \ldots, x_n\}$, a fuzzy set A can be represented using the ordered pairs concept and written as

$$A = \{(x_1, \mu_A(x_1)), (x_2, \mu_A(x_2)), \ldots, (x_n, \mu_A(x_n))\}. \tag{2.8}$$

For example, in Example 2.2,

B = "Medium Score" = {(10, 0), (20, 0), (30, 0.1), (40, 0.5), (50, 0.8), (60, 1), (70, 0.8), (80, 0.5), (90, 0), (100, 0)}.

Using the support of a fuzzy set A, we can simplify the representation of a fuzzy set A as

$$A = \mu_1/x_1 + \mu_2/x_2 + \cdots + \mu_i/x_i + \cdots + \mu_n/x_n = \sum_{i=1}^{n} \mu_i/x_i, \tag{2.9}$$

where + indicates the union of the elements and μ_i is the grade of membership of x_i, that is, $\mu_i = \mu_A(x_i) > 0$. For example, the above fuzzy set B can be represented as

$$B = 0.1/30 + 0.5/40 + 0.8/50 + 1/60 + 0.8/70 + 0.5/80.$$

Note that in using the support of a fuzzy set to represent a fuzzy set, we consider only those elements in the universe of discourse that have a nonzero degree of membership grade in the fuzzy set. If U is not discrete, but is an interval of real numbers, we can use the notation

$$A = \int_U \mu_A(x)/x, \tag{2.10}$$

where $\int$ indicates the union of the elements in A. For example, the fuzzy set A in Example 2.1 can be written as

$$A = \int_{\mathbb{R}} \frac{1}{1 + 10\,(x - 5)^2} \bigg/ x.$$

Another important notion and property of fuzzy sets is the resolution principle which requires us to understand α-cuts or α-level sets. An α-*cut* (or α-*level set*) of a fuzzy set A is a crisp set A_α that contains all the elements of the universal set U that have a membership grade in A greater than or equal to α. That is,

$$A_\alpha = \{x \in U \mid \mu_A(x) \geq \alpha\}, \qquad \alpha \in (0,\,1]. \tag{2.11}$$

If $A_\alpha = \{x \in U \mid \mu_A(x) > \alpha\}$, then A_α is called a *strong α-cut*. Furthermore, the set of all levels $\alpha \in (0,\,1]$ that represents distinct α-cuts of a given fuzzy set A is called a *level set* of A. That is,

$$\Lambda_A = \{\alpha \mid \mu_A(x) = \alpha, \qquad \text{for some } x \in U\}. \tag{2.12}$$

Example 2.3

Consider the test score example in Example 2.2 again (Table 2.1). We have

$$A_{0.5} = \text{High\_Score}_{0.5} = \{70, 80, 90, 100\},$$

$$B_{0.8} = \text{Medium\_Score}_{0.8} = \{50, 60, 70\},$$

$$C_{0.2} = \text{Low\_Score}_{0.2} = \{10, 20, 30, 40, 50, 60\},$$

and

$$\Lambda_A = \Lambda_{\text{High\_Score}} = \{0.1, 0.3, 0.5, 0.8, 1\},$$

$$\Lambda_C = \Lambda_{\text{Low\_Score}} = \{0.1, 0.3, 0.5, 0.7, 0.9, 1\}.$$

It is clear that if $\alpha \leq \beta$, then $A_\beta \subseteq A_\alpha$.

With this understanding of α-cuts, we shall introduce an important property of fuzzy set theory, called the *resolution principle*, which indicates that a fuzzy set A can be expanded in terms of its α-cuts.

Theorem 2.1

Let A be a fuzzy set in the universe of discourse U. Then the membership function of A can be expressed in terms of the characteristic functions of its α-cuts according to

$$\mu_A(x) = \sup_{\alpha \in (0,1]} [\alpha \wedge \mu_{A_\alpha}(x)] \qquad \forall x \in U, \tag{2.13}$$

where $\wedge$ denotes the min operation and $\mu_{A_\alpha}(x)$ is the characteristic function of the crisp set A_α,

$$\mu_{A_\alpha}(x) = \begin{cases} 1 & \text{if and only if } x \in A_\alpha \\ 0 & \text{otherwise.} \end{cases} \tag{2.14}$$

Proof: Let $\vee$ denote the max operation. Since $\mu_{A_\alpha}(x) = 1$ [i.e., $\mu_A(x) \geq \alpha$] if $x \in A_\alpha$, and $\mu_{A_\alpha}(x) = 0$ [i.e., $\mu_A(x) < \alpha$] if $x \notin A_\alpha$, we have

$$\sup_{\alpha \in (0,1]} [\alpha \wedge \mu_{A_\alpha}(x)] = \sup_{\alpha \in (0,\mu_A(x)]} [\alpha \wedge \mu_{A_\alpha}(x)] \vee \sup_{\alpha \in (\mu_A(x),1]} [\alpha \wedge \mu_{A_\alpha}(x)]$$

$$= \sup_{\alpha \in (0,\mu_A(x)]} [\alpha \wedge 1] \vee \sup_{\alpha \in (\mu_A(x),1]} [\alpha \wedge 0]$$

$$= \sup_{\alpha \in (0,\mu_A(x)]} \alpha$$

$$= \mu_A(x).$$

Theorem 2.1 leads to the following representation of a fuzzy set A using the resolution principle. Let A be a fuzzy set in the universe of discourse U. Let αA_α denote a fuzzy set with the membership function

$$\mu_{\alpha A_\alpha}(x) = [\alpha \wedge \mu_{A_\alpha}(x)] \qquad \forall x \in U. \tag{2.15}$$

Then the *resolution principle* states that the fuzzy set A can be expressed in the form

$$A = \bigcup_{\alpha \in \Lambda_A} \alpha A_\alpha \qquad \text{or} \qquad A = \int_0^1 \alpha A_\alpha. \tag{2.16}$$

The resolution principle indicates that a fuzzy set A can be decomposed into αA_α, $\alpha \in (0, 1]$. On the other hand, a fuzzy set A can be retrieved as a union of its αA_α, which is called the *representation theorem*. In other words, a fuzzy set can be expressed in terms of its α-cuts without resorting to the membership function. This concept is illustrated in Fig. 2.2.

Example 2.4

Consider the fuzzy set A in Example 2.2. That is,

$$A = 0.1/50 + 0.3/60 + 0.5/70 + 0.8/80 + 1/90 + 1/100.$$

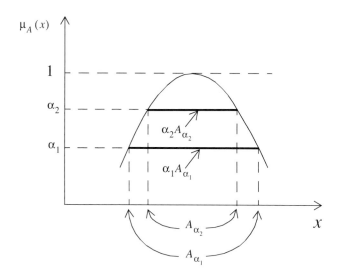

Figure 2.2 Decomposition of a fuzzy set.

Using the resolution principle, A can be written as

$$A = 0.1/50 + 0.3/60 + 0.5/70 + 0.8/80 + 1/90 + 1/100$$
$$= 0.1/50 + 0.1/60 + 0.1/70 + 0.1/80 + 0.1/90 + 0.1/100$$
$$+ 0.3/60 + 0.3/70 + 0.3/80 + 0.3/90 + 0.3/100$$
$$+ 0.5/70 + 0.5/80 + 0.5/90 + 0.5/100$$
$$+ 0.8/80 + 0.8/90 + 0.8/100$$
$$+ 1/90 + 1/100$$

or, in terms of αA_α,

$$A = 0.1/50 + 0.3/60 + 0.5/70 + 0.8/80 + 1/90 + 1/100$$
$$= 0.1(1/50 + 1/60 + 1/70 + 1/80 + 1/90 + 1/100)$$
$$+ 0.3\,(1/60 + 1/70 + 1/80 + 1/90 + 1/100)$$
$$+ 0.5\,(1/70 + 1/80 + 1/90 + 1/100)$$
$$+ 0.8\,(1/80 + 1/90 + 1/100)$$
$$+ 1\,(1/90 + 1/100)$$
$$= 0.1A_{0.1} + 0.3A_{0.3} + 0.5A_{0.5} + 0.8A_{0.8} + 1A_1$$
$$= \bigcup_{\alpha \in \Lambda_A} \alpha A_\alpha, \qquad \text{where } \Lambda_A = \{0.1, 0.3, 0.5, 0.8, 1\},$$

where

$$0.1A_{0.1} = 0.1\,(1/50 + 1/60 + 1/70 + 1/80 + 1/90 + 1/100)\,,$$

$$0.3A_{0.3} = 0.3\,(1/60 + 1/70 + 1/80 + 1/90 + 1/100)\,,$$

$$0.5A_{0.5} = 0.5\,(1/70 + 1/80 + 1/90 + 1/100)\,,$$

$$0.8A_{0.8} = 0.8\,(1/80 + 1/90 + 1/100)\,,$$

$$1A_1 = 1\,(1/90 + 1/100)\,.$$

On the other hand, if we are given $A_{0.1} = \{1, 2, 3, 4, 5\}$, $A_{0.4} = \{2, 3, 5\}$, $A_{0.8} = \{2, 3\}$, and $A_1 = \{3\}$, then using the representation theorem, A can be expressed as

$$A = \bigcup_{\alpha \in \Lambda_A} \alpha A_\alpha = \bigcup_{\alpha \in \{0.1, 0.4, 0.8, 1\}} \alpha A_\alpha$$

$$= 0.1A_{0.1} + 0.4A_{0.4} + 0.8A_{0.8} + 1A_1$$

$$= 0.1\,(1/1 + 1/2 + 1/3 + 1/4 + 1/5) + 0.4\,(1/2 + 1/3 + 1/5)$$

$$+ 0.8\,(1/2 + 1/3) + 1\,(1/3)$$

$$= 0.1/1 + 0.8/2 + 1/3 + 0.1/4 + 0.4/5.$$

Basics of Fuzzy Sets　　　Chap. 2

Convexity of fuzzy sets plays an important role in fuzzy set theory, and it can be defined in terms of α-cuts or membership functions. A fuzzy set is convex if and only if each of its α-cuts is a convex set. Or, equivalently, a fuzzy set A is convex if and only if

$$\mu_A(\lambda x_1 + (1 - \lambda)x_2) \geq \min(\mu_A(x_1), \mu_A(x_2)), \qquad (2.17)$$

where $x_1, x_2 \in U$, $\lambda \in [0, 1]$. Equation (2.17) can be interpreted as: Take two elements x_1 and x_2 in a fuzzy set A and draw a connecting straight line between them; then the membership grade of all the points on the line must be greater than or equal to the minimum of $\mu_A(x_1)$ and $\mu_A(x_2)$. For example, the fuzzy set A in Fig. 2.3(a) is convex, but it is not normalized. The fuzzy set B in Fig. 2.3(b) is not convex, but it is normalized. Note that the convexity definition does not imply that the membership function of a convex fuzzy set is a convex function [see Fig. 2.3(c)].

A convex, normalized fuzzy set defined on the real line $\Re$ whose membership function is piecewise continuous or, equivalently, each α-cut is a closed interval, is called a *fuzzy number*. Two typical fuzzy numbers are the *S function* and the *π function*, which are, respectively, defined by

$$S(x; a, b) = \begin{cases} 0 & \text{for } x < a \\ 2\left(\dfrac{x-a}{b-a}\right)^2 & \text{for } a \leq x < \dfrac{a+b}{2} \\ 1 - 2\left(\dfrac{x-b}{b-a}\right)^2 & \text{for } \dfrac{a+b}{2} \leq x < b \\ 1 & \text{for } x \geq b, \end{cases} \qquad (2.18)$$

$$\pi(x; a, b) = \begin{cases} S(x; b - a, b) & \text{for } x < b \\ 1 - S(x; b, b + a) & \text{for } x \geq b. \end{cases} \qquad (2.19)$$

These two functions are shown in Fig. 2.4(a) and (b), respectively. In $S(x; a, b)$, the crossover point is $(a + b)/2$. In $\pi(x; a, b)$, b is the point at which π is unity, while the two crossover points are $b - a/2$ and $b + a/2$. The separation between these two crossover points, a, is the bandwidth. Sometimes the π function is simply defined as

$$\pi'(x; a, b) = \dfrac{1}{1 + [x - a/b]^2}, \qquad (2.20)$$

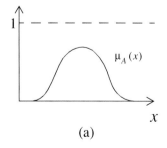 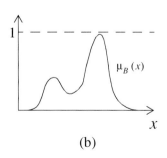 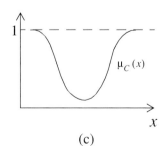

(a)   (b)   (c)

Figure 2.3   Convex and nonconvex fuzzy sets.

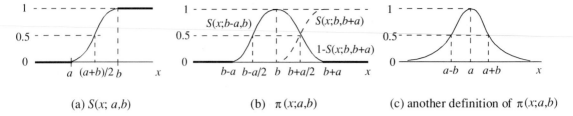

(a) $S(x; a,b)$ (b) $\pi(x;a,b)$ (c) another definition of $\pi(x;a,b)$

Figure 2.4   The S function and the π function.

which is shown in Fig. 2.4(c), where $2b$ is the bandwidth. With the S function and the π function, it is convenient to express the membership function of a fuzzy subset of the real line in terms of one of these "standard" functions whose parameters can be adjusted accordingly to fit a specified membership function approximately. More details on fuzzy numbers, including the arithmetic operations (e.g., addition and subtraction) of two fuzzy numbers, will be presented in Sec. 5.2.

Similar to the cardinality of a crisp set, which is defined as the number of elements in the crisp set, the *cardinality* (or *scalar cardinality*) of a fuzzy set A is the summation of the membership grades of all the elements of x in A. That is,

$$|A| = \sum_{x \in U} \mu_A(x). \tag{2.21}$$

The *relative* cardinality of A is

$$|A|_{\text{rel}} = \frac{|A|}{|U|}, \tag{2.22}$$

where $|U|$ is finite. The relative cardinality evaluates the proportion of elements of U having the property A when U is finite. When a fuzzy set A has a finite support, its cardinality can be defined as a fuzzy set. This *fuzzy* cardinality is denoted as $|A|_f$ and defined by Zadeh [1978a] as

$$|A|_f = \sum_{\alpha \in \Lambda_A} \frac{\alpha}{|A_\alpha|}. \tag{2.23}$$

Example 2.5

Consider the fuzzy set A in Table 2.1 (Example 2.2). We have

$$|A| = |\text{High\_Score}| = 0.1 + 0.3 + 0.5 + 0.8 + 1 + 1 = 3.7,$$

$$|A|_{\text{rel}} = \frac{|A|}{|U|} = \frac{|A|}{10} = 0.37,$$

$$|A|_f = 0.1/6 + 0.3/5 + 0.5/4 + 0.8/3 + 1/2,$$

where the fuzzy cardinality of A can be interpreted as "approximately 3."

With these basic notations and definitions for fuzzy sets, we are now ready to introduce some basic set-theoretic definitions and operations for fuzzy sets. Let A and B be fuzzy sets in the universe of discourse U.

1. Complement: When $\mu_A(x) \in [0, 1]$, the complement of A, denoted as $\bar{A}$, is defined by its membership function as [see Fig. 2.5(a)]

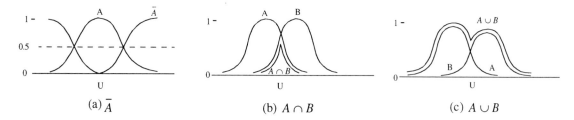

Figure 2.5   Complement, intersection, and union of two fuzzy sets A and B.

(a) $\bar{A}$ (b) $A \cap B$ (c) $A \cup B$

$$\mu_{\bar{A}}(x) \triangleq 1 - \mu_A(x) \qquad \forall x \in U. \qquad (2.24)$$

2. Intersection: The intersection of fuzzy sets A and B, denoted as $A \cap B$, is defined by [see Fig. 2.5(b)]

$$\mu_{A \cap B}(x) \triangleq \min [\mu_A(x), \mu_B(x)] \equiv \mu_A(x) \wedge \mu_B(x) \qquad \forall x \in U, \qquad (2.25)$$

where $\wedge$ indicates the min operation. It is clear that

$$A \cap B \subseteq A \qquad \text{and} \qquad A \cap B \subseteq B. \qquad (2.26)$$

3. Union: The union of fuzzy sets A and B, denoted as $A \cup B$, is defined by [see Fig. 2.5(c)]

$$\mu_{A \cup B}(x) \triangleq \max [\mu_A(x), \mu_B(x)] \equiv \mu_A(x) \vee \mu_B(x) \qquad \forall x \in U, \qquad (2.27)$$

where $\vee$ indicates the max operation. It is clear that

$$A \subseteq A \cup B \qquad \text{and} \qquad B \subseteq A \cup B. \qquad (2.28)$$

4. Equality: A and B are *equal* if and only if

$$\mu_A(x) = \mu_B(x) \qquad \forall x \in U. \qquad (2.29)$$

Hence, if $\mu_A(x) \neq \mu_B(x)$ for some $x \in U$, then $A \neq B$. This definition of "equality" is *crisp*. To check the *degree of equality* of two fuzzy sets, we can use the *similarity measure* [Lin and Lee, 1992]:

$$E(A, B) \equiv \text{degree}(A = B) \triangleq \frac{|A \cap B|}{|A \cup B|}, \qquad (2.30)$$

where $\cap$ and $\cup$ denote intersection and union of A and B, respectively. When $A = B$, $E(A, B) = 1$; when $|A \cap B| = 0$ (i.e., A and B do not overlap at all), $E(A, B) = 0$. In most general cases, $0 \leq E(A, B) \leq 1$.

5. Subset: A is a *subset* of B; that is, $A \subseteq B$ if and only if

$$\mu_A(x) \leq \mu_B(x) \qquad \forall x \in U. \qquad (2.31)$$

If $A \subseteq B$ and $A \neq B$, then A is a *proper subset* of B; that is, $A \subset B$. Again, the definition of subset is crisp. To check the degree that A is a subset of B, we can use the *subsethood measure* [Kosko, 1992a]:

$$S(A, B) \equiv \text{degree}(A \subseteq B) \triangleq \frac{|A \cap B|}{|A|}. \qquad (2.32)$$

Example 2.6

Consider the two membership functions of the fuzzy sets A and B in Table 2.1. Obviously, $A \neq B$, A is not a subset of B, and B is not a subset of A either. Moreover, we have

$$\overline{A} = 1/10 + 1/20 + 1/30 + 1/40 + 0.9/50 + 0.7/60 + 0.5/70 + 0.2/80,$$

$$A \cap B = 0.1/50 + 0.3/60 + 0.5/70 + 0.5/80,$$

$$A \cup B = 0.1/30 + 0.5/40 + 0.8/50 + 1/60 + 0.8/70 + 0.8/80 + 1/90 + 1/100,$$

$$E(A, B) = \frac{|A \cap B|}{|A \cup B|} = \frac{0.1 + 0.3 + 0.5 + 0.5}{0.1 + 0.5 + 0.8 + 1 + 0.8 + 0.8 + 1 + 1} = \frac{1.4}{6} = 0.23,$$

$$S(A, B) = \frac{|A \cap B|}{|A|} = \frac{0.1 + 0.3 + 0.5 + 0.5}{0.1 + 0.3 + 0.5 + 0.8 + 1 + 1} = \frac{1.4}{3.7} = 0.38.$$

A justification of the choice of negation, min, and max as complement, intersection, and union operators, respectively, was given in Bellman and Giertz [1973] where these operators were shown to be the only operators that meet a set of requirements (axioms). With the above definitions, the reader can verify the following facts [refer to Eqs. (2.29) and (2.31) for definitions of "equality" and "subset"].

$$(A \cap B)_\alpha = A_\alpha \cap B_\alpha \quad \text{and} \quad (A \cup B)_\alpha = A_\alpha \cup B_\alpha, \quad \text{but } (\overline{A})_\alpha \neq \overline{A}_\alpha. \quad (2.33)$$

As in the case of crisp sets, we have the double-negation law (involution) and DeMorgan's laws for fuzzy sets.

6. Double-negation law (involution):

$$\overline{\overline{A}} = A. \quad (2.34)$$

7. DeMorgan's laws:

$$\overline{A \cup B} = \overline{A} \cap \overline{B}, \quad (2.35)$$

$$\overline{A \cap B} = \overline{A} \cup \overline{B}. \quad (2.36)$$

However, the *law of the excluded middle* (i.e., $E \cup \overline{E} = U$) and the *law of contradiction* (i.e., $E \cap \overline{E} = \varnothing$) of the crisp set E are no longer true and valid in fuzzy sets. That is, for fuzzy set A,

$$A \cup \overline{A} \neq U \quad \text{and} \quad A \cap \overline{A} \neq \varnothing, \quad (2.37)$$

which means that because of the lack of precise boundaries, complementary sets are overlapping and cannot cover the universal set U perfectly. On the contrary, these two laws are the necessary characteristics of crisp sets, which bring together a crisp set E and its complement $\overline{E}$ to provide the whole set; that is, nothing exists between E and $\overline{E}$.

The other properties of fuzzy set operations that are common to crisp set operations are listed in Table 2.2. However, it is noted that the above discussion about the properties of fuzzy set operations is based on the definitions of complement, intersection, and union operations in Eqs. (2.24), (2.25), and (2.27), respectively. As we will see in the next section, there are other definitions of these operations and hence some properties mentioned above may fail to hold while others may become true for various definitions. As a matter of fact, it has been shown that if the *excluded-middle laws* hold for fuzzy sets, then union and intersection cannot be *idempotent* and are no longer *mutually distributive* [Kandel, 1986; Klir

TABLE 2.2 Properties of Fuzzy Set Operations

Idempotence	$A \cup A = A, A \cap A = A$
Distributivity	$A \cap (B \cup C) = (A \cap B) \cup (A \cap C)$
	$A \cup (B \cap C) = (A \cup B) \cap (A \cup C)$
Commutativity	$A \cup B = B \cup A, \quad A \cap B = B \cap A$
Associativity	$(A \cup B) \cup C = A \cup (B \cup C)$
	$(A \cap B) \cap C = A \cap (B \cap C)$
Absorption	$A \cup (A \cap B) = A, \quad A \cap (A \cup B) = A$
Law of zero	$A \cup U = U, \quad A \cap \varnothing = \varnothing$
Law of identity	$A \cup \varnothing = A, \quad A \cap U = A$
Double-negation law	$\overline{\overline{A}} = A$
De Morgan's laws	$\overline{A \cup B} = \overline{A} \cap \overline{B}, \quad \overline{A \cap B} = \overline{A} \cup \overline{B}$

and Folger, 1988]. Hence, when we choose union and intersection to combine fuzzy sets, we have to give up either excluded-middle laws or distributivity and idempotence.

Next, we shall introduce some popular algebraic operations on fuzzy sets. Further fuzzy set operations will be discussed in the next section.

8. Cartesian product: Let $A_1, A_2, \ldots, A_n$ be fuzzy sets in $U_1, U_2, \ldots, U_n$, respectively. The Cartesian product of $A_1, A_2, \ldots, A_n$ is a fuzzy set in the product space $U_1 \times U_2 \times \cdots \times U_n$ with the membership function as

$$\mu_{A_1 \times A_2 \times \cdots \times A_n}(x_1, x_2, \ldots, x_n) \triangleq \min[\mu_{A_1}(x_1), \mu_{A_2}(x_2), \ldots, \mu_{A_n}(x_n)],$$
$$x_1 \in U_1, x_2 \in U_2, \ldots, x_n \in U_n. \tag{2.38}$$

9. Algebraic sum: The algebraic sum of two fuzzy sets, $A + B$, is defined by

$$\mu_{A+B}(x) \triangleq \mu_A(x) + \mu_B(x) - \mu_A(x) \cdot \mu_B(x). \tag{2.39}$$

10. Algebraic product: The algebraic product of two fuzzy sets, $A \cdot B$, is defined by

$$\mu_{A \cdot B}(x) \triangleq \mu_A(x) \cdot \mu_B(x). \tag{2.40}$$

11. Bounded sum: The bounded sum of two fuzzy sets, $A \oplus B$, is defined by

$$\mu_{A \oplus B}(x) \triangleq \min\{1, \mu_A(x) + \mu_B(x)\}. \tag{2.41}$$

12. Bounded difference: The bounded difference of two fuzzy sets, $A \ominus B$, is defined by

$$\mu_{A \ominus B}(x) \triangleq \max\{0, \mu_A(x) - \mu_B(x)\}. \tag{2.42}$$

Example 2.7

Let $A = \{(3, 0.5), (5, 1), (7, 0.6)\}$ and $B = \{(3, 1), (5, 0.6)\}$. Then we can obtain

$$A \times B = \{[(3, 3), 0.5], [(5, 3), 1], [(7, 3), 0.6], [(3, 5), 0.5], [(5, 5), 0.6],$$
$$[(7, 5), 0.6]\},$$

$$A + B = \{(3, 1), (5, 1), (7, 0.6)\},$$

$$A \cdot B = \{(3, 0.5), (5, 0.6), (7, 0)\},$$

$$A \oplus B = \{(3, 1), (5, 1), (7, 0.6)\},$$

$$A \ominus B = \{(3, 0), (5, 0.4), (7, 0.6)\}.$$

2.2 EXTENSIONS OF FUZZY SET CONCEPTS

In the previous section, we introduced basic definitions and operations on fuzzy sets. The membership functions were assumed to be crisp, and the membership space M was restricted to the space of real numbers. Specific operations of set complement, intersection, and union were given in Eqs. (2.24), (2.25), and (2.27), where negation, min, and max operators were adopted in these operations, respectively. These specific operations are called the *standard operations* of fuzzy sets that are always used in *possibility theory* [Zadeh, 1978a]. More on possibility theory will be presented in Chaps. 4 and 5.

The basic concept covered in Sec. 2.1 can be extended in two possible directions. The first one concerns other kinds of fuzzy sets including different structures of the membership space and different assumptions about the membership functions. This extension is treated in Sec. 2.2.1. The second extension concerns the operations of fuzzy sets. It is understood that the standard operations of fuzzy sets are not the only possible generalization of crisp set operations. Several different classes of functions, which possess proper properties, have been proposed. These will be discussed in Sec. 2.2.2.

2.2.1 Other Kinds of Fuzzy Sets

An extension of ordinary fuzzy sets is to allow the membership values to be a fuzzy set instead of a crisply defined degree. A fuzzy set whose membership function is itself a fuzzy set is called a *type-2* fuzzy set. A *type-1* fuzzy set is an ordinary fuzzy set. Hence, a type-2 fuzzy set is a fuzzy set whose membership values are type-1 fuzzy sets on $[0, 1]$. A type-2 fuzzy set in a universe of discourse U is characterized by a *fuzzy membership function* μ_A as [Mizumoto and Tanaka, 1976]

$$\mu_A: U \rightarrow [0, 1]^{[0, 1]}, \tag{2.43}$$

where $\mu_A(x)$ is the *fuzzy grade* and is a fuzzy set in $[0, 1]$ represented by

$$\mu_A(x) = \int f(u)/u, \qquad u \in [0, 1], \tag{2.44}$$

where f is a membership function for the fuzzy grade $\mu_A(x)$ and is defined as

$$f: [0, 1] \rightarrow [0, 1]. \tag{2.45}$$

For example, we may define a type-2 fuzzy set "Beautiful" with membership values as type-1 fuzzy sets such as *Below average, Average, Above average, Superior,* and so on. We can recursively define a *type-m* fuzzy set ($m > 1$) in U whose membership values are type-$(m - 1)$ fuzzy sets on $[0, 1]$.

A different extension of the concept of fuzzy sets is to consider a fuzzy set of fuzzy sets of U, that is, a fuzzy set whose elements are fuzzy sets. Such fuzzy sets are called *level-2* fuzzy sets. For example, a level-2 fuzzy set is the collection of desired attributes for an electric razor. The elements of this level-2 fuzzy set are ordinary (level-1) fuzzy sets such as *Reliable, Inexpensive, Good appearance,* and so on. Recursively, a *level-k* ($k > 1$) fuzzy set can be defined, where k indicates the depth of nesting. Given a universe of discourse U, let $\tilde{\mathcal{P}}(U)$ denote the set of all fuzzy subsets of U and let $\tilde{\mathcal{P}}^k(U)$ be defined by

$$\tilde{\mathcal{P}}^k(U) = \tilde{\mathcal{P}}(\tilde{\mathcal{P}}^{k-1}(U)), \tag{2.46}$$

for all integers $k \geq 2$. Then, a level-k fuzzy set A is defined by

$$\mu_A: \tilde{\mathcal{P}}^{k-1}(U) \rightarrow [0, 1]. \qquad (2.47)$$

2.2.2 Further Operations on Fuzzy Sets

As we have mentioned, the standard operations, that is, negation, min, and max operations in Eqs. (2.24), (2.25), and (2.27), respectively, are not the only possible generalization of the crisp set complement, intersection, and union operations. This raises a question concerning the requirements, specifications, and properties of other functions that can be viewed as a generalization of the crisp set operations. We shall first discuss several different classes of functions for each of the above three standard set operators. These functions will possess appropriate properties. For each operation, the corresponding functions can be divided into two categories. One is nonparametric functions such as Eqs. (2.24), (2.25), and (2.27), and the other is parametric functions in which parameters are used to adjust the "strength" of the corresponding operations. Based on these functions, we will introduce other kinds of fuzzy set operations. Let us consider the fuzzy complement first.

A complement of a fuzzy set A, denoted as $\bar{A}$, is specified by a function

$$c: [0, 1] \rightarrow [0, 1], \qquad (2.48)$$

such that

$$\mu_{\bar{A}}(x) = c(\mu_A(x)), \qquad (2.49)$$

where the function $c(\cdot)$ satisfies the following conditions:

c1. *Boundary conditions:* $c(0) = 1$ and $c(1) = 0$.
c2. *Monotonic property:* For any $x_1, x_2 \in U$, if $\mu_A(x_1) \leq \mu_A(x_2)$, then $c(\mu_A(x_1)) \geq c(\mu_A(x_2))$; that is, $c(\cdot)$ is monotonic nonincreasing.
c3. *Continuity:* $c(\cdot)$ is a continuous function.
c4. *Involution:* $c(\cdot)$ is involutive, which means that

$$c(c(\mu_A(x))) = \mu_A(x), \qquad \forall x \in U. \qquad (2.50)$$

Based on the above conditions, typical examples of nonparametric and parametric fuzzy complements are

1. *Negation complement:* The complement of A using this operation is denoted as $\bar{A}$ and is defined as in Eq. (2.24), that is,

$$\mu_{\bar{A}}(x) = c(\mu_A(x)) \triangleq 1 - \mu_A(x) \qquad \forall x \in U. \qquad (2.51)$$

2. λ *Complement (Sugeno class):* This complement is denoted as $\bar{A}^\lambda$ and is defined by

$$\mu_{\bar{A}^\lambda}(x) = c(\mu_A(x)) \triangleq \frac{1 - \mu_A(x)}{1 + \lambda\mu_A(x)}, \qquad -1 < \lambda < \infty. \qquad (2.52)$$

λ is a parameter that gives the degree of complementation. When $\lambda = 0$, the function becomes $c(\mu_A(x)) = 1 - \mu_A(x)$, the standard fuzzy complement, and as λ approaches -1, $\bar{A}^\lambda$ approaches the universal set U. When λ approaches infinity, $\bar{A}^\lambda$

approaches the empty set. It is noted that the double-negation law [Eq. (2.34)] and DeMorgan's laws [Eqs. (2.35) and (2.36)] hold for the λ-complement.

3. *w Complement (Yager class):* This complement is denoted as $\bar{A}^w$ and is defined by

$$\mu_{\bar{A}^w}(x) = c\,(\mu_A\,(x)\,) \triangleq (1 - \mu_A^w\,(x)\,)^{1/w}, \qquad 0 < w < \infty. \qquad (2.53)$$

Again, the parameter w adjusts the degree of complementation. When $w = 1$, the w-complement function becomes the standard fuzzy complement of $c\,(\mu_A\,(x)\,) = 1 - \mu_A\,(x)$.

The *equilibrium* of a fuzzy complement c is defined as any value a for which $c\,(a) = a$. For example, the equilibrium of the standard complement operation is 0.5, which is the solution of the equation $1 - a = a$. An important property shared by all fuzzy complements is that every fuzzy complement has at most one equilibrium due to the monotonic nonincreasing nature of fuzzy complements.

Next, let us discuss the intersection and union operations of fuzzy sets, which are often referred to as *triangular norms (t-norms)* and *triangular conorms (t-conorms),* respectively [Dubois and Prade, 1980, 1985b]. *t*-norms are two-parameter functions of the form

$$t: [0, 1] \times [0, 1] \rightarrow [0, 1], \qquad (2.54)$$

such that

$$\mu_{A \cap B}(x) = t\,[\mu_A\,(x)\,, \mu_B\,(x)\,], \qquad (2.55)$$

where the function $t\,(\cdot, \cdot)$ satisfies the following conditions:

t1. *Boundary conditions:* $t\,(0, 0) = 0; t\,(\mu_A\,(x)\,, 1) = t\,(1, \mu_A\,(x)\,) = \mu_A\,(x)$.
t2. *Commutativity:* $t\,(\mu_A\,(x)\,, \mu_B\,(x)\,) = t\,(\mu_B\,(x)\,, \mu_A\,(x)\,)$.
t3. *Monotonicity:* If $\mu_A\,(x) \le \mu_C\,(x)$ and $\mu_B\,(x) \le \mu_D\,(x)$, then $t\,(\mu_A\,(x)\,, \mu_B\,(x)\,) \le t\,(\mu_C\,(x)\,, \mu_D\,(x)\,)$.
t4. *Associativity:* $t\,(\mu_A\,(x)\,, t\,(\mu_B\,(x)\,, \mu_C\,(x)\,)\,) = t\,(t\,(\mu_A\,(x)\,, \mu_B\,(x)\,)\,, \mu_C\,(x)\,)$.

The *t*-norms and *t*-conorms are also used to define other operations. Typical nonparametric *t*-norms are [to simplify the notation, we use $a \equiv \mu_A\,(x)$ and $b = \mu_B\,(x)$ for the remainder of this section only]:

1. Intersection: $a \wedge b = \min\,(a, b)$. $\qquad (2.56)$
2. Algebraic product: $a \cdot b = ab$. $\qquad (2.57)$
3. Bounded product: $a \odot b = \max\,(0, a + b - 1)$. $\qquad (2.58)$
4. Drastic product: $a \stackrel{\wedge}{\cdot} b = \begin{cases} a, & b = 1, \\ b, & a = 1, \\ 0, & a, b < 1. \end{cases}$ $\qquad (2.59)$

One representative parametric *t*-norm is the *Yager intersection* which is defined by the function

$$t_w\,(a, b) = 1 - \min\,[1,\,(\,(1 - a)^w + (1 - b)^w\,)^{1/w}\,], \qquad (2.60)$$

where $w \in (0, \infty)$. For $w = 1$, the Yager intersection becomes the bounded product of Eq. (2.58). It can be shown that when $w \rightarrow \infty$, $t_w\,(a, b) = \min\,(a, b)$, and when $w \rightarrow 0$, $t_w\,(a, b)$ becomes the drastic product [Klir and Folger, 1988]. That is, the Yager intersection becomes the min operator when $w \rightarrow \infty$. It is observed that the membership grade increases as w

increases. Hence, the parameter w can be interpreted as the degree of strength of intersection performed. Some other classes of parametric t-norms are shown in Table 2.3.

t-conorms (also called s-norms) are two-parameter functions of the form

$$s: [0, 1] \times [0, 1] \rightarrow [0, 1], \tag{2.61}$$

such that

$$\mu_{A \cup B}(x) = s[\mu_A(x), \mu_B(x)], \tag{2.62}$$

where the function $s(\cdot, \cdot)$ satisfies the following conditions:

s1. *Boundary conditions:* $s(1, 1) = 1$, $s(\mu_A(x), 0) = s(0, \mu_A(x)) = \mu_A(x)$.
s2. *Commutativity:* $s(\mu_A(x), \mu_B(x)) = s(\mu_B(x), \mu_A(x))$.
s3. *Monotonicity:* If $\mu_A(x) \leq \mu_C(x)$ and $\mu_B(x) \leq \mu_D(x)$, then $s(\mu_A(x), \mu_B(x)) \leq s(\mu_C(x), \mu_D(x))$.
s4. *Associativity:* $s(\mu_A(x), s(\mu_B(x), \mu_C(x))) = s(s(\mu_A(x), \mu_B(x)), \mu_C(x))$.

Based on the above conditions, typical nonparametric t-conorms are

1. Union: $a \vee b = \max(a, b)$. $\qquad\qquad$ (2.63)
2. Algebraic sum: $a \mathbin{\hat{+}} b = a + b - ab$. $\qquad\qquad$ (2.64)

TABLE 2.3 Some Parameterized t-Norms (Fuzzy Intersections) and t Conorms (Fuzzy Unions), where $a \equiv \mu_A(x)$ and $b \equiv \mu_B(x)$.

References	t norms (Fuzzy Intersections)	t conorms (Fuzzy Unions)	Range
Schweizer and Sklar [1961]	$\max\left\{0, a^{-r} + b^{-r} - 1\right\}^{-\frac{1}{r}}$	$1 - \max\left\{0, (1-a)^{-r} + (1-b)^{-r} - 1\right\}^{-\frac{1}{r}}$	$r \in (-\infty, \infty)$
Hamacher [1978]	$\dfrac{ab}{\gamma + (1-\gamma)(a+b-ab)}$	$\dfrac{a+b-(2-\gamma)ab}{1-(1-\gamma)ab}$	$\gamma \in (0, \infty)$
Frank [1979]	$\log_s\left[1 + \dfrac{(s^a - 1)(s^b - 1)}{s - 1}\right]$	$1 - \log_s\left[1 + \dfrac{(s^{1-a} - 1)(s^{1-b} - 1)}{s - 1}\right]$	$s \in (0, \infty)$
Yager [1980]	$1 - \min\left\{1, (1-a)^w + (1-b)^w)^{\frac{1}{w}}\right\}$	$\min\left\{1, (a^w + b^w)^{\frac{1}{w}}\right\}$	$w \in (0, \infty)$
Dubois and Prade [1980]	$\dfrac{ab}{\max\{a, b, \alpha\}}$	$\dfrac{a+b-ab-\min\{a, b, 1-\alpha\}}{\max\{1-a, 1-b, \alpha\}}$	$\alpha \in (0, 1)$
Dombi [1982]	$1/1 + \left[\left(\frac{1}{a} - 1\right)^\lambda + \left(\frac{1}{b} - 1\right)^\lambda\right]^{\frac{1}{\lambda}}$	$1/1 + \left[\left(\frac{1}{a} - 1\right)^{-\lambda} + \left(\frac{1}{b} - 1\right)^{-\lambda}\right]^{-\frac{1}{\lambda}}$	$\lambda \in (0, \infty)$
Werners [1988]	$\beta \min\{a, b\} + \dfrac{(1-\beta)(a+b)}{2}$	$\beta \max\{a, b\} + \dfrac{(1-\beta)(a+b)}{2}$	$\beta \in [0, 1]$
Zimmermann and Zysno [1980]	$(ab)^{(1-\gamma)}[1 - (1-a)(1-b)]^\gamma$	γ parameter indicates compensation between intersection and union	$\gamma \in [0, 1]$

3. Bounded sum: $a \oplus b = \min(1, a + b)$.   (2.65)

4. Drastic sum: $a \,\dot{\vee}\, b = \begin{cases} a, & b = 0, \\ b, & a = 0, \\ 1, & a, b > 0. \end{cases}$ (2.66)

One typical parametric t-conorm is the *Yager union* which is defined by the function

$$s_w(a, b) = \min\left[1, (a^w + b^w)^{1/w}\right],\qquad\qquad (2.68)$$

where $w \in (0, \infty)$. For $w = 1$, the Yager union becomes the bounded sum of Eq. (2.65). We can show that when $w \to \infty$, $s_w(a, b) = \max(a, b)$, and when $w \to 0$, $s_w(a, b)$ becomes the drastic sum [Klir and Folger, 1988]. It is observed that the membership grade decreases as w increases. Some other classes of parametric t-conorms are also shown in Table 2.3.

The relations among various t-norms (fuzzy intersections) and t-conorms (fuzzy unions) are characterized by the following theorem.

Theorem 2.2

Let A and B be fuzzy sets in the universe of discourse U. The t-norms [Eqs. (2.56)–(2.59)] are bounded by the inequalities

$$t_{dp}(a, b) = t_{\min}(a, b) \leq t(a, b) \leq t_{\max}(a, b) = \min(a, b),\qquad (2.69)$$

where $t_{dp}(a, b)$ is the drastic product in Eq. (2.59). Similarly, the t-conorms [Eqs. (2.63)–(2.67)] are bounded by the inequalities

$$\max(a, b) = s_{\min}(a, b) \leq s(a, b) \leq s_{\max}(a, b) = s_{ds}(a, b),\qquad (2.70)$$

where $s_{ds}(a, b)$ is the drastic sum in Eq. (2.66).

Proof: Since the proof of Eq. (2.70) is similar to that of Eq. (2.69), we shall prove only Eq. (2.69). Using the boundary condition of the t-norm, we have $t(a, 1) = a$ and $t(1, b) = b$. Then by the monotonicity condition of the t-norm, we obtain

$$t(a, b) \leq t(a, 1) = a \qquad \text{and} \qquad t(a, b) \leq t(1, b) = b.$$

Hence, we conclude that

$$t(a, b) \leq \min(a, b),$$

which is the second inequality in Eq. (2.69). For the first inequality in Eq. (2.69), when $b = 1$, $t(a, b) = a$, and when $a = 1$, $t(a, b) = b$ (boundary conditions). Hence, the first inequality holds when $a = 1$ or $b = 1$. Since $t(a, b) \in [0, 1]$, it follows from the second inequality in Eq. (2.69) that $t(a, 0) = t(0, b) = 0$. By the monotonicity condition, we have

$$t(a, b) \geq t(0, b) = t(a, 0) = 0,$$

which completes the proof of the first inequality in Eq. (2.69).

Hence, the standard min and max operations are, respectively, the upper bound of t-norms (the weakest intersection) and the lower bound of t-conorms (the strongest union). As mentioned before, the Yager intersection [Eq. (2.60)] and the Yager union [Eq. (2.68)] become the standard min and max operations, respectively, as $w \to \infty$, and become the $t_{\min}$ and $s_{\max}$ operations, respectively, as $w \to 0$. Hence, the Yager class of fuzzy intersections and unions covers the entire range of the operations as given by the inequalities in Eqs. (2.69) and (2.70).

As discussed in Sec. 2.1, the standard operations of fuzzy sets in Eqs. (2.24), (2.25), and (2.27) do not satisfy the law of the excluded middle and the law of contradiction, although they satisfy the properties in Table 2.2. If it is desired, we may preserve these two laws in our choice of fuzzy union and intersection operations by sacrificing idempotency and distributivity. We can easily verify that the standard complements t_{min} and s_{max} satisfy the law of the excluded middle and the law of contradiction. Another combination of these properties involves standard complement, bounded product, and bounded sum.

The t-norms and t-conorms are a kind of *aggregation operations* on fuzzy sets, which are operations by which several fuzzy sets are combined to produce a single set. Such operations play an important role in the context of decision making in a fuzzy environment. In general, an aggregation operation is defined by [Klir and Folger, 1988]

$$h: [0, 1]^n \rightarrow [0, 1], \qquad n \geq 2, \qquad (2.71)$$

such that

$$\mu_A(x) = h(\mu_{A_1}(x), \mu_{A_2}(x), \ldots, \mu_{A_n}(x)) \qquad \forall x \in U. \qquad (2.72)$$

As indicated by Eqs. (2.69) and (2.70), all t-norms are smaller than the min operator intersection function and all t-conorms are greater than the max operator union function. Naturally, there is a class of aggregation operators lying between the min operator and the max operator. These operators are called *averaging operators* since they realize the idea of trade-offs between the minimum and the maximum degree of membership of the aggregated sets. Hence, averaging operators are aggregation operators for which

$$\min(a_1, a_2, \ldots, a_n) \leq h(a_1, a_2, \ldots, a_n) \leq \max(a_1, a_2, \ldots, a_n), \qquad (2.73)$$

where $a_i = \mu_{A_i}(x)$, $i = 1, \ldots, n$. One typical parametric averaging operator is the *generalized means* which is defined as

$$h_\alpha(a_1, a_2, \ldots, a_n) \triangleq \left(\frac{a_1^\alpha + a_2^\alpha + \cdots + a_1^\alpha}{n} \right)^{1/\alpha}, \qquad (2.74)$$

where $\alpha \in \mathcal{R}$ but $\alpha \neq 0$. It can be verified that when α approaches $-\infty$, $h_\alpha(a_1, a_2, \ldots, a_n)$ becomes $\min(a_1, a_2, \ldots, a_n)$, and when α approaches ∞, $h_\alpha(a_1, a_2, \ldots, a_n)$ becomes $\max(a_1, a_2, \ldots, a_n)$. Hence, the generalized means covers the entire interval between the min and the max operators. The full scope of fuzzy aggregation operators is shown in Fig. 2.6.

An important extension of the generalized means is the *weighted generalized means* defined by

$$h_\alpha(a_1, a_2, \ldots, a_n; w_1, w_2, \ldots, w_n) \triangleq (w_1 a_1^\alpha + w_2 a_2^\alpha + \cdots + w_n a_n^\alpha)^{1/\alpha}, \qquad (2.75)$$

where $w_i \geq 0$ and $\sum_{i=1}^n w_i = 1$. The w_i are weights expressing the relative importance of the aggregated sets. The weighted generalized means are useful in decision-making problems where different criteria differ in importance (weights). More averaging operators can be found in [Zimmerman, 1991].

Finally, based on t-norms and t-conorms, we shall further introduce some operations of fuzzy sets that are central to fuzzy logic and fuzzy reasoning. They will be useful in Chaps. 6 and 7. In the following, let A and B be fuzzy sets in universal sets U and V, respectively.

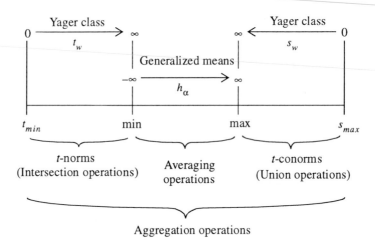

Figure 2.6 The full scope of fuzzy aggregation operators.

1. *Fuzzy conjunction:* The fuzzy conjunction of A and B is denoted as $A \wedge B$ and defined by

$$\mu_{A \wedge B}(x, y) \triangleq t(\mu_A(x), \mu_B(y)), \qquad \text{where } t \text{ is a } t\text{-norm.} \qquad (2.76)$$

2. *Fuzzy disjunction:* The fuzzy disjunction of A and B is denoted as $A \vee B$ and defined by

$$\mu_{A \vee B}(x, y) \triangleq s(\mu_A(x), \mu_B(y)), \qquad \text{where } s \text{ is a } t\text{-conorm.} \qquad (2.77)$$

3. *Fuzzy implication:* The fuzzy implication of A and B is denoted as $A \rightarrow B$ and has five different definitions [Lee, 1990]. In the following, t is a t-norm, s is a t-conorm, and the complement is the standard complement.

Material implication: $A \rightarrow B = s(\overline{A}, B)$. $\qquad (2.78)$

Propositional calculus: $A \rightarrow B = s(\overline{A}, t(A, B))$. $\qquad (2.79)$

Extended propositional calculus: $A \rightarrow B = s(\overline{A} \times \overline{B}, B)$. $\qquad (2.80)$

Generalization of modus ponens: $A \rightarrow B = \sup\{k \in [0, 1], t(A, k) \leq B\}$. $\qquad (2.81)$

Generalization of modus tollens: $A \rightarrow B = \inf\{k \in [0, 1], s(B, k) \leq A\}$. $\qquad (2.82)$

Example 2.8

Let us see some special cases of the above operations. If t = min operator, s = max operator, and the material implication is adopted, then we have

$$\mu_{A \wedge B}(x, y) = \min(\mu_A(x), \mu_B(y)),$$

$$\mu_{A \vee B}(x, y) = \max(\mu_A(x), \mu_B(y)), \qquad (2.83)$$

$$\mu_{A \rightarrow B}(x, y) = \max(1 - \mu_A(x), \mu_B(y)).$$

If t = algebraic product, s = algebraic sum, and the material implication is adopted, then we have

$$\mu_{A \wedge B}(x, y) = \mu_A(x) \mu_B(y),$$

$$\mu_{A \vee B}(x, y) = \mu_A(x) + \mu_B(y) - \mu_A(x) \mu_B(y), \qquad (2.84)$$

$$\mu_{A \rightarrow B}(x, y) = 1 - \mu_A(x) + \mu_A(x) \mu_B(y).$$

Basics of Fuzzy Sets   Chap. 2

If t = bounded product, s = bounded sum, and the material implication is adopted, then we obtain

$$\mu_{A \wedge B}(x, y) = \max[0, \mu_A(x) + \mu_B(y) - 1],$$

$$\mu_{A \vee B}(x, y) = \min[1, \mu_A(x) + \mu_B(y)], \tag{2.85}$$

$$\mu_{A \to B}(x, y) = \min[1, 1 - \mu_A(x) + \mu_B(y)].$$

2.3 EXTENSION PRINCIPLE AND ITS APPLICATIONS

The *extension principle,* introduced by Zadeh [1978a], is one of the most important tools of fuzzy set theory. This principle allows the generalization of crisp mathematical concepts to the fuzzy set framework and extends point-to-point mappings to mappings for fuzzy sets. It provides a means for any function f that maps an n-tuple $(x_1, x_2, \ldots, x_n)$ in the crisp set U to a point in the crisp set V to be generalized to mapping n fuzzy subsets in U to a fuzzy subset in V. Hence, any mathematical relationship between nonfuzzy elements can be extended to deal with fuzzy entities. Furthermore, the extension principle is very useful for dealing with set-theoretic operations for higher-order fuzzy sets. We shall first state the extension principle and then show some of its applications.

Given a function $f: U \to V$ and a fuzzy set A in U, where $A = \mu_1/x_1 + \mu_2/x_2 + \cdots + \mu_n/x_n$, the extension principle states that

$$f(A) = f(\mu_1/x_1 + \mu_2/x_2 + \cdots + \mu_n/x_n)$$
$$= \mu_1/f(x_1) + \mu_2/f(x_2) + \cdots + \mu_n/f(x_n). \tag{2.86}$$

If more than one element of U is mapped to the same element y in V by f (i.e., a many-to-one mapping), then the maximum among their membership grades is taken. That is,

$$\mu_{f(A)}(y) = \max_{\substack{x_i \in U \\ f(x_i) = y}} [\mu_A(x_i)], \tag{2.87}$$

where x_i are the elements that are mapped to the same y. Quite often, the function f that is of interest maps n-tuples in U to a point in V. Let U be a Cartesian product of universes $U = U_1 \times U_2 \times \cdots \times U_n$ and $A_1, A_2, \ldots, A_n$ be n fuzzy sets in $U_1, U_2, \ldots, U_n$, respectively. The function f maps an n-tuple $(x_1, x_2, \ldots, x_n)$ in the crisp set U to a point y in the crisp set V; that is, $y = f(x_1, x_2, \ldots, x_n)$. The extension principle allows the function $f(x_1, x_2, \ldots, x_n)$ to be extended to act on the n fuzzy subsets of $U, A_1, A_2, \ldots, A_n$, such that

$$B = f(A), \tag{2.88}$$

where B is the fuzzy image (fuzzy set) of $A_1, A_2, \ldots, A_n$ through $f(\cdot)$. The fuzzy set B is defined by

$$B = \{(y, \mu_B(y)) \mid y = f(x_1, x_2, \ldots, x_n), (x_1, x_2, \ldots, x_n) \in U\}, \tag{2.89}$$

where

$$\mu_B(y) = \sup_{\substack{(x_1, x_2, \ldots, x_n) \in U \\ y = f(x_1, x_2, \ldots, x_n)}} \min[\mu_{A_1}(x_1), \mu_{A_2}(x_2), \ldots, \mu_{A_n}(x_n)], \tag{2.90}$$

with an additional condition that $\mu_B(y) = 0$ if there exists no $(x_1, x_2, \ldots, x_n) \in U$ such that $y = f(x_1, x_2, \ldots, x_n)$. Let us consider several numerical examples to illustrate this important extension principle.

Example 2.9

Let $U = \{1, 2, 3, 4, 5, 6, 7, 8, 9, 10\}$. A fuzzy set $A = $ "Large" is given as

$$A = \text{"Large"} = 0.5/6 + 0.7/7 + 0.8/8 + 0.9/9 + 1/10.$$

If the function f is a squaring operation and is indicated by $y = f(x) = x^2$, then by the extension principle, the fuzzy set $B = $ "Large"^{2} can be easily calculated as

$$B = \text{"Large"}^2 = 0.5/36 + 0.7/49 + 0.8/64 + 0.9/81 + 1/100.$$

Example 2.10

We are given $U = \{-2, -1, 0, 1, 2\}$ and a fuzzy set $A = \{(-1, 0.5), (0, 0.8), (1, 1), (2, 0.4)\}$. The function f is a squaring operation and is indicated by $y = f(x) = x^2$. It is easier to see if one constructs a table listing all the relevant information and calculations:

x	$\mu_A(x)$	$y = f(x) = x^2$	$\mu_B(y)$
-1	0.5	1	$\max\{0.5, 1.0\} = 1.0$
0	0.8	0	$\max\{0.8\} = 0.8$
1	1.0	1	$\max\{0.5, 1.0\} = 1.0$
2	0.4	4	$\max\{0.4\} = 0.4$

From the above calculations, it is obvious that we have two points (-1 and 1) in U mapped into a single point $y = 1$. The membership grade of $y = 1$ is taken as the maximum membership grade of $x = -1$ and $x = 1$, which gives us 1. Hence, the fuzzy image B is

$$B = 1/1 + 0.8/0 + 0.4/4.$$

Example 2.11

Suppose f is a function mapping ordered pairs from $U_1 = \{-1, 0, 1\}$ and $U_2 = \{-2, 2\}$ to $V = \{-2, -1, 2, 3\}$, and $f(x_1, x_2) = x_1^2 + x_2$. Let A_1 and A_2 be fuzzy sets defined on U_1 and U_2, respectively, such that $A_1 = 0.5/-1 + 0.1/0 + 0.9/1$ and $A_2 = 0.4/-2 + 1.0/2$. Use the extension principle to derive $f(A_1, A_2)$. The calculation process can be illustrated in the following table.

x_1	μ_{A_1}	x_2	μ_{A_2}	$\mu_{A_1 \times A_2}(x_1, x_2)$	$y = f(x_1, x_2) = x_1^2 + x_2$
-1	0.5	-2	0.4	$\min\{0.5, 0.4\}$	-1
-1	0.5	2	1.0	$\min\{0.5, 1.0\}$	3
0	0.1	-2	0.4	$\min\{0.1, 0.4\}$	-2
0	0.1	2	1.0	$\min\{0.1, 1.0\}$	2
1	0.9	-2	0.4	$\min\{0.9, 0.4\}$	-1
1	0.9	2	1.0	$\min\{0.9, 1.0\}$	3

From these table calculations, it is clear that we have two ordered pairs (-1, -2) and (1, -2) that map to the same point $y = -1$, and (-1, 2) and (1, 2) are mapped to the same point $y = 3$. Thus, their respective maximum membership grades must be taken.

$$\mu_B(y = -1) = \max\left[\min\left(\mu_{A_1}(x_1 = -1), \mu_{A_2}(x_2 = -2)\right), \min\left(\mu_{A_1}(x_1 = 1), \mu_{A_2}(x_2 = -2)\right)\right]$$

$$= \max\left[\min(0.5, 0.4), \min(0.9, 0.4)\right] = 0.4,$$

$$\mu_B(-2) = \max\left[\min\left(\mu_{A_1}(0), \mu_{A_2}(-2)\right)\right]$$

$$= \max\left[\min(0.1, 0.4)\right] = 0.1,$$

$$\mu_B(2) = \max\left[\min\left(\mu_{A_1}(0), \mu_{A_2}(2)\right)\right] = \max\left[\min(0.1, 1)\right] = 0.1,$$

$$\mu_B(3) = \max\left[\min\left(\mu_{A_1}(-1), \mu_{A_2}(2)\right), \min\left(\mu_{A_1}(1), \mu_{A_2}(2)\right)\right]$$

$$= \max\left[\min(0.5, 1), \min(0.9, 1)\right] = 0.9.$$

The fuzzy set B obtained from the extension principle is

$$B = 0.1/-2 + 0.4/-1 + 0.1/2 + 0.9/3.$$

Justification or proof of the extension principle based on Zadeh's rule of fuzzy compositional inference can be found in [Yager, 1986]. We shall next show some applications of the extension principle.

2.3.1 Operations of Type-2 Fuzzy Sets

The extension principle can be used to define the operations of intersections (e.g., an algebraic product), union (e.g., an algebraic sum), and complement of type-2 fuzzy sets. Let $\mu_A(x)$ and $\mu_B(x)$ be fuzzy grades for type-2 fuzzy sets A and B, respectively, and they are defined by

$$\mu_A(x) = \int f(u)/u, \qquad u \in [0, 1], \qquad \mu_B(x) = \int g(w)/w, \qquad w \in [0, 1], \qquad (2.91)$$

where f and g depend on x as well as on u or w. Using the extension principle, we have the following:

1. Min operator [$A \cap B$; see Eq. (2.56)]:

$$\mu_{A \cap B}(x) = \mu_A(x) \cap \mu_B(x) = \int f(u)/u \cap \int g(w)/w$$

$$= \int f(u) \wedge g(w)/u \wedge w. \qquad (2.92)$$

2. Max operator [$A \cup B$; see Eq. (2.63)]:

$$\mu_{A \cup B}(x) = \mu_A(x) \cup \mu_B(x) = \int f(u)/u \cup \int g(w)/w$$

$$= \int f(u) \wedge g(w)/u \vee w. \qquad (2.93)$$

3. Algebraic product [AB; see Eq. (2.57)]:

$$\mu_{AB}(x) = \mu_A(x) \cdot \mu_B(x) = \int f(u)/u \cdot \int g(w)/w$$

$$= \int f(u) \wedge g(w)/uw. \qquad (2.94)$$

4. Algebraic sum [$A \stackrel{+}{\wedge} B$; see Eq. (2.64)]:

$$\mu_{A \stackrel{+}{\wedge} B}(x) = \mu_A(x) \stackrel{+}{\wedge} \mu_B(x) = \int f(u) \wedge g(w)/u \stackrel{+}{\wedge} w$$

$$= \int f(u) \wedge g(w)/u + w - uw. \tag{2.95}$$

5. Complement ($\overline{A}$):

$$\mu_{\overline{A}}(x) = \overline{\mu_A(x)} = \int f(u)/(1 - u). \tag{2.96}$$

Example 2.12

Let $\mu_A(x) = 0.3/0.4 + 0.7/0.8$ and $\mu_B(x) = 0.1/0.1 + 0.5/0.2 + 1/0.4$. Then,

$$\mu_{AB}(x) = 0.3 \wedge 0.1/0.4 \times 0.1 + 0.3 \wedge 0.5/0.4 \times 0.2 + 0.3 \wedge 1/0.4 \times 0.4$$

$$+ 0.7 \wedge 0.1/0.8 \times 0.1 + 0.7 \wedge 0.5/0.8 \times 0.2 + 0.7 \wedge 1/0.8 \times 0.4$$

$$= 0.1/0.04 + 0.3/0.08 + 0.3/0.16 + 0.1/0.08 + 0.5/0.16 + 0.7/0.32$$

$$= 0.1/0.04 + 0.3/0.08 + 0.5/0.16 + 0.7/0.32.$$

2.3.2 Consistency Degree of Two Fuzzy Sets

By applying the extension principle to the equality of two fuzzy sets, we can define the consistency degree of two fuzzy sets A and B as

$$\sup_{x=y} \min (\mu_A(x), \mu_B(y)) = \text{Height}(A \cap B). \tag{2.97}$$

Example 2.13

Suppose John and Mary made an appointment to meet at 6:00 P.M. Let John's concept about six o'clock be denoted by the fuzzy set "6_{John}" which is shown in Fig. 2.7(a). Also, let Mary's concept about six o'clock be denoted by "6_{Mary}" which is shown in Fig. 2.7(b). Then the possibility that John and Mary will see each other can be determined by the consistency degree of "6_{John}" and "6_{Mary}" which is shown in Fig. 2.7(c).

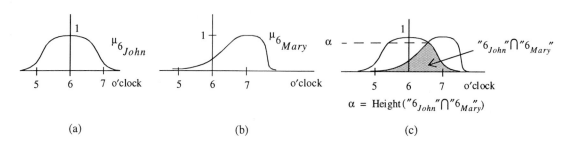

Figure 2.7 Membership functions used in Example 2.13.

Let fuzzy set A (B) denote the degree of membership of fuzzy set B in fuzzy set A. Using the extension principle, we have

$$\mu_{A(B)}(i) = \sup_{\substack{x \in U \\ \mu_A(x)=i}} (\mu_B(x)) \qquad \forall i \in [0, 1]. \qquad (2.98)$$

There are still many important applications of the extension principle such as *fuzzy arithmetic* in which the binary arithmetic operations of addition, subtraction, multiplication, and division are extended from simply operating on numbers to be applicable to fuzzy numbers (see Chap. 5). Such applications will appear in the proper context of this book from time to time. For example, the fuzzy cardinality of a fuzzy set defined in Eq. (2.23) is also an application of the extension principle.

2.4 CONCLUDING REMARKS

This chapter focuses on the basic concepts and notation of fuzzy sets. Fuzzy sets are introduced to establish a mathematical framework to deal with problems in which the source of imprecision is the absence of sharply defined criteria for defining class membership. This mathematical framework provides a solid foundation for studying vague conceptual phenomena precisely and vigorously.

It is important to know that fuzzy sets satisfy all the properties listed in Table 2.2. However, because of the unsharp boundary, fuzzy sets and their complements are overlapping and do not satisfy the excluded-middle laws (i.e., $A \cup \bar{A} \neq U$ and $A \cap \bar{A} \neq \varnothing$). Thus, if we want to choose fuzzy intersection and union operations that satisfy the excluded-middle laws, then the operations do not satisfy distributivity and idempotency.

Basic concepts in fuzzy sets are further extended to cover *t*-norms, *t*-conorms, and other types of fuzzy sets. Type-2 and level-2 fuzzy sets are briefly discussed. Other types of fuzzy sets that are not discussed but may be of interest include interval-valued fuzzy sets [Klir and Folger, 1988], probabilistic sets [Hirota, 1981], intuitionistic fuzzy sets [Atanassov, 1986], rough sets [Pawlak et al., 1988], and hybrid numbers [Kaufmann and Gupta, 1991].

t-norms and *t*-conorms are a class of fuzzy intersection and union operations that satisfy boundary conditions, commutativity, monotonicity, and associativity conditions. Several parameterized and nonparameterized *t*-norms and *t*-conorms are discussed. It is interesting to note that the *t*-norms are bounded above by the standard min operator and below by the drastic product, while the *t*-conorms are bounded above by the drastic sum operator and below by the standard max operator. Considering *t*-norms and *t*-conorms as aggregation operations on fuzzy sets, other aggregation operations that are bounded in between the standard min and max operators are discussed. Two such averaging operations are discussed: generalized means and weighted generalized means. Another effective averaging operator is the *multiplicative* γ *model* proposed by Zimmermann and Zysno [1980, 1983]. Finally, fuzzy set operations that are central to fuzzy logic and fuzzy reasoning are discussed, including fuzzy conjunction, fuzzy disjunction, and various fuzzy implications.

One of the most important tools of fuzzy set theory introduced by Zadeh is the extension principle, which allows any mathematical relationship between nonfuzzy elements to be extended to deal with fuzzy entities. This extension principle was applied to algebraic operations and used to define set-theoretic operations for higher-order fuzzy sets.

A thorough understanding of the topics covered in this chapter is essential to understanding future topics on fuzzy relations, fuzzy relation equations, fuzzy measures, possibility theory, fuzzy logic and approximate reasoning, and fuzzy logic control systems.

2.5 PROBLEMS

2.1 Determine the α-cuts of the following fuzzy sets A, B, and C.

$$A = \{(2,1),\ (3,0.8),\ (4,0.6),\ (5,0.4),\ (6,0.2),\ (7,0.4),\ (8,0.6),\ (9,0.8),\ (10,1)\},$$

$$\mu_B(x) = \frac{1}{1 + (x-10)^2} \qquad \text{for } \alpha = 0.2, 0.5;\ X = [0,\infty],$$

$$\mu_C(x) = \begin{cases} 0 & \text{for } x \le 10 \\ (1 + (x-10)^{-2})^{-1} & \text{for } x > 10 \end{cases} \qquad \text{for } \alpha = 0.2, 0.5;\ X = [0,\infty].$$

2.2 Using the resolution principle, express the following fuzzy sets in the form of Eq. (2.16):
   (a) $A = 0.1/2 + 0.4/3 + 0.5/4 + 0.6/5 + 1/7 + 1/8 + 0.5/9$,
   (b) $B = 0.1/-2 + 0.4/-1 + 0.1/2 + 0.9/3$,
   (c) $C = 0.1/0.04 + 0.3/0.08 + 0.5/0.16 + 0.7/0.32$.

2.3 Determine the convexity of the fuzzy sets A, B, and C in Prob. 2.1.

2.4 Show that a fuzzy set A is convex if and only if

$$\mu_A(\lambda x_1 + [1 - \lambda] x_2) \ge \min[\mu_A(x_1),\ \mu_A(x_2)],$$

where $x_1, x_2 \in U$, $\lambda \in [0,1]$.

2.5 Given the following fuzzy sets, verify whether they are also fuzzy numbers:
   (a) $0.1/1 + 0.8/2 + 0.9/3 + 0.4/4 + 0.5/5$,
   (b) $0.1/7 + 0.1/8 + 1/9 + 0.2/10 + 0.2/11$,
   (c) $\int_U \mu(x)/x$, where $\mu(x) = x$, $x \in U$, $U = [0,1]$,
   (d) $\int_U \mu(x)/x$, where $\mu(x) = x^2$, $x \in U$, $U = [0,1]$.

2.6 Show that the S function and the π function, defined in Eqs. (2.18) and (2.19), respectively, are fuzzy numbers.

2.7 Given fuzzy sets A and B as $A = 0.2/1 + 0.9/2 + 0.7/3 + 0.6/4 + 0.1/5$ and $B = 0.3/1 + 1.0/2 + 0.5/3 + 0.4/4 + 0.1/5$, compute:
   (a) The subsethood value $S(A,B)$ and $S(B,A)$,
   (b) Their fuzzy similarity measure $E(A,B)$,
   (c) Their difference, Difference $(A,B) \triangleq 1 - E(A,B)$.

2.8 Repeat the calculations in Prob. 2.7 for the following fuzzy sets A and B:

$$\mu_A(x) = \begin{cases} 2 - x & \text{if } 1 \le x < 2 \\ x & \text{if } 0 \le x < 1 \\ 0 & \text{otherwise,} \end{cases}$$

$$\mu_B(x) = \begin{cases} 3 - 2x & \text{if } 1 \le x < 1.5 \\ 1 & \text{if } -2 \le x < 1 \\ 0.5x + 2 & \text{if } -4 \le x < -2 \\ 0 & \text{otherwise.} \end{cases}$$

2.9 Given that A and B are fuzzy sets, prove the modular equality of fuzzy counting:

$$|A| + |B| = |A \cap B| + |A \cup B|.$$

2.10 Prove for fuzzy sets A and B,

$$E(A, B) = \frac{1}{[1/S(A,B)] + [1/S(B,A)] - 1}.$$

2.11 From Prob. 2.10, show that $0 \leq E(A, B) \leq 1$.

2.12 Show that the following fuzzy sets satisfy DeMorgan's laws:

(a) $\mu_A(x) = \dfrac{1}{1 + 2|x|}$,

(b) $\mu_B(x) = \left(\dfrac{1}{1 + 2|x|}\right)^{1/2}$.

2.13 Show that the double-negation law [Eq. (2.34)] and DeMorgan's laws [Eqs. (2.35)–(2.36)] hold for the λ complement and w complement [see Eqs. (2.52) and (2.53), respectively].

2.14 Show that the following complements, t-norms, and t-conorms satisfy the law of the excluded middle and the law of contradiction: [Note that $a \equiv \mu_A(x)$ and $b \equiv \mu_B(x)$. For fuzzy sets, the law of the excluded middle is $s(a, \bar{a}) = 1$ and the law of contradiction is $t(a, \bar{a}) = 0$.]
(a) $c(a) = 1 - a$; $t(a, b) = \max(0, a + b - 1)$, and $s(a, b) = \min(1, a + b)$,
(b) $c(a) = 1 - a$; $t(a, b) =$ drastic product, and $s(a, b) =$ drastic sum.

2.15 Find the equilibrium of λ complement and w complement operations.

2.16 Show that the Sugeno class complement defined in Eq. (2.52) is a fuzzy complement since it satisfies the four conditions: boundary conditions, monotonic property, continuity, and involution.

2.17 We are given six fuzzy sets A, B, C, D, E, and F as follows:

$$\mu_A(x) = \begin{cases} (x-2)/3 & 2 \leq x \leq 5 \\ (8-x)/3 & 5 < x \leq 8, \end{cases} \qquad \mu_B(x) = \begin{cases} (x-3)/3 & 3 \leq x \leq 6 \\ (9-x)/3 & 6 < x \leq 9, \end{cases}$$

$$\mu_C(y) = \begin{cases} (y-5)/3 & 5 \leq y \leq 8 \\ (11-y)/3 & 8 < y \leq 11, \end{cases} \qquad \mu_D(y) = \begin{cases} (y-4)/3 & 4 \leq y \leq 7 \\ (10-y)/3 & 7 < y \leq 10, \end{cases}$$

$$\mu_E(z) = \begin{cases} (z-1)/3 & 1 \leq z \leq 4 \\ (7-z)/3 & 4 < z \leq 7, \end{cases} \qquad \mu_F(z) = \begin{cases} (z-3)/3 & 3 \leq z \leq 6 \\ (9-z)/3 & 6 < z \leq 9. \end{cases}$$

Assume discrete universes for these fuzzy sets:
(a) Determine $A \cap B, C \cap D, E \cap F, A \cup B, C \cup D, E \cup F$.
(b) Calculate all the nonparametric t-norms such as intersection, algebraic product, bounded product, and drastic product for fuzzy sets A and B, C and D, and E and F.
(c) Calculate all the nonparametric t-conorms such as union, algebraic sum, bounded sum, and drastic sum for fuzzy sets A and B, C and D, and E and F.

2.18 Show that the Yager intersection defined by

$$t_w(a, b) = 1 - \min[1, ((1-a)^w + (1-b)^w)^{1/w}]$$

satisfies the following conditions: (a) $t_w(a, 0) = 0$, (b) $t_w(a, 1) = a$, (c) $t_w(a, a) \leq a$, (d) if $w_1 \leq w_2$, then $t_{w_1}(a, b) \leq t_{w_2}(a, b)$, (e) $\lim_{w \to 0} t_w(a, b) = t_{\min}(a, b)$.

2.19 Show that the Yager union defined by Eq. (2.68) satisfies the following properties:
(a) $\mu_{A \cup B}(x) = \mu_A(x)$ for $\mu_B(x) = 0$,
(b) $\mu_{A \cup B}(x) = 1$ for $\mu_B(x) = 1$,

(c) $\mu_{A \cup B}(x) \geq \mu_A(x)$ for $\mu_A(x) = \mu_B(x)$,

(d) The Yager union reduces to a drastic sum as $w \to 0$.

2.20 Show that the nonparametric t-conorms defined in Eqs. (2.63)–(2.67) are bounded by Eq. (2.70).

2.21 Various fuzzy implications are defined in Eqs. (2.78)–(2.82). Derive the formula for $\mu_{A \to B}(x, y)$ using the following t-norms and t-conorms:

(a) t = min operation, s = max operation,

(b) t = algebraic product, s = algebraic sum,

(c) t = bounded product, s = bounded sum.

2.22 Suppose f is a function mapping ordered pairs from $U_1 = \{-1, 0, 1\}$ and $U_2 = \{-2, 2\}$ to $V = \{-2, -1, 0, 1, 2, 4, 6, 9\}$, and $f(x_1, x_2) = x_1^2 + x_2^2 - 2x_1 x_2$. Let A_1 and A_2 be fuzzy sets defined on U_1 and U_2, respectively, such that $A_1 = 0.5/-1 + 0.1/0 + 0.9/1$ and $A_2 = 0.4/-2 + 1.0/2$. Use the extension principle to derive $B = f(A_1, A_2)$.

2.23 Suppose f_1 and f_2 are functions mapping ordered pairs from $U_1 = \{0, 0.1, 0.2, \ldots, 0.9, 1\}$ and $U_2 = \{0, 0.1, 0.2, \ldots, 0.9, 1\}$ to $V = \{0, 0.1, 0.2, \ldots, 0.9, 1\}$ where

$$f_1(x_1, x_2) = \max(1 - x_1, x_2),$$

$$f_2(x_1, x_2) = \max[1 - x_1, \min(x_1, x_2)],$$

and $x_1 \in U_1, x_2 \in U_2$. Let A_1 and A_2 be fuzzy sets defined on U_1 and U_2, respectively, such that

$$A_1 = 0.5/0.2 + 0.7/0.4 + 1/0.6,$$

$$A_2 = 0.8/0.5 + 0.5/0.7 + 0.7/0.9.$$

Use the extension principle to derive $f_1(A_1, A_2)$ and $f_2(A_1, A_2)$

2.24 Let the function f map ordered pairs from $U_1 = \{a, b, c\}$ and $U_2 = \{x, y, z\}$ to $V = \{p, q, r\}$. Let the function f be specified by a mapping matrix as follows:

$$f: \begin{array}{c} \\ a \\ b \\ c \end{array} \begin{array}{ccc} x & y & z \\ \left(\begin{array}{ccc} r & r & p \\ p & q & q \\ q & r & p \end{array}\right) \end{array}$$

From the elements of the mapping matrix f, we can identify the mapping function that results in the elements of the mapping matrix. Let A_1 and A_2 be fuzzy sets defined on U_1 and U_2, respectively,

$$A_1 = 0.2/a + 0.6/b + 0.8/c \qquad \text{and} \qquad A_2 = 0.5/x + 1/y + 0.3/z.$$

Use the extension principle to find the membership function of the fuzzy set $B = f(A_1, A_2)$.

2.25 Given $\mu_A(x)$ and $\mu_B(x)$ as in Example 2.12, calculate:

(a) $\mu_{A \cup B}(x)$, **(b)** $\mu_{A \cap B}(x)$, **(c)** $\mu_{A \hat{+} B}(x)$, **(d)** $\mu_{\bar{A}}(x)$.

3

Fuzzy Relations

A crisp binary relation represents the presence or absence of association, interaction, or interconnectedness between the elements of two sets. Fuzzy binary relations are a generalization of crisp binary relations to allow for various degrees of association between elements. Degrees of association can be represented by membership grades in a fuzzy binary relation in the same way that degrees of set membership are represented in the fuzzy set. Thus, fuzzy binary relations are in fact fuzzy sets. This chapter introduces basic concepts and operations on fuzzy relations, and both the relation-relation composition and the set-relation composition are studied via the max-min and min-max compositions. This eventually leads us to fuzzy relation equations which play an important role in areas such as fuzzy system analysis, design of fuzzy controllers, and fuzzy pattern recognition. Various notions of crisp relations such as equivalence and partial ordering are generalized to fuzzy similarity and fuzzy partial ordering.

3.1 BASICS OF FUZZY RELATIONS

The notion of relations is basic in science and engineering, which is essentially the discovery of relations between observations and variables. The traditional *crisp relation* is based on the concept that everything is either related or unrelated. Hence, a crisp relation represents the presence or absence of interactions between the elements of two or more sets. By generalizing this concept to allow for various degrees of interactions between elements, we obtain the *fuzzy relation*. Hence, a fuzzy relation is based on the philosophy that everything is related to some extent or unrelated. More specifically, crisp relations and fuzzy relations can be defined in terms of subsets.

A crisp relation among crisp sets $X_1, X_2, \ldots, X_n$ is a crisp subset on the Cartesian product $X_1 \times X_2 \times \cdots \times X_n$. This relation is denoted by $R(X_1, X_2, \ldots, X_n)$. Hence

$$R(X_1, X_2, \ldots, X_n) \subset X_1 \times X_2 \times \cdots \times X_n, \tag{3.1}$$

where

$$X_1 \times X_2 \times \cdots \times X_n = \{(x_1, x_2, \ldots, x_n) \mid x_i \in X_i \quad \text{for all } i \in \{1, \ldots, n\}\}. \tag{3.2}$$

It is interpreted that the relation R exists among $\{X_1, X_2, \ldots, X_n\}$ if the tuple $(x_1, x_2, \ldots, x_n)$ is in the set $R(X_1, X_2, \ldots, X_n)$; otherwise the relation R does not exist among $\{X_1, X_2, \ldots, X_n\}$. A fuzzy relation is a fuzzy set defined on the Cartesian product of crisp sets $\{X_1, X_2, \ldots, X_n\}$, where tuples $(x_1, x_2, \ldots, x_n)$ may have varying degrees of membership $\mu_R(x_1, x_2, \ldots, x_n)$ within the relation. That is,

$$R(X_1, X_2, \ldots, X_n) = \int_{X_1 \times X_2 \times \cdots \times X_n} \mu_R(x_1, x_2, \ldots, x_n)/(x_1, x_2, \ldots, x_n), \quad x_i \in X_i. \tag{3.3}$$

In the simplest case, consider two crisp sets X_1, X_2. Then

$$R(X_1, X_2) = \{((x_1, x_2), \mu_R(x_1, x_2)) \mid (x_1, x_2) \in X_1 \times X_2\} \tag{3.4}$$

is a fuzzy relation on $X_1 \times X_2$. It is clear that a fuzzy relation is basically a fuzzy set.

Example 3.1

Let $X = \{x_1, x_2\} = \{$New York City (NYC), Tokyo (TKO)$\}$ and $Y = \{y_1, y_2, y_3\} = \{$Taipei (TPE), Hong Kong (HKG), Bejing (BJI)$\}$. Let R represent the relation, "very close." If R is a crisp relation, it might be defined by the following characteristic function $\mu_R(x_i, y_j)$:

		y_1	y_2	y_3
		TPE	HKG	BJI
x_1	NYC	0	0	0
x_2	TKO	1	1	1

However, if R is considered a fuzzy relation, it may be defined as having the following membership function $\mu_R(x_i, y_j)$:

		y_1	y_2	y_3
		TPE	HKG	BJI
x_1	NYC	0.3	0.1	0.1
x_2	TKO	1	0.7	0.8

That is,

$$R(X, Y) = 0.3/(\text{NYC, TPE}) + 0.1/(\text{NYC, HKG}) + 0.1/(\text{NYC, BJI})$$

$$+ 1/(\text{TKO, TPE}) + 0.7/(\text{TKO, HKG}) + 0.8/(\text{TKO, BJI}).$$

Example 3.2

Let $X = Y = \Re^1$, the real line. For $x \in X, y \in Y$, the fuzzy relation $R \equiv$ "y is much larger than x" on $X \times Y$ can be defined by the following membership function:

$$\mu_R(x, y) = \begin{cases} 0 & \text{for } x \geq y \\ \dfrac{1}{1 + [5/(y - x)^2]} & \text{for } x < y. \end{cases}$$

A special fuzzy relation called a *binary (fuzzy) relation* plays an important role in fuzzy set theory. A binary fuzzy relation is a fuzzy relation between two sets X and Y and is denoted by $R(X, Y)$. When $X \neq Y$, binary relations $R(X, Y)$ are referred to as *bipartite graphs*. When $X = Y$, R is a binary fuzzy relation on a single set X, and the relations are referred to as *directed graphs,* or *digraphs,* and are denoted by $R(X, X)$ or $R(X^2)$. The relations defined in Examples 3.1 and 3.2 are both binary fuzzy relations. There are convenient forms of representation of binary fuzzy relations $R(X, Y)$ in addition to the membership function. Let $X = \{x_1, x_2, \ldots, x_n\}$ and $Y = \{y_1, y_2, \ldots, y_m\}$. First, the fuzzy relation $R(X, Y)$ can be expressed by an $n \times m$ matrix as

$$R(X, Y) = \begin{bmatrix} \mu_R(x_1, y_1) & \mu_R(x_1, y_2) & \cdots & \mu_R(x_1, y_m) \\ \mu_R(x_2, y_1) & \mu_R(x_2, y_2) & \cdots & \mu_R(x_2, y_m) \\ \vdots & \vdots & \ddots & \vdots \\ \mu_R(x_n, y_1) & \mu_R(x_n, y_2) & \cdots & \mu_R(x_n, y_m) \end{bmatrix}. \tag{3.5}$$

Such a matrix is called a *fuzzy matrix* and is used in Examples 3.1 and 3.2.

A binary fuzzy relation can also be expressed by a graph called a *fuzzy graph*. Each element in X and Y (denoted by x_i and y_j, respectively) corresponds to a vertex (node) in the fuzzy graph. Elements of $X \times Y$ with nonzero membership grades in $R(X, Y)$ are represented in the graph by links (arcs) connecting the respective vertices. These links are labeled with the value of the membership grade $\mu_R(x_i, y_j)$. When $X \neq Y$, each of the sets X and Y can be represented by a set of vertices such that vertices corresponding to one set are clearly distinguished from nodes representing the other set. In this case, the link connecting two vertices is an undirected link and the fuzzy graph is an undirected binary graph, which is called a *bipartite graph* in graph theory. On the other hand, when $X = Y$, the fuzzy graph can be reduced to a simpler graph in which only one set of vertices corresponding to set X is used. In this case, directed links are used and a vertex is possibly connected to itself. Such graphs are called *directed graphs.*

Example 3.3

Let $X = \{x_1, x_2, x_3, x_4\}$. Consider the following binary fuzzy relation on X:

$$R(X, X) = \begin{array}{c} \\ x_1 \\ x_2 \\ x_3 \\ x_4 \end{array} \begin{pmatrix} x_1 & x_2 & x_3 & x_4 \\ 0.3 & 0 & 0.7 & 0 \\ 0 & 1 & 0.9 & 0.6 \\ 0.2 & 0 & 0.5 & 0 \\ 0 & 0.3 & 0 & 1 \end{pmatrix}.$$

Then the bipartite graph and simple fuzzy graph of $R(X, X)$ are shown in Fig. 3.1(a) and (b), respectively.

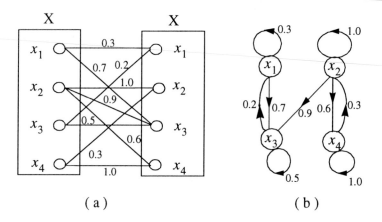

Figure 3.1 Graph representations of a binary fuzzy relation in Example 3.3. (a) Bipartite graph. (b) Simple fuzzy graph.

The *domain* of a binary fuzzy relation $R(X, Y)$ is the fuzzy set "dom $R(X, Y)$" with the membership function

$$\mu_{\text{domR}}(x) = \max_{y \in Y} \mu_R(x, y) \qquad \text{for each } x \in X. \tag{3.6}$$

The *range* of a binary fuzzy relation $R(X, Y)$ is the fuzzy set "ran $R(X, Y)$" with the membership function

$$\mu_{\text{ranR}}(y) = \max_{x \in X} \mu_R(x, y) \qquad \text{for each } y \in Y. \tag{3.7}$$

Analogous to the height of a fuzzy set, the *height* of a fuzzy relation R is a number $H(R)$ defined by

$$H(R) = \sup_{y \in Y} \sup_{x \in X} \mu_R(x, y). \tag{3.8}$$

If $H(R) = 1$, then R is a *normal* fuzzy relation; otherwise it is a *subnormal* fuzzy relation.

Similar to the resolution principle for fuzzy sets, every binary fuzzy relation $R(X, Y)$ can be represented in its *resolution form*

$$R = \bigcup_{\alpha \in \Lambda_R} \alpha R_\alpha, \tag{3.9}$$

where Λ_R is the level set of R and αR_α is defined as in Eq. (2.15). Hence, a fuzzy relation can be represented as a series of crisp relations comprising its α-cuts, each scaled by the value α.

Example 3.4

Consider the fuzzy relation

$$R = \begin{bmatrix} 0.4 & 0.5 & 0 \\ 0.9 & 0.5 & 0 \\ 0 & 0 & 0.3 \\ 0.3 & 0.9 & 0.4 \end{bmatrix}.$$

Using the resolution principle, R can be expressed as

$$R = 0.3R_{0.3} + 0.4R_{0.4} + 0.5R_{0.5} + 0.9R_{0.9}$$

$$= 0.3 \begin{bmatrix} 1 & 1 & 0 \\ 1 & 1 & 0 \\ 0 & 0 & 1 \\ 1 & 1 & 1 \end{bmatrix} + 0.4 \begin{bmatrix} 1 & 1 & 0 \\ 1 & 1 & 0 \\ 0 & 0 & 0 \\ 0 & 1 & 1 \end{bmatrix} + 0.5 \begin{bmatrix} 0 & 1 & 0 \\ 1 & 1 & 0 \\ 0 & 0 & 0 \\ 0 & 1 & 0 \end{bmatrix} + 0.9 \begin{bmatrix} 0 & 0 & 0 \\ 1 & 0 & 0 \\ 0 & 0 & 0 \\ 0 & 1 & 0 \end{bmatrix}.$$

3.2 OPERATIONS ON FUZZY RELATIONS

Since the fuzzy relation from X to Y is a fuzzy set in $X \times Y$, the operations for fuzzy sets discussed in Sec. 2.1 can be extended to fuzzy relations. In this section, we shall introduce some operations that are specific for fuzzy relations. Given a fuzzy relation $R(X, Y)$, let $[R \downarrow Y]$ denote the *projection* of R onto Y. Then $[R \downarrow Y]$ is a fuzzy set (relation) in Y whose membership function is defined by

$$\mu_{[R \downarrow Y]}(y) = \max_x \mu_R(x, y). \tag{3.10}$$

Since the standard max operation is a *t*-conorm, the above projection can be generalized by replacing the max operator with any *t*-conorm [see Eqs. (2.63)–(2.67)]. This projection concept can be extended to an *n*-ary relation $R(X_1, X_2, \ldots, X_n)$.

Example 3.5

Consider the fuzzy relation

$$
\begin{array}{c}
 & \begin{array}{ccccc} y_1 & y_2 & y_3 & y_4 & y_5 \end{array} \\
R(X, Y) = \begin{array}{c} x_1 \\ x_2 \\ x_3 \end{array} & \begin{pmatrix} 0.2 & 0.5 & 1 & 0 & 0.6 \\ 0.1 & 0 & 0.7 & 0.4 & 0 \\ 0.9 & 0.2 & 0 & 0.2 & 1 \end{pmatrix}.
\end{array}
$$

Then

$$[R \downarrow X] = 1/x_1 + 0.7/x_2 + 1/x_3,$$

$$[R \downarrow Y] = 0.9/y_1 + 0.5/y_2 + 1/y_3 + 0.4/y_4 + 1/y_5.$$

Consider a 3-ary (ternary) fuzzy relation. Let $X_1 = \{a, b\}$, $X_2 = \{c, d\}$, $X_3 = \{f, g\}$, and

$$R(X_1, X_2, X_3) = 0.3/acf + 0.7/adf + 0.1/bcg + 0.8/bdf + 1/bdg.$$

Then

$$R_{1,2} \equiv \left[R \downarrow \{X_1, X_2\} \right] = 0.3/ac + 0.7/ad + 0.1/bc + 1/bd,$$

$$R_{1,3} \equiv \left[R \downarrow \{X_1, X_3\} \right] = 0.7/af + 0.8/bf + 1/bg,$$

$$R_{2,3} \equiv \left[R \downarrow \{X_2, X_3\} \right] = 0.3/cf + 0.1/cg + 0.8/df + 1/dg,$$

$$R_1 \equiv [R{\downarrow}X_1] = 0.7/a + 1/b,$$

$$R_2 \equiv [R{\downarrow}X_2] = 0.3/c + 1/d,$$

$$R_3 \equiv [R{\downarrow}X_3] = 0.8/f + 1/g.$$

Given a fuzzy relation $R(X)$ or a fuzzy set R on X, let $[R{\uparrow}Y]$ denote the *cylindric extension* of R into Y. Then $[R{\uparrow}Y]$ is a fuzzy relation in $X \times Y$ with the membership function defined by

$$\mu_{[R{\uparrow}Y]}(x, y) = \mu_R(x) \qquad \text{for every } x \in X, y \in Y. \tag{3.11}$$

Equivalently, we can use the Cartesian product to define the cylindric extension. Assume $X \times Y$ is the whole Cartesian product space. Let R be a fuzzy set on X, where $X = \{x_1, x_2, ..., x_n\}$. Then the cylindric extension of R into $Y = \{y_1, y_2, ..., y_m\}$ can be obtained by

$$[R{\uparrow}Y] = R \times Y, \tag{3.12}$$

where we consider that $Y = 1/y_1 + 1/y_2 + \cdots + 1/y_m$. Similarly, if R is a fuzzy set on Y, then

$$[R{\uparrow}X] = X \times R. \tag{3.13}$$

For example, assume $X = \{x_1, x_2\}$ and $Y = \{y_1, y_2\}$. Let $R = \mu_R(x_1)/x_1 + \mu_R(x_2)/x_2$ and $Y = 1/y_1 + 1/y_2$. Then

$$[R{\uparrow}Y] = R \times Y = \mu_R(x_1)/(x_1, y_1) + \mu_R(x_1)/(x_1, y_2)$$
$$+ \mu_R(x_2)/(x_2, y_1) + \mu_R(x_2)/(x_2, y_2),$$

which is exactly what Eq. (3.11) states. The concept of cylindric extension can be used to extend an *r*-ary relation $R(X_1, X_2, ..., X_r)$ to an *n*-ary relation $R(X_1, X_2, ..., X_r, ..., X_n)$, where $n > r$.

Example 3.6

Continuing from Example 3.5, we have

$$[[R{\downarrow}X]{\uparrow}Y] = \begin{bmatrix} 1 & 1 & 1 & 1 & 1 \\ 0.7 & 0.7 & 0.7 & 0.7 & 0.7 \\ 1 & 1 & 1 & 1 & 1 \end{bmatrix},$$

$$[[R{\downarrow}Y]{\uparrow}X] = \begin{bmatrix} 0.9 & 0.5 & 1 & 0.4 & 1 \\ 0.9 & 0.5 & 1 & 0.4 & 1 \\ 0.9 & 0.5 & 1 & 0.4 & 1 \end{bmatrix}.$$

Also, the membership functions of the cylindric extension of $R_{1,2}$, $R_{1,3}$, $R_{2,3}$, and R_1 in Example 3.5 are

For example,

$$\mu_{[R_{1,2}{\uparrow}X_3]}(a, d, f) = \mu_{[R_{1,2}{\uparrow}X_3]}(a, d, g) = \mu_{R_{1,2}}(a, d) = 0.7.$$

	$[R_{1,2}\uparrow X_3]$	$[R_{1,3}\uparrow X_2]$	$[R_{2,3}\uparrow X_1]$	$[R_1\uparrow\{X_2, X_3\}]$
(a,c,f)	0.3	0.7	0.3	0.7
(a,c,g)	0.3	0	0.1	0.7
(a,d,f)	0.7	0.7	0.8	0.7
(a,d,g)	0.7	0	1	0.7
(b,c,f)	0.1	0.8	0.3	1
(b,c,g)	0.1	1	0.1	1
(b,d,f)	1	0.8	0.8	1
(b,d,g)	1	1	1	1

From Eq. (3.12), it is clear that the cylindric extension produces the "largest" fuzzy relation (in the sense of membership grades of elements of the extended Cartesian product) that is compatible with the given projection. The cylindric extension thus derives its *most nonspecific n*-dimensional relation from one of its *r*-dimensional projections, where $n > r$.

When we compare the fuzzy relation $R(X, Y)$ in Example 3.5 and $\big[[R\downarrow X]\uparrow Y\big]$ in Example 3.6, we find that they are quite different. In fact, fuzzy relations that can be reconstructed from one of their projections by cylindric extension are rather rare. In order to reconstruct a fuzzy relation that will be as close to its original relation as possible, it is desirable to reconstruct the fuzzy relation from several of its projections. The *cylindric closure* provides an approximate solution to this problem. Let $Y = Y_1 \times Y_2 \times \cdots \times Y_n$ be the whole Cartesian product space, where Y_i may be more than one dimension. Given a set of projections of a fuzzy relation $\{R_i | R_i$ is a projection on $Y_i, i \in [1, n]\}$, the *cylindric closure* of these projections, denoted as $\text{cyl}\{R_i\}$, is defined by

$$\text{cyl}\{R_i\} = \big[R_1\uparrow(Y - Y_1)\big] \cap \big[R_2\uparrow(Y - Y_2)\big] \cap \cdots \cap \big[R_n\uparrow(Y - Y_n)\big], \qquad (3.14)$$

where $(Y - Y_i)$ is the Cartesian product space without Y_i (i.e., $Y_1 \times Y_2 \times \cdots \times Y_{i-1} \times Y_{i+1} \times \cdots \times Y_n$) and the intersection $\cap$ can be any *t*-norm operator. However, the min operator is used if the max operator is used to determine the projections.

Example 3.7

The cylindric closures of $R_{1,2}, R_{1,3}$, and $R_{2,3}$ in Examples 3.5 and 3.6 are

$$\text{cyl}\{R_{1,2}, R_{1,3}, R_{2,3}\} = [R_{1,2}\uparrow X_3] \cap [R_{1,3}\uparrow X_2] \cap [R_{2,3}\uparrow X_1]$$
$$= 0.3/acf + 0.7/adf + 0.1/bcf + 0.1/bcg + 0.8/bdf + 1/bdg,$$

which is very close to the original relation $R(X_1, X_2, X_3)$ in Example 3.5.

It is noted that when we are restricted to the binary fuzzy relation $R(X, Y)$, the cylindric closure reduces to the Cartesian product in Eq. (2.38). That is, let $R_X \triangleq [R\downarrow X]$ and $R_Y \triangleq [R\downarrow Y]$, and then

$$\text{cyl}\{R_X, R_Y\} = [R_X\uparrow Y] \cap [R_Y\uparrow X]$$
$$= [R_X \times Y] \cap [X \times R_Y] \qquad (3.15)$$
$$= R_X \times R_Y.$$

It is clear that we have the relation $R(X, Y) \subseteq R_X \times R_Y$.

Example 3.8

Consider the relation $R(X, Y)$ used in Examples 3.5 and 3.6. We have

$$R_X \times R_Y = \left[[R \downarrow X] \uparrow Y\right] \cap \left[[R \downarrow Y] \uparrow X\right] = \begin{bmatrix} 0.9 & 0.5 & 1 & 0.4 & 1 \\ 0.7 & 0.5 & 0.7 & 0.4 & 0.7 \\ 0.9 & 0.5 & 1 & 0.4 & 1 \end{bmatrix}.$$

Comparing $R_X \times R_Y$ with $R(X, Y)$ in Example 3.5, we find that $R(X, Y) \subset R_X \times R_Y$.

For a fuzzy relation $R(X, Y)$, the *inverse* fuzzy relation $R^{-1}(X, Y)$ is defined by

$$\mu_{R^{-1}}(y, x) \triangleq \mu_R(x, y) \qquad \text{for all } (x, y) \in X \times Y. \tag{3.16}$$

Example 3.9

Let $R(X, Y)$ be a fuzzy relation on $X = \{x_1, x_2, x_3\}$ and $Y = \{y_1, y_2\}$ such that

$$R(X, Y) = \begin{array}{c} \\ x_1 \\ x_2 \\ x_3 \end{array} \begin{array}{cc} y_1 & y_2 \\ \begin{pmatrix} 0.2 & 1 \\ 0 & 0.4 \\ 0.8 & 0 \end{pmatrix} \end{array}.$$

Then

$$R^{-1}(X, Y) = R^T(X, Y) = \begin{array}{c} \\ y_1 \\ y_2 \end{array} \begin{array}{ccc} x_1 & x_2 & x_3 \\ \begin{pmatrix} 0.2 & 0 & 0.8 \\ 1 & 0.4 & 0 \end{pmatrix} \end{array}.$$

Another important operation of fuzzy relations is the composition of fuzzy relations. Basically, there are two types of composition operators: *max-min* and *min-max* compositions. These compositions can be applied to both *relation-relation* compositions and *set-relation* compositions. We shall first consider relation-relation compositions. Let $P(X, Y)$ and $Q(Y, Z)$ be two fuzzy relations on $X \times Y$ and $Y \times Z$, respectively. The *max-min composition* of $P(X, Y)$ and $Q(Y, Z)$, denoted as $P(X, Y) \circ Q(Y, Z)$, is defined by

$$\mu_{P \circ Q}(x, z) \triangleq \max_{y \in Y} \min \left[\mu_P(x, y), \mu_Q(y, z) \right] \qquad \text{for all } x \in X, z \in Z. \tag{3.17}$$

Dual to the max-min composition is the min-max composition. The min-max composition of $P(X, Y)$ and $Q(Y, Z)$, denoted as $P(X, Y) \square Q(Y, Z)$, is defined by

$$\mu_{P \square Q}(x, z) \triangleq \min_{y \in Y} \max \left[\mu_P(x, y), \mu_Q(y, z) \right] \qquad \text{for all } x \in X, z \in Z. \tag{3.18}$$

From the above definition, it is clear that the following relation holds:

$$\overline{P(X, Y) \square Q(Y, Z)} = \overline{P(X, Y)} \circ \overline{Q(Y, Z)}. \tag{3.19}$$

The max-min composition is the most commonly used. Equation (3.17) indicates that the max-min composition for fuzzy relations can be interpreted as indicating the strength of the existence of a relational chain between the elements of X and Z.

Example 3.10

Let $X = \{x_1, x_2\}$, $Y = \{y_1, y_2, y_3\}$, and $Z = \{z_1, z_2\}$. Given two fuzzy relations $P(X, Y)$ and $Q(Y, Z)$ as

$$P(X, Y) = \begin{array}{c} \\ x_1 \\ x_2 \end{array}\begin{array}{c} y_1 \quad y_2 \quad y_3 \\ \begin{pmatrix} 0.3 & 0 & 0.7 \\ 0.8 & 1 & 0.4 \end{pmatrix} \end{array}, \qquad Q(Y, Z) = \begin{array}{c} \\ y_1 \\ y_2 \\ y_3 \end{array}\begin{array}{c} z_1 \quad z_2 \\ \begin{pmatrix} 0.5 & 1 \\ 0 & 0.9 \\ 0.2 & 0.6 \end{pmatrix} \end{array}.$$

Then

$$P \circ Q = \begin{bmatrix} 0.3 & 0 & 0.7 \\ 0.8 & 1 & 0.4 \end{bmatrix} \circ \begin{bmatrix} 0.5 & 1 \\ 0 & 0.9 \\ 0.2 & 0.6 \end{bmatrix}$$

$$= \begin{bmatrix} (0.3 \wedge 0.5) \vee (0 \wedge 0) \vee (0.7 \wedge 0.2) & (0.3 \wedge 1) \vee (0 \wedge 0.9) \vee (0.7 \wedge 0.6) \\ (0.8 \wedge 0.5) \vee (1 \wedge 0) \vee (0.4 \wedge 0.2) & (0.8 \wedge 1) \vee (1 \wedge 0.9) \vee (0.4 \wedge 0.6) \end{bmatrix}$$

$$= \begin{array}{c} \\ x_1 \\ x_2 \end{array}\begin{array}{c} z_1 \quad z_2 \\ \begin{pmatrix} 0.3 & 0.6 \\ 0.5 & 0.9 \end{pmatrix} \end{array}.$$

The max-min composition can be generalized to other compositions by replacing the min operator with any t-norm operator. In particular, when the algebraic product of Eq. (2.57) is adopted, we have the *max product composition* denoted as $P(X, Y) \odot Q(Y, Z)$ and defined by

$$\mu_{P \odot Q}(x, z) \triangleq \max_{y \in Y} \left[\mu_P(x, y) \cdot \mu_Q(y, z) \right] \qquad \text{for all } x \in X, z \in Z. \tag{3.20}$$

Similarly, the min-max composition can be generalized to other compositions by replacing the max operator with any t-conorm operator. Since from Eqs. (2.69) and (2.70), the min operator is a maximal t-norm and the max operator is the smallest t-conorm, we obtain the following inequalities characterizing the range of all possible results of compositions:

$$\max_{y \in Y} t[\mu_P(x, y), \mu_Q(y, z)] \leq \max_{y \in Y} \min [\mu_P(x, y), \mu_Q(y, z)], \tag{3.21}$$

$$\min_{y \in Y} s[\mu_P(x, y), \mu_Q(y, z)] \geq \min_{y \in Y} \max [\mu_P(x, y), \mu_Q(y, z)]. \tag{3.22}$$

Similar to the properties of the composition of crisp binary relations, the max-min, max product, and min-max compositions have the following properties:

$$P \circ Q \neq Q \circ P, \tag{3.23}$$

$$(P \circ Q)^{-1} = Q^{-1} \circ P^{-1}, \tag{3.24}$$

$$(P \circ Q) \circ R = P \circ (Q \circ R). \tag{3.25}$$

Example 3.11

Assume there are four courses offered: fuzzy theory (FT), fuzzy control (FC), neural networks (NNs), and expert systems (ESs). Three students, Peter, Mary, and John, are planning to take one of these courses based on their different preferences for theory, application, hardware, and programming. We shall show that the composition of fuzzy relations can help them in their decision making.

Let $X = \{$Peter, Mary, John$\}$, $Y = \{y_1, y_2, y_3, y_4\} = \{$ theory, application, hardware, programming $\}$, and $Z = \{$FT, FC, NN, ES$\}$. Assume the student's interest is represented by the fuzzy relation $P(X, Y)$:

$$P(X, Y) = \begin{array}{c} \\ \text{Peter} \\ \text{Mary} \\ \text{John} \end{array} \begin{pmatrix} \begin{array}{cccc} y_1 & y_2 & y_3 & y_4 \\ 0.2 & 1 & 0.8 & 0.1 \\ 1 & 0.1 & 0 & 0.5 \\ 0.5 & 0.9 & 0.5 & 1 \end{array} \end{pmatrix}.$$

The properties of the courses are indicated by the fuzzy relation $Q(Y, Z)$:

$$Q(Y, Z) = \begin{array}{c} \\ y_1 \\ y_2 \\ y_3 \\ y_4 \end{array} \begin{pmatrix} \begin{array}{cccc} \text{FT} & \text{FC} & \text{NN} & \text{ES} \\ 1 & 0.5 & 0.6 & 0.1 \\ 0.2 & 1 & 0.8 & 0.8 \\ 0 & 0.3 & 0.7 & 0 \\ 0.1 & 0.5 & 0.8 & 1 \end{array} \end{pmatrix}.$$

Then, the max-min composition of $P(X, Y)$ and $Q(Y, Z)$ can help these students to choose the proper courses:

$$P \circ Q = \begin{array}{c} \\ \text{Peter} \\ \text{Mary} \\ \text{John} \end{array} \begin{pmatrix} \begin{array}{cccc} \text{FT} & \text{FC} & \text{NN} & \text{ES} \\ 0.2 & 1 & 0.8 & 0.8 \\ 1 & 0.5 & 0.6 & 0.5 \\ 0.5 & 0.9 & 0.8 & 1 \end{array} \end{pmatrix}.$$

Hence, Peter is encouraged to take the fuzzy control course, Mary should take the fuzzy theory course, and John should take the expert systems course.

As in the case of relation-relation compositions, we have max-min and min-max compositions for set-relation compositions. Let A be a fuzzy set on X and $R(X, Y)$ be a fuzzy relation on $X \times Y$. The *max-min composition* of A and $R(X, Y)$, denoted as $A \circ R(X, Y)$, is defined by

$$\mu_{A \circ R}(y) \triangleq \max_{x \in X} \min [\mu_A(x), \mu_R(x, y)] \qquad \text{for all } y \in Y. \qquad (3.26)$$

The dual composition, the *min-max composition* of A and $R(X, Y)$, is denoted as $A \,\square\, R(X, Y)$ and is defined by

$$\mu_{A \square R}(y) \triangleq \min_{x \in X} \max [\mu_A(x), \mu_R(x, y)] \qquad \text{for all } y \in Y. \qquad (3.27)$$

Again in more general definitions, the min operator of the max-min composition and the max operator of the min-max composition can be replaced by any *t*-norm and *t*-conorm, respectively. Furthermore, similar inequalities in Eqs. (3.21) and (3.22) can be obtained for set-relation compositions.

Finally, a similar operator on two binary fuzzy relations, called a *relational joint*, is introduced. It differs from the relation-relation composition in that it yields triples instead of pairs. Let $P(X, Y)$ and $Q(Y, Z)$ be two binary fuzzy relations. The relational joint of P and Q, denoted as $P \,\star\, Q$, is defined by

$$\mu_{P \star Q}(x, y, z) \triangleq \min [\mu_P(x, y), \mu_Q(y, z)]$$
$$\text{for each } x \in X, y \in Y, \text{ and } z \in Z. \qquad (3.28)$$

Like the max-min compositions, the min operator can be generalized by replacing it with any *t*-norm operator.

Example 3.12

Let fuzzy relations P and Q be defined as in Example 3.10. Then $P \star Q$ is defined as in the accompanying table

x	y	z	$\mu_{P \star Q}(x, y, z)$
x_1	y_1	z_1	0.3
x_1	y_1	z_2	0.3
x_1	y_3	z_1	0.2
x_1	y_3	z_2	0.6
x_2	y_1	z_1	0.5
x_2	y_1	z_2	0.8
x_2	y_2	z_2	0.9
x_2	y_3	z_1	0.2
x_2	y_3	z_2	0.4

3.3 VARIOUS TYPES OF BINARY FUZZY RELATIONS

In this section, we are concerned with binary fuzzy relations on a single set X. Various important types of binary fuzzy relations are distinguished on the basis of three different characteristic properties: reflexivity, symmetry, and transitivity. A fuzzy relation $R(X, X)$ is *reflexive* if and only if

$$\mu_R(x, x) = 1 \qquad \text{for all } x \in X. \tag{3.29}$$

If this is not the case for some $x \in X$, then $R(X, X)$ is *irreflexive*. If Eq. (3.29) is not satisfied for all $x \in X$, then the relation is called *antireflexive*.

A fuzzy relation $R(X, X)$ is *symmetric* if and only if

$$\mu_R(x, y) = \mu_R(y, x) \qquad \text{for all } x, y \in X. \tag{3.30}$$

If it is not satisfied for some $x, y \in X$, then the relation is called *asymmetric*. If the equality is not satisfied for all members of the support of the relation, then the relation is called *antisymmetric*. If Eq. (3.30) is not satisfied for all $x, y \in X$, then $R(X, X)$ is called *strictly antisymmetric*.

A fuzzy relation $R(X, X)$ is *transitive* (or, more specifically, *max-min transitive*) if and only if

$$\mu_R(x, z) \geq \max_{y \in X} \min [\mu_R(x, y), \mu_R(y, z)] \qquad \text{for all } (x, z) \in X^2. \tag{3.31}$$

If this is not true for some members of X, $R(X, X)$ is called *nontransitive*. If the inequality of Eq. (3.31) does not hold for all $(x, z) \in X^2$, then $R(X, X)$ is called *antitransitive*.

The max-min transitive can be generalized to alternative transitives by replacing the min operator with any *t*-norm. For example, using the algebraic product, we obtain the *max product transitive* which is defined by

$$\mu_R(x, z) \geq \max_{y \in X} [\mu_R(x, y) \mu_R(y, z)] \qquad \text{for all } (x, z) \in X^2. \tag{3.32}$$

Example 3.13

The following are examples of fuzzy relations that satisfy the above properties.

$$R_a = \begin{bmatrix} 1 & 0.8 & 0.3 \\ 0.3 & 1 & 0.6 \\ 0.4 & 0 & 1 \end{bmatrix}, \quad R_b = \begin{bmatrix} 0.3 & 1 & 0.9 \\ 0 & 0.7 & 0.2 \\ 0.5 & 0 & 0.3 \end{bmatrix}, \quad R_c = \begin{bmatrix} 1 & 0.5 & 0.7 \\ 0.5 & 0.3 & 0.1 \\ 0.7 & 0.1 & 0 \end{bmatrix},$$

$$R_d = \begin{bmatrix} 1 & 0 & 0.6 \\ 0 & 0.3 & 0.8 \\ 0.5 & 0.7 & 0.5 \end{bmatrix}, \quad R_e = \begin{bmatrix} 1 & 0 & 0.6 \\ 0.1 & 0.3 & 0.8 \\ 0.5 & 0 & 0.5 \end{bmatrix}, \quad R_f = \begin{bmatrix} 0.1 & 0.5 & 0.7 \\ 0 & 1 & 0.2 \\ 0 & 0.3 & 0.2 \end{bmatrix}.$$

It is clear that R_a is reflexive, R_b is antireflexive, R_c is symmetric, R_d is antisymmetric, R_e is strictly antisymmetric, and R_f is transitive. The fuzzy relation in R_f is transitive because

$$R_f = \begin{bmatrix} 0.1 & 0.5 & 0.7 \\ 0 & 1 & 0.2 \\ 0 & 0.3 & 0.2 \end{bmatrix} \supseteq \begin{bmatrix} 0.1 & 0.5 & 0.2 \\ 0 & 1 & 0.2 \\ 0 & 0.3 & 0.2 \end{bmatrix} = R_f \circ R_f.$$

Example 3.14

The fuzzy relation "x and y are very near" is reflexive, symmetric, and nontransitive. The fuzzy relation "x and y do not look alike" is antireflexive, symmetric, and nontransitive. The fuzzy relation "x is greatly smaller than y" is antireflexive, strictly antisymmetric, and transitive.

When a fuzzy relation $R(X, X)$ is nontransitive or antitransitive, we may want to find a transitive fuzzy relation that contains $R(X, X)$ and is minimum in the sense of membership grade. This is the transitive closure of a fuzzy relation. The *transitive closure* of a fuzzy relation $R(X, X)$ is denoted by $R_T(X, X)$; it is a fuzzy relation that is transitive and contains $R(X, X)$, and its elements have the smallest possible membership grades. When X has n elements, the transitive closure $R_T(X, X)$ can be obtained by

$$R_T(X, X) = R \cup R^2 \cup \cdots \cup R^n, \qquad \text{where } R^i = R^{i-1} \circ R, \ i \geq 2. \qquad (3.33)$$

Example 3.15

Let $X = \{x_1, x_2, x_3\}$ and let a fuzzy relation $R(X, X)$ be given as

$$R = \begin{bmatrix} 0.1 & 0.5 & 0.2 \\ 0.4 & 0.7 & 0.8 \\ 0 & 0.1 & 0.4 \end{bmatrix}.$$

Then the fuzzy closure of R can be obtained as follows:

$$R^2 = R \circ R = \begin{bmatrix} 0.4 & 0.5 & 0.5 \\ 0.4 & 0.7 & 0.7 \\ 0.1 & 0.1 & 0.4 \end{bmatrix}, \quad R^3 = \begin{bmatrix} 0.4 & 0.5 & 0.5 \\ 0.4 & 0.7 & 0.7 \\ 0.1 & 0.1 & 0.4 \end{bmatrix},$$

$$R_T(X, X) = R \cup R^2 \cup R^3 = \begin{bmatrix} 0.4 & 0.5 & 0.5 \\ 0.4 & 0.7 & 0.8 \\ 0.1 & 0.1 & 0.4 \end{bmatrix}.$$

From this example, it is noted that we do not need to calculate all the R^i, $i = 2, 3, \ldots, n$, in deriving the transitive closure of R. We can unify only the terms $R, R^2, \ldots, R^k$, when $R^{k+1} = R^k$.

We have discussed three variants of reflexivity, four variants of symmetry, and three variants of transitivity. By considering their combinations, a total of $3 \times 4 \times 3 = 36$ different types of binary fuzzy relations on a single set can be identified. Some important ones with their properties are shown in Table 3.1 and will be discussed in the following sections.

TABLE 3.1   Various Types of Binary Fuzzy Relations on a Single Set

	Property				
Fuzzy Relation	Reflexive	Antireflexive	Symmetric	Antisymmetric	Transitive
Similarity	X		X		X
Resemblance	X		X		
Partial ordering	X			X	X
Preordering	X				X
Strict ordering		X		X	X

3.3.1 Similarity Relations

A binary fuzzy relation that is reflexive, symmetric, and transitive is known as a *similarity relation*. Similarity relations are the generalization of *equivalence relations* in binary crisp relations to binary fuzzy relations. In order to understand similarity relations, we need to understand equivalence relations in binary crisp relations and then extend them to similarity relations.

A binary crisp relation $C(X, X)$ is called an equivalence relation if it satisfies the following conditions:

$$Reflexivity: \ (x, x) \in C(X, X) \ \text{for every } x \in X. \tag{3.34}$$

$$Symmetry: \ \text{If } (x, y) \in C(X, X), \text{ then } (y, x) \in C(X, X), \ x, y \in X. \tag{3.35}$$

$$Transitivity: \ \text{If } (x, y) \in C(X, X) \text{ and } (y, z) \in C(X, X),$$

$$\text{then } (x, z) \in C(X, X), \ x, y, z, \in X. \tag{3.36}$$

For each element x in X, one can define a crisp set A_x that contains all the elements of X that are related to x by the equivalence relation. That is,

$$A_x = \{ y \mid (x, y) \in C(X, X) \}. \tag{3.37}$$

Here, A_x is a subset of X. The element x is itself contained in A_x because of the reflexivity. Because $C(X, X)$ is transitive and symmetric, each member of A_x is related to all the other members of A_x. This set A_x is called an *equivalence class* of $C(X, X)$ with respect to x. Furthermore, the family of all such equivalence classes defined by the relation forms a *partition* on X and is denoted by $\pi(C)$.

Example 3.16

Let $X = \{-10, -9, \ldots, -1, 0, 1, \ldots, 10, 11, 12, 13, 14\}$. Let $C(X, X) = \{(x, y) \mid x = y \,(\text{mod } 5)\}$; that is, $(x - y)$ is divisible by 5. Then, clearly, $C(X, X)$ is an equivalence relation. There are exactly five equivalence classes in X:

$$A_0 = A_{-10} = A_{-5} = A_5 = A_{10} = \{-10, -5, 0, 5, 10\},$$

$$A_1 = A_{-9} = A_{-4} = A_6 = A_{11} = \{-9, -4, 1, 6, 11\},$$

$$A_2 = A_{-8} = A_{-3} = A_7 = A_{12} = \{-8, -3, 2, 7, 12\},$$

$$A_3 = A_{-7} = A_{-2} = A_8 = A_{13} = \{-7, -2, 3, 8, 13\},$$

$$A_4 = A_{-6} = A_{-1} = A_9 = A_{14} = \{-6, -1, 4, 9, 14\}.$$

The partition of X with respect to $C(X, X)$ is $\pi(C) = \{A_0, A_1, A_2, A_3, A_4\}$.

Hence, an equivalence relation $C(X, X)$ partitions the set X by putting those elements that are related to each other in the same equivalence class.

A similarity relation can be considered to effectively group elements into crisp sets whose members are "similar" to each other to some specified degree. Note that when this degree of similarity is 1, the grouping is then an equivalence class. This concept is clear when the similarity relation is represented in its resolution form [Eq. (3.9)], that is, $R = \bigcup_{\alpha \in \Lambda_R} \alpha R_\alpha$. Then each α-cut R_α is an equivalence relation representing the presence of similarity between the elements to the degree α. For this equivalence relation R_α, there is a partition on X, πR_α. Hence, each similarity relation is associated with the set

$$\pi(R) = \{\pi(R_\alpha) \mid \alpha \in \Lambda_R\} \tag{3.38}$$

of partitions.

Example 3.17

Let $X = \{x_1, x_2, x_3, x_4, x_5\}$. Consider the similarity relation $R(X, X)$:

$$
R = \begin{array}{c c} & \begin{array}{c c c c c} x_1 & x_2 & x_3 & x_4 & x_5 \end{array} \\
\begin{array}{c} x_1 \\ x_2 \\ x_3 \\ x_4 \\ x_5 \end{array} &
\left(\begin{array}{c c c c c}
1 & 0.7 & 0.3 & 0.6 & 0.7 \\
0.7 & 1 & 0.3 & 0.6 & 0.9 \\
0.3 & 0.3 & 1 & 0.3 & 0.3 \\
0.6 & 0.6 & 0.3 & 1 & 0.6 \\
0.7 & 0.9 & 0.3 & 0.6 & 1
\end{array}\right).
\end{array}
$$

Note that the relation matrix is symmetric. The level set $\Lambda_R = \{0.3, 0.6, 0.7, 0.9, 1\}$, and its associated R_α are

$$R_{0.3} = \begin{bmatrix} 1 & 1 & 1 & 1 & 1 \\ 1 & 1 & 1 & 1 & 1 \\ 1 & 1 & 1 & 1 & 1 \\ 1 & 1 & 1 & 1 & 1 \\ 1 & 1 & 1 & 1 & 1 \end{bmatrix}, \quad R_{0.6} = \begin{bmatrix} 1 & 1 & 0 & 1 & 1 \\ 1 & 1 & 0 & 1 & 1 \\ 0 & 0 & 1 & 0 & 0 \\ 1 & 1 & 0 & 1 & 1 \\ 1 & 1 & 0 & 1 & 1 \end{bmatrix}, \quad R_{0.7} = \begin{bmatrix} 1 & 1 & 0 & 0 & 1 \\ 1 & 1 & 0 & 0 & 1 \\ 0 & 0 & 1 & 0 & 0 \\ 0 & 0 & 0 & 1 & 0 \\ 1 & 1 & 0 & 0 & 1 \end{bmatrix},$$

$$R_{0.9} = \begin{bmatrix} 1 & 0 & 0 & 0 & 0 \\ 0 & 1 & 0 & 0 & 1 \\ 0 & 0 & 1 & 0 & 0 \\ 0 & 0 & 0 & 1 & 0 \\ 0 & 1 & 0 & 0 & 1 \end{bmatrix}, \quad R_1 = \begin{bmatrix} 1 & 0 & 0 & 0 & 0 \\ 0 & 1 & 0 & 0 & 0 \\ 0 & 0 & 1 & 0 & 0 \\ 0 & 0 & 0 & 1 & 0 \\ 0 & 0 & 0 & 0 & 1 \end{bmatrix}.$$

Hence, the equivalence classes for these equivalence relations are

$$\pi(R_1) = \{\{x_1\}, \{x_2\}, \{x_3\}, \{x_4\}, \{x_5\}\},$$
$$\pi(R_{0.9}) = \{\{x_1\}, \{x_2, x_5\}, \{x_3\}, \{x_4\}\},$$
$$\pi(R_{0.7}) = \{\{x_1, x_2, x_5\}, \{x_3\}, \{x_4\}\},$$
$$\pi(R_{0.6}) = \{\{x_1, x_2, x_4, x_5\}, \{x_3\}\},$$
$$\pi(R_{0.3}) = \{\{x_1, x_2, x_3, x_4, x_5\}\}.$$

The collection of these partitions, $\pi(R) = \{\pi(R_1), \pi(R_{0.9}), \pi(R_{0.7}), \pi(R_{0.6}), \pi(R_{0.3})\}$, can be shown in a treelike structure, called a *partition tree,* as in Fig. 3.2.

Similar to the equivalence class in an equivalence relation, we can also define a *similarity class* in a similarity relation. Let R be a similarity relation for $X = \{x_1, x_2, \ldots, x_n\}$. Then the similarity class for X_i, A_{x_i} is a fuzzy set in X with a membership function of

$$\mu_{A_{x_i}}(x_j) = \mu_R(x_i, x_j). \tag{3.39}$$

Hence, the similarity class for an element x represents the degree to which all the other members of X are similar to x.

3.3.2 Resemblance Relations

A binary fuzzy relation that is reflexive and symmetric is called a *resemblance relation.* It is obvious that similarity relations are a special case of resemblance relations. For example, the binary relation "look-alike" is reflexive and symmetric but not transitive, and so it is not a similarity relation but a resemblance relation.

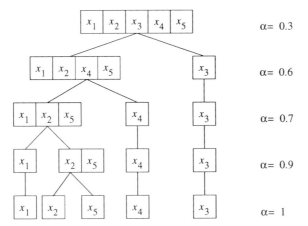

$\alpha = 0.3$

$\alpha = 0.6$

$\alpha = 0.7$

$\alpha = 0.9$

$\alpha = 1$ 　　**Figure 3.2** Partition tree in Example 3.17.

Let us express a resemblance relation $R(X, X)$ in its resolution form $R = \bigcup_{\alpha \in \Lambda_R} \alpha R_\alpha$. Similar to the equivalence class in equivalence relations, a *resemblance class* A_α corresponding to the α-cut R_α of the resemblance relation R can be defined as: A_α is a subset of X such that $\mu_R(x, y) \geq \alpha$ for all $x, y \in A_\alpha$ and it is not properly contained within any other resemblance class. The family consisting of all the resemblance classes A_α is called an α *cover* of X with respect to R_α. Hence, for each α-cut R_α there is an α cover of X that corresponds to the *partition* $\pi(C)$ of an equivalence relation C. However, because of the lack of transitivity, the resemblance classes in an α cover might not be disjoint. Furthermore, corresponding to the partition tree in similarity relations, there is a *complete α-cover tree* consisting of all α covers, $\alpha \in \Lambda_R$.

Example 3.18

Let $X = \{x_1, x_2, x_3, x_4, x_5\}$. Consider the following resemblance relation $R(X, X)$:

$$R(X, X) = \begin{array}{c} \\ x_1 \\ x_2 \\ x_3 \\ x_4 \\ x_5 \end{array} \begin{pmatrix} x_1 & x_2 & x_3 & x_4 & x_5 \\ 1 & 0.6 & 0.3 & 0.3 & 0.7 \\ 0.6 & 1 & 0.3 & 0.3 & 0.9 \\ 0.3 & 0.3 & 1 & 0.3 & 0.3 \\ 0.3 & 0.3 & 0.3 & 1 & 0.7 \\ 0.7 & 0.9 & 0.3 & 0.7 & 1 \end{pmatrix}.$$

Then the complete α-cover tree of R is shown in Fig. 3.3.

Since the only difference between resemblance relations and similarity relations is transitivity, we can obtain a similarity relation from a resemblance relation by applying the transitive closure R_T to the resemblance relation R.

3.3.3 Fuzzy Partial Ordering

A binary fuzzy relation R on a set X is a *fuzzy partial ordering* if and only if it is reflexive, antisymmetric, and transitive. A relation like "slightly less than or equal to" is a fuzzy partial ordering. Every partial ordering R can be conveniently represented by a directed graph called a *Hasse diagram*. This diagram can be derived from the simple fuzzy graph repre-

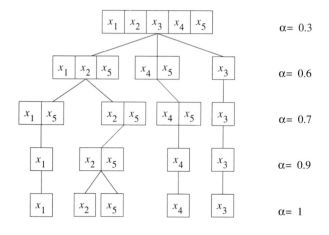

| $\alpha = 0.3$ |
| $\alpha = 0.6$ |
| $\alpha = 0.7$ |
| $\alpha = 0.9$ |
| $\alpha = 1$ |

Figure 3.3 Complete α-cover tree in Example 3.18.

sentation of R [see Fig. 3.1(b)] by omitting the directed link connecting a node to itself and the link $x_i \rightarrow x_j$ if there exist other nodes $x_{k_1}, x_{k_2}, \ldots, x_{k_n}$ such that $x_i \rightarrow x_{k_1} \rightarrow x_{k_i} \rightarrow \cdots \rightarrow x_{k_n} \rightarrow x_j$, where n can be equal to 1. Hence in a Hasse diagram, if there is a link from x_i to x_j, then x_j is called an *immediate successor* of x_i and x_i is an *immediate predecessor of x_j*.

Example 3.19

Consider the following fuzzy partial ordering $R(X, X)$ on X:

$$
R = \begin{array}{c@{\ }c}
& \begin{array}{cccccc} x_1 & x_2 & x_3 & x_4 & x_5 & x_6 \end{array} \\
\begin{array}{c} x_1 \\ x_2 \\ x_3 \\ x_4 \\ x_5 \\ x_6 \end{array} &
\left(\begin{array}{cccccc}
1 & 0.9 & 0.7 & 0.6 & 0.3 & 0.8 \\
0 & 1 & 0 & 0 & 0.3 & 0 \\
0 & 0 & 1 & 0 & 0.5 & 0 \\
0 & 0 & 0 & 1 & 0.6 & 0.8 \\
0 & 0 & 0 & 0 & 1 & 0 \\
0 & 0 & 0 & 0 & 0 & 1
\end{array} \right)
\end{array}.
$$

The simple fuzzy graph and Hasse diagram of R are shown in Fig. 3.4(a) and (b), respectively.

For a given partial ordering $R(X, X)$, two important fuzzy sets are associated with each element x in X. They are the dominating class of x and the dominated class of x. Given a fuzzy partial ordering $R(X, X)$ on X, the dominating class for an element x of X is denoted by $R_{\geq [x]}$ and is a fuzzy set in X defined by

$$\mu_{R_{\geq [x]}}(y) = \mu_R(x, y) \qquad y \in Y. \tag{3.40}$$

Similarly, the dominated class for element x of X is denoted by $R_{\leq [x]}$ and is a fuzzy set in X defined by

$$\mu_{R_{\leq [x]}}(y) = \mu_R(y, x) \qquad y \in Y. \tag{3.41}$$

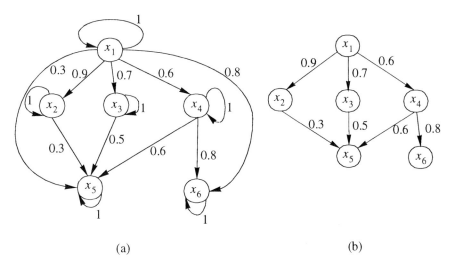

(a)   (b)

Figure 3.4   The simple fuzzy graph and Hasse diagram of a fuzzy ordering. (a) Simple fuzzy graph. (b) Hasse diagram.

Element x is called a *maximal* or *undominated element* if

$$\mu_R(x, y) = 0 \qquad \text{for all } y \in X \text{ and } y \neq x. \tag{3.42}$$

Element x is called a *minimal* or *undominating element* if

$$\mu_R(y, x) = 0 \qquad \text{for all } y \in X \text{ and } y \neq x. \tag{3.43}$$

For example, considering the fuzzy partial ordering in Fig. 3.4, x_5 and x_6 are maximal elements and x_1 is a minimal element.

Let R be a fuzzy partial ordering on X and let A be a crisp subset of X. The *fuzzy upper bound* of A is the fuzzy set $U(A)$ defined by

$$U(A) = \bigcap_{x \in A} R_{\geq [x]}, \tag{3.44}$$

where $\bigcap$ is a fuzzy intersection (t-norm) operation. The *least upper bound* of the set A, if it exists, is the unique element in $U(A)$ such that

$$\mu_{U(A)}(x) > 0 \qquad \text{and} \qquad \mu_R(x, y) > 0 \tag{3.45}$$

for all elements y in the support of $U(A)$. That is, the least upper bound of A is the smallest element of $U(A)$. In the same way, the *fuzzy lower bound* of A is the fuzzy set $L(A)$ defined by

$$L(A) = \bigcap_{x \in A} R_{\leq [x]}. \tag{3.46}$$

The *greatest lower bound* of the set A, if it exists, is the unique element in $L(A)$ such that

$$\mu_{L(A)}(x) > 0 \qquad \text{and} \qquad \mu_R(y, x) > 0$$

for all elements y in the support of $L(A)$. In other words, the greatest lower bound of A is the largest element of $L(A)$.

Example 3.20

Consider the fuzzy ordering in Example 3.19 (Fig. 3.4). Let $A = \{x_2, x_3, x_4\}$. Then we have

$$U(A) = R_{\geq [x_2]} \cap R_{\geq [x_3]} \cap R_{\geq [x_4]}$$

$$= (1/x_2 + 0.3/x_5) \cap (1/x_3 + 0.5/x_5) \cap (1/x_4 + 0.6/x_5 + 0.8/x_6)$$

$$= 0.3/x_5,$$

$$L(A) = R_{\leq [x_2]} \cap R_{\leq [x_3]} \cap R_{\leq [x_4]}$$

$$= (0.9/x_1 + 1/x_2) \cap (0.7/x_1 + 1/x_3) \cap (0.6/x_1 + 1/x_4)$$

$$= 0.6/x_1.$$

3.4 FUZZY RELATION EQUATIONS

The notion of fuzzy relation equations was first recognized and studied by Sanchez [1976]. Since then, many further studies have been done [Klir and Folger, 1988; Pedrycz, 1989]. Fuzzy relation equations play an important role in areas such as fuzzy system analysis, design of fuzzy controllers, decision-making processes, and fuzzy pattern recognition.

The notion of fuzzy relation equations is associated with the concept of composition of binary fuzzy relations, which includes both the set-relation composition and the relation-relation composition. Here we shall focus on the max-min composition because it has been studied extensively and has been utilized in numerous applications. Let A be a fuzzy set in X and $R(X, Y)$ be a binary fuzzy relation in $X \times Y$. The set-relation composition of A and R, $A \circ R$, results in a fuzzy set in Y. Let us denote the resulting fuzzy set as B. Then we have

$$A \circ R = B, \tag{3.47}$$

whose membership function, from Eq. (3.26), is

$$\mu_B(y) = \mu_{A \circ R}(y) \triangleq \max_{x \in X} \min \left[\mu_A(x), \mu_R(x, y) \right]. \tag{3.48}$$

Equation (3.47) is a so-called fuzzy relation equation. If we view R as a fuzzy system, A as a fuzzy input, and B as a fuzzy output, then we can consider Eq. (3.47) as describing the characteristics of a fuzzy system via its fuzzy input-output relation. This concept is shown in Fig. 3.5. Hence, given a fuzzy input A to a fuzzy system R, a fuzzy output B can be decided by Eq. (3.47). The basic problem concerning the fuzzy relation equation in Eq. (3.47) is that given any two items of A, B, and R, one can find the third. When A and R are given, the fuzzy set B can be easily determined using Eq. (3.48).

Example 3.21

Given a fuzzy set A in X and a fuzzy relation R in $X \times Y$ as follows,

$$A = 0.2/x_1 + 0.8/x_2 + 1/x_3 \equiv \begin{matrix} x_1 & x_2 & x_3 \\ (0.2 & 0.8 & 1) \end{matrix},$$

$$R = \begin{matrix} & y_1 & y_2 & y_3 \\ x_1 & \begin{pmatrix} 0.7 & 1 & 0.4 \\ x_2 & 0.5 & 0.9 & 0.6 \\ x_3 & 0.2 & 0.6 & 0.3 \end{pmatrix} \end{matrix},$$

we then have

$$B = A \circ R = \begin{matrix} x_1 & x_2 & x_3 \\ (0.2 & 0.8 & 1) \end{matrix} \circ \begin{matrix} & y_1 & y_2 & y_3 \\ x_1 & \begin{pmatrix} 0.7 & 1 & 0.4 \\ x_2 & 0.5 & 0.9 & 0.6 \\ x_3 & 0.2 & 0.6 & 0.3 \end{pmatrix} \end{matrix} = \begin{matrix} y_1 & y_2 & y_3 \\ (0.5 & 0.8 & 0.6) \end{matrix}$$

$$= 0.5/y_1 + 0.8/y_2 + 0.6/y_3.$$

Next, we shall study the following more difficult problems:

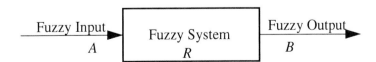

Figure 3.5 Fuzzy system with fuzzy input and fuzzy output.

Next, we shall study the following more difficult problems:

P1: Given A and B, determine R such that $A \circ R = B$.
P2: Given R and B, determine A such that $A \circ R = B$.

Since the solutions for the preceding problems may not exist, we first need to check the solvability of these equations or the existence of their solutions. Let us study P1 first.

Theorem 3.1

Problem P1 has solution(s) if and only if the height of the fuzzy set A is greater than or equal to the height of the fuzzy set B, that is,

$$\max_{x \in X} \mu_A(x) \geq \mu_B(y) \qquad \text{for all } y \in Y. \qquad (3.49)$$

Proof: If Eq. (3.49) does not hold, that is,

$$\max_{x \in X} \mu_A(x) < \mu_B(y) \qquad \text{for some } y \in Y,$$

then it is clear that we cannot find a $\mu_R(x, y)$ that will satisfy Eq. (3.48). Hence, a solution R does not exist. On the other hand, assume that Eq. (3.49) holds. Let $x^* \in X$ be the element at which $\mu_A(x^*)$ is maximal, that is, $\mu_A(x^*) = \max_{x \in X} \mu_A(x)$. If we define the membership function of R as $\mu_R(x^*, y) = \mu_B(y)$ for all $y \in Y$, and $\mu_R(x, y) = 0$ for all $x \in X$ and $x \neq x^*$ and for all $y \in Y$, then this R clearly satisfies Eq. (3.48). Hence, R is a solution to problem P1 and we can conclude that problem P1 has solution(s) if the inequality of Eq. (3.49) holds.

In order to solve problem P1 (and problem P2 later), we need to introduce the α-operation. For any $a, b \in [0, 1]$, the α-*operator* is defined as

$$a \, \alpha \, b \triangleq \begin{cases} 1 & \text{if } a \leq b \\ b & \text{if } a > b. \end{cases} \qquad (3.50)$$

For fuzzy sets A and B in X and Y, respectively, the α-composition of A and B forms a fuzzy relation $A \overset{\alpha}{\to} B$ in $X \times Y$ which is defined by

$$\mu_{A \overset{\alpha}{\to} B}(x, y) \triangleq \mu_A(x) \, \alpha \, \mu_B(y) = \begin{cases} 1 & \text{if } \mu_A(x) \leq \mu_B(y) \\ \mu_B(y) & \text{if } \mu_A(x) > \mu_B(y). \end{cases} \qquad (3.51)$$

Furthermore, the α-composition of a fuzzy relation R and a fuzzy set B is denoted by $R \overset{\alpha}{\to} B$ and is defined by

$$\mu_{R \overset{\alpha}{\to} B}(x) \triangleq \min_{y \in Y} [\mu_R(x, y) \, \alpha \, \mu_B(y)]. \qquad (3.52)$$

With the above α-operator and α-composition, the following properties will be useful for determining the solutions of problem P1.

Theorem 3.2

Let R be a fuzzy relation on $X \times Y$. For any fuzzy sets A and B in X and Y, respectively, we have

$$R \subseteq A \overset{\alpha}{\to} (A \circ R), \qquad (3.53)$$

$$A \circ (A \overset{\alpha}{\to} B) \subseteq B. \qquad (3.54)$$

Proof: Let us prove Eq. (3.53) first. Rewriting the right-hand side of Eq. (3.53) in terms of membership functions, we have

$$\mu_{A \overset{\alpha}{\hookrightarrow} (A \circ R)}(x, y) = \mu_A(x)\, \alpha \mu_{A \circ R}(y) = \mu_A(x)\, \alpha \left[\max_{z \in X} (\mu_A(z) \wedge \mu_R(z, y)) \right]$$

$$= \mu_A(x)\, \alpha \left\{ \max \left[\max_{z \in X,\, z \neq x} (\mu_A(z) \wedge \mu_R(z, y)),\, \mu_A(x) \wedge \mu_R(x, y) \right] \right\}$$

$$\geq \mu_A(x)\, \alpha\, [\mu_A(x) \wedge \mu_R(x, y)]$$

$$\geq \mu_R(x, y),$$

where $\wedge$ is used here for the min operation to simplify the notation. This proves Eq. (3.53). For Eq. (3.54), we have

$$\mu_{A \circ (A \overset{\alpha}{\hookrightarrow} B)}(y) = \max_{x \in X} [\mu_A(x) \wedge \mu_{A \overset{\alpha}{\hookrightarrow} B}(x, y)]$$

$$= \max_{x \in X} \{\mu_A(x) \wedge [\mu_A(x)\, \alpha \mu_B(y)]\}$$

$$\leq \mu_B(y).$$

Hence, Eq. (3.54) holds.

With the above properties, we can derive the following theorem.

Theorem 3.3

If the solution of problem P1 exists, then the largest R (in the sense of set-theoretic inclusion) that satisfies the fuzzy relation equation $A \circ R = B$ is $\hat{R}$

$$\hat{R} = A \overset{\alpha}{\hookrightarrow} B, \qquad (3.55)$$

whose membership function is given by Eq. (3.51).

Proof: From Eq. (3.54) in Theorem 3.2, we know that $A \circ \hat{R} \subseteq B$. From Eq. (3.53), we have $R \subseteq \hat{R}$. Then because of the monotonicity of max-min composition, we obtain $A \circ R \subseteq A \circ \hat{R}$, that is, $B \subseteq A \circ \hat{R}$. Since $A \circ \hat{R} \subseteq B$ from Eq. (3.54), we come up with the final equality $A \circ \hat{R} = B$. Moreover, since $R \subseteq \hat{R}$, $\hat{R}$ is the largest solution to the fuzzy relation equation $A \circ R = B$.

Example 3.22

From Example 3.21, we are given $A = 0.2/x_1 + 0.8/x_2 + 1/x_3$ and $B = 0.5/y_1 + 0.8/y_2 + 0.6/y_3$. Then we have

$$\hat{R} = A \overset{\alpha}{\hookrightarrow} B = \begin{matrix} x_1 \\ x_2 \\ x_3 \end{matrix} \begin{pmatrix} 0.2 \\ 0.8 \\ 1 \end{pmatrix} \overset{\alpha}{\hookrightarrow} \begin{matrix} y_1 & y_2 & y_3 \\ (0.5 & 0.8 & 0.6) \end{matrix} = \begin{matrix} & y_1 & y_2 & y_3 \\ x_1 & 1 & 1 & 1 \\ x_2 & 0.5 & 1 & 0.6 \\ x_3 & 0.5 & 0.8 & 0.6 \end{matrix}.$$

With the solution $\hat{R}$, it can be checked that $A \circ \hat{R} = B$ and $R \subset \hat{R}$, where R is given in Example 3.21.

Next, consider problem P2; that is, given R and B, determine A such that $A \circ R = B$. Similar to Theorems 3.1–3.3 for problem P1, the next three theorems characterize the solutions of problem P2.

Theorem 3.4

Problem P2 has no solution if the following inequality holds:

$$\max_{x \in X} \mu_R(x, y) < \mu_B(y) \qquad \text{for some } y \in Y. \tag{3.56}$$

The proof of this theorem is obvious by observing Eq. (3.48). This theorem allows us, in certain cases, to determine quickly that problem P2 has no solution. However, the converse of Eq. (3.56) is only a necessary and not a sufficient condition for the existence of a solution to problem P2.

Example 3.23

Consider the max-min composition of $A \circ R$:

$$A \circ R = [x_1, x_2, x_3] \circ \begin{array}{c} \\ x_1 \\ x_2 \\ x_3 \end{array} \overset{\begin{array}{cc} y_1 & y_2 \end{array}}{\begin{pmatrix} 0.8 & 0.5 \\ 1 & 0.7 \\ 0.3 & 0.2 \end{pmatrix}} = [0.5, 1] = B.$$

Since $\max_{x \in X} \mu_R(x, y_2) = \max[0.5, 0.7, 0.2] = 0.7 < \mu_B(y_2) = 1$, this set-relation equation has no solution. Consider another fuzzy set-relation equation:

$$A \circ R = [x_1, x_2, x_3] \circ \begin{array}{c} \\ x_1 \\ x_2 \\ x_3 \end{array} \overset{\begin{array}{cc} y_1 & y_2 \end{array}}{\begin{pmatrix} 1 & 1 \\ 1 & 1 \\ 1 & 1 \end{pmatrix}} = [0.5, 0.7] = B.$$

Although $\max_{x \in X} \mu_R(x, y_1) = 1 > \mu_B(y_1) = 0.5$ and $\max_{x \in X} \mu_R(x, y_2) = 1 > \mu_B(y_2) = 0.7$, there is obviously no solution to the above set-relation equation.

Theorem 3.5

Let R be a fuzzy relation on $X \times Y$. For any fuzzy sets A and B in X and Y, respectively, we have

$$(R \overset{\alpha}{\leftharpoonup} B) \circ R \subseteq B, \tag{3.57}$$

$$A \subseteq R \overset{\alpha}{\leftharpoonup} (A \circ R). \tag{3.58}$$

Proof: Let us prove Eq. (3.57) first [refer Eq. (3.52)]:

$$\mu_{(R \overset{\alpha}{\leftharpoonup} B) \circ R}(y) = \max_{x \in X} \left\{ \min_{y \in Y} \left[\mu_R(x, y) \, \alpha \mu_B(y) \right] \wedge \mu_R(x, y) \right\}$$

$$= \max_{x \in X} \left\{ \left[\min_{z \in Y, z \neq y} (\mu_R(x, z) \, \alpha \mu_B(z)) \wedge (\mu_R(x, y) \, \alpha \mu_B(y)) \right] \wedge \mu_R(x, y) \right\}$$

$$\leq \max_{x \in X} \left\{ [\mu_R(x, y) \, \alpha \mu_B(y)] \wedge [\mu_R(x, y)] \right\}$$

$$\leq \mu_B(y) \qquad \text{for all } y \in Y,$$

which completes the proof of Eq. (3.57). Again $\wedge$ is used in the above proof for the min operation to simplify the notation. For Eq. (3.58), we have

$$\mu_{R \overset{\alpha}{\leftrightarrow} (A \circ R)} (x)$$

$$= \min_{y \in Y} \left\{ \mu_R (x, y) \alpha \max_{x \in X} [\mu_A (x) \wedge \mu_R (x, y)] \right\}$$

$$= \min_{y \in Y} \left\{ \mu_R (x, y) \alpha \max \left[\max_{z \in X, z \neq x} (\mu_A (z) \wedge \mu_R (z, y)), \mu_A (x) \wedge \mu_R (x, y) \right] \right\}$$

$$\geq \min_{y \in Y} \left\{ \mu_R (x, y) \alpha [\mu_A (x) \wedge \mu_R (x, y)] \right\}$$

$$\geq \mu_A (x) \qquad \text{for every } x \in X,$$

which completes the proof of Eq. (3.58).

We are ready to derive the following theorem for the solution of problem P2.

Theorem 3.6

If a solution to problem P2 exists, then the largest fuzzy set A that satisfies $A \circ R = B$ is $\hat{A}$:

$$\hat{A} = R \overset{\alpha}{\leftrightarrow} B, \tag{3.59}$$

whose membership function is given by Eq. (3.52).

Proof: From Eq. (3.58), we have the relationship $A \subseteq R \overset{\alpha}{\leftrightarrow} B = \hat{A}$. Then because of the monotonicity of the max-min composition, we have $B = A \circ R \subseteq \hat{A} \circ R$. From Eq. (3.57), we obtain $\hat{A} \circ R \subseteq B$. Hence, $\hat{A} \circ R = B$. Moreover, since $A \subseteq \hat{A}$, $\hat{A}$ is the largest solution to $A \circ R = B$.

Example 3.24

From Example 3.21, we are given R and B. Then, have

$$\hat{A} = R \overset{\alpha}{\leftrightarrow} B = \begin{matrix} & y_1 & y_2 & y_3 \\ x_1 \\ x_2 \\ x_3 \end{matrix} \begin{pmatrix} 0.7 & 1 & 0.4 \\ 0.5 & 0.9 & 0.6 \\ 0.2 & 0.6 & 0.3 \end{pmatrix} \overset{\alpha}{\leftrightarrow} \begin{matrix} y_1 \\ y_2 \\ y_3 \end{matrix} \begin{pmatrix} 0.5 \\ 0.8 \\ 0.6 \end{pmatrix}$$

$$= \begin{pmatrix} 0.5 \wedge 0.8 \wedge 1 \\ 1 \wedge 0.8 \wedge 1 \\ 1 \wedge 1 \wedge 1 \end{pmatrix} = \begin{matrix} x_1 \\ x_2 \\ x_3 \end{matrix} \begin{pmatrix} 0.5 \\ 0.8 \\ 1 \end{pmatrix}.$$

From the solution $\hat{A}$ that we obtained, we can confirm that $\hat{A} \circ R = B$ and $A \subseteq \hat{A}$, where A is given in Example 3.21.

3.5 CONCLUDING REMARKS

In this chapter, the notion of fuzzy relations is introduced as a generalization of crisp relations. We mainly focus on the operations and compositions of fuzzy binary relations. Max-min and min-max compositions of both the relation-relation composition and the set-relation composition are addressed. The fuzzy relation equations addressed are based on the max-min composition, and the solution obtained is based on α composition. Several generalizations based on max t-norm composition and min s-norm composition can be found in [Pedrycz, 1989, 1990b, 1991], and the solutions can be obtained via π composition [Tsukamoto and Terano, 1977] and ω composition [Togai and Wang, 1985]. The methods for solving fuzzy relation equations introduced in this chapter strongly rely on a fundamental assumption that the family of solutions is nonempty. However, this assumption may not be easily satisfied in practical applications. When this assumption is violated, *approximate* solutions to fuzzy relation equations can be obtained. Details can be found in [Pedrycz, 1989, 1990b, 1991].

Another topic related to this chapter is *fuzzy functions*. A fuzzy function is a generalization of classical functions. There are several ways to view a fuzzy function, according to what is assumed to be fuzzy. There are crisp functions with a fuzzy domain and/or range, and fuzzy functions with crisp variables (i.e., blurring functions). Details on fuzzy functions can be found in [Dubois and Prade, 1979b] and [Zimmermann, 1991].

3.6 PROBLEMS

3.1 Consider the fuzzy relation

$$R\,(X,Y) = \begin{bmatrix} 0.3 & 0 & 0.7 & 0 \\ 0 & 1 & 0.9 & 0.6 \\ 0.2 & 0 & 0.5 & 0 \\ 0 & 0.3 & 0 & 1 \end{bmatrix}.$$

(a) What are the domain, range, and height of $R\,(X,Y)$?
(b) Express $R\,(X,Y)$ in its resolution form.

3.2 The following binary fuzzy relations are given:

$$R_1 = \begin{bmatrix} 0.4 & 0.5 & 0 \\ 0.9 & 0.5 & 0 \\ 0 & 0 & 0.3 \end{bmatrix}, \quad R_2 = \begin{bmatrix} 0.3 & 0 & 0.7 & 0 \\ 0 & 0.1 & 0.9 & 0.6 \\ 0.2 & 0 & 0.5 & 0 \\ 0 & 0.3 & 0 & 1 \end{bmatrix}.$$

Determine
(a) The domain, range, and height of the relations.
(b) The resolution forms of the relations.
(c) The inverse of the relations.

3.3 The following fuzzy relations are given:

$$M_1 = \begin{bmatrix} 0.5 & 1 & 0 \\ 0 & 0.7 & 0.3 \\ 0.2 & 0 & 1 \end{bmatrix} \quad M_2 = \begin{bmatrix} 0.4 & 0 & 0.4 \\ 0.3 & 1 & 0 \\ 0 & 0 & 1 \end{bmatrix} \quad M_3 = \begin{bmatrix} 1 & 0 & 0 \\ 0.8 & 0 & 1 \\ 0.9 & 0 & 0.3 \end{bmatrix}.$$

(a) Determine the domain of all the fuzzy relations.
(b) Determine the height of all the fuzzy relations.
(c) Express the domains and ranges in their resolution forms.

3.4 Draw a bipartite graph of the fuzzy relation R given in Example 3.5.

3.5 As in Example 3.5, what are the projections of the fuzzy relation R onto Y if other t-conorms such as algebraic sum, bounded sum, and drastic sum are used?

3.6 For the fuzzy relations given in Prob. 3.3, determine
  (a) All the projections.
  (b) Cylindric extensions and cylindric closure of the projections.

3.7 Prove that the max-min composition on binary fuzzy relations is associative.

3.8 Show that Eq. (3.19) holds.

3.9 Obtain the solution to min s-type fuzzy relation equations, which are counterparts of the max t-type fuzzy relation equations in Sec. 3.4.

3.10 Two fuzzy relations are given as

$$R_1 = \begin{bmatrix} 0 & 0.6 & 0.3 \\ 0 & 0.6 & 0.4 \\ 0 & 0 & 0.5 \end{bmatrix} \quad \text{and} \quad R_2 = \begin{bmatrix} 0.7 & 0.4 & 0.5 \\ 0 & 0.2 & 0.3 \\ 0 & 0 & 0 \end{bmatrix}.$$

Are these two fuzzy relations transitive?

3.11 Prove that under the inversion for both crisp and fuzzy relations, the symmetric, reflexivity, and transitivity properties are preserved.

3.12 Show that if R is transitive and reflexive, then $R \circ R = R$.

3.13 Show that if R is an $n \times n$ transitive relation and $\max_{x \in X} \max [\mu_R (x, y), \mu_R (y, x)] \le \mu_R (y, y)$ for any y, then $R^{n-1} = R^n$.

3.14 Prove the following statements:
  (a) If $R (X, X)$ is a strictly antisymmetric crisp relation, then $R \cap R^{-1} = \varnothing$.
  (b) If $R (X, X)$ is max-min transitive, then $R \circ R \subseteq R$.

3.15 Given is a similarity relation $R (X, X)$ on $X = \{a, b, c, d, e, f, g\}$, where its membership matrix is

$$
R (X, X) =
\begin{array}{c c}
& \begin{array}{c c c c c c c} a & b & c & d & e & f & g \end{array} \\
\begin{array}{c} a \\ b \\ c \\ d \\ e \\ f \\ g \end{array} &
\begin{bmatrix}
1 & 0.7 & 0.2 & 0.4 & 0.3 & 0.2 & 0.2 \\
0.7 & 1 & 0.2 & 0.4 & 0.3 & 0.2 & 0.2 \\
0.2 & 0.2 & 1 & 0.2 & 0.2 & 0.7 & 0.4 \\
0.4 & 0.4 & 0.2 & 1 & 0.3 & 0.2 & 0.2 \\
0.3 & 0.3 & 0.2 & 0.3 & 1 & 0.2 & 0.2 \\
0.2 & 0.2 & 0.7 & 0.2 & 0.2 & 1 & 0.4 \\
0.2 & 0.2 & 0.4 & 0.2 & 0.2 & 0.4 & 1
\end{bmatrix}.
\end{array}
$$

Draw its partition tree.

3.16 Given is a resemblance (or compatibility) relation $R (X, X)$ on a set X, where $X = \{x_1, x_2, x_3, x_4\}$ and its membership matrix is

$$
R (X, X) =
\begin{array}{c c}
& \begin{array}{c c c c} x_1 & x_2 & x_3 & x_4 \end{array} \\
\begin{array}{c} x_1 \\ x_2 \\ x_3 \\ x_4 \end{array} &
\begin{pmatrix}
1 & 0.8 & 0.3 & 0.3 \\
0.8 & 1 & 0.5 & 0.5 \\
0.3 & 0.5 & 1 & 0.3 \\
0.3 & 0.5 & 0.3 & 1
\end{pmatrix}.
\end{array}
$$

  (a) Find the α covers of the relation.
  (b) The transitive closure of R is a similarity relation. Find the α partitions and its partition tree.

3.17 Given is a fuzzy partial ordering $R(X, X)$ on a set X, where $X = \{x_1, x_2, x_3, x_4, x_5, x_6\}$ and its membership matrix is

$$
R(X, X) = \begin{array}{c} \\ x_1 \\ x_2 \\ x_3 \\ x_4 \\ x_5 \\ x_6 \end{array}
\begin{array}{cccccc}
x_1 & x_2 & x_3 & x_4 & x_5 & x_6 \\
\left(\begin{array}{cccccc}
1 & 0.8 & 0.3 & 0.6 & 0.6 & 0.4 \\
0 & 1 & 0.2 & 0.5 & 0.6 & 0.4 \\
0 & 0 & 1 & 0 & 0.5 & 0.6 \\
0 & 0 & 0 & 1 & 0.6 & 0.4 \\
0 & 0 & 0 & 0 & 1 & 0 \\
0 & 0 & 0 & 0 & 0 & 1
\end{array} \right)
\end{array}.
$$

(a) Find the fuzzy Hasse diagram.
(b) Find the fuzzy upper bound and lower bound of $\{x_2, x_3, x_4\}$.
(c) Find the least upper bound and the greatest lower bound if they exist.

3.18 Solve the following fuzzy relation equations, where $\circ$ indicates the max-min composition.

(a)
$$
A \circ \begin{array}{c} \\ x_1 \\ x_2 \\ x_3 \end{array}
\begin{array}{ccc}
y_1 & y_2 & y_3 \\
\left(\begin{array}{ccc}
0.9 & 0.6 & 1 \\
0.8 & 0.8 & 0.5 \\
0.6 & 0.4 & 0.6
\end{array} \right)
\end{array} = [0.6, 0.6, 0.5],
$$

(b)
$$
\begin{array}{c} x_1 \\ x_2 \\ x_3 \\ x_4 \end{array}
\left(\begin{array}{c}
0.5 \\ 0.6 \\ 0.4 \\ 0.2
\end{array} \right) \circ R =
\begin{array}{cccc}
y_1 & y_2 & y_3 & y_4 \\
(0.3 & 0.5 & 0.4 & 0.2).
\end{array}
$$

3.19 Given are two fuzzy sets A and B whose membership functions are

$$A = 0.2/x_1 + 0.8/x_2 + 1/x_3,$$
$$B = 0.5/y_1 + 0.8/y_2 + 0.6/y_3.$$

Determine R such that $A \circ R = B$.

3.20 Given is a fuzzy set B whose membership function is

$$B = 0.5/y_1 + 0.2/y_2 + 0.4/y_3 + 0.5/y_4.$$

If $A \circ R = B$, where the fuzzy relation R is

$$
R = \begin{array}{c} \\ x_1 \\ x_2 \\ x_3 \\ x_4 \end{array}
\begin{array}{cccc}
y_1 & y_2 & y_3 & y_4 \\
\left(\begin{array}{cccc}
0.4 & 0.7 & 0 & 0.2 \\
0 & 0.3 & 0 & 0.8 \\
0.2 & 0.8 & 0.5 & 0.6 \\
0.3 & 0.7 & 1 & 0
\end{array} \right)
\end{array},
$$

find the fuzzy set A.

4

Fuzzy Measures

Previous chapters have focused on the basic concepts and operations of fuzzy sets. The fuzzy set concept provides us with an intuitive method of representing one form of uncertainty, vagueness, by eliminating the sharp boundary that divides members of the class from nonmembers. In fuzzy sets, a value is assigned to each element x of the universal set X signifying its degree of membership in a particular set with unsharp (fuzzy) boundaries. This is useful in situations where it is not possible to draw crisp boundaries in deciding if a person is tall and in observing the shape of a growing animal cell in biology. However, in some decision-making situations such as judging if a defendant is guilty or not guilty, and in most measurements in physics such as measurements of length, area, and weight, classes are defined with sharp boundaries. In the trial example, it is obvious that the group of guilty persons and the group of innocent persons are crisp sets. For the length measurement case, represented by an interval of real numbers $[a, b]$ into n disjoint subintervals $[a, a_1)$, $[a_1, a_2)$, ..., $[a_{n-1}, b]$ according to the desired accuracy, we want to fit a measured length into one of the disjoint subintervals. Since the evidence for trial judgment is rarely perfect and measurement error is unavoidable in most physical sciences, some uncertainty usually prevails. To represent this kind of uncertainty, known as *ambiguity,* we assign a value in the unit interval $[0, 1]$ to each possible crisp set to which the element in question might belong. This value represents the degree of evidence or belief or certainty of the element's membership in the set. Such a representation of uncertainty is known as a *fuzzy measure*. Thus, a fuzzy measure assigns a value in the unit interval $[0, 1]$ to each crisp set of the universal set signifying the degree of evidence or belief that a particular element x belongs in the crisp set. Several different measures such as belief measures, plausibility measures, necessity measures, and possibility measures will be covered in this chapter. They are all functions applied to *crisp subsets,* instead of *elements,* of a universal set.

Let us discuss an example to distinguish the differences between fuzzy sets and fuzzy measures. Consider a group of people X. For fuzzy sets, the age of a person $x \in X$ is *known,* and consider x to be "Old" with a membership grade of $\mu_A(x)$, where A is a fuzzy set of "Old" people. On the other hand, for fuzzy measures, the age of the person $x \in X$ is unknown, and by looking at that person, we can consider him or her to be in the crisp set A consisting of people who are more than 50 years old with a measure of $g_x(A)$. The measure $g_x(A)$ is a fuzzy measure that assigns a value to each possible crisp set (i.e., each age group of people) to which the person in question might belong. So, in fuzzy sets, a value is assigned to each element of the universal set signifying its degree of membership in a particular set with an unsharp boundary, while in fuzzy measures, a value is assigned to each crisp set of the universal set signifying the degree of evidence or belief that a particular element belongs in the set. Thus, fuzzy sets are used to solve *vagueness* associated with the difficulty of making sharp or precise distinctions of objects in the world. On the other hand, fuzzy measures are used to solve *ambiguity* associated with making a choice between two or more alternatives. Note that the element x in a fuzzy set A has been *located* to A, while the element x in a fuzzy measure has *not* been previously located to the crisp set A. We shall study two important and well-developed special types of fuzzy measures, namely, belief and plausibility measures. These two measures are complementary and mutually dual, and one can be derived from the other. Then three special types of belief and plausibility measures—the well-known probability measure, the possibility measure, and the necessity measure will be discussed. Since the possibility measure has a strong relationship to fuzzy set theory, we shall briefly discuss their connection. We then study one related important topic, the fuzzy integral, based on which fuzzy measures of fuzzy sets are defined. Finally, measures of fuzziness, which evaluate the degree of fuzziness of fuzzy sets, will be discussed.

4.1 FUZZY MEASURES

In general, a fuzzy measure is defined by a (set) function

$$g: \quad \mathcal{P}(X) \rightarrow [0, 1], \tag{4.1}$$

which assigns to each crisp subset of a universe of discourse X a number in the unit interval $[0, 1]$, where $\mathcal{P}(X)$ is the power set of X. When this number is assigned to a crisp subset $A \in \mathcal{P}(X)$, $g(A)$ represents the degree of evidence or our belief that a given element $x \in X$ (which has not been previously located in any crisp subset of X) belongs to the crisp subset A. Notice that the domain of the function g is the power set $\mathcal{P}(X)$ of *crisp* subsets of X and not the power set $\mathcal{P}(X)$ of fuzzy subsets of X. A fuzzy measure as defined is obviously a set function. In order to qualify as a fuzzy measure, the function g must have certain properties; thus, a fuzzy measure is formally described as follows.

A fuzzy measure is a (set) function

$$g: \quad \mathcal{B} \rightarrow [0, 1], \tag{4.2}$$

where $\mathcal{B} \subset \mathcal{P}(X)$ is a family of crisp subsets of X and is a Borel field or a σ field and g satisfies the following three axioms of fuzzy measures:

Axiom g1 (*Boundary conditions*): $g(\varnothing) = 0$ and $g(X) = 1$.

Axiom g2 (*Monotonicity*): For every crisp set $A,B \in \mathcal{P}(X)$, if $A \subseteq B$, then $g(A) \leq g(B)$.

Axiom g3 (*Continuity*): For every sequence $(A_i \in \mathcal{P}(X) \mid i \in \mathcal{N})$ of subsets of X, if either $A_1 \subseteq A_2 \subseteq \cdots$ or $A_1 \supseteq A_2 \supseteq \cdots$ (i.e., the sequence is monotonic), then

$$\lim_{i \to \infty} g(A_i) = g\left(\lim_{i \to \infty} A_i\right) \tag{4.3}$$

where $\mathcal{N}$ is the set of all positive integers. A Borel field $\mathcal{B}$ or a σ field satisfies these properties: (1) $\varnothing \in \mathcal{B}$ and $X \in \mathcal{B}$; (2) if $A \in \mathcal{B}$, then $\overline{A} \in \mathcal{B}$; and (3) $\mathcal{B}$ is closed under the operation of set union; that is, if $A \in \mathcal{B}$ and $B \in \mathcal{B}$, then $A \cup B \in \mathcal{B}$.

In the above axioms, Axiom g1 states that we always know that the element in question definitely does not belong to the empty set and definitely does belong to the universal set. Axiom g2 requires that the degree of evidence of an element in a set (i.e., B) must be at least as great as the evidence that the element belongs to any subset of that set. Axiom g3 is applicable only to an infinite universal set and can be disregarded when we are dealing with a finite universal set. This axiom requires that function g is a continuous function.

The concept of fuzzy measures was introduced by Sugeno [1977] to exclude the *additivity* requirement of standard measures, h. The additivity requirement indicates that when two sets A and B are disjoint (i.e., $A \cap B = \varnothing$), then $h(A \cup B) = h(A) + h(B)$. The well-known probability measure has this additivity property. However, additivity is a strict condition that does not exist in many practical measures. Hence, fuzzy measures are defined by a weaker axiom of *subadditivity*, thus subsuming probability measures as a special type of fuzzy measure.

Let us explore some basic properties of fuzzy measures. Since $A \subseteq A \cup B$ and $B \subseteq A \cup B$, and because of the required monotonic property of the fuzzy measure g, we have

$$\max[g(A), g(B)] \leq g(A \cup B). \tag{4.4}$$

Similarly, since $A \cap B \subseteq A$ and $A \cap B \subseteq B$ and because of Axiom g2, we have

$$g(A \cap B) \leq \min[g(A), g(B)]. \tag{4.5}$$

4.1.1 Belief and Plausibility Measures

The belief measure is a special type of fuzzy measure that satisfies Axioms g1–g3 and an axiom of subadditivity. A belief measure is a function

$$\text{Bel:} \quad \mathcal{B} \to [0, 1] \tag{4.6}$$

that satisfies Axioms g1–g3 of fuzzy measures and the following *subadditivity* axiom (Axiom g4):

$$\text{Bel}(A_1 \cup A_2 \cup \cdots \cup A_n) \geq \sum_i \text{Bel}(A_i) - \sum_{i<j} \text{Bel}(A_i \cap A_j)$$
$$+ \cdots + (-1)^{n-1} \text{Bel}(A_1 \cap A_2 \cap \cdots \cap A_n) \tag{4.7}$$

for every $n \in \mathcal{N}$ and every collection of subsets of X, where $\mathcal{N}$ is the set of all positive integers.

For each crisp set $A \in \mathcal{B}(\subset \mathcal{P}(X))$, Bel($A$) is interpreted as the degree of belief that a given element of X belongs to the set A. Axiom g4 indicates that knowledge of Bel(A) and Bel(B) is not always sufficient to calculate Bel($A \cup B$). For $n = 2$, Axiom g4 has the form of

$$\text{Bel}(A_1 \cup A_2) \geq \text{Bel}(A_1) + \text{Bel}(A_2) - \text{Bel}(A_1 \cap A_2). \qquad (4.8)$$

Let us observe some properties of the belief measure. First, when the sets $A_1, A_2, \cdots$, A_n in X are pairwise disjoint (i.e., $A_i \cap A_j = \emptyset$ for all $i, j \in \{1, 2, ..., n\}, i \neq j$), Axiom g4 requires that

$$\text{Bel}(A_1 \cup A_2 \cup \cdots \cup A_n) \geq \text{Bel}(A_1) + \text{Bel}(A_2) + \cdots + \text{Bel}(A_n). \qquad (4.9)$$

This shows the *nonadditivity* (or *subadditivity*) of belief measures. Second, for $n = 2$, let $A_1 \equiv A$ and $A_2 \equiv \overline{A}$, and then Axiom g4 indicates

$$\text{Bel}(A_1 \cup A_2) = \text{Bel}(A \cup \overline{A}),$$

$$\text{Bel}(A \cup \overline{A}) \geq \text{Bel}(A) + \text{Bel}(\overline{A}) - \text{Bel}(A \cap \overline{A}).$$

Since $A \cup \overline{A} = X$ and $A \cap \overline{A} = \emptyset$, we have

$$\text{Bel}(X) \geq \text{Bel}(A) + \text{Bel}(\overline{A}) \qquad \text{or} \qquad \text{Bel}(A) + \text{Bel}(\overline{A}) \leq 1. \qquad (4.10)$$

Equation (4.10) indicates that a lack of belief in $x \in A$ does not imply a strong belief in $x \in \overline{A}$.

Associated with each belief measure one can define a plausibility measure Pl as

$$\text{Pl}(A) = 1 - \text{Bel}(\overline{A}) \qquad (4.11)$$

for all $A \in \mathcal{B}(\subset \mathcal{P}(X))$. Similarly, a belief measure can be defined in terms of plausibility measures,

$$\text{Bel}(A) = 1 - \text{Pl}(\overline{A}). \qquad (4.12)$$

Equations (4.11) and (4.12) show that belief measures and plausibility measures are mutually dual and that one can be derived from the other. However, plausibility measures can also be defined independently of belief measures.

A plausibility measure is a function

$$\text{Pl}: \quad \mathcal{B} \rightarrow [0, 1] \qquad (4.13)$$

that satisfies Axioms g1–g3 of fuzzy measures and the following additional *subadditivity* axiom (Axiom g5):

$$\text{Pl}(A_1 \cap A_2 \cap \cdots \cap A_n) \leq \sum_i \text{Pl}(A_i) - \sum_{i<j} \text{Pl}(A_i \cup A_j)$$

$$+ \cdots + (-1)^{n-1} \text{Pl}(A_1 \cup A_2 \cup \cdots \cup A_n), \qquad (4.14)$$

for every $n \in \mathcal{N}$ and every collection of subsets of X.

For $n = 2$, consider $A_1 \equiv A$ and $A_2 \equiv \overline{A}$; then we have

$$\text{Pl}(A \cap \overline{A}) \leq \text{Pl}(A) + \text{Pl}(\overline{A}) - \text{Pl}(A \cup \overline{A}), \qquad (4.15)$$

which leads to

$$\text{Pl}(A) + \text{Pl}(\overline{A}) \geq 1. \qquad (4.16)$$

This property can be compared with the property of belief measures expressed in Eq. (4.10).

Since the belief measure and the plausibility measure are mutually dual, it will be beneficial to express both of them in terms of a set function m, called a *basic probability assignment* (or simply a *basic assignment*).

The basic probability assignment m is a set function,

$$m: \; \mathcal{B} \rightarrow [0, 1], \tag{4.17}$$

such that

$$m(\varnothing) = 0 \qquad \text{and} \qquad \sum_{A \in \mathcal{B}} m(A) = 1. \tag{4.18}$$

The quantity $m(A) \in [0, 1]$, $A \in \mathcal{B}(\subset \mathcal{P}(X))$, is called A's basic probability number and is interpreted as the degree of evidence indicating that a specific element of X belongs to the set A but not to any special subset of A. It is interesting to point out that basic probability assignments are not fuzzy measures.

Since $m(A)$ measures the belief that one commits to the set A exactly and not the total belief that one commits to A, to obtain the total belief committed to A, one must add to $m(A)$ the quantities $m(B)$ for all proper subsets B of A. Thus, given a basic assignment m, a belief measure and a plausibility measure can be uniquely determined by

$$\text{Bel}(A) = \sum_{B \subseteq A} m(B) \tag{4.19}$$

and

$$\text{Pl}(A) = \sum_{B \cap A \neq \varnothing} m(B) \tag{4.20}$$

for all $A \in \mathcal{B}(\subset \mathcal{P}(X))$. It can be shown that the belief measure and the plausibility measure obtained from Eqs. (4.19) and (4.20) meet their respective requirements [Shafer, 1976]. From Eqs. (4.19) and (4.20), we can interpret the relationships among $m(A)$, Bel(A), and Pl(A) as follows:

1. $m(A)$ measures the belief that the element in question ($x \in X$) belongs to the set A *alone*, not the total belief that the element commits to A.
2. Bel(A) indicates the total evidence that the element ($x \in X$) belongs to the set A and to the various *special subsets* of A.
3. Pl(A) represents the total evidence or belief that the element ($x \in X$) belongs to the set A or to any of the various special subsets of A plus the additional evidence or belief associated with sets that *overlap* with A.

Hence, we have

$$\text{Pl}(A) \geq \text{Bel}(A) \geq m(A) \qquad \forall A \in \mathcal{B}. \tag{4.21}$$

Given a basic probability assignment m, one can uniquely find the corresponding belief and plausibility measures from Eqs. (4.19) and (4.20), respectively. Conversely, given a belief measure Bel, the corresponding basic assignment m can be recovered from the given belief measure [Shafer, 1976]:

$$m(A) = \sum_{B \subseteq A} (-1)^{|A-B|} \text{Bel}(B) \qquad \forall A \in \mathcal{B}, \tag{4.22}$$

where $|A - B|$ is the size or cardinality of $(A - B)$. Since Bel and Pl are mutually dual by Eq. (4.12), the corresponding basic assignment m can also be obtained from a given plausibility measure Pl:

$$m(A) = \sum_{B \subseteq A} (-1)^{|A-B|}[1 - \text{Pl}(\overline{B})] \qquad \forall A \in \mathcal{B}. \qquad (4.23)$$

Every set $A \in \mathcal{B}(\subset \mathcal{P}(X))$ for which $m(A) > 0$ is called a focal element of m. Focal elements are subsets of X on which the available evidence focuses. When X is finite, m can be fully characterized by a list of its focal elements A with the corresponding values $m(A)$. The pair $(\mathcal{F}, m)$ denotes a *body of evidence*, where $\mathcal{F}$ denotes a set of focal elements and m its associated basic assignment. Total ignorance is expressed in terms of the basic assignment by $m(X) = 1$ and $m(A) = 0$ for all $A \neq X$. That is, we know that the element is in the universal set, but we have no evidence about its location in any subset of X.

Example 4.1

Assume a doctor is trying to diagnose a disease. He or she is trying to determine whether the patient belongs to one of the sets of people with pneumonia (P), bronchitis (B), or emphysema (E). Let the universal set X denote the set of all possible diseases, and let P, B, and E be subsets of X (i.e., $X = P \cup B \cup E$). First, assume that the doctor, after examining the patient, provides the basic assignment as in the following table. Determine the corresponding belief measure and plausibility measure.

Focal Elements	$m(\cdot)$
P	0.05
B	0.05
E	0.05
$P \cup B$	0.15
$P \cup E$	0.1
$B \cup E$	0.05
$P \cup B \cup E$	0.55

Note that the summation of the given basic probability numbers must be equal to unity. Then, from Eq. (4.19), we can obtain the corresponding belief measure. For instance,

$\text{Bel}(P) = m(P) = 0.05, \text{Bel}(B) = m(B) = 0.05, \text{Bel}(E) = m(E) = 0.05,$

$\text{Bel}(P \cup B) = m(P \cup B) + m(P) + m(B) = 0.15 + 0.05 + 0.05 = 0.25,$

$\text{Bel}(P \cup E) = m(P \cup E) + m(P) + m(E) = 0.1 + 0.05 + 0.05 = 0.2,$

$\text{Bel}(B \cup E) = m(B \cup E) + m(B) + m(E) = 0.05 + 0.05 + 0.05 = 0.15,$

$\text{Bel}(P \cup B \cup E) = m(P \cup B \cup E) + m(P \cup B) + m(P \cup E) + m(B \cup E) + m(P) + m(B) + m(E) = 1.$

Note that $\text{Bel}(X = P \cup B \cup E) = 1$. Similarly, from Eq. (4.20), we can obtain the corresponding plausibility measure. For instance,

$\text{Pl}(P) = m(P) + m(P \cup B) + m(P \cup E) + m(P \cup B \cup E)$

$= 0.05 + 0.15 + 0.1 + 0.55 = 0.85,$

$\text{Pl}(B) = m(B) + m(P \cup B) + m(B \cup E) + m(P \cup B \cup E)$

$= 0.05 + 0.15 + 0.05 + 0.55 = 0.8,$

$$\text{Pl}(P \cup B) = m(P \cup B) + m(P) + m(B) + m(P \cup E) + m(B \cup E) + m(P \cup B \cup E)$$

$$= 0.15 + 0.05 + 0.05 + 0.1 + 0.05 + 0.55 = 0.95,$$

$$\text{Pl}(P \cup B \cup E) = m(P \cup B \cup E) + m(P) + m(B) + m(E)$$

$$+ m(P \cup B) + m(P \cup E) + m(B \cup E) = 1.$$

From the belief and plausibility measures that we have just obtained, Bel $(\overline{A})$ and Pl $(\overline{A})$ can be obtained using Eqs. (4.11) and (4.12), respectively. The corresponding belief and plausibility measures that we obtained are listed in the accompanying table.

Focal Elements	$m(A)$	Bel(A)	Pl(A)	Bel($\overline{A}$)	Pl($\overline{A}$)
P	0.05	0.05	0.85	0.15	0.95
B	0.05	0.05	0.8	0.2	0.95
E	0.05	0.05	0.75	0.25	0.95
$P \cup B$	0.15	0.25	0.95	0.05	0.75
$P \cup E$	0.1	0.2	0.95	0.05	0.8
$B \cup E$	0.05	0.15	0.95	0.05	0.85
$P \cup B \cup E$	0.55	1	1	0	0

Conversely, if the doctor provides the belief measure as in the third column of the above table, then we can obtain the basic assignment as in the second column of the above table using Eq. (4.22). For instance,

$$m(P) = (-1)^{|\varnothing|} \text{Bel}(P) = \text{Bel}(P) = 0.05,$$

$$m(P \cup E) = (-1)^{|\varnothing|} \text{Bel}(P \cup E) + (-1)^{|\{E\}|} \text{Bel}(P) + (-1)^{|\{P\}|} \text{Bel}(E)$$

$$= \text{Bel}(P \cup E) + (-1)\text{Bel}(P) + (-1)\text{Bel}(E)$$

$$= 0.2 - 0.05 - 0.05 = 0.1,$$

$$m(P \cup B \cup E) = (-1)^{|\varnothing|} \text{Bel}(P \cup B \cup E) + (-1)^{|\{E\}|} \text{Bel}(P \cup B) + (-1)^{|\{B\}|} \text{Bel}(P \cup E)$$

$$+ (-1)^{|\{P\}|} \text{Bel}(B \cup E) + (-1)^{|\{B, E\}|} \text{Bel}(P)$$

$$+ (-1)^{|\{P, E\}|} \text{Bel}(B) + (-1)^{|\{P, B\}|} \text{Bel}(E)$$

$$= \text{Bel}(P \cup B \cup E) - \text{Bel}(P \cup B) - \text{Bel}(P \cup E) - \text{Bel}(B \cup E) + \text{Bel}(P)$$

$$+ \text{Bel}(B) + \text{Bel}(E)$$

$$= 1 - 0.25 - 0.2 - 0.15 + 0.05 + 0.05 + 0.05 = 0.55.$$

The above discussion focuses on obtaining the belief and plausibility measures from given basic assignments, and vice versa, from a single source (or expert). Occasionally, for important decisions, we like to have a second opinion (or assessment) from another independent source or expert in the same area. Hence, it is important to be able to combine two basic assignments m_1 and m_2 on some power set $\mathcal{P}(X)$ that are evidence from two independent sources to obtain a joint basic probability assignment $m_{1,2}$. That is, we want to obtain a group decision from various experts based on the evidence or belief obtained by each expert independently. Then from the joint basic assignment $m_{1,2}$, the joint belief and joint plausibility measures can be computed using Eqs. (4.19) and (4.20), respectively. A standard way of combining evidence from two independent sources was proposed by Dempster and is called *Dempster's rule of combination* or the *Dempster-Shafer theory* [Shafer, 1976; Pearl, 1988].

Given two basic assignments m_1 and m_2 on $\mathcal{P}(X)$ from two independent sources, the Dempster-Shafer rule of combining two pieces of evidence is

$$m_{1,2}(C_k) = \frac{\displaystyle\sum_{A_i \cap B_j = C_k} m_1(A_i)\, m_2(B_j)}{1 - \displaystyle\sum_{A_i \cap B_j = \varnothing} m_1(A_i)\, m_2(B_j)} \qquad (4.24)$$

for $C_k \neq \varnothing$ and $m_{1,2}(\varnothing) = 0$, where A_i and B_j $(i, j = 1, 2, \ldots, n)$ are the focal points of m_1 and m_2, respectively. The denominator of Eq. (4.24) is a normalization factor, which is equal to the sum of products $m_1(A_i)\, m_2(B_j)$ for all focal elements A_i of m_1 and all focal elements B_j of m_2 such that their intersections $A_i \cap B_j \neq \varnothing$ (See Fig. 4.1). The numerator of Eq. (4.24) indicates that the degree of evidence $m_1(A_i)$ from the first source or expert that focuses on set $A_i \in \mathcal{P}(X)$ and the degree of evidence $m_2(B_j)$ from the second source or expert that focuses on set B_j are combined by taking the product $m_1(A_i)\, m_2(B_j)$, which focuses on their intersection $A_i \cap B_j$. Since some of these intersections may result in the same set C_k, we add all the corresponding products to obtain $m_{1,2}(C_k)$. To obtain a normalized joint basic assignment $m_{1,2}(C_k)$ as required, each of these products $m_1(A_i)\, m_2(B_j)$ must be divided by the normalization factor. When two or more basic assignments that have been inferred from independent evidence are combined, Eq. (4.24) is then used successively to obtain their joint basic assignment.

Example 4.2

Suppose two basic assignments m_1 and m_2, from two independent experts, are as given in the accompanying table. Determine the joint basic assignment.

Focal Elements	Expert 1 m_1	Expert 2 m_2	Combined Evidence $m_{1,2}$
A	0.1	0.3	0.276
B	0.3	0.4	0.517
$A \cup B$	0.6	0.3	0.207

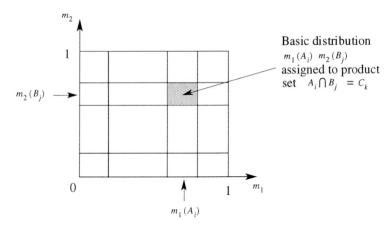

Figure 4.1   Dempster's combination rule for basic probability distribution.

To compute $m_{1,2}(C_k)$, we first need to calculate the normalization factor of Eq. (4.24):

$$1 - \sum_{A_i \cap B_j = \varnothing} m_1(A_i) m_2(B_j) = 1 - m_1(A) m_2(B) - m_1(B) m_2(A)$$

$$= 1 - (0.1)(0.4) - (0.3)(0.3) = 0.87.$$

Then the joint basic assignment of each crisp subset in $\mathscr{B}$ can be computed:

$$m_{1,2}(A) = \frac{1}{0.87}[m_1(A) m_2(A) + m_1(A) m_2(A \cup B) + m_1(A \cup B) m_2(A)]$$

$$= \frac{1}{0.87}(0.03 + 0.03 + 0.18) = 0.276,$$

$$m_{1,2}(B) = \frac{1}{0.87}[m_1(B) m_2(B) + m_1(B) m_2(A \cup B) + m_1(A \cup B) m_2(B)]$$

$$= \frac{1}{0.87}(0.12 + 0.09 + 0.24) = 0.517,$$

$$m_{1,2}(A \cup B) = \frac{1}{0.87}[m_1(A \cup B) m_2(A \cup B)] = \frac{1}{0.87}(0.18) = 0.207.$$

This example can also be explained "graphically" using Fig. 4.1. Using a matrix notation to represent Fig. 4.1 for this example and the data from the above table, we arrive at the following matrix:

$$A_i \cap B_j / m_1(A_i) \cdot m_2(B_j) \quad\quad A \quad\quad\quad\quad B \quad\quad\quad\quad A \cup B$$

$$\begin{array}{c} A \\ B \\ A \cup B \end{array} \begin{pmatrix} A/0.03 & \varnothing/0.04 & A/0.03 \\ \varnothing/0.09 & B/0.12 & B/0.09 \\ A/0.18 & B/0.24 & A \cup B/0.18 \end{pmatrix}$$

The nine elements in the above matrix correspond to all the possible intersections of all the focal elements $A_i \cap B_j$ and their corresponding products $m_1(A_i) \cdot m_2(B_j)$. Out of these nine cells, we have two cells with an empty set, three cells whose intersection results in set A, three cells whose intersection results in set B, and one cell whose intersection results in set $A \cup B$. The normalization factor can be obtained by subtracting the summation of the product of $m_1(\cdot)$ and $m_2(\cdot)$ from cells with empty sets from unity. To calculate the joint basic probability assignment for set A, $m_{1,2}(A)$, we sum the product of $m_1(\cdot)$ and $m_2(\cdot)$ from cells whose intersection results in set A; in this example, we have three such cells. Similarly, for $m_{1,2}(B)$, we sum the product of $m_1(\cdot)$ and $m_2(\cdot)$ from cells whose intersection results in set B, and again we have three such cells. Finally, to calculate $m_{1,2}(A \cup B)$, we have only one cell whose intersection results in set $A \cup B$. Note that to obtain the correct joint basic probability assignment, these products must be divided by the normalization factor.

In Eq. (4.24), A_i and B_j $(i, j = 1, 2, \ldots, n)$ are crisp subsets in $\mathscr{B}$. Without losing its essence, the Dempster-Shafer theory can be extended to handle fuzzy sets in X using the *similarity measure* $E(A, B)$ [in Eq. (2.30)] and the *subsethood measure* $S(A, B)$ [in Eq. (2.32)]. The similarity measure indicates the degree to which fuzzy sets A and B overlap each other, and the subsethood measure indicates the degree to which fuzzy set A is a subset of fuzzy set B. The similarity measure and the subsethood measure can be easily adopted into the Dempster-Shafer theory, and the belief and plausibility measures in Eqs. (4.19) and (4.20), respectively, can be extended to

$$\text{Bel}(A) = \sum_{B \subseteq X} S(B, A) m(B) \tag{4.25}$$

and

$$\text{Pl}(A) = \sum_{B \subseteq X} E(A, B) m(B). \tag{4.26}$$

Furthermore, the Dempster-Shafer rule of combination can be extended to handle evidence from fuzzy sets:

$$m_{1,2}(C_k) = \frac{\displaystyle\sum_{A_i, B_j} E(C_k, A_i \cap B_j) m_1(A_i) m_2(B_j)}{1 - \displaystyle\sum_{A_i, B_j} (1 - E(A_i, B_j)) m_1(A_i) m_2(B_j)}, \tag{4.27}$$

where $C_k \neq \varnothing$ and $m_{1,2}(\varnothing) = 0$. Another study on the extension of the Dempster-Shafer rule of combination to fuzzy sets can be found in [Yen, 1990a].

4.1.2 Probability Measures

When the axiom of subadditivity [Axiom g4 in Eq. (4.7)] for belief measures is replaced with a stronger axiom of additivity (Axiom g6),

$$\text{Bel}(A \cup B) = \text{Bel}(A) + \text{Bel}(B) \qquad \text{whenever } A \cap B = \varnothing; A, B \in \mathcal{B}, \tag{4.28}$$

we obtain the classical probability measures (or Bayesian belief measures). In other words, the belief measure becomes the classical probability measure under the axiom of additivity.

A probability measure is a function

$$P: \quad \mathcal{B} \to [0, 1], \tag{4.29}$$

that satisfies Axioms g1–g3 of fuzzy measures and the following axiom of *additivity* (Axiom g6):

$$P(A \cup B) = P(A) + P(B) \qquad \text{whenever } A \cap B = \varnothing; A, B \in \mathcal{B}. \tag{4.30}$$

With this axiom of additivity (Axiom g6), the following important theorem relates the belief measure and the basic assignment to the probability measure [Klir and Folger, 1988].

Theorem 4.1

A belief measure Bel on a finite Borel field $\mathcal{B}$, which is a subset of $\mathcal{P}(X)$, is a probability measure if and only if its basic probability assignment m is given by $m(\{x\}) = \text{Bel}(\{x\})$ and $m(A) = 0$ for all subsets of X that are not singletons.

Proof: The proof follows Klir and Folger [1988]. First, assume that Bel is a probability measure. It is trivial that $m(\varnothing) = 0$ from the definition of m. If set A is a singleton, from Eq. (4.19) we can easily obtain that $m(\{x\}) = \text{Bel}(\{x\})$. Now consider that A is not a singleton and let $A = \{x_1, x_2, \ldots, x_n\}$. Then from Axiom g6 [Eq. (4.28)], we obtain

$$\begin{aligned}
\text{Bel}(A) &= \text{Bel}(\{x_1\}) + \text{Bel}(\{x_2, x_3, \ldots, x_n\}) \\
&= \text{Bel}(\{x_1\}) + \text{Bel}(\{x_2\}) + \text{Bel}(\{x_3, x_4, \ldots, x_n\}) \\
&= \cdots = \text{Bel}(\{x_1\}) + \text{Bel}(\{x_2\}) + \cdots + \text{Bel}(\{x_n\}) \\
&= m(\{x_1\}) + m(\{x_2\}) + \cdots + m(\{x_n\}).
\end{aligned}$$

By comparing the above result with Eq. (4.19), we can conclude that the basic assignments of nonsingletons are zero since Bel is defined in terms of a basic assignment that focuses only on singletons.

Second, assume that a basic assignment m is given and that it focuses only on singletons. Then for any set A, $B \in \mathcal{B}$ such that $A \cap B = \emptyset$, we have

$$\text{Bel}(A) + \text{Bel}(B) = \sum_{x \in A} m(\{x\}) + \sum_{x \in B} m(\{x\})$$

$$= \sum_{x \in A \cup B} m(\{x\}) = \text{Bel}(A \cup B).$$

So Bel is a probability measure. This completes the proof.

Theorem 4.1 is very significant. It indicates that a probability measure on finite sets can be uniquely represented by a function defined on the elements of the universal set X rather than its subsets. That is, probability measures on finite sets can be fully represented by a function

$$p: X \rightarrow [0, 1] \qquad \text{such that } p(x) = m(\{x\}). \qquad (4.31)$$

This function $p(x)$ is called a *probability distribution function*.

When the basic assignments focus only on singletons, it can be shown, from Eqs. (4.19) and (4.20), that

$$\text{Bel}(A) = \sum_{B \subseteq A} m(B) = \sum_{x \in A} m(\{x\}) \quad \text{and} \quad \text{Pl}(A) = \sum_{B \cap A \neq 0} m(B) = \sum_{x \in A} m(\{x\}). \qquad (4.32)$$

Using Theorem 4.1 and Eq. (4.32), we have

$$P(A) = \text{Bel}(A) = \text{Pl}(A) = \sum_{x \in A} m(\{x\}) = \sum_{x \in A} p(x) \qquad \forall A \in \mathcal{B}. \qquad (4.33)$$

Hence, the dual belief and plausible measures merge under the axiom of additivity (Axiom g6) to the classical probability measure, and the probability measure can be computed from a given basic assignment (or from a given probability distribution function) using Eq. (4.33).

The above discussion shows that if a doctor diagnoses an illness as in Example 4.1 based on the probability measure, he or she will give only a probability value to each possible disease and will not consider the probability of a set of diseases. Within probability measures, total ignorance is expressed by the uniform probability distribution function (or basic assignment) $p(x) = m(\{x\}) = 1/|X|$ for all $x \in X$.

Given an arbitrary body of evidence $(\mathcal{F}, m)$, where the basic assignment m does not necessarily focus only on singletons, the corresponding plausibility and belief measures can be viewed as *upper* and *lower probabilities* that characterize a set of probability measures. Individual probability measures in this set can be defined by the following procedure:

1. Choose a particular element $x_A \in A$ for each $A \in \mathcal{F}$.
2. Set $P(\{x\}) = p(x) = \sum_{A \text{ with } x_A = x} m(A)$ for all $x \in X$.

For all the probability measures P that can be assigned according to the above procedure, the inequalities

$$\text{Bel}(A) \leq P(A) \leq \text{Pl}(A) \qquad (4.34)$$

hold for all $A \in \mathcal{F}$. Thus, the plausibility measure and the belief measure can be viewed as upper and lower probabilities, respectively [Dempster, 1967]. A body of evidence thus represents for each $A \in \mathcal{P}(X)$ the range [Bel(A), Pl(A)] of feasible probabilities.

4.1.3 Possibility and Necessity Measures

In the previous section, we discussed the probability measure as a special class of belief and plausibility measures by relaxing the axiom of subadditivity and replacing it with a stronger axiom of additivity. In this section, we shall discuss two subclasses of belief and plausibility measures that focus on *nested* focal elements.

A family of subsets of a universal set is *nested* if these subsets can be ordered in such a way that each is contained within the next; that is, $A_1 \subset A_2 \subset A_3 \subset \cdots \subset A_n, A_i \in \mathcal{P}(X)$, are nested sets. When the focal elements of a body of evidence $(\mathcal{F}, m)$ are nested, the associated belief and plausibility measures are called *consonant* since in this case the degrees of evidence allocated to them do not conflict with each other and the belief and plausibility measures are characterized by the following theorem [Klir and Folger, 1988].

Theorem 4.2

Given a consonant body of evidence $(\mathcal{F}, m)$, the associated consonant belief and plausibility measures possess the following properties:

$$\mathrm{Bel}(A \cap B) = \min [\, \mathrm{Bel}(A),\ \mathrm{Bel}(B)\,], \tag{4.35}$$

$$\mathrm{Pl}(A \cup B) = \max [\, \mathrm{Pl}(A),\ \mathrm{Pl}(B)\,], \tag{4.36}$$

for all $A, B \in \mathcal{B}\ (\subset \mathcal{P}(X))$.

Detailed proof of this theorem can be found in Klir and Folger [1988]. Let us illustrate this theorem by an example.

Example 4.3

We have $X = \{p, q, r, s\}$ and $\mathcal{B} = \mathcal{P}(X)$. The basic assignment m is given in the accompanying table. The focal elements of m are $\{q\}$, $\{q, s\}$, $\{q, r, s\}$, and $\{p, q, r, s\}$. Since $\{q\} \subset \{q, s\} \subset \{q, r, s\} \subset \{p, q, r, s\}$, the associated belief and plausibility measures are consonant, and they are computed using Eqs. (4.19) and (4.20), respectively. We can see that the properties in Theorem 4.2 hold. For instance,

	$m\,(\cdot)$	Bel $(\cdot)$	Pl $(\cdot)$
$\{p\}$	0	0	0.6
$\{q\}$	0.15	0.15	1
$\{r\}$	0	0	0.7
$\{s\}$	0	0	0.85
$\{p, q\}$	0	0.15	1
$\{p, r\}$	0	0	0.7
$\{p, s\}$	0	0	0.85
$\{q, r\}$	0	0.15	1
$\{q, s\}$	0.15	0.3	1
$\{r, s\}$	0	0	0.85
$\{p, q, r\}$	0	0.15	1
$\{p, q, s\}$	0	0.3	1
$\{q, r, s\}$	0.1	0.4	1
$\{p, r, s\}$	0	0	0.85
$\{p, q, r, s\}$	0.6	1	1

$$Bel(\{q\}) = Bel(\{q\} \cap \{q, r, s\}) = \min\left[Bel(\{q\}), Bel(\{q, r, s\})\right]$$
$$= \min\,(0.15, 0.4) = 0.15$$
$$Bel(\{q, s\}) = Bel(\{p, q, s\} \cap \{q, r, s\}) = \min\left[Bel(\{p, q, s\}), Bel(\{q, r, s\})\right]$$
$$= \min\,(0.3, 0.4) = 0.3$$
$$Pl(\{p, q\}) = Pl(\{p\} \cup \{q\}) = \max\left[Pl(\{p\}), Pl(\{q\})\right]$$
$$= \max\,(0.6, 1) = 1$$
$$Pl(\{p, r, s\}) = Pl(\{p\} \cup \{r, s\}) = \max\left[Pl(\{p\}), Pl(\{r, s\})\right]$$
$$= \max\,(0.6, 0.85) = 0.85$$

Consonant belief and plausibility measures are usually referred to as necessity and possibility measures and are denoted as N and Π, respectively. The possibility and necessity measures can also be defined independently.

The necessity measure N and the possibility measure Π are functions

$$N\colon\ \mathscr{B} \longrightarrow [0, 1], \tag{4.37}$$

$$\Pi\colon\ \mathscr{B} \longrightarrow [0, 1], \tag{4.38}$$

such that both N and Π satisfy Axioms g1–g3 of fuzzy measures and the following additional axiom (Axiom g7):

$$N(A \cap B) = \min\,(N(A), N(B)),$$
$$\Pi(A \cup B) = \max\,(\Pi(A), \Pi(B)) \qquad \forall A, B \in \mathscr{B}. \tag{4.39}$$

Since necessity and possibility measures are special subclasses of belief and plausibility measures, respectively, they are related to each other by [see Eqs. (4.11) and (4.12)]

$$\Pi(A) = 1 - N(\overline{A}) \qquad \text{and} \qquad N(A) = 1 - \Pi(\overline{A}) \qquad \forall A \in \mathscr{B}. \tag{4.40}$$

From Eqs. (4.39) and (4.40), the following properties can be easily obtained:

1.
$$\max\left(\Pi(A), \Pi(\overline{A})\right) = \Pi(A \cup \overline{A}) = \Pi(X) = 1, \tag{4.41}$$

   which expresses the fact that either A or $\overline{A}$ is completely possible.

2.
$$\min\left(N(A), N(\overline{A})\right) = N(A \cap \overline{A}) = 0, \tag{4.42}$$

   which expresses the fact that either A or $\overline{A}$ is not necessary at all or that a positive belief is never granted to both sides of a dichotomy at the same time.

3.
$$\Pi(A) \geq N(A) \qquad \forall A \subseteq \mathscr{B}, \tag{4.43}$$

   which follows from Eq. (4.21) and agrees with the intuition that an event becomes possible before becoming necessary.

4.
$$\text{If } N(A) > 0, \text{ then } \Pi(A) = 1,$$
$$\text{If } \Pi(A) < 1, \text{ then } N(A) = 0, \tag{4.44}$$

   which come from Eqs. (4.40)–(4.42). These two equations indicate that if an event is necessary, then it is completely possible. If it is not completely possible, then it is not necessary.

We shall study possibility measures only because necessity and possibility measures are mutually dual and one can be derived from the other using Eq. (4.40).

Like the probability measure and the probability distribution function, a possibility measure on finite sets can be uniquely represented by a possibility distribution function defined on the elements of the universal set rather than its subsets.

Theorem 4.3

Every possibility measure Π on $\mathcal{B} \subset \mathcal{P}(X)$ can be uniquely determined by a possibility distribution function

$$\pi: X \rightarrow [0, 1] \tag{4.45}$$

using the formula

$$\Pi(A) = \max_{x \in A} \pi(x) \qquad \forall A \in \mathcal{B}. \tag{4.46}$$

Proof: This can be proved by induction. Let $|A| = 1$, $A = \{x\}$, $x \in X$, and then Eq. (4.46) is trivially satisfied. Assume now that Eq. (4.46) is true for $|A| = n - 1$, and consider $|A| = n$ when $A = \{x_1, x_2, \ldots, x_n\}$. Then by Eq. (4.39),

$$\Pi(A) = \max[\Pi(\{x_1, x_2, \ldots, x_{n-1}\}), \Pi(\{x_n\})]$$

$$= \max\{\max[\Pi(\{x_1\}), \Pi(\{x_2\}), \ldots, \Pi(\{x_{n-1}\})], \Pi(\{x_n\})\}$$

$$= \max[\Pi(\{x_1\}), \Pi(\{x_2\}), \ldots, \Pi(\{x_n\})]$$

$$= \max_{x \in A} \pi(x).$$

Since the necessity and possibility measures are mutually dual, we can obtain the necessity measure from the possibility distribution function. From Eq. (4.40) and using Eq. (4.46), we have

$$N(A) = (1 - \Pi(\overline{A})) = 1 - \max_{x \notin A} \pi(x) = \min_{x \notin A} (1 - \pi(x)) = \min_{x \in \overline{A}} (1 - \pi(x)). \tag{4.47}$$

Equation (4.47) indicates the logic that "A is necessary" is equivalent to "non-A is not possible."

Example 4.4

Let $X = \{0, 1, 2, \ldots, 10\}$ and let $\pi(x)$ be the possibility distribution function that x is close to 8 and is defined by

x	0	1	2	3	4	5	6	7	8	9	10
$\pi(x)$	0	0	0	0	0	0.1	0.5	0.8	1	0.8	0.5

Note that it is not required that $\sum_{x \in X} \pi(x) = 1$. $\Pi(A)$ and $N(A)$ are the possibility and necessity measures that set A contains an integer close to 8, respectively, where $A \subset X$. For instance, when $A = \{2, 5, 9\}$, we have

$$\Pi(A) = \max_{x \in A} \pi(x) = \max\{\pi(2), \pi(5), \pi(9)\} = \max\{0, 0.1, 0.8\} = 0.8,$$

$$N(A) = \min_{x \in A} (1 - \pi(x)) = \min\{1 - \pi(0), 1 - \pi(1), 1 - \pi(3), 1 - \pi(4), 1 - \pi(6),$$

$$1 - \pi(7), 1 - \pi(8), 1 - \pi(10)\} = \min\{1, 1, 1, 1, 0.5, 0.2, 0, 0.5\} = 0.$$

Equations (4.20) and (4.23) show the relationships between plausibility measures and basic assignments. Next, we would like to find the relationship between the possibility distribution function and the basic assignment so that the possibility measure can be obtained from the basic assignment.

Let a possibility distribution function π be defined on a universal set $X = \{x_1, x_2, ..., x_n\}$. Then $\boldsymbol{\pi}_X = (\pi(x_1), \pi(x_2), ..., \pi(x_n))$ is called a possibility distribution associated with the function π. For convenience, the elements of X have been ordered in such a way that $\pi(x_i) \geq \pi(x_j)$ when $i < j$. We further assume that a possibility measure has been defined in $\mathcal{P}(X)$ in terms of its basic assignment m. This requires that the focal elements are nested, or without any loss of generality, that the focal elements are some or all of the subsets in the complete sequence of nested subsets

$$A_1 \subset A_2 \subset \cdots \subset A_n (=X),\qquad(4.48)$$

where $A_i = \{x_1, x_2, ..., x_i\}$, $i \in \{1, 2, ..., n\}$, and $\sum_{i=1}^{n} m(A_i) = 1$. Notice that it is not required that $m(A_i) \neq 0$ for all $i \in \{1, 2, ..., n\}$ (See Fig. 4.2). It follows from Eq. (4.46) and from the definition of possibility measures as consonant plausibility measures that

$$\pi(x_i) = \Pi(\{x_i\}) = \text{Pl}(\{x_i\}),\qquad(4.49)$$

for all $x_i \in X$. From Eq. (4.20) and because of the nested sets, we obtain a set of equations

$$\pi(x_i) = \text{Pl}(\{x_i\}) = \sum_{k=i}^{n} m(A_k),\qquad(4.50)$$

with one equation for each $i \in \{1, 2, ..., n\}$. Notice that from Eq. (4.50) and the definition of a basic assignment that $\sum_{i=1}^{n} m(A_i) = 1$, $\pi(x_1) = 1$ is true all the time. Expanding Eq. (4.50) explicitly for each $i \in \{1, 2, ..., n\}$ and solving the equations for $m(A_i)$ for each $i \in \{1, 2, ..., n\}$ by back substitution, we obtain

$$m(A_i) = \pi(x_i) - \pi(x_{i+1})\qquad(4.51)$$

for all $i \in \{1, 2, ..., n\}$, where $\pi(x_{n+1}) = 0$ by convention. Equations (4.46)–(4.51) show the relationship between possibility and necessity measures and basic assignments. Given a

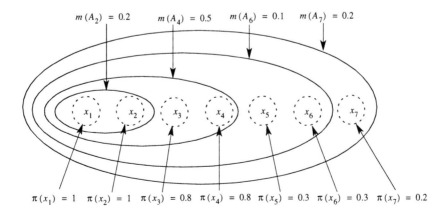

Figure 4.2 Nested focal elements of possibility measure in Example 4.5.

basic assignment, Eq. (4.50) can be used to compute the corresponding possibility distribution and Eqs. (4.46) and (4.47) can be used to calculate the possibility and necessity measures, respectively. Conversely, given a possibility distribution π_X, Eq. (4.51) can be used to calculate the corresponding basic assignment $m(A_i)$ for each $i \in \{1, 2, \ldots, n\}$.

Example 4.5

Let $X = \{x_1, x_2, \ldots, x_7\}$ and $A_1, A_2, \ldots, A_7$ be the complete sequence of nested subsets such that $A_1 \subset A_2 \subset \cdots \subset A_7$. The basic assignment is given as (see Fig. 4.2)

	A_1	A_2	A_3	A_4	A_5	A_6	A_7
$m(A_i)$	0	0.2	0	0.5	0	0.1	0.2

Using Eq. (4.50), we obtain the corresponding possibility distribution as in Fig. 4.2. For instance,

$$\pi(x_1) = \sum_{i=1}^{7} m(A_i) = 1, \qquad \pi(x_2) = \sum_{i=2}^{7} m(A_i) = 1,$$

$$\pi(x_3) = \sum_{i=3}^{7} m(A_i) = 0.8, \qquad \pi(x_4) = \sum_{i=4}^{7} m(A_i) = 0.8,$$

$$\pi(x_5) = \sum_{i=5}^{7} m(A_i) = 0.3, \qquad \pi(x_6) = \sum_{i=6}^{7} m(A_i) = 0.3,$$

$$\pi(x_7) = \sum_{i=7}^{7} m(A_i) = 0.2.$$

Then using Eq. (4.46), the possibility measure of a subset can be determined. For instance,

$$\Pi(\{x_1, x_2, x_3\}) = \max(\pi(x_1), \pi(x_2), \pi(x_3)) = \max\{1, 1, 0.7\} = 1,$$

$$\Pi(\{x_3, x_4, x_5\}) = \max(\pi(x_3), \pi(x_4), \pi(x_5)) = \max\{0.8, 0.8, 0.3\} = 0.8.$$

Conversely, if the possibility distribution $\pi_X = \{\pi(x_1), \pi(x_2), \ldots, \pi(x_7)\} = \{1, 1, 0.8, 0.8, 0.3, 0.3, 0.2\}$ is given, then using Eq. (4.51), the corresponding basic assignments can be obtained. For instance,

$$m(A_1) = \pi(x_1) - \pi(x_2) = 1 - 1 = 0,$$

$$m(A_2) = \pi(x_2) - \pi(x_3) = 1 - 0.8 = 0.2,$$

$$m(A_3) = \pi(x_3) - \pi(x_4) = 0.8 - 0.8 = 0,$$

$$m(A_4) = \pi(x_4) - \pi(x_5) = 0.8 - 0.3 = 0.5,$$

$$m(A_5) = \pi(x_5) - \pi(x_6) = 0.3 - 0.3 = 0,$$

$$m(A_6) = \pi(x_6) - \pi(x_7) = 0.3 - 0.2 = 0.1,$$

$$m(A_7) = \pi(x_7) - \pi(x_8) = 0.2 - 0 = 0.2,$$

where $\pi(x_8) = 0$ by convention.

The total ignorance is expressed in terms of the possibility distribution by $\pi(x_n) = 1$ and $\pi(x_i) = 0$ for $i = 1, \ldots, n - 1$, which corresponds to $\Pi(A_n) = \Pi(X) = 1$ and $\Pi(A) = 0$ for $A \neq A_n$ as described before.

In 1977 Zadeh developed the theory of possibility that relates fuzzy set theory to possibility distribution by defining a possibility distribution as a fuzzy restriction that acts as an elastic constraint on the values that may be assigned to a (fuzzy) variable [Zadeh, 1977]. Let F be a fuzzy set of a universe of discourse U with membership function $\mu_F(u)$ and let X be a (fuzzy) variable that takes values in U. F is a *fuzzy restriction* $R(X)$ associated with X if F acts as an elastic constraint on the values that may be assigned to X. Then the proposition "X is F," which translates into $R(X) = F$, associates a possibility distribution π_X with X, which is postulated to be equal to $R(X)$; that is,

$$\pi_X = R(X) = F. \tag{4.52}$$

$R(X) = F$ is called a *relational assignment equation* which assigns the fuzzy set F to the fuzzy restriction $R(X)$. In general, a relational assignment equation represents the assignment of a fuzzy set (or a fuzzy relation) to the restriction associated with X. The possibility distribution function associated with X (or the possibility distribution function of π_X) is denoted $\pi_X(u)$ and is defined to be numerically equal to the membership function $\mu_F(u)$ of F; that is,

$$\pi_X(u) = \mu_F(u) \qquad \forall u \in U. \tag{4.53}$$

Thus, $\pi_X(u)$, the possibility that $X = u$, is postulated to be equal to $\mu_F(u)$.

As a simple illustration, let U be the set of the integers $\{10, 20, \ldots, 80\}$, let F_1 be the fuzzy set "Young" defined by

$$\text{Young} = 1/10 + 0.8/20 + 0.5/30 + 0.2/40 + 0.1/50,$$

and let F_2 be the fuzzy set "Very Young" defined by

$$\text{Very Young} = 1/10 + 0.64/20 + 0.25/30 + 0.04/40 + 0.01/50.$$

Then the proposition "John is Young" (i.e., X is F_1) associates with $X \equiv \text{Age (John)}$ the possibility distribution

$$\pi_X = \pi_{\text{Age(John)}} = 1/10 + 0.8/20 + 0.5/30 + 0.2/40 + 0.1/50,$$

in which $\pi_X(30) = 0.5$ indicates that the possibility that "John is 30," given that John is Young, is 0.5. If the proposition is "John is Very Young" (i.e., X is F_2), then the possibility distribution is

$$\pi_X = \pi_{\text{Age(John)}} = 1/10 + 0.64/20 + 0.25/30 + 0.04/40 + 0.01/50,$$

in which $\pi_X(30) = 0.25$ indicates that the possibility that "John is 30," given that John is Very Young, is 0.25.

The concept of fuzzy restriction and the relational assignment equation are used to link fuzzy set theory with possibility theory by Zadeh [1978a]. Further discussions on the theory of possibility will continue in Chap. 5.

Finally, we shall briefly introduce another fuzzy measure g_λ, called a Sugeno measure. The motivation for defining this measure is that the specification of a fuzzy measure g requires the knowledge of $g(A)$ for all subsets A in X. In order to reduce the quantity of primary data, an extra axiom can be added to Axioms g1–g3 of fuzzy measures, which allows the calculation of $g(A)$ from $\{g(\{x\}) \mid x \in A\}$. This extra axiom proposed by Sugeno [1977] is: For all $A, B \in \mathcal{B}(\subset \mathcal{P}(X))$, if $A \cap B = \emptyset$, then

$$g_\lambda(A \cup B) = g_\lambda(A) + g_\lambda(B) + \lambda g_\lambda(A) g_\lambda(B), \tag{4.54}$$

where $\lambda > -1$ is a parameter by which different types of Sugeno measures are distinguished. It has been shown that Sugeno measures are belief measures for $\lambda > 0$, plausibility measures for $-1 < \lambda < 0$, and probability measures for $\lambda = 0$ [Wierzchon, 1982].

4.2 FUZZY INTEGRALS

Similar to an ordinary integral, a Lebesque integral, which is defined based on "measures," is used by Sugeno [1977] to define a fuzzy integral using fuzzy measures.

Let h be a mapping from X to $[0, 1]$. The fuzzy integral, in the sense of the fuzzy measure g, of h over a subset A of X is

$$\int_A h(x) \circ g = \sup_{\alpha \in [0, 1]} \min [\alpha, g(A \cap H_\alpha)], \qquad (4.55)$$

where $H_\alpha = \{x \in X \mid h(x) \geq \alpha\}$. In this definition, A is called the domain of integration. If $h = a \in [0, 1]$ is a constant, then its fuzzy integral over X is a itself since $g(X \cap H_\alpha) = 1$ for $\alpha \leq a$ and $g(X \cap H_\alpha) = 0$ for $\alpha > a$. That is,

$$\int_X a \circ g = a, \qquad a \in [0, 1]. \qquad (4.56)$$

Since the fuzzy measure g is monotonic (Axiom g2 of fuzzy measures), we have the following monotonic properties for fuzzy integrals, which come from the properties of fuzzy measures:

$$\text{If } A \subset B, \text{ then } \int_A h(x) \circ g \leq \int_B h(x) \circ g. \qquad (4.57)$$

$$\text{If } h_1 \leq h_2, \text{ then } \int_X h_1(x) \circ g \leq \int_X h_2(x) \circ g. \qquad (4.58)$$

Equations (4.57) and (4.58) show the monotonic feature of fuzzy integrals. On the other hand, the characteristics of Lebesque integrals are their additivity. That is, let u be a Lebesque measure, and then we have

$$\text{If } A \cap B = \varnothing, \text{ then } \int_{A \cup B} h(x) \, du = \int_A h(x) \, du + \int_B h(x) \, du \qquad (4.59)$$

$$\int_X (h_1(x) + h_2(x)) \, du = \int_X h_1(x) \, du + \int_X h_2(x) \, du. \qquad (4.60)$$

These properties come from the additivity of Lebesque measures. Fuzzy integrals are thus the generalization of Lebesque integrals. The latter are a kind of linear function, and the former are merely a kind of nonlinear or monotonous function.

Let us see how the fuzzy integration in Eq. (4.55) can be performed. Let X be a finite set such that $X = \{x_1, x_2, \ldots, x_n\}$. Without loss of generality, assume the function to be integrated, h, is $h(x_1) \geq h(x_2) \geq \cdots \geq h(x_n)$. This can be achieved after proper ordering. Then the fuzzy integral in Eq. (4.55) becomes

$$\int_X h(x) \circ g = \max_{i=1,\ldots,n} \min [h(x_i), g(H_i)], \qquad (4.61)$$

$$H_i = \{x_1, x_2, \ldots, x_i\}. \tag{4.62}$$

The results of the integration are shown in Fig. 4.3. It is clear that calculation of the fuzzy measure g is a key point in performing a fuzzy integration. So, it is convenient if we can obtain an equation that gives the value of g for any given subset of X. With this consideration, the Sugeno fuzzy measure g_λ [see Eq. (4.54)] can provide us with this convenience [Sugeno, 1977]. Let us work out an example to illustrate the practical meaning of fuzzy integrals.

Example 4.6

Consider an evaluation of the desirability of houses. The attributes of the houses that we shall consider are $x_1 \equiv$ price, $x_2 \equiv$ size, $x_3 \equiv$ facilities, $x_4 \equiv$ location, and $x_5 \equiv$ living environment. Let $X = \{x_1, x_2, x_3, x_4, x_5\}$ express the set of attributes of the houses, let m be the number of houses, and let

$$h_j: \; X \rightarrow [0, 1], \qquad j = 1, \ldots, m,$$

be the evaluation function for houses such that $h_j(x_i)$ represents the evaluation value of attribute x_i of the jth house, where $i = 1, \ldots, 5$. For example, $h_3(x_1)$ is the evaluation value given for the price of the third house, and $h_1(x_5)$ is the evaluation value for the living environment of the first house. According to our definition, the evaluation value $h_j(x_i)$ is a number within the interval $[0, 1]$. Then let the fuzzy measure

$$g: \; \mathcal{P}(X) \rightarrow [0, 1]$$

be the degree of consideration of an attribute in the evaluation process. For example, $g(\{x_2\})$ is the degree to which we consider the size of a house and $g(\{x_3, x_4\})$ is the degree to which we consider facilities and location simultaneously. Under these assumptions, the desirability of the jth house, e_j, can be computed using a fuzzy integral as in Eq. (4.55):

$$e_j = \int_X h_j \circ g.$$

In Sec. 4.1, we introduced the fuzzy measures of crisp sets. We shall now consider the fuzzy measures of fuzzy sets which are defined by means of fuzzy integrals. The fuzzy measure of the fuzzy set $A \subset \tilde{\mathcal{P}}(X)$ is

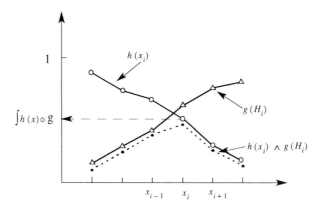

Figure 4.3   Calculation of the fuzzy integration.

$$g(A) = \int_X \mu_A(x) \circ g = \sup_{a \in [0,\, 1]} \min[\alpha, g(A_\alpha)], \qquad (4.63)$$

where A_α is the α-cut of A and $\tilde{\mathcal{P}}(X)$ is the power set of all fuzzy sets of X.

The $g(A)$ in Eq. (4.63) can be interpreted as the grade of certainty of the fuzzy event "x belongs to the fuzzy set A," where x is the element in question. The right-hand side of Eq. (4.63) is very similar to the α-cuts expansion formula in Eq. (2.13). Hence, Dubois and Prade [1980] gave the fuzzy measure of fuzzy sets, $g(A)$, another interpretation that $g(A)$ is the grade of membership of x in the fuzzy set of elements that more or less surely belong to A. This is different from the membership value $\mu_A(x)$, which indicates the grade of membership of x in the fuzzy set A.

Now we can consider a special type of fuzzy measure of fuzzy sets, the *possibility measure of fuzzy sets*. Let A be a fuzzy set in the universe U and let π_X be a possibility distribution associated with a variable X that takes values in U. The possibility measure $\Pi(A)$ of A is defined by

$$\Pi(A) = \sup_{u \in U} \min\{\mu_A(u), \pi_X(u)\}, \qquad (4.64)$$

and the necessity measure $N(A)$ of A is defined by

$$N(A) = \inf_{u \in U} \max\{\mu_A(u), 1 - \pi_X(u)\}. \qquad (4.65)$$

It should be noticed that Axiom g7 in Eq. (4.39) still holds for fuzzy sets $A, B \subseteq U$.

Example 4.7

Assume the possibility distribution induced by the proposition "X is a small integer" is

$$\pi_X = \{(1, 1), (2, 1), (3, 0.8), (4, 0.6), (5, 0.4), (6, 0.2)\}.$$

Now if $A = \{3, 4, 5\}$ is a crisp set, then the possibility and necessity measures of A are [from Eq. (4.46)]

$$\Pi(A) = \max\{0.8, 0.6, 0.4\} = 0.8.$$

If A is assumed to be the fuzzy set "Integers that are not small" and is defined as

$$A = \{(3, 0.2), (4, 0.4), (5, 0.6), (6, 0.8), (7, 1), \ldots\},$$

then the possibility measure of "X is not a small integer" is

$$\Pi(A) = \max\{\min(0.2, 0.8), \min(0.4, 0.6), \min(0.6, 0.4), \min(0.8, 0.2)\}$$
$$= \max\{0.2, 0.4, 0.4, 0.2\} = 0.4,$$
$$N(A) = \min\{\max(0.2, 0.2), \max(0.4, 0.4), \max(0.6, 0.6), \max(0.8, 0.8)\}$$
$$= \min\{0.2, 0.4, 0.6, 0.8\} = 0.2.$$

Another useful definition involving the possibility measure is the possibility measure of fuzzy set B given fuzzy set A, which is denoted by $\Pi(B \mid A)$ and defined by

$$\Pi(B \mid A) \triangleq \sup_{x \in X} \{\min[\mu_B(x), \mu_A(x)]\}, \qquad (4.66)$$

where A and B are fuzzy sets on X. Hence, the possibility measure between fuzzy sets A and B gives the maximum of their intersection, and it measures the extent to which they overlap. That is, $\Pi(B \mid A)$ expresses the degree of matching of two fuzzy sets.

As in Eq. (4.40), the necessity measure of fuzzy set B give fuzzy set A is denoted by

$$N(B \mid A) = 1 - \Pi(\overline{B} \mid A). \tag{4.67}$$

The possibility and necessity measures of fuzzy set B given fuzzy set A are useful when we need to determine the similarity of two fuzzy sets. They have been used, for example, in fuzzy expert systems (Sec. 6.4) and in fuzzy pattern recognition (Sec. 8.1).

4.3 MEASURES OF FUZZINESS

Two categories of uncertainty can be recognized: vagueness and ambiguity. In general, *vagueness* is the uncertainty associated with the difficulty of making a sharp or precise boundary in grouping objects of interest, while *ambiguity* is the uncertainty associated with choice, that is, difficulty in making a choice between two or more alternatives (one-to-many relations). Clearly, the concept of fuzzy sets provides a basic mathematical framework for dealing with vagueness. On the other hand, the concept of fuzzy measures provides a general mathematical framework for dealing with ambiguity. Hence, fuzzy sets and fuzzy measures are tools for representing these two distinct forms of uncertainty. Measures of uncertainty related to vagueness are referred to as measures of fuzziness. This subsection focuses on measures of fuzziness used to evaluate the degree of fuzziness of a fuzzy set. For the measures of uncertainty related to ambiguity, the reader is encouraged to read Klir and Folger's book [1988, Chap. 5].

In general, a measure of fuzziness is a function

$$f\colon \tilde{\mathcal{P}}(X) \to \mathfrak{R}, \tag{4.68}$$

where $\tilde{\mathcal{P}}(X)$ denotes the set of all fuzzy subsets of X, $\mathfrak{R}$ is the real line, and the function f satisfies the following axioms:

Axiom f1: $f(A) = 0$ if and only if A is a crisp set.
Axiom f2: If $A \prec B$, then $f(A) \leq f(B)$, where $A \prec B$ denotes that A is *sharper* than B.
Axiom f3: $f(A)$ assumes the maximum value if and only if A is *maximally fuzzy.*

Axiom f1 indicates that a crisp set has zero degree of fuzziness. Since there are different definitions of "sharper" in Axiom f2 and "maximally fuzzy" in Axiom f3, several different measures of fuzziness exist in the literature. We shall discuss only three measures of fuzziness, and two of them are based on the following concept of "sharper" and "maximally fuzzy":

1. $A \prec B$ (A is sharper than B) is defined by

$$\begin{cases} \mu_A(x) \leq \mu_B(x), & \text{for } \mu_B(x) \leq \tfrac{1}{2} \\ \mu_A(x) \geq \mu_B(x), & \text{for } \mu_B(x) \geq \tfrac{1}{2} \end{cases} \quad \text{for all } x \in X. \tag{4.69}$$

2. A is maximally fuzzy if $\mu_A(x) = \tfrac{1}{2}$ for all $x \in X$.

The first type of measure of fuzziness that we want to introduce is defined by this function:

$$f(A) = -\sum_{x \in x} \{\mu_A(x)\log_2 [\mu_A(x)] + [1 - \mu_A(x)]\log_2 [1 - \mu_A(x)]\}, \tag{4.70}$$

and it can be normalized as

$$\hat{f}(A) = \frac{f(A)}{|X|}, \tag{4.71}$$

where $|X|$ denotes the cardinality of the universal set X. This measure of fuzziness can be considered as the entropy of a fuzzy set [De Luca and Termini, 1972].

Example 4.8
Let $A = $ "small positive integer" be defined by $A = \{(1, 1.0), (2, 1.0), (3, 0.8), (4, 0.6), (5, 0.4), (6, 0.2)\}$. Then

$$f(A) = 0 + 0 + 0.72 + 0.97 + 0.97 + 0.72 = 3.38.$$

Another measure of fuzziness, referred to as an *index of fuzziness* [Kaufmann, 1975] based on the definition in Eq. (4.69), is defined in terms of a metric distance (e.g., the Hamming or Euclidean distance) of A from any of the nearest crisp set C for which

$$\mu_C(x) = \begin{cases} 0 & \text{if } \mu_A(X) \leq \frac{1}{2} \\ 1 & \text{if } \mu_A(X) > \frac{1}{2}. \end{cases} \tag{4.72}$$

Hence, when the Hamming distance is used, the measure of fuzziness is

$$f(A) = \sum_{x \in X} |\mu_A(x) - \mu_C(x)|, \tag{4.73}$$

and for the Euclidean distance, we have

$$f(A) = \left\{ \sum_{x \in X} |\mu_A(x) - \mu_C(x)|^w \right\}^{1/w}, \quad w \in [1, \infty). \tag{4.74}$$

Example 4.9
Let A be defined as in Example 4.8, and the nearest crisp set C is

$$C = \{(1, 1), (2, 1), (3, 1), (4, 1), (5, 0), (6, 0)\}. \tag{4.75}$$

Following Eq. (4.73), we obtain

$$f(A) = |1 - 1| + |1 - 1| + |0.8 - 1| + |0.6 - 1| + |0.4 - 0| + |0.2 - 0| = 1.2.$$

The third measure of fuzziness is based on the degree of distinction between the fuzzy set and its complement [Yager, 1979b; Higashi and Klir, 1982]. This approach utilizes the following definitions for "sharper" and "maximally fuzzy":

1. $A \prec B$ if and only if

$$\left| \mu_A(x) - \mu_{\bar{A}}(x) \right| \geq \left| \mu_B(x) - \mu_{\bar{B}}(x) \right| \qquad \text{for all } x \in X. \tag{4.76}$$

2. A is maximally fuzzy if $\mu_A(x) = e_c$ for all $x \in X$, provided that the complement employed has an equilibrium e_c.

This type of measure of fuzziness is defined as

$$f(A) = 1 - \frac{D_w(A, \bar{A})}{|X|^{1/w}}, \tag{4.77}$$

where

$$D_w(A, \overline{A}) = \left\{ \sum_{x \in X} | \mu_A(x) - \mu_{\overline{A}}(x) |^w \right\}^{1/w}, \qquad w \in [1, \infty). \qquad (4.78)$$

In this definition, if $w = 1$, the Hamming metric is used; if $w = 2$, the Euclidean metric is used.

Example 4.10

Let A be defined as in Example 4.8, $X = \{1, 2, 3, 4, 5, 6\}$, $\mu_{\overline{A}}(x) = 1 - \mu_A(x)$, and $w = 1$. Then according to Eq. (4.77),

$$f(A) = 1 - \frac{D_1(A, \overline{A})}{6} = 1 - \frac{\sum_{x \in X} | 2\mu_A(x) - 1 |}{6} = 0.4.$$

4.4 CONCLUDING REMARKS

In this chapter, we discuss the concept of fuzzy measures and the axioms that must be satisfied by a set function in order for it to be a fuzzy measure. Belief and plausibility measures, which are mutually dual, are characterized by a pair of dual axioms of subadditivity (Axioms g4 and g5). Moreover, a belief measure and its dual plausibility measure can be represented by a simple set function—the basic probability assignment m, which assigns degrees of evidence or belief indicating that a specific element of X belongs only to the set A and not to any special subset of A. Focal elements are subsets that are assigned with non-zero degrees of evidence. When all focal elements are singletons, the corresponding belief measure is equal to its dual plausibility measure and the dual properties of subadditivity merge into a single property of additivity, Bel($A \cup B$) = Bel(A) + Bel(B), which is a fundamental property of the classical probability measure (Bayesian belief measures). The Dempster-Shafer rule for combining two pieces of evidence from two independent sources to obtain a joint consensus is also discussed.

An important property of probability measures is that each of them can be uniquely represented by a probability distribution function defined on the elements of a universal set rather than on its subsets. Similarly, possibility and necessity measures, which are consonant plausibility measures and consonant belief measures, respectively, can also be uniquely characterized by functions defined on the elements of the universal set rather than on its subsets.

An important development is the theory of possibility, developed by Zadeh in 1977 [Zadeh, 1977], which relates fuzzy set theory to possibility distribution by defining a possibility distribution as a fuzzy restriction. This concept will be further explored in the next chapter.

The fuzzy integrals defined and used by Sugeno [1977] are also discussed. An interesting problem in fuzzy integration involves fuzzy integral evaluation models. Details of fuzzy integral evaluation models can be found in [Sugeno, 1977; Terano and Sugeno, 1975]. Besides being used to define the fuzzy measures of a fuzzy set, fuzzy integrals are also used to perform integration of fuzzy functions [Dubois and Prade, 1982d,e; Zimmermann, 1991]. In analogy with integration, approaches to extending ordinary differentiation to fuzzy differentiation have also been pursued [Dubois and Prade, 1980, 1982b; Aumann, 1965; and Nguyen, 1978].

Finally, measures of fuzziness are discussed. Other measures of fuzziness can also be defined for different definitions of the complement and metric [Yager, 1979b; Knopfmacher, 1975]. Furthermore, the definitions of measures of fuzziness in this chapter can be extended to nonfinite supports by replacing the summation by integration properly [Klir and Folger, 1988].

4.5 PROBLEMS

4.1 Show that Bel (A) and Pl (A) given in Eqs. (4.19) and (4.20) are belief and plausibility measures, respectively.

4.2 Given that $X = \{a, b, c, d\}$ and the basic assignments of $m(\{a, b\}) = 0.1$, $m(\{b, c\}) = 0.1$, $m(\{a, c, d\}) = 0.3$, $m(\{a, b, d\}) = 0.4$, and $m(\{a, b, c\ d\}) = 0.1$, compute the corresponding belief and plausibility measures.

4.3 Determine the corresponding belief and plausibility measures from the accompanying table.

Focal Elements	m	Bel	Pl
P	0.15		
B	0.05		
E	0.1		
$P \cup B$	0.1		
$P \cup E$	0.15		
$B \cup E$	0.1		
$P \cup B \cup E$	0.35		

4.4 Using the basic assignments given in Example 4.2, compute $\text{Bel}_1(A \cup B)$, $\text{Bel}_2(A \cup B)$, $\text{Pl}_1 (A \cup B)$, $\text{Pl}_2 (A \cup B)$, $\text{Bel}_{1,2}(A \cup B)$, and $\text{Pl}_{1,2}(A \cup B)$].

4.5 Given $X = \{a, b, c, d\}$ and its belief measures as $\text{Bel}(\{a\}) = 0.2$, $\text{Bel}(\{a, b\}) = 0.3$, $\text{Bel}(\{a, c\}) = 0.3$, $\text{Bel}(\{a, d\}) = 0.2$, $\text{Bel}(\{c, d\}) = 0.1$, $\text{Bel}(\{a, b, c\}) = 0.4$, $\text{Bel}(\{a, b, d\}) = 0.3$, $\text{Bel}(\{a, c, d\}) = 0.4$, $\text{Bel}(\{b, c, d\}) = 0.6$, and $\text{Bel}(\{a, b, c, d\}) = 1$, determine the corresponding basic assignments.

4.6 $X = \{a, b, c, d\}$ and the basic assignments on X are as follows: $m(a) = 0.1$, $m(b) = 0$, $m(c) = 0$, $m(d) = 0.2$, $m(a, b) = 0$, $m(a, c) = 0.1$, $m(a, d) = 0$, $m(b, c) = 0.3$, $m(b, d) = 0$, $m(c, d) = 0$, $m(a, b, c) = 0.1$, $m(a, b, d) = 0.2$, $m(a, c, d) = 0$, $m(b, c, d) = 0$, $m(a, b, c, d) = 0$. Find the corresponding belief and plausibility measures.

4.7 The function

$$Q(A) = \sum_{A \subseteq B \subseteq X} m(B)$$

is called a *commonality number*. For each $A \in \mathcal{P}(X)$, the value $Q(A)$ represents the total portion of belief that can move freely to every point of A. Given X and the basic assignment on X as in the above problem, calculate the corresponding commonality number and verify that

$$\text{Pl}(A) = \sum_{\varnothing \neq B \subseteq A} (-1)^{|B|+1} Q(B).$$

4.8 Derive the formula

$$Q(A) = \sum_{B \subseteq A \neq \varnothing} (-1)^{|B|+1} \text{Pl}(B).$$

4.9 Suppose three basic assignments, $m_1, m_2,$ and m_3, from three independent experts are given as in the accompanying table.

Focal Element	Expert 1 m_1	Expert 2 m_2	Expert 3 m_3	Combined Evidence $m_{1,2,3}$
A	0.1	0.3	0.2	
B	0.3	0.4	0.3	
$A \cup B$	0.6	0.3	0.5	

(a) Determine the joint basic assignment $m_{1,2,3}$.

(b) Is the order of combining the evidence from three experts important? Justify your answer.

4.10 Let ν and μ be two measures. Show that if for all $A \subset X$, $\mu(A) + \nu(\overline{A}) = 1$, then μ is a consonant belief function if and only if ν is a possibility measure.

4.11 Given two basic assignment m_1 and m_2 on $\mathcal{P}(X)$ from two independent sources, the Dempster-Shafer rule of combining two pieces of evidence is given by Eq. (4.24). Suppose the denominator of Eq. (4.24) is positive, show the Eq. (4.24) is a basic probability assignment.

4.12 Show that $m(A)$ given in Eq. (4.22) can be recovered from the given belief measure.

4.13 Show that a belief measure that satisfies Eq. (4.35) is based on nested focal elements.

4.14 Show that a plausibility measure that satisfies Eq. (4.36) is based on nested focal elements.

4.15 A possibility distribution function $\pi(x)$ with $X = \{1, 2, 3, 4, 5, 6\}$ is given as shown:

x	1	2	3	4	5	6
$\pi(x)$	0.2	0.5	1	0.8	0.6	0.5

(a) Determine the relationship between the above possibility distribution function $\pi(\cdot)$ and the basic probability assignment $m(\cdot)$.

(b) If $A = \{1, 2, 4\}$, determine Pl (A) from the basic probability assignment obtained in part (a).

4.16 Let $X = \{1, 2, \ldots, 10\}$ and let $\pi(x)$ be the possibility distribution function that x is close to 8 and is defined by

x	1	2	3	4	5	6	7	8	9	10
$\pi(x)$	0	0	0	0	0.1	0.5	0.8	1	0.8	0.5

(a) Determine the relationship between the above possibility distribution function and the basic assignment.

(b) If $B = \{5, 6, 9\}$, determine Pl (B) from the basic assignment.

(c) Repeat part (b) for $B = \{6, 9, 10\}$.

4.17 A possibility distribution function $\pi(x)$ is given as shown, with $X = \{1, 2, 3, 4, 5\}$.

x	1	2	3	4	5
$\pi(x)$	0.25	0.625	1	0.5	0.75

(a) Determine the relationship between the above possibility distribution function and the basic probability assignment.

(b) If $A = \{1, 4, 5\}$, determine Pl (A) from the basic assignment obtained in part (a).

4.18 $X = \{a, b, c\}$ and its possibility distributions from two experts, expert A and expert B, are $\pi_A (a) = 1$, $\pi_A (b) = 0.7$, $\pi_A (c) = 0.5$, and $\pi_B (a) = 1$, $\pi_B (b) = 0.75$, $\pi_B (c) = 0.5$, respectively. Calculate the joint basic assignment by the Dempster-Shafer rule.

4.19 Let us extend Example 4.1 to include the diagnosis of an illness by two doctors. Both doctors are trying to make an independent diagnosis and to determine whether the patient belongs to one of the sets of people with pneumonia (P), bronchitis (B), or emphysema (E). Let the universal set X denote the set of all possible diseases and let P, B, and E be subsets of X (i.e., $X = P \cup B \cup E$). Assume that the doctors, after examining the patient, provide their basic assignments as in the accompanying table. Use the Dempster-Shafer rule of combination to determine the joint basic assignments and the corresponding joint belief measure and joint plausibility measure (i.e., fill in the blanks in the following table).

Focal Elements	Expert 1		Expert 2		Combined Evidence		
	m_1	Bel_1	m_2	Bel_2	$m_{1,2}$	$Bel_{1,2}$	$Pl_{1,2}$
P	0.05	0.05	0.15	0.15			
B	0.05	0.05	0.05	0.05			
E	0.05	0.05	0.05	0.05			
$P \cup B$	0.15	0.25	0.05	0.25			
$P \cup E$	0.1	0.2	0.2	0.4			
$B \cup E$	0.05	0.15	0.05	0.15			
$P \cup B \cup E$	0.55	1	0.45	1			

4.20 Give two fuzzy sets A and B, where A is *sharper* than B [using the definition of "sharper" in Eqs. (4.69) and (4.76)]. Draw graphs of A and B to illustrate your example.

4.21 Show that the maximum measure of fuzziness defined by Eq. (4.70) is $|X|$.

4.22 Verify that the three measures of fuzziness given in Eqs. (4.70), (4.74), and (4.77) satisfy the axiom saying that if A is sharper than B, then $f(A) \leq f(B)$.

5

Possibility Theory and Fuzzy Arithmetic

This chapter continues to explore the important concepts of possibility theory. Joint, marginal, and conditional possibility distributions will be discussed with examples. Then we shall focus on one of the major topics in possibility theory—fuzzy arithmetic, which is concerned with the operations and computations of fuzzy numbers. Fuzzy numbers are essential for expressing fuzzy cardinalities and fuzzy quantifiers, and fuzzy arithmetic is a basic tool in dealing with fuzzy quantifiers in approximate reasoning (see Chap. 6). Also, fuzzy arithmetic is useful for computations in physical sciences and engineering when only imprecise or uncertain sensory data are available for computations.

5.1 BASICS OF POSSIBILITY THEORY

Possibility theory can be related to fuzzy set theory by defining possibility distribution as a fuzzy restriction that acts as an elastic constraint on values that may be assigned to a (fuzzy) variable. The distribution function associated with this fuzzy restriction is a possibility distribution function π_X. In other words, the membership function μ_A of a fuzzy set A can be interpreted as a possibility distribution function π_X of the variable X, and A is viewed as the set of more or less possible values for X; that is, $\pi_X = \mu_A$ [Eq. (4.53)]. While fuzzy set theory has different operators for intersection and union (e.g., t-norms and t-conorms), possibility theory is well developed and uniquely defined with respect to operation and structure [Zadeh, 1978a, 1983b; Dubois and Prade, 1988b]. Most importantly, the intersection and union in possibility theory are restricted only to min and max operators, respectively, and there exists a value u of the universe U that can be assigned to X such that $\pi_X(u) = 1$ or, more generally,

$$\max_{u \in U} \pi_X(u) = 1, \qquad (5.1)$$

which is formally equivalent to a normalized fuzzy set. The requirement in Eq. (5.1) is similar to the condition that the summation of probabilities of all elements is equal to 1 in probability theory.

Possibility theory is analogous, yet different from probability theory. One of the major differences between possibility and probability can be seen from the following:

$$P(A) + P(\overline{A}) = 1, \qquad (5.2)$$

$$\Pi(A) + \Pi(\overline{A}) \geq 1, \qquad (5.3)$$

$$N(A) + N(\overline{A}) \leq 1, \qquad (5.4)$$

which are the direct results of the conditions of probability, possibility, and necessity measures. These equations indicate that the probability of an event completely determines the probability of the contrary event, while the possibility (or the necessity) of an event is weakly linked with the contrary event. In fact, as a special case of Eq. (4.34),

$$N(A) \leq P(A) \leq \Pi(A), \qquad (5.5)$$

the possibility and necessity measures can be considered as limiting cases of probability measures [Dempster, 1967]. Hence, possibility corresponds more to evidence theory than to classical probability theory.

To illustrate the difference between probability and possibility in a more straightforward way, Zedah [1978a] proposed a simple but impressive example as follows.

Example 5.1

[Zadeh, 1978a]. Consider the statement "Hans ate X eggs for breakfast," with X taking values in $U = \{1, 2, ..., 8\}$. We may associate a possibility distribution function with X by interpreting $\pi_X(u)$ as the "degree of ease" with which Hans can eat u eggs. We may also associate a probability distribution function with X, $p_X(u)$, which might have been determined by observing Hans at breakfast for hundreds of days. The values of $\pi_X(u)$ and $p_X(u)$ might be shown in the accompanying table.

u	1	2	3	4	5	6	7	8
$\pi_X(u)$	1	1	1	1	0.8	0.6	0.4	0.2
$p_X(u)$	0.1	0.8	0.1	0	0	0	0	0

Thus, a high degree of possibility does not imply a high degree of probability, nor does a low degree of probability imply a low degree of possibility. However, if an event is impossible, it is bound to be improbable. This coincides with Eq. (5.5) where possibility is an upper bound of probability. This heuristic connection between possibility and probability is stated by Zadeh [1978a] in his *possibility/probability consistency principle.*

Possibility-probability consistency principle: If a variable X can take the values $u_1, u_2, ..., u_n$ with respective possibility distribution $\boldsymbol{\pi}_X = (\pi_1, \pi_2, ..., \pi_n)$ and probability distribution $\mathbf{p}_X = (p_1, p_2, ..., p_n)$, then the degree of consistency of the probability distribution $\mathbf{p}_X$ with the possibility distribution $\boldsymbol{\pi}_X$ is expressed by

$$\gamma = \pi_1 p_1 + \pi_2 p_2 + \cdots + \pi_n p_n = \sum_{i=1}^{n} \pi_i p_i, \qquad (5.6)$$

where + indicates an arithmetic sum.

It should be noted that the above principle is not a precise law but a heuristic connection between possibilities and probabilities. Since in most situations what is known about a variable X is its possibility distribution rather than its probability distribution, this principle is of great use in such cases; it indicates that high probabilities should not be assigned to values of X with low degrees of possibility. It is worth pointing out that a possibility distribution π_X, in the context of possibility theory, is a fuzzy restriction (i.e., it is a fuzzy set or relation) with an associated possibility distribution function $\pi_X(u)$.

As in the case of probability, one can define joint and marginal possibility distributions. Let $X = (X_1, X_2, \ldots, X_n)$ be n-ary fuzzy variables taking values in $U = U_1 \times U_2 \times \cdots \times U_n$ and let π_X be a possibility distribution associated with X, with $\pi_X(u_1, u_2, \ldots, u_n)$ denoting the possibility distribution function of π_X. Here, π_X is also called the *joint possibility distribution* of $X_1, X_2, \ldots, X_n$. Let $q = (i_1, i_2, \ldots, i_k)$ be a subsequence of the index sequence $(1, 2, \ldots, n)$ and let $X_{(q)}$ be the q-ary fuzzy variable $X_{(q)} = (X_{i_1}, X_{i_2}, \ldots, X_{i_k})$. The *marginal possibility distribution* $\pi_{X_{(q)}}$ is a possibility distribution associated with $X_{(q)}$ which is induced by π_X as the projection of π_X on $U_{(q)} = U_{i_1} \times U_{i_2} \times \cdots \times U_{i_k}$; that is,

$$\pi_{X_{(q)}} \triangleq [\pi_X \downarrow U_{(q)}], \qquad (5.7)$$

where $[\pi_X \downarrow U_{(q)}]$ is the projection of π_X on $U_{(q)}$ as defined in Sec. 3.2. Note that the joint possibility distribution π_X is equivalent to a fuzzy relation defined on the Cartesian product of $X_1, X_2, \ldots, X_n$.

Example 5.2

Let $X = (X_1, X_2, X_3)$ and $U_1 = U_2 = U_3 = \{a, b\}$. The joint possibility distribution of X_1, X_2, X_3 is defined as

$$\pi_X = 0.8/aaa + 1/aab + 0.6/baa + 0.2/bab + 0.5/bbb.$$

Then if $X_{(2)} = (X_2, X_3)$, the marginal possibility distribution with $X_{(2)}$ is

$$\pi_{X_{(2)}} \equiv [\pi_X \downarrow (X_2, X_3)] = 0.8/aa + 1/ab + 0.5/bb.$$

By analogy with the concept of independence of a random variable, we can define the joint possibility distribution. Two fuzzy variables X_1 and X_2 are noninteractive if and only if their joint possibility distribution associated with $X = (X_1, X_2)$ is equal to the Cartesian product of the possibility distributions associated with X_1 and X_2; that is,

$$\pi_X = \pi_{X_1} \times \pi_{X_2}, \qquad (5.8)$$

or, equivalently

$$\pi_X(u_1, u_2) = \min(\pi_{X_1}(u_1), \pi_{X_2}(u_2)), \qquad u_1 \in U_1, u_2 \in U_2. \qquad (5.9)$$

In general, the fuzzy variables $X_1, X_2, \ldots, X_n$ are noninteractive if and only if

$$\boldsymbol{\pi}_X = \boldsymbol{\pi}_{X_1} \times \boldsymbol{\pi}_{X_2} \times \cdots \times \boldsymbol{\pi}_{X_n}. \tag{5.10}$$

In essence, noninteraction [Eq. (5.9)] means that a variation in one or more components of a possibility distribution cannot be compensated for by variations in the complementary components. From the point of view of fuzzy relations, Eq. (5.9) defines the largest fuzzy relation (in the sense of inclusion) or, equivalently, the least specific possibility function, that can have A_1 and A_2 as projections, where A_1 and A_2 are the fuzzy restrictions of X_1 and X_2, respectively. Moreover, from Eq. (5.9), if X_1 and X_2 are noninteractive, then the possibility measure of their corresponding fuzzy restrictions A_1 and A_2 has the following properties:

$$\Pi_X(A_1 \times A_2) = \min \left(\Pi_{X_1}(A_1), \Pi_{X_2}(A_2) \right). \tag{5.11}$$

Again, analogous to the conditional probability distribution in probability theory, the conditional possibility distribution can be defined. Let X_1 and X_2 be fuzzy variables in the universes U_1 and U_2, respectively. The conditional possibility distribution of X_1 given $X_2 = u_2 \in U_2$ is defined as

$$\boldsymbol{\pi}_{(X_1 | X_2)} \triangleq \boldsymbol{\pi}_{X_1}[X_2 = u_2] \equiv \boldsymbol{\pi}_X \mid_{X_2 = u_2}, \tag{5.12}$$

where $\boldsymbol{\pi}_X$ is the joint possibility distribution of X_1 and X_2. Equation (5.12) can be extended to more than two fuzzy variables. For example, if $\boldsymbol{\pi}_X$ is as defined in Example 5.2, then $\boldsymbol{\pi}_{(X_2, X_3)}[X_1 = a] = 0.8/aa + 1/ab$.

If what we know is the possibility distribution of a fuzzy variable instead of its value, then the conditional possibility distribution has the following definition. Let X_1 and X_2 be fuzzy variables in the universes U_1 and U_2, respectively. The conditional possibility distribution X_1 given $\boldsymbol{\pi}_{X_2} = B$ is defined (according to [Zadeh, 1978a]) as

$$\boldsymbol{\pi}_{(X_1 | X_2)} = \boldsymbol{\pi}_{X_1}[\boldsymbol{\pi}_{X_2} = B] \triangleq [(\boldsymbol{\pi}_X \cap [B \uparrow X_1]) \downarrow X_1], \tag{5.13}$$

where $[B \uparrow X_1]$ is the cylindric extension of B as defined in Sec. 3.2. Again, this definition can be extended to more than two fuzzy variables.

Example 5.3
Continuing from Example 5.2, if we are given

$$\boldsymbol{\pi}_{(X_1, X_2)} = B = 1/aa + 0.6/ba + 0.5/bb,$$

then

$$[B \uparrow X_3] = 1/aaa + 1/aab + 0.6/baa + 0.6/bab + 0.5/bba + 0.5/bbb.$$

So we have

$$\boldsymbol{\pi}_X \cap [B \uparrow X_3] = 0.8/aaa + 1/aab + 0.6/baa + 0.2/bab + 0.5/bbb$$

and

$$\boldsymbol{\pi}_{X_3}[\boldsymbol{\pi}_{(X_1, X_2)} = B] = [(\boldsymbol{\pi}_X \cap [B \uparrow X_3]) \downarrow X_3] = 0.8/a + 1/b.$$

If we know the possibility distribution of X_1, π_{X_1}, and the conditional possibility distribution of X_2 given X_1, $\pi_{X_2|X_1}$, then we can construct the joint possibility distribution of X_1 and X_2 from the following equation:

$$\pi_{(X_1, X_2)} = \left(\pi_{X_1} \uparrow X_2\right) \cap \left(\pi_{X_2|X_1} \uparrow X_1\right). \tag{5.14}$$

Let us examine a practical application of the above concept.

Example 5.4

Consider the statement "John is Big," where Big = (Height, Weight) with joint possibility distribution

$$\pi_{\text{Big}} = 0.7/ (170, 70) + 0.8/ (170, 80) + 0.9/ (180, 80) + 1/ (190, 90).$$

Notice that, for simplicity, we consider only the four possible (Height, Weight) combinations, (170, 70), (170, 80), (180, 80), (190, 90) in this example. Now in addition to knowing that "John is Big," we also know that "John is Tall." Here the possibility distribution associated with "Tall" is

$$\pi_{\text{Height}} = 0.8/170 + 0.9/180 + 1/190.$$

Then the answer to the question What is the weight of John? can be obtained from Eq. (5.13):

$$\pi_{(\text{Weight|Height})} = \left[\left(\pi_{\text{Big}} \cap [\pi_{\text{Height}} \uparrow \text{Weight}]\right) \downarrow \text{Weight}\right],$$

$$[\pi_{\text{Height}} \uparrow \text{Weight}] = 0.8/ (170, 70) + 0.8/ (170, 80) +$$
$$0.9/ (180, 80) + 1/ (190, 90),$$

$$\pi_{\text{Big}} \cap [\pi_{\text{Height}} \uparrow \text{Weight}] = 0.7/ (170, 70) + 0.8/ (170, 80) +$$
$$0.9/ (180, 80) + 1/ (190, 90).$$

So,

$$\pi_{(\text{Weight|Height})} = 0.7/70 + 0.9/80 + 1/90.$$

Now, assume that $\pi_{(\text{Weight|Height})}$ and π_{Height} are given as above; then the joint possibility distribution can be derived from Eq. (5.14):

$$\pi_{(\text{Height,Weight})} = \left(\pi_{\text{Height}} \uparrow \text{Weight}\right) \cap \left(\pi_{(\text{Weight|Height})} \uparrow \text{Height}\right)$$

$$= \left(0.8/ (170, 70) + 0.8/ (170, 80) + 0.9/ (180, 80) + 1/ (190, 90)\right)$$

$$\cap \left(0.7/ (170, 70) + 0.9/ (170, 80) + 0.9/ (180, 80) + 1/ (190, 90)\right)$$

$$= 0.7/ (170, 70) + 0.8/ (170, 80) + 0.9/ (180, 80) + 1/ (190, 90)$$

5.2 FUZZY ARITHMETIC

In the physical sciences and in engineering we are often faced with computations using imprecise data. In these computations, the uncertain value or the inaccurate data from measuring instruments are usually expressed in the form of intervals, and mathematical operations are then performed on these intervals to obtain a reliable estimate of the measurements (again in the form of intervals). This branch of mathematical computations is called *interval analysis* or *interval arithmetic* [Moore, 1966, 1979].

Fuzzy numbers, as defined in Sec. 2.1, are normal, convex fuzzy sets of the real line. Recent developments involving operations and computations on fuzzy numbers have evolved into what has come to be called *fuzzy arithmetic,* which is one of the major topics in possibility theory and, equivalently, one of the major branches of fuzzy set theory. Among many applications, fuzzy numbers are essential for expressing fuzzy cardinalities and fuzzy quantifiers [Dubois and Prade, 1985c]. Thus, fuzzy arithmetic is a basic tool in dealing with fuzzy quantifiers in approximate reasoning (see Chap. 6). Because the concept of fuzzy numbers includes the interval as a special case, fuzzy arithmetic subsumes interval arithmetic. Interval analysis, commonly applied in physics, merely serves to throw the inaccuracies of measuring instruments, in the form of intervals, back onto the magnitudes estimated by the measurements. In this section, we shall consider a fuzzy number an extension of the concept of intervals. By virtue of the gradation of membership in a fuzzy set, fuzzy arithmetic has far greater expressive power than interval arithmetic. Instead of considering intervals at only one unique level, fuzzy numbers consider them at several levels or, more generally, at all levels from 0 to 1. Major references on this topic are [Dubois and Prade, 1988b; Kaufmann and Gupta, 1991].

In the next section, we shall briefly discuss the representation of uncertain data by intervals and their basic mathematical operations. Then we shall extend this concept of intervals to fuzzy numbers and their computations.

5.2.1 Interval Representation of Uncertain Values

Consider that values or data obtained from a scientific instrument are uncertain and that we can accept or locate this uncertain value as belonging to the real line. In many situations, it is possible to locate this uncertain value inside a closed interval on the real line $\Re$; that is, this uncertain value is inside an interval of confidence of $\Re$, $x \in [a_1, a_2]$, where $a_1 \leq a_2$. This indicates that we are certain that the value x is greater than or equal to a_1 and smaller than or equal to a_2. In other words, we limit the uncertainty of the data to an interval specified by the lower and upper bounds.

Symbolically, we represent an interval by $A = [a_1, a_2]$, and if an uncertain value x is inside this closed interval, we can also use set notation to express it as

$$A = [a_1, a_2] = \{x \mid a_1 \leq x \leq a_2\}. \tag{5.15}$$

In general, the numbers a_1 and a_2 are finite. However in some cases, $a_1 = -\infty$ and/or $a_2 = +\infty$. If the value x that we obtained is certain and is a singleton in $\Re$, it can be expressed in the form of intervals as $x = [x, x]$. For instance, $0 = [0, 0]$. In other words, an ordinary number $k \in \Re$ can be written in the form of an interval as $k = [k, k]$.

When considering intervals, we have four types:

$[a_1, a_2] = \{x \mid a_1 \leq x \leq a_2\}$: closed interval.

$[a_1, a_2) = \{x \mid a_1 \leq x < a_2\}$: closed at left end point and open at right end point.

$(a_1, a_2] = \{x \mid a_1 < x \leq a_2\}$: open at left end point and closed at right end point.

$(a_1, a_2) = \{x \mid a_1 < x < a_2\}$: open interval.

Here brackets and parentheses are used to denote closed and open end points, respectively.

Let us discuss some mathematical operations on intervals of confidence such as addition $(+)$, subtraction $(-)$, multiplication $(\cdot)$, division $(:)$, max operation $(\vee)$, and min operation $(\wedge)$.

- **Addition $(+)$ and subtraction $(-)$:** Let $A = [a_1, a_2]$ and $B = [b_1, b_2]$ be two intervals of confidence in $\Re$. If $x \in [a_1, a_2]$ and $y \in [b_1, b_2]$, then $x + y \in [a_1 + b_1, a_2 + b_2]$. Symbolically, we write

$$A(+)B = [a_1, a_2](+)[b_1, b_2] = [a_1 + b_1, a_2 + b_2]. \qquad (5.16)$$

For the same two intervals of confidence, their subtraction is

$$A(-)B = [a_1, a_2](-)[b_1, b_2] = [a_1 - b_2, a_2 - b_1]; \qquad (5.17)$$

that is, we subtract the larger value in $[b_1, b_2]$ from a_1, and the smaller value in $[b_1, b_2]$ from a_2.

- **Image $\overline{A}$:** If $x \in [a_1, a_2]$, then its image $-x \in [-a_2, -a_1]$. That is, if $A = [a_1, a_2]$, then its image is $\overline{A} = [-a_2, -a_1]$. Note that

$$A(+)\overline{A} = [a_1, a_2](+)[-a_2, -a_1] = [a_1 - a_2, a_2 - a_1] \neq 0. \qquad (5.18)$$

Using the concept of image, subtraction becomes addition of an image. That is,

$$A(-)B \equiv A(+)\overline{B} = [a_1, a_2](+)[-b_2, -b_1] = [a_1 - b_2, a_2 - b_1]. \qquad (5.19)$$

- **Multiplication $(\cdot)$ and division $(:)$:** Consider two intervals of confidence, $A = [a_1, a_2]$ and $B = [b_1, b_2]$ in $\Re^+$, where $\Re^+$ is the nonnegative real line. The multiplication of these two intervals is

$$A(\cdot)B = [a_1, a_2](\cdot)[b_1, b_2] = [a_1 \cdot b_1, a_2 \cdot b_2]. \qquad (5.20)$$

If $A, B \subset \Re$, then $A(\cdot)B$ is more complicated and has nine possible combinations. Details of the multiplication of intervals in $\Re$ can be found in [Kaufmann and Gupta, 1991]. If we multiply an interval by a nonnegative number $k \in \Re^+$, then for all $A \subset \Re^+$, we have

$$k(\cdot)A = [k, k](\cdot)[a_1, a_2] = [k\,a_1, k\,a_2]. \qquad (5.21)$$

For the division of two intervals of confidence in $\Re^+$, we have

$$A(:)B = [a_1, a_2](:)[b_1, b_2] = \left[\frac{a_1}{b_2}, \frac{a_2}{b_1} \right]. \qquad (5.22)$$

If $b_1 = 0$, then the upper bound increases to $+\infty$. If $b_1 = b_2 = 0$, then the interval of confidence is extended to $+\infty$.

- **Inverse A^{-1}:** If $x \in [a_1, a_2] \subset \Re_0^+$, where $\Re_0^+$ is the positive real line, then its inverse is $(1/x) \in [1/a_2, 1/a_1]$ and

$$A^{-1} = [a_1, a_2]^{-1} = \left[\frac{1}{a_2}, \frac{1}{a_1} \right]. \qquad (5.23)$$

Using the concept of inverse, division becomes multiplication of an inverse. That is,

$$A(:)B \equiv A(\cdot)B^{-1} = [a_1, a_2](\cdot)\left[\frac{1}{b_2}, \frac{1}{b_1} \right] = \left[\frac{a_1}{b_2}, \frac{a_2}{b_1} \right]. \qquad (5.24)$$

For division by a nonnegative number $k > 0$, it is equivalent to $(1/k)(\cdot)A$. That is,

$$A(:)k \equiv A(\cdot)\left[\frac{1}{k}, \frac{1}{k}\right] = \left[\frac{a_1}{k}, \frac{a_2}{k}\right].\tag{5.25}$$

- **Max ($\vee$) and min ($\wedge$) operations:** Consider two intervals of confidence $A, B \subset \Re$. Their max and min operations are, respectively, defined as

$$A(\vee)B = [a_1, a_2](\vee)[b_1, b_2] = [a_1 \vee b_1, a_2 \vee b_2].\tag{5.26}$$

$$A(\wedge)B = [a_1, a_2](\wedge)[b_1, b_2] = [a_1 \wedge b_1, a_2 \wedge b_2].\tag{5.27}$$

There are several interesting algebraic properties associated with the operations on intervals of confidence which are listed in Table 5.1 It is obvious that subtraction and division are neither commutative nor associative. Let us illustrate the above concepts of interval arithmetic with some numerical examples.

TABLE 5.1 Algebraic Properties of Addition and Multiplication on Intervals

Property	Addition, $(+)$	Multiplication, $(\cdot)$
Intervals	For all $A, B, C \subset \Re$	For all $A, B, C \subset \Re^+$
Commutativity	$A(+)B = B(+)A$	$A(\cdot)B = B(\cdot)A$
Associativity	$(A(+)B)(+)C = A(+)(B(+)C)$	$(A(\cdot)B)(\cdot)C = A(\cdot)(B(\cdot)C)$
Neutral number	$A(+)0 = 0(+)A = A$	$A(\cdot)1 = 1(\cdot)A = A$
Image and inverse	$A(+)\overline{A} = \overline{A}(+)A \neq 0$	$A(\cdot)A^{-1} = A^{-1}(\cdot)A \neq 1$

Example 5.5

Consider $A = [1.23, 4.56]$, $B = [2.45, 6.26]$, $C = [-3.12, 5.64]$, $D = [-4.02, -1.27]$, $E = [2, 4]$, $F = [-4, 6]$, and $G = [-6, -2]$. Then we have

$$A(+)B = [1.23, 4.56](+)[2.45, 6.26] = [1.23 + 2.45, 4.56 + 6.26] = [3.68, 10.82],$$

$$A(-)C = [1.23, 4.56](-)[-3.12, 5.64] = [1.23 - 5.64, 4.56 + 3.12] = [-4.41, 7.68],$$

$$\overline{C} = [-5.64, 3.12],$$

$$C(+)\overline{C} = [-3.12, 5.64](+)[-5.64, 3.12] = [-8.76, 8.76] \neq 0,$$

$$(A(+)B)(-)C = [3.68, 10.82](-)[-3.12, 5.64] = [-1.96, 13.94],$$

$$A(\cdot)B = [1.23, 4.56](\cdot)[2.45, 6.26] = [3.0135, 28.5456],$$

$$A(:)B = [1.23, 4.56](:)[2.45, 6.26] = [1.23/6.26, 4.56/2.45] = [0.1965, 1.8612],$$

$$A^{-1} = [1/4.56, 1/1.23] = [0.2193, 0.8130],$$

$$A(\cdot)A^{-1} = [1.23, 4.56](\cdot)[0.2193, 0.8130] = [0.2697, 3.7073] \neq 1,$$

$$E(\wedge)F = [2, 4](\wedge)[-4, 6] = [2 \wedge -4, 4 \wedge 6] = [-4, 4],$$

$$E(\vee)F = [2 \vee -4, 4 \vee 6] = [2, 6],$$

$$F(\wedge)G = [-4 \wedge -6, 6 \wedge -2] = [-6, -2],$$

$$F(\vee)G = [-4 \vee -6, 6 \vee -2] = [-4, 6].$$

5.2.2 Operations and Properties of Fuzzy Numbers

A fuzzy number is a normal, convex fuzzy subset on the real line $\Re$ whose membership function is piecewise continuous. That is, every α-cut A_α, $\alpha \in [0, 1]$, of a fuzzy number A is a closed interval of $\Re$, and the highest value of μ_A is equal to unity. Thus, given two fuzzy numbers A and B in $\Re$, for a specific $\alpha_1 \in [0, 1]$, we will obtain two closed intervals, $A_{\alpha_1} \triangleq [a_1^{(\alpha_1)}, a_2^{(\alpha_1)}]$ from fuzzy number A and $B_{\alpha_1} \triangleq [b_1^{(\alpha_1)}, b_2^{(\alpha_1)}]$ from fuzzy number B. The interval arithmetic that we have discussed can be applied to these two closed intervals. Hence, a fuzzy number can be considered an extension of the concept of intervals. Instead of considering intervals at only one unique level, fuzzy numbers consider them at several levels with each of these levels corresponding to each α-cut of the fuzzy numbers. To indicate that we are considering or dealing with arithmetic operations on all levels of the closed interval of fuzzy numbers, we shall use the notation $A_\alpha \triangleq [a_1^{(\alpha)}, a_2^{(\alpha)}]$ to represent a closed interval of a fuzzy number A at an α level.

Let us extend the discussion of interval arithmetic for closed intervals to fuzzy numbers. Let ($\star$) denote an arithmetic operation on fuzzy numbers such as addition ($+$), subtraction ($-$), multiplication ($\cdot$), or division ($:$). Using the extension principle, the result $A(\star)B$, where A and B are two fuzzy numbers can be obtained:

$$\mu_{A(\star)B}(z) = \sup_{z=x\star y} \min\{\mu_A(x), \mu_B(y)\}, \tag{5.28}$$

where $x, y \in \Re$. For min operation (i.e., ($\star$) = ($\wedge$)) and max operation (i.e., ($\star$) = ($\vee$)), we have

$$\mu_{A(\star)B}(z) = \sup_{z=x\star y} (\mu_A(x) \star \mu_B(y)), \tag{5.29}$$

Using the α-cuts, Eqs. (5.28) and (5.29) become

$$(A(\star)B)_\alpha = A_\alpha(\star)B_\alpha \qquad \text{for all } \alpha \in [0, 1], \tag{5.30}$$

where $A_\alpha = [a_1^{(\alpha)}, a_2^{(\alpha)}]$ and $B_\alpha = [b_1^{(\alpha)}, b_2^{(\alpha)}]$. Note that for $\alpha_1, \alpha_2 \in [0, 1]$, if $\alpha_1 > \alpha_2$, then $A_{\alpha_1} \subset A_{\alpha_2}$. The right-hand side of Eq. (5.30) denotes the arithmetic operation on the α-cuts of A and B (or closed intervals of $\Re$).

Extending the addition and subtraction operations on intervals to two fuzzy numbers A and B in $\Re$, we have [from Eqs. (5.16) and (5.17)]

$$A_\alpha(+)B_\alpha = [a_1^{(\alpha)} + b_1^{(\alpha)}, a_2^{(\alpha)} + b_2^{(\alpha)}], \tag{5.31}$$

$$A_\alpha(-)B_\alpha = [a_1^{(\alpha)} - b_2^{(\alpha)}, a_2^{(\alpha)} - b_1^{(\alpha)}], \tag{5.32}$$

Extending Eqs. (5.20) and (5.22) to multiplication and division on two fuzzy numbers A, B in $\Re^+ = [0, \infty)$, we have

$$A_\alpha(\cdot)B_\alpha = [a_1^{(\alpha)} \cdot b_1^{(\alpha)}, a_2^{(\alpha)} \cdot b_2^{(\alpha)}], \tag{5.33}$$

$$A_\alpha (:) B_\alpha = \left[\frac{a_1^{(\alpha)}}{b_2^{(\alpha)}}, \frac{a_2^{(\alpha)}}{b_1^{(\alpha)}} \right] \qquad b_2^{(\alpha)} > 0. \tag{5.34}$$

The multiplication of a fuzzy number $A \subset \Re$ by an ordinary number $k \in \Re^+$ can also be defined as

$$(k \, (\cdot) \, A)_\alpha = k \, (\cdot) \, A_\alpha = \left[k a_1^{(\alpha)}, k a_2^{(\alpha)} \right] \tag{5.35}$$

or, equivalently,

$$\mu_{k \, (\cdot) \, A}(x) = \mu_A \left(\frac{x}{k} \right) \qquad \text{for all } x \in \Re. \tag{5.36}$$

Example 5.6

Compute the sum and difference of the two triangular fuzzy numbers A and B shown in Fig. 5.1, where their membership functions are defined as

$$\mu_A (x) = \begin{cases} 0, & x \le -6 \\ (x+6)/4, & -6 < x \le -2 \\ (-x+3)/5, & -2 < x \le 3 \\ 0, & x > 3 \end{cases} \quad \text{and} \quad \mu_B (x) = \begin{cases} 0, & x \le -1 \\ (x+1)/5, & -1 < x \le 4 \\ (-x+10)/6, & 4 < x \le 10 \\ 0, & x > 10. \end{cases}$$

First, we need to find their α-cuts or closed intervals $[a_1^{(\alpha)}, a_2^{(\alpha)}]$ and $[b_1^{(\alpha)}, b_2^{(\alpha)}]$; that is, we need to find $a_1^{(\alpha)}, a_2^{(\alpha)}, b_1^{(\alpha)},$ and $b_2^{(\alpha)}$. To find $a_1^{(\alpha)}$ and $a_2^{(\alpha)}$, we respectively set x to the lower and upper bounds in $\mu_A (x)$. Thus, we have

$$\frac{a_1^{(\alpha)} + 6}{4} = \alpha \qquad \text{and} \qquad \frac{-a_2^{(\alpha)} + 3}{5} = \alpha. \tag{5.37}$$

Solving $a_1^{(\alpha)}$ and $a_2^{(\alpha)}$ in Eq. (5.37), we obtain

$$A_\alpha = [a_1^{(\alpha)}, a_2^{(\alpha)}] = [4\alpha - 6, -5\alpha + 3] . \tag{5.38}$$

Similarly, we can find $b_1^{(\alpha)}$ and $b_2^{(\alpha)}$ from the membership function $\mu_B (x)$:

$$B_\alpha = [b_1^{(\alpha)}, b_2^{(\alpha)}] = [5\alpha - 1, -6\alpha + 10] . \tag{5.39}$$

Then using Eq. (5.31) on Eqs. (5.38) and (5.39), we obtain their sum

$$A_\alpha (+) B_\alpha = [9\alpha - 7, -11\alpha + 13] \triangleq [c_1^{(\alpha)}, c_2^{(\alpha)}]. \tag{5.40}$$

To find the membership function $\mu_{A (+) B} (x)$, we need to find the ranges of $x \in \Re$ where the α-cuts are valid. Thus, from $c_1^{(\alpha)}$, we have

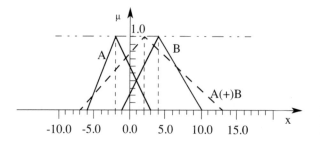

Figure 5.1   Addition of two triangular fuzzy numbers in Example 5.6.

Possibility Theory and Fuzzy Arithmetic   Chap. 5

$$x = 9\alpha - 7,$$

from which we obtain

$$\alpha = \frac{x+7}{9}. \tag{5.41}$$

Similarly, from $c_2^{(\alpha)}$, we have

$$x = -11\alpha + 13,$$

from which we obtain

$$\alpha = \frac{-x+13}{11}. \tag{5.42}$$

Thus, Eqs. (5.41) and (5.42) provide the membership function for $A\,(+)\,B$:

$$\mu_{A\,(+)\,B}\,(x) = \begin{cases} 0, & x \le -7, \\ (x+7)/9, & -7 < x \le 2 \\ (-x+13)/11, & 2 < x \le 13 \\ 0, & x > 13. \end{cases}$$

The result is shown in Fig. 5.1. Note that the ranges of x where $\alpha \ge 0$ are obtained by adding the ranges of x from $\mu_A\,(x)$ and $\mu_B\,(x)$.

For $A\,(-)\,B$, using Eq. (5.32) and A_α from Eq. (5.38) and B_α from Eq. (5.39), we have

$$A_\alpha\,(-)\,B_\alpha = [10\alpha - 16, -10\alpha + 4],$$

which leads us to the following membership function

$$\mu_{A\,(-)\,B}\,(x) = \begin{cases} 0, & x \le -16, \\ (x+16)/10, & -16 < x \le -6 \\ (-x+4)/10, & -6 < x \le 4 \\ 0, & x > 4. \end{cases}$$

Note that the ranges of x where $\alpha \ge 0$ are obtained by correspondingly subtracting the ranges of x in $\mu_B\,(x)$ from the ranges of x in $\mu_A\,(x)$.

Example 5.7

Compute the multiplication and division of the two triangular fuzzy numbers shown in Fig. 5.2, where their membership functions are

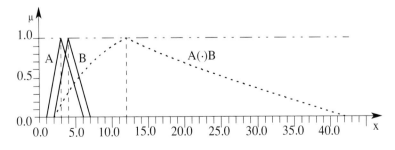

Figure 5.2 Multiplication of two fuzzy numbers in Example 5.7.

$$\mu_A(x) = \begin{cases} 0, & x \le 1 \\ (x-1)/2, & 1 < x \le 3 \\ (-x+6)/3, & 3 < x \le 6 \\ 0, & x > 6 \end{cases} \quad \text{and} \quad \mu_B(x) = \begin{cases} 0, & x \le 2 \\ (x-2)/2, & 2 < x \le 4 \\ (-x+7)/3, & 4 < x \le 7 \\ 0, & x > 7. \end{cases}$$

First, we compute the α-cuts from $\mu_A(x)$:

$$\alpha = \frac{(a_1^{(\alpha)} - 1)}{2} \qquad \text{or} \qquad a_1^{(\alpha)} = 2\alpha + 1,$$

$$\alpha = \frac{(-a_2^{(\alpha)} + 6)}{3} \qquad \text{or} \qquad a_2^{(\alpha)} = -3\alpha + 6,$$

from which we obtain the α-cuts of A:

$$A_\alpha = [2\alpha + 1, -3\alpha + 6]. \tag{5.43}$$

Similarly, from $\mu_B(x)$, we obtain the α-cuts of B:

$$B_\alpha = [2\alpha + 2, -3\alpha + 7]. \tag{5.44}$$

Then from Eq. (5.33), we obtain their multiplication:

$$A_\alpha(\cdot)B_\alpha = [(2\alpha + 1)(2\alpha + 2), (-3\alpha + 6)(-3\alpha + 7)]$$
$$= [4\alpha^2 + 6\alpha + 2, 9\alpha^2 - 39\alpha + 42].$$

To find the membership function $\mu_{A(\cdot)B}(x)$, we again need to find the ranges of $x \in \Re^+$ where the α-cuts are valid. This can be accomplished by solving the following equations for α:

$$4\alpha^2 + 6\alpha + 2 = x$$
$$9\alpha^2 - 39\alpha + 42 = x.$$

Solving these equations for α gives us $\alpha = (-3 \pm \sqrt{1 + 4x})/4$ and $\alpha = (13 \pm \sqrt{1 + 4x})/6$. This leads to the membership function $\mu_{A(\cdot)B}(x)$ as shown in Fig. 5.2.

$$\mu_{A(\cdot)B}(x) = \begin{cases} 0, & x \le 2 \\ (-3 + \sqrt{1 + 4x})/4, & 2 < x \le 12 \\ (13 - \sqrt{1 + 4x})/6, & 12 < x \le 42 \\ 0, & x > 42. \end{cases}$$

The appropriate sign for the square root is determined by satisfying $\alpha \in [0, 1]$ within the appropriate ranges of x. The ranges of $x \in \Re^+$ are determined from the products of ranges of x from $\mu_A(x)$ and $\mu_B(x)$.

For $A(:)B$, using Eq. (5.34) and A_α from Eq. (5.43) and B_α from Eq. (5.44), we have

$$A_\alpha(:)B_\alpha = \left[\frac{2\alpha + 1}{-3\alpha + 7}, \frac{-3\alpha + 6}{2\alpha + 2} \right],$$

which, using a similar technique to find the ranges of x where the α-cuts are valid, leads to the following membership function

$$\mu_{A\,(:)\,B}(x) = \begin{cases} 0, & x \le \dfrac{1}{7} \\[2mm] (7x-1)/(3x+2), & \dfrac{1}{7} < x \le \dfrac{3}{4} \\[2mm] (-2x+6)/(2x+3), & \dfrac{3}{4} < x \le 3 \\[2mm] 0, & x > 3. \end{cases}$$

Again the appropriate ranges of $x \in \Re^+$ for the above membership function are obtained by dividing the appropriate ranges of x in $\mu_A(x)$ by the appropriate ranges of x in $\mu_B(x)$.

Finally, let us find $k\,(\cdot)\,A$ for $k = 5$. Using Eq. (5.36), the membership function of $\mu_{k\,(\cdot)\,A}(x)$ is

$$\mu_{k\,(\cdot)\,A}(x) = \mu_A\!\left(\dfrac{x}{5}\right) = \begin{cases} 0, & x \le 5 \\[2mm] (x-5)/10, & 5 < x \le 15 \\[2mm] (-x+30)/15, & 15 < x \le 30 \\[2mm] 0, & x > 30. \end{cases}$$

The operations on fuzzy numbers have properties similar to those listed in Table 5.1, and they are summarized in Table 5.2. Again, subtraction and division are neither commutative nor associative. In addition to the above algebraic properties, the operations on fuzzy numbers have the following properties:

1. If A and B are fuzzy numbers in $\Re$, then $A(+)B$ and $A(-)B$ are also fuzzy numbers.
2. If A and B are fuzzy numbers in $\Re^+$, then $A(\cdot)B$ and $A(:)B$ are also fuzzy numbers.
3. There are no image and inverse fuzzy numbers $\overline{A}$ and A^{-1}, respectively, such that [Yager, 1979a]

$$A(+)\overline{A} = 0 \qquad \text{and} \qquad A(\cdot)A^{-1} = 1. \tag{5.45}$$

4. The following inequalities are true:

$$(A(-)B)(+)B \ne A \qquad \text{and} \qquad (A(:)B)(\cdot)B \ne A. \tag{5.46}$$

To prove the above properties, the concept of α-cuts is usually used. The techniques are similar to what will be employed in the proof of the following theorem.

TABLE 5.2 Algebraic Properties of Addition and Multiplication on Fuzzy Numbers

Property	Addition, $(+)$	Multiplication, $(\cdot)$
Fuzzy numbers	For all $A, B, C \subset \Re$	For all $A, B, C \subset \Re^+$
Commutativity	$A(+)B = B(+)A$	$A(\cdot)B = B(\cdot)A$
Associativity	$(A(+)B)(+)C = A(+)(B(+)C)$	$(A(\cdot)B)(\cdot)C = A(\cdot)(B(\cdot)C)$
Ordinary number	$A(+)0 = 0(+)A = A$	$A(\cdot)1 = 1(\cdot)A = A$
Image and inverse	$A(+)\overline{A} = \overline{A}(+)A \ne 0$	$A(\cdot)A^{-1} = A^{-1}(\cdot)A \ne 1$

Theorem 5.1

Let A, B, C be fuzzy numbers in $\mathfrak{R}^+$; then the following distributivity holds

$$(A\,(+)\,B)\,(\cdot)\,C = (A\,(\cdot)\,C)\,(+)\,(B\,(\cdot)\,C)\,. \qquad (5.47)$$

Proof

$$((A\,(+)\,B)\,(\cdot)\,C)_\alpha = \left([a_1^{(\alpha)}, a_2^{(\alpha)}]\,(+)\,[b_1^{(\alpha)}, b_2^{(\alpha)}]\right)(\cdot)\,[c_1^{(\alpha)}, c_2^{(\alpha)}]$$

$$= [a_1^{(\alpha)} + b_1^{(\alpha)}, a_2^{(\alpha)} + b_2^{(\alpha)}]\,(\cdot)\,[c_1^{(\alpha)}, c_2^{(\alpha)}]$$

$$= [a_1^{(\alpha)} \cdot c_1^{(\alpha)} + b_1^{(\alpha)} \cdot c_1^{(\alpha)}, a_2^{(\alpha)} \cdot c_2^{(\alpha)} + b_2^{(\alpha)} \cdot c_2^{(\alpha)}],$$

and

$$((A\,(\cdot)\,C)\,(+)\,(B\,(\cdot)\,C))_\alpha = \left([a_1^{(\alpha)}, a_2^{(\alpha)}]\,(\cdot)\,[c_1^{(\alpha)}, c_2^{(\alpha)}]\right)(+)\left([b_1^{(\alpha)}, b_2^{(\alpha)}]\,(\cdot)\,[c_1^{(\alpha)}, c_2^{(\alpha)}]\right)$$

$$= [a_1^{(\alpha)} \cdot c_1^{(\alpha)} + b_1^{(\alpha)} \cdot c_1^{(\alpha)}, a_2^{(\alpha)} \cdot c_2^{(\alpha)} + b_2^{(\alpha)} \cdot c_2^{(\alpha)}].$$

So Eq. (5.47) is obtained.

Note that distributivity does not hold for $(A\,(\cdot)\,B)(+)C \neq (A(+)C)(\cdot)(B(+)C)$.

It is worth noting from property 3 that equations with fuzzy numbers cannot be solved in the usual manner. This is because of the lack of additive and multiplicative inverses. Under this circumstance, we can only try to find the degree of truth associated with a given solution [Yager, 1979a; Kandel, 1986] in some less complicated cases. For instance, given fuzzy numbers A and C, find B such that $A(+)B = C$ or find B such that $A(\cdot)B = C$. However, if some conditions are met by A and C, then the solution B can be obtained. Details on the solution of fuzzy number equations can be found in [Kaufmann and Gupta, 1991].

Let us extend the min and max operations of intervals [Eqs. (5.26) and (5.27)] to fuzzy numbers. Two fuzzy numbers A and B in $\mathfrak{R}$ are comparable if

$$a_1^{(\alpha)} \leq b_1^{(\alpha)} \qquad \text{and} \qquad a_2^{(\alpha)} \leq b_2^{(\alpha)} \qquad \text{for all } \alpha \in [0, 1], \qquad (5.48)$$

and we can write $A \leq B$. The *fuzzy minimum* and *fuzzy maximum* of two fuzzy numbers A and B in $\mathfrak{R}$ are denoted as $A(\wedge)B$ and $A(\vee)B$, respectively, and are defined, respectively, by

$$A_\alpha(\wedge)B_\alpha \equiv [\min(a_1^{(\alpha)}, b_1^{(\alpha)}), \min(a_2^{(\alpha)}, b_2^{(\alpha)})] = [a_1^{(\alpha)} \wedge b_1^{(\alpha)}, a_2^{(\alpha)} \wedge b_2^{(\alpha)}]. \qquad (5.49)$$

$$A_\alpha(\vee)B_\alpha \equiv [\max(a_1^{(\alpha)}, b_1^{(\alpha)}), \max(a_2^{(\alpha)}, b_2^{(\alpha)})] = [a_1^{(\alpha)} \vee b_1^{(\alpha)}, a_2^{(\alpha)} \vee b_2^{(\alpha)}]. \qquad (5.50)$$

Example 5.8

Compute the fuzzy minimum and fuzzy maximum of the two triangular fuzzy numbers shown in Fig. 5.3, where their membership functions are

$$\mu_A(x) = \begin{cases} 0, & x \leq -3 \\ x+3, & -3 < x \leq -2 \\ (-x+5)/7, & -2 < x \leq 5 \\ 0, & x > 5, \end{cases} \qquad \text{and} \qquad \mu_B(x) = \begin{cases} 0, & x \leq -4 \\ (x+4)/5, & -4 < x \leq 1 \\ -x+2, & 1 < x \leq 2 \\ 0, & x > 2. \end{cases}$$

The α-cuts from $\mu_A(x)$ and $\mu_B(x)$ are computed:

$$A_\alpha = [\alpha - 3, -7\alpha + 5] \qquad \text{and} \qquad B_\alpha = [5\alpha - 4, -\alpha + 2]\,. \qquad (5.51)$$

Thus, the minimum of $A\,(\wedge)\,B$ is

Possibility Theory and Fuzzy Arithmetic   Chap. 5

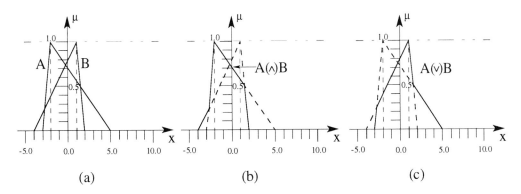

Figure 5.3 Triangular fuzzy numbers in Example 5.8. (a) Two triangular fuzzy numbers A and B. (b) Minimum of fuzzy numbers A and B. (c) Maximum of fuzzy numbers A and B.

$$A_\alpha (\wedge) B_\alpha = [\,(\alpha - 3) \wedge (5\alpha - 4),\ (-7\alpha + 5) \wedge (-\alpha + 2)\,] \equiv [c_1^{(\alpha)}, c_2^{(\alpha)}]. \tag{5.52}$$

Equation (5.52) indicates that it is possible to have four combinations of the above α-cuts when evaluating their minimum, namely, $\{[a_1^{(\alpha)}, a_2^{(\alpha)}], [a_1^{(\alpha)}, b_2^{(\alpha)}], [b_1^{(\alpha)}, a_2^{(\alpha)}], [b_1^{(\alpha)}, b_2^{(\alpha)}]\}$. To determine these combinations, we need to find the α values at which the membership functions $\mu_A(x)$ and $\mu_B(x)$ cross each other. These α values can be obtained by solving the following equations from the $c_1^{(\alpha)}$ and $c_2^{(\alpha)}$ in Eq. (5.52):

$$\alpha - 3 = 5\alpha - 4,$$

$$-7\alpha + 5 = -\alpha + 2.$$

Solving these equations indicates that the membership functions $\mu_A(x)$ and $\mu_B(x)$ cross at $\alpha = 0.25$ and $\alpha = 0.50$. With these α values, we can evaluate the minimum of Eq. (5.52):

$$A_\alpha (\wedge) B_\alpha = \begin{cases} [5\alpha - 4, -\alpha + 2], & 0 \le \alpha \le 0.25 \\ [\alpha - 3, -\alpha + 2], & 0.25 < \alpha \le 0.50 \\ [\alpha - 3, -7\alpha + 5], & 0.50 < \alpha \le 1. \end{cases} \tag{5.53}$$

Using these α-cuts, we can find the membership function of $\mu_{A_\alpha (\wedge) B_\alpha}(x)$ by evaluating the appropriate ranges of x in each α-cut as before.

$$\mu_{A_\alpha (\wedge) B_\alpha}(x) = \begin{cases} 0, & x \le -4 \\ (x + 4)/5, & -4 < x \le -2.75 \\ x + 3, & -2.75 < x \le -2.0 \\ (-x + 5)/7, & -2.0 < x \le 1.5 \\ -x + 2, & 1.5 < x \le 2 \\ 0, & x > 2. \end{cases}$$

Similarly, for the maximum of $A \, (\vee) \, B$, we have [from Eqs. (5.50) and (5.51)]

$$A_\alpha (\vee) B_\alpha = [\,(\alpha - 3) \vee (5\alpha - 4),\ (-7\alpha + 5) \vee (-\alpha + 2)\,] \equiv [c_1^{(\alpha)}, c_2^{(\alpha)}]. \tag{5.54}$$

Since the membership functions $\mu_A(x)$ and $\mu_B(x)$ cross at $\alpha = 0.25$ and $\alpha = 0.50$, we can evaluate the maximum of Eq. (5.54):

$$A_\alpha(\vee)B_\alpha = \begin{cases} [\alpha - 3, -7\alpha + 5], & 0 \le \alpha \le 0.25 \\ [5\alpha - 4, -7\alpha + 5], & 0.25 < \alpha \le 0.50 \\ [5\alpha - 4, -\alpha + 2], & 0.50 < \alpha \le 1. \end{cases} \tag{5.55}$$

Using these α-cuts, we can find the membership function of $\mu_{A_\alpha(\vee)B_\alpha}(x)$ by evaluating the appropriate ranges of x in each α-cut as before:

$$\mu_{A_\alpha(\vee)B_\alpha}(x) = \begin{cases} 0, & x \le -3 \\ x + 3, & -3 < x \le -2.75 \\ (x+4)/5, & -2.75 < x \le 1 \\ -x + 2, & 1 < x \le 1.5 \\ (-x+5)/7, & 1.5 < x \le 5 \\ 0, & x > 5. \end{cases}$$

L-R Fuzzy Numbers

From the above discussion of mathematical operations on fuzzy numbers, it is obvious that they are computationally intensive, which hinders their applicability to real-world problems. To increase the computational efficiency, Dubois and Prade [1980] proposed the L-R representation of fuzzy numbers, which increases the computational efficiency without limiting its generality. In essence, the L-R representation of fuzzy numbers is a parametric representation of fuzzy numbers, and the computational efficiency in L-R fuzzy numbers is achieved by calculating their parametric representation (and with some approximations in some cases).

Consider, in general, an L-R reference (or shape) function $\phi(x) \in [0, 1]$:

$$\phi(x) = \begin{cases} L(x), & -\infty < x < 0 \\ 1, & x = 0 \\ R(x), & 0 < x < \infty \end{cases} \qquad \text{for all } x \in \mathcal{R}. \tag{5.56}$$

Both reference functions $L(x)$ and $R(x)$ map $\mathcal{R}^+ \rightarrow [0, 1]$ and are monotonic nonincreasing functions. L (or R) is a reference function of fuzzy numbers if and only if (i) $L(x) = L(-x)$, (ii) $L(0) = 1$, and (iii) L is nonincreasing on $[0, +\infty)$. Hence, $\phi(x)$ is a normal convex function; however, $L(x)$ and $R(x)$ are not necessarily symmetric. Thus, an L-R fuzzy number is represented by a pair of functions $L(x)$ and $R(x)$ with nonincreasing monotonicity. Different functions can be chosen for $L(x)$ (a decreasing function). For instance, $L(x) = \max(0, 1 - x^p)$ for $p > 0$, $L(x) = e^{-x}$ or $L(x) = e^{-x^2}$, and $L(x) = 1$ for $x \in [-1, +1]$ and 0 otherwise.

A fuzzy number M is called an L-R fuzzy number if its membership function is defined by

$$\mu_M(x) = \begin{cases} L[(m - x)/\alpha], & x < m, \ \alpha > 0 \\ 1, & x = m \\ R[(x - m)/\beta], & x > m, \ \beta > 0, \end{cases} \tag{5.57}$$

where L and R are monotonic nonincreasing functions, m is the mean value of M, and α and β are called the left and right *spreads*, respectively. When the spreads are zero, M is a non-fuzzy number. As the spreads increase, M becomes fuzzier. If $m < 0$, we have a left translation (i.e., the fuzzy number is moved to the left); If $m > 0$, we have a right translation. If $\alpha < 1$ and $\beta < 1$, we have a contraction; if $\alpha > 1$ and $\beta > 1$, we have a dilation on their respective reference function. Symbolically, the *L-R* fuzzy number M is represented by three parameters (m, α, β) and is denoted by

$$M = (m, \alpha, \beta)_{LR}. \tag{5.58}$$

Because of the parametric representation of the L and R functions, the mathematical operations on two *L-R* fuzzy numbers are much simpler. Consider two *L-R* fuzzy numbers $A = (m, \alpha, \beta)_{LR}$ and $B = (n, \gamma, \delta)_{LR}$ in $\Re$ with nonincreasing L and R reference functions. We have

- **Addition:**

$$A(+)B = (m, \alpha, \beta)_{LR}(+)(n, \gamma, \delta)_{LR} = (m + n, \alpha + \gamma, \beta + \delta)_{LR}. \tag{5.59}$$

- **Image:** The opposite or an image of an *L-R* fuzzy number A is

$$\overline{A} = -(m, \alpha, \beta)_{LR} = (-m, \beta, \alpha)_{RL}. \tag{5.60}$$

Note that the L and R are exchanged. That is, the image of A can be obtained from A by a left translation of $-m$; it uses the R reference function as its left reference function with a spread value of β and uses the L reference function as its right reference function with a spread value of α.

- **Subtraction:** Because $L(x)$ and $R(x)$ are not necessarily symmetric, subtraction of two *L-R* fuzzy numbers must conform to their reference functions. That is, for $A = (m, \alpha, \beta)_{LR}$ and $B = (n, \gamma, \delta)_{RL}$ in $\Re$, we have

$$A(-)B = (m, \alpha, \beta)_{LR}(-)(n, \gamma, \delta)_{RL} = (m - n, \alpha + \delta, \beta + \gamma)_{LR}. \tag{5.61}$$

- **Multiplication:** When multiplying by an ordinary number $k \in \Re$, we have

$$k(\cdot)A = k(\cdot)(m, \alpha, \beta)_{LR} = \begin{cases} (km, k\alpha, k\beta)_{LR}, & k > 0 \\ (km, -k\beta, -k\alpha)_{RL}, & k < 0. \end{cases} \tag{5.62}$$

It is noted that the multiplication of two *L-R* fuzzy numbers is not an *L-R* fuzzy number. Neither the inverse of an *L-R* fuzzy number or the division of two *L-R* fuzzy numbers is an *L-R* fuzzy number. However, the results of these operations can be approximated to be *L-R* fuzzy numbers. The reader is referred to [Dubois and Prade, 1980] for details.

Example 5.9

Consider the left and right reference functions as (see Fig. 5.4)

$$L(x) = \begin{cases} 0, & x < -1 \\ \sqrt{1 + x}, & -1 \leq x \leq 0 \end{cases} \quad \text{and} \quad R(x) = \begin{cases} 1 - x^2, & 0 \leq x \leq 1 \\ 0, & x > 1. \end{cases}$$

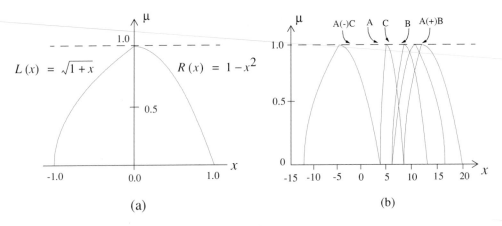

Figure 5.4 Left and right reference functions in Example 5.9. (a) An *L-R* fuzzy number. (b) Fuzzy addition and subtraction of two *L-R* fuzzy numbers.

Three *L-R* fuzzy numbers *A*, *B*, and *C*, with their means and left and right spreads, are given as

$$A = (m, \alpha, \beta)_{LR} = (3, 1, 3)_{LR},$$

$$B = (n, \gamma, \delta)_{LR} = (6, 2, 4)_{LR},$$

$$C = (p, \zeta, \lambda)_{RL} = (8, 4, 5)_{RL}.$$

Using Eq. (5.59) for adding fuzzy numbers *A* and *B*, we have

$$A(+)B = (m + n, \alpha + \gamma, \beta + \delta)_{LR} = (3 + 6, 1 + 2, 3 + 4)_{LR} = (9, 3, 7)_{LR}.$$

Using Eq. (5.61) to subtract *C* from *A*, we have

$$A(-)C = (m, \alpha, \beta)_{LR} (-) (p, \zeta, \lambda)_{RL} = (m - p, \alpha + \lambda, \beta + \zeta)_{LR}$$
$$= (3 - 8, 1 + 5, 3 + 4)_{LR} = (-5, 6, 7)_{LR}.$$

Quite often we may have an *L-R* fuzzy number whose mean value *m* does not occur at one single value of $x \in \Re$ but rather has a "flat interval" at $\alpha = 1$. This is called an *L-R fuzzy interval* instead of an *L-R* fuzzy number.

An *L-R* fuzzy interval *M* has a membership function defined by

$$\mu_M(x) = \begin{cases} L[(m_1 - x)/\alpha], & x < m_1, \alpha > 0 \\ 1, & x \in [m_1, m_2] \\ R[(x - m_2)/\beta], & x > m_2, \beta > 0, \end{cases} \quad (5.63)$$

where m_1 and m_2 indicate the starting and ending flat interval of the mean value of the *L-R* fuzzy interval, respectively, and *L* and *R* reference functions are nonincreasing functions. If *L* and *R* are monotonic increasing and decreasing functions, respectively, then the *L-R* fuzzy interval *M* has a membership function defined by

$$\mu_M(x) = \begin{cases} L[(x - m_1)/\alpha], & x < m_1, \alpha > 0 \\ 1, & x \in [m_1, m_2] \\ R[(x - m_2)/\beta], & x > m_2, \beta > 0. \end{cases} \qquad (5.64)$$

We denote such an L-R fuzzy interval as $M \equiv (m_1, m_2, \alpha, \beta)_{LR}$.

Let us now consider the arithmetic operations on L-R fuzzy intervals. The use of L-R fuzzy intervals is mainly for addition, subtraction, and multiplication by an ordinary number. For other operations, some approximations must be used. Consider two L-R fuzzy intervals $M = (m_1, m_2, \alpha, \beta)_{LR}$ and $N = (n_1, n_2, \gamma, \delta)_{LR}$ in $\Re$ with nonincreasing L and R reference functions. We have

- **Addition:**

$$M(+)N \equiv (m_1, m_2, \alpha, \beta)_{LR}(+)(n_1, n_2, \gamma, \delta)_{LR}$$
$$= (m_1 + n_1, m_2 + n_2, \alpha + \gamma, \beta + \delta)_{LR}. \qquad (5.65)$$

- **Image:** The image of an L-R fuzzy interval M is

$$\overline{M} = -(m_1, m_2, \alpha, \beta)_{LR} = (-m_2, -m_1, \beta, \alpha)_{RL}. \qquad (5.66)$$

- **Subtraction:** Again because $L(x)$ and $R(x)$ are not necessarily symmetric, subtraction of two L-R fuzzy intervals must conform to their reference functions. That is, M and N must be of opposite type, $M = (m_1, m_2, \alpha, \beta)_{LR}$ and $N = (n_1, n_2, \gamma, \delta)_{RL}$. Then

$$M(-)N \equiv (m_1, m_2, \alpha, \beta)_{LR}(-)(n_1, n_2, \gamma, \delta)_{RL}$$
$$= (m_1 - n_2, m_2 - n_1, \alpha + \delta, \beta + \gamma)_{LR}. \qquad (5.67)$$

- **Multiplication:** When $M > 0$ is multiplied by an ordinary number $k \in \Re$, we have

$$k(\cdot)M = k(\cdot)(m_1, m_2, \alpha, \beta)_{LR}$$
$$= \begin{cases} (km_1, km_2, k\alpha, k\beta)_{LR}, & k > 0 \\ (km_2, km_1, |k|\beta, |k|\alpha)_{RL}, & k < 0. \end{cases} \qquad (5.68)$$

As in the case of L-R fuzzy numbers, the multiplication of two L-R fuzzy intervals is not an L-R fuzzy interval. Neither the inverse of an L-R fuzzy interval or the division of two L-R fuzzy intervals is an L-R fuzzy interval. However, the results of these operations can be approximated to be L-R fuzzy intervals. Details can be found in [Dubois and Prade, 1980].

Example 5.10

Consider the setting up of a research budget forecast from various funding sources or agencies. The sources are referred to as A, B, and C:

Source A: A certain and precise amount of $60,000 is expected from the National Science Foundation (NSF).

Source B: Funding from the Office of Naval Research (ONR) may range from $60,000 to $120,000, but it is reasonable to expect an amount of $70,000 to $100,000.

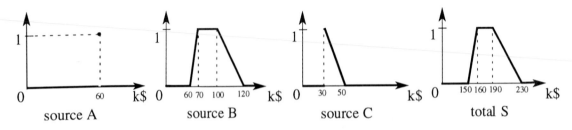

Figure 5.5 Fuzzy numbers in Example 5.10.

Source C: Funding from the Army Research Office (ARO) may amount to $30,000 but may not be more than $50,000.

These three sources of finance can be represented as three *L-R* fuzzy intervals (unit is in thousands): $A = (60, 60, 0, 0)_{LR}$, $B = (70, 100, 10, 20)_{LR}$, and $C = (30, 30, 0, 20)_{LR}$, with the functions L and R defined by $L(x) = R(x) = \max(0, 1 - x), x \in \mathbb{R}^+$. These three *L-R* fuzzy intervals are shown in Fig. 5.5. Then the total amount S can be estimated as

$$S = A(+)B(+)C = (60, 60, 0, 0)_{LR}(+)(70, 100, 10, 20)_{LR}(+)(30, 30, 0, 20)_{LR}$$

$$= (160, 190, 10, 40)_{LR},$$

which is also shown in Fig. 5.5. So the possible amount is $150,000 to $230,000 and the expected amount is $160,000 to $190,000.

5.2.3 Ordering of Fuzzy Numbers

Several methods have been developed to compare two fuzzy numbers or to rank a set of n fuzzy numbers [Bortolan and Degani, 1985]. We shall introduce a technique based on the concept of possibility measure of a fuzzy set developed in Sec. 4.1 [Dubois and Prade, 1988b]. First, associated with a fuzzy number A, two fuzzy sets, denoted as A_P and A_N, are defined. For a fuzzy number A, the set of numbers that are possibly greater than or equal to A is denoted as A_P and is defined as

$$\mu_{A_P}(w) \equiv \Pi_A((-\infty, w)) = \sup_{u \leq w} \mu_A(u). \tag{5.69}$$

Similarly, the set of numbers that are necessarily greater than A is denoted as A_N and is defined as

$$\mu_{A_N}(w) \equiv N_A((-\infty, w)) = \inf_{u \geq w}(1 - \mu_A(u)), \tag{5.70}$$

where Π_A and N_A are the possibility and necessity measures defined in Eqs. (4.46) and (4.47), respectively. Examples of A, A_P, and A_N are shown in Fig. 5.6, from which μ_{A_P} and μ_{A_N} can be viewed as the upper and lower possibility distribution functions of A, respectively. Then we try to compare two fuzzy numbers A and B to see whether A is greater than B. To achieve this, we can compare A with B_P and B_N by means of an index of comparison such as the possibility or necessity measure of a fuzzy set. That is, we can calculate the possibility and the necessity measures, in the sense of μ_A, of the fuzzy sets B_P and B_N. In this way we obtain four fundamental indices of comparison. (In the following explanation, we assume that X and Y are variables whose domains are constrained by μ_A and μ_B, respectively.)

Possibility Theory and Fuzzy Arithmetic   Chap. 5

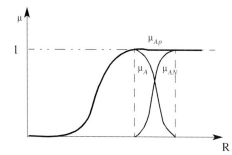

Figure 5.6 Fuzzy number A and its associated A_P.

1.
$$\Pi_A(B_P) = \sup_u \min\left(\mu_A(u), \sup_{v \leq u} \mu_B(v)\right)$$
$$= \sup_{u \geq v} \min\left(\mu_A(u), \mu_B(v)\right), \tag{5.71}$$

which indicates the possibility that the largest value X can take is at least equal to the smallest value that Y can take.

2.
$$\Pi_A(B_N) = \sup_u \min\left(\mu_A(u), \inf_{v \geq u} [1 - \mu_B(v)]\right)$$
$$= \sup_u \inf_{v \geq u} \min\left(\mu_A(u), 1 - \mu_B(v)\right), \tag{5.72}$$

which indicates the possibility that the largest value X can take is greater than the largest value that Y can take.

3.
$$N_A(B_P) = \inf_u \max\left(1 - \mu_A(u), \sup_{v \leq u} \mu_B(v)\right)$$
$$= \inf_u \sup_{v \leq u} \max\left(1 - \mu_A(u), \mu_B(v)\right), \tag{5.73}$$

which indicates the necessity that the smallest value X can take is at least equal to the smallest value that Y can take.

4.
$$N_A(B_N) = \inf_u \max\left(1 - \mu_A(u), \inf_{v \geq u} [1 - \mu_B(v)]\right)$$
$$= 1 - \sup_{u \leq v} \min\left(\mu_A(u), \mu_B(v)\right), \tag{5.74}$$

which indicates the necessity that the smallest value X can take is greater than the largest value that Y can take.

An example of computation of the above four indices is shown in Fig. 5.7. It shows that the four comparison indices of two triangular or trapezoidal fuzzy numbers can be obtained graphically. That is,

1. $\Pi_A(B_P)$ corresponds to the intersection of the right-hand spread of μ_A and the left-hand spread of μ_B.
2. $\Pi_A(B_N)$ corresponds to the intersection of the right-hand spreads of μ_A and $(1 - \mu_B)$.
3. $N_A(B_p)$ corresponds to the intersection of the left-hand spread of $1 - \mu_A$ and the left-hand spread of μ_B.

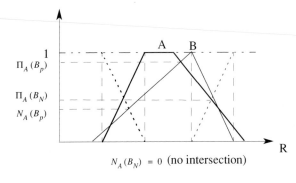

$N_A(B_N) = 0$ (no intersection)

Figure 5.7 Four comparison indices of two fuzzy numbers.

With these four indices, we are ready to order a set of n fuzzy numbers $\{M_1, M_2, \ldots, M_n\}$. For such an ordering problem, four indices can be assigned to each M_i as a comparison with the others:

$$\text{PSE}(M_i) = \min_{j \neq i} \Pi_{M_i}\big((M_j)_P\big),$$

$$\text{PS}(M_i) = \min_{j \neq i} \Pi_{M_i}\big((M_j)_N\big),$$

$$\text{NSE}(M_i) = \min_{j \neq i} N_{M_i}\big((M_j)_P\big),$$

$$\text{NS}(M_i) = \min_{j \neq i} N_{M_i}\big((M_j)_N\big),$$

(5.75)

where PSE indicates the possibility that the largest value M_i can take is at least equal to the smallest value that the other fuzzy numbers can take, PS indicates the possibility that the largest value M_i can take is greater than the largest value that the other fuzzy numbers can take, NSE indicates the necessity that the smallest value M_i can take is at least equal to the smallest value that the other fuzzy numbers can take, and NS indicates the necessity that the smallest value M_i can take is greater than the largest value that the other fuzzy numbers can take.

Example 5.11

Consider the three fuzzy numbers N_1, N_2, and N_3 in Fig. 5.8. We want to find the largest fuzzy number among them. The four indices in Eq. (5.75) can be obtained in the way indicated in Fig. 5.7 as follows.

	PSE	PS	NSE	NS
N_1	1	1/3	2/7	0
N_2	8/9	2/5	1/2	0
N_3	1	3/5	1/2	0

From the result we can determine the largest one. Because the intervals overlap each other, none strictly dominates the others with respect to necessity (NS = 0). Ordering by the index PS shows that the largest values that X_3 can take are greater than those the other variables can take. Ordering by the index NSE shows that N_1 is out of consideration for the largest number, and ordering by index PSE puts N_2 aside. Thus, we conclude that N_3 can be considered the largest of these fuzzy numbers.

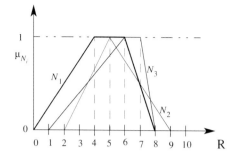

Figure 5.8   Three fuzzy numbers in Example 5.11.

5.3 CONCLUDING REMARKS

Differences between possibility theory and probability theory are briefly discussed in this chapter, and marginal, joint, and conditional possibility distributions are explored with numerical examples. Fuzzy arithmetic, which can be considered an extension of interval arithmetic, is thoroughly discussed. Operations and computations on fuzzy numbers are worked out with illustrative examples.

In practical situations, the fuzziness that arises from human thinking processes and the randomness associated with experiments are often mixed together. Kaufmann and Gupta [1991] thus proposed hybrid numbers to combine fuzzy and random data. This can also be viewed as a way of combining possibility and probability. For the properties of hybrid numbers and some advanced topics in fuzzy arithmetic, the reader is referred to [Kaufmann and Gupta, 1991].

Another way of combining possibility and probability is to define the probability of a fuzzy event. Based on the probability measure, Zadeh [1968] defined the probability of a fuzzy event as the expectation of its membership function. The probability of fuzzy events has the same properties as in the case of ordinary probability. We can also derive the fuzzy total probability formula and the fuzzy Bayes formula, which are similar to their counterparts in classical probability theory. The fuzzy Bayes formula can be used for fuzzy decision making that involves fuzzy conditions. [Terano et al., 1992]. Other applications of fuzzy probability include *fuzzy discrimination methods* that choose the decision that minimizes the average probability of error discrimination, and *fuzzy quantification theory,* which can quantify qualitative judgments and evaluations by replacing qualitative expressions with numerical expressions [Terano et al., 1992]. Kandel [1986] extended Zadeh's definition of the probability of fuzzy events to the probability of *time-dependent* fuzzy events, in which the membership function is a function of time. Unlike Zadeh, Yager [1984b] defined the probability of a fuzzy event using the probability of an α-cut.

5.4 PROBLEMS

5.1   Find the degree of consistency of the probability distribution p_X with the possibility distribution π_X in Example 5.1.

5.2   In Example 5.4, what is the possibility distribution $\pi_{(\text{Weight,Height})}$ derived from π_{Weight}?

5.3 **(a)** Prove that there are no image and inverse fuzzy numbers $\overline{A}$ and A^{-1} such that $A\,(+)$ $\overline{A} = 0, A\,(\cdot)\,A^{(-1)} = 1$.

(b) Prove that the following inequalities are true:

$$(A\,(-)\,B)\,(+)\,B \neq A \qquad \text{and} \qquad (A\,(:)\,B)\,(\cdot)\,B \neq A.$$

(c) Prove that distributivity does not hold for

$$(A\,(\cdot)\,B)\,(+)\,C \neq (A\,(+)\,C)\,(\cdot)\,(B\,(+)\,C).$$

5.4 Let $A = 0.3/0 + 0.7/1 + 1/2 + 0.7/3 + 0.3/4$ and $B = 0.3/2 + 0.7/3 + 1/4 + 0.7/5 + 0.3/0.6$. Calculate $A\,(+)\,B, A\,(-)\,B, A\,(\cdot)\,B$, and $A\,(:)\,B$.

5.5 Let $A = B = \int_0^1 x/x$. What are the algebraic sum and algebraic product of A and B?

5.6 Two triangular fuzzy numbers A and B are given, whose membership functions are, respectively,

$$\mu_A(x) = \begin{cases} x/3, & \text{if } 0 \le x \le 3 \\ 4 - x, & \text{if } 3 \le x \le 4 \\ 0, & \text{otherwise,} \end{cases} \qquad \mu_B(x) = \begin{cases} x - 1, & \text{if } 1 \le x \le 2 \\ (-x + 6)/4, & \text{if } 2 \le x \le 6 \\ 0, & \text{otherwise.} \end{cases}$$

(a) Compute $A\,(+)\,B$ and $A\,(-)\,B$.

(b) Compute $A\,(:)\,B$ and $A\,(\cdot)\,B$.

(c) Compute $A\,(\wedge)\,B$ and $A\,(\vee)\,B$.

5.7 Two triangular fuzzy numbers A and B are given, whose membership functions are, respectively:

$$\mu_A(x) = \begin{cases} 0, & \text{if } x \le 0 \\ x/4, & \text{if } 0 \le x \le 4 \\ (-x + 12)/8, & \text{if } 4 \le x \le 12 \\ 0, & \text{if } x \ge 12, \end{cases} \qquad \mu_B(x) = \begin{cases} 0, & x \le 1 \\ (x - 1)/2, & 1 \le x \le 3 \\ -x/12 + 5/4, & 3 \le x \le 15 \\ 0, & x \ge 15. \end{cases}$$

(a) Compute $A\,(+)\,B$ and $A\,(-)\,B$.

(b) Compute $A\,(:)\,B$ and $A\,(\cdot)\,B$.

(c) Compute $A\,(\wedge)\,B$ and $A\,(\vee)\,B$.

5.8 Given an L-R fuzzy number in Example 5.9 represented by $M = (m, \alpha, \beta)_{LR}$, sketch M if (a) $M = (3, 1, 2)_{LR}$, (b) $M = (-1, 5, 5)_{LR}$, and (c) $M = (4, 10, 6)_{LR}$.

5.9 Given two L-R fuzzy numbers $M = (3, 4, 2)_{LR}$ and $N = (2, 2, 3)_{LR}$, compute $M\,(+)\,N$, $M\,(-)\,\overline{N}, M\,(\cdot)\,N, M\,(:)\,N, M\,(\wedge)\,N$, and $M\,(\vee)\,N$.

5.10 Given two L-R fuzzy numbers $M = (4, 0.3, 0.2)$ and $N = (2, 0.1, 0.2)$, with

$$L(x) = R(x) = \begin{cases} 1, & -1 \le x \le 1 \\ 0, & \text{otherwise,} \end{cases}$$

what is the L-R representations of $M\,(\cdot)\,N$?

5.11 Which of the following functions can be used for L-R reference functions?

(a) $f_1(x) = e^{-x}$

(b) $f_2(x) = \dfrac{1}{1 + 2x^2}$

(c) $f_3(x) = |3x + 1|$

(d) $f_4(x) = \dfrac{1}{1 + 3|x|^2}$

(e) $f_5(x) = \begin{cases} x/3 + 1, & -3 \le x \le 0 \\ -3x + 1, & 0 < x < \frac{1}{3} \\ 0, & \text{otherwise.} \end{cases}$

5.12 Prove that the addition of $A = (m, \alpha, \beta)_{LR}$ and $B = (n, r, \delta)_{LR}$ is equal to $A(+)B = (m + n, \alpha + r, \beta + \delta)_{LR}$ using the extension principle, i.e.,

$$\mu_{A(+)B}(z) = \bigvee_{z=x+y} (\mu_A(x) \wedge \mu_B(y)).$$

5.13 Using the fuzzy numbers N_1 and N_2 in Example 5.11, verify the following properties:
  (a) $\Pi_A(B_P) \ge \max(\Pi_A(B_N), N_A(B_P))$,
  (b) $N_A(B_N) \le \min(\Pi_A(B_N), N_A(B_P))$,
  (c) $\max(\Pi_A(B_P), \Pi_B(A_P)) = 1$.

5.14 The performance of five students on some exams is listed in the accompanying table. The table shows the possibility for the grades A to E that the students may receive.

Student	A	B	C	D	E
John	0.4	0.5	0.7	0.3	0.2
Jim	0.1	0.6	0.5	0.2	0
Peter	0.3	0.4	0.8	0.5	0.1
Mary	0.9	0.8	0.2	0.1	0
Tracy	0.2	0.8	0.3	0.2	0.1

  (a) What is the necessity that Mary will get a B on her next exam?
  (b) How reliable is it that Jim or Peter will get a B or a C on the next exam?

5.15 Given three fuzzy sets A, B, C and their membership functions

$$\mu_A(x) = \frac{1}{1 + 20x}, \qquad \mu_B(x) = \left(\frac{1}{1 + x}\right)^2, \qquad \mu_C(x) = \left(\frac{1}{1 + x}\right)^{1/2},$$

order the fuzzy sets. (Assume $x \ge 0$.)

6

Fuzzy Logic and Approximate Reasoning

As fuzzy sets are extensions of classical crisp sets, fuzzy logic is an extension of classical two-valued logic. As there is a correspondence between classical crisp sets and classical logic, so is there a correspondence between fuzzy set theory and fuzzy logic. For instance, we have the "union" operator corresponding to the logic OR, "intersection" to AND, and "complement" to NOT. Furthermore, the degree of an element in a fuzzy set may correspond to the truth value of a proposition in fuzzy logic. This chapter focuses on fuzzy logic operations and reasoning. Linguistic variables are first introduced with fuzzy proposition and linguistic truth values. They are then used in fuzzy reasoning, where both the preconditions and the consequents of the rules of inference are fuzzy propositions. Four principal modes of fuzzy reasoning in fuzzy logic are then explored and discussed.

6.1 LINGUISTIC VARIABLES

Linguistic variable is an important concept in fuzzy logic and approximate reasoning and plays a key role in many of its applications, especially in the realm of fuzzy expert systems and fuzzy logic control. Basically, a linguistic variable is a variable whose values are words or sentences in a natural or artificial language. For example, *speed* is a linguistic variable if it takes the values such as *slow, fast, very fast,* and so on. The concept of linguistic variables was introduced by Zadeh [1975a] to provide a means of approximate characterization of phenomena that are too complex or too ill-defined to be amenable to description in conventional quantitative terms. Before we introduce the formal definition of a linguistic variable, let us define a *fuzzy variable* first.

A fuzzy variable is characterized by a triple $(X, U, R(X))$ in which X is the name of the variable, U is a universe of discourse, and $R(X)$ is a fuzzy subset of U which represents a *fuzzy restriction* imposed by X. As an example, $X =$ "Old" with $U = \{10, 20, ..., 80\}$, and $R(X) = 0.1/20 + 0.2/30 + 0.4/40 + 0.5/50 + 0.8/60 + 1/70 + 1/80$ is a fuzzy restriction on "Old."

A linguistic variable is a variable of a higher order than a fuzzy variable, and it takes fuzzy variables as its values. A linguistic variable is characterized by a quintuple $(x, T(x), U, G, M)$ in which x is the name of the variable; $T(x)$ is the term set of x, that is, the set of names of linguistic values of x with each value being a fuzzy variable defined on U; G is a syntactic rule for generating the names of values of x; and M is a semantic rule for associating each value of x with its meaning.

Example 6.1

If *speed* is interpreted as a linguistic variable with $U = [0, 100]$, that is, $x =$ "*speed*," then its term set $T(speed)$ could be

$$T(speed) = \{\text{VERY Slow, Slow, Moderate, Fast}, ...\}.$$

Here the syntactic rule G for generating the names (or the labels) of the elements in $T(speed)$ is quite intuitive. The semantic rule M could be defined as

$M(\text{Slow}) =$ the fuzzy set for "a speed below about 40 miles per hour (mph)" with membership function μ_{Slow}.

$M(\text{Moderate}) =$ the fuzzy set for a "speed close to 55 mph" with membership function μ_{Moderate}.

$M(\text{Fast}) =$ the fuzzy set for "a speed above about 70 mph" with membership function μ_{Fast}.

These terms can be characterized by the fuzzy sets whose membership functions are shown in Fig. 6.1.

In the above example, the term set contains only a small number of terms, and so it is practicable to list the elements of $T(x)$ and set up a direct association between each element and its meaning M. A linguistic variable x is said to be *structured* if its term set $T(x)$ and its semantic rule M can be characterized algorithmically such that they can be viewed as algorithmic procedures for generating the elements of $T(x)$ and computing the meaning of each term in $T(x)$. Before going any further on the structured linguistic variable, let us first intro-

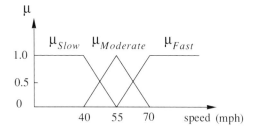

Figure 6.1 Terms of the linguistic variable *speed.*

duce the *linguistic hedge* (or *modifier*) h, which is an operator for modifying the meaning of its operator or, more generally, of a fuzzy set A to create a new fuzzy set $h(A)$. For example, in the fuzzy set "VERY Young," "VERY" is a linguistic hedge. The following fuzzy set operations are frequently used in defining a linguistic hedge:

Concentration: CON(A)

$$\mu_{\text{CON}_{(A)}}(u) = (\mu_A(u))^2. \tag{6.1}$$

Dilation: DIL(A)

$$\mu_{\text{DIL}_{(A)}}(u) = (\mu_A(u))^{1/2}. \tag{6.2}$$

Intensification: INT(A)

$$\mu_{\text{INT}_{(A)}}(u) = \begin{cases} 2(\mu_A(u))^2, & \mu_A(u) \in [0, 0.5] \\ 1 - 2(1 - \mu_A(u))^2, & \text{otherwise.} \end{cases} \tag{6.3}$$

Some popular linguistic hedges are

$$\begin{aligned}
\text{VERY}(A) &= \text{CON}(A) = A^2, \\
\text{HIGHLY}(A) &= A^3, \\
\text{FAIRLY (MORE OR LESS)}(A) &= \text{DIL}(A) = A^{1/2}, \\
\text{ROUGHLY}(A) &= \text{DIL}[\text{DIL}(A)], \\
\text{PLUS}(A) &= A^{1.25}, \\
\text{MINUS}(A) &= A^{0.75}, \\
\text{RATHER}(A) &= \text{INT}[\text{CON}(A)] \text{ AND NOT}[\text{CON}(A)], \\
\text{SLIGHTLY}(A) &= \text{INT}[\text{PLUS}(A) \text{ AND NOT}(\text{VERY}(A))], \\
\text{SORT OF}(A) &= \text{INT}[\text{DIL}(A)] \text{ AND INT}[\text{DIL}(\text{NOT}(A))], \\
\text{PRETTY}(A) &= \text{INT}(A) \text{ AND NOT}[\text{INT}(\text{CON}(A))].
\end{aligned} \tag{6.4}$$

where AND and NOT are the fuzzy conjunction and complement operators defined in Section 2.2.2. The resulting fuzzy sets in Eq. (6.4) should be normalized if the height is not equal to 1. An example is shown in Fig. 6.2 [Lakoff, 1973].

With the aid of linguistic hedges, one can define a term set of a linguistic variable such as

$$T(age) = \{\text{Old, VERY Old, VERY VERY Old},\dots\}, \tag{6.5}$$

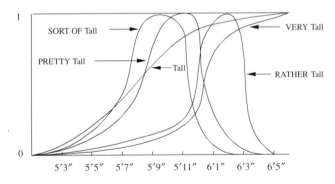

Figure 6.2 Hedges acting on the fuzzy set "Tall." (From *Fuzzy Sets Natural Language Computations and Risk Analysis* by Schmucker. Copyright © 1983 by Computer Science Press. Used with permission of W.H. Freeman and Company.)

in which "Old" is called the *primary term* and the corresponding syntactic rule G, which can generate the term set $T(age)$ recursively, could be the following recursive algorithm:

$$T^{i+1} = \{\text{Old}\} \cup \{\text{VERY } T^i\}, \qquad i = 0, 1, 2, \ldots, \tag{6.6}$$

where $T^0 = \varnothing$. For example, for $i = 0, 1, 2, 3$, we have

$$T^0 = \varnothing,$$
$$T^1 = \{\text{Old}\},$$
$$T^2 = \{\text{Old, VERY Old}\},$$
$$T^3 = \{\text{Old, VERY Old, VERY VERY Old}\}.$$

Furthermore, the semantic rule M that can associate with each T^i a meaning can be the following recursive algorithm:

$$M(T^{i+1}) = M(T^i) \cup \text{Old}^{i+1}, \qquad i = 1, 2, 3, \ldots. \tag{6.7}$$

With Eqs. (6.6) and (6.7), "age" is a *structured linguistic variable.*

One important linguistic variable is "truth," which is of particular interest in fuzzy logic. Some of the terms of "truth" defined by Baldwin [1979] are shown in Fig. 6.3, where the linguistic hedges in Eq. (6.4) are adopted.

Another important topic involving linguistic variables is *linguistic approximation* [Zadeh, 1975a,; Mamdani and Gaines, 1981]. This is a procedure for determining a term from the term set of a linguistic variable such that the meaning of this term is closest to a given fuzzy set. A solution to this problem might be quite intuitive; however, since this a very nontrivial problem, there is a lack of general theory [Novák, 1989]. A very interesting and successful algorithm for linguistic approximation is based on the idea proposed by Esragh and Mamdani [1979]. The computational complexity of their approach is quite high; however, it can be simplified for some special types of fuzzy sets. We shall intuitively solve

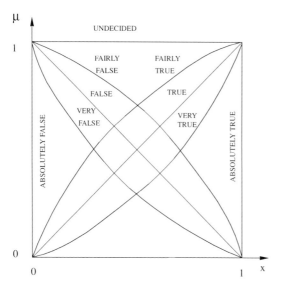

Figure 6.3 Linguistic variable "truth" defined by Baldwin [1979].

the linguistic approximation problem based on the *similarity measure* of two fuzzy sets $E(A, B)$, which indicates the degree of equality of two fuzzy sets A and B and is defined in Eq. (2.30):

$$E(A, B) = \frac{|A \cap B|}{|A \cup B|}, \qquad (6.8)$$

where $|A|$ indicates the cardinality of fuzzy set A and $0 \le E(A, B) \le 1$. One important property of $E(A, B)$ is that when $E(A, B)$ approaches 1, A and B are more similar. The idea that the linguistic approximation of a given fuzzy set A is the term $T_A \in T(x)$, which is the *most similar* to A compared to the other terms in the term set $T(x)$ of a given linguistic variable; that is,

$$E(A, T_A) = \max_{T_i \in T(x)} E(A, T_i). \qquad (6.9)$$

Example 6.2

Given $U = \{0, 0.1, 0.2, ..., 1\}$ and the term set $\{A, B, C\}$ of the linguistic variable "truth," where

$$A = \text{"True"} = 0.7/0.8 + 1/0.9 + 1/1,$$

$$B = \text{"MORE OR LESS True"} = 0.5/0.6 + 0.7/0.7 + 1/0.8 + 1/0.9 + 1/1,$$

$$C = \text{"ALMOST True"} = 0.6/0.8 + 1/0.9 + 0.6/1,$$

find the linguistic approximation of the fuzzy set D defined by

$$D = 0.6/0.8 + 1/0.9 + 1/1.$$

Since $E(D, A) = 2.6/2.7 = 0.96$, $E(D, B) = 2.6/4.2 = 0.62$, and $E(D, C) = 2.2/2.6 = 0.85$, the linguistic approximation of the fuzzy set D is the term A, "True." One application of the linguistic approximation is to set up a *fuzzy truth table*, which will be introduced in the next section (see Example 6.3).

6.2 FUZZY LOGIC

Logic is a basis for *reasoning*. Classical bivalence logic deals with *propositions* that are required to be either *true* (with a logical value of 1) or *false* (with a logical value of 0), which is called the *truth value* of the propositions. Propositions are sentences expressed in some language and can be expressed, in general, in a *canonical form*,

$$x \text{ is } P, \qquad (6.10)$$

where x is a symbol of the *subject* and P designates the *predicate* which characterizes a property of the subject. For example, "Indianapolis is in Indiana" is a proposition in which "Indianapolis" is the subject and "in Indiana" is the predicate that specifies a property of "Indianapolis," namely, its geographical location in Indiana. Each proposition A has an opposite called a *negation* of the proposition and is denoted as $\overline{A}$. A proposition and its negation are required to assume opposite truth values. We shall mainly focus on two major concerns of logic: logic operations and logic reasoning.

Logic operations are (logic) functions of two propositions and are defined via *truth tables*. Consider two propositions A and B, either of which can be true or false. Then the four basic logic operations are conjunction ($\wedge$), disjunction ($\vee$), implication (or conditional) ($\Rightarrow$), and equivalence (or bidirectional) ($\Leftrightarrow$) and are interpreted as "*A* and *B*," "*A* or *B*," "if *A* then *B*," and "*A* if and only if *B*," respectively.

Another major concern of logic systems is the reasoning procedure which is performed through some *inference rules.* Some important inference rules are

$$(A \wedge (A \Rightarrow B)) \Rightarrow B \qquad \text{(modus ponens)}$$
$$(\overline{B} \wedge (A \Rightarrow B)) \Rightarrow \overline{A} \qquad \text{(modus tollens)} \qquad (6.11)$$
$$((A \Rightarrow B) \wedge (B \Rightarrow C)) \Rightarrow (A \Rightarrow C) \qquad \text{(hypothetical syllogism).}$$

The resulting propositions in Eq. (6.11) are always true no matter what the truth values of propositions *A* and *B* are. They are called *tautologies.* The use of Eq. (6.11) for reasoning is clear if, for example, we interpret the modus ponens as: If *A* is true and if the proposition "If *A* is true then *B* is true" is also true, then proposition *B* is true. The modus ponens is closely related to the forward data-driven inference which, when extended to fuzzy logic, is particularly useful for fuzzy logic control. On the other hand, the modus tollens is closely related to the backward goal-driven inference which is usually used in expert systems.

Fuzzy logic is an extension of set-theoretic bivalence logic in which the truth values are terms of the linguistic variable "truth." Its goal is to provide foundations for approximate reasoning with an imprecise proposition using fuzzy set theory. In the following sections we shall show the main features of fuzzy logic that differentiate it from traditional logic systems [Zadeh, 1992]. One feature concerns the truth value in fuzzy logic, and the others concern the proposition in fuzzy logic, called the fuzzy proposition.

6.2.1 Truth Values and Truth Tables in Fuzzy Logic

Unlike the situation in two-valued logic, the truth values of propositions in fuzzy logic are allowed to range over the fuzzy subsets of unit interval [0, 1] or a point in the interval. For example, a truth value in fuzzy logic, "VERY True," may be interpreted as a fuzzy set in [0, 1] and defined as in Fig. 6.3. The *truth value* of the proposition "*X* is *A*," or simply the *truth value* of *A*, which is denoted by $v(A)$ is defined to be a point in [0, 1] (called the *numerical truth value*) or a fuzzy set in [0, 1] (called the *linguistic truth values*).

Next we shall attempt to obtain the truth value of a proposition that comes from the logic operations (i.e., negation, conjunction, disjunction, and implication) of other propositions whose truth values are known. If $v(A)$ and $v(B)$ are numerical truth values of propositions *A* and *B*, respectively, then

$$v(\text{NOT } A) \triangleq 1 - v(A), \qquad (6.12)$$
$$v(A \text{ AND } B) \triangleq v(A) \wedge v(B) = \min\{v(A), v(B)\}, \qquad (6.13)$$
$$v(A \text{ OR } B) \triangleq v(A) \vee v(B) = \max\{v(A), v(B)\}, \qquad (6.14)$$
$$v(A \Rightarrow B) \triangleq v(A) \Rightarrow v(B) = \max\{1 - v(A), \min(v(A), v(B))\}. \qquad (6.15)$$

Equation (6.15) is based on Zadeh's [1975ab] definition of implication. Other definitions of implication can also be applied (see Table 7.1).

If $v(A)$ and $v(B)$ are linguistic truth values of propositions *A* and *B*, respectively, and are expressed as $v(A) = \alpha_1/v_1 + \alpha_2/v_2 + \cdots + \alpha_n/v_n$ and $v(B) = \beta_1/w_1 + \beta_2/w_2 + \cdots + \beta_m/w_m$, where $\alpha_i, \beta_i, v_i, w_i \in [0,1]$, then using the extension principle on Eqs. (6.12)–(6.15), we have

$$v\,(\text{NOT } A) \equiv \alpha_1/(1 - v_1) + \cdots + \alpha_n/(1 - v_n), \tag{6.16}$$

$$v\,(A \text{ AND } B) \equiv v\,(A) \land v\,(B) = \sum_{ij} \min(\alpha_i, \beta_j)/\min(v_i, w_j), \tag{6.17}$$

$$v\,(A \text{ OR } B) \equiv v\,(A) \lor v\,(B) = \sum_{ij} \min(\alpha_i, \beta_j)/\max(v_i, w_j), \tag{6.18}$$

$$v\,(A \Rightarrow B) \equiv v\,(A) \Rightarrow v\,(B) = \sum_{ij} \min(\alpha_i, \beta_j)/\max\{1 - v_i, \min(v_i, w_j)\} \tag{6.19}$$

Note that various definitions of "implication" can be applied to obtain $v\,(A \Rightarrow B)$ other than Eq. (6.19).

Example 6.3

Let the linguistic truth values of two propositions P and Q be $v\,(P) = $ "MORE OR LESS True" and $v\,(Q) = $ "ALMOST True," which are defined as the fuzzy sets B and C, respectively, in Example 6.2. Then we have

$$v\,(\text{NOT } P) = v\,(\text{NOT MORE OR LESS True})$$

$$= 0.5/0.4 + 0.7/0.3 + 1/0.2 + 1/0.1 + 1/0,$$

$$v\,(P \text{ AND } Q) = v\,(P) \land v\,(Q) = \text{"MORE OR LESS True"} \land \text{"ALMOST True"}$$

$$= 0.5/0.6 + 0.7/0.7 + 1/0.8 + 1/0.9 + 0.6/1$$

$$v\,(P \text{ OR } Q) = v\,(P) \lor v\,(Q) = \text{"MORE OR LESS True"} \lor \text{"ALMOST True"}$$

$$= 0.6/0.8 + 1/0.9 + 1/1.$$

In the above example, we observe that "MORE OR LESS True" $\lor$ "ALMOST True" is equal to the fuzzy set D defined in Example 6.2. There we found that its linguistic approximation was the fuzzy set "True" defined in Example 6.2. This leads us to define the *truth table* in fuzzy logic. Consider the truth table for $\lor$. Assume that the ith row label is "MORE OR LESS True" and the jth column label is "ALMOST True." Then the (i, j)th entry in the truth table can be decided as "True" from the linguistic approximation. This is the basic idea behind Zadeh's truth table for fuzzy logic. For example, if we consider three truth values, "True" $\equiv$ T, "False" $\equiv$ F, "UNKNOWN" $\equiv$ T + F, then we obtain the accompanying truth table for conjunction and disjunction.

TABLE 6.1 Zadeh's Truth Table for Conjunction and Disjunction

Truth Value	Conjunction ($\land$)			Disjunction ($\lor$)		
	T	F	T + F	T	F	T + F
T	T	F	T + F	T	T	T
F	F	F	F	T	F	T + F
T + F	T + F	F	T + F	T	T + F	T + F

Fuzzy Logic and Approximate Reasoning   Chap. 6

6.2.2 Fuzzy Propositions

To provide the capability of approximate reasoning, fuzzy logic allows the use of *fuzzy predicates, fuzzy predicate modifiers, fuzzy quantifiers,* and *fuzzy qualifiers* in the propositions. These also represent some of the principal differences between fuzzy logic and classical logic [Zadeh, 1992].

- *Fuzzy predicates:* In fuzzy logic, the predicates can be fuzzy, for example, *Tall, Ill, Young, Soon, MUCH Heavier, Friend of.* Hence, we can have a (fuzzy) proposition like "Mary is Young." It is clear that most of the predicates in natural language are fuzzy rather than crisp.
- *Fuzzy predicate modifiers:* In classical logic, the only widely used predicate modifier is the negation NOT. In fuzzy logic, in addition to the negation modifier, there are a variety of predicate modifiers that act as *hedges,* for example, *VERY, RATHER, MORE OR LESS, SLIGHTLY, A LITTLE, EXTREMELY.* As mentioned in Sec. 6.1 [especially Eq. (6.4)], such predicate modifiers are essential in generating the values of a linguistic variable. Here we can have a fuzzy proposition like "This house is EXTREMELY Expensive."
- *Fuzzy quantifiers:* Fuzzy logic allows the use of fuzzy quantifiers exemplified by *Most, Many, Several, Few, Much of, Frequently, Occasionally, About Five.* Hence, we can have a fuzzy proposition like "Many students are happy." In fuzzy logic, a fuzzy quantifier is interpreted as a fuzzy number or a *fuzzy proportion* that provides an imprecise characterization of the cardinality of one or more fuzzy or nonfuzzy sets. For example, a fuzzy quantifier such as *Most* in the fuzzy proposition "Most big men are kind" is interpreted as a fuzzily defined proportion of the fuzzy set of "kind men" in the fuzzy set of "big men." Based on this view, fuzzy quantifiers may be used to represent the meaning of propositions containing probabilities and hence make it possible to manipulate probabilities within fuzzy logic. For example, a proposition of the form $p \equiv Q$ A's are B's, where Q is a fuzzy quantifier (e.g., "Most professors are very tall"), implies that the conditional probability of the event B given the event A is a fuzzy probability equal to Q. Because of the interchangeability between fuzzy probabilities and fuzzy quantifiers, any proposition involving fuzzy probabilities may be replaced by a semantically equivalent proposition involving fuzzy quantifiers (i.e., identical possibility distributions can be induced). Propositions involving fuzzy probabilities will be discussed in the following as "fuzzy probability qualifications."
- *Fuzzy qualifiers:* Fuzzy logic has four major modes of qualification as in the following:
    Fuzzy truth qualification, expressed as "*p* is τ," in which τ is a fuzzy truth value. It is used to claim the degree of truth of a (fuzzy) proposition. For example,

    (John is Old) is NOT VERY True,

    in which the qualified proposition is (John is Old) and the qualifying fuzzy truth value is "NOT VERY True."
    Fuzzy probability qualification, expressed as "*p* is λ," in which λ is a fuzzy probability. In classical logic, probability is numerical or interval-valued. In fuzzy

logic, one has the additional option of employing fuzzy probabilities exemplified by *Likely, Unlikely, VERY Likely, Around 0.5,* and so on. For example,

(John is Old) is VERY Likely,

in which the qualifying fuzzy probability is "VERY Likely." Such probabilities may be interpreted as fuzzy numbers that may be manipulated through the use of fuzzy arithmetic. In addition to fuzzy probability, fuzzy logic makes it possible to deal with fuzzy events. For example, "Tomorrow will be a Warm day," is a fuzzy event, where "Warm" is a fuzzy predicate. The probability of a fuzzy event may be a crisp or a fuzzy number.

Fuzzy possibility qualification, expressed "*p* is π," in which π is a fuzzy possibility, for example, *Possible, QUITE Possible, ALMOST Impossible.* Such values may be interpreted as labels of fuzzy subsets of the real line. For example,

(John is Old) is ALMOST Impossible,

in which the qualifying fuzzy possibility is "ALMOST Impossible."

Fuzzy usuality qualification, expressed as "Usually(*p*) = Usually(*X* is *F*)," in which the subject *X* is a variable taking values in a universe of discourse *U* and the predicate *F* is a fuzzy subset of *U* which may be interpreted as a *usual value* of *X* denoted as $U(X) = F$. The concept of usuality relates to propositions that are usually true or to events that have a high probability of occurrence. As a simple illustration, consider the proposition, *p* = "a loaf of bread usually costs about a dollar." In *p*, *X* is the cost of a loaf of bread, *U* is an interval of prices, and *F* is a fuzzy subset of *U* described by the label "about a dollar" whose membership function is shown in Fig. 6.4. The membership function of "Usually" is also shown in Fig. 6.4. A usuality qualified proposition in which *usually* is implicit rather than explicit is said to be a *disposition.* Simple examples of dispositions are *a loaf of bread costs about a dollar, snow is white,* and *a TV set weighs about 50 pounds.* The concept of usuality, especially dispositions, underlies much of what is commonly referred to as commonsense knowledge and governs most of our decision making in the course of a day.

In the formalization of commonsense reasoning, it is important to note the close connection among *fuzzy probability qualification, fuzzy usuality qualification,* and *fuzzy quantifiers.* For example, the disposition "women are considerate" may be in-

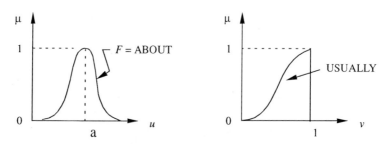

Figure 6.4   Representation of Usually (*X* is about a dollar).

terpreted as "Most women are considerate" or, equivalently, as "(a woman is considerate) is Likely" or, equivalently, as "Usually (a woman is considerate)."

6.3 APPROXIMATE REASONING

As in any other logic, the rules of inference in fuzzy logic govern the deduction of a proposition q from a set of premises $\{p_1, p_2, \ldots, p_n\}$. In fuzzy logic, both the premises and the conclusion are allowed to be fuzzy propositions. Furthermore, since the inferred results usually must be translated into more meaningful terms (fuzzy sets) by the use of linguistic approximation, the final conclusion drawn from the premises $p_1, p_2, \ldots, p_n$ is, in general, an approximate rather than an exact consequence of $p_1, p_2, \ldots, p_n$. There are four principal modes of fuzzy reasoning (or approximate reasoning) in fuzzy logic. They are *categorical reasoning, qualitative reasoning, syllogistic reasoning,* and *dispositional reasoning* and will be introduced in the following sections.

6.3.1 Categorical Reasoning

In this mode of reasoning, the premises contain no fuzzy quantifiers and no fuzzy probabilities. Moreover, the premises are assumed to be in the canonical form of "X is A" or in the conditional canonical form of "IF X is A, THEN Y is B," where A and B are fuzzy predicates. To study the principal rules of inference of categorical reasoning in fuzzy logic [Zadeh, 1978a, 1992], we shall use these notations:

$X, Y, Z, \ldots \equiv$ (fuzzy) variables taking values in the universes $U, V, W, \ldots$

$A, B, C, \ldots \equiv$ fuzzy predicates.

• *Projection rule of inference:*

$$\frac{(X, Y) \text{ is } R}{X \text{ is } [R \downarrow X],} \tag{6.20}$$

where $[R \downarrow X]$ denotes the projection of fuzzy relation R on X. For example,

$$\frac{(X, Y) \text{ is Close to } (3, 2)}{X \text{ is Close to } 3.}$$

• *Conjunction or particularization rule of inference:*

$$\frac{\begin{array}{l}X \text{ is } A \\ X \text{ is } B\end{array}}{X \text{ is } A \cap B,} \quad \frac{\begin{array}{l}(X, Y) \text{ is } A \\ X \text{ is } B\end{array}}{(X, Y) \text{ is } A \cap (B \times V),} \quad \frac{\begin{array}{l}(X, Y) \text{ is } A \\ (Y, Z) \text{ is } B\end{array}}{(X, Y, Z) = (A \times W) \cap (U \times B).} \tag{6.21}$$

For example,

$$\frac{\begin{array}{c}\text{pressure is NOT VERY High} \\ \text{pressure is NOT VERY Low}\end{array}}{\text{pressure is NOT VERY High AND NOT VERY Low;}}$$

$$\frac{\begin{array}{c}X \text{ and } Y \text{ are APPROXIMATELY Equal} \\ X \text{ is Small}\end{array}}{X \text{ and } Y \text{ are (APPROXIMATELY Equal)} \cap \text{(Small} \times V)).}$$

- *Disjunction or Cartesian product rule of inference:*

$$\frac{\begin{array}{l} X \text{ is } A \\ \text{OR } X \text{ is } B \end{array}}{X \text{ is } A \cup B,} \qquad \frac{\begin{array}{l} X \text{ is } A \\ Y \text{ is } B \end{array}}{(X, Y) \text{ is } A \times B} \qquad (6.22)$$

- *Negation rule:*

$$\frac{\text{NOT } (X \text{ is } A)}{X \text{ is } \bar{A}.} \qquad (6.23)$$

For example,

$$\frac{\text{NOT (John is Tall)}}{\text{John is NOT Tall.}}$$

- *Entailment rule of inference:*
  The entailment rule of inference, also called the *entailment principle,* asserts that from any fuzzy proposition p we can infer a fuzzy proposition q if the possibility distribution induced by p is contained in the possibility distribution induced by q. Thus, schematically, we have

$$\frac{\begin{array}{l} X \text{ is } A \\ A \subset B \end{array}}{X \text{ is } B.} \qquad (6.24)$$

For example,

$$\frac{\begin{array}{l} \text{Mary is VERY Young} \\ \text{VERY Young} \subset \text{Young} \end{array}}{\text{Mary is Young.}}$$

- *Compositional rule of inference:*

$$\frac{\begin{array}{l} X \text{ is } A \\ (X, Y) \text{ is } R \end{array}}{Y \text{ is } A \circ R,} \qquad (6.25)$$

where $A \circ R$ indicates the max-min composition of a fuzzy set A and a fuzzy relation R and is defined by [see Eq. (3.26)]

$$\mu_{A \circ R}(v) = \max_u \min\left(\mu_A(u), \mu_R(u, v)\right). \qquad (6.26)$$

The compositional rule of inference may be viewed as a combination of the conjunctive and projection rules. An example of using this rule will be illustrated later.

- *Generalized modus ponens:*

$$\frac{\begin{array}{l} X \text{ is } A \\ \text{IF } X \text{ is } B, \ \text{THEN } Y \text{ is } C \end{array}}{Y \text{ is } A \circ (\bar{B} \oplus C),} \qquad (6.27)$$

where

$$\mu_{\bar{B} \oplus C}(u, v) = \min\left(1, 1 - \mu_B(u) + \mu_C(v)\right). \qquad (6.28)$$

Actually, the generalized modus ponens is a special case of the compositional rule of inference. Unlike the modus ponens in classical logic [Eq.(6.11)], the generalized modus ponens does not require that the precondition "X is B" be identical to the premise "X is A." The generalized modus ponens is related to the *interpolation rule* for solving the important problem of "partial" matching of preconditions of rules that arises in the operation of any rule-based system. Details about the fuzzy interpolation can be found in [Zadeh, 1983b, 1988; Lowen, 1990]. The generalized modus ponens plays a very important role in fuzzy control and fuzzy expert systems. Various different definitions in addition to Eq. (6.27) exist, and we shall present more details about the generalized modus ponens in the next chapter.

- *Extension principle:*

$$\frac{X \text{ is } A}{f(X) \text{ is } f(A),} \tag{6.29}$$

where f is a mapping from U to V so that X is mapped into $f(X)$, and according to the extension principle in Sec. 2.3, the membership function of $f(A)$ is defined by

$$\mu_{f(A)}(v) = \sup_{v=f(u)} \mu_A(u), \qquad u \in U, v \in V. \tag{6.30}$$

The extension principle can answer a question like, Assuming that X taking values in U is constrained by the proposition "X is A," what is the constraint on $f(X)$ that is induced by the constraint on X? For example,

$$\frac{X \text{ is Small}}{X^2 \text{ is Small}^2, \text{ where } \mu_{\text{Small}^2}(u) = (\mu_{\text{Small}}(u))^2.}$$

Example 6.4

Consider the premises

$$p = \text{John is VERY Big,}$$

$$q = \text{John is VERY Tall,}$$

where "Big" is a given fuzzy subset of $U \times V$ (i.e., values of *Height* × values of *Weight*) and "Tall" is a given fuzzy subset of U (values of *Height*). How heavy is John? This question can be answered by employing the particularization rule of inference [Eq. (6.21)] and then the projection rule of inference [Eq. (6.20)] as follows:

$$\frac{(\text{height (John), weight (John)}) \text{ is Big}^2}{\frac{(\text{height (John)}) \text{ is Tall}^2}{\frac{(\text{height (John), weight (John)}) \text{ is Big}^2 \cap (\text{Tall}^2 \times V)}{\text{weight (John) is } [(\text{Big}^2 \cap (\text{Tall}^2 \times V)) \downarrow \text{Weight}].}}}$$

Example 6.5

Consider the premises

$$p = X \text{ is Small}$$

$$q = X \text{ and } Y \text{ are APPROXIMATELY Equal}$$

in which X and Y range over the set $U = \{1, 2, 3, 4\}$ and Small and APPROXIMATELY Equal are, respectively, defined by

$$\text{Small} = 1/1 + 0.6/2 + 0.2/3,$$

$$\text{APPROXIMATELY Equal} = 1/(1, 1) + 1/(2, 2) + 1/(3, 3) + 1/(4, 4) +$$
$$0.5/(1, 2) + 0.5/(2, 1) + 0.5/(2, 3) + 0.5/(3, 2) +$$
$$0.5/(3, 4) + 0.5/(4, 3).$$

Using the compositional rule of inference [Eq. (6.25)], we have the conclusion premise r:

$$r = X \text{ is Small } \circ \text{ APPROXIMATELY\_Equal,}$$

in which the composition can be performed as

$$[1, 0.6, 0.2, 0] \circ \begin{bmatrix} 1 & 0.5 & 0 & 0 \\ 0.5 & 1 & 0.5 & 0 \\ 0 & 0.5 & 1 & 0.5 \\ 0 & 0 & 0.5 & 1 \end{bmatrix} = [1, 0.6, 0.5, 0.2].$$

Hence, $\pi_Y = 1/1 + 0.6/2 + 0.5/3 + 0.2/4$. Through the linguistic approximation, we can say, for example, $r =$ "Y is MORE OR LESS Small," which is inferred from propositions p and q.

6.3.2 Qualitative Reasoning

In fuzzy logic, qualitative reasoning refers to a mode of reasoning in which the input-output relation of a system is expressed as a collection of fuzzy IF-THEN rules in which the pre-conditions and consequents involve fuzzy or linguistic variables [Zadeh, 1975a,b, 1989a,b, 1992]. For example, if X and Y are input variables and Z is the output variable, the relation among X, Y, and Z may be expressed as

$$\text{IF } X \text{ is } A_1 \text{ AND } Y \text{ is } B_1, \text{ THEN } Z \text{ is } C_1$$

$$\text{IF } X \text{ is } A_2 \text{ AND } Y \text{ is } B_2, \text{ THEN } Z \text{ is } C_2$$

$$\cdots \quad \cdots \quad \cdots \tag{6.31}$$

$$\text{IF } X \text{ is } A_n \text{ AND } Y \text{ is } B_n, \text{ THEN } Z \text{ is } C_n,$$

where A_i, B_i, and C_i, $i = 1, \ldots, n$, are fuzzy subsets of their respective universe of discourse.

Given the dependence of Z on X and Y in the form of Eq. (6.31), we can employ the compositional rule of inference to compute the value of Z given the values of X and Y. A very simple example of qualitative reasoning is

IF pressure is High, THEN volume is Small

IF pressure is Low, THEN volume is Large

IF pressure is Medium, THEN volume is $\max\{w_1 \wedge \text{Small}, w_2 \wedge \text{Large}\}$,

where $w_1 = \sup(\text{High} \wedge \text{Medium})$, $w_2 = \sup(\text{Low} \wedge \text{Medium})$, and $\wedge$ represents the min operation. w_1 and w_2 in the above equations can be considered weighting coefficients that represent, respectively, the degrees to which the preconditions "High" and "Low" match the input "Medium."

Qualitative reasoning plays a key role in many applications of fuzzy logic in the realms of control and systems analysis [Mamdani and Gaines, 1981; Sugeno, 1985a; Pospelov, 1987; Lee, 1990]. Chapter 7 will provide more details on qualitative reasoning along with the compositional rule of inference or, more specifically, the generalized modus ponens.

6.3.3 Syllogistic Reasoning

In contrast to categorical reasoning, syllogistic reasoning relates to inference from premises containing fuzzy quantifiers [Zadeh, 1983a,b, 1985, 1992; Dubois and Prade, 1988a]. In its generic form, a fuzzy syllogism may be expressed as the inference scheme

$$\begin{aligned} p &= Q_1 A\text{'s are } B\text{'s} \\ q &= Q_2 C\text{'s are } D\text{'s} \\ \hline r &= Q_3 E\text{'s are } F\text{'s,} \end{aligned} \tag{6.32}$$

where A, B, C, D, E, and F are interrelated fuzzy predicates, Q_1, Q_2 are given fuzzy quantifiers, and Q_3 is the fuzzy quantifier to be decided. The interrelations among A, B, C, D, E, and F provide a collection of fuzzy syllogisms. These syllogisms create a set of inference rules for combining evidence through conjunction ($\wedge$), disjunction ($\vee$), and chaining in fuzzy expert systems. The six most important fuzzy syllogisms are

- *Intersection or product syllogism:* $C = A \wedge B$, $\quad E = A$, $\quad F = C \wedge D$.
- *Chaining syllogism:* $C = B$, $\quad E = A$, $\quad F = D$.
- *Consequent conjunction syllogism:* $A = C = E$, $\quad F = B \wedge D$.
- *Consequent disjunction syllogism:* $A = C = E$, $\quad F = B \vee D$.
- *Precondition conjunction syllogism:* $B = D = F$, $\quad E = A \wedge C$.
- *Precondition disjunction syllogism:* $B = D = F$, $\quad E = A \vee C$.

We shall discuss only the first three basic fuzzy syllogisms.

- *Intersection or product syllogism:*

$$\begin{aligned} & Q_1 A\text{'s are } B\text{'s} \\ & \underline{Q_2 (A \text{ and } B)\text{'s are } C\text{'s}} \\ & (Q_1 (\cdot) Q_2) A\text{'s are } (B \text{ and } C)\text{'s,} \end{aligned} \tag{6.33}$$

where $Q_1 (\cdot) Q_2$ is the product of the fuzzy numbers Q_1 and Q_2 in fuzzy arithmetic and is shown in Fig. 6.5. The intersection or product syllogism is a basic fuzzy syllogism that is of considerable relevance to the rules of combination of evidence. Let us consider a simple example of Eq. (6.33):

$$\begin{aligned} & \text{Most students are Young} \\ & \underline{\text{Most Young students are single}} \\ & \text{Most}^2 \text{ students are Young and single} \end{aligned}$$

where "Most^2" denotes the product of the fuzzy quantifier *Most* with itself.

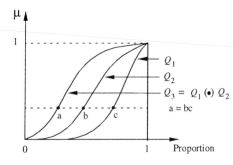

Figure 6.5 Representation of fuzzy quantifiers in the intersection or product syllogism.

- *Chaining syllogism:*

$$\begin{array}{l} Q_1 A\text{'s are } B\text{'s} \\ \underline{Q_2 B\text{'s are } C\text{'s}} \\ QA\text{'s are } C\text{'s,} \end{array} \qquad (6.34)$$

where $Q = Q_1 (\cdot) Q_2$ when $B \subset A$ and Q_1, Q_2 are monotonic increasing (e.g., *Most*). The chaining syllogism is basically a special case of the intersection or product syllogism. First, since the intersection of B and C is contained in C, an immediate consequence of Eq. (6.33) is

$$\begin{array}{l} Q_1 A\text{'s are } B\text{'s} \\ \underline{Q_2 (A \text{ and } B) \text{'s are } C\text{'s}} \\ \geq (Q_1 (\cdot) Q_2) A\text{'s are } C\text{'s,} \end{array} \qquad (6.35)$$

where the fuzzy number $(\geq (Q_1 (\cdot) Q_2))$ is read as "at least $(Q_1 (\cdot) Q_2)$," which represents the composition of the binary relation $\geq$ with the unary relation $Q_1 (\cdot) Q_2$, that is,

$$\mu_{\geq (Q_1 (\cdot) Q_2)} (x) = \max_y \min\{ \mu_\geq (x, y), \mu_{Q_1 (\cdot) Q_2} (y)\}, \qquad (6.36)$$

where $x, y \in V = [0, 1]$ and $\mu_\geq(x, y) = 1$ if $x \geq y$; otherwise $\mu_\geq(x, y) = 0$. An example of $\geq (Q_1 (\cdot) Q_2)$ is shown in Fig. 6.6. It is clear that $(\geq (Q_1 (\cdot) Q_2))$ can be written as $(Q_1 (\cdot) Q_2)_P$, representing the fuzzy set of numbers that are possibly greater than or equal to $Q_1 (\cdot) Q_2$. Now, since Q_1 and Q_2 are monotonic increasing, that is, $\geq Q_1 = Q_1$, $\geq Q_2 = Q_2$, we can easily obtain $\geq (Q_1 (\cdot) Q_2) = Q_1 (\cdot) Q_2$. In addition, since $B \subset A$ and thus $(A \text{ AND } B)$'s $= B$'s, Eq. (6.35) becomes the chaining syllogism as in Eq. (6.34). Let us show a simple example to illustrate the chaining syllogism:

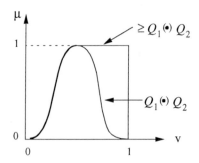

Figure 6.6 Representation of the "at least" quantifier.

$$\frac{\text{Most students are undergraduates}}{\text{Most}^2 \text{ students are single,}}$$

where $undergraduate \subset students$.

- *Consequent conjunction syllogism:*

$$\frac{\begin{array}{c}Q_1A\text{'s are }B\text{'s}\\ Q_2A\text{'s are }C\text{'s}\end{array}}{QA\text{'s are }(B\text{ and }C)\text{'s,}} \qquad (6.37)$$

where Q is a fuzzy quantifier defined by the inequalities

$$0(\vee)(Q_1(+)Q_2(-)1) < Q < Q_1(\wedge)Q_2, \qquad (6.38)$$

in which $(+)$, $(-)$, $(\vee)$, and $(\wedge)$ are, respectively, addition, subtraction, maximum, and minimum operations on fuzzy numbers in fuzzy arithmetic. The consequent conjunction syllogism provides a formal basis for combining rules in an expert system through a conjunctive combination of hypotheses. An illustration is as follows:

$$\frac{\begin{array}{c}\text{Most students are Young}\\ \text{Most students are single}\end{array}}{Q \text{ students are single and Young,}}$$

where $2\,\text{Most}(-)1 \le Q \le \text{Most}$, which comes from Eq. (6.38) since $\text{Most}(\wedge)\text{Most} = \text{Most}$, and $0(\vee)(2\text{Most}(-)1) = 2\text{Most}(-)1$.

6.3.4 Dispositional Reasoning

In dispositional reasoning, the premises are dispositions that may contain, explicitly or implicitly, the fuzzy quantifier "Usually"; that is, the propositions are preponderantly but not necessarily always true. The concept of usuality plays a key role in dispositional reasoning and is the concept that links together the dispositional and syllogistic modes of reasoning. In a more general setting, reasoning with disposition may be viewed as part of the *theory of usuality*—a theory that provides a computational framework for commonsense reasoning [Zadeh, 1986, 1992]. We shall introduce some principal rules of inference of dispositional reasoning.

- *Dispositional projection rule of inference:*

$$\frac{\text{Usually }((X, Y)\text{ is }R)}{\text{Usually }(X\text{ is }[R\downarrow X]),} \qquad (6.39)$$

where $[R\downarrow X]$ is the projection of fuzzy relation R on X. Let us illustrate this with a simple example.

$$\frac{\text{Heavy smoking is a leading cause of cancer}}{\text{To avoid lung cancer avoid Heavy smoking,}}$$

in which "Usually" is implicit in the proposition.

- *Dispositional entailment rule of inference:*

$$\frac{\begin{array}{c}\text{Usually } (X \text{ is } A)\\ A \subset B\end{array}}{\text{Usually } (X \text{ is } B),} \qquad \frac{\begin{array}{c}X \text{ is } A\\ \text{Usually } (A \subset B)\end{array}}{\text{Usually } (X \text{ is } B),} \qquad \frac{\begin{array}{c}\text{Usually } (X \text{ is } A)\\ \text{Usually } (A \subset B)\end{array}}{\text{Usually}^2 \ (X \text{ is } B).} \qquad (6.40)$$

Here "Usually^2" is less specific than "Usually" (see Fig. 6.7). In the limiting case where "Usually" becomes "Always," Eq. (6.40) becomes Eq. (6.24), the ordinary entailment rule of inference.

- *Dispositional modus ponens:*

$$\frac{\begin{array}{c}\text{Usually } (X \text{ is } A)\\ \text{Usually } (\text{IF } X \text{ is } A, \text{ THEN } Y \text{ is } B)\end{array}}{\text{Usually}^2 \ (Y \text{ is } B),} \qquad (6.41)$$

where the conditional proposition is interpreted as the statement, "The value of the fuzzy conditional probability of B given A is the fuzzy number Usually."

- *Dispositional chaining hypersyllogism:*

$$\frac{\begin{array}{c}Q_1 A\text{'s are } B\text{'s}\\ Q_2 B\text{'s are } C\text{'s}\\ \text{Usually } (B \subset A)\end{array}}{\text{Usually } (\geq (Q_1 \, (\cdot) \, Q_2) \, A\text{'s are } C\text{'s}).} \qquad (6.42)$$

The prefix *hyper-* signifies that the fuzzy quantifier "Usually" as applied to the containment relation $B \subset A$ is a higher-order fuzzy quantifier.

- *Dispositional consequent conjunction syllogism:*

$$\frac{\begin{array}{c}\text{Usually } (A\text{'s are } B\text{'s})\\ \text{Usually } (A\text{'s are } C\text{'s})\end{array}}{(2 \text{ Usually } (\text{-}) \, 1) \, (A\text{'s are } (B \text{ and } C)\text{'s}),} \qquad (6.43)$$

which can be viewed as a special case of Eq. (6.37). For example,

$$\frac{\begin{array}{c}\text{Usually the probability of failure is NOT VERY Low}\\ \text{Usually the probability of failure is NOT VERY High}\end{array}}{\begin{array}{c}(2 \text{ Usually } (\text{-}) \, 1) \text{ the probability of failure}\\ \text{is NOT VERY Low AND NOT VERY High.}\end{array}}$$

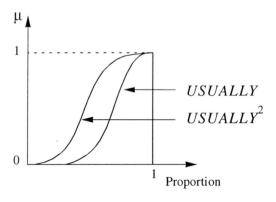

USUALLY

USUALLY^2

Figure 6.7 Representation of the fuzzy quantifiers "Usually" and "Usually^2". (Adapted from Zadeh [1988], © 1988 IEEE.)

6.4 FUZZY EXPERT SYSTEMS

An expert system is a program that behaves like an expert for some problem domain. An expert system basically has two major functions. The first is the problem-solving function capable of using domain-specific knowledge. For this function, an expert system is often expected to be able to deal with uncertain and incomplete information. This is our focus in this section. The second is the user interaction function, which includes an explanation of the system's intentions and decisions during and after the problem-solving process. The basic structure of an expert system, as show in Fig. 6.8, consists of three major blocks: a knowledge base, an inference engine, and a user interface. A *knowledge base* comprises the knowledge specific to the domain of application, including such things as facts about the domain and rules that describe relations in the domain. IF-THEN rules are by far the most popular formalism for representing knowledge. An *inference engine* can actively use the knowledge in the knowledge base to perform reasoning to obtain answers for users' queries. A *user interface* provides smooth communication between the user and the system; it also provides the user with an insight into the problem-solving process carried out by the inference engine.

It is important for an expert system to handle imprecision in order for it to be a useful tool. Most methods of handling imprecision are probability-based. An important example is the MYCIN expert system [Shortliffe, 1976] which introduces the concept of *certainty factors* to deal with uncertainty. Each rule in MYCIN has a strength, called a certainty factor, associated with it. The certainty factor lies in the unit interval $[0, 1]$. When a rule is fired, its precondition is evaluated and a numerical value between -1 and 1, called the firing strength, is associated with the precondition. If the firing strength is great enough, that is, the value is outside the previously specified threshold interval (e.g., $[-0.2, 0.2]$), then the consequent of the rule is evaluated and the conclusion is made with a certainty that is the firing strength times the certainty factor of the rule. The resulting conclusion and its certainty are the evidence provided by this fired rule for the hypotheses given by the user. Evidence for hypotheses from different rules is combined into measures of belief and disbelief which are values in the intervals $[0, 1]$ and $[-1, 0]$, respectively. A hypothesis is believed if its belief measure is above a threshold value. Similarly, a hypothesis is disbelieved if its disbelief measure is below a threshold value. This concept has been widely applied, in several different forms, to the handling of imprecision in expert systems.

The above method and others are reasonably effective in specific cases. However, it is interesting that experts often do not think in terms of probability values but in terms of

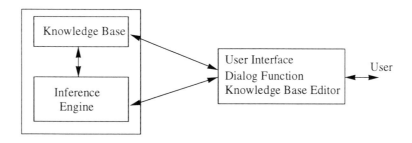

Figure 6.8   Basic structure of an expert system.

such expressions as "much", "usually", "always", and so on. This motivates the use of fuzzy logic in traditional expert systems and forms so-called *fuzzy expert systems*. Hence, where the domain is not amenable to the estimation or measurement of probabilities, or where fuzzy sets and linguistic terms best describe items in the domain, fuzzy set theory or possibility theory offers an alternative and may be applied more naturally than probability theory.

By fuzzy expert systems we mean expert systems that incorporate fuzzy sets and/or fuzzy logic into their reasoning process and/or knowledge representation scheme. Hence, the approximate reasoning introduced in the last section can provide a unified theoretical approach with various methods for handling uncertainty in expert systems. The application of fuzzy sets and possibility theory to rule-based expert systems has been mainly developed along two lines: (1) generalization of the certainty factor approach in MYCIN by enlarging the possible operations to be used for combining the uncertainty coefficients or by allowing the use of *linguistic-certainty values,* (e.g., Possible, ALMOST-Impossible) in addition to the conventional numerical certainty values, and (2) the handling of vague predicates in the expression of expert rules or available information. The second trend has motivated an impressive surge of research interest in fuzzy expert systems. The techniques proposed in the previous sections are fundamental tools for handling vague predicates in expert rules as well as for the linguistic-certainty-value approach. In addition to these two kinds of fuzzy expert systems, we can also combine the techniques in these two trends into a fuzzy expert system that can effectively deal with both uncertainty and vagueness (imprecision). We shall consider two kinds of fuzzy expert systems by presenting two practical, representative examples.

6.4.1 MILORD

MILORD is a fuzzy expert system building tool containing two inference engines (forward and backward) with uncertainty reasoning capabilities based on fuzzy logic [Godo et al., 1988; López de Mántaras et al., 1992a,b]. It allows the user to express the degree of certainty by means of expert-defined linguistic statements. Associated with the two inference engines are two types of control strategies: one consists of a lookahead technique that allows the user to detect in advance whether or not the linguistic certainty value of a conclusion will reach a minimal threshold acceptance value; the other concerns the selection of rules according to some criteria. We shall briefly introduce some major features of MILORD.

The knowledge base of MILORD consists of *facts* and *rules*. The facts are associated with a linguistic value of certainty ([VC]). For example, the fact, "A cat is bigger than a mouse is almost true," can be represented as

IS-BIGGER-THAN (CAT, MOUSE) [VC = ALMOST True].

A nonevaluated fact will have the certainty value *NIL,* and therefore, whether a given fact is known can be quickly checked, that is, if a certainty value has been assigned to it.

The rules in MILORD are externally represented as follows:

Rule-*N* IF (preconditions), THEN (consequents) WITH CERTAINTY [VC],

where N is the number of rules and [VC] is the linguistic-certainty value of the rule. For example, a rule may look like

Rule-1: IF Alcoholic and Cavitation,
THEN tuberculosis
WITH CERTAINTY ALMOST-Impossible.

The precondition of a rule can also include a certainty value, for example,

IF the pneumonia is bacterial WITH CERTAINTY QUITE-Possible
AND the pneumonia is atypical WITH CERTAINTY Possible,

THEN consider Mycoplasm, Virus, Clamidia, Tuberculosis,
Nocardia, Criptococcus, Pneumocystis carinii
WITH CERTAINTY QUITE Possible.

Hence, every rule has a set of preconditions which, when evaluated with degrees of linguistic certainty, lead to a consequent whose degree of linguistic certainty depends on the degrees of linguistic certainty of the preconditions. In order to enable fast access to the rules, MILORD translates a rule into the following internal representation:

$$\text{Rule-}N \rightarrow \text{VAL[VC] IF } (p_1, \ldots, p_N), \text{THEN } (c_1, \ldots, c_M), \tag{6.44}$$

where VAL, IF, and THEN are properties of a rule and p_i and c_j are preconditions and consequents, respectively. Access to the preconditions and consequents of a rule is then access to the properties of the rule. To further speed up the inference process, MILORD builds a *property list* for each consequent. A property list of a consequent is the list of rules (Rule-i) that deduce this consequent together with the linguistic-certainty value (VC_i) of each rule, that is,

$$\text{Consequent} \rightarrow \text{Rules ((Rule-1, } VC_1), \text{(Rule-2, } VC_2), \ldots, \text{(Rule-}k, VC_k)), \tag{6.45}$$

where the rules on the list are in decreasing order of their linguistic-certainty values. This ordering will be used by the lookahead control strategy and the rule selection strategy.

Each linguistic value is represented internally by a fuzzy number in the truth space or interval [0, 1] in MILORD. Although the expert can define its own term set together with its internal representation, MILORD provides the following default term set:

$$\{\text{False, ALMOST-False, Maybe, ALMOST-True, True}\}. \tag{6.46}$$

Each term in the above term set is represented by a trapezoidal membership function $T_i = (a_i, b_i, c_i, d_i)$, defined by the four parameters a_i, b_i, c_i, d_i as in Fig. 6.9. These membership functions are shown in Fig. 6.10.

According to fuzzy arithmetics with trapezoidal membership functions, we have the following formulas which speed up the rule inference. Given two linguistic-certainty values $VC_1 = (a, b, c, d)$ and $VC_2 = (a', b', c', d')$, we have

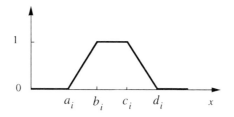

Figure 6.9 Trapezoidal membership function.

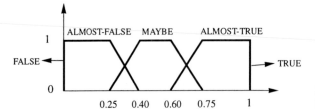

Figure 6.10 Default term set of the linguistic-certainty value in MILORD.

$$VC_1 \, (+) \, VC_2 = (a + a', b + b', c + c', d + d'),$$

$$VC_1 \, (\text{-}) \, VC_2 = (a - d', b - c', c - b', d - a'),$$

$$VC_1 \, (\cdot) \, VC_2 = (aa', bb', cc', dd'), \tag{6.47}$$

$$VC_1 \, (\wedge) \, VC_2 = (\min(a, a'), \min(b, b'), \min(c, c'), \min(d, d')),$$

$$VC_1 \, (\vee) \, VC_2 = (\max(a, a'), \max(b, b'), \max(c, c'), \max(d, d')).$$

We shall next introduce the forward and backward inference engines of MILORD. The fundamental problem for rule inference is the operation (and the interpretation) of the AND, OR, and implication connectives. In MILORD, t-norms are used for AND and implication connectives, and t-conorms are used for an OR connective. In particular, [see Eqs. (2.56)–(2.59) and Eqs. (2.63)–(2.67)], the dual t-norm and t-conorm pairs $(\wedge, \vee)$, $(\cdot, \triangle)$, and $(\odot, \oplus)$ have been implemented in MILORD. For example, when the pair $(\wedge, \vee)$ is used, proper (linguistic) certainty values $VC(\cdot)$ can be determined by the following formulas:

$$VC(A \text{ AND } B) = \min(VC(A), VC(B)),$$

$$VC(C_{R1} \text{ OR } C_{R2}) = \max(VC(C_{R1}), VC(C_{R2})), \tag{6.48}$$

$$VC(C) = \min(VC(R), VC(P)),$$

where A and B are preconditions of the same rule, C_{R1} and C_{R2} represent the same consequent deduced by the two rules $R1$ and $R2$, and C is the consequent of rule R whose precondition is P. The above formulas are used, respectively, in evaluating the satisfaction of the precondition, in combining several rules with the same consequent, and in propagating the uncertainty from the precondition to the consequent of a rule. Now, we are ready to see how the forward and backward inference engines work.

In MILORD, the forward reasoning starts with a set of given facts, and its goal is to deduce a hypothesis (conclusion) whose linguistic-certainty value computed by Eq. (6.48) reaches a given acceptance threshold. If the forward reasoning gets to a hypothesis whose certainty value is below the threshold, then the backward reasoning is used to try to increase the certainty value of the hypothesis by considering, through a *lookahead control strategy,* other rule paths that would conclude the same hypothesis with a higher certainty. The lookahead process in the backward reasoning starts assuming that all the nonevaluated preconditions of the rules leading to the same consequent have the highest linguistic-certainty value (e.g., "True" in the default term set). This allows computation of the highest possible certainty value that this consequent can reach. If this value is higher than the acceptance threshold, then the backward reasoning proceeds to ask the user to assign a linguistic-certainty value to the nonevaluated, *nondeducible* preconditions one by one. Each time a precondition reaches its certainty value, it is propagated to the consequent using Eq. (6.48), and if its certainty value is still higher than the threshold, the process proceeds to ask for the value of the next nondeducible precondition, and so on until either all the nondeducible preconditions have been assigned a certainty value (in which case, MILORD has successfully found an alternative rule path such that the conclusion has an acceptable certainty value) or the certainty value of the conclusion falls below the threshold (in which case, MILORD recalls the forward reasoning mode to deduce another hypothesis). As far as the nonevaluated but *deducible* conditions are concerned, the lookahead process is applied recursively to each one of them as described, and its certainty value is also propagated toward the conclusion in order to keep checking if its certainty value is higher than the threshold, in which case the process resumes. Otherwise, the forward reasoning mode is called to deduce a new hypothesis.

The backward reasoning mode can also be used directly when the user initially gives a set of hypotheses instead of a set of facts. These hypotheses can be tried to validate with a linguistic-certainty value higher than the threshold one by one via backward reasoning until either one of them succeeds or all of them fail.

Besides the lookahead control strategy, another control strategy in the inference engine of MILORD is for the selection of rules for reasoning. The rule selection criteria available in MILORD include (1) the order of the rules, (2) the linguistic-certainty values, (3) the number of preconditions, (4) the number of consequents, (5) the rule most recently used, and (6) the rule containing the most recently deduced fact in its preconditions.

During the reasoning process, t-norms and t-conorms are applied to the membership functions of linguistic-certainty values to produce another membership function which will have to be matched to a term in the term set to keep the term set closed. In MILORD, the results of linguistic approximation under the operation of t-norms such as $\odot$, $\cdot$, and $\wedge$ on the default term set as in Fig. 6.10 are shown in Fig. 6.11(a), (b), and (c), respectively. In this way, once the linguistic values have been defined by the expert, the system computes and stores the matrices corresponding to the different conjunction and disjunction operations on all the pairs of terms in the term set. Later, when MILORD is run on a particular application, the propagation and combination of uncertainty are performed by simply accessing these precomputed matrices.

MILORD also contains a knowledge elicitation module for aiding engineers in knowledge base design and has an explanation module as well as a rule editor which are not described here. MILORD has been applied successfully to medical diagnoses [Godo et al.,

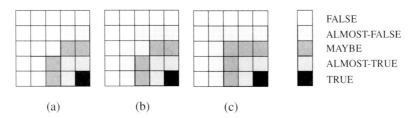

	FALSE
	ALMOST-FALSE
	MAYBE
	ALMOST-TRUE
	TRUE

(a)   (b)   (c)

Figure 6.11 The results of linguistic approximation in MILORD.

1988]. More details on MILORD can be found in [Godo et al., 1988; López de Mántaras et al., 1992a,b].

6.4.2 Z-II

The Z-II system is a fuzzy expert system shell that effectively deals with both uncertainty and imprecision [Leung and Lam, 1988]. In this system, four types of inexact information have been classified:

1. When one is not absolutely certain about a piece of information, uncertainty occurs and a numerical value is used to represent the degree of certainty. For example, "If X is a bird, then it can fly (0.9)."
2. When the boundary of a piece of information is not crisp, fuzziness occurs and fuzzy terms are adopted. For example, "If the price is High, then the profit should be Good," and "Mary is VERY Pretty."
3. Uncertainty and fuzziness may occur simultaneously. For example, "John is RATHER Tall (0.8)."
4. The uncertainty can also be fuzzy. For example, "John is VERY Heavy (Around 0.7)," where "Around 0.7" is a fuzzy uncertainty and "VERY Heavy" is a fuzzy term.

The system architecture of Z-II is shown in Fig 6.12. Basically, it consists of three subsystems: the knowledge acquisition subsystem, the consultation driver, and the fuzzy knowledge base. The components of the knowledge acquisition subsystem include management modules for objects, facts, fuzzy terms, rules, and system properties. These modules are responsible for acquiring and managing rules and facts, which may contain any mix of fuzzy and normal terms and uncertainty. The fuzzy knowledge base stores all these knowledge entities. An object is a basic entity in Z-II and is uniquely identified by two elements: an object name and an attribute. For example, the term "the weight of the body" is represented by the object "BODY WEIGHT," with BODY being the object name and WEIGHT being the attribute. A fuzzy term is defined by a fuzzy set which is usually a trapezoidal membership function. A fact is actually a data proposition of the form

$$\langle \text{OBJECT} \rangle \text{ is } \langle \text{VALUE} \rangle \langle \text{fuzzy / nonfuzzy uncertainty} \rangle. \qquad (6.49)$$

A rule is defined as an implication statement with single or multiple propositions connected by either a logical AND or a logical OR in its precondition part and a single proposition in the consequent. It is noted that a rule with multiple propositions connected by a logical AND in its consequent can be treated as multiple rules with a single consequent. For example,

Rule-1: IF (the body is Well-built OR the height is Tall)
AND the person is Healthy,
THEN the weight of the person is Heavy
WITH CERTAINTY (Close to 1.0).

The consultation driver consists of three modules: the inference engine, the linguistic approximation routine, and the review management module. The function of the inference engine is to extract the knowledge stored in the fuzzy knowledge base and to make infer-

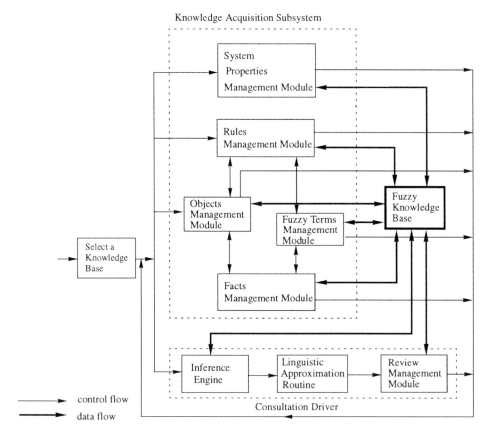

Knowledge Acquisition Subsystem

System
Properties
Management Module

Rules
Management Module

Objects
Management
Module

Fuzzy Terms
Management
Module

Fuzzy
Knowledge
Base

Select a
Knowledge
Base

Facts
Management Module

Inference
Engine

Linguistic
Approximation
Routine

Review
Management
Module

control flow

data flow

Consultation Driver

Figure 6.12 Architecture of the Z-II System. (Adapted from Leung and Lam [1988], © 1988 IEEE.)

ences from the respective rules and facts. The linguistic approximation routine maps a set of fuzzy sets onto a set of linguistic expressions or descriptions such that a fuzzy set (conclusion) drawn by Z-II is translated into natural language. The review management module provides two types of explanations: *why* a fact is required by the system and *how* a fact is established. We shall discuss the details of the inference engine.

The inference engine of Z-II uses backward *chaining* to build the appropriate reasoning trees but uses *forward evaluation* of the values of the fuzzy terms. It also uses *evidence combination* for cases in which two or more rules have the same consequent proposition.

- *Backward reasoning chain:* Z-II adopts backward reasoning during the consultation process such that the questioning is guaranteed to follow the focused goal conclusion. The user may issue queries of the form

$$\text{What should } \langle \text{OBJECT} \rangle \text{ be?} \tag{6.50}$$

For example, What should the weight of the person be? Then, the object in the query becomes the current top-level goal and the system begins the reasoning by searching those rules whose consequent propositions have the goal object. For example, if the goal object is *the weight of the person,* the system will trigger Rule-1 described above and start to examine its precondition propositions. Thus, the objects (BODY WELL-BUILT), (HEIGHT TALL), and (PERSON HEALTHY) then become subgoal objects and the system tries to obtain the values of the subgoal objects one by one by asking a question or by deducing from other rules and facts. Finally, the rule is fired if the precondition part is satisfied completely. In this way, Z-II can find the value of the goal object by evaluating the rule and the matched fact.

If the objects involved are fuzzy, the inference engine uses fuzzy logic operations to calculate the fuzzy uncertainty of the goal object from the fuzzy uncertainties of the facts and rules.

- *Forward rule evaluation:* The typical rule evaluation problem is as follows:

$$
\begin{array}{lll}
\text{Rule:} & \text{IF } A \text{ is } V_1, \text{THEN } C \text{ is } V_2 & (FN_1) \\
\text{Fact:} & A \text{ is } V_1' & (FN_2) \\
\hline
\text{Conclusion:} & C \text{ is } V_2' & (FN_3),
\end{array}
\tag{6.51}
$$

where A and C are precondition object and consequent object, respectively, and FN_i is a fuzzy number denoting corresponding uncertainty. Three possible cases are considered:

1. If A is nonfuzzy, V_1 and V_1' must be the same ($V_1 = V_1'$) in order to apply this rule. In this case, the conclusion V_2' is equal to V_2 and the fuzzy uncertainty FN_3 of the conclusion is obtained by

$$
FN_3 = FN_1 \, (\cdot) \, FN_2.
\tag{6.52}
$$

2. If both A and C are fuzzy objects (accordingly, V_1, V_1', V_2, and V_2' are fuzzy sets), then the conclusion V_2' can be derived via a compositional rule of inference [Eq. (6.25)] or generalized modus ponens [Eq. (6.27)]. In this case, calculation of the fuzzy uncertainty FN_3 of the conclusion is the same as that in Eq. (6.52).

3. If A is fuzzy and C is nonfuzzy (accordingly, V_1 and V_1' are fuzzy sets), V_2' in the conclusion must equal V_2. However, the fuzzy uncertainty FN_3 is obtained by the formula

$$
FN_3 = m \cdot [FN_1 \, (\cdot) \, FN_2],
\tag{6.53}
$$

where m is a scalar representing the similarity between V_1 and V_1'. The first product in Eq. (6.53) represents the multiplications of an ordinary number and a fuzzy number, which are defined in Eqs. (5.35) and (5.36), respectively. The similarity m is defined by

$$
m = \begin{cases}
\Pi \, (V_1 \mid V_1') & \text{if } N \, (V_1 \mid V_1') > 0.5 \\
(N \, (V_1 \mid V_1') + 0.5) \cdot \Pi \, (V_1 \mid V_1') & \text{otherwise,}
\end{cases}
\tag{6.54}
$$

where $\Pi \, (V_1 \mid V_1')$ and $N \, (V_1 \mid V_1')$ are, respectively, the possibility measure and necessity measure of V_1 and V_1', which are defined in Eq. (4.66).

- *Evidence combination:* In some cases, two or more rules have the same consequent proposition. Each of these rules with matched facts can be treated as contributing evi-

Fuzzy Logic and Approximate Reasoning   Chap. 6

dence to the conclusion. The way to combine the evidence is as follows. Assume we have the following single-rule inference results:

Rule:	IF A_1 is V_1, THEN C is V_3	(FN_i)	
Fact:	A_1 is V_1'	(FN_j)	(6.55)
Conclusion:	C is C'	(FN_1),	
Rule:	IF A_2 is V_2, THEN C is V_3	(FN_k)	
Fact:	A_2 is V_2'	(FN_ℓ)	(6.56)
Conclusion:	C is C''	(FN_2).	

Then the final conclusion of the evaluation of the above two rules and facts is

$$C_R = C' \cap C''. \tag{6.57}$$

The fuzzy uncertainty of the final conclusion is obtained by

$$FN_R = FN_1\,(+)\,FN_2\,(-)\,[FN_1\,(\cdot)\,FN_2]. \tag{6.58}$$

The Z-II system has been used to construct several expert systems. The useful application domains have been college selection for graduating high-school students, medical diagnosis, psychoanalysis, and risk analysis.

6.5 CONCLUDING REMARKS

Many attempts have been made to relax classical two-valued logic and extend it to three-valued logic and to many-valued logic [Klir and Folger, 1988]. Fuzzy logic is in fact an extension of set-theoretic multivalued logic. The linguistic variable "truth" plays an important role in fuzzy logic. We have introduced Baldwin's [1979] definition of the linguistic variable "truth"; other researchers have proposed different definitions [Zadeh, 1975a], and other definitions of fuzzy truth tables can also be found in [Baldwin, 1979; Zimmermann, 1991]. One related topic not covered in this chapter is representation of the meaning of fuzzy propositions. This is basically a process by which the implicit constraints and variables in the fuzzy proposition are made explicit. In fuzzy logic, it is accomplished by representing fuzzy propositions in the *canonical form* [Zadeh, 1988]. Some meaning translation rules corresponding to different kinds of fuzzy propositions introduced in this chapter can be found in [Zadeh, 1979, 1983a, 1986a, 1992].

We have introduced several important rules of inference of approximate reasoning. Direct applications of approximate reasoning are the fuzzy algorithm and the fuzzy flow chart. Another related topic is *fuzzy languages* which are formal languages based on fuzzy logic and approximate reasoning. Several fuzzy languages have been developed [Zimmermann, 1991]. Among them, the most notable are Zadeh's Possibilistic Relational Universal Fuzzy (PRUF) [1978b] and Baldwin's Support Logic Programming (SLOP) [1986, 1987]. An excellent introduction to PRUF and SLOP can be found in [Zimmermann, 1991].

The approximate reasoning introduced in this chapter mainly follows Zadeh's approach. A different but closely related approach is the *certainty factor* approach in which two distinct ways of specifying a possibility distribution, either by *possibility* [Zadeh, 1978b] or by *certainty* (or *confidence*) qualification [Yager, 1984a, Prade, 1985], are used.

Details of the certainty factor approach can be found in [Yager, 1992b; Dubois and Prade, 1992]. Also, see [Dubois and Prade, 1991] and [Dubois et al., 1991] for an extensive overview of fuzzy logic and approximate reasoning for the past 20 years and a discussion of the generalized modus ponens and of the certainty factor approaches.

Two fuzzy expert systems, MILORD and Z-II, are introduced in this chapter. Another representative fuzzy expert system, called *SPERIL*, is a special-purpose fuzzy expert system for assessing earthquake damage sustained by buildings [Ishizuka, Fu, and Yao, 1982; Ogawa, Fu, and Yao, 1985].

6.6 PROBLEMS

6.1 Provide several examples of linguistic variables that are characterized by a quintuple $(X, T(X), U, G, M)$.

6.2 Given $U = \{0, 0.1, 0.2, ..., 1\}$ and the fuzzy variable A, where $A =$ "large" $= 0.7/0.7 + 0.8/0.8 + 0.9/0.9 + 1/1$, derive the following values: VERY(A), RATHER(A), ROUGHLY(A), PRETTY(A).

6.3 Consider the linguistic variable "Old." If the variable is defined by

$$\mu_{Old}(x) = \begin{cases} 0 & 0 \leq x < 50 \\ [1 + (x - 50/5)^{-2}]^{-1} & 50 \leq x < 100. \end{cases}$$

Determine the membership function of the terms NOT VERY Old, MORE OR LESS Old, VERY Old.

6.4 Consider two linguistic truth values of two propositions, True and False, which are defined as follows:

$$v(True) = 0.6/0.6 + 0.7/0.7 + 0.8/0.8 + 0.9/0.9 + 1/1$$

$$v(False) = 0.4/0.6 + 0.3/0.7 + 0.2/0.8 + 0.1/0.9$$

Determine the linguistic truth values of "VERY True" and "VERY False," and "MORE OR LESS True" ∨ "RATHER True."

6.5 We are given the membership function of the linguistic variable "True" defined by

$$T(x) = \begin{cases} 0 & \text{if } x \leq 3 \\ 2[(x - 3)/7]^2 & \text{if } 3 \leq x \leq 6 \\ 1 - 2[(x - 10)/7]^2 & \text{if } 6 \leq x \leq 10 \\ 1 & \text{if } x \geq 10. \end{cases}$$

(a) Sketch the membership function.
(b) Determine the membership function of "VERY True."
(c) Determine the membership function of "VERY False" where "False" = "NOT True."

6.6 Show, by a truth table, that Eq. (6.11) is always true.

6.7 As in Example 6.3, what are the values of $v(P \Rightarrow Q)$ and $v[NOT(P) OR Q]$?

6.8 Consider the linguistic truth values "True (T)," "False (F)," "VERY True (T^2)," "FAIRLY True ($T^{1/2}$)," and an extra term "Undecided (U)," which is defined by $\mu_{Undecided}(x) = 1$ for all $x \in [0, 1]$. Complete the following fuzzy truth table. (*Hint:* Refer to [Baldwin, 1979; Zimmermann, 1991].)

$v(P)$	$v(Q)$	$v(P) \wedge v(Q)$	$v(P) \vee v(Q)$
F	F		
T	F		
T	T		
U	F		
U	T		
U	U		
T	T^2		
T	$T^{1/2}$		

6.9 Give an example of each of the following proposition principles:
   (a) Fuzzy truth qualification.
   (b) Fuzzy probability qualification.
   (c) Fuzzy possibility qualification.
   (d) Fuzzy usuality qualification.

6.10 Let X and Y be variables taking values in U and V, respectively, where $U = V = [0, 1]$, and let A and B be fuzzy sets defined as follows:

$$A = \int_U s\,(x; 0, 1) \Big/ x, \qquad B = \int_V \pi\,(y; 0.5, 0.5) \Big/ y.$$

Determine the results of (a) X is A AND Y is B, i.e., $\pi_{(X \text{ and } Y)}$, (b) X is A OR Y is B, i.e., $\pi_{(X \text{ or } Y)}$, (c) IF X is A, THEN Y is B, i.e., $\pi_{(Y|X)}$.

6.11 Provide several examples of fuzzy propositions including fuzzy predicates, fuzzy predicate modifiers, fuzzy quantifiers, and fuzzy qualifiers.

6.12 Consider the premises "The weather today is Very Good." and "IF the weather is Not Good THEN the temperature is Low." What can we say about the temperature today using the generalized modus ponens in Eq. (6.27)?

6.13 Let the universe be $U = \{1, 2, 3, 4\}$. Given a linguistic variable "Small" $= 1/1 + 0.7/2 + 0.3/3 + 0.1/4$ and a fuzzy relation $R =$ "ALMOST equal," be defined as

$$R: \quad \begin{array}{c} \\ 1 \\ 2 \\ 3 \\ 4 \end{array} \begin{array}{cccc} 1 & 2 & 3 & 4 \\ \begin{pmatrix} 1 & 0.6 & 0.1 & 0 \\ 0.6 & 1 & 0.6 & 0.1 \\ 0.1 & 0.6 & 1 & 0.6 \\ 0 & 0.1 & 0.6 & 1 \end{pmatrix} \end{array}.$$

Use the max-min composition to compute $R\,(y) = X$ is Small $\circ$ ALMOST equal.

6.14 Provide an example of each of the following approximate reasoning rules:
   (a) Conjunction and disjunction rule of inference.
   (b) Entailment rule of inference.
   (c) Compositional rule of inference.

6.15 Let the trapezoidal membership functions in MILORD be defined by False $= (0, 0, 0, 0)$, ALMOST-False $= (0, 0, 0.25, 0.40)$, Maybe $= (0.25, 0.40, 0.60, 0.75)$, ALMOST-True $= (0.60, 0.75, 1, 1)$, and True $= (1, 1, 1, 1)$. Verify the linguistic approximation shown in Fig. 6.11.

6.16 In discussing the forward rule evaluation of the Z-II fuzzy expert system, we focused on the rule with a single precondition proposition. Figure out the forward rule evaluation scheme for rules with multiple propositions in the precondition parts. (*Hint:* Refer to [Leung and Lam, 1988].)

7

Fuzzy Logic
Control Systems

During the past decade, fuzzy logic control (FLC), initiated by the pioneering work of Mamdani and Assilian [1975], has emerged as one of the most active and fruitful areas for research in the application of fuzzy set theory, fuzzy logic, and fuzzy reasoning. Its application ranges from industrial process control to medical diagnosis and securities trading. Many industrial and consumer products using this technology have been built, especially in Japan where FLC has achieved considerable success. In contrast to conventional control techniques, FLC is best utilized in complex ill-defined processes that can be controlled by a skilled human operator without much knowledge of their underlying dynamics.

The basic idea behind FLC is to incorporate the "expert experience" of a human operator in the design of the controller in controlling a process whose input-output relationship is described by a collection of fuzzy control rules (e.g., IF-THEN rules) involving linguistic variables rather than a complicated dynamic model. This utilization of linguistic variables, fuzzy control rules, and approximate reasoning provides a means to incorporate human expert experience in designing the controller.

In this chapter, we shall introduce the basic architecture, the design methodology, and the stability analysis of fuzzy logic controllers. Some practical application examples will also be discussed. We will find that FLC is strongly based on the concepts of fuzzy sets and relations, linguistic variables, and approximate reasoning introduced in the previous chapters.

7.1 BASIC STRUCTURE AND OPERATION OF FUZZY LOGIC CONTROL SYSTEMS

The typical architecture of a FLC is shown in Fig. 7.1, which is comprised of four principal components: *a fuzzifier, a fuzzy rule base, an inference engine,* and *a defuzzifier.* If the out-

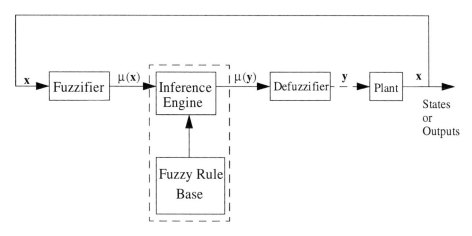

Figure 7.1 Basic architecture of a fuzzy logic controller (FLC).

put from the defuzzifier is not a control action for a plant, then the system is a fuzzy logic *decision* system. The fuzzifier has the effect of transforming crisp measured data (e.g., speed is 10 miles per hour) into suitable linguistic values (i.e., fuzzy sets, for example, speed is *too slow*). The fuzzy rule base stores the empirical knowledge of the operation of the process of the domain experts. The inference engine is the kernel of a FLC, and it has the capability of simulating human decision making by performing approximate reasoning to achieve a desired control strategy. The defuzzifier is utilized to yield a nonfuzzy decision or control action from an inferred fuzzy control action by the inference engine. More details about the operations of these components are described in the following sections.

7.1.1 Input-Output Spaces

The purpose of fuzzy logic controllers is to compute values of control (or action) variables from the observation or measurement of state variables of the controlled process such that a desired system performance is achieved. Thus, a proper choice of process state variables and control variables is essential to characterization of the operation of a fuzzy logic control system (FLCS) and has a substantial effect on the performance of a FLC. Expert experience and engineering knowledge play an important role during this state variables and control variables selection process. Typically, the input variables in a FLC are the state, state error, state error derivative, state error integral, and so on. Following the definition of linguistic variables, the input vector $\mathbf{x}$ which includes the input state linguistic variables x_i and the output state vector $\mathbf{y}$ which includes the output state (or control) linguistic variables y_i in Fig. 7.1 can be defined, respectively, as

$$\mathbf{x} = \{(x_i, U_i, \{T_{x_i}^1, T_{x_i}^2, \ldots, T_{x_i}^{k_i}\}, \{\mu_{x_i}^1, \mu_{x_i}^2, \ldots, \mu_{x_i}^{k_i}\}) |_{i=1,\ldots,n}\}, \tag{7.1}$$

$$\mathbf{y} = \{(y_i, V_i, \{T_{y_i}^1, T_{y_i}^2, \ldots, T_{y_i}^{l_i}\}, \{\mu_{y_i}^1, \mu_{y_i}^2, \ldots, \mu_{y_i}^{l_i}\}) |_{i=1,\ldots,m}\}, \tag{7.2}$$

where the input linguistic variables x_i form a fuzzy input space $U = U_1 \times U_2 \times \cdots \times U_n$ and the output linguistic variables y_i form a fuzzy output space $V = V_1 \times V_2 \times \cdots \times V_m$.

From Eqs. (7.1) and (7.2), we observe that an input linguistic variable x_i in a universe of discourse U_i is characterized by $T(x_i) = \{T_{x_i}^1, T_{x_i}^2, \ldots, T_{x_i}^{k_i}\}$ and $\mu(x_i) = \{\mu_{x_i}^1, \mu_{x_i}^2, \ldots, \mu_{x_i}^{k_i}\}$, where $T(x_i)$ is the *term set* of x_i, that is, the set of names of linguistic values of x_i with each value $T_{x_i}^{k_i}$ being a fuzzy number with membership function $\mu_{x_i}^{k_i}$ defined on U_i. So $\mu(x_i)$ is a semantic rule for associating each value with its meaning. For example, if x_i indicates speed, then $T(x_i) = \{T_{x_i}^1, T_{x_i}^2, T_{x_i}^3\}$ may be "Slow," "Medium," and "Fast." Similarly, an output linguistic variable y_i is associated with a term set $T(y_i) = \{T_{y_i}^1, T_{y_i}^2, \ldots, T_{y_i}^{l_i}\}$ and $\mu(y_i) = \{\mu_{y_i}^1, \mu_{y_i}^2, \ldots, \mu_{y_i}^{l_i}\}$. The size (or cardinality) of a term set $|T(x_i)| = k_i$ is called the *fuzzy partition* of x_i. The fuzzy partition determines the granularity of the control obtainable from a FLC. Figure 7.2(a) depicts two fuzzy partitions in the same normalized universe $[-1, +1]$. For a two-input FLC, the fuzzy input space is divided into many overlapping grids [see Fig. 7.2(b)]. Furthermore, the fuzzy partitions in a fuzzy input space determine the *maximum* number of fuzzy control rules in a FLCS. For example, in the case of a two-input–one-output fuzzy logic control system, if $|T(x_1)| = 3$ and $|T(x_2)| = 7$, then the maximum number of fuzzy control rules is $|T(x_1)| \times |T(x_2)| = 21$. The input membership functions $\mu_{x_i}^k$, $k = 1, 2, \ldots, k_i$, and the output membership functions $\mu_{y_i}^l$, $l = 1, 2, \ldots, l_i$, used in a FLC are usually parametric functions such as triangular functions, trapezoidal functions, and bell-shaped functions. Triangular functions and the trapezoidal functions can be represented by L-R fuzzy numbers, while bell-shaped membership functions can be defined as

$$\mu_{x_i}(x) = \exp\left(\frac{-(x - m_i)^2}{2\sigma_i^2}\right), \tag{7.3}$$

where m_i and σ_i specify the mean location and the width of the bell-shaped function, respectively. Proper fuzzy partitioning of input and output spaces and a correct choice of membership functions play an essential role in achieving a successful FLC design. Unfortunately, they are not deterministic and have no unique solutions. Traditionally, a heuristic trial-and-error procedure is usually used to determine an optimal fuzzy partition. Furthermore, the choice of input and output membership functions is based on subjective decision criteria and relies heavily on time-consuming trial and error. A promising approach to automating and speeding up these design choices is to provide a FLC with the ability to learn its input and output membership functions and the fuzzy control rules. This will be explored later in Part III of this book (see Chap. 19).

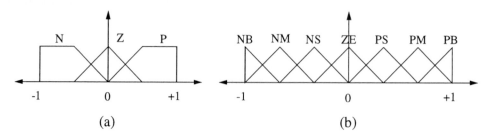

(a)   (b)

Figure 7.2 Diagrammatic representation of a fuzzy partition. (a) Coarse fuzzy partition with three terms: N, negative; ZE, zero; P, positive. (b) Finer fuzzy partition with seven terms: NB, negative big; NM, negative medium; NS, negative small; ZE, zero; PS, positive small; PM, positive medium; PB, positive big.

7.1.2 Fuzzifier

A fuzzifier performs the function of fuzzification which is a subjective valuation to transform measurement data into valuation of a subjective value. Hence, it can be defined as a mapping from an observed input space to labels of fuzzy sets in a specified input universe of discourse. Since the data manipulation in a FLC is based on fuzzy set theory, fuzzification is necessary and desirable at an early stage. In fuzzy control applications, the observed data are usually crisp (though they may be corrupted by noise). A natural and simple fuzzification approach is to convert a crisp value x_0 into a fuzzy singleton A within the specified universe of discourse. That is, the membership function of A, $\mu_A(x)$, is equal to 1 at the point x_0, and zero at other places. In this case, for a specific value $x_i(t)$ at time t, it is mapped to the fuzzy set $T_{x_i}^1$ with degree $\mu_{x_i}^1(x_i(t))$ and to the fuzzy set $T_{x_i}^2$ with degree $\mu_{x_i}^2(x_i(t))$, and so on. This approach is widely used in FLC applications because it greatly simplifies the fuzzy reasoning process. In a more complex case where observed data are disturbed by random noise, a fuzzifier should convert the probabilistic data into fuzzy numbers, that is, fuzzy (possibility) data. For this, Dubois and Prade [1985a] defined a bijective transformation which transforms a probability measure into a possibility measure by using the concept of the degree of necessity. In large-scale systems, some observations relating to the behavior of such systems are precise, others are measurable only in a statistical sense, and some, referred to as "hybrids," require both probabilistic and possibilistic modes of characterization.

7.1.3 Fuzzy Rule Base

Fuzzy control rules are characterized by a collection of fuzzy IF-THEN rules in which the preconditions and consequents involve linguistic variables. This collection of fuzzy control rules (or fuzzy control statements) characterizes the simple input-output relation of the system. The general form of the fuzzy control rules in the case of multi-input–single-output systems (MISO) is:

$$R^i: \text{IF } x \text{ is } A_i,\ldots,\ \text{AND } y \text{ is } B_i, \text{THEN } z = C_i, \qquad i = 1, 2,\ldots, n, \qquad (7.4)$$

where $x,\ldots, y$, and z are linguistic variables representing the process state variables and the control variable, respectively, and $A_i,\ldots, B_i$, and C_i are the linguistic values of the linguistic variables $x,\ldots, y$, and z in the universes of discourse $U,\ldots, V$, and W, respectively. A variant of this type is that the consequent is represented as a function of the process state variables $x,\ldots, y$, that is

$$R^i: \text{IF } x \text{ is } A_i,\ldots,\ \text{AND } y \text{ is } B_i, \text{THEN } z = f_i(x,\ldots, y), \qquad (7.5)$$

where $f_i(x,\ldots, y)$ is a function of the process state variables $x,\ldots, y$. The fuzzy control rules in Eqs. (7.4) and (7.5) evaluate the process state (i.e., state, state error, state error integral, and so on) at time t and compute and decide the control actions as a function of the state variables $(x,\ldots, y)$. It is worthwhile to point out that both fuzzy control rules have linguistic values as inputs and either linguistic values [as in Eq. (7.4)] or crisp values [as in Eq. (7.5)] as outputs.

7.1.4 Inference Engine

This is the kernel of the FLC in modeling human decision making within the conceptual framework of fuzzy logic and approximate reasoning. As mentioned in Section 6.3.1, the generalized modus ponens (forward data-driven inference) in Eq. (6.27) plays an especially important role in this context. For application to fuzzy reasoning in FLCs, the generalized modus ponens in Eq. (6.27) can be rewritten as follows:

Premise 1:	IF x is A, THEN y is B	
Premise 2:	x is A'	(7.6)
Conclusion:	y is B'.	

where A, A', B, and B' are fuzzy predicates (fuzzy sets or relations) in the universal sets U, U, V, and V, respectively. In general, a fuzzy control rule [e.g., premise 1 in Eq. (7.6)] is a fuzzy relation which is expressed as a fuzzy implication $R = A \rightarrow B$. According to the compositional rule of inference in Eq. (6.25), conclusion B' in Eq. (7.6) can be obtained by taking the composition of fuzzy set A' and the fuzzy relation (here the fuzzy relation is a fuzzy implication) $A \rightarrow B$:

$$B' = A' \circ R = A' \circ (A \rightarrow B).$$

(7.7)

In addition to the definitions of fuzzy composition and implication given in Eqs. (6.26) and (6.28), there are four types of compositional operators that can be used in the compositional rule of inference. These correspond to the four operations associated with the t-norms:

- Max-min operation [Zadeh, 1973],
- Max product operation [Kaufmann, 1975],
- Max bounded product (max $- \odot$) operation [Mizumoto, 1981],
- Max drastic product (max $- \wedge$) operation [Mizumoto, 1981],

where bounded product and drastic product operations are stated in Eqs. (2.58) and (2.59), respectively. In FLC applications, max-min and max product compositional operators are the most commonly and frequently used because of their computational simplicity and efficiency. Let max $- \star$ represent any one of the above four composition operations. Then Eq. (7.7) becomes

$$B' = A' \star R = A' \star (A \rightarrow B),$$

$$\mu_{B'}(v) = \sup_u \{ \mu_{A'}(u) \star \mu_{A \rightarrow B}(u, v) \},$$

(7.8)

where $*$ denotes the t-norm operations such as min, product, bounded product, and drastic product operations. As for the fuzzy implication $A \rightarrow B$, there are nearly 40 distinct fuzzy implication functions described in the existing literature. Table 7.1 provides a list of several fuzzy implication rules commonly used in a FLC [Mizumoto, 1988].

It is observed that the fuzzy implication rules defined in Table 7.1 are generated from the *fuzzy conjunction, fuzzy disjunction,* or *fuzzy implication* by employing various t-norms or t-conorms. The first four fuzzy implications, R_c, R_p, R_{bp}, and R_{dp}, are all t-norms. For example, Mamdani's min fuzzy implication R_c is obtained if the intersection operator is used in the fuzzy conjunction. Larsen's product fuzzy implication R_p is obtained if the algebraic product is used in the fuzzy conjunction. R_{bp} and R_{dp} are obtained if the bounded product and the drastic product are used in the fuzzy conjunction,

TABLE 7.1 Various Fuzzy Implication Rules

Rule of Fuzzy Implication	Implication Formulas	Fuzzy Implication: $\mu_{A \rightarrow B}(u, v)$
R_c: min operation [Mamdani]	$a \rightarrow b = a \wedge b$	$= \mu_A(u) \wedge \mu_B(v)$
R_p: product operation [Larsen]	$a \rightarrow b = a \cdot b$	$= \mu_A(u) \cdot \mu_B(v)$
R_{bp}: bounded product	$a \rightarrow b = 0 \vee (a + b - 1)$	$= 0 \vee [\mu_A(u) + \mu_B(v) - 1]$
R_{dp}: drastic product	$a \rightarrow b = \begin{cases} a, & b = 1 \\ b, & a = 1 \\ 0, & a, b < 1 \end{cases}$	$= \begin{cases} \mu_A(u), & \mu_B(v) = 1 \\ \mu_B(v), & \mu_A(u) = 1 \\ 0, & \mu_A(u), \mu_B(v) < 1 \end{cases}$
R_a: arithmetic rule [Zadeh]	$a \rightarrow b = 1 \wedge (1 - a + b)$	$= 1 \wedge (1 - \mu_A(u) + \mu_B(v))$
R_m: max-min rule [Zadeh]	$a \rightarrow b = (a \wedge b) \vee (1 - a)$	$= (\mu_A(u) \wedge \mu_B(v)) \vee (1 - \mu_A(u))$
R_s: standard sequence	$a \rightarrow b = \begin{cases} 1, & a \leq b \\ 0, & a > b \end{cases}$	$= \begin{cases} 1, & \mu_A(u) \leq \mu_B(v) \\ 0, & \mu_A(u) > \mu_B(v) \end{cases}$
R_b: Boolean fuzzy implication	$a \rightarrow b = (1 - a) \vee b$	$= ((1 - \mu_A(u)) \vee \mu_B(v))$
R_g: Gödelian logic	$a \rightarrow b = \begin{cases} 1, & a \leq b \\ b, & a > b \end{cases}$	$= \begin{cases} 1, & \mu_A(u) \leq \mu_B(v) \\ \mu_B(v), & \mu_A(u) > \mu_B(v) \end{cases}$
R_Δ: Goguen's fuzzy implication	$a \rightarrow b = \begin{cases} 1, & a \leq b \\ b/a, & a > b \end{cases}$	$= \begin{cases} 1, & \mu_A(u) \leq \mu_B(v) \\ \mu_B(v)/\mu_A(u), & \mu_A(u) > \mu_B(v) \end{cases}$

respectively. Furthermore, we note that Zadeh's arithmetic rule R_a follows Eq. (2.78) by using the bounded sum operator, and Zadeh's max-min rule R_m follows Eq. (2.79) by using the intersection and union operators. Other fuzzy implication rules in Table 7.1 can be obtained employing fuzzy implication definitions in Eqs. (2.78)–(2.82) using various t-norms and t-conorms.

Example 7.1

This example illustrates the various fuzzy implications in Table 7.1 graphically. Assume fuzzy set A' is a singleton at u_0; that is, $\mu_{A'}(u_0) = 1$ and $\mu_{A'}(u) = 0$ for $u \neq u_0$. Let A and B be fuzzy sets in U and V, respectively, as in Fig. 7.3. Then the consequent B' of Eq. (7.6) at $A' = u_0$ under the fuzzy implications $A \rightarrow B$ in Table 7.1 is depicted in Fig. 7.4, where $\mu_A(u_0) = a$ with $a = 0.3$ (dotted line) and $a = 0.7$ (solid line). Figure 7.4 is obtained from the equations in the third column of Table 7.1 by setting $\mu_A(u) = \mu_A(u_0)$ in those equations.

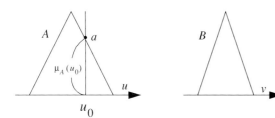

Figure 7.3 Fuzzy sets A and B in Example 7.1.

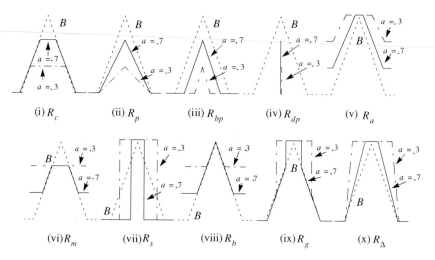

(i) R_c (ii) R_p (iii) R_{bp} (iv) R_{dp} (v) R_a

(vi) R_m (vii) R_s (viii) R_b (ix) R_g (x) R_Δ

Figure 7.4 Inference results $\mu_{B'}(v) = \mu_{A \to B}(u_0, v) = \mu_A(u_0) \to \mu_B(v)$ at $\mu_A(u_0) = a$ in Example 7.1.

Among the various fuzzy implications in Table 7.1, Mamdani's fuzzy implication method R_c associated with the max-min composition is the most frequently used in fuzzy logic control. Let us consider an example of this.

Example 7.2

In this example, we will derive the conclusion B' in Eq. (7.6) using Eq. (7.8) when $A' = A$, when $A' = $ VERY A, when $A' = $ MORE OR LESS A, and when $A' = $ NOT A [see Eq. (6.4)]. Here, Mamdani's method R_c and max-min composition are adopted.

(a) For $A' = A$:

$$\mu_{B'}(v) = \bigvee_u \{\mu_A(u) \wedge (\mu_A(u) \wedge \mu_B(v))\} = \bigvee_u \{\mu_A(u) \wedge \mu_B(v)\}$$

$$= \bigvee_u \mu_A(u) \wedge \mu_B(v) = 1 \wedge \mu_B(v) = \mu_B(v),$$

where we assume that A is normal.

(b) For $A' = A^2$ (i.e., VERY A):

$$\mu_{B'}(v) = \bigvee_u \{\mu_A^2(u) \wedge (\mu_A(u) \wedge \mu_B(v))\} = \bigvee_u \{\mu_A^2(u) \wedge \mu_B(v)\} = 1 \wedge \mu_B(v) = \mu_B(v).$$

(c) For $A' = A^{1/2}$ (i.e., MORE OR LESS A):

$$\mu_{B'}(v) = \bigvee_u \{\mu_A^{1/2}(u) \wedge (\mu_A(u) \wedge \mu_B(v))\} = \bigvee_u \{\mu_A(u) \wedge \mu_B(v)\} = \mu_B(v).$$

(d) For $A' = 1 - A$ (i.e., NOT A):

$$\mu_{B'}(v) = \bigvee_u \{(1 - \mu_A(u)) \wedge (\mu_A(u) \wedge \mu_B(v))\}$$

$$= \bigvee_u \{(1 - \mu_A(u)) \wedge \mu_A(u)\} \wedge \mu_B(v) = 0.5 \wedge \mu_B(v).$$

The results in the above example are shown in the first row of Table 7.2 in which the corresponding results of some other implication operators in Table 7.1 also appear. From Table 7.2, we observe that although R_c and R_p do not have a well-defined logical structure, the results indicate that they are well suited for the generalized modus ponens. R_m and R_a are not well suited for approximate reasoning since the inferred consequents do not always fit our intuition. Furthermore, for fuzzy logical systems, R_b and $R_\triangle$ have significant shortcomings. Overall, R_s yields reasonable results and thus constitutes an appropriate choice for use in the compositional rules of inference. The above observations are all based on the max-min composition. We found from Table 7.2 that, for example, for $A' = A$, $B' = A \circ R_a = (1 + B)/2 \neq B$. Thus, R_a does not satisfy the normal modus ponens in Eq. (6.11). Let us explore what the inferred results will be from other composition operators. Let $\square$ and $\triangle$ denote the max bounded product and the max drastic product compositions, respectively. Then we have

$$B' = A \ \square \ R_a = A \ \triangle \ R_a = B, \qquad (7.9)$$

that is, it satisfies the modus ponens. It should be clear that using the max bounded product and the max drastic product compositions, we can obtain inference results that match intuition even for the R_a method, which was unsatisfactory when based on the max-min composition.

In the above discussion, we considered various possible operations for obtaining the conclusion B' using the generalized modus ponens in Eq. (7.6). Next, we will show an exact application of the generalized modus ponens in the inference engine of a FLC. In most general cases, the fuzzy rule base has the form of a multi-input–multi-output (MIMO) system

$$R = \{ R_{\mathrm{MIMO}}^1, R_{\mathrm{MIMO}}^2, \dots, R_{\mathrm{MIMO}}^n \}, \qquad (7.10)$$

where R_{MIMO}^i represents the ith rule:

TABLE 7.2 Summary of Inference Results for Generalized Modus Ponens

	A	Very A (A^2)	More or Less A $(A^{1/2})$	Not A
R_c	μ_B	μ_B	μ_B	$0.5 \wedge \mu_B$
R_p	μ_B	μ_B	μ_B	$\mu_B/(1 + \mu_B)$
R_a	$\dfrac{1 + \mu_B}{2}$	$\dfrac{3 + 2\mu_B - \sqrt{5 + 4\mu_B}}{2}$	$\dfrac{\sqrt{5 + 4\mu_B} - 1}{2}$	1
R_m	$0.5 \vee \mu_B$	$(3 - \sqrt{5})/2 \vee \mu_B$	$(\sqrt{5} - 1)/2 \vee \mu_B$	1
R_s	μ_B	μ_B^2	$\sqrt{\mu_B}$	1
R_b	$0.5 \vee \mu_B$	$(3 - \sqrt{5})/2 \vee \mu_B$	$(\sqrt{5} - 1)/2 \vee \mu_B$	1
R_g	μ_B	μ_B	$\sqrt{\mu_B}$	1
$R_\triangle$	$\sqrt{\mu_B}$	$\mu_B^{2/3}$	$\mu_B^{1/3}$	1

$$\text{IF } (x \text{ is } A_i \text{ AND } \cdots \text{ AND } y \text{ is } B_i), \text{ THEN } (z_1 \text{ is } C_i^1, \ldots, z_q \text{ is } C_i^q), \qquad (7.11)$$

where z_q indicates the qth control variable and C_i^q denotes the output predicate of the qth control variable. The precondition of R_{MIMO}^i forms a fuzzy set $A_i \times \cdots \times B_i$ in the product space $U \times \cdots \times V$, and the consequent is the union of q *independent* control actions. Thus the ith rule R_{MIMO}^i may be represented as a fuzzy implication,

$$R_{\text{MIMO}}^i : (A_i \times \cdots \times B_i) \rightarrow (C_i^1 + \cdots + C_i^q) = \bigcup_{k=1}^q (A_i \times \cdots \times B_i) \rightarrow C_i^k, \qquad (7.12)$$

where $+$ represents the union of q independent control variables or actions. Equation (7.12) indicates that the rule base R in Eq. (7.10) can be represented as the union of all the n rules:

$$
\begin{aligned}
R &= \left\{ \bigcup_{i=1}^n R_{\text{MIMO}}^i \right\} = \left\{ \bigcup_{i=1}^n [(A_i \times \cdots \times B_i) \rightarrow (C_i^1 + \cdots + C_i^q)] \right\} \\
&= \left\{ \bigcup_{k=1}^q \bigcup_{i=1}^n [(A_i \times \cdots \times B_i) \rightarrow C_i^k] \right\} \\
&= \{ RB_{\text{MISO}}^1, RB_{\text{MISO}}^2, \ldots, RB_{\text{MISO}}^q \}.
\end{aligned}
\qquad (7.13)
$$

The above equation shows that the fuzzy rule base R of a FLC is composed of a set of q subrule bases RB_{MISO}^i, with each subrule base RB_{MISO}^i consisting of n fuzzy control rules with multiple process state variables and a single control variable. Thus, a MIMO system with n inputs and q outputs can be decomposed into q n-input–single-output subsystems, and each of these q subsystems has a set of subrule base $\{RB_{\text{MISO}}^i\}$. Hence, instead of considering fuzzy control rules for a MIMO system, we will consider fuzzy control rules only for a MISO system. The general form of MISO fuzzy control rules in the case of two-input–single-output fuzzy systems is

Input	:	x is A' AND y is B'
R^1	:	IF x is A_1 AND y is B_1, THEN z is C_1
ALSO R^2	:	IF x is A_2 AND y is B_2, THEN z is C_2
$\cdots$	$\cdots$ $\cdots$	
$\cdots$	$\cdots$ $\cdots$	
ALSO R^n	:	IF x is A_n AND y is B_n, THEN z is C_n

$$(7.14)$$

Conclusion : z is C'.

In the above rules, the connectives AND and ALSO may be interpreted as either *intersection* ($\cap$) or *union* ($\cup$) for different definitions of fuzzy implication in Table 7.1. Let $\circ$ denote the max-min compositional operator and let $\cdot$ denote the max product compositional operator. Then we have the following theorem governing the connective AND with one fuzzy control rule to obtain the conclusion.

Theorem 7.1

Let us assume that there is only one rule, say R_i, in Eq. (7.14). With Mamdani's min fuzzy implication R_c, the conclusion C' can be expressed as the intersection of the individual conclusions of input linguistic variables. That is,

$$C' = (A', B') \circ R_c(A_i, B_i; C_i)$$
$$= [A' \circ R_c(A_i; C_i)] \cap [B' \circ R_c(B_i; C_i)], \tag{7.15}$$

where $R_c(A_i, B_i; C_i) \equiv (A_i \text{ AND } B_i) \rightarrow C_i$, $R_c(A_i; C_i) \equiv A_i \rightarrow C_i$ and $R_c(B_i; C_i) \equiv B_i \rightarrow C_i$ are fuzzy implications by Mamdani's method R_c.

Proof

$$C' = (A', B') \circ R_c(A_i, B_i; C_i)$$

$$\mu_{C'}(w) = \bigvee_{u, v} \{[\mu_{A'}(u) \wedge \mu_{B'}(v)] \wedge [\mu_{A_i}(u) \wedge \mu_{B_i}(v) \wedge \mu_{C_i}(w)]\}$$

$$= \bigvee_u \left\{ [\mu_{A'}(u) \wedge \mu_{A_i}(u) \wedge \mu_{C_i}(w)] \wedge \left[\bigvee_v \{\mu_{B'}(v) \wedge \mu_{B_i}(v) \wedge \mu_{C_i}(w)\} \right] \right\}$$

$$= \bigvee_u \{\mu_{A'}(u) \wedge \mu_{A_i}(u) \wedge \mu_{C_i}(w) \wedge \mu_{B' \circ R_c(B_i; C_i)}(w)\}$$

$$= \mu_{A' \circ R_c(A_i; C_i)}(w) \wedge \mu_{B' \circ R_c(B_i; C_i)}(w).$$

That is,

$$C' = [A' \circ R_c(A_i; C_i)] \cap [B' \circ R_c(B_i; C_i)].$$

It can be shown that Theorem 7.1 is also true for the fuzzy implications R_p, R_{bp}, and R_{dp} in Table 7.1. However, if we try other fuzzy implication rules in Table 7.1, it can be shown that we should interpret the connective AND as the union operator ($\cup$). That is, the conclusion is expressed as the union ($\cup$) of the individual conclusions. For example,

$$C' = (A', B') \circ R_a(A_i, B_i; C_i)$$
$$= [A' \circ R_a(A_i; C_i)] \cup [B' \circ R_a(B_i; C_i)], \tag{7.16}$$

where $R_a(A_i, B_i; C_i) \equiv (A_i \text{ AND } B_i) \rightarrow C_i$, $R_a(A_i; C_i) \equiv A_i \rightarrow C_i$ and $R_a(B_i; C_i) \equiv B_i \rightarrow C_i$ are fuzzy implications by Zadeh's arithmetic rule R_a. Equation (7.16) is also true for the fuzzy implication methods R_m, R_s, R_b, R_g, and $R_\triangle$ in Table 7.1.

Notice that Eqs. (7.15) and (7.16) are also true for the max product compositional operator; that is, we can replace $\circ$ in Eqs. (7.15) and (7.16) by $\cdot$ and the results will still be valid.

The next theorem concerns the whole set of rules in Eq. (7.14) and the interpretation of the connective ALSO in the control rules in obtaining the conclusion.

Theorem 7.2

Consider the whole set of rules in Eq. (7.14). With Mamdani's min fuzzy implication R_c, the conclusion C' can be expressed as a unification of the individual conclusions of fuzzy control rules. That is,

$$C' = (A', B') \circ \bigcup_{i=1}^{n} R_c(A_i, B_i; C_i) = \bigcup_{i=1}^{n} (A', B') \circ R_c(A_i, B_i; C_i). \tag{7.17}$$

Proof: The membership function $\mu_{C'}$ of the fuzzy set C' is pointwise defined for all $w \in W$ by

$$\mu_{C'}(w) = (\mu_{A'}(u) \wedge \mu_{B'}(v)) \circ \bigvee_{u,v,w} (\mu_{R_1}(u,v,w), \ldots, \mu_{R_n}(u,v,w))$$

$$= \bigvee_{u,v} \left\{ (\mu_{A'}(u) \wedge \mu_{B'}(v)) \wedge \left[\bigvee_{u,v,w} (\mu_{R_1}(u,v,w), \ldots, \mu_{R_n}(u,v,w)) \right] \right\}$$

$$= \bigvee_{u,v,w} \bigvee_{u,v} \left\{ [(\mu_{A'}(u) \wedge \mu_{B'}(v)) \wedge \mu_{R_1}(u,v,w,)], \right.$$

$$\left. \ldots, [(\mu_{A'}(u) \wedge \mu_{B'}(v)) \wedge \mu_{R_n}(u,v,w)] \right\}$$

$$= \bigvee_{u,v,w} \left\{ [(\mu_{A'}(u) \wedge \mu_{B'}(v)) \circ \mu_{R_1}(u,v,w)], \right.$$

$$\left. \ldots, [(\mu_{A'}(u), \mu_{B'}(v)) \circ \mu_{R_n}(u,v,w)] \right\},$$

where $\mu_{R_i}(u,v,w) \equiv \mu_{A_i}(u) \wedge \mu_{B_i}(v) \wedge \mu_{C_i}(w)$. This completes the proof.

We can also show that Eq. (7.17) is also true for Larsen's product fuzzy implication R_p, bounded product implication R_{bp}, and drastic product implication R_{dp}. That is, we can simply replace R_c by R_p, R_{bp}, or R_{dp} in Eq. (7.17) and Theorem 7.2 will still be valid. This is equivalent to saying that the rule connective ALSO is interpreted as the union operator ($\cup$) for R_c, R_p, R_{bp}, and R_{dp} fuzzy implications. On the other hand, the connective ALSO is also interpreted as the intersection operator ($\cap$) for R_a, R_m, R_s, R_b, R_g, and $R_\triangle$ fuzzy implications in Table 7.1. So, we have

$$C' = (A', B') \circ \bigcap_{i=1}^{n} R_a(A_i, B_i; C_i) = \bigcap_{i=1}^{n} (A', B') \circ R_a(A_i, B_i; C_i), \tag{7.18}$$

where R_a can be replaced by R_m, R_s, R_b, R_g, or $R_\triangle$. It should be noted that Eqs. (7.17) and (7.18) still hold if we use the max product composition instead of the max-min composition. By combining Theorems 7.1 and 7.2, the above discussion can be summarized as follows:

- If any one of the fuzzy implication rules R_c, R_p, R_{bp}, or R_{dp} is used, then the conclusion in Eq. (7.14) is given by

$$C' = (A' \cap B') \circ [(A_1 \cap B_1 \to C_1) \cup (A_2 \cap B_2 \to C_2)$$

$$\cup \cdots \cup (A_n \cap B_n \to C_n)]$$

$$= [(A' \circ (A_1 \to C_1)) \cap (B' \circ (B_1 \to C_1))]$$

$$\cup [(A' \circ (A_2 \to C_2)) \cap (B' \circ (B_2 \to C_2))] \tag{7.19}$$

$$\cup \cdots \cup [(A' \circ (A_n \to C_n)) \cap (B' \circ (B_n \to C_n))]$$

$$= \bigcup_{i=1}^{n} \left\{ [A' \circ R_i(A_i; C_i)] \cap [B' \circ R_i(B_i; C_i)] \right\}.$$

where $R_i(\cdot)$ is one of the fuzzy implication rules of R_c, R_p, R_{bp}, or R_{dp}.

- If any one of the fuzzy implication rules R_a, R_m, R_s, R_b, R_g, or R_Δ is used, then the conclusion in Eq. (7.14) is given by

$$C' = (A' \cup B') \circ [(A_1 \cup B_1 \to C_1) \cap (A_2 \cup B_2 \to C_2)$$
$$\cap \cdots \cap (A_n \cup B_n \to C_n)]$$
$$= [(A' \circ (A_1 \to C_1)) \cup (B' \circ (B_1 \to C_1))]$$
$$\cap [(A' \circ (A_2 \to C_2)) \cup (B' \circ (B_2 \to C_2))] \qquad (7.20)$$
$$\cap \cdots \cap [(A' \circ (A_n \to C_n)) \cup (B' \circ (B_n \to C_n))]$$
$$= \bigcap_{i=1}^{n} \{ [A' \circ R_i(A_i; C_i)] \cup [B' \circ R_i(B_i; C_i)] \}.$$

where $R_i(\cdot)$ is one of the fuzzy implication rules of R_a, R_m, R_s, R_b, R_g, or R_Δ.

Again, Eqs. (7.19) and (7.20) are still true if the max-min composition is replaced by the max product composition.

Next, we shall focus on two special fuzzy implication rules R_c and R_p, which are most commonly used in FLCs. Since in fuzzy control the inputs are usually fuzzy singletons, namely, $A' = u_0$ and $B' = v_0$ in Eq. (7.14), the following theorem plays an important role in FLC applications.

Theorem 7.3

Consider the max-min compositional operator $\circ$. If the inputs are fuzzy singletons, namely, $A' = u_0$ and $B' = v_0$, then the results C' in Eq. (7.14) derived by employing Mamdani's minimum operation rule R_c and Larsen's product operation rule R_p, respectively, may be expressed simply as

$$R_c: \ \mu_{C'}(w) = \bigvee_{i=1}^{n} \alpha_i \wedge \mu_{C_i}(w) \equiv \bigvee_{i=1}^{n} \left[\mu_{A_i}(u_0) \wedge \mu_{B_i}(v_0) \right] \wedge \mu_{C_i}(w), \qquad (7.21)$$

$$R_p: \ \mu_{C'}(w) = \bigvee_{i=1}^{n} \alpha_i \cdot \mu_{C_i}(w) \equiv \bigvee_{i=1}^{n} \left[\mu_{A_i}(u_0) \wedge \mu_{B_i}(v_0) \right] \cdot \mu_{C_i}(w), \qquad (7.22)$$

where α_i denotes the firing strength (or weighting factor) of the ith rule, which is a measure of the contribution of the ith rule to the fuzzy control action. If the max product compositional operator $\cdot$ is considered, then the corresponding R_c and R_p are the same as Eqs. (7.21) and (7.22), respectively.

Proof: For R_c:

$$C'_i = [A' \circ R_c(A_i; C_i)] \cap [B' \circ R_c(B_i; C_i)], \qquad i = 1, 2, \dots, n.$$

$$\mu_{C'_i}(w) = \left[\mu_{A'}(u_0) \wedge (\mu_{A_i}(u) \wedge \mu_{C_i}(w)) \right] \wedge \left[\mu_{B'}(v_0) \wedge (\mu_{B_i}(v) \wedge \mu_{C_i}(w)) \right]$$

$$= \left[\mu_{A_i}(u_0) \wedge \mu_{B_i}(v_0) \right] \wedge \mu_{C_i}(w), \qquad i = 1, 2, \dots, n.$$

$$\mu_{C'}(w) = \bigvee_{i=1}^{n} \mu_{C'_i}(w) = \bigvee_{i=1}^{n} \left[\mu_{A_i}(u_0) \wedge \mu_{B_i}(v_0) \right] \wedge \mu_{C_i}(w).$$

For R_p:

$$C_i' = [A' \circ R_p(A_i; C_i)] \cap [B' \circ R_p(B_i; C_i)], \qquad i = 1, 2, \ldots, n.$$

$$\mu_{C_i'}(w) = \left[\mu_{A'}(u_0) \wedge (\mu_{A_i}(u) \cdot \mu_{C_i}(w))\right] \wedge \left[\mu_{B'}(v_0) \wedge (\mu_{B_i}(v) \cdot \mu_{C_i}(w))\right]$$

$$= \left[\mu_{A_i}(u_0) \wedge \mu_{B_i}(v_0)\right] \cdot \mu_{C_i}(w), \qquad i = 1, 2, \ldots, n.$$

$$\mu_{C'}(w) = \bigvee_{i=1}^{n} \mu_{C_i'}(w) = \bigvee_{i=1}^{n} \left[\mu_{A_i}(u_0) \wedge \mu_{B_i}(v_0)\right] \cdot \mu_{C_i}(w).$$

The proof for the max product compositional operator is similar and is left as an exercise for the reader.

Equations (7.21) and (7.22) are the most frequently used in fuzzy control applications. They not only simplify computations but also provide a graphical interpretation of the fuzzy inference mechanism in the FLC. Next, we shall summarize the three types of fuzzy reasoning currently employed in FLC applications. For simplicity, let us assume that we have two fuzzy control rules as follows:

$$R^1: \text{ IF } x \text{ is } A_1 \text{ AND } y \text{ is } B_1, \text{ THEN } z \text{ is } C_1,$$

$$R^2: \text{ IF } x \text{ is } A_2 \text{ AND } y \text{ is } B_2, \text{ THEN } z \text{ is } C_2.$$

Then the firing strengths α_1 and α_2 of the first and second rules may be expressed as

$$\alpha_1 = \mu_{A_1}(x_0) \wedge \mu_{B_1}(y_0) \qquad \text{and} \qquad \alpha_2 = \mu_{A_2}(x_0) \wedge \mu_{B_2}(y_0), \qquad (7.23)$$

where $\mu_{A_1}(x_0)$ and $\mu_{B_1}(y_0)$ indicate the degrees of partial match between the user-supplied data and the data in the fuzzy rule base.

1. *Fuzzy reasoning of the first type—Mamdani's minimum fuzzy implication rule, R_c:* In this mode of reasoning, the ith fuzzy control rule leads to the control decision

$$\mu_{C_i'}(w) = \alpha_i \wedge \mu_{C_i}(w). \qquad (7.24)$$

The final inferred consequent C is given by

$$\mu_C(w) = \mu_{C_1'} \vee \mu_{C_2'} = \left[\alpha_1 \wedge \mu_{C_1}(w)\right] \vee \left[\alpha_2 \wedge \mu_{C_2}(w)\right]. \qquad (7.25)$$

This fuzzy reasoning process is illustrated in Fig. 7.5.

2. *Fuzzy reasoning of the first type—Larsen's product fuzzy implication rule, R_p:* In this case, the ith fuzzy control rule leads to the control decision

$$\mu_{C_i'}(w) = \alpha_i \cdot \mu_{C_i}(w). \qquad (7.26)$$

Consequently, the membership function μ_C of the inferred consequent C is given by

$$\mu_C(w) = \mu_{C_1'} \vee \mu_{C_2'} = \left[\alpha_1 \cdot \mu_{C_1}(w)\right] \vee \left[\alpha_2 \cdot \mu_{C_2}(w)\right]. \qquad (7.27)$$

This fuzzy reasoning process is illustrated in Fig. 7.6.

3. *Fuzzy reasoning of the second type—Tsukamoto's method with linguistic terms as monotonic membership functions* [Tsukamoto, 1979]: This is a simplified method based on fuzzy reasoning of the first type in which the consequent C_i is required to

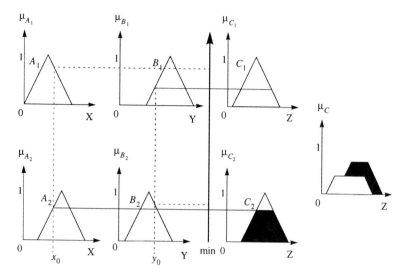

Figure 7.5 Diagrammatic representation of fuzzy reasoning of the first type, R_c.

be monotonic; that is, μ_{C_i} is required to be a monotonic function such that $\mu_{C_i}^{-1}$ exists. In this method, the results inferred from the first rule and the second rule are $z_1 = \mu_{C_1}^{-1}(\alpha_1)$ and $z_2 = \mu_{C_2}^{-1}(\alpha_2)$, respectively (see Fig. 7.7). Correspondingly, a crisp control action may be expressed as the weighted combination

$$z_0 = \frac{\alpha_1 z_1 + \alpha_2 z_2}{\alpha_1 + \alpha_2}.$$ (7.28)

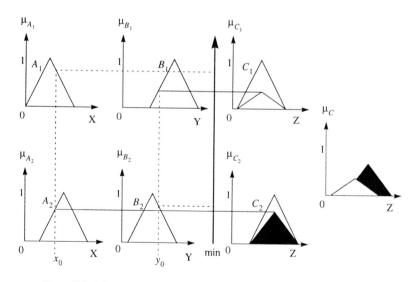

Figure 7.6 Diagrammatic representation of fuzzy reasoning of the first type, R_p.

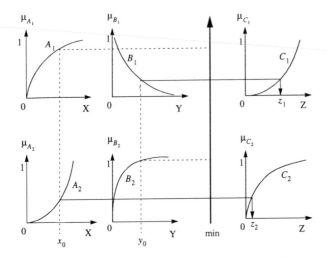

Figure 7.7 Diagrammatic representation of fuzzy reasoning of the second type.

4. *Fuzzy reasoning of the third type—The consequent of a rule is a function of input linguistic variables*: In this mode of reasoning, the ith fuzzy control rule is of the form of Eq. (7.5). For simplicity, assume that we have two fuzzy control rules as follows:

$$R^1: \text{ IF } x \text{ is } A_1 \text{ AND } y \text{ is } B_1, \text{ THEN } z \text{ is } f_1(x, y),$$

$$R^2: \text{ IF } x \text{ is } A_2 \text{ AND } y \text{ is } B_2, \text{ THEN } z \text{ is } f_2(x, y).$$

The inferred values of the control action from the first and second rules are $\alpha_1 f_1(x_0, y_0)$ and $\alpha_2 f_2(x_0, y_0)$, respectively. Consequently, a crisp control action is given by

$$z_0 = \frac{\alpha_1 f_1(x_0, y_0) + \alpha_2 f_2(x_0, y_0)}{\alpha_1 + \alpha_2}. \tag{7.29}$$

This method was proposed by Takagi and Sugeno [1983] and has been applied to guide a model car smoothly along a crank-shaped track [Sugeno and Nishida, 1985] and to park a model car in a garage [Sugeno and Murakami, 1985].

7.1.5 Defuzzifier

Defuzzification is a mapping from a space of fuzzy control actions defined over an output universe of discourse into a space of nonfuzzy (crisp) control actions. This process is necessary because in many practical applications crisp control action is required to actuate the control. Thus, a defuzzifier is necessary when fuzzy reasoning of the first type [Eqs. (7.24) and (7.26)] is used.

A defuzzification strategy is aimed at producing a nonfuzzy control action that best represents the possibility distribution of an inferred fuzzy control action. Unfortunately, there is no systematic procedure for choosing a defuzzification strategy. Two commonly used methods of defuzzification are the *center of area* (COA) method and the *mean of maximum* (MOM) method.

The widely used COA strategy generates the center of gravity of the possibility distribution of a control action. In the case of a discrete universe, this method yields

$$z_{\text{COA}}^* = \frac{\sum_{j=1}^n \mu_C(z_j) z_j}{\sum_{j=1}^n \mu_C(z_j)}, \tag{7.30}$$

where n is the number of quantization levels of the output, z_j is the amount of control output at the quantization level j, and $\mu_C(z_j)$ represents its membership value in the output fuzzy set C. If the universe of discourse is continuous, then the COA strategy generates an output control action of

$$z_{\text{COA}}^* = \frac{\int_z \mu_C(z) z \, dz}{\int_z \mu_C(z) \, dz}. \tag{7.31}$$

The MOM strategy generates a control action that represents the mean value of all local control actions whose membership functions reach the maximum. In the case of a discrete universe, the control action may be expressed as

$$z_{\text{MOM}}^* = \sum_{j=1}^m \frac{z_j}{m}, \tag{7.32}$$

where z_j is the support value at which the membership function reaches the maximum value $\mu_C(z_j)$ and m is the number of such support values.

Of these two commonly used defuzzification strategies, the COA strategy has been shown to yield superior results [Braae and Rutherford, 1978]. Furthermore, the MOM strategy yields a better transient performance, while the COA strategy yields a better steady-state performance (lower mean square error) [Lee, 1990].

Yager and Filev [Yager, 1992c; Filev and Yager, 1991] proposed a generalized approach to defuzzification based on the basic defuzzification distribution (BADD) transform. They view the defuzzification process as first converting the inferred fuzzy control actions on z into a probability distribution, BADD, on z and then taking the expected value. More specifically, in the case of a discrete universe, the control action is expressed as

$$z_0 = \sum_{i=1}^n z_i p_i, \tag{7.33}$$

where p_i is the BADD defined as

$$p_i = \frac{\mu_C^\alpha(z_i)}{\sum_{j=1}^n \mu_C^\alpha(z_j)} \tag{7.34}$$

and is parameterized by a parameter $\alpha \in [0, \infty]$. For different values of α, one obtains different defuzzification strategies: (1) If $\alpha = 1$, then the defuzzification strategy is reduced to the COA method. (2) If $\alpha \to \infty$, then the defuzzification strategy is reduced to the MOM method. (3) If $\alpha = 0$, then $p_i = 1/n$; where n is the cardinality of z.

One immediate implication of the introduction of BADD is that we can provide an adaptive learning scheme to obtain the optimal defuzzification parameter α. The value of α can be interpreted as some kind of measure of confidence in the controller rule base output. We see that $\alpha = 0$ corresponds to no confidence, and the information supplied by the rule base is completely discounted. If $\alpha = 1$, we take the information supplied by the controller at face value. This can be interpreted as normal confidence. If $\alpha = \infty$, then we place extremely high confidence in the information supplied by the controller.

Let us conclude this section with a simple example to illustrate the basic structure and operation of a FLC.

Example 7.3

We are given a fuzzy logic control system with the following two fuzzy control rules [Berenji, 1992a]:

$$\text{Rule 1: IF } x \text{ is } A_1 \text{ AND } y \text{ is } B_1, \text{ THEN } z \text{ is } C_1.$$

$$\text{Rule 2: IF } x \text{ is } A_2 \text{ AND } y \text{ is } B_2, \text{ THEN } z \text{ is } C_2.$$

Suppose x_0 and y_0 are the sensor readings for linguistic input variables x and y and the following membership functions for fuzzy predicates $A_1, A_2, B_1, B_2, C_1,$ and C_2 are given:

$$\mu_{A_1}(x) = \begin{cases} \dfrac{x-2}{3} & 2 \leq x \leq 5 \\[2mm] \dfrac{8-x}{3} & 5 < x \leq 8, \end{cases} \qquad \mu_{A_2}(x) = \begin{cases} \dfrac{x-3}{3} & 3 \leq x \leq 6 \\[2mm] \dfrac{9-x}{3} & 6 < x \leq 9, \end{cases}$$

$$\mu_{B_1}(y) = \begin{cases} \dfrac{y-5}{3} & 5 \leq y \leq 8 \\[2mm] \dfrac{11-y}{3} & 8 < y \leq 11, \end{cases} \qquad \mu_{B_2}(y) = \begin{cases} \dfrac{y-4}{3} & 4 \leq y \leq 7 \\[2mm] \dfrac{10-y}{3} & 7 < y \leq 10, \end{cases}$$

$$\mu_{C_1}(z) = \begin{cases} \dfrac{z-1}{3} & 1 \leq z \leq 4 \\[2mm] \dfrac{7-z}{3} & 4 < z \leq 7, \end{cases} \qquad \mu_{C_2}(z) = \begin{cases} \dfrac{z-3}{3} & 3 \leq z \leq 6 \\[2mm] \dfrac{9-z}{3} & 6 < z \leq 9. \end{cases}$$

Further assume that at time t_1 we are reading the sensor values at $x_0(t_1) = 4$ and $y_0(t_1) = 8$. Let us illustrate how the final control output is computed.

First, the sensor readings $x_0(t_1)$ and $y_0(t_1)$ have to be matched against the preconditions A_1 and B_1 of rule 1, respectively. This will produce $\mu_{A_1}(x_0 = 4) = \frac{2}{3}$ and $\mu_{B_1}(y_0 = 8) = 1$. Similarly, for rule 2, we have $\mu_{A_2}(x_0) = \frac{1}{3}$ and $\mu_{B_2}(y_0) = \frac{2}{3}$. The firing strength of rule 1 is calculated by

$$\alpha_1 = \min\left(\mu_{A_1}(x_0), \mu_{B_1}(y_0)\right) = \min\left(\frac{2}{3}, 1\right) = \frac{2}{3},$$

and similarly for rule 2, the firing strength is

$$\alpha_2 = \min\left(\mu_{A_2}(x_0), \mu_{B_2}(y_0)\right) = \min\left(\frac{1}{3}, \frac{2}{3}\right) = \frac{1}{3}.$$

Applying α_1 to the consequent of rule 1 results in the shaded trapezoid figure shown in Fig. 7.8 for C_1. Similarly, applying α_2 to the consequent of rule 2 results in the dashed trapezoid shown in Fig. 7.8 for C_2. By superimposing the resulting memberships over each other and using the max operator, the membership function for the combined conclusion of these rules is found. Furthermore, using the COA method [in Eq. (7.30)], the defuzzified value for the conclusion is obtained:

$$z_{\text{COA}}^* = \frac{2\left(\frac{1}{3}\right) + 3\left(\frac{2}{3}\right) + 4\left(\frac{2}{3}\right) + 5\left(\frac{2}{3}\right) + 6\left(\frac{1}{3}\right) + 7\left(\frac{1}{3}\right) + 8\left(\frac{1}{3}\right)}{\frac{1}{3} + \frac{2}{3} + \frac{2}{3} + \frac{2}{3} + \frac{1}{3} + \frac{1}{3} + \frac{1}{3}} = 4.7.$$

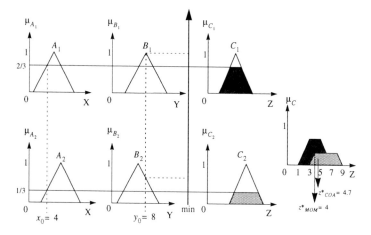

Figure 7.8 Fuzzy reasoning process in Example 7.3.

Using the MOM defuzzification strategy, three quantized values reach their maximum memberships in the combined membership function (i.e., 3, 4, and 5 with membership values of $\frac{2}{3}$). Therefore,

$$z^*_{MOM} = (3 + 4 + 5)/3 = 4.0.$$

7.2 DESIGN METHODOLOGY OF FUZZY CONTROL SYSTEMS

From the previous discussions, we can see that the principal elements of designing a FLC include (1) defining input and output variables, (2) deciding on the fuzzy partition of the input and output spaces and choosing the membership functions for the input and output linguistic variables, (3) deciding on the types and the derivation of fuzzy control rules, (4) designing the inference mechanism, which includes choosing a fuzzy implication and a compositional operator, and the interpretation of sentence connectives AND and ALSO, and (5) choosing a defuzzification operator.

The first two design principles indicate that, in the design of a FLC, one must identify the main process state variables and control variables and determine a term set that is at the right level of granularity for describing the values of each (linguistic) variable. For example, a three-term set such as {Small, Medium, Large} may not be satisfactory in some domains, and the use of a finer five-term set such as {VERY Small, Small, Medium, Large, and VERY Large} may be required instead. Hence, the number of fuzzy partitions of the input-output spaces should be large enough to provide an adequate approximation and yet be small enough to save memory space. This number has an essential effect on how fine a control can be obtained. Moreover, different types of fuzzy membership functions, for example, monotonic, triangular, trapezoidal, and bell-shaped functions, may be used for the linguistic values of each linguistic variable. There are two methods for making these choices. First, we can use experience and engineering (domain) knowledge to select the possible and proper input-output variables and then use a heuristic cut-and-try procedure to find a proper fuzzy partition and a trial-and-error approach to find suitable membership functions. Although this method is rather time-consuming and nontrivial, it has been widely employed and has been used in many successful industrial applications. A rule of thumb of this method is concerned with the ϵ completeness of input-output membership functions; that is, the union of the supports of the fuzzy sets in a term set should cover the related universe of discourse in relation to some level set ϵ. In general, we choose the level ϵ at the crossover point as shown in Fig. 7.2, implying that a dominant rule always exists and is associated with a degree of belief greater than 0.5. In the extreme case, two dominant rules are activated with an equal belief of 0.5. Second, we can use learning or self-organization techniques. The idea is to decide on and adjust the fuzzy partitions and membership functions and to select important, useful input-output variables from a group of candidates automatically and systematically, and/or dynamically through learning techniques. In this methodology, the use of neural network–based learning techniques and genetic learning algorithms has proved to be a very promising approach. They will be discussed further in detail in Part III of this book.

For the fourth and fifth design principles of a FLC, there is no systematic methodology for realizing the design of an inference engine and the choice of a defuzzification operator. Most practitioners use empirical studies and results to provide guidelines for these choices.

The third design principle in determining fuzzy control rules depends heavily on the nature of the controlled plant. In general, there are four methods for the derivation of fuzzy control rules [Sugeno, 1985a; Lee, 1990], and these methods are not mutually exclusive. A combination of them may be necessary to construct an effective method for the derivation of fuzzy control rules.

1. **Expert experience and control engineering knowledge:** Fuzzy control rules are designed by referring to a human operator's and/or a control engineer's knowledge. More specifically, we can ask a human expert to express his or her knowledge in terms of fuzzy implications, that is, to express this know-how in fuzzy IF-THEN rules. We can also ask a control engineer to list a number of protocols based on his or her knowledge about the process to be controlled. Finally, a heuristic cut-and-try procedure is used to fine-tune the fuzzy control rules. This method is the least structured of the four methods, and yet it is the most widely used. A typical example is the operating manual for a cement kiln [King and Karonis, 1988; Zimmermann, 1991]. The kiln production process is complex and nonlinear, it contains time lags and interrelationships, and the kiln's response to control inputs depends on the prevailing kiln conditions. These factors are certainly the reason why a fuzzy controller was designed and used. The aim is to automate the routine control strategy of an experienced kiln operator. The strategies are based on detailed studies of the process operator experiences which include a qualitative model of influence of the control variables on the measured variables, for example, "If the air flow is increased, then the temperature in the smoke chamber will increase, while the kiln drive load and the oxygen percentage will decrease." From this kind of verbal statement, we can derive the following rule:

   IF drive load gradient is *Normal*

   AND drive load is *SLIGHTLY High*

   AND smoke chamber temperature is *Low,*

THEN change oxygen percentage is *Positive*

AND change airflow is *Positive.*

More details on this example can be found in [Holmblad and Ostergaard, 1982].

The disadvantages of this mode of derivation of fuzzy control rules are that (i) an operator may not be able to verbalize his or her knowledge, and (ii) it may be difficult for a control engineer to write down control rules because the controlled process is too complex.

2. **Modeling an operator's control actions:** We can model an operator's skilled actions or control behavior in terms of fuzzy implications using the input-output data connected with his control actions. Then we can use the obtained "input-output model" as a fuzzy controller. The idea behind this mode of derivation is that it is easier to model an operator's actions than to model a process since the input variables of the model are likely found by asking the operator what kind of information he uses in his control actions or by watching these actions.

A typical and interesting example is Sugeno's fuzzy car [Sugeno and Murakami, 1985; Sugeno and Nishida, 1985]. His model car has successfully followed a crank-shaped track and parked itself in a garage. The training process involves a skilled operator guiding the fuzzy model car under different driving conditions. The control policy incorporated is represented by a set of state-evaluation fuzzy control rules:

$$R^i: \text{ IF } x \text{ is } A_i \text{ AND } \ldots \text{ AND } y \text{ is } B_i, \text{ THEN } z = a_0^i + a_1^i x + \cdots + a_n^i y, \quad (7.35)$$

where $x, \ldots,$ and y are linguistic variables representing the distance and orientation in relation to the boundaries of the track, z is the next steering angle decided by the ith control rule, and $a_0^i, \ldots, a_n^i$ are the parameters entering in the identification process of a skilled driver's actions. This identification is made by optimizing a least squares performance index via a weighted linear regression method (a weighted recursive least squares algorithm) [Tong, 1978a; Takagi and Sugeno, 1983, 1985; Sugeno and Kang, 1986, 1988]. In addition to modeling an operator's actions, this method is also used to model (identify) controlled processes according to their input-output data, which involves parameter learning as well as structure learning [Sugeno and Tanaka, 1991]. These are called *linguistic control rule* approaches to fuzzy modeling or fuzzy identification. The Takagi and Sugeno fuzzy model has the following form:

$$\begin{aligned} L^i: \text{ IF } x\,(k) \text{ is } A_1^i \text{ AND } \ldots \text{ AND } x\,(k - n + 1) \text{ is } A_n^i \\ \text{AND } u\,(k) \text{ is } B_1^i \text{ AND } \cdots \text{ AND } u\,(k - m + 1) \text{ is } B_m^i, \\ \text{THEN } x^i\,(k + 1) = a_0^i + a_1^i x\,(k) + \cdots + a_n^i x\,(k - n + 1) \\ + b_1^i u\,(k) + \cdots + b_m^i u\,(k - m + 1), \end{aligned} \quad (7.36)$$

where $x\,(\cdot)$ is the state variable, $x^i\,(k + 1)$ is the output of rule L^i, and $u\,(\cdot)$ is the input variable. The output of the fuzzy model can be obtained by fuzzy reasoning of the third type [Eq. (7.29)]. The design of a FLC based on the derived fuzzy model is called a "model-based" FLC design and is representative of the third mode of design methodology described below.

3. **Based on a fuzzy model or behavior analysis of a controlled process:** In this mode, fuzzy control rules are derived or justified based on either the fuzzy model or the behavior analysis of a controlled process. If we have a fuzzy model of the process or if we know some useful properties of the process, we can design or generate a set of fuzzy control rules for attaining optimal performance. By fuzzy modeling, we mean representation of the dynamic characteristics of the process by a set of fuzzy implications with inputs, state variables, and outputs. There are two methods for designing fuzzy control rules in this mode.

   (a) *Heuristic method*: We set a fuzzy control rule to compensate for an undesirable system behavior by considering the control objective. This is done by analyzing the behavior of a controlled process. Such behavior analysis techniques include the phase-plane approach [King and Mamdani, 1975], the linguistic phase-plane approach [Braae and Rutherford, 1979a], the pole placement approach [Braae and Rutherford, 1979b], a fuzzy Proportional-Integral-Derivative (PID) control approach [Peng et al., 1988; Abdelnour et al., 1991], and other approaches [Baaklini and Mamdani, 1975; Mamdani and Assilian, 1975]. These techniques usually have their counterparts in conventional control theory.

   (b) *Optimal control method*: This is basically a deterministic method which can systematically determine the linguistic structure and/or parameters of fuzzy control rules that satisfy the control objectives and constraints (of minimizing a performance index) based on the fuzzy model of a process. Such systematic methods are usually studied by means of *fuzzy relational equations* and *linguistic control rules* for fuzzy modeling which are comprised of two phases, namely, structure identification and parameter estimation. The linguistic control rule approaches were mentioned above. For the fuzzy relational equation approach, structure identification requires determination of the system order and time delays of discrete-time fuzzy models, while parameter estimation reduces to determination of the overall fuzzy relation matrix from the input-output data of the system [Czogala and Pedrycz, 1981, 1982; Pedrycz, 1981, 1984, 1989; Togai and Wang, 1985; Xu and Zailu, 1987; Sugeno and Tanaka, 1991]. Let us use an example to illustrate the fuzzy relational equation approach to the fuzzy controller design.

Example 7.4

[Togai and Wang, 1985] Consider the fuzzy dynamical system in Fig. 7.9, where X and Y are fuzzy subsets on U and V, respectively, R is a ternary relation on $V \times U \times V$, and D is a delay unit. The fuzzy relation R represents the transition relation for the closed-loop system with a first-order delay unit D. Thus, we have

$$Y_{t+1} = (Y_t \cap X_t) \circ R = X_t \circ (Y_t \circ R), \tag{7.37}$$

where the second equality holds for the min operation ($\cap$) and the max-min composition ($\circ$). Then it is possible to derive the input X_t, which drives the state from Y_t to Y_{t+1}, by solving the fuzzy relational equation in Eq. (7.37) (see Sect. 3.4) as shown below:

$$X_t = (Y_t \circ R) \overset{\alpha}{\leftrightarrow} Y_{t+1}, \tag{7.38}$$

where $\overset{\alpha}{\leftrightarrow}$ indicates the α operator and is defined in Eq. (3.52).

4. **Based on learning (or self-organizing).** Many FLCs have been built to emulate human decision-making behavior. Currently, many research efforts are focused on

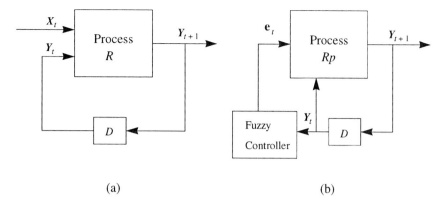

(a)   (b)

Figure 7.9 Block diagram of the fuzzy dynamical system in Example 7.4. (a) Original system. (b) Original system with a fuzzy controller.

emulating human learning, mainly on the ability to create fuzzy control rules and to modify them based on experience. Procyk and Mamdani [1979] proposed the first self-organizing controller (SOC). The SOC has a hierarchical structure which consists of two rule bases (see Fig. 7.10). The first one is the general control rule base of a FLC. The second one is constructed by "meta rules" which can create and modify the control rule base based on the desired overall performance of the system. Let us consider an example [Scharf and Mandic, 1985; Transcheit and Scharf, 1988] in which a SOC is used for robot control. This example also illustrates a very popular method of representing fuzzy logic rules in terms of a *lookup table.*

Example 7.5

[Scharf and Mandic, 1985]. Consider the control system shown in Fig. 7.10. The inputs to the FLC are the error between a set point and an actual output e and the rate of change of this error $\dot{e}$. The fuzzy control rule base (lookup table), denoted as R_1, in the FLC is shown in Fig. 7.11. Each nonzero entry in the lookup table corresponds to one control rule; the two axes of the

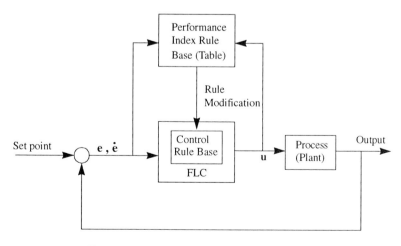

Figure 7.10 Structure of a self-organizing controller.

$$\dot{e}$$

e \ $\dot{e}$	-6	-5	-4	-3	-2	-1	0	+1	+2	+3	+4	+5	+6
-6	·	·	·	·	·	·	-6	·	·	·	·	·	·
-5	·	·	·	·	·	-6	·	·	·	·	·	·	·
-4	·	·	·	·	·	·	·	·	·	·	·	·	·
-3	·	·	·	·	·	·	-3	·	·	·	·	·	·
-2	·	·	·	·	·	·	-5	+1	·	·	·	·	·
-1	·	·	·	+1	+1	-1	-2	+2	·	·	·	·	·
0	·	·	+2	+4	+3	·	0	+5	+5	·	·	·	·
+1	·	·	·	·	+5	·	·	+6	·	·	·	·	·
+2	·	·	·	·	·	+6	·	·	·	·	·	·	·
+3	·	·	·	·	·	+6	+6	·	·	·	·	·	·
+4	·	·	·	·	·	·	·	·	·	·	·	·	·
+5	·	·	·	·	·	·	·	·	·	·	·	·	·
+6	·	·	·	·	·	·	·	·	·	·	·	·	·

Figure 7.11   Control lookup table in Example 7.5.

lookup table are for e and $\dot{e}$. Each axis and entry has 13 possible values from -6 through 0 to +6. The values 1 to 6 can be taken to mean "VERY Small," "Small," "Medium," "QUITE Large," "Large," and "VERY Large." The membership functions for these fuzzy sets are properly defined in advance. Thus, the rule $R_1 (e, \dot{e}) = R_1 (+1, -2) = +5$ is interpreted as: "IF e is *positive VERY Small* AND $\dot{e}$ is *negative Small,* Then u is *positive Large,*" where u is the control output (consequent of a rule). It is noted that the · in the lookup table in Fig. 7.11 means "undecided." Such rules will be determined (or "created") during the learning process. Hence, the lookup table R_1 in Fig. 7.11 can be considered an initial rule base.

Next, let us see how the learning takes place. Learning occurs by referring to a performance index table (Fig. 7.12) that has the same size and axes as the fuzzy control lookup table. The performance index table, denoted as R_2, consists of a set of performance "critic" rules which relate the state of the process $(e, \dot{e})$ to the cost of the deviation from its desired behavior. The larger the deviation that we are willing to accept, the lower the associated cost. A performance index table has integer entries ranging from -6 to +6. These entries are the costs or *reinforcements,* positive or negative, that are given to the rule corresponding to a given $(e, \dot{e})$ pair in the control lookup table. Note that reinforcement also implies rule creation.

With the initial setup of these two tables, learning proceeds as follows. Assume that the current observed e_k and $\dot{e}_k$ at time k are mainly due to the control output u_{k-1} at time k - 1 and that u_{k-1} is mainly caused by the rule $R_1 (e_{k-1}, \dot{e}_{k-1})$. Then the new fuzzy control lookup table at time k is obtained by the following equation:

$$R_1 (e_k, \dot{e}_k) = R_1 (e_{k-1}, \dot{e}_{k-1}) + R_2 (e_k, \dot{e}_k). \qquad (7.39)$$

This update process continues until it converges.

Like the learning concept of a SOC, introducing the learning abilities of neural networks into FLCs has shown to be a very promising approach recently [Lin and Lee, 1991b]. This so-called neuro-fuzzy control will be covered in Chap. 19.

In addition to the four modes of derivation of fuzzy control rules, there are two hierarchical approaches to the design of FLCs. The first approach is the *windowing* technique. Windowing relies on refining the control rules when the process appears in a prescribed region, as shown in Fig. 7.13 [Pedrycz, 1989]. FLCs can be applied to multivariable control systems where the precondition part of each rule is expanded to cover conditions relevant

Fuzzy Logic Control Systems   Chap. 7

ė

e \ ė	-6	-5	-4	-3	-2	-1	0	+1	+2	+3	+4	+5	+6
-6	0	0	-1	-2	-3	-4	-6	-6	-6	-6	-6	-6	-6
-5	0	0	0	-1	-2	-3	-4	-4	-5	-5	-6	-6	-6
-4	0	0	0	0	-1	-2	-3	-3	-4	-5	-5	-6	-6
-3	+1	0	0	0	0	-1	-2	-2	-3	-4	-5	-5	-6
-2	+2	+1	0	0	0	0	-1	-1	-2	-3	-4	-5	-6
-1	+3	+2	+1	0	0	0	-1	-1	-1	-2	-3	-4	-5
0	+4	+3	+2	+1	+1	0	0	0	-1	-1	-2	-3	-4
+1	+5	+4	+3	+2	+1	+1	+1	0	0	0	-1	-2	-3
+2	+6	+5	+4	+3	+2	+1	+1	0	0	0	0	-1	-2
+3	+6	+5	+5	+4	+3	+2	+2	+1	0	0	0	0	-1
+4	+6	+6	+5	+5	+4	+3	+3	+2	+1	0	0	0	0
+5	+6	+6	+6	+5	+5	+4	+4	+3	+2	+1	0	0	0
+6	+6	+6	+6	+6	+6	+6	+6	+4	+3	+2	+1	0	0

Figure 7.12 Performance index table in Example 7.5.

to each input of the controller (subconditions). Hence, we may have a higher-level lookup table for coarse control and a lower-level lookup table for fine control. The rules at each level may be derived by the methods that we discussed previously. Applications of the windowing technique can be found in [Li and Lan, 1989].

The second hierarchical FLC design approach has been proposed by Berenji et al. [1990] for a controller design problem with multiple goals. In this approach, priorities can be assigned among the goals. Let $G = \{g_1, g_2, \ldots, g_n\}$ be a set of n goals that the system should achieve and maintain. Notice that if $n = 1$ (i.e., there are no interacting goals), then the problem becomes simpler and may be handled using the methods mentioned previously. Assume that the priorities of the goals can be ordered as $g_1, g_2, \ldots, g_n$. As an example, in the simple problem of balancing a pole on the palm of a hand and also moving the pole to a predetermined location, we can set the goal of keeping the pole balance as the first priority and the goal of moving to the desired location as the second priority. Furthermore, assuming that x_i is the input linguistic variable related to achieving goal g_i, we can derive the control rules recursively by the following steps:

Step 1: Acquire the rule set R_1 of appropriate control rules directly related to the highest priority goal. These rules are in the general form of

$$\text{IF } x_1 \text{ is } A_1, \text{ THEN } z \text{ is } C_1.$$

Step 2: Subsequently form the rule set R_i for $i = 2$ to n. The format of the rules in these rule sets is similar to the ones in the previous step except that it

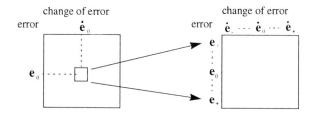

Figure 7.13 Windowing technique.

includes aspects of approximately achieving the previous goal, that is, "IF g_{i-1} is approximately achieved AND x_i is A_i, THEN z is C_i." We can see that the interactions between the goals g_i and g_{i-1} are handled by forming rules that include more preconditions on the left-hand side. For example, assume that we have acquired a set of rules for keeping a pole vertical. In deriving the second rule set R_2 for moving to a pre-specified location, a precondition such as *the pole is almost balanced* can be added. The linguistic hedge, *concentration* [Eq. (6.1)], can be used here to systematically obtain a more focused membership function for the parameters representing the achievement of previous goals.

We have discussed general methodologies for the design of FLCs with four modes of deriving fuzzy control rules and two hierarchical design approaches. These design approaches and the derivation of fuzzy control rules are used in many industrial and consumer product applications. A few of these applications will be discussed in Sect. 7.4, and further applications of fuzzy sets and fuzzy logic will be considered in Chap. 8.

7.3 STABILITY ANALYSIS OF FUZZY CONTROL SYSTEMS

One of the most important concepts concerning the properties of control systems is stability. This is also true for fuzzy control systems. As fuzzy control has been successfully applied to many practical industrial applications, stability analysis of fuzzy control systems is gaining much attention. Of various existing methodologies for stability analysis of fuzzy systems [Mamdani, 1976; Kickert and Mamdani, 1978; Tong, 1978b, 1980; Braae and Rutherford, 1979a,b; Kania et al., 1980; Pedrycz, 1981; Kiszka et al., 1985; Chen, 1989; Yamashita, 1991; Langari and Tomizuka 1990b, 1991], the one proposed by Tanaka et al. is introduced in this section.

Tanaka and Sugeno [1992] and Tanaka and Sano [1992] used Lyapunov's direct method to perform stability analysis of fuzzy control systems where the fuzzy rules are in the form of Eqs. (7.35) and (7.36). They used Takagi and Sugeno's fuzzy control rule [Eq. (7.35)] and fuzzy model [Eq. (7.36)] and assumed that the membership functions of the fuzzy sets in these rules (e.g., A_i, B_i, A_k^i, B_k^i) are *continuous piecewise polynomial functions* (e.g., triangular type or trapezoidal type). Let us consider the following fuzzy system with zero input:

$$L^i: \text{ IF } x(k) \text{ is } A_1^i \text{ AND } \cdots \text{ AND } x(k-n+1) \text{ is } A_n^i,$$
$$\text{THEN } x^i(k+1) = a_1^i x(k) + \cdots + a_n^i x(k-n+1),$$

$$(7.40)$$

where $i = 1, 2, \ldots, l$. The consequent of Eq. (7.40) can be written in matrix form as

$$\mathbf{x}^i(k+1) = \mathbf{A}_i \mathbf{x}(k),$$

$$(7.41)$$

where $\mathbf{x}(k) = [x(k), x(k-1), \ldots, x(k-n+1)]^T$ and

$$\mathbf{A}_i = \begin{bmatrix} a_1^i & a_2^i & \cdots & a_{n-1}^i & a_n^i \\ 1 & 0 & \cdots & 0 & 0 \\ 0 & 1 & \cdots & 0 & 0 \\ \vdots & \vdots & \ddots & \vdots & \vdots \\ 0 & 0 & \cdots & 1 & 0 \end{bmatrix}. \tag{7.42}$$

The output of the fuzzy system is inferred by fuzzy reasoning of the third type [Eq. (7.29)] as follows:

$$\mathbf{x}(k+1) = \frac{\sum_{i=1}^{l} \alpha_i \mathbf{A}_i \mathbf{x}(k)}{\sum_{i=1}^{l} \alpha_i}, \tag{7.43}$$

where α_i is the firing strength, which is defined as [the min operator in Eq. (7.23) is replaced by the product operation]

$$\alpha_i = \mu_{A_1^i}(x_0(k)) \cdot \mu_{A_2^i}(x_0(k-1)) \cdots \mu_{A_n^i}(x_0(k-n+1)), \tag{7.44}$$

where $x_0(\cdot)$ denotes the crisp value of $x(\cdot)$ at a specific instance. With this formulation, we have the following theorems of stability analysis. The first one is the well-known Lyapunov's stability theorem [Kuo, 1980].

Theorem 7.4

Consider a discrete system

$$\mathbf{x}(k+1) = \mathbf{f}(\mathbf{x}(k)), \tag{7.45}$$

where $\mathbf{x}(k) \in \Re^n$, $\mathbf{f}(\mathbf{x}(k))$ is an $n \times 1$ function vector with the property that $\mathbf{f}(\mathbf{0}) = \mathbf{0}$ for all k. Suppose that there exists a scalar function $V(\mathbf{x}(k))$ continuous in $\mathbf{x}(k)$ such that

  (a) $V(\mathbf{0}) = 0$,
  (b) $V(\mathbf{x}(k)) > 0$ for $\mathbf{x}(k) \neq \mathbf{0}$,
  (c) $V(\mathbf{x}(k))$ approaches infinity as $\|\mathbf{x}(k)\| \to \infty$,
  (d) $\Delta V(\mathbf{x}(k)) < 0$ for $\mathbf{x}(k) \neq \mathbf{0}$.

Then the equilibrium state $\mathbf{x}(k) = \mathbf{0}$ for all k is asymptotically stable in the large, and $V(\mathbf{x}(k))$ is a Lyapunov function.

Theorem 7.5

If $\mathbf{P}$ is a positive-definite matrix such that

$$\mathbf{A}^T \mathbf{P} \mathbf{A} - \mathbf{P} < \mathbf{0} \quad \text{and} \quad \mathbf{B}^T \mathbf{P} \mathbf{B} - \mathbf{P} < \mathbf{0}, \tag{7.46}$$

where $\mathbf{A}, \mathbf{B}, \mathbf{P} \in \Re^{n \times n}$, then

$$\mathbf{A}^T \mathbf{P} \mathbf{B} + \mathbf{B}^T \mathbf{P} \mathbf{A} - 2\mathbf{P} < \mathbf{0}. \tag{7.47}$$

Proof: We have

$$\mathbf{A}^T \mathbf{P} \mathbf{B} + \mathbf{B}^T \mathbf{P} \mathbf{A} - 2\mathbf{P} = -(\mathbf{A} - \mathbf{B})^T \mathbf{P}(\mathbf{A} - \mathbf{B}) + \mathbf{A}^T \mathbf{P} \mathbf{A} + \mathbf{B}^T \mathbf{P} \mathbf{B} - 2\mathbf{P}$$

$$= -(\mathbf{A} - \mathbf{B})^T \mathbf{P}(\mathbf{A} - \mathbf{B}) + \mathbf{A}^T \mathbf{P} \mathbf{A} - \mathbf{P} + \mathbf{B}^T \mathbf{P} \mathbf{B} - \mathbf{P}.$$

Since $\mathbf{P}$ is a positive-definite matrix,

$$- (\mathbf{A} - \mathbf{B})^T \mathbf{P} (\mathbf{A} - \mathbf{B}) \le 0.$$

Therefore the conclusion of the theorem follows.

Using the results of these two theorems, we are ready to present the important theorem with respect to the stability of a fuzzy system.

Theorem 7.6

[Tanaka and Sugeno, 1992]. The equilibrium of a fuzzy system described by Eq. (7.43) is globally asymptotically stable if there exists a common positive-definite matrix $\mathbf{P}$ for all the subsystems such that

$$\mathbf{A}_i^T \mathbf{P} \mathbf{A}_i - \mathbf{P} < 0 \qquad \text{for } i \in \{1, 2, ..., l\}. \tag{7.48}$$

Proof: Consider a scalar function $V(\mathbf{x}(k))$ such that

$$V(\mathbf{x}(k)) = \mathbf{x}^T(k) \mathbf{P} \mathbf{x}(k), \tag{7.49}$$

where $\mathbf{P}$ is a positive-definite matrix. This function satisfies the following properties:

   (a) $V(0) = 0,$
   (b) $V(\mathbf{x}(k)) > 0$ for $\mathbf{x}(k) \ne \mathbf{0},$
   (c) $V(\mathbf{x}(k))$ approaches infinity as $\|\mathbf{x}(k)\| \to \infty.$
      Next, condition (d) of Theorem 7.4 is

$$\Delta V(\mathbf{x}(k)) = V(\mathbf{x}(k+1)) - V(\mathbf{x}(k))$$

$$= \mathbf{x}^T(k+1) \mathbf{P} \mathbf{x}(k+1) - \mathbf{x}^T(k) \mathbf{P} \mathbf{x}(k)$$

$$= \left(\frac{\sum_{i=1}^{l} \alpha_i \mathbf{A}_i \mathbf{x}(k)}{\sum_{i=1}^{l} \alpha_i} \right)^T \mathbf{P} \left(\frac{\sum_{i=1}^{l} \alpha_i \mathbf{A}_i \mathbf{x}(k)}{\sum_{i=1}^{l} \alpha_i} \right) - \mathbf{x}^T(k) \mathbf{P} \mathbf{x}(k)$$

$$= \mathbf{x}^T(k) \left\{ \left(\frac{\sum_{i=1}^{l} \alpha_i \mathbf{A}_i^T}{\sum_{i=1}^{l} \alpha_i} \right) \mathbf{P} \left(\frac{\sum_{i=1}^{l} \alpha_i \mathbf{A}_i}{\sum_{i=1}^{l} \alpha_i} \right) - \mathbf{P} \right\} \mathbf{x}(k)$$

$$= \frac{\sum_{i,j=1}^{l} \alpha_i \alpha_j \mathbf{x}^T(k) \{ \mathbf{A}_i^T \mathbf{P} \mathbf{A}_j - \mathbf{P} \} \mathbf{x}(k)}{\sum_{i,j=1}^{l} \alpha_i \alpha_j}$$

$$= \frac{\sum_{i=1}^{l} (\alpha_i)^2 \mathbf{x}^T(k) \{ \mathbf{A}_i^T \mathbf{P} \mathbf{A}_i - \mathbf{P} \} \mathbf{x}(k) + \sum_{i<j} \alpha_i \alpha_j \mathbf{x}^T(k) \{ \mathbf{A}_i^T \mathbf{P} \mathbf{A}_j + \mathbf{A}_j^T \mathbf{P} \mathbf{A}_i - 2\mathbf{P} \} \mathbf{x}(k)}{\sum_{i,j=1}^{l} \alpha_i \alpha_j},$$

where $\alpha_i \ge 0$ for $i \in \{1, 2, ..., l\}$ and $\sum_{i=1}^{l} \alpha_i > 0.$
   (d) From Theorem 7.5 and Eq. (7.48), we obtain $\Delta V(\mathbf{x}(k)) < 0.$

By Theorem 7.4, $V(\mathbf{x}(k))$ is a Lyapunov function and the fuzzy system described by Eq. (7.43) is globally asymptotically stable.

This theorem is reduced to the Lyapunov stability theorem for a linear discrete system when $l = 1$. The following example demonstrates the use of Theorem 7.6 to check the stability of a fuzzy control feedback system.

Example 7.6

Consider the following fuzzy model of a process in the form of Eq. (7.36):

$$L^1: \text{ IF } x(k) \text{ is } A^1, \text{ THEN } x^1(k+1) = 2.178x(k) - 0.588x(k-1) + 0.603u(k) \qquad (7.50)$$

$$L^2: \text{ IF } x(k) \text{ is } A^2, \text{ THEN } x^2(k+1) = 2.256x(k) - 0.361x(k-1) + 1.120u(k) \qquad (7.51)$$

Then the output of the fuzzy model is

$$x(k+1) = \frac{\alpha_1 x^1(k+1) + \alpha_2 x^2(k+1)}{\alpha_1 + \alpha_2}, \qquad (7.52)$$

where α_1 and α_2 are firing strengths defined by Eq. (7.44). Also, we are given a FLC expressed in the form of Eq. (7.35):

$$R^1: \text{ IF } x(k) \text{ is } A^1, \text{ THEN } u^1(k) = -2.109x(k) + 0.475x(k-1) \qquad (7.53)$$

$$R^2: \text{ IF } x(k) \text{ is } A^2, \text{ THEN } u^2(k) = -1.205x(k) + 0.053x(k-1). \qquad (7.54)$$

Then the output of the FLC is

$$u(k) = \frac{\alpha_1 u^1(k) + \alpha_2 u^2(k)}{\alpha_1 + \alpha_2}. \qquad (7.55)$$

Substituting Eq. (7.55) into Eq. (7.52) and using Eqs. (7.50), (7.51), (7.53), and (7.54), we obtain

$$x^1(k+1) = \frac{0.906\alpha_1 + 1.451\alpha_2}{\alpha_1 + \alpha_2} x(k) + \frac{-0.302\alpha_1 - 0.556\alpha_2}{\alpha_1 + \alpha_2} x(k-1)$$

$$x^2(k+1) = \frac{-0.106\alpha_1 + 0.906\alpha_2}{\alpha_1 + \alpha_2} x(k) + \frac{0.171\alpha_1 - 0.302\alpha_2}{\alpha_1 + \alpha_2} x(k-1).$$

Hence

$$x(k+1) = \frac{\alpha_1 x^1(k+1) + \alpha_2 x^2(k+1)}{\alpha_1 + \alpha_2}$$

$$= \frac{0.906\alpha_1^2 + 1.345\alpha_1\alpha_2 + 0.906\alpha_2^2}{(\alpha_1 + \alpha_2)^2} x(k)$$

$$- \frac{0.302\alpha_1^2 + 0.385\alpha_1\alpha_2 + 0.302\alpha_2^2}{(\alpha_1 + \alpha_2)^2} x(k-1)$$

$$= \frac{\left[0.906\alpha_1^2 x(k) - 0.302\alpha_1^2 x(k-1)\right] + \left[1.345\alpha_1\alpha_2 x(k) - 0.385\alpha_1\alpha_2 x(k-1)\right] + \left[0.906\alpha_2^2 x(k) - 0.302\alpha_2^2 x(k-1)\right]}{\alpha_1^2 + 2\alpha_1\alpha_2 + \alpha_2^2}$$

Comparing the above equation with Eq. (7.43), the fuzzy feedback control system created by Eqs. (7.50) and (7.51) and the FLC in Eqs. (7.53) and (7.54) can be represented by the following rules:

$$S^{11}: \text{ IF } x(k) \text{ is } (A^1 \text{ AND } A^1), \text{ THEN } \mathbf{x}^{11}(k+1) = \mathbf{A}_{11}\mathbf{x}(k),$$

$$S^{12}: \text{ IF } x(k) \text{ is } (A^1 \text{ AND } A^2), \text{ THEN } \mathbf{x}^{12}(k+1) = \mathbf{A}_{12}\mathbf{x}(k), \qquad (7.56)$$

$$S^{22}: \text{ IF } x(k) \text{ is } (A^2 \text{ AND } A^2), \text{ THEN } \mathbf{x}^{22}(k+1) = \mathbf{A}_{22}\mathbf{x}(k),$$

where

$$\mathbf{A}_{11} = \begin{bmatrix} 0.906 & -0.302 \\ 1 & 0 \end{bmatrix}, \qquad \mathbf{A}_{12} = \begin{bmatrix} 0.672 & -0.193 \\ 1 & 0 \end{bmatrix}, \qquad \mathbf{A}_{22} = \begin{bmatrix} 0.906 & -0.302 \\ 1 & 0 \end{bmatrix}.$$

Let

$$\mathbf{P} = \begin{bmatrix} 4.19 & -0.88 \\ -0.88 & 1.38. \end{bmatrix}.$$

Then we can verify that

$$\mathbf{A}_{11}^T \mathbf{P} \mathbf{A}_{11} - \mathbf{P} < 0, \qquad \mathbf{A}_{12}^T \mathbf{P} \mathbf{A}_{12} - \mathbf{P} < 0, \qquad \mathbf{A}_{22}^T \mathbf{P} \mathbf{A}_{22} - \mathbf{P} < 0.$$

So from Theorem 7.6, the total fuzzy system, Eq. (7.56), is globally asymptotically stable.

All the $\mathbf{A}_i$ matrices are stable matrices if there exists a common positive-definite matrix $\mathbf{P}$. However, a common positive-definite matrix $\mathbf{P}$ obviously does not always exist even if all the $\mathbf{A}_i$ matrices are stable matrices, and a fuzzy system may be globally asymptotically stable even if there does not exist a common positive-definite matrix $\mathbf{P}$. We further note that a fuzzy system is not always globally asymptotically stable even if all the $\mathbf{A}_i$ matrices are stable matrices. In the following theorem, a necessary condition for ensuring the existence of a common positive-definite matrix $\mathbf{P}$ is given.

Theorem 7.7

[Tanaka and Sugeno, 1992]. Assume that $\mathbf{A}_i$ is a stable, nonsingular matrix for $i = 1, 2,..., l$. $\mathbf{A}_i \mathbf{A}_j$ is a stable matrix for $i, j = 1, 2,..., l$ if there exists a common positive-definite matrix $\mathbf{P}$ such that

$$\mathbf{A}_i^T \mathbf{P} \mathbf{A}_i - \mathbf{P} < 0. \tag{7.57}$$

Proof: From Eq. (7.57), we obtain

$$\mathbf{P} - (\mathbf{A}_i^{-1})^T \mathbf{P} \mathbf{A}_i^{-1} < 0$$

since $(\mathbf{A}_i^{-1})^T = (\mathbf{A}_i^T)^{-1}$. Therefore, $\mathbf{P} < (\mathbf{A}_i^{-1})^T \mathbf{P}(\mathbf{A}_i^{-1})$ for $i = 1, 2,..., l$. Since $\mathbf{A}_i^T \mathbf{P} \mathbf{A}_i < \mathbf{P}$ from Eq. (7.57), the following inequality holds for $i, j = 1, 2,..., l$:

$$\mathbf{A}_i^T \mathbf{P} \mathbf{A}_i < (\mathbf{A}_j^{-1})^T \mathbf{P}(\mathbf{A}_j^{-1}).$$

From the inequality, we obtain $\mathbf{A}_j^T \mathbf{A}_i^T \mathbf{P} \mathbf{A}_i \mathbf{A}_j - \mathbf{P} < 0$. Therefore, $\mathbf{A}_i \mathbf{A}_j$ must be a stable matrix for $i, j = 1, 2,..., l$.

Theorem 7.7 shows that if one of the $\mathbf{A}_i \mathbf{A}_j$ matrices is not a stable matrix, then there does not exist a common positive-definite matrix $\mathbf{P}$. In order to check the stability of a fuzzy system, we must find a common positive-definite matrix $\mathbf{P}$. It is difficult to find a common positive-definite matrix $\mathbf{P}$ as effectively as possible. The following simple two-step procedure can be used to find a common positive-definite matrix $\mathbf{P}$.

Step 1: Find a positive-definite matrix $\mathbf{P}_i$ such that

$$\mathbf{A}_i^T \mathbf{P}_i \mathbf{A}_i - \mathbf{P}_i < 0 \qquad i = 1, 2,..., l.$$

It is possible to find a positive-definite matrix $\mathbf{P}_i$ if $\mathbf{A}_i$ is a stable matrix.

Step 2: If there exists $\mathbf{P}_j$ in $\{\mathbf{P}_i \mid i = 1, 2, ..., l\}$ such that

$$\mathbf{A}_i^T \mathbf{P}_j \mathbf{A}_i - \mathbf{P}_j < 0 \qquad i = 1, 2, ..., l,$$

then $\mathbf{P}_j$ is selected as a common positive-definite matrix $\mathbf{P}$. If step 2 is not successful, then go back to step 1.

It is observed that the stability condition of Eq. (7.48) in Theorem 7.6 depends only on $\mathbf{A}_i$. A weaker stability condition depending both on $\mathbf{A}_i$ and on the firing strengths $\alpha_i(k)$ (and thus on the membership functions of preconditions of fuzzy rules) has been derived by Tanaka and Sano [1992].

We next introduce a method of representing a *parameter region* (PR) for Eq. (7.43). The PR representation graphically shows locations of fuzzy IF-THEN rules in consequent parameter space. It is easier to understand the PR representation through the examples that follow.

Example 7.7

Consider the following fuzzy system (fuzzy system 1):

Rule 1: IF $x(k)$ is A_1, THEN $x_1(k + 1) = 0.1x(k) + 0.1x(k - 1)$.

Rule 2: IF $x(k)$ is A_2, THEN $x_2(k + 1) = 0.3x(k) + 0.1x(k - 1)$.

Rule 3: IF $x(k)$ is A_3, THEN $x_3(k + 1) = 0.1x(k) + 0.3x(k - 1)$.

We can obtain

$$\mathbf{A}_1 = \begin{bmatrix} 0.1 & 0.1 \\ 1 & 0 \end{bmatrix}, \qquad \mathbf{A}_2 = \begin{bmatrix} 0.3 & 0.1 \\ 1 & 0 \end{bmatrix}, \qquad \mathbf{A}_3 = \begin{bmatrix} 0.1 & 0.3 \\ 1 & 0 \end{bmatrix}$$

from the consequent equations. Figure 7.14(a) shows the PR of this fuzzy system.

Consider another fuzzy system (fuzzy system 2):

Rule 1: IF $x(k)$ is B_1, THEN $x_1(k + 1) = 0.1x(k) + 0.1x(k - 1)$.

Rule 2: IF $x(k)$ is B_2, THEN $x_2(k + 1) = 0.3x(k) + 0.1x(k - 1)$.

Rule 3: IF $x(k)$ is B_3, THEN $x_3(k + 1) = 0.1x(k) + 0.3x(k - 1)$.

Rule 4: IF $x(k)$ is B_4, THEN $x_4(k + 1) = 0.2x(k) + 0.2x(k - 1)$.

Rule 5: IF $x(k)$ is B_5, THEN $x_5(k + 1) = 0.15x(k) + 0.15x(k - 1)$.

We can obtain

$$\mathbf{A}_1 = \begin{bmatrix} 0.1 & 0.1 \\ 1 & 0 \end{bmatrix}, \qquad \mathbf{A}_2 = \begin{bmatrix} 0.3 & 0.1 \\ 1 & 0 \end{bmatrix}, \qquad \mathbf{A}_3 = \begin{bmatrix} 0.1 & 0.3 \\ 1 & 0 \end{bmatrix},$$

$$\mathbf{A}_4 = \begin{bmatrix} 0.2 & 0.2 \\ 1 & 0 \end{bmatrix}, \qquad \mathbf{A}_5 = \begin{bmatrix} 0.15 & 0.15 \\ 1 & 0 \end{bmatrix}$$

from the consequent equations. Figure 7.14(b) shows the PR of this fuzzy system.

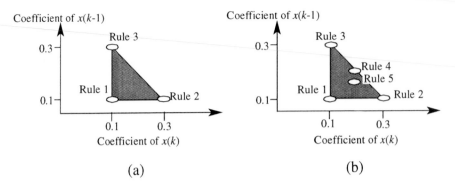

Figure 7.14 Parameter region (PR) representations of the fuzzy systems in Example 7.7. (a) PR of fuzzy system 1. (b) PR of fuzzy system 2.

We notice a difference between the PR of fuzzy system 1 and that of fuzzy system 2. In the former [Fig. 7.14(a)], each plotted point corresponds to each edge of the parameter region. Conversely, in the latter [Fig. 7.14(b)], the parameter region constructed using the plotted points of rules 1–3 includes the plotted points of rules 4 and 5. This observation implies that rules 1–3 of fuzzy system 1 or fuzzy system 2 are edges of the PR; they are said to be *edge rules*. The consequent matrices A_1, A_2, and A_3 in *edge rules* are said to be *edge matrices*. A fuzzy system that consists only of *edge rules* is said to be a *minimum representation*. Obviously, fuzzy system 1 in Example 7.7 is a minimum representation, while fuzzy system 2 is not a minimum representation. The following theorem is important for checking stability in the case of nonminimum representation.

Theorem 7.8

[Tanaka and Sano, 1993]. Assume that P is a positive-definite matrix. If $A_i^T P A_i - P < 0$ for $i = 1, 2, \dots, l$, then $A^{*T} P A^* - P < 0$, where A^* is a nonedge matrix such that

$$A^* = \sum_{i=1}^{l} s_i A_i, \qquad \text{where } \sum_{i=1}^{l} s_i = 1 \text{ and } s_i \geq 0. \tag{7.58}$$

The above theorem indicates that the stability of a fuzzy system can be checked by applying the Tanaka-Sugeno theorem (Theorem 7.6) to a minimum representation of the fuzzy system. For example, in fuzzy system 2 in Example 7.7, $A_4 = 0.5A_2 + 0.5A_3$ and $A_5 = 0.5A_1 + 0.25A_2 + 0.25A_3$. Therefore, a minimum representation of fuzzy system 2 is equivalent to fuzzy system 1. Hence, it is found from Theorem 7.8 that fuzzy system 2 is stable if fuzzy system 1 is stable.

7.4 APPLICATIONS OF FUZZY CONTROLLERS

Over the past decade, we have witnessed a very significant increase in the number of applications of fuzzy logic–based techniques to various commercial and industrial products and systems. In many applications, especially in controlling nonlinear, time-varying, ill-defined systems and in managing complex systems with multiple independent decision-making processes, FLC-based systems have proved to be superior in performance when compared to conventional control systems.

Notable applications of FLC include a steam engine [Mamdani and Assilian, 1975; Ray and Majumder, 1985]; a warm water process [Kickert and Van Nauta Lemke, 1976]; heat exchange [Ostergaard, 1977]; activated sludge wastewater treatment [Tong et al., 1980; Itoh et al., 1987; Yu et al., 1990]; traffic junction control [Pappis and Mamdani, 1977]; a cement kiln [Larsen, 1980; Umbers and King, 1980]; aircraft flight control [Larkin, 1985; Chaudhary, 1990; Chiu et al., 1991]; autonomous orbital operations [Lea and Jani, 1992]; a turning process [Sakai, 1985]; robot control [Uragami et al., 1976; Scharf and Mandic, 1985; Tanscheit and Scharf, 1988; Ciliz et al., 1987; Isik, 1987; Palm 1989]; model car parking and turning [Sugeno and Murakami, 1984, 1985; Sugeno and Nishida, 1985; Sugeno et al., 1989]; automobile speed control [Murakami, 1983; Murakami and Maeda, 1985]; a water purification process [Yagishita et al., 1985]; elevator control [Fujitec, 1988]; automobile transmission and braking control [Kasai and Morimoto, 1988]; power systems and nuclear reactor control [Bernard, 1988; Kinoshita et al., 1988]; arc welding [Murakami et al., 1989; Langari and Tomizuka, 1990a]; refuse incineration [Ono et al., 1989]; process control [Efstathiou, 1987]; adaptive control [Graham and Newell, 1989]; automatic tuning [Ollero and Garcia-Cerezo, 1989]; control of a liquid level rig [Graham and Newell, 1988]; gasoline refinery catalytic reformer control [Bare et al., 1990]; a ping-pong game [Hirota et al., 1989]; biological processes [Czogala and Rawlik, 1989]; knowledge structure [Van Der Rhee et al., 1990]; a model helicopter [Sugeno, 1990]; a walking machine [DeYoung et al., 1992]; a rigid disk drive [Yoshida and Wakabayashi, 1992]; highway incident detection [Hsiao et al., 1993]; gas cooling plant control [Tobi et al., 1989]; control theory [Tang and Mulholland, 1987; Berenji et al., 1989; Li and Lan, 1989]; fuzzy hardware devices [Togai and Watanabe, 1986; Togai and Chiu, 1987; Watanabe and Dettloff, 1988; Yamakawa and Miki, 1986; Yamakawa and Sasaki, 1987; Yamakawa, 1988a,b, 1989; Yamakawa and Kabuo, 1988; Hirota and Ozawa, 1988, 1989]; and fuzzy computers [Yamakawa, 1987].

Among these applications, the cement kiln control system was the first successful industrial application of a FLC. In contrast to previous analog fuzzy logic controllers which were designed based on a continuous state-space model, a discrete-event fuzzy controller was intended for airport control [Clymer et al., 1992]. Fuzzy control has also been successfully applied to automatic train operation systems and automatic container crane operation systems [Yasunobu and Miyamoto, 1985; Yasunobu and Hasegawa, 1986, 1987; Yasunobu et al., 1987]. Fuzzy logic control systems have also found application in household appliances such as air conditioners (Mitsubishi); washing machines (Matsushita, Hitachi); video recorders (Sanyo, Matsushita); television autocontrast and brightness control cameras (Canon), autofocusing and jitter control [Shingu and Nishimori, 1989; Egusa et al., 1992]; vacuum cleaners (Matsushita); microwave ovens (Toshiba); palmtop computers (Sony); and many others. In the remainder of this section, the application of fuzzy logic in camera tracking control is discussed in more detail as an illustration of fuzzy control.

An interesting application of fuzzy control is the camera tracking control system at the Software Technology Laboratory, NASA/Johnson Space Center, used to investigate fuzzy logic approaches in autonomous orbital operations [Lea and Jani, 1992]. The camera tracking control system utilizes the tracked object's pixel position on the image as input and controls the gimbal drives to keep the object in the field of view (FOV) of the camera as shown in Fig. 7.15(a). Thus, tracking an object means aligning the pointing axis of a camera along the object's line of sight (LOS). The LOS vector is estimated from the sensory measurements.

In this camera tracking control system, the monitoring camera is mounted on the pan and tilt gimbal drives, which can rotate the camera or, equivalently, the pointing axis of the camera within a certain range. The *camera frame* (viewing plane) consists of three axes: vertical, horizontal, and pointing vectors. This plane is a Cartesian coordinate plane of 170×170 pixels with the origin at the upper left corner as shown in Fig. 7.15(a). When an image is received, it is processed to determine the location of the object in the camera frame. Using an appropriate image processing technique, the centroid of the image is computed and used as the current location of the object in the viewing plane.

As shown in Fig. 7.15(b), the inputs to a fuzzy logic–based tracking controller are the LOS vector and the range of the object (the distance of the object from the camera), and the outputs are the command pan and tilt rates. The LOS vector is expressed in terms of pixel position (x, y) in the camera's FOV. The range of the object is received from the laser range finder as a measurement. With these three inputs, the task of the FLC is to determine the proper pan and tilt rates for the gimbal drives so that the pointing axis of the camera is along the LOS vector of the object and the image location is at the center of the viewing plane [i.e., at (85, 84)]. In the camera's FOV, tilt upward is negative and pan right is positive.

Membership functions of the input variables (i.e., range, horizontal, and vertical positions) are shown in Fig. 7.16(a). Membership functions of the scale-factor and the output variables (i.e., pan rate and tilt rate) are shown in Fig. 7.16(b). The scale-factor parameter is used as an intermediate step to indicate the degree that a control action should propose to reflect the distance of the tracked object from the camera. The basic concept is that the movement of the object in the FOV caused by the movement of the camera is greater when the object is closer to the camera than when it is farther from the camera.

Three sets of fuzzy control rules are used [see Table (7.3)]. The first set of rules is for finding the scale factor, which will be used in the next two sets of rules. For example, one rule in the second rule set may read: "If the horizontal position of the object is to the far left

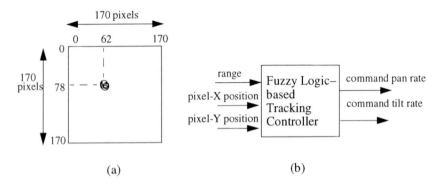

(a) (b)

Figure 7.15   Camera tracking system. (a) Camera field of view. (b) Input-output of fuzzy logic–based tracking controller.

Fuzzy Logic Control Systems   Chap. 7

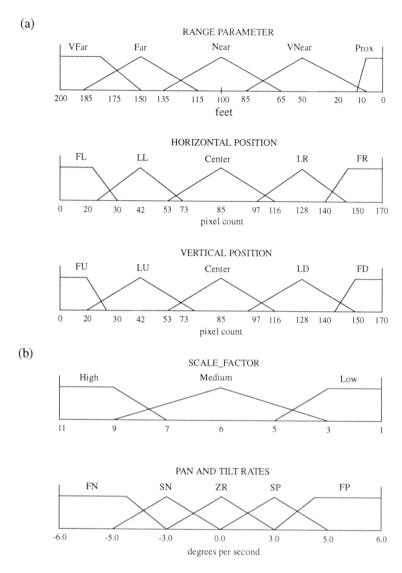

(a)

RANGE PARAMETER

VFar   Far   Near   VNear   Prox

200 185 175 150 135 115 100 85 65 50 20 10 0
feet

HORIZONTAL POSITION

FL   LL   Center   LR   FR

0 20 30 42 53 73 85 97 116 128 140 150 170
pixel count

VERTICAL POSITION

FU   LU   Center   LD   FD

0 20 30 42 53 73 85 97 116 128 140 150 170
pixel count

(b)

SCALE_FACTOR

High   Medium   Low

11   9   7   6   5   3   1

PAN AND TILT RATES

FN   SN   ZR   SP   FP

-6.0   -5.0   -3.0   0.0   3.0   5.0   6.0
degrees per second

Figure 7.16 (a) Membership functions for input parameters. VFar, Very far; VNear, Very near; Prox, Proximity zone; FL, far left; LL, little left; LR, little right; FR, far right; FU far up; LU, little up; LD, little down; FD, far down. (b) Membership functions for Scale_Factor and Output parameters for camera tracking system. FN, Fast negative; SN, slow negative; ZR, zero; FP, fast positive; SP, slow positive. (Reprinted by permission of the publisher from "Fuzzy Logic in Autonomous Orbital Operations," by R. N. Lea and Y. Jani, *International Journal of Approximate Reasoning,* Vol. 6, No. 2, pages 151–184. Copyright 1992 by Elsevier Science Inc.)

of the center of the viewing plane and the scale factor is low (i.e., the distance of the object is far), then set the pan rate fast negative (left)." This example also illustrates application of the *chain rule* technique of expert systems in FLC design; that is, the firing of a rule causes the firing of another rule. Normally, a FLC has only single-layer-rule firing.

TABLE 7.3 Base Rule for a Camera Tracking Control System

	Distance Membership Functions				
	VFar	Far	Near	VNear	Prox
Scale_Factor	Low	Low	Med	High	High

	Horizontal Position Membership Functions				
Scale_Factor	FL	LL	Center	LR	FR

	Pan_Rate Membership Functions				
Low	FN	SN	ZR	SP	FP
Med	SN	SN	ZR	SP	SP
High	SN	ZR	ZR	ZR	SP

	Vertical Position Membership Functions				
Scale_Factor	FD	LD	Center	LU	FU

	Tilt_Rate Membership Functions				
Low	FP	SP	ZR	SN	FN
Med	SP	SP	ZR	SN	SN
High	SP	ZR	ZR	ZR	SN

7.5 CONCLUDING REMARKS

The basic architecture, design methodology, and stability analysis of fuzzy logic controllers are discussed in this chapter. In addition, an interesting application of fuzzy control to the camera tracking control problem at the NASA/Johnson Space Center is described. Utilization of fuzzy set theory in other practical applications will be discussed in Chap. 8.

An important component of FLCs is the set of fuzzy control rules that describe the input-output relationship of a controlled system. Two types of fuzzy control rules are currently being used in the design of FLCs. They are *state evaluation* and *object evaluation* fuzzy control rules. In this chapter, we focus on state evaluation fuzzy control rules since they are widely used in various applications. Object evaluation fuzzy control rules predict present and future control actions and evaluate the control objectives; if the control objectives are satisfied, then the control action is applied to the process. A typical application of such control rules is in the automatic train operation (ATO) system in Japan [Yasunobu and Miyamoto, 1985].

SOCs have been applied in generating rule bases with limited success [Lembessis, 1984; Bartolini et al., 1985; Sugiyama, 1986; Shao, 1988; Peng et al., 1988; Sugiyama, 1988; Langari and Tomizuka, 1990a], and some problems still remain unsolved. In particular, convergence has yet to be established, and membership functions are still chosen subjectively.

The notion of stability, controllability, and observability is well established in modern control theory. However, because of the complexity of mathematical analysis of fuzzy logic controllers, stability analysis requires further study and controllability and observability issues need to be defined and studied for fuzzy control systems. Hence, there is no theoretical guarantee that a general fuzzy control system will not become chaotic, although such a possibility appears to be extremely slim based on practical experience. Currently, much attention is being focused on the stability analysis of fuzzy systems. Some recent results can be found in [Wang, 1993b, 1994; Kang, 1993]. As for the most recent applications of fuzzy control, a thorough review can be found in [Marks, 1994].

7.6 PROBLEMS

7.1 If the fuzzy partition of X, denoted by $|T(X_i)|$, is $|T(x_i)| = 4$ for all $i = 1,\ldots,4$, what is the maximum number of fuzzy control rules in the FLC?

7.2 Write a computer program for an inference engine to simulate Example 7.1 and verify the results.

7.3 Repeat Example 7.2 by using Larsen's method and max product composition.

7.4 Show that Theorems 7.1 and 7.2 are valid for the fuzzy implications R_p, R_{bp}, and R_{dp} in Table 7.1.

7.5 Show that Eqs. (7.16) and (7.18) are valid for R_a, R_m, R_s, R_b, R_g, and $R_\triangle$ in Table 7.1.

7.6 Show that Eqs. (7.15)–(7.18) are valid for the max product compositional operator, that is, we can replace $\circ$ in Eqs. (7.15)–(7.18) by $\cdot$ and the results will still be valid.

7.7 Complete the proof of Theorem 7.3.

7.8 Verify the statement that the COA and MOM defuzzification methods are two special cases of the defuzzification strategy based on BADD introduced in Sec. 7.1.5.

7.9 The input-output relation of a fuzzy system is described by a fuzzy relation $R(X, Y)$, where $X = \{0, 0.1,\ldots,0.9, 1\}$ and $Y = \{0, 0.1,\ldots,0.9, 1\}$. This fuzzy relation is realized by a fuzzy implication and, in particular, the material implication is used; that is, $A \rightarrow B = \max(\bar{A}, B)$, where $A \subset X$ and $B \subset Y$. We are given A and B as follows:

$$A = 0.5/0.2 + 0.6/0.5 + 1/0.7,$$
$$B = 0.8/0.2 + 0.5/0.5 + 0.7/0.7,$$

and the input is A', where

$$A' = 0.2/0.2 + 0.9/0.5 + 1/0.7.$$

(a) Determine the output (i.e., B') of the fuzzy system if the max-min compositional rule is used, that is, if

$$B' = A' \circ (A \rightarrow B).$$

(b) Determine the output of the fuzzy system if the max-min compositional rule is used and the fuzzy implication $A \rightarrow B = \min(A, B)$ is used instead.

7.10 $v(A)$ and $v(B)$ are linguistic truth values of propositions A and B, respectively, and their implication is defined as

$$v(A \Rightarrow B) \triangleq v(A) \Rightarrow v(B) = \sum_{ij} \min(\alpha_i, \beta_j)/\max\{1 - v_i, \min(v_i, w_j)\},$$

where $\alpha_i, \beta_j, v_i, w_j \in [0, 1]$ and

$$v(A) = \alpha_1/v_1 + \alpha_2/v_2 + \cdots + \alpha_n/v_n,$$
$$v(B) = \beta_1/w_1 + \beta_2/w_2 + \cdots + \beta_m/w_m.$$

Use the above implication operation on the linguistic truth values

$$v(A) = 0.5/0.6 + 0.7/0.7 + 0.8/0.8 + 0.9/0.9 + 1/1,$$
$$v(B) = 0.6/0.3 + 1/0.5 + 0.6/0.7.$$

7.11 Show that for any given input and output membership functions of a fuzzy logic controller, using the max product composition rule of inference and R_c implication will result in a smaller control action than using the max-min composition rule of inference and R_c implication.

7.12 Write a computer program for fuzzy inference including defuzzification schemes and try to solve Example 7.3 using your program.

7.13 For a given fuzzy logic controller, we have the following three fuzzy control rules:

Rule 1: IF X is A_1 and Y is B_1, THEN Z is C_1.

Rule 2: IF X is A_2 and Y is B_2, THEN Z is C_2.

Rule 3: IF X is A_3 and Y is B_3, THEN Z is C_3.

Suppose x_0 and y_0 are the sensor readings for fuzzy variables X and Y and the following input and output membership functions are given:

$$\mu_{A_1}(x) = \begin{cases} \dfrac{3+x}{3} & -3 \le x \le 0 \\ 1 & 0 \le x \le 3 \\ \dfrac{6-x}{3} & 3 \le x \le 6, \end{cases}$$

$$\mu_{A_2}(x) = \begin{cases} \dfrac{x-2}{3} & 2 \le x \le 5 \\ \dfrac{9-x}{4} & 5 \le x \le 9, \end{cases}$$

$$\mu_{A_3}(x) = \begin{cases} \dfrac{x-6}{4} & 6 \le x \le 10 \\ \dfrac{13-x}{3} & 10 \le x \le 13, \end{cases}$$

$$\mu_{B_1}(y) = \begin{cases} \dfrac{y-1}{4} & 1 \le y \le 5 \\ \dfrac{7-y}{2} & 5 \le y \le 7, \end{cases}$$

$$\mu_{B_2}(y) = \begin{cases} \dfrac{y-5}{3} & 5 \le y \le 8 \\ \dfrac{12-y}{4} & 8 \le y \le 12, \end{cases}$$

$$\mu_{B_3}(y) = \begin{cases} \dfrac{y-8}{4} & 8 \le y \le 12 \\ \dfrac{15-y}{3} & 12 \le y \le 15, \end{cases}$$

$$\mu_{C_1}(z) = \begin{cases} \dfrac{z+3}{2} & -3 \le z \le -1 \\ 1 & -1 \le z \le +1 \\ \dfrac{3-z}{2} & 1 \le z \le 3, \end{cases}$$

$$\mu_{C_2}(z) = \begin{cases} \dfrac{z-1}{3} & 1 \le z \le 4 \\ \dfrac{7-z}{3} & 4 \le z \le 7, \end{cases}$$

$$\mu_{C_3}(z) = \begin{cases} \dfrac{z-5}{2} & 5 \le z \le 7 \\ 1 & 7 \le z \le 9 \\ \dfrac{11-z}{2} & 9 \le z \le 11 \end{cases}$$

Assume discrete universes for $X, Y,$ and Z; that is $x, y, z = 1, 2, \ldots$. If the sensor values are $x_0 = 3$ and $y_0 = 6$, then

(a) Use the max-min composition rule of inference and R_p for fuzzy implication to determine the resultant control action.

(b) Sketch the resultant output membership functions.

(c) Use the COA method of defuzzification to determine the control action.

7.14 What are the differences between fuzzy logic control systems and expert systems as discussed in Chap. 6?

7.15 Briefly show that each of the following statements is true or false.

(a) The algebraic product of two fuzzy sets will be greater than the union of the same two fuzzy sets.

(b) A fuzzy logic control system is always stable.

7.16 Consider the following fuzzy system:

$$L^1: \text{IF } x(k-1) \text{ is } A^1, \text{THEN } x^1(k+1) = x(k) - 0.5x(k-1),$$

$$L^2: \text{IF } x(k-1) \text{ is } A^2, \text{THEN } x^2(k+1) = -x(k) - 0.5x(k-1),$$

where the membership functions of fuzzy sets A^1 and A^2 are shown in Fig. P7.16.

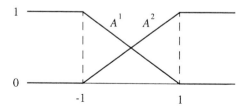

Figure P7.16 Membership functions of fuzzy sets A^1 and A^2 in Problem 7.16.

(a) Show that the two linear subsystems L^1 and L^2 are stable.

(b) Show that the fuzzy system consisting of the linear subsystems is unstable by observing the behavior of the fuzzy system starting from the initial condition $x(0) = 0.9$ and $x(1) = -0.7$.

(c) Show that there does not exist a common positive-definite matrix $\mathbf{P}$ for the fuzzy system (see Theorem 7.7).

7.17 Write a computer program to simulate the camera tracking control system in Sec. 7.4.

8

Applications
of Fuzzy Theory

This chapter explores the application of fuzzy set theory to various application domains such as pattern recognition, optimization, mathematical programming, database systems, and human-machine interactions. In some applications, the incorporation of fuzzy set concepts into existing methodologies or techniques broadens their flexibility and robustness. Examples are worked out to illustrate the improved performance. Because of space limitations, this chapter samples only some important applications.

8.1 FUZZY PATTERN RECOGNITION

Much of the information that we have to deal with in real life is in the form of complex patterns. Pattern recognition involves the search for structure in these complex patterns. The methodologies used for recognition schemes include linear classification, statistical (probabilistic) approaches, fuzzy set theory (possibility approaches), perceptrons (neural networks), knowledge-based classification based on artificial intelligence techniques, and many others. Among these, fuzzy set theory has long been considered a suitable framework for pattern recognition, especially classification procedures, because of the inherent fuzziness involved in the definition of a class or a cluster. Indeed, fuzzy set theory has introduced several new methods of pattern recognition which have led to successful realizations in various areas including speech recognition, intelligent robots, image processing, character recognition, scene analysis, recognition of geometric objects, signal classification, and medical applications. Major references include [Bezdek, 1981; Kandel, 1982; Pal and Dutta Majumder, 1986; Pedrycz, 1990a; Bezdek and Pal, 1992].

As shown in Fig. 8.1, pattern recognition usually consists of three steps: (1) data acquisition, (2) feature selection, and (3) classification. First, the data for classification are gathered from the environment via a set of sensors. They can be numerical, linguistic, or both. Afterward, feature selection is usually performed to search for internal structure in the data. It is desirable that the dimensions of the feature space be much smaller than those of the data space so that classification techniques can be efficiently applied. Finally, classification is performed via a classifier and is actually a transformation between classes and features.

The concept of fuzzy set theory can be introduced into the pattern recognition process in Fig. 8.1 to cope with uncertainty in several different ways. Two of them are in evidence: (i) fuzziness involving the feature space, and (ii) fuzziness involving the classification space. It is understood that most of the information gathered in the recognition processes of a human being is of a nonnumerical type. Even if numerical data are available, the process is worked out by the human mind at a level of nonnumerical labels. This indicates that the classification is performed not on the basis of a mass of numbers but by elicitation relationships between the classes and linguistic labels attached to the object for recognition. These linguistic labels can be represented by fuzzy sets specified in appropriate spaces. Thus, we may have, for example, a classification rule like, "If an object is *heavy* and *small* and it moves *fast,* then it belongs to the class ω_i." A second important way of introducing fuzziness is about class assignment ("labeling") in the classification space. Unlike "hard" labeling in which an object is classified as belonging to only one class crisply, "fuzzy" labeling allows an object to be identified as belonging to different classes to different degrees. That is, the boundaries of the classes are vague. For example, we can say, "If an object is black and cubic, then it *possibly* belongs to the class ω_i." Obviously, the above two approaches can be merged into a classification rule like, "If an object is heavy and small and it moves fast, then it very possibly belongs to the class ω_i."

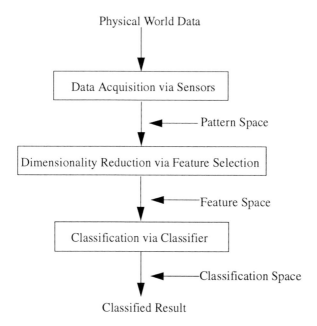

Physical World Data

Data Acquisition via Sensors

Pattern Space

Dimensionality Reduction via Feature Selection

Feature Space

Classification via Classifier

Classification Space

Classified Result

Figure 8.1   General scheme of pattern recognition.

Fuzziness and probability can handle different facets of uncertainty in pattern recognition. Statistical (probabilistic) methods have a long history in pattern recognition. Some well-known reference sources include [Fu, 1968; Fukunaga, 1972; Patrick, 1972; Duda and Hart, 1973]. The difference between these two methods, possibility-based (fuzzy set theory) and probability-based, can be seen from the following two statements indicating the outcomes of classifiers:

1. The grade of membership of the pattern in the class ω_i is α, where $\alpha \in [0, 1]$.
2. The probability that the pattern belongs to the class ω_i is α, where $\alpha \in [0, 1]$.

The α in the first statement indicates the degree of the pattern's similarity to the "prototype" of the class ω_i. The second statement tells us that if the pattern with the same feature vector appears N times, then for αN times it belongs to the class ω_i.

In the following sections, we shall introduce some fuzzy pattern recognition approaches based on fuzzy relations and fuzzy clustering. The issue of feature selection is also discussed.

8.1.1 Classification Methods Based on Fuzzy Relations

In this section, we consider pattern classification performed in a fuzzy environment, assuming both features represented by fuzzy labels and class assignment are fuzzy, such as "If the object is light and large and it moves fast, then it possibly belongs to the class ω_i."

Let X denote the pattern from the environment observed via the data acquisition process. The pattern is described in linguistic terms rather than in numerical fashion. Therefore, the ith feature of X, X_i, is represented as a fuzzy set with membership function μ_{X_i}. We further assume that there exists finite number of classes $W = \{\omega_1, \omega_2, ..., \omega_c\}$. The goal is to find a fuzzy set Ω with membership function μ_Ω such that the value $\mu_\Omega(\omega_i)$, $i = 1, 2, ..., c$, denotes the grade of membership of the pattern X in the ith class.

To solve the above problem, we first need to define the feature space. We assume that the feature space χ consists of n coordinates, that is,

$$\chi = \chi_1 \times \chi_2 \times \cdots \times \chi_n, \tag{8.1}$$

where each χ_i, $i = 1, 2, ..., n$, is a linguistic variable consisting of a term set,

$$T(\chi_i) = \{\chi_{i1}, \chi_{i2}, ..., \chi_{in_i}\}, \tag{8.2}$$

where each term χ_{iji} in a term set is a fuzzy set with membership function $\mu_{\chi_{iji}}$. For example, let the classified object be characterized by two features: *length* (χ_1) and *width* (χ_2) with term sets, respectively, defined by

$$T(\chi_1) = T(length) = \{\chi_{11}, \chi_{12}, \chi_{13}\} = \{\text{Short, Medium, Long}\},$$

$$T(\chi_2) = T(width) = \{\chi_{21}, \chi_{22}\} = \{\text{Narrow, Wide}\}. \tag{8.3}$$

These fuzzy sets form a partition of the feature space χ_1 and χ_2, respectively. Sometimes, it is additionally assumed that these fuzzy sets satisfy the orthogonal condition, that is, that their membership degrees sum up to 1 at each element of the universe of discourse.

After the feature space is defined, the next step is to transform the input pattern X into this feature space. One convenient way to accomplish such a transformation is to use the possibility measure defined in Eq. (4.66), which indicates the degree of matching of two fuzzy sets,

$$\Pi\left(X_i \mid \chi_{ij_i}\right) = \sup_{x \in X_i} \left[\min\left(\mu_{X_i}(x), \mu_{\chi_{ij_i}}(x)\right)\right], \tag{8.4}$$

for all $i = 1, 2, \ldots, n$ and $j_i = 1, 2, \ldots, n_i$. For the simple example used above [Eq. (8.3)], $\Pi(X_i \mid \chi_{ij_i})$ is defined for $i = 1, 2$, $j_1 = 1, 2, 3$, and $j_2 = 1, 2$. The higher the value of the possibility measure, the better the fuzzy set X_i fits the label expressed by the fuzzy set χ_{ij_i}. Note that if the ith feature of the pattern X can be precisely measured and represented by the real number z_i instead of the fuzzy set X_i, then Eq. (8.4) is simplified to

$$\Pi(z_i \mid \chi_{ij_i}) = \mu_{\chi_{ij_i}}(z_i). \tag{8.5}$$

By such a transformation, the pattern X is represented by the Cartesian product of the (row) vectors $\chi^{(1)}, \chi^{(2)}, \ldots, \chi^{(n)}$,

$$\chi = \chi^{(1)} \times \chi^{(2)} \times \cdots \times \chi^{(n)}, \tag{8.6}$$

where each vector $\chi^{(i)}$, $i = 1, 2, \ldots, n$, is derived from Eq. (8.4) and is defined as

$$\chi^{(i)} \triangleq \left[\Pi(X_i \mid \chi_{i1}), \Pi(X_i \mid \chi_{i2}), \ldots, \Pi(X_i \mid \chi_{in_i})\right]. \tag{8.7}$$

Hence, χ is viewed as a fuzzy relation defined in the Cartesian product of the reference fuzzy sets, $\chi = \chi_1 \times \chi_2 \times \cdots \times \chi_n$; that is, $\chi : \chi \to [0, 1]$.

The next step is to perform classification, that is, to transform the fuzzy set (fuzzy relation) χ in the feature space to a fuzzy set Ω in the classification space W. There should be a dependence between χ and Ω if the selected features have enough discriminant power; that is, χ and Ω are related via a certain relation $R(\chi, W)$, which is exactly the *classifier* that we want to design. Such a transformation can be conveniently expressed by a fuzzy relation equation as

$$\Omega = \chi \circ R, \tag{8.8}$$

where the max-min composition $\circ$ can be replaced by any max-t or min-s composition. In the following derivation, we shall use the only max-min composition for clarity. From Eq. (3.48), we have

$$\mu_\Omega(\omega_j) = \max_{x \in \chi} \min\left[\mu_\chi(x), \mu_R(x, \omega_j)\right], \tag{8.9}$$

for $j = 1, 2, \ldots, c$. The above equation indicates that the degree of membership $\mu_\Omega(\omega_j)$ in the given class ω_j results from the intersection of the features of the pattern and the fuzzy relation R. The more similar χ is to the fuzzy relation R, the higher the value of $\mu_\Omega(\omega_j)$ will be.

Next, we need to design the classifier R in Eq. (8.8). The design of the classifier requires a set of training patterns,

$$(\chi_1, \Omega_1), (\chi_2, \Omega_2), \ldots, (\chi_L, \Omega_L), \tag{8.10}$$

that satisfy the fuzzy relation equation in Eq. (8.8),

$$\Omega_i = \chi_i \circ R, \qquad i = 1, 2, \ldots, L. \tag{8.11}$$

Then, according to Theorem 3.3, the fuzzy relation of the classifier is given by

$$R = \bigcap_{i=1}^{L} (\chi_i \overset{\alpha}{\rightharpoonup} \Omega_i),$$

(8.12)

where $\overset{\alpha}{\rightharpoonup}$ indicates the α operator as defined in Eq. (3.52).

The system of equations in Eq. (8.11) may not always produce solutions. In such cases, approximate solutions of the system of equations must be pursued. Details on obtaining approximate solutions can be found in [Pedrycz, 1991c].

Example 8.1

[Pedrycz, 1990a]. Let the feature space consist of two coordinates, *length* and *width,* as defined in Eq. (8.3). The membership functions of the terms $\{\chi_{11}, \chi_{12}, \chi_{13}\}$ and $\{\chi_{21}, \chi_{22}\}$ are shown in Fig. 8.2. Two classes of patterns, $\Omega = \{\omega_1, \omega_2\} = \{(a, d), (b, c)\}$ are established in the feature space in Fig. 8.2. The problem is to design a classifier R to classify these two classes by using the given patterns as the training data. First, Eq. (8.6) is used to obtain the fuzzy relations of patterns as follows:

$$\chi_1 = \chi^{(1)} \times \chi^{(2)} = [1, 0, 0] \times [1, 0] = \begin{bmatrix} 1.0 & 0.0 \\ 0.0 & 0.0 \\ 0.0 & 0.0 \end{bmatrix},$$

$$\chi_2 = \chi^{(1)} \times \chi^{(2)} = [1, 0, 0] \times [0, 1] = \begin{bmatrix} 0.0 & 1.0 \\ 0.0 & 0.0 \\ 0.0 & 0.0 \end{bmatrix},$$

$$\chi_3 = \chi^{(1)} \times \chi^{(2)} = [0, 0, 1] \times [0, 1] = \begin{bmatrix} 0.0 & 0.0 \\ 0.0 & 0.0 \\ 0.0 & 1.0 \end{bmatrix},$$

$$\chi_4 = \chi^{(1)} \times \chi^{(2)} = [0, 0, 1] \times [1, 0] = \begin{bmatrix} 0.0 & 0.0 \\ 0.0 & 0.0 \\ 1.0 & 0.0 \end{bmatrix}.$$

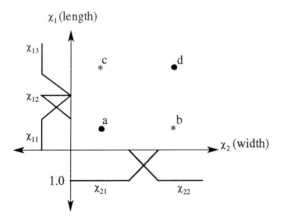

Figure 8.2 Feature space in Example 8.1.

The corresponding training patterns in the classification space are $\Omega_1 = [1.0, 0.0]$, $\Omega_2 = [0.0, 1.0]$, $\Omega_3 = [1.0, 0.0]$, and $\Omega_4 = [0.0, 1.0]$. Then, according to Eq. (8.12), we can derive the classifier as

$$ R = \left\{ \begin{bmatrix} 1 & 0 \\ 1 & 1 \\ 0 & 1 \end{bmatrix}_{\omega_1} \begin{bmatrix} 0 & 1 \\ 1 & 1 \\ 1 & 0 \end{bmatrix}_{\omega_2} \right\}. $$

It can be checked using Eq. (8.9) that $\Omega_i = \chi_i \circ R$ for all the training patterns. This means that the fuzzy classifier is characterized by zero classification error.

The classification equation in Eq. (8.8) leads to a natural ordering of the features with respect to their ability to discriminate among the specified classes. To check the discrimination power of the jth feature, $\chi^{(j)}$, of χ, we first create a new fuzzy relation χ^j which is equal to the relation χ, but the jth coordinate $\chi^{(j)}$ is modeled as the fuzzy set UNKNOWN with all the elements of the membership function equal to 1. In this way, there is a χ_i^j for each training pattern χ_i. Let Ω_i^j be the fuzzy set of the class assignment given by

$$ \Omega_i^j = \chi_i^j \circ R. \tag{8.13} $$

Then the discrimination power of $\chi^{(j)}$ can be decided by the difference between Ω_i^j and Ω_i, $i = 1, 2, \ldots, L$, to see its influence on the fuzzy set of belongingness to classes. For this purpose, the following sum of distances is defined as an index:

$$ D_j = \sum_{i=1}^{L} \frac{d(\Omega_i^j, \Omega_i)}{c}, \tag{8.14} $$

where $d(\cdot, \cdot)$ is any distance measure such as the Hamming distance and c is a normalization factor. This index indicates to what extent the jth feature is important for the classification results. The higher the value of D_j, the more significant the jth feature. Hence, we can say that the jth feature is preferred to the kth one, denoting $\chi_j > \chi_k$, if $D_j \geq D_k$.

Example 8.2
Let us continue with Example 8.1. The fuzzy relations χ_i^j are created as follows:

$$ \chi_1^1 = [1, 1, 1] \times [1, 0], \qquad \chi_1^2 = [1, 0, 0] \times [1, 1], $$
$$ \chi_2^1 = [1, 1, 1] \times [0, 1], \qquad \chi_2^2 = [1, 0, 0] \times [1, 1], $$
$$ \chi_3^1 = [1, 1, 1] \times [0, 1], \qquad \chi_3^2 = [0, 0, 1] \times [1, 1], $$
$$ \chi_4^1 = [1, 1, 1] \times [1, 0], \qquad \chi_4^2 = [0, 0, 1] \times [1, 1]. $$

Then from Eq. (8.13), we have

$$ \Omega_1^1 = \Omega_1^2 = \Omega_2^1 = \Omega_2^2 = \Omega_3^1 = \Omega_3^2 = \Omega_4^1 = \Omega_4^2 = [1.0, 1.0]. $$

From Eq. (8.14),

$$ D_1 = D_2 = \tfrac{1}{2}(1.0 + 1.0 + 1.0 + 1.0) = 2.0. $$

So, features χ_1 (*length*) and χ_2 (*width*) have the same discrimination power.

8.1.2 Fuzzy Clustering

Clustering essentially deals with the task of splitting a set of patterns into a number of more-or-less homogeneous classes (clusters) with respect to a suitable similarity measure such that the patterns belonging to any one of the clusters are similar and the patterns of different clusters are as dissimilar as possible. The similarity measure used has an important effect on the clustering results since it indicates which mathematical properties of the data set, for example, distance, connectivity, and intensity, should be used and in what way they should be used in order to identify the clusters. In nonfuzzy "hard" clustering, the boundary of different clusters is crisp, such that one pattern is assigned to exactly one cluster. On the contrary, fuzzy clustering provides partitioning results with additional information supplied by the cluster membership values indicating different degrees of belongingness.

Let us formulate the fuzzy clustering problem formally. Consider a finite set of elements $X = \{x_1, x_2, \ldots, x_n\}$ as being elements of the p-dimensional Euclidean space $\mathbb{R}^p$, that is, $x_j \in \mathbb{R}^p$, $j = 1, 2, \ldots, n$. The problem is to perform a partition of this collection of elements into c fuzzy sets with respect to a given criterion, where c is a given number of clusters. The criterion is usually to optimize an *objective function* that acts as a performance index of clustering. The end result of fuzzy clustering can be expressed by a *partition matrix U* such that

$$U = [u_{ij}]_{i=1\ldots c,\ j=1\ldots n},\qquad (8.15)$$

where u_{ij} is a numerical value in $[0, 1]$ and expresses the degree to which the element x_j belongs to the ith cluster. However, there are two additional constraints on the value of u_{ij}. First, a total membership of the element $x_j \in X$ in all classes is equal to 1.0; that is,

$$\sum_{i=1}^{c} u_{ij} = 1 \qquad \text{for all } j = 1, 2, \ldots, n. \qquad (8.16)$$

Second, every constructed cluster is nonempty and different from the entire set; that is,

$$0 < \sum_{j=1}^{n} u_{ij} < n \qquad \text{for all } i = 1, 2, \ldots, c. \qquad (8.17)$$

A general form of the objective function is

$$J(u_{ij}, \mathbf{v}_k) = \sum_{i=1}^{c} \sum_{j=1}^{n} \sum_{k=1}^{c} g[w(\mathbf{x}_j), u_{ij}]\, d(\mathbf{x}_j, \mathbf{v}_k), \qquad (8.18)$$

where $w(\mathbf{x}_j)$ is the a priori weight for each $\mathbf{x}_j$, $g[w(\mathbf{x}_j), u_{ij}]$ influences the degree of fuzziness of the partition matrix, and $d(\mathbf{x}_j, \mathbf{v}_k)$ is the degree of dissimilarity between the data $\mathbf{x}_j$ and the supplemental element $\mathbf{v}_k$, which can be considered the central vector of the kth cluster. The degree of dissimilarity is defined as a measure that satisfies two axioms:

$$\begin{aligned}&\text{(i)} \quad d(\mathbf{x}_j, \mathbf{v}_k) \geq 0, \\ &\text{(ii)} \quad d(\mathbf{x}_j, \mathbf{v}_k) = d(\mathbf{v}_k, \mathbf{x}_j),\end{aligned} \qquad (8.19)$$

and thus it is a concept weaker than distance measures.

With the above background, fuzzy clustering can be precisely formulated as an optimization problem:

$$\text{Minimize} \quad J(u_{ij}, \mathbf{v}_k), \qquad i, k = 1, 2, \ldots, c; \; j = 1, 2, \ldots, n$$

$$\text{subject to Eqs. (8.16) and (8.17).} \tag{8.20}$$

One of the widely used clustering methods based on Eq. (8.20) is the fuzzy c-means (FCM) algorithm developed by Bezdek [1981]. This objective function of the FCM algorithm takes the form of

$$J(u_{ij}, \mathbf{v}_i) = \sum_{i=1}^{c} \sum_{j=1}^{n} (u_{ij})^m \| \mathbf{x}_j - \mathbf{v}_i \|^2, \qquad m > 1, \tag{8.21}$$

where m is called the exponential weight which influences the degree of fuzziness of the membership (partition) matrix. To solve this minimization problem, we first differentiate the objective function in Eq. (8.21) with respect to $\mathbf{v}_i$ (for fixed u_{ij}, $i = 1, \ldots, c$, $j = 1, \ldots, n$) and to u_{ij} (for fixed $\mathbf{v}_i$, $i = 1, \ldots, c$) and apply the conditions of Eq. (8.16), obtaining

$$\mathbf{v}_i = \frac{1}{\sum_{j=1}^{n} (u_{ij})^m} \sum_{j=1}^{n} (u_{ij})^m \mathbf{x}_j, \qquad i = 1, 2, \ldots, c, \tag{8.22}$$

$$u_{ij} = \frac{(1/\| \mathbf{x}_j - \mathbf{v}_i \|^2)^{1/(m-1)}}{\sum_{k=1}^{c} (1/\| \mathbf{x}_j - \mathbf{v}_k \|^2)^{1/(m-1)}}, \qquad i = 1, 2, \ldots, c; \; j = 1, 2, \ldots, n. \tag{8.23}$$

The system described by Eqs. (8.22) and (8.23) cannot be solved analytically. However, the FCM algorithm provides an iterative approach to approximating the minimum of the objective function starting from a given position. This algorithm is summarized in the following.

Algorithm FCM: Fuzzy c-Means Algorithm

Step 1: Select a number of clusters $c (2 \leq c \leq n)$ and exponential weight $m(1 < m < \infty)$. Choose an initial partition matrix $U^{(0)}$ and a termination criterion ϵ. Set the iteration index l to 0.

Step 2: Calculate the fuzzy cluster centers $\{ \mathbf{v}_i^{(l)} \mid i = 1, 2, \ldots, c \}$ by using $U^{(l)}$ and Eq. (8.22).

Step 3: Calculate the new partition matrix $U^{(l+1)}$ by using $\{ \mathbf{v}_i^{(l)} \mid i = 1, 2, \ldots, c \}$ and Eq. (8.23).

Step 4: Calculate $\triangle = \| U^{(l+1)} - U^{(l)} \| = \max_{i,j} |u_{ij}^{(l+1)} - u_{ij}^{(l)}|$. If $\triangle > \epsilon$, then set $l = l + 1$ and go to step 2. If $\triangle \leq \epsilon$, then stop.

END FCM

The iterative procedure described above minimizes the objective function in Eq. (8.21) and leads to any of its local minima. Let us consider the famous "butterfly" example in Bezdek [1981].

Example 8.3

The data for the butterfly shown in Fig. 8.3 are processed by a fuzzy 2-means algorithm with the starting partition matrix

$$U^{(0)} = \begin{bmatrix} 0.854 & 0.146 & 0.854 & 0.854 & \cdots & 0.854 \\ 0.146 & 0.854 & 0.146 & 0.146 & \cdots & 0.146 \end{bmatrix}_{2 \times 15}.$$

The termination criterion ϵ is chosen to be 0.01, and the value of m is chosen as $m = 1.25$. The calculated membership values are shown in Fig. 8.4.

It is noted that the larger the exponential weight m is, the more fuzzy the partition matrix becomes. In fact, as $m \to \infty$, U approaches $U = [1/c]$. In practice, it is reasonable to choose any value of m from the range $[1.5, 30]$.

An important question for the FCM algorithm is how to determine the "correct" number of clusters, c. Since there is no exact solution to this question, some scalar measures of partitioning fuzziness have been used as synthetic indices, called *validity indicators,* to point out the most *plausible* number of clusters in the data set. Some of these scalar measures are:

1. Partitioning entropy:

$$H(U, c) = \frac{1}{n} \sum_{j=1}^{n} \sum_{i=1}^{c} |u_{ij} \ln u_{ij}|; \tag{8.24}$$

2. Partitioning coefficient:

$$F(U, c) = \frac{1}{n} \sum_{i=1}^{c} \sum_{j=1}^{n} u_{ij}^{2}; \tag{8.25}$$

3. Proportion exponent:

$$P(U, c) = -\ln \left\{ \prod_{j=1}^{n} \left[\sum_{k=1}^{u_j^{-1}} (-1)^{k+1} \binom{c}{k} (1 - ku_j)^{(c-1)} \right] \right\}, \tag{8.26}$$

where

$$u_j = \max_{1 \leq i \leq c} u_{ij} \quad \text{and} \quad [u_j^{-1}] = \text{greatest integer} \leq \left(\frac{1}{u_j} \right). \tag{8.27}$$

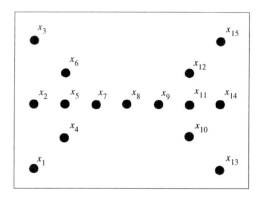

Figure 8.3 Data for the "butterfly" in Example 8.3.

Applications of Fuzzy Theory   Chap. 8

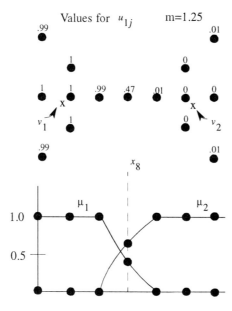

Figure 8.4 Clustering result for $m = 1.25$ in Example 8.3.

These indices have the properties that $H = 0$ and $F = 1$ if $u_{ij} \in \{0, 1\}$ (hard partitioning); $H = \ln c$ and $F = 1/c$ if $u_{ij} = 1/c$ for all i and j; that is, $0 \le H \le \ln c$ and $1/c \le F \le 1$. It is noted that while H and F depend on all cn elements, P depends on the maximum degree of membership of n elements and $0 \le P < \infty$. The value of P converges toward infinity with increasing u_j in Eq. (8.26). To determine the proper number of clusters c according to the above indices, one assumes that the clustering structure is better identified when more points concentrate around the cluster centers, that is, the crisper the partitioning matrix is. According to this assumption, the heuristic rules for selecting (by direct search) the best partitioning number c are:

$$\min_{c=2}^{n-1} \left\{ \min_{U \in \Omega_c} [H(U, c)] \right\}, \tag{8.28}$$

$$\max_{c=2}^{n-1} \left\{ \max_{U \in \Omega_c} [F(U, c)] \right\}, \tag{8.29}$$

$$\max_{c=2}^{n-1} \left\{ \max_{U \in \Omega_c} [P(U, c)] \right\}, \tag{8.30}$$

where Ω_c is the set of all optimal solutions for a given c. Although simulation experiments confirmed the utility of the above equations, their behavior has not been theoretically justified [Bezdek, 1981].

Example 8.4

This example concerns *Iris* data, which are well known and widely treated as the reference data set for pattern recognition [Duda and Hart, 1973]. It contains three categories of the species *Iris*, including *Iris sestosa* (A_1), *Iris versicolor* (A_2), and *Iris virginica* (A_3). These data are represented in a two-dimensional space with coordinates petal length and petal width (see Fig. 8.5.) This data set is processed by the FCM algorithm using a Euclidean distance $\epsilon = 0.05$, $m = 4.0$,

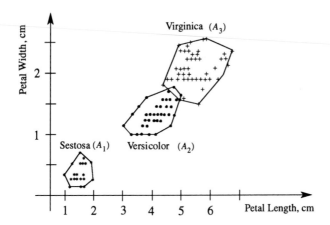

Petal Width, cm

2

1

Virginica (A_3)

Sestosa (A_1)   Versicolor (A_2)

1   2   3   4   5   6   Petal Length, cm   **Figure 8.5**   *Iris* data set in Example 8.4

and $c = 2, 3, 4, 5, 6$. Only one initial guess is used for $U^{(0)}$. Consequently, Ω_c contains one opti-mal pair $(U, \mathbf{v})$ for the objective function Q at each c value. Values of the three validity indica-tors are listed in Table 8.1. Note that H and F are, respectively, monotonic decreasing and increasing functions of c (this fact is also the limitation of these two indicators) but that P is not monotonic. From this table we find that H and F indicate the same solution $c_{best} = 2$, while P indicates $c_{best} = 3$. When validity indicators are at odds with each other, one is forced to turn elsewhere, namely, to the data themselves. There is usually more than one useful interpretation of substructure in a data set. In this example, $c_{best} = 2$ results in a *coarse* substructure and $c_{best} = 3$ results in a *finer (botanical)* substructure of *Iris* data.

TABLE 8.1   Validity Indicators In Example 8.4

c	Partition entropy H(U;c)	Partition coefficient F(U;c)	Proportion exponent P(U;c)
2	0.55←	0.63←	109
3	0.92	0.45	113←
4	1.21	0.35	111
5	1.43	0.27	62
6	1.60	0.23	68

8.2 FUZZY MATHEMATICAL PROGRAMMING

In mathematical programming, a real problem is described in terms of a mathematical model and then an optimal solution is found from the model. Specifically, mathematical programming is an algorithmic-based approach to solving the following type of optimiza-tion problem:

$$\text{Maximize } f(x)$$
$$\text{subject to } g_i(x) = 0 \qquad \text{for } i = 1, 2, \ldots, m, \tag{8.31}$$

where $f(x)$ and $g_i(x)$ are, respectively, the *objective function* (goal) and the *constraints* of the problem to be solved. One of the most simple and most commonly used types of mathematical programming of Eq. (8.31) is *linear programming*. It focuses on the following problem

$$\text{Maximize } f(\mathbf{x}) = \mathbf{c}^T\mathbf{x}, \qquad \mathbf{c}, \mathbf{x} \in \mathfrak{R}^n$$
$$\text{such that } \mathbf{Ax} \le \mathbf{b}, \qquad \mathbf{b} \in \mathfrak{R}^m, \mathbf{A} \in \mathfrak{R}^{m \times n}, \mathbf{x} \ge \mathbf{0}. \tag{8.32}$$

Traditionally, it is assumed that each element and operation in Eqs. (8.31) and (8.32) is crisp, that all the constraints are of equal importance, and that the violation of any single constraint renders the solution infeasible. These crisp assumptions and constraints are usually nonexistent in real-world problems. For example, the stated goal may be to maximize our gain to about \$1 million with the constraint to keep investments to about \$10,000 or less. This problem would be difficult to formulate using crisp mathematical programming. Fuzzy linear programming, which expresses a kind of ambiguity in terms of fuzzy sets, better describes our understanding about the problems that we want to optimize than crisp mathematical programming. Several types of fuzzy linear programming problems can be defined by partly relaxing the crisp assumptions in classical linear programming problems [Zimmermann, 1992]. For example, one might just want to improve one's present income considerably instead of maximizing it, a decision maker might accept small violations of different constraints, or one may only have fuzzy data (fuzzy numbers) instead of precise numerical data in this optimization problem. In this section, we shall discuss a simple type of fuzzy linear programming problem.

The problem to be considered is a type of symmetric fuzzy linear programming problem in the form of Eq. (8.32), called a linear programming problem with fuzzy inequality [Zimmermann, 1991, 1992]. The objectives and constraints are given by the following fuzzy inequalities:

$$\mathbf{c}^T\mathbf{x} \succeq z,$$
$$\mathbf{Ax} \preceq \mathbf{b}, \tag{8.33}$$
$$\mathbf{x} \ge \mathbf{0},$$

where $\succeq$ means "essentially greater than or equal" and $\preceq$ means "essentially smaller than or equal." In Eq. (8.33), it is assumed that the decision maker can give an aspiration level z for the objective function, which he or she wants to achieve as far as possible, and that the constraints can be slightly violated.

Since Eq. (8.33) is fully symmetric with respect to the objective function and constraints, we can consolidate and write

$$\mathbf{Bx} \preceq \mathbf{d},$$
$$\mathbf{x} \ge \mathbf{0}, \tag{8.34}$$

where

$$\mathbf{B} = \begin{bmatrix} -\mathbf{c}^T \\ \mathbf{A} \end{bmatrix} \quad \text{and} \quad \mathbf{d} = \begin{bmatrix} -z \\ \mathbf{b} \end{bmatrix}. \tag{8.35}$$

The ith inequality [i.e., the ith row of Eq. (8.34)] is defined by the following membership functions

$$\mu_i([\mathbf{Bx}]_i) = \begin{cases} 1 & \text{if } [\mathbf{Bx}]_i \leq d_i \\ \in [0, 1] & \text{if } d_i < [\mathbf{Bx}]_i \leq d_i + p_i, \quad i = 1, 2,\dots, m+1 \\ 0 & \text{if } [\mathbf{Bx}]_i > d_i + p_i, \end{cases} \qquad (8.36)$$

where $[\mathbf{Bx}]_i$ is the ith element of the vector $\mathbf{Bx}$, $\mu_i(\cdot)$ is the membership function of the ith inequality, d_i is the ith element of the vector $\mathbf{d}$, and p_i is the maximum possible value of the right-hand side of the ith inequality. Using the simplest type of membership function, we assume it to be linearly decreasing over the *tolerance interval* p_i (see Fig. 8.6):

$$\mu_i([\mathbf{Bx}]_i) = \begin{cases} 1 & \text{if } [\mathbf{Bx}]_i \leq d_i \\ 1 - ([\mathbf{Bx}]_i - d_i)/p_i & \text{if } d_i < [\mathbf{Bx}]_i \leq d_i + p_i, \quad i = 1, 2,\dots, m+1 \\ 0 & \text{if } [\mathbf{Bx}]_i > d_i + p_i. \end{cases} \qquad (8.37)$$

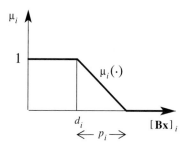

Figure 8.6 Example of the fuzzy set "Essentially smaller than or equal."

Then the maximizing decision is the $\mathbf{x}$ that satisfies

$$\max_{\mathbf{x} \geq 0} \min_i \{\mu_i([\mathbf{Bx}]_i)\} = \max_{\mathbf{x} \geq 0} \min_i \left(1 - \frac{[\mathbf{Bx}]_i - d_i}{p_i}\right). \qquad (8.38)$$

By introducing a new variable λ and performing normalization, we can transform Eq. (8.38) into the following standard linear programming problem:

Maximize λ

such that $\lambda p_i + [\mathbf{Bx}]_i \leq d_i + p_i, \qquad i = 1, 2,\dots, m+1,$ (8.39)

$\qquad \mathbf{x} \geq \mathbf{0},$

which can be solved using conventional approaches.

Example 8.5

[Zimmermann, 1976]. A company wants to decide on the size and structure of its truck fleet. Four trucks, x_1, x_2, x_3, x_4, of different sizes are considered. The objective is to minimize cost, and the constraints are to supply all customers who have a strong seasonally fluctuating demand. At first, the standard linear programming problem is formulated as follows:

$$\text{Minimize } f(\mathbf{x}) = 41{,}400x_1 + 44{,}300x_2 + 48{,}100x_3 + 49{,}100x_4$$

$$\text{such that } 0.84x_1 + 1.44x_2 + 2.16x_3 + 2.4x_4 \geq 170$$

$$16x_1 + 16x_2 + 16x_3 + 16x_4 \geq 1{,}300$$

$$x_1 \geq 6, \, x_2, x_3, x_4 \geq 0.$$

Then, the corresponding fuzzy linear programming problem is formulated based on the aspiration level $z = 3.7$ million and the following parameters:

Low bounds of the tolerance intervals: $d_1 = 3{,}700{,}000$, $d_2 = 170$, $d_3 = 1{,}300$, and $d_4 = 6$, Spreads of tolerance intervals: $p_1 = 500{,}000$, $p_2 = 10$, $p_3 = 100$, and $p_4 = 6$.

After dividing all the rows in Eq. (8.39) by their respective p_i values and rearranging the position λ, the fuzzy linear programming problem becomes

$$\text{Maximize } \lambda$$

$$\text{such that } 0.083x_1 + 0.089x_2 + 0.096x_3 + 0.098x_4 + \lambda \leq 8.4$$

$$0.084x_1 + 0.144x_2 + 0.216x_3 + 0.240x_4 - \lambda \geq 16$$

$$0.160x_1 + 0.160x_2 + 0.160x_3 + 0.160x_4 - \lambda \geq 12$$

$$0.167x_1 - \lambda \geq 0$$

$$\lambda, x_1, x_2, x_3, x_4 \geq 0.$$

The solutions for the above nonfuzzy and fuzzy linear programming problems are

Nonfuzzy	Fuzzy
$x_1 = 6$	$x_1 = 17.414$
$x_2 = 16.29$	$x_2 = 0$
$x_3 = 0$	$x_3 = 0$
$x_4 = 58.96$	$x_4 = 66.54$
$z = 3{,}864{,}975$	$z = 3{,}988{,}250$

The values for the constraints are

	Nonfuzzy	Fuzzy
1.	170	174.33
2.	1,300	1,343.328
3.	6	17.414

From the solution, we find that "leeway" has been provided to all constraints at an additional cost of 3.2% using fuzzy linear programming.

8.3 FUZZY DATABASES

In real-world applications, because of the need for data integrity and independence, data from measurement devices or sensors must be efficiently stored and then processed. Because of these requirements, research on database systems has been very active since the

1960s. Database systems have traditionally modeled a precise universe where all values are known. However, in many real-world situations, especially in fields directly involving people, such as human-machine systems, decision making, and natural language processing, there is a great deal of ambiguous data whose values are imprecise with fuzzy connotations and are sometimes even missing. To use this ambiguous data constructively, people have tried to incorporate fuzzy set theory into standard databases and have built *fuzzy databases.*

There are important benefits in extending data models to incorporate fuzzy and imprecise information. First, it provides a more accurate representation of the database universe. Second, it allows for data retrieval based on *similarity* of values and thus provides the user with considerably more flexibility in data manipulation. Third, it provides much help in the coupling of artificial intelligence and databases, which has attracted growing research interest in improving the functionality and applicability of database systems.

The first generation of databases consisted of *network* and *hierarchical* data models. Because of the lack of physical independence of these models, *relational* databases, developed in the early 1970s, dominated research efforts in the 1980s and became the second generation of databases. The growing complexity of data modeling requirements, especially those involving complex objects and large amounts of data in scientific databases, led to the development of *extended relational models, semantic database models,* and *object-oriented databases.* Among these, object-oriented database systems mark the genesis of the third generation.

In general, there are two approaches to incorporating fuzzy information into databases. The first is to maintain the standard data model and allows fuzzy queries, and the second is to retain the standard database language (e.g., SQL in a relational database) and extends the data model. First-generation databases, network data models, have not received much attention in fuzzy database research because of the obstacle caused by the functionality condition of network databases indicating that the same record cannot appear in more than one set. In this section, we shall introduce some examples of fuzzy relational databases and fuzzy object-oriented databases [Petry et al., 1992].

8.3.1 Fuzzy Relational Databases

In a relational model, the database is a group of *relations.* The relations are essentially the same as the relations of set theory and are expressed in the form of two-dimensional tables. The columns of a table (relation) are called *attributes;* thus each row (called a *tuple*) is a sequence of attribute values. For each attribute, there is a prescribed set of values, called the *domain,* from which values may be selected. Each element of the domain set has the same structure, for example, integers, real numbers, or character strings.

Almost all fuzzy databases are extensions of relational models. Approaches to the representation of inexact information in relational data models include simply adding a membership attribute value to each relation by substituting similarity for equality in the application of query terms and relational calculus and by allowing data values to be possibility distributions. More than one of these approaches can be applied at the same time. Let us consider an example of a similarity-relational model [Petry et al., 1992].

Example 8.6

Consider the relation BOOKS' in Table 8.2 of a library information system. The similarity relation for the attribute COLOR and its domain D_{COLOR} is shown in Table 8.3. Assume the following query is asked:

"Print the titles of the books which are red or close to red and written by author A2."

This query is expressed as

```
BOOKS" = MERGE (BOOKS') WITH Level (COLOR) ≥ 0.6,
         Level (BNO, PRICE) ≥ 0.0, Level (AUTHOR, TITLE) = 1.0,
```

where MERGE is a relational algebra operation for picking up data for the indicated domain only. What follows WITH indicates the threshold value, meaning that we view elements with a similarity of 0.6 or more for the domain COLOR as being the same. We can now use the SQL-like language to answer the query:

```
SELECT TITLE FROM BOOKS" WHERE AUTHOR = {A2} AND COLOR = {RED}.
```

TABLE 8.2 Relation BOOKS' as a Book Inventory Used in the Library Information Systems in Example 8.6

BOOKS'				
BNO	AUTHOR	TITLE	PRICE	COLOR
1	A1	T1	P1	RED
1	A2	T1	P1	RED
1	A1	T1	P1	RED
1	A2	T1	P1	RED
2	A1	T2	P2	LIGHT RED
2	A1	T2	P2	LIGHT RED
3	A1	T3	P3	ORANGE
3	A1	T3	P3	ORANGE
3	A1	T3	P3	ORANGE
4	A2	T4	P4	BLUE

TABLE 8.3 The Similarity Relation for the Attribute COLOR in Example 8.6

	Red	Reddish	Orange	Light Red	Blue
Red	1	0.8	0.4	0.6	0
Reddish	0.8	1	0.5	0.5	0
Orange	0.4	0.5	1	0.3	0
Light Red	0.6	0.5	0.3	1	0
Blue	0	0	0	0	1

$D_{COLOR} = \{$Red, Reddish, Orange, Light Red, Blue$\}$

Here, the minimum threshold value for the domain COLOR is set as 0.6, meaning that if two colors in COLOR have a similarity of 0.6 or more, then they are viewed as the same color. The resulting solution is shown in Table 8.4, and the answer to the query is {T1, T2}. If one chooses the threshold value for COLOR as 0.3, then the query is

```
BOOKS" = MERGE (BOOKS') WITH Level (COLOR) ≥ 0.3,
         Level (BNO, PRICE) = 0.0, Level (AUTHOR, TITLE) = 1.0
```

Then the result is shown in Table 8.5, and the answer to the query is $\{T_1, T_2, T_3\}$. Note that two kinds of brackets are used to designate attribute values in Tables 8.4 and 8.5. The bracket { } is a multivalued expression which uses AND semantics among its elements. This means that each member of the set necessarily and precisely belongs to the set. The bracket [ ] is a fuzzy expression which has elements with an imprecise relationship among them. This relationship is interpreted as XOR here, which means that exactly only one element of the set can possibly belong. In addition to MERGE, other relational algebra operations such as *selection, projection, union, difference, unmerge,* and *Cartesian product* have also been defined [Yazici et al., 1990].

8.3.2 Fuzzy Object-Oriented Databases

The object-oriented approach to data modeling views the universe as consisting of a collection of interacting objects, each of which represents an entity or an event of interest. An object is completely specified by its *identity, state,* and *behavior.* An object identifier maintains the identity of an object, thus distinguishing it from all others. The state of an object consists of the values of its attributes, where every attribute takes a value from a domain. The behavior of an object is specified by the set of methods that operate on the state. The

TABLE 8.4 The BOOKS" Relation, Where Similar Tuples are Merged and the Level Value of the Attribute COLOR = 0.6 in Example 8.6

		BOOKS"		
BNO	AUTHOR	TITLE	PRICE	COLOR
[1, 2]	{A1, A2}	{T1, T2}	[P1, P2]	[RED, LIGHT RED]
[3]	{A1}	{T3}	[P3]	[ORANGE]
[4]	{A2}	{T4}	[P4]	[BLUE]

TABLE 8.5 The BOOKS''' Relation, Where Similar Tuples are Merged and the Level Value of the Attribute COLOR = 0.3 in Example 8.6

		BOOKS'''		
BNO	AUTHOR	TITLE	PRICE	COLOR
[1, 2, 3]	{A1, A2}	{T1, T2, T3}	[P1, P2, P3]	[RED, LIGHT RED, ORANGE]
[4]	{A2}	{T4}	[P4]	[BLUE]

most powerful aspect of an object-oriented database (OODB) is its ability to model *inheritance*. Similar objects are grouped together into a *type* which is completely specified by its structure and a set of methods. A type with its extension (data) constitutes a *class*. A class may inherit all the methods and attributes of its *superclass*. Class-subclass relationships form a class hierarchy which is similar to a generalization-specification relationship. Class-subclass relationships can be represented as follows:

$$C_i \subseteq_s C_{i+1} \subseteq_s \cdots \subseteq_s C_n, \tag{8.40}$$

where C_n is the root (basic) class and C_i is the most refined (leaf) class.

Object-oriented databases offer considerable representational capability with respect to fuzzy information. Two levels of fuzziness may be represented. The first is the fuzziness of object attribute values, which is also adopted in fuzzy relational databases. The second is the impreciseness of object membership in class values; that is, the class hierarchy is generalized to include the concept of membership. A subclass is represented now by a pair $(C_i, \mu(C_{i+1}))$, the second element of which represents the membership of C_i in its immediate subclass C_{i+1}. Hence, Eq. (8.40) becomes

$$(o_i, \mu(C_i)) \subseteq_s (C_i, \mu(C_{i+1})) \subseteq_s (C_{i+1}, \mu(C_{i+2})) \subseteq_s \cdots \subseteq_s (C_n, \mu(C_{n+1})), \tag{8.41}$$

which indicates that the object o_i belongs to the class C_i with degree $\mu(C_i)$, the class C_i belongs to its immediate subclass C_{i+1} with degree $\mu(C_{i+1})$, and so on.

An object o in a fuzzy OODB is expressed as

$$o = (i, \langle a_{k1} : i_{k1}, a_{k2} : i_{k2}, \ldots, a_{km} : i_{km} \rangle, \langle \mu_o(C_i), \mu_o(C_{i+1}), \ldots, \mu_o(C_n) \rangle), \tag{8.42}$$

where i is the identity of the object, a_{kj} is its jth attribute with a value coming from the object with identity i_{kj}, $\mu_o(C_i)$ is the degree to which object o belongs to class C_i, and $\mu_o(C_{i+1})$ is the degree to which object o belongs to class C_{i+1}, and so on. An important data manipulation operator MERGE in fuzzy OODB can combine two object instances of a class into a single object instance according to the similarity of an attribute value. The MERGE operator at the same time maintains the membership relationship existing between the object or class and its class or subclass.

Example 8.7

[Petry et al., 1992]. Consider the fuzzy OODB shown in Fig. 8.7. Two classes considered here are Educational (C_1) and Toy (C_2). We assume the following instances of Toy in Fig. 8.7.

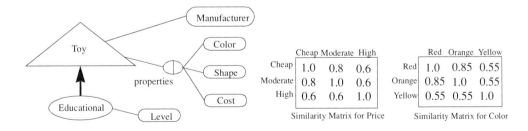

	Cheap	Moderate	High
Cheap	1.0	0.8	0.6
Moderate	0.8	1.0	0.6
High	0.6	0.6	1.0

Similarity Matrix for Price

	Red	Orange	Yellow
Red	1.0	0.85	0.55
Orange	0.85	1.0	0.55
Yellow	0.55	0.55	1.0

Similarity Matrix for Color

Figure 8.7 Schematic representation of a database of Toys with similarity matrices for "price" and "color" in Example 8.7.

$$o_1 = (i_1, \langle manufacturer : i_{11}, properties : i_{12} \rangle, \langle 1 \rangle)$$

$$o_2 = (i_2, \langle manufacturer : i_{11}, properties : i_{13} \rangle, \langle 1 \rangle)$$

$$o_3 = (i_3, \langle manufacturer : i_{14}, properties : i_{15} \rangle, \langle 1 \rangle)$$

$$o_4 = (i_4, \langle manufacturer : i_{14}, properties : i_{16} \rangle, \langle 1 \rangle)$$

$$o_5 = (i_{12}, \langle shape : i_{17}, color : i_{19}, cost : i_{22} \rangle)$$

$$o_6 = (i_{13}, \langle shape : i_{18}, color : i_{20}, cost : i_{22} \rangle)$$

$$o_7 = (i_{15}, \langle shape : i_{17}, color : i_{19}, cost : i_{22} \rangle)$$

$$o_8 = (i_{16}, \langle shape : i_{18}, color : i_{21}, cost : i_{22} \rangle)$$

$$o_9 = (i_{11}, \text{`}KiddyKars\text{'}), \quad o_{10} = (i_{14}, \text{`}TinkerToys\text{'})$$

$$o_{11} = (i_{17}, \text{`}spheroid\text{'}), \quad o_{12} = (i_{18}, \text{`}parallelopiped\text{'})$$

$$o_{13} = (i_{19}, \text{`}red\text{'}), \quad o_{14} = (i_{20}, \text{`}orange\text{'}), \quad o_{15} = (i_{72}, \text{`}red\text{'})$$

$$o_{16} = (i_{21}, \text{`}yellow\text{'}), \quad o_{17} = (i_{22}, \text{`}cheap\text{'})$$

$$o_{23} = (i_{23}, \langle manufacturer : i_{11}, properties : i_{12}, level : i_{27} \rangle, \langle 0.95, 1 \rangle)$$

$$o_{24} = (i_{24}, \langle manufacturer : i_{11}, properties : i_{13}, level : i_{28} \rangle, \langle 0.75, 1 \rangle)$$

$$o_{25} = (i_{25}, \langle manufacturer : i_{14}, properties : i_{13}, level : i_{29} \rangle, \langle 0.9, 1 \rangle)$$

$$o_{26} = (i_{26}, \langle manufacturer : i_{14}, properties : i_{16}, level : i_{30} \rangle, \langle 0.8, 1 \rangle)$$

$$o_{27} = (i_{27}, \text{`}sophomore\text{'}), \quad o_{28} = (i_{28}, \text{`}junior\text{'})$$

$$o_{29} = (i_{29}, \text{`}freshman\text{'}), \quad o_{30} = (i_{30}, \text{`}senior\text{'})$$

where for objects o_1 to o_4, $\mu_{o_1}(C_2) = \mu_{o_2}(C_2) = \mu_{o_3}(C_2) = \mu_{o_4}(C_2) = 1$; for objects o_{23} to o_{26}, $\mu_{o_{23}}(C_1) = 0.95$, $\mu_{o_{24}}(C_1) = 0.75$, $\mu_{o_{25}}(C_1) = 0.9$, $\mu_{o_{26}}(C_1) = 0.8$, and $\mu_{o_{23}}(C_2) = \mu_{o_{24}}(C_2) = \mu_{o_{25}}(C_2) = \mu_{o_{26}}(C_2) = 1$. Now suppose the following query is proposed: "Retrieve educational toys that are red in color."

```
Red_Toys = MERGE (Toys) WITH Level (Toy.Properties.Color) ≥ 0.85,
Level(Toy.Manufacturer) ≥ 0.0, Level (Toy.Properties.Shape) ≥ 0.0,
Level(Toy.Properties.Cost) ≥ 0.0, Membership(Toys.Educational) ≥
0.85.
```

The query asks for toys that are "near" red in color, with the corresponding values of manufacturer, shape, and cost being immaterial. The red and the educational levels are based on the attribute level and object membership grade values supplied. This query will give the following new objects:

$$o'_1 = (i'_1, \langle manufacturer : i'_{11}, properties : i'_{12}, level : i'_{27} \rangle, \langle 0.95, 1 \rangle)$$

$$o'_{11} = (i'_{11}, \{i_{11}, i_{14}\})$$

$$o'_{12} = (i'_{12}, \langle shape : i'_{13}, color : i'_{14}, cost : i'_{15} \rangle)$$

$$o'_{13} = (i'_{13}, \{i_{17}, i_{18}\}), \quad o'_{14} = (i'_{14}, \{i_{19}, i_{20}\})$$

$$o'_{15} = (i'_{15}, \{i_{22}\}), \quad o'_{27} = (i'_{27}, \{i_{27}, i_{29}\}),$$

where we assume the combination function used for object membership levels is the max operator. The result for the query retrieves the answer that the manufacturers are Kiddy Kars and Tinker Toys and that the toys are parallelopiped and spherical in shape, are all cheap in price, and are suitable for the educational levels of freshmen and sophomores. Note that the new membership level has the maximum of the individual object membership levels.

8.4 HUMAN-MACHINE INTERACTIONS

Human-machine studies involve the investigation of complex and ill-defined relationships among people, machines, and physical environments. The main goal is to remove the incompatibilities between humans and tasks and to optimize the human-machine system with respect to the physical and psychological characteristics of the users. Such human-centered systems are very complex and difficult to analyze because of a variety of interacting factors and their inherent uncertainty. The uncertainty includes the vagueness of the natural language, the vagueness of the relationships between people and their working environments, and the fuzziness inherent in human thinking processes and subjective perceptions of the outside world. Figure 8.8 shows human-machine interactions and the fuzziness in them. In this figure, the human operator interpretation block represents traditional human-machine interfaces, which include (1) information sensing and receiving, (2) information processing, (3) decision making, and (4) control actions. The complex work systems block includes environmental and situational variables. In this connection, fuzzy set theory offers a useful approach to the analysis and design of human-machine interactions [Karwowski and Salvendy, 1992; Karwowski and Mital, 1986]. In this section, we shall introduce the fuzzy modeling of human-machine interactions.

Fuzzy methodologies can be very useful in the modeling of human-machine interactions in general, and of human-computer interactions systems (HCISs) in particular, by

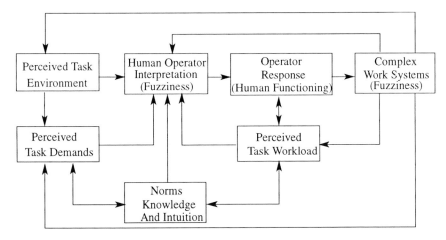

Figure 8.8 Fuzziness in human-machine interactions. (Adapted from Evans and Karwowski [1986], Copyright 1986 Elsevier Science Publishers B.V.)

modeling vague and imprecise relationships between the user and the computer. A HCIS is formally defined as a quintuple [Karwowski et al., 1990]:

$$\text{HCIS} = (T, U, C, E, I), \tag{8.43}$$

where T is task requirements (physical and cognitive), U is user characteristics (physical and cognitive), C is computer characteristics (hardware and software, including computer interfaces), E is an environment, and I is a set of interactions. The set of interactions I embodies all possible interactions among T, U, and C in E, for example, the interaction between the data stored in the computer memory and the corresponding knowledge of the user. The interaction between U and C reflects the narrow concept of the traditional human-computer interface.

Recently, there have been some initial attempts to incorporate fuzziness in HCIS research. One of the models of computer user information processing is the GOMS concept [Card et al., 1983; Karwowski et al., 1989, 1990]. According to the GOMS model, the user's cognitive structure consists of four components: (1) a set of *Goals*, (2) a set of *Operators*, (3) a set of *Methods* for achieving the goals, and (4) a set of *Selection* rules for choosing among competing methods for goals.

Fuzziness can be introduced into any one or more of the four components to result in a fuzzy GOMS model. In particular, the selection rules (reasoning process) can be either probabilistic or fuzzy. The example presented below refers to the fuzzy GOMS model in which the goals (description) and the operators (nature of acts) are precise and the methods (description) and the selection rules (reasoning processes) are fuzzy.

Example 8.8

[Karwowski et al., 1989]. This example uses a fuzzy GOMS model for a text editing task. The experiment performed for such modeling consists of the following steps:

1. The subject performed a familiar text editing task using a screen editor.
2. The methods by which the subject achieved her goals (word location) as well as the selection rules were elicited.
3. It was established that many of the rules had fuzzy components.
4. Several membership functions for fuzzy terms used by the subject were derived.
5. The possibility measure was used to predict the methods that the subject would use.
6. The selected methods were compared to nonfuzzy predictions and actual experimental data.

The subject did not know the contents of the file to be edited and was familiar with and regularly used the visual screen editor. In terms of the GOMS model, the goal (G) here is to place the cursor on the word to be changed; the operators (O) include (1) Control-D: scrolls down one half of the screen; (2) Control-F: jumps to the next page; (3) Return key: moves the cursor to the left side of the page and down one line; (4) Arrow up or down: moves the cursor directly up or down; and (5) Pattern search: places the cursor on the first occurrence of the pattern.

The methods (M) in the GOMS model were obtained by *knowledge elicitation:* the subject was asked to describe why she chose a particular method, for example,

Subject: The word (to be changed) is more than half a screen down, so I will use the Control-D method and then Return-key to reach the word.

Knowledge Engineer: How strongly do you feel that it is more than half?

Subject: Very strong, by, say 0.8.

In this way, the methods used and the membership function of fuzzy terms can be found by having the subject perform many tasks while verbalizing the rules. As a result, the subject verbalized five cursor placement rules and seven fuzzy descriptors. The following rules were used:

1. If the word is *more than half a screen* from the cursor and on the same screen, or if the word is *more than half a screen* from the cursor and across the printed page, use operator 1.
2. If the word is *more than 70 lines* and the pattern is *not distinct,* use operator 2.
3. If the word is *less than half a screen* and *on the left half of the page,* use operator 3.
4. If the word is *less than half a screen* and *on the right half of the page,* use operator 4.
5. If the word is distinct and *more than 70 lines away,* use operator 5.

An example of the membership function for the "right-hand side of the screen" elicited in the experiment is given in Fig. 8.9.

Having the G and O Components defined and the M component elicited, what remains to be specified in the GOMS model is its S component—the rule selection (reasoning processes). Rule matching and selection as introduced in the fuzzy control techniques in Sec. 7.1.4 were adopted as the S component here. For example, consider the goal to be achieved: "Move down 27 lines to a position in column 20." First, the following membership grades were obtained:

For rule 1: μ (*more than half a screen*) = 0.4
For rule 2: μ (*more than 70 lines*) = 0.0
For rule 3: μ (*less than half a screen*) = 0.3 and μ (*left half of the page*) = 0.4
For rule 4: μ (*less than half a screen*) = 0.3 and μ (*right half of the page*) = 0.9
For rule 5: μ (*more than 70 lines away*) = 0.0.

Then since $\max\{0.4, 0.0, (0.3 \wedge 0.4), (0.9 \wedge 0.3), 0.0\} = 0.4$, the most applicable one is rule 1 and thus operator 1, that is, Control-D method will be selected. All the fuzzy GOMS model predictions in the experiment were checked against the selection rule decisions made by the subject. Out of 17 decisions, the fuzzy GOMS model predicted 76% correctly, but the nonfuzzy GOMS model predicted only 47% correctly.

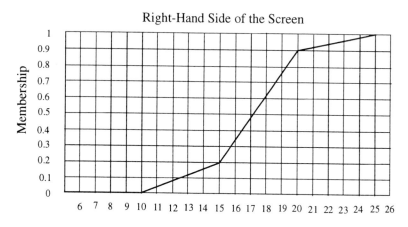

Figure 8.9 Membership function for the fuzzy set "Right-hand side of screen" in Example 8.8. (Adapted from Karowski et al. [1990], © Ablex Publishing Corporation.)

8.5 CONCLUDING REMARKS

Besides the fuzzy classification methods discussed in this chapter, a practical example of pattern recognition based on fuzzy relations can be found in [López de Mántaras and Aguilar Martin, 1983]. One approach not covered in this chapter is pattern classification methods based on fuzzy pattern matching [Grabisch and Sugeno, 1992]. In these methods, pattern recognition is performed by matching fuzzy patterns; that is, finding the similarity between two fuzzy sets. One important concept involving fuzzy clustering is the *core* of a cluster. Since each pattern in fuzzy clustering is characterized by the degree of membership in a given cluster, we can distinguish between patterns forming the main structure of the cluster (i.e., the core) and those that are outliers [Pedrycz, 1990a]. Other important topics in fuzzy pattern recognition include fuzzy image processing [Pal, 1992], fuzzy computer vision [Krishnapuram and Keller, 1992], fuzzy geometry [Rosenfeld, 1992], and so on. A complete and comprehensive collection of papers on fuzzy pattern recognition can be found in [Bezdek and Pal, 1992].

Symmetric fuzzy linear programming problems are discussed under fuzzy mathematical programming. Other important problems include linear programming with fuzzy constraints and crisp objectives [Zimmermann, 1992], fuzzy mathematical programming with fuzzy parameters [Negoita and Sularia, 1976; Ramík and Rímánek, 1985; Tanaka and Asai, 1984; Rommelfanger et al., 1989; Delgado et al., 1989; Dubois, 1987; Orlovsky, 1985], fuzzy multicriteria decision making [Yager, 1978, 1992b], and fuzzy dynamic programming [Terano et al., 1992; Zimmermann, 1991; Kacprzyk, 1983]. The reader is referred to [Zimmermann, 1991; Dubois, 1987; Sakawa, 1984; Kickert, 1978] for further studies and more references on fuzzy mathematical programming. Real applications of fuzzy mathematical programming include logistics, which is the determination of time schedules for containerships [Ernst, 1982; Zimmermann, 1992], and operations research [Zimmermann 1991].

For fuzzy databases, fuzzy relational databases and fuzzy object-oriented databases are discussed in this chapter. A representative fuzzy relational database is called a *possibility distribution-relational model* [Umano et al., 1978; Umano, 1982]. This model has possibility distributions as attributive values. Other approaches to fuzzy databases utilizing possibility distributions include [Umano, 1983; Prade and Testemale, 1984, 1985; Zemankova-Leech and Kandel, 1984]. Another important topic related to databases is *information retrieval*. The reader is referred to [Kraft and Buell, 1983; Terano et al., 1992] for details on fuzzy information retrieval.

One of the most important problems in human-machine systems is the exchange of information between humans and machines (computers). Hirota et al. [1986] proposed a data entry system based on extended fuzzy expressions such as type II fuzzy sets and probabilistic sets. Further references on human-machine communication describe using color scales to model subjectively defined categories [Benson, 1982], using a linguistic approach to pragmatic communication in graphic displays [Simcox, 1984], and using a fuzzy graphic rating scale [Hesketh et al., 1988]. The reader is referred to [Karwowski and Mital, 1986] for extensive research on the applications of fuzzy set theory to human-machine interactions. Other research on the modeling of human-machine interactions includes the type of fuzziness in layperson perception [Saaty, 1977], the perception of visual and vestibular in industrial inspection tasks [Willaeys and Malvache, 1979], human vocal patterns [Hirsh et al., 1981], a fuzzy model of driver behavior in lane control [Kramer and Rohr, 1982], a human reliability model [Terano et al., 1983], fuzzy models in information retrieval tasks [Boy and Kuss, 1986], and a fuzzy model that assesses the acceptability of stresses in manual lifting tasks [Karwowski et al., 1992].

8.6 PROBLEMS

8.1 Verify Eq. (8.12) by referring to the related results derived in Sec. 3.4.

8.2 Three classes of patterns, $\Omega = \{\omega_1, \omega_2, \omega_3\} = \{(a, b), (c, d), (e, f)\}$, are established in the feature space in Fig. 8.2 with the pattern e lying in the middle of the line connecting a and c, and the pattern f lying in the middle of the line connecting a and b. Repeat Examples 8.1 and 8.2 for designing a classifier R to classify these three classes by using the given patterns as the training data, and determine the discrimination power of the two features on the given patterns.

8.3 Derive Eqs. (8.22) and (8.23) in detail by differentiating the objective function in Eq. (8.21) with respective to v_i and u_{ij}.

8.4 Show the convergence of the FCM algorithm. (*Hint:* Refer to [Bezdek, 1981].)

8.5 Write a computer program for implementing the FCM algorithm and redo Example 8.3 using the following starting partition matrix:

$$U^{(0)} = \begin{bmatrix} 0.8 & 0.2 & 0.8 & 0.8 & \cdots & 0.8 \\ 0.2 & 0.8 & 0.2 & 0.2 & \cdots & 0.2 \end{bmatrix}_{2 \times 15}.$$

Sketch the resulting graphs corresponding to Fig. 8.4.

8.6 With reference to Example 8.4, compute the values of the three validity indicators in Eqs. (8.24)–(8.27) of the butterfly example in Example 8.3.

8.7 Consider the constraints with crisp inequality in addition to the constraints with fuzzy inequality in Eq. (8.33). Write down the corresponding standard linear programming problem like the one in Eq. (8.39).

8.8 Repeat Example 8.5 but set the low bounds of the tolerance intervals as $d_1 = 4,200,000$, $d_2 = 100$, $d_3 = 1,000$, and $d_4 = 10$, and the spreads of tolerance intervals as $p_1 = 550,000$, $p_2 = 8, p_3 = 90$, and $p_4 = 8$.

8.9 Consider the following linear programming problem:

$$\text{Minimize } 3x_1 + 5x_2 + x_3$$

$$\text{such that } 4x_1 + 3x_2 + 3x_3 \leq 50$$

$$4x_1 + x_2 + x_3 \leq 7$$

$$2x_2 + x_3 \geq 3 \qquad x_1, x_2, x_3 \geq 0.$$

(a) Find the (crisp) optimal solution.

(b) Assume the low bounds of the tolerance intervals for the fuzzy constraints are $d_1 = 50$, $d_2 = 7, d_3 = 3$, and the spreads of tolerance intervals are $p_1 = 10, p_2 = 14, p_3 = 5$. Use the model in Eq. (8.39) to determine the optimal solution of the resulting (symmetric) fuzzy linear programming problem with crispy ojbective and compare it with the crisp optimal solution obtained in part (a).

8.10 Replace the following linear interval programming problem by a standard linear programming problem by considering the worst case in which the constraints are guaranteed to be satisfied:

$$\text{Minimize } 6x_1 + 5x_2$$

$$\text{such that } [0.03, 0.06]\, x_1 + [0.07, 0.09]\, x_2 \subseteq [1.37, 6.5]$$

$$[0.2, 0.7]\, x_1 - [0.01, 0.05]\, x_2 \subseteq [0.42, 5]$$

$$x_1, x_2 \geq 0.$$

Solve the resulting standard linear programming problem and check whether the constraints in the original linear interval programming problem are satisfied.

8.11 Consider the fuzzy database in Example 8.6. Assume the following query is asked: "Print the titles of the books that are close to orange and written by author A1." The threshold value for COLOR is chosen as 0.4.

(a) Express this query in the SQR language.

(b) Express the answer to this query in a table like Table 8.4 or 8.5.

8.12 Consider the fuzzy OODB shown in Fig. 8.7. Suppose the following query is proposed. "Retrieve educational toys that are cheap and yellow in color."

```
Yellow_Toys = MERGE (Toys) WITH Level (Toy.Properties.Color) ≥ 0.75,
Level (Toy.Manufacturer) ≥ 0.0, Level (Toy.Properties.Shape) ≥ 0.0,
Level (Toy.Properties.Cost) ≥ 0.6, Membership(Toys.Educational) ≥ 0.75.
```

What new objects will be added for this query?

8.13 Consider the block diagram of human-machine interactions shown in Fig. 8.8. Discuss what and how fuzziness could be incorporated in each functional block; that is, how each functional block could be fuzzified.

8.14 Formulate the problem described in Example 8.8 as a quintuple: HCIS $= (T, U, C, E, I)$; that is, specify the five constituents, T, U, C, E, I, in this problem.

8.15 Consider the GOMS model introduced in Example 8.8. If the goal to be achieved is "Move down 50 lines to a position in column 17," which rule and operator should be selected?

9

Introduction to Artificial Neural Networks

Neural networks are a promising new generation of information processing systems that demonstrate the ability to learn, recall, and generalize from training patterns or data. In Part II of this book (Chaps. 9–16), we shall explore and study their fundamental architectures, operations, properties, learning ability, and applications. Basic models, learning rules, and distributed representations of neural networks are discussed in this chapter, and the material covered here will be used extensively in the next seven chapters.

9.1 FUNDAMENTAL CONCEPTS OF ARTIFICIAL NEURAL NETWORKS

Artificial neural networks (ANNs) are systems that are deliberately constructed to make use of some organizational principles resembling those of the human brain. They represent the promising new generation of information processing systems. ANNs are good at tasks such as pattern matching and classification, function approximation, optimization, vector quantization, and data clustering, while traditional computers, because of their architecture, are inefficient at these tasks, especially pattern-matching tasks. However, traditional computers are faster in algorithmic computational tasks and precise arithmetic operations.

ANNs have a large number of highly interconnected *processing elements* (*nodes* or *units*) that usually operate in parallel and are configured in regular architectures. The *collective* behavior of an ANN, like a human brain, demonstrates the ability to learn, recall, and generalize from training patterns or data. ANNs are inspired by modeling networks of real (biological) neurons in the brain. Hence, the processing elements in ANNs are also called *artificial neurons,* or simply *neurons.* A human brain consists of approximately 10^{11} neurons of many different types. A schematic diagram of a typical biological neuron is shown in Fig. 9.1(a). A typical neuron has three major parts: the *cell body* or *soma*, where the cell nucleus is located, the *dendrites*, and the *axon*. Dendrites are treelike networks of nerve fiber connected to the cell body. An axon is a single, long, cylindric connection extending from the cell body and carrying impulses (signals) from the neuron. The end of an axon splits into strands or a fine arborization. Each strand terminates in a small bulblike organ called a *synapse*, where the neuron introduces its signal to the neighboring neurons. The receiving ends of these junctions on the neighboring neurons can be found both on the dendrites and on the cell bodies themselves. There are approximately 10^4 synapses per neuron in a human brain.

The signals reaching a synapse and received by dendrites are electric impulses. Such signal transmission involves a complex chemical process in which specific transmitter substances are released from the sending side of the junction. This raises or lowers the electric potential inside the body of the receiving cell. The receiving cell *fires* if its electric potential reaches a *threshold*, and a pulse or *action potential* of fixed strength and duration is sent out through the axon to the axonal arborization to synaptic junctions to other neurons. After firing, a neuron has to wait for a period of time called the *refractory period* before it can fire again. Synapses are *excitatory* if they let passing impulses cause the firing of the receiving neuron, or *inhibitory* if they let passing impulses hinder the firing of the neuron.

Figure 9.1(b) shows a simple mathematical model of the above-mentioned biological neuron proposed by McCulloch and Pitts [1943], usually called an *M-P neuron*. In this model, the ith processing element computes a weighted sum of its inputs and outputs $y_i = 1$ (firing) or 0 (not firing) according to whether this weighted input sum is above or below a certain threshold θ_i:

$$y_i(t+1) = a\left(\sum_{j=1}^{m} w_{ij} x_j(t) - \theta_i \right),\tag{9.1}$$

where the activation function $a(f)$ is a unit step function:

$$a(f) = \begin{cases} 1 & \text{if } f \geq 0 \\ 0 & \text{otherwise.} \end{cases}\tag{9.2}$$

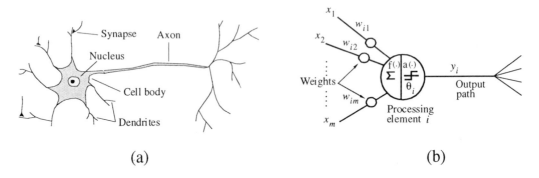

(a) (b)

Figure 9.1 Correspondence between a biological neuron and an artificial neuron. (a) Schematic diagram of a biological neuron. (b) Schematic diagram of a McCulloch and Pitts neuron.

Introduction to Artificial Neural Networks   Chap. 9

The weight w_{ij} represents the strength of the synapse (called the *connection* or *link*) connecting neuron j (source) to neuron i (destination). A positive weight corresponds to an excitatory synapse, and a negative weight corresponds to an inhibitory synapse. If $w_{ij} = 0$, then there is no connection between the two neurons. In Eq. (9.1), it is assumed that a unit relay elapses between the time instants t and $(t + 1)$. This assumption will also be used in our further discussion of this subject.

Although simplicity models a biological neuron as a binary threshold unit, a McCulloch-Pitts neuron has substantial computing potential. It can perform the basic logic operations NOT, OR, and AND when weights and thresholds are selected accordingly. Since any multivariable combinational function can be implemented by these basic logic operations, a synchronous assembly of such neurons is capable of performing universal computations, much like an ordinary digital computer. Several generalizations or variations of the M-P neuron, which is the basic component of ANNs, will be introduced later.

In summary, an ANN is a parallel distributed information processing structure with the following characteristics:

1. It is a neurally inspired mathematical model.
2. It consists of a large number of highly interconnected processing elements.
3. Its connections (weights) hold the knowledge.
4. A processing element can dynamically respond to its input stimulus, and the response completely depends on its local information; that is, the input signals arrive at the processing element via impinging connections and connection weights.
5. It has the ability to learn, recall, and generalize from training data by assigning or adjusting the connection weights.
6. Its collective behavior demonstrates the computational power, and no single neuron carries specific information (*distributed representation* property).

Because of these characteristics, other commonly used names for ANNs are *parallel distributed processing models, connectionist models, self-organizing systems, neurocomputing systems,* and *neuromorphic systems.*

9.2 BASIC MODELS AND LEARNING RULES OF ANNS

Models of ANNs are specified by three basic entities: models of the neurons themselves, models of synaptic interconnections and structures, and the training or learning rules for updating the connecting weights. We shall introduce the basics of these three entities in the following sections.

9.2.1 Processing Elements

The function of a M-P neuron expressed in Eqs. (9.1) and (9.2) can be extended to a general model of a processing element (PE). As shown in Fig. 9.1(b), the information processing of a PE can be viewed as consisting of two parts: input and output. Associated with the input of a PE is an integration function f which serves to combine information, activation, or evidence from an external source or other PEs into a *net input* to the PE. This is usually a linear function of the inputs x_j to the PE as in the case of a M-P neuron:

$$f_i \triangleq \text{net}_i = \sum_{j=1}^{m} w_{ij} x_j - \theta_i, \tag{9.3}$$

where θ_i is the threshold of the *i*th PE. More-complex integration functions can also be considered as follows.

- *Quadratic function*:

$$f_i = \sum_{j=1}^{m} w_{ij} x_j^2 - \theta_i, \tag{9.4}$$

- *Spherical function*:

$$f_i = \rho^{-2} \sum_{j=1}^{m} (x_j - w_{ij})^2 - \theta_i, \tag{9.5}$$

where ρ and w_{ij} are the radius and the center of the sphere, respectively. The *spherical hole* integration function is just the reciprocal of Eq. (9.5).

- *Polynomial function*:

$$f_i = \sum_{j=1}^{m} \sum_{k=1}^{m} w_{ijk} x_j x_k + x_j^{\alpha_j} + x_k^{\alpha_k} - \theta_i, \tag{9.6}$$

where w_{ijk} is the weight on the conjunctive link connecting PE *j* and PE *k* to PE *i*, and α_j and α_k are real constants. Equation (9.6) can be extended to include higher-order terms. A PE with a polynomial integration function is also called a sigma-pi ($\Sigma\Pi$) unit.

A second action of each PE is to output an activation value as a function of its net input through an *activation function* or *transfer function* $a(f)$. Some commonly used activation functions are as follows.

- *Step function*:

$$a(f) = \begin{cases} 1 & \text{if } f \geq 0 \\ 0 & \text{otherwise,} \end{cases} \tag{9.7}$$

- *Hard limiter (threshold function)*:

$$a(f) = \text{sgn}(f) = \begin{cases} 1 & \text{if } f \geq 0 \\ -1 & \text{if } f < 0, \end{cases} \tag{9.8}$$

where sgn($\cdot$) is the signum function.

- *Ramp function*:

$$a(f) = \begin{cases} 1 & \text{if } f > 1 \\ f & \text{if } 0 \leq f \leq 1 \\ 0 & \text{if } f < 0, \end{cases} \tag{9.9}$$

- *Unipolar sigmoid function*:

$$a(f) = \frac{1}{1 + e^{-\lambda f}},$$
(9.10)

- *Bipolar sigmoid function*:

$$a(f) = \frac{2}{1 + e^{-\lambda f}} - 1,$$
(9.11)

where $\lambda > 0$ in Eqs. (9.10) and (9.11) determines the steepness of the continuous function $a(f)$ near $f = 0$. The shapes of the above functions are shown in Fig. 9.2, where it is observed that as $\lambda \to \infty$, Eq. (9.10) reduces to Eq. (9.7) and Eq. (9.11) reduces to Eq. (9.8). A PE with a linear integration function and a hard limiter activation function [Eq. (9.8)] is called a *linear threshold unit* (LTU), and a PE with a linear integration function and a graded activation function [Eq. (9.10) or (9.11)] is called a *linear graded unit* (LGU). The LTU and the LGU are the most frequently used models in ANNs.

The nonlinear integration functions of the input allow the formation of complex partitions of the feature space called *decision boundaries*. However, as the integration functions become more complex and powerful, more complex interactions are required in ANNs. The activation function of a PE can also be varied, but with less effect. What seems to be the most importance is the smoothness of the individual PE response. Let us consider the following example for a graphical demonstration.

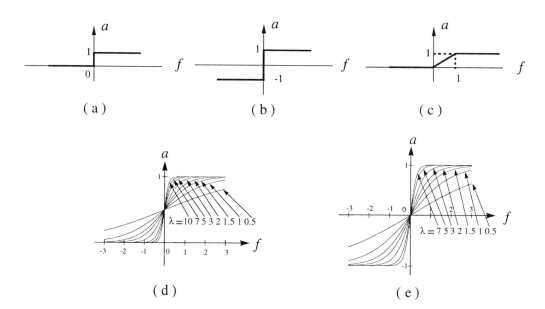

Figure 9.2 Sample activation (transfer) functions. (a) Step function. (b) Hard limiter. (c) Ramp function. (d) Unipolar sigmoid function. (e) Bipolar sigmoid function.

Example 9.1

[Hanson and Burr, 1990]. A four-neuron network is used to illustrate how neurons act together and produce linear or nonlinear boundaries. Assume first that each neuron is a LTU. In Fig. 9.3(a), the neurons L1, L2, and L3 correspond to the lines in Fig. 9.3(b), and the weights and threshold (the values in circles) of each neuron define the corresponding line. Each neuron decides on which side of its line the input point lies. When a point in the region interior to the triangle formed by the lines L1, L2, and L3 is inputed, neurons L1, L2, and L3 turn on. Then, since the combined input to neuron L4 is 3.0 and it exceeds its threshold value of 2.3, neuron L4 also turns on. Any point exterior to the triangle turns L4 off. Hence, neuron L4 acts like an AND gate in Fig. 9.3(a). Activation surfaces of the whole network are shown in Fig. 9.3(c) and (d), where Fig. 9.3(c) is the net input to neuron L4 and Fig. 9.3(d) is the threshold output of neuron L4. Now if LGUs are adopted, the activation surfaces corresponding to Fig. 9.3(c) and

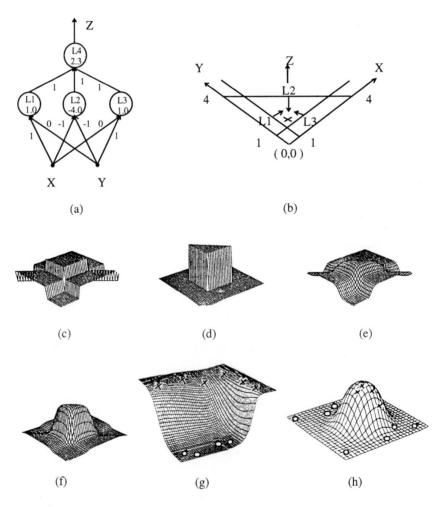

Figure 9.3 Simple two-layer network and its various activation surfaces as in Example 9.1. (Adapted from Hanson and Burr [1990]. Reprinted with permission of © Cambridge University Press.)

(d) are shown in Fig. 9.3(e) and (f), respectively, in which the output change is smooth but with ripples in the floor region of Fig. 9.3(f), which are are absent in Fig. 9.3(d).

If a neuron with a nonlinear integration function is used, a single neuron can produce a rather complex activation surface. Figure 9.3(g) shows the activation surface of a polynomial unit performing the categorization task of separating X's from O's located arbitrarily in a feature space. Figure 9.3(h) performs the same task using a spherical unit.

The above demonstration shows that ANNs are capable of spatial partitioning and of constructing arbitrary continuous regions. Since ANNs can use such arbitrary partitioning to solve problems and create associative maps, multiple units are often involved in representing spatial regions. Hence, knowledge is properly represented as distributed patterns of activation. This *distributed representation* concept is usually adopted in ANNs and will be discussed in Section 9.3.

9.2.2 Connections

An ANN consists of a set of highly interconnected PEs such that each PE output is connected, through weights, to other PEs or to itself; both delay and lag-free connections are allowed. Hence, the structure that organizes these PEs and the connection geometry among them should be specified for an ANN. It is also important to point out where the connection originates and terminates in addition to specifying the function of each PE in an ANN. Besides the simplest single-node neural network as shown in Fig. 9.1(b), Fig. 9.4 shows five other basic types of connection geometries [Nelson and Illingworth, 1991].

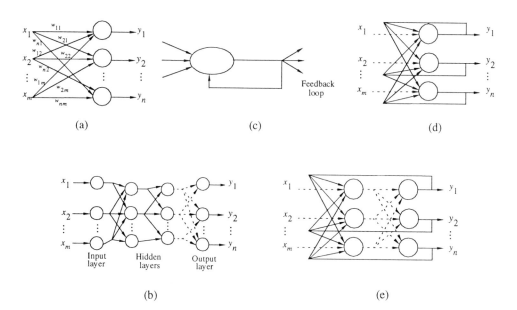

Figure 9.4 Five basic network connection geometries. (a) Single-layer feedforward network. (b) Multilayer feedforward network. (c) Single node with feedback to itself. (d) Single-layer recurrent network. (e) Multilayer recurrent network.

We can first take a PE and combine it with other PEs to make a *layer* of these nodes. Inputs can be connected to these nodes with various weights, resulting in a series of outputs, one per node. This results in a *single-layer feedforward network* as shown in Fig. 9.4(a). We can further interconnect several layers to form a *multilayer feedforward network* as shown in Fig. 9.4(b). The layer that receives inputs is called the *input layer* and typically performs no function other than buffering of the input signal. The outputs of the network are generated from the *output layer.* Any layer between the input and output layers is called a *hidden layer* because it is internal to the network and has no direct contact with the external environment. There may be from zero to several hidden layers in an ANN. The network is said to be *fully connected* if every output from one layer is connected to every node in the next layer. It is clear that the network in Fig. 9.4(b) is not fully connected.

The two types of networks mentioned above (single-layer and multilayer) are *feedforward networks* since no PE output is an input to a node in the same layer or in a preceding layer. When outputs can be directed back as inputs to same- or preceding-layer nodes, the network is a *feedback network.* The feedback in which PE output is directed back as input to PEs in the same layer is called *lateral feedback.* Feedback networks that have closed loops are called *recurrent networks.* Figure 9.4(c) shows the simplest recurrent neural network—a single node with feedback to itself. A single-layer network with a feedback connection is shown in Fig. 9.4(d) in which PE output can be directed back to the PE itself, to other PEs, or to both. An important type of connection with lateral feedback is the *on-center–off-surround* or *lateral-inhibition* structure. In this structure, each PE receives two different classes of inputs—"excitatory" inputs from nearby PEs and "inhibitory" inputs from more distant PEs. The connections of the lateral-inhibition structure are shown in Fig. 9.5, where the links with open circles are excitatory connections and the links with solid circles are inhibitory connections. Only the lateral feedback of one PE (the base PE) is shown in Fig. 9.5. In a multilayer recurrent network, a PE output can be directed back to the nodes in the preceding layers as shown in Fig. 9.4(e). Of course, in such networks, a PE output can be also directed back to the PE itself and to the other PEs in the same layer. More than one of the basic connection geometries summarized in Fig. 9.4 can be used together in an ANN.

9.2.3 Learning Rules

The third important element in specifying an ANN is the learning rules. Broadly speaking, there are two kinds of learning in ANNs: *parameter learning* which is concerned with updating of the connecting weights in an ANN, and *structure learning* which focuses on the change in the network structure, including the number of PEs and their connection types. These two kinds of learning can be performed simultaneously or separately. We shall first focus on the parameter learning rules since most of the existing learning rules are of this type. The structure learning rules will be explored in Chap. 15.

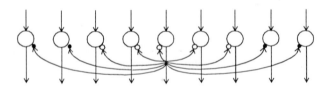

Figure 9.5 The interconnections of a lateral-inhibition structure.

Introduction to Artificial Neural Networks   Chap. 9

To keep the mathematical notation simple, it is assumed that there are n PEs in an ANN and each PE has exactly m adaptive weights. The *weight matrix* (or the *connection matrix*) $\mathbf{W}$ is defined by

$$\mathbf{W} \triangleq \begin{bmatrix} \mathbf{w}_1^T \\ \mathbf{w}_2^T \\ \vdots \\ \mathbf{w}_n^T \end{bmatrix} = \begin{bmatrix} w_{11} & w_{12} & \cdots & w_{1m} \\ w_{21} & w_{22} & \cdots & w_{2m} \\ \vdots & \vdots & \ddots & \vdots \\ w_{n1} & w_{n2} & \cdots & w_{nm} \end{bmatrix}, \tag{9.12}$$

where $\mathbf{w}_i = (w_{i1}, w_{i2}, \ldots, w_{im})^T$, $i = 1, 2, \ldots, n$, is the *weight vector* of PE i and w_{ij} is the weight on the link from PE j (source node) to PE i (destination node).

Suppose that the weight matrix $\mathbf{W}$ contains all the adaptive elements of an ANN. Then the set of all possible $\mathbf{W}$ matrices determines the set of all possible information processing configurations for this ANN. In other words, if the information processing performance we desire is to be realized by this ANN, then the ANN can be realized by finding an appropriate matrix $\mathbf{W}$. In this connection, we say that the weights encode *long-term memory* (LTM) and the activation states of neurons encode *short-term memory* (STM) in neural networks. Hence, for ANNs that utilize weight learning, we have to develop learning rules to efficiently guide the weight matrix $\mathbf{W}$ in approaching a desired matrix that yields the desired network performance. In general, learning rules are classified into three categories: *supervised learning, reinforcement learning,* and *unsupervised learning.*

In supervised learning, at each instant of time when input is applied to an ANN, the corresponding desired response $\mathbf{d}$ of the system is given. The network is thus told precisely what it should be emitting as output. More clearly, in the supervised learning mode, an ANN is supplied with a sequence of examples, $(\mathbf{x}^{(1)}, \mathbf{d}^{(1)}), (\mathbf{x}^{(2)}, \mathbf{d}^{(2)}), \ldots, (\mathbf{x}^{(k)}, \mathbf{d}^{(k)}), \ldots,$ of desired input-output pairs. When each input $\mathbf{x}^{(k)}$ is put into the ANN, the corresponding desired output $\mathbf{d}^{(k)}$ is also supplied to the ANN. As shown in Fig. 9.6(a), the difference

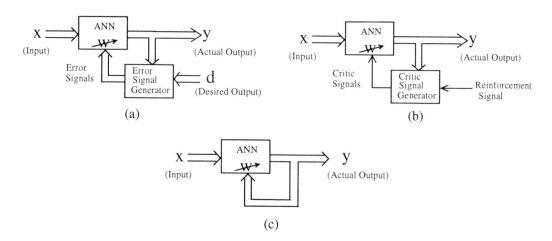

Figure 9.6 Three categories of learning. (a) Supervised learning. (b) Reinforcement learning. (c) Unsupervised learning.

between the actual output $\mathbf{y}^{(k)}$ and the desired output $\mathbf{d}^{(k)}$ is measured in the error signal generator which then produces error signals for the ANN to correct its weights in such a way that the actual output will move closer to the desired output.

In supervised learning, it is assumed that the correct "target" output values are known for each input pattern. But in some situations only less detailed information is available. For example, the ANN may only be told that its current actual output is "too high" or "50% correct." In the extreme case, there is only a single bit of feedback information indicating whether the output is *right* or *wrong*. Learning based on this kind of critic information is called *reinforcement learning,* and the feedback information is called the *reinforcement signal.* As shown in Fig. 9.6(b), reinforcement learning is a form of supervised learning because the network still receives some feedback from its environment. But the feedback (i.e., the reinforcement signal) is only *evaluative (critic)* rather than instructive. That is, it just says how good or how bad a particular output is and provides no hint as to what the right answer should be. The external reinforcement signal is usually processed by the critic signal generator [see Fig. 9.6(b)] to produce a more informative critic signal for the ANN to adjust its weights properly with the hope of getting better critic feedback in the future. Reinforcement learning is also called *learning with a critic* as opposed to *learning with a teacher,* which describes supervised learning.

In unsupervised learning, there is no teacher to provide any feedback information [see Fig. 9.6(c)]. There is no feedback from the environment to say what the outputs should be or whether they are correct. The network must discover for itself patterns, features, regularities, correlations, or categories in the input data and code for them in the output. While discovering these features, the network undergoes changes in its parameters; this process is called *self-organizing.* A typical example is making an unsupervised classification of objects without providing information about the actual classes. The proper clusters are formed by discovering the similarities and dissimilarities among the objects.

Referring the three basic learning modes shown in Fig. 9.6, we next consider a general training structure for a PE in an ANN as shown in Fig. 9.7. In this figure, the input x_j, $j = 1, 2, \ldots, m$, can be an output from another PE or can be an external input. Note that the threshold parameter θ may be included in the learning as one of the weights by fixing

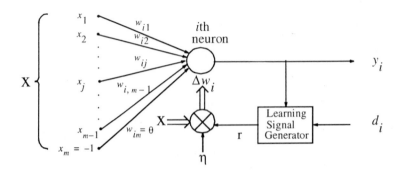

Figure 9.7 The general weight learning rule (d_i is not provided for the unsupervised learning mode).

Introduction to Artificial Neural Networks   Chap. 9

one of the inputs, say, x_m, at a value of -1. The desired signal d_i is available only in the supervised learning mode or in the reinforcement learning mode, where d_i is the reinforcement signal. Hence, in these two learning modes, the weights of PE i are modified according to the input signal it receives, its output value, and the associated teaching response. However, in the unsupervised learning mode, the PE modifies its weights based only on the input and/or output values.

A general form of the weight learning rule in neural networks indicates that the increment of the weight vector $\mathbf{w}_i$ produced by the learning step at time t is proportional to the product of the learning signal r and the input $\mathbf{x}(t)$; that is (see Fig. 9.7),

$$\Delta \mathbf{w}_i(t) \propto r\mathbf{x}(t) \qquad \text{or} \qquad \Delta \mathbf{w}_i(t) = \eta r\mathbf{x}(t), \qquad (9.13)$$

where η is a positive number called the *learning constant* which determines the rate of learning and r is the learning signal which is in general a function of $\mathbf{w}_i$, $\mathbf{x}$ and, if available, a teacher's signal d_i; that is,

$$r = f_r(\mathbf{w}_i, \mathbf{x}, d_i). \qquad (9.14)$$

Hence, the general weight learning rule in Eq. (9.13) indicates that the weight vector $\mathbf{w}_i = (w_{i1}, w_{i2}, \ldots, w_{im})^T$ increases in proportion to the product of input $\mathbf{x}$ and learning signal r. According to Eqs. (9.13) and (9.14), the weight vector at learning time step $(t + 1)$ is

$$\mathbf{w}_i(t + 1) = \mathbf{w}_i(t) + \eta f_r(\mathbf{w}_i(t), \mathbf{x}(t), d_i(t))\mathbf{x}(t), \qquad (9.15)$$

which can also be written as

$$\mathbf{w}_i^{(t+1)} = \mathbf{w}_i^{(t)} + \eta f_r\left(\mathbf{w}_i^{(t)}, \mathbf{x}^{(t)}, d_i^{(t)}\right)\mathbf{x}^{(t)}, \qquad (9.16)$$

where the superscript indicates the learning time instant. Equation (9.16) is concerned with a sequence of discrete-time weight modifications, and its counterpart for continuous-time weight modifications can be expressed as

$$\frac{d\mathbf{w}_i(t)}{dt} = \eta r\mathbf{x}(t). \qquad (9.17)$$

For Eqs. (9.16) and (9.17), the weights should be properly initialized (e.g., by assigning the initial weights randomly) before the learning precedes.

Using the general weight learning rule in Eq. (9.16), several supervised and unsupervised weight learning and training rules have been developed. The major distinguishing factor of these supervised and unsupervised weight learning rules focuses on how the learning signal r is being generated to modify or update the weights of an ANN.

We shall first discuss Hebb's learning law in the form of the general weight learning rule. Hebb [1949] hypothesized that when an axonal input from neuron A to neuron B causes neuron B to immediately emit a pulse (fire) and this situation happens repeatedly or persistently, then the efficacy of that axonal input, in terms of its ability to help neuron B to fire in the future, is somehow increased. Hence, he suggested that synaptic strengths in the brain change proportionally to the correlation between the firing of the pre- and postsynaptic neurons. This concept brought pioneering contributions to neuroscience and neurocomputing. Many other neural network learning rules often reflect the Hebbian rule principle.

Following the Hebbian hypothesis that the weights are adjusted according to the pre- and postcorrelations, the learning signal r in the general weight learning rule is set as

$$r \triangleq a(\mathbf{w}_i^T \mathbf{x}) = y_i, \qquad (9.18)$$

where $a(\cdot)$ is the activation function of the PE. Hence, in the Hebbian learning rule, the learning signal r is simply set as the PE's current output. Then, according to Eq. (9.13), the increment $\Delta \mathbf{w}_i$ of the weight vector becomes

$$\Delta \mathbf{w}_i = \eta a(\mathbf{w}_i^T \mathbf{x})\mathbf{x} = \eta y_i \mathbf{x}. \qquad (9.19)$$

That is, the components of the weight vector are updated by an amount of

$$\Delta w_{ij} = \eta a(\mathbf{w}_i^T \mathbf{x})x_j = \eta y_i x_j, \qquad i = 1, 2, \ldots, n; j = 1, 2, \ldots, m. \qquad (9.20)$$

Thus, the Hebbian learning rule is an unsupervised learning rule for a feedforward network since it uses only the product of inputs and actual outputs to modify the weights. No desired outputs are given to generate the learning signal to update the weights. This learning rule requires weight initialization at small random values around zero before learning. Equation (9.20) indicates that if the input-output correlation term $y_i x_j$ is positive, the weight w_{ij} will increase; otherwise the weight w_{ij} will decrease. Furthermore, since the output is strengthened in turn for each input presented, frequently occurring input patterns will have the most influence on the weights and will eventually produce the largest output. Hence, the learning rule in Eq. (9.20) captures the idea of the Hebbian hypothesis.

Example 9.2

Consider the Hebbian learning rule for an ANN with a single PE which is a LTU. There are four inputs, x_1, x_2, x_3, and x_4, to this PE. The corresponding weight vector is $\mathbf{w} = (w_1, w_2, w_3, w_4)^T$. Assume that this ANN is to be trained using the following three input vectors:

$$\mathbf{x}^{(1)} = \begin{pmatrix} 1 \\ 1.5 \\ 0.5 \\ 0 \end{pmatrix}, \qquad \mathbf{x}^{(2)} = \begin{pmatrix} -0.5 \\ 1 \\ 0 \\ 1.5 \end{pmatrix}, \qquad \mathbf{x}^{(3)} = \begin{pmatrix} -1 \\ 0 \\ -1 \\ -0.5 \end{pmatrix}.$$

The initial weight vector is selected as

$$\mathbf{w}^{(1)} = \begin{pmatrix} 1 \\ 0 \\ -1 \\ 0 \end{pmatrix},$$

and the learning constant is set to $\eta = 1$. Then according to the Hebbian learning rule, the following steps are taken:

Step 1: Consider the first input pattern $\mathbf{x}^{(1)}$ to update the weight vector:

$$\mathbf{w}^{(2)} = \mathbf{w}^{(1)} + \text{sgn}((\mathbf{w}^{(1)})^T \mathbf{x}^{(1)})\mathbf{x}^{(1)} = \begin{pmatrix} 1 \\ 0 \\ -1 \\ 0 \end{pmatrix} + \text{sgn}(0.5)\begin{pmatrix} 1 \\ 1.5 \\ 0.5 \\ 0 \end{pmatrix} = \begin{pmatrix} 2 \\ 1.5 \\ -0.5 \\ 0 \end{pmatrix}.$$

Introduction to Artificial Neural Networks   Chap. 9

Step 2: Consider the second input pattern $\mathbf{x}^{(2)}$:

$$\mathbf{w}^{(3)} = \mathbf{w}^{(2)} + \text{sgn}((\mathbf{w}^{(2)})^T \mathbf{x}^{(2)}) \mathbf{x}^{(2)} = \begin{pmatrix} 2 \\ 1.5 \\ -0.5 \\ 0 \end{pmatrix} + \text{sgn}\,(0.5) \begin{pmatrix} -0.5 \\ 1 \\ 0 \\ 1.5 \end{pmatrix} = \begin{pmatrix} 1.5 \\ 2.5 \\ -0.5 \\ 1.5 \end{pmatrix}.$$

Step 3: Consider the third input pattern $\mathbf{x}^{(3)}$:

$$\mathbf{w}^{(4)} = \mathbf{w}^{(3)} + \text{sgn}((\mathbf{w}^{(3)})^T \mathbf{x}^{(3)}) \mathbf{x}^{(3)} = \begin{pmatrix} 1.5 \\ 2.5 \\ -0.5 \\ 1.5 \end{pmatrix} + \text{sgn}\,(-1.75) \begin{pmatrix} -1 \\ 0 \\ -1 \\ -0.5 \end{pmatrix} = \begin{pmatrix} 2.5 \\ 2.5 \\ 0.5 \\ 2 \end{pmatrix}.$$

It can be verified that $\text{sgn}((\mathbf{w}^{(4)})^T \mathbf{x}^{(1)}) = \text{sgn}((\mathbf{w}^{(4)})^T \mathbf{x}^{(2)}) = 1$ and $\text{sgn}((\mathbf{w}^{(4)})^T \mathbf{x}^{(3)}) = -1$. This means that the inputs ($\mathbf{x}^{(1)}$ and $\mathbf{x}^{(2)}$) that caused the PE to fire previously will cause it to fire again in the future with the final learned weights. This is also true for the input $\mathbf{x}^{(3)}$ which inhibits the firing of the PE. Thus, the final weights have captured the coincidence relationship of input-output training pairs.

Other weight learning rules in the form of Eq. (9.13), such as the perceptron learning rule, the delta learning rule, the Widrow-Hoff learning rule, and the generalized delta learning rule will be covered in Chap. 10, while the winner-take-all learning rule, the instar-outstar learning rule, and other unsupervised learning rules will be discussed in Chaps. 11 and 12.

9.3 DISTRIBUTED REPRESENTATIONS

In distributed representations, an entity is represented by a pattern of activity distributed over many processing elements, and each processing element is involved in representing many different entities. This is in contrast to the familiar *local* representation in which each entity is represented by one processing element. For example, there are 16 PEs with a + or – output and three entities, "Dog," "Cat," and "Bread." The distributed representation for the three entities might be as follows:

	P_0	P_1	P_2	P_3	P_4	P_5	P_6	P_7	P_8	P_9	P_{10}	P_{11}	P_{12}	P_{13}	P_{14}	P_{15}
Dog	+	–	+	+	–	–	–	–	+	+	+	+	+	–	–	–
Cat	+	–	+	+	–	–	–	–	+	–	+	–	+	+	–	+
Bread	+	+	–	+	–	+	+	–	+	–	–	+	+	+	+	–

There are several advantages of distributed representation. First, it provides an efficient way of using parallel hardware to implement best-fit searches and act as a content-addressable memory. For example, if we know $P_8 = P_9 = P_{10} = P_{11} = +$, then the entity "Dog" can be easily retrieved by fitting the activation patterns. Second, it is easy for generalization based on similarity. For example, if another entity, "Fido," with the following distributed representation is given,

	P_0	P_1	P_2	P_3	P_4	P_5	P_6	P_7	P_8	P_9	P_{10}	P_{11}	P_{12}	P_{13}	P_{14}	P_{15}
Fido	+	−	−	+	−	−	−	−	+	+	+	+	+	+	−	−

then we can say "Fido" is a "Dog" since its distributed representation is very similar to that of the entity "Dog." Another example is that if we know a dog has four legs, because of the similarity of their patterns, we induce that a cat also has four legs. The third advantage of distributed representation is that it makes the creation of new entities or concepts easy. We just need to change the weights in networks accordingly without allocating new hardware. Ideally, the distributed representation chosen for a new concept should be the one that requires the least modification of weights to make the new pattern stable and to make it have the required effects on other representations, for example, to remain similar to related concepts. For example, if a new entity "Doughnut" is to be added, its distributed representation could be

	P_0	P_1	P_2	P_3	P_4	P_5	P_6	P_7	P_8	P_9	P_{10}	P_{11}	P_{12}	P_{13}	P_{14}	P_{15}
Doughnut	+	+	−	−	−	+	+	−	+	−	−	−	+	+	+	−

which is quite similar to that of "Bread." Finally, distributed representation has the capability of fault tolerance. For example, if two PEs, say PE3 and PE10, break down, we still have a high probability of identifying the patterns of different entities. However, distributed representations also have some disadvantages. The main disadvantage is that they are difficult for an outside observer to understand or modify. Hence, learning procedures and special mechanisms are usually necessary for formulation or modification and storing or retrieval of data with distributed representation.

A useful technique in the implementation of distributed representation is the *coarse coding* technique [Hinton et al., 1986; Rosenfeld and Touretzky, 1988; Hinton, 1991]. In this technique, each PE has a *receptive field* which is the set of all values including all the patterns it represents. For example, in the above distributed representations for "Dog," "Cat," and "Bread," we can say that the receptive fields of P_0, P_1, and P_2 are {Dog, Cat, Bread}, {Bread}, and {Dog, Cat}, respectively. The receptive field of each PE is coarsely tuned to cover a considerable range of values, and a particular value is represented by activities in a number of PEs with overlapping receptive fields. In other words, coarse coding uses overlapping codes to store multiple items simultaneously. In this connection, we find the correspondence between ANNs and fuzzy logic systems: Each PE with an overlapping receptive field in ANNs corresponds to a fuzzy set, and its receptive field corresponds to the membership function of the fuzzy set.

A fundamental task in the distributed representation of structured knowledge is to build up a relationship (i.e., implement an arbitrary mapping) between two distributed representations in two domains. Let us use an example to illustrate how a distributed representation on one group of units can cause an appropriate distributed representation on another group of units.

Example 9.3

[Hinton et al., 1986]. This example sets up the association between the visual form (grapheme-position) of a word and its meaning. Consider some three-letter English words: "bat," "cat," "mat," "can," and "car." Figure 9.8(a) and (b) shows two three-layer networks implementing the grapheme-position—meaning association using the local representation and the distributed representation, respectively. In Fig. 9.8(a), the bottom layer contains PEs that represent particular graphemes in particular positions (grapheme-position) within the word. The hidden layer contains PEs that recognize complete words. The local representations of words are used in this layer because each PE represents exactly one word and one word is exactly represented by one PE. The top layer contains PEs that represent semantic features (sememes) of the meaning of the word.

In Fig. 9.8(b), the top and bottom layers are the same as those in Fig. 9.8(a), but the hidden layer uses distributed representations. Each PE in this layer has a receptive field with a set of words as indicated in the figure. Hence, a PE in the hidden layer can be activated by the graphemic representation of any one of the whole set of words associated with it. The PE then provides input to every semantic feature that occurs in the meaning of any of the words that activate it. In Fig. 9.8(b), only those word sets containing the word "cat" are shown. Only the semantic features that receive input from all these word sets are the semantic features of "cat."

From Example 9.3, it is clear that the word set (receptive field) of a PE in the hidden layer should be chosen such that each word's meaning contains only a small fraction of the total set of sememes such that the distributed representations in which each word set PE participates in the representation of many words do not lead to errors. Actually, finding

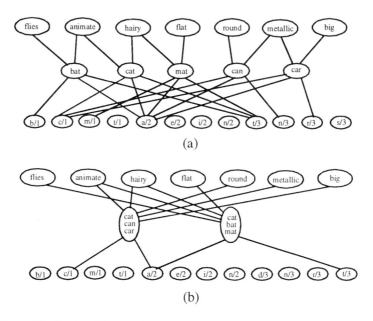

Figure 9.8 Local and distributed representations of the mapping from strings of graphemes onto meanings in Example 9.3. (a) Local representation. (b) Distributed representation. (From "Distributed Representation" by G. E. Hinton J. L. McClelland, and D. E. Rumelhart, in *Parallel Distributed Processing,* by D. E. Rumelhart and J. L. McClelland (editors), Vol. 1, Chapter 3, 1986. Copyright 1986 MIT Press.)

proper distributed representations is not an easy task in most cases. It is better to search for a learning scheme that can find distributed representations that are adequate. In fact, one central problem in the development of the theory of distributed representation is the problem of specifying the exact procedures by which distributed representations are to be learned. All such procedures involve connection weight modification as seen in the following example.

Example 9.4

[Rumelhart et al., 1986a]. In this example, we want to classify input binary strings of length six as to whether or not they are symmetric about their center. For example, the strings "101101," "010010," and "110011" are symmetric, but the strings "110110," "001111," and "000111" are not. The network shown in Fig. 9.9 can serve this purpose, where each PE is a LTU and the numbers inside the circles are threshold values. The output PE signals whether or not the input string is symmetric about its center. We observe that each hidden PE has weights that are symmetric about the middle and are equal in magnitude but opposite in sign. Hence, if a symmetric string is the input, both hidden PEs will receive a net input of zero and both will be off (output -1). This will turn on the output PE (output +1). We further observe that the weights on each side of the midpoint of the string are in the ratio of $1:2:4$. This ensures that each of the eight patterns that can occur on each side of the midpoint sends a unique integrated sum to the hidden PE. This ensures that there is no pattern on the left that will exactly balance a nonsymmetric string on the right. Hence, for every nonsymmetric string, at least one of the two hidden PEs will come on and turn off the output PE because the two hidden PEs have identical patterns of weights from input PEs except for the sign.

The network in Fig. 9.9 was arrived at after 1208 presentations of each six-bit pattern using the back-propagation learning algorithm which will be introduced in Chap. 10. This learning process can automatically find the internal distributed representations (i.e., the hidden PE patterns) of the six-bit strings, which are very helpful for purposes of classification. The distributed representation for a symmetric string is $(-1, -1)$, and that for a nonsymmetric string is $(+1, -1)$, $(-1, +1)$, or $(+1, +1)$.

From the above example, we observe that in ANNs, it is the weights of the connections between PEs that do the representation. Everything the system has learned at any point is encoded in its weights. Furthermore, the main reason why distributed representations dif-

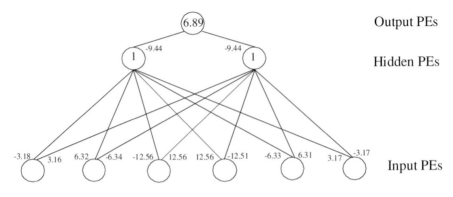

Figure 9.9 Network for solving the symmetry problem in Example 9.4.

Introduction to Artificial Neural Networks Chap. 9

fer from local representations is that the feature representations for inputs are chosen a priori in local representations but are determined through the learning process in distributed representations. Based on the connection weights, it will become obvious (to the network, at least) what makes up the input stimulus. So the real difference between the symbolic and the connectionist approach is not in the type of representation but in the distributed representation's commitment to learning. In connectionism, a network has the freedom to choose its internal representation. In other words, instead of asking what the representation for a cup or a table is, connectionists want to know under what conditions a *useful* representation for a cup or a table will be learned.

9.4 CONCLUDING REMARKS

An interesting account of the historical development of artificial neural networks and their relationship to traditional artificial intelligence can be found in [Haykin, 1994; Lin, 1994]. Besides the basic structure of multilayer feedforward networks and recurrent networks, a commonly encountered architectural arrangement of neural networks is an *on-center–off-surround* or *lateral-inhibition* structure [Kohonen, 1989]. In this structure, the effect of a single PE output on surrounding PEs is in the shape of the "Mexican hat function."

Concepts of supervised learning, unsupervised learning, and reinforcement learning are briefly considered in this chapter. The general weight learning rule discussed here will be followed when other learning rules are developed in later chapters. The Hebbian learning rule is quite simple in concept and principle and is often reflected in other learning rules.

Distributed representation is an important property of neural networks. A useful technique in the implementation of distributed representation, called *coarse coding* technique, is described in [Hinton et al., 1986; Rosenfeld and Touretzky, 1988; Hinton, 1991]. Mathematical analysis of coarse-coded symbol representation has been by Rosenfeld and Touretzky [1988]. Coarse-coded memories have been used for storing symbols in several neural network symbol processing models [Rosenfeld and Touretzky, 1988; Hinton, 1991]. An interesting extension of distributed representations is *recursive* distributed representations [Pollack, 1991b]. They are able to represent variable-sized recursive data structures, such as trees and lists, in fixed-width patterns on a connectionist architecture. Further advanced topics on connectionist symbol processing can be found in [Hinton, 1991].

9.5 PROBLEMS

9.1 (a) Design neural networks with only one *M-P* neuron that implement the three basic logic operations: (i) NOT (x_1), (ii) OR (x_1, x_2), (iii) AND (x_1, x_2), where x_1 and $x_2 \in \{0, 1\}$.

  (b) Explain why a single-layer neural network consisting of *M-P* neurons cannot perform the XOR logic operation.

9.2 (a) Show that the derivative of the unipolar sigmoid function $a(f)$ in Eq. (9.10) with respect to f is given by

$$a'(f) = \frac{da(f)}{df} = \lambda a(f)[1 - a(f)].$$

(b) Show that the derivative of the bipolar sigmoid function $a(f)$ in Eq. (9.11) with respect to f is given by

$$a'(f) = \frac{da(f)}{df} = \frac{\lambda}{2}[1 - a^2(f)].$$

9.3 The outputs of activation functions used for PEs are usually bounded in a range [e.g., see Eqs. (9.7)–(9.11)]. Explain the advantage(s) and disadvantage(s) caused by this limitation.

9.4 Refer to Example 9.1 to design a five-LTU network that produces an output of +1 when a two-dimensional input pattern (x, y) falls inside the rectangle whose four corners are at $(1, 1)$, $(-2, 1)$, $(-2, -3)$, and $(1, -3)$ on the x-y space and produces an output of -1 when (x, y) falls outside the rectangle. Sketch the activation surface of the designed network.

9.5 Patterns from two classes C_1 and $C_2 \in \mathcal{R}^2$ are to be classified. Design a three-LTU network to perform the task such that
  (a) The input (x, y) belongs to C_1 if $y - 2x - 2 > 0$ and $y + 3x - 3 > 0$; otherwise it belongs to C_2.
  (b) The input (x, y) belongs to C_1 if $y - 2x - 2 > 0$ or $y + 3x - 3 > 0$; otherwise it belongs to C_2.

9.6 Given a discrete-time two-LTU fully connected recurrent network with the weight matrix

$$\mathbf{W} = \begin{bmatrix} k & 1 \\ -1 & k \end{bmatrix}.$$

Find k such that
  (a) The state sequence doesn't converge.
  (b) The state sequence is convergent.

9.7 Obtain the equations of the integration (spherical) function and the activation function of the spherical unit with the activation surface shown in Fig. 9.3(h). Compare the number of connection weights in this single-node network with that in the network shown in Fig. 9.3(a) and explain why these two networks have a compatible pattern classification capability.

9.8 **(a)** Construct a feedforward network with four input nodes, three hidden nodes, and four output nodes that has lateral-inhibition structure in the output layer.
  (b) Construct a recurrent network with five input nodes, three hidden nodes, and two output nodes that has feedback links from the hidden layer to the input layer.
  (c) Figure out a neural network structure that is not totally constructed from the five basic connection geometries shown in Fig. 9.4.

9.9 Consider a multilayer feedforward network with all neurons having a linear integration function and a linear activation function. Justify that this network is equivalent to a single-layer feedforward network with all neurons having a linear integration function and a linear activation function.

9.10 For the Hebbian learning rule, frequently occurring input patterns have the most influence on the PEs weights and eventually produce the largest output. Using the Hebbian learning rule with the same input vector $\mathbf{x}^{(k)}$ at the successive time steps of k and $(k + 1)$, show that the output,

$$\left| y^{(k+1)} \right| \geq \left| y^{(k)} \right|,$$

if the input-output correlation term at time step k is positive and that an increasing activation function is used.

9.11 Consider the general weight learning rule in Eq. (9.13) and assume that all the neurons are LTUs. If the learning signal r is given by

$$r \triangleq d_i - y_i,$$

where $y_i = \text{sgn}(\mathbf{w}_i^T\mathbf{x})$ and d_i is the desired output, then we obtain the *perceptron learning rule* as follows:

$$\Delta w_{ij} = \eta[d_i - \text{sgn}(\mathbf{w}_i^T\mathbf{x})]x_j, \qquad i = 1, 2,\ldots, n; j = 1, 2,\ldots, m.$$

Train a single-LTU network (see Fig. 9.7) using the perceptron learning rule. The set of input and desired output training vectors is

$$\left(\mathbf{x}^{(1)} = [1, -2, 0, -1]^T; d_1 = -1\right),$$

$$\left(\mathbf{x}^{(2)} = [0, 1.5, -0.5, -1]^T; d_2 = -1\right),$$

$$\left(\mathbf{x}^{(3)} = [-1, 1, 0.5, -1]^T; d_3 = +1\right),$$

and the initial weight vector is $\mathbf{w}^{(1)} = [1, -1, 0, 0.5]^T$. The learning constant is set as $\eta = 0.1$. Show the learning process step by step by recycling the training data until the network can recognize and classify all the input vectors correctly. Reuse the training data set if necessary.

9.12 Consider the general weight learning rule in Eq. (9.13) and assume that all the neurons are LGUs. If the learning signal r is given by

$$r \triangleq [d_i - a(\mathbf{w}_i^T\mathbf{x})]a'(\mathbf{w}_i^T\mathbf{x}),$$

where $a(\cdot)$ is the bipolar sigmoid function with $\lambda = 1$, $a'(\cdot)$ is the derivative of $a(\cdot)$ with respect to its input, and d_i is the desired output, then we obtain the *delta learning rule* as follows:

$$\Delta w_{ij} = \eta[d_i - a(\mathbf{w}_i^T\mathbf{x})]a'(\mathbf{w}_i^T\mathbf{x})x_j \qquad i = 1, 2,\ldots, n; \; j = 1, 2,\ldots, m.$$

Train a single-LGU network (see Fig. 9.7) using the delta learning rule. The training data pairs are

$$\left[\mathbf{x}^{(1)} = (2, 0, -1)^T, \quad d_1 = -1\right],$$

$$\left[\mathbf{x}^{(2)} = (1, -2, -1)^T, \quad d_2 = +1\right],$$

and the initial weight vector is $\mathbf{w}^{(1)} = (1, 0, 1)^T$. The learning constant is selected as $\eta = 0.25$. Perform two training cycles of this learning process.

9.13 Consider the general learning rule in Eq. (9.13). If the learning signal r is given by

$$r \triangleq d_i - \mathbf{w}_i^T\mathbf{x},$$

then we have the Widrow-Hoff learning rule or the least mean square (LMS) learning rule as follows:

$$\Delta w_{ij} = \eta(d_i - \mathbf{w}^T\mathbf{x})x_j, \qquad i = 1, 2,\ldots, n; j = 1, 2,\ldots, m.$$

Note that this learning rule is independent of the activation function used. Using the same training data as in Prob. 9.12, perform two training cycles for the network shown in Fig. 9.7 using the Widrow-Hoff learning rule.

9.14 Redraw Fig. 9.8(b) for distributed representations of the mapping from the strings of graphemes onto the meanings for the words "car" and "mat."

9.15 Consider the neural network in Fig. 9.3(a). Identify the internal distributed representations of the points falling in different regions partitioned by the lines L1, L2, and L3 shown in Fig. 9.3(b).

10

Feedforward Networks and Supervised Learning

This chapter covers the important topics involving single-layer and multilayer feedforward networks and their associated supervised learning rules. In particular, we shall discuss the perceptron learning rule for simple perceptrons, the Widrow-Hoff learning rule for Adaline, the delta learning rule for single-layer feedforward networks with continuous activation functions, and the back-propagation learning algorithm for multilayer feedforward networks with continuous activation functions. The factors that affect convergence of the back-propagation algorithm will also be considered. Finally, some interesting feedforward networks will be explored.

10.1 SINGLE-LAYER PERCEPTRON NETWORKS

In this section, we shall focus on single-layer feedforward networks, known as *simple perceptrons*. Figure 10.1 shows an example of such networks and defines some notation. As in Fig. 9.7, the thresholds are treated as the weights connected to an input terminal which is permanently clamped at -1. The learning problem that is of interest belongs to the class of supervised learning. Thus, we ask for a particular output pattern $\mathbf{d}^{(k)} = [\, d_1^{(k)}, d_2^{(k)}, \ldots, d_n^{(k)}]^T$ in response to an input pattern $\mathbf{x}^{(k)} = [\, x_1^{(k)}, x_2^{(k)}, \ldots, x_m^{(k)}]^T$, $k = 1, 2, \ldots, p$, m is the number of inputs, n is the number of outputs, and p is the number of input-output pairs in the training set. That is, we want the *actual* output pattern $\mathbf{y}^{(k)} = [\, y_1^{(k)}, y_2^{(k)}, \ldots, y_n^{(k)}]^T$ to be equal to the target pattern $\mathbf{d}^{(k)}$ after the learning process:

$$y_i^{(k)} = a\big(\mathbf{w}_i^T \mathbf{x}^{(k)}\big) = a\left(\sum_{j=1}^{m} w_{ij} x_j^{(k)} \right) = d_i^{(k)}, \qquad i = 1, 2, \ldots, n;\ k = 1, 2, \ldots, p, \qquad (10.1)$$

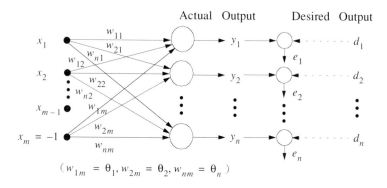

Actual Output   Desired Output

$(w_{1m} = \theta_1, w_{2m} = \theta_2, w_{nm} = \theta_n)$

Figure 10.1   A simple perceptron.

where $\mathbf{w}_i^T = [w_{i1}, w_{i2}, ..., w_{im}]$ is the weight vector associated with PE i and $a(\cdot)$ is the activation function of the ith PE, which can be, for example, a threshold function [Eq. (9.8)] or a continuous sigmoid function [Eqs. (9.10) and (9.11)]. We shall discuss some simple learning rules that will determine the set of weights w_{ij} needed to achieve the desired performance stated in Eq. (10.1) for simple perceptrons. In general, these learning rules start with a general initial guess at the weight values and then make successive adjustments based on the evaluation of an objective function. They eventually reach a near-optimal or optimal solution in a finite number of steps.

In the following sections, we shall first discuss simple perceptrons with linear threshold units {LTUs} and their corresponding *perceptron learning rule*. We shall then introduce simple perceptrons with linear graded units (LGUs) and their corresponding *Widrow-Hoff learning rule*.

10.1.1 Perceptron Learning Rule

For simple perceptrons with LTUs, the desired outputs $d_i^{(k)}$ can take only ± 1 values. Then Eq. (10.1) becomes

$$y_i^{(k)} = \text{sgn}(\mathbf{w}_i^T \mathbf{x}^{(k)}) = d_i^{(k)}, \qquad i = 1, 2, ..., n; \; k = 1, 2, ..., p, \qquad (10.2)$$

which indicates that the weight vector $\mathbf{w}_i$ of the ith PE must be chosen so that the projection of pattern $\mathbf{x}^{(k)}$ onto it has the same sign as $d_i^{(k)}$. Since the boundary between positive and negative projections onto $\mathbf{w}_i$ is the hyperplane $\mathbf{w}_i^T \mathbf{x}^{(k)} = 0$ (called the *decision plane*) through the origin perpendicular to $\mathbf{w}_i$, the requirement in Eq. (10.2) is equivalent to finding a hyperplane that divides inputs that have positive and negative targets (or outputs). Let us clarify this projection concept with an example.

Example 10.1

In this example, we shall design a single-LTU perceptron that can classify the six patterns in a two-dimensional pattern space shown in Fig. 10.2(a) into two classes as follows:

$$\{[-1, 0]^T, [-1.5, -1]^T, [-1, -2]^T\} : \text{class 1},$$

$$\{[2, 0]^T, [2.5, -1]^T, [1, -2]^T\} : \text{class 2}.$$

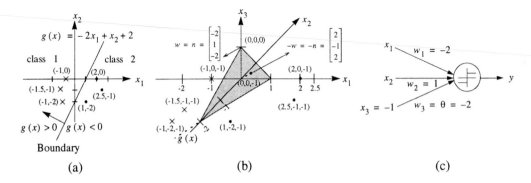

Figure 10.2 Classification problem using single-LTU perception in Example 10.1.

Inspection of the patterns indicates that the equation for the decision boundary can be arbitrarily chosen as shown in Fig. 10.2(a):

$$g(\mathbf{x}) = -2x_1 + x_2 + 2 = 0,$$

which divides the pattern space into two contiguous regions called *decision regions*. It is clear that $g(\mathbf{x}) > 0$ and $g(\mathbf{x}) < 0$ in each of the half-planes containing patterns of classes 1 and 2, respectively. We shall design a single-LTU perceptron such that it will respond with a $+1$ when patterns of class 1 are fed into it and respond with a -1 when patterns of class 2 are fed into it. If we consider the threshold of the LTU *explicitly,* that is,

$$y^{(k)} = \text{sgn}(w_1 x_1^{(k)} + w_2 x_2^{(k)} - \theta), \tag{10.3}$$

where θ is the threshold and $[x_1^{(k)}, x_2^{(k)}]^T$, $k = 1, 2, \ldots, 6$, are the six input patterns, then the boundary (decision surface) does not pass through the origin of the input space. By equating the above equation with $g(\mathbf{x})$, we obtain $w_1 = -2$, $w_2 = 1$, and $\theta = -2$ as the parameters for the single-LTU perceptron classifier shown in Fig. 10.2(c).

We shall now consider the threshold of the LTU *implicitly.* That is, the simple perceptron to be designed should function as

$$y^{(k)} = \text{sgn}(\mathbf{w}^T \mathbf{x}^{(k)}) = d^{(k)}, \tag{10.4}$$

where

$$\mathbf{x}^{(1)} = \begin{pmatrix} -1 \\ 0 \\ -1 \end{pmatrix}, \quad \mathbf{x}^{(2)} = \begin{pmatrix} -1.5 \\ -1 \\ -1 \end{pmatrix}, \quad \mathbf{x}^{(3)} = \begin{pmatrix} -1 \\ -2 \\ -1 \end{pmatrix}, \quad \mathbf{x}^{(4)} = \begin{pmatrix} 2 \\ 0 \\ -1 \end{pmatrix}, \quad \mathbf{x}^{(5)} = \begin{pmatrix} 2.5 \\ -1 \\ -1 \end{pmatrix}, \quad \mathbf{x}^{(6)} = \begin{pmatrix} 1 \\ -2 \\ -1 \end{pmatrix},$$

$$d^{(1)} = d^{(2)} = d^{(3)} = +1, \qquad d^{(4)} = d^{(5)} = d^{(6)} = -1, \qquad \mathbf{w} = [w_1, w_2, w_3]^T.$$

In the above, the threshold of the LTU is viewed as a weight ($\theta = w_3$), and the augmented input vectors, each of which contains a fixed input $x_3 = -1$, are used as inputs. The augmented three-dimensional input space is shown in Fig. 10.2(b) in which a plane $\mathbf{w}^T \mathbf{x} = 0$ passes through the origin and cuts the plane $x_3 = -1$ at the line $g(\mathbf{x}) = -2x_1 + x_2 + 2 = 0$. Since the plane divides the inputs that have positive and negative targets, it is a decision plane for this classification problem. Hence its normal vector $\mathbf{n} = [-2, 1, -2]^T$ is used as the weight vector $\mathbf{w}$ of the single-LTU perceptron. This simple perceptron is shown in Fig. 10.2(c).

The decision-plane dichotomization mentioned above does not always exist for a given set of patterns. A famous example is the XOR problem. As shown in Fig. 10.3, the

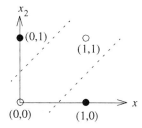

Figure 10.3 The XOR problem.

desired output is $+1$ when one or the other of the inputs is 1, and the desired output is -1 when both inputs are $+1$ or 0. Figure 10.3 makes it clear that there exists no plane (line) that can separate these patterns into two classes; thus we cannot represent the XOR function with a simple perceptron. Hence, the condition for solvability of a pattern classification problem by a simple perceptron with LTUs depends on whether the problem is *linearly separable* or not. A linearly separable (classification) problem is one in which a decision plane can be found in the input space separating the input patterns with desired output $= +1$ from those with desired output $= -1$. If there is more than one output PE, we must be able to find one such plane for *each* output. More precisely, if a (classification) problem is linearly separable by a simple perceptron as shown in Fig. 10.1, then we can find the weight vectors $\mathbf{w}_i$, $i = 1, 2, \ldots, n$, such that

$$\mathbf{w}_i^T \mathbf{x} > 0 \qquad \text{for each } \mathbf{x} \text{ with desired output} = +1,$$
$$\mathbf{w}_i^T \mathbf{x} < 0 \qquad \text{for each } \mathbf{x} \text{ with desired output} = -1, \tag{10.5}$$

The above is true for each output PE i, $i = 1, 2, \ldots, n$.

In the following, we shall consider only linearly separable problems. Example 10.1 illustrates the design of a simple perceptron by a simple analytical method. We shall next introduce a learning procedure for finding appropriate weights of a simple perceptron so that it can find a decision plane. This is called the *perceptron learning rule* and processes the training data one by one and adjusts the weights incrementally. For the perceptron learning rule, the learning signal in the general weight learning rule in Eq. (9.14) is set as the difference between the desired and actual PE responses [Rosenblatt, 1958]. That is,

$$r \triangleq d_i - y_i, \tag{10.6}$$

where $y_i = \text{sgn}(\mathbf{w}_i^T \mathbf{x})$ and d_i are the actual and desired outputs of the ith PE, respectively. Since the desired output d_i takes the values of ± 1, using Eq. (9.13), we have

$$\Delta w_{ij} = \eta[d_i - \text{sgn}(\mathbf{w}_i^T \mathbf{x})]x_j = \begin{cases} 2\eta d_i x_j & \text{if } y_i \neq d_i \\ 0, & \text{otherwise} \end{cases} \quad \text{for } j = 1, 2, \ldots, m, \tag{10.7}$$

which indicates that weights are adjusted only when the actual output y_i disagrees with d_i. The weights are initialized at any value in this method.

An example of weight updating by the perceptron learning rule is shown in Figure 10.4. Here, for convenience, the learning constant η is set to 0.5. Successive values of the weight vector are shown by $\mathbf{w}^{(1)}$, $\mathbf{w}^{(2)}$, $\mathbf{w}^{(3)}$, and $\mathbf{w}^{(4)}$, where the superscript indicates the weight vector after each learning step. There are four input patterns from two classes: patterns $\mathbf{x}^{(1)}$ and $\mathbf{x}^{(2)}$ belong to class 1, and patterns $\mathbf{x}^{(3)}$ and $\mathbf{x}^{(4)}$ belong to class 2. The desired output for class

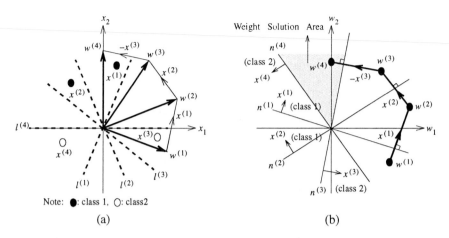

Figure 10.4 Evolvement of the weight vectors under the perceptron learning rule.

1 patterns is $+1$, while for class 2 patterns it is -1. That is, the input patterns presented to the perceptron learning rule are in the order $\mathbf{x}^{(1)}$, $\mathbf{x}^{(2)}$, $\mathbf{x}^{(3)}$, $\mathbf{x}^{(4)}$, and we want to find the weight vector $\mathbf{w}^*$ such that $\text{sgn}\big((\mathbf{w}^*)^T \mathbf{x}^{(1)}\big) = \text{sgn}\big((\mathbf{w}^*)^T \mathbf{x}^{(2)}\big) = +1$ and $\text{sgn}\big((\mathbf{w}^*)^T \mathbf{x}^{(3)}\big) = \text{sgn}\big((\mathbf{w}^*)^T \mathbf{x}^{(4)}\big) = -1$. Figure 10.4(a) illustrates the weight updating in the input space. In this figure, the line $l^{(i)}$ with the normal vector $\mathbf{w}^{(i)}$, $i = 1, 2, 3, 4$, is the decision line at the ith time step. It is observed that no further weight updating is performed when $\mathbf{x}^{(4)}$ is presented since no classification error occurred with the weight vector $\mathbf{w}^{(4)}$. Figure 10.4(b) shows the weight space in which the normal vector of line $n^{(i)}$ is the input pattern $\mathbf{x}^{(i)}$, $i = 1$, 2, 3, 4. It is observed that the weights in the shaded region provide the solution for this two-class classification problem.

Example 10.2

Let us consider another simple classification problem where the input space is a one-dimensional space, that is, a real line:

$$\text{Class 1: } x^{(1)} = 0.5, \qquad x^{(3)} = 2; \qquad d^{(1)} = d^{(3)} = +1.$$
$$\text{Class 2: } x^{(2)} = -1, \qquad x^{(4)} = -2; \qquad d^{(2)} = d^{(4)} = -1.$$

The simple perceptron with a single LTU for solving this problem is shown in Figure 10.5(a). The unknown weights w_1 and w_2 in this figure are trained using the following augmented input vectors:

$$\mathbf{x}^{(1)} = \begin{pmatrix} x^{(1)} \\ -1 \end{pmatrix} = \begin{pmatrix} 0.5 \\ -1 \end{pmatrix}, \qquad \mathbf{x}^{(2)} = \begin{pmatrix} -1 \\ -1 \end{pmatrix}, \qquad \mathbf{x}^{(3)} = \begin{pmatrix} 2 \\ -1 \end{pmatrix}, \qquad \mathbf{x}^{(4)} = \begin{pmatrix} -2 \\ -1 \end{pmatrix},$$

which will be "recycled" for training if necessary. For convenience, let us arbitrarily choose $\eta = 0.5$ and an initial weight $\mathbf{w}^{(1)} = [-2, 1.5]^T$. Then the training proceeds as follows.

Step 1: When $\mathbf{x}^{(1)}$ is the input, the corresponding actual output and weights are, respectively,

$$y^{(1)} = \text{sgn}\left([-2, 1.5] \begin{pmatrix} 0.5 \\ -1 \end{pmatrix} \right) = -1 \neq d^{(1)},$$

$$\mathbf{w}^{(2)} = \mathbf{w}^{(1)} + \mathbf{x}^{(1)} = \begin{pmatrix} -1.5 \\ 0.5 \end{pmatrix}.$$

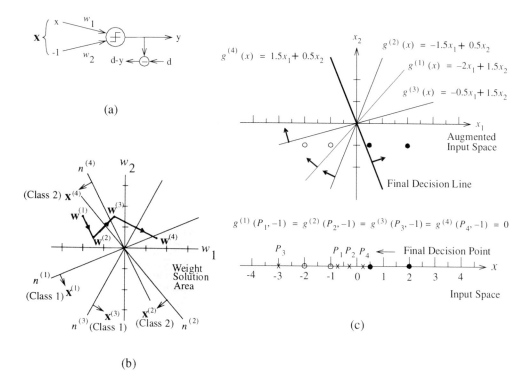

(a)

(b)

(c)

$$g^{(4)}(x) = 1.5x_1 + 0.5x_2$$

$$g^{(2)}(x) = -1.5x_1 + 0.5x_2$$

$$g^{(1)}(x) = -2x_1 + 1.5x_2$$

$$g^{(3)}(x) = -0.5x_1 + 1.5x_2$$

Augmented Input Space

Final Decision Line

$$g^{(1)}(P_1, -1) = g^{(2)}(P_2, -1) = g^{(3)}(P_3, -1) = g^{(4)}(P_4, -1) = 0$$

Final Decision Point

Input Space

Figure 10.5 Single-LTU perceptron in Example 10.2.

Step 2: When $\mathbf{x}^{(2)}$ is the input, the corresponding actual output and weights are, respectively,

$$y^{(2)} = \text{sgn}\left([-1.5, 0.5] \begin{pmatrix} -1 \\ -1 \end{pmatrix} \right) = 1 \neq d^{(2)},$$

$$\mathbf{w}^{(3)} = \mathbf{w}^{(2)} - \mathbf{x}^{(2)} = \begin{pmatrix} -0.5 \\ 1.5 \end{pmatrix}.$$

Step 3: Similarly, when $\mathbf{x}^{(3)}$ is the input, the corresponding actual output and weights are, respectively,

$$y^{(3)} = \text{sgn}\left([-0.5, 1.5] \begin{pmatrix} 2 \\ -1 \end{pmatrix} \right) = -1 \neq d^{(3)},$$

$$\mathbf{w}^{(4)} = \mathbf{w}^{(3)} + \mathbf{x}^{(3)} = \begin{pmatrix} 1.5 \\ 0.5 \end{pmatrix}.$$

Step 4: Finally, when $\mathbf{x}^{(4)}$ is the input, the corresponding actual output and weights are, respectively,

$$y^{(4)} = \text{sgn}\left([1.5, 0.5] \begin{pmatrix} -2 \\ -1 \end{pmatrix} \right) = -1 = d^{(4)},$$

$$\mathbf{w}^{(5)} = \mathbf{w}^{(4)}.$$

Now, we will reuse the training data $\mathbf{x}^{(1)}$, $\mathbf{x}^{(2)}$, $\mathbf{x}^{(3)}$, and $\mathbf{x}^{(4)}$ as a new set of training data, that is, $\mathbf{x}^{(5)} = \mathbf{x}^{(1)}$, $\mathbf{x}^{(6)} = \mathbf{x}^{(2)}$, $\mathbf{x}^{(7)} = \mathbf{x}^{(3)}$, and $\mathbf{x}^{(8)} = \mathbf{x}^{(4)}$, and repeat the above training procedure by updating the weights when the actual and desired outputs are not equal. It can be easily checked that $\mathbf{w}^{(8)} = \mathbf{w}^{(7)} = \mathbf{w}^{(6)} = \mathbf{w}^{(5)} = \mathbf{w}^{(4)}$. Hence, $\mathbf{w}^{(4)}$ is the solution of this problem; that is, $w_1 = 1.5$ and $w_2 = 0.5$ in Fig. 10.5(a). The evolvement of weight vectors in the weight space is shown in Fig. 10.5(b), and the decision surfaces (lines or points) at various time steps are shown in Fig. 10.5(c).

The above example showed that the perceptron learning rule converges to a correct set of weights in a finite number of training steps. We thus arrive at an important theorem governing the convergence property of the perceptron learning rule.

Theorem 10.1

(*Perceptron convergence theorem*). The perceptron learning rule in Eq. (10.7) will converge to a set of weights that accomplish the desired association of Eq. (10.5) in a finite number of steps provided that the solution exists.

Proof: We shall assume that the solution weight vector $\mathbf{w}^*$ exists and prove that the perceptron learning rule in Eq. (10.7) reaches it in a finite number of steps [Zurada, 1992]. Because of the assumption that the solution weight vector $\mathbf{w}^*$ exists, the following inequalities hold for a small, arbitrarily selected constant $0 < \delta < 1$ [see Eq. (10.5)]:

$$\begin{aligned} (\mathbf{w}^*)^T \mathbf{x} > +\delta > 0 \qquad & \text{for each pattern } \mathbf{x} \text{ in class 1,} \\ (\mathbf{w}^*)^T \mathbf{x} < -\delta < 0 \qquad & \text{for each pattern } \mathbf{x} \text{ in class 2.} \end{aligned} \qquad (10.8)$$

Consider the following normalized scalar product:

$$\phi(\mathbf{w}) = \frac{(\mathbf{w}^*)^T \mathbf{w}}{\|\mathbf{w}^*\| \|\mathbf{w}\|}, \qquad (10.9)$$

where $\mathbf{w}$ is the weight vector at some instance of the learning process. Since $\phi(\mathbf{w})$ is the cosine of the angle between the weight vectors $\mathbf{w}^*$ and $\mathbf{w}$, it is obviously less than or equal to 1. The essence of this proof is that the weight update will stop eventually; otherwise the function $\phi(\mathbf{w})$ would get arbitrarily large, which would contradict the fact that $0 \leq \phi(\mathbf{w}) \leq 1$. To prove this, let us consider the numerator and denominator of $\phi(\mathbf{w})$ at the kth learning step as follows [assume that the weight was updated at the kth learning step, that is, $(\mathbf{w}^{(k)})^T \mathbf{x} < 0$ when pattern $\mathbf{x}$ is in class 1 and $(\mathbf{w}^{(k)})^T \mathbf{x} > 0$ when pattern $\mathbf{x}$ is in class 2]:

$$(\mathbf{w}^*)^T \mathbf{w}^{(k+1)} = \begin{cases} (\mathbf{w}^*)^T \mathbf{w}^{(k)} + \eta (\mathbf{w}^*)^T \mathbf{x}, & \text{if } \mathbf{x} \in \text{class 1} \\ (\mathbf{w}^*)^T \mathbf{w}^{(k)} - \eta (\mathbf{w}^*)^T \mathbf{x}, & \text{if } \mathbf{x} \in \text{class 2.} \end{cases}$$

$$\|\mathbf{w}^{(k+1)}\|^2 = \begin{cases} (\mathbf{w}^{(k)} + \eta \mathbf{x})^T (\mathbf{w}^{(k)} + \eta \mathbf{x}), & \text{if } \mathbf{x} \in \text{class 1} \\ (\mathbf{w}^{(k)} - \eta \mathbf{x})^T (\mathbf{w}^{(k)} - \eta \mathbf{x}), & \text{if } \mathbf{x} \in \text{class 2.} \end{cases}$$

Then from Eq. (10.8) and the fact that the weight was updated at the kth learning step, we have

$$(\mathbf{w}^*)^T \mathbf{w}^{(k+1)} > (\mathbf{w}^*)^T \mathbf{w}^{(k)} + \eta\delta \qquad \text{and} \qquad \|\mathbf{w}^{(k+1)}\|^2 < \|\mathbf{w}^{(k)}\|^2 + \eta^2 \|\mathbf{x}\|^2. \qquad (10.10)$$

Upon performing a total of k_0 training steps, Eq. (10.10) tells us that

$$(\mathbf{w}^*)^T \mathbf{w}^{(k_0+1)} > \eta k_0 \delta \qquad \text{and} \qquad \|\mathbf{w}^{(k_0+1)}\|^2 < \eta^2 k_0 \|\mathbf{x}\|^2_{\min}, \qquad (10.11)$$

where the initial weights are all assumed to be zero and $\|\mathbf{x}\|_{\min}$ represents the minimum of $\|\mathbf{x}\|$ for all input $\mathbf{x}$ patterns. Equation (10.9) now becomes, for $\mathbf{w} = \mathbf{w}^{(k_0+1)}$,

$$\phi\left(\mathbf{w}^{(k_0+1)}\right) = \frac{(\mathbf{w}^*)^T \mathbf{w}^{(k_0+1)}}{\|\mathbf{w}^*\| \|\mathbf{w}^{(k_0+1)}\|} > \frac{k_0 \delta}{\sqrt{k_0} \|\mathbf{x}\|_{\min} \|\mathbf{w}^*\|} = \sqrt{k_0} \delta', \tag{10.12}$$

where $\delta' = \delta/(\|\mathbf{x}\|_{\min} \|\mathbf{w}^*\|)$ is a constant between 0 and 1. Since $\phi\left(\mathbf{w}^{(k_0+1)}\right)$ has an upper bound of 1, the inequality in Eq. (10.12) would be violated if a solution were not found after k_0 steps, where $\sqrt{k_0} \delta' < 1$. Thus, we conclude that the perceptron learning rule is convergent.

In the above proof, the number of steps k_0 needed to find a solution weight vector depends strongly on the η value and on the sequence of training patterns presented. Since the PEs in a simple perceptron are independent, the theorem is applied to a general simple perceptron with n PEs (Fig. 10.1). Hence, the convergence theorem can also be applied to the *multicategory* classification problem provided that pattern classes are linearly pairwise separable or that each class is linearly separable from each other class. A simple perceptron with n PEs can be trained to solve an n-category classification problem by a set of training pairs $\left(\mathbf{x}^{(k)}, \mathbf{d}^{(k)}\right)$, $k = 1, 2, \ldots, p$, where all the components of $\mathbf{d}^{(k)}$ are -1 except the ith component $d_i^{(k)}$, is $+1$ if the pattern $\mathbf{x}^{(k)}$ belongs to the ith class (category). For example, if $n = 5$ and $\mathbf{x}^{(k)}$ belongs to the fourth class, then set the corresponding desired output vector as $\mathbf{d}^{(k)} = [-1, -1, -1, +1, -1]^T$.

10.1.2 Adaline

In the last section, we focused on simple perceptrons with linear threshold units. We now turn to PEs with continuous and differentiable activation functions, that is, linear graded units. We shall first consider units with a linear activation function, called *linear units*.

A network with a single linear unit is called an *Adaline* (*Adaptive Linear Element*) [Widrow, 1962]. That is, in an Adaline the input-output relationship is linear. The problem to be solved here is again a supervised learning problem as indicated in Eq. (10.1). For a given set of p training patterns, $\left\{\left(\mathbf{x}^{(1)}, d^{(1)}\right), \left(\mathbf{x}^{(2)}, d^{(2)}\right), \ldots, \left(\mathbf{x}^{(p)}, d^{(p)}\right)\right\}$, the goal is to find a correct set of weights w_i such that

$$\sum_{j=1}^{m} w_j x_j^{(k)} = d^{(k)}, \qquad k = 1, 2, \ldots, p. \tag{10.13}$$

The above equation is actually a combination of linear equations whose solutions $\mathbf{w}^*$ exist if the input patterns $\mathbf{x}^{(1)}, \mathbf{x}^{(2)}, \ldots, \mathbf{x}^{(p)}$ are *linearly independent*. A set of p input patterns, each of which is an m-dimensional vector, can be linearly independent only if $p \leq m$, and so we can store at most m arbitrary associations in an Adaline. The linear independence condition for linear units is compatible with the linear separability condition for threshold units. Linear independence implies linear separability, but the reverse is not true.

To find the weights from Eq. (10.13), we define a *cost function* $E(\mathbf{w})$, which measures the system's performance error by

$$E(\mathbf{w}) = \tfrac{1}{2} \sum_{k=1}^{p} (d^{(k)} - y^{(k)})^2 = \tfrac{1}{2} \sum_{k=1}^{p} (d^{(k)} - \mathbf{w}^T \mathbf{x}^{(k)})^2$$

$$= \tfrac{1}{2} \sum_{k=1}^{p} \left(d^{(k)} - \sum_{j=1}^{m} w_j x_j^{(k)} \right)^2. \tag{10.14}$$

Clearly, if $E(\mathbf{w})$ is smaller, the better w_j will be; $E(\mathbf{w})$ is normally positive but approaches zero when $y^{(k)}$ approaches $d^{(k)}$ for $k = 1, 2, \ldots, p$. Thus, we try to find the weights that will minimize the mean squared error $E(\mathbf{w})$. Instead of obtaining an analytical solution, we are interested in finding a learning rule that can find such a set of weights by successive improvement from an arbitrary starting point. Given the cost function $E(\mathbf{w})$ in Eq. (10.14), we can improve on a set of weights w_j by sliding downhill on the surface it defines in the weight space. More specifically, the usual *gradient-descent algorithm* suggests adjusting each weight w_i by an amount Δw_i proportional to the negative of the gradient of $E(\mathbf{w})$ at the current location:

$$\Delta \mathbf{w} = -\eta \nabla_{\mathbf{w}} E(\mathbf{w}). \tag{10.15}$$

That is,

$$\Delta w_j = -\eta \frac{\partial E}{\partial w_j} = \eta \sum_{k=1}^{p} (d^{(k)} - \mathbf{w}^T \mathbf{x}^{(k)}) x_j^{(k)}, \qquad j = 1, 2, \ldots, m. \tag{10.16}$$

If these changes are made individually for each input pattern $\mathbf{x}^{(k)}$ in turn, then the change in response to pattern $\mathbf{x}^{(k)}$ is simply

$$\Delta w_j = \eta (d^{(k)} - \mathbf{w}^T \mathbf{x}^{(k)}) x_j^{(k)}, \tag{10.17}$$

The learning rule in Eq. (10.17) is called the *Adaline learning rule* or the *Widrow-Hoff learning rule* [Widrow and Hoff, 1960]. It is also referred to as the *least mean square* (LMS) rule. In this method, weights are initialized at any value. As compared to the general weight learning rule in Eq. (9.13), the learning signal r here is set as $r = d - y = d - \mathbf{w}^T \mathbf{x}$.

The Widrow-Hoff learning rule is very similar to the perceptron learning rule in Eq. (10.7). The major difference is that the perceptron learning rule originated in an empirical Hebbian assumption, while the Widrow-Hoff learning rule was derived from the gradient-descent method which can be easily generalized to more than one layer. Furthermore, the perceptron learning rule stops after a finite number of learning steps, while, in principle, the gradient-descent approach continues forever, converging only asymptotically to the solution. Since the cost function in Eq. (10.14) is in quadratic form in the weights, in the subspace spanned by the patterns, the surface is a parabolic or hyperparabolic curve with a single minimum, and the minimum (solution) is at $E(\mathbf{w}) = 0$. Hence, within the pattern subspace, the gradient-descent rule necessarily decreases the error if η is small enough because it approaches the minimum in the downhill gradient direction. Thus, from any starting point, we can approach the bottom of the valley arbitrarily close with enough iterations and obtain the solution with required precision.

The above discussion and analysis of the Adaline can also be applied to a single-layer network consisting of an array of Adalines (called a *linear network*) since each Adaline in such a linear network is independent of the others.

So far in this section, we have focused on PEs with a linear activation function a (net) = net. Such a linear unit is the basic element of an Adaline and a linear network. It is straightforward to generalize the gradient-descent learning rule from simple perceptrons with linear units to those with LGUs whose activation functions are differentiable. In this case, the cost function in Eq. (10.14) becomes

$$E(\mathbf{w}) = \frac{1}{2}\sum_{k=1}^{p}\sum_{i=1}^{n}(d_i^{(k)} - y_i^{(k)})^2 = \frac{1}{2}\sum_{k=1}^{p}\sum_{i=1}^{n}[d_i^{(k)} - a(\mathbf{w}_i^T\mathbf{x}^{(k)})]^2$$
$$= \frac{1}{2}\sum_{k=1}^{p}\sum_{i=1}^{n}\left[d_i^{(k)} - a\left(\sum_{j=1}^{m}w_{ij}x_j^{(k)}\right)\right]^2,$$

(10.18)

where the superscript k indicates the kth training data and p is the total number of training data.

Applying the gradient-descent algorithm in Eq. (10.15) to Eq. (10.18), we obtain

$$\frac{\partial E}{\partial w_{ij}} = -\sum_{k=1}^{p}[d_i^{(k)} - a(\text{net}_i^{(k)})]a'(\text{net}_i^{(k)})x_j^{(k)},$$

(10.19)

where $\text{net}_i^{(k)} \triangleq \mathbf{w}_i^T\mathbf{x}^{(k)}$ is the net input to the ith PE when the kth input pattern is presented and $a'(\text{net}_i^{(k)}) = \partial a(\text{net}_i^{(k)})/\partial \text{net}_i^{(k)}$. If we apply the above equation to weight updating, we find that the *true* gradient involves a summation over all the patterns in the training set. However, in most cases, estimates of the gradient from individual samples are usually used. To compensate for the use of gradient estimates rather than true gradients, the learning constant η is chosen to be relatively small. Hence, the gradient-descent correction to w_{ij} after the kth pattern is presented is

$$\Delta w_{ij} = -\eta\frac{\partial E}{\partial w_{ij}} = \eta[d_i^{(k)} - a(\text{net}_i^{(k)})]a'(\text{net}_i^{(k)})x_j^{(k)}.$$

(10.20)

Equation (10.20) is usually called the *delta learning rule* which, in the form of the general learning rule in Eq. (9.13), is obtained by setting the learning signal r as

$$r \triangleq [d_i - a(\mathbf{w}_i^T\mathbf{x})]a'(\mathbf{w}_i^T\mathbf{x}).$$

(10.21)

Example 10.3

[Zurada, 1992]. Consider a four-input, single-node perceptron with a bipolar sigmoid function:

$$a(\text{net}) = \frac{2}{1 + \exp(-\text{net})} - 1,$$

(10.22)

where the λ in Eq. (9.11) is set to 1. The set of input and desired output training patterns is as follows: $\{\mathbf{x}^{(1)} = (1, -2, 0, -1)^T, \ d^{(1)} = -1\}$, $\{\mathbf{x}^{(2)} = (0, 1.5, -0.5, -1)^T, \ d^{(2)} = -1\}$, $\{\mathbf{x}^{(3)} = (-1, 1, 0.5, -1)^T, d^{(3)} = 1\}$. The initial weight is chosen as $\mathbf{w}^{(1)} = [1, -1, 0, 0.5]^T$, and the learning constant is set as $\eta = 0.1$. To apply the delta learning rule, we need to find a' (net) first:

$$a'(\text{net}) = \frac{\partial a(\text{net})}{\partial \text{net}} = \frac{1}{2}[1 - a^2(\text{net})] = \frac{1}{2}(1 - y^2).$$

(10.23)

The learning process is performed as follows:

Step 1: The input pattern is $\mathbf{x}^{(1)}$, and the weight vector is $\mathbf{w}^{(1)}$:

$$\text{net}^{(1)} = \left(\mathbf{w}^{(1)}\right)^T \mathbf{x}^{(1)} = 2.5 \qquad \text{and} \qquad y^{(1)} = a\!\left(\text{net}^{(1)}\right) = 0.848,$$

$$a'\!\left(\text{net}^{(1)}\right) = \tfrac{1}{2}\!\left[1 - \left(y^{(1)}\right)^2\right] = 0.14,$$

$$\mathbf{w}^{(2)} = \eta\!\left(d^{(1)} - y^{(1)}\right)a'\!\left(\text{net}^{(1)}\right)\mathbf{x}^{(1)} + \mathbf{w}^{(1)}$$

$$= [0.974, -0.948, 0, 0.526]^T.$$

Step 2: The input pattern is $\mathbf{x}^{(2)}$, and the weight vector is $\mathbf{w}^{(2)}$:

$$\text{net}^{(2)} = \left(\mathbf{w}^{(2)}\right)^T \mathbf{x}^{(2)} = -1.948 \qquad \text{and} \qquad y^{(2)} = a\!\left(\text{net}^{(2)}\right) = -0.75,$$

$$a'\!\left(\text{net}^{(2)}\right) = \tfrac{1}{2}\!\left[1 - \left(y^{(2)}\right)^2\right] = 0.218,$$

$$\mathbf{w}^{(3)} = \eta\!\left(d^{(2)} - y^{(2)}\right)a'\!\left(\text{net}^{(2)}\right)\mathbf{x}^{(2)} + \mathbf{w}^{(2)}$$

$$= [0.974, -0.956, 0.002, 0.531]^T.$$

Step 3: The input pattern is $\mathbf{x}^{(3)}$, and the weight vector is $\mathbf{w}^{(3)}$:

$$\text{net}^{(3)} = \left(\mathbf{w}^{(3)}\right)^T \mathbf{x}^{(3)} = -2.46 \qquad \text{and} \qquad y^{(3)} = a\!\left(\text{net}^{(3)}\right) = -0.842,$$

$$a'\!\left(\text{net}^{(3)}\right) = \tfrac{1}{2}\!\left[1 - \left(y^{(3)}\right)^2\right] = 0.145,$$

$$\mathbf{w}^{(4)} = \eta\!\left(d^{(3)} - y^{(3)}\right)a'\!\left(\text{net}^{(3)}\right)\mathbf{x}^{(3)} + \mathbf{w}^{(3)}$$

$$= [0.947, -0.929, 0.016, 0.505]^T.$$

Up to now, all the training patterns have been used for training *once*. This is called one *epoch*. The input patterns need to be "recycled" to train the network continuously for more epochs until satisfactory outputs are obtained.

The conditions for the existence of a solution of simple perceptrons with LGUs are exactly the same as for those with linear units—linear independence of the input patterns if we consider only monotonic activation functions. The reason is that the solution to our present problem is equivalent to that for the linear one with targets $d_i^{(k)}$ replaced by $a^{-1}\!\left(d_i^{(k)}\right)$. But their convergence properties are different—the question of whether the delta learning rule finds the solution for nonlinear networks (assuming it exists) is not the same as in the case of the Widrow-Hoff learning rule for the linear networks. If the targets lie outside the range of a (net) [e.g., ± 1 targets with a bipolar sigmoid function in Eq. (10.22)], it is possible that in the nonlinear case the cost function may have *local minima* besides the global minimum at $E(\mathbf{w}) = 0$. In this case, the delta learning rule may then become stuck at such a local minimum.

In simple perceptrons, there are two main advantages of using nonlinear activation functions. First, they keep the outputs between fixed bounds (e.g., ± 1 for a bipolar sigmoid function). This makes a feedforward network structure with an arbitrary number of layers feasible. Second, they introduce nonlinearity into networks, where they make possible the solutions of problems that are not possible with linear units. The computation performed by a multilayer linear feedforward network is exactly equivalent to that performed by a single-layer linear network since a linear transformation of a linear transformation is a linear transformation. Hence, a multilayer linear feedforward network has the same limitations as a single-layer linear feedforward network. In particular, it works only if the input patterns are linearly independent. But a multilayer nonlinear feedforward network does not have this restriction. Since the nonlinear activation functions that we are considering here are differentiable, the delta learning rule can be easily generalized to multilayer networks with such units. We shall next introduce the generalized delta learning rule for multilayer feedforward networks.

10.2 MULTILAYER FEEDFORWARD NETWORKS

Our study thus far has focused on simple perceptrons whose ability to solve a problem depends on the condition that the input patterns of the problem be linearly separable (for threshold units) or linearly independent (for continuous and differentiable units). These limitations of simple perceptrons do not apply to feedforward networks with intermediate or "hidden" layers between the input and output layers. Let us look at an example to understand why multilayer networks can solve problems that cannot be solved by single-layer networks. For the remainder of this book, we shall slightly misuse the notation by counting the input layer as one layer in our discussion of multilayer networks. This is not the case when we consider single-layer networks.

Example 10.4

This example illustrates how a linearly nonseparable problem is transformed to a linearly separable problem by a space transformation and thus can be solved by a multilayer perceptron network with LTUs. The problem we consider is the XOR problem. As shown in Fig. 10.6(a), the input patterns and the corresponding desired outputs are

$$\left(\mathbf{x}^{(1)} = \begin{pmatrix} 0 \\ 0 \end{pmatrix}, d^{(1)} = 1\right); \qquad \left(\mathbf{x}^{(2)} = \begin{pmatrix} 0 \\ 1 \end{pmatrix}, d^{(2)} = -1\right);$$

$$\left(\mathbf{x}^{(3)} = \begin{pmatrix} 1 \\ 0 \end{pmatrix}, d^{(3)} = -1\right); \qquad \left(\mathbf{x}^{(4)} = \begin{pmatrix} 1 \\ 1 \end{pmatrix}, d^{(4)} = 1\right).$$

Obviously, the four input patterns are not linearly separable in the input space (or the *pattern space*). We arbitrarily use two lines to partition the input space into three subspaces [see Fig.

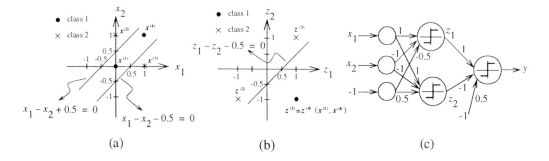

(a) (b) (c)

Figure 10.6 Multilayer perceptron for the XOR problem in Example 10.4. (a) Input (pattern) space (linearly nonseparable). (b) Image space (linearly separable). (c) A multilayer perceptron network for the XOR problem.

10.6(a)] in such a way that each subspace contains patterns belonging to the same class. The two selected lines are

$$x_1 - x_2 + 0.5 = 0 \qquad \text{and} \qquad x_1 - x_2 - 0.5 = 0.$$

Two LTUs are used to perform the partitioning created by these two selected lines. Hence, their respective outputs are

$$z_1 = \text{sgn}(x_1 - x_2 + 0.5) \qquad \text{and} \qquad z_2 = \text{sgn}(x_1 - x_2 - 0.5).$$

These two LTUs are put in the hidden layer of the final network in Fig. 10.6(c). Looking at the z_1-z_2 space, also called the *image space*, the original training patterns become

$$\left(\mathbf{z}^{(1)} = \begin{pmatrix} 1 \\ -1 \end{pmatrix}, d^{(1)} = 1 \right); \qquad \left(\mathbf{z}^{(2)} = \begin{pmatrix} -1 \\ -1 \end{pmatrix}, d^{(2)} = -1 \right);$$

$$\left(\mathbf{z}^{(3)} = \begin{pmatrix} 1 \\ 1 \end{pmatrix}, d^{(3)} = -1 \right); \qquad \left(\mathbf{z}^{(4)} = \begin{pmatrix} 1 \\ -1 \end{pmatrix}, d^{(4)} = 1 \right).$$

The transformed training patterns in the image space are shown in Fig. 10.6(b). It is observed that the original input patterns $\mathbf{x}^{(1)}$ and $\mathbf{x}^{(4)}$ coincide in the image space and that the transformed training patterns also become linearly separable in the image space. The remaining classification problem becomes what we have dealt with previously. A boundary can be chosen arbitrarily, say $z_1 - z_2 - 0.5 = 0$ [see Fig. 10.6(b)], to separate these patterns. The function of the selected line is performed by the third LTU in the output layer, whose output is

$$y = \text{sgn}(z_1 - z_2 - 0.5).$$

The final network for solving the XOR problem is shown in Fig. 10.6(c).

The above example illustrates that the original pattern space is mapped into the image space so that a three-layer network can eventually classify the patterns that are linearly non-separable in the original pattern space. Although the greater solving power of multilayer networks was realized long ago, it was only recently shown how they can be utilized to *learn* a particular function. In the next section, we shall study an important learning algorithm called *back propagation* for training multilayer feedforward networks.

10.2.1 Back Propagation

The back-propagation learning algorithm is one of the most important historical developments in neural networks [Bryson and Ho, 1969; Werbos, 1974; LeCun, 1985; Parker, 1985; Rumelhart et al., 1986a,b]. It has reawakened the scientific and engineering community to the modeling and processing of many quantitative phenomena using neural networks. This learning algorithm is applied to multilayer feedforward networks consisting of processing elements with continuous differentiable activation functions. Such networks associated with the back-propagation learning algorithm are also called *back-propagation networks*. Given a training set of input-output pairs $\{(\mathbf{x}^{(k)}, \mathbf{d}^{(k)})\}$, $k = 1, 2, ..., p$, the algorithm provides a procedure for changing the weights in a back-propagation network to classify the given input patterns correctly. The basis for this weight update algorithm is simply the gradient-descent method as used for simple perceptrons with differentiable units.

For a given input-output pair $(\mathbf{x}^{(k)}, \mathbf{d}^{(k)})$, the back-propagation algorithm performs two phases of data flow. First, the input pattern $\mathbf{x}^{(k)}$ is propagated from the input layer to the output layer and, as a result of this forward flow of data, it produces an actual output $\mathbf{y}^{(k)}$. Then the error signals resulting from the difference between $\mathbf{d}^{(k)}$ and $\mathbf{y}^{(k)}$ are *back-propagated* from the output layer to the previous layers for them to update their weights. Let us consider a three-layer network as shown in Fig. 10.7 to illustrate the details of the back-propagation learning algorithm. The result can be easily extended to networks with any number of layers. In Fig. 10.7, we have m PEs in the input layer, l PEs in the hidden layer, and n PEs in the output layer; the solid lines show the forward propagation of signals, and the dashed lines show the backward propagation of errors.

First, let us consider an input-output training pair $(\mathbf{x}, \mathbf{d})$, where the superscript k is omitted for notation simplification. Given an input pattern $\mathbf{x}$, a PE q in the hidden layer receives a net input of

$$\text{net}_q = \sum_{j=1}^{m} v_{qj} x_j \tag{10.24}$$

and produces an output of

$$z_q = a\,(\text{net}_q) = a\left(\sum_{j=1}^{m} v_{qj} x_j\right). \tag{10.25}$$

The net input for a PE i in the output layer is then

$$\text{net}_i = \sum_{q=1}^{l} w_{iq} z_q = \sum_{q=1}^{l} w_{iq} a\left(\sum_{j=1}^{m} v_{qj} x_j\right), \tag{10.26}$$

and it produces an output of

$$y_i = a\,(\text{net}_i) = a\left(\sum_{q=1}^{l} w_{iq} z_q\right) = a\left(\sum_{q=1}^{l} w_{iq} a\left(\sum_{j=1}^{m} v_{qj} x_j\right)\right). \tag{10.27}$$

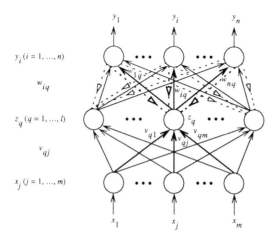

Figure 10.7 Three-layer back-propagation network.

The above equations indicate the forward propagation of input signals through the layers of neurons. Next, we shall consider the error signals and their back propagation. We first define a cost function as in Eq. (10.14):

$$E(\mathbf{w}) = \tfrac{1}{2}\sum_{i=1}^{n}(d_i - y_i)^2 = \tfrac{1}{2}\sum_{i=1}^{n}[d_i - a(\text{net}_i)]^2$$

$$= \tfrac{1}{2}\sum_{i=1}^{n}\left[d_i - a\left(\sum_{q=1}^{l}w_{iq}z_q\right)\right]^2. \qquad (10.28)$$

Then according to the gradient-descent method, the weights in the hidden-to-output connections are updated by

$$\Delta w_{iq} = -\eta\frac{\partial E}{\partial w_{iq}}. \qquad (10.29)$$

Using Eqs. (10.26)–(10.28) and the chain rule for $\partial E/\partial w_{iq}$, we have

$$\Delta w_{iq} = -\eta\left[\frac{\partial E}{\partial y_i}\right]\left[\frac{\partial y_i}{\partial \text{net}_i}\right]\left[\frac{\partial \text{net}_i}{\partial w_{iq}}\right] = \eta[d_i - y_i][a'(\text{net}_i)][z_q] \triangleq \eta\delta_{oi}z_q, \qquad (10.30)$$

where δ_{oi} is the *error signal* and its double subscript indicates the ith node in the output layer. The error signal is defined by

$$\delta_{oi} \triangleq -\frac{\partial E}{\partial \text{net}_i} = -\left[\frac{\partial E}{\partial y_i}\right]\left[\frac{\partial y_i}{\partial \text{net}_i}\right] = [d_i - y_i][a'(\text{net}_i)], \qquad (10.31)$$

where net_i is the net input to PE i of the output layer and $a'(\text{net}_i) = \partial a(\text{net}_i)/\partial \text{net}_i$. The result thus far is identical to the delta learning rule obtained in Eq. (10.20) for a single-layer perceptron whose input is now the output z_q of the hidden layer.

For the weight update on the input-to-hidden connections, we use the chain rule with the gradient-descent method and obtain the weight update on the link weight connecting PE j in the input layer to PE q in the hidden layer,

$$\Delta v_{qj} = -\eta\left[\frac{\partial E}{\partial v_{qj}}\right] = -\eta\left[\frac{\partial E}{\partial \text{net}_q}\right]\left[\frac{\partial \text{net}_q}{\partial v_{qj}}\right]$$

$$= -\eta\left[\frac{\partial E}{\partial z_q}\right]\left[\frac{\partial z_q}{\partial \text{net}_q}\right]\left[\frac{\partial \text{net}_q}{\partial v_{qj}}\right]. \qquad (10.32)$$

From Eq. (10.28), it is clear that each error term $[d_i - y_i]$, $i = 1, 2,\dots, n$, is a function of z_q. Evaluating the chain rule, we have

$$\Delta v_{qj} = \eta\sum_{i=1}^{n}[(d_i - y_i)a'(\text{net}_i)w_{iq}]a'(\text{net}_q)x_j. \qquad (10.33)$$

Using Eq. (10.31), we can rewrite Eq. (10.33) as

$$\Delta v_{qj} = \eta\sum_{i=1}^{n}[\delta_{oi}w_{iq}]a'(\text{net}_q)x_j = \eta\delta_{hq}x_j, \qquad (10.34)$$

where δ_{hq} is the error signal of PE q in the hidden layer and is defined as

$$\delta_{hq} \overset{\triangle}{=} -\frac{\partial E}{\partial \text{net}_q} = -\left[\frac{\partial E}{\partial z_q}\right]\left[\frac{\partial z_q}{\partial \text{net}_q}\right] = a'(\text{net}_q)\sum_{i=1}^{n}\delta_{oi}w_{iq}, \qquad (10.35)$$

where net_q is the net input to the hidden PE q [Eq. (10.24)]. The error signal of a PE in a hidden layer is different from the error signal of a PE in the output layer, as seen in Eqs. (10.31) and (10.35). Because of this difference, the above weight update procedure is called the *generalized delta learning rule*. We observe from Eq. (10.35) that the error signal δ_{hq} of a hidden PE q can be determined in terms of the error signals δ_{oi} of the PEs, y_i, that it feeds. The coefficients are just the weights used for the forward propagation, but here they are propagating error signals (δ_{oi}) backward instead of propagating signals forward. This is shown by the dashed lines in Fig. 10.7. This also demonstrates one important feature of the back-propagation algorithm—the update rule is local; that is, to compute the weight change for a given connection, we need only quantities available at both ends of that connection.

Note that both Eqs. (10.30) and (10.34) are in the same form of the general weight learning rule in Eq. (9.13) except that the learning signals, $r = \delta$, are different. The above derivation can be easily extended to the network with more than one hidden layer by using the chain rule continuously. In general, with an arbitrary number of layers, the back-propagation update rule is in the form

$$\Delta w_{ij} = \eta\delta_i x_j = \eta\delta_{\text{output-}i} \cdot x_{\text{input-}j}, \qquad (10.36)$$

where "output-i" and "input-j" refer to the two ends of the connection from PE j to PE i, x_j is the proper input-end activation from a hidden PE or an external input, and δ_i is the learning signal which is defined by Eq. (10.31) for the last (or output) layer of connection weights and defined by Eq. (10.35) for all the other layers. When the bipolar sigmoid function is used as the activation function, then using Eq. (10.23), Eqs. (10.31) and (10.35), respectively, become

$$\delta_{oi} = \tfrac{1}{2}(1 - y_i^2)\,[d_i - y_i], \qquad (10.37)$$

and

$$\delta_{hq} = \tfrac{1}{2}(1 - z_q^2)\sum_{i=1}^{n}\delta_{oi}w_{iq}. \qquad (10.38)$$

In summary, the error back-propagation learning algorithm can be outlined in the following algorithm BP.

Algorithm BP: Back-propagation Learning Rule

Consider a network with Q feedforward layers, $q = 1, 2,\ldots, Q$, and let $^q\text{net}_i$ and ^qy_i denote the net input and output of the ith unit in the qth layer, respectively. The network has m input nodes and n output nodes. Let $^qw_{ij}$ denote the connection weight from $^{q-1}y_j$ to ^qy_i.

Input: A set of training pairs $\{(\mathbf{x}^{(k)}, \mathbf{d}^{(k)}) \mid k = 1, 2,\ldots,p\}$, where the input vectors are augmented with the last elements as -1, that is, $x_{m+1}^{(k)} = -1$.

Step 0 (Initialization): Choose $\eta > 0$ and $E_{\max}$ (maximum tolerable error). Initialize the weights to small random values. Set $E = 0$ and $k = 1$.

Step 1 (Training loop): Apply the kth input pattern to the input layer $(q = 1)$:

$$^qy_i = {}^1y_i = x_i^{(k)} \qquad \text{for all } i. \qquad (10.39)$$

Step 2 (Forward propagation): Propagate the signal forward through the network using

$$^q y_i = a(^q \mathrm{net}_i) = a\left(\sum_j {}^q w_{ij} \, {}^{q-1} y_j\right)$$ (10.40)

for each i and q until the outputs of the output layer $^Q y_i$ have all been obtained.

Step 3 (Output error measure): Compute the error value and error signals $^Q \delta_i$ for the output layer:

$$E = \frac{1}{2} \sum_{i=1}^{n} (d_i^{(k)} - {}^Q y_i)^2 + E,$$ (10.41)

$$^Q \delta_i = (d_i^{(k)} - {}^Q y_i) a'(^Q \mathrm{net}_i).$$ (10.42)

Step 4 (Error back-propagation): Propagate the errors backward to update the weights and compute the error signals $^{q-1} \delta_i$ for the preceding layers:

$$\Delta^q w_{ij} = \eta \, {}^q \delta_i \, {}^{q-1} y_j \quad \text{and} \quad {}^q w_{ij}^{\mathrm{new}} = {}^q w_{ij}^{\mathrm{old}} + \Delta^q w_{ij},$$ (10.43)

$$^{q-1} \delta_i = a'(^{q-1} \mathrm{net}_i) \sum_j {}^q w_{ji} \, {}^q \delta_j \quad \text{for } q = Q, Q-1, \dots, 2.$$ (10.44)

Step 5 (One epoch looping): Check whether the whole set of training data has been cycled once. If $k < p$, then $k = k + 1$ and go to step 1; otherwise, go to step 6.

Step 6 (Total error checking): Check whether the current total error is acceptable: If $E < E_{\max}$, then terminate the training process and output the final weights; otherwise, $E = 0$, $k = 1$, and initiate the new training epoch by going to step 1.

End BP

The above algorithm adopts the *incremental* approach in updating the weights; that is, the weights are changed immediately after a training pattern is presented. The alternative is *batch-mode* training—where the weights are changed only after all the training patterns have been presented. The relative effectiveness of the two approaches depends on the problem, but batch-mode training requires additional local storage for each connection to maintain the immediate weight changes. Furthermore, for best results, patterns should be chosen at random from the training set instead of following a fixed order as in step 1 of the algorithm BP.

Example 10.5

Consider a simple back-propagation network as in Fig. 10.8. For clarity, simplified notations are shown in the figure. Each PE in this network has an unipolar sigmoid activation function defined in Eq. (9.10); that is,

$$y = a(\mathrm{net}) = \frac{1}{1 + e^{-\lambda \mathrm{net}}},$$ (10.45)

where "net" is the net input defined as the weighted summation of the input values and $\lambda = 1$. It can be shown that

$$a'(\mathrm{net}) = y(1 - y).$$ (10.46)

From Eq. (10.42), we have

$$\delta_9 = a_9'(\mathrm{net}_9)(d - y_9) = y_9(1 - y_9)(d - y_9).$$

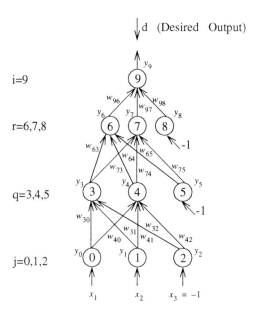

i=9

r=6,7,8

q=3,4,5

j=0,1,2

d (Desired Output)

x_1 x_2 $x_3 = -1$

Figure 10.8 Back-propagation network in Example 10.5.

For hidden layers, from Eq. (10.44) we have the following error signals:

$$\delta_6 = a_6' \, (\text{net}_6) \sum_{i=9}^{9} w_{i6}\delta_i = y_6 \, (1 - y_6) \, w_{96}\delta_9,$$

$$\delta_7 = a_7' \, (\text{net}_7) \sum_{i=9}^{9} w_{i7}\delta_i = y_7 \, (1 - y_7) \, w_{97}\delta_9,$$

$$\delta_3 = a_3' \, (\text{net}_3) \sum_{r=6}^{7} w_{r3}\delta_r = y_3 \, (1 - y_3) \, (w_{63}\delta_6 + w_{73}\delta_7),$$

$$\delta_4 = a_4' \, (\text{net}_4) \sum_{r=6}^{7} w_{r4}\delta_r = y_4 \, (1 - y_4) \, (w_{64}\delta_6 + w_{74}\delta_7).$$

Then the weight update rules are [see Eq. (10.43)]

$$\Delta w_{96} = \eta\delta_9 y_6, \qquad \Delta w_{97} = \eta\delta_9 y_7, \qquad \Delta w_{98} = \eta\delta_9 y_8 = -\eta\delta_9,$$

$$\Delta w_{63} = \eta\delta_6 y_3, \qquad \Delta w_{64} = \eta\delta_6 y_4, \qquad \Delta w_{65} = \eta\delta_6 y_5 = -\eta\delta_6,$$

$$\Delta w_{73} = \eta\delta_7 y_3, \qquad \Delta w_{74} = \eta\delta_7 y_4, \qquad \Delta w_{75} = \eta\delta_7 y_5 = -\eta\delta_7,$$

$$\Delta w_{30} = \eta\delta_3 y_0, \qquad \Delta w_{31} = \eta\delta_3 y_1, \qquad \Delta w_{32} = \eta\delta_3 y_2 = -\eta\delta_3,$$

$$\Delta w_{40} = \eta\delta_4 y_0, \qquad \Delta w_{41} = \eta\delta_4 y_1, \qquad \Delta w_{42} = \eta\delta_4 y_2 = -\eta\delta_4.$$

The above weight changes are performed for a single training pattern, called a *learning step*. After a learning step is finished, the next training pattern is submitted and the learning step is repeated. The learning steps proceed until all the patterns in the training set have been exhausted. This terminates the complete learning cycle known as one epoch. The cumulative cycle error is computed for the complete learning cycle using Eq. (10.28) and then compared with the maximum error allowed. If the total error is not satisfied, a new learning cycle will be initiated.

Before discussing the convergence property of the back-propagation learning algorithm, we first take a look at the function approximation capability of multilayer feedforward networks. The following theorem addresses this issue, which is presented and proved in [Hornik et al., 1989].

Theorem 10.2

Multilayer feedforward network architectures with as few as one hidden layer using arbitrary *squashing activation functions* and linear or polynomial integration functions can approximate virtually any (Borel-measurable) function of interest to any desired degree of accuracy provided sufficiently many hidden units are available. A function $a: \Re \rightarrow [0, 1]$ (or $[-1, 1]$) is a squashing function if it is nondecreasing, $\lim_{\lambda \to \infty} a(\lambda) = 1$, and $\lim_{\lambda \to -\infty} a(\lambda) = 0$ (or -1), where λ is a parameter in the squashing function.

It is clear that the activation functions defined in Eqs. (9.7)–(9.11), including step functions, threshold functions, ramp functions, and sigmoid functions, are all squashing functions. The integration functions in Eq. (9.3) (linear) and Eq. (9.6) (polynomial) fit the requirement of the above theorem. Hence, this theorem applies not only to a multilayer network with LGU units (called a *Madaline* network), but also to a multilayer network with LTU units.

Theorem 10.2 establishes multilayer feedforward networks as a class of universal approximators. This implies that any lack of success in application must arise from *inadequate learning, insufficient numbers of hidden units,* or *lack of a deterministic relationship between input and desired output.* Although this theorem indicates that three layers are always enough, it is often essential to have four, five, or even more layers in solving real-world problems. This is because an approximation with three layers would require an impractically large number of hidden units for many problems, whereas an adequate solution can be obtained with a tractable network size by using more than three layers. In fact, it has been shown that single-hidden-layer networks are not sufficient for stabilization, especially in discontinuous mapping, but that two-hidden-layer networks are enough assuming that threshold units are used [Sontag, 1992].

Back-propagation networks are multilayer feedforward networks with the back-propagation learning algorithm. Hence, Theorem 10.2 ensures the representation capability of the *structures* of back-propagation networks if the hidden units are enough. Actually, it has been shown that a back-propagation network, when used as a classifier, is equivalent to the optimal Bayesian discriminant function for asymptotically large sets of statistically independent training patterns [Hampshire and Pearlmutter, 1990; Ruck et al., 1990]. The problem remaining is whether the back-propagation learning algorithm can always converge and find proper weights for the network after enough learning. Intuitively, it will converge since it implements a gradient descent on the error surface in the weight space, and the "state-space ball" will roll down the error surface to the nearest error minimum and stop. But this is true only when the relationship between input and output training patterns is deterministic and the error surface is deterministic. Unfortunately, this rarely happens in the real world, where the produced square-error surfaces are always random. This is the stochastic nature of the back-propagation algorithm, which is actually based on the stochastic gradient-descent method. In fact, the back-propagation algorithm has been shown to be a special case of stochastic approximation [White, 1989]. Another problem if that is the back-propagation algorithm converges at all, it may become stuck at local minima and be unable to find satisfactory solutions. This inspires us to examine back-propagation error surfaces. Let us look at an example.

Example 10.6

[Hush et al., 1992]. In this example, we consider the shapes of the error surfaces formed by a three-layer back-propagation network with LGUs as shown in Fig. 10.9(a). This network has a total of 13 weights. The training data are drawn from a four-dimensional, two-class Gaussian distribution with the mean vectors and the covariance matrices given by

$$\mathbf{m}_1 = [1, 1, 1, 1]^T, \qquad \mathbf{m}_2 = [-1, -1, -1, -1]^T,$$

$$\mathbf{C}_1 = \begin{bmatrix} 3 & 0 & 0 & 0 \\ 0 & 3 & 0 & 0 \\ 0 & 0 & 3 & 0 \\ 0 & 0 & 0 & 3 \end{bmatrix}, \qquad \mathbf{C}_2 = \begin{bmatrix} 1 & 0 & 0 & 0 \\ 0 & 1 & 0 & 0 \\ 0 & 0 & 1 & 0 \\ 0 & 0 & 0 & 1 \end{bmatrix}.$$

Ten training patterns for each class are used to train the network. The network is first trained using the back-propagation algorithm to obtain a set of weights corresponding to a minimum of the surface. The plots in Fig. 10.9(b) correspond to plots of $E(w_i, w_j)$ as a function of two selected weights in the network, while the other 11 weights are kept fixed at the minimum. It is observed that most of what we see are plateaus and troughs. There are many flat surfaces with different heights.

The above example indicates the three basic known facts about back-propagation error surfaces. First, the error functions typically have large numbers of global minima because of combinatoric permutations of weights that keep the network input-output function unchanged. This causes the error surfaces to have numerous troughs. Second, there are local minima at error levels above the levels of the global minima of the surfaces. This causes the back-propagation learning to become stuck at the local minima. However, from empirical studies, we know that this does not happen often if we use more (redundant) hidden units than are necessary. This is because of the stochastic nature of the algorithm. The randomness helps it get out of local minima. The larger the neural networks, the greater the number of stochastic factors. Third, error surfaces have a multitude of areas with shallow slopes in multiple dimensions. This usually happens because the outputs of some nodes are large and insensitive to small weight changes and takes place on the shallow tails of the sigmoid function. The existence of many areas with shallow slopes on the error surfaces always causes the back propagation to converge rather slowly. Figure 10.10 shows the curves that indicate the rate of convergence at long times in the back-propagation learning algorithm for networks with and without hidden units [Tesauro et al., 1989]. The network used has 23 input units and varying numbers of hidden units in a single hidden layer. The training set contained 200 patterns generated from a uniform random distribution. The straight-line behavior at the end of the learning indicates power-low decay of the error function. In each case, the slope is approximately -1, indicating that $E \approx 1/t$. Some variations of the back-propagation learning algorithm for improving learning speed and avoiding local minima will be discussed next.

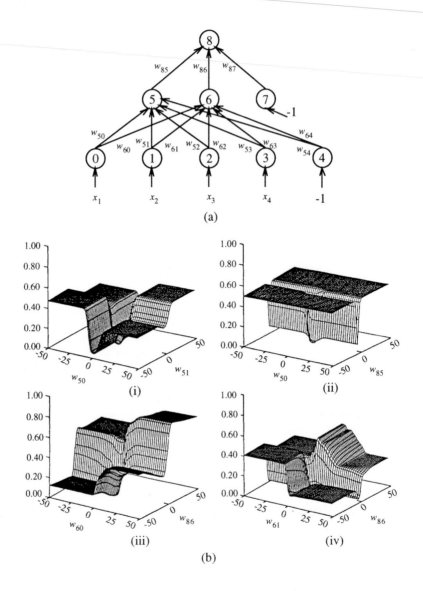

(a)

(i)

(ii)

(iii)

(iv)

(b)

Figure 10.9 Three-layer back-propagation network in Example 10.6 and its error surfaces. (a) The tested back-propagation network. (b) Two-dimensional projections of the error surface for the network in (a) formed by fixing 11 weights at the minimum and varying the other two. (i) $E(w_{50}, w_{51})$. (ii) $E(w_{50}, w_{85})$. (iii) $E(w_{60}, w_{86})$. (iv) $E(w_{61}, w_{86})$. (Adapted from Hush et al. [1992], © 1992 IEEE.)

10.2.2 Learning Factors of Back Propagation

We shall address the issue of convergence of the back-propagation algorithm based on some important learning factors such as the initial weights, the learning constant, the cost function, the update rule, the size and nature of the training set, and the architecture (number of

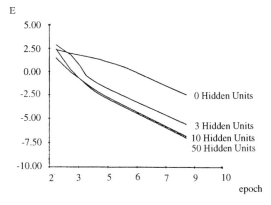

E

5.00	
2.50	
0.00	
-2.50	0 Hidden Units
-5.00	3 Hidden Units
-7.50	10 Hidden Units
	50 Hidden Units
-10.00	

2   3   5   6   7   9   10

epoch

Figure 10.10   Plot of total training set error versus epochs of training time on a log-log scale for networks learning the majority function using back propagation. (From Gerald Tesauro, Yu He and Su Ahmad, "Asymptotic Convergence of Backpropagation," *Neural Computation*, Vol. 1, No. 3, pp. 389. © 1989 by the Massachusetts Institute of Technology.)

layers and number of nodes per layer). Our concern will focus on the problems of learning speed, local minima, and the generalization capability of back-propagation networks. Some variations on back propagation will also be introduced.

Initial weights.   The initial weights of a multilayer feedforward network strongly affect the ultimate solution. They are typically initialized at *small random* values. Equal initial weight values cannot train the network properly if the solution requires unequal weights to be developed. The initial weights cannot be large, otherwise the sigmoids will saturate from the beginning and the system will become stuck at a local minimum or in a very flat plateau near the starting point. One proper way is to choose the weight w_{ij} in the range of $\left[-3/\sqrt{k_i}, 3/\sqrt{k_i}\right]$, where k_i is the number of PE j that feedforward to PE i (the number of input links of PE i) [Wessels and Barnard, 1992].

Learning constant.   Another important factor that affects the effectiveness and convergence of the back-propagation learning algorithm significantly is the learning constant η. There is no single learning constant value suitable for different training cases and η is usually chosen experimentally for each problem. A larger value of η could speed up the convergence but might result in overshooting, while a smaller value of η has a complementary effect. Values of η ranging from 10^{-3} to 10 have been used successfully for many computational back-propagation experiments.

Another problem is that the best values of the learning constant at the beginning of training may not be as good in later training. Thus, a more efficient approach is to use an adaptive learning constant [Vogl et al., 1988; Jacobs, 1988]. The intuitive method is to check whether a particular weight update has decreased the cost function. If it has not, then the process has overshot and η should be reduced. On the other hand, if several steps in a row have decreased the cost function, then we may be too conservative and should try increasing η. More precisely, the learning constant should be updated according to the following rule [Hertz et al., 1991]:

$$\Delta\eta = \begin{cases} +a & \text{if } \Delta E < 0 \text{ consistently} \\ -b\eta & \text{if } \Delta E > 0 \\ 0 & \text{otherwise,} \end{cases} \tag{10.47}$$

where ΔE is the change in the cost function and a and b are positive constants. The meaning of "consistently" in Eq. (10.47) can be judged based on the last k learning steps or on a weighted moving average of the observed ΔE. For the latter approach, we have the following *delta-bar-delta* rule:

$$\Delta\eta\,(t+1) = \begin{cases} +a & \text{if } \overline{\lambda}\,(t-1)\,\lambda\,(t) > 0 \\ -b\eta\,(t) & \text{if } \overline{\lambda}\,(t-1)\,\lambda\,(t) < 0 \\ 0 & \text{otherwise,} \end{cases} \qquad (10.48)$$

where

$$\lambda\,(t) = \frac{\partial E}{\partial w_{ij}} \qquad \text{and} \qquad \overline{\lambda}\,(t) = (1-c)\,\lambda\,(t) + c\overline{\lambda}\,(t-1)\,, \qquad (10.49)$$

where $c \in [0, 1]$ is a constant. Even without an adaptive rule, it may be appropriate to have different η for each pattern or each connection weight according to the fan-in of the corresponding node [Tesauro and Janssens, 1988].

Cost functions. The quadratic cost function in Eq. (10.28) is not the only possible choice. The squared error term $(d_i - y_i)^2$ can be replaced by any other differentiable function $F\,(d_i, y_i)$ which is minimized when its arguments are equal. Based on this new cost function, we can derive a corresponding update rule. It can be easily seen that only the error signal δ_{oi} in Eq. (10.31) for the output layer changes for different cost functions, while all the other equations of the back-propagation algorithm remain unchanged.

The cost functions usually used are those based on L_p norm $(1 \le p \le \infty)$ because of the advantage of easier mathematical formulation. Such cost functions are in the form of [see Eq. (10.28) for comparison]

$$E = \frac{1}{p}\sum_i (d_i - y_i)^p \qquad \text{where } 1 \le p < \infty. \qquad (10.50)$$

In particular, the least squares criteria (L_2 norm) used in the quadratic cost function is widely employed because of its simplicity. Let us now consider the L_∞ norm, which is also called the *Chebyshev norm*. Analogous to the least squares norm in Eq. (10.28), the L_∞ norm defines the error per pattern as

$$E^\infty = \sup_i \left| d_i - y_i \right|, \qquad (10.51)$$

where $\sup| \cdot |$ denotes a function selecting the largest component in the vector. The above definition implies that the overall error measure E^∞ equals the largest component of the error vector, while all the other error components are negligible. From the cost function in Eq. (10.51), we can derive the error signal δ_{oi} of the output layer as [see Eq. (10.31) for comparison]

$$\delta_{oi} = -\frac{\partial E^\infty}{\partial net_i} = \begin{cases} 0 & \text{if } i \ne i^* \\ a'\,(net_i^*)\,\text{sgn}\,(d_i^* - y_i^*) & \text{if } i = i^*, \end{cases} \qquad (10.52)$$

where i^* is the index of the largest component of the output error vector. This error signal indicates that the only error with the back propagation is the largest one among the errors of all output nodes and that it is propagated from the i*th output node, where it occurs, back to the preceding layers. No error component is back-propagated from the other output nodes. The reader is referred to [Burrascano, 1991a] for a norm selection criterion via the analysis of a correspondence between L_p norms and the error distribution at the output of a back-propagation network.

Momentum. The gradient descent can be very slow if the learning constant η is small and can oscillate widely if η is too large. This problem essentially results from error-surface valleys with steep sides but a shallow slope along the valley floor. One efficient and commonly used method that allows a larger learning constant without divergent oscillations occurring is the addition of a momentum term to the normal gradient-descent method [Plaut et al., 1986]. The idea is to give each weight some inertia or momentum so that it tends to change in the direction of the average downhill force that it feels. This scheme is implemented by giving a contribution from the previous time step to each weight change:

$$\Delta w(t) = -\eta \nabla E(t) + \alpha \Delta w(t-1), \qquad (10.53)$$

where $\alpha \in [0, 1]$ is a momentum parameter and a value of 0.9 is often used. Figure 10.11 shows the trajectories of gradient descent with and without momentum on a simple quadratic surface. Note that the trajectory without momentum (the left curve) has larger oscillations than the one with momentum (the right curves). We further observe from the right curves in Fig. 10.11 that the momentum can enhance progress toward the target point if the weight update is in the right direction (point A to A' in Fig. 10.11). On the other hand, it can redirect movement in a better direction toward the target point in the case of overshooting (point B to B' in Fig. 10.11). This observation indicates that the momentum term typically helps to speed up the convergence and to achieve an efficient and more reliable learning profile.

A momentum term is useful with either pattern-by-pattern or batch-mode updating. In the batch mode, it has the effect of complete averaging over the patterns. Although the averaging is only partial in the pattern-by-pattern case, it can leave some beneficial fluctuations in the trajectory.

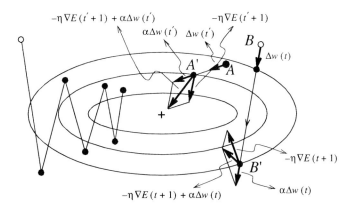

Figure 10.11 Gradient descent on a simple quadratic surface. There is no momentum term on the left trajectory, while on the right there is a momentum term.

Update rules. Although the gradient-descent (or steepest-descent) method is one of the simplest optimization techniques, it is not a very effective one. Further numerical optimization theory [Luenberger, 1976] can be applied to make convergence of the back-propagation algorithm significantly faster. Numerical optimization theory provides a rich and robust set of techniques which can be applied to neural networks to improve learning rates. Although some of them are not well suited for network implementation, they are nevertheless worth considering for off-line training a network for later implementation as a physical network with predetermined weights.

The gradient-descent method considers only the first-order derivative of an error function. It is helpful to take into account higher-order derivatives. Using Taylor's series expansion on $E(\mathbf{w})$ around the current point $\mathbf{w}_0$, we have

$$E(\mathbf{w}) = E(\mathbf{w}_0) + (\mathbf{w} - \mathbf{w}_0)^T \nabla E(\mathbf{w}_0) + \tfrac{1}{2}(\mathbf{w} - \mathbf{w}_0)^T \mathbf{H}(\mathbf{w})(\mathbf{w} - \mathbf{w}_0) + \cdots, \qquad (10.54)$$

where $\mathbf{H}(\mathbf{w})$ is called a *Hessian matrix* and is the second derivative evaluated at $\mathbf{w}_0$:

$$\mathbf{H}(\mathbf{w}) \triangleq \nabla^2 E(\mathbf{w}) \qquad \text{or} \qquad H_{ij} = \frac{\partial^2 E}{\partial w_i \partial w_j}. \qquad (10.55)$$

To find the minimum of $E(\mathbf{w})$, we set its gradient to zero:

$$\nabla E(\mathbf{w}) = \nabla E(\mathbf{w}_0) + \mathbf{H}(\mathbf{w})(\mathbf{w} - \mathbf{w}_0) + \cdots = 0. \qquad (10.56)$$

If we ignore the third- and higher-order terms, we obtain

$$\mathbf{w} = \mathbf{w}_0 - \mathbf{H}^{-1}(\mathbf{w}) \nabla E(\mathbf{w}_0), \qquad (10.57)$$

or use k to indicate the kth step of learning, we obtain

$$\mathbf{w}^{(k+1)} = \mathbf{w}^{(k)} - \mathbf{H}^{-1}(\mathbf{w}^{(k)}) \nabla E(\mathbf{w}^{(k)}). \qquad (10.58)$$

This is called *Newton's method* of weight updating. Newton's method uses the second derivative in addition to the gradient to determine the next step direction and step size. It can converge quadratically when close to the solution of a convex function. However, there are several drawbacks in Newton's method. First, in order to converge, it requires a good initial estimate of the solution. Second, for a convex function, it can converge quickly; however, for a nonconvex function, it may easily converge to a local minimum or a saddle point. And third, the key drawback is that each iteration requires computation of the Hessian matrix and also its inversion, and so the method is expensive in terms of both storage and computation requirements. Hence, it is not a practical technique, and alternatives or revised methods have been proposed. These include the conjugate-direction method and the quasi-Newton method [Luenberger, 1976].

Training data and generalization. We always require that training data be *sufficient* and *proper*. However, there is no procedure or rule suitable for all cases in choosing training data. One rule of thumb is that training data should cover the entire expected input space and then during the training process select training-vector pairs randomly from the set. More precisely, assume that the input space is linearly separable into M disjoint regions with boundaries being part of the hyperplanes. Let P be the lower bound on the number of training patterns. Then choosing P such that $P/M \gg 1$ hopefully allows the network to discriminate pattern classes using fine piecewise hyperplane partitioning. In some situations, *scaling* or *normalization* is necessary to help the learning. For example, if the output function is sigmoidal, then the output values need to be scaled properly.

The back-propagation network is good at generalization. The network is said to generalize well when it sensibly interpolates input patterns that are new to the network. Networks with too many trainable parameters for the given amount of training data learn well but do not generalize well. This phenomenon is usually called *overfitting*. With too few trainable parameters, the network fails to learn the training data and performs very poorly on the test data. In order to improve the ability of a network to generalize from a training data set to a test data set, it is desirable that small changes in the input space of a pattern do not change the output components. This can be done by including variations in the input space of training patterns as part of the training set—but this is computationally very expensive. One way is to form a cost function that is the sum of the normal cost term E_f found in the back-propagation algorithm [Eq. (10.28)] and an additional term that is a function of the Jacobian:

$$E_b = \frac{1}{2}\left(\frac{\partial E_f}{\partial x_1}\right)^2 + \frac{1}{2}\left(\frac{\partial E_f}{\partial x_2}\right)^2 + \cdots + \frac{1}{2}\left(\frac{\partial E_f}{\partial x_m}\right)^2, \qquad (10.59)$$

where x_j refers to the jth input. The rationale for this approach is that if the input changes slightly, the cost function E_f should not change. To minimize the new cost function, a *double back-propagation* network was constructed [Drucker and LeCun, 1992] such that one back propagation was for $\partial E_f/\partial w_j$ and the other for $\partial E_b/\partial w_j$. This technique has been shown to improve the generalization capability of a trained network by forcing the output to be insensitive to incremental changes in the input.

Number of hidden nodes. The size of a hidden layer is a fundamental question often raised in the application of multilayer feedforward networks to real-world problems. The exact analysis of this issue is rather difficult because of the complexity of the network mapping and the nondeterministic nature of many successfully completed training procedures. Hence, the size of a hidden layer is usually determined experimentally. One empirical guideline is as follows. For a network of reasonable size (e.g., hundreds or thousands of inputs), the size of hidden nodes needs to be only a relatively small fraction of the input layer. If the network fails to converge to a solution, it may be that more hidden nodes are required. If it does converge, you may try fewer hidden nodes and then settle on a size based on overall system performance [Freeman and Skapura, 1991].

There are also some guidelines based on analytical analysis. An often asked question is: How many hidden nodes are required to partition the input space such that different inputs will be contained in different regions? Assume that an m-dimensional nonaugmented input space is linearly separable into M disjoint regions with boundaries being part of the hyperplanes such that elements in the same region have the same outputs (i.e., belong to the same class). Since single-hidden-layer networks (see Fig. 10.7) can form arbitrary decision regions in the m-dimensional input space, the problem here is finding the proper number of hidden neurons N_m needed for the network to perform properly. The relationship among M, N_m, and m was shown to be [Mirchandini and Cao, 1989; Huang and Huang, 1991]

$$N_m + 1 \le M \le \sum_{j=0}^{m} \binom{N_m}{j}, \qquad \text{where} \quad \binom{N_m}{j} = 0 \quad \text{for } N_m < j. \tag{10.60}$$

That is, the maximum number of regions linearly separable using N_m hidden nodes in the m-dimensional input space is $M_{\max}$ defined by

$$M_{\max} = \sum_{j=0}^{m} \binom{N_m}{j}$$
$$= 1 + N_m + \frac{N_m(N_m - 1)}{2!} + \cdots + \frac{N_m(N_m - 1) \cdots (N_m - m + 1)}{m!}, \tag{10.61}$$

for $N_m > m$. For the case $N_m \le m$, we have

$$M_{\max} = 2^{N_m} \qquad \text{and} \qquad N_m = \log_2 M_{\max}. \tag{10.62}$$

For example, consider the XOR problem in Fig. 10.6. There are $M = 3$ disjoint regions for the two-dimensional input patterns. A simple computation shows that a single-hidden-layer network with two hidden nodes can solve the XOR problem.

10.2.3 Time-Delay Neural Networks

Many practical applications require neural networks to respond to a sequence of patterns. That is, the network is required to produce a particular output sequence in response to a particular sequence on inputs. Speech signals, measured waveform data, and control signals are typical examples of discrete-time sequences.

A well-known benchmark signal usually adopted to test a network's time sequence prediction capability (e.g., [Tenorio and Lee, 1990]) is the signal $x(t)$ produced by the numerical solution of the Mackey-Glass differential-delay equation [Mackey and Glass, 1977]

$$\frac{dx(t)}{dt} = \frac{ax(t - \tau)}{1 + x^{10}(t - \tau)} - bx(t). \tag{10.63}$$

By setting $a = 0.2$, $b = 0.1$, and $\tau = 17$, a chaotic time series with a strange attractor of fractal dimension about 3.5 can be produced. Part of such a signal is shown in Fig. 10.12.

To use back-propagation networks to perform a time sequence prediction, we simply turn the temporal sequence into a spatial input pattern. In this way, the given set of samples in a sequence can be fed simultaneously to a network. As illustrated in Fig. 10.13, a series connection of delay elements (called a tapped delay line) are attached to the input of a neuron, and thus the inputs to the neurons are samples $x_i(t - j\Delta)$ for $i = 0, 1, \ldots, m$, and $j = 0$, $1, \ldots, d$, where d is the maximum number of delay. A neuron with a tapped delay line is called a *time-delay neural network (TDNN) unit*, and a network consisting of TDNN units is called a TDNN.

A typical application of TDNNs is speech recognition. A TDNN has been designed for the recognition of phonemes, in particular, the voiced stops B, D, and G [Waibel et al., 1989]. A two-hidden-layer network was built for this purpose. Its overall architecture and a typical set of activities in the units are shown in Fig. 10.14. At the lowest level, 16 normalized mel scale spectral coefficients serve as inputs to the network, where a *mel* is a

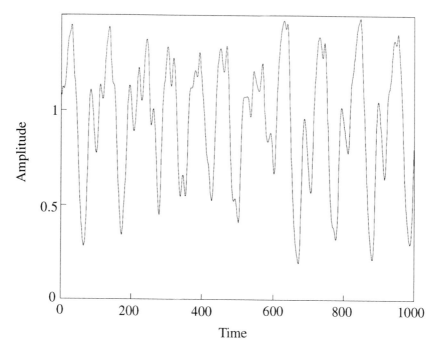

Figure 10.12 Plot of a chaotic time series.

unit of measure of perceived pitch or frequency of a tone. Input speech, sampled at 12 kilohertz, was Hamming-windowed, and a 256-point fast Fourier transform (FFT) was computed every 5 milliseconds. Mel scale coefficients were computed from the power spectrum by calculating log energies in each mel scale energy band properly. Adjacent

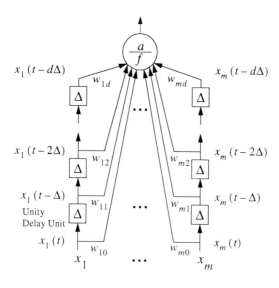

Figure 10.13 Time-delay neural network (TDNN) unit.

coefficients in time were collapsed for further data reduction, resulting in an overall 10-millisecond frame rate. All coefficients of an input token (in this case, 15 frames of speech centered around the hand-labeled vowel onset) were then normalized to lie between −1 and +1. Figure 10.14 shows the resulting coefficients for the speech token BA as inputs to the network, where positive and negative values are shown as black and gray squares, respectively.

The input layer is fully interconnected to the first hidden layer which has 8 TDNN units with $m = 16$ and $d = 2$ (see Fig. 10.13). Hence, there are 16 coefficients over 3 frames with time delay 0, 1, and 2. An alternative way of seeing this is depicted in Fig. 10.14, which shows the inputs to these TDNN units expanded spatially into a 3-frame window which is passed over the input spectrogram. Each unit in the first hidden layer now receives input from the coefficients in the 3-frame window. In the second hidden layer, each of three TDNN units looks at a 5-frame window of activity levels in hidden layer 1 (i.e., $m = 8$, $d = 4$). Finally, the output is obtained by summing the evidence from each of the three units in hidden layer 2 over time and connecting it to the pertinent output unit.

The TDNN was trained using the back-propagation learning rule with a momentum term on the training set of 780 tokens. Performance evaluation over 1946 testing tokens from three speakers showed that the TDNN achieved a recognition rate of 98.5% correct, while the rate obtained by the best of the traditional hidden Markov models (HMM) was only 93.7%.

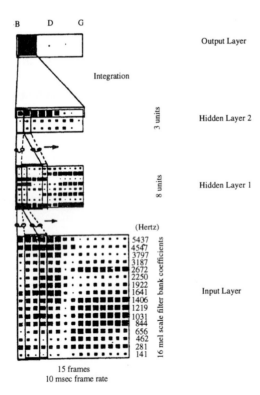

Figure 10.14 Architecture of the TDNN for phoneme recognition. (From Alex Waibel, "Modular Construction of Time-Delay Neural Networks for Speech Recognition," *Neural Computation*, Vol. 1, No. 1, pp. 41. © 1989 by the Massachusetts Institute of Technology.)

10.3 OTHER FEEDFORWARD NETWORKS

In this section, we shall introduce several different types of single-layer and multilayer feedforward networks that have also attracted much attention for various applications.

10.3.1 Functional-Link Networks

Functional-link networks [Pao, 1989] are single-layer neural networks that are able to handle linearly nonseparable tasks using the appropriately enhanced input representation. Thus, finding a suitably enhanced representation of the input data is the key point of the method. Additional input data used in the scheme usually incorporate higher-order effects and thus artificially increase the dimensions of the input space. The expanded input data, instead of the actual input data, are then used for training. The additional higher-order input terms are chosen such that they are linearly independent of the original pattern components. In this way, the input representation is enhanced and linear separability can be achieved in the extended space.

Figure 10.15 shows two examples of functional-link networks. Figure 10.15(a) shows the *tensor model* which is suitable for handling input patterns in the form of vectors. In this model, additional input terms are obtained for each m-dimensional input pattern as the product $x_i x_j$ for all $1 \le i$ and $j \le m$ such that $i < j \le m$, and as the product $x_i x_j x_k$ for all $1 \le i, j, k, \le m$ such that $i < j < k \le m$. Figure 10.15(b) illustrates another kind of functional-link network known as the *functional model*. This model is suitable for learning continuous functions. In this model, the higher-order input terms are generated using orthogonal basis functions such as $\sin \pi x$, $\cos \pi x$, $\sin 2\pi x$, and $\cos 2\pi x$. The power of functional-link networks can be illustrated by solving the XOR problem which is known to be linearly nonseparable. The augmented inputs are now $(x_1, x_2, x_1 x_2) = (-1, -1, 1)$, $(-1, 1, -1)$, $(1, -1, -1)$, and $(1, 1, 1)$, and the desired outputs are 1, -1, -1, and 1, respectively. Hence, it is easily seen that the simple functional-link network in Fig. 10.15(c) can solve this problem.

Since the functional-link network has only one layer, it can be trained using the simple delta learning rule instead of the generalized delta learning rule (back propagation). Hence, the learning speed of functional-link networks is much faster than that of back-propagation networks.

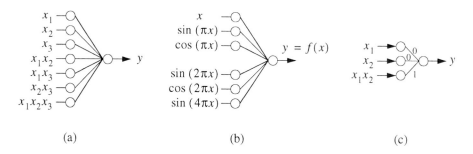

(a)   (b)   (c)

Figure 10.15   Functional-link networks. (a) The tensor model. (b) The functional model. (c) The XOR problem.

10.3.2 Tree Neural Networks

The classification tree, like multilayer feedforward neural networks, is a popular approach to the pattern recognition problem. The tree neural network (TNN) is a technique combining these two approaches [Sankar and Mammone, 1991; Guo and Gelfand, 1992]. The basic idea is to use a small multilayer network at each decision node of a binary classification tree to extract nonlinear features. TNNs exploit the power of tree classifiers to use appropriate local features at different levels and nodes of the tree.

The classification tree is an increasingly popular form of the multistage or sequential decision rule. A binary classification tree is shown in Fig. 10.16. The circular nodes are decision nodes, and the square nodes are terminal nodes. Each terminal node has a class label $\hat{c}$ associated with it. Each decision node has a *splitting rule* $f(\mathbf{x}) < \theta$ associated with it. The splitting rule determines whether the pattern goes to the left or right descendant, where $f(\mathbf{x})$ and θ are the associated feature and threshold, respectively. The pattern is assigned the class label of the terminal node it lands on. The power of the classification tree approach lies in the fact that appropriate features can be selected at different nodes and levels in the tree. Difficult pattern recognition problems with complex-decision boundaries usually require nonlinear features; thus, in a TNN, a small multilayer network is used at each decision node to extract a feature. A feature $y = f(\mathbf{x})$ generated by a multilayer network at decision node t is used in the following manner. If $y < 0$, then $\mathbf{x}$ is directed to its left-child node t_L; if $y \geq 0$, then $\mathbf{x}$ is directed to its right-child node t_R. The (learning) algorithm for constructing a TNN consists of two phases. In the *tree-growing* phase, a large tree is grown by recursively finding splitting rules until all terminal nodes have pure or nearly pure class membership or cannot be split further. In the *tree-pruning* phase, a smaller tree is selected from the pruned subtrees to avoid overfitting the data.

The idea of the learning algorithm in the tree-growing phase is, at each decision node, to partition the classes attached to it into two groups, to find a good split between the two groups, and then to find two good groups and hence a good overall split. Let $C = \{c_1, \ldots, c_M\}$ be the set of M classes at node t. The training involves two nested optimization problems. In the inner optimization problem, the back-propagation algorithm is used to train the network for a given pair of aggregate classes, C_L and C_R of C, to find a good split between C_L and C_R, where C_L and C_R are current (expected) sets of classes attached to the

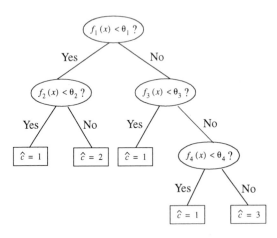

Figure 10.16 Binary classification tree for a three-class problem.

left-child node t_L and the right-child node t_R, respectively. In the outer optimization problem, a heuristic search is used to find a good pair of aggregate classes C'_L and C'_R and hence a good overall split. When the tree-growing phase is finished, the resulting large tree T is processed by a pruning algorithm. Starting from the bottom, the pruning algorithm tests each node to determine how pruning the branch stemming from the node would affect the estimated error rate. The branch is pruned if and only if the error rate will not increase. The algorithm tests each child node before it tests the parent node, and the smallest optimally pruned subtree T^* is generated in one bottom-up pass [Guo and Gelfand, 1992].

When tested on a waveform recognition problem and a handwritten character recognition problem, the TNN demonstrated significant decreases in error rate and tree size relative to standard classification tree design methods. The TNN also yielded comparable error rates and shorter training times than a large back-propagation network on the same problem. Furthermore, it provides a structured approach to neural network classifier design, including the selection of optimal network size.

10.3.3 Wavelet Neural Networks

The wavelet neural network (WNN) is constructed based on the wavelet transform theory [Zhang and Benveniste, 1992] and is an alternative to feedforward neural networks for approximating arbitrary nonlinear functions. *Wavelet decomposition* [Chui, 1992] is a powerful tool for function approximation. Let $f(\mathbf{x})$ be a piecewise continuous function. Wavelet decomposition allows us to decompose $f(\mathbf{x})$ using a family of functions obtained by dilating and translating a single wavelet function $\psi : \Re^n \rightarrow \Re$ as

$$f(\mathbf{x}) = \sum_{i=1}^{N} w_i \det[\,\mathbf{D}_i^{1/2}\,] \psi\,[\mathbf{D}_i\,(\mathbf{x} - \mathbf{t}_i)\,]\,, \qquad (10.64)$$

where $\mathbf{D}_i = \mathrm{diag}\,(\mathbf{d}_i)$, $\mathbf{d}_i \in \Re^n_+$ are dilation vectors specifying the diagonal dilation matrices $\mathbf{D}_i$, $\mathbf{t}_i$ are translation vectors, and $\det[\cdot]$ is the determinant operator. The selected wavelet function ψ must satisfy some properties. One example for selecting $\psi : \Re^n \rightarrow \Re$ is

$$\psi\,(\mathbf{x}) = \psi_s\,(x_1) \cdots \psi_s\,(x_n) \qquad \text{for } \mathbf{x} = (x_1, \ldots, x_n)\,, \qquad (10.65)$$

where

$$\psi_s\,(x) = -xe^{-x^2/2} \qquad (10.66)$$

is a scalar wavelet.

Based on the wavelet decomposition, we can construct a network structure of the form [refer to Eq. (10.64)]

$$y\,(\mathbf{x}) = \sum_{i=1}^{N} w_i \psi\,[\mathbf{D}_i\,(\mathbf{x} - \mathbf{t}_i)\,] + \bar{y}, \qquad (10.67)$$

where the additional parameter $\bar{y}$ is introduced to help deal with nonzero mean functions on finite domains. Furthermore, to compensate for the orientation selective nature of the dilations in Eq. (10.67), a rotation is added to make the network more flexible:

$$y\,(\mathbf{x}) = \sum_{i=1}^{N} w_i \psi\,[\mathbf{D}_i\,\mathbf{R}_i\,(\mathbf{x} - \mathbf{t}_i)\,] + \bar{y}, \qquad (10.68)$$

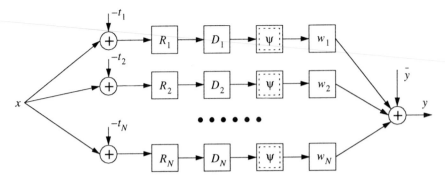

Figure 10.17 Wavelet neural network.

where $\mathbf{R}_i$ are rotation matrices. The network performing Eq. (10.68) is called the wavelet neural network as shown in Fig. 10.17, in which the combination of translation, rotation, dilation, and wavelet lying on the same line is called a *wavelon* in contrast to the *neuron* in general neural networks.

An algorithm of the back-propagation type has been derived for adjusting the parameters of the WNN. Learning is based on a sample of *random* input-output pairs $(\mathbf{x}, f(\mathbf{x}))$, where $f(\mathbf{x})$ is the function to be approximated. More precisely, the training data are a sequence of random pairs $\{\mathbf{x}^{(k)}, d^{(k)} = f(\mathbf{x}^{(k)}) + v^{(k)}\}$, where $\{v^{(k)}\}$ is the observation noise. The objective of learning is to minimize the cost function

$$E(\boldsymbol{\theta}) = \frac{1}{2} \sum_k \{[y_{\boldsymbol{\theta}}(\mathbf{x}^{(k)}) - d^{(k)}]^2\}, \tag{10.69}$$

where the vector $\boldsymbol{\theta}$ consists of all the parameters $\bar{y}$, $\mathbf{w}_i$, $\mathbf{t}_i$, $\mathbf{D}_i$, $\mathbf{R}_i$, and $y_{\boldsymbol{\theta}}(\mathbf{x})$ is the network output defined by Eq. (10.68) with the parameter vector $\boldsymbol{\theta}$. Details of the derivation of the learning rule can be found in [Zhang and Benveniste, 1992].

10.4 CONCLUDING REMARKS

This chapter focuses on various supervised learning rules for single-layer and multilayer feedforward networks. These learning rules assume that a set of input–desired-output training data are available for training the networks.

For simple perceptrons, there are some alternative perceptron learning rules that can be viewed as *steepest-descent* (gradient-descent) methods by defining an appropriate performance function [Shynk, 1990]. The *capacity* of simple perceptrons, that is, the number of random input-output pairs that can be stored reliably in a given perceptron network of known size, was analyzed in [Hertz et al., 1991]. For the Adaline, it has been successfully used as an adaptive filter in several applications [Widrow and Stearns, 1985; Widrow and Winter, 1988]. Not much information on Madaline is included here, and details on Madaline and its associated learning rule, called Madaline rule II (MRII), can be found in [Winter and Widrow, 1988]. Andes et al. [1990] proposed a new version of MRII, called MRIII, which is similar to MRII but the threshold function on the output of each Adaline is replaced by a continuous function. Bartlett and Downs [1992] have proposed the concept of *random weights* such that the back-propagation learning rule can be applied to Madalines. Another network called a binary feedforward neural network (BFNN) [Gray and Michel, 1992] is very similar to a Madaline except that the threshold function is replaced by a step function.

For multilayer feedforward networks, their solving power was first recognized by the well-known *Kolmogorov's mapping neural network existence theorem* [Kolmogorov, 1957; Hecht-Nielsen, 1990]. Theorems similar to Theorem 10.2 were also established in [Funahashi, 1989; Hecht-Nielsen, 1989; Poggio and Girosi, 1990]. For the learning factors of back propagation, Wessels and Barnard [1992] proposed a better method of weight initialization to avoid local minima. Drago and Ridella [1992] proposed an optimum weight initialization process to minimize the time needed to reach the minimum of the cost function by statistical analysis. Choi and Choi [1992] indicated that the *sensitivity* of a neural network depends on the set of weights. The effects of the shapes of activation functions on the learning performance of back-propagation networks were studied in [Syu and Tsao, 1993]. Other output learning signals different from Eq. (10.31) can be found in [Solla et al., 1988; Fahlman, 1988; Makram-Ebeid et al., 1989]. Studies on gradient-descent methods with higher-order derivatives can be found in [Ricotti et al., 1988; Becker and LeCun, 1988; Makram-Ebeid et al., 1989; Bello, 1992]. Saratchandran [1991] derived a *dynamical programming* approach for performing optimal weight selection. The issue of the proper number of training data was studied in [Mehrotra et al., 1991]. In [Holmström and Koistinen, 1992; Matsuoka, 1992], the generalization capability of a neural network was improved by introducing additive noise to the training samples. Issues involving the representation of input training data can be found in [Denker et al., 1987; Solla, 1988; Birx and Pipenberg, 1993].

Interesting applications of back-propagation networks include handwritten character recognition [LeCun et al., 1989; English et al., 1993], temperature control [Khalid and Omatu, 1992], diagnosis of liver cancer [Maclin and Dempsey, 1993], and fluorescent diagnostics of organic pollution in natural waters [Orlov et al., 1993]. As for the TDNN for phoneme recognition, Bodenhausen and Waibel [1993] proposed an automatic structure optimization (ASO) algorithm that can automatically optimize the network structure and the total number of parameters of a TDNN synergetically. LeCun et al. [1989] used the weight decay and/or *optimal brain damage* (OBD) to further refine the ASO architecture to achieve optimal performance.

Other interesting and useful feedforward networks include the probabilistic neural network (PNN) [Specht, 1990a,b; Burrascano, 1991b], which is a direct implementation of the Bayes strategy for pattern classification tasks, expert neural networks (ENNs) [Lacher et al., 1992] that can perform inference and knowledge acquisition for rule-based expert systems, and Ho-Kashyap neural networks [Hassoun and Song, 1992], which are simple perceptrons with linear threshold units or linear graded units but use the *adaptive Ho-Kashyap* (AHK) training rules [Ho and Kashyap, 1965]. The WNNs introduced in this chapter were also described in [Pati and Krishnaprasad, 1993].

10.5 PROBLEMS

10.1 Use (a) the analytical approach and (b) the perceptron learning rule to design and train a single-LTU perceptron that can classify the following six patterns in a two-dimensional pattern space into two classes as follows:

$$\{[2, 1.5]^T, [3, 3]^T, [-0.5, 4]^T\}: \text{class 1 with } d^{(i)} = +1,$$

$$\{[3, -1.5]^T, [-1, 2.5]^T, [-2, -1]^T\}: \text{class 2 with } d^{(i)} = -1.$$

10.2 Consider the following six patterns from two classes in a two-dimensional pattern space:

$$\left\{\mathbf{x}^{(1)}, \mathbf{x}^{(3)}, \mathbf{x}^{(5)}\right\} = \left\{[2, 1.5]^T, [-2, -1]^T, [-0.5, 4]^T\right\}: \text{class 1} \ (d^{(i)} = +1),$$

$$\left\{\mathbf{x}^{(2)}, \mathbf{x}^{(4)}, \mathbf{x}^{(6)}\right\} = \left\{[3, -1.5]^T, [-1, 2.5]^T, [2.5, 3]^T\right\}: \text{class 2} \ (d^{(i)} = -1).$$

(a) Determine if the two classes of patterns are linearly separable.
(b) Use the perceptron learning rule to train a single-LTU perceptron to classify these patterns by recycling the training patterns for 10 epochs. After each epoch, determine the "goodness" or the performance of the trained perceptron using the following two performance measures:

(i) Classification error: $J_1 = \sum_{k=1}^{6} \left|d^{(k)} - y^{(k)}\right|,$

(ii) Shynk's measure [Shynk, 1990]: $J_2 = -\sum_{k=1}^{6} [d^{(k)} - y^{(k)}]\text{net}^{(k)},$

where $\text{net}^{(k)} = \mathbf{w}^T\mathbf{x}^{(k)}$ is the net input to the LTU and $\mathbf{w}$ is the weight vector of the single-LTU perceptron. (*Note:* You may want to use the MATLAB neural network toolbox for the above calculations.)

(c) Which performance measure in part (b) is better for the perceptron learning rule? Justify your answer.

10.3 The learning constant η of the perceptron learning rule in Eq. (10.7) can be meaningfully controlled by the equation:

$$\eta^{(k)} = \beta\frac{\left|(\mathbf{w}^{(k)})^T\mathbf{x}^{(k)}\right|}{\mathbf{x}^T\mathbf{x}},$$

where β, $0 < \beta \leq 2$, is a constant. Then the perceptron learning rule becomes

$$\mathbf{w}^{(k+1)} = \mathbf{w}^{(k)} + \eta^{(k)}[\mathbf{d}^{(k)} - \text{sgn}((\mathbf{w}^{(k)})^T\mathbf{x}^{(k)})]\mathbf{x}^{(k)},$$

where $\mathbf{x}^{(k)}$ is the input vector and $\mathbf{d}^{(k)}$ is the corresponding desired output vector. This way, the correction increment η is therefore not constant and depends on the current training pattern.

(a) Let β be the ratio of the distance between the old weight vector $\mathbf{w}^{(k)}$ and the new weight vector $\mathbf{w}^{(k+1)}$ to the distance from $\mathbf{w}^{(k)}$ to the pattern hyperplane in the weight space. Justify the following facts with illustrations in the weight space: (i) For $\beta = 1$, the new weights $\mathbf{w}^{(k+1)}$ displace exactly onto the decision plane $(\mathbf{w}^{(k)})^T\mathbf{x}^{(k)} = 0$. (ii) For $\beta = 2$, the new weights are reflected symmetrically with respect to the decision plane. (iii) For $0 < \beta < 1$, we have *fractional weight corrections*. (iv) For $1 < \beta < 2$, we have *absolute weight corrections*.
(b) Write a program for implementing the perceptron learning rule with the above adaptive learning constants for training a single-LTU perceptron that can classify the six patterns in a three-dimensional pattern space into two classes as follows:

$$\left\{[0.7, 0.4, 0]^T, [1.1, 0.8, 0.4]^T, [0.9, 0.8, 0.3]^T\right\}: \text{class 1} \ (d^{(i)} = +1),$$

$$\left\{[0.2, 0.8, 0.7]^T, [0.2, 0.1, 1.5]^T, [0, 0.1, 0.3]^T\right\}: \text{class 2} \ (d^{(i)} = -1),$$

Perform the training task for $\beta = 1$ and $\beta = 2$ and compare the performance (learning speed) in these two cases. Note that the same nonzero initial weight vector should be used.
(c) Repeat part (b) using the traditional perceptron learning rule with learning constant $\eta = 1$. Compare its performance with that in part (b). Perform this training task with zero initial weight vector $\mathbf{w} = 0$, and also with the same nonzero initial weight vector as in part (b).

10.4 (a) Use the perceptron learning rule to train a simple perceptron with three LTUs that can classify the following three prototype points of three classes in a two-dimensional pattern space:

$$\mathbf{x}^{(1)} = (10, 2)^T \text{ (class 1)},$$

$$\mathbf{x}^{(2)} = (2, -5)^T \text{ (class 2)},$$

$$\mathbf{x}^{(3)} = (-5, 5)^T \text{ (class 3)}.$$

(b) Repeat part (a) using the LMS learning rule to train a linear network with three Adalines.

(c) Repeat part (a) using the delta learning rule to train a simple perceptron with three LGUs (assume $\lambda = 1$).

10.5 The *normalized LMS* learning rule is described by the following update rule:

$$\hat{\mathbf{w}}^{(k+1)} = \hat{\mathbf{w}}^{(k)} + \eta[d^{(k)} - (\hat{\mathbf{w}}^{(k)})^T \mathbf{x}^{(k)}]\frac{\mathbf{x}^{(k)}}{\|\mathbf{x}^{(k)}\|^2},$$

where $\eta, 0 < \eta < 1$, is a learning constant and $\|\mathbf{x}^{(k)}\|$ is the Euclidean norm of the input vector $\mathbf{x}^{(k)}$. Assume that the $(k + 1)$ th step requires weight adaptation. Show that after the weight correction is made in the kth step and the same input vector $\mathbf{x}^{(k+1)} = \mathbf{x}^{(k)}$ is presented again, the error is reduced $(1 - \eta)$ times.

10.6 The LMS learning rule is known for its application to echo cancellation in telephone circuits. Figure P10.6 is a block diagram of a telephone circuit with a dual-input single-weight Adaline used as an echo-suppression device. Describe how the LMS learning rule can be used here by writing down the equations that describe the operation of this device.

10.7 Six patterns from two categories are give as follows:

$$\{[3, 2]^T, [1, -2]^T, [-2, 0]^T\}: \text{class 1,}$$

$$\{[2, 1]^T, [0, -1]^T \ [-1, 2]^T\}: \text{class 2.}$$

With appropriate pattern-image transformation, plot patterns in the image space and design a single-hidden-layer classifier with LTUs to perform the classification.

10.8 Given the following patterns from two classes:

$$\{[0, 0]^T, [1, 0]^T, [0, 1]^T\}: \text{class 1,}$$

$$\{[0.5, 0.5]^T, [0.3, 0.3]^T\}: \text{class 2.}$$

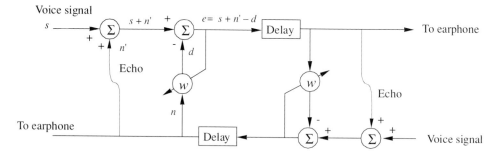

Figure P10.6 Echo cancellation in telephone circuit in Problem 10.6.

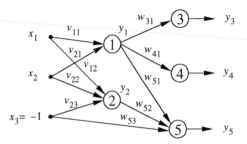

Figure P10.10 Back-propagation network in Problem 10.10.

(a) Design a multilayer perceptron network (with a maximum of three LTUs) to classify these patterns such that an output of $+1$ from the network indicates class 1 patterns while an output of -1 indicates patterns from class 2.

(b) Draw the complete resultant perceptron network with weights.

10.9 Repeat Prob. 10.8 with the following patterns from two classes:

$$\{[0, 0]^T, [1, 0]^T, [0, 1]^T\}: \text{class 1},$$

$$\{[0.5, 0]^T, [0, 0.5]^T\}: \text{class 2}.$$

10.10 We are given a three-layer back-propagation network as shown in Fig. P10.10.

(a) Derive the weight update rules for $\{v_{ij}\}$ and $\{w_{ij}\}$ for all i and j. Assume that the activation function for all the nodes is an unipolar sigmoid function with $\lambda = 1$ and that the learning constant is $\eta = 0.2$.

(b) Use the equations derived in part (a) to update the weights in the network for one step with input vector $\mathbf{x} = [1.2, 0.5, -1]^T$, desired output vector $\mathbf{d} = [0, 1, 0]^T$, and small random initial weights.

10.11 Given a multilayer feedforward neural network as shown in Fig. P10.11, derive the weight update rule for $\{w_{ij}\}$ for all i and j. Assume that the activation function for all the neurons is a bipolar sigmoid function with $\lambda = 4$ and that the learning constant is $\eta = 0.2$.

10.12 Write a program for implementing algorithm BP for training a single-hidden-layer back-propagation network with bipolar sigmoidal units ($\lambda = 1$) to achieve the following two-to-one mappings:

$$\text{(i)} \quad y = 4 \sin(\pi x_1) + 2 \cos(\pi x_2),$$

$$\text{(ii)} \quad y = \sin(\pi x_1) \cos(0.5\pi x_2).$$

(a) Set up two sets of data, each of which consists of 20 input-output pairs, one for network training and the other for network testing. The input-output data are obtained by varying the input variables (x_1, x_2) within $[-1, 1]$ randomly. The desired output data d is normalized within $[-1, 1]$.

(b) Apply the training data to the program to find proper weights in the network.

(c) Evaluate the accuracy (generalization capability) of the trained network using the test data.

(d) Investigate how the network performance is affected by varying the size of (or the number of hidden nodes in) the hidden layer.

(e) Repeat part (b) using the delta learning rule with the momentum term in Eq. (10.53). Compare the new learning speed (in epochs) with that in part (b).

(f) Repeat part (b) using the delta-bar-delta learning rule in Eq. (10.48). Compare the new learning speed (in epochs) with that in parts (b) and (e).

(g) Repeat part (b) using the double back-propagation technique [see Eq. (10.59)]. Compare the new generalization capability with that in part (c).

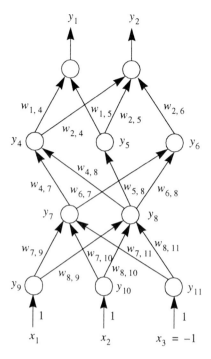

Figure P10.11 Back-propagation network in Problem 10.11.

10.13 The delta learning rule with the inclusion of a momentum term can be written as

$$\Delta w_{ij}(t) = -\eta \frac{\partial E}{\partial w_{ij}} + \alpha \Delta w_{ij}(t-1).$$

(a) If the initial weight $w_{ij}(0)$ is zero, show that for Δw_{ij} to be convergent, α must satisfy $0 \le |\alpha| < 1$.

(b) Use Fig. 10.11 to describe the situations that occur when the momentum parameter α is negative.

(c) If $\partial E / \partial w_{ij}$ has the same algebraic sign in consecutive iterations, show that inclusion of the momentum term can accelerate descent in steady downhill directions.

(d) If $\partial E / \partial w_{ij}$ has the opposite signs in consecutive iterations, what is the effect of the momentum term?

10.14 The delta learning rule with the momentum term and with the delta-bar-delta learning rule are both for accelerating the convergence of back propagation. Describe the similarities and differences between these two rules.

10.15 Consider the guideline for determining the number of hidden nodes in a hidden layer in Eq. (10.61).

(a) A single-hidden-layer network with two-dimensional input space is used to partition a space into M disjoint regions. What is the minimum number of hidden nodes N_m needed for this network?

(b) Assume that a two-class classification problem of two-dimensional patterns ($m = 2$) needs to be solved using six hidden nodes ($N_m = 6$). Determine the lower bound on p, the number of training patterns. Note that this number is equal to the maximum number of separable regions M.

(c) Repeat part (b) for $m = 50$ and $N_m = 8$.

10.16 The problem of time-series prediction can be formulated as: Given $x(k-m+1), x(k-m+2)$, $..., x(k)$, determine $x(k+\ell)$, where m and ℓ are fixed positive integers; that is, determine a mapping from $[x(k-m+1)], x(k-m+2)],..., [x(k)]^T \in \mathfrak{R}^m$ to $[x(k+\ell)] \in \mathfrak{R}$.

   (a) Write a program for training TDNN to predict the Mackey-Glass chaotic time sequence described by Eq. (10.63), where $a = 0.2$, $b = 0.1$, and $\tau = 30$. Use $m = 9$, $\ell = 1$, and 500 training patterns in the simulation. The learning constant is set as $\eta = 0.001$, and the momentum parameter as $\alpha = 0.9$. Show the learning curve for 200 epochs.

   (b) Repeat part (a) using the LMS algorithm designed to perform a linear prediction (linear network). The learning constant is set as $\eta = 0.1$. Show the learning curve for 200 epochs and compare it with that in part (a).

10.17 Use a functional link network similar to Fig. 10.15(b) to solve the two-to-one mapping problems described in Prob. 10.12. Compare the learning speed with that in part (b) of Prob. 10.12 by drawing the learning curves.

11

Single-Layer Feedback Networks and Associative Memories

This chapter considers the famous Hopfield networks which are single-layer feedback networks with symmetric weights. Both continuous and discrete Hopfield networks will be discussed with their update rules, properties, and characteristics. Hopfield networks have been used in many applications. We shall focus only their application in associative memory and optimization problems. Boltzmann machines, a variant of Hopfield networks with simulated annealing, will also be discussed.

11.1 HOPFIELD NETWORKS

The publication of Hopfield's seminal papers [1982, 1984] started the modern era in neural networks. His proposed networks are known as *Hopfield networks,* and his work also promoted construction of the first analog VLSI neural chip [Howard et al., 1988]. Hopfield networks have found many useful applications, especially in associative memory and optimization problems. In this section, we shall discuss two versions of this network: *discrete* and *continuous* Hopfield networks.

11.1.1 Discrete Hopfield Networks

The Hopfield network is a single-layer feedback network as shown in Fig. 9.4(d); its detailed network configuration is shown in Fig. 11.1. When operated in discrete-time fashion, it is called a discrete Hopfield network and its structure as a single-layer feedback network can also be termed *recurrent.* This chapter mainly focuses on single-layer recurrent networks, and multilayer recurrent networks will be discussed in Chap. 13. When a single-

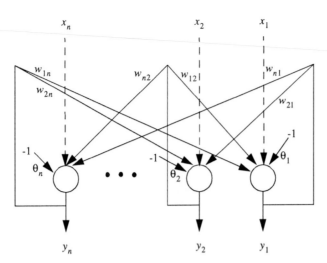

x_n x_2 x_1

w_{1n} w_{n2} w_{12} w_{n1}

w_{2n} w_{21}

-1 -1

-1 θ_1

θ_n θ_2

y_n y_2 y_1

Figure 11.1 Structure of the Hopfield network.

layer recurrent network performs a sequential updating process, an input pattern is first applied to the network, and the network's output is initialized accordingly. Then, the initializing pattern is removed and the initialized output becomes the new, updated input through the feedback connections. The first updated input forces the first updated output; this in turn acts as the second updated input through the feedback links and produces the second updated output. The transition process continues until no new, updated responses are produced and the network has reached its equilibrium.

Consider the Hopfield network shown in Fig. 11.1. Each node has an external input x_j and a threshold θ_j, where $j = 1, 2,..., n$. It is important to point out that there is no self-feedback in a Hopfield network. The jth node output is connected to each of the other nodes' inputs through a multiplicative weight w_{ij} for $i = 1, 2,..., n$, $i \neq j$; that is, $w_{ii} = 0$ for $i = 1, 2,..., n$. Furthermore, it is required that the network weights be *symmetric,* that is, $w_{ij} = w_{ji}$, $i, j = 1, 2,..., n$. The evolving rule (or update rule) for each node in a discrete Hopfield network is

$$y_i^{(k+1)} = \text{sgn}\left(\sum_{\substack{j=1 \\ j\neq i}}^{n} w_{ij} y_j^{(k)} + x_i - \theta_i \right), \qquad i = 1, 2,..., n, \tag{11.1}$$

where sgn($\cdot$) is the signum function defined in Eq. (9.8) and the superscript k denotes the index of recursive update. It is required that the above update rule be applied in an *asynchronous* fashion. This means that for a given time only a single node is allowed to update its output. The next update on a randomly chosen node in a series uses the already updated output. In other words, under asynchronous operation of the network, each output node is updated separately, while taking into account the most recent values that have already been updated. This update rule is referred to as an *asynchronous stochastic recursion* of the discrete Hopfield network. The following example illustrates the difference between synchronous and asynchronous updates.

Example 11.1

Consider a two-node discrete Hopfield network with $w_{12} = w_{21} = -1$, $w_{11} = w_{22} = 0$, $x_1 = x_2 = 0$, and $\theta_1 = \theta_2 = 0$. Set the initial output vector as $\mathbf{y}^{(0)} = [-1, -1]^T$. According to the asynchronous update rule, only one node is considered at a time. Assume now that the first node is chosen for update. Then

$$y_1^{(1)} = \text{sgn}\left(w_{12}y_2^{(0)}\right) = \text{sgn}\left[(-1)(-1)\right] = 1.$$

Hence, $\mathbf{y}^{(1)} = [1, -1]^T$. Next, the second node is considered for update; that is,

$$y_2^{(2)} = \text{sgn}\left(w_{21}y_1^{(1)}\right) = \text{sgn}\left((-1)(1)\right) = -1.$$

Hence, $\mathbf{y}^{(2)} = [1, -1]^T$. It can be easily found that no further output state changes will occur and that the state $[1, -1]^T$ is an equilibrium state of the network. Using different initial outputs, we can obtain the state transition diagram in Fig. 11.2 in which the vectors $[1, -1]^T$ and $[-1, -1]^T$ are the two equilibria of the system. Note that the asynchronous update allows for one single-component update of an n-tuple vector at a time.

For the case of synchronous update of the initial output vector $[-1, -1]^T$, using Eq. (11.1) we have

$$\mathbf{y}^{(1)} = \begin{pmatrix} \text{sgn}\left[w_{12}y_2^{(0)}\right] \\ \text{sgn}\left[w_{21}y_1^{(0)}\right] \end{pmatrix} = \begin{pmatrix} \text{sgn}\left[(-1)(-1)\right] \\ \text{sgn}\left[(-1)(-1)\right] \end{pmatrix} = \begin{pmatrix} 1 \\ 1 \end{pmatrix}.$$

In the next update, we obtain

$$\mathbf{y}^{(2)} = \begin{pmatrix} \text{sgn}\left[w_{12}y_2^{(1)}\right] \\ \text{sgn}\left[w_{21}y_1^{(1)}\right] \end{pmatrix} = \begin{pmatrix} \text{sgn}\left[(-1)(1)\right] \\ \text{sgn}\left[(-1)(1)\right] \end{pmatrix} = \begin{pmatrix} -1 \\ -1 \end{pmatrix}.$$

Thus, the result gives back the same vector as $\mathbf{y}^{(0)}$. Hence, the synchronous update produces a cycle of two states rather than a single equilibrium state. This example thus indicates that the synchronous update may cause the networks to converge to either fixed points or limit cycles.

We shall next evaluate the stability property of a discrete Hopfield network. For this purpose, we can characterize the behavior of this network by an energy function E as

$$E = -\frac{1}{2}\sum_{\substack{i=1 \\ j \neq i}}^{n}\sum_{j=1}^{n} w_{ij}y_iy_j - \sum_{i=1}^{n} x_iy_i + \sum_{i=1}^{n} \theta_iy_i. \tag{11.2}$$

The idea is to show that if the network is stable, then the above energy function always decreases whenever the state of any node changes. Let us assume that node i has just

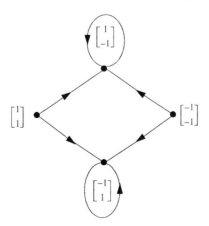

Figure 11.2 State transition diagram in Example 11.1.

changed its state from $y_i^{(k)}$ to $y_i^{(k+1)}$. In other words, its output has changed from $+1$ to -1, or vice versa. The change in energy ΔE is then

$$\Delta E = E\left(y_i^{(k+1)}\right) - E\left(y_i^{(k)}\right)$$

$$= -\left(\sum_{\substack{j=1 \\ j \neq i}}^{n} w_{ij} y_j^{(k)} + x_i - \theta_i\right)\left(y_i^{(k+1)} - y_i^{(k)}\right), \tag{11.3}$$

or briefly

$$\Delta E = -(\text{net}_i)\,\Delta y_i, \tag{11.4}$$

where $\Delta y_i = y_i^{(k+1)} - y_i^{(k)}$. The derivation of Eq. (11.3) exploits the fact that $y_j^{(k+1)} = y_j^{(k)}$ for $j \neq i$, and $w_{ij} = w_{ji}$ and $w_{ii} = 0$ (symmetric weight property).

From Eq. (11.1), if y_i has changed from $y_i^{(k)} = -1$ to $y_i^{(k+1)} = +1$ (i.e., $\Delta y_i = 2$), then net_i must have been positive and ΔE will be negative. Similarly, if y_i has changed from $y_i^{(k)} = +1$ to $y_i^{(k+1)} = -1$ (i.e., $\Delta y_i = -2$), then net_i must have been negative and ΔE will again be negative. If y_i has not changed, then $\Delta y_i = y_i^{(k+1)} - y_i^{(k)} = 0$, in which case ΔE will be zero. Thus,

$$\Delta E \leq 0. \tag{11.5}$$

Since the energy function E in Eq. (11.2) is in quadratic form and is bounded in an n-dimensional space consisting of 2^n vertices of the n-dimensional hypercube, E must have an absolute minimum value. Moreover, the minimum of E must lie at the corners of the hypercube. Hence, the energy function, under the update rule in Eq. (11.1), has to reach its minimum (probably a local minimum). Thus, starting at any initial state, a Hopfield network always converges to a stable state in a finite number of node-updating steps, where every stable state lies at a local minimum of the energy function E. In the above discussion, the connection weights are required to be symmetric. The asymmetry of the weights, that is, $w_{ij} \neq w_{ji}$ for some i, j, may lead to a modified Hopfield network which has also been shown to be stable [Roska, 1988].

The above proving process actually employs the well-known Lyapunov stability theorem [Banks, 1989], which is usually used to prove the stability of a dynamic system defined with arbitrarily many interlocked differential or difference equations. We have introduced this theorem as Theorem 7.4 for discrete systems. Since it provides a powerful tool in the theoretical study of neural networks, we state it for continuous systems as follows [Zurada, 1992].

Theorem 11.1

(Lyapunov Theorem). Consider the autonomous (i.e., unforced) system described with a system of n first-order linear or nonlinear differential equations:

$$\dot{y}_1 = f_1(\mathbf{y})$$

$$\dot{y}_2 = f_2(\mathbf{y})$$

$$\vdots \tag{11.6}$$

$$\dot{y}_n = f_n(\mathbf{y}),$$

or in vector-matrix notation:

$$\dot{\mathbf{y}}(t) = \mathbf{f}(\mathbf{y}), \tag{11.7}$$

where $\mathbf{y}(t) = (y_1, y_2, \ldots, y_n)^T$ is the state vector of the system and $\mathbf{f}(\mathbf{y}) = (f_1, f_2, \ldots, f_n)^T$ is a nonlinear vector function. Without loss of generality, we assume that the equations have been written so that $\mathbf{y} = \mathbf{0}$ is an equilibrium state that satisfies $\mathbf{f}(\mathbf{0}) = \mathbf{0}$. We formulate a condition for the equilibrium $\mathbf{y} = \mathbf{0}$ to be asymptotically stable, which means that the state vector converges to zero as time goes to infinity. This can be accomplished if a positive-definite (energy) function $E(\mathbf{y})$ can be found such that

1. $E(\mathbf{y})$ is continuous with respect to all the components y_i for $i = 1, 2, \ldots, n$, and
2. $dE[\mathbf{y}(t)]/dt < 0$, which indicates that the energy function is decreasing in time, and hence the origin of the state space is asymptotically stable.

A positive-definite (energy) function $E(\mathbf{y})$ satisfying the above requirements is called a *Lyapunov function*. This function is *not* unique for a given system. If at least one such function can be found for the system, then the system is asymptotically stable. However, the converse is not true; that is, the inability to find a satisfactory Lyapunov function does not mean that the evaluated system is unstable. If the derivative of the Lyapunov function is modified to be nonpositive rather than strictly negative, then the evaluated system is allowed for the *limit cycles,* which correspond to limited but undamped and steady oscillations. According to the Lyapunov theorem, the energy function associated with a Hopfield network and defined in Eq. (11.2) is a Lyapunov function; thus, the discrete Hopfield network is asymptotically stable. This theorem is more important in analyzing the continuous Hopfield networks that we shall focus on next.

11.1.2 Continuous Hopfield Networks

A discrete Hopfield network can be generalized to a continuous model in which time is assumed to be a continuous variable and the nodes have a continuous, graded output rather than a two-state binary output. Hence, the energy of the network decreases continuously in time. Hopfield showed that continuous Hopfield networks have the same useful properties of a discrete model. Moreover, there is an analogous electronic circuit that uses nonlinear amplifiers and resistors for realizing continuous Hopfield networks. This suggests the possibility of building a Hopfield network using analog VLSI technology [Mead, 1989].

The model of a continuous Hopfield network using electrical components is shown in Fig. 11.3(a). It consists of n amplifiers (nodes), each mapping its input voltage u_i into an output voltage y_i through the activation function $a(u_i)$, which can be considered, for example, as a sigmoid function [Eq. (9.10)] $a(\lambda u_i) = 1/(1 + e^{-\lambda u_i})$, where λ is called the *gain parameter.* When $\lambda \to \infty$, a continuous model becomes a discrete one. Each amplifier has an input conductance g_i and an input capacitance C_i as shown. Also shown are the external input signals x_i. For an actual circuit, the external input signals supply a constant current to each amplifier. Conductance w_{ij} connects the output of the jth node to the input of the ith node. Since all real resistor values are positive, inverted node outputs $\bar{y}_i$ are used to simulate inhibitory signals. If the output of a particular node excites some other node, then the connection is made with the signal from the noninverted output. If the connection is inhibitory,

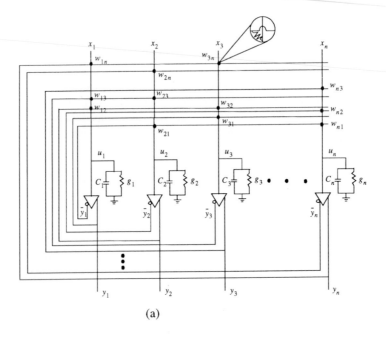

(a)

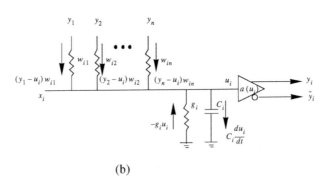

(b)

Figure 11.3 Continuous Hopfield network using electrical components. (a) The whole network structure. (b) The inputs of a node in (a).

it is made from the inverted output. Again, the important symmetric weight requirement for Hopfield networks is imposed, that is, $w_{ij} = w_{ji}$ and $w_{ii} = 0$.

The evolving rule of each node in a continuous Hopfield network can be derived as follows. Consider the input of a node as shown in Fig. 11.3(b). Using the Kirchhoff current law which states that the total current entering a junction is equal to that leaving the same junction, we obtain

$$C_i \frac{du_i}{dt} = \sum_{\substack{j=1 \\ j \neq i}}^{n} w_{ij}(y_j - u_i) - g_i u_i + x_i = \sum_{\substack{j=1 \\ j \neq i}}^{n} w_{ij} y_j - G_i u_i + x_i, \qquad (11.8)$$

where

$$G_i \triangleq \sum_{\substack{j=1 \\ j \neq i}}^{n} w_{ij} + g_i. \qquad (11.9)$$

Equation (11.8) completely describes the time evolution of the system. If each node is given an initial value $u_i(0)$, then the value $u_i(t)$ and thus the amplifier output $y_i(t) = a(u_i(t))$ at time t can be known by solving the differential equation in Eq. (11.8).

To evaluate the stability property of continuous Hopfield networks, we will define a continuous-energy function such that the evolution of the system is in the general direction of the negative gradient of the energy function and finally converges to one of the stable minima in the state space. A suitable Lyapunov energy function for the network in Fig. 11.3 is

$$E = -\frac{1}{2}\sum_{i=1}^{n}\sum_{\substack{j=1 \\ j \neq i}}^{n} w_{ij} y_i y_j - \sum_{i=1}^{n} x_i y_i + \frac{1}{\lambda}\sum_{i=1}^{n} G_i \int_0^{y_i} a^{-1}(y)\, dy, \qquad (11.10)$$

where $a^{-1}(y) = \lambda u$ is the inverse of the function $y = a(\lambda u)$. It is graphed in Fig. 11.4 along with the integral of $a^{-1}(y)$ as a function of y.

To show that Eq. (11.10) is a Lyapunov function for the network, we take the time derivative of Eq. (11.10) assuming w_{ij} is symmetric:

$$\frac{dE}{dt} = \sum_{i=1}^{n} \frac{dE}{dy_i}\frac{dy_i}{dt} = \sum_{i=1}^{n}\left(-\sum_{\substack{j=1 \\ j \neq i}}^{n} w_{ij} y_j + G_i u_i - x_i\right)\frac{dy_i}{dt}$$

$$= -\sum_{i} C_i \frac{du_i}{dt}\frac{dy_i}{dt}, \qquad (11.11)$$

where the last equality comes from Eq. (11.8). Since $u_i = (1/\lambda)a^{-1}(y_i)$, we have

$$\frac{du_i}{dt} = \frac{1}{\lambda}\frac{da^{-1}(y_i)}{dy_i}\frac{dy_i}{dt} = \frac{1}{\lambda}a^{-1'}(y_i)\frac{dy_i}{dt}, \qquad (11.12)$$

where $a^{-1'}(y)$ is the derivative of $a^{-1}(y)$. Hence, Eq. (11.11) becomes

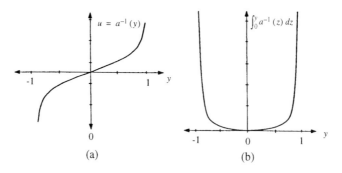

(a) (b)

Figure 11.4 (a) The inverse of the nonlinear activation function (sigmoid function). (b) The integral of (a).

$$\frac{dE}{dt} = -\sum_i \frac{C_i}{\lambda} a^{-1'}(y_i) \left(\frac{dy_i}{dt}\right)^2. \tag{11.13}$$

Figure 11.4(a) shows that $a^{-1}(y_i)$ is a monotonically increasing function of y_i and thus its derivative $a^{-1'}(y_i)$ is positive everywhere. This indicates that dE/dt is negative, and thus the energy function E must decrease as the system evolves. Hence, if E is bounded, the system will eventually reach a stable state where $dE/dt = dy_i/dt = 0$.

Assume that all the threshold values are zero; then the continuous-energy function in Eq. (11.10) is identical to the discrete-energy function in Eq. (11.2) except for the term

$$\frac{1}{\lambda} \sum_{i=1}^{n} G_i \int_0^{y_i} a^{-1}(y)\, dy. \tag{11.14}$$

As shown in Fig. 11.4(b), this integral is zero for $y_i = 0$ and positive otherwise and becomes very large as y_i approaches ± 1. Hence, the energy function E is bounded from below and is a Lyapunov function. Furthermore, the term in Eq. (11.14) alters the energy landscape such that the stable point of the system no long lies exactly at the corners of the hypercube. In the limit of very high gain $\lambda \to \infty$, this term [Eq. (11.14)] is driven to zero and the continuous-energy model becomes identical to the discrete-energy model. For a finite gain, the stable points move toward the interior of the hypercube. Hence, the value of the gain parameter λ determines how close the stable points get to the corners of the hypercube.

Example 11.2

Consider a two-node continuous Hopfield network with $w_{12} = w_{21} = 1$, $\lambda = 1.4$, and $a(\lambda u) = (2/\pi) \tan^{-1}(\lambda u \pi/2)$. As in example 11.1, this system has two stable states. The energy contour map for this system is illustrated in Fig. 11.5, where the two axes are the outputs of the two nodes (amplifiers). The upper right and lower left corners are stable minima for infinite gain (i.e., $\lambda \to \infty$), and the minima are displaced inward by the finite gain $\lambda = 1.4$. The arrows in the figure show the motion of the state from Eq. (11.8). Note that this motion is not in general perpendicular to the energy contours.

The continuous Hopfield network is in fact a special case of a broader class of continuous-time associative networks introduced by Cohen and Grossberg [1983], and thus the

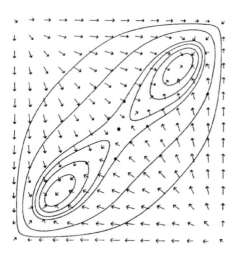

Figure 11.5 Energy contour map for the two-node two-stable-state continuous Hopfield network in Example 11.2. (From *Proc. Nat. Acad. Sci.*, Vol. 81, page 3091, 1984, © John J. Hopfield. Reproduced by kind permission of the author.)

above discussion about the stability of a continuous Hopfield network is subsumed by the following Cohen-Grossberg theorem [Hecht-Nielsen, 1990].

Theorem 11.2

(Cohen-Grossberg Theorem). Given is an associative neural network with n nodes having output signals u_i and an evolving rule of the form

$$\dot{u}_i = a_i(u_i)\left[b_i(u_i) - \sum_{j=1}^{n} w_{ij}f_j(u_j)\right]$$ (11.15)

such that

1. Matrix $[w_{ij}]$ is symmetric (i.e., $w_{ij} = w_{ji}$) and all $w_{ij} \geq 0$.
2. Function $a_i(u)$ is continuous for $u \geq 0$, and $a_i(u) > 0$ for $u > 0$.
3. Function $b_i(u)$ is continuous and never "levels out" over an open interval for $u > 0$.
4. Function $f_i(u)$ is differentiable, and $f_i'(u) > 0$ for $u \geq 0$.
5. $[b_i(u) - w_{ii}f_i(u)] < 0$ as $u \rightarrow \infty$.
6. Either $\lim_{u \to 0^+} b_i(u) = \infty$ or $\lim_{u \to 0^+} b_i(u) < \infty$ and $\int_0^u [1/a_i(s)]\,ds = \infty$ for some $u > 0$.

If state $\mathbf{u}(0)$ of the network at time 0 is in the positive orthant of $\mathfrak{R}^n$ [i.e., $u_i(0) > 0$ for $i = 1, 2, \ldots, n$], then the network will almost certainly converge to some stable point [i.e., a point $\mathbf{p}$ such that $\dot{\mathbf{u}}(\mathbf{p}) = \mathbf{0}$] also in the positive orthant. Furthermore, there will be at most a countable number of such stable points.

Notice that the actual output of a node to other nodes is $f_j(u_j)$ instead of u_j. The statement that b_i does not level out in condition 3 of the theorem means that none of the sets $S(c) = \{u > 0 \mid b_i(u) = c\}$ contains an open interval $\{u \mid \alpha < u < \beta\}$. The statement that the network will "almost certainly" converge to a stable point means that this will happen except for certain rare choices of the weight matrix.

If we set $a_i(u_i) = 1/C_i$, $b_i(u_i) = -G_i u_i + x_i$, $f_j(u_j) = a(u_j) = y_j$, $w_{ij} = -m_{ij}$ and $w_{ii} = 0$, then Eq. (11.15) becomes

$$\dot{u}_i = \frac{1}{C_i}\left[-G_i u_i + x_i + \sum_{\substack{j=1 \\ j \neq i}}^{n} m_{ij} y_j\right],$$ (11.16)

which is exactly the activation equation of the Hopfield network in Eq. (11.8). The Cohen-Grossberg theorem can be proved using the Lyapunov theorem. The Lyapunov function for the associated neural network defined in Eq. (11.15) can be defined as

$$E(\mathbf{u}) = \sum_{i=1}^{n}\sum_{j=1}^{n} w_{ij}f_i(u_i)f_j(u_j) - 2\sum_{i=1}^{n}\int_0^{u_i} b_i(u)f_i'(u)\,du,$$ (11.17)

which is quite similar to Eq. (11.10). It can be easily shown that

$$\dot{E}(\mathbf{u}(t)) = -2\sum_{i=1}^{n} a_i(u_i)f_i'(u_i)\left[b_i(u_i) - \sum_{j=1}^{n} w_{ij}f_j(u_j)\right]^2.$$ (11.18)

Hence, $\dot{E}(\mathbf{u}) \leq 0$ along trajectories when every function $f_i(u_i)$ is monotonic nondecreasing. The difficulty of proving this theorem arises in showing that the solution always stays in a positive orthant and in satisfying some other detailed mathematical requirements. A detailed proof of the Cohen-Grossberg theorem can be found in [Cohen and Grossberg, 1983]. This theorem will frequently be used in this book.

In the following sections, we shall introduce associative memories and optimization problems as two major applications of Hopfield networks. We shall explore how the connection weights of a Hopfield network are determined.

11.2 ASSOCIATIVE MEMORIES

An associative memory can store a set of patterns as memories. When the associative memory is presented with a *key pattern,* it responds by producing whichever one of the stored patterns most closely resembles or relates to the key pattern. Hence, the recall is through association of the key pattern with the information memorized. Such memories are also called *content-addressable memories* in contrast to the traditional *address-addressable memories* in digital computers in which a stored pattern (in bytes) is recalled by its address. The basic concept of using Hopfield networks as associative memories is to interpret the system's evolution as a movement of an input pattern toward the one stored pattern most resembling the input pattern.

Two types of associative memories can be distinguished. They are *autoassociative memory* and *heteroassociative memory.* Suppose we have p pairs of vectors $\{(\mathbf{x}^1, \mathbf{y}^1), (\mathbf{x}^2, \mathbf{y}^2), ..., (\mathbf{x}^p, \mathbf{y}^p)\}$ with $\mathbf{x}^i \in \Re^n$ and $\mathbf{y}^i \in \Re^m$. In the autoassociative memory, it is assumed that $\mathbf{x}^i = \mathbf{y}^i$ and that the network implements a mapping Φ of $\Re^n$ to $\Re^n$ such that $\Phi(\mathbf{x}^i) = \mathbf{x}^i$. If some arbitrary pattern $\mathbf{x}$ is *closer* to $\mathbf{x}^i$ than to any other $\mathbf{x}^j$, $j = 1, 2,..., p, j \neq i$, then $\Phi(\mathbf{x}) = \mathbf{x}^i$; that is, the network will produce the stored pattern $\mathbf{x}^i$ when the key pattern $\mathbf{x}$ is presented as input. In the heteroassociative memory, the network implements a mapping Φ of $\Re^n$ to $\Re^m$ such that $\Phi(\mathbf{x}^i) = \mathbf{y}^i$, and if some arbitrary pattern $\mathbf{x}$ is *closer* to $\mathbf{x}^i$ than to any other $\mathbf{x}^j$, $j = 1, 2,..., p, j \neq i$, then $\Phi(\mathbf{x}) = \mathbf{y}^i$. In the above, "closer" means with respect to some proper distance measure, for example, the Euclidean distance or the Hamming distance (HD). The *Euclidean distance d* between two vectors $\mathbf{x} = (x_1, x_2,..., x_n)^T$ and $\mathbf{x}' = (x_1', x_2',..., x_n')^T$ is defined as $d = [(x_1 - x_1')^2 + \cdots + (x_n - x_n')^2]^{1/2}$, and the *Hamming distance* is defined as the number of mismatched components of $\mathbf{x}$ and $\mathbf{x}'$ vectors. More specifically,

$$\text{HD}(\mathbf{x}, \mathbf{x}') = \begin{cases} \sum_{i=1}^{n} |x_i - x_i'| & \text{if } x_i, x_i' \in \{0, 1\} \\ \frac{1}{2}\sum_{i=1}^{n} |x_i - x_i'| & \text{if } x_i, x_i' \in \{-1, 1\}. \end{cases} \tag{11.19}$$

For example, if $\mathbf{x} = (1, 1, 0, 1)^T$ and $\mathbf{x}' = (0, 1, 0, 0)^T$, then $\text{HD}(\mathbf{x}, \mathbf{x}') = 2$. Similarly, if $\mathbf{x} = (1, -1, -1, -1)^T$ and $\mathbf{x}' = (1, 1, -1, -1)^T$, then $\text{HD}(\mathbf{x}, \mathbf{x}') = 1$.

In a special case where the vectors $\mathbf{x}^i$, $i = 1, 2,..., p$, form an orthonormal set, the associative memory can be defined as

$$\Phi(\mathbf{x}) = \mathbf{W}\mathbf{x} \triangleq (\mathbf{y}^1(\mathbf{x}^1)^T + \mathbf{y}^2(\mathbf{x}^2)^T + \cdots + \mathbf{y}^p(\mathbf{x}^p)^T)\mathbf{x}, \tag{11.20}$$

where $\mathbf{W}$ can be considered a weight matrix, called a *cross-correlation* matrix, of the network. It is easily seen that $\Phi(\mathbf{x}^i) = \mathbf{W}\mathbf{x}^i = \mathbf{y}^i$ since the set of $\mathbf{x}^i$ vectors is orthonormal.

The associative network with the weight matrix defined as in Eq. (11.20) is called a *linear associator.*

If the input vector $\mathbf{x}$ to a linear associator is different from any $\mathbf{x}^i$, $i = 1, 2,...,p$, such that $\mathbf{x} = \mathbf{x}^i + \mathbf{d}$, then the output is $\Phi(\mathbf{x}) = \Phi(\mathbf{x}^i + \mathbf{d}) = \mathbf{y}^i + \mathbf{Wd}$, where $\mathbf{Wd}$ is the kind of *cross-talk noise* caused by distortion of the input pattern. The cross-talk noise in a linear associator contains all the elements of the memory cross-correlation matrix weighted by a distortion term $\mathbf{d}$, even in the case of stored orthonormal patterns. It is clear that the linear associator provides no means for the suppression of cross-talk noise, and hence its use for accurate retrieval of the originally stored association is quite limited.

The restriction that the set of $\mathbf{x}$ vectors is orthonormal in the linear associator can be relaxed to the case that the vectors $\mathbf{x}^1, \mathbf{x}^2,..., \mathbf{x}^p$ are linearly independent. In this case, the weight matrix in Eq. (11.20) can be defined by [Kohonen, 1977, 1989]

$$\mathbf{W} = \mathbf{Y}\mathbf{X}^+ = \mathbf{Y}(\mathbf{X}^T\mathbf{X})^{-1}\mathbf{X}^T, \tag{11.21}$$

where $\mathbf{Y} = [\mathbf{y}^1, \mathbf{y}^2,..., \mathbf{y}^p]$, $\mathbf{X} = [\mathbf{x}^1, \mathbf{x}^2,..., \mathbf{x}^p]$, and $\mathbf{X}^+$ is the Moore-Penrose pseudoinverse matrix of $\mathbf{X}$. This weight matrix minimizes the squared output error in the case of linearly independent vectors $\mathbf{x}^i$.

The linear associators are *static* or *nonrecurrent* memory networks since they implement a feedforward operation of mapping without a feedback, or recursive update, operation. We shall next introduce the *dynamic* or recurrent memory networks that exhibit dynamic evolution in the sense that they converge to a equilibrium state according to the recursive formula $\mathbf{y}^{(k+1)} = \Phi(\mathbf{x}^{(k)}, \mathbf{y}^{(k)})$, where k is the time step and Φ is a nonlinear mapping in the form of thresholding. Recurrent memory networks, because they threshold the output and recycle the output to input, are able to suppress the output noise at the memory output to produce an improved association.

11.2.1 Recurrent Autoassociative Memory— Hopfield Memory

We shall first introduce *Hopfield autoassociative memory* (or *Hopfield memory* for short), that is, Hopfield networks utilized as autoassociative memories. A Hopfield memory is able to recover an original stored vector when presented with a probe vector close to it. Here, we focus on discrete Hopfield networks and consider continuous Hopfield networks as the former's hardware implementation with continuous transient responses. In Hopfield memory, Eq. (11.1) is the data *retrieval rule* that is applied asynchronously and stochastically. The remaining problem is how to store data in memory. Assume bipolar binary vectors that need to be stored are $\mathbf{x}^k$ for $k = 1, 2,...,p$. The *storage algorithm* for finding the weight matrix is

$$\mathbf{W} = \sum_{k=1}^{p} \mathbf{x}^k (\mathbf{x}^k)^T - p\mathbf{I}, \tag{11.22}$$

or

$$w_{ij} = \sum_{k=1}^{p} x_i^k x_j^k, \qquad i \neq j; \ w_{ii} = 0, \tag{11.23}$$

where $\mathbf{x}^k = (x_1^k, x_2^k, \ldots, x_n^k)^T$ and $\mathbf{I}$ is an appropriate identity matrix. If $\mathbf{x}^i$ are unipolar binary vectors, that is, $x_i^k \in \{0, 1\}$, then the storage rule is

$$w_{ij} = \sum_{k=1}^{p} (2x_i^k - 1)(2x_j^k - 1), \qquad i \neq j; \; w_{ii} = 0. \tag{11.24}$$

The weight assignment rule in Eq. (11.22) is basically the Hebbian learning rule in Eq. (9.20) with zero initial weights. Hence, this rule is called a *Hebbian-type* learning rule or an *outer-product* learning rule. Additional autoassociations can be added to the existing memory at any time by superimposing new, incremental weight matrices. Autoassociations can also be removed by respective weight matrix subtraction. Moreover, the storage rule in Eq. (11.22) is invariant with respect to the sequence of storing patterns and also is invariant under the binary complement operation.

Example 11.3

[Lippmann, 1987]. In this example, a Hopfield memory with 120 nodes and thus 14,400 weights is used to store the eight examplar patterns shown in Fig. 11.6(a). Input elements to the network take on the value $+1$ for black pixels and -1 for white pixels. In a test of recalling capability, the pattern for the digit 3 is corrupted by randomly reversing each bit independently from $+1$ to -1, and vice versa, with a probability of 0.25. This corrupted pattern is then used as a key pattern and applied to the Hopfield network at time zero. The states of the network for iterations 0 to 7 are shown in Fig. 11.6(b). It is clear that the network converges to the digit 3 pattern correctly.

Example 11.4

[Zurada, 1992]. Consider the use of a Hopfield memory to store the two vectors $\mathbf{x}^1$ and $\mathbf{x}^2$:

$$\mathbf{x}^1 = [1, -1, -1, 1]^T \qquad \text{and} \qquad \mathbf{x}^2 = [-1, 1, -1, 1]^T.$$

From Eq. (11.22), we obtain the weight matrix as

$$\mathbf{W} = \sum_{k=1}^{2} \mathbf{x}^k (\mathbf{x}^k)^T - 2\mathbf{I} = \begin{bmatrix} 0 & -2 & 0 & 0 \\ -2 & 0 & 0 & 0 \\ 0 & 0 & 0 & -2 \\ 0 & 0 & -2 & 0 \end{bmatrix},$$

(a)   (b)

Figure 11.6 Patterns stored by Hopfield memory in Example 11.3. (a) Eight examplar patterns. (b) Output patterns for noisy "3" input. (Adapted from Lippmann [1987], © 1987 IEEE.)

and from Eq. (11.2), the energy function is

$$E(\mathbf{x}) = -\tfrac{1}{2}\mathbf{x}^T\mathbf{W}\mathbf{x} = 2\,(x_1 x_2 + x_3 x_4).$$

The state transition diagram is shown in Fig. 11.7. There are a total of 16 states, each of which corresponds to *one vertex*. This figure shows all possible asynchronous transitions and their directions. Note that every vertex is connected only to the neighboring vertex differing by a single bit because of asynchronous transitions. In Fig. 11.7, each state is associated with its energy value. It is observed that transitions are toward lower energy values. We further find that there are two extra stable states $\bar{\mathbf{x}}^1 = [-1, 1, 1, -1]^T$ and $\bar{\mathbf{x}}^2 = [1, -1, 1, -1]^T$ in addition to the two states $\mathbf{x}^1$ and $\mathbf{x}^2$ that we want to store.

Let us consider some transition examples. Starting at the state $[1, 1, 1, 1]^T$ and with nodes updating asynchronously in ascending order, we have state transitions $[1, 1, 1, 1]^T \rightarrow [-1, 1, 1, 1]^T \rightarrow [-1, 1, 1, 1]^T \rightarrow [-1, 1, -1, 1]^T \cdots$. Hence, the state will converge at the stored pattern $\mathbf{x}^2$. However, it is possible (with a different updating order) that the state $[1, 1, 1, 1]^T$ will converge to $\mathbf{x}^1 = [1, -1, -1, 1]^T$, $\bar{\mathbf{x}}^1 = [-1, 1, 1, -1]^T$ or $\bar{\mathbf{x}}^2 = [1, -1, 1, -1]^T$. This happens because the Hamming distance between the initial state, $[1, 1, 1, 1]^T$ and any of $\mathbf{x}^1, \mathbf{x}^2, \bar{\mathbf{x}}^1,$ or $\bar{\mathbf{x}}^2$ is of the same value 2.

The above example indicates an important fact about the Hopfield memory—that the *complement* of a stored vector is also a stored vector. The reason is that they have the same energy value $E(\mathbf{x}) = E(\bar{\mathbf{x}})$. Hence, the memory of transitions may terminate as easily at $\mathbf{x}$ as at $\bar{\mathbf{x}}$. The crucial factor determining the convergence is the "similarity" between the initializing output vector and $\mathbf{x}$ and $\bar{\mathbf{x}}$.

Two major problems of Hopfield memories are observed from the above example. The first is the unplanned stable states, called *spurious stable states,* which are caused by

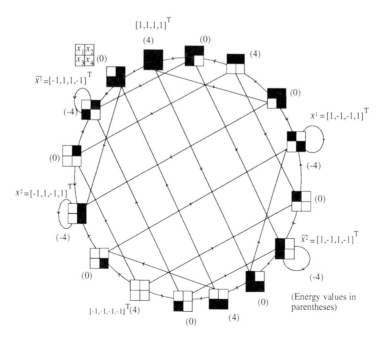

Figure 11.7 State transition diagram for Example 11.4.

the minima of the energy function in addition to the ones we want. The second is uncertain recovery, which concerns the *capacity* of a Hopfield memory. Overloaded memory may result in a small Hamming distance between stored patterns and hence does not provide error-free or efficient recovery of stored patterns. It has been observed that the relative number of spurious states decreases as the dimensionality of the stored vectors (i.e., the number of neurons n) increases with respect to the number of stored vectors. Eventually, a point is reached where there are relatively so few within a certain Hamming radius of each original stored vector that it becomes valid to consider each memory as having a fixed radius of convergence.

It is natural to ask what the *capacity* of a Hopfield memory is, that is, what the relationship between the number of storable memories and the size of the network is. Indeed, capacity is the most important performance parameter or index of an associative memory. The capacity of a Hopfield memory has been widely studied both experimentally [Hopfield, 1983] and from a probabilistic and information-theoretic point of view [McEliece et al., 1987; Venkatesh and Psaltis, 1989; Dembo, 1989]. We shall summarize some of the results here.

A useful measure for associative memory capacity evaluation is the *radius of attraction* ρ, which is defined in terms of the distance ρn from a stable state $\mathbf{x}$ such that every vector within this distance eventually reaches the stable state $\mathbf{x}$. The distance ρn is conveniently measured as a Hamming distance and therefore is of integer value. Since the stored vectors should not be too close, each of the p distinct stored vectors used for a capacity study is usually selected at random. The asymptotic capacity c of a Hopfield autoassociative memory consisting of n neurons was estimated in [McEliece et al., 1987] as

$$c = \frac{(1 - 2\rho)^2 n}{4 \ln n}, \qquad 0 \le \rho < \frac{1}{2}. \tag{11.25}$$

When the number of stored vectors p is below the capacity c in Eq. (11.25), all the stored memories will be stable with a probability near 1. If we allow that a small fraction of the stored memories are unrecoverable and not stable, then the capacity is derived as

$$c = \frac{(1 - 2\rho)^2 n}{2 \ln n}, \qquad 0 \le \rho < \frac{1}{2}. \tag{11.26}$$

In summary, regardless of the radius of attraction $0 \le \rho < \frac{1}{2}$, the capacity of the Hopfield memory is bounded as follows

$$\frac{n}{4 \ln n} < c < \frac{n}{2 \ln n}. \tag{11.27}$$

For example, the capacity of a 100-node Hopfield network is from 5.4 to 10.8 memory vectors. From an experimental study [Hopfield, 1983; Amit et al., 1985], it was found that when the number of stored vectors is less than $0.14n$ ($p \le 0.14n$), stable states are found very close to the stored memories at a distance of $0.03n$. Hence, memory retrieval is mostly accurate for $p \le 0.14n$ if a small percentage of error is tolerable.

It can be shown that the Hebbian-type learning rule for the Hopfield memory has the following two desirable properties if the stored vectors are orthogonal [Aiyer et al., 1990]. First, the original stored vectors are stable states of the network. Second, these memory stable states have a radius of attraction such that initial states of the network lying within this radius can then be corrected to the corresponding stored memory vector. Similar to the case for linear associators, the restriction that the stored vectors $\mathbf{x}^k$ are orthogonal can be relaxed to the restriction that they are linearly independent. In this case, similar to Eq. (11.21), by using a pseudoinverse matrix, the weight learning rule can be written [Personnza et al., 1985, 1986; Venkatesh and Psaltis, 1989; Dembo, 1989]

$$\mathbf{W} = \mathbf{X}\mathbf{X}^+ = \mathbf{X}(\mathbf{X}^T\mathbf{X})^{-1}\mathbf{X}^T, \qquad (11.28)$$

where $\mathbf{X} = [\mathbf{x}^1, \mathbf{x}^2, \ldots, \mathbf{x}^p]^T$. This rule is called the *projection learning rule* and also has the above two properties if the stored vectors are linearly independent. However, the disadvantages of the projection learning rule are that it is computationally complex and that the regions of attraction for each pattern become significantly smaller for a larger number of stored vectors p stored within a network of a given size as compared to the Hebbian-type learning rule in Eq. (11.22). The decrease in memory convergence quality is rather drastic when p approaches $n/2$.

11.2.2 Bidirectional Associative Memory

Bidirectional associative memory (BAM) is a recurrent heteroassociative memory consisting of two layers and can be considered an extension of a Hopfield network. It performs forward and backward associative searches for stored stimulus-response associations [Kosko, 1987, 1988]. Similar to a Hopfield network, we can have discrete and continuous BAMs. We shall first introduce a discrete BAM because of its simplicity.

The structure of a discrete BAM is shown in Fig. 11.8. When the memory neurons are activated by putting an initial vector at the input of a layer, the network evolves to a two-pattern stable state with each pattern at the output of one layer. The network's dynamics involves two layers of interaction. More precisely, assume that an initializing vector $\mathbf{x}$ is applied at the input of neuron layer Y. The input is processed and transferred to the output of layer Y as follows:

$$\mathbf{y}' = a(\mathbf{Wx}) \qquad \text{or} \qquad y_i' = a\left(\sum_{j=1}^{m} w_{ij}x_j \right), \qquad i = 1, 2, \ldots, n, \qquad (11.29)$$

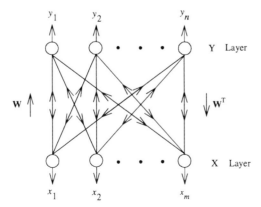

Figure 11.8 Structure of a bidirectional associative memory.

where $a(\cdot)$ is a threshold function. The vector $\mathbf{y}'$ now feeds to neuron layer X and produces the following output:

$$\mathbf{x}' = a(\mathbf{W}^T\mathbf{y}') \qquad \text{or} \qquad x'_j = a\left(\sum_{i=1}^n w_{ji} y'_i\right), \qquad j = 1, 2, \dots, m. \qquad (11.30)$$

Then $\mathbf{x}'$ feeds into the input of layer Y and produces $\mathbf{y}''$ according to Eq. (11.29). The process continues until further updates of $\mathbf{x}$ and $\mathbf{y}$ stop. This recursive retrieval process consists of the following steps:

$$
\begin{aligned}
\mathbf{y}^{(1)} &= a(\mathbf{W}\mathbf{x}^{(0)}) && \text{(first forward pass),} \\
\mathbf{x}^{(2)} &= a(\mathbf{W}^T\mathbf{y}^{(1)}) && \text{(first backward pass),} \\
\mathbf{y}^{(3)} &= a(\mathbf{W}\mathbf{x}^{(2)}) && \text{(second forward pass),} \\
\mathbf{x}^{(4)} &= a(\mathbf{W}^T\mathbf{y}^{(3)}) && \text{(second backward pass),} && (11.31) \\
&\vdots \\
\mathbf{y}^{(k-1)} &= a(\mathbf{W}\mathbf{x}^{(k-2)}) && [(k/2)\text{th forward pass],} \\
\mathbf{x}^{(k)} &= a(\mathbf{W}^T\mathbf{y}^{(k-1)}) && [(k/2)\text{th backward pass].}
\end{aligned}
$$

Note that the state update in Eq. (11.31) is synchronous following Eqs. (11.29) and (11.30). The state update can also be asynchronous following Eqs. (11.29) and (11.30) for randomly chosen nodes i and j. It can be shown that the system is stable under either a synchronous or an asynchronous operation. Hence, a synchronous operation is usually used in a BAM for its larger energy changes and thus much faster convergence.

Consider that there are p vector association pairs to be stored in a BAM:

$$\{(\mathbf{x}^1, \mathbf{y}^1), (\mathbf{x}^2, \mathbf{y}^2), \dots, (\mathbf{x}^P, \mathbf{y}^P)\}, \qquad (11.32)$$

where $\mathbf{x}^k = (x_1^k, x_2^k, \dots, x_m^k)^T$ and $\mathbf{y}^k = (y_1^k, y_2^k, \dots, y_n^k)^T$ are either unipolar or bipolar vectors. Using the outer-product learning rule, the weight learning (assignment) rule for the BAM is

$$\mathbf{W} = \begin{cases} \sum_{k=1}^P \mathbf{y}^k (\mathbf{x}^k)^T & \text{for bipolar vectors} \\ \sum_{k=1}^P (2\mathbf{y}^k - 1)(2\mathbf{x}^k - 1)^T & \text{for unipolar vectors.} \end{cases} \qquad (11.33)$$

or

$$w_{ij} = \begin{cases} \sum_{k=1}^P y_i^k x_j^k & \text{for bipolar vectors} \\ \sum_{k=1}^P (2y_i^k - 1)(2x_j^k - 1) & \text{for unipolar vectors.} \end{cases} \qquad (11.34)$$

Assume one of the stored vectors $\mathbf{x}^{k'}$ is presented to the BAM. Then, according to Eq. (11.29),

$$y = a \left(\sum_{k=1}^{p} (\mathbf{y}^k (\mathbf{x}^k)^T) \mathbf{x}^{k'} \right)$$

$$= a \left(m\mathbf{y}^{k'} + \sum_{\substack{k=1 \\ k \neq k'}}^{p} \mathbf{y}^k (\mathbf{x}^k)^T \mathbf{x}^{k'} \right) \tag{11.35}$$

$$= a(m\mathbf{y}^{k'} + \boldsymbol{\eta}),$$

where $\boldsymbol{\eta}$ is the noise term. Hence, if the vectors $\mathbf{x}^k$ are orthogonal (i.e., HD $(\mathbf{x}^k, \mathbf{x}^l) = m/2$ for $k, l = 1, 2,..., p, k \neq l$), then the noise term $\boldsymbol{\eta}$ is zero, and thus immediate stabilization and exact association $\mathbf{y} = \mathbf{y}^{k'}$ occur within only a single pass through layer Y. Note that two vectors containing ± 1 elements are orthogonal if and only if they differ in exactly $m/2$ bits. If the input vector is a distorted version of pattern $\mathbf{x}^{k'}$, the stabilization at $\mathbf{y}^{k'}$ depends on factors such as the HD between the input vector and stored $\mathbf{x}^k$ vectors, the orthogonality of vectors $\mathbf{y}^k$, and the HD between vectors $\mathbf{y}^k$.

The stability analysis of a BAM is based on defining a Lyapunov (energy) function. A BAM is said to be *bidirectionally stable* if the state converges to a stable point: $\mathbf{y}^{(k)} \rightarrow \mathbf{x}^{(k+1)} \rightarrow \mathbf{y}^{(k+2)}$ and $\mathbf{y}^{(k+2)} = \mathbf{y}^{(k)}$. This corresponds to the minimum of the energy function. The energy function or Lyapunov function of a discrete BAM is defined by

$$E(\mathbf{x}, \mathbf{y}) \equiv -\tfrac{1}{2}\mathbf{x}^T \mathbf{W}^T \mathbf{y} - \tfrac{1}{2}\mathbf{y}^T \mathbf{W}\mathbf{x} = -\mathbf{y}^T \mathbf{W}\mathbf{x}. \tag{11.36}$$

The energy changes due to the single bit changes in Δy_i and Δx_i can be found as

$$\Delta E_{y_i} = \nabla_{\mathbf{y}} E \, \Delta y_i = -\mathbf{W}\mathbf{x}\Delta y_i = -\left(\sum_{j=1}^{m} w_{ij} x_j \right) \Delta y_i, \qquad i = 1, 2,..., n, \tag{11.37}$$

$$\Delta E_{x_j} = \nabla_{\mathbf{x}} E \, \Delta x_j = -\mathbf{W}^T \mathbf{y}\Delta x_j = -\left(\sum_{i=1}^{n} w_{ji} y_i \right) \Delta x_j, \qquad j = 1, 2,..., m. \tag{11.38}$$

From Eqs. (11.29) and (11.30), we have

$$\Delta y_i = \begin{cases} 2 & \text{for } \sum_{j=1}^{m} w_{ij} x_j > 0 \\ 0 & \text{for } \sum_{j=1}^{m} w_{ij} x_j = 0 \\ -2 & \text{for } \sum_{j=1}^{m} w_{ij} x_j < 0, \end{cases} \tag{11.39}$$

$$\Delta x_j = \begin{cases} 2 & \text{for } \sum_{i=1}^{n} w_{ji} y_i > 0 \\ 0 & \text{for } \sum_{i=1}^{n} w_{ji} y_i = 0 \\ -2 & \text{for } \sum_{i=1}^{n} w_{ji} y_i < 0. \end{cases} \tag{11.40}$$

Hence, it is obvious that $\Delta E \leq 0$ for either synchronous or asynchronous update rules. Since the energy function is bounded below by $E(\mathbf{x}, \mathbf{y}) \geq -\sum_{i=1}^{n}\sum_{j=1}^{m} |w_{ij}|$, the discrete BAM will converge to a stable state.

Example 11.5

Given the following two pairs of vectors to be stored in a BAM:

$$\mathbf{x}^1 = [1, -1, -1, 1, 1, -1, 1, -1, -1, 1]^T, \qquad \mathbf{y}^1 = [-1, -1, 1, 1, 1, 1]^T,$$
$$\mathbf{x}^2 = [1, 1, 1, -1, 1, 1, 1, -1, 1, -1]^T, \qquad \mathbf{y}^2 = [-1, -1, 1, 1, -1, -1]^T.$$

From Eq. (11.33) we have

$$\mathbf{W} = \begin{bmatrix} -2 & 0 & 0 & 0 & -2 & 0 & -2 & 2 & 0 & 0 \\ -2 & 0 & 0 & 0 & -2 & 0 & -2 & 2 & 0 & 0 \\ 2 & 0 & 0 & 0 & 2 & 0 & 2 & -2 & 0 & 0 \\ 2 & 0 & 0 & 0 & 2 & 0 & 2 & -2 & 0 & 0 \\ 0 & -2 & -2 & 2 & 0 & -2 & 0 & 0 & -2 & 2 \\ 0 & -2 & -2 & 2 & 0 & -2 & 0 & 0 & -2 & 2 \end{bmatrix}.$$

For testing, we first choose a vector $\mathbf{x}$ with a HD of 2 from $\mathbf{x}^1$: $\mathbf{x}^{(0)} = [-1, 1, -1, 1, 1, -1, 1, -1, -1, 1]^T$. From Eq. (11.31), we obtain

$$\mathbf{y}^{(1)} = a([-4, -4, 4, 4, 8, 8]^T) = [-1, -1, 1, 1, 1, 1]^T,$$
$$\mathbf{x}^{(2)} = a([8, -4, -4, 4, 8, -4, 8, -8, -4, 4]^T) = [1, -1, -1, 1, 1, -1, 1, -1, -1, 1]^T,$$
$$\mathbf{y}^{(3)} = [-1, -1, 1, 1, 1, 1]^T = \mathbf{y}^{(1)}.$$

Hence it is bidirectionally stable and recalls the first-stored pair successfully. Let us perform another trial by choosing $\mathbf{x}^{(0)} = [-1, 1, 1, -1, 1, -1, -1, 1, 1, 1]^T$. Since $HD(\mathbf{x}^{(0)}, \mathbf{x}^1) = 7$ and $HD(\mathbf{x}^{(0)}, \mathbf{x}^2) = 5$, it is expected that the second-stored pair will be recalled. Using Eq. (11.31), we have

$$\mathbf{y}^{(1)} = a([4, 4, -4, -4, -4, -4]^T) = [1, 1, -1, -1, -1, -1]^T,$$
$$\mathbf{x}^{(2)} = a([-8, 4, 4, -4, -8, 4, -8, 8, 4, -4]^T) = [-1, 1, 1, -1, -1, 1, -1, 1, 1, -1]^T,$$
$$\mathbf{y}^{(3)} = [1, 1, -1, -1, -1, -1]^T = \mathbf{y}^{(1)}.$$

Further propagation does not change the states. The achieved stable state does not match any of the stored pairs. However, it is actually the complement of the first-stored pair: $(\mathbf{x}^{(2)}, \mathbf{y}^{(3)}) = (\overline{\mathbf{x}}^1, \overline{\mathbf{y}}^1)$. This illustrates the fact that if a pair $(\mathbf{x}, \mathbf{y})$ is stored in a BAM, then its complement $(\overline{\mathbf{x}}, \overline{\mathbf{y}})$ is also stored.

The capacity of a BAM can be roughly estimated as follows. From Eq. (11.35), we can statistically expect that if $p > m$, the noise term $\boldsymbol{\eta}$ in Eq. (11.35) exceeds the signal term. This estimation can also apply to the other direction, that is, back propagation of the signal from layer Y to layer X. Hence, a rough estimate of the BAM storage capacity is [Kosko, 1988]

$$p \leq \min(m, n). \tag{11.41}$$

A more conservative capacity measure can be obtained by observing Eq. (11.35) in another way. The noise term $\boldsymbol{\eta}$ in Eq. (11.35) can be rewritten in a bipolar mode as

$$\boldsymbol{\eta} = \sum_{\substack{k=1 \\ k \neq k'}}^{p} \mathbf{y}^k (\mathbf{x}^k)^T \mathbf{x}^{k'} = \sum_{\substack{k=1 \\ k \neq k'}}^{p} \mathbf{y}^k [m - 2\mathrm{HD}(\mathbf{x}^k, \mathbf{x}^{k'})]. \tag{11.42}$$

Roughly speaking, if we store more pairs in a BAM, the average Hamming distance between any two points becomes shorter, which makes $(\mathbf{x}^k)^T \mathbf{x}^{k'} = m - 2\mathrm{HD}(\mathbf{x}^k, \mathbf{x}^{k'})$ larger. Hence, $(\mathbf{x}^k)^T \mathbf{x}^{k'}$ is proportional to the number of training pairs, p. Since there are $(p-1)$ terms in the summation of Eq. (11.42), the noise term $\boldsymbol{\eta}$ is approximately of order $O(p^2)$. To cancel the effects of $\boldsymbol{\eta}$, basically [see Eq. (11.35)] $p^2 < m$ is preferred. Again, when considering the reverse information flow direction in a BAM, we prefer $p^2 < n$. Thus, we have a more conservative capacity estimation as follows:

$$p = \sqrt{\min(m, n)}. \tag{11.43}$$

A BAM can be generalized to enable multiple associations $(\mathbf{x}^k, \mathbf{y}^k, \mathbf{z}^k, \dots)$, $k = 1, 2, \dots, p$. This multiple-association memory is called *multidirectional associative memory* [Hagiwara, 1990]. A multidirectional associative memory for storing vectors with triple associations is shown in Fig. 11.9. It is a three-layer structure. Let $\mathbf{x}^k, \mathbf{y}^k, \mathbf{z}^k$, $k = 1, 2, \dots, p$, be the bipolar vectors of associations to be stored. The weight learning rules are generalized from Eq. (11.33) as follows:

$$\mathbf{W}_{YX} = \sum_{k=1}^{p} \mathbf{y}^k (\mathbf{x}^k)^T, \qquad \mathbf{W}_{ZX} = \sum_{k=1}^{p} \mathbf{z}^k (\mathbf{x}^k)^T, \qquad \mathbf{W}_{YZ} = \sum_{k=1}^{p} \mathbf{y}^k (\mathbf{z}^k)^T. \tag{11.44}$$

The recall proceeds as follows. Each node independently and synchronously updates its output according to the following update rules until a multidirectionally stable state is reached:

$$\mathbf{y}' = a[\mathbf{W}_{YX}\mathbf{x} + \mathbf{W}_{YZ}\mathbf{z}]$$
$$\mathbf{z}' = a[\mathbf{W}_{ZX}\mathbf{x} + \mathbf{W}_{YZ}^T\mathbf{y}] \tag{11.45}$$
$$\mathbf{x}' = a[\mathbf{W}_{YX}^T\mathbf{y} + \mathbf{W}_{ZX}^T\mathbf{z}].$$

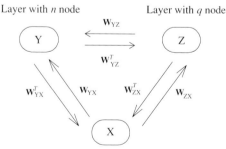

Figure 11.9 Structure of a triple-directional associative memory.

Extending the above discussion of discrete BAMs to continuous BAMs, the state update rules of the nodes in the two layers (layers X and Y) are

$$\dot{y}_i = -a_i y_i + \sum_{j=1}^{m} w_{ij} a(x_j) + s_i,$$

$$\dot{x}_j = -c_j x_j + \sum_{i=1}^{n} w_{ij} a(y_i) + t_j,$$

(11.46)

where a_i, c_j, s_i, and t_j are positive constants, $i = 1, 2, ..., n$, $j = 1, 2, ..., m$, $a(\cdot)$ is a sigmoid function, and w_{ij} is the ijth element of an $n \times m$ real matrix. It can be easily proved, using the Cohen-Grossberg theorem (Theorem 11.2), that given any starting state $(\mathbf{x}^{(0)}, \mathbf{y}^{(0)})$, a continuous BAM will converge to a stable state $(\mathbf{x}^{(\infty)}, \mathbf{y}^{(\infty)})$.

If the activation function $a(\cdot)$ in Eq. (11.46) is taken as a bipolar sigmoid function with sufficiently high gain and we set $a_i = 1$ for all i and $c_j = 1$ for all j, then an empirical study has shown that the continuous BAM will converge to a state such that the vectors $a(\mathbf{x}) = [a(x_1), a(x_2), ..., a(x_m)]^T$ and $a(\mathbf{y}) = [a(y_1), a(y_2), ..., a(y_n)]^T$ will approach vertices of the cubes $\{-1, 1\}^m$ and $\{-1, 1\}^n$, respectively. In this case, it acts like a discrete BAM.

11.2.3 Temporal Associative Memory

We have so far been concerned with associative networks that evolve to a stable state and then stay there. They can thus act as content-addressable memories for a set of static patterns. It is also interesting to investigate the possibility of storing sequences of patterns in the form of dynamic state transitions [Amari, 1972]. Such patterns are called *temporal* patterns, and an associative memory with such a capability is called a *temporal associative memory*. In this section, we shall see how the Hopfield network and the BAM act as temporal associative memories. We assume all temporal patterns are bipolar binary vectors given by an ordered set (or a sequence) S containing p vectors:

$$S = \{\mathbf{s}^1, \mathbf{s}^2, ..., \mathbf{s}^p\},$$

(11.47)

where column vectors $\mathbf{s}^k$ are n-dimensional. If unipolar vectors are considered, they should be transferred to bipolar vectors for weight learning as we did for associative memories above. It is hoped that the neural network can memorize the sequence S in its dynamic state transitions such that the recalled sequence is $\mathbf{s}^1 \to \mathbf{s}^2 \to \cdots \to \mathbf{s}^p \to \mathbf{s}^1 \to \mathbf{s}^2 ...$, or in the reverse order. We shall take $\mathbf{s}^{p+1}$ to mean $\mathbf{s}^1$ in the following.

To use Hopfield networks as temporal associative memories, we want the network to go through a predetermined sequence, usually in a closed *limit cycle*. Hopfield [1982] suggested that asymmetric weights

$$w_{ij} = \frac{1}{n} \sum_{k=1}^{p} s_i^k s_j^k + \frac{\lambda}{n} \sum_{k=1}^{p} s_i^{k+1} s_j^k$$

(11.48)

for an n-node Hopfield network might solve this problem, where λ is a constant that governs the relative strength of symmetric and asymmetric terms. If such a network is in the state $\mathbf{s}^{k'}$, then the net input $(\text{net}_i^{k'})$ to node i is

$$\text{net}_i^{k'} = \sum_{j=1}^{n} w_{ij} s_j^{k'} = \frac{1}{n} \sum_{j=1}^{n} \sum_{k=1}^{p} s_i^k s_j^k s_j^{k'} + \frac{\lambda}{n} \sum_{j=1}^{n} \sum_{k=1}^{p} s_i^{k+1} s_j^k s_j^{k'}$$

(11.49)

$$= s_i^{k'} + \lambda s_i^{k'+1} + \text{cross-terms}.$$

The cross-terms are small if the patterns are uncorrelated and there are not too many of them. If $\lambda > 1$, then the second term dominates and tends to move the system to the next pattern s_i^{k+1}. As Eq. (11.28) did for correlated patterns, the Hebbian-type learning rule in Eq. (11.48) may be replaced by the pseudoinverse rule:

$$w_{ij} = \frac{1}{n} \sum_{k=1}^{p} \sum_{l=1}^{p} s_i^k (\mathbf{S}^T \mathbf{S})_{kl}^{-1} s_j^l + \frac{\lambda}{n} \sum_{k=1}^{p} \sum_{l=1}^{p} s_i^{k+1} (\mathbf{S}^T \mathbf{S})_{kl}^{-1} s_j^l,$$

(11.50)

where $\mathbf{S} = [\mathbf{s}^1, \mathbf{s}^2, \ldots, \mathbf{s}^p]^T$.

Unfortunately, these schemes may not work very well in practice. The asynchronous updating tends to dephase the system such that the states that overlap several consecutive patterns are usually obtained. It works well only if the length of the sequence is very small ($p \ll n$) [Nishimori et al., 1990]. Even so, Eq. (11.48) provides the fundamental concept of using Hopfield networks as temporal associative memories.

A BAM can also be used to generate the sequence S in Eq. (11.47). The idea is to treat the pair of consecutive vectors $\mathbf{s}^k$ and $\mathbf{s}^{k+1}$ as heteroassociative. From this point of view, $\mathbf{s}^1$ is associated with $\mathbf{s}^2$, $\mathbf{s}^2$ with $\mathbf{s}^3, \ldots$, and $\mathbf{s}^p$ with $\mathbf{s}^1$. Then the outer-product learning rule for the weight assignment is

$$\mathbf{W} = \sum_{k=1}^{p} \mathbf{s}^{k+1} (\mathbf{s}^k)^T.$$

(11.51)

A BAM for temporal patterns can be modified in such a way that both layers X and Y are now described by identical weight matrices $\mathbf{W}$. Hence, the recall formulas become

$$\mathbf{x} = a(\mathbf{Wy}) \qquad \text{and} \qquad \mathbf{y} = a(\mathbf{Wx}),$$

(11.52)

where $a(\cdot)$ is a threshold function. Obviously, a reverse order recall can be implemented using the transposed weight matrices in both layers X and Y. In the temporal BAM, layers X and Y update nonsimultaneously and in an alternate circular fashion. The Lyapunov energy function for the temporal BAM can be defined by

$$E = -\sum_{k=1}^{p} \mathbf{s}^{k+1} \mathbf{W} \mathbf{s}^k.$$

(11.53)

The reader can check that E decreases during the temporal sequence retrieval $\mathbf{s}^1 \rightarrow \mathbf{s}^2 \rightarrow \cdots \rightarrow \mathbf{s}^p$. However, the energy increases stepwise at the transition, $\mathbf{s}^p \rightarrow \mathbf{s}^1$ [Kosko, 1988], and then it continues to decrease in the following cycle of $(p-1)$ retrievals. The storage capacity of the temporal BAM can be estimated using Eq. (11.41). Hence, the maximum length sequence is bounded by $p < n$.

Example 11.6

Let the temporal sequence to be stored be

$$S = \{\mathbf{s}^1, \mathbf{s}^2, \mathbf{s}^3\} = \{[1, -1, 1, -1, -1]^T, [-1, 1, 1, 1, -1, 1]^T, [1, 1, -1, -1, 1]^T\}.$$

From Eq. (11.51), we have

$$\mathbf{W} = \mathbf{s}^2 (\mathbf{s}^1)^T + \mathbf{s}^3 (\mathbf{s}^2)^T + \mathbf{s}^1 (\mathbf{s}^3)^T$$

$$= \begin{bmatrix} -1 & 3 & -1 & -1 & 3 \\ -1 & -1 & 3 & -1 & -1 \\ 3 & -1 & -1 & -1 & -1 \\ -1 & -1 & -1 & 3 & -1 \\ -1 & -1 & 3 & -1 & -1 \end{bmatrix}.$$

We can check that

$$a(\mathbf{Ws}^1) = a([-8, 5, 5, -3, 5]^T) = [-1, 1, 1, -1, 1]^T = \mathbf{s}^2,$$
$$a(\mathbf{Ws}^2) = a([5, 3, -5, -5, 3]^T) = [1, 1, -1, -1, 1]^T = \mathbf{s}^3,$$
$$a(\mathbf{Ws}^3) = a([9, -5, 3, -5, -5]^T) = [1, -1, 1, -1, -1]^T = \mathbf{s}^1.$$

Hence, it can recall the sequence $\mathbf{s}^2, \mathbf{s}^3, \mathbf{s}^1$ successfully.

11.3 OPTIMIZATION PROBLEMS

Besides being used as associative memories to perform information retrieval or recognition of a task, Hopfield networks are also widely employed in another important application area of solving optimization problems. That is, the network is expected to find a configuration for minimizing an energy function which acts as the cost function of the optimization problem. We shall also explore another network, the Boltzmann machine, for solving optimization problems. Boltzmann machines can be viewed as the stochastic version of Hopfield networks, and they have some advantages over Hopfield networks for optimization problems.

11.3.1 Hopfield Networks for Optimization Problems

Typically, in using Hopfield networks for solving optimization problems, the energy function of the Hopfield network is made equivalent to a certain *objective* (*cost*) function that needs to be minimized. The search for a minimum energy performed by the Hopfield network corresponds to the search for a solution to the optimization problem. Hence, the key concept here is to formulate an optimization problem with a proper objective function that can be used to construct a Hopfield network, especially for finding its weights. When we formulate the optimization problems to be solved by Hopfield networks, we are in reality constructing a particular kind of parallel algorithm for their solution. These algorithms lend themselves to a direct implementation in terms of the Hopfield networks that we have been studying, including the analog circuits in Sec. 11.1.2. Methodologies for formulating optimization problems in terms of Hopfield networks are quite problem-oriented. Some typical examples are used here to illustrate the methodology for problem formulation.

Example 11.7

In this example, we shall design a four-bit analog-to-digital (A/D) converter using a continuous unipolar Hopfield network. This application was first proposed by Tank and Hopfield [1986]. The goal is to convert an analog input value x, $0 \leq x \leq 15$, to a binary representation $y = [y_3, y_2, y_1, y_0]^T$, where y_0, y_1, y_2, and $y_3 \in \{0, 1\}$ such that the decimal value of the binary vector $8y_3 + 4y_2 + 2y_1 + y_0$ and the value x are as close as possible. The A/D conversion error E_c can be considered as an energy function as follows:

$$E_c = \frac{1}{2} \left(x - \sum_{i=0}^{3} 2^i y_i \right)^2. \tag{11.54}$$

Obviously, minimizing this energy function is equivalent to minimizing the conversion error of the A/D converter. Our objective here is to construct a four-node continuous Hopfield network with a unipolar activation function to perform this minimization. For this purpose, we need to find proper parameters, including weights and external inputs, of the Hopfield network. This can be done by comparing E_c with the general formula for the energy function of a continuous Hopfield network [i.e., comparing Eq. (11.54) with Eq. (11.10)]. However, our first observation indicates that the energy function E_c contains terms y_i^2, $i = 0, 1, 2, 3$, with nonzero coefficients which will make the w_{ii} terms of the Hopfield network nonzero. This contradicts the definition of Hopfield networks. Hence, a supplemental energy term E_a should be added to eliminate these terms. Furthermore, E_a should be minimized close to the corners of the cube $[0, 1]^4$. This is a requirement of the A/D converter and is also a characteristic of the Hopfield network. A suitable choice for E_a is thus

$$E_a = -\frac{1}{2} \sum_{i=0}^{3} 2^{2i} y_i (y_i - 1), \tag{11.55}$$

and the resultant total energy function will be

$$E = E_c + E_a = \frac{1}{2} \left(x - \sum_{i=0}^{3} 2^i y_i \right)^2 - \frac{1}{2} \sum_{i=0}^{3} 2^{2i} y_i (y_i - 1). \tag{11.56}$$

Note that the supplemental term E_a is nonnegative and has the lowest value when $y_i = 0$ or $y_i = 1$. Hence, E_a can force the network state to the corners of the hypercube when the total energy E is minimized.

The expression for total energy in Eq. (11.56) should now be equated to the general formula for energy as in Eq. (11.10), which is equal to

$$E = -\frac{1}{2} \sum_{i=0}^{3} \sum_{\substack{j=0 \\ j \neq i}}^{3} w_{ij} y_i y_j - \sum_{i=0}^{3} x_i y_i \tag{11.57}$$

in the case of high-gain neurons. Note that the term with the integral in Eq. (11.10) vanishes because of the high-gain neurons used here. Comparing coefficients of Eqs. (11.56) and (11.57), we have

$$w_{ij} = -2^{i+j} \qquad \text{and} \qquad x_i = -2^{2i-1} + 2^i x, \qquad i, j = 0, 1, 2, 3; i \neq j. \tag{11.58}$$

That is,

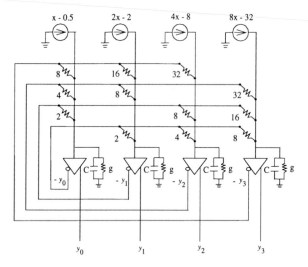

x - 0.5   2x - 2   4x - 8   8x - 32

Figure 11.10 Hopfield network as a four-bit A/D converter.

$$\mathbf{W} = -\begin{bmatrix} 0 & 2 & 4 & 8 \\ 2 & 0 & 8 & 16 \\ 4 & 8 & 0 & 32 \\ 8 & 16 & 32 & 0 \end{bmatrix} \quad \text{and} \quad \mathbf{x} = -\begin{bmatrix} 0.5 - x \\ 2 - 2x \\ 8 - 4x \\ 32 - 8x \end{bmatrix}. \tag{11.59}$$

With the above weight matrix, the Hopfield network designed as a four-bit A/D converter is shown in Fig. 11.10.

Example 11.8

In this example, we will solve the traveling saleseperson problem [Lawler et al., 1985] using a discrete unipolar Hopfield network. The problem is to find the minimum-length closed tour that visits each city once and returns to its starting point. This is a classical combinatorial optimization problem, and if it is of size n (n cities), there are order e^n or $n!$ possible solutions of which we want the one that minimizes the cost function. Hence, instead of using conventional combinational optimization approaches, we consider a solution for the problem using continuous Hopfield networks [Hopfield and Tank, 1985].

An example of five cities, A, B, C, D, E, and their shortest tour, $B \to C \to E \to D \to A \to B$, are shown in Fig. 11.11(a). For an n-city tour, there are $n!$ possible paths. However, since it does not matter which of n cities is the starting point and which of the two directions is followed on the tour, there are actually $n!/2n$ paths. A Hopfield network consisting of n^2 unipolar continuous neurons, arranged in the form of an $n \times n$ matrix, is designed to solve this problem. The ith row in the matrix corresponds to the ith city, and the ith column corresponds to the ith order of visiting. Let the output of the node at row x and column i be denoted by $y_{x,i}$ where x represents a city and i represents a visiting order. One example network output representing the shortest path $B \to C \to E \to D \to A \to B$ is shown in Fig. 11.11(b), where solid and open circles denote nodes with outputs $+1$ (on) and 0 (off), respectively. A node at row x and column i (i.e., $y_{x,i} = 1$) means visiting city x at the order i. Since each city can be visited only once and only one city can be visited at a time, the solution matrix can have only a single 1 in each column and a single 1 in each row.

An energy function should be constructed that favors states that (i) have each city on the tour only once,(ii) have each order number on the tour only once, (iii) include all n cities, and

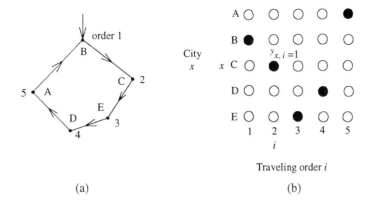

Figure 11.11 Traveling salesperson problem solution. (a) Shortest path. (b) Neuron matrix representation.

(iv) have the shortest total distances. Assume that the distance between city x and city y is $d_{xy} = d_{yx}$, where $x, y \in \{A, B, C, D, E\}$. A proper energy function is defined as

$$E = \frac{p}{2}\sum_{x=1}^{n}\sum_{i=1}^{n}\sum_{\substack{j=1 \\ j\neq i}}^{n} y_{x,i}y_{x,j} + \frac{q}{2}\sum_{i=1}^{n}\sum_{x=1}^{n}\sum_{\substack{y=1 \\ y\neq x}}^{n} y_{x,i}y_{y,i} +$$

$$\frac{r}{2}\left(\sum_{x=1}^{n}\sum_{i=1}^{n} y_{x,i} - n\right)^{2} + \frac{s}{2}\sum_{x=1}^{n}\sum_{\substack{y=1 \\ y\neq x}}^{n}\sum_{i=1}^{n} d_{xy}y_{x,i}(y_{y,i+1} + y_{y,i-1}) \qquad (11.60)$$

$$= E_1 + E_2 + E_3 + E_4,$$

where $y_{x,n+1} = y_{x,1}, y_{x,0} = y_{x,n}$, and p, q, r, and s are positive constants. For the first term (E_1) in Eq. (11.60), the product terms $y_{x,i}y_{x,j}$ refer to a single city x. The inner two sums result in a sum of products $y_{x,i}y_{x,j}$ for all combinations of i and j except $i = j$. Hence, this term is zero if there is a single neuron in each row, that is, if each city is visited only once. Otherwise, this term is greater than zero. Similarly, the second term (E_2) in Eq. (11.60) is zero if and only if there is a single neuron in each column, that is, only one city is visited at a time. The third term (E_3) in Eq. (11.60) ensures that exactly n cities are visited on a tour. Up to this point, we see that minimization of the energy function $E_1 + E_2 + E_3$ favors generation of one of the valid tours. Finally, the fourth term (E_4) computes a value proportional to the distance traveled on the tour. Here we need to make sure that only the distances between adjacent cities are counted. Thus, a minimum-distance tour results in a minimum contribution of this term to the energy function.

The energy function [Eq. (11.60)] is now equated to the general form of a Hopfield network [Eq. (11.2)], which we repeat here for the two-dimensional $n \times n$ neuron matrix:

$$E = -\frac{1}{2}\sum_{(x,i)=(1,1)}^{(n,n)}\sum_{\substack{(y,j)=(1,1) \\ (y,j)\neq(x,i)}}^{(n,n)} w_{(x,i),(y,j)}y_{x,i}y_{y,j} - \sum_{(x,i)=(1,1)}^{(n,n)} x_{x,i}y_{x,i}. \qquad (11.61)$$

By comparing the coefficients of Eqs. (11.60) and (11.61), we have the weights and external input currents as

$$w_{(x,i),(y,j)} = -2p\delta_{xy}(1 - \delta_{ij}) - 2q\delta_{ij}(1 - \delta_{xy}) - 2y - 2sd_{xy}(\delta_{j,i+1} + \delta_{j,i-1}), \qquad (11.62)$$

$$x_{x,i} = 2rn, \tag{11.63}$$

where δ_{ij} is the Kronecker delta and is defined as

$$\delta_{ij} \triangleq \begin{cases} 1 & \text{for } i = j \\ 0 & \text{for } i \neq j. \end{cases} \tag{11.64}$$

Note that the energy functions E_1, E_2, E_3, and E_4 produce corresponding terms in Eq. (11.62). The term E_1 leads to an inhibitory (negative) connection of value $-2p$ within each row. Similarly, the term E_2 causes an inhibitory connection of value $-2q$ within each column. In the first term of Eq. (11.62), the first delta ensures that this inhibition is confined to each row, where $x = y$. The second delta ensures that each node does not inhibit itself. The term E_3 results in global inhibition provided by each weight. Finally, the fourth term in Eq. (11.62) is caused by E_4. For a given column j (i.e., for a given visiting order on the tour), the two delta terms ensure that inhibitory connections are made only to nodes in adjacent columns. Nodes in adjacent columns represent cities that might come either before or after the cities in column j. The factor $-2sd_{xy}$ ensures that the nodes representing cities farther apart will receive larger inhibitory signals.

Substituting $w_{(x,i),(y,j)}$ from Eq. (11.62) into Eq. (11.8), we obtain the following update rule:

$$\frac{dy_{x,i}}{dt} = -\frac{y_{x,i}}{\tau} - 2p \sum_{\substack{j=1 \\ j \neq i}}^{n} y_{x,j} - 2q \sum_{\substack{y=1 \\ y \neq x}}^{n} y_{y,i} -$$

$$\tag{11.65}$$

$$2r \left(\sum_{x=1}^{n} \sum_{j=1}^{n} y_{x,j} - n \right) - 2s \sum_{\substack{y=1 \\ y \neq x}}^{n} d_{xy} (y_{y,i+1} + y_{y,i-1}).$$

It is important to choose proper parameters p, q, r, and s. In [Hopfield and Tank, 1985], $p = q = 500$, $r = 200$, $s = 500$, $\tau = 1$, $\lambda = 50$, and $n = 15$ were used for a 10-city problem, where λ is the gain parameter of the sigmoidal activation function. Notice that it is not necessary to choose $n = 10$ even for a 10-city problem. Simulation using Eq. (11.65) showed that 50% of the trials produced the two best paths among 181,440 distinct paths.

Example 11.9

This example uses a continuous unipolar Hopfield network to solve the problem of reconstructing a smooth surface from the sparse data of a camera image while preserving its discontinuities [Koch et al., 1986]. To solve this problem, the nodes in a Hopfield network are arranged in a two-dimensional lattice as shown in Fig. 11.12(a) The neurons are divided into three groups: *depth* neurons (the crosses in the figure), horizontal-line (*h*-line) neurons (the horizontal lines in the figure), and vertical-line (*v*-line) neurons (the vertical lines in the figure). Each depth neuron is enclosed on all four sides by a *h*-line or *v*-line neuron. The depth neurons use linear activation functions, while the *h*-line and *v*-line neurons have sigmoidal activation functions. The output of the depth neuron at coordinate (i, j) is denoted by y_{ij}, which is a continuous value representing the depth of the surface at that position. The output of the *h*-line (*v*-line) neuron at coordinate (i, j) is denoted by h_{ij} (v_{ij}), which is a unipolar value indicating the existence (h_{ij} or $v_{ij} = 1$) or absence (h_{ij} or $v_{ij} = 0$) of an edge (discontinuity) at position (i, j) between two adjacent depth neurons. Let d_{ij} be the measured depth of position (i, j). A suitable energy function is composed of five terms: the term implementing a membrane type of surface

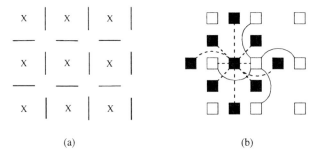

Figure 11.12 Structure of the Hopfield network for surface reconstruction. (a) The two-dimensional lattice of depth neurons (crosses), h-line neurons (horizontal lines), and v-line neurons (vertical lines). (b) The local connections between neighboring line (h-line and v-line) neurons (filled squares) and the depth neuron (open squares).

interpolation E_I together with the data term E_D, the line potential terms E_{HL} and E_{VL}, and the gain term E_G:

$$E_I = \sum_{ij} (y_{i,j+1} - y_{ij})^2 (1 - h_{ij}) + C_C \sum_{ij} h_{ij} \tag{11.66}$$
$$+ \sum_{ij} (y_{i+1,j} - y_{ij})^2 (1 - v_{ij}) + C_C \sum_{ij} v_{ij},$$

$$E_D = C_D \sum_{ij} (y_{ij} - d_{ij})^2, \tag{11.67}$$

$$E_{HL} = C_V \sum_{ij} h_{ij} (1 - h_{ij}) + C_P \sum_{ij} h_{ij} h_{i,j+1} \tag{11.68}$$
$$+ C_L \sum_{ij} h_{ij} [(1 - h_{i+1,j} - v_{ij} - v_{i,j+1})^2 + (1 - h_{i-1,j} - v_{i-1,j} - v_{i-1,j+1})^2],$$

$$E_{VL} = C_V \sum_{ij} v_{ij} (1 - v_{ij}) + C_P \sum_{ij} v_{ij} v_{i+1,j} \tag{11.69}$$
$$+ C_L \sum_{ij} v_{ij} [(1 - v_{i,j+1} - h_{ij} - h_{i+1,j})^2 + (1 - v_{i,j-1} - h_{i,j-1} - h_{i+1,j-1})^2],$$

$$E_G = C_G \sum_{ij} \int_0^{h_{ij}} a_{ij}^{-1}(h_{ij}) \, dh_{ij} + C_G \sum_{ij} \int_0^{v_{ij}} a_{ij}^{-1}(v_{ij}) \, dv_{ij}. \tag{11.70}$$

The E_I term means that if the gradient of y becomes too large [i.e., $(y_{i,j+1} - y_{ij})^2 > C_C$], it becomes less costly to break the surface and put in a line—paying the "price" C_C—rather than to interpolate smoothly. The line neurons h_{ij} and v_{ij} introduce local minima into the energy function, making the problem nonquadratic—the energy function contains cubic terms (e.g., $y_{i,j+1} y_{ij} h_{ij}$). The energy E_D that describes the weighted difference between the measured data d_{ij} and the approximate surface value y_{ij} is weighted by C_D, which depends on the signal-to-noise ratio. If d_{ij} is very reliable, then $C_D \gg 1$. Note that the summation in E_D includes nodes only where measurements are available.

The two energy terms E_{HL} and E_{VL}, one for h-line neurons and the other for v-line neurons, have a similar meaning. We shall explain E_{HL} only. The first term in E_{HL} forces the h-line neuron to the corners of the hypercube, that is, to either 0 or 1. The second term penalizes the formation of adjacent parallel lines. The third term is an interaction term that favors continuous lines and penalizes both multiple-line intersections and discontinuous-line segments. The gain energy E_G forces the outputs of the h-line and v-line neurons inside the hypercube $[0, 1]^n$. Figure 11.12(b) illustrates the connections required to implement the above total energy function within the line and the depth lattices.

Let the total energy function be $E(\mathbf{y}, \mathbf{h}, \mathbf{v}) = E_I + E_D + E_{HL} + E_{VL} + E_G$. Then the update rules for each of the three kinds of neurons can be derived from Eq. (11.11) as

$$\frac{dy_{ij}}{dt} = -\frac{\partial E}{\partial y_{ij}},$$

$$\frac{dh_{ij}}{dt} = -\frac{1}{C_{ij} a_{ij}^{-1'}(h_{ij})} \frac{\partial E}{\partial h_{ij}}, \qquad (11.71)$$

$$\frac{dv_{ij}}{dt} = -\frac{1}{C_{ij} a_{ij}^{-1'}(v_{ij})} \frac{\partial E}{\partial v_{ij}}.$$

It is easy to see that for these updates, the total energy will always decrease and the system will evolve in this way to find a minimum of E.

An analog network for a 32×32 image was simulated. The parameters were set as $C_V = 0.5$, $C_L = 4.0$, $C_P = 5.0$, $C_C = 1.0$, $C_G = 0.5$, and $\lambda = 16$, where λ is the gain of the activation functions of the line neurons. As boundary conditions h_{ij} and v_{ij} are set to 1 along the boundaries of the square, the initial values of the line neurons are set as $h_{ij} = v_{ij} = 0.5$ for all i, j, assuming that the line neurons are substantially slower than the depth neurons. Figure 11.13 shows the temporal evolution of the states of the network for a sparsely sampled synthetic scene containing three slanting rectangles. On the average, every third point is sampled. Again, these measurements are corrupted by Gaussian noise. Figure 11.13 represents the changing state of the network with time specified in terms of $\tau = C_{ij}/G_{ij} = C/G$ [see Eq. (11.8)].

From the above examples, the major problem of Hopfield networks appears to be the local minimum problem. That is, the stable solution reached does not represent, in general, a global optimal solution to the problem of energy function minimization. This is due to the often highly complex shape of the multidimensional energy function. The presence of many local minima is responsible for trapping the evolution of the network states. However, the solutions achieved, although not optimal, are acceptable in a statistical sense since global solutions of real, large-scale minimization problems are often mathematically difficult to track anyway. In the following section, we shall introduce one major approach to solving the local minimum problem in Hopfield networks.

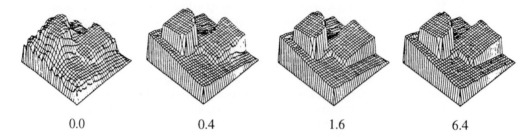

| 0.0 | 0.4 | 1.6 | 6.4 |

Figure 11.13 Temporal evolution of the states of the network for surface reconstruction. (From *Proc. Nat. Acad. Sci.*, Vol. 83, page 4265, 1986, © C. Koch, J. Marroquin, and A. Yuille. Reproduced by kind permission of the authors.)

11.3.2 Boltzmann Machines

A Boltzmann machine is simply a discrete Hopfield network in which each node performs a *simulated annealing* process such that it has the ability to escape from local minima to achieve the global minimum [Ackley et al., 1985]. The idea of simulated annealing comes from the physical annealing process done on metals and other substances. In metallurgical annealing, a metal body is heated to near its melting point and then slowly cooled back down to room temperature. This process will cause the global energy function of the metal to reach an absolute minimum value eventually. If the temperature is dropped too quickly, the energy of the metallic lattice will be much higher than this minimum because of the existence of frozen lattice dislocations that would otherwise eventually disappear because of thermal agitation. Analogous to this physical behavior, simulated annealing allows a system to change its state to a higher energy state occasionally such that it has a chance to jump out of local minima and seek the global minimum [Kirkpatrick et al., 1983; Geman and Geman, 1984]. Moreover, there is a *cooling procedure* in the simulated annealing process such that the system has a higher probability of achieving an increasing-energy state change in the early phase of convergence. Then, as time goes by, the system becomes stable and always changes its state in the direction of decreasing system energy as in normal minimization procedures (e.g., the gradient-descent method).

More precisely, using simulated annealing, a system changes its state from the original state $\mathbf{s}^{\text{old}}$ to a new state $\mathbf{s}^{\text{new}}$ with a probability p given by

$$p = \frac{1}{1 + \exp\left(-\Delta E / T\right)}, \tag{11.72}$$

where $\Delta E = E^{\text{old}} - E^{\text{new}}$ is the corresponding energy change and T is a nonnegative parameter that acts like the temperature of a physical system. Figure 11.14 shows the probability p as a function of ΔE for different values of the temperature T. This figure illustrates what we have mentioned above. Note that the probability with $\Delta E > 0$ is always higher than the probability with $\Delta E < 0$ for any temperature since we hope the system energy decreases after all.

When the simulated annealing process is applied to the discrete Hopfield network, it becomes a Boltzmann machine. Hence, the Boltzmann machine is basically a single-layer,

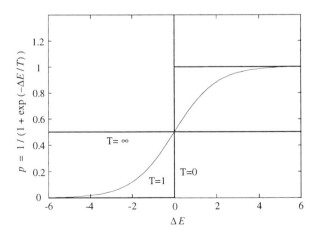

Figure 11.14 State change probability p in Eq. (11.72) as a function of ΔE for different values of the temperature T.

fully connected recurrent network with the following stochastic update rule [compare with Eq. (11.1)]:

$$
y_i^{\text{new}} = \begin{cases} 1 & \text{if } z \le p_i = \dfrac{1}{1 + \exp(-\Delta E_i/T)} \\ y_i^{\text{old}} & \text{otherwise,} \end{cases}
\tag{11.73}
$$

where y_i is 1 or 0 for $i = 1, 2, \ldots, n$, T is the temperature, z is a random number between 0 and 1 chosen by means of a uniform probability density function, and ΔE_i is defined by

$$
\Delta E_i = E_{y_i=0} - E_{y_i=1} = \sum_{\substack{j=1 \\ j \ne i}}^{n} w_{ij} y_j = \text{net}_i,
\tag{11.74}
$$

which is derived from Eq. (11.4). As in a discrete Hopfield network, the above update is performed asynchronously and randomly. As in the simulated annealing procedure described above, the temperature T is lowered either when the energy has dropped quite a bit or when a sufficiently large number of updates has occurred. For example, a cooling procedure may look like this: two time steps at $T = 10$, two time steps at $T = 8$, four time steps at $T = 6$, four time steps at $T = 4$, eight time steps at $T = 2$. Here, one time step is defined as the time required for each node to be given, on average, one chance to change its state. This means that if there are n unclamped nodes (i.e., nodes that can change states freely), then a time step involves n random probes in which some node is given a chance to change its state. Unlike the Hopfield network, which is guaranteed to converge to a local minimum of the energy function E in a finite number of update steps, the Boltzmann machine may or may not converge to a final stable state. However, the state achieved by the Boltzmann machine at the point where the stopping criterion ends its operation is usually very close to the global minimum of the energy function E.

The update rule in Eq. (11.73) ensures that in thermal equilibrium the relative probability of two global states is determined solely by their energy difference and follows a *Boltzmann distribution:*

$$
\frac{P_\alpha}{P_\beta} = e^{-(E_\alpha - E_\beta)/T} \qquad \text{and} \qquad P_\alpha = C e^{-E_\alpha/T},
\tag{11.75}
$$

where P_α is the probability of being in the αth global state, E_α is the energy of that state, and C is a constant that can be derived from the fact that $\sum_\alpha P_\alpha = 1$ as $C = (\sum_\alpha e^{-E_\alpha/T})^{-1}$. Since a Boltzmann machine is basically a discrete Hopfield network, it can be quite useful for solving certain types of optimization problems. Finding the proper weights of a Boltzmann machine required to solve optimization problems is exactly the same as for Hopfield networks.

In addition to solving combinatorial optimization problems, a Boltzmann machine can also be used as an associative memory. In this case, it allows some nodes to be hidden nodes. Hence, Boltzmann machines may also be seen as an extension of Hopfield networks to include hidden nodes. The nodes y_i in a Boltzmann machine are divided into *visible* and *hidden* nodes as shown in Fig. 11.15(a). This corresponds to an autoassociative memory.

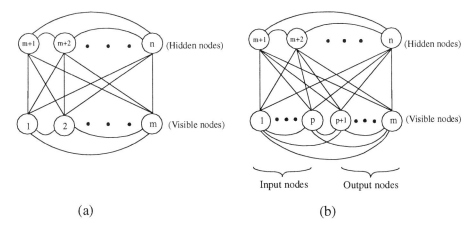

Figure 11.15 Structures of a Boltzmann machine with hidden nodes. (a) The nodes are divided into visible ones and hidden ones. (b) The visible nodes can be divided into input and output nodes.

The visible nodes can be further divided into separate input and output nodes as in Fig. 11.15(b). In this case, it is a heteroassociative memory. The hidden nodes have no connection to the outside world. The connections between nodes may be complete (fully connected as shown in the figure) or structured in some convenient way. Whatever the choice, all weights must be symmetric (i.e., $w_{ij} = w_{ji}$). Just as in feedforward networks with hidden nodes, the problem is to find the proper weights for the hidden nodes without knowing what the hidden nodes should represent from training patterns. The learning of Boltzmann machines is discussed next.

Equation (11.73) can be considered the retrieval rule for a Boltzmann machine–based associative memory. Let us consider first the problem of storing the patterns in the memory, that is, the weight learning rule of Boltzmann machines. In Boltzmann learning, we attempt to adjust the weight w_{ij} to give the states of the visible nodes a particular desired probability distribution. As was the case with pattern recall, learning in Boltzmann machines is accomplished using a simulated annealing technique. The learning rule for Boltzmann machines employs a gradient-descent method, but the function being minimized is no longer identified with the energy of the network. We shall simply summarize the learning rule here [Amari et al., 1992]. Let us consider the simplest case where no hidden elements exist. Let $q(\mathbf{y})$ be a probability distribution over $\mathbf{y}$ at which an environmental information source emits a signal $\mathbf{y}$. Signals are generated independently subject to $q(\mathbf{y})$ and presented to the Boltzmann machine. This machine is expected to modify its weights and thresholds so that it can simulate the environmental information source. That is, it is required that the stationary distribution $p(\mathbf{y})$ of the Boltzmann machine becomes as close to $q(\mathbf{y})$ as possible.

The learning rule derived by Ackley et al. [1985] is given by

$$\Delta w_{ij} = \Delta w_{ji} = \eta \, (q_{ij} - p_{ij}), \tag{11.76}$$

where η is a small constant and q_{ij} and p_{ij} are, respectively, defined by

$$q_{ij} = E_q \, [y_i y_j] = \sum_{\mathbf{y}} q \, (\mathbf{y}) \, y_i y_j, \tag{11.77}$$

$$p_{ij} = E_p[y_i y_j] = \sum_{\mathbf{y}} p(\mathbf{y}) y_i y_j, \qquad (11.78)$$

where E_q and E_p denote, respectively, the expectation operation with respect to the probability distributions $q(\mathbf{y})$ and $p(\mathbf{y})$. Hence, q_{ij} is the relative frequency at which both y_i and y_j are jointly excited under the probability distribution $q(\mathbf{y})$ (called the q phase), and p_{ij} is the relative frequency at which both y_i and y_j are jointly excited under $p(\mathbf{y})$, that is, when the Boltzmann machine is running freely (called the p phase).

The learning rule can be realized by the Hebbian synaptic modification method in two phases. In the first phase, the input learning phase, the connection weight w_{ij} is increased by a small amount whenever both y_i and y_j are excited by an input $\mathbf{y}$; hence on average the increment of w_{ij} is proportional to q_{ij}. In the second phase, the free or unlearning phase, w_{ij} is decreased by the same small amount whenever both y_i and y_j are excited by a free state transition; hence the decrement of w_{ij} is proportional to p_{ij} on average.

Let us now consider a more general case where nodes are divided into two parts: visible nodes and hidden nodes. Visible nodes are further divided into input and output nodes [Fig. 11.15(b)]. Input patterns are represented by a vector $\mathbf{y}_V = (\mathbf{y}_I, \mathbf{y}_O)$ on visible nodes where $\mathbf{y}_I$ and $\mathbf{y}_O$ correspond to the states on the input and output nodes, respectively. Let $q(\mathbf{y}_I, \mathbf{y}_O)$ be the joint probability distribution with which an environmental information source emits the signal $\mathbf{y}_V$. The conditional distribution of $\mathbf{y}_O$ given $\mathbf{y}_I$ is written as

$$q(\mathbf{y}_O \mid \mathbf{y}_I) = \frac{q(\mathbf{y}_I, \mathbf{y}_O)}{q(\mathbf{y}_I)}, \qquad (11.79)$$

where

$$q(\mathbf{y}_I) = \sum_{\mathbf{y}_O} q(\mathbf{y}_I, \mathbf{y}_O). \qquad (11.80)$$

In the learning phase, input patterns $\mathbf{y}_V$ are applied directly to visible nodes. The Boltzmann machine is required to realize the conditional probability distribution $q(\mathbf{y}_O \mid \mathbf{y}_I)$ of the environment as faithfully as possible by learning. The distribution of the state of the hidden nodes is of no concern, but $p(\mathbf{y}_O, \mathbf{y}_I)$ should be as close to $q(\mathbf{y}_O, \mathbf{y}_I)$ as possible. The derived weight learning rule is the same as Eq. (11.76) except that q_{ij} now denotes the relative frequency of $y_i = y_j = 1$ under the condition that $\mathbf{y}_I$ and $\mathbf{y}_O$ be fixed (q phase) and p_{ij} is the relative frequency in the restricted free run when only $\mathbf{y}_I$ is fixed (p phase). In this more general case, only input $\mathbf{y}_I$ of $\mathbf{y}_V$ is applied. Then, the update rule in Eq. (11.73) is performed under this condition of fixed $\mathbf{y}_I$ (i.e., the input nodes are *clamped* at the value $\mathbf{y}_I$) so that the conditional stationary distribution $p(\mathbf{y}_H, \mathbf{y}_O \mid \mathbf{y}_I)$ is realized, where $\mathbf{y}_H$ denotes the states of the hidden nodes.

In practice, the quantity q_{ij} in Eq. (11.76) can be estimated in the following steps [Freeman and Skapura, 1991]:

Step 1: Clamp one training vector to the visible nodes of the network.

Step 2: Anneal the network according to the annealing schedule until an equilibrium is reached at the desired minimum temperature.

Step 3: Continue to run the network for several more processing cycles. After each cycle, determine which pairs of connected nodes are on simultaneously.

Step 4: Average the cooccurrence results from step 3.

Step 5: Repeat steps 1 through 4 for all training vectors and average the cooccurrence results to obtain an estimate of q_{ij} for each pair of connected nodes.

The quantity p_{ij} in Eq. (11.76) is estimated in the same way except that the input vector $\mathbf{y}_l$ is taken away from the input nodes (i.e., the input nodes are *unclamped*) in step 1 of the above estimation steps. When q_{ij} and p_{ij} are available, the weight can be updated according to Eq. (11.76). All the above steps (called a *sweep*) should be repeated until $(q_{ij} - p_{ij})$ is sufficiently small. Another important factor in this learning procedure is to determine the proper cooling procedure. Geman and Geman [1984] showed that the temperature must be reduced in proportion to the inverse log of the time

$$T(t_n) = \frac{T_0}{1 + \ln t_n}, \tag{11.81}$$

where T_0 is the starting temperature and t_n is the nth time step. However, this rule usually requires an impractical number of time steps. The practical cooling procedure is usually chosen experimentally as in the next example.

Example 11.10

[Ackley et al., 1985]. In this example, a Boltzmann machine with four input visible nodes, four output visible nodes, and two hidden nodes is used to solve the 4-2-4 encoder problem. The structure of the network is shown in Fig. 11.16. Note that the network is not fully connected. The four-bit binary input vectors are $[1\,0\,0\,0]^T$, $[0\,1\,0\,0]^T$, $[0\,0\,1\,0]^T$, and $[0\,0\,0\,1]^T$. Each time, one of these vectors is clamped to the input visible nodes. The problem is to train the network to reproduce the identical vector on the output visible nodes. In this way, the two hidden nodes learned a two-digital binary code, 00,01,10,11 for the four possible input vectors. The annealing schedule used was for two time steps at $T = 20$, two at $T = 15$, two at $T = 12$, and four at $T = 10$. On the average, 110 sweeps were required to train the network to perform the encoding task.

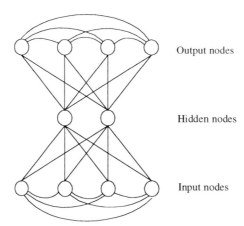

Output nodes

Hidden nodes

Input nodes

Figure 11.16   Boltzmann machine used in Example 11.10.

The simulated annealing technique is also used in the *Cauchy machine* proposed by Szu [1986] which is based on the Cauchy distribution rather than the Boltzmann distribution. The Cauchy distribution is

$$p = \frac{T}{T^2 + \Delta E^2} \, ,$$ (11.82)

which has the same general shape as the Boltzmann distribution but does not fall off as sharply at large energies such that the Cauchy machine may occasionally take a rather large jump out of a local minimum. Hence, this approach can reach the global minimum with a much shorter cooling schedule. In contrast to Eq. (11.81), the annealing temperature for the Cauchy machine follows the inverse of the time:

$$T(t_n) = \frac{T_0}{1 + t_n} \, ,$$ (11.83)

where T_0 is the starting temperature and t_n is the nth time step. This cooling schedule is much faster than the one for the corresponding Boltzmann machine, and thus the Cauchy machine is also called *fast simulated annealing*.

11.4 CONCLUDING REMARKS

The basic idea of the Hopfield networks, and thus the Boltzmann machines, is based on the *Ising spin-glass model* used to investigate the collective properties of physical systems made from a large number of simple elements [Edwards and Anderson, 1975; Kirkpatrick and Sherrington, 1978; Tanaka and Edwards, 1980a]. The properties of discrete Hopfield networks with synchronous update rules were studied in [Goles-Chacc et al., 1985; Michel et al., 1991; Shrivastava et al., 1992]. In particular, the *block sequential iteration* method was investigated in [Goles-Chacc et al., 1985].

For associative memories, in addition to the linear associator, there is another nonrecurrent associative memory called the *learn matrix network* [Steinbuch, 1961; Hecht-Nielsen, 1990, Section 4.3] which forms associations between pairs of binary patterns. A good theoretical study of Hopfield networks can be found in [Aiyer et al., 1990], where the relationships among the fixed points (stable states) of the network, the Hopfield Lyapunov functions, and the eigenvalues of the weight matrix are explored. The capacity of the Hopfield memory when the weights have limited precision after *discretizing* and limited range after *clipping* was studied in [van Hemmen and Kühn, 1988]. The performance of a Hopfield memory using the outer-product learning rule in the presence of faulty interconnections was examined and equations for predicting network reliability were developed in [Chung and Krile, 1992]. In addition to the outer-product learning rule in Eq. (11.22) and the projection learning rule in Eq. (11.28), an *eigenstructure method* was proposed in [Michel et al., 1991] to design a Hopfield memory. Several improvements on the Hopfield networks used for temporal associative memories can be found in [Sompolinsky and Kanter, 1986; Kleinfeld, 1986; Buhmann and Schulten, 1987ab; Amit, 1988]. An important neural network similar to the Hopfield networks is the brain-state-in-a-box (BSB) network [Anderson et al., 1977]. The idea of the BSB is that the state of the network can lie anywhere within the closed solid cube $[-1, 1]^n$ that contains the cube $\{-1, 1\}^n$ instead of being confined to the vertices of the discrete cube $\{-1, 1\}^n$ as in the Hopfield memory. A generalized BSB network model with a stability analysis was proposed by Hui and Zak [1992].

An exact capacity measure of the BAM was done by Haines and Hecht-Nielsen [1988]. The major problem of the outer-product weight learning rule in Eqs. (11.33) and (11.34) is that it does not ensure that the stored pairs correspond to local energy minima. Wang et al.[1990] solved this problem by proposing the *multiple-training encoding strategy* and the *dummy augmentation encoding strategy* to determine the weight matrix. The multiple-training concept was further extended to ensure recall of multiple pairs for a discrete BAM [Wang et al., 1991]. Wang et al. [1992] also proposed a weighted learning rule emphasizing the degree of association among patterns for a BAM where each desired pattern is weighted.

For applications of Hopfield networks to optimization problems, Lee and Sheu [1991] proposed a modified Hopfield network–based A/D converter that involved putting another amplifier at each node to provide correction of current feedback and thus eliminate the local minima. Several improvements on the use of Hopfield networks for the traveling salesperson problem can be found in [Tagliarini and Page, 1987; Wilson and Pawley, 1988; Abe, 1989; Kahng, 1989; Aiyer et al., 1990]. Hopfield networks have also been used in other combinatorial optimization problems, especially in graph theory. The reader is referred to [Takefuji, 1992] for details. For problems in early vision, Hutchinson et al. [1988] constructed a three-dimensional Hopfield network to compute optical flow in the presence of discontinuities for motion analysis. Lin et al.[1991] developed a hierarchical approach for three-dimensional object recognition. Another interesting application of Hopfield networks is in solving linear programming problems [Tank and Hopfield, 1986; Kennedy and Chua, 1987, 1988; Maa and Shanblatt, 1992ab; Ingman and Merlis, 1992].

For Boltzmann machines, some modified Boltzmann learning rules have been proposed based on concepts of *information geometry* [Amari, 1991; Amari et al., 1992; Byrne, 1992]. The properties of Boltzmann machines with asymmetric weights were described in [Allen and Alspector, 1990]. To attack the long-learning-time problem of the Boltzmann machine, a mean-field approximation [Glauber, 1963; Hopfield, 1984] was used to replace the stochastic nodes of the original Boltzmann machine with deterministic analog nodes [Peterson and Anderson, 1987; Hinton, 1989]. This technique is called *mean-field annealing* [Bilbro et al., 1988, 1992; Van den Bout and Miller III, 1990]. The resultant network, called a *deterministic Boltzmann machine* (DBM), has a significant improvement in learning efficiency. A DBM with asymmetric connection weights was investigated by Galland and Hinton [1989]. By generalizing the original two-valued Boltzmann machine, Lin and Lee [1995] proposed a multivalued Boltzmann machine; each node in this network can take one of m directions in a plane discretely. A multivalued Boltzmann machine with 100×100 nodes arranged in a two-dimensional grid was applied to the mobile robot navigation problem [Lin and Lee, 1991, 1995]. Another network similar to the Boltzmann machine, called a harmonium, has been introduced by Smolensky [1986]. A harmonium is effectively a two-layer version of a Boltzmann machine with connections only between the layers.

11.5 PROBLEMS

11.1 (a) Consider a four-node discrete Hopfield network with weight matrix

$$W = \begin{bmatrix} 0 & 1 & 1 & -1 \\ 1 & 0 & 1 & -1 \\ 1 & 1 & 0 & -1 \\ -1 & -1 & -1 & 0 \end{bmatrix}.$$

Examine the energy distribution and state updating process of the network by drawing a state transition diagram like the one shown in Fig. 11.7. Identify the potential attractors that may have been encoded in the system described by the weight matrix W by comparing the energy values at each of the $[-1, +1]$ cube vertices. Implement five sample asynchronous discrete-time transitions from high- to low-energy vertices.

(b) Based on the energy values, determine the stored patterns. Verify these patterns by comparing the resulting weight matrix and the above weight matrix.

(c) Repeat part (a) but perform the recall synchronously. Determine if the energy value decreases in this update mode.

11.2 Consider the two-node continuous Hopfield network studied in Example 11.2. Assume the conductance is $g_1 = g_2 = 1$ mho. The gain parameter is $\lambda = 1.4$, and the external inputs are zero. Calculate the accurate energy value of the state $y = [0.01, 0.01]^T$ using Eq. (11.10).

11.3 Design a linear associator that associates the following pairs of vectors:

$$x^1 = \left[\frac{1}{6}, -\frac{5}{6}, -\frac{1}{6}, \frac{1}{2} \right]^T, \qquad y^1 = [1, 0, 0]^T,$$

$$x^2 = \left[\frac{1}{2}, \frac{1}{2}, -\frac{1}{2}, \frac{1}{2} \right]^T, \qquad y^2 = [0, 1, 1]^T,$$

$$x^3 = \left[-\frac{5}{6}, \frac{1}{6}, -\frac{1}{6}, \frac{1}{2} \right]^T, \qquad y^3 = [0, 0, 0]^T.$$

(a) Verify that vectors x^1, x^2, and x^3 are orthonormal.

(b) Compute the weight matrix of the linear associator.

(c) Verify the association performed by the network for each of x^1, x^2, and x^3.

(d) Distort one specific pattern x^i by setting one of its components to zero and compute the resulting noise vector.

11.4 Design a linear associator that associates the following pairs of vectors:

$$x^1 = [1, 3, -4, 2]^T \qquad y^1 = [0, 1, 0]^T,$$
$$x^2 = [2, 2, -4, 0]^T \qquad y^2 = [0, 0, 0]^T,$$
$$x^3 = [1, -3, 2, -3]^T \qquad y^3 = [1, 0, 1]^T.$$

(a) Verify that vectors x^1, x^2, and x^3 are linearly independent.

(b) Repeat parts (b)–(d) in Prob. 11.3 for the above patterns.

11.5 Consider a linear associator that has been designed using a cross-correlation matrix for heteroassociative association of p orthonormal patterns. Suppose another orthonormal pattern x^{p+1} is associated with y^{p+1} must be stored subsequently. This is achieved by performing an incremental change in the weight matrix using the cross-correlation concept. Show that the association $(\mathbf{x}^{p+1}, \mathbf{y}^{p+1})$ results in no noise term being present at the output.

11.6 Write a program for implementing the Hopfield memory that performs the task in Example 11.3 and reproduces the results in Fig. 11.6. (Note that in the recall mode, the node can be updated asynchronously in ascending order starting at node 1.)

11.7 Consider a discrete Hopfield network with a synchronous update.

    (a) Show that if all the pattern vectors are orthogonal, then every original pattern is an attractor and a global minimum.

    (b) Show that every complement of the stored orthogonal patterns is also an attractor and a global minimum.

    (c) Show that in general other global minima exist.

    (d) Show that parts (a) and (c) are also true for a discrete Hopfield network with an asynchronous update.

11.8 Based on Eq. (11.27), determine how many more patterns, if there are any, can be stored in the Hopfield memory studied in Example 11.3.

11.9 You are given the following three pairs of vectors to be stored in a BAM:

$$\mathbf{x}^1 = [1, -1, -1, 1, 1, 1, -1, -1, -1]^T, \qquad \mathbf{y}^1 = [1, 1, 1, -1, -1, -1, -1, 1, -1]^T,$$

$$\mathbf{x}^2 = [-1, 1, 1, 1, -1, -1, 1, 1, 1]^T, \qquad \mathbf{y}^2 = [1, -1, -1, -1, -1, -1, -1, -1, 1]^T,$$

$$\mathbf{x}^3 = [1, -1, 1, -1, 1, 1, -1, 1, 1]^T, \qquad \mathbf{y}^3 = [-1, 1, -1, 1, -1, -1, 1, -1, 1]^T,$$

    (a) Compute the weight matrix of the BAM.

    (b) Present $\mathbf{x}^2$ to the BAM and perform memory recall. Assume the recalling cycle terminates with the state $(\mathbf{x}^2, \mathbf{y}^1)$. Is $\mathbf{y}^1$ equal to $\mathbf{y}^2$? In other words, can the pattern pair $(\mathbf{x}^2, \mathbf{y}^2)$ be recalled correctly?

    (c) Compute and compare the energy values of the states $(\mathbf{x}^2, \mathbf{y}^2)$ and $(\mathbf{x}^2, \mathbf{y}^1)$.

    (d) Demonstrate that $(\mathbf{x}^2, \mathbf{y}^2)$ is not a local minimum by evaluating the energy value at a point that is one Hamming distance away from $\mathbf{y}^2$.

    (e) Use the multiple-training method to make the pair $(\mathbf{x}^2, \mathbf{y}^2)$ recoverable. Try a multiplicity of 2 or 3 and determine the minimum number of multiplicity.

11.10 Prove the stability of the continuous BAM described by Eq. (11.46) using (a) the Cohen-Grossberg theorem and (b) the Lyapunov theorem. [*Hint:* Consider the following Lyapunov function for the continuous BAM.

$$E(\mathbf{x}, \mathbf{y}) = -\sum_{i=1}^{n}\sum_{j=1}^{m} w_{ij} a(y_i) a(x_j) + \sum_{i=1}^{n} a_i \int_0^{y_i} a'(u_i) u_i \, du_i$$

$$+ \sum_{j=1}^{m} c_j \int_0^{x_j} a'(v_j) v_j \, dv_j - \sum_{i=1}^{n} a(y_i) s_i - \sum_{j=1}^{m} a(x_j) t_j.$$

11.11 **(a)** Design a Hopfield temporal associative memory with a threshold activation function for recall of the following sequence:

$$S = \{\mathbf{s}^1, \mathbf{s}^2, \mathbf{s}^3\} = \{[-1, 1, 1, 1, -1, -1]^T, [1, -1, -1, -1, 1, -1]^T, [-1, -1, 1, -1, 1, 1]^T\}.$$

    Compute the weight matrix $\mathbf{W}$ and check the recall of patterns in the forward and backward directions.

    (b) Design a BAM-based temporal associative memory with a threshold activation function for performing the same job described in part (a).

11.12 Emulate Example 11.7 in the design of a two-bit A/D converter using a two-node continuous Hopfield network. [Note that the values of resistance (conductance) should be positive.]

11.13 Based on the four-bit A/D converter in Example 11.7, design a summing network with four-bit digital outputs. This network needs to compute the sum of N analog voltages x_k with corresponding weighting coefficients a_k as follows:

$$x = \sum_{k=0}^{N-1} a_k x_k,$$

where we assume that $0 \le x \le 16$. This network should then find the digital representation of the sum x using four digital bits. The latter part is actually a four-bit A/D converter that has been designed and is shown in Fig. 11.10. Design an analog summing network and attach it to the input end (the current sources) of the circuit in Fig. 11.10 to realize the summing network with digital outputs. (*Hint:* Replace x in the total energy function in Eq. (11.56) by the summation term in the above equation. Expand and rearrange the resultant expression of total energy function. Equate this expression to the general formula for energy as in Eq. (11.57) to compare the coefficients and set up the *whole* network.)

11.14 Show that when the temperature parameter T in a Boltzmann machine is equal to zero, the Boltzmann machine reduces into a Hopfield network.

11.15 Train a Boltzmann machine with two input nodes, one output node, and one hidden node to solve the XOR problem.

12

Unsupervised Learning Networks

In this chapter, we shall study the second major learning paradigm—unsupervised learning, where there is no feedback from the environment to indicate what the desired outputs of a network should be or whether they are correct. The network must discover for itself any relationships of interest, such as patterns, features, regularities, correlations, or categories in the input data, and translate the discovered relationship into outputs. Four unsupervised learning rules, signal Hebbian, competitive, differential Hebbian, and differential competitive learning rules, will be studied. Then various important existing unsupervised learning networks, such as Hamming networks, Kohonen's self-organizing feature maps, Grossberg's ART networks, counterpropagation networks, adaptive BAM, and a hierarchical network for pattern recognition, called neocognitron, will be explored. These unsupervised learning rules will be useful in determining the presence of fuzzy logic rules and fuzzy partitioning of the input and output spaces of a neuro-fuzzy system.

12.1 UNSUPERVISED LEARNING RULES

In unsupervised learning there is no feedback from the environment to indicate what the outputs of a network should be or whether they are correct. The network must discover for itself any relationships of interest that may exist in the input data and translate the discovered relationship into outputs. Such networks are also called *self-organizing networks*. The relationships in the input data include features, regularities, correlations, and categories. For example, an unsupervised learning network could tell us how similar a new input pattern is to typical patterns seen in the past, and the network would gradually learn what is typical (*similarity*); the network could construct a set of axes along which to measure similarity to previous examples (*principal component analysis*); the network might form categories on the basis of correlations in the input patterns and then tell us which of several categories an input pattern belong to (*clustering*) or give us as output a prototype or examplar for the appropriate class (*adaptive vector quantization,* AVQ); or the network could make a topographic map of the input such that similar input patterns would trigger nearby output nodes (*feature mapping*).

In this section, we shall examine four typical unsupervised learning rules: signal Hebbian, competitive, differential Hebbian, and differential competitive [Kosko, 1990], and other related ones. They are in the form of first-order differential (or difference) equations. The concepts of these learning rules are adopted in several neural network models, some of which will be introduced in other sections. In the following sections, we shall consider a single-layer network with input $\mathbf{x} = (x_1, x_2, \ldots, x_m)^T$ and output $\mathbf{y} = (y_1, y_2, \ldots, y_n)^T$. The weight from input j *to node* i is denoted by w_{ij}. The function $s(\cdot)$ is a monotonic nondecreasing signal function that transforms x and y to the bounded signals $s(x)$ and $s(y)$, respectively.

12.1.1 Signal Hebbian Learning Rule

The *signal Hebbian learning rule* is

$$\dot{w}_{ij} = -w_{ij} + s_i(y_i) s_j(x_j), \tag{12.1}$$

which is similar to the Hebbian learning rule in Eq. (9.20) (called *plain Hebbian learning*) except for the *forgetting term* $-w_{ij}$ and the signal functions that keep the weight values bounded. This rule learns an exponentially weighted average of sampled patterns and washes away the prior learned pattern information $w_{ij}(0)$ exponentially. Synaptic equilibrium in the signal Hebbian rule occurs when the weights stop changing, that is, $\dot{w}_{ij} = 0$, $i = 1, 2, \ldots, n$, $j = 1, 2, \ldots, m$. The signal Hebbian learning rule is usually used for measuring familiarity or projecting onto the principal components of the input data.

A common method from statistics for analyzing data is *principal component analysis* (PCA) [Jolliffe, 1986], which is equivalent to maximizing the information content of the output signal in situations where there is a Gaussian distribution. The aim is to find a set of n orthogonal vectors in the data space that accounts for as much as possible of the data's variance and then projects the data from their original m-dimensional space onto the n-dimensional subspace spanned by these vectors, where typically $n \ll m$. Figure 12.1 illustrates the principal component analysis. In this figure, OA is the first principal component direction of the distribution that generates the cloud of points, and OB is the second princi-

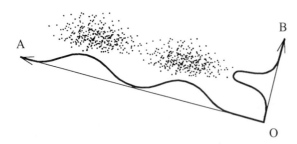

Figure 12.1 Principal component analysis.

pal component. Observe that the projection onto OA shows more structure than the projection onto OB. Clusters are thus more likely to be distinguished by projection in a high-variance direction than in a low-variance one. Hence, the *dimensionality reduction* in the PCA could retain most of the intrinsic information in the data. In PCA, the kth principal component direction is along an eigenvector direction belonging to the kth largest eigenvalue of the *correlation matrix* $\mathbf{C}$ of the input data defined by

$$\mathbf{C} = E\{\mathbf{xx}^T\} \quad \text{or} \quad c_{ij} = E\{x_i x_j\}, \qquad i, j = 1, 2, \ldots, m, \qquad (12.2)$$

where $E\{\cdot\}$ is the expectation operator [i.e., the average over the input distribution $p(\mathbf{x})$] and we assume that the data are zero mean.

It will be desirable to have an n-output network that extracts the first n principal components of the input data. Variant modified signal Hebbian learning rules have been proposed for a single-layer feedforward network for this purpose, called the *principal component network* [Oja, 1982, 1989; Sanger, 1989b]. Among these, Sanger's learning rule is expressed as

$$\dot{w}_{ij} = \eta y_i \left(x_j - \sum_{k=1}^{i} y_k w_{kj} \right), \qquad (12.3)$$

where $y_i = \sum_j w_{ij} x_j$; that is, the networks are linear. With Sanger's rule, it can be shown that the weight vectors become exactly the first n principal component directions in order $\mathbf{w}_i \to \pm \mathbf{c}^i$, where $\mathbf{c}^i$ is a normalized eigenvector of the correlation matrix $\mathbf{C}$ belonging to the ith largest eigenvalue. Furthermore, Eq. (12.3) makes the weight vector approach a constant length $|\mathbf{w}_i| = 1$, $i = 1, 2, \ldots, n$, without having to do any normalization. Also, when $n = 1$ (i.e., there is a single output y), the single weight vector $\mathbf{w}$ lies in a maximal eigenvector direction of $\mathbf{c}$, which is also a direction that maximizes $E\{y^2\}$. Sanger's learning rule is not local. Updating weight w_{ij} requires more information than is available at input j and output i. However, it can be localized by proper reformulation and particular input connections [Sanger, 1989b].

Another modified Hebbian learning rule is Grossberg's learning rule [Grossberg, 1971, 1982a], which is expressed by the equation

$$\dot{w}_i = \eta \left[yx_i - w_i \right] u(x_i), \qquad (12.4)$$

where $0 < \eta < 1$, $u(x_i) = 1$ if $x_i \geq 0$, and $u(x_i) = 0$ otherwise; that is, $u(\cdot)$ is a unit step function. The basic idea is that the weight will not change unless $x_i > 0$. This learning rule is used in the *instar* structure as shown in Fig. 12.2. A node of unspecified transfer function

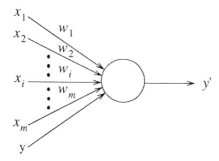

Figure 12.2 Structure of an instar.

receives multiple input signals, including x_i and y. The x_i input is a nonnegative real value and has a weight w_i associated with it. In Grossberg's original neurological model, it was assumed that $x_i = 0$ most of the time and takes on a large fixed positive value when it becomes active. Hence, the idea of the learning rule in Eq. (12.4) is that whenever the x_i input is *active,* its weight w_i learns the average value of the concurrent y input multiplicatively weighted by x_i. In some situations, it is desirable to replace y by $\dot{y}$ in Eq. (12.4) [Grossberg, 1982a].

12.1.2 Competitive Learning Rule

The competitive learning rule [Grossberg, 1969b; Rumelhart and Zipser, 1986] is described by

$$\dot{w}_{ij} = s_i(y_i)[s_j(x_j) - w_{ij}],\tag{12.5}$$

where

$$s_i(y_i) = \frac{1}{1 + e^{-cy_i}}, \qquad c > 0.\tag{12.6}$$

This learning rule modulates the difference $[s_j(x_j) - w_{ij}]$ with the competitive signal $s_i(y_i)$, which can approximate a binary win-lose indicator with large c. We say that the ith neuron "wins" the competition at time t if $s_i(y_i(t)) = 1$, and "loses" if $s_i(y_i(t)) = 0$. Hence, the theme of competitive learning is *learn if win.* The output nodes compete for being the one to fire and therefore are often called *winner-take-all* nodes. In practice, if we use $s_j(x_j) = x_j$, then the competitive learning rule reduces to the *linear competitive learning rule:*

$$\dot{w}_{ij} = s_i(y_i)[x_j - w_{ij}].\tag{12.7}$$

Competitive learning systems adaptively quantize the pattern space $\aleph^n$. Each weight vector $\mathbf{w}_i$ behaves like a quantization vector. Hence, competitive learning can be called *adaptive vector quantization.* Competitive learning distributes the n weight vectors $\mathbf{w}_1, \mathbf{w}_2,..., \mathbf{w}_n$ in $\aleph^n$ to approximate the unknown probability density function $p(\mathbf{x})$ of the random pattern vector $\mathbf{x}$. It can be shown using the Lyapunov theorem that the competitive weight vectors converge exponentially to the centroids of the sampled decision classes in a competitive AVQ system [Kosko, 1991].

We shall now introduce a simple but important competitive learning rule: the *Kohonen learning rule* [Kohonen, 1989] or the *winner-take-all learning rule.* Learning is based on the *clustering* of input data to group similar objects and separate dissimilar ones. It is assumed in this clustering technique that the number of classes is n, which is known a priori. The network to be trained is called the *Kohonen network* or the *winner-take-all network* and is shown in Fig. 12.3. The output y_i is computed by $y_i = a(\mathbf{w}_i^T \mathbf{x})$, where $a(\cdot)$ is a continuous activation function and $\mathbf{w}_i = (w_{i1}, w_{i2},..., w_{im})^T$. The training set is $\{\mathbf{x}^1, \mathbf{x}^2,..., \mathbf{x}^p\}$ which represents n clusters, but there is no information indicating which input vector belongs to which cluster. Hence, the Kohonen network classifies input vectors into one of the specified n categories according to the clusters detected in the training set.

The Kohonen learning rule is in a specific form of Eq. (12.7) and is described by a two-stage computation:

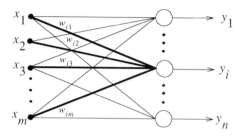

Figure 12.3 Kohonen (winner-take-all) network. (Adapted weights are highlighted.)

Similarity matching: $\|\mathbf{x} - \hat{\mathbf{w}}_i^{(k)}\| = \min_{1 \le j \le n} \{\|\mathbf{x} - \hat{\mathbf{w}}_j^{(k)}\|\},$

Updating: $\qquad \hat{\mathbf{w}}_i^{(k+1)} = \hat{\mathbf{w}}_i^{(k)} + \alpha^{(k)}(\mathbf{x} - \hat{\mathbf{w}}_i^{(k)})$ (12.8)

$$\hat{\mathbf{w}}_j^{(k+1)} = \hat{\mathbf{w}}_j^{(k)}, \qquad \text{for } j = 1, 2, \dots n; \, j \ne i,$$

where $\alpha^{(k)}$ is a suitable learning constant at the kth time step and $\hat{\mathbf{w}}_i$ denotes the normalized vector $\mathbf{w}_i$, that is,

$$\hat{\mathbf{w}}_i = \frac{\mathbf{w}_i}{\|\mathbf{w}_i\|}. \qquad (12.9)$$

Note that the neuron's activation function is of no relevance to the learning. The above learning process stops when two consecutive weight changes are small enough. The exact meaning of the updating part of Eq. (12.8) is that the sum on the right-hand side is normalized to produce the new normalized vector $\hat{\mathbf{w}}_i^{(k+1)}$. Such normalization requires that we renormalize the winning node's weight vector $\mathbf{w}_i$ at each iteration. Normalization is required so that similarity matching is meaningful. The similarity-matching part of Eq. (12.8) finds the "winner" $\hat{\mathbf{w}}_i^{(k)}$, which is the pattern closest to the current input pattern. Since

$$\arg\min_j \|\mathbf{x} - \hat{\mathbf{w}}_j\|^2 = \arg\min_j (\mathbf{x} - \hat{\mathbf{w}}_j)^T (\mathbf{x} - \hat{\mathbf{w}}_j)$$

$$= \arg\min_j (\mathbf{x}^T\mathbf{x} + \hat{\mathbf{w}}_j^T\hat{\mathbf{w}}_j - 2\mathbf{x}^T\hat{\mathbf{w}}_j) \qquad (12.10)$$

$$= \arg\max_j (\mathbf{x}^T\hat{\mathbf{w}}_j) = \arg\max_j (\hat{\mathbf{w}}_j^T\mathbf{x}),$$

the ith competing neuron wins if it has the largest net input (net$_i = \hat{\mathbf{w}}_i^T\mathbf{x}$), that is, if the input pattern $\mathbf{x}$ correlates maximally with $\hat{\mathbf{w}}_i$. From the cosine law,

$$\text{net}_i = \hat{\mathbf{w}}_i^T\mathbf{x} = \|\hat{\mathbf{w}}_i\| \|\mathbf{x}\| \cos(\hat{\mathbf{w}}_i, \mathbf{x}), \qquad (12.11)$$

we can obtain the geometric interpretation of the Kohonen learning rule. The term $\cos(\hat{\mathbf{w}}_i, \mathbf{x})$ denotes the cosine of the angle between the two vectors $\hat{\mathbf{w}}_i$ and $\mathbf{x}$. Equation (12.11) implies that the ith node wins if the input pattern $\mathbf{x}$ is more *parallel* to its weight vector $\hat{\mathbf{w}}_i$ than to any other $\hat{\mathbf{w}}_j$, $j \ne i$. The result of weight adjustment in Eq. (12.8) is mainly rotation of the winning weight vector $\hat{\mathbf{w}}_i$ toward the input vector.

The learning rule in Eq. (12.8) will gradually lead to weight vectors that approximate the centroids of past winning input vectors. However, since the weights are adjusted in proportion to the number of events that end up with weight adjustments, the network reacts to the probability of occurrence of input patterns. In fact, this is true for networks trained in the self-organizing mode—such networks react not only to values of inputs but also to their statistical parameters; that is, rare inputs have less impact on learning than those that occur frequently. Let us now consider an example illustrating Kohonen learning.

Example 12.1

[Zurada, 1992, Example 7.2]. In this example, a two-node Kohonen network is used to identify two possible clusters of training patterns; that is, $n = 2$. The normalized training patterns are

$$\{\mathbf{x}^1, \mathbf{x}^2, \mathbf{x}^3, \mathbf{x}^4, \mathbf{x}^5\} = \left\{ \begin{pmatrix} 0.8 \\ 0.6 \end{pmatrix}, \begin{pmatrix} 0.1736 \\ -0.9848 \end{pmatrix}, \begin{pmatrix} 0.707 \\ 0.707 \end{pmatrix}, \begin{pmatrix} 0.342 \\ -0.9397 \end{pmatrix}, \begin{pmatrix} 0.6 \\ 0.8 \end{pmatrix} \right\},$$

which in polar coordinate form are

$$\{\mathbf{x}^1, \mathbf{x}^2, \mathbf{x}^3, \mathbf{x}^4, \mathbf{x}^5\} = \{1 \angle 36.87°; 1 \angle -80°; 1 \angle 45°; 1 \angle -70°; 1 \angle 53.13°\}.$$

The training vectors are shown in Fig. 12.4(a). The selected normalized initial weights are

$$\hat{\mathbf{w}}_1^{(0)} = \begin{pmatrix} 1 \\ 0 \end{pmatrix} \qquad \text{and} \qquad \hat{\mathbf{w}}_2^{(0)} = \begin{pmatrix} -1 \\ 0 \end{pmatrix}.$$

The inputs presented to the network are in the recycled order $\mathbf{x}^1, \mathbf{x}^2, \ldots, \mathbf{x}^5, \mathbf{x}^1, \mathbf{x}^2, \ldots$ The parameter $\alpha^{(k)}$ in Eq. (12.8) is set to a constant of $\frac{1}{2}$. After the first time step (i.e., after $\mathbf{x}^1$ is presented to the network), we have

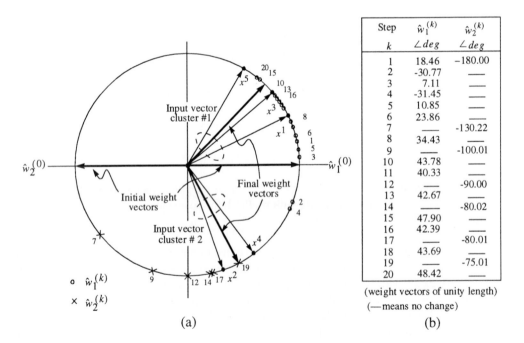

Step	$\hat{w}_1^{(k)}$	$\hat{w}_2^{(k)}$
k	$\angle deg$	$\angle deg$
1	18.46	−180.00
2	−30.77	——
3	7.11	——
4	−31.45	——
5	10.85	——
6	23.86	——
7	——	−130.22
8	34.43	——
9	——	−100.01
10	43.78	——
11	40.33	——
12	——	−90.00
13	42.67	——
14	——	−80.02
15	47.90	——
16	42.39	——
17	——	−80.01
18	43.69	——
19	——	−75.01
20	48.42	——

(weight vectors of unity length)
(—means no change)

(a)　　　　　　　　　　(b)

Figure 12.4 Kohonen learning in Example 12.1. (Reprinted by permission from page 408 of *Introduction to Artificial Neural Systems* by J. M. Zurada; Copyright © 1992 by West Publishing Company. All rights reserved.)

$$\hat{\mathbf{w}}_1^{(1)} = \begin{pmatrix} 0.948 \\ 0.316 \end{pmatrix} \qquad \text{and} \qquad \hat{\mathbf{w}}_2^{(1)} = \begin{pmatrix} -1 \\ 0 \end{pmatrix}$$

since the first neuron is the winner. Hence, $\hat{\mathbf{w}}_1$ moves closer to $\mathbf{x}^1$. The iterative weight adjustments continue in this way. Figure 12.4(b) shows the tabulated results of weight iterations for $k \le 20$. The geometric interpretation of weight vector displacement during learning is shown on the unity circle in Fig. 12.4(a). For large k, $\hat{\mathbf{w}}_1$ centers around $1 \angle 45°$ and $\hat{\mathbf{w}}_2$ centers around $1 \angle \text{-}75°$. This coincides with the fact that the center of the first quadrant cluster composed of $\mathbf{x}^1, \mathbf{x}^3$, and $\mathbf{x}^5$ is $(\mathbf{x}^1 + \mathbf{x}^3 + \mathbf{x}^5)/3 = 1 \angle 45°$ and the center of another cluster is $(\mathbf{x}^2 + \mathbf{x}^4)/2 = 1 \angle \text{-}75°$.

In the Kohonen learning rule [Eq. (12.8)] there are two factors that affect learning: the initial weights and the $\alpha^{(k)}$ parameters. The weights are usually initialized randomly; that is, they are uniformly distributed on the unity hypersphere in the n-dimensional pattern space. Another method is to assign the n weight vectors to be the first n training vectors initially, that is, $\hat{\mathbf{w}}_1^{(0)} = \mathbf{x}^1/\|\mathbf{x}^1\|$, $\hat{\mathbf{w}}_2^{(0)} = \mathbf{x}^2/\|\mathbf{x}^2\|,\dots, \hat{\mathbf{w}}_n^{(0)} = \mathbf{x}^n/\|\mathbf{x}^n\|$, thus ensuring that they are all in the right domain. Improper initial weights may cause weights to get stuck in isolated regions without forming adequate clusters. In such cases the training must be reinitialized with new initial weights. As for the learning constant $\alpha^{(k)}$, it should be selected such that it begins with a large value and then decreases gradually as learning goes on. In this way, the weights are trained to provide coarse clustering first, and then they are finely tuned within each cluster. More precisely, the sequence $\{\alpha^{(k)}; k = 0, 1,\dots; 0 < \alpha^{(k)} < 1\}$ is usually a slowly decreasing function of time. It is conjectured that $\{\alpha^{(k)}\}$ should satisfy the following conditions [Kohonen, 1989]:

$$\sum_{k=0}^{\infty} \alpha^{(k)} = \infty, \qquad \sum_{k=0}^{\infty} (\alpha^{(k)})^2 < \infty. \tag{12.12}$$

For example, the sequence could be $\{\alpha^{(k)}\} = \{1, \frac{1}{2}, \frac{1}{3},\dots\}$, $\alpha^{(k)} = \alpha_0 k^{-\beta}$ (with $0 < \beta \le 1$) or $\alpha^{(k)} = \alpha_0 (1 - \beta k)$. Practically, we can take, for instance, $\alpha^{(k)} = 0.1 (1 - k/10{,}000)$ for 10,000 samples $\mathbf{x}(k)$.

There are some modifications of the Kohonen learning rule that are of interest:

1. We can update the weights of all the losers as well as those of the winners, but with a much smaller α [Rumelhart and Zipser, 1986]. Then a neuron that is always losing will gradually move toward the average input direction until it eventually succeeds in winning a competition. This is called *leaky competitive learning* and can be helpful in cases where clusters are hard to distinguish.
2. Since the similarity matching in Eq. (12.8) is equivalent to finding the maximum net input, net_i in Eq. (12.11), we can subtract a threshold θ_i from net_i and dynamically adjust the thresholds properly to make it easier for frequently losing neurons to win [Grossberg, 1976b; DeSieno, 1988].
3. We can select K winners instead of a single winner in the competition for weight updating, and the winning K neurons will be the ones best matching the input vector. This is called a *K-winners-take-all network* [Majani et al., 1989; Wolfe et al., 1991].
4. The above two approaches of using a threshold and selecting K winners can be combined to form *generalized winner-take-all* (g-WTA) *activation* [Lemmon and Vijaya Kumar, 1992]. In this approach, all the neurons whose net input exceeds the *sliding*

threshold are viewed as winners and their weights are updated. The sliding threshold allows each neuron to have a different threshold.

5. The Kohonen learning rule can be used as supervised learning when the proper class for some pattern is known a priori [Simpson, 1990]. In this supervised learning mode, the learning constant α is set as $\alpha > 0$ [see Eq. (12.8)] for correct classifications, and $\alpha < 0$ otherwise. More generally, the *supervised competitive learning* rule is given by [Kohonen, 1989]

$$\dot{w}_{ij} = r_i(\mathbf{x}) s_i(y_i) [x_j - w_{ij}], \tag{12.13}$$

where $s_i(y_i) = 1$ if y_i is the winner and $s_i(y_i) = 0$ otherwise; $r_i(\mathbf{x}) = 1$ if $\mathbf{x}$ is in the cluster denoted by y_i and $r_i(\mathbf{x}) = -1$ otherwise. This learning rule is also called *learning vector quantization* (LVQ) [Kohonen, 1989].

12.1.3 Differential Hebbian Learning Rule

The differential Hebbian learning rule correlates signal velocities as well as neuronal signals:

$$\dot{w}_{ij} = -w_{ij} + s_i(y_i) s_j(x_j) + \dot{s}_i(y_i) \dot{s}_j(x_j), \tag{12.14}$$

where

$$\dot{s}_i(y_i) = \frac{ds_i(y_i)}{dt} = \frac{ds_i}{dy_i} \frac{dy_i}{dt} = s_i' \dot{y}_i. \tag{12.15}$$

Since time derivatives measure changes, products of derivatives correlate changes. This leads to the simplest differential Hebbian learning rule as follows:

$$\dot{w}_{ij} = -w_{ij} + \dot{s}_i(y_i) \dot{s}_j(x_j), \tag{12.16}$$

where the passive decay term $-w_{ij}$ forces zero causality between unchanging concepts. The signal velocities may be positive or negative even though the signals may take only nonnegative values. This makes differential Hebbian learning suitable for real-time causal inference. Intuitively, Hebbian correlations may catch spurious causal associations among concurrently active nodes. Differential correlations estimate the concurrent and presumably causal variation among active nodes. Hence, differential Hebbian learning allows the weights to represent temporal aspects of the network's dynamics and is a kind of *spatiotemporal learning*.

Another differential Hebbian learning rule is the Kosko-Klopf learning rule [Hecht-Nielsen 1990], which uses the same idea to include time derivatives of signals in the learning. The Kosko-Klopf learning rule is somewhat similar to Grossberg's learning rule in Eq. (12.4) and is expressed by the following equation:

$$\dot{w}_{ij} = -aw_{ij} + [by_i x_j - cw_{ij}] u(\dot{y}_i) u(\dot{x}_j), \tag{12.17}$$

where $u(\cdot)$ is the unit step function and a, b, and c are positive constants with a typically much smaller than c. The purpose of a is to cause weights that are never or almost never increased to eventually go to zero. Hence, the first term in Eq. (12.17) causes a slow decay of infrequently increased weights but does not interface with the learning of weights that are frequently reinforced. This term can be left out if all the weights are started at zero. The terms inside the bracket $[by_i x_j - cw_{ij}]$ are essentially similar to the terms in Eq. (12.4). Thus, as compared to Grossberg's learning rule in Eq. (12.4), the main difference is that here it is *gated* by the product of the derivatives of signals instead of the signal itself. The gating term $u(\dot{y}_i) u(\dot{x}_j)$ ensures that the weight increase takes place only during the period when the target neuron y_i is increasing its output signal and the source neuron x_j is increasing its output signal. In this way, the learning catches the temporal correlation that the "pulse" x_j causes the occurrence of the "pulse" y_i.

12.1.4 Differential Competitive Learning Rule

The differential competitive learning rule combines competitive and differential Hebbian learning as follows:

$$\dot{w}_{ij} = \dot{s}_i(y_i)[s_j(x_j) - w_{ij}], \qquad (12.18)$$

which means *learn only if change;* that is, the system learns only if the competing neurons change their competitive signal. The signal velocity $\dot{s}_i(y_i)$ provides local reward-punish reinforcement and resembles the term $r_i(\cdot)$ in the supervised competitive learning rule in Eq. (12.13). In nondifferential competitive learning, winning neurons may tend to keep winning. However, in differential competitive learning, the winning signal $s_i(y_i)$ rapidly stops changing once the *i*th neuron has secured its competitive victory. In practice, the following *linear differential competitive learning rule* is used for pattern recognition and probability-density function estimation:

$$\dot{w}_{ij} = \dot{s}_i(y_i)[x_j - w_{ij}]. \qquad (12.19)$$

The discrete (or pulse-coded) differential competitive learning rule is

$$w_{ij}(k+1) = w_{ij}(k) + \Delta s_i(y_i(k))[x_j(k) - w_{ij}(k)], \qquad (12.20)$$

which represents a neural version of the *adaptive delta modulation* technique used in communication theory [Hambly, 1990].

The discrete differential competitive learning rule has been applied to centroid estimation and phoneme recognition [Kong and Kosko, 1991]. Simulations showed that weight vectors trained by differential competitive learning converged to class centroids quickly and wandered about these centroids less than weight vectors trained by supervised competitive learning.

12.2 HAMMING NETWORKS

The Hamming network is for selecting stored classes that are at a minimum Hamming distance (HD) from the noisy or incomplete argument vector presented at the input [Steinbuch and Piske, 1963; Lippmann, 1987]. The vectors involved are all binary and bipolar. As shown in Fig. 12.5, the Hamming network consist of two parts (layers). The first layer calculates the $(m - HD)$ between the input vector **x** and the stored n prototype vectors $\mathbf{s}^1, \mathbf{s}^2, ..., \mathbf{s}^n$ in the feedforward pass. The strongest response of a neuron in this layer is indicative of the minimum HD value between the input and the category this neuron represents. The second layer of the Hamming network is a MAXNET or a winner-take-all network which is a recurrent network. The MAXNET suppresses values at MAXNET output nodes other than the initially maximum output node of the first layer.

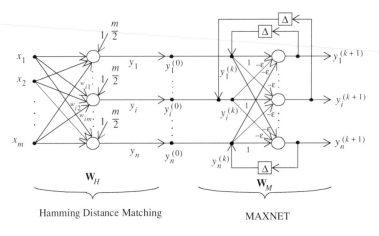

Figure 12.5 Hamming network.

Let us first see how to design the first layer of the Hamming network. It is desirable to have the ith node in the first layer compute $[m - HD(\mathbf{x}, \mathbf{s}^i)]$ for a given input vector $\mathbf{x}$, where $HD(\mathbf{x}, \mathbf{s}^i)$ is the Hamming distance between vectors $\mathbf{x}$ and $\mathbf{s}^i$. Since

$$\mathbf{x}^T \mathbf{s}^i = [m - HD(\mathbf{x}, \mathbf{s}^i)] - HD(\mathbf{x}, \mathbf{s}^i), \qquad (12.21)$$

we have

$$\frac{1}{2}\mathbf{x}^T \mathbf{s}^i = \frac{m}{2} - HD(\mathbf{x}, \mathbf{s}^i). \qquad (12.22)$$

Hence, if the weight matrix $\mathbf{W}_H$ of the first layer is set to

$$\mathbf{W}_H = \frac{1}{2}\begin{bmatrix} s_1^1 & s_2^1 & \cdots & s_m^1 \\ s_1^2 & s_2^2 & \cdots & s_m^2 \\ \vdots & \vdots & \ddots & \vdots \\ s_1^n & s_2^n & \cdots & s_m^n \end{bmatrix}, \qquad (12.23)$$

then the net input of node i becomes

$$\text{net}_i = \frac{1}{2}\mathbf{x}^T \mathbf{s}^i + \frac{m}{2} = m - HD(\mathbf{x}, \mathbf{s}^i), \qquad i = 1, 2, \ldots, n, \qquad (12.24)$$

where $m/2$ is the threshold value for every node. This design of the first layer can achieve our goal. To keep the output value between 0 and 1, the activation function is chosen as $a(\text{net}_i) = (1/m)\,\text{net}_i$, $i = 1, 2, \ldots, n$.

The second layer of the Hamming network is the MAXNET, whose purpose is to enhance the initial dominant response of the ith node and suppress the others. As a result of MAXNET recurrent processing, the ith node responds positively while the responses of all remaining nodes decay to zero. This requires positive self-feedback connections and negative lateral inhibition connections (see Fig. 9.5). The $n \times n$ weight matrix $\mathbf{W}_M$ of the MAXNET is thus taken as

$$\mathbf{W}_M = \begin{bmatrix} 1 & -\epsilon & -\epsilon & \cdots & -\epsilon \\ -\epsilon & 1 & -\epsilon & \cdots & -\epsilon \\ -\epsilon & -\epsilon & 1 & \cdots & -\epsilon \\ \vdots & \vdots & \vdots & \ddots & \vdots \\ -\epsilon & -\epsilon & -\epsilon & \cdots & 1 \end{bmatrix}, \tag{12.25}$$

where $0 < \epsilon < 1/n$ is called the lateral interaction coefficient. The activation function is given by

$$a\,(\text{net}) = \begin{cases} \text{net}, & \text{net} \geq 0 \\ 0, & \text{net} < 0, \end{cases} \tag{12.26}$$

and the recurrent update rule of the MAXNET is

$$\mathbf{y}^{k+1} = a\big[\mathbf{W}_M\,\mathbf{y}^{(k)}\big], \tag{12.27}$$

where $a\,(\cdot)$ is applied to each entry in the column vector $\mathbf{W}_M\,\mathbf{y}^{(k)}$. Each updated vector $\mathbf{y}^{(k+1)}$ entry decreases at the kth recursion step, with the largest entry decreasing the slowest because of the condition that $0 < \epsilon < 1/n$. Hence, when the MAXNET stabilizes, the only nonzero output response node is the node closest to the input vector argument in the sense of the Hamming distance.

It is noted that the Hamming network retrieves only the closest class index and not the entire prototype vector. Hence, it is a classifier rather than an associative memory. However, it can be modified to be an associative memory by simply adding an extra layer after the MAXNET such that the winner, $y_i^{(k+1)}$, in the MAXNET will trigger a corresponding stored vector (weight) $\hat{\mathbf{s}}_i$. Such an associative memory is called a Hamming memory network. It can be autoassociative ($\hat{\mathbf{s}}_i = \mathbf{s}_i$) or heteroassociative ($\hat{\mathbf{s}}_i \neq \mathbf{s}_i$).

12.3 SELF-ORGANIZING FEATURE MAPS

Feature mapping converts patterns of arbitrary dimensionality (the pattern space) into the responses of one- or two-dimensional arrays of neurons (the feature space). A network that performs such a mapping is called a *feature map*. In addition to achieving dimensionality reduction, another major goal is to obtain a *topology-preserving map* that preserves neighborhood relations of the input pattern. That is, we ask for nearby outputs of a feature map corresponding to nearby input patterns. To obtain such feature maps, we would like to find a self-organizing neural array that consists of neurons arranged in a virtual one-dimensional segment or in a two-dimensional array. One typical network structure is shown in Fig. 12.6(a). Note that each component of the input vector $\mathbf{x}$ is connected to each of the nodes. If the input vector is two-dimensional, the inputs x_{kl} can themselves be arranged in a two-dimensional array that defines the input space (k, l) as shown in Fig. 12.6(b). Again, the connections between two layers are fully connected.

One approach to designing a self-organizing feature map network is to use the Kohonen learning rule [Eq. (12.8)], with updated weights going to the neighbors of the winning neuron as well as to the winning neuron itself. This is the well-known Kohonen's

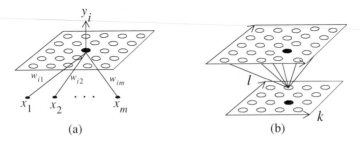

Figure 12.6 Two basic types of feature mapping networks.

self-organizing feature map. The learning rule of the Kohonen feature map is [consider the network structure in Fig. 12.6(a)]

$$\| \mathbf{x} - \hat{\mathbf{w}}_{i*} \| = \min_{j} \{ \| \mathbf{x} - \hat{\mathbf{w}}_{j} \| \} \qquad \text{(similarity matching)}$$

$$w_{ij}^{(k+1)} = \begin{cases} w_{ij}^{(k)} + \alpha^{(k)} [x_j^{(k)} - w_{ij}^{(k)}] & \text{for } i \in N_{i*}^{(k)} \\ w_{ij}^{(k)}, & \text{otherwise} \end{cases} \qquad \text{(updating)} \qquad (12.28)$$

for all i and j, where $N_{i*}^{(k)} = N_{i*}(k)$ is the *neighborhood set* of the winner node i^* at time step k. With this learning rule, nearby nodes receive similar updates and thus end up responding to nearby input patterns. Practically, the neighborhood set $N_{i*}(k)$ and the learning constant α in Eq. (12.28) are changed dynamically during learning. We start with a wide range for $N_{i*}(k)$ and a large α and then reduce both the range of $N_{i*}(k)$ and the value of α gradually as learning proceeds. This allows the network to perform an initial global ordering of weights and then refine them slowly with respect to the input patterns. The selection of proper sequences of $\alpha(k)$ has been discussed in Sec. 12.1.1 [see Eq. (12.12)]. Figure 12.7 shows two sequences of shrinking neighborhood sets, $N_{i*}(k_1) \supset N_{i*}(k_2) \supset N_{i*}(k_3) \supset \cdots$, where $k_1 < k_2 < k_3 \cdots$.

As a result of weight adjustment using Eq. (12.28), a planar neuron map is obtained with weights coding the stationary probability density function $p(\mathbf{x})$ of the pattern vectors used for training. The ordered image of patterns forms the weights w_{ij}.

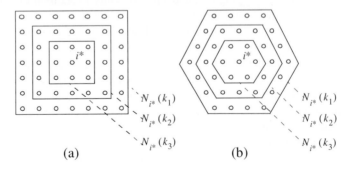

Figure 12.7 Two examples of a topological neighborhood

Example 12.2

[Ritter et al., 1992]. In this example, a neural network creates a map or an image of an unknown region G with a curved boundary. There is a source of sound moving around in G. From time to time, the sound source emits a sound signal of constant intensity and the position in G of each sound emission is random. The sound signal is received by two microphones, each connected to an amplifier with logarithmic characteristics [see Fig. 12.8(a)]. The relationship between the sound source position x, y and the output signals v_1 and v_2 of the two amplifiers is given by

$$v_1 = -\log[(x - a)^2 + y^2] \qquad \text{and} \qquad v_2 = -\log[(x + a)^2 + y^2],$$

where $2a$ is the separation of the microphones. The two signals, v_1 and v_2, are fed into each of 1600 neurons arranged in a planar 40×40 lattice as shown in Fig. 12.6(a). Every neuron i has two weights, w_{i1} and w_{i2}, on the connections to inputs v_1 and v_2, respectively. According to Eq. (12.28), each node updates its weights gradually in such a way as to become sensitive to a small subset of input signals $(v_1, v_2)^T$. This subset corresponds to a small subarea of G within which the moving source may be located. This subarea constitutes the *receptive field* of the particular neuron in the environment G. Figure 12.8(b) and (c) displays the different distributions of weights during training. The horizontal and vertical coordinates of the plots are the resulting values w_{i1} and w_{i2}, respectively, for an array of 40×40 neurons. Line intersections on the maps

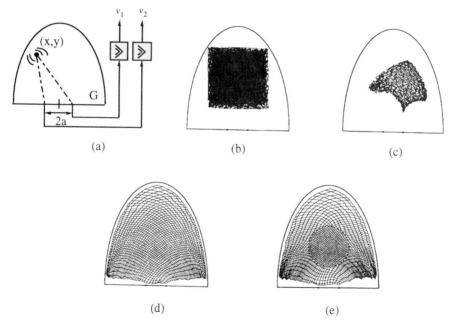

(a) (b) (c)

(d) (e)

Figure 12.8 Map created by the neural network in Example 12.2. (a) Region G containing a sound source. The two microphone positions are marked at the lower boundary of G. The microphone signals are fed into two logarithmic amplifiers, whose output signals v_1, v_2 serve as input for the network. (b) Initial feature map. (c) Feature map after 100 learning steps. (d) Feature map after 40,000 learning steps. (e) Result of the same simulation as in (d) but using nonuniform random sound source positions. (Martinetz/Ritter/Schulten, *Neural Computation and Self-Organizing Maps: An Introduction.* © 1992 Addison-Wesley Publishing Company, Inc. Reprinted by permission of Addison-Wesley Publishing Company, Inc.)

specify weight values for a single *i*th neuron. Lines between the nodes on the graph merely connect weight points for neurons that are topological nearest neighbors. Figure 12.8(b) shows the initial distribution of weights which are selected randomly. The final weights of the neurons after 40,000 learning iterations are shown in Fig. 12.8(d), which is a topology-preserving map of the area *G*. The feature maps, Fig. 12.8(b)–(d), also indicate the assignment of neurons to positions in *G*. From this point of view, for each neuron *i* the location (x, y) of its receptive field in *G* is marked as a line intersection. Marked locations are connected by a line if their corresponding neurons are adjacent on the lattice. Then it is observed that Fig. 12.8(d) forms a good correspondence between lattice neurons and points of *G*.

In the above discussion, we used a uniform probability distribution for the random sound source positions. If the distribution is nonuniform, we will find more grid points of the weight network where the probability is higher. This phenomenon is illustrated in Fig. 12.8(e) in which, within the circular region marked by dots, signals are emitted with a probability three times higher than in the remaining region of *G*. In this case, more neurons code positions in the circular region, which corresponds to a higher resolution of the map created for this region.

The Kohonen feature map can be extended to a multilayer network by adding an association layer (output layer) to the output of the self-organizing map layer (see Figure 12.9). The output nodes associate desired output values with certain input vectors. This structure is referred to as a *self-organizing motor map* [Ritter et al., 1992], and the added layer is called a *motor map* in which movement commands are mapped to two-dimensional locations of excitation. In this structure, the feature map is a hidden layer and acts as a competitive network that classifies input vectors. The training of the feature map is exactly the same as discussed above. The formation of a motor map corresponds to the learning of a control task. Such learning can be supervised or unsupervised and can be achieved by several methods including the delta learning rule and the outstar procedure described later. The learning of a motor map acts as an extension of Kohonen's original learning algorithm.

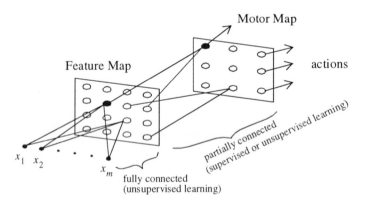

Figure 12.9   Structure of a self-organizing motor map.

12.4 ADAPTIVE RESONANCE THEORY

Adaptive resonance theory (ART) neural networks were developed by Carpenter and Grossberg [1987a,b, 1988, 1990] and serve the purpose of cluster discovery through unsupervised learning. The novel property of ART networks is the controlled discovery of clusters. They produce clusters by themselves without a priori information about the possible number and type of clusters. ART first emerged from an analysis of the instability of a three-layer feedforward network called the *instar-outstar model* [Grossberg, 1976ab]. Because of its generality, we shall first introduce the instar-outstar model before considering ART networks.

12.4.1 The Instar-Outstar Model—Shunting Activation Equations

The instar-outstar model is a three-layer neural network that performs input-output data mapping, producing an output vector **y** in response to an input vector **x**, based on competitive learning. Several neural networks are examples of instar-outstar competitive learning models. These include Kohonen's self-organizing motor map, (see Fig. 12.9), ART networks, and counterpropagation networks which will be introduced in the next section.

As shown in Fig. 12.10, there are three layers in an instar-outstar model: the input layer, the competitive layer (hidden layer), and the output layer. The connections between the input layer and the competitive layer form the *instar* structure, and the connections between the competitive layer and the output layer form the *outstar* structure. The competitive layer is actually a winner-take-all network or a MAXNET with lateral feedback connections. There is no lateral connection within the input layer and the output layer. The connections between layers are usually fully connected, but only parts of the connections are shown in Fig. 12.10. The four major components of the instar-outstar model are the input layer, the instar, the competitive layer, and the outstar. Before discussing each of these four components, we first introduce a general neuron activation equation called the *shunting activation equation* [Grossberg, 1988b], which describes the *dynamic behavior* of a neuron.

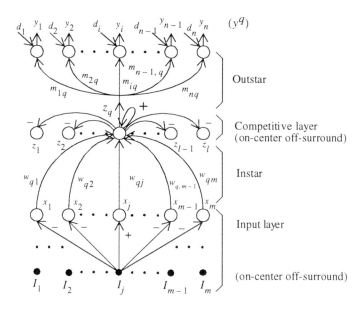

Figure 12.10 Structure of the instar-outstar model.

Shunting activation equations. The shunting or *multiplicative* activation equation is an important generalization of the normal *additive* activation equation. In an additive dynamic model (i.e., a neural network described by additive activation equations), the activity of a node is proportional to the difference between the net excitatory input and the net inhibitory input [Grossberg, 1988b]. More precisely, the additive activation equation looks like

$$\dot{y}_i = -y_i + \left[\sum_j w_{ij} x_j + \theta_i \right] - [\text{inhibition}], \tag{12.29}$$

where y_i is the activity of node i, θ_i is its threshold value, and x_j is the jth input component. The first term on the right-hand side of Eq. (12.29) is the *passive decay* term, which causes the neuron's activity y_i to decay exponentially to its zero resting potential when there is no external input. In general, the right-hand side of an additive activation equation has the form of: *decay + excitation – inhibition*. In fact, the continuous Hopfield network described by Eq. (11.8) and the continuous bidirectional associative memory described by Eq. (11.46) are both additive dynamical models and can be called the *additive Hopfield network* and the *additive BAM,* respectively. Additive dynamics resemble linear dynamics since the change in neuronal activation equals the sum of activations and signals. Hence, activations may be huge in the presence of large inputs. To attack this problem, Grossberg [1982a] proposed a generalization of the additive model called the *shunting model.* In a shunting network, excitatory inputs drive activity toward a finite maximum, while inhibitory inputs drive activity toward a finite minimum:

$$\dot{y}_i = -y_i + (A - y_i) \sum_i \left[\begin{array}{c} \text{excitatory} \\ \text{inputs} \end{array} \right] - (B + y_i) \sum \left[\begin{array}{c} \text{inhibitory} \\ \text{inputs} \end{array} \right]. \tag{12.30}$$

In Eq. (12.30), activity y_i remains in the bounded range of $(-B, A)$ and decays to the resting level 0 in the absence of all inputs. Furthermore, shunting equations display other crucial properties such as normalization and automatic gain control. These properties will be further explained later.

A general shunting activation equation in the form of Eq. (12.30) was introduced by Grossberg [1988b] as

$$\dot{y}_i = -A_i y_i + (B_i - C_i y_i)[I_i + f_i(y_i)] - (D_i y_i + E_i) \left[J_i + \sum_{k=1}^{n} F_{ik} g_k(y_k) \right], \tag{12.31}$$

$$i = 1, 2, \ldots, n,$$

where y_i is the potential or short-term memory activity of the ith neuron in the network, $-A_i y_i$ describes the passive decay of activity at a rate of $-A_i$, and

$$(B_i - C_i y_i)[I_i + f_i(y_i)] \tag{12.32}$$

describes how an excitatory input I_i and an excitatory feedback signal $f_i(y_i)$ increase the activity y_i. If $C_i = 0$, then Eq. (12.32) describes an additive effect of input and feedback signals on activity. If $C_i > 0$, this term describes a shunting or multiplicative effect of input and feedback signals on activity y_i, and the input and feedback signal become ineffective when $y_i = B_i C_i^{-1}$ since then $B_i - C_i y_i = 0$. In a shunting network, the initial value inequality $y_i(0) \le B_i C_i^{-1}$ implies that $y_i(t) \le B_i C_i^{-1}$ for all $t \ge 0$. The third term in Eq. (12.31),

$$- (D_i y_i + E_i) \left[J_i + \sum_{k=1}^{n} F_{ik} g_k (y_k) \right], \tag{12.33}$$

describes how an inhibitory input J_i and inhibitory feedback signals $F_{ik} g_k (y_k)$ from neuron k to neuron i decrease the activity y_i of neuron i. If $D_i = 0$, then Eq. (12.33) describes an additive effect of input and feedback signals on activity y_i. If $D_i > 0$, then Eq. (12.33) describes a shunting effect of input and feedback signals on activity y_i, and the input and feedback signals become ineffective when $y_i = -D_i^{-1} E_i$ since then $D_i y_i + E_i = 0$. An initial value choice of $y_i(0) \geq -D_i^{-1} E_i$ implies that $y_i(t) \geq -D_i^{-1} E_i$ for all $t \geq 0$. Thus, in a shunting network, but not an additive network, each activity $y_i(t)$ is restricted to a finite interval (i.e., $[-D_i^{-1} E_i, B_i C_i^{-1}]$) for all time $t \geq 0$. The interval can be determined by finding the equilibrium points for Eq. (12.31), that is, by setting $\dot{y}_i = 0$. This will be demonstrated when we discuss the instar-outstar model. Suitably designed shunting networks can automatically adjust their sensitivity to maintain a sensitive response within these finite intervals even if their inputs fluctuate in size over a much broader dynamical range.

From the above discussion, we note that Eq. (12.31) describes an *on-center–off-surround* shunting network structure in which a neuron i receives a self-excitatory feedback signal $f_i(y_i)$ as well as the lateral inhibitory feedback signals $g_k(y_k)$ from other neurons $k \neq i$. This structure is like that of the MAXNET shown in Fig. 12.5. The general shunting activation equation [Eq. (12.31)] is in the form of the Cohen-Grossberg activation equation [see Eq. (11.15)]. Hence, the stability of the shunting networks is guaranteed by the Cohen-Grossberg theorem (Theorem 11.2).

Using Eq. (12.31), an additive neural network can be changed to a shunting neural network. For example, a *shunting BAM* was defined by Kosko [1987] [see Eq. (11.46) for the additive BAM for comparison]

$$\dot{y}_i = -a_i y_i + (b_i - y_i)[a(y_i) + s_i^+] - y_i \left[\sum_j w_{ij} a(x_j) + s_i^- \right],$$
$$\dot{x}_j = -c_j x_j + (b_j - x_j)[a(x_j) + t_j^+] - x_j \left[\sum_i w_{ij} a(y_i) + t_j^- \right], \tag{12.34}$$

where s_i^+ and s_i^- are, respectively, the excitatory and inhibitory inputs to node y_i and t_j^+ and t_j^- are those to node x_j. The shunting activation equation in Eq. (12.31) will be used in the instar-outstar model described next.

Instar-outstar models. We shall consider the four key components of the instar-outstar model (see Fig. 12.10) (i.e., the input layer, the instar, the competitive layer, and the outstar) one by one in the following discussion.

1. *Input Layer*

   For each node j in the input layer, there is an input value I_j. The outputs x_j of the nodes in this layer are governed by the set of shunting activation equations

$$\dot{x}_j = -A x_j + (B - x_j) I_j - x_j \sum_{k \neq j} I_k, \qquad j = 1, 2, \ldots, m, \tag{12.35}$$

where $0 < x_i(0) < B$ and $A, B > 0$. Each node receives a net excitation (on-center) of $(B - x_j)I_j$ from its corresponding input value I_j. It also receives inhibitory signals (off-surround) $-x_jI_k$ from other nodes. The inhibitory signals can prevent the activity of the node j from rising in proportion to the absolute pattern intensity I_j.

Once an input pattern is applied, the node j quickly reaches an equilibrium state x_j^{eq}, which can be determined by setting $\dot{x}_j = 0$ in Eq. (12.35) as

$$x_j^{eq} = I_j \frac{B}{A + \sum_k I_k} = \frac{I_j}{I} \frac{BI}{A + I} = P_j \frac{BI}{A + I}, \qquad (12.36)$$

where $I \equiv \sum_k I_k$ and $P_j \equiv I_j/I$. The vector $(P_1, P_2, \dots, P_m)^T$ is called a *reflectance pattern*. We find that x_j^{eq} is less than B and approaches P_jB as $I \to \infty$. Hence, the activity is bounded in $[0, B]$. Furthermore, the output pattern is normalized since

$$\sum_{j=1}^m x_j = \frac{BI}{A + I} \qquad (12.37)$$

is always less than B and approaches B as $I \to \infty$. Thus, the activity pattern is proportional to the reflectance pattern rather than to the original input pattern. After the input pattern is removed, because of the passive decay term $-Ax_j$, the activity is reduced gradually back to zero. Thus, we have observed that the input layer with the on-center–off-surround arrangement and shunting activation equations in Eq. (12.35) can normalize the input patterns within a bound automatically. In computer simulations, this is always done in preprocessing, and the input nodes are viewed as simply pass-through units.

2. *Instar*

In Fig. 12.10, nodes $x_1, x_2, \dots, x_m, z_q$ and the connections between them constitute an instar. It is basically a node z_q with its fan-in. However, use of the term "instar" is usually restricted to those units whose processing and learning are governed by the equations for the instar-outstar model. Usually, an instar responds maximally to the input vectors from a particular cluster. A typical learning rule for an instar is given by

$$\dot{w}_{qj} = -\alpha w_{qj}x_j + \beta z_q x_j, \qquad (12.38)$$

where node z_q is the output of the instar and $\alpha, \beta > 0$. Equation (12.38) is in fact a modified signal Hebbian learning rule in Eq. (12.4). It differs from the signal Hebbian learning rule in Eq. (12.1) in the passive decay term $-\alpha w_{qj}x_j$, which keeps the weight vector unchanged when a different category representation is active, that is, $x_j = 0$. The input x_j thus buffers, or gates, the weights w_{qj} against undesirable changes, including memory loss due to passive decay. This rule will lead the final weight to the average position of the input vector I; that is $\mathbf{w}_{final} = \bar{\mathbf{I}}$, where $\bar{\mathbf{I}}$ is the average (mean) position of input vectors. Obviously, other unsupervised learning rules [Eqs. (12.5), (12.14), and (12.18)] introduced in Sec. 12.1 can be applied here if the passive decay terms are properly managed and included.

3. *Competitive Layer*

As shown in Fig. 12.10, l instars are grouped into a layer called the competitive layer. Each instar responds maximally to a group of input vectors in a different region of space. Then this layer of instars can classify any input vector since, for a given input, the instar (winning instar) with the strongest response identifies the region of space in which the input vector lies. For this purpose, we want the competitive layer to single out the winning instar by setting its output to a nonzero value and suppressing the other outputs to zero. That is, it is a winner-take-all or a MAXNET-type network. Here, on-center–off-surround connections are used to implement competitions among the instars, and the following shunting activation equation is used:

$$\dot{z}_q = -Az_q + (B - z_q)[a(z_q) + \text{net}_q] - z_q\left[\sum_{k \neq q} a(z_k) + \sum_{k \neq q} \text{net}_k\right],$$

(12.39)

$$q = 1, 2, \ldots, l,$$

where $A, B > 0$, $\text{net}_q = \sum_j w_{qj} x_j$, and $a(z_q)$ is an activation function such as the sigmoid function [Grossberg, 1982a].

4. *Outstar*

An outstar is composed of all the nodes in the output layer and a single node in the competitive layer. The outstar q, corresponding to the node z_q, is shown in Fig. 12.10, which shows l independent outstars. The outstar looks like the fan-out of a node (in the competitive layer). However, use of the term "outstar" is restricted to the structure having the functions and properties discussed in the following. It is desirable for the output vector of an outstar q to be equal to the desired vector $\mathbf{d}^q$ (i.e., $\mathbf{y}^q \approx \mathbf{d}^q$) when its corresponding node in the competitive layer (node z_q in Fig. 12.10) turns on (i.e., when z_q is a winner). In the training phase, the desired output $\mathbf{d}$ is fed into the output layer and the processing of the output node i takes place according to a simple additive activation equation:

$$\dot{y}_i = -ay_i + bd_i + c \, \text{net}_i,$$

(12.40)

where net_i is the net input to output node i from the competitive layer and $a, b, c > 0$. If there is one nonzero node in the competitive layer and its output value is equal to 1 (e.g., $z_q = 1$), then Eq. (12.40) becomes

$$\dot{y}_i = -ay_i + bd_i + cm_{iq},$$

(12.41)

where m_{iq} is the connection weight from z_q to y_i. When the weights have been trained to reach equilibrium m_{iq}^{eq}, the activity of the outstar becomes

$$\dot{y}_i = -ay_i + cm_{iq}^{eq}$$

(12.42)

and the equilibrium state of y_i is

$$y_i^{eq} = \frac{c}{a} m_{iq}^{eq}.$$

(12.43)

Since it is desirable to have $y_i^{eq} = d_i$, the weights should be trained to store the desired output patterns $\mathbf{d}$. Again, the learning rules in Sec. 12.1 can be utilized to perform this. A typical learning rule for outstar pattern learning is given by

$$\dot{m}_{iq} = -gm_{iq} z_q + hd_i z_q,$$

(12.44)

where $g, h > 0$. Equation (12.44) is similar to the signal Hebbian learning rule in Eq. (12.1) with the modified passive decay term in Eq. (12.38) for the instar. Then $m_{iq}^{eq} = (h/g) d_i$, assuming $z_q = 1$ when it is a winner. In this case, $y_i^{eq} = (c/a)(h/g)d_i$ and thus if $a = c$ and $g = h$, then $y_i^{eq} = d_i$. Strictly speaking, the weight learning in the outstar is supervised learning since the desired output **d** is given. Hence, other appropriate supervised learning rules can also be applied here.

Let us summarize the above discussion. In the instar-outstar model, the competitive layer participates in both the instar and outstar structures of the network. The function of the competitive instars is to recognize an input pattern through a winner-take-all competition. The winner will activate a corresponding outstar which associates some desired output pattern with the input pattern. The instar and outstar complement each other in the way that the instar recognizes an input pattern and classifies it; the outstar identifies or labels the selected class. The learning of the instar-outstar model usually takes place in the unsupervised-supervised mixed mode of learning—unsupervised learning for the instar and supervised learning for the outstar. However, it may be a purely unsupervised learning network in some special cases, for example, if we require the desired outputs **d** to be equal to the inputs **x**.

Most of the neural networks that we have discussed so far require external control of system dynamics and have individual learning modes and performance modes. For example, the back-propagation network needs external control of the forward and backward information flow in the learning phase. After the learning phase, the learned neural network is put to use to evaluate its performance. In this performance phase, weight changes are suppressed and only forward propagation is performed. The instar-outstar model described in this section, however, is a *real-time* model. Here the phrase "real-time" describes neural network models that require no external control of system dynamics. (Real-time is alternatively used to describe any system that is able to process inputs as fast as they arrive and respond to the inputs as desired.) Differential equations are usually used to describe real-time models. A real-time model may or may not have an external teaching input, and learning may or may not be shut down after a finite time interval. The dynamics of performance are described by the same set of equations as the dynamics of learning, and there is no externally imposed distinction between a learning mode and a performance mode. In real-time models, fast nodal activation and slow weight adaptation are always assumed. Real-time modeling has characterized most of the work of Grossberg [1988a], and ART neural networks are representative examples of real-time models.

Several neural networks resemble the instar-outstar model in structure or concept, such as the self-organizing motor map in Fig. 12.9. In the following sections, we shall introduce other network models that resemble the instar-outstar model in structure. In describing these networks, we may omit the detailed dynamical behavior of the neurons as we did for the input layer and the competitive layer of the instar-outstar model. As a result, complex shunting activation equations such as Eq. (12.31) may be replaced by simpler discrete-time activation functions ignoring the time-transient terms. Although this replacement makes them look less like real-time models, they are easier to understand and can be more easily simulated by digital computers.

12.4.2 Adaptive Resonance Theory

The major problem of an instar-outstar model is its instability, which arises from two sources. First, even if a chosen category is the best match for a given input, that match may nevertheless be a poor one, chosen only because all the others are even worse. Second, a learning rule such as Eq. (12.38) implies that recently learned patterns tend to erode past learning. It was the analysis of the instability of the feedforward instar-outstar model that led to the discovery of adaptive resonance theory [Grossberg, 1976b] and to development of the neural network systems ART1, ART2, and ART3 [Carpenter and Grossberg, 1987a,b, 1988, 1990]. The instability of instar-outstar networks could be solved by reducing the learning rate gradually to zero, thus freezing the learned categories. But then the network would lose its *plasticity,* or the ability to react to any new data. It is obviously difficult to have both stability and plasticity. ART networks are designed, in particular, to resolve the *stability-plasticity dilemma;* that is, they are stable enough to preserve significant past learning but nevertheless remain adaptable enough to incorporate new information (clusters) whenever it might appear.

ART networks overcome the stability-plasticity dilemma by accepting and adapting the stored prototype of a category only when the input is sufficiently similar to it. The input and stored prototype are said to be *resonate* when they are sufficiently similar. When an input pattern is not sufficiently similar to any existing prototype, a new node is then created to represent a new category with the input patterns as the prototype. The meaning of "sufficiently similar" depends on a *vigilance* parameter ρ, with $0 < \rho \leq 1$. If ρ is small, the similarity condition is easier to meet, resulting in a coarse categorization. On the other hand, if ρ is chosen to be close to 1, many finely divided categories are formed. The vigilance parameter value can be changed during learning such that increasing it can prompt subdivision of existing categories.

Since ART networks are for cluster discovery instead of data mapping, the above concept for resolving the stability-plasticity dilemma can be implemented by using an instar-outstar network with the desired output set equal to input, $\mathbf{d} = \mathbf{x}$ (see Fig. 12.10). In this way, for an input pattern $\mathbf{x}$, the instar part of the instar-outstar model determines the closest category that $\mathbf{x}$ belongs to, and then the outstar part checks the similarity between the prototype of the selected category and the input $\mathbf{x}$ to see if they will resonate. This is equivalent to folding the feedforward three-layer instar-outstar network in Fig. 12.10 back on itself, identifying the output layer and the input layer. Hence, the competitive layer becomes the output layer, and its nonzero output indicates the category a given input lies in. Thus, the minimal ART module, ART1, includes a bottom-up competitive learning system combined with a top-down outstar pattern-learning system. ART1 is designed for binary $0/1$ inputs, whereas ART2 is for continuous-valued inputs. We shall introduce ART1 first and then consider ART2.

A schematic representation of ART1 is shown in Fig. 12.11. Each input vector $\mathbf{x}$ has m binary $0/1$ components. Let the weights on the bottom-up links, x_j to y_i, be denoted by $\overline{w}_{ij}$, and the weights on the top-down links, y_i to x_j, be denoted by w_{ij}. Note that the first subscript of a top-down weight indicates the source node and that the second subscript indicates the destination node. This notation is different from the traditional notation used in previous chapters. Then the weight vectors $\mathbf{w}_i = (w_{i1}, w_{i2}, ..., w_{im})^T$, $i = 1, 2, ..., n$, repre-

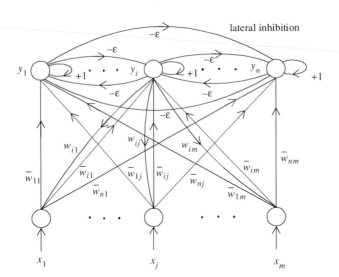

lateral inhibition

Figure 12.11 Schematic representation of ART1 network (top-down links shown for only one of the top nodes).

sent stored prototype vectors and thus are also binary $0/1$ vectors, where i indexes the output nodes or categories, each of which can be *enabled* or *disabled*. The algorithm characterizing ART1 is as follows:

Algorithm ART1: Adaptive Resonance Theory for Binary Inputs

This algorithm discovers clusters of a set of pattern vectors.

Input: A set of pattern vector $\mathbf{x}$ to be clustered, where $\mathbf{x} \in \{0, 1\}^m$.

Output: A set of weight vectors $\mathbf{w}_i = (w_{i1}, w_{i2}, \dots, w_{im})^T$, $i = 1, 2, \dots, n$, representing the prototype vectors of the discovered clusters, where n is the number of clusters found.

Step 0: (Initialization): Set $w_{ij}(0) = 1$, $\overline{w}_{ij}(0) = 1/(1 + m)$, for $0 < \rho \le 1$.

Step 1: Present a new pattern $\mathbf{x}$ to the input nodes.

Step 2: Enable all the output nodes.

Step 3: Use bottom-up processing to obtain a weighted sum

$$y_i = (\overline{\mathbf{w}}_i)^T \mathbf{x} = \sum_{j=1}^{m} \overline{w}_{ij} x_j, \tag{12.45}$$

where $\overline{w}_{ij}$ is the normalization of w_{ij} given by

$$\overline{w}_{ij} = \frac{w_{ij}}{\epsilon + \sum_j w_{ij}}, \qquad j = 1, 2, \dots, m. \tag{12.46}$$

The small number ϵ (usually $\epsilon = 0.5$) is included to break ties, selecting the longer of two $\mathbf{w}_i$ that both have all their bits in $\mathbf{x}$.

Step 4: Use the MAXNET procedure to find the output node i with the largest y_i value.

Step 5: Verify that $\mathbf{x}$ truly belongs to the ith cluster by performing top-down processing and form the weighted sum $\sum_j w_{ij} x_j$. Then perform the following checking:

$$\text{IF} \qquad r = \frac{\sum_{j=1}^{m} w_{ij} x_j}{\|\mathbf{x}\|} > \rho, \qquad \text{where } \|\mathbf{x}\| = \sum_{j=1}^{m} |x_j|, \tag{12.47}$$

Unsupervised Learning Networks   Chap. 12

THEN **x** belongs to the ith cluster; proceed to step 6;

ELSE IF the top layer has more than a single enabled node left, then go to step 7;

ELSE create a new output node i with its initial weights set as in step 0 and go to step 6.

Step 6: Update the weights as follows:

$$w_{ij}(t+1) = w_{ij}(t)x_j, \qquad j = 1, 2, \ldots, m, \qquad (12.48)$$

which updates the weights of the ith cluster (newly created or the existing one). Then go to step 1.

Step 7: The output node i is disabled by clamping y_i to 0. Thus, this node does not participate in the current cluster search. The algorithm goes back to step 3, and it will attempt to establish a new cluster different from i for the pattern **x.**

END ART1

We observe that the above ART1 algorithm includes both a learning mode and a performance mode. For a given input vector **x,** the algorithm can terminate in two ways. First, if a matching prototype vector $\mathbf{w}_i$ is found, then it is adjusted in step 6 according to Eq. (12.48) and the category i is outputed. Second, if no suitable prototype vector is found among the stored categories, then a new output node i^* is created, which represents a new category with a prototype vector $\mathbf{w}_i^*$ made equal to the input **x** in step 6 by Eq. (12.48); again the new category i^* is outputed. In practice, there may be a finite number of *free* output nodes available. Hence, when we cannot find a matching prototype vector and are running out of free output nodes, we end up with all the nodes disabled and hence no output. The adaptation rule in Eq. (12.48) actually deletes any bits in $\mathbf{w}_i(t)$ that are not in **x.** This is equivalent to a logical AND operation, and the input vector is said to be *masked.* Since this adaptation rule only removes bits from the prototype vector and never adds any, a given prototype vector can never cycle back to a previous value. This ensures the stability of the algorithm; that is, all weight changes cease after a finite number of presentations of any fixed set of inputs. On the other hand, the node-growing capability of ART1 allows it to have plasticity until all the free output nodes are used up. This explains why ART1 can resolve the stability-plasticity dilemma.

It is worth pointing out that the loop from step 7 back to step 3 constitutes a *search* throughout the prototype vectors based on the two criteria in Eqs. (12.45) and (12.47). This search looks at the closest prototype vector, the next closest prototype vector, and so on, by the maximum $(\overline{\mathbf{w}}_i)^T\mathbf{x}$ criterion (the first criterion) until one is found that satisfies the $r \geq \rho$ criterion (the second criterion). From Eq. (12.46), we know that $\overline{\mathbf{w}}_i$ is a normalized weight of $\mathbf{w}_i$. Hence, the first criterion is concerned with the fraction of bits in $\mathbf{w}_i$ that are also in **x.** However, the second criterion of r is concerned with the fraction of bits in **x** that are also in $\mathbf{w}_i$ because of the normalization factor $\|\mathbf{x}\|$ in Eq. (12.47). Hence, these two criteria are different; large $(\overline{\mathbf{w}}_i)^T\mathbf{x}$ cannot guarantee large r, and vice versa. The best matching prototype vector $\mathbf{w}_i^*$ should be the one with the largest $(\overline{\mathbf{w}}_{i*})^T\mathbf{x}$ and the largest r. However, such best matching is difficult to find. Thus, the strategy here is that going further away by the first criterion may actually bring us closer by the second criterion. Let us illustrate the ART1 algorithm with an example.

Example 12.3

[Stork, 1989]. In this example, an ART1 network is used to cluster four input patterns as shown in Fig. 12.12. Each input pattern is of size 5×5 mask with the black (or white) grid indicating

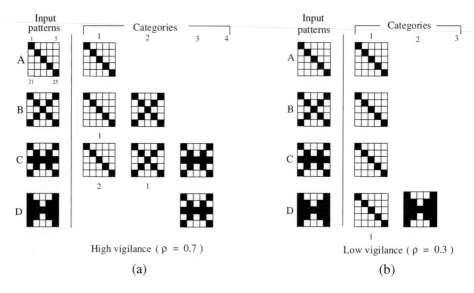

Figure 12.12 Discrete-time learning simulation of an example ART1 network. (Adapted from Carpenter and Grossberg [1987a], Copyright 1987 Academic Press, Inc.)

1 (or 0), and thus there are 25 nodes in the input layer ($m = 25$). Assume that there are four free output nodes available.

According to the initialization process of ART1, the initial weights are

$$w_{ij} = 1 \qquad \text{and} \qquad \overline{w}_{ij} = \frac{1}{26}, \qquad j = 1, 2, \ldots, 25; \ i = 1, 2, 3, 4.$$

The vigilance parameter ρ is set as 0.7. The input patterns are then fed to the ART1 algorithm one by one.

1. *Pattern A*: When pattern A is presented, one of the four output nodes has the largest output. It is denoted as number 1. Since $w_{ij} = 1$ for all i, j at this time, $r = 1$ in Eq. (12.47) and the vigilance test is passed unconditionally. This results in an unconditional definition of the first cluster. The weights are then changed according to Eqs. (12.48) and (12.46):

$$w_{1,1} = w_{1,7} = w_{1,13} = w_{1,19} = w_{1,25} = 1,$$

$$w_{1,j} = 0, \qquad j \neq 1, 7, 13, 19, 25,$$

$$\overline{w}_{1,1} = \overline{w}_{1,7} = \overline{w}_{1,13} = \overline{w}_{1,19} = \overline{w}_{1,25} = \frac{1}{0.5 + 5} = \frac{2}{11},$$

$$\overline{w}_{1,j} = 0, \qquad j \neq 1, 7, 13, 19, 25.$$

2. *Pattern B*: When pattern B is presented, there is no top-layer node competing for clustering since there is only one active node; that is, node 1 is the unconditional winner. The vigilance test indicates that

$$r = \frac{1}{\|\mathbf{x}\|} \sum_{j=1}^{25} w_{1j} x_j = \frac{1}{9} \cdot 5 = \frac{5}{9} < 0.7.$$

Hence, it fails the test. Since output node i is the single enabled node now, there is no need to search further, and pattern B is treated as a new cluster represented by another output node numbered 2. Then the corresponding weights $\mathbf{w}_2$ and $\overline{\mathbf{w}}_2$ are computed as

$$w_{2,1} = w_{2,5} = w_{2,7} = w_{2,9} = w_{2,13} = w_{2,17} = w_{2,19} = w_{2,21} = w_{2,25} = 1,$$

and the remaining weights are set as $w_2, j = 0$;

$$\overline{w}_{2,1} = \overline{w}_{2,5} = \overline{w}_{2,7} = \overline{w}_{2,9} = \overline{w}_{2,13} = \overline{w}_{2,17} = \overline{w}_{2,19} = \overline{w}_{2,21} = \overline{w}_{2,25} = \frac{2}{19},$$

and the remaining weights are set as $\overline{w}_{2,j} = 0$.

3. *Pattern C:* When pattern C is presented, the following output values are computed according to Eq. (12.45):

$$y_1 = 5\left(\frac{2}{11}\right) + 8\,(0) = 0.91 \qquad \text{and} \qquad y_2 = 9\left(\frac{2}{19}\right) + 4\,(0) = 0.95.$$

Hence, output node 2 is a winner. But the vigilance test fails since

$$r = \frac{1}{\|\mathbf{x}\|} \sum_{j=1}^{25} w_{2,j} x_j = \frac{9}{13} < 0.7.$$

Hence, output node 2 is disabled. Then since output node 1 is the only enabled node left, it is the winner. However, it also does not pass the vigilance test either since

$$r = \frac{1}{\|\mathbf{x}\|} \sum_{j=1}^{25} w_{1,j} x_j = \frac{5}{13} < 0.7.$$

Since output node 1 is the single enabled node, pattern C is considered a new cluster represented by a new output node. Following this procedure, pattern D is classified as category 3, the category that pattern C lies in. The weights $\mathbf{w}_3$ and $\overline{\mathbf{w}}_3$ are then updated to account for the new member of category 3. Figure 12.12(a) demonstrates the whole process.

Figure 12.12(b) shows the same process but with a low vigilance parameter $\rho = 0.3$. Only two categories are found: one contains patterns A, B, and C, and the other contains pattern D.

In the above discussion, we introduced the algorithm ART1 for ART1 networks. In fact, Carpenter and Grossberg designed the ART1 network as a *real-time* system. The input layer, the selection of a winner, the enable-disable mechanism, and the weight changes are all described by differential equations such as the shunting activation equation [Eq. (12.31)]and the unsupervised learning rules in Sec. 12.1. Hence, the ART1 network can be implemented by analog circuits governed by these differential equations. In this way, the ART1 network runs entirely autonomously. It does not need any external sequencing or control signals and can cope stably with an infinite stream of input data. The details of the real-time ART1 network can be found in [Freeman and Skapura, Chap. 8, 1991].

The ART1 network performs very well with perfect binary input patterns, but it is sensitive to noise in the input data. From the weight update rule in Eq. (12.48), it is understood that if random bits are sometimes missing from input patterns, the stored prototype vectors will be gradually degraded. A generalized system, the ART2 network [Carpenter and Grossberg, 1987b], was developed to self-organize recognition categories for analog as well as binary input sequences. The major difference between ART1 and ART2 networks is the input layer. Because of the stability criterion for analog inputs, a three-layer feedback system in the input layer of ART2 is required: a bottom layer where input patterns are read in, a top layer where inputs from the output layer are read in, and a middle layer where the top and bottom patterns are brought together to form a matched pattern which is then fed back to the top and bottom input layers. Furthermore, unlike the situation in Eqs. (12.45) and (12.46), the similarity between the input vector $\mathbf{x}$ and the prototypes (weights), $\mathbf{w}_i$ (or $\overline{\mathbf{w}}_i$), is measured by their Euclidean distance $\|\mathbf{x} - \mathbf{w}_i\|$ (or $\|\mathbf{x} - \overline{\mathbf{w}}_i\|$) in ART2. An illustrative example is shown in Fig. 12.13. These results were obtained by Carpenter and Grossberg [1987b] for 50 analog input patterns using ART2. Figure 12.13(a) shows that the 50 patterns were grouped into 34 different categories with a high value of the vigilance parameter, while with a lower vigilance value the 50 input patterns were organized into 20 categories as shown in Fig. 12.13(b).

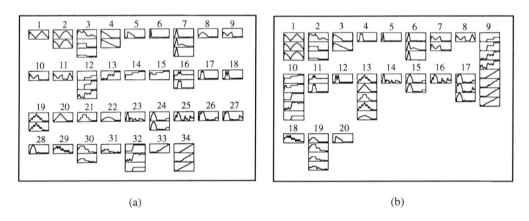

(a)   (b)

Figure 12.13 ART2 network. (a) Category grouping of 50 analog input patterns into 34 recognition categories. (b) Category grouping of 50 analog input patterns into 20 recognition categories with a lower vigilance value. (Adapted from Carpenter and Grossberg [1987b], © Optical Society of America.)

12.5 COUNTERPROPAGATION NETWORKS

The counterpropagation network, proposed by Hecht-Nielsen [1987a,b, 1988], is composed of two sets of instar-outstar models as shown in Fig. 12.14. More precisely, the instar is actually a Kohonen network. The network is designed to approximate a continuous function $f: A \subset \mathbb{R}^m \to B \subset \mathbb{R}^n$ defined on a compact set A. The full network works best if the inverse function f^{-1} exists and is continuous. It is assumed that the $\mathbf{x}$ vectors are drawn from A in accordance with a fixed probability density function $p(\mathbf{x})$. During the training, training examples $(\mathbf{x}^k, \mathbf{y}^k)$ of f [where $\mathbf{y}^k = f(\mathbf{x}^k)$] are presented to the network from both sides as shown in Fig. 12.14(b). These $\mathbf{x}$ and $\mathbf{y}$ vectors then propagate through the network in a *counterflow* manner to yield output vectors $\mathbf{x}^*$ and $\mathbf{y}^*$ which are intended to be approximations of $\mathbf{x}$ and $\mathbf{y}$, respectively.

Consider the forward-only counterpropagation network in Fig. 12.14(a). The first layer is the Kohonen network (i.e., a winner-take-all network). For a given input vector $\mathbf{x}$, a

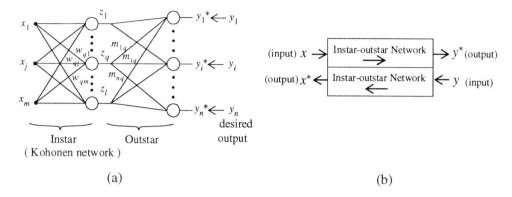

Figure 12.14 Structure of the counterpropagation network. (a) The forward-only counterpropagation network. (b) Full counterpropagation network.

competition is held among the hidden nodes to determine which node's weight vector lies closest to the input vector **x.** The winning node (e.g., node q) has its output signal set to 1 (i.e., $z_q = 1$), and all other nodes have their output signals set to 0. At the same time, the winner's weight vector (i.e., $\mathbf{w}_q$) is updated according to the Kohonen learning rule in Eq. (12.8). After training with a large number of training data, the $\mathbf{w}_i$ vectors arrange themselves in $\mathfrak{R}^n$ in such a way that they are approximately equiprobable in a nearest-neighbor sense with respect to **x** vectors drawn from A in accordance with the probability density function $p(\mathbf{x})$. The output layer of the counterpropagation network is an outstar. It receives the **z**-vector signals from the hidden layer ($z_q = 1$ and $z_i = 0$ for $i \neq q$). The output y_i^* of output node i is governed by

$$y_i^* = \sum_{q=1}^{l} m_{iq} z_q, \qquad (12.49)$$

which simply selects the weight associated with the input to node i from the winning node of the hidden layer and emits this weight value as the node output signal y_i^*. The weights m_{iq}, $i = 1, 2,\ldots, n$, are updated according to the outstar learning rule in Eq. (12.44) to determine the averages of the y_i values associated with the **x** inputs within the equiprobable "win regions" of the nodes of the hidden layer.

The counterpropagation network is statistically optimal in two ways: First, the $\mathbf{w}_i$ vectors are equiprobable. Second, the vector $\mathbf{m}_q = (m_{1q},\ldots, m_{iq},\ldots, m_{nq})^T$ is the statistical average of the **y** vectors associated with the **x** vectors that activate the associated hidden layer node z_q. When this goal is achieved, the training can be terminated and the network functions exactly as a *lookup table*. The input vector is compared with the instar weight vectors to find the closest match $\mathbf{w}_q$, and the outstar weight vector $\mathbf{m}_q$ associated with $\mathbf{w}_q$ is then emitted by the network. The mean squared error of the network can be made as small as desired by choosing a sufficiently large number (l) of hidden nodes. Hence, for continuous functions, the counterpropagation network is in principle just as effective as the back-propagation network; that is, it is a universal continuous-function approximator. However, it appears to be less efficient since the number of hidden nodes needed to achieve a particular level of accuracy is often much greater than that required by the back-propagation network. Nevertheless, the greatest appeal of counterpropagation networks is their learning speed. Compared to other mapping networks, it typically requires orders of magnitude fewer training steps to achieve its best performance. This is usually true for any *hybrid learning scheme* that combines unsupervised learning (e.g., instar learning) and supervised learning (e.g., outstar learning). We shall examine another important neural network model of this kind in the next section.

One important variant of the counterpropagation network is operating it in an *interpolation* mode after training has been completed. In this mode, more than one hidden node is allowed to win the competition. Thus, we have the first winner, second winner, third winner, and so on, with nonzero output values. If the total strength $\sum_q z_q$ of these multiple winners is normalized to 1, then the total output will interpolate linearly among the individual $\mathbf{m}_q$ vectors. To select which nodes to fire, we can choose all those with weight vectors within a certain radius of the input $\mathbf{x}$ or just the k closest ones for some fixed k.

12.6 RADIAL BASIS FUNCTION NETWORKS

Another hybrid network, which also has the architecture of the instar-outstar model and uses the hybrid unsupervised and supervised learning scheme, is the *radial basis function network* (RBFN) suggested by Moody and Darken [1989]. Like the counterpropagation network, the RBFN is designed to perform input-output mapping trained by examples $(\mathbf{x}^k, \mathbf{d}^k)$, $k = 1, 2,..., p$. The RBFN is based on the concept of the locally tuned and overlapping receptive field structure studied in the cerebral cortex, the visual cortex, and so on. Figure 12.15 is a schematic diagram of the RBFN. Unlike the instar-outstar model in which the hidden nodes are linear winner-take-all nodes, the hidden nodes in the RBFN have normalized Gaussian activation function

$$z_q = g_q(\mathbf{x}) \triangleq \frac{R_q(\mathbf{x})}{\sum_{k=1}^{l} R_k(\mathbf{x})} = \frac{\exp\left[-|\mathbf{x} - \mathbf{m}_q|^2/2\sigma_q^2\right]}{\sum_{k=1}^{l} \exp\left[-|\mathbf{x} - \mathbf{m}_k|^2/2\sigma_k^2\right]}, \qquad (12.50)$$

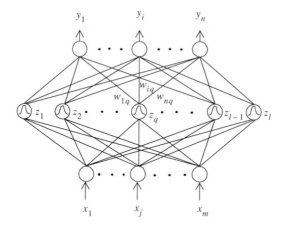

Figure 12.15 Structure of the RBFN.

where $\mathbf{x}$ is the input vector. Thus, hidden node q gives a maximum response to input vectors close to $\mathbf{m}_q$. Each hidden node q is said to have its own *receptive field* $R_q(\mathbf{x})$ in the input space, which is a region centered on $\mathbf{m}_q$ with size proportional to σ_q, where $\mathbf{m}_q$ and σ_q^2 are the mean (an m-dimensional vector) and variance of the qth Gaussian function. Gaussian functions are a particular example of *radial basis functions*. The output of the RBFN is simply the weighted sum of the hidden node output:

$$y_i = a_i \left(\sum_{q=1}^{l} w_{iq} z_q + \theta_i \right), \tag{12.51}$$

where $a_i(\cdot)$ is the output activation function and θ_i is the threshold value. Generally, $a_i(\cdot)$ is an identity function (i.e., the output node is a linear unit) and $\theta_i = 0$.

The purpose of the RBFN is to pave the input space with overlapping receptive fields. For an input vector $\mathbf{x}$ lying somewhere in the input space, the receptive fields with centers close to it will be appreciably activated. The output of the RBFN is then the weighted sum of the activations of these receptive fields. In the extreme case, if $\mathbf{x}$ lies in the center of the receptive field for hidden node q, then $\mathbf{x} = \mathbf{m}_q$. If we ignore the overlaps between different receptive fields, then only hidden node q is activated (a winner) and the corresponding weight vector $\mathbf{w}_q = (w_{1q}, w_{2q}, \ldots, w_{nq})^T$ is chosen as the output, assuming linear output units. Hence, the RBFN acts like a *gradient-type* forward-only counterpropagation network.

The RBFN is basically trained by the hybrid learning rule: unsupervised learning in the input layer and supervised learning in the output layer. The weights in the output layer can be updated simply by using the delta learning rule:

$$\Delta w_{iq} = \eta (d_i - y_i) z_q, \tag{12.52}$$

assuming linear output units. When averaged over the p training pairs, this minimizes the following mean squared error cost function:

$$\begin{aligned} E(w_{iq}) &= \frac{1}{2} \sum_k \sum_i [d_i^k - y_i^k]^2 \\ &= \frac{1}{2} \sum_k \sum_i \left[d_i^k - \sum_{q=1}^{l} w_{iq} z_q^k \right]^2 \\ &= \frac{1}{2} \sum_k \sum_i \left[d_i^k - \sum_{q=1}^{l} w_{iq} g_q(\mathbf{x}^k) \right]^2 . \end{aligned} \tag{12.53}$$

The unsupervised part of the learning involves the determination of the receptive field centers $\mathbf{m}_q$ and widths σ_q, $q = 1, 2, \ldots, l$. The proper centers $\mathbf{m}_q$ can be found by unsupervised learning rules such as the vector quantization approach, competitive learning rules, or simply the Kohonen learning rule in Eq. (12.8); that is,

$$\Delta \mathbf{m}_{\text{closest}} = \eta (\mathbf{x} - \mathbf{m}_{\text{closest}}), \tag{12.54}$$

where $\mathbf{m}_{\text{closest}}$ is the center of the receptive field closest to the input vector $\mathbf{x}$ and the other centers are kept unchanged. We can also emulate the Kohonen feature map approach in Eq. (12.28) to adjust all the centers with the update value tuned by the relative "distance" between a center $\mathbf{m}_q$ and an input vector $\mathbf{x}$. Then, once the receptive field centers $\mathbf{m}_q$ have been found, their widths can be determined by minimizing the following objective function with respect to the σ_q:

$$E = \frac{1}{2} \sum_{q=1}^{l} \left[\left| \sum_{r=1}^{l} R_q\left(\mathbf{m}_r\right) \left| \frac{\mathbf{m}_q - \mathbf{m}_r}{2\sigma_q} \right|^2 - \gamma \right]^2 \right], \qquad (12.55)$$

where γ is an overlap parameter. The effect of minimizing this function is to ensure that the receptive field nodes form a smooth, contiguous interpolation over those regions of the input space that they represent. In practice, the widths σ_q are usually determined by an ad hoc choice such as the mean distance to the first few nearest neighbors $\mathbf{m}$ (the γ-nearest-neighbors heuristic). In the simplest case, the following *first-nearest-neighbor* heuristic can be used [Lin and Lee, 1991b]:

$$\sigma_q = \frac{\left| \mathbf{m}_q - \mathbf{m}_{\text{closest}} \right|}{\gamma}, \qquad (12.56)$$

where $\mathbf{m}_{\text{closest}}$ is the closest vector to $\mathbf{m}_q$.

The RBFN offers a viable alternative to the two-layer neural network in many applications of signal processing, pattern recognition, control, and function approximation. As an example, a RBFN was used to learn and predict a chaotic time series resulting from integrating the Mackey-Glass differential delay equation in Eq. (10.63) (see Fig. 10.12) [Moody and Darken, 1989] with satisfactory results. In fact, it has been shown that the RBFN can fit an arbitrary function with just one hidden layer [Hartman et al., 1990]. Also, it has been shown that a Gaussian sum density estimator can approximate any probability density function to any desired degree of accuracy [Sorenson and Alspach, 1971]. Although the RBFN generally cannot quite achieve the accuracy of the back-propagation network, it can be trained several orders of magnitude faster than the back-propagation network. This is again due to the advantage of hybrid-learning networks which have only one layer of connections trained by supervised learning.

The RBFN can also be trained by the error back-propagation rule and becomes a purely supervised learning network. The goal is to minimize the cost function in Eq. (12.53) globally. In this approach, the output layer is still trained by Eq. (12.52). The output error (i.e., the difference between the desired output and the actual output) is then back-propagated to the layer of receptive fields to update their centers and widths. According to the chain rule, the supervised learning rule for the RBFN can be derived as

$$\Delta w_{iq} = \eta_w \left(d_i - y_i \right) z_q,$$

$$\Delta \mathbf{m}_q = \eta_m \sum_i \left(d_i - y_i \right) \frac{\partial y_i}{\partial \mathbf{m}_q}, \qquad (12.57)$$

$$\Delta \sigma_q = \eta_\sigma \sum_i \left(d_i - y_i \right) \frac{\partial y_i}{\partial \sigma_q},$$

where the derivatives $\partial y_i / \partial \mathbf{m}_q$ and $\partial y_i / \partial \sigma_q$ can be obtained using the chain rule on Eqs. (12.50) and (12.51). In this way, the centers and widths of the receptive fields can be adjusted dynamically. This technique has been used to form a proper input space representation for learning control [Franklin, 1989]. Unfortunately, the RBFN with back-propagation learning does not learn appreciably faster than the back-propagation network. Also, it may happen that the Gaussians learn large widths and lose the locality intended in the RBFN. One solution to the *large-width* problem is to control the effective radius of receptive fields [Lee and Kil, 1988]. The idea is that when an input pattern lies far away from the existing receptive fields, a new receptive field (i.e., a new hidden node) is added to account for this new pattern. This also provides the RBFN with node-growing capability, and thus the minimally necessary number of receptive fields (hidden nodes) of the RBFN can be determined. Such a learning scheme is usually composed of two phases. In phase one, the proper number of hidden nodes is determined (structure-learning phase). In phase two, the weights, centers, and widths are fine-tuned by a purely back-propagation rule and the hidden nodes are not generated anymore (parameter learning phase).

Another learning rule for the RBFN with node-growing capability is based on the *orthogonal least squares learning algorithm* [Chen et al., 1991]. This procedure chooses the centers of radial basis functions one by one in a rational way until an adequate network has been constructed. This technique has been used to train the RBFN as a communication channel equalizer to filter out channel noise [Chen et al., 1991]. In [Leonard et al., 1992], the RBFN is extended by adding additional output nodes indicating the confidence or correctness of the RBFN's predictions. It is not easy for conventional neural networks to warn the user when they make predications without adequate training data (extrapolating), and furthermore, they do not provide error estimates for their predictions. However, the RBFN has an intrinsic ability to indicate when it is extrapolating since activation of the receptive field is directly related to the proximity of the test point to the training data.

12.7 ADAPTIVE BIDIRECTIONAL ASSOCIATIVE MEMORIES

Previously we introduced both discrete bidirectional associative memory (BAM) [Eqs. (11.29) and (11.30)] and continuous BAM [Eq. (11.46) or (12.34)]. However, thus far, we have not incorporated adaptive learning abilities into BAMs. In fact, any of the four basic unsupervised learning rules can be used as learning rules for BAMs. A BAM with such a learning ability is called an *adaptive bidirectional associative memory* (ABAM) [Kosko, 1987, 1992a]. Hence, an ABAM can be specified by either Eq. (11.46) (additive BAM) or Eq. (12.34) (shunting BAM) associated with one of the four basic unsupervised learning rules. For simplicity of notation, both additive BAM and shunting BAM can be specified by the following general dynamic formula adopted from the Cohen-Grossberg activation dynamics of Eq. (11.15) in Theorem 11.2:

$$
\dot{y}_i = -a_i(y_i)\left[b_i(y_i) - \sum_{j=1}^{m} w_{ij}s_j(x_j)\right],
$$

$$
\dot{x}_j = -a_j(x_j)\left[b_j(x_j) - \sum_{i=1}^{n} w_{ij}s_i(y_i)\right],
$$

(12.58)

where $a_i(y_i)$, $a_j(x_j)$, $b_i(y_i)$, and $b_j(x_j)$ are coefficient functions and $s(\cdot)$ is a monotonic nondecreasing signal function that transforms x_j and y_i to the bounded signals $s_j(x_j)$ and $s_i(y_i)$, respectively [see Eq. (12.6)]. Note that Eq. (12.58) can be reduced to Eqs. (11.46) and (12.34) by setting the coefficient functions $a_i(y_i)$, $a_j(x_j)$, $b_i(y_i)$, and $b_j(x_j)$ properly.

With the general dynamics formula in Eq. (12.58), the *Hebbian ABAM* can be specified by

$$\dot{y}_i = -a_i(y_i) \left[b_i(y_i) - \sum_{j=1}^{m} w_{ij} s_j(x_j) \right], \tag{12.59}$$

$$\dot{x}_j = -a_j(x_j) \left[b_j(x_j) - \sum_{i=1}^{n} w_{ij} s_i(y_i) \right], \tag{12.60}$$

$$\dot{w}_{ij} = -w_{ij} + s_i(y_i) s_j(x_j), \tag{12.61}$$

which are a combination of Eqs. (12.58) and (12.1). This ABAM model reduces to the Cohen-Grossberg model if no learning occurs, if the two *X* and *Y* layers collapse into one autoassociative layer, and if the constant weight matrix **W** is symmetric. Similarly, we have a *competitive ABAM* (CABAM) which uses the competitive learning rule in Eq. (12.5) in place of Eq. (12.61):

$$\dot{w}_{ij} = s_i(y_i) [s_j(x_j) - w_{ij}]. \tag{12.62}$$

CABAMs are topologically equivalent to ART systems. Similarly, the *differential Hebbian ABAM* uses the differential Hebbian learning rule in Eq. (12.14) in place of Eq. (12.61):

$$\dot{w}_{ij} = -w_{ij} + s_i(y_i) s_j(x_j) + \dot{s}_i(y_i) \dot{s}_j(x_j). \tag{12.63}$$

The *differential competitive ABAM* uses the differential competitive learning rule in Eq. (12.18) in place of Eq. (12.61):

$$\dot{w}_{ij} = \dot{s}_i(y_i) [s_j(x_j) - w_{ij}]. \tag{12.64}$$

The stability of these ABAMs is guaranteed by the ABAM theorem, which can be proved by finding a Lyapunov function *E* for the above ABAM dynamical systems [Kosko, 1992a].

12.8 HIERARCHICAL NETWORKS—NEOCOGNITRON

The competitive learning models discussed so far have a single layer in which exactly one node wins for each input pattern. To form a *multilayer unsupervised* (or competitive) *network,* we need to allow several winners per layer so that input patterns are analyzed by subsequent layers to detect successively higher-order patterns in the data. This multilayer competitive learning network approach is illustrated in Fig. 12.16. Competitive learning takes place in the context of sets of hierarchically layered nodes. The nodes in a given layer are broken into a set of nonoverlapping clusters, in each of which one node will win. In other words, each cluster is a winner-take-all cluster, and thus each node within a cluster inhibits every other node in that cluster. Also, every node in every cluster receives inputs from the same sources. One can think of the configuration of active nodes on any given layer as representing the input pattern for the next higher level, and there can be an arbitrary number of such layers. One important characteristic of hierarchical networks is that the connections between layers are usually *sparse* and *local.* Hence, a node on each layer

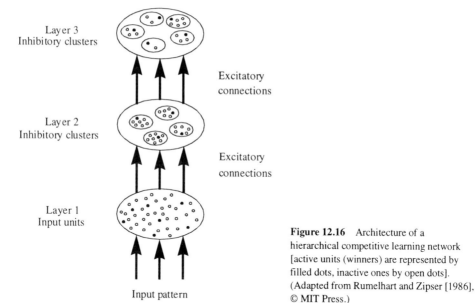

Layer 3
Inhibitory clusters

Excitatory
connections

Layer 2
Inhibitory clusters

Excitatory
connections

Layer 1
Input units

Figure 12.16 Architecture of a
hierarchical competitive learning network
[active units (winners) are represented by
filled dots, inactive ones by open dots].
(Adapted from Rumelhart and Zipser [1986],
© MIT Press.)

Input pattern

receives connections only from a restricted localized subset (receptive field) of the previous layer's nodes. The sparse local connections between the layers indicate the advantage that the nodes of each layer have in to concern with the processing of only a limited amount of information. The total global situation is then pieced together as one ascends from one hierarchical layer to the next. In this section, we shall briefly describe a representative hierarchical neural network—the *neocognitron,* proposed by Fukushima and Miyaka [1980, 1984; Fukushima, 1988, 1989; Fukushima and Wake, 1991; Fukushima et al., 1983]. We shall provide only a functional description of this network, while detailed equations of the neocognitron can be found in [Fukushima and Wake, 1991].

The hierarchical structure of the neocognitron is illustrated in Fig. 12.17 in which each rectangle represents a two-dimensional array of cells and is called a cell plane. There are nine layers, each with a varying number of planes. The size of each layer, in terms of the number of nodes, is given below each layer in the figure. For example, layer U_{S1} has 12 planes of 19×19 nodes arranged in a square matrix. The input layer U_0, called the retina, consists of a two-dimensional array of receptor cells. Each succeeding stage has a layer consisting of cells called S cells, followed by another layer of cells called C cells. Thus, in the whole network, layers of S cells and C cells are arranged alternately, and the pair U_{Sl} and U_{Cl} constitutes the lth stage. In layer U_{S1}, each S cell receives input connections from a small region of the retina. Nodes in the corresponding positions on all planes receive input connections from the same region of the retina, and the region from which an S cell receives input connections defines the receptive field of the cell. In intermediate layers, each node on an S plane receives input connections from the corresponding locations on all C planes in the previous stage. C cells have connections from a region of S cells on the C plane in the preceding layer. If the number of C planes is the same as that of S planes at that stage, then each C cell has connections from S cells on a single S plane. If there are fewer C planes than S planes, some C cells may receive connections from more than one S plane. The output

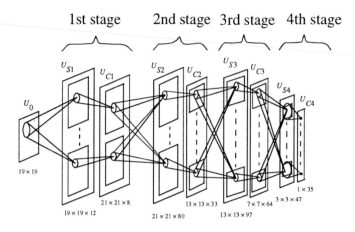

1st stage   2nd stage 3rd stage 4th stage

U_{S1} U_{C1} U_{S2} U_{C2} U_{S3} U_{C3} U_{S4} U_{C4}

U_0

19 × 19

1 × 35

3 × 3 × 47

21 × 21 × 8   13 × 13 × 33   7 × 7 × 64

19 × 19 × 12   21 × 21 × 80   13 × 13 × 97

Figure 12.17   Hierarchical network structure of the neocognitron. The numerals at the bottom of the figure show the total numbers of S and C cells in individual layers of the network.

layer U_{C4} is the recognition layer representing the final result of the pattern recognition by the neocognitron. The neocognitron shown in Fig. 12.17 is for the recognition of 35 handwritten alphanumeric characters. Hence, the output layer U_{C4} has 35 nodes, each of which represents a number or a character.

S cells are feature-extracting cells. Each S cell on a single plane is sensitive to the same feature but at different locations on its input (previous) layer. S cells on different planes respond to different features, and S cells at higher layers respond to features at higher levels of abstraction. C cells integrate the response of groups of S cells. Because each S cell is looking for the same feature in a different location, the C cell's response is less sensitive to the exact location of the feature on the input layer. This gives the neocognitron its capacity for position-invariant recognition. The connections converging on the cells in a cell plane are homogeneous; that is, all the cells in a cell plane receive input connections of the same spatial distribution, in which only the positions of the preceding cells shift in parallel with the position of the cells in the cell plane. The density of cells in each layer is designed to decrease with the order of the stage because the cells in higher stages usually have larger receptive fields and the neighboring cells receive similar signals.

Figure 12.18 shows the details of the connections between cells in the network. Each S cell is associated with a subsidiary cell called a V cell which has the same receptive field as the S cell. The output of the V cell has an inhibitory effect on the S cells. The weights on the connections to S cells are variable and are adjusted by training (or learning). After the training of S cells with the aid of the subsidiary V cells, they can extract features from the input pattern. The features the S cells extract are determined by training patterns given to the input layer. On the other hand, the weights on connections from S cells to C cells are fixed and invariable. The training of the network will be discussed later. Since this learning is in the form of Hebbian learning, the weights can only increase without upper bound. However, the inhibitory input from the V cells keeps the output value of S cells finite even for large weight values.

In summary, the process of feature extraction by S cells and the tolerance of positional shift by C cells are repeated in the neocognitron. Tolerating positional errors a little

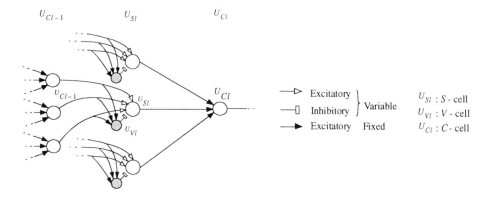

Figure 12.18 Connections between cells in the neocognitron.

at a time at each stage is effective in deformation-invariant pattern recognition. During this process, local features that are extracted at a lower stage are gradually integrated into more global features. Finally, each C cell of the recognition layer at the highest stage integrates all the information of the input pattern and responds to only one specific pattern. Figure 12.19 illustrates some of the details of how the neocognitron operates. The neocognitron decomposes the input pattern into elemental parts consisting of line segments at various angles of rotation, and the system then integrates these elements into higher-order structures at each successive level in the network. Cells at each level integrate the responses of cells in the previous level over a finite area. This behavior gives the neocognitron its ability to identify characters regardless of their exact position or size in the field of view of the retina.

The neocognitron can be trained by either supervised learning or unsupervised learning. Let us consider only the unsupervised learning approach because of its simplicity. In unsupervised learning, the network is simply presented with a large number of character examples and is not told which numeral each example corresponds to. Hence, a competition mechanism is used to select the S cells that will have their weights modified. To understand how this works, we can think of the S planes on a given layer as being stacked vertically on top of one another, aligned so that cells at corresponding locations are directly on top of one another. We can now imagine many overlapping columns running perpendicular to this stack. These columns define groups of S cells, where all of the members in a group have receptive fields in approximately the same location of the input layer. With this model in mind, we now apply an input pattern and examine the response of the S cells in each column. To ensure that each S cell provides a distinct response, we can initialize the excitatory weights to small, positive random values, and the inhibitory weights (on the connection from the C cell) to zero. We first choose the winning S cell whose response is the strongest in each column. This is the first competition. Then we examine the individual planes so that if a plane contains two or more winning S cells, we will disregard all but the cell responding the strongest. This is the second competition. With these two parts of competition, we can locate the S cell on each plane whose response is the strongest, subject to the condition that each of these cells is in a different column. In other words, each of the final winning S cells has different receptive fields. Only the weights of the final winning S cells are

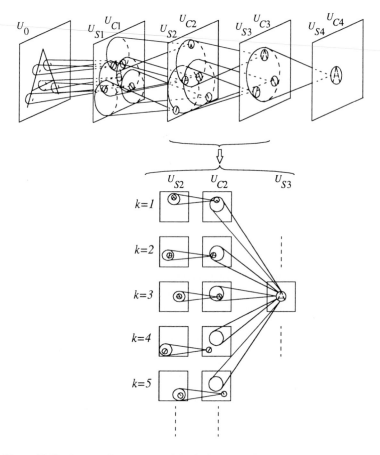

Figure 12.19 Process of pattern recognition in the neocognitron.

increased proportional to their input signals from the previous layer. Note that the weights can only increase and that there is no upper bound on the weight value. Once the cells on a plane begin to respond to a certain feature, they tend to respond less to other features. After a short time, each plane develops a strong response to a particular feature. A characteristic of the neocognitron training process is its *weight-sharing mechanism*. This mechanism is arranged so that whenever a cell, the seed cell, in a plane has its weights modified, all the cells of the plane immediately adopt these new weights. Therefore, the homogeneity of connections within cell planes is always preserved, and all the cells in the cell plane come to extract the same feature at different locations.

12.9 CONCLUDING REMARKS

There are other interesting unsupervised learning rules that were not discussed in this chapter because of space limitations. For principal component analysis, there is also *self-supervised back propagation* [Sanger, 1989a], *anti-Hebbian learning* [Rubner and Tavan, 1989;

Rubner and Schulten, 1990], and the *multilayer Hebbian learning network* [Linsker, 1988]. For the Kohonen learning rule, Hecht-Nielsen [1987c] proposed another weight initialization method called *convex combination* and another learning procedure called *radial sprouting*. The theoretical issues of AVQ can be found in [Kosko, 1991]. With the same notion of including the time derivatives of signals into learning as in differential competitive learning, Klopf [1986, 1988] independently proposed another differential Hebbian learning scheme called the *drive-reinforcement model*.

The convergence properties, the convergence time, and the capacity of the Hamming memory were studied in [Floréen, 1991]. Willshaw and von der Malsburg [1976] proposed another way to design an unsupervised learning network that self-organizes into a feature map. They used ordinary competitive learning with the addition of lateral connections within the output layer. Kohonen [1988] used the Kohonen feature map for speech recognition and built a so-called *neural phonetic typewriter*. The convergence property of the Kohonen feature map was analyzed in [Kohonen, 1989; Ritter et al., 1992]. Other variants of the Kohonen feature map can be found in [Kangas et al., 1990]. Details about the applications of Kohonen feature maps can be found in [Ritter et al., 1992]. In [Bauer and Pawelzik, 1992], the degree of neighborhood preservation of the Kohonen feature map from the input space to the output space is measured quantitatively by a *topographic product*. Another technique closely related to the Kohonen feature mapping approach is the *elastic net* method, which has shown its computational power on the traveling salesperson problem [Durbin and Willshaw, 1987; Burr 1988].

For ART networks, more details on the instar-outstar model can be found in Grossberg [1982a]. Caudell [1992] implemented a real-time ART1 model by a hybrid optoelectronic technique. Improved ART2 models were proposed in [Carpenter et al., 1991a; Peper et al., 1993]. ART3 and its modification can be found in [Carpenter and Grossberg, 1990; Healy et al., 1993]. For counterpropagation networks, many applications have been investigated, including pattern classification, data compression, speech recognition, function approximation, and statistical analysis [Hecht-Nielsen, 1988; Huang and Lippmann, 1987; Lippmann, 1989a,b; Freeman and Skapura, 1991]. The applications of RBFNs include speech recognition [Moody and Darken, 1989] and control [Sanner and Slotine, 1992]. The theoretic details of the ABAM and its generalization can be found in [Kosko, 1990, 1992]. VLSI implementation of the neocognitron has been proposed in [White and Elmasry, 1992].

12.10 PROBLEMS

12.1 Show that in Sanger's learning rule in Eq. (12.3), the weight vector becomes exactly the first n principal component directions in order of the input data. (*Hint*: See [Sanger, 1989b].)

12.2 Randomly generate 50 two-dimensional pattern vectors from each of the following Gaussian distributions:

$$p_1(\mathbf{x}) = \frac{1}{\sigma_1\sqrt{2\pi}}\exp\frac{-\left|\mathbf{x}-\mathbf{m}_1\right|^2}{2\sigma_1^2}, \qquad p_2(\mathbf{x}) = \frac{1}{\sigma_2\sqrt{2\pi}}\exp\frac{-\left|\mathbf{x}-\mathbf{m}_2\right|^2}{2\sigma_2^2},$$

where $\mathbf{m}_1 = [0.5, 0.5]^T$, $\mathbf{m}_2 = [-0.5, -0.5]^T$, and $\sigma_1 = \sigma_2 = 1$. Use Sanger's learning rule to train a two-node principal component network using the generated 100 pattern vectors to obtain stable final weight vectors. Comment on the relationship of the final weight vectors and the distribution of training patterns.

12.3 Show that if the weight vectors in the Kohonen learning rule are not normalized, then it is possible that the weight vector closest to the input vector (i.e., the winner) will not be chosen when the dot product metric [Eq. (12.10)] is used.

12.4 Repeat Example 12.1 (redraw Fig. 12.4) but use the following training patterns:

$$\{x^1, x^2, x^3, x^4, x^5\} = \{1 \angle 15°; 1 \angle 70°; 1 \angle 55°; 1 \angle -60°; 1 \angle -30°\}.$$

12.5 Construct a 4×3 ABAM [see Eqs. (12.59)–(12.61)]. Randomly generate 100 four-dimensional X-layer pattern vectors and 100 three-dimensional associated Y-layer pattern vectors. Train the ABAM using the four unsupervised learning rules in Sec. 12.1 and draw the squared-error curves of the four learning schemes for 5000 iterations.

12.6 Consider a four-node MAXNET receiving an input vector

$$y^0 = [0.4, 0.8, 0.7, 0.5]^T .$$

(a) Find the ϵ value in Eq. (12.25) that can suppress the output of the weakest node exactly to zero after the first cycle.
(b) Find the subsequent responses of the network using the ϵ value in part (a).

12.7 Design a Hamming network to classify the following three bipolar binary class prototype vectors:

$$s^1 = [1, 1, 1, 1, -1, -1, 1, 1, 1]^T ,$$

$$s^2 = [-1, 1, -1, -1, 1, -1, -1, 1, -1]^T ,$$

$$s^3 = [1, 1, 1, -1, 1, -1, -1, 1, -1]^T .$$

Check the sample responses of both layers of the designed network using the test input vector $x = [1, 1, 1, 1, 1, 1, 1, 1, 1]^T$.

12.8 Consider the following pattern pairs:

$$\begin{array}{ll} x^1 = [1, 1, 1, 1, 1]^T , & y^1 = [1, 0, 1]^T ; \\ x^2 = [0, 1, 1, 1, 0]^T , & y^2 = [1, 0, 0]^T ; \\ x^3 = [1, 0, 1, 0, 1]^T , & y^3 = [0, 1, 0]^T ; \\ x^4 = [0, 0, 1, 1, 0]^T , & y^4 = [1, 1, 1]^T ; \\ x^5 = [1, 0, 0, 0, 0]^T , & y^5 = [0, 1, 1]^T . \end{array}$$

(a) Use the self-organizing feature map algorithm to map the above x^i vectors with cyclic repetition onto a 5×5 array of nodes. In the training, adopt the discrete neighborhood function shown in Fig. 12.7(a) and decrease the neighborhood radius from covering the entire array initially (radius of 2 units) to a radius of zero after 1000 steps. For the learning constant, decrease α linearly from 0.5 to 0.04 for the first 1000 steps and then decrease it from 0.04 to 0 for steps 1000 to 10,000. Draw the feature maps at different learning steps as shown in Fig. 12.8.
(b) Based on the self-organizing feature map constructed in part (a), set up a self-organizing motor map to obtain the $(x^i - y^i)$ mapping given above.
(c) Assume that x_1, x_2, and x_3 belong to class 1 and that x_4 and x_5 belong to class 2. Use the LVQ technique to perform this supervised pattern classification task.

12.9 Train a 10×10 self-organizing feature map on a set of two-dimensional pattern vectors uniformly distributed in a disk centered at $(0, 0)$ with radius 1. Permit the neighborhood function around the winner to decay much faster than normally. Try several such neighborhood functions to obtain a "folded (twisted)" feature map that fails to preserve the topological ordering of the training data.

12.10 Solve the differential equation in Eq. (12.35), which is the shunting activation equation for the input layer of the instar-outstar model.

12.11 Consider the four noise-free unipolar binary pattern vectors A, B, C, and D shown in Fig. 12.12 and the distorted versions of them.

(a) Set the vigilance level at 0.95. Train the ART1 network with patterns 1 through 4 first and then submit the distorted patterns one by one as inputs to the network. Record the output of the network for each input presentation.

(b) Repeat part (a) with the vigilance level set at 0.9.

(c) Repeat part (a) with the vigilance level set at 0.85.

(d) Comment on the limitations of an ART1 network trained with noisy versions of the prototype vectors.

12.12 Design a counterpropagation network to perform the following vector-to-vector mapping:

$$\mathbf{x}^1 = [1,-1,-1,1,1,1,-1,-1,-1]^T, \qquad \mathbf{y}^1 = [1,1,1,-1,-1,-1,-1,1,-1]^T,$$
$$\mathbf{x}^2 = [-1,1,1,1,-1,-1,1,1,1]^T, \qquad \mathbf{y}^2 = [1,-1,-1,-1,-1,-1,-1,-1,1]^T,$$
$$\mathbf{x}^3 = [1,-1,1,-1,1,1,-1,1,1]^T, \qquad \mathbf{y}^3 = [-1,1,-1,1,-1,-1,1,-1,1]^T.$$

Check the functionality of the designed network.

12.13 (a) Train an RBF network with three hidden nodes to solve the XOR problem using (i) the hybrid learning rule and (ii) the purely supervised learning rule.

(b) Train an RBF network with four hidden nodes to solve the XOR problem using the purely supervised learning rule, where each radial basis function center is determined by each piece of input data.

(c) State the differences between an RBF network and a back-propagation network and explain why the former can learn much faster than the latter.

12.14 Justify the comment that the output of an RBF network in response to a random input vector may be approximated by a Gaussian distribution and that the approximation improves as the number of hidden nodes (centers) is increased. (*Hint*: Consider the central limit theorem in the probability theorem.)

12.15 Prove the stability of the Hebbian ABAM described by Eqs. (12.59)–(12.61) using the Lyapunov theorem. [*Hint*: Consider the following Lyapunov function for the Hebbian ABAM:

$$E = -\sum_i \sum_j s_i(y_i) s_j(x_j) w_{ij} + \sum_i \int_0^{y_i} s_i'(\theta_i) b_i(\theta_i) d\theta_i + \sum_j \int_0^{x_j} s_j'(\epsilon_j) b_j(\epsilon_j) d\epsilon_j + \frac{1}{2} \sum_i \sum_j w_{ij}^2.$$

13

Recurrent Neural Networks

A *recurrent neural network,* also called a *feedback network,* is one in which self-loops and backward connections between nodes are allowed. One of the consequences of these connections is that dynamical behaviors not possible with strictly feedforward networks, such as *limit cycles* and *chaos,* can be produced with recurrent networks. Recurrent networks with symmetric weight connections always converge to a stable state as we have seen in Hopfield networks. In this chapter, we consider recurrent neural networks without the symmetry constraint. Such networks have more complex dynamical behaviors than both feedforward networks and symmetric recurrent networks. Asymmetric recurrent networks will, in general, lead to spatiotemporal (space-time) behavior, such as cyclic output (limit cycles) rather than a steady state. The diversity of dynamical behaviors suggests that recurrent networks may be well suited to the problem of time series (i.e., spatiotemporal signal) prediction. We have already seen how back-propagation networks, Hopfield networks, and bidirectional associative memory (BAM) are modified to handle spatiotemporal signals (see Secs. 10.2.3 and 11.2.3). We shall explore the powerful capability of recurrent networks in connection with spatiotemporal patterns, signals recognition, and prediction. Another possible benefit of recurrent networks is that smaller networks may provide the functionality of much larger feedforward networks. This will ease complexity analysis which traditionally assumes a large number of nodes. Several recurrent networks and learning algorithms will be discussed in this chapter, and we will conclude with a discussion of reinforcement learning which usually requires the prediction of a time series signal.

13.1 FEEDBACK BACK-PROPAGATION NETWORKS

13.1.1 Recurrent Back-propagation Networks

The back-propagation network and algorithm can be generalized to the recurrent neural network by adding feedback connections such that the recurrent network will converge to a stable state [Pineda, 1987, 1988, 1989; Almeida, 1987, 1988; Rohwer and Forrest, 1987; Hertz et al., 1991]. The algorithm for training the resultant recurrent network is called *recurrent back propagation* (RBP). An example of such a network is shown in Fig. 13.1(a) in which nodes 1 and 2 are output nodes with desired outputs d_1 and d_2; nodes 1, 5, 6, and 7 are input nodes; and nodes 3 and 4 are hidden nodes. Note that node 1 is both an input and an output node.

In the general case, consider n continuous-valued nodes y_i with activation function $a(\cdot)$ and weights w_{ij} on the connections from node j. Some of these nodes are input nodes receiving external input x_i. We define $x_i = 0$ for the noninput nodes. Also, some are output nodes with the desired value d_i. The activation of each node can be expressed by the following differential equation:

$$\tau \dot{y}_i = -y_i + a\left(\sum_j w_{ij} y_j + x_i\right), \tag{13.1}$$

where τ is the relaxation time scale. Note that when the weights are symmetric, $w_{ij} = w_{ji}$, and $w_{ii} = 0$, then this system reduces to the Hopfield model with graded neurons, which is guaranteed to be stable. In general, the solutions of Eq. (13.1) exhibit oscillations and converge to isolated fixed points, limit cycles, or chaos. For our current discussion, convergence to isolated fixed points is the desired behavior because we use the value of the fixed

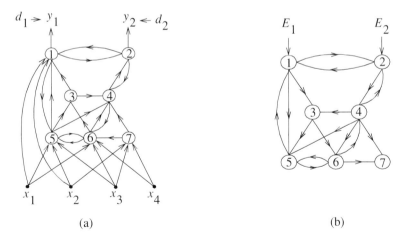

(a)   (b)

Figure 13.1 Example of a recurrent back-propagation network (RBP). (a) A seven-node recurrent back-propagation network with desired outputs d_1 and d_2. (b) The corresponding error propagation network with reversed connections and error inputs E_1 and E_2.

point as the output of the system. Recurrent networks for such purpose are also called *set-tling* networks. The fixed point can be calculated by setting $\dot{y}_i = 0$ in Eq. (13.1) as

$$y_i = a(h_i) = a\left(\sum_j w_{ij} y_j + x_i\right), \tag{13.2}$$

where $h_i = \sum_j w_{ij} y_j + x_i$ is the net input to node i when the network is at the attractor. Hence, we shall assume that at least one such fixed point exists and is a stable attractor. Alternatives such as limit cycles and chaotic trajectories for spatiotemporal pattern recognition or prediction will be considered in later sections.

As in normal back-propagation learning, the cost function to be minimized by the recurrent network is

$$E = \frac{1}{2}\sum_{k=1}^{n} E_k^2, \tag{13.3}$$

where

$$E_k = \begin{cases} d_k - y_k & \text{if } k \text{ is an output node} \\ 0, & \text{otherwise.} \end{cases} \tag{13.4}$$

Using the gradient-descent method, the weight is updated by

$$\Delta w_{pq} = -\eta \frac{\partial E}{\partial w_{pq}} = \eta \sum_k E_k \frac{\partial y_k}{\partial w_{pq}}. \tag{13.5}$$

To evaluate $\partial y_k / \partial w_{pq}$, we differentiate the fixed point equation in Eq. (13.2) to obtain

$$\frac{\partial y_i}{\partial w_{pq}} = a'(h_i)\left[\delta_{ip} y_q + \sum_j w_{ij} \frac{\partial y_j}{\partial w_{pq}}\right], \tag{13.6}$$

which can be rewritten as

$$\frac{\partial y_i}{\partial w_{pq}} - \sum_j a'(h_i) w_{ij} \frac{\partial y_j}{\partial w_{pq}} = \sum_j [\delta_{ij} - a'(h_i) w_{ij}] \frac{\partial y_j}{\partial w_{pq}} = \delta_{ip} a'(h_i) y_q, \tag{13.7}$$

where $\delta_{ij} = 1$ if $i = j$ and $\delta_{ij} = 0$ if $i \neq j$. To simplify the notation, we have

$$\sum_j L_{ij} \frac{\partial y_j}{\partial w_{pq}} = \delta_{ip} a'(h_i) y_q, \tag{13.8}$$

where

$$L_{ij} = \delta_{ij} - a'(h_i) w_{ij}. \tag{13.9}$$

Now, the term $\partial y_k / \partial w_{pq}$ in Eq. (13.5) can be obtained by solving the linear equations in Eq. (13.8). Using matrix inversion, we have

$$\frac{\partial y_k}{\partial w_{pq}} = [\mathbf{L}^{-1}]_{kp} a'(h_p) y_q, \tag{13.10}$$

and the learning rule in Eq. (13.5) becomes

$$\Delta w_{pq} = \eta \sum_k E_k [\mathbf{L}^{-1}]_{kp} a'(h_p) y_q = \eta \delta_p y_q, \tag{13.11}$$

where

$$\delta_p \triangleq a'(h_p)\sum_k E_k [\mathbf{L}^{-1}]_{kp}. \tag{13.12}$$

Note that the learning rule for the RBP network requires matrix inversion for δ_p, which can be done numerically [Rohwer and Forrest, 1987].

To avoid matrix inversion in the learning rule in Eq. (13.11), we rewrite Eq. (13.12) as

$$\delta_p = a'(h_p) z_p, \tag{13.13}$$

where

$$z_p = \sum_k E_k [\mathbf{L}^{-1}]_{kp}, \tag{13.14}$$

which comes from the following linear equations for z_p:

$$\sum_p \mathbf{L}_{pi} z_p = E_i. \tag{13.15}$$

Then from Eq. (13.9), we have

$$z_i - \sum_p a'(h_p) w_{pi} z_p = E_i, \tag{13.16}$$

which has the same form as the fixed point equation in Eq. (13.2). Once z_i are obtained, δ_p can be calculated from Eq. (13.13) and the weight can be updated according to Eq. (13.11). From Eq. (13.16), we observe that z_i is in fact the fixed point of the differential equation

$$\tau \dot{z}_i = -z_i + \sum_p a'(h_p) w_{pi} z_p + E_i, \tag{13.17}$$

which resembles the node evolution equation in Eq. (13.1). Hence, the values z_p in Eq. (13.13) can be obtained by evolution of a new *error-propagation network* with the above dynamical equation in Eq. (13.17). By comparing Eqs. (13.17) and (13.1), we can *construct* this error-propagation network as follows. The topology of the required error-propagation network is the same as that of the original network, with the coupling ω_{ij} from j to i replaced by $a'(h_i) w_{ij}$ from i to j, a simple linear transfer function $a(x) = x$, and an input term E_i (the error at node i in the original network) instead of x_i. Figure 13.1(b) shows the error-propagation network corresponding to Fig. 13.1(a). In electrical network theory, the two networks are called *network transpositions* of one another.

In summary, the learning procedure involving only local operations (i.e., without matrix inversion) for a RBP network includes the following four steps [Hertz et al., 1991]:

Step 1: Relax the RBP network with Eq. (13.1) to find the fixed points y_i.

Step 2: Calculate the error of each node E_i using Eq. (13.4).

Step 3: Relax the error-propagation network of the RBP network using Eq. (13.17) to find the fixed points z_i.

Step 4: Update the weights using Eqs. (13.11) and (13.13).

We have the following theorem concerning the stability of the RBP learning rule.

Theorem 13.1

If a RBP network has a stable attractor in Eq. (13.2) (as we assumed), then its corresponding error-propagation network has a stable attractor in Eq. (13.16). In other words, Eq. (13.16) is a stable attractor of Eq. (13.17) if Eq. (13.2) is a stable attractor of Eq. (13.1).

Proof: Let us linearize the dynamical equations about their respective fixed points. Writing $y_i = y_i^* + \epsilon_i$ in Eq. (13.1) and $z_i = z_i^* + \delta_i$ in Eq. (13.17), where y_i^* and z_i^* are the fixed points of Eqs. (13.1) and (13.17), respectively [i.e., y_i^* and z_i^* are, respectively, the solutions of Eqs. (13.2) and (13.16)], we obtain two linear differential equations:

$$\tau \dot{\epsilon}_i = -\epsilon_i + a'(h_i) \sum_j w_{ij} \epsilon_j = -\sum_j \mathbf{L}_{ij} \epsilon_j, \tag{13.18}$$

$$\tau \dot{\delta}_i = -\delta_i + \sum_p a'(h_p) w_{pi} \delta_p = -\sum_p \mathbf{L}_{ip}^T \delta_p. \tag{13.19}$$

Since $\mathbf{L}$ and $\mathbf{L}^T$ have the same eigenvalues, the local stability of the two equations is the same. Thus, both attractors are stable (i.e., eigenvalues of $\mathbf{L}$ are all positive) if one is.

Further analysis of stability and convergence properties of RPB networks can be found in Simard et al. [1989].

Example 13.1

In this example, a simple RBP network [Fig. 13.2(a)] is used for learning the XOR problem. In this simulation, we approximate Eq. (13.1) [and, similarly, Eq. (13.17)] by

$$y_i(t + \Delta t) = y_i(t) + \frac{\Delta t}{\tau} (-y_i(t) + a(h_i(t)))$$

and set $\tau = \Delta t = 1$. According to Eq. (13.2), we first obtain the following fixed points of this RBP network:

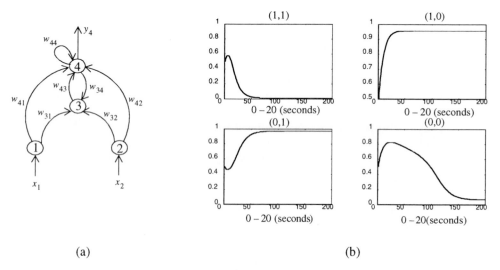

(a)   (b)

Figure 13.2 RBP network in Example 13.1. (a) The RBP network for the XOR problem. (b) The outputs y_4 of the trained RBP network in (a) when inputs (x_1, x_2) are $(1, 1)$, $(1, 0)$, $(0, 0)$, $(0, 1)$, respectively.

$$y_1 = a(x_1),$$

$$y_2 = a(x_2),$$

$$y_3 = a(h_3) = a(w_{31}y_1 + w_{32}y_2 + w_{34}y_4 - 0.5),$$

$$y_4 = a(h_4) = a(w_{41}y_1 + w_{42}y_2 + w_{43}y_3 + w_{44}y_4 - 0.5),$$

where y_i denotes the output value of node i, the activation function is $a(x) = (1 + e^{-x})^{-1}$, and the threshold values of nodes 3 and 4 are 0.5. Also from Eq. (13.16) and the fact that $E_4 = d_4 - y_4$, $E_1 = E_2 = E_3 = 0$, we have the following fixed points of the corresponding error-propagation network:

$$z_4 = E_4 + a'(h_4)w_{44}z_4 + a'(h_3)w_{34}z_3,$$

$$z_3 = a'(h_4)w_{43}z_4.$$

Then the weight update rules can be derived from Eq. (13.11) as follows:

$$\Delta w_{41} = \eta\delta_4 y_1, \qquad \Delta w_{42} = \eta\delta_4 y_2, \qquad \Delta w_{43} = \eta\delta_4 y_3, \qquad \Delta w_{44} = \eta\delta_4 y_4,$$

$$\Delta w_{31} = \eta\delta_3 y_1, \qquad \Delta w_{32} = \eta\delta_3 y_2, \qquad \Delta w_{34} = \eta\delta_3 y_4,$$

where [see Eq. (13.13)]

$$\delta_4 = a'(h_4)z_4, \qquad \delta_3 = a'(h_3)z_3.$$

After the network is trained using the above update rules with $\eta = 0.5$, it is tested by setting inputs (x_1, x_2) as $(1, 1)$, $(1, 0)$, $(0, 0)$, and $(0, 1)$, respectively. The results as shown in Fig. 13.2(b) indicate that the RBP network has learned the XOR function.

13.1.2 Partially Recurrent Networks

In this section, we shall focus on ways of training a recurrent network to recognize or reproduce a temporal sequence of states (i.e., a spatiotemporal pattern), usually in a limit cycle, instead of merely converging to fixed points as in RBP networks. This naturally requires a recurrent network with asymmetric connections; neither a feedforward network nor a recurrent network with symmetric connections will do because they necessarily go to a stationary state. In this connection, we shall introduce *partially recurrent networks* [Hertz et al., 1991] which have been popularly used for sequence recognition and reproduction. These networks are basically back-propagation networks with proper feedback links. In other words, the connections in the partially recurrent networks are mainly feedforward but include a carefully chosen set of feedback connections. The main function of partially recurrent networks is to deal with time explicitly as opposed to representing temporal information spatially, as in the TDNN (Sec. 10.2.3) for example. The recurrency in the partially recurrent network allows the network to remember cues from the recent past but does not appreciably complicate the structure and training of the whole network. In most cases, the weights on the feedback links are fixed, and so the general back-propagation learning rule may be easily used for training. Such networks are also referred to as *sequential networks,* and the nodes receiving feedback signals are called *context units.* In these networks, forward propagation is assumed to occur quickly or without reference to time, while the feedback signal is clocked. Hence, at time t the context units have signals coming from part of the network state at time $(t - 1)$. In this way, the context units remember some aspects of the past, which forms a context for processing at time t. Thus, the state of the whole network at a particular time depends on an aggregate of previous states as well as on the current input. The network can therefore recognize sequences on the basis of its state at the end of the sequence or even predict (reproduce) the successor of a given token in a temporal sequence. Since a partially recurrent network is basically a multilayer feedforward network, feedback links can come from either the output nodes or the hidden-layer nodes, and the destinations of the feedback links (i.e., the context units) can be either input nodes or hidden-layer nodes. Because of these various possibilities, there are several different models of partially recurrent networks [Hertz et al., 1991]. We shall discuss two major models here.

Jordan's sequential network. The first partially recurrent network was proposed by Jordan [1986, 1989] and is called *Jordan's sequential network*. This model is realized by adding recurrent links from the network's output to a set of context units C_i, which form a context layer, and from the context units to themselves. Figure 13.3(a) shows the general structure of the Jordan model. In this figure, single arrows represent connections only from the ith node in the source layer to the ith context unit in the destination (context) layer, whereas wide arrows represent feedforward connections which are usually fully connected as in the general back-propagation network. One example of the Jordan model is shown in Fig. 13.3(b). In such a network, the output associated with each state is fed back to the context units and blended with the input representing the next state on the input nodes. The whole constitutes the new network state for processing at the next time step. After several steps of processing, the pattern present on the context units together with input units are characteristics of the particular sequence of the states that the network has traversed. In other words, context units copy the activations of output nodes from the previous time step through the feedback links with unit weights. The self-connections in the context layer give the context units C_i themselves some individual memory or inertia. The activations of the context units are governed by

$$\dot{C}_i(t) = -\alpha C_i(t) + y_i(t), \qquad (13.20)$$

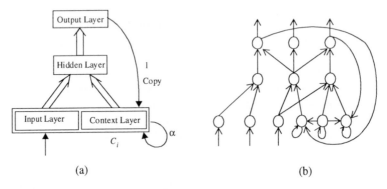

(a)

(b)

Figure 13.3 Structure of Jordan's sequential network. (a) The general model. (b) An example.

Recurrent Neural Networks   Chap. 13

where the y_i are the activations of the output nodes and α $(0 < \alpha < 1)$ is the strength of the self-connections. The solution to Eq. (13.20) is

$$C_i(t) = C_i(0) e^{-\alpha t} + \int_0^t e^{-\alpha(t-s)} y_i(s)\, ds. \qquad (13.21)$$

We can see that if the activations y_i were fixed, then C_i would clearly decay exponentially toward y_i/α, thus gradually forgetting their previous values. Such units are called *decay units*. Moreover, Eq. (13.21) indicates that context units in general accumulate a weighted moving average or *trace* of the past value y_i that they see. When α is chosen to be 0, the memory is made to extend further back into the past, but at the same time it becomes less sensitive to detail. The value of α should be chosen so that the decay rate matches the characteristic time scale of the input sequence [Stornetta et al., 1988]. In discrete time, the evolving rule of the context units is

$$C_i(t + 1) = (1 - \alpha)\, C_i(t) + y_i(t). \qquad (13.22)$$

Since the modifiable connections of the Jordan model are all feedforward, it can be trained by the conventional back-propagation method by treating the context units like inputs without introducing terms like $\partial C_k/\partial w_{ij}$ into the derivation. With fixed inputs, the network is trained to generate a set of output sequences with different input patterns triggering different output sequences. The network has been applied to categorize a class of English syllables [Anderson et al., 1989].

Simple recurrent networks.   Jordan's sequential network can be trained to recognize and distinguish different input sequences. However, with sequences of increasing length, the network encounters more difficulty in discriminating on the basis of the first cues presented, although the architecture does not rigidly constrain the length of input sequences. Moreover, while such a network learns *how to use* the representation of successive states, it does not *discover* a representation for the sequence.

Elman [1990] has introduced an architecture called the simple recurrent network (SRN) which has the potential to master an infinite corpus of sequences with the limited means of a learning procedure that is *completely local in time*. In an SRN, the feedback links are from the hidden layer to the context layer as shown in Fig. 13.4. The input layer can be considered to be divided into two parts: true input units and context units. Context

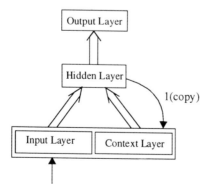

Figure 13.4   Structure of the simple recurrent network.

units simply hold a copy of the activations of the hidden nodes from the previous time step. They thus provide the system with memory in the form of a trace of processing in the previous time slice. Like Jordan's sequential network, the conventional back-propagation method can be applied to train an SRN since the modifiable connections are all feedforward. As mentioned in Sec. 9.3, the pattern of activation on the hidden nodes corresponds to the *encoding of an internal (distributed) representation* of the input pattern. By the nature of back propagation, such representations correspond to the input pattern partially processed into features relevant to the task. In an SRN, internal representations encode not only the prior event but also relevant aspects of the representation that was constructed in predicting the prior event from its predecessor. Hence, when they are fed into the hidden layer as inputs, these representations can provide information that allows the network to maintain prediction-relevant features of an entire sequence. In other words, since the hidden-layer activation is a function of both current and past input, the recurrency in the SRN allows the internal representation to be time-dependent as well as task-dependent. As compared to Jordan's sequential network, the importance of internalizing the recurrent link is that whereas activation in the input and output layers is explicitly determined by the user, the internal layer's activation is only indirectly constrained through learning.

It has been shown that an SRN can learn to mimic closely a finite-state automaton, with different states of the hidden nodes representing the internal states of the automaton [Cleeremans et al., 1989; Elman, 1991; Servan-Schreiber et al., 1991]. In fact, this is a prediction task; that is, given a token in a temporal sequence, the network is required to predict its successor. The following example illustrates the learning of a finite-state grammar.

Example 13.2

[Servan-Schreiber et al., 1991]. In this example, an SRN is employed to learn the contingencies implied by a small finite-state grammar used by Reber [1967]. As shown in Fig. 13.5, a finite-state grammar consists of nodes connected by labeled arcs. A grammatical string is generated by entering the network through the "Begin" node and by moving from node to node until the "End" node is reached. Each transition from one node to another produces a letter corresponding to the label of the arc linking these two nodes. Examples of strings that can be generated by this grammar are "PVV," "TSXS," and "TSXXTVPS." The difficulty in mastering the prediction task when letters of a string are presented individually is that two instances of the same letter may lead to different nodes and therefore different predictions about its successors. Hence, the network needs to encode more than just the identity of the current letter.

As shown in Fig. 13.6, an SRN with seven true input nodes, three context units, three hidden nodes, and seven output nodes is used in this example. On each trial, the network is pre-

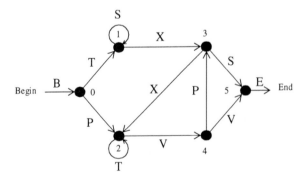

Figure 13.5 Finite-state grammar used by Reber [1967].

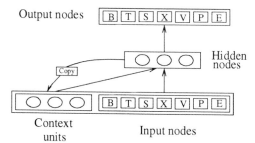

Output nodes

Hidden nodes

Copy

Context units

Input nodes

Figure 13.6 Simple recurrent network used in Example 13.2.

sented with an element of the string and is supposed to produce the next element on the output layer. In both the input and the output layers, letters are represented by the activation of a single node. Five nodes therefore are coded for the five different possible letters in each of these two layers. In addition, two nodes are coded for *begin* and *end* bits. These two bits are needed so that the network can be trained to predict the first element and the end of a string (although only one *transition* bit is strictly necessary). Hence, a string of n letters is coded as a series of $(n + 1)$ training patterns. Each pattern consists of two input vectors and one target vector. The target vector is a seven-bit vector representing element $(t + 1)$ of the string. The two input vectors are a three-bit vector representing the activation of the hidden nodes at time $(t - 1)$ and a seven-bit vector representing element t of the string.

A total of 60,000 randomly generated strings ranging from 3 to 30 letters are used to train the network. Each string is generated from the grammar, starting with "B," and successive arcs are then selected randomly from the possible continuations with a probability of 0.5. The activations of the context units are reset to 0 at the beginning of each string. For a string, each letter is presented sequentially to the network, and then the back-propagation algorithm with a momentum term is applied to adjust the weights according to the error between the network's prediction and the *actual successor* specified by the string.

After training, the network is tested on various situations. A prediction is considered accurate if, for every letter in a given string, activation of its successor is above 0.3. If this criterion is not met, presentation of the string is stopped and the string is considered "rejected." Extensive tests show that a trained SRN correctly accepted all of the 20,000 strings derived randomly from the grammar. In another test, the network was presented with 130,000 strings, of which 0.2% were grammatical and 99.7% were nongrammatical. The network performed flawlessly, accepting all the grammatical strings and rejecting all the others. Finally, the network can even correctly predict the legal successor of several extremely long strings (e.g., a 100-letter string).

13.2 FULLY RECURRENT NETWORKS

The networks discussed in Sec.13.1.2 are partially recurrent. We shall now turn to fully recurrent networks in which any node y_i may be connected to any other nodes. The recurrent back-propagation network (RBP) is an example of a fully recurrent network; however, it is required to converge to an attractor (fixed point). The fully recurrent networks discussed in this section will emphasize more about the stable states of limit cycles or chaos and thus will be used for recognizing and reproducing spatiotemporal signals. In this connection, the view of neural networks as nonlinear dynamical systems can help us to explore the dynamical complexity such as the limit cycle and chaotic behavior which can be exploited for a useful purpose in neural networks [Huberman and Hogg, 1987; Derrida and

Meir, 1988; Van der Maas et al., 1990; Hendin et al., 1991; Pollack, 1991a]. Thus, it is helpful to have some background knowledge about nonlinear systems.

Nonlinear dynamical systems have some interesting properties—their behavior in the limit reaches a steady state (fixed point), an oscillation (limit cycle), or an aperiodic instability (chaos). When the state space of a nonlinear dynamical system is plotted, these three regimes have characteristic figures called *attractors*—fixed points show up as *point attractors*, limit cycles as *periodic attractors*, and chaos as *strange attractors* which usually have a *fractal* nature. Small changes in the controlling parameters (e.g., the weights in neural networks) can lead through *phase transitions* to these qualitatively different behavioral regimes. A *bifurcation* is a change in the periodicity of the limit behavior of a system; the route from steady-state to periodic to aperiodic behavior follows a universal pattern. As for chaotic systems, one of their characteristics is that they can be very sensitive to initial conditions and a slight change in the initial condition can lead to radically different outcomes. Further details of nonlinear systems can be found in [Devaney, 1987; Gleick, 1987; Grebogi et al., 1987; Perko, 1991].

The general temporal association task for a fully recurrent network is to produce particular (desired) output sequences $\mathbf{d}(t)$ in response to specific input sequences $\mathbf{x}(t)$. As in the RBP network, individual nodes may be input nodes, output nodes, neither, or both; a desired output (target) $d_i(t)$ is usually defined on only certain nodes at certain times. This task is also called a *sequential supervised learning* task, which means that the output values of certain nodes in the network are to match specified target values at specified times. In the following sections we shall consider several different approaches to accomplishing this task.

13.2.1 Real-Time Recurrent Learning

Real-time recurrent learning (RTRL) is a general approach to training an arbitrary fully recurrent network by adjusting weights along the error gradient [Robinson and Fallside, 1987; Williams and Zipser, 1989a,b]. RTRL can be run *on-line*; that is, learning occurs while sequences are being presented rather than after they are complete and can thus deal with sequences of arbitrary length. This on-line learning rule is derived as follows.

Assume that the activation of each node in a fully recurrent network is described by the equation

$$y_i(t) = a\left(h_i(t-1)\right) = a\left(\sum_j w_{ij} y_j(t-1) + x_i(t-1)\right), \tag{13.23}$$

where $a(\cdot)$ is the activation function, $h_i(t)$ is the net input to node i at time t, and $x_i(t)$ is the input, if any, to node i at time t. If there is no such input at that node at that time, then we put $x_i(t) = 0$. As in Eq. (13.3), the total cost function to be minimized is

$$E = \sum_{t=0}^{T} E(t) = \sum_{t=0}^{T} \left[\tfrac{1}{2} \sum_k (E_k(t))^2 \right] \tag{13.24}$$

if the domain of interest is $t = 0, 1, \ldots, T$, where

$$E_k(t) = \begin{cases} d_k(t) - y_k(t) & \text{if node } k \text{ has a desired output } d_k \text{ at time } t \\ 0, & \text{otherwise.} \end{cases} \tag{13.25}$$

Equation (13.25) is an appropriate error measure for node k at time t. Since the gradient of E separates in time, the gradient-descent method can be performed by defining

$$\Delta w_{pq}(t) = -\eta \, \frac{\partial E(t)}{\partial w_{pq}} = \eta \sum_{k} E_k(t) \, \frac{\partial y_k(t)}{\partial w_{pq}} \tag{13.26}$$

and by taking the full change in w_{pq} as the time summation of $\Delta w_{pq}(t)$. The last derivative in Eq. (13.26) can now be found by differentiating the dynamical rule in Eq. (13.23) just as in Eq. (13.6):

$$\frac{\partial y_i(t)}{\partial w_{pq}} = a' \, (h_i(t-1)) \left[\delta_{ip} y_q (t-1) + \sum_{j} w_{ij} \, \frac{\partial y_j(t-1)}{\partial w_{pq}} \right]. \tag{13.27}$$

This relates the derivatives $\partial y_i / \partial w_{pq}$ at time t to those at time $(t-1)$. If we were interested in only a stable attractor, we could set the derivatives at different time steps equal and then solve the resulting linear equations, exactly as we did in recurrent back propagation in Section 13.1.1. Here we can instead iterate it forward from the initial condition

$$\frac{\partial y_i(0)}{\partial w_{pq}} = 0 \tag{13.28}$$

at $t = 0$, which is based on the reasonable assumption that the initial state of the network has no functional dependence on the weights.

From Eq. (13.27), a dynamical system with variables $\{z_{pq}^i\}$ is created, and the dynamics are given by

$$z_{pq}^i(t) = a' \, (h_i(t-1)) \left[\delta_{ip} y_q (t-1) + \sum_{j} w_{ij} z_{pq}^j (t-1) \right], \tag{13.29}$$

with the initial condition $z_{pq}^i(0) = 0$, where

$$z_{pq}^i(t) \triangleq \frac{\partial y_i(t)}{\partial w_{pq}} \tag{13.30}$$

for every time step t and all appropriate indices i, j, and k. The precise algorithm then consists of computing, at each time step t from 0 to T, the quantities $z_{pq}^i(t)$ using Eq. (13.29) and then using the difference $E_k(t)$ in Eq. (13.25) between the desired and actual outputs to compute the weight changes

$$\Delta w_{pq}(t) = \eta \sum_{k} E_k(t) z_{pq}^k(t). \tag{13.31}$$

The overall correction to be applied to each weight w_{pq} in the network is then simply the summation of these individual $\Delta w_{pq}(t)$ values for each time step t along the trajectory. The whole procedure has to be repeated until the system remembers the correct temporal associations. One may use various methods known from back propagation to speed up the learning, such as momentum terms. The time and memory requirements for the above algorithm are nevertheless very large; for n fully recurrent nodes there are n^3 derivatives to maintain, and updating each takes time proportional to n for each derivation and thus requires $O(n^4)$ computations per time step.

In order to allow on-line training, the weights can be updated according to Eq. (13.31) after each time step instead of waiting until the sequence is ended ($t = T$) if the learning constant η is sufficiently small. The resulting algorithm is called on-line recurrent learning since the weight changes occur on-line during the presentation of the input and output sequences. This method is very simple to implement and avoids the memory size requirement which depends on the maximum time T. The potential disadvantage of RTRL is that it no longer follows the precise negative gradient of the total error along a trajectory; however, it is found that RTRL stays very close to the true gradient descent if the learning rate is made very small.

An interesting technique that is frequently used in temporal supervised learning tasks [Jordan, 1986; Pineda, 1988] is to replace the actual output $y_k(t)$ of a node by the desired signal $d_k(t)$ in subsequent computation of the behavior of the network, whenever such a value exists. This must be done after computing the error $E_k(t)$ and the set of derivatives. This technique is called *teacher forcing*. Using this method, the appropriate modification of the RTRL algorithm is to set $\partial y_i(t) / \partial w_{pq}$ in Eq. (13.27) [or $z_{pq}^i(t)$ in Eq. (13.29)] to zero for all p and q in the iterative use of Eq. (13.27) [or Eq. (13.29)] whenever node i is forced to its target value after they have been used to compute the Δw_{pq} values. The teacher forcing procedure keeps the network closer to the desired track and usually seems to speed up learning considerably. This method can also be applied to other recurrent networks introduced in this chapter.

Example 13.3

[Tsung and Cottrell, 1993]. This example illustrates the dynamical behavior of a simple two-node fully recurrent network. We study its dynamics as it is trained to produce sine-wave oscillations autonomously (i.e., without eternal inputs). The two-node network is described by

$$y_i(t+1) = a(x_i), \qquad i = 1, 2, \tag{13.32}$$

where

$$a(x_i) = \frac{1}{1 + e^{-x_i}} \qquad \text{and} \qquad x_i = \sum_j w_{ij} y_j. \tag{13.33}$$

Both nodes receive teacher signals, which are sine waves with a $\pi/4$ phase difference and discretized at 30 samples per period. That is, the network is trained to oscillate with a period of 30 iterations [$x(t+30) = x(t)$]. The learning algorithm used is the *teacher-forcing* RTRL.

The dynamics of system activations through the learning process can be visualized by the phase space. The phase space is the space of the activations of the nodes with time represented as movement through this space. A *nullcline* is a curve in the phase space where one of the derivatives vanishes; therefore, the nullclines of y_1 and y_2 show where y_1 or y_2 changes direction, either from increasing to decreasing, or vice versa. The intersection of the nullclines is a fixed point of the network. Having plotted the nullclines for a particular network, it is possible to approximately trace out the asymptotic behavior of any trajectory. In particular, one can determine whether the system goes to a fixed point or if a limit cycle exists.

Figure 13.7 shows the evolution of the nullclines during one typical training session. One trajectory with initial conditions $(y_1, y_2) = (0.4, 0.4)$ is also shown. Initially, the network heads straight to the fixed point, where the nullclines intersect. At approximately 700 iterations, the trajectory of the network visibly spirals into the fixed point. Note that the fixed point shifts position as the nullclines are changed by the training. Between 1000 and 1100 iterations, a stable limit cycle appears. Once the limit cycle is created, it grows quickly to fit the target sine waves. This exchange between a stable fixed point and a stable limit cycle is the main charac-

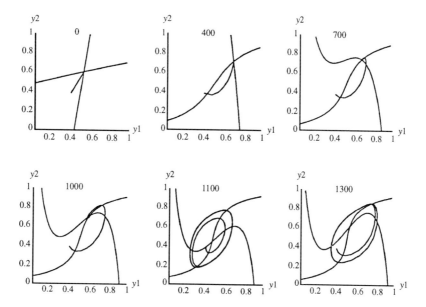

Figure 13.7 Evolution of the nullclines as the network learns to oscillate. For each phase diagram, one trajectory starting from (0.4, 0.4) is also plotted. The number above each diagram shows how many iterations the network has been trained in (Example 13.3). (Adapted from Tsung and Cottrell [1993], © 1993 IEEE.)

teristic of a phenomenon called *Hopf bifurcation* [Marsden and McCracken, 1976; Perko, 1991]. The basic Hopf bifurcation theorem, translated into a geometric description, states that when trajectories that formerly have spiraled into a fixed point suddenly spiral out as a small adjustment on a system parameter (i.e., a weight in a neural network) is made, then a bifurcation has occurred. At this time, not only has the fixed point changed from being stable (spiraling in) to unstable (spiraling out), but a stable limit cycle is also starting from the fixed point and its radius grows larger with the system parameters.

13.2.2 Time-Dependent Recurrent Back Propagation

A related algorithm, called *time-dependent recurrent back propagation* (TDRB), for training a general *continuous-time* recurrent network was developed by Pearlmutter [1989] (see also Werbos [1988] and Sato [1990]). Similar to the recurrent back-propagation dynamics in Eq. (13.1), the nodes in TDRB evolve according to

$$\tau_i \dot{y}_i = -y_i + a\left(\sum_j w_{ij} y_j\right) + x_i, \tag{13.34}$$

where τ_i is the relaxation time scale and the inputs $x_i(t)$ are continuous functions of time. The desired outputs $d_i(t)$ are also continuous functions of time. A proper cost function for an overall time domain $[t_0, t_1]$ is

$$E = \frac{1}{2} \int_{t_0}^{t_1} \sum_{i \in O} [\, y_i(t) - d_i(t)\,]^2 \, dt, \tag{13.35}$$

where O denotes the set of output nodes and the summation is over only those output nodes with specified values of $d_i(t)$. The cost function E measures the deviation of the network outputs $y_i(t)$ from the desired functions $d_i(t)$ from $t = t_0$ to $t = t_1$ for $i \in O$. Minimizing this E would yield a network having $y_i(t)$ to imitate or follow $d_i(t)$. In the following, the technique of *finite-difference approximation* is used to compute $\partial E/\partial w_{ij}$ and $\partial E/\partial \tau_i$, thus allowing gradient descent in the weights and time constants so as to minimize E.

First, approximating the derivative in Eq. (13.34) with $\dot{y}_i(t) = [y_i(t + \Delta t) - y_i(t)]/\Delta t$ yields a first-order difference approximation to Eq. (13.34) as

$$y_i(t + \Delta t) = \left(1 - \frac{\Delta t}{\tau_i}\right) y_i(t) + \frac{\Delta t}{\tau_i} a(h_i(t)) + \frac{\Delta t}{\tau_i} x_i(t), \qquad (13.36)$$

where $h_i(t) = \sum_j w_{ij} y_j(t)$ is the net input to node i. Let us define the *functional derivatives*:

$$E_i(t) = \frac{\delta E}{\delta y_i(t)} = [y_i(t) - d_i(t)]. \qquad (13.37)$$

Intuitively, $E_i(t)$ measures how much a small change in y_i at time t affects E if everything else is left unchanged.

Let us define a continuous function $z_i(t)$ that measures how much a small change in $y_i(t)$ at time t affects E when this change is propagated forward through time and influences the remainder of the trajectory. This function can be expressed as $z_i(t) = \partial E(t)/\partial y_i(t)$. We can use the chain rule concept to derive $z_i(t)$ in terms of $z_i(t + \Delta t)$. According to the chain rule, we add all the separate influences that varying $y_i(t)$ has on E. It has a direct contribution of $\Delta t E_i(t)$ [see Eq. (13.37)], which comprises the first term in the equation for $z_i(t)$. From the first term on the right-hand side of Eq. (13.36), we find that varying $y_i(t)$ by ϵ has an effect on $y_i(t + \Delta t)$ of $\epsilon(1 - \Delta t/\tau_i)$, giving us a second term, namely, $(1 - \Delta t/\tau_i) z_i(t + \Delta t)$. Each weight w_{ij} allows $y_i(t)$ to influence $y_i(t + \Delta t)$. Let us compute this influence in stages; varying $y_i(t)$ by ϵ varies $h_j(t)$ by ϵw_{ji}, which in turn varies $a(h_j(t))$ by $\epsilon w_{ji} a'(h_j(t))$, which in turn varies $y_j(t + \Delta t)$ by $\epsilon w_{ji} a'(h_j(t)) \Delta t/\tau_j$ [see the second term on the right-hand side of Eq. (13.36)]. This gives us our third and final term, $\sum_j w_{ji} a'(h_j(t)) z_j(t + \Delta t) \Delta t/\tau_j$. Combining these terms, we have

$$z_i(t) = \Delta t E_i(t) + \left(1 - \frac{\Delta t}{\tau_i}\right) z_i(t + \Delta t) + \sum_j w_{ji} a'(h_j(t)) \frac{\Delta t}{\tau_j} z_j(t + \Delta t). \qquad (13.38)$$

If we use the approximation $\dot{z}_i(t) = [z_i(t + \Delta t) - z_i(t)]/\Delta t$ and take the limit as $\Delta t \to 0$, we obtain the differential equation

$$\dot{z}_i = \frac{1}{\tau_i} z_i - \sum_j \frac{1}{\tau_j} w_{ji} a'(h_j) z_j - E_i. \qquad (13.39)$$

For boundary conditions, note that $z_i(t_1) = \Delta t E_i(t_1)$, and so in the limit as $\Delta t \to 0$, we have $z_i(t_1) = 0$ for all i at the end point.

We are now ready to derive $\partial E/\partial w_{ij}$ and $\partial E/\partial \tau_i$. Consider making an infinitesimal change dw_{ij} in w_{ij} for a period Δt starting at t. This will cause a corresponding infinitesimal change in E of

$$y_j(t) a'(h_i(t)) \frac{\Delta t}{\tau_i} z_i(t) dw_{ij}. \qquad (13.40)$$

Since we wish to know the effect of making this infinitesimal change in w_{ij} through time, we integrate over the entire interval, obtaining

$$\frac{\partial E}{\partial w_{ij}} = \frac{1}{\tau_i} \int_{t_0}^{t_1} y_j a'(h_i) z_i \, dt. \tag{13.41}$$

If we substitute $\rho_i = 1/\tau_i$ into Eq. (13.36), find $\partial E/\partial \rho_i$ by proceeding analogously, and substitute τ_i back in, we obtain

$$\frac{\partial E}{\partial \tau_i} = -\frac{1}{\tau_i} \int_{t_0}^{t_1} z_i \frac{dy_i}{dt} \, dt. \tag{13.42}$$

These results [Eqs. (13.41) and (13.42)] can also be derived using the calculus of variations and Lagrange multipliers or from the continuous form of dynamical programming [Pearlmutter, 1989].

The steps in using the above equations in the learning algorithm are as follows. We need a forward-backward technique. We first integrate Eq. (13.34) forward from $t = t_0$ to $t = t_1$ and store the resulting $y_i(t)$. Then we integrate Eq. (13.39) backward from $t = t_1$ to $t = t_0$ to obtain the $z_i(t)$ based on the boundary condition $z_i(t_1) = 0$ while numerically integrating $y_j a'(h_i) z_i$ [Eq. (13.41)] and $z_i \, dy_i/dt$ [Eq. (13.42)], thus computing the proper gradient descent increments $\Delta w_{ij} = -\eta_1 \partial E/\partial w_{ij}$ and $\Delta \tau_i = -\eta_2 \partial E/\partial \tau_i$. These integrations can be done by finite difference approximations in practice. Since computing dz_i/dt requires knowing $a'(h_i)$, we can store it and retrieve it backward as well. We can also store and retrieve y_i as it is used in expressions being numerically integrated. The TDRB method can be used to derive the RTRL approach and, in particular, it can be considered an extension of recurrent back propagation to dynamical sequences instead of only stable attractors. This is observed from the similarity of the backward equation in Eq. (13.39) to the transposed equation in Eq. (13.17) in recurrent back propagation. This accounts for the name "time-dependent recurrent back propagation."

The time and space complexities of the TDRB method are great but are generally less than those of the RTRL approach. Assume that there are n fully recurrent nodes and k time steps between 0 and T. Then the time complexity per forward-backward pass is $O(kn^2)$ compared to $O(kn^4)$ for RTRL. However, the proper k is often much larger in TDRB where continuous time is discretized. The space (memory) complexity of TDRB is $O(ank + bn^2)$ compared to $O(n^3)$ for RTRL. The following example illustrates the use of TDRB in generating stable limit cycles.

Example 13.4

In this example, TDRB is used to train three recurrent networks of different sizes to follow three desired trajectories as shown in Fig. 13.8(a), (c), and (e). There is no external input to these networks; that is, $x_i(t) = 0$ in Eq. (13.34). In these simulations, the unipolar sigmoid function is used as the activation function; that is, $a(h) = 1/(1 + e^{-h})$. Each node has a threshold value of -0.5 or, equivalently, the input $x_i(t)$ is not zero but fixed at -0.5 [i.e., $x_i(t) = -0.5$ for all $t \in [t_0, t_1]$]. We only perform weight updating using Eq. (13.41) and keep the time constants fixed as $\tau_i = 1$. Hence, we do not use Eq. (13.42) in this example. The discrete-time step $\Delta t = 0.1$ is used. Weights are initialized to uniform random values between 1 and -1, and the initial values of $y_i(0)$ are set to 0.5. Each simulation is performed as follows. In the forward path, $y_i(t)$ is computed and stored from $t = 0$ to $t = t_1$ using Eq. (13.36) at each time step Δt. In the backward path, we compute $z_i(t)$ from $t = t_1$ to $t = 0$ using Eq. (13.38) at each time step Δt. Here, the functional derivative $E_i(t)$ in Eq. (13.37) is computed by

$$E_i(t) = \begin{cases} y_i(t) - d_i(t) & \text{for } t \geq t_0 \text{ and } i \in O \\ 0 & \text{otherwise,} \end{cases} \tag{13.43}$$

where O denotes the set of output nodes. We then store $z_i(t)$ and $a'(h_i)$. After the forward and backward passes are computed, we are ready to calculate the gradient $\partial E / \partial w_{ij}$ using Eq. (13.41). This is approximated by

$$\frac{\partial E(t + \Delta t)}{\partial w_{ij}} \approx \frac{\partial E(t)}{\partial w_{ij}} + \frac{1}{\tau_i} y_j(t) a'(h_i(t)) z_i(t), \tag{13.44}$$

where $\partial E(0) / \partial w_{ij} = 0$ initially. Finally, the weights are updated at each time step Δt by $w_{ij}(t + \Delta t) = w_{ij}(t) - \eta [\partial E(t + \Delta t) / \partial w_{ij}]$.

In the first simulation, a network with no input node, four hidden nodes, and two output nodes, all fully connected, is trained to follow the trajectory in Fig. 13.8(a). The parameters used are $\eta = 0.1$, $t_0 = 6$, and $t_1 = 22$. Hence, the network output state is required to be on the desired trajectory at $t = 6$ and to go around the circle taking 16 units of time. Figure 13.8(b) shows the state trajectory of the trained network after 7100 iterations. As shown in the figure, the network moves from its initial position at $(0.5, 0.5)$ to the correct location on the desired trajectory and then goes around the first desired trajectory.

In the second simulation, an enlarged network with 10 hidden nodes (12 nodes totally) is trained to follow the figure-eight shape shown in Fig. 13.8(c). The parameters used are $\eta = 0.3$, $t_0 = 4$, and $t_1 = 20$. Again, after the network is well trained after 5000 iterations, we observe [see Fig. 13.8(d)] that before $t = 4$, while unconstrained by the environment, the net-

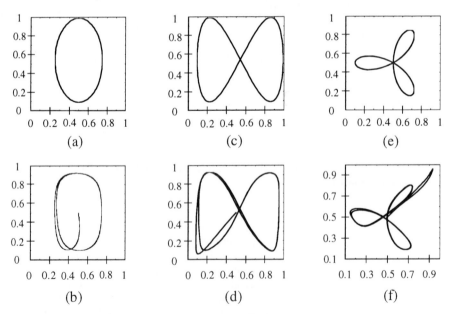

Figure 13.8 Training of three recurrent networks in Example 13.4. (a), (c), and (e) Desired states d_1 and d_2 are plotted against each other. (b), (d), and (f) Corresponding actual states y_1 and y_2 are plotted against each other at epochs (b) 7100, (d) 5000, and (f) 5000.

work moves in a short loop from the initial position at (0.5, 0.5) to where it should be on the limit cycle at $t = 5$ and then correctly follows the desired trajectory.

In the third simulation, an even enlarged network with 23 hidden nodes is trained to follow the more complex trajectory shown in Fig. 13.8(e). The parameters used are $\eta = 0.3$, $t_0 = 4$, and $t_1 = 20$. The state trajectories of the network, which is trained after 5000 iterations, are shown in Fig. 13.8(f). Again it can follow the desired trajectory quite well.

13.2.3 Second-Order Recurrent Networks

Previously, we have shown that (*first-order*) recurrent neural networks have the ability to learn finite-state automata (FSA) or finite-state languages (see Example 13.2). Generally speaking, these results were obtained by training a network to predict the next symbol rather than by training it to accept or reject strings of different lengths. That is, we previously assumed that a teacher could supply a consistent and generalizable final output for each member of a set of strings, which turned out to be a significant overconstraint. In learning a two-state machine like parity, this does not matter, as the one-bit state fully determines the output. However, for the case of higher-dimensional systems, we may know what the final output of the system should be, but we don't care what its final state is. This is a problem in training with *don't care* conditions; that is, there is no specific target for an output node during a particular training example. This problem has been attacked by second-order recurrent networks. In this section, we shall mainly introduce the second-order recurrent networks proposed by Pollack [1987, 1990, 1991b] and Giles et al. [1992].

Pollack's sequential cascaded recurrent networks. The sequential cascaded recurrent network (SCRN) proposed by Pollack [1987, 1990, 1991b] is a well-behaved higher-order (sigma-pi) [see Eq. (9.6)] connectionist architecture to which the back-propagation learning rule can be applied. As shown in Fig. 13.9, it basically consists of two subnetworks in a master-slave relationship. The *function (slave)* network is a standard feedforward network with or without hidden layers; however, the weights on the function network are dynamically computed by the linear *context (master)* network. A context network has as many outputs as there are weights in the function network, and the outputs of the function network are used as recurrent inputs to the context network. Such a structure can be trained to associate specific outputs with variable-length input sequences. The problem is that given a sequence $x_j(t)$, $t = 1, 2, \ldots, n$, the output of the output node l at time

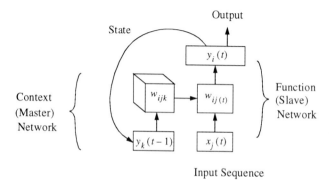

Figure 13.9 Sequential cascaded recurrent network. The outputs of the master net (left) are the weights in the slave net (right), and the outputs of the slave net are recurrent inputs to the master net.

$t = n$ is required to be equal to d_l; that is, $y_l(n) = d_l$ for some specific l. For clarity, assume no hidden nodes, and then the forward-pass computation is

$$w_{ij}(t) = \sum_k w_{ijk} y_k(t-1) \quad \text{and} \quad y_i(t) = a\left(\sum_j w_{ij}(t) x_j(t)\right), \quad (13.45)$$

which reduces to

$$y_i(t) = a\left(\sum_{j,k} w_{ijk} y_k(t-1) x_j(t)\right), \quad (13.46)$$

where $x_j(t)$, $t = 1, 2, \ldots, n$, is a sequence of inputs and $y_i(t)$, $t = 1, 2, \ldots, n$, is the sequence of outputs from the network. Equation (13.46) indicates the multiplicative connections in the SCRN.

The basic idea of SCRN learning is to unroll a recurrent loop. However, the learning rule here involves only a single *backspace,* unrolling the loop only once instead of completely unrolling the loop. This is a *truncated* approximation to a gradient descent and leads to the calculation of only one error term for each weight. As usual, let us first define the cost function to be

$$E = \tfrac{1}{2}[y_l(n) - d_l]^2. \quad (13.47)$$

Then the following derivatives related to output node l can be obtained:

$$\frac{\partial E}{\partial w_{lj}(n)} = [y_l(n) - d_l] a'\left(\sum_k w_{lk}(n) x_k(n)\right) x_j(n), \quad (13.48)$$

$$\frac{\partial E}{\partial w_{ljk}} = \frac{\partial E}{\partial w_{lj}(n)} y_k(n-1). \quad (13.49)$$

The error on the remaining weights $(\partial E/\partial w_{ij}, \partial E/\partial w_{ijk}, i \neq l)$ is calculated using values from the penultimate time step:

$$\frac{\partial E}{\partial y_k(n-1)} = \sum_l \sum_j \frac{\partial E}{\partial w_{ljk}} \frac{\partial E}{\partial w_{lj}(n)}, \quad (13.50)$$

$$\frac{\partial E}{\partial w_{ij}(n-1)} = \frac{\partial E}{\partial y_k(n-1)} x_j(n-1), \quad (13.51)$$

$$\frac{\partial E}{\partial w_{ijk}} = \frac{\partial E}{\partial w_{ij}(n-1)} y_k(n-2). \quad (13.52)$$

A schematic of the backspace trick is shown in Fig. 13.10, where the gradient calculations for the weights are highlighted. The above learning rules can be easily generalized to situations where there are hidden nodes in the function or context network and/or the system is trained with more than one bit of desired output. The key point is that the gradients to a subset of the outputs with available targets are calculated directly, but the gradients connected to don't-care recurrent states are calculated one step back in time. The forward and backward calculations are performed over a corpus of variable-length input patterns, and then all the weights are updated. As the overall squared sum of errors approaches zero, the network improves its calculation of final outputs for the set of sequences (strings) in the training set. At some threshold, for example, when the network responds with a value above 0.8 for

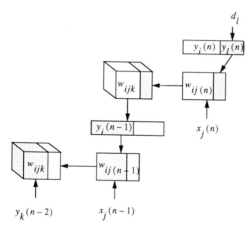

Figure 13.10 The backspace trick. Only partial information is available for computing error gradients on the weights, and so the penultimate configuration is used to calculate gradients for the remaining weights.

accept sequences (strings) and a value below 0.2 for reject sequences (strings), training is halted. The network now classifies the training set and can be tested on its generalization to a testing set.

The following example illustrates the use of the SCRN for the inference of seven relatively simple grammars originally created and studied by Tomita [1982]. These grammars, called *regular grammars*, are the simplest type of grammar in the Chomsky hierarchy and have a one-to-one correspondence with finite-state machines [Hopcroft and Ullman, 1979]. These grammars have been generally used as benchmarking tests in the recurrent networks community. The FSA for the seven Tomita's grammars are shown in Fig. 13.11, where

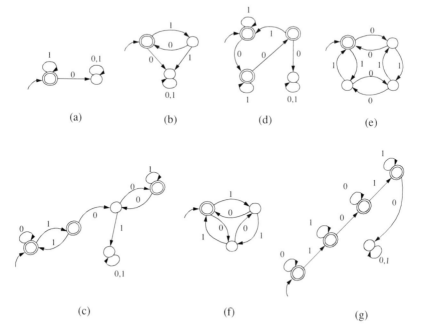

Figure 13.11 Finite state automata (FSA) for Tomita's seven grammars (the final-state nodes are double-circled).

final-state nodes are drawn with double circles. For each language, there are two sets of training strings coming from the corresponding FSA. As an example, the training data for Tomita's fourth grammar are shown in Table 13.1, which corresponds to the FSA in Fig. 13.11(d). The network is trained to *accept* the strings in the "accept" set and to *reject* the strings in the "reject" set in the training data.

TABLE 13.1   Training Data for Tomita's Fourth Grammar

Set 4 Accept	Set 4 Reject
1	0 0 0
0	1 1 0 0 0
1 0	0 0 0 1
0 1	0 0 0 0 0 0 0 0
0 0	1 1 1 1 1 0 0 0 0 1 1
1 0 0 1 0 0	1 1 0 1 0 1 0 0 0 0 0 1 0 1 1 1
0 0 1 1 1 1 1 0 1 0 0	1 0 1 0 0 1 0 0 0 1
0 1 0 0 1 0 0 1 0 0	0 0 0 0
1 1 1 0 0	0 0 0 0 0
0 0 1 0	

Example 13.5

[Pollack, 1991b]. In this example, an SCRN learns to recognize and generate Tomita's fourth language by the training data in Table 13.1. This language includes any string not containing "000" as a substring. The SCRN used is a one-input–four-output function network (with bias connections, making eight weights for the context network to compute) and a three-input–eight-output context network with bias connections. Only three of the outputs of the function net are fed back to the context network, while the fourth output unit is used as the accept bit. The standard back-propagation learning rate is set to 0.3, and the momentum to 0.7. All 32 weights are set to random numbers between ±0.5 for each run. Training is halted when all accept strings return output bits above 0.8 and reject strings below 0.2. The results show that the SCRN converges in about 250 epochs with 100% correctness in separating the accept and reject strings.

Giles' second-order recurrent network.   Giles et al. [1990, 1991, 1992] also proposed a second-order recurrent network to learn regular grammars (languages). Their network can learn various grammars well, and in addition, it has been shown to learn regular grammars more easily than the simple recurrent network, which does not use second-order nodes. Henceforth, we will refer to Giles' network as a *second-order recurrent network*. This network has n recurrent state nodes labeled s_j, m special, nonrecurrent input nodes labeled x_k, and n^2m real-valued weights labeled w_{ijk}. As long as the number of input nodes is small compared to the number of state nodes, the complexity of the network grows only as $O(n^2)$. The weights w_{ijk} modify a product of state node s_j and input node x_k. This quadratic form directly represents the state transition diagrams of a state process—{input_state} $\Rightarrow$ {next_state}. A second-order recurrent network with $n = 3$ and $m = 2$ is shown in Fig. 13.12. A second-order recurrent network accepts a time-ordered sequence of inputs and evolves with dynamics defined by the following equations:

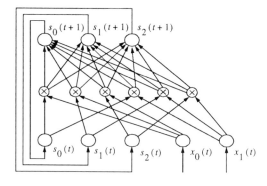

Figure 13.12 Second-order, single-layer recurrent neural network. $s_j(t)$ represents the value of the ith state node at time t, and $x_k(t)$ represents the value of the kth input node at time t. The nodes marked $\times$ represent the operation $w_{ijk} \cdot s_j(t) \cdot x_k(t)$.

$$s_i(t+1) = a\,(h_i(t)) \qquad \text{and} \qquad h_i(t) = \sum_{j,\,k} w_{ijk} s_j(t)\,x_k(t)\,, \qquad (13.53)$$

where $a\,(\cdot)$ is an activation function (usually, it is a sigmoid function). Each input string (sequence) is encoded in the input nodes one character (element) per discrete time step t. The above equation is then evaluated for each state node s_i to compute the next state $s_i(t+1)$ at the next time step $t+1$. Note that Eq. (13.53) is equivalent to Eq. (13.46), and so the second-order recurrent network is equivalent to Pollack's SCRN without any hidden layers.

A convenient way to view a second-order recurrent network that deals with binary sequences is to decompose the network structure into two separate component networks, net0 and net1, controlled by an "enabling" or "gating" signal as shown in Fig. 13.13 [Zeng et al., 1993]. The network consists of two first-order recurrent networks with shared state

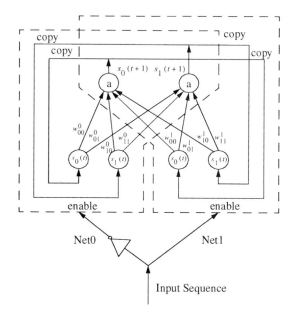

Figure 13.13 Equivalent first-order structure of a second-order recurrent network.

nodes. The common state node values are copied back to both net0 and net1 after each time step, and the input sequence acts as a switching control to enable or disable one of the two nets. For example, when the current input is 1, net1 is enabled while net0 is disabled. The state node values are then determined by the state node values from the previous time step weighted by the weights in net1. Note that this representation of a second-order recurrent network, as two networks with a gating function, provides insight into the nature of second-order nets; that is, they clearly have greater representational power than a single simple recurrent network, given the same number of state (context) nodes.

The training of a second-order recurrent network is based on a *complete* gradient descent in contrast to the *truncated approximation* to the gradient descent used in the SCRN. The cost function E is defined by selecting a special state node s_l as the output or response node, which is either on ($s_l > 1 - \epsilon$) if an input sequence is accepted or off ($s_l < \epsilon$) if an input sequence is rejected, where ϵ is the response tolerance of the response node. The acceptance or rejection of an input string is determined only at the end, say at time $t = n$, of the presentation of each sequence $x(1), x(2), \ldots, x(n)$. The cost function is defined as

$$E = \tfrac{1}{2}[s_l(n) - d_l]^2, \tag{13.54}$$

where d_l is the desired output for the response node s_l. The target response is defined as $d_l = 0.8$ for "accept" sequences and $d_l = 0.2$ for "reject" sequences (see Table 13.1). Note that the cost function in Eq. (13.54) is the same as Eq. (13.47). The training is an on-line algorithm which updates the weights at the end of each sample sequence presentation with a gradient-descent weight update rule

$$\Delta w_{ijk} = -\eta \, \frac{\partial E}{\partial w_{ijk}} = \eta \, (d_l - s_l(n)) \, \frac{\partial s_l(n)}{\partial w_{ijk}}, \tag{13.55}$$

in which the momentum term can be added to speed up the convergence. The last derivative in Eq. (13.55) can be evaluated from Eq. (13.53) as

$$\frac{\partial s_r(n)}{\partial w_{ijk}} = a'(h_r(n-1)) \left[\delta_{ri} s_j(n-1) x_k(n-1) + \sum_{p,q} w_{rpq} x_q(n-1) \frac{\partial s_p(n-1)}{\partial w_{ijk}} \right]. \tag{13.56}$$

In general,

$$\frac{\partial s_r(t)}{\partial w_{ijk}} = a'(h_r(t-1)) \left[\delta_{ri} s_j(t-1) x_k(t-1) + \sum_{p,q} w_{rpq} x_q(t-1) \frac{\partial s_p(t-1)}{\partial w_{ijk}} \right]. \tag{13.57}$$

These partial derivative terms are calculated iteratively as the equation suggests, with one iteration per input symbol, and the initial terms $\partial s_r(0)/\partial w_{ijk}$ are set to zero. The precise learning procedure is as follows. After the initial weight values are selected, $\partial s_r(t)/\partial w_{ijk}$ can be evaluated on-line as each input $x_k(t)$ enters the network. In this way, the error term is forward-propagated and accumulated at each time step t. The time complexity for each

Recurrent Neural Networks   Chap. 13

update of $\partial s_r(t) / \partial w_{ijk}$ is $O\left(n^4 m^2\right)$, which becomes $O\left(n^4\right)$ if $n \gg m$. Comparing Eq. (13.57) to Eq. (13.27), we find out that the above on-line learning rule is in fact a second-order form of the real-time recurrent learning rule in Sec. 13.2.1. Second-order recurrent networks have been used successfully to learn Tomita's grammars by Giles et al. [1992] and Zeng et al. [1993], as SCRNs have.

13.2.4 The Extended Kalman Filter

Up to this point, we have focused on simpler gradient-based training algorithms for recurrent networks. In this section, we shall introduce the use of a more complex but relatively effective approach, called the *extended Kalman filter* (EKF), as an on-line learning algorithm for determining the weights in a recurrent network given target outputs as it runs. The EKF can provide a substantial speed-up in the number of training time steps when compared with other simpler on-line gradient-based algorithms at the expense of higher computational cost at each step.

The *Kalman filter* is a well-known linear recursive technique for estimating a system state vector $\mathbf{x}$ from a set of noisy measurements $\mathbf{z}$. The basic Kalman filter is optimal in the mean squared error sense given certain assumptions and is the best possible of all filters (including nonlinear filters) if $\mathbf{x}$ and $\mathbf{z}$ are Gaussian vectors and the additive noise is white and has zero mean. The EKF can be thought of as a gradient-based, on-line information processing algorithm that is used for smoothing, filtering, or predicting the states of a nonlinear dynamical system. For background knowledge, we shall briefly review the EKF algorithm in general terms. Complete treatment of the Kalman filter and the EKF can be found in several excellent textbooks [Gelb, 1974; Anderson and Moore, 1979; Brown 1983; Goodwin and Sin, 1984]. Specifically, the following assumptions are inherent in the discrete-time Kalman filter. Assume a plant model

$$\mathbf{x}(k+1) = \mathbf{f}_k(\mathbf{x}(k)) + \text{noise} \tag{13.58}$$

and a measurement model

$$\mathbf{z}(k) = \mathbf{h}_k(\mathbf{x}(k)) + \text{noise}, \tag{13.59}$$

where $\mathbf{x}(k)$ is the n-dimensional state vector of the system and $\mathbf{z}(k)$ is the m-dimensional measurement vector at time step k. The functions $\mathbf{f}_k = \left[f_k^1, f_k^2, \ldots, f_k^n\right]$ and $\mathbf{h}_k = \left[h_k^1, h_k^2, \ldots, h_k^m\right]$ are assumed to be differentiable and possibly time-varying. The plant noise and measurement noise are uncorrelated white Gaussian zero-mean noise. Let $\mathbf{Q}(k)$ represent the covariance of the plant noise, and $\mathbf{R}(k)$ the covariance of the measurement noise. The effect of external input to the system can be taken into account through $\mathbf{f}_k$. The internal variables of the filter are an $n \times m$ gain matrix $\mathbf{K}$ and an $n \times n$ *approximate* error covariance matrix $\mathbf{P}$, which is used to model the correlations or interactions between each pair of weights in the network. Both $\mathbf{K}$ and $\mathbf{P}$ approach limiting values as the filter runs, independently of the filter input. If, however, the system and/or the noise deviates from the above assumptions, then there is no guarantee that $\mathbf{K}$ and $\mathbf{P}$ will settle to appropriate values; as a result, the filter output may diverge from the true system state vector. The EKF algorithm then consists of the following steps for each time step $k > 0$.

Algorithm EKF: Extended Kalman Filter

(Williams, 1992b). At time step $k > 0$, perform the following steps:

Step 1: Compute the linearized state transition matrix:

$$\mathbf{F}(k-1) = \left. \frac{\partial \mathbf{f}_{k-1}}{\partial \mathbf{x}} \right|_{\mathbf{x} = \hat{\mathbf{x}}(k-1|k-1)}, \qquad (13.60)$$

where $\hat{\mathbf{x}}(k-1|k-1)$ is the estimate of the state vector $\mathbf{x}(k-1)$ at time step $(k-1)$.

Step 2: Perform a *time update:*

$$\hat{\mathbf{x}}(k|k-1) = \mathbf{f}_{k-1}(\hat{\mathbf{x}}(k-1|k-1)), \qquad (13.61)$$

$$\mathbf{P}(k|k-1) = \mathbf{F}(k-1)\mathbf{P}(k-1|k-1)\mathbf{F}^T(k-1) + \mathbf{Q}(k-1). \qquad (13.62)$$

Step 3: If measurement $\mathbf{z}(k)$ is available, compute the linearized measurement matrix:

$$\mathbf{H}(k) = \left. \frac{\partial \mathbf{h}_k}{\partial \mathbf{x}} \right|_{\mathbf{x} = \hat{\mathbf{x}}(k|k-1)}, \qquad (13.63)$$

where $\hat{\mathbf{x}}(k|k-1)$ is the estimate of the state vector $\mathbf{x}(k)$ at time step $(k-1)$. Then compute the *Kalman gain matrix:*

$$\mathbf{K}(k) = \mathbf{P}(k|k-1)\mathbf{H}^T(k)[\mathbf{H}(k)\mathbf{P}(k|k-1)\mathbf{H}^T(k) + \mathbf{R}(k)]^{-1}, \qquad (13.64)$$

and perform a *measurement update:*

$$\hat{\mathbf{x}}(k|k) = \hat{\mathbf{x}}(k|k-1) + \mathbf{K}(k)[\mathbf{z}(k) - \mathbf{h}_k(\hat{\mathbf{x}}(k|k-1))], \qquad (13.65)$$

$$\mathbf{P}(k|k) = \mathbf{P}(k|k-1) + \mathbf{K}(k)\mathbf{H}(k)\mathbf{P}(k|k-1), \qquad (13.66)$$

else

$$\hat{\mathbf{x}}(k|k) = \hat{\mathbf{x}}(k|k-1), \qquad (13.67)$$

$$\mathbf{P}(k|k) = \mathbf{P}(k|k-1). \qquad (13.68)$$

END EKF

This algorithm maintains an n-dimensional state estimate $\hat{\mathbf{x}}$ and an $n \times n$ approximate error covariance estimate $\mathbf{P}$. The notation used in the above algorithm distinguishes an estimate for time k based on earlier measurements [e.g., $\hat{\mathbf{x}}(k|k-1)$] from the corresponding estimate after the current measurement has been taken into account [e.g., $\hat{\mathbf{x}}(k|k)$]. The process is initialized with some appropriate choice of $\hat{\mathbf{x}}(0|0)$ and $\mathbf{P}(0|0)$. Successful application of the EKF in nonlinear problems generally requires judicious choice of the noise covariance matrices $\mathbf{Q}$ and $\mathbf{R}$ at each time step even if the underlying nonlinear model is deterministic.

Now, let us see how the EKF algorithm can be extended and applied to recurrent networks. We consider an arbitrary recurrent network given target values for specified nodes at specified times, and the objective is to find weights that allow optimal matching between target and actual values in a least mean-squared-error sense. For simplicity, all connections are assumed to have a one-time-step delay. Let the network have n_u nodes and n_w weights, with n_o nodes serving as output units (i.e., units that are ever given target values). Let $\mathbf{u}(k)$ denote the input vector presented to the network at time k and let $\mathbf{y}(k)$ denote the n_u-dimensional vector of activations of the n_u nodes at time k. Moreover, let $\mathbf{w}(k)$

denote the network weight matrix at time k, but treat it as an n_w-dimensional vector rather than a matrix. However, we will still use w_{ij} to denote the weight from the jth node to the ith node.

To apply the EKF, the measurement vector $\mathbf{z}$ in Eq. (13.59) is treated as the target value of the differentiable functions $\mathbf{h}_k(\cdot)$ at the activation values of the network's output nodes, and the state vector $\mathbf{x}$ in Eq. (13.58) is taken as the $(n_u + n_w)$-dimensional column vector

$$\mathbf{x} = \begin{bmatrix} \mathbf{y} \\ \mathbf{w} \end{bmatrix}. \tag{13.69}$$

For convenience, assume that the indexes of the output nodes are lower than the indexes of all other (i.e., hidden) nodes. Then the output nodes (values) are $y_1, y_2, \ldots, y_{n_o}$, and Eq. (13.59) becomes

$$\mathbf{z}(k) = \mathbf{h}_k(\mathbf{x}(k)) = [h_k^1(\mathbf{x}(k)), h_k^2(\mathbf{x}(k)), \ldots, h_k^{n_o}(\mathbf{x}(k)), 0, 0, \ldots, 0]^T. \tag{13.70}$$

Thus, the linearized measurement matrix in Eq. (13.63) becomes

$$\mathbf{H}(k) = \left[\frac{\partial h_k^1}{\partial \mathbf{x}}, \frac{\partial h_k^2}{\partial \mathbf{x}}, \ldots, \frac{\partial h_k^{n_o}}{\partial \mathbf{x}}, 0, 0, \ldots, 0 \right] \Bigg|_{\mathbf{x} = \hat{\mathbf{x}}(k|k-1)} \tag{13.71}$$

$$\triangleq [\mathbf{H}^o(k), \mathbf{0}, \mathbf{0}], \tag{13.72}$$

where the columns in the first block correspond to output nodes, the columns in the second block correspond to hidden nodes, and the columns in the third block correspond to weights. In general cases, $\mathbf{z}$ is directly the target output vector of the network, and thus $\mathbf{z}(k) = [y_1, y_2, \ldots, y_{h_o}, 0, 0, \ldots, 0]^T$, which implies that

$$\mathbf{H}(k) = [\mathbf{I}, \mathbf{0}, \mathbf{0}]. \tag{13.73}$$

The dynamics of the network are given by

$$\mathbf{y}(k+1) = \mathbf{f}(\mathbf{y}(k), \mathbf{w}(k), \mathbf{u}(k)), \tag{13.74}$$

$$\mathbf{w}(k+1) = \mathbf{w}(k) \qquad \text{for all } k, \tag{13.75}$$

where $\mathbf{f}$ represents the overall state transition mapping performed by the network as a function of node activities, weights, and input. The linearization of this mapping [i.e., Eq. (13.60)] thus has the block structure

$$\mathbf{F} = \begin{bmatrix} \mathbf{F}_1 & \mathbf{F}_2 \\ \mathbf{0} & \mathbf{I} \end{bmatrix}, \tag{13.76}$$

where $\mathbf{F}_1$ is an $n_u \times n_u$ block and $\mathbf{F}_2$ is an $n_u \times n_w$ block. The block structure of the state vector naturally leads to corresponding block decompositions of all other matrices in an EKF, so that the approximate error covariance matrix becomes

$$\mathbf{P} = \begin{bmatrix} \mathbf{P}_1 & \mathbf{P}_2 \\ \mathbf{P}_3 & \mathbf{P}_4 \end{bmatrix}, \tag{13.77}$$

where $\mathbf{P}_1(k)$ models the interactions between the recurrent node outputs, $\mathbf{P}_4(k)$ models the interactions between the weights of the network, and $\mathbf{P}_2(k) = \mathbf{P}_3^T(k)$ models the cross-correlations between the network's weights and recurrent node outputs. The Kalman gain matrix is also decomposed into

$$\mathbf{K} = \begin{bmatrix} \mathbf{K}_1 \\ \mathbf{K}_2 \end{bmatrix}, \tag{13.78}$$

where $\mathbf{K}_1$ prescribes changes in the network activity and $\mathbf{K}_2$ prescribes weight changes in response to errors. The full algorithm is then obtained by substituting these block decompositions into the EKF algorithm and differentiating the particular dynamical equations representing the computation performed at each node to obtain $\mathbf{F}_1$ and $\mathbf{F}_2$.

Let us summarize the learning procedure briefly. According to the algorithm, in applying the EKF to the recurrent network, there are two distinct steps, the *time* update and the *measurement* update. The time update step involves propagating input signals and time-delayed recurrent node outputs through the recurrent network, computing the linearized dynamics by computing the *partial* derivatives of recurrent node outputs with respect to both the recurrent node outputs from the previous time step and the network's weight estimates, and then propagating the error covariance. The measurement update step involves computing the linearized measurement matrix, which is trivial if Eq. (13.73) is used, computing the Kalman gain matrix using the error covariance obtained in the time update step, and finally performing the measurement updates.

Training of recurrent networks by RTRL usually requires that very low learning rates be employed because of the inherent correlations between successive node outputs. On the other hand, the EKF is a second-order algorithm that in effect processes and uses information about the shape of the training problem's error surface in updating the states of the system, thus providing an effective mechanism of dealing with temporal and spatial correlations in input signals and successive node outputs in recurrent neural networks. Hence, the EKF demonstrates fast learning as a function of the number of training data presented. However, the computation in each training instance is quite complex. The reason is that, in the time update step in the EKF algorithm, the partial derivatives of recurrent node outputs are *not* recursively defined as a function of ordered derivatives from the previous time step. As a result, the ordered derivatives of recurrent node outputs with respect to the network's weight parameters become embedded in the submatrices $\mathbf{P}_2(k)$ and $\mathbf{P}_3(k)$. However, these ordered derivatives are coupled with evolution of the error covariance matrix and do not appear to be directly accessible. This greatly increases the EKF's computational expense.

Let us consider the time and space complexity of the EKF. Assume fixed input and output dimensions and full connectivity with one weight per connection. Let the total number of nodes be n. The storage requirements are dominated by the need to store the $\mathbf{P}$ matrix, which contains $O(n^4)$ elements, each of which must be updated at every time step. One interesting fact is that of the $O(n^2)$ elements in each row of the matrix $\mathbf{F}_2$, only $O(n)$ are nonzero. Careful arrangement of just one particular matrix multiplication computation taking this into account can thus be shown to lead to an algorithm requiring $O(n^4)$ arithmetic operations per time step.

The EKF algorithm has been successfully applied to signal processing [Matthews, 1990] and system identification in control problems. It has also been used to train a recurrent network to emulate a finite-state machine with Boolean input and output on problems similar to the examples described previously in this chapter. Simulations showed that the EKF found solutions to these problems often requiring up to 10 fewer time steps than RTRL. Note that just as in the case of simple gradient-descent algorithms, it is important to ensure that the gain at each time step is small enough so that the learning trajectory in the weight space moves reasonably slowly along the nonlinearities.

13.3 REINFORCEMENT LEARNING

In all the supervised learning problems that we have discussed so far, we have assumed that correct target output values are known for each input pattern. But for some real-world applications, such detailed information is usually difficult and expensive, if not impossible, to obtain. For this reason, there are *reinforcement learning* algorithms for either recurrent or nonrecurrent neural networks. For a reinforcement learning problem, training data are very rough and coarse, and they are just "evaluative" as compared with the "instructive" feedback in a supervised learning problem. Training a network with this kind of evaluative feedback is called *reinforcement learning,* and this simple evaluative feedback, called a reinforcement signal, is a scalar. In the extreme case, there is only a single bit of information to indicate whether the output is right or wrong. Reinforcement learning is thus the learning of a mapping from situations to actions so as to maximize the scalar reward or reinforcement signal. Since the learner is not told which action to take, it must discover which actions yield the highest reward by trying them. In addition to the roughness and noninstructive nature of the reinforcement signal, a more challenging problem in reinforcement learning is that a reinforcement signal may be available only at a time long after a sequence of actions has occurred. To solve the long-delay problem, prediction capabilities are necessary in a reinforcement learning system. Reinforcement learning with prediction capabilities is much more useful than the supervised learning schemes in dynamical control problems and artificial intelligence because the success or failure signal might be known only after a long sequence of control actions have taken place. These two characteristics (*trial-and-error search* and *delayed reward*) are the two most important distinguishing features of reinforcement learning.

Figure 13.14 shows how a network and its training environment interact in a reinforcement learning problem. The environment supplies a time-varying vector of input to the

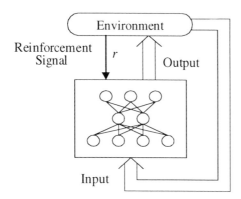

Figure 13.14 A neural network and its training environment interact in a reinforcement learning problem.

network, receives its time-varying vector of outputs or actions from the network, and then provides a time-varying scalar reinforcement signal to the network. In the general case, the reinforcement signal $r(t)$ can be in one of the following forms: (1) a two-valued number, $r(t) \in \{-1, 1\}$ or $\{0, 1\}$, such that $r(t) = 1$ means "success" and $r(t) = -1$ (or 0) means "failure"; (2) a multivalued discrete number in the range of $[-1, 1]$ or $[0, 1]$, for example, $r(t) \in \{-1, -0.5, 0, 0.5, 1\}$ which corresponds to different discrete degrees of failure or success; or (3) a real number, $r(t) \in [-1, 1]$ or $[0, 1]$, which represents a more detailed and continuous degree of failure or success. We also assume that $r(t)$ is the reinforcement signal available at time step t and is caused by the input and actions chosen at time step $(t - 1)$ or even affected by earlier input and actions. The objective of learning is to maximize a function of this reinforcement signal, such as the expectation of its value at the upcoming time step or the expectation of some integral of its values over all future time.

Precise computation of the reinforcement signal greatly depends on the nature of the environment and is assumed to be unknown to the learning system. It can be a deterministic or a stochastic function of the input produced by the environment and the output it receives from the network. There are three classes of reinforcement learning problems [Hertz et al., 1991]. First, for the simplest case, the reinforcement signal is always the *same* for a given input-output pair; hence, the network can learn a definite input-output mapping. Moreover, the reinforcement signal and input patterns do not depend on previous network output. For example, the parity learning problem and the symmetry learning problem are typical of this class. Second, in a stochastic environment, a particular input-output pair determines only the probability of positive reinforcement. However, this probability is fixed for each input-output pair, and again, the reinforcement signal and input sequence do not refer to past history. This class includes the nonassociative reinforcement learning problem in which there is no input, and we need to determine the best output pattern with the highest probability of positive reinforcement from only a finite set of trials. A typical example is the two-armed bandit problem, in which we imagine being able to pull either handle of a two-armed slot machine without prior knowledge of the payoff probabilities. Third, for the most general case, the environment is itself governed by a complicated dynamical process, and both the reinforcement signal and input patterns may depend on past network output. For example, in a chess game, the environment is actually another player, and the network receives a reinforcement signal (win or loss) only after a long sequence of moves. In such situations, we should know how to assign credit or blame, for an eventual success or failure, individually to each move in such a sequence. This is the *credit assignment problem,* which belongs to the temporal credit assignment problem in contrast to the more familiar *structure* credit assignment problem of attributing network error to different weights. To resolve the three different classes of reinforcement learning problems, we shall discuss in the following sections several different neural network models and learning algorithms which will provide solutions to these problems.

13.3.1 Associative Reward-Penalty

We shall first introduce the *associative reward-penalty* (A_{R-P}) algorithm for adaptive elements called A_{R-P} elements [Barto and Anandan, 1985] and its generalizations [Barto and Jordan, 1987; Hertz et al., 1991]. This learning procedure is applicable to the first and second classes of reinforcement learning problems. In this section, we assume that the reinforcement signal is a two-valued number $r(t) \in \{-1, 1\}$.

The goal of reinforcement learning is to adjust the weights of the network such that the reinforcement signal is a maximum, that is,

$$\Delta w_i = \eta \frac{\partial r}{\partial w_i} . \tag{13.79}$$

In other words, the objective of a reinforcement learning system is to search the space of all possible weight vectors (matrices) $\mathbf{w}$ for a point where $E(r \mid \mathbf{w})$ is maximum and E denotes the expectation operator. We need to use the expectation value here because of the potential randomness in any of the following: (a) the environment's choice of input to the network, (b) the network's choice of output corresponding to any particular input, and (c) the environment's choice of reinforcement value for any particular input-output pair. To determine $\partial r / \partial w_i$, we need to know $\partial r / \partial y_j$, where y_j is the output of the network. Because the reinforcement signal does not provide any hint as to what the right answer should be in terms of a cost function, there is no gradient information. Hence, one needs to estimate the gradient $\partial r / \partial y$. If we can estimate $\partial r / \partial y$, then the output weights can be trained by the usual delta rule and the remaining weights (if there are any) can be trained by the usual gradient-based supervised learning algorithms (e.g., back propagation, recurrent back propagation). In this way, a reinforcement learning problem is transformed into a supervised learning problem. To estimate the gradient information in a reinforcement learning network, there needs to be some source of randomness in the manner in which output actions are chosen by the network such that the space of possible output can be explored to find a correct value. Thus, the output nodes of the network are now designed to be *stochastic* units which compute their output as a stochastic function of their input; the rest of the network architecture is arbitrary and can be chosen to suit the problem at hand.

Let the ith output node $y_i = \pm 1$ be governed by the following stochastic dynamical rule:

$$\text{Prob}(y_i = \pm 1) = a(\pm h_i) = f_\beta(\pm h_i) = \frac{1}{1 + \exp(\mp 2\beta h_i)} , \tag{13.80}$$

where the parameter β controls the steepness of the function $f_\beta(\pm h_i)$ near $h_i = 0$ and $h_i = \sum_j w_{ij} x_j$ is the net input to the output node i, where x_j might be the activations of some hidden nodes or might be the network inputs. The problem now is to determine an appropriate error estimate δ_i^k for each of the output nodes when their inputs are set to a particular pattern x_j^k. Since the target patterns are unknown, we can construct our own target patterns d_i^k as [Widrow et al., 1973]

$$d_i^k = \begin{cases} y_i^k & \text{if } r^k = +1 \text{ (reward)} \\ -y_i^k & \text{if } r^k = -1 \text{ (penalty)}, \end{cases} \tag{13.81}$$

where the superscript k denotes the kth pattern. Equation (13.81) indicates that the network is more likely to do what it just did if that was rewarded, and more likely to do the opposite if that was penalized. Note that for 0/1 reinforcement signals instead of ± 1, the $-y_i^k$ in the penalty case is replaced by $(1 - y_i^k)$. The error δ_i^k can then be estimated by comparing the target d_i^k with the average output value $\bar{y}_i^k$:

$$\delta_i^k = d_i^k - \bar{y}_i^k, \tag{13.82}$$

where $\bar{y}_i^k$ can be found by averaging for a while or simply by calculation from Eq. (13.80) as

$$\bar{y}_i^k = (+1)\, a(h_i^k) + (-1)[\, 1 - a(h_i^k)] = \tanh(\beta h_i^k). \tag{13.83}$$

According to the delta rule, the update rule for the output weights is then

$$\Delta w_{ij} = \eta\, (r^k)\, \delta_i^k x_j^k, \tag{13.84}$$

where the learning rate η depends on whether the output was right or wrong. Typically $\eta^+ \triangleq \eta\,(+1)$ is taken as 10 to 100 times larger than $\eta^- \triangleq \eta\,(-1)$. Hence, the standard form of the $A_{R\text{-}P}$ learning rule is

$$\Delta w_{ij} = \begin{cases} \eta^+ [\, y_i^k - \bar{y}_i^k] x_j^k & \text{if } r^k = +1 \text{ (reward)} \\ \eta^- [\, -y_i^k - \bar{y}_i^k] x_j^k & \text{if } r^k = -1 \text{ (penalty)}, \end{cases} \tag{13.85}$$

which indicates how to adjust the weights going to the output nodes. It is understandable that such learning is very slow compared to supervised learning because of the nature of trial-and-error search. When learning converges to a correct solution, the $\bar{y}_i^k$ approach ± 1 and converge to the state that provides the largest *average* reinforcement. The convergence of $A_{R\text{-}P}$ for the case of a single binary output node and a set of linearly independent patterns x_j^k with the learning rates η^+ and η^- decaying to zero has been proved [Barto and Anandan, 1985]. Detailed theoretical analysis of $A_{R\text{-}P}$ can be found in Hertz et al. [1991]. The learning speed of $A_{R\text{-}P}$ can be improved if a given pattern is presented several times before moving on to the next one [Ackley and Littman, 1990]. Moreover, this should be done in *batch mode,* that is, accumulating all the weight changes and then adding the accumulated sum to the weights at the end. This batch-mode procedure provides a better estimate of the output errors.

  If we consider the continuous-valued scalar reinforcement signal, $0 \le r \le 1$, with 0 meaning failure and 1 meaning success, we can generalize Eq. (13.85) to

$$\Delta w_{ij} = \eta\, (r^k)(\, r^k [\, y_i^k - \bar{y}_i^k] + (1 - r^k)[\, -y_i^k - \bar{y}_i^k]) x_j^k, \tag{13.86}$$

where $\eta\,(r^k)$ indicates the dependence of η on r. Another variation is to use $(\bar{y}_i^k - y_i^k)$ instead of $(-y_i^k - \bar{y}_i^k)$ for the penalty case. Then Eq. (13.85) becomes

$$\Delta w_{ij} = \eta r^k [\, y_i^k - \bar{y}_i^k] x_j^k, \tag{13.87}$$

where the dependence of η on r is left out. Note that, on receipt of $r = -1$, Eq. (13.87) tells the network not to do what it is doing while Eq. (13.85) tells it to do the opposite of what it is doing. In practice, Eq. (13.85) seems to work better. However, Eq. (13.87) is more amenable to theoretical analysis. It has been shown to have the property [Hertz et al., 1991]

$$\Delta \bar{w}_{ij} = \frac{\eta}{\beta} \frac{\partial \bar{r}}{\partial w_{ij}}, \tag{13.88}$$

where the averages are across all patterns and outcomes. Hence, the learning rule in Eq. (13.87) continues to increase the average reinforcement until a maximum is reached. Another variation with a similar concept is to set η^- to 0 in Eq. (13.85). This is equivalent to modifying the reinforcement signal from ± 1 to $0/1$, meaning failures are not penalized. The resulting rule is called the *associative reward-inaction rule* or A_{R-I}.

13.3.2 REINFORCE Algorithms

A wider class of algorithms that possess the statistical gradient-following property of Eq. (13.88) has been identified by Williams [1987, 1988, 1992a]. These algorithms, called REINFORCE algorithms, are for tasks that are associative, and they involve *immediate reinforcement* (meaning that the reinforcement provided to the network is determined by the most recent input-output pair only, as in the first and second classes of reinforcement learning problems). The general form of REINFORCE learning algorithms is

$$\Delta w_{ij} = \alpha_{ij} (r - b_{ij}) e_{ij}, \qquad (13.89)$$

where α_{ij} is a *learning rate factor,* b_{ij} is a *reinforcement baseline* which is conditionally independent of y_i, and

$$e_{ij} = \frac{\partial \ln a_i(y_i, h_i)}{\partial w_{ij}} = \frac{\partial \ln a_i(y_i, \mathbf{w}_i, \mathbf{x}_i)}{\partial w_{ij}} \qquad (13.90)$$

is called the *characteristic eligibility* of w_{ij}, where $a_i(y_i, h_i) = \text{Prob}(y_i \mid h_i)$ with h_i the net input to node i. The following theorem characterizes this class of algorithms.

Theorem 13.2

(Williams, 1992a). For any REINFORCE algorithm, the inner product of $E(\Delta\mathbf{W} \mid \mathbf{W})$ and $\nabla_\mathbf{W} E(r \mid \mathbf{W})$ is nonnegative, where $\mathbf{W}$ is the weight matrix and $E(\cdot)$ is the expectation operator. Furthermore, if $\alpha_{ij} > 0$ for all i and j, then this inner product is zero only when $\nabla_\mathbf{W} E(r \mid \mathbf{W}) = \mathbf{0}$. Also, if $\alpha_{ij} = \alpha$ is independent of i and j, then $E(\Delta\mathbf{W} \mid \mathbf{W}) = \alpha \nabla_\mathbf{W} E(r \mid \mathbf{W})$.

This theorem says that for any REINFORCE algorithm, the average update vector in the weight space lies in a direction in which the average reinforcement is increasing. There are a number of interesting special cases of such algorithms. It is easily checked that if $a_i(\cdot)$ is as defined in Eq. (13.80) and $\beta = 0.5$, then e_{ij} in Eq. (13.90) becomes $e_{ij} = (y_i - p_i) x_j$, where $p_i = \text{Prob}(y_i = 1)$. Here we consider $0/1$ reinforcement signals. Then setting $\alpha_{ij} = \alpha$ and $b_{ij} = 0$ for all i and j yields a REINFORCE algorithm having the general learning rule

$$\Delta w_{ij} = \alpha r (y_i - p_i) x_j, \qquad (13.91)$$

which is exactly the same as the A_{R-I} algorithm with a $0/1$ reinforcement signal and a continuous-valued r. Thus, A_{R-I} is a REINFORCE algorithm. However, note that REINFORCE algorithms do not include full A_{R-P} algorithms.

When the reinforcement baseline b_{ij} in Eq. (13.89) is nonzero, REINFORCE algorithms become a kind of *reinforcement comparison* [Sutton, 1984] strategy. For this strategy, one maintains an adaptive estimate $\hat{r}$ of upcoming reinforcement based on past experience. As a particular example, the A_{R-I} algorithm in Eq. (13.91) can be extended to

$$\Delta w_{ij} = \alpha \, (r - \hat{r}) \, (y_i - p_i) \, x_j, \tag{13.92}$$

which is then a REINFORCE algorithm as long as the computation of $\hat{r}$ is never based on the current value of y_i or r. One common approach to computing $\hat{r}$ is to use an exponential averaging scheme

$$\hat{r}(t) = \gamma r(t-1) + (1-\gamma) \hat{r}(t-1), \tag{13.93}$$

where $0 < \gamma \le 1$. An alternative algorithm is given by the rule

$$\Delta w_{ij} = \alpha \, (r - \hat{r}) \, (y_i - \bar{y}_i) \, x_j, \tag{13.94}$$

where $\bar{y}_i$ is updated by

$$\bar{y}_i = \gamma y_i(t-1) + (1-\gamma) \bar{y}_i(t-1) \tag{13.95}$$

using the same γ used for updating $\hat{r}$. This particular algorithm has been found generally to converge faster and more reliably than the corresponding REINFORCE algorithm.

An interesting application of the REINFORCE framework is in developing learning algorithms for units that determine their scalar output stochastically from multiparameter distributions rather than single-parameter distributions as in Eq. (13.80). One general example is the *Gaussian* unit:

$$a(y_i, m_i, \sigma_i) = \text{Prob}(y_i \mid m_i, \sigma_i) = \frac{1}{\sqrt{2\pi}\sigma_i} \exp\left(\frac{-(y_i - m_i)^2}{2\sigma_i^2}\right), \tag{13.96}$$

where m_i and σ_i are the mean and the variance of the normal distribution, respectively. Such a unit first computes values of m_i and σ_i deterministically based on its weights and input and then draws its output y_i stochastically from the normal distribution with mean m_i and variance σ_i. One potentially useful feature of the Gaussian unit is that the mean and variance of its output are individually controllable as long as separate weights or inputs are used to determine these two parameters. Then the exploratory behavior of the random unit can be controlled in such a way that m_i indicates the search center and σ_i describes the search range.

Rather than commit to a particular means of determining the mean and variance of a Gaussian unit's output from its input and weights, we will simply treat this unit as if the mean and variance themselves serve as the adaptable parameters of the unit. Any more general functional dependence of these parameters on the actual adaptable parameters and input to the unit simply requires application of the chain rule. Hence, the characteristic eligibilities of m_i and σ_i as defined in Eq. (13.90) are, respectively,

$$\frac{\partial \ln a}{\partial m_i} = \frac{y_i - m_i}{\sigma_i^2} \quad \text{and} \quad \frac{\partial \ln a}{\partial \sigma_i} = \frac{(y_i - m_i)^2 - \sigma_i^2}{\sigma_i^3}. \tag{13.97}$$

A REINFORCE algorithm for this unit thus has the form

$$\Delta m_i = \alpha_m \, (r - b_m) \frac{y_i - m_i}{\sigma_i^2} \quad \text{and} \quad \Delta \sigma_i = \alpha_\sigma \, (r - b_\sigma) \frac{(y_i - m_i)^2 - \sigma_i^2}{\sigma_i^3}, \tag{13.98}$$

where α_m, b_m, α_σ, and b_σ are chosen appropriately. The use of multiparameter distributions in reinforcement learning will be demonstrated in Chap. 19.

REINFORCE algorithms may serve as a sound basis for developing other more effective reinforcement learning algorithms. Since they involve a gradient-based approach, they integrate well with other gradient computation techniques such as back propagation. More thorough discussions of REINFORCE algorithms can be found in Williams [1992a].

13.3.3 Temporal Difference Methods

Thus far, we have focused on the first and second classes of reinforcement learning problems, that is, immediate reinforcement tasks. We shall next focus on *delayed reinforcement* tasks in which there is a long time delay between a reinforcement signal and the actions that caused it. In such cases, a *temporal credit assignment* problem results because we need to assign credit or blame, for an eventual success or failure, to each step individually in a long sequence. Hence, for this class of reinforcement learning problems, we need to solve the temporal credit assignment problem together with the original structure credit assignment problem of attributing network error to different connections or weights. A widely used approach in developing algorithms for such tasks is to combine an immediate-reinforcement learner (network) with an adaptive predictor or *critic* to perform the task of predicting reinforcement based on the use of *temporal difference* (TD) methods [Sutton, 1988]. In Fig. 13.15 [where the structure shown is sometimes called *adaptive heuristic critic* (AHC) learning architecture], the critic receives the raw reinforcement signal r from the environment and sends a processed signal, called an internal reinforcement signal ρ, on to the main network, called the *action network*. The internal reinforcement signal ρ represents an evaluation of the current behavior of the action network, whereas r typically involves the past history. If the critic can produce a prediction p of r, then we can set, for example, $\rho = r - p$, such that the action network performs a reinforcement comparison so that it will be rewarded when r exceeds expectations and penalized when r falls short of expectations [see Eq. (13.92)]. The critic itself is normally adaptive and improves with experience. It usually learns to predict the reinforcement signal by TD methods.

TD methods consist of a class of incremental learning procedures specialized for prediction. Conventional prediction-learning methods assign credit based on the difference between predicted and actual outcomes, while TD methods assign credit based on the difference between *temporally successive predictions*. In TD methods, learning occurs whenever there is a change in prediction over time and does not wait for an external teaching (reinforcement or supervised) signal. We can distinguish two kinds of prediction-learning problems. In *single-step* prediction problems, all information about the correctness of each

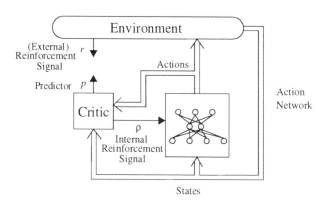

Figure 13.15 Reinforcement learning network with a critic—adaptive heuristic critic (AHC) learning architecture.

prediction is revealed at once. In *multistep* prediction problems, correctness is not revealed until more than one step after the prediction is made. That is, the function of the single-step predictor (critic) is to predict the external reinforcement signal $r(t)$ one time step ahead, that is, at time $(t-1)$. Here, $r(t)$ is the real reinforcement signal resulting from the inputs and actions chosen at time step $(t-1)$, but it can be known only at time step t in the first and second classes of reinforcement learning problems. Since data naturally come in observation-outcome pairs in single-step prediction problems, the training of a single-step predictor is a simple supervised learning problem with a cost function $E = \frac{1}{2}[r(t) - p(t)]^2$. Hence, TD methods cannot be distinguished from supervised learning methods in this case. In fact, reinforcement learning problems with single-step prediction are considered immediate reinforcement problems and can be solved by, for example, REINFORCE algorithms without a critic. However, with a correct predicted signal $p(t)$, a better action can be chosen by the action network at time step $(t-1)$ in its stochastic exploration, and the corresponding learning can be performed on the action network at time step t upon receiving the external reinforcement signal $r(t)$. In other words, the predicted reinforcement signal (from either a single-step or a multistep predictor) can help the action network to do a more efficient random search. To achieve this purpose, we need to make use of stochastic units with multiparameter distribution [see Chap. 19 and also [Franklin, 1989]]. Single-step prediction is the extreme case of the multistep prediction discussed in the following.

The function of a multistep predictor is to predict the reinforcement signal at each time step within two successive external reinforcement signals which may be separated by many time steps. It can thus ensure that both the predictor and the action network do not have to wait until the actual outcome is known and can update their parameters within the period without any evaluative feedback from the environment. There are three important cases of TD methods in multistep prediction [Sutton, 1988; Lin and Lee, 1994]:

Case 1: *Prediction of final outcome.* Given are the observation-outcome sequences of the form $\mathbf{x}_1, \mathbf{x}_2, \ldots, \mathbf{x}_m, z$, where each $\mathbf{x}_t$ is an input vector available at time step t from the environment and z is the external reinforcement signal available at time step $(m+1)$. For each observation-outcome sequence, the predictor produces a corresponding sequence of predictions $p_1, p_2, \ldots, p_m$, each of which is an estimate of z. Since p_t is the output of the evaluation network (critic) at time t, p_t is a function of the network's input $\mathbf{x}_t$ and the network's adjustable parameters (weights) w_t and thus can be denoted as $p(\mathbf{x}_t, w_t)$. For this prediction problem, the learning rule, which is called a TD(λ) family of learning procedures, is

$$\Delta w_t = \eta (p_t - p_{t-1}) \sum_{k=1}^{t-1} \lambda^{t-k-1} \nabla_w p_k, \tag{13.99}$$

where $p_{m+1} \equiv z$, $0 \leq \lambda \leq 1$, η is the learning rate, and λ is the recency weighting factor with which alternations in the predictions of observation vectors occurring k steps in the past are weighted by λ^k. In the extreme case that $\lambda = 1$, all the proceeding predictions $p_1, p_2, \ldots, p_{t-1}$ are altered properly according to the current temporal difference $(p_t - p_{t-1})$ to an "equal" extent. In this case, Eq. (13.99) reduces to a supervised learning approach, and if p_t is a linear function of $\mathbf{x}_t$ and w_t, called a *linear TD(1) procedure,* then it is the same as the Widrow-Hoff procedure in Eq. (10.17) as indicated in Theorem 13.3 (we shall discuss Theorem 13.3 after all three cases are identified). In the other extreme case, $\lambda = 0$, the increment of the parameter w is determined only by its effect on the prediction associated with the most recent observation.

Case 2: *Prediction of finite cumulative outcomes.* In this case, p_t predicts the remaining cumulative cost given the tth observation $\mathbf{x}_t$ rather than the overall cost for the sequence. This happens when we are more concerned with the sum of future predictions than the prediction of what will happen at a specific future time. Let r_t be the actual cost incurred between time steps $(t-1)$ and t. Then p_{t-1} must predict $z_{t-1} = \sum_{k=t}^{m+1} r_k$. Hence, the prediction error is $z_{t-1} - p_{t-1} = \sum_{k=t}^{m+1} r_k - p_{t-1} = \sum_{k=t}^{m+1} (r_k + p_k - p_{k-1})$, where p_{m+1} is defined as 0. Thus, the learning rule is

$$\Delta w_t = \eta\,(r_t + p_t - p_{t-1}) \sum_{k=1}^{t-1} \lambda^{t-k-1} \nabla_w p_k. \tag{13.100}$$

Case 3: *Prediction of infinite discounted cumulative outcomes.* In this case, p_{t-1} predicts $z_{t-1} = \sum_{k=0}^{\infty} \gamma^k r_{t+k} = r_t + \gamma p_t$, where the discount rate parameter γ, $0 \le \gamma < 1$, determines the extent to which we are concerned with short- or long-range prediction. This method is used for prediction problems in which exact success or failure may never become completely known. In this case, the prediction error is $(r_t + \gamma p_t) - p_{t-1}$ and the learning rule is

$$\Delta w_t = \eta\,(r_t + \gamma p_t - p_{t-1}) \sum_{k=1}^{t-1} \lambda^{t-k-1} \nabla_w p_k. \tag{13.101}$$

Let us now state the important Theorem 13.3 which relates the particular TD procedure, TD(1), to the general gradient-based supervised learning rule.

Theorem 13.3

For multistep prediction problems, the TD(1) procedure produces the same per-sequence weight changes as the general gradient-based supervised learning rule.

Proof: To solve the multistep prediction problem defined in case 1, the supervised learning approach treats each sequence of observations and its outcome as an observation-outcome pair, that is, as the pairs $(\mathbf{x}_1, z)$, $(\mathbf{x}_2, z)$,..., $(\mathbf{x}_m, z)$. Then the weight increment at time t has the general form

$$\Delta w_t = \alpha\,(z - p_t)\,\nabla_w p_t, \tag{13.102}$$

where all Δw_t depend critically on z and thus cannot be determined until the end of the sequence when z becomes known. Hence, this equation cannot be computed incrementally. However, we can represent the error $(z - p_t)$ as a sum of changes in predictions, that is, as

$$z - p_t = \sum_{k=t}^{m} (p_{k+1} - p_k), \qquad \text{where } p_{m+1} \triangleq z. \tag{13.103}$$

Then the total weight change can be written as

$$\sum_{t=1}^{m} \alpha\,(z - p_t)\,\nabla_w p_t = \sum_{t=1}^{m} \alpha \sum_{k=t}^{m} (p_{k+1} - p_k)\,\nabla_w p_t$$

$$= \sum_{k=1}^{m} \alpha \sum_{t=1}^{k} (p_{k+1} - p_k)\,\nabla_w p_t \tag{13.104}$$

$$= \sum_{t=1}^{m} \alpha\,(p_{t+1} - p_t) \sum_{k=1}^{t} \nabla_w p_k.$$

Hence, the update rule becomes

$$\Delta w_t = \alpha \, (p_{k+1} - p_k) \sum_{k=1}^{t} \nabla_w p_k,\qquad(13.105)$$

which is the TD(1) procedure.

Theorem 13.3 shows that the TD(1) procedure and the gradient-based supervised learning rule produce exactly the same weight changes, but that the TD(1) procedure can be implemented incrementally and therefore requires far less computational power. The TD(1) procedure can be considered a conceptual bridge to the larger family of TD procedures in Eqs. (13.99)–(13.101) that produce weight changes different from those produced by any supervised learning method. The following example illustrates that TD methods can learn more efficiently than supervised learning methods even on very simple prediction problems. This was argued to be true for any predicted system that is dynamical and has a state that can be observed to be evolving over time.

Example 13.6

(Sutton, 1988). This example uses TD methods on a simple dynamic system that generates *bounded random walks*. A bounded random walk is a state sequence generated by taking random steps to the right or to the left until a boundary is reached. Figure 13.16 shows a system that generates such state sequences. Each walk begins in the center state D. The walk moves to a neighboring state, either to the right or to the left with equal probability at each step. The walk terminates if either edge state (A or G) is entered. A typical walk might be $DCBCDEFG$. The problem here is to estimate the probability of a walk ending in the rightmost state G, given that it is in each of the other states. This problem can be easily formulated as a reinforcement learning problem as follows. A walk's outcome is defined to be $z = 0$ for a walk ending on the left at A and $z = 1$ for a walk ending on the right at G. The learning methods estimate the expected value of z, which is equal to the probability of a right-side termination. If the walk is in state i at time t, then $\mathbf{x}_t = \mathbf{x}_i$, which is the corresponding observation vector. For example, the learning procedure is given the sequence $\mathbf{x}_D, \mathbf{x}_C, \mathbf{x}_B, \mathbf{x}_C, \mathbf{x}_D, \mathbf{x}_E, \mathbf{x}_F, 1$ for the walk $DCBCDEFG$. The vector $\mathbf{x}_i$ is a $0/1$ vector of length 5, with a single 1 in the component corresponding to i (e.g., $\mathbf{x}_D = [0, 0, 1, 0, 0]^T$).

A total of 100 training sets, each consisting of 10 sequences are constructed for use by all learning procedures. For all procedures, weight increments are computed according to a linear TD(λ), that is, Eq. (13.99) with $p = \mathbf{w}^T \mathbf{x}$. Seven different values are used for λ. They are $\lambda = 1$, resulting in the Widrow-Hoff learning procedure, $\lambda = 0$, resulting in a linear TD(0), and $\lambda = 0.1, 0.3, 0.5, 0.7$, and 0.9, resulting in a range of intermediate TD procedures. In training, each training set is presented once to each procedure. Weight updates are performed after each sequence. Moreover, each learning procedure is applied with a range of values for the learning rate parameter α to find its minimum error value. The result is shown in Fig. 13.17 which is a plot of the best error level achieved for each λ value. It is found that the Widrow-Hoff procedure, TD(1), produces the worst estimates. All TD methods with $\lambda < 1$ perform better than the supervised learning method.

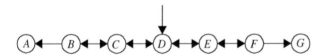

Figure 13.16   Generator of bounded random walks. This Markov process generates the data sequences in Example 13.6.

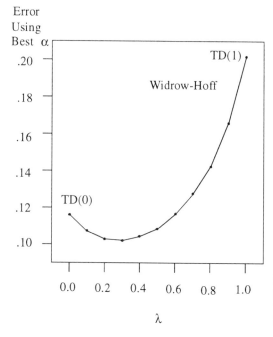

Error Using Best α

Figure 13.17 Average error at best α value for the random-walk problem in Example 13.6. (Adapted from Sutton [1988], © 1988 Kluwer Academic Publisher.)

The above example shows that although the Widrow-Hoff procedure minimizes error on the training set, it does not necessarily minimize error for future experience. The advantages of TD methods over supervised learning approaches in prediction problems were further discussed in [Tesauro, 1992]. In fact, it has been proved that the linear TD(0) converges to what can be considered the optimal estimates for matching future experience, which is consistent with the maximum-likelihood estimate of the underlying Markov process [Sutton, 1988].

Barto et al. [1983] constructed a network consisting of an *adaptive critic element* (ACE) and an *associative search element* (ASE) which resembles the A_{R-P} unit to learn the problem of balancing a pole on a movable cart. The system was able to learn the task even though the "failure" reinforcement signal r typically came long after the mistakes that produced it, where r remains zero throughout a run and becomes -1 when a failure occurs. This network, as shown in Fig. 13.18, is representative of the AHC architecture in Fig. 13.15 with the ACE acting as the predictor and the ASE as the action network. The decoder in the figure digitizes the continuous input space in such a way that each state vector $[x, \dot{x}, \theta, \dot{\theta}]^T$ is transformed into an n-component binary vector $[x_1, x_2, \ldots, x_n]^T$ whose components are all zero except for a single 1 in the position corresponding to the "lattice" (or "box") containing the state vector. Since we hope the system never fails (i.e., the failure reinforcement signal r never comes up), the ACE must predict infinite discounted cumulative outcomes and thus we should use case 3 of the TD methods [Eq. (13.101)]. That is, the ACE performs the following functions:

$$p(t) = \sum_{i=1}^{n} v_i(t)x_i(t), \qquad (13.106)$$

$$\Delta v_i(t) = \eta[r(t) + \gamma p(t) - p(t-1)]\hat{x}_i(t), \qquad (13.107)$$

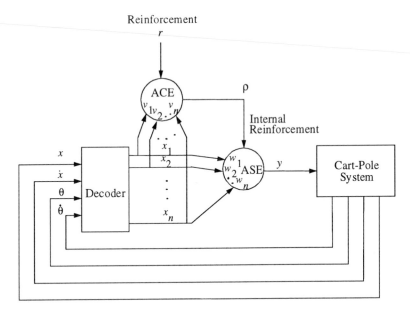

Reinforcement

r

Figure 13.18   ASE and ACE configured for a pole-balancing task. ACE receives the same state input as ASE and uses it to compute an improved or internal reinforcement signal to be used by ASE.

where

$$\hat{x}_i(t+1) = \lambda \hat{x}_i(t) + (1-\lambda) x_i(t), \tag{13.108}$$

which indicates the value at time t of the trace of x_i. Since the output of the ACE, $p(t)$, is to predict the value $r(t+1) + \lambda p(t+1)$, the internal reinforcement signal to the ASE is set to

$$\rho(t) = [r(t) + \gamma p(t)] - p(t-1). \tag{13.109}$$

The ASE resembles an A_{R-P} unit and performs the REINFORCE learning algorithm in Eq. (13.89). It is governed by the following equations:

$$y(t) = \text{sgn}\left[\sum_{i=1}^{n} w_i(t) x_i(t) + \text{noise}(t)\right], \tag{13.110}$$

$$\Delta w_i(t) = \alpha \rho(t) e_i(t), \tag{13.111}$$

where for computational simplicity, the exponentially decaying eligibility trace $e_i(t)$ is defined similarly to Eq. (13.108) as

$$e_i(t+1) = \delta e_i(t) + (1-\delta) y(t) x_i(t), \tag{13.112}$$

where δ, $0 \le \delta < 1$, determines the trace decay rate. The system has been shown to solve a difficult learning control problem such as the cart-pole balancing problem. Details of this problem and improved reinforcement learning systems will be addressed in Chap. 19.

13.4 CONCLUDING REMARKS

One of the first recurrent neural networks was the avalanche network developed by Grossberg [1969c, 1982a] for learning and performing an arbitrary spatiotemporal pattern. This network was constructed from the instar-outstar model. To generalize the avalanche network to recognizing more than one spatiotemporal pattern, a fully recurrent avalanche network, called a *sequential competitive avalanche field* (SCAF), was proposed [Hecht-Nielsen, 1986; Freeman and Skapura, 1991]. North [1988] applied a layered avalanche network in identifying each of seven civilian boats from the boats' passive sonar signatures.

RBP networks have shown a considerable improvement in performance over normal feedforward BP networks for a number of problems such as pattern completion [Almeida, 1987], stereo disparity [Qian and Sejnowski, 1988], skeletonization and thinning of binary images [Krishnapuram and Chen, 1993], and robot control [Barhen et al., 1989]. An interesting approach to the analysis of internal representations of the SRN based on principal component analysis can be found in [Elman, 1991], which describes an SRN trained to predict the order of words in simple (two- and three-word) sentences. Systematic empirical analysis of the SRN applied to the prediction task has been done by Jodouin [1993]. Mozer [1989] proposed another partially recurrent network, called a *focused back-propagation network*. In this network, the context layer is itself a hidden layer and each context unit has feedback to itself. Other partially recurrent networks can be found in [Watrous and Shastri, 1987; Morgan and Scofield, 1991].

For fully recurrent networks, an intuitive idea for implementing or training recurrent networks is to unfold an arbitrary recurrent network into a multilayer feedforward network that grows by one layer for each time step. This idea, called *back propagation through time* (BPTT) or *unfolding of time* [Rumelhart et al., 1986a,b], is suitable when we are interested in sequences with a small maximum length T. It has been used for learning for a shift register, for a sequence-completion task [Rumelhart et al., 1986b], and for a constraint-satisfaction problem [Nowlan, 1988]. It also has the potential to be applied to control problems such as adaptive state estimation [Miller et al., 1990]. The power and generality of the RTRL method have been demonstrated by several tasks in [Williams and Zipser, 1989a]. One modification of RTRL was reported by Sun et al. [1992]. They proposed a method for speeding up the calculations involved in a RTRL-style on-line network by using a Green's function approach. Another modification was made by Schmidhuber [1992a] who proposed an algorithm that is a cross between the BPTT and the RTRL algorithms. Li and Haykin [1993] used the RTRL algorithm to train a recurrent network with a specific structure for real-time nonlinear adaptive filtering. The performance of the three recurrent network training algorithms, TDRB, RTRL, and Green's function method [Sun et al., 1992], has been compared with respect to speed and accuracy for a given problem [Logar et al., 1993]. The learning and recall properties of TDRB on recurrent back-propagation networks for spatio-temporal signal recognition were studied by Sterzing and Schürmann [1993]. The algorithms for supervised sequential learning introduced in this chapter (such as RTRL, TDRB) are all based on *dynamical* recurrent networks. An alternative class of gradient-based systems consisting of two *feedforward* networks that learn to deal with temporal sequences using *fast weights* was proposed by Schmidhuber [1992b].

For second-order recurrent networks, Giles et al. [1992] suggested procedures for extracting what the network has learned. Second-order recurrent networks were also used by

Watrous and Kuhn [1992] to learn Tomita's grammars; however, they used a different learning rule which was also a fully gradient-based method. Zeng et al. [1993] proposed a modified second-order recurrent network, called a *self-clustering recurrent network*, which can learn long strings. Issues on the use of recurrent networks for recognizing formal grammars were discussed in [Pollack, 1989; Sun et al. 1990; Morgan and Scofield, 1991]. It has been shown that RTRL and RTRL with teacher forcing are two simplified versions of the EKF [Williams, 1992b]. Discussions of more advanced topics on the EKF can be found in [Singhal and Wu, 1989; Douglas and Meng, 1991; Puskorius and Feldkamp, 1991, 1992, 1993; Shah et al., 1992].

A detailed historical review of reinforcement learning can be found in [Narendra and Thathachar, 1989; Lin, 1994]. Detailed theoretical studies on the convergence of TD(λ) for general λ can be found in [Dayan, 1992]. Another form of TD-based reinforcement learning (besides the AHC learning architecture) is Q-learning [Watkins, 1989; Watkins and Dayan, 1992]. A thorough comparison of AHC learning and Q-learning was made in [Lin, 1992]. Sutton [1990, 1991] introduced the *Dyna* class of reinforcement learning architectures in which a form of *planning* is involved in addition to Q-learning. This approach and its modifications have been applied to the problem of mobile robot navigation in an unknown environment [Peng and Williams, 1993; Lin, 1993].

13.5 PROBLEMS

13.1 Write a program for implementing the RBP network in Example 13.1 and reproduce the results in Fig. 13.2(b).

13.2 (a) What is the dimension of the weight space and the phase space of the RBP network shown in Fig. 13.1?
   (b) Referring to the weight update equations derived in Example 13.1, derive the exact weight update rule for each weight in the RBP network shown in Fig. 13.1.

13.3 Consider a pattern-completion problem. There are 10 binary random vectors, and each of them has 10 elements. The problem is to find the values of two randomly selected, missing elements, given the other 8 elements. Solve this problem using (a) standard back propagation, and (b) a recurrent back-propagation algorithm on a multilayer (feedforward or recurrent) network with 10 hidden nodes.

13.4 Design a recurrent neural network that combines the characteristics of Jordan's sequential network and a simple recurrent network. Describe the interesting properties of the designed network. What kind of problems could it be best applied to?

13.5 (a) Explain why the SRN has difficulty in dealing with embedded loops in sequences.
   (b) Develop a strategy that can make the SRN retain information across a longer period than only two time steps.

13.6 (a) Derive the exact learning formula for the RTRL method with teacher forcing by modifying Eqs. (13.27) and (13.29) properly.
   (b) Derive the learning rules for the RTRL network which is expected to converge to a stable attractor.

13.7 Write a program for implementing the TDRB networks in Example 13.4 and reproduce the results in Fig. 13.8, where Fig. 13.8(a) is governed by $d_1(t) = 0.25(\sin(\pi t/8) + 1.2) + 0.2$, $d_2(t) = 0.45(\cos(\pi t/8) + 1.2)$. Figure 13.8(c) is governed by $d_1(t) = 0.45(\sin(\pi t/4) + 1.2)$, $d_2(t) = 0.45(\cos(\pi t/8) + 1.2)$. Figure 13.8(e) is governed by $d_1(t) = 0.4\sin(0.5t)\sin(1.5t) + 0.5$, $d_2(t) = 0.4\cos(0.5t)\sin(1.5t) + 0.5$.

13.8 Indicate how the TDRB method can be used to derive the RTRL method.

13.9 Generalize the SCRN learning rules derived in Sec. 13.2.3 to the case of higher-order recurrent networks with one hidden layer and draw a schematic of the corresponding backspace trick like the one in Fig. 13.10.

13.10 Write a program to train an SCRN to recognize Tomita's fourth language using the training data in Table 13.1. Use the SCRN described in Example 13.5. Test the recognition rate of the trained network by 10 "accept" strings (any string not containing "000" as a substring) and 10 "reject" strings (any string containing "000" as a substring).

13.11 Derive the derivative in Eq. (13.57) for the second-order recurrent network.

13.12 Show how to apply the EKF to a multilayer feedforward network and compare its performance (learning speed) with the standard error back-propagation rule on the function approximation problem in Problem 10.12.

13.13 **(a)** Consider the problem in assigning credit for the outcome (win, loss, or draw) of a game of chess. Describe the temporal credit assignment problem and the structural credit assignment problem in the context of this game.
(b) Figure out a way to transfer a supervised learning problem to a reinforcement learning problem by defining the reinforcement signal properly.

13.14 Verify that the REINFORCE algorithm does not include the full A_{R-P} algorithm.

13.15 **(a)** Show that the linear TD(1) procedure is exactly the Widrow-Hoff procedure.
(b) Write down a general rule for the three kinds of TD methods for multistep prediction given in Eqs. (13.99)–(13.101).

13.16 Consider the ASE and ACE configurations in Fig. 13.18. Verify that the ACE performs the TD method and that the ASE performs the REINFORCE learning algorithm.

14

Genetic Algorithms

Genetic algorithms (GAs) are developed to mimic some of the processes observed in natural evolution. The underlying principles of GAs were first published by Holland [1962]. The mathematical framework was developed in the 1960s and is presented in his pioneering book [Holland, 1975]. Genetic algorithms have been employed primarily in two major areas: optimization and machine learning. In optimization applications, they have been used in many diverse fields such as function optimization, image processing, the traveling salesperson problem, system identification, and control. In machine learning, GAs have been used to learn syntactically simple string IF-THEN rules in an arbitrary environment. Excellent references on GAs and their implementation and application are [Goldberg, 1989; Davis, 1991; Michalewicz, 1992].

This chapter focuses on the study of genetic algorithms as an important tool in the structure and parameter learning of neural networks. Structure and parameter learning problems of neural networks are coded as genes (or chromosomes), and GAs are then used to search for better solutions (optimal structure and parameters). Furthermore, GAs can be used to find the membership functions and fuzzy rules of a fuzzy logic system. Fundamental concepts of genetic operators, evolution schemes, hybrid genetic algorithms, and genetic programming will be discussed. Some applications of GAs to neural network learning, robotic path planning, and system identification and control will also be explored.

14.1 BASICS OF GENETIC ALGORITHMS

Genetic algorithms are search algorithms based on the mechanics of natural selection, genetics, and evolution. It is widely accepted that the evolution of living beings is a process that operates on *chromosomes*—organic devices for encoding the structure of living beings. Natural selection is the link between chromosomes and the performance of their decoded structures. Processes of natural selection cause chromosomes that encode successful structures to reproduce more often than those that do not. In addition to *reproduction, mutations* may cause the chromosomes of children to be different from those of their biological parents, and *recombination* processes may create quite different chromosomes in children by combining material from the chromosomes of their two parents. These features of natural evolution inspired the development of GAs. Roughly speaking, through a proper encoding mechanism GAs manipulate strings of binary digits (1s and 0s) called chromosomes, which represent multiple points in the search space. Each bit in a string is called an *allele*. They carry out simulated evolution on populations of chromosomes. Like nature, GAs solve the problem of finding good chromosomes by manipulating the material in the chromosomes blindly without any knowledge about the type of problem they are solving. The only information they are given is an evaluation of each chromosome they produce. This evaluation is used to bias the selection of chromosomes so that those with the best evaluations tend to reproduce more often than those with bad evaluations. Genetic algorithms, using simple manipulations of chromosomes such as simple encodings and reproduction mechanisms, can display complicated behavior and solve some extremely difficult problems without knowledge of the decoded world.

A high-level description of a GA is as follows [Davis, 1991].

Algorithm GA: Genetic Algorithm.

Given a way or a method of *encoding* solutions of a problem into the form of chromosomes and given an *evaluation function* that returns a measurement of the cost value of any chromosome in the context of the problem, a GA consists of the following steps (see Fig. 14.1):

Step 1: Initialize a population of chromosomes.

Step 2: Evaluate each chromosome in the population.

Step 3: Create new chromosomes by mating current chromosomes; apply mutation and recombination as the parent chromosomes mate.

Step 4: Delete members of the population to make room for new chromosomes.

Step 5: Evaluate the new chromosomes and insert them into the population.

Step 6: If the stopping criterion is satisfied, then stop and return the best chromosome; otherwise, go to step 3.

END GA

The encoding mechanisms and the evaluation function form the links between the GA and the specific problem to be solved. The technique for encoding solutions may vary from problem to problem and from GA to GA. Generally, encoding is carried out using bit strings. The coding that has been shown to be optimal is binary coding [Holland, 1975]. Intuitively, it is better to have a few possible options for many bits than to have many possible options for a few bits. An evaluation function takes a chromosome as input and returns a number or a list of numbers that are a measure of the chromosome's performance on the problem to be solved. Evaluation functions play the same role in GAs as the environment plays in natural evolution. The interaction of an individual with its environment provides a measure of fitness. Similarly, the interaction of a chromosome with an evaluation function provides a measure of fitness that the GA uses when carrying out reproduction.

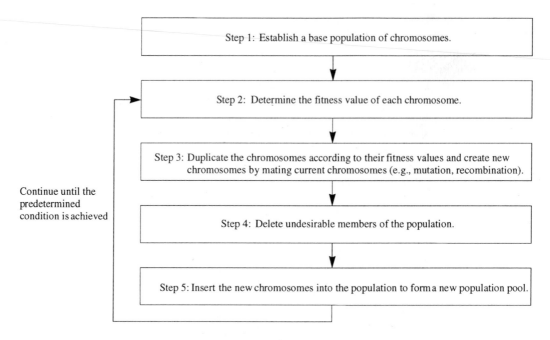

Figure 14.1 Basic steps of genetic algorithm.

The GA is a general-purpose stochastic optimization method for solving search problems. GAs differ from normal optimization and search procedures in several ways. First, the algorithm works with a population of strings, searching many peaks in parallel. By employing genetic operators, it exchanges information between the peaks, thus lessening the possibility of ending at a local minimum and missing the global minimum. Second, it works with a coding of the parameters, not the parameters themselves. Third, the algorithm needs to evaluate only the objective function to guide its search, and there is no requirement for derivatives or other auxiliary knowledge. The only available feedback from the system is the value of the performance measure (fitness) of the current population. Finally, as in the Boltzmann machine, the transition rules are probabilistic rather than deterministic. The randomized search is guided by the fitness value of each string and how it compares to the others. Using the operators on chromosomes taken from the population, the algorithm efficiently explores parts of the search space where the probability of finding improved performance is high.

The basic element processed by a GA is the string formed by concatenating substrings, each of which is a binary coding of a parameter of the search space. Thus, each string represents a point in the search space and hence a possible solution to the problem. Each string is decoded by an evaluator to obtain the objective function value of an individual point in the search space. This function value, which should be maximized or minimized by this algorithm, is then converted to a fitness value which determines the probability of the individual being acted on genetic operators. The population then evolves from generation to generation through the application of genetic operators. The total number of strings included in a population is kept unchanged throughout generations. A GA in its simplest form uses three operators: *reproduction, crossover,* and *mutation.*

Reproduction. Reproduction is a process in which individual strings are copied according to their fitness value. This operator is an artificial version of natural selection. A fitness $f(i)$ is assigned to each individual in the population, where high numbers denote good fit. The fitness function can be any nonlinear, nondifferentiable, discontinuous, positive function because the algorithm only needs a fitness assigned to each string. The reproduction (parent selection) process is conducted by spinning a simulated biased roulette wheel whose slots have different sizes proportional to the fitness values of the individuals. This technique is called *roulette-wheel parent selection.* Each time an offspring is needed, a simple spin of the weighted roulette wheel yields the reproduction candidate. This technique can be implemented algorithmically as in the following steps:

1. Sum the fitnesses of all the population members and call this result the total fitness.
2. Generate n, a random number between 0 and total fitness.
3. Return the first population member whose fitness, added to the fitnesses of the preceding population members (running total), is greater than or equal to n.

The following example illustrates the roulette-wheel parent selection technique.

Example 14.1

Consider a population of six chromosomes (strings) with a set of fitness values totaling 50 as shown in Table 14.1. The corresponding weighted roulette wheel is shown in Fig. 14.2. We then generate numbers randomly from the interval 0 and 50. For each number, the roulette-wheel parent selection technique chooses the first chromosome for which the running total of fitness is greater than or equal to the random number. Seven randomly generated numbers together with the indices of the chosen strings are shown in the accompanying table.

Random number	26	2	49	15	40	36	9
Chromosome chosen	4	1	6	2	5	5	2

This example indicates that more highly fit strings have a higher number of offspring in the succeeding generation. On balance over a number of generations, this method will eliminate the least fit members and contribute to the spread of genetic material in the fittest population members. Once a string has been selected for reproduction, an exact replica of it is made. This string is then entered into a mating pool, a tentative new population, for further genetic operator action.

Crossover. Reproduction directs the search toward the best existing individuals but does not create any new individuals. In nature, an offspring has two parents and inherits

TABLE 14.1 Sample Problem Strings and Fitness Values in Example 14.1

No.	String (Chromosome)	Fitness	% of Total	Running Total
1	01110	8	16	8
2	11000	15	30	23
3	00100	2	4	25
4	10010	5	10	30
5	01100	12	24	42
6	00011	8	16	50

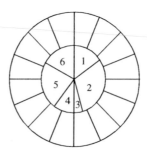

Figure 14.2 Weighted roulette wheel in Example 14.1.

genes from both. The main operator working on the parents is crossover, which happens for a selected pair with a crossover probability p_c. At first, two strings from the reproduced population are mated at random, and a crossover site (a bit position) is randomly selected. Then the strings are crossed and separated at the site (see Fig. 14.3). This process produces two new strings, each of which takes after both parents. Reproduction and crossover provide GAs with considerable power by directing the search toward better areas using already existing knowledge.

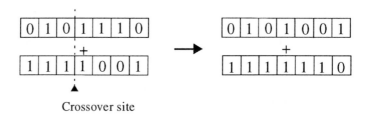

Crossover site

Figure 14.3 Crossover in a standard genetic algorithm. Two mating individuals (left) and their offspring (right).

Mutation. Although reproduction and crossover produce many new strings, they do not introduce any new information into the population at the bit level. As a source of new bits, mutation is introduced and is applied with a low probability p_m. It inverts a randomly chosen bit on a string. Mutation should be used sparingly because it is a random search operator; otherwise, with high mutation rates, the algorithm will become little more than a random search.

These three operators are applied repeatedly until the offspring take over the entire population. The next generation is thus made up of offspring of three types: mutated after crossover, crossed over but not mutated, and neither crossed over nor mutated, but just selected.

In a simple GA, we need to specify the following four parameters:

n = population size,

p_c = crossover probability,

p_m = mutation probability,

G = generation gap.

The generation gap G was introduced by De Jong [1975] to permit overlapping populations. It is defined between 0 and 1 as follows:

Genetic Algorithms   Chap. 14

$G = 1$, nonoverlapping populations,

$0 < G < 1$, overlapping populations.

In overlapping populations, nG individuals are selected for further genetic action. Resulting offspring are placed in the existing population by choosing nG population slots uniformly at random. When $G = 1$, all members of the old population will be deleted and only new children will be provided through genetic operators.

Example 14.2

Consider the problem of maximizing the function $f(x) = x^2$, where x is between 0 and 31. To use a GA, we code the variable x simply as a binary unsigned integer of length 5; for example, the string "11000" represents the integer $x = 24$. The fitness function is simply defined as the function $f(x)$. We shall simulate a single generation of a GA with reproduction, crossover, and mutation. The reproduction process is shown in Table 14.2(a). At first, an initial population of size 4 is randomly selected. Then the mating pool of the next generation is chosen by spinning the weighted roulette wheel four times. Actual simulation has resulted in string 1 and string 4 receiving one copy in the mating pool, string 2 receiving two copies, and string 3 receiving no copy. The resulting mating pool is presented in Table 14.2(b) which shows the crossover process. The crossover probability is assumed to be unity, $p_c = 1.0$. A random choice of mates has selected the second string in the mating pool to be mated with the first at crossing site 4. The remaining two strings in the mating pool are crossed at site 2. The last operator, mutation, is performed on a bit-by-bit basis. The mutation probability p_m is assumed to be 0.001, and thus the expected mutation is $5 \cdot 4 \cdot 0.001 = 0.02$ bits. In other words, we expect 0.02 bits to undergo mutation in a given generation. Simulation of this process indicates that no bits

TABLE 14.2 GA in Example 14.2: Reproduction Process and Crossover Process

(a) Reproduction Process

No.	Initial Population	x	Fitness $f(x) = x^2$	P_{select_i}, $f_i/\sum f$	No. of Copies from Roulette Wheel
1	01001	9	81	0.08	1
2	11000	24	576	0.55	2
3	00100	4	16	0.02	0
4	10011	19	361	0.35	1
	Sum		1034		
	Average		259		

(b) Crossover Process

Mating Pool after Reproduction	Mate	Crossover Site	New Population	x	x^2
0100|1	2	4	01000	8	64
1100|0	1	4	11001	25	625
11|000	4	2	11011	27	729
10|011	2	2	10000	16	256
			Sum		1674
			Average		419

undergo mutation at this probability value during a single generation. As shown in Table 14.2, the population average fitness has improved from 259 to 419 in one generation and the maximum fitness has increased from 576 to 729 during the same period.

In the above example, we observe that the combination of two above-average bit patterns, namely, the substrings $11---$ and $---11$, produces good strings. This illustrates the concept of *schemata* in GAs. A schema is a similarity template describing a subset of strings with similarities at certain string positions. For example, the schema $*111*$ describes a subset with four members $\{01110, 01111, 11110, 11111\}$, where $*$ indicates "don't care." Two quantities are defined for a schema: schema *order* and schema *length*. The order of a schema H, denoted by $o(H)$, is simply the number of fixed positions; for example, $o(*111*) = 3$ and $o(*1***) = 1$. The defining length of a schema H, denoted by $\delta(H)$, is the distance between the first and the last specific string position; for example, $\delta(011*1**) = 5 - 1 = 4$ and $\delta(0******) = 1 - 1 = 0$. In GAs, highly fit, short, length-defining schemata (called *building blocks*) are propagated from one generation to the next by giving exponentially increasing samples to the observed best. All this takes place in parallel without special bookkeeping or special memory other than the population of n strings, and this processing leverage is called *implicit parallelism*. An important schema theorem and a building-block hypothesis about schemata are outlined here, while other theoretical treatments of schemata can be found in Goldberg [1989].

Theorem 14.1

Schema Theorem (*Fundamental Theorem of Genetic Algorithms*). Short, low-order, above-average schemata receive exponentially increasing trials in subsequent generations.

The Building Block Hypothesis

Short, low-order, highly fit schemata (building blocks) are sampled, recombined, and resampled to form strings of potentially higher fitness. In other words, building blocks are combined to form better strings.

This hypothesis indicates that in a way, by working with these building blocks, we reduce the complexity of our problem; instead of building high-performance strings by trying every conceivable combination, we construct better and better strings from the best partial solutions of past samplings. There is a growing body of empirical evidence supporting this claim in regard to a variety of problem classes [Goldberg, 1989].

We shall next discuss some practical issues in applying GAs to optimization problems.

Mapping objective function values to fitness. Since a fitness function must be a nonnegative figure of merit, it is often necessary to map the underlying natural objective function to a fitness function form through one or more mappings. If the optimization problem is to minimize a cost function $g(x)$, then the following cost-to-fitness transformation is commonly used with GAs:

$$f(x) = \begin{cases} C_{\max} - g(x) & \text{when } g(x) < C_{\max} \\ 0, & \text{otherwise,} \end{cases} \quad (14.1)$$

where $C_{\max}$ may be taken as an input coefficient, for example, as the largest g value observed thus far, the largest g value in the current population, or the largest of the last k generations. Perhaps more appropriately, $C_{\max}$ should vary depending on the population variance.

When the original objective function is a profit or utility function $u(x)$ that is to be maximized, we simply transform fitness according to the equation

$$f(x) = \begin{cases} u(x) + C_{min} & \text{when } u(x) + C_{min} > 0 \\ 0 & \text{otherwise,} \end{cases} \quad (14.2)$$

where C_{min} can be chosen as an input coefficient such as the absolute value of the worst u value in the current or last k generations or as a function of the population variance.

Fitness scaling. It is important to regulate the number of offspring that an individual can have to maintain diversity in the population. This is especially important for the first few generations when a few "super" individuals can potentially take over a large part of the population, thereby reducing its diversity and leading to *premature convergence*. Fitness scaling can help with this problem. One useful scaling procedure is linear scaling. Let us denote the raw fitness as f and the scaled fitness as f'. Linear scaling requires a linear relationship between f' and f as follows:

$$f' = af + b, \quad (14.3)$$

where the coefficients a and b are chosen such that

$$f'_{avg} = f_{avg} \quad (14.4)$$

and

$$f'_{max} = C_{mult} f_{avg}, \quad (14.5)$$

where C_{mult} is the number of expected copies desired for the best population member. For typically small populations ($n = 50$ to 100), $C_{mult} = 1.2$ to 2 has been used successfully. Equation (14.4) ensures that each population member with average fitness contributes one expected offspring to the next generation. Equation (14.5) controls the number of offspring given to the population member with maximum raw fitness. Note that the linear scaling in Eqs. (14.3)–(14.5) may cause the low fitness values to go negative after scaling, violating the nonnegativity requirement. One solution is to replace the condition in Eq. (14.5) by the condition $f'_{min} = 0$.

Coding. The first step in GAs is coding, which maps a finite-length string to the parameters of an optimization problem. The two fundamental guidelines for choosing a GA coding are:

1. *Meaningful building blocks:* The user should select a coding such that short, low-order schemata are relevant to the underlying problem and relatively unrelated to schemata over other fixed positions.
2. *Minimal alphabets:* The user should select the smallest alphabet that permits natural expression of the problem.

For the second guideline, it is easy to show that the binary alphabet offers the maximum number of schemata per bit of information in any coding. Recall that one of our original motivations for considering schemata is the natural attempt to associate high fitness with similarities among strings in the population. Since finding schemata with many similarities is essential to GAs, when we design a code, we should maximize the number of schemata available for the GA to exploit.

The above two guidelines provide us with some clues for designing effective coding for simple GAs. In practice, one successfully used method of coding multiparameter optimization problems involving real parameters is *concatenated, multiparameter, mapped, fixed-point coding*. For a parameter $x \in [U_{min}, U_{max}]$, we map the decoded unsigned integer linearly from $[0, 2^l]$ to the specified interval $[U_{min}, U_{max}]$. In this way, we can carefully control the range and precision of the decision variables. The precision of this mapped coding is

$$\pi = \frac{U_{max} - U_{min}}{2^l - 1}.$$ (14.6)

To construct a multiparameter coding, we simply concatenate as many single-parameter codes as we require. Each code can have its own sublength and its own U_{max} and U_{min} values. An example of such coding for 10 parameters is shown in Fig. 14.4.

Many optimization problems have not only a single control parameter but also a control function that must be specified at every point in some continuum—a functional. To apply GAs to these problems, they first must be reduced to finite parameter form before parameter coding can be performed. In other words, we must transform the search for an optimal continuous function to the search for multiple points on the function through discretization. For example, suppose we wish to minimize the time of bicycle travel between two points and suppose further that we can apply a force f as a function of time $f(t)$ between limits $|f(t)| \leq f_{max}$. In this problem, we would attempt to calculate the schedule of force application as a continuous function of time as shown in Fig. 14.5. To apply the GA to find such a function, the continuous schedule is discretized into a finite parameter representation by spacing force values f_i at regular intervals of time. For example, in the force control problem, the search for the optimal continuous function $f(t)$ is reduced to a search for the six parameters $f_0, f_1, \ldots, f_5$, as shown in Fig. 14.5. Then the finite number of parameters is encoded in string form through some coding process. When the optimal values f_i^* of the finite parameters are found, we then assume some functional form, such as a step function, linear interpolant, piecewise quadratic, or cubic spline, to fit through the points f_i^*. Figure 14.5 shows a linear interpolating function approximation to the continuous force schedule in the bicycle control problem.

Single U_1 Parameter ($l_1 = 4$)

0 0 0 0 $\rightarrow U_{min}$

1 1 1 1 $\rightarrow U_{min}$

Others map linearly in between

Multiparameter Coding (10 parameters)

0 0 0 1	0 1 0 1	...	1 1 0 0	1 1 1 1
U_1	U_2	...	U_9	U_{10}

Figure 14.4 Multiparameter code constructed from concatenated, mapped, fixed-point codes.

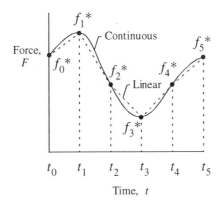

Force, F

Continuous

f_1^*
f_0^*
f_2^*
f_4^*
f_5^*
f_3^*

Linear

t_0 t_1 t_2 t_3 t_4 t_5

Time, t

Figure 14.5 Discretized force control schedule.

Optimization problems with constraints.   To incorporate constraints into a GA search, we can use the *penalty method* which degrades the fitness ranking in relation to the degree of constraint violation. In the penalty method, a constrained problem in optimization is transformed to an unconstrained problem by associating a cost or penalty with all constraint violations. This cost is included in the objective function evaluation. For example, the constrained problem in minimization form:

$$\text{Minimize } g(\mathbf{x})$$
$$\text{subject to } h_i(\mathbf{x}) \geq 0, \qquad i = 1, 2, \cdots, n, \tag{14.7}$$

can be transformed to an unconstrained form:

$$\text{Minimize } g(\mathbf{x}) + \sum_{i=1}^{n} r \, \Phi \, [h_i(\mathbf{x})], \tag{14.8}$$

where $\Phi(\cdot)$ is a proper penalty function and r is the penalty coefficient. An example of a penalty function is $\Phi[h_i(\mathbf{x})] = h_i^2(\mathbf{x})$ for all violated constraints i. The r values in GAs are often sized separately for each type of constraint so that moderate violations of the constraints yield a penalty that is a significant percentage of a nominal operating cost. The following example illustrates the use of a GA on a difficult optimization problem.

Example 14.3
    The problem here is to maximize the function [Schaffer et al., 1989]

$$f(x, y) = 0.5 - \frac{\sin^2 \sqrt{x^2 + y^2} - 0.5}{[1.0 + 0.001 \, (x^2 + y^2)]^2}, \tag{14.9}$$

where $x, y \in [-100, 100]$. This function has a single optimal solution, seen at the center of Fig. 14.6, in which the y value of the function has been fixed at its optimal point. Since the function is symmetric in x and y, a graph of y values holding the x value at its optimum would look the same. Equation (14.9) is a function that describes a very hilly two-dimensional landscape, with an optimal region that occupies a tiny fraction of the total area. It is difficult for many function optimization strategies such as *hill-climbing* techniques because of its oscillation.
    We shall now describe a way of using a GA on this problem. Since the objective function $f(x, y)$ is positive and to be maximized, it is used as the fitness function directly. In the decoding process, a chromosome, which is a string of 44 bits, is converted to two real numbers x and y, each of which lies in the interval [-100, 100]. This is done in three steps. First, the ini-

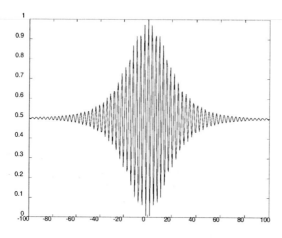

Figure 14.6 Graph of the function varying x when y is held constant at its optimal value (see Example 14.3).

tial 22 bits of the chromosome are interpreted as a representation of an integer x in base-2 notation and the last 22 bits as an integer y in base-2 notation. Then x and y are multiplied by $200/2^{22}$ to map the values of x and y from the range $[0, 2^{22} - 1]$ to the range $[0, 200]$. Finally, 100 is subtracted from x and y and become real numbers between -100 and 100. As an illustration, the following chromosome

$$0000101000011000000001100010101010001110111011$$

is first partitioned into two strings

$$0000101000011000000001 \quad \text{and} \quad 1000101010001110111011$$

which represent two unsigned integers $x = 165{,}377$ and $y = 2{,}270{,}139$, respectively. After multiplying by $200/2^{22}$ and then subtracting 100, we have $x = -92.11$ and $y = 8.25$. The corresponding fitness value is $f(-92.11, 8.25) = 0.495$.

The GA creates an initial population consisting of randomly generated bit strings. Three operators are adopted here: roulette-wheel parent selection, simple crossover with random mating, and simple mutation. The parameters are set as n (population size) $= 100$, p_c (crossover probability) $= 0.65$, p_m (mutation probability) $= 0.008$, and G (generation gap) $= 1$. After generating a population of 100 random bit strings as the first generation of chromosomes initially, the GA begins a series of cycles replacing its current population of chromosomes with a new population. In each cycle, according to the fitness values, the roulette-wheel parent selection technique is first applied to form a mating pool consisting of 100 chromosomes. Then 50 pairs of parents are selected randomly. The crossover and mutation operators are then applied to these two parents to generate two new chromosomes (children) according to the probabilities p_c and p_m. The resulting 100 chromosomes form the next generation. These generational cycles continue until 4000 individuals have been produced at the fortieth generation. At this point, the top five chromosomes are very similar and obtain fitness values above 0.99 as shown below:

0111100101100010110101100010000110010001011	.99304112
0111101111100010110111100010100011011010010	.99261288
0111101111000010010101100010100011011010011	.99254826
0111101111000000010101100010100011011010001	.99254438
0111101111100010110101100010100111011010011	.99229856.

The above example indicates that in the initial phase of GA runs, the population is *heterogeneous* in that it consists of randomly generated chromosomes that are quite dissimilar. As time goes by, the chromosomes become similar because of reproduction or recombination of the best chromosomes. At this point, the population converges somewhat on a single solution. Thereafter, the GA searches throughout the region of that solution to introduce diversity through mutation. When a population consists of primarily similar individuals, then we say that it has converged.

14.2 FURTHER EVOLUTION OF GENETIC ALGORITHMS

Thus far, we have discussed the basic concepts of GAs. There are various improvements on this basic technique. This section first examines improvements in the selection scheme and then introduces more advanced genetic operators.

14.2.1 Improved Selection Schemes

The selection scheme used in a standard GA is roulette-wheel selection. This scheme has the potential problem that the best member of the population may fail to produce offspring in the next generation and may cause a so-called stochastic error. Several alternate selection schemes that can reduce the stochastic errors associated with roulette-wheel selection will be introduced [De Jong, 1975; Brindle, 1981; Goldberg, 1989; Davis, 1991].

Elitism. The elitist strategy copies the best member of each generation into the succeeding generation. This strategy may increase the speed of domination of a population by a super individual and thus improves the local search at the expense of a global perspective, but on balance it appears to improve GA performance.

Deterministic Sampling. In this scheme, the probabilities of selection are calculated as usual $p_{\text{select}_i} = f_i / \sum f_j$. Then the expected number e_i of offspring for string A_i is calculated by $e_i = n p_{\text{select}_i}$. Each string is allocated offspring according to the integer part of the e_i value. The remaining strings needed to fill out the population are drawn from the top of the sorted list.

Remainder Stochastic Sampling with Replacement. This scheme starts in a manner identical to the above deterministic sampling scheme. Expected individual count values are calculated as before, and integer parts are assigned. Then the fractional parts of the expected number values are used to calculate weights in a roulette-wheel selection procedure to fill the remaining population slots.

Remainder Stochastic Sampling Without Replacement. This scheme again starts in a manner identical to the deterministic scheme, and the fractional parts of the expected number values are treated as probabilities. In other words, the strings receive a number of offspring at least equal to the integer value of their expected individual counts. Then the population is filled out by choosing another offspring for each of the strings with probability equal to the fractional part of the expected individual count until the total number of offspring equals the population size n. For example, a string with an expected number of copies equal to 1.5 would surely receive one copy and another copy with probability 0.5.

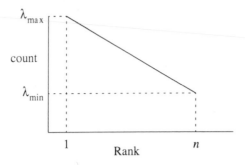

Figure 14.7 Baker's ranking procedure.

Empirical studies have demonstrated the superiority of this scheme over the expected-value scheme. As a result, the stochastic remainder selection procedure without replacement has been widely used in many applications.

Ranking Procedure. The ranking procedure is a nonparametric procedure for selection. In this method, the population is sorted according to an objective function (fitness) value. Individuals are then assigned an offspring count that is solely a function of their rank. One such function proposed by Baker [1985] is shown in Fig. 14.7. Specifically, the expected number of individuals i is computed according to

$$e_i = -\frac{2(\lambda_{max} - 1)}{n - 1} \text{ rank }(i) + 1 + (\lambda_{max} - 1)\frac{n + 1}{n - 1}, \qquad (14.10)$$

where λ_{max} is a user-defined value, $1 \le \lambda_{max} \le 2$, and n is the population size. The range of e_i will then be $[2 - \lambda_{max}, \lambda_{max}]$. The function in Eq. (14.10) is a special case of the function in Fig. 14.7 obtained by setting the minimum count to $(2 - \lambda_{max})$; that is, $\lambda_{min} = 2 - \lambda_{max}$ in Fig. 14.7.

14.2.2 Advanced Operators

Simple GAs are guided largely by the action of three operators: reproduction, crossover, and mutation. There are several other interesting natural operators and phenomena. Two types of genetic operators are considered here that can improve the robustness of simple GAs. They are micro operators, which are genetic operators operating at a chromosonal level, and macro operators, which are genetic operators acting at a population level. We shall first examine some micro operators: multiple-point crossover and reordering operators.

Multiple-point crossover. The crossover operation used thus far is one-point crossover since only one crossover site is chosen. This simple crossover can be generalized to multiple-point crossover in which the number of crossover points N_c is defined. When N_c is set to 1, generalized crossover reduces to simple crossover. With even N_c values, the string is treated as a ring with no beginning and no end, and N_c crossover points are selected around the circle uniformly at random. An example with $N_c = 4$ is shown in Fig. 14.8(a). With odd N_c values, a default crossing point is always assumed at position 0 (the beginning of the string) as illustrated in Fig. 14.8(b) with $N_c = 3$. Multiple-point crossover can solve certain combinations of features encoded on chromosomes that one-point crossover cannot solve. Consider the following two chromosomes:

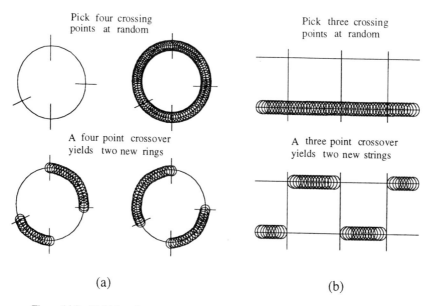

Pick four crossing points at random

A four point crossover yields two new rings

Pick three crossing points at random

A three point crossover yields two new strings

(a)   (b)

Figure 14.8 Multiple-point crossover operations. (a) Even-numbered cross point (CP = 4).
(b) Odd-numbered cross point (CP = 3).

Chromosome 1:   10110001100

Chromosome 2:   00101101001,

where the underlined bits represent two high-performance schemata. Assume that if either of these schemata is altered, its beneficial effects are lost. Obviously one-point crossover cannot avoid this, since no matter where the crossover point is selected, the first schema will be broken up and will not be passed on. This problem can be solved by, for example, two-point crossover as follows:

Parent 1:   1 0 1 1 | 0 0 0 1 | 1 0 0

Parent 2:   0 0 1 0 | 1 1 0 1 | 0 0 1

Child 1:   1 0 1 1   1 1 0 1   1 0 0

Child 2:   0 0 1 0   0 0 0 1   0 0 1,

where vertical lines indicate the two crossover points. Hence, with two-point crossover the problematic schemata are combined in one of the children.

Another way to implement multiple-point crossover is the *uniform crossover* operator proposed by Syswerda [1989]. In this scheme, two parents are selected and two children are produced. For each bit position on the two children, we decide randomly which parent contributes its bit value to which child according to a randomly generated template. This action is illustrated as follows.

Parent 1:   0 1 1 0 0 1 1 1

Parent 2:   1 1 0 1 0 0 0 1

Template: 0 1 1 0 1 0 0 1

yields

$$\text{Child 1:} \quad 1\,1\,1\,1\,0\,0\,0\,1$$

$$\text{Child 2:} \quad 0\,1\,0\,0\,0\,1\,1\,1.$$

Even though multiple-point crossover has the advantage mentioned above, it should be used with caution. Empirical studies have shown that multiple-point crossover degrades the performance of GAs increasingly with an increasing number of crossover points N_c. The reason is that, with increasing N_c values, multiple-point crossover causes more mixing and less structure. Hence, it becomes more like a random shuffle and fewer important schemata can be preserved.

Reordering operators. Unlike the operators discussed so far that search for better sets of allele values, reordering operators search for better codes as well as better allele sets. These operators are appropriate for problems where fitness values depend on string arrangement, such as where fitness f depends on some combination of allele value v and ordering o, $f = f(v, o)$. A string incorporating both allele values and ordering information can be expressed, for example, by

$$1\,2\,3\,4\,5\,6\,7\,8$$

$$1\,0\,0\,1\,0\,0\,0\,1$$

where $1, 2, \ldots, 8$ represent positions or *gene names*. One commonly used reordering operator in GAs is the *inversion operator*. Under this operator, two points are chosen along the length of the chromosome, the chromosome is then cut at these points, and the end points of the cut section switch places. For example, consider the following eight-position string where two inversion sites are chosen at random:

$$1\ 2\,|\,3\ 4\ 5\ 6\,|\,7\ 8$$

$$0\ 1\,|\,1\ 1\ 0\,|\,1\ 0$$

Then after inversion, it becomes

$$1\,2\,6\,5\,4\,3\,7\,8$$

$$0\,1\,0\,1\,1\,1\,1\,0$$

Next, we shall introduce a macro operator that acts at a population level in GAs. This operator accounts for the phenomenon of interspecies differentiation (specialization) in nature. Interspecies differentiation is carried out in nature through *speciation* and *niche exploitation*. A scheme that can encourage the formation of niche exploitation and speciation in GAs is the *sharing function* [Goldberg and Richardson, 1987]. A sharing function determines the neighborhood and degree of sharing for each string in the population. A simple sharing function $s(d(x_i, x_j))$ is shown in Fig. 14.9, where $d(x_i, x_j)$ is the (Hamming) distance between the two strings x_i and x_j. For a given individual, the degree of sharing is determined by summing the sharing function values contributed by all other strings in the population. Strings close to an individual require a high degree of sharing (close to 1), and strings far from the individual require a very small degree of sharing (close to 0). After accumulating the total number of shares in this manner, an individual's derated fitness is

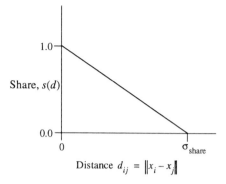

Figure 14.9 Triangular sharing function.

calculated by taking the potential (unshared) fitness and dividing by the accumulated number of shares:

$$f_s(x_i) = \frac{f(x_i)}{\sum_{j=1}^{n} s(d(x_i, x_j))}.$$

(14.11)

Hence, when many individuals are in the same neighborhood, they derate one another's fitness values. As a result, this mechanism limits the uncontrolled growth of particular species within a population.

The effects of the sharing function are shown in Fig. 14.10. Using the triangular sharing function in Fig. 14.9, an even distribution of points is found at each peak after 100 generations as shown in Fig. 14.10(a). For comparison, the results from a simple GA with no sharing are shown in Fig. 14.10(b).

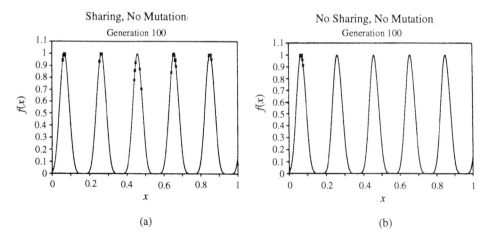

Figure 14.10 Simple genetic algorithm performance on equal peaks (a) with sharing and (b) without sharing. Population distribution at generation 100. (Goldberg, *Genetic Algorithms in Search, Optimization, and Machine Learning,* © 1989 Addison-Wesley Publishing Company, Inc. Reprinted by permission of Addison-Wesley.)

14.3 HYBRID GENETIC ALGORITHMS

Traditional simple GAs, though robust, are generally not the most successful optimization algorithms for any particular domain. Hybridizing a GA with algorithms currently in use can produce an algorithm better than both the GA and the current algorithms. Hence, for an optimization problem, when there are algorithms, optimization heuristics, or domain knowledge that can aid in optimization, it may be advantageous to consider a hybrid GA. A GA may be crossed with various problem-specific search techniques to form a hybrid that exploits the global perspective of the GA (*global search*) and the convergence of the problem-specific technique (*local search*).

There are numerous gradient techniques (e.g., the gradient-descent method, the conjugate gradient method) and gradientless techniques (e.g., the golden search, the simplex method) available for finding local optima in a calculus-friendly function (e.g., a continuous function) [Luenberger, 1976]. Even without a calculus-friendly function, there are well-developed heuristic search schemes for many popular problems. For example, the greedy algorithms in combinatorial optimization are a form of local search [Lawler, 1976]. The result of hybridizing GAs with local search techniques is that the GA finds the hills and the local searcher goes and climbs them. Thus, in this approach, we simply allow the GA to run to substantial convergence and then permit the local optimization procedure to take over, perhaps searching from the top 5 or 10% of points in the last generation. With this approach, the niche exploitation and speciation technique of the previous section may be useful in maintaining diversity within the GA population, thereby allowing stable subpopulations to form at different peaks in the function domain.

In some situations, hybridization entails employing the representation as well as the optimization techniques already in use in the domain while tailoring the GA operators to the new representation. Moreover, hybridization can involve adding domain-based optimization heuristics to the GA operator set. In these cases, we can no longer apply the familiar GA operators directly and must create their analogs to account for new representations and/or added optimization schemes. As an illustration, we describe an approach to hybridizing a simple GA with the simulated annealing algorithm considered in the following.

Genetic algorithms and simulated annealing (SA) introduced in Sec. 11.3.2 have emerged as the leading methodologies for search and optimization problems in high-dimensional spaces [Davis, 1987]. There have been several attempts to hybridize these two algorithms [Adler, 1993]. A simple scheme for combining SA with GA is to replace all or some of the mutation and crossover (recombination) operators in standard GAs with SA operators: SA mutation (SAM) and SA recombination (SAR). The SAM operator works exactly like a standard mutation operator: It receives a solution as input, mutates it, and returns a solution as output. The difference is that internally the SAM operator can call the evaluation function and use the result to decide whether to accept the mutated solution or just stay with the previous solution:

```
SAM(s, T){
        s' = mutate(s, T)
        if (accept(s', s, T)) return s'
        else return s
              }.
```

The function *accept* checks the acceptance condition of the mutated string s' according to its fitness and current annealing temperature T. The annealing temperature is lowered in a nonhomogeneous way between generations. Thus, in every (or more) generation, the temperature is lowered, making the SA operator more selective about the mutations it accepts. The SAR operator is very similar. First crossover is applied, and then each of the children is compared to the best of the two parents for acceptance.

As GA operators, SAM and SAR can completely replace existing operators or coexist with them. This can be controlled by their relative probabilities of selection. If we set the probability of the SAM or SAR operator to 0, we will obtain the standard GA. On the other hand, setting all the other operator probabilities to zero leaves us with a standard SA algorithm. Between these two extreme cases, we can easily and continuously obtain a variety of intermediate situations.

14.4 APPLICATIONS OF GENETIC ALGORITHMS

We shall now present some applications of GAs to optimization problems in the following sections. From these applications, the reader can also learn some innovative techniques of interest involving GAs, such as real number representation of chromosomes and variable-length chromosomes.

14.4.1 Genetic Algorithms for Neural Network Parameter Learning

Genetic algorithms have been used to search the weight space of a multilayer feedforward neural network without the use of any gradient information [Montana and Davis, 1989; Whitley and Hanson, 1989, Ichikawa and Sawa, 1992; Ichikawa and Ishii, 1993]. The basic concept behind this technique is as follows. A complete set of weights is coded in a (binary or real number) string, which has an associated "fitness" indicating its effectiveness. For example, the fitness can be simply given by $-E$, where E is the value of the cost function for that set of weights. Starting with a random population of such strings, successive generations are constructed using genetic operators to construct new strings out of old ones such that fitter strings (weights) are more likely to survive and to participate in crossover operations. The crossover operation can in principle bring together good building blocks—such as hidden units that compute certain logical functions—found by chance in different members of the population. Unlike the back-propagation learning rule, GAs perform a global search and are thus not easily fooled by local minima. Furthermore, since the fitness function does not have to be differentiable, we can, for example, start with threshold units in Boolean problems instead of having to use sigmoids that are later trained to saturation. However, for neural networks with continuous activation functions, it is an appropriate compromise to hybridize GAs with gradient methods such as the back-propagation algorithm: An initial genetic search followed by a gradient method [McInerney and Dhawan, 1993] or a gradient-descent step can be included as one of the genetic operators [Montana and Davis, 1989].

The weights and biases in a neural network are encoded in order as a list. An example is shown in Fig. 14.11. Thus, each chromosome (individual) completely describes a neural network. To evaluate the fitness of a chromosome, the weights on the chromosome

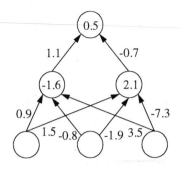

Encoding : (1.1, -0.7, 0.5, 0.9, 1.5, -0.8, -1.9, 3.5, -7.3, -1.6, 2.1)

Figure 14.11   Encoding a network on a chromosome.

are assigned to the links in a network of a given architecture (decoding process), the network is then run over the training set of examples, and the sum of the squares of the errors is returned from each example. In other words, the network plays the role of an evaluation function in our GAs. The entries (i.e., weights) of the initial members of the population are chosen at random within some interval, for example, [-1, 1]. An efficient initialization scheme can be used to choose the weights randomly with a probability distribution given by $e^{-\|x\|}$, that is, a two-sided exponential distribution with a mean of 0 and a mean absolute value of 1. This probability distribution reflects the empirical observation that optimal solutions tend to contain predominantly weights with small absolute values but that they can also have weights with arbitrarily large absolute values. Hence, this special initialization allows the GA to explore the range of all possible solutions, and this tends to favor the most likely solutions.

Mutation crossover and gradient genetic operators are used to search for the optimal weight set solutions. The following mutation operators take one parent and randomly change some of the entries in its chromosome to create a child.

> *Unbiased-mutate-weights*: For each entry in the chromosome, this operator with fixed probability ($p = 0.1$) replaces it with a random value chosen from the initialization probability distribution.
>
> *Biased-mutate-weights*: For each entry in the chromosome, this operator with fixed probability distribution ($p = 0.1$) adds to it a random value chosen from the initialization probability distribution.
>
> *Mutate-nodes*: This operator selects n (e.g., $n = 2$) noninput nodes of the network that the parent chromosome represents. For each input link to these n nodes, the operator adds to the link's weight a random value from the initialization probability distribution. It then encodes this new network on the child's chromosome. Since the input links to a node form a logical subgroup of all links, confining the random weight changes to these subgroups seems more likely to result in a good evaluation.

Simulation results from comparing the performance of the above three mutation operators show that mutate-nodes were better than biased-mutate-weights, which were better than unbiased-mutate-weights.

A crossover operator takes two parents and creates one or two children containing some of the genetic material of each parent. The following crossover operators are used in this application to search for optimal weight sets. Empirical studies have shown that they performed equally well.

Crossover-weights: This operator puts a value into each position (weight) on the child's chromosome by randomly selecting one of the two parents and using the value in the same position on the parent's chromosome.

Crossover-nodes: For each node in the network encoded by the child's chromosome, this operator selects one of the two parents' networks and finds the corresponding node in this network. It then puts the weight of each input link to the parent's node into the corresponding link in the child's network. The intuition here is similar to that for the mutate-nodes operator; logical subgroups should stay together as genetic material is passed around.

A gradient operator that takes one parent and produces a child by adding to its entries a multiple of the gradient with respect to the evaluation function is also used in the search for optimal weight sets.

Hill-climb: This operator calculates the gradient for each member of the training set and sums them together to obtain a total gradient. It then normalizes this gradient by dividing it by the magnitude. The child is obtained from the parent by taking a step in the direction determined by the normalized gradient of size η, where η is a changing parameter that adapts throughout the run. If the child's evaluation is worse than the parent's, η is multiplied by a decaying rate, 0.4; otherwise, it is multiplied by an expanding rate, 1.4.

Several parameters must be defined for the above genetic operators, and the values of these parameters can greatly influence the performance of the algorithm. Some of the important parameters are discussed here. The parameter "PARENT-SCALAR" determines the probability that each individual will be chosen as a parent. This value can be linearly interpolated between 0.92 and 0.89 over the course of a run. The list of parameters "OPERATOR-PROBABILITIES" determines the probability that each operator in the operator pool will be selected. These values are initialized so that mutation and crossover have equal probabilities of selection. Of course, we still have the parameter "POPULATION-SIZE" to determine the number of children in a generation. Furthermore, we can have the parameter "GENERATION-SIZE" which tells how many children to generate (and thus how many current population members to delete) for each generation. Having the generation size as small as possible (e.g., set to 1) has the advantage that when better individuals are created they can be immediately incorporated into the reproductive process as potential parents.

Example 14.4

In this example, a specific GA used to train a multilayer feedforward network is first described and then used to train the network shown in Fig. 14.12 for the XOR problem [Ichikawa and Sawa, 1992]. The activation function in the network is the unipolar sigmoid function. The string (chromosome) of the network is encoded as $(w_1, w_2, \cdots, w_9)$, where each allele is a weight value that is not binary-coded. The smallest element that crossover and mutation han-

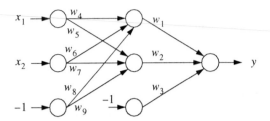

Figure 14.12 Network structure for the XOR problem in Example 14.4.

dle is the weight. The crossover operator used here is the uniform crossover; at first, n_c allele positions are randomly chosen, and then alleles at these positions are exchanged with each other. The number of alleles to be exchanged, n_c, is usually half the total number of alleles possessed by an individual. Mutation occurs with a probability of 1.0 on selected individuals who have not crossed over. Thus, if selected, the probability that a pair will undergo crossover is p_c, and the probability of mutation is $(1 - p_c)$. All the alleles are increased by a mutation with Δw, which is randomly chosen within an interval determined in advance.

Two types of selection are used here, one for choosing pairs to apply genetic operators, and the other for choosing survivors for the next generation. While the first is the same as the standard algorithm, the second is somewhat special. After genetic operators create new individuals, survivors are selected from the doubled tentative population which includes current and newly created individuals. In this process, newly created individuals are evaluated to obtain their objective function values, and fitness values are assigned to all the individuals in the tentative population. Then the individuals for the next generation are selected from the tentative population with probabilities proportional to their fitness values. Furthermore, the elitist strategy is adopted here; that is, the individual that has the highest objective function value is chosen regardless of its fitness value. The population size of the next generation is also kept constant by choosing half of the tentative population.

Scaling and sharing schemes are also adopted in this GA. The linear scaling in Eqs. (14.3)–(14.5) is used, where the expected number of offspring created from the most fit individual, C_{mult}, is set as 2. In order to check diversity in allele values, a kind of minimal distance between all the individuals in a population is determined. The distance between two individuals q_1 and q_2, denoted by $d[q_1, q_2]$, is defined as

$$d[q_1, q_2] = \min_i \{|q_1 \,(\text{allele } i) - q_2 \,(\text{allele } i)|\}, \tag{14.12}$$

where q_1 (allele i) indicates the ith allele (weight) of individual q_1. "Sharing" of a fitness value occurs after the scaling such that the fitness of individual q is divided by the total number of individuals in the population whose distance from q is less than 1.0. This sharing function is similar to Eq. (14.11).

Now we are ready to apply the GA described above to the network in Fig. 14.12 to solve the XOR problem, where x_1, x_2, and y take either 0.1 or 0.9 corresponding to FALSE or TRUE, respectively. The size of the population is 20, and these 20 networks with different weights and different behaviors evolve over generations. Initial values given to them are randomly chosen from integers within an interval $[-10, 10]$. The crossover probability p_c is 0.7, and the number of crossover positions N_c is 4. The mutation width Δw is an integer randomly chosen from -3 to 3. The mutation is adjusted such that each weight does not exceed the bounds -10 and 10, in order to maintain the size of the search space. The fitness value is defined as the reciprocal of the error, which is the absolute sum of the output differences over the four XOR patterns. After 30 generations of iteration, a satisfactory network has been created whose error is less than 0.05 (the fitness value is more than 20).

Genetic Algorithms   Chap. 14

Example 14.5

In this more complex example, the GA developed in the last example is used to train a neural controller [Ichikawa and Sawa, 1992]. The (nonlinear) plant to be controlled is described by the following equation of motion:

$$\frac{d^2x}{dt^2} = u \, \text{sgn} \, (x), \tag{14.13}$$

where x is a position variable and u is the external applied force. The mission of the controller is to regulate the displacement $x(t)$, which is either $+1$ or -1 initially, to zero. The network configuration in Fig. 14.13 is used, where the bipolar sigmoid activation function is used. The state variables are chosen such that $x_1 = x$, $x_2 = dx/dt$. The output y scaled by 0.1 is fed into the plant as a driving force.

To evaluate the fitness of a chromosome q, using the corresponding network weights, the system's dynamical response is simulated from time 0 to N_{max}, where the simulation length N_{max} is 10. Two such simulations are assigned to each individual with initial conditions $x(0) = 1$ and $x(0) = -1$. Then the fitness value F of individual q is given by

$$F = -\log\left(P\big|_{x(0)=1.0} + P\big|_{x(0)=-1.0}\right), \tag{14.14}$$

where

$$P = \left|x_1 \left(N_{max}\right)\right| + 10\left|x_2 \left(N_{max}\right)\right| + Q,$$

$$Q = 10^4 \qquad \text{if max} \left\{\left|u\left(n\right)\right|\right\} \text{ is less than } 5 \times 10^{-2} \text{ and } 0.0 \text{ if not.}$$

In the above fitness function, P stands for a penalty value which is an absolute weighted sum of x_1 and x_2 at the final sampling time and Q is an additional penalty for removing a local minimum into which deactivated networks are prone to fall.

The population size is 20 with $p_c = 0.7$ and $N_c = 8$. For Δw, integers randomly selected from -5 to 5 have been used. The results after 100 generations are shown in Fig. 14.14. Both responses starting from 1.0 and -1.0 are successfully regulated.

Among other applications, a GA was used to select features for neural network classifiers, especially for the counterpropagation network [Brill et al., 1992]. In this feature-selection formulation of GAs, individuals are composed of bit strings: A 1 in bit position i indicates that feature i should be used; 0 indicates that this feature should not be used. A proper fitness function was defined according to this representation. Peck et al. [1993] used a GA to select the input variables to a neural network function approximator. In modeling

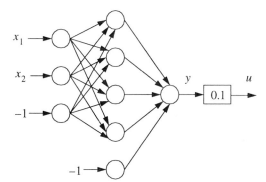

Figure 14.13 Network structure for nonlinear control in Example 14.5.

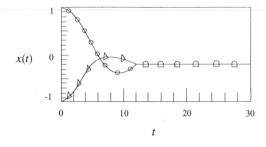

Figure 14.14 Nonlinear control results in Example 14.5. Responses with $x(0) = 1$ (marked $\bigcirc$) and $x(0) = -1$ (marked $\triangle$).

critical parameters of the space shuttle main engine, the functional relationships among measured parameters are unknown and complex. Furthermore, the number of possible input parameters is quite large. A GA was employed to systematize the input selection process. The results suggested that a GA can generate parameter lists of high quality without explicit use of problem domain knowledge.

14.4.2 Genetic Algorithms for Path Planning

Genetic algorithms have also been used for robot path planning and trajectory generation. A characteristic of these applications is the use of *variable-length* and *order-based* chromosomes. The following example illustrates this point.

Example 14.6

In this example, a GA is used to find the optimal paths for a robot to move in a known environment with a static map expressed by nodes and links in the graph shown in Fig. 14.15 [Shibata and Fukuda, 1993]. In the GA, a path for a mobile robot is encoded based on an order of via points. The robot has a starting point and a target point on the graph under the assumption that in a path each robot passes each point only once or not at all. Each node has a number in Fig. 14.15 and the nodes are used to encode a path as a string expressed by the order of numbers, for example, 0-4-8-10-17-22-25-26. In this string, 0 is the starting point and 26 is the target point for a mobile robot. The via points are selected randomly at first, while adjacent numbers must be connected with a link on the graph. Since variable-length and order-based strings are used, special crossover and mutation operators are adopted.

During the crossover, a string that has an efficient fitness is randomly selected as a parent, and a number in the string is also randomly selected. Then, one more string that also has an efficient fitness is selected as a second parent at random. If the second parent contains the same number selected in the first parent, both strings exchange the part of their strings following that number. If not, another string is selected as the second parent, and the same procedure is followed. For example,

Parent 1:   0-1-2-3-6-9-11-15-16-21-24-26

Parent 2:   0-4-8-10-15-20-23-26.

Since each parent has the point 15, the underlined parts of each string are exchanged, yielding:

Child 1:   0-1-2-3-6-9-11-15-20-23-26

Child 2:   0-4-8-10-15-16-21-24-26.

After the crossover, children are checked to determine whether each string has repeated numbers. If so, the part of the string between the repeated numbers is cut off as follows:

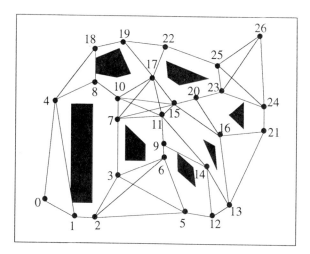

Figure 14.15 Graph for a static map of the mobile robot's environment in Example 14.6.

Child 3:   0-1-2-3-6-9-11-15-10-7-11-17-22-25-26,

and after the cutoff operation,

Child 3':   0-1-2-3-6-9-11-17-22-25-26.

In mutation, a position in each string is selected at random based on the probability of mutation, which is low. Then, the number of nodes is selected randomly for the following positions which are connected sequentially. The distance of a path indicated by a string is used to calculate the *fitness* of each string. Since the fitness should increase as the distance decreases, the fitness $F(q)$ of the string $q = 0\text{-}4\text{-}8\text{-}10\text{-}15\text{-}20\text{-}23\text{-}26$ can be given by

$$F(q) = 1/(d_{0-4} + d_{4-8} + \cdots + d_{23-26}),\qquad (14.15)$$

where d_{i-j} is the distance between nodes i and j, which is equal to the length of a corresponding link on the static map.

In the simulation, the starting point was 0, the target point was 26, and the size of the search space was about 620,000. The GA used 50 strings for a population and calculated 100 generations with an 80% probability of crossover and a 20% probability of mutation for each string. Fifty cases of random parameters were investigated. The GA succeeded in obtaining the optimal path at a rate of 22% and a feasible path in the remaining cases.

14.4.3 Genetic Algorithms for System Identification and Controls

Genetic algorithms have also been applied in system identification and adaptive control of both continuous- and discrete-time systems [Kristinsson and Dumont, 1992], as well as to optimal control problems with or without constraints [Krishnakumar and Goldberg, 1992; Michalewicz and Krawezyk, 1992]. The following example illustrates the use of GA on an optimal control problem with constraints [Michalewicz and Janikow, 1991; Liu, 1993].

Example 14.7

Consider the following discrete-time system:

$$\begin{bmatrix} x_1(k+1) \\ x_2(k+1) \end{bmatrix} = \begin{bmatrix} 1 & 0.05 \\ -0.05 & 1.05 \end{bmatrix}\begin{bmatrix} x_1(k) \\ x_2(k) \end{bmatrix} + \begin{bmatrix} 0.0013 \\ 0.0513 \end{bmatrix} u(k),\qquad (14.16)$$

with

$$\begin{bmatrix} x_1(0) \\ x_2(0) \end{bmatrix} = \begin{bmatrix} 0 \\ -1 \end{bmatrix}, \qquad \text{where } k = 0, 1, \cdots, K.$$

The goal is to find a sequence of inputs $\{u(0), u(1), \ldots, u(K)\}$ to the sytem such that the objective function

$$g = \sum_{k=0}^{K} \left[x_1^2(k) + x_2^2(k) + 0.005u^2(k) \right] \qquad (14.17)$$

is minimized and, moreover, the following constraint is satisfied:

$$h_k = x_2(k) - \left[0.02(k-10)^2 - 0.5 \right] \le 0, \qquad k = 1, 2, \cdots, K. \qquad (14.18)$$

Using a GA to find the optimal input sequence, the chromosome is set as the list $(u(0), u(1), \cdots, u(K))$. The concept of a penalty function in Eq. (14.8) is used to transform the constrained problem to an unconstrained form. First, the *violation index* v is calculated by

$$v = \sum_{k=1}^{K} \langle h_k \rangle, \qquad \text{where } \langle h \rangle = \begin{cases} h & \text{if } h > 0 \\ 0 & \text{if } h \le 0. \end{cases} \qquad (14.19)$$

The violation index of a given chromosome indicates the degree to which the constraints are violated during the whole running period controlled by the corresponding input sequence. Let v_{max} and v_{min} denote, respectively, the maximum and minimum values of violation indices in a population. Let g_{max} indicate the worst objective value among those of the individuals that are admissible solutions. Set $g_{max} = v_{min}$ if all the individuals in a population are nonadmissible solutions. Then, according to the violation index v of a chromosome, its objective value is adjusted using the following equation:

$$\hat{g} = m_1 g_{max} + \frac{m_2 g_{max} - m_1 g_{max}}{v_{max} - v_{min}} (v - v_{min}), \qquad m_2 > m_1 > 1. \qquad (14.20)$$

The above equation has the property that adjusted objective values of the individuals that are not admissible solutions will fall in the interval $[m_1 g_{max}, m_2 g_{max}]$ linearly. Larger m_1 and m_2 values can make the probability of selecting nonadmissible solutions lower. However, if this probability is too low (i.e., m_1 and m_2 are too large), the admissible solutions might converge prematurely because of less competition, and also, some useful alleles on these nonadmissible chromosomes might be lost. In this simulation, $m_1 = 1.1$ and $m_2 = 1.5$ are used.

Having the adjusted objective values available, the corresponding fitness values are calculated by Eq. (14.1), and then the standard GA can be performed. We set the search space $u(k)$ as $-5 < u(k) < 15$ and use these parameters: $p_c = 0.7$, $p_m = 0.01$, and population size $= 50$. Simulation results showed that the best objective value (0.175) obtained by the GA is very close to the theoretic optimal value (0.171). Moreover, the best solution obtained by the GA in each generation is an admissible solution.

14.5 GENETIC PROGRAMMING

The GA has proven successful at finding an optimal point in a search space for a wide variety of problems. However, for many problems the most natural representation for the solution to the problem is not merely a single numerical point in the search space of the problem but an entire function, that is, a composite of primitive functions (e.g., addition, subtraction) and terminals (e.g., time, real numbers). The size, shape, and contents of the composite needed to solve the problem are generally not known in advance. *Genetic programming* (GP) provides a way to search the space of all possible functions composed of certain terminals and primitive functions to find a function that solves a problem [Koza, 1992a–c]. GP is an extension of the GA: It uses analogies of GA genetic operators directly on tree-structured programs (typically LISP functions which are symbolic expressions called S-expressions). In other words, in GP, individuals in the genetic population are composites of primitive functions and terminals appropriate to the particular problem domain, and these composites are typically in the form of S-expressions.

GP, like the conventional GA, is a domain-independent method. GP proceeds by genetically breeding populations of primitive functions and terminals (i.e., computer programs) to solve problems by executing the following three steps:

Step 1: Generate an initial population of random computer programs composed of the primitive functions and terminals of the problem.

Step 2: Iteratively perform the following substeps until the termination criterion is satisfied:

    a. Execute each program in the population and assign it a fitness value according to how well it solves the problem.

    b. Create a new population of programs by applying the following two genetic operations. These operations are applied to program(s) in the population selected with a probability based on fitness (i.e., the fitter the program is, the more likely it is to be selected).

        (i) *Reproduction:* Copy existing programs to the new population.

        (ii) *Crossover:* Create two new offspring programs for the new population by genetically recombining randomly chosen parts of two existing programs. The genetic crossover operation (described below) operates on two parental computer programs and produces two offspring programs using parts of each parent.

Step 3: The single best computer program in the population produced during the run is designated the result of the GP run. This result may be a solution (or approximate solution) to the problem.

The crossover operation in GP is best understood by example. Consider the following computer program (S-expression):

$$(+(*0.123z)\,(-x\,0.547))\,,$$

which, in ordinary form, is $0.123z + x - 0.547$. This program (function) takes two points (x and z) and produces a floating-point output. Also, consider a second program:

$$(*\,(*zy)\,(+y\,(*0.725z)))\,,$$

which is equivalent to $zy\,(y + 0.725z)$. In Fig. 14.16(a), these two programs are depicted as trees with ordered branches. Internal nodes of the tree correspond to functions, and leaf nodes correspond to terminals. These nodes are numbered in a depth-first way starting at the left. The crossover operation creates new offspring by exchanging subtrees between the two

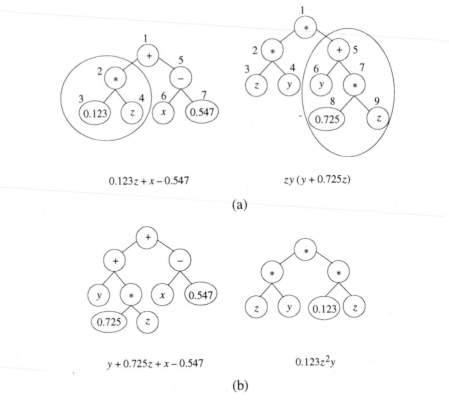

$$0.123z + x - 0.547 \qquad\qquad zy\,(y + 0.725z)$$

(a)

$$y + 0.725z + x - 0.547 \qquad\qquad 0.123z^2 y$$

(b)

Figure 14.16 Crossover operation in genetic programming. (a) Two parental computer programs. (b) Two offspring.

parents. Suppose node 2 is randomly chosen as the crossover point for the first parent and node 5 is randomly chosen as the crossover point for the second parent. The two crossover fragments (corresponding to the underlined subprograms) are the two subtrees indicated in Fig. 14.16(a). The two offspring, shown in Fig. 14.16(b), resulting from the crossover are

$$(+(+y\,(*0.725z)\,)\,(-x\,0.547)\,) \qquad \text{and} \qquad (*\,(*zy)\,(*0.123z)\,)\,.$$

Hence, crossover creates new computer programs using parts of existing parental programs. Because entire subtrees are exchanged, this crossover operation always produces syntactically and semantically valid programs as offspring regardless of the choice of the two crossover points. Because programs are selected to participate in the crossover operation with a probability based on fitness, crossover allocates future trials to regions of the search space whose programs contain parts form promising programs.

From the above discussion, we can see that there are five major steps in preparing to use GP, namely, determining (1) the set of terminals, (2) the set of primitive functions, (3) the fitness measure, (4) the parameters for controlling the run, and (5) the method for designating a result and the criterion for terminating a run.

The following example illustrates the use of GP to find the impulse response function in an S-expression for a linear time-invariant system [Koza et al., 1993].

Example 14.8

In this example, GP is used to find the symbolic form of the impulse response function for a linear time-invariant system using only the observed response of the system to a particular known forcing function. Figure 14.17 shows the linear time-invariant testing system (plant) which sums the output of three major components, each consisting of a pure time-delay element, a lag circuit containing a resistor and a capacitor, and a gain element. For example, for the first component in this system, the time delay is 6, the gain is $+3$, and the time constant RC is 5. We shall consider the discrete-time version of this system.

The known forcing function is a unit square input $i(t)$ that arises from an amplitude of 0 to 1 at time step 3 and falls back to zero amplitude at time step 23. The response of the unknown system to the square forcing function is given to the GP. The response along with the forcing input function is shown in Fig. 14.18. In fact, the output of a linear time-invariant system is the discrete-time convolution of the input $i(t)$ and the impulse response function $H(t)$. That is,

$$o(t) = \sum_{\tau=-\infty}^{t} i(t-\tau) H(\tau). \tag{14.21}$$

The impulse response function $H(t)$ for the system shown in Fig. 14.17 is known to be

$$H(t) = \begin{cases} 0 & \text{if } t \le 6, \\ a(t) = [3(1-\tfrac{1}{5})^{t-6}]/5 & \text{if } t > 6 \end{cases}$$

$$+ \begin{cases} 0 & \text{if } t \le 15 \\ b(t) = [-8(1-\tfrac{1}{12})^{t-15}]/12 & \text{if } t > 15, \end{cases} \tag{14.22}$$

$$+ \begin{cases} 0 & \text{if } t \le 25 \\ c(t) = [6(1-\tfrac{1}{9})^{t-25}]/9 & \text{if } t > 25. \end{cases}$$

We now show how an approximation to this impulse response function can be discovered via GP using just the observed output from the square forcing function. In other words, given only Fig. 14.18, the GP is expected to find the S-expression of the impulse response function in Eq. (14.22). Hence, the goal is to produce the following S-expression (program) or an approximation to it:

$$(+(+\text{IFLTE}(T\,6\,0\,a(t))\ \text{IFLTE}(T\,15\,0\,b(t))\,)\ \text{IFLTE}(T\,25\,0\,c(t))\,), \tag{14.23}$$

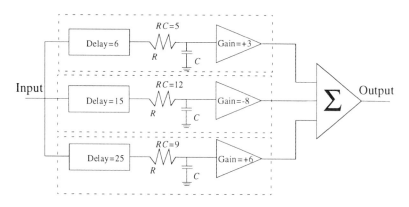

Figure 14.17 Linear time-invariant system in Example 14.8.

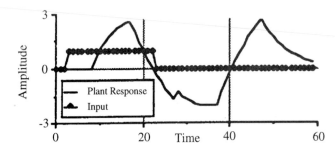

Figure 14.18 Plant square input response in Example 14.8. (Adapted from Koza et al. [1993], © 1993 IEEE.)

where we omit the exact S-expressions of $a(t)$, $b(t)$, and $c(t)$ in Eq. (14.22). The four-argument conditional branching function IFLTE (if less than or equal) evaluates and returns its third argument if its first argument is less than or equal to its second argument and otherwise evaluates and returns its fourth argument.

In preparing to use GP to find the impulse response function, we use the following setting:

1. The terminal set is $\{T, R\}$, that is, time and real constants.
2. The set of primitive functions is $\{+, -, *, /, \text{EXP}, \text{IFLTE}\}$, which includes the four arithmetic operations, the exponential function EXP, and the decision function IFLTE. Decision functions permit alternative calculations to be performed within a computer program, and the exponential function seems relevant to this problem.
3. The fitness of an individual impulse response function in the population is measured in terms of the difference between the known observed response of the system to a particular forcing function and the response computed by convoluting the individual impulse response function and the forcing function. The smaller the difference, the better. An exact impulse response of the system would have a difference of zero. The use of the convolution operation applied to the forcing function and the impulse response function is a common technique employed in control engineering to compute the time-domain response. Specifically, each individual in the population is tested against a simulated environment consisting of $N_{\text{fc}} = 60$ fitness cases, each representing the output $o(t)$ of the given system for various discrete times between 0 and 59 when the square input $i(t)$ described above is used as the forcing function for the system. The fitness of any given genetically produced individual impulse response function $G(t)$ in the population is the sum, over the $N_{\text{fc}} = 60$ fitness cases, of the squares of the differences between the observed response $o(t)$ of the system to the forcing function $i(t)$ and the response computed by convoluting the forcing function and the given genetically produced impulse response $G(t)$. That is, the fitness is

$$f(G) = \sum_{i=1}^{N_{\text{fc}}} [o(t_i) - \sum_{\tau=-\infty}^{t} i(t_i - \tau) G(\tau)]^2. \tag{14.24}$$

4. The population size is set at 4000, and the maximum number of generations is selected as 50.
5. A run is terminated after 51 generations, and then the best-so-far individual is designated the result of a run.

In computer simulations, an individual (S-expression) is said to solve the problem (i.e., is considered a good approximation of the impulse response function) if its fitness value is 20 or less over the 60 fitness cases. Results show that if this problem is run through to generation 46, processing a total of 940,000 individuals is sufficient to yield a solution with 98% probability.

14.6 CONCLUDING REMARKS

In addition to being described in Holland's pioneering book [Holland, 1975], the mathematical foundations of GAs can be found in [Goldberg, 1989; Bethke, 1981; Holland, 1987]. Another useful scheme for GAs is Holland-Hollstien's *triallelic dominance-diploidy scheme* [Hollstien, 1971; Holland, 1975] which originates from the concepts of diploidy (pairs of chromosomes) and dominance (an important genotype-to-phenotype mapping) in natural genetics. Detailed theoretical and empirical results comparing various reordering operators in GAs can be found in [Oliver et al., 1987]. Schemes that encourage the formation of niches and species in GAs were described in [Goldberg and Richardson, 1987; Booker, 1982, 1985]. An *operator fitness* technique in which each evolving stage in a GA consists of selection of an operator from the operator list is described in [Davis, 1991]. The steps in hybridizing a greedy algorithm with a simple GA for solving the graph coloring problem were proposed in [Davis, 1991].

One major application area of GAs is machine learning. Genetic-based machine learning (GBML) systems are machine learning systems that use genetic search as their primary discovery heuristic. The most common GBML architecture is the so-called *classifier system* [Holland and Reitman, 1978], which learns syntactically simple string IF-THEN rules (called *classifiers*) to guide its performance in an arbitrary environment. Complete and detailed material about GBML systems as well as classifier systems can be found in [Goldberg, 1989]. In other applications of GAs in optimization problems, Davidor [1990] used GAs to solve the robot trajectory generation problem, Grefenstette et al. [1990] employed variable-length chromosomes for the optimization of policies for sequential decision tasks, Shimamoto et al. [1993] applied a GA to a dynamical routing problem in communications, and Kristinsson and Dumont [1992] used a GA to directly identify physical parameters (poles and zeroes) of a continuous system.

The computational effort of simple genetic programming can be greatly reduced by employing the technique of *automatic function definition* [Koza, 1992a; Koza et al., 1993]. GP has been applied in solving a variety of different problems in a wide variety of fields [Koza, 1992a; Koza and Rice, 1992]. Kinnear [1993] described the use of GP in evolving iterative sorting algorithms.

14.7 PROBLEMS

14.1 What kind of learning does the GA best represent (supervised, unsupervised, or reinforcement learning)? Justify your answer.

14.2 In Example 14.1, if the seven randomly generated numbers are 27, 40, 8, 35, 11, 22, and 4, what are the corresponding indices of the chosen strings?

14.3 Find the combination of two variables (x_1, x_2) such that its score (fitness) is the highest, where $x_1, x_2 \in \{1, 2,..., 9\}$ and the fitness value (score) for each possible x_1 and x_2 combination is given in Fig. P14.3. Evidently, the highest score combination is $(x_1, x_2) = (5, 5)$, whose score is 9. Let the chromosome in this problem consist of two numbers acting as gene analogs. The

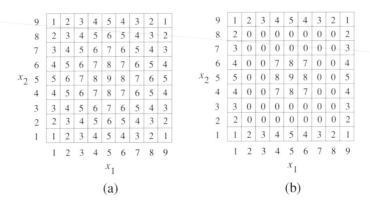

(a)   (b)

Figure P14.3 Scoring table for Problem 14.3.

first determines the x_1 value, and the second determines the x_2 value. The population size of each generation is kept at 4 ($n = 4$).

(a) Consider the scoring table in Fig. P14.3(a). Perform a GA search to find the optimal (x_1, x_2) using only mutation operations. Let the initial chromosomes be $\{(1, 1), (1, 9), (9, 1), (9, 9)\}$, the mutation probability p_m be 1, and the generation gap G be 1. Notice that the mutation operator changes one gene by adding or subtracting 1.

(b) Repeat part (a) but allow the use of crossover operator with the crossover probability set as unity, $p_c = 1.0$, and the crossover site falling between x_1 and x_2.

(c) Repeat parts (a) and (b) but consider the scoring table in Fig. P14.3(b).

(d) Comment on the effects of crossover in the two scoring tables, respectively.

(e) Explain why crossover can help the GA search in the scoring table in Fig. P14.3(b) but could hinder the GA search in the scoring table in Fig. P14.3(a).

14.4 Write a program for redoing Example 14.3 and compare the results with those in Example 14.3.

14.5 Assume that a function of three variables $f(x_1, x_2, x_3)$ is to be maximized. The domain of each variable is as follows: $x_1 \in [-30, 150]$, $x_2 \in [-0.5, 0.5]$, and $x_3 \in [0, 10^5]$. The desired precision values for $x_1, x_2,$ and x_3 are 0.1, 0.001, and 1000, respectively.

(a) Design concatenated multiparameter-mapping fixed-point coding for this problem.

(b) What is the minimum number of bits required to obtain the desired precision?

(c) With the designed coding method, write down the strings that represent each of the following points (x_1, x_2, x_3): (−30, −0.5, 0), (10.5, 0.008, 52,000), (72.8, 0.359, 72,000), (150, 0.5, 100,000).

14.6 Consider a search space containing 16,777,216 points. Compare a binary-coded GA to an octal-coded GA by calculating and comparing the following quantities using both coding methods:

(a) Total number of schemata.

(b) Number of schemata contained within a single individual.

(c) Upper and lower bounds on the number of schemata in a population of size $n = 100$.

14.7 Consider the following schemata of length 10: (i) *1********1, (ii) ********11, (iii) *1**1*****, (iv) ****1*00**, (v) *100010*11.

(a) What are the order and the defining length of each of the schemata?

(b) Estimate the probability of surviving mutation for each schema if the probability of mutation p_m is 0.1 at a single bit position.

14.8 Another method for mapping profit (utility) values u_i to fitness values $f(u_i)$, called the *fixed-ratio method,* is to keep a constant ratio r beween the fitness of the chromosome producing the highest profit result and that of the chromosome producing the lowest profit result. More specifically, we want the mapping to meet the following conditions:

$$f(u_{max}) = rf(u_{min}),$$

$$f(u_i) = f(u_{min}) + [f(u_{max}) - f(u_{min})] \frac{u_i - u_{min}}{u_{max} - u_{min}},$$

$$\sum_i f(u_i) = 1.$$

Determine a formula for $f(u_i)$.

14.9 Consider seven chromosomes with the following fitness values: 5, 15, 30, 45, 55, 70, and 100.
   (a) Use the roulette-wheel selection method to calculate the expected number of copies of each chromosome in the mating pool if a constant population size, $n = 7$, is maintained.
   (b) Repeat part (a) but use the selection method of remainder stochastic sampling without replacement.
   (c) In what ways are these two selection methods different? In what ways are they similar?

14.10 Another rank-based selection method similar to Baker's ranking procedure (Fig. 14.7) is stated as follows. First, sort the n individuals (chromosomes) by fitness values. The probability of picking the first-ranked individual is p. If the first individual is not picked, the probability of picking the second-ranked individual is p, and so on, until one individual is left, in which case it is selected.
   (a) Assume there are five individuals and $p = 0.2$ in the above. Calculate the probability of being selected for each of the five as a function of rank.
   (b) What probability should we use to pick the first-ranked individual from among those still under consideration such that all will have an equal chance of being selected?

14.11 Apply the inversion operator on the following two strings and show the resulting strings:

$$A = 1 \ 9 \ 7 \mid 8 \ 6 \ 2 \mid 5 \ 3 \ 10 \ 4$$
$$B = 10 \ 5 \ 3 \mid 1 \ 9 \ 4 \mid 7 \ 6 \ 2 \ 8,$$

where | indicates the site where the operator acts.

14.12 Describe a way of using GA in designing the analog-to-digital (A/D) converter discussed in Example 11.7. Specify the coding scheme, fitness function, and genetic operators clearly.

14.13 Describe a way of using a hybrid GA in training a multilayer feedforward network. The idea is that we can hybridize a GA with back-propagation learning such that the former can find a good network structure (i.e., find the number of hidden layers and number of hidden nodes) and the latter can find proper weights (parameter learning).

14.14 Describe a way of using a GA to solve the traveling salesperson problem in Example 11.8.

14.15 Consider these two functions:

$$0.2xy + \underline{0.15z \, (x - 4.22)} + 5.4 \qquad \text{and} \qquad x(x + \underline{0.8yz}) - 7.125z + 9.6.$$

   (a) Write down the S-expressions for these two functions and draw the corresponding tree graphs (see Fig. 14.16).
   (b) Perform the crossover operation in GP on the underlined parts of these two functions. Illustrate this operation with tree graphs and write down the resultant functions (offspring).

15

Structure-Adaptive Neural Networks

In previous chapters on neural networks, we focused mainly on parameter learning; that is, we assumed that the structure of the network was given and then proposed learning algorithms to fine-tune the parameters (or the connection weights) of the network so that the trained network would perform as desired. In this chapter, we shall focus on methods for learning the structures as well as the parameters of neural networks. We first investigate simulated evolution in which techniques involving genetic algorithms (GAs) and evolutionary programming (EP) will be explored for structure-level learning. The search schemes in GAs and EP are quite time-consuming, even for a medium-size network. Thus, techniques employing incremental modification or construction of a network from an initial network structure will be studied. These include pruning neural networks, growing neural networks, and growing and pruning neural networks.

15.1 SIMULATED EVOLUTION FOR NEURAL NETWORK STRUCTURE LEARNING

All intelligent systems are evolutionary. Simulated evolution provides a method for generating machine intelligence, and *genetic algorithms* and *evolutionary programming* are two major approaches in simulated evolution. They have been applied in learning the structures as well as the weights of neural networks, and we shall discuss such techniques in this section.

15.1.1 Genetic Algorithms for Designing Neural Networks

In Sec. 14.4.1, we discussed methods of using genetic algorithms to learn the parameters of neural networks. Another potential application of GAs for neural networks is in synthesizing network architectures. The basic idea is to conduct a genetic search in the space of possible architectures. We first train each architecture separately by using a suitable learning rule such as the back-propagation rule and then evaluate it with an appropriate cost function that incorporates both performance and number of nodes. Then a search is carried out by a GA, so that good building blocks found in one trial architecture are likely to survive and can be combined with good building blocks from others. In this section, we shall describe some techniques for encoding neural network architectures on variable-length binary chromosomes and corresponding genetic operators. These procedures can also be viewed as a way of realizing and combining neural networks with GAs.

A system developed by Harp et al. [1989, 1990] and Harp and Samad [1991], called NeuroGENESYS, is able to synthesize appropriate network structures and parameters in learning algorithms. Compared with other approaches to structure-level learning in neural networks, which will be introduced in the following sections, this system deals more with relationships between sets of nodes and bundles of connections than with determining each individual node or connection. The system begins with a population of randomly generated networks. The structure of each network is described by a chromosome, which is a collection of genes that determine the anatomical properties of the network structure and the parameter values of the learning algorithm. The back-propagation rule is used to train each of these networks to solve the problem, and then the fitness of each network in a population is evaluated. The fitness values pertain to learning speed, accuracy, and cost factors such as the size and complexity of the network. Network chromosomes from a given generation produce offspring according to a GA based on the relative fitness of individuals. A network spawned in this fashion tends to contain some attributes from both of its parents, but a new network may also be a mutant. This process of training individual networks, measuring their fitness, and applying genetic operators to produce a new population of networks is repeated over many generations. The basic cycle is shown in Fig. 15.1 for a network trained to identify digits. Each key part of this process, including encoding, search space, special genetic operators, and the fitness function, will be considered in the following discussion.

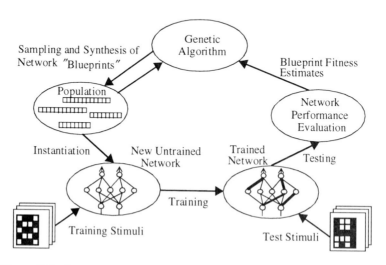

Figure 15.1 Basic cycle of using genetic algorithms for designing neural networks. (Adapted from Harp and Samad [1991], Copyright © 1991 Van Nostrand Reinhold.)

Sec. 15.1   Simulated Evolution for Neural Network Structure Learning   **415**

Encoding. There are, of course, many different ways to parameterize network organization and operation. These parameters might include the number of layers, the number of nodes in a layer, the number of feedback connections allowed, the degree of connectivity from one layer to another, the learning rate, and the error term utilized by the learning rule. An important consideration in choosing encoding strategy is that the representation scheme be *closed* under the genetic operations. In other words, the recombination or mutation of network chromosomes should always yield new, meaningful network chromosomes. One proper network representation is illustrated in Fig. 15.2, in which all the network's parameters are encoded in one long string of bits. The bit string is composed of one or more segments, each of which represents an area and its efferent connectivity or projections. Unlike most feedforward neural networks, areas need not be simply ordered. Each segment is an area specification substring consisting of two parts: (a) an *area parameter specification* (APS) which is of fixed length and parameterizes the area in terms of its address, the number of nodes in it, how they are organized, and the learning parameters associated with its threshold weights; and (b) one or more *projection specification fields* (PSFs), each of fixed length. Each field describes a projection from one area to another. As the number of layers is not fixed in the architecture (although it is bounded), the number of PSFs in an area segment is not fixed either. Hence, the chromosomes used here are of variable length. A projection is indicated by the address of the target area, the degree of connectivity, the dimension of the projection to the area, and so on.

There are markers on the bit string designating the start and the end of area segments and the start of PSFs. The markers enable any well-formed string to be parsed into a meaningful neural network architecture. They also allow a special genetic crossover operator to discover new networks without generating "nonsense" strings. Each parameter is encoded with a field three bits wide, allowing eight possible values.

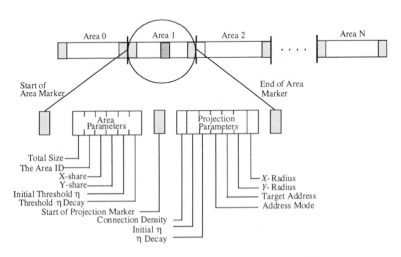

Figure 15.2 Overview of a prototype bit string representation of a neural network architecture (top). The patterned bars are markers indicating the start and end of area segments. Detail shows the mapping of network parameters in the area specification fields and projection fields. (Adapted from Harp and Samad [1991], Copyright © 1991 Van Nostrand Reinhold.)

In the APS, each area has an identification number that serves as a name, which need not be unique among the bit string areas. The input and output areas have the fixed identifiers 0 and 7, and an area has a size and a spatial organization. The total size parameter determines how many nodes the area will have. It ranges from 0 to 7 and is interpreted as the logarithm (base 2) of the actual number of nodes; for example, if the total size is 5, then there are 32 nodes. The two dimension share parameters, X-share and Y-share, which are also base-2 logarithms, impose a spatial organization on the nodes. The nodes of areas may have a one- or a two-dimensional rectilinear extent (X-share × Y-share); in other words, they may be arrayed in a line or in a rectangle.

The PSFs in an area's segment of the bit string determine where the nodes in that area will make efferent connections and how. Different nodes within an area can be connected to different portions of a target area, and even to different target areas. Each PSF indicates the identity of the target area, and there are two ways to specify the target. In the absolute mode (address mode, A), the PSF's address parameter is taken to be the identification number of the target area. The relative mode (address mode, R) indicates that the address bits hold the position of the target area in the bit string relative to the *current area*. A relative address of zero refers to the area immediately following the one containing the projection; a relative address of *n* refers to the *n*th area beyond this. Relative addresses indicating areas beyond the end of the chromosome are taken to refer to the final area of the chromosome—the output area. Figure 15.3 shows examples of absolute and relative addressing schemes. The addressing schemes are designed to assist the relationships between areas in surviving the crossover operator—either intact or with potentially useful modifications. Absolute addressing allows a projection to indicate a target no matter where that target winds up on the chromosome of a new individual. Relative addressing helps areas that are close on the bit string to maintain projections even if their identifications change.

The dimension radius parameters (also base-2 logarithms), X-radius and Y-radius, allow nodes in an area to project only to a localized group of nodes in the target area. This feature permits the target nodes to have localized receptive fields. Even within receptive fields, projections between one area and another do not necessarily imply full connectivity. The connection density parameter for the projection may stipulate one of eight degrees of connectivity between 30 and 100%.

Projections subsume one or more weight matrices, which contain the weights on the projection links. The weights are adjusted by the back-propagation learning rule. There are two learning parameters in the PSF. The η parameter controls the learning rate and may take on one of eight values between 0.1 and 12.8. The η-decay parameter controls the rate of exponential decay for η as a function of the training epoch. Separate η and η-decay parameters are included in the ASF for the learning of threshold values.

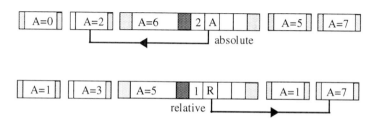

Figure 15.3 Examples of absolute and relative addressing in projections.

An example of the above bit string representation of neural network structures is presented in Fig. 15.4, which shows a fully connected single-hidden-layer feedforward network. The corresponding chromosome as shown has three areas, with each layer specified by one area. Since every layer is a one-dimensional array, the parameters Y-share in APSs and Y-radius in PSFs are all zero ($2^0 = 1$).

Genetic operators. The genetic operators here are quite straightforward, including reproduction, mutation, and modified crossover. The reproduction and mutation operators are much like those in standard GAs, where mutation is performed on an area of the network chromosome. During crossover, because the chromosomes are of variable length, care must be taken to ensure that meaningful building blocks (homologous segments) from the chromosomes of the two networks are exchanged. This can be accomplished by performing modified crossover in three steps: (a) alignment, (b) site selection, and (c) exchange. This differs from simple crossover in addition of the alignment step. In this step, homologous segments are identified on two individuals by referring to the string's markers. Suppose we have two neural network structures NS_1 and NS_2 as follows:

$$NS_1 = : A0 : A1 : A2 : A7,$$

$$NS_2 = : A0 : A4 : A6 : A5 : A3 : A7,$$

where the A's stand for different areas and the :'s are starting area markers. During the alignment process, a random starting area marker is selected for each chromosome and the chromosomes slide along until these two markers are aligned. For example, suppose we pick an alignment site of 1 for NS_1 and a site of 3 for NS_2. The resulting alignment before crossover is as follows:

$$NS_1 = \qquad\qquad : A0 : A1 : A2 : A7,$$

$$NS_2 = \ : A0 : A4 : A6 : A5 : A3 : A7.$$

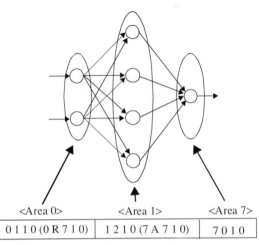

<Area 0>   <Area 1>   <Area 7>

0 1 1 0 (0 R 7 1 0)	1 2 1 0 (7 A 7 1 0)	7 0 1 0

<area> = = <id> <size> <dim1> <dim2> <proj>

<proj> = = (<target> <mode> <density> <dim1> <dim2>)

Figure 15.4 Example of a chromosome for a network with a single hidden layer.

Then a crossing site or (or multiple crossing sites) can be selected at any of the aligned markers. The crossing site can also be chosen at the starting projection marker within some aligned area. When the crossing site is selected, exchange of substructures proceeds as with the simple crossover operator described in the last chapter.

Even though the bit string representation space is designed with closure under the genetic operators in mind, it is still possible for the GA to generate individuals that are unacceptable. Possible situations include (a) a network that has no projection pathways from input to output, (b) a network that has areas with no projections, or projections that lead nowhere, and (c) a network that has areas that are not the targets of any projection. Two strategies can be employed for minimizing the burden of these misfits. First, the individuals with fatal abnormalities [as in situation (a)] are deleted. Second, individuals with minor abnormalities [as in situations (b) and (c)] are *purified* in their network implementation by ignoring (excising) their defects (useless areas). Hence, modified crossover is associated with the purification process.

The fitness function should be defined to account for different performance and cost factors. The relative interest in these factors may change from one application to another. Hence, the fitness function can be defined as a weighted sum of these performance metrics, P_j, optionally transformed by a function ψ_j. The fitness function $F(i)$ for individual i is expressed by

$$F(i) = \sum_{j=1}^{n} a_j \psi_j (P_j(i)), \qquad (15.1)$$

where the coefficients a_j are adjusted to express the desired character of the network. The general metrics include performance factors such as observed learning speed and accuracy of the network on noisy inputs, cost factors such as the size of the network in terms of nodes and weights, and the maximal and average density of the connections formed. The transformation, typically a sigmoid function, serves to normalize or expand the dynamical range of the raw metric. Because the relative weight on each metric can be modified, the network structure can be tuned for different optimization criteria. For example, if one of our goals is to synthesize networks that are computationally efficient, size metrics might be given a higher weight. On the other hand, if accuracy and noise tolerance are more crucial, then performance on noisy input patterns will be given a higher weight.

Example 15.1

[Harp and Samad, 1991]. This example shows the results of using NeuroGENESYS to synthesize neural networks for the XOR problem and the sine function approximation problem. The population size is 30 with initial architectures generated at random, and the system is set to run for a fixed number of generations. Figure 15.5(a) shows a typical discovered network for solving the XOR problem, where accuracy is weighted at 0.75 and the number-of-connections measure has a weight of 0.25. This network is a near-minimal configuration. Figure 15.5(b) shows results obtained for the sine function approximation problem. The fitness function for this problem is chosen to depend on the accuracy of the trained network.

The basic approach we have described in exploring neural network architecture is very flexible. Other learning algorithms can be employed to train networks with recurrent projections. Also, through suitable alterations in the representation, the same genetic scheme can be applied to a wide range of neural networks.

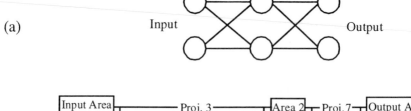

(a)   Input   Output

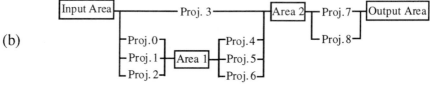

(b)

Figure 15.5 Neural network in Example 15.1. (a) A typical architecture discovered for solving the XOR problem with few connections. (b) An individual that exhibited high accuracy on the sine function approximation problem.

15.1.2 Evolutionary Programming for Designing Neural Networks

Similar to GAs, evolutionary programming is a neo-Darwinian search paradigm suggested by Fogel et al. [1966]. This multiagent search paradigm provides a systematic means for employing stochastic optimization techniques using an arbitrary objective function. The EP optimization algorithm can be described by the following steps [Fogel, 1991a]:

Step 1: Form an initial population $\{P_0(\mathbf{x}), P_1(\mathbf{x}), \ldots, P_{2N-1}(\mathbf{x})\}$ of size $2N$. The parameter vector $\mathbf{x}$ associated with parent element P_i is randomly initialized from a user-specified search domain.

Step 2: Assign a cost J_i to each element $P_i(\mathbf{x})$ in the population based on the objective function.

Step 3: Reorder the population based on the number of wins generated from a stochastic competition process.

Step 4: Generate offspring $(P_N, \ldots, P_{2N-1})$ from the highest ranked N elements $(P_0, \ldots, P_{N-1})$ in the population by perturbing $\mathbf{x}$.

Step 5: Loop to step 2.

Although both EP and GAs operate on a population of candidate solutions and employ a selection criterion to determine which solution should be maintained for future generations, EP differs from GAs in the following ways [Fogel, 1993]: (a) The representation of a problem follows in a top-down fashion from the problem. Rather than trying to fit a single coding structure to every problem, each problem is regarded as unique; (b) the number of offspring per parent is generally unimportant, and successful simulations need not create more than a single offspring per parent; (c) offspring are created through various mutation operations that follow naturally from the chosen problem representation. No emphasis is put on specific genetic operations such as crossover and inversion. Selection is then made based on a probabilistic function of fitness.

EP has been found well-suited for evolving both neural network structures and weights [Fogel et al., 1990]. McDonnell and Waagen [1993] suggested an approach restricted to feedforward networks. In their procedure for the determination of network weights using EP, a population of $2N$ feedforward networks is first generated with weights instantiated from a uniform distribution of $U(-0.5; 0.5)$. Then each network i is assigned a cost J_i, which is typically the sum squared error $E = 0.5\sum_{k=1}^{p}\sum_{j=1}^{n}(d_j^{(k)} - y_j^{(k)})^2$ over all p patterns for n output nodes, where $d_j^{(k)}$ is the desired output value of the jth output node for the kth input pattern and $y_j^{(k)}$ is the corresponding actual output value. The *best* N members of the population generate offspring (perturbed weight sets, $\mathbf{W}_O$) according to

$$\mathbf{W}_O = \mathbf{W}_P + \delta\mathbf{W}_P, \tag{15.2}$$

where $\mathbf{W}_P$ is the parent weight matrix and $\delta\mathbf{W}_P$ is a multivariate random variable with normal distribution $N(0, \delta_f E_P)$, where δ_f is a scaling coefficient and E_P is the sum squared error for each parent network. The scaling factor is a probabilistic analog to the learning rate used in gradient-based methods and can even be treated as a random variable within the EP search strategy. The variance of the weight perturbations is bounded by the total system error using this approach. To emulate the probabilistic nature of survival, a pairwise competition is held where individual elements compete against randomly chosen members of the population. This is the so-called *stochastic competition* process. For example, if network j is randomly selected to compete against network i, a "win" is awarded to network i if $J_i < J_j$. The N networks with the most wins are kept and the process is repeated.

Next, we investigate the structure-level adaptation of neural networks using EP. First, the objective function is modified to account for the existence of a connection:

$$J = \alpha E_P + \beta N_C, \tag{15.3}$$

where E_P is the sum squared error as before and N_C is the number of connections. Let C_{ij}^l denote the connection from node j at layer $(l-1)$ to node i at layer l, where $C_{ij}^l = 1$ if a connection exists or $C_{ij}^l = 0$ if no connection is present. Before going through the EP search, the designer must specify the number of hidden nodes over which the search is conducted. This number determines the maximum number of connections.

Two kinds of probabilities are defined based on the variance of a neuron's activation level to bias the connection selection process within the EP search. The probability of connecting a synapse C_{ij}^l [(i.e., for a node j at layer $(l-1)$, the probability of setting up the link from it to some node i at layer l.] is given by

$$P_c(C_{ij}^l) = \frac{\sigma_{li}^2}{n_{li}^{(u)}\sum_{k\in l}\sigma_{lk}^2}, \tag{15.4}$$

where $n_{li}^{(u)}$ is the number of unconnected synapses available for propagating the signal from node i at layer l to the next layer and σ_{li} is the standard deviation of the activation level of node i at layer l over all input patterns for a fixed set of weights. Of course, this probability is applied only to the nonexisting connection $C_{ij}^l = 0$. According to Eq. (15.4), synapses propagating signals to very active nodes tend to be chosen more than synapses that propa-

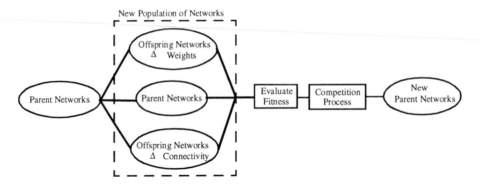

Figure 15.6 One generation of the evolutionary programming search process in design-ing neural networks. (Adapted from McDonnell and Waagen [1993], © 1993 IEEE.)

gate signals to relatively inactive neurons. Likewise, the probability of disconnecting a synapse $C_{ij}^l = 1$ is

$$
P_d(C_{ij}^l) = \begin{cases} 1 & \text{if } \sigma_{li}^2 = 0 \\[2ex] \dfrac{\sigma_{li}^{-2}}{n_{li}^{(c)} \sum_{k \in l} \sigma_{lk}^{-2}} & \text{if } \sigma_{li}^2 \neq 0, \end{cases} \tag{15.5}
$$

where $n_{li}^{(c)}$ is the number of synapses connected from node i at layer l to the subsequent layer. Connections emanating from neurons with zero variance are always disconnected. According to the probability in Eq. (15.5), the synapses propagating signals to neurons with relatively high activity levels have a lower probability of being chosen to become disconnected. As in parameter learning using EP, offspring with changed connectivity are evaluated according to the objective function in Eq. (15.3).

To facilitate both structure-level evolution and optimization of the weights, a strategy is employed that generates one set of offspring with a perturbed weight set in parallel with another set of offspring that has a modified connectivity structure. Figure 15.6 illustrates the evolutionary search process over a single generation.

Example 15.2

In this example, EP is used for a three-bit parity problem. The training starts from a fully connected 3–16–1 network with $\delta_f = 1$, $\alpha = 100$, $\beta = 0.05$, and 10 parent networks. The weight sets are perturbed using a normally distributed $N(0, E_p)$ random variable. The best (least-cost) evolved network after 2000 generations has achieved a mean sum squared error of 0.000018 and has 10 connections as shown in Fig. 15.7.

In addition to the objective function defined in Eq. (15.3), other more complex objective functions can be defined as the criteria for optimal network selection. These criteria should provide a tradeoff between the accuracy and the complexity of the network. Since the problem of choosing the optimal number of nodes and layers is analogous to choosing an optimal subset of regressor variables in statistical model building, some criteria developed for selecting optimal statistical models in information theory can be adopted here. One of the most commonly accepted methods is *Mallows's* C_p *statistic* [Mallows, 1973]:

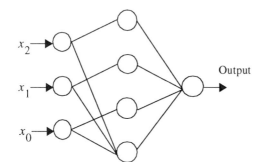

Input

Output

Figure 15.7 Three-bit parity mapping network resulting from evolutionary programming search in Example 15.2.

$$J = \frac{E}{\hat{\sigma}^2} - p + 2N, \qquad (15.6)$$

where E is the sum squared error, p is the number of patterns (observations), N is the number of parameters in the model [corresponding to the number of connections N_C in Eq. (15.3)], and $\hat{\sigma}^2$ is an unbiased estimate of the variance of an error term. The expected value of J is N if the fitted network has negligible bias and is greater otherwise. Generally, small values of J that are close to N are desirable. While this statistic has a good theoretical development, it requires subjective judgment in the use of an estimated $\hat{\sigma}^2$.

Another popular criterion is *Akaike's information criterion* (AIC) based on maximizing the mean log-likelihood of a model [Akaike, 1974]. A simplified version of this criterion for linear polynomial models is

$$J = p \ln\left(\frac{E}{p}\right) + 2N. \qquad (15.7)$$

In spite of the success of the AIC estimator in various applications, this estimator has been proven inconsistent [Kashyap, 1980]. Finally, there is the *minimal description length* (MDL) information criterion [Rissanen, 1978, 1980] for a consistent estimate of the number of parameters while achieving minimum error. The MDL for linear polynomial models is

$$J = 0.5p \ln\left(\frac{E}{p}\right) + 0.5N \ln p. \qquad (15.8)$$

Although Eqs. (15.7) and (15.8) are restricted to linear polynomial models (e.g., $y = a_0 + a_1x_1 + a_2x_2 + a_3x_1x_2$), they can be used to replace Eq. (15.3) as approximations of AIC and MDL criteria for selecting optimal neural networks.

The search schemes introduced in this section are quite time-consuming, especially for applications requiring large networks, where training just one architecture often requires massive computation power. In the following sections, we shall introduce several approaches in which constructing or modifying an architecture to suit a particular task proceeds incrementally. Basically, there are three ways to modify an architecture with the objective of modifying as few nodes (connections) as possible: (a) starting with a network with too many nodes and then pruning excess nodes (*pruning networks*); (b) starting with a network with too few nodes and then adding more nodes as needed (*growing networks*);

(c) starting with a network with too few nodes and then adding more nodes and deleting some nonuseful nodes as well (*growing and pruning networks*). We shall discuss these approaches in the following three sections.

15.2 PRUNING NEURAL NETWORKS

One possible method of obtaining a neural network of appropriate size for a particular problem is to start with a larger network and then prune it to the desired size. In this section, we introduce some network-pruning techniques for general feedforward or recurrent networks.

15.2.1 Weight Decay

One approach to having the network itself remove nonuseful connections during training is called *weight decay*. This is to give each connection w_{ij} a tendency to decay to zero so that connections disappear unless reinforced [Scalettar and Zee, 1988; Hanson and Pratt, 1989]. Consider a back-propagation network. The weight update rule [Eq. (10.16)] is modified to

$$w_{ij}(k+1) = -\eta \frac{\partial E}{\partial w_{ij}}(k) + \beta w_{ij}(k) \tag{15.9}$$

for some positive $\beta < 1$. The same weight decay term was introduced in Chap. 12 when we discussed the basic unsupervised learning rules. With the weight decay term, weights that do not have much influence on decreasing the error while learning (i.e., have $\partial E/\partial w_{ij} \approx 0$) experience an exponential time decay:

$$w_{ij}(k) \simeq \beta^n w_{ij}(0). \tag{15.10}$$

This is equivalent to adding a penalty term w_{ij}^2 to the original cost function E, changing it to

$$E' = E + \gamma \sum_{ij} w_{ij}^2 \tag{15.11}$$

and performing gradient descent $\Delta w_{ij} = -\eta \, \partial E'/\partial w_{ij}$ on the resulting total E'. The β parameter in Eq. (15.9) is then just $1 - 2\gamma\eta$.

Although Eq. (15.11) penalizes the use of more weights than necessary, it discourages the use of only large weights. That is, one large weight costs much more than many small ones. To solve this problem, the following different penalty term [Weigend et al., 1990] can be used:

$$E' = E + \gamma \sum_{ij} \frac{w_{ij}^2}{1 + w_{ij}^2}, \tag{15.12}$$

which is equivalent to making β in Eq. (15.9) dependent on w_{ij}:

$$\beta_{ij} = 1 - \frac{2\gamma\eta}{(1 + w_{ij}^2)^2}, \tag{15.13}$$

so that the small w_{ij} decay more rapidly than the large ones. It is noted that Eq. (15.12) is reduced to Eq. (15.3) when w_{ij} is large.

The above weight decay rules aim at removing unnecessary weights (i.e., *connections*). However, we often want to remove whole nodes so that we can start with an excess of hidden nodes and later discard those not needed. This can be achieved by making weight decay rates larger for nodes that have small outputs or that already have small incoming weights [Chauvin, 1989]. For example, Eq. (15.13) can be replaced by

$$\beta_i = 1 - \frac{2\gamma\eta}{\left(1 + \sum_j w_{ij}^2\right)^2},$$
(15.14)

and the same β_i is used for all connections feeding node i,

15.2.2 Connection and Node Pruning

Instead of waiting for weight decay in the learning process, we can trim the trained network by removing unimportant connections and/or nodes. With this approach, it is necessary to *retrain* the network after the "brain damage," but this retraining is usually rather fast. When a network has learned, then an arbitrary setting of a weight w_{ij} to zero (which is equivalent to eliminating the connection from node j to node i) typically results in an increase in the error E. Hence, efficient pruning means finding the subset of weights that, when set to zero, lead to the smallest increase in E. The same concept is applied to node elimination. Sietsma and Dow [1988] proposed that all nodes of a network are examined when the entire set of training data is presented and that each node (along with its synaptic connections) that does not change state or replicate another node is removed. Thus, they found a subset of the network that had the same performance (i.e., no increase in E) as the complete network for the given training data. The major problem with this technique is that scaling it up to large networks and many patterns will result in a prohibitively long learning process.

Another approach to connection and/or node pruning is based on estimation of the *sensitivity* of the global cost function to the elimination of each connection [Mozer and Smolensky, 1989; Karnin, 1990]. The idea is to keep track of the incremental changes in the connection weights during the learning process. The connections are then ordered by decreasing sensitivity values, and so the network can be efficiently pruned by discarding the last items on the sorted list. In terms of possible connection elimination, the sensitivity with respect to w_{ij}, denoted by S_{ij}, is defined as

$$S_{ij} = E\left(w_{ij} = 0\right) - E\left(w_{ij} = w_{ij}^f\right),$$
(15.15)

where w_{ij}^f is the final value of the connection on completion of the training phase and all other weights are fixed at their final states. To calculate the sensitivity value S_{ij} according to Eq. (15.15) after training, we need to present all the training patterns to the network for each special weight setting $w_{ij} = 0$. It is better if we can calculate it incrementally during the learning process and obtain it as a by-product of network training. To achieve this goal, the sensitivity S_{ij}, defined in Eq. (15.15), can be rewritten as

$$S_{ij} = - \frac{E\left(w_{ij} = w_{ij}^f\right) - E\left(w_{ij} = 0\right)}{w_{ij}^f - 0} w_{ij}^f.$$
(15.16)

Since a typical learning process does not start with $w_{ij} = 0$ but rather with some small, randomly chosen initial value w_{ij}^i, Eq. (15.16) is approximated by

$$S_{ij} \simeq - \frac{E(w_{ij} = w_{ij}^f) - E(w_{ij} = w_{ij}^i)}{w_{ij}^f - w_{ij}^i} w_{ij}^f. \tag{15.17}$$

Furthermore, the numerator in Eq. (15.17) can be approximated by

$$E(w_{ij} = w_{ij}^f) - E(w_{ij} = w_{ij}^i) \simeq \int_I^F \frac{\partial E}{\partial w_{ij}} dw_{ij}, \tag{15.18}$$

where the integration is along the line from an initial point I in the weight space to the final weight state F. This expression can be further approximated by replacing the integral by a summation over the discrete steps that the network takes while learning. Thus, from Eq. (15.17), the estimated sensitivity to the removal of connection w_{ij} is evaluated as

$$\hat{S}_{ij} = - \sum_{k=0}^{N-1} \frac{\partial E}{\partial w_{ij}}(k) \, \Delta w_{ij}(k) \frac{w_{ij}^f}{w_{ij}^f - w_{ij}^i}, \tag{15.19}$$

where N is the number of training epochs. The terms used in Eq. (15.19) are readily available during the normal course of training using gradient-descent methods (e.g., steepest descent, conjugate gradient, Newton's method).

For the special case of back propagation, weights are updated according to $\Delta w_{ij} = -\eta \, \partial E / \partial w_{ij}$. Hence, Eq. (15.19) reduces to

$$\hat{S}_{ij} = \sum_{k=0}^{N-1} [\Delta w_{ij}(k)]^2 \frac{w_{ij}^f}{\eta(w_{ij}^f - w_{ij}^i)}. \tag{15.20}$$

Note that for back propagation with a momentum term, the general form of Eq. (15.19) should be used. Upon completion of training, we have a list of sensitivity values, one per each connection. They are created by a process that runs concurrently with, but does not interface with, the learning process. At this point a decision can be made on pruning the connections with the smallest sensitivity values as demonstrated in the following example.

Example 15.3

[Karnin, 1990]. Consider the pattern classification problem in two-dimensional feature space illustrated in Fig. 15.8. The feature vectors (x, y) are uniformly distributed in $[-1, 1] \times [-1, 1]$, and the two nonoverlapping classes are equally probable (i.e., $b = 2/(a + 1) - 1$; see

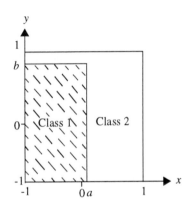
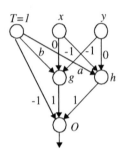

Figure 15.8 Pattern classification problem in Example 15.3.

Structure-Adaptive Neural Networks   Chap. 15

Fig. 15.8). The problem is to train a neural net classifier such that its output is 1 for patterns in class 1 and -1 for patterns in class 2. An ideal two-input, two-hidden-node, one-output network is shown in Fig. 15.8, where node T stands for the constant 1 input used to set the threshold for all internal and output nodes.

We set $a = 0.1$ in Fig. 15.8, where it is clear that x is a more important feature than y as far as a minimum decision error is concerned. Hence, we expect the sensitivity analysis to indicate this fact. After training with $\eta = 0.05$, momentum coefficient $\alpha = 0.5$, weights updating every 24 presentations of random patterns, and 10,000 training epochs, the following weights are obtained:

First-Layer Weight					Second-Layer Weight			
	T	x	y			T	g	h
g	2.96	0.57	-4.43		O	-4.32	5.44	5.31
h	1.56	-7.39	0.80					

The hidden node h roughly learned to produce the decision line $x = a$, while the decision of the other hidden node was mainly based on y. Now, suppose we want to eliminate one of the hidden nodes by pruning its connection to the output. The sensitivities obtained are:

Sensitivities			
	T	g	h
O	0.67	0.15	0.33

The connection from node g to the output has the lowest sensitivity, hence w_{og} is to be pruned. As expected, the result is a network that produces a decision boundary that is roughly a vertical line through $x = a$ in Fig. 15.8.

15.3 GROWING NEURAL NETWORKS

Rather than starting with too large a network and performing some pruning, it is more appealing to start with a small network and gradually increase it to an appropriate size. The ART network introduced in Sec. 12.4 is representative of growing neural networks. In this section, we shall introduce two approaches to growing neural networks: *input space partitioning* and *prototype selection*. ART networks belong to the second category.

15.3.1 Input Space Partitioning

In this section, we consider constructing a multilayer perceptron that correctly evaluates a Boolean function from m binary inputs to a single binary output given by a training set of p input-output pairs. The training set is assumed to have no internal conflicts (i.e., different outputs for the same input). Since threshold units are used in all the layers, each node functions as a hyperplane that partitions the input (pattern) space. This concept has been illustrated in Sec. 10.1. The problem here concerns how to partition the input space to separate different patterns using as few hyperplanes as possible. This is equivalent to constructing a network using as few nodes as possible. The following algorithms provide such construction schemes to get around this problem, and Fig. 15.9 illustrates the ways that different algorithms construct networks [Hertz et al., 1991].

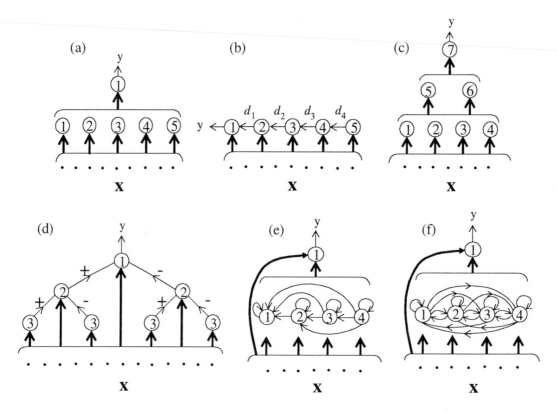

Figure 15.9 Network construction algorithms. The dots are inputs, while the numbered circles are threshold units numbered in order of their creation. Shaded arrows represent connections from all the units or inputs at the arrow's tail. (a) Marchand's algorithm. (b) Cascade perceptron. (c) Tiling algorithm. (d) Upstart algorithm. (e) Recurrent cascade correlation network. (f) Simple expanding recurrent network.

Marchand's algorithm. Marchand et al. [1990] proposed an algorithm that constructs a single-hidden-layer network for solving the Boolean function problem mentioned above [see Fig. 15.9(a)]. Hidden nodes are added one by one, each separating out one or more of the p patterns. The separated pattern(s) are then removed from consideration for the following hidden nodes. That is, each hidden node is chosen so that it has the same output (say $+1$) for *all* remaining patterns with one target (say $+1$) and the opposite output (-1) for *at least one* of the remaining patterns with the opposite target (-1). The latter one or more patterns are then removed from consideration for the following hidden nodes. We can always find such hidden nodes, unless all remaining patterns have the same target. When this does happen, the node-adding process terminates. The resulting transformed patterns on the hidden layer each have a unique target ± 1. These patterns can be considered the *internal representation* of the original input patterns. It can be shown that the heteroassociation problem which associates the transformed patterns to their targets is linearly separable. It can therefore be performed with just one more layer using the perceptron learning rule in Sec. 10.1.1.

Cascade perceptron algorithm.   Using a concept similar to that of the above algorithm, Martinelli et al. [1993] proposed an algorithm that constructs a solution for the Boolean (binary mapping) problem using a series of cascaded hidden units as shown in Fig. 15.9(b). The constructed network is called a *cascade perceptron* (CP) because of its form. Each CP node receives all the inputs, sends its output to the preceding node, and has the threshold controlled by the neuron of the successive nodes. This threshold can be excitatory (when the connection weight d_i is positive) or inhibitory (when d_i is negative). For two succeeding nodes, node i and node $(i + 1)$, in a CP, node $(i + 1)$ is called the *controlling node* of node i and node i is called the *controlled node* of node $(i + 1)$. Then, when a controlling node is active (i.e., its output is 1), the threshold of the controlled node changes depending on the sign and value of the connection weight d_i. The resulting architecture is a feedforward cascade.

At each step of the CP-generating algorithm (CPA), we need to determine a hyperplane (i.e., a node) that divides the input space (hypercube) into two hyperregions. The first hyperregion must contain all positive vertices (corresponding to the patterns with a target value of $+1$) together with some negative vertices (violated constraints), and the second must contain only negative vertices. The optimal choice requires maximization of the number of vertices contained in the second region. This has been formulated as a linear programming (LP) problem with constraints and has been solved by the simplex algorithm [Martinelli et al., 1990, 1993; Luenberger, 1976]. Hence, at each step in the CPA, we solve an LP problem. In general binary mappings, after solving the first LP problem to find the first hyperplane, some negative constraints are violated. This means that the first neuron needs a successive controlling neuron. The latter modifies the threshold of the first in order to solve the violated constraints. The same considerations apply to the new neuron. In this way, at each step a new node is added and at least one of the negative constraints is solved. Since the training patterns corresponding to the solved constraints are disregarded, the number of training patterns to be considered decreases with successive steps; consequently, CPA is always convergent.

Tiling algorithm.   Mézard and Nadal [1989; Nadal, 1989] proposed a *tiling algorithm* that constructs multilayer perceptrons as shown in Fig. 15.9(c), starting from the bottom and working upward. Each successive layer has fewer nodes than the previous one, and the process eventually terminates with a single output node.

It is clear that if two input patterns have different targets at the output layer, then their internal representations must be different on every hidden layer. Such internal representations are called *faithful representations* of the input patterns. The idea of the tiling algorithm is to start each layer with a *master unit* that does well in classifying the input patterns with minimum error and then add further *ancillary units* until the representation at that layer is faithful. Figure 15.10 illustrates this concept. The next layer is constructed in the same way, using the output of the previous layer as its input. Eventually, a master unit itself classifies all patterns correctly and becomes the final output node.

The master unit in each layer is trained to produce the correct target output on as many of its input patterns as possible. If its input patterns are linearly separable, then the perceptron learning rule can be used to train it to classify all its input patterns and the tiling algorithm terminates. However, in normal situations, when its input patterns are not linearly separable, the perceptron learning rule wanders through the weight space, spending the

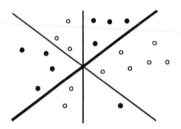

Figure 15.10 Input space partition by tiling algorithm. The heavy line corresponds to the master unit, and the thinner lines to the ancillary units.

most time in regions giving the fewest errors but not staying there. So we can use a variant of the perceptron learning rule, called the *pocket algorithm* [Gallant, 1986, 1990], which simply stores (or "puts in your pocket") the set of weights that has had the longest unmodified run of success so far. The algorithm is stopped after some chosen time *t,* which is the only free parameter in the tiling algorithm.

Whenever the internal representation on the latest layer is not faithful, then the layer has at least one activation pattern without a unique target; the subset of its input patterns that produces the ambiguous pattern includes both targets. So we train a new ancillary unit on this subset, also using the tiling algorithm and trying to separate it as much as possible. Then we look again for ambiguous patterns and repeat this process until the representation is faithful as shown in Fig. 15.10. The convergence of the tiling algorithm has been proved in [Hertz et al., 1991].

Upstart algorithm.   Figure 15.9(d) shows the kind of architecture generated by the *upstart algorithm* proposed by Frean [1990]. It is specifically for off/on (0/1) units. First, a single node (layer-1 node in the figure), directly connected to the input, is used to classify the input patterns as well as possible. Then we identify all the cases in which the output is wrong and create two more layer-2 nodes if necessary, one to correct the *wrongly "on"* cases and the other to correct the *wrongly "off"* ones. The subsidiary nodes 2 are also directly connected to the input and are trained to do their best with their own problem of correcting the wrongly on or wrongly off patterns without upsetting the correct patterns. Their outputs are connected to output node 1 with large positive or negative weights so that they override the previous output when activated. If necessary, layer-3 nodes are further created to correct the mistakes of layer-2 nodes, and so on. The process eventually ceases, since each additional node created reduces the number of incorrectly classified patterns by at least 1.

The unusual hierarchical architecture created by the upstart algorithm can be converted to an equivalent two-layer network. This can be done by placing all the nodes of the hierarchical arrangement in the hidden layer, removing the connections between them. Then a new output node is added and fully connected to the hidden layer. Proper weights on these connections can be found to regenerate the desired targets.

Cascade-correlation algorithm.   The *cascade-correlation algorithm,* proposed by Fahlman and Lebiere [1990], also builds a hierarchy of hidden nodes similar to the one in Fig. 15.9(d). The cascade architecture is shown in Fig. 15.11. It begins with some inputs and one or more output nodes, but with no hidden nodes. Every input is connected to every output node. The output nodes may be linear units, or they may employ some nonlinear

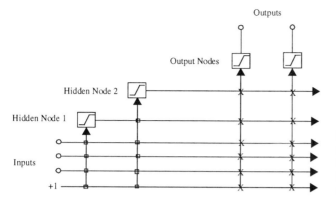

Outputs

Output Nodes

Hidden Node 2

Hidden Node 1

Inputs

+1

Figure 15.11 Cascade architecture after two hidden nodes have been added. The vertical lines sum all incoming activation. Boxed connections are frozen, and X connections are trained repeatedly.

activation function such as a bipolar sigmoidal activation function. New hidden nodes are added to the network one by one in the learning process. For each new hidden node, the magnitude of the *correlation* between the new node's output and the residual error signal is maximized. Each node receives a connection from each of the network's original inputs and also from every preexisting hidden node. The hidden node's input weights are frozen at the time the node is added to the network, and only the output connections are trained repeatedly. Each new node thus adds a new one-node layer to the network.

The learning algorithm begins with no hidden nodes, and the network is trained over the entire training set. Since there is no hidden node, a simple learning rule such as the Widrow-Hoff learning rule can be used. When no significant error reduction has occurred after a certain number of training cycles and the final error is unsatisfactory, we attempt to reduce the residual errors further by adding a new hidden node. To do this, we begin with a *candidate node* that receives trainable input connections from all the network's external inputs and from all preexisting hidden nodes. The output of this candidate node is not yet connected to the active network. We then run a number of passes over the examples in the training set, adjusting the candidate node's input weights after each pass to maximize S defined as

$$S = \sum_o \left| \sum_p (v_p - \overline{v})(E_{p,o} - \overline{E}_o) \right|, \tag{15.21}$$

where o is the network output at which the error is measured, p is the training pattern, v is the candidate node's output value, E_o is the residual output error observed at node o, and $\overline{v}$ and $\overline{E}_o$ are the values of v and E_o averaged over all patterns. The quantity S measures the correlation (or the covariance) between the candidate node's output value and the residual output error. In order to maximize S, the gradient $\partial S/\partial w_i$ is derived as

$$\frac{\partial S}{\partial w_i} = \sum_{p,o} \sigma_o (E_{p,o} - \overline{E}_o) a'_p I_{i,p}, \tag{15.22}$$

where σ_o is the sign of the correlation between the candidate's value and output o, a'_p is the derivative for pattern p of the candidate node's activation function with respect to the sum of its inputs, and $I_{i,p}$ is the input the candidate node receives from node i for pattern p. Once the gradient $\partial S/\partial w_i$ is available, we can perform a gradient ascent to maximize S. Again we are training only a single layer of weights, and the simple delta learning rule can be applied.

When S stops improving, we install the new candidate as a node in the active network and freeze its input weights. Then all the output weights are once again trained by the simple learning rule used previously, the whole cycle repeating itself until the error is acceptably small.

Based on the cascade-correlation network, Fahlman [1991] further proposed a constructive training method for creating a recurrent network called the *recurrent cascade-correlation* (RCC) network. Its structure is the same as that in Fig. 15.11 except that each hidden node is a recurrent node; that is, each hidden node has a connection to itself. The self-recurrent link is trained along with the node's other input weights to maximize S with the same procedure as in the cascade-correlation algorithm. When a candidate node is added to the active network as a new hidden node, the self-recurrent weight is frozen along with all the other input weights. Each new hidden node is in effect a single state variable in a finite-state machine built specifically for the task at hand.

The RCC network is topologically viewed as in Fig. 15.9(e). The hidden recurrent layer is activated by both the input neurons and the recurrent layer itself. The output neurons are in general activated by the input and recurrent neurons or, in a special case, by only the recurrent neurons. It differs from a fully connected recurrent network in the sense that the recurrent connections between the old neurons and the newly added neurons are restricted, that is, nonexistent. This self-recurrent restriction simplifies the training in a way that each neuron can be trained sequentially. However, this structure restriction significantly restricts the representational power of the network. It has been shown that this type of structure with a threshold or sigmoidal activation function is not capable of representing all finite-state automata [Chen et al., 1993]. We shall next introduce a more general approach.

Simple expanding recurrent neural network. As discussed in Chap. 13, recurrent neural networks have been shown to be both theoretically and experimentally capable of learning finite-state automata. Furthermore, it has been shown theoretically that a fully connected recurrent network is capable of representing any finite-state automaton [Minsky, 1967]. However, it is difficult to determine the minimal neural network structure for a particular automaton. Alon et al. [1991] has given an upper limit on the size of the first-order network needed to represent a regular grammar or a state automaton. However, in practice, we often do not have enough information about the nature of the target sequence to decide on the network size before training. In addition, for a particular problem, a much smaller network than that given by the theoretical upper bound solution usually exists. Constructive or destructive recurrent network training methods might offer a solution to this problem. Chen et al. [1993] devised a simple constructive training method that adds neurons during training while still preserving the powerful fully recurrent structure. This scheme is called the *simple expanding recurrent neural network*.

With this method, the network created is shown in Fig. 15.9(f) and is a standard fully recurrent network. The number of neurons in the recurrent layer is allowed to expand whenever needed. Whenever a new node is added, the resulting network should be retrained using one of the proper recurrent network learning algorithms introduced in Chap. 13. To speed up the training, we need to satisfy the principle that the network preserves previously acquired knowledge while the network undergoes changes. To do this, the network is required to be expanded smoothly; that is, the newly added weights should remain zero or very small random numbers. Then, the new network behaves very similarly to the old one immediately after the expansion.

Choosing a criterion for deciding when the network is to expand is very important. A simple method is to determine if the training error reaches the local minimum. More-complex methods based on information criteria (introduced in Sec. 15.1.2), entropy measure, network capacity, or neuron activity distribution would be more feasible. This simple constructive method has been used to create recurrent networks that learn some small Tomita grammars (see, for example, Fig. 13.11). It was found that the constructive method converges very quickly when the network reaches the minimal size required.

15.3.2 Prototype Selection

In this section, we shall explore neural networks for pattern classification. The general configuration of a pattern classification network is depicted in Fig. 15.12. It consists of a cascade of two subnetworks. The first subnetwork, called a matching score (MS) net, maps an input vector $\mathbf{x} = [x_1, x_2, \ldots, x_m]^T \in \mathfrak{R}^m$ into n real numbers $y_1, y_2, \ldots, y_n$ called matching scores (one for each category of patterns) and appearing at the n output nodes of that network. The second subnetwork, usually implemented in the form of the MAXNET, then assigns the input pattern to the class for which the matching score is the highest. Models such as Hamming networks, self-organizing feature map networks, instar networks, and ART networks have the kind of structure shown in Fig. 15.12. Furthermore, some mapping networks such as instar-outstar networks, counterpropagation networks, and multilayer self-organizing feature map networks have this configuration as their input parts.

To train a pattern classification network, we are usually given a large set of exemplars of different categories. From these exemplars, the network creates (using one or more learning rules) a smaller set of prototypes that statistically represent patterns of different categories. These prototypes are stored in the MS net for matching with an input testing pattern to decide its matching score. The prototype selection is important in reducing the complexity (numbers of nodes and connections) and increasing the generalization ability of a classification network. Since in many practical situations, the exact number of categories in a classification problem is unknown and/or the training exemplars are produced on-line or in real time, it is desired that the classification network select or create a new prototype incrementally in the training process. This is equivalent to the process of node growing, since a prototype is usually represented by a node in the MS net. The ART network introduced in Sec. 12.4 is representative of a classification network with a node-growing capability. In this section, we shall explore another representative network, the restricted Coulomb energy neural network.

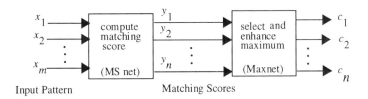

Figure 15.12 General configuration of a pattern classifier network.

The restricted Coulomb energy (RCE) neural network, developed by Reilly et al. [1982], is a single-hidden-layer neural network for supervised learning of pattern categories that can resolve pattern classes separated by nonlinear, essentially arbitrary boundaries. In the RCE network, pattern classification is accomplished through *prototype formation.* It has four major salient characteristics. First, the hidden layer of the network is not preconfigured but dynamically constructed during training. Second, learning in the RCE network is through the commitment of prototypes and modification of a scalar weighting variable associated with each prototype that defines the threshold of categorization. Third, learning stops when there is no new prototype created and no modification of a prototype. Finally, the RCE network is not forced to make a decision on novel patterns. If the testing pattern presented does not belong to any previous training class, the RCE network responds with "unidentified." We shall next describe the RCE network.

The architecture of the RCE network is shown in Fig. 15.13, where input patterns from input layer X are mapped, through weight matrix $\mathbf{A}$, to prototype layer G, which in turn projects onto classification layer H through the weight matrix $\mathbf{B}$. If an input pattern $\mathbf{x}$ causes activity in a single H node, it is classified as belonging to the category associated with that node; otherwise, $\mathbf{x}$ is unidentified. In the learning process, a prototype for a class is *imprinted* on the connections between a G node and the X set, thus becoming the most effective stimulus for that G node. For any given class, there may be more than one prototype; each corresponds to a different G node. The function of the mapping B (realized by the weight matrix $\mathbf{B}$) between layers G and H is to map a subset of G nodes, consisting of prototypes representing the same class, to a given H node, causing it to fire. A stimulus sufficient for an H node to fire is supraliminal activity in any member of its corresponding G node subset.

Each H node is a 0/1 threshold unit. The firing rate of a G node, g_i, is the weighted sum of inputs gated by some threshold function:

$$g_i = a\left(\sum_j A_{ij} x_j\right), \tag{15.23}$$

where

$$a(s) = \begin{cases} 0 & \text{if } s \le \theta \\ s - b & \text{if } s > \theta, \end{cases} \tag{15.24}$$

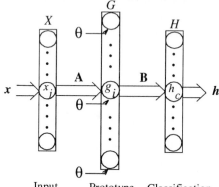

Input Nodes   Prototype Nodes   Classification Nodes

Figure 15.13 Architecture of the RCE neural network.

where b is a constant and θ is the threshold value. Given a prototype $\mathbf{p}(c)$ representing a class c of inputs, the setting $A_{ij} = p_j(c)$, for all j, establishes a correspondence between node g_i and a particular class of patterns, c. The weight vector of g_i takes on the values of the prototype.

Each prototype cell has a "region of influence" in the input pattern space, which is defined as the set of input patterns that satisfies the threshold condition for node firing. For convenience, assume input patterns are normalized ($\mathbf{x}^T\mathbf{x} = 1$) in our discussion. The region of influence defined by node g_i with threshold θ is the intersection of the surface of a unit hypersphere with a cone of angular width $\gamma = \cos^{-1}\theta$, where γ is the angle between $\mathbf{p}(c)$ and an input $\mathbf{x}$ at threshold. The RCE network can develop by itself a set of prototypes whose influence regions map out the areas belonging to different categories in the pattern space without prior information about what these areas are. We shall next discuss prototype formation in the RCE network.

Associated with each prototype is a modifiable scalar weighting factor λ, which effectively defines the threshold for categorization of an input with the class of the given prototype. That is, each committed prototype node g_i has a weight vector $\mathbf{A}_i$ of the form

$$\mathbf{A}_i = \lambda_i \mathbf{p}^i, \tag{15.25}$$

where $\mathbf{A}_i$ is the ith row of matrix $\mathbf{A}$, $\mathbf{p}^i$ is a normalized prototype vector, and $\lambda_i > 1$. The vector $\mathbf{p}^i$ corresponds to some previously seen input pattern whose presentation failed to excite the H node of the appropriate class. Learning in the RCE network involves (a) commitment of prototypes to memory and (b) adjustment of the various λ factors to eliminate classification errors. That is, modification of prototype node connections is governed by the following conditions, where $\mathbf{x}(c)$ represents the input pattern from class c.

1. *New classification:* If $\mathbf{x}(c)$ is presented and the H node h_c for the cth class does not fire, then a new G node (call it g_k) is committed to $\mathbf{x}(c)$ and the connection between g_k and h_c is assigned a weight of 1. The connection weights of g_k with input nodes are modified according to

$$A_{kj} = \lambda_0 x_j \qquad \text{for all } j, \text{ where } \lambda_0 > \theta. \tag{15.26}$$

2. *Confusion:* If the presentation of $\mathbf{x}(c)$ causes some H node, say h_w, to fire, where $w \neq c$, the λ factors of each currently active G node associated with h_w should be reduced. The quantity λ is diminished until the response of the node to $\mathbf{x}(c)$ lies at threshold. That is, if g_r is such a node, then set λ_r as λ_r', where

$$\lambda_r' \mathbf{p}^r \cdot \mathbf{x}(c) = \theta. \tag{15.27}$$

These two rules for prototype acquisition and modification will allow the network to learn the geography of the pattern classes.

Let us go through a few steps in constructing a RCE network to illustrate the above rules. Initially, all G nodes are uncommitted, and the weights between G nodes and H nodes are all zero or some arbitrarily small number. When a pattern $\mathbf{x}^1(c)$ is presented to this system, no H node fires. A single G node g_1 is committed to $\mathbf{x}^1(c)$ as a prototype for the class $\mathbf{p}^1(c) = \mathbf{x}^1(c)$, and the weight between g_1 and h_c is set equal to 1. We can check that if the same pattern were to be presented again to the system, the response of g_1 would be $\lambda_0 \mathbf{p}^1(c) \cdot \mathbf{x}^1(c) = \lambda_0 > \theta$. Then g_c would cause h_c to fire. Now suppose a second pattern $\mathbf{x}^2(c')$ is presented to the system. Assume $c' = c$. If $\lambda_0 \mathbf{p}^1(c) \cdot \mathbf{x}^2(c) > \theta$, then h_c will fire and the pattern will be correctly classified. Thus, no change occurs. If $\lambda_0 \mathbf{p}^1(c) \cdot \mathbf{x}^2(c) < \theta$, then $\mathbf{x}^2(c)$ will be committed to the new G node g_2 with prototype $\mathbf{p}^2(c) = \mathbf{x}^2(c)$, and the weight between g_2 and h_c is set to 1. In this case, a class is characterized by more than one prototype. Finally, consider the situation in which $c' \neq c$. Since there will be no active H nodes of class c', a new prototype node g_2 is committed to $\mathbf{x}^2(c')$ with $\mathbf{p}^2(c') = \mathbf{x}^2(c')$, and the weight between g_2 and h'_c is set to 1. If in addition, $\lambda_0 \mathbf{p}^1(c) \cdot \mathbf{x}^2(c') > \theta$, then λ_0 is reduced to λ_1 such that $\lambda_1 \mathbf{p}^1(c) \cdot \mathbf{x}^2(c') = \theta$. Hence, as the system learns, the λ factors associated with any active incorrect class prototypes will be reduced, leaving only the correct H node to respond to the pattern.

Multiple RCE networks can be cascaded together to form a multistage RCE network [Reilly et al., 1987]. The following example illustrates the use of a RCE net and a multistage RCE net for the classification of seismic signals [Shyu et al., 1990].

Example 15.4

It is known that seismic signals carry critical information for target identification. This example uses the RCE network to classify seismic signals. Seismic data collected from a geophone consist of three categories of signals: the track vehicle's seismic signal, the wheeled vehicle's seismic signal, and the helicopter's seismic signal. A short-term Fourier transform was used to extract the power spectrum of seismic signal. The spectral envelope was composed of 64 spectral samples normalized between 0.0 and 100.0. The power spectrum was then presented to the input layer for training and testing of the RCE neural network. Each of the spectral samples was fed to each node in the input layer. Data sets of 1770 seismic signals were used, 1180 of them for training and the remaining 590 for performance testing.

First, a basic RCE network was used as shown in Fig. 15.14(a). The input layer has 64 nodes, each receiving the power spectral density associated with a given frequency, and the

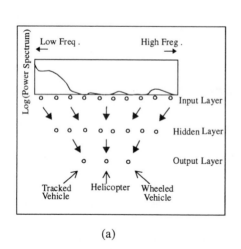

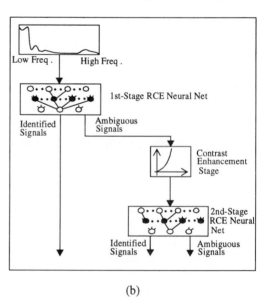

(a)   (b)

Figure 15.14   RCE networks in Example 15.4. (a) Single-stage RCE network. The input layer has 64 nodes, and the output layer has 3 nodes. After training, the hidden layer has 126 nodes. (b) Multistage RCE network. Each stage has 64 nodes in the input layer and 3 nodes in the output layer. After training, there are 177 nodes in the two hidden layers. (Adapted from Shyu et al. [1990], © 1990 IEEE.)

classification (output) layer has 3 nodes. After training, the prototype (hidden) layer had 126 nodes, and 87.9% correct identification on the testing data set was recorded.

To increase accuracy, a two-stage RCE network was used as shown in Fig. 15.14(b). Each stage is a basic RCE network. Correctly identified signals processed in the first stage are passed to the output layer without further processing. Signals processed in the first stage that are ambiguous (unidentified or uncertain) are processed in a *contrast-enhancement stage* to encode their features. Then these enhanced signals are sent to the second RCE network. The reason for this procedure is that ambiguities in the signal are due to low contrast in the medium- and high-frequency regions of the spectra. In other words, the dynamical range of the power spectral density in these frequency regions is too small to provide enough difference for the RCE network to perform pattern recognition. The most basic solution to this kind of problem is to amplify the difference between signals—contrast enhancement. The amplification must be large enough for classification but not so large that the signal will be saturated. With this approach, the classification accuracy is increased to 91.7%.

15.4 GROWING AND PRUNING NEURAL NETWORKS

In this section, we shall study neural networks that have both growing and pruning capabilities. These two actions can be performed simultaneously or sequentially, growing first and then pruning.

15.4.1 Activity-Based Structural Adaptation

Activity-based structure-level adaptation (ASLA) is a paradigm introduced by Lee [1991b] and serves as a general guideline for structure-level adaptation of neural networks. Three major structure-level operators (SOPs) in neural networks are proposed: *node generation operator* (for generating a new node), *node annihilation operator* (for killing a node), and *structural relationship modification operator* (for changing the structural relationship between nodes). We need to determine the rules for applying these SOPs to a network structure. In ASLA, these rules are based on the *activities* of the objects (nodes or weights) in the network as described in the following.

Node generation. It is observed that if a neural network has enough nodes to process a class of problems, then during the training phase the weights of each node will converge to a small neighborhood region around a certain value in the weight space. On the contrary, if a neural network does not have enough nodes to learn a class of problems, then the weights will tend to fluctuate greatly even after a long training period. These observations are used as the basis for determining criteria for the node generation process in ASLA. The activity of a node can be characterized by the time variation of its weights. Hence, a measure, called the *walking distance* (WD), is defined for nodes:

$$\text{WD}_i(n) = \sum_{m=n-L+1}^{n} \| \mathbf{w}_i(m) - \mathbf{w}_i(m-1) \|, \qquad (15.28)$$

where $\text{WD}_i(n)$ is the WD for node i at time step n and $\mathbf{w}_i(m)$ is the input weight vector to node i at time m. WD_i measures the short-term average length of the movement of the input weight vector of node i in the weight space within a temporal window of size L. If WD_i is too high, then the processing capability of node i is insufficient and a new node is needed to share its load. To avoid the storage of L numbers for WD calculations, Eq. (15.28) can be approximated by the exponential averaging scheme in Eq. (13.93). Then we have

$$\text{WD}_i(n) \simeq \gamma \text{WD}_i(n-1) + (1-\gamma) \| \mathbf{w}_i(n) - \mathbf{w}_i(n-1) \|, \qquad (15.29)$$

where $0 < \gamma \leq 1$ controls the effective temporal window size in the averaging process. Equation (15.29) represents a weighted average of the distance between temporally adjacent weight vectors.

With this definition, the criteria for node generation can be defined by the following guidelines:

1. Node i should generate another node if

$$\epsilon_i \triangleq \frac{\partial E}{\partial \text{WD}_i} \text{WD}_i > \theta, \qquad (15.30)$$

where E is the overall system error or cost function and θ is some threshold value. The resulting ϵ_i represents the contribution of node i to the overall system error owing to its weight fluctuation.

2. The newly generated node should inherit the same structure-level attributes as its parent node.

Node annihilation. The criteria for node annihilation are quite straightforward. We can kill a node if

1. It is not a functioning element in the network.
2. It is a redundant element in the network.

The first criterion can be checked by monitoring the output activity of a node during the weight adaptation process. If the output activity is fixed over a very long period of time, then it does not contribute to the function of the network since it does not generate any information in its output. Hence, the first criterion can be measured by the variance of the output activity, called *activity variance* (VA) and defined by

$$\text{VA}_i \triangleq \left\langle \| y_i - \bar{y}_i \|^2 \right\rangle, \qquad (15.31)$$

where y_i is the output of node i, $\bar{y}_i$ is the average of y_i, and $\langle \cdot \rangle$ denotes the expected value. Like Eq. (15.29), this equation can be approximated by

$$\text{VA}_i(n) \simeq \gamma \text{VA}_i(n-1) + (1-\gamma) \| y_i(n) - \bar{y}_i(n) \|^2, \qquad (15.32)$$

where

$$\bar{y}_i(n) = \gamma' \bar{y}_i(n-1) + (1-\gamma') y_i(n) \qquad (15.33)$$

and $0 < \gamma' \leq 1$. Note that zero VA_i for a given node i means that no information is generated from that node; hence, this node is not performing any signal processing function and can be eliminated from the network.

For the second criterion, we need to identify the redundancy in the network. This can be done by observing the dependency between the output values of nodes. If two nodes are totally dependent (which means that given the output value of one node, the output of the other node can be determined with a probability of 1), then one of the nodes can be annihilated without affecting the performance of the network. A sufficient condition for two nodes to be highly dependent is that the values of their weight vectors are very similar to each other. Hence, we can monitor the input weight vectors of nodes in the network, and whenever the weight vectors of two nodes are "very close" to each other, one of them can be eliminated. Identifying the closeness between the input weight vectors of two nodes is a fairly easy job for *topological neural networks* (like Kohonen's feature map in Sec. 12.3) and requires only local operations; however, it is necessary to search through a substantial subset of nodes in neural networks without topological relationships between nodes (like multilayer feedforward networks).

Structural relationship modification. The criteria for modifying the structural relationship between nodes (i.e., changing the connection types) can be defined based on the activity of nodes. Such criteria are model-dependent since the structural relationships between nodes differ among different models. However, the activity-based approach can still be used. First, we need to define the structural relations in the network as objects and then, based on the activities of these relational objects and the attribute objects of these relations, we can define the firing criteria of the structure operators for any specific neural network model.

The general framework outlined above allows us to specify structure-level adaptation for a broad spectrum of neural networks. We shall introduce one such example in the next section.

15.4.2 Function Networks

In this section, the ASLA scheme is applied to a multilayer feedforward network. The resulting network is called a function network (FUNNET) [Lee, 1991b]. As discussed in Chap. 10, the appropriate weights of a multilayer feedforward network can be found using the error back-propagation algorithm. However, a suitable number of nodes in the hidden layers are usually chosen experimentally. To solve this problem, the FUNNET provides both parameter-level and structure-level learning capabilities.

The FUNNET extends the back-propagation network model to include structure-level adaptation. Hence, in the FUNNET, weight learning is still performed by the back-propagation algorithm. For the structure-level adaptation, we consider two kinds of operators: $a^+(l)$, the operator for generating a node in layer l; and $a^-(l, i)$, the operator for removing node i from layer l. Now, we need to specify the rules for firing these two sets of operators.

Node generation process. Node generation is required when the representation power of the network is insufficient. We use the stabilized error after learning as an index to determine whether the network needs to generate a new node. If after a certain period of parameter adaptation the error is stabilized but is larger than the desired value, then a new node can be generated. If a node is to be generated, then the next question is where in the network the new node should be placed. According to the guidelines for node generation, we first need to evaluate Eq. (15.30). The following theorem serves this purpose.

Theorem 15.1

(*Fluctuated Distortion Measure*) [Lee, 1991b]. In a multilayer feedforward network, the contribution of the fluctuation of the input weight vector of the ith node at layer l (measured by $WD_i^{(l)}$) to the total system distortion can be measured by the following *fluctuated distortion measure:*

$$FD_i^{(l)} = \left| \delta_i^{(l)} \right| \left\| Q^{(l-1)} \right\| WD_i^{(l)}, \tag{15.34}$$

where $WD_i^{(l)}$ is given by Eq. (15.29), $Q^{(l-1)}$ is the vector formed by the output values of the nodes at the $(l-1)$th layer, and $\delta_i^{(l)}$ is the *presigmoidal error* for node i at layer l; that is,

$$\delta_i^{(l)} \triangleq a'(net_i^{(l)}) e_i^{(l)}, \tag{15.35}$$

where $a(\cdot)$ is the sigmoidal activation function, $net_i^{(l)}$ is the net input of node i at layer l, and $e_i^{(l)}$ is the *postsigmoidal* error propagated to the ith node at layer l.

Proof: According to Eq. (15.30), we first find the derivative of the overall system error with respect to the walking distance of the ith node at layer l:

$$
\begin{aligned}
\frac{\partial E}{\partial WD_i^{(l)}} &= \left| \frac{\partial E}{\partial WD_i^{(l)}} \right| = \left| \frac{\partial \langle \| \mathbf{y}^d - \mathbf{y} \|^2 \rangle}{\partial net_i^{(l)}} \frac{\partial net_i^{(l)}}{\partial WD_i^{(l)}} \right| \\
&= \left\langle \left| \frac{\partial \| \mathbf{y}^d - \mathbf{y} \|^2}{\partial net_i^{(l)}} \right| \left| \frac{\partial net_i^{(l)}}{\partial WD_i^{(l)}} \right| \right\rangle \\
&= \left\langle \left| \delta_i^{(l)} \right| \left| \frac{\partial net_i^{(l)}}{\partial WD_i^{(l)}} \right| \right\rangle,
\end{aligned}
\tag{15.36}
$$

where $\mathbf{y}^d$ is the desired output vector, $\mathbf{y}$ is the system output vector, and $\delta_i^{(l)}$ is defined in Eq. (15.35). Notice that the net input $net_i^{(l)}$ can be written as

$$net_i^{(l)} = \sum_j y_j^{(l-1)} w_{ij}^{(l,l-1)} = (Q^{(l-1)})^T W_i^{(l,l-1)}, \tag{15.37}$$

where $y_j^{(l-1)}$ is the output of node j at layer $(l-1)$ and $w_{ij}^{(l,l-1)}$ is the weight from node j at layer $(l-1)$ to node i at layer l. Let

$$W_i^{(l,l-1)} = \hat{W}_i^{(l,l-1)} + \Delta W_i^{(l,l-1)}, \tag{15.38}$$

where $\hat{W}_i^{(l,l-1)}$ is the optimal value of $W_i^{(l,l-1)}$ and $\Delta W_i^{(l,l-1)}$ is its fluctuation. $\Delta W_i^{(l,l-1)}$ can be modeled by

$$\Delta W_i^{(l,l-1)} = WD_i^{(l,l-1)} \hat{\mathbf{w}}, \tag{15.39}$$

where $\hat{\mathbf{w}}$ is some normalized random variable. Then we have

$$
\begin{aligned}
\frac{\partial net_i^{(l)}}{\partial WD_i^{(l)}} &= \frac{\partial ((Q^{(l-1)})^T W_i^{(l,l-1)})}{\partial WD_i^{(l)}} \\
&= (Q^{(l-1)})^T \frac{\partial W_i^{(l,l-1)}}{\partial WD_i^{(l)}} \\
&= (Q^{(l-1)})^T \hat{\mathbf{w}}.
\end{aligned}
\tag{15.40}
$$

Substituting Eq. (15.40) into Eq. (15.36), we have

Substituting Eq. (15.40) into Eq. (15.36), we have

$$\frac{\partial E}{\partial \text{WD}_i^{(l)}} = \left\langle \left| \delta_i^{(l)} \right| \left| (Q^{(l-1)})^T \hat{\mathbf{w}} \right| \right\rangle$$

$$\propto \left\langle \left| \delta_i^{(l)} \right| \left\| Q^{(l-1)} \right\| \right\rangle. \tag{15.41}$$

Then from Eq. (15.30), we have

$$\epsilon_i^l = \frac{\partial E}{\partial \text{WD}_i^{(l)}} \, \text{WD}_i^{(l)}$$

$$\propto \left\langle \left| \delta_i^{(l)} \right| \left\| Q^{(l-1)} \right\| \right\rangle \text{WD}_i^{(l)} \tag{15.42}$$

$$= \left\langle \left| \delta_i^{(l)} \right| \left\| Q^{(l-1)} \right\| \text{WD}_i^{(l)} \right\rangle.$$

Since ϵ_i^l is the contribution from the WD of the ith neuron at layer l to the total system output error, the distortion measure $\text{FD}_i^{(l)}$, defined in Eq. (15.34), is a measure of the contribution of node i at layer l to the total system distortion.

From the above theorem we know that, according to the measure $\text{FD}_i^{(l)}$ in Eq. (15.34), we can find the node that contributes most to the output distortion of the network. The node with the highest $\text{FD}_i^{(l)}$ is selected to be split into two when node generation is required (not including the input and output nodes). Furthermore, according to the second guideline for node generation, the new node is added to the network with exactly the same connections as its parent node.

Node annihilation process. In the FUNNET, the criteria for killing a node are exactly based on the guidelines for node annihilation introduced in the last section. According to Eqs. (15.32) and (15.33), the activity variance $\text{VA}_i^l(n)$ is calculated to measure the activity variation of each node i at layer l. If it is very close to zero, then this node is annihilated. To find redundant nodes in a multilayer feedforward network, we can monitor the input weight vectors of nodes at the same layer. If two of them are linearly dependent, then they represent the same hyperplane and one node can be annihilated. However, checking the redundancy in a certain layer would require comparing every pair of nodes within the layer; hence, a computational complexity of $O(N^2/L)$ is required for an N-node network with L layers. The following example illustrates the structure-learning capability of the FUNNET.

Example 15.5

In this example, a three-layer network initialized with two nodes in the hidden layer is used to test the structure-level adaptation behavior for a problem with time-varying statistics. The test problem is a two-class classification problem with two-dimensional input feature vectors. The time-varying statistics of the input pattern are shown in Fig. 15.15. The input vectors are randomly selected from the distribution regions of the two classes. There are two output nodes in the network, with node 1 representing class 1 and node 2 representing class 2. For iterations 0 to 1000 as shown in Fig. 15.15(a), only two hyperplanes are needed to separate the decision regions; thus two hidden nodes are enough. For iterations 1001 to 5000 as shown in

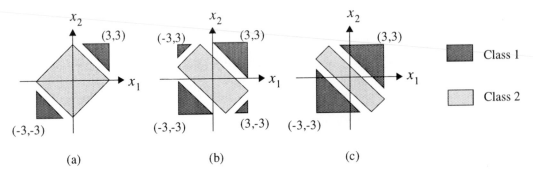

Figure 15.15 Input pattern distribution for Example 15.5. (a) Iterations 0 to 1000. (b) Iterations 1001 to 5000. (c) Iterations 5001 to 7000.

Fig. 15.15(b), class 1 becomes four disconnected regions, and four nodes are needed. As a result, the network can find the desired number of nodes in the hidden layer. For iterations 5001 to 7000 as shown in Fig. 15.15(c), class 1 again becomes two regions. Now because two hidden nodes are enough, the network annihilates the two unnecessary nodes.

15.5 CONCLUDING REMARKS

In this chapter, techniques of genetic algorithms and evolutionary programming are explored for the design of neural networks through appropriate search schemes. Other search schemes that are suitable for designing neural networks but are not discussed in this chapter can be found in [Miller et al., 1989; Harp et al., 1989, 1990; Harp and Samad, 1991; Bornholdt and Graudenz, 1992]. In particular, Oliker et al. [1993] proposed a *distributed genetic algorithm* that can reduce the search space drastically. In EP, a precise AIC information criterion has been formulated by Fogel [1991b] for the selection of an optimal general feedforward network. A modified MDL information criterion has also been used as a structure estimation criterion for feedforward networks [Tenorio and Lee, 1990].

For pruning neural networks, Ivankhnenko [1968, 1971] proposed the group method of data handling (GMDH) network, which is a feedforward multilayer *polynomial* neural network (see also [Farlow, 1984; Hecht-Nielsen, 1990]). The power of GMDH neural networks comes from the use of simple elementary functions and the ability to discard unpromising nodes. Some improved versions can be found in [Duffy and Franklin, 1975; Ikeda et al., 1976; Tamura and Kondo, 1980].

For growing neural networks, Martinelli et al. [1990] proposed an algorithm called the *pyramidal delayed perceptron,* which is similar to the CP-generating algorithm. Sirat and Nadal [1990] independently proposed exactly the same way of dividing up the input space as that of the upstart algorithm. Their procedure, called the *neural tree,* corresponds to traversing a binary tree. deFigueiredo [1990, 1992; Sin and deFigueiredo, 1993] proposed an optimal interpolative (OI) network. The OI network can easily adapt to new exemplars by growing its hidden layers (i.e., increasing the number of hidden nodes).

For growing and pruning neural networks, Lee [1991] proposed the space partition network (SPAN) which is an extension of Kohonen's self-organizing feature map to include structure-level adaptation. Another growing and pruning neural network is the *decision tree network* [Fisher and McKusick, 1989; Dietterich et al., 1990; Cios and Liu, 1992]. The idea is to construct a neural network as a decision tree and then apply machine learning techniques in traditional AI for tree growing and pruning.

In addition to the FUNNET scheme and the pruning methods discussed in this chapter, there are several other approaches, either analytical or constructive, that can find proper size and/or number of hidden layers of a multilayer feedforward network. For example, in [Kung and Hwang, 1988], the algebraic projection approach was used to analyze the optimal hidden-layer size in back-propagation learning. In [Bichsel and Seitz, 1989], a maximum information entropy approach was used to determine the generation of nodes and hidden layers. Ash [1989] noted that nodes can also be created dynamically in the back-propagation network. Azimi-Sadjadi et al. [1993] proposed a method for simultaneous recursive weight adaptation and node creation in back-propagation networks.

15.6 PROBLEMS

15.1 Discuss the advantages and disadvantages of absolute and relative addressing schemes for GA encoding as shown in Fig. 15.3.

15.2 Suppose we have two neural network structures NS_1 and NS_2:

$$NS_1 = : A0 : A3 : A4 : A2 : A7 : A9 : A1 : A6 : A11,$$

$$NS_2 = : A0 : A1 : A4 : A3 : A7 : A2,$$

where the A's stand for different areas and the :'s are starting area markers.
(a) Suppose we pick an alignment site of 5 for NS_1 and a site of 2 for NS_2. What is the resulting alignment before crossover?
(b) If we select the crossover site as the fifth area, what will the resulting networks be after the crossover operation?

15.3 It is possible for the genetic operators introduced in Sec. 15.1.1 to generate individuals (neural networks) that are unacceptable. Illustrate your answer by giving examples of how the following undesirable situations may occur:
(a) A network that has no projection pathway from input to output.
(b) A network that has areas with no projections or projections that lead nowhere.
(c) A network that has areas that are not the targets of any projection.

15.4 Consider the two kinds of probabilities defined for biasing the connection selection process within the EP search.
(a) Explain why, according to Eq. (15.4), synapses propagating signals to very active nodes tend to be chosen more than synapses propagating signals to relatively inactive nodes.
(b) Explain why, according to the probability in Eq. (15.5), synapses propagating signals to nodes with relatively high activity levels have a lower probability of being chosen to become disconnected.

15.5 Verify the statement that the AIC estimator in Eq. (15.7) is inconsistent and the MDL estimator in Eq. (15.8) is consistent. (*Hint*: Refer to [Kayshap, 1980] and [Rissanen, 1978, 1980])

15.6 (a) Derive the weight update rules corresponding to the energy functions E' in Eqs. (15.11) and (15.12).
(b) Verify the energy function E' that results in the β_i value in Eq. (15.13).

15.7 Write a program for redoing Example 15.3 and compare the results with those in Example 15.3.

15.8 Illustrate the use of the following node-growing algorithms to solve the XOR problem step by step: (a) Marchand's algorithm, (b) the cascade perceptron algorithm, (c) the tiling algorithm, and (d) the upstart algorithm.

15.9 Sketch the structure of the cascade-correlation network at each of the following evolving stages. Label the weights and indicate which weights are fixed and which are updated at each stage.

Stage 1: The initial network has four input nodes, two output nodes, and no hidden node.

Stage 2: One hidden node is added to the initial network.

Stage 3: A second hidden node is added to the network in stage 2.

15.10 Explain how the RCE network handles the following problems: (a) separating disjoint regions, (b) separating nonlinear separable decision regions, (c) learning new categories that are introduced at a later stage.

15.11 Two or more RCE networks can be combined into a multiple network, arbitrated by a controller. For this problem, use such a multiple network as a waveform classifier. Assume that three different attributes of the waveform patterns under study are used to create the input vectors. These attributes (parameters) are related in some specific way to frequencies, slopes, and peaks in the waveform patterns. Each of these parameters has certain advantages in performing classification, and thus their combination will be more effective than any one taken alone. Sketch a multiple RCE network for this classification task and describe the (logic) functions that the arbitrator (controller) should have.

15.12 Explain why the ϵ_i in Eq. (15.30) represents the contribution of node i to the overall system error owing to its weight fluctuation.

15.13 Write a program for redoing Example 15.5 and compare the results with those in Example 15.5.

15.14 Use the FUNNET to solve the problem described in Example 15.3.

15.15 Describe how the ASLA scheme can be applied to the radial basis function network (in Sec. 12.6).

16

Applications of Neural Networks

Neural networks have been used successfully in various areas including control systems, vision, speech processing, optimization, communication, signal classification, robotics, medical applications, power systems, and many others. We have mentioned a few applications of some neural network models in previous chapters. Examples of other diverse applications are presented in this chapter. Since the field of neural networks is expanding very rapidly and new uses are emerging every day, we have made no attempt to provide complete coverage for all applications. Therefore, instead of merely enumerating many successful applications in an encyclopedic manner, the approach adopted in this chapter is to consider several examples in detail. This presentation hopefully will stimulate the reader to pursue the development of his or her own application project.

16.1 NEURAL NETWORKS IN CONTROL SYSTEMS

The need to meet demanding control requirements in increasingly complex dynamical control systems under significant uncertainty makes the use of neural networks in control systems very attractive because of their ability to learn, to approximate functions, and to classify patterns and because of their potential for massively parallel hardware implementation. They are able to implement many functions essential to controlling systems with a higher degree of autonomy. The type of neural network most commonly used is the feedforward multilayer neural network with supervised learning. A major property of these networks for control systems is their ability to generate input-output maps that can approximate any function with any desired accuracy. Neural networks have been used mainly in control systems for *system identification* and *control*. In system identification, to model the input-output behavior of a dynamical system, the network is trained using input-output data and the weights are adjusted using the back-propagation algorithm. The underlying assumption is that the nonlinear static map generated by the network can adequately represent the system's dynamical behavior in the ranges of interest for a particular application. For this to be possible one must provide the neural network with information about the history of the system—typically delayed inputs and outputs. How much history is needed depends on the desired accuracy. One may start with as many delayed input signals as the order of the system and then modify the neural network accordingly; it also appears that using a two-hidden-layer network, instead of a one-hidden-layer network, will result in a better performance.

When a multilayer neural network is trained as a controller, either as an open-loop controller or a closed-loop controller, most of the issues are similar to the above. The difference is that the desired output of the network (the appropriate controller-generated control input to the plant) is not readily available but has to be induced from the known desired plant output. For this, one uses either approximations based on a mathematical model of the plant, if available, or a neural model of the dynamics of the plant or even of the dynamics of the inverse of the plant. In the latter case, it is assumed that the inverse dynamics can be represented by a neural network. It is also possible to adaptively change the neural controller based on a critic signal that indicates how well the system is performing. This is the reinforcement learning problem discussed in Sec. 13.3. Neural networks can be combined to both identify and control the plant, thus implementing an adaptive controller.

Neural networks can also be used to detect and identify system failures and to help store information for decision making—thus providing the ability to decide when to switch to a different controller among a finite number of controllers, to classify patterns, and so on. Theoretical developments of neural control are, of course, very important. However, in a control system containing neural networks, it is difficult to prove typical control system properties such as stability. This is due to the mathematical difficulties associated with nonlinear systems controlled by highly nonlinear neural network controllers. Some progress has been made in this area, and it is expected successful applications of neural networks in control systems will provide clues and guidelines for the corresponding theoretical development.

In general, there are potential applications of neural networks at all levels of hierarchical intelligent controllers that provide a higher degree of autonomy to systems. Neural networks are useful at the lowest execution level, where conventional control algorithms are implemented via hardware and software, through the coordination level, to the highest organizational level where decisions are made based on possibly uncertain and/or incomplete information. At the execution level, the ability of neural networks in function approximation and massively parallel computation appears to be of paramount importance. On the other hand, at higher levels, abilities such as pattern classification and storing information in associative memory appear to be of most interest.

We shall introduce some basic ways in which neural network training data can be obtained in tasks relevant to control (see Fig. 16.1) [Miller et al., 1990]. In Fig. 16.1, we do not consider possible time-delay elements in the connections.

Copying from an Existing Controller. If there is a controller capable of controlling the plant, then the information required to train a neural network can be obtained from this controller as shown in Fig. 16.1(a). The target network output for a given input is the

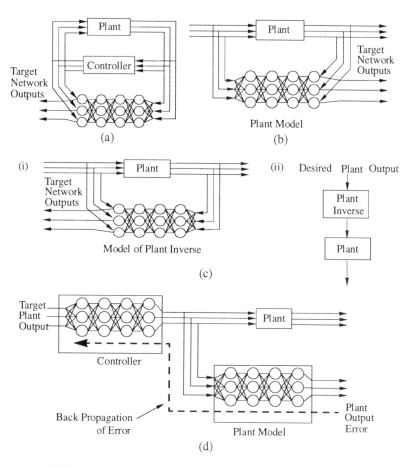

Figure 16.1 Basic configurations for training neural network–based control-identification systems. (a) Copying an existing controller with a neural network. (b) Using a neural network for system identification. (c) Using a neural network to identify a system inverse. (d) Back propagation through a forward model of the plant to determine controller errors. (From "Connectionist Learning for Control: An Overview," by A. G. Barto, in *Neural Networks for Control,* by W. T. Miller, R. S. Sutton, and P. J. Werbos (editors), 1990. Copyright © 1990 MIT Press.)

output of the existing controller for that input. Then the network learns to copy the existing controller. One reason for copying an existing controller is that the latter may be a device that is impractical to use, such as a person (expert). Furthermore, in some cases we may know only some finite input-command pairs of a desired controller. Then a neural network can be trained to emulate the desired controller by interpolating these input-command pairs.

System Identification.   In using neural networks for system identification, training data can be obtained by observing the input-output behavior of a plant as shown in Fig. 16.1(b), where the network receives the same input as the plant and plant output is the target network output. Notice that, in more complex cases, the input to the model may consist of various delayed values of plant inputs and the network model may be a recursive model. When a plant has been identified by a neural network, a proper controller can be designed based on this network. We shall describe a design scheme for such controller.

Identification of System Inverse. Figure 16.1(c)(i) shows how a neural network can be used to identify the inverse of a plant, where the input to the network is the output of the plant and the target output of the network is the plant input. Once one has such an inverse, it can be used for control purposes as shown in Fig. 16.1(c)(ii). The desired plant output is provided as input to the network, and the resulting network output is then used as input to the plant. Since the network is a plant inverse, this plant input causes the desired plant output. Hence, an inverse model of a nonlinear plant, unlike a forward model, has immediate utility for control. A major problem with inverse identification is that the plant's inverse is not always well-defined; that is, more than one plant input produces the same output. In this case, the network attempts to map the same network input to many different target responses. As a result, it tends to average over the various targets, thereby producing a mapping that is not necessarily an inverse.

Differentiating a Model. In this scheme, a multilayer network is first trained to identify the plant's forward model as shown in Fig. 16.1(b). Then this network and another multilayer network used as the controller are configured as in Fig. 16.1(d). The advantage of a forward model having this form is that one can efficiently compute the derivative of the model's output with respect to its input by means of the back-propagation process, which evaluates the transpose of the network Jacobian at the network's current input vector. As a result, propagating errors between actual and desired plant outputs back through the forward model produces error in the control signal, which can be used to train another network to be a controller. This error back-propagation path is illustrated by the dashed line in Fig. 16.1(d). This method has advantages over the direct identification of a plant inverse when the inverse is not well-defined.

Obviously, the configurations shown in Fig. 16.1 are very basic ones. There are many advanced networks for more complex system identification and control problems. The reader is referred to [Miller et al., 1990; Antsaklis, 1990, 1992] for excellent references. In the following sections, we shall discuss some specific techniques and applications of neural networks for control.

16.1.1 Dynamical Back Propagation for System Identification and Control

In this section, we shall introduce models for system identification and control of unknown nonlinear dynamical systems using neural networks [Narendra and Parthasarathy 1990, 1991, 1992]. These models illustrate that well-established adaptive identification and control techniques can be applied to the analysis and synthesis of dynamical systems containing neural networks as subsystems. In the following discussion, we first introduce the basic elements in these models—*generalized neural networks* and *dynamical back propagation*—and then illustrate the models for system identification and control, respectively.

In the models to be considered, multilayer and recurrent networks are interconnected in novel configurations. For convenience in the following discussion, each layer of a typical multilayer network is represented by the operator

$$N_i[\mathbf{u}] = \Gamma[\mathbf{W}^i\mathbf{u}], \tag{16.1}$$

where **u** is the input vector to the considered layer, $\mathbf{W}^i$ represents the associated weight matrix, and Γ is a diagonal nonlinear operator with identical sigmoid functions. Hence, for example, the input-output mapping of a typical multilayer network with two hidden layers is represented by

$$\mathbf{y} = N\,[\mathbf{u}] = \Gamma\,[\mathbf{W}^3\Gamma\,[\mathbf{W}^2\Gamma\,[\mathbf{W}^1\mathbf{u}]\,]\,] = N_3 N_2 N_1\,[\mathbf{u}]. \qquad (16.2)$$

From a system-theoretic point of view, multilayer networks represent versatile static nonlinear maps, while recurrent networks represent nonlinear dynamical feedback systems. In system analysis, both types of operators play an important role. Hence, it is desirable to study the properties of feedback systems having both types of networks as components.

From the above discussion, it follows that the basic element in a multilayer network is the mapping $N_i\,[\cdot] = \Gamma\,[\mathbf{W}^i]$, while addition of the time-delay element z^{-1} to the feedback path results in a recurrent network. In fact, general recurrent networks can be constructed composed of only the basic operations of (a) delay, (b) summation, and (c) the nonlinear operator $N_i\,[\cdot]$. In continuous-time networks, the delay operator is replaced by an integrator, and in some cases multiplication by a constant is also allowed. Hence, such networks, called *generalized neural networks,* are nonlinear feedback systems consisting only of elements $N_i\,[\cdot]$ in addition to the usual operations found in linear systems.

Since arbitrary linear time-invariant dynamical systems can be constructed using the operations of summation, multiplication by a constant, and time delay, the classes of nonlinear dynamical systems that can be generated using generalized neural networks can be represented in terms of transfer matrices of linear systems [i.e., $W(z)$] and nonlinear operators $N\,[\cdot]$. Figure 16.2 shows these operators connected in cascade and feedback in four configurations representing the building blocks for more-complex systems. The superscript notation N^i is used to distinguish among different multilayer networks in any specific representation. Examples of the $W(z)$ functions are

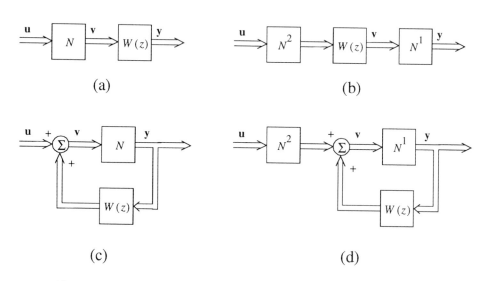

(a) (b)

(c) (d)

Figure 16.2 Building blocks for identification and control models. (a) Representation 1. (b) Representation 2. (c) Representation 3. (d) Representation 4.

1. $W(z) = z^{-d}$: the simplest situation where the linear dynamical transfer function is a pure delay of d units.
2. $W(z) = \sum_{i=1}^{d} \alpha_i z^{-i}$: $W(z)$ is assumed to have a finite plus response of duration d units.
3. $W(z)$ is a *stable rational transfer function* [e.g., $W(z) = (z + 0.8)/(z^2 - 0.5z - 0.6)$]: the most general case, where $W(z)$ has a pulse response that lasts for all $k > 0$.

Since a single-hidden-layer network with an arbitrary large number of hidden nodes can approximate any continuous function, we can assume that the generalized neural networks described above are adequate to deal with a large class of problems in nonlinear system theory. In fact, the structures and configurations shown in Fig. 16.2 represent the basic building blocks of identification and control models for nonlinear systems.

With these generalized neural networks, our next problem involves how to adjust the weights based on a given set of input-output pairs. The learning in these models is based on the back-propagation algorithm and its extension, called *dynamical back propagation,* to dynamical systems.

For a typical multilayer network, the cost function (performance criterion) E is defined as $E = \sum_k \|e\|^2$, where the summation is carried out over all patterns in the training set. If the input patterns are assumed to be presented at each time step, the performance criterion E may be interpreted as the sum squared error over an interval of time. It is this interpretation that is found to be relevant in dynamical systems. When the inputs and outputs are time sequences, the performance criterion E can be defined as $(1/T) \sum_{i=k-T+1}^{k} e^2(i)$, where T is a suitably chosen integer.

In a dynamical system, the change in a parameter at time k produces a change in the output $y(t)$ for all $t \geq k$. If neural networks are to be used for identification or control of such systems, the overall system must include dynamical elements. Hence, extension of the back-propagation algorithm to dynamical systems to adjust the weights of the network is called *dynamical back propagation.* Since complex dynamical systems can be expressed in terms of the four representations of generalized neural networks shown in Fig. 16.2, the back-propagation method can be extended to such systems if the partial derivatives of the outputs with respect to the parameters can be determined for each of the representations. In the following discussion, we shall explore how this can be done in these four cases. In all the cases, it is assumed that the partial derivative of the output of a multilayer neural network with respect to one of the parameters can be computed using static back propagation. Since the performance criterion E can be expressed as a functional of e, our interest is in determining $\partial e(k)/\partial w$ as a function of time, where w denotes the adjustable parameter (weight) of the network.

- **Representation 1:** $\mathbf{y} = W(z)\mathbf{v} = W(z)N[\mathbf{u}]$.

  In this representation, the desired output $y_d(k)$ as well as the error $e(k) = y(k) - y_d(k)$ are functions of time. The desired partial derivative can be obtained from

$$\frac{\partial e(k)}{\partial w_j} = \frac{\partial y(k)}{\partial w_j} = W(z) \frac{\partial v}{\partial w_j}, \tag{16.3}$$

where w_j is a typical parameter of the network N and v is the output of network N. Since $\partial v/\partial w_j$ can be computed at every time step using static back propagation,

$\partial e\,(k)/\partial w_j$ can be realized as the output of a dynamical system $W(z)$ whose inputs are the partial derivatives generated.

- **Representation 2:** $\mathbf{y} = N^1[\mathbf{v}] = N^1[W(z)N^2[\mathbf{u}]]$.

If w_j is a typical parameter of N^1, the partial derivative $\partial e\,(k)/\partial w_j$ can be computed by static back propagation. However, if w_j is a typical parameter of N^2, then we have

$$\frac{\partial y_i}{\partial w_j} = \sum_l \frac{\partial y_i}{\partial v_l}\frac{\partial v_l}{\partial w_j}, \tag{16.4}$$

where v_l is the input of network N^1. Since $\partial v_l/\partial w_j$ can be computed using the method described for representation 1 and $\partial y_i/\partial v_l$ can be obtained by static back propagation, the product of the two yields the partial derivative of the signal y_i with respect to the parameter w_j.

- **Representation 3:** $\mathbf{y} = N[\mathbf{v}] = N[\mathbf{u} + W(z)\mathbf{y}]$.

Before considering this representation, we describe briefly a notational difficulty that arises in it but has not been encountered in earlier representations or in static systems. It concerns situations where the performance index involves time functions [e.g., $f[x(k,w), w]$] that are dependent on parameters w_j, $j = 1, 2,\ldots$, both implicitly in terms of $x(k, w)$ and explicitly. In such cases, our interest is in the total derivative of f with respect to w_j, denoted by $\overline{\partial} f/\overline{\partial} w_j$. Hence,

$$\frac{\overline{\partial} f}{\overline{\partial} w_j} = \frac{\partial f}{\partial x}\frac{\partial x}{\partial w_j} + \frac{\partial f}{\partial w_j}, \tag{16.5}$$

where $\partial f/\partial w_j$ is the partial derivative of f with respect to w_j. The notation $\overline{\partial}/\overline{\partial} w_j$ is used to denote the total derivative, in place of the usual notation d/dw_j, to emphasize the vector nature of the parameter w.

This representation shows a neural network connected in feedback with a transfer matrix $W(z)$. The input to the nonlinear feedback system is a vector $\mathbf{u}(k)$. If w_j is a typical parameter of the neural network, then the aim is to determine the derivatives $\overline{\partial} y_i\,(k)/\overline{\partial} w_j$ for $i = 1, 2,\ldots, m$ and all $k \geq 0$. We observe from the following equation that $\partial y_i(k)/\overline{\partial} w_j$ is the solution of a difference equation; that is, $\overline{\partial} y_i\,(k)/\overline{\partial} w_j$ is affected by its own past values:

$$\frac{\overline{\partial}\mathbf{y}}{\overline{\partial} w_j} = \frac{\partial N\,[\mathbf{v}]}{\partial \mathbf{v}}\frac{\partial \mathbf{v}}{\partial w_j} + \frac{\partial N\,[\mathbf{v}]}{\partial w_j}$$

$$= \frac{\partial N\,[\mathbf{v}]}{\partial \mathbf{v}}\,W(z)\,\frac{\overline{\partial}\mathbf{y}}{\overline{\partial} w_j} + \frac{\partial N\,[\mathbf{v}]}{\partial w_j}, \tag{16.6}$$

where $\overline{\partial}\mathbf{y}/\overline{\partial} w_j$ is a vector and $\partial N[\mathbf{v}]/\partial \mathbf{v}$ and $\partial N\,[\mathbf{v}]/\partial w_j$ are the Jacobian matrix and a vector, respectively, which are evaluated around the nominal trajectory. Hence, it represents a linearized difference equation in the variables $\overline{\partial} y_i/\overline{\partial} w_j$. $\partial N[\mathbf{v}]/\partial \mathbf{v}$ and $\partial N\,[\mathbf{v}]/\partial w_j$ can be computed at every time step as described earlier.

- **Representation 4:** $\mathbf{y} = N^1[\mathbf{v}] = N^1[N^2[\mathbf{u}] + W(z)\mathbf{y}]$.

The feedback system described in the previous representation is preceded in this case by a neural network N^2. The presence of N^2 does not affect the computation of the partial derivatives of the outputs with respect to the parameters of N^1; hence the same method as in representation 3 can be adopted. However, to compute the partial derivative with respect to the parameters of the network N^2, the following procedure is used:

$$\frac{\partial \mathbf{y}}{\partial w_j} = \frac{\partial N^1 [\mathbf{v}]}{\partial \mathbf{v}} \frac{\partial \mathbf{v}}{\partial w_j}$$

$$= \frac{\partial N^1 [\mathbf{v}]}{\partial \mathbf{v}} \left[\frac{\partial N^2 [\mathbf{u}]}{\partial w_j} + W(z) \frac{\partial \mathbf{y}}{\partial w_j} \right]. \quad (16.7)$$

This can be expressed as the input $\partial N^2 [\mathbf{u}] / \partial w_j$ to a nonlinear system obtained using representation 3. Once again, the Jacobian matrix $\partial N^1 [\mathbf{v}] / \partial \mathbf{v}$ and the vector $\partial N^2 [\mathbf{u}] / \partial w_j$ can be computed at every time step in in the same way as described earlier.

The following example illustrates some of the above concepts [Narendra and Parthasarathy, 1991].

Example 16.1

In this example, we consider representation 3 in Figure 16.2(c). Consider a feedback system with $f [v] = v / (1 + 4v^2)$ in the forward loop and $W(z) = (-1.12z + 0.33) / (z^2 - 0.8z + 0.15)$ in the feedback path. The input to the system is $u(k) = 2 \sin(\pi k / 25)$. The aim is to determine a feedback system, with a neural network N in the forward path and $W(z)$ in the feedback path, whose output $y(k)$ approximates the output of the unknown system $y_d(k)$ asymptotically.

The neural network N used here has a single input-output node, 20 first-hidden-layer nodes, and 10 second-hidden-layer nodes. The parameters of N are adjusted within the feedback system using the method described above with a step size of $\eta = 0.01$, and the adjustments are carried out every 10 steps for 500,000 time steps; the results are shown in Fig. 16.3. While N does not approximate f satisfactorily over the entire interval $[-2, 2]$, the output error $y(k) - y_d(k)$ shown in Fig. 16.3(a) is found to be small.

We shall now apply the above techniques to system identification problems. Four models of discrete-time single-input–single-output (SISO) plants were suggested [Narendra and Parthasarathy, 1990]. These models have been chosen for their generality as well as

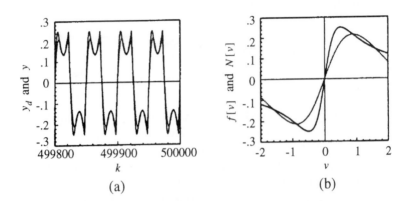

(a)   (b)

Figure 16.3 Results for neural network in Example 16.1. (a) Outputs $y_d(k)$ and $y(k)$. (b) Plots of $f[v]$ and $N[v]$. (Adapted from Narendra and Parthasarathy [1991], © 1991

for their analytical tractability. Use of these models is motivated by corresponding models that have been used in the adaptive systems literature for the identification of linear systems and can be considered generalizations to nonlinear systems. The models of the four classes of plants introduced here can be described by the following nonlinear difference equations:

Model I:

$$y_p(k+1) = \sum_{i=0}^{n-1} \alpha_i y_p(k-i) + g[u(k),...,u(k-m+1)], \qquad (16.8)$$

Model II:

$$y_p(k+1) = f[y_p(k),...,y_p(k-n+1)] + \sum_{i=0}^{m-1} \beta_i u(k-i), \qquad (16.9)$$

Model III:

$$y_p(k+1) = f[y_p(k),...,y_p(k-n+1)] + g[u(k),...,u(k-m+1)], \qquad (16.10)$$

Model IV:

$$y_p(k+1) = f[y_p(k),...,y_p(k-n+1); u(k),...,u(k-m+1)],$$
$$m \leq n, \qquad (16.11)$$

where $[u(k), y_p(k)]$ represents the input-output pair of the plant at time k and $f: \mathbb{R}^n \to \mathbb{R}$ and $g: \mathbb{R}^m \to \mathbb{R}$ are assumed to be differentiable functions of their arguments. It is further assumed that f and g can be approximated to the desired degree of accuracy on compact sets by the multilayer networks used. In model I, the output of the unknown nonlinear plant is assumed to depend linearly on its past values and nonlinearly on the past values of the input. In model II, the output depends linearly on the input $u(k)$ and its past values but nonlinearly on its own past values. The advantage of this model is that it readily lends itself to control in practical situations. In model III, the output depends nonlinearly on its past values as well as those of the input. However, the effects of the input and output values are additive as shown in Eq. (16.10). Model IV is the most general model introduced here. The output is a nonlinear function of the past values of both the input and the output.

Since we have assumed that f and g in the plant models can be approximated by multilayer networks to the desired degree of accuracy, the plant can be represented by a generalized neural network. This assumption motivates the choice of the identification models and allows the statement of well-posed identification problems. The identification model of the plant is composed of neural networks and tapped delay lines (TDLs). In each case, the neural network is assumed to contain a sufficient number of layers, and nodes in each layer, so as to be able to match exactly the input-output characteristics of the corresponding nonlinear mapping in the given plant. In essence, the identification models have the same structure as the plant but contain neural networks with adjustable parameters.

To identify the plant, an identification model is chosen based on prior information concerning the class to which it belongs. For example, assuming that the plant has a structure described by model III, then the model is chosen to have the form shown in

Fig. 16.4, where the sensitivity network is the part for computing the gradient in the learning rules. The aim then is to determine the weights of the two neural networks N^1 and N^2 so that the mapping N^1 is equal to $g[\cdot]$ and the mapping N^2 is equal to $f[\cdot]$. If $y_p(k+1)$ and $\hat{y}_p(k+1)$ are, respectively, the outputs at time step $(k+1)$ for the plant and the identification model, the error $e(k+1) = \hat{y}_p(k+1) - y_p(k+1)$ is used to update the weights of N^1 and N^2. As mentioned above, either static or dynamical back propagation is used, depending on the structure of the identifier. We have the following two models of identifiers.

1. **Parallel model:** In this case, the structure of the identifier is identical to that of the plant with f and g replaced by N^2 and N^1, respectively. This is shown in Fig. 16.4. This implies that the model is described by the equation

$$\hat{y}_p(k+1) = N^2[\hat{y}_p(k),\ldots,\hat{y}_p(k-n+1)] + \tag{16.12}$$
$$N^1[u(k),\ldots,u(k-m+1)].$$

Since N^2 is in a dynamical feedback loop, the parameters of N^1 and N^2 have to be adjusted using dynamical back propagation.

2. **Series-parallel model:** In this case, $y_p(k+1)$ rather than $\hat{y}_p(k+1)$ is used to generate the output of the model. This implies that the model is described by the equation

$$\hat{y}_p(k+1) = N^2[y_p(k),\ldots,y_p(k-n+1)] + \tag{16.13}$$
$$N^1[u(k),\ldots,u(k-m+1)].$$

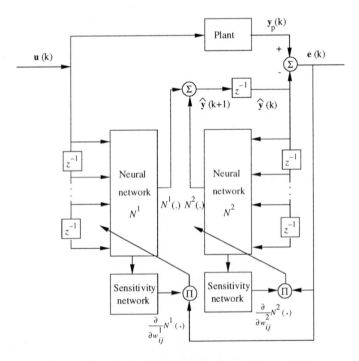

Figure 16.4 Structure of the identification model for model III.

Since the model does not include a feedback loop containing a nonlinear element, static back propagation of the error can be used to adjust the weights of the neural network.

Extensive computer simulations have revealed that a large class of nonlinear plants can be identified using the above procedure. The following example presents some of the simulation results.

Example 16.2

In this example, we consider a simple first-order nonlinear system which is identified using the dynamical back-propagation method. The nonlinear plant is described by the difference equation

$$y_p(k+1) = 0.8y_p(k) + f[u(k)], \tag{16.14}$$

where the function $f(u) = (u - 0.8)u(u + 0.5)$ is unknown. However, it is assumed that f can be approximated to the desired degree of accuracy by a multilayer neural network.

The identification model used is described by the difference equation

$$\hat{y}_p(k+1) = 0.8\hat{y}_p(k) + N[u(k)], \tag{16.15}$$

and the neural network has a single input node, a single output node, 20 first-hidden-layer nodes, and 10 second-hidden-layer nodes. The model chosen corresponds to representation 1 in Fig. 16.2(a). The objective is to adjust a total of 261 weights in the neural network so that $e(k) = \hat{y}_p(k) - y_p(k)$ approaches 0 asymptotically. Defining the performance criterion to be minimized as $E = (1/2T)\sum_{i=k-T+1}^{k} e^2(i)$, the partial derivative of E with respect to a weight w_j in the neural network can be computed as $\partial E/\partial w_j = (1/T)\sum_{i=k-T+1}^{k} e(i)(\partial e(i)/\partial w_j)$. The quantity $\partial e(i)/\partial w_j$ can be computed in the dynamical back propagation [Eq. (16.3)] and used in the gradient rule, $\Delta w_j = -\eta \partial E/\partial w_j$, to update w.

Figure 16.5(a) shows the outputs of the plant and the identification model when the weights in the neural network were adjusted after an interval of 10 times steps using a step size of $\eta = 0.01$. The input to the plant (and the model) was $u(k) = \sin(2\pi k/25)$. In Fig. 16.5(b),

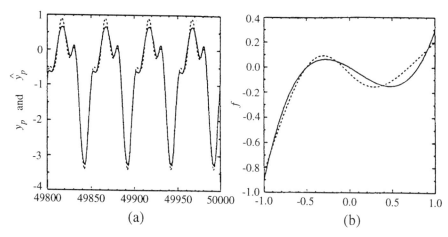

(a) (b)

Figure 16.5 Results for neural network in Example 16.2. (a) Outputs of the plant and identification model. (b) $f[u]$ and $N[u]$ for $u \in [-1, 1]$. (Adapted from Narendra and Parthasarathy [1990], © 1990 IEEE.)

the function $f(u) = (u - 0.8) u (u + 0.5)$ as well as the function realized by the three-layer neural network after 50,000 steps for $u \in [-1, 1]$ are shown. As seen in the figure, the neural network approximates the given function quite accurately.

When a plant is identified, a proper controller can be designed based on the identification model as illustrated in Fig. 16.1(d). In this control scheme, called *indirect adaptive control*, the system identification methods described above must first be used on-line to identify the input-output behavior of the plant. Using the resulting identification model N^i, which contains neural networks and linear dynamical elements as subsystems, the parameters of the controller N^c are adjusted by back-propagating the error e_c, (between the identified model and the reference model outputs) through the identified model. In short, once the plant has been identified to the desired level of accuracy, control action is initiated so that the output of the plant follows the output of a stable reference model. A block diagram of such an adaptive system is shown in Fig. 16.6, where TDL represents the tapped delay line, and the reference model, which is usually linear, specifies the desired overall system performance. Both identification and control can be carried out at every time step or after processing the data over finite intervals. When external disturbances and/or noise are not present in the system, it is reasonable to adjust the control and identification parameters synchronously. However, when sensor noise or external disturbances are present, identification is carried out at every time step while control parameter updating is carried out over a slower time scale to ensure robustness (i.e., control parameters are adjusted with a lower frequency than identification parameters). Hence, the time intervals T_i and T_c over which the identification and control parameters, respectively, are to be updated have to be judiciously chosen in such cases.

The following example illustrates some of the empirical studies on the above neural network–based indirect adaptive control scheme [Narendra and Parthasarathy, 1990].

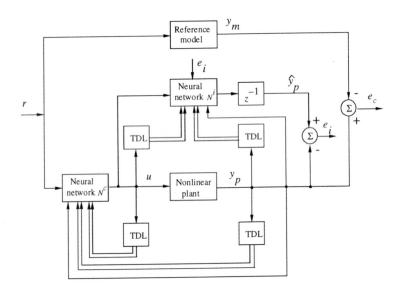

Figure 16.6 Indirect adaptive control using neural networks. (Adapted from Narendra and Parthasarathy [1990], © 1990 IEEE.)

Applications of Neural Networks   Chap. 16

Example 16.3

In this example, the plant to be controlled is described by the second-order difference equation

$$y_p(k+1) = f[y_p(k), y_p(k-1)] + u(k), \qquad (16.16)$$

where

$$f[y_p(k), y_p(k-1)] = \frac{y_p(k)y_p(k-1)[y_p(k)+2.5]}{1+y_p^2(k)+y_p^2(k-1)}. \qquad (16.17)$$

This corresponds to model II in Eq. (16.9). The function f in Eq. (16.17) is assumed to be unknown. A reference model is described by the second-order difference equation

$$y_m(k+1) = 0.6y_m(k) + 0.2y_m(k-1) + r(k), \qquad (16.18)$$

where $r(k)$ is a bounded reference input. If the output error $e_c(k)$ is defined as $e_c(k) = y_p(k) - y_m(k)$, the objective of control is to determine a bounded control input $u(k)$ such that $\lim_{k \to \infty} e_c(k) = 0$. If $f(\cdot)$ in Eq. (16.17) is known, it follows directly from Eqs. (16.16) and (16.18) that at time step k, $u(k)$ can be computed from $y_p(k)$ and its past values as

$$u(k) = -f[y_p(k), y_p(k-1)] + 0.6y_p(k) + 0.2y_p(k-1) + r(k), \qquad (16.19)$$

resulting in the error difference equation $e_c(k+1) = 0.6e_c(k) + 0.2e_c(k-1)$. Since the reference model is asymptotically stable, it follows that $\lim_{k \to \infty} e_c(k) = 0$ for arbitrary initial conditions. However, since $f(\cdot)$ is assumed to be unknown, it can be identified on-line using a neural network N and the series-parallel method. Then Eq. (16.19) becomes

$$u(k) = -N[y_p(k), y_p(k-1)] + 0.6y_p(k) + 0.2y_p(k-1) + r(k). \qquad (16.20)$$

This results in the nonlinear difference equation

$$y_p(k+1) = f[y_p(k), y_p(k-1)] - N[y_p(k), y_p(k-1)] + 0.6y_p(k) + \\ 0.2y_p(k-1) + r(k) \qquad (16.21)$$

governing the behavior of the plant.

In the first simulation, the unknown plant is identified off-line using the system identification methods mentioned before. Following this, Eq. (16.20) is used to generate the control input. The response of the controlled system with a reference input $v(k) = \sin(2\pi k/25)$ is shown in Fig. 16.7(a). In the second simulation, both identification and control are implemented simultaneously using different values of T_i and T_c. The asymptotic response of the system when identification and control start at $k = 0$ with $T_i = 1$ and $T_c = 3$ is shown in Fig. 16.7(b).

16.1.2 Cerebellar Model Articulation Controller

The cerebellar model articulation controller (CMAC) was proposed by Albus [1975]. It is a perceptron-like associative memory with an overlapping receptive field that is capable of learning multidimensional nonlinear functions. It has found applications in function approximation, pattern recognition, and robotic control problem domains. The basic idea of the CMAC approach is to learn an approximation of the system characteristics and then use it to generate the appropriate control signal. The approximation of the system characteristics is understood as gradual learning based on the observations of plant input-output data in real time. As a demonstration, consider the difference equation

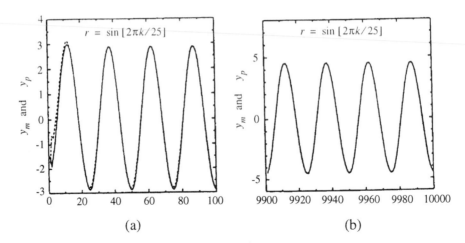

Figure 16.7 Response of control system in Example 16.3. (a) Response when control is initiated after the plant is identified. (b) Response when control is initiated at $k = 0$ with $T_i = 1$ and $T_c = 3$. (Adapted from Narendra and Parthasarathy [1990], © 1990 IEEE.)

$$x(k + 1) = x(k) + [u(k)]^{1/3}, \qquad (16.22)$$

which represents the input-output relationship of a nonlinear system. An alternative way to interpret the system input-output characteristics is to view this equation as a three-dimensional diagram as shown in Fig. 16.8. The horizontal axes are $x(k + 1)$, $x(k)$, and the vertical axis is the system input $u(k)$. Each point $x(k)$ and $x(k + 1)$ corresponds to one system input $u(k)$.

The basic idea behind the CMAC approach is to generate an approximation to this characteristic system surface from input-output measurements and then use the surface as feedforward information to calculate the appropriate control signal according to the measured current system state $x(k)$ and the desired next state $x(k + 1)$. If the values of the system parameters are known, the surface can be precalculated and stored in memory by dividing the input space into disjointed grids. Then, given the control objective (i.e., the desired position in memory), it would be possible to look up in memory the correct control signal. The more interesting problem is when the system parameters are unknown and the

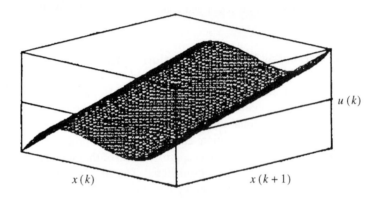

Figure 16.8 Characteristic surface of a nonlinear system.

Applications of Neural Networks   Chap. 16

surface must be learned form input-output data in real time. One relatively simple and robust technique for solving this problem is to iteratively improve the values in memory representing the surface according to the following delta-type learning rule:

$$w(k + 1) = w(k) + \eta [u(k) - w(k)], \tag{16.23}$$

where $w(k)$ is the present value of the memory location corresponding to the system state $(x(k), x(k + 1))$.

The learning rule in Eq. (16.23) updates only one memory location during each control cycle. Hence, no information is extrapolated to "nearby" memory locations. In order to speed up learning and increase the information spread to adjacent memory cells, the concept of *generalization* is used [Kraft and Campagna, 1990ab]. The idea is to update a group of memory cells *close* to the selected memory cell, based on the assumption that similar states require similar control effort for well-behaved systems. The concept of generalization is equivalent to the idea of overlapping receptive fields. For the above two-dimensional example, the generalization region becomes a square of memory locations $(2c + 1)$ locations wide and centered at the selected location. The update rule becomes

$$w_{ij} (k + 1) = w_{ij} (k) + \eta [u (k) - w_{ij} (k)], \tag{16.24}$$

where $w_{ij} (k)$ is the value of the selected memory location and i and j range from $-c$ to c. The value of the system input needed for control is found by averaging over the generalization region according to the equation

$$u (k) = \sum_{i=-c}^{c} \sum_{j=-c}^{c} \frac{w_{ij} (k)}{(2c + 1)^2}. \tag{16.25}$$

The difference between learning with and without generalization is illustrated in Fig. 16.9. Without generalization, the surface is updated one point at a time, whereas with generalization several memory locations are corrected during each control cycle. It is also important to realize that the particular regions of memory trained correspond to particular reference inputs. According to the above discussion, the standard CMAC is just like a lookup table. In the following, we shall introduce more advanced and practical models—

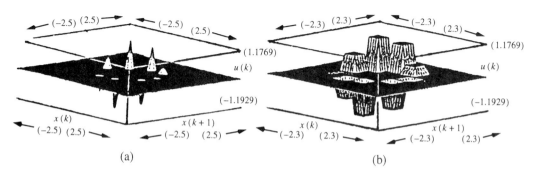

Figure 16.9 Learning of the characteristic surface. (a) Pointwise learning mode (without generalization). (b) Neighborhood learning mode (with generalization). (Adapted from Kraft and Campagna [1990a], © 1990 IEEE.)

higher-order CMAC neural networks [Lane et al., 1992] which include the standard CMAC as a special case.

Let us consider the CMAC in a formal way. A CMAC represents a nonlinear function

$$y = f(\mathbf{x}) \tag{16.26}$$

using two primary mappings,

$$S: \ X \Rightarrow A, \tag{16.27}$$

$$P: \ A \Rightarrow Y, \tag{16.28}$$

where X is a continuous s-dimensional input space, A is an N_A-dimensional association space, and Y is a one-dimensional output space. Figure 16.10 is a schematic of the basic CMAC architecture. The function $S(\mathbf{x})$ is usually fixed and maps each point $\mathbf{x}$ in the input space onto an association vector $\mathbf{a} = S(\mathbf{x}) \in A$ that has N_L nonzero elements. In Fig. 16.10, $N_L = 4$ (corresponding to the bold lines in the figure). Normally (as in the case of the standard CMAC), the association vectors contain binary elements, with 1 indicating excitation and 0 no excitation. However, it will be shown subsequently that this need not be the case. The function $P(\mathbf{a})$ computes a scalar output y by projecting the association vector onto a vector of adjustable weights such that

$$y = P(\mathbf{a}) = \mathbf{a}^T \mathbf{w} = \sum_{i=1}^{N_A} w_i S_i(\mathbf{x}), \tag{16.29}$$

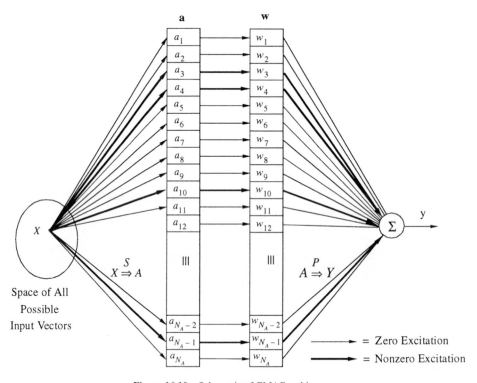

Figure 16.10   Schematic of CMAC architecture.

where w_i is the weight associated with the ith element of $\mathbf{a}$ and $S_i(\mathbf{x}) = a_i$ is the ith element of $\mathbf{a}$.

The CMAC neural network further decomposes the mapping $S(\mathbf{x})$ of Eq. (16.27) into three submappings,

$$R: \; X \Rightarrow M, \tag{16.30}$$

$$Q: \; M \Rightarrow L, \tag{16.31}$$

$$E: \; L, M \Rightarrow A, \tag{16.32}$$

through the use of receptive field functions $R(\mathbf{x})$, a quantization function Q, and an embedding function E, where M is a matrix of receptive field activation values and L is an array of column vectors used to identify the locations of maximally active receptive fields along each input dimension.

The learning rule associated with Eqs. (16.26)–(16.32) involves determining the weights w_i such that when summed according to Eq. (16.29) they approximate the desired function $f(\mathbf{x})$ over the regions of interest. The learning rule is similar to Eq. (16.24) and is given by

$$w_i(k+1) = w_i(k) + \eta \, \frac{(y_d - y)S_i(\mathbf{x})}{\sum_{j=1}^{N_A} S_j^2(\mathbf{x})}, \tag{16.33}$$

where y_d is the desired output. In Eq. (16.33), the term $S_i(\mathbf{x})$ determines which weights are to be updated; only the weights with corresponding nonzero elements of $\mathbf{a} = S(\mathbf{x})$ are updated. We shall next describe the three submappings in Eqs. (16.30)–(16.32).

Receptive field functions. Standard CMACs with generalization have G nonzero (active) rectangular receptive field functions $\{r_j(x_i), r_{j+1}(x_i), r_{j+2}(x_i), \ldots, r_{j+G-1}(x_i)\}$ for each input element, x_i lying in the interval $[\lambda_{j-1}, \lambda_j)$ on the input dimension X_i, where x_i is bounded and is discretized into a fixed number of levels in natural order indexed by integers $\lambda_0, \lambda_1, \lambda_2, \ldots$. Figure 16.11 shows the nonzero receptive fields for $G = 4$ and $x \in [\lambda_4, \lambda_5)$ on the dimension X. Notice that when $G = 1$, it is reduced to the standard CMACs without generalization as illustrated in Fig. 16.9. CMAC output generalization is controlled mainly by the width of the receptive fields, while the offset between adjacent receptive fields determines the input quantization and the output resolution.

Standard CMAC receptive field functions output 1s as long as the input remains within its domain of excitation; otherwise they output 0s. Because of the rectangular shape

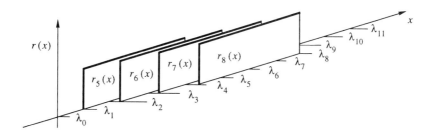

Figure 16.11 Standard CMAC receptive field functions ($G = 4$, $x \in [\lambda_4, \lambda_5)$).

of the receptive field functions, standard CMACs construct discontinuous (staircase) function approximations to multi-input-output data without inherent analytical derivatives. However, the ability to learn both functions and function derivatives is important in the development of many on-line adaptive filter, estimation, and control algorithms. To solve this discontinuous function approximation problem, the use of B-spline receptive field functions allows a higher-order CMAC to be developed that can learn both functions and function derivatives. The resulting higher-order CMAC, developed by Lane et al. [1992], is called the *B-spline CMAC* (BMAC). As an example, Fig. 16.12 shows the linear B-spline receptive field functions for the BMAC.

Using a tensor product to fully interconnect the receptive fields between each input, multidimensional receptive fields can be constructed that represent the interior of a hypercube in the input space X. Multidimensional receptive field functions are then obtained by multiplying the respective one-dimensional receptive field functions contained in each tensor product term as follows:

$$R(\mathbf{x}) = {}^1\mathbf{R}(x_1) \otimes {}^2\mathbf{R}(x_2) \otimes \cdots \otimes {}^s\mathbf{R}(x_s),$$ (16.34)

where $\otimes$ is the tensor product operator and ${}^i\mathbf{R}(x_i) = [{}^ir_1(x_i), {}^ir_2(x_i), \ldots, {}^ir_j(x_i), \ldots]^T$ is the vector containing the receptive field activation values on the ith input x_i. For example, when the number of inputs $s = 2$ and $G = 4$, Fig. 16.13 shows the linear B-spline receptive field functions that are active (nonzero) when the input values (x_1, x_2) are in the shaded region. The 16 nonzero tensor product terms are represented by grid elements with dots in the upper right corner. The indices of these grid elements correspond to the combination of active receptive field B splines in the product term basis element; for example, the grid element index (6,5) corresponds to the tensor product term $({}^1r_6\,{}^2r_5)$.

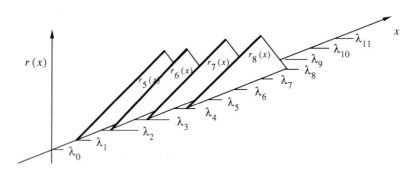

Figure 16.12   Linear B-spline receptive field functions $(G = 4, x \in [\lambda_4, \lambda_5))$.

Quantization function.   The mapping Q of Eq. (16.31) is a quantization function that determines the locations of the nonzero receptive field functions in the s-dimensional input space. The output of Q is a matrix,

$$\mathbf{L} = [\mathbf{l}_1 | \mathbf{l}_2 | \ldots | \mathbf{l}_s],$$ (16.35)

where each column vector $\mathbf{l}_i$, $i = 1, 2, \ldots, s$, contains G elements corresponding to the indices $j_i, j_i + 1, \ldots, j_i + G - 1$ of the nonzero receptive field functions active on the ith input. For example, the $\mathbf{L}$ matrix for Fig. 16.13 is

Applications of Neural Networks   Chap. 16

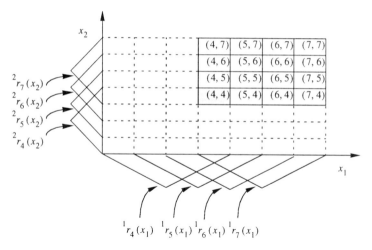

Figure 16.13 Multidimensional linear B-spline receptive field functions $(s = 2, G = 4)$. (Adapted from Lane et al. [1992], © 1992 IEEE.)

$$\mathbf{L} = \begin{bmatrix} 4 & 4 \\ 5 & 5 \\ 6 & 6 \\ 7 & 7 \end{bmatrix}.$$

As in Eq. (16.34), the locations of nonzero receptive fields in the input space X can be determined using the tensor product of $\mathbf{l}_1, \mathbf{l}_2, \ldots, \mathbf{l}_s$ as follows:

$$\wedge \triangleq \mathbf{l}_1 \otimes \mathbf{l}_2 \otimes \ldots \otimes \mathbf{l}_s. \tag{16.36}$$

Embedding function. The embedding function E in Eq. (16.32) maps the nonzero receptive field activation values R in Eq. (16.34), and the nonzero receptive field locations $\wedge$ in Eq. (16.36) onto an association vector

$$\mathbf{a} = S(\mathbf{x}) = E(\wedge, R) \in A, \tag{16.37}$$

which has N_L nonzero elements, by constructing a set of N_L active indices of $\mathbf{a}$:

$$\mathbf{w}_I = \{\alpha_1, \alpha_2, \ldots, \alpha_{N_L}\}, \tag{16.38}$$

which is called the *weight address vector*. For example, the weight address vector in Fig. 16.10 is $\mathbf{w}_I = \{3, 4, 10, N_A - 1\}$. Elements of $\mathbf{a}$ not addressed by $\mathbf{w}_I$ are assumed to be equal to zero.

When the weight address vector $\mathbf{w}_I$ in Eq. (16.38) is determined, the embedding function (for either CMAC or BMAC) *hash-codes* the set of weight addresses contained in $\mathbf{w}_I$ with random mapping to compress the large virtual memory address space of A onto a smaller, more manageable physical address space A_p called *hash memory*. The hash memory is not shown in Fig. 16.10. It should exist between the $\mathbf{a}$ vector and the $\mathbf{w}$ vector in Fig. 16.10. Hash coding is done to take advantage of the fact that most real-world function approximation problems need not represent every point in the input space. The probability of hash collisions can be made small by properly choosing the relationship between the physical memory size $|A_p|$ and the number of elements in $\mathbf{w}_I$, N_L [Albus, 1975, 1981; Wong and Sideris, 1992].

16.2 NEURAL NETWORKS IN SENSOR PROCESSING

Neural networks have been recognized as being well-suited for solving problems in *sensor processing*. Major application areas include pattern recognition, filtering, and sensory data compression. In particular, neural networks are often reputed to enjoy four major advantages over many classical low-level computational techniques for pattern recognition. They are adaptivity (adjustment for new data or information from a changing environment), speed (via massive parallelism), fault tolerance (of missing, confusing, and noisy data), and optimality (regarding error rates in classification systems) [Bezdek, 1992b]. Sensor processing problems usually involve one of two different classes of sensor data: images and time series. In previous chapters in Part II, we saw several application examples in these areas using different neural network models. We shall explore some other interesting examples here.

PSRI object recognition. The objective of the position-, scale-, and rotation-invariant (PSRI) object recognition domain is to recognize an object despite changes in the object's position in the input field, size, or in-plane rotation. Various techniques have previously been applied to achieve this goal, including a number of neural network techniques. Three of the more successful of these methods are back-propagation networks (Chap. 10), the neocognitron (Sec. 12.8), and higher-order networks. We now introduce a higher-order network approach developed by Spirkovska and Reid [1993].

The output of a node, denoted by y_i for node i, in a general higher-order neural network (HONN) is given by

$$y_i = a\left(\sum_j w_{ij} x_j + \sum_j \sum_k w_{ijk} x_j x_k + \sum_j \sum_k \sum_l w_{ijkl} x_j x_k x_l + \cdots \right), \quad (16.39)$$

where $a(\cdot)$ is an activation function and x_j, x_k, x_l are its inputs. These higher-order terms can be used to build transformation invariance directly into the architecture of the network by employing information about the relationships expected between the input nodes. For example, a strictly third-order network can be used to build simultaneous invariance to translation, scale, and in-plane rotation as follows. The output of a strictly third-order network is given by

$$y_i = a\left(\sum_j \sum_k \sum_l w_{ijkl} x_j x_k x_l \right). \quad (16.40)$$

As illustrated in Fig. 16.14, in a third-order network the input pixels are first combined in triplets and then the output is determined from a weighted sum of these products. These triplets of input pixels represent triangles with certain included angles (α, β, γ). In order to build invariance to all three transformations into the architecture of the network, the weights are constrained such that all combinations of three pixels that define similar triangles are connected to the output with the same weight. That is,

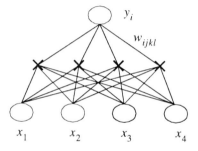

Figure 16.14 Third-order network with four inputs and one output. Inputs are first multiplied together (at X) and then multiplied by a weight before being summed.

$$w_{ijkl} = w_{imno},\qquad (16.41)$$

if the ordered included angles of the triangle formed by connecting pixels (j, k, l) are equal to the ordered included angles of the triangle formed by connecting pixels (m, n, o). This is illustrated in Fig. 16.15. This in effect extracts all triangles that are geometrically similar. These similar triangle features are invariant to all geometric transformations. Note that the connections for similar triangles and equivalence of weights are established before any images are drawn in the input field. Since these invariances are contained in the network architecture before any input vectors are presented, the network needs to learn to distinguish between just one view of each object, not numerous transformed views. As a result, fewer training passes and a smaller training set are required to learn to distinguish between the objects.

Example 16.4

In this example, a third-order network is trained to distinguish between pattern A and pattern B as shown in Fig. 12.12. A third-order network with 25 input nodes and a single output node is set up to associate the first pattern with one output value and the second with a different output value. That is, the network is trained on the vectors:

(1000001000001000001000001, 0)

(1000101010001000101010001, 1)

where the first 25 components represent the input pixel values and the last component represents the desired output value. Training of the network then proceeds in the usual way under

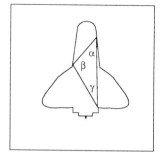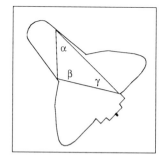

Figure 16.15 Because the included angles are invariant over scale, rotation, and translation, invariance is built into the network by using the same weight for all similar triangles formed by input pixel triplets. (Adapted from Spirkovska and Reid [1993], © 1993 IEEE.)

the constraint of Eq. (16.41); that is, the training vectors are applied and the weights are modified until the network produces the desired output values. The output is determined using a hard limiting transfer function given by

$$y = \begin{cases} 1 & \text{if } \sum_j \sum_k \sum_l w_{jkl} x_j x_k x_l > 0 \\ 0 & \text{otherwise,} \end{cases} \tag{16.42}$$

where j, k, and l range from 1 to the number of pixels (25), x represent pixel values, and w_{jkl} represents the weight associated with the triplet of inputs (j, k, l). Moreover, since HONNs are capable of providing nonlinear separation using only a single layer, the network can be trained using a simple perceptron-like rule of the form

$$\Delta w_{jkl} = (y^d - y) x_j x_k x_l, \tag{16.43}$$

where the expected training output y^d, the actual output y, and the inputs x are all binary. During testing, an input image is presented to the network and an output value is determined using Eq. (16.42). The simulation results achieved 100% accuracy on all test images with various translation, in-place rotation, and scaling up to 40% of reduction and enlargement of the original size.

Spectral feature identification. In this application example, a time-delayed neural network (TDNN) is applied to spectra from the digitized acoustic vibration signals of moving trains in order to identify features of the rail cars for traffic statistics [Mackay and Bozich, 1993]. The goal is to classify the parts of the rail cars, such as the wheels, the coupling, and the car body, based on the acoustic signals (sound or vibration) of the passing trains using a microphone or accelerometer as a transducer. This problem is illustrated in Fig. 16.16. Because of the similarities between rail car identification and speech analysis, the TDNN is used for this application. The input layer is a time-delayed series of mel-

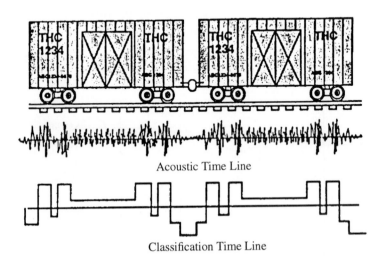

Acoustic Time Line

Classification Time Line

Figure 16.16 Simplified view of rail car identification problem. (Adapted from Mackay and Bozich [1993]. Copyright © 1993 ASME Press. Reprinted by permission of ASME Press.)

Applications of Neural Networks   Chap. 16

scaled frequency spectra arranged in columns consisting of 15 spectral time slices of 16 spectral values each. There are four nodes in the output layer allowing the classification of four features: wheel, car body, coupling, and no train. The network weights are trained using the back-propagation algorithm.

The training data are collected from two different geographical locations with differing railside conditions. The microphone is an omnidirection electrofet placed 10 feet from the rail bed, while the accelerometer is attached to a metal stake driven a foot into the ground near the microphone. On the side nearest the acoustic sensors, a strain gauge is glued to the underside of the rail. All three signals are recorded simultaneously on a multi-track analog tape recorder. The microphone and accelerometer channels are later digitized with 12-bit resolution, and their spectral time series are created using a 256-point FFT with a Hamming window with 50% overlapping between spectra. The resulting spectra are condensed using the mel scale into 16 spectral bins and normalized by the maximum amplitude of the spectra to values between 0.5 and -0.5. The final spectral bins are used as the TDNN inputs. The strain gauge outputs a simple spike with amplitude proportional to the weight as a train wheel rolls over it (making its data easy to understand and interpret in the time domain) and thus correlate with the time sequence of the microphone or accelerometer spectra to create the training data.

Training required some 40,000 spectral samples before the error leveled out. The test results at site 1 are shown in Fig. 16.17. The top trace shows a spectrogram of the input sequence. The next trace is the total root-mean-square (RMS) error, and the last four traces compare the expected output (solid line) with the actual output. The wheel and the rail car body classifications are reasonably well learned, but the RMS error remains high for both the coupling and the no-train classifications. This can be attributed partly to the lower percentage of time the training pattern contains these signals.

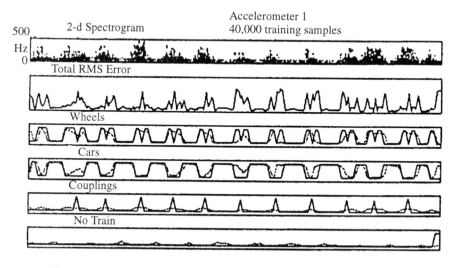

Figure 16.17 Results for the accelerometer from site 1 in the rail car identification problem. (Adapted from Mackay and Bozich [1993]. Copyright © 1993 ASME Press. Reprinted by permission of ASME Press.)

16.3 NEURAL NETWORKS IN COMMUNICATIONS

This section describes the use of neural networks for service quality control in the asynchronous transfer mode (ATM) communication network proposed by Hiramatsu [1990]. The broad-band integrated services digital network (B-ISDN) is a future communication network expected to provide multimedia services including voice, video, and data communications. The ATM is intended to be a key technology that will help in realization of the B-ISDN. An ATM is a high-speed packet-switching network in which all information is segmented into a series of short, fixed-size data packets called *cells*. The network has extensive flexibility; a wide variety of arbitrary bit-rate communication is allowed, and various communication media can be easily combined into one service by cell multiplexing. A flexible control of service quality is needed for a flexible network. There are service quality parameters to be controlled in the ATM network such as cell transmission delay and cell loss rate, and requirements differ among users and services. The network controller has to satisfy all these requirements while using the network efficiently. It also has to adapt to changes in traffic characteristics since many new services will be introduced after the network is designed and installed. Neural networks seem quite suitable to ATM service quality control; they can learn the relation between the offered traffic characteristics and resulting service quality.

Figure 16.18 shows an ATM network structure. The ATM node combines all cells from user terminals into output trunks by cell multiplexing. Users can send cells at arbitrary bit rates after negotiation with the network in the call setup procedure. Each call's characteristics, such as the maximum bit rate, average bit rate, and frequency of bit-rate change, vary with the user and the service. Hence, the statistical characteristics of the multiplexed calls change broadly according to the connected calls' characteristics. At the multiplexer, received cells are sent to output trunks sequentially. Cells must wait in buffers for the available output cycle when too many cells arrive simultaneously. Some cells may be lost when the buffers are full. The job of the network controller is to adjust service quality, such as delay time and cell loss rate, to the proper values for users by observing the total bit rates and keeping them within the trunk capacity. To achieve effective control, the ATM network control function is divided into three control levels by the control cycle: cell trans-

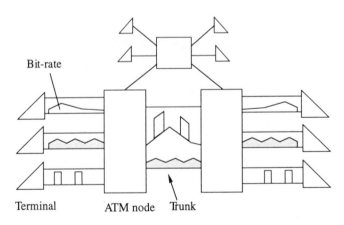

Figure 16.18   Structure of the ATM network.

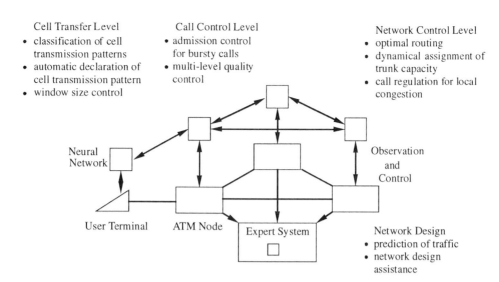

Cell Transfer Level
- classification of cell transmission patterns
- automatic declaration of cell transmission pattern
- window size control

Call Control Level
- admission control for bursty calls
- multi-level quality control

Network Control Level
- optimal routing
- dynamical assignment of trunk capacity
- call regulation for local congestion

Neural Network

Observation and Control

User Terminal   ATM Node

Expert System

Network Design
- prediction of traffic
- network design assistance

Figure 16.19   ATM network control with neural networks. (Adapted from Hiramatsu [1990], © 1990 IEEE.)

fer level, call control level, and network control level. Effective integration of the three levels is important.

An overview of an ATM network learning control using neural networks is shown in Fig. 16.19. Neural networks are expected to be applied to network control such as call admission control and routing, and to expert systems for network design by predicting service quality from observed traffic. Neural networks can approximate the complicated input-output relations by selecting significant inputs and deriving feature parameters from input data autonomously. Thus, a neural controller can accurately control an ATM network with changing characteristics by learning. Furthermore, the global training of many neural networks interconnected to each other is expected to be able to integrate all three control levels mentioned above. Also, the ability of a neural network to solve optimization problems can resolve optimal link capacity assignment.

As an example, consider the use of a back-propagation network in call admission control. The objective of call admission control is to keep the service quality under the requested values by rejecting some of the call setup requests while connecting as many calls as possible. User terminals send a call setup request to the admission controller before they start sending data cells. The request states the traffic characteristics of the call (such as service type, maximum bit rate, and average bit rate) and the required service quality (such as maximum cell loss rate and maximum cell transmission delay). The admission controller accepts the request when the network can ensure the requested service quality and rejects it otherwise.

The model ATM node consists of a single multiplexer and a controller as shown in Fig. 16.20, where a three-layered fully connected back-propagation network is used as the admission controller. Input signals to the neural network are the observed multiplexer status (such as cell arrival rate, cell loss rate, call generation rate, trunk utilization rate, number of connected calls) and the declared parameters contained in a call setup request (such

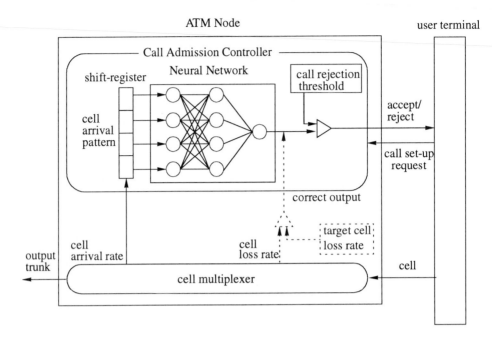

ATM Node   user terminal

Figure 16.20 Structure of a call admission controller. (Adapted from Hiramatsu [1990], © 1990 IEEE.)

as average bit rate and bit-rate fluctuation of the call and holding time). Also a history of the past observed status is inputed to the neural network in parallel format when the sequence of data is expected to contain significant information. Output signals are the predicted service quality parameters and the decision values for acceptance or rejection (such as predicted values of cell arrival rate and cell loss rate, and the call rejection rate).

16.4 NEURAL KNOWLEDGE-BASED SYSTEMS

Integration of domain knowledge into empirical learning is important in building a useful intelligent system in practical domains since the existing knowledge is not always perfect and the training data are not always adequate. In this connection, an integrated neural network–based, knowledge-based hybrid intelligent system is highly desirable [Holden and Suddarth, 1993]. Such a combination can be a close one where knowledge bases are embedded in neural networks, or vice versa. On the other hand, the combination can be a loose one where knowledge bases and neural networks work in a hierarchical manner. We shall explore two examples, one for each type of combination, in this section.

Knowledge-based neural networks. A system combining connectionist and symbolic reasoning models is known as a hybrid intelligent system. One major line of research on hybrid intelligent systems involves knowledge-based neural networks (KBNNs) which utilize domain knowledge to determine the initial structure of the neural network. It is highly desirable that a KBNN provides bidirectional linkage between neural networks and rule-based systems [Fu, 1992, 1993]. On the one hand, a rule-based system can be mapped into a neural network. On the other hand, neural network knowledge can be transferred back to the rule-based system. Thus, domain knowledge can be fed into the network, revised empirically over time, and decoded in symbolic form. Hence, the KBNN model for the rule-based refinement consists of the following major steps: (a) mapping the rule base into a neural network, (b) training the neural network at parameter level and/or structure level with the training data, (c) translating the trained neural network into rules.

Basically, an IF-THEN-type rule-based inference system can be mapped into a three-layer neural network architecture in a way that the first layer is the attributes of the IF part, the next layer is the conjunction of these attributes to form the precondition, and the third layer is the consequent in the THEN part. Furthermore, the rule strength (certainty factor) corresponds to the weight associated with the connection from the precondition (conjunction) node to the consequent node. In an expert or knowledge-based system, rules are often organized in a multilevel hierarchy which can be mapped onto a neural network of three or more layers. An example network is shown in Fig. 16.21.

The next step is to train the network according to a given set of training data. The training could include structure-level adaptation in addition to parameter adjustment. This corresponds to rule base refinement as discussed later. There are five basic operators for rule base maintenance: *modification of strengths, deletion, generalization, specialization,* and *creation.* The first operator is directly implemented by modifying weights in the neural network version. This can be achieved by using a suitable parameter learning algorithm such as the back-propagation learning rule. All other operators are implemented by deleting or adding connections in the neural network. This can be performed, for example, by the structure learning schemes introduced in Chap. 15; for example, in pruning a network, small weights are nullified such that different hidden nodes encode noninteracting patterns. Also, hidden nodes with similar input weight vectors can be considered a cluster. Then a new hidden node with the average input weight vector and the average output weight vector replaces the hidden nodes in the same cluster within a layer. This is the technique of *clustering of hidden nodes* described in [Fu, 1993]. Deletion of connections in a KBNN may have different meanings. Deletion of a connection pointing from a conjunction node to a disjunction node means deletion of a rule because the path between the rule's precondition

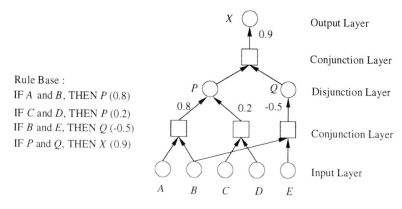

Figure 16.21 Example of a knowledge-based neural network.

and rule's consequent is cut. However, deletion of a connection from a disjunction node or an input node to a conjunction node corresponds to generalization of a rule because removing an input connection from the conjunction node makes the rule's precondition more general. Likewise, addition of a connection pointing from a conjunction node to a disjunction node creates a rule, but addition of a connection from a disjunction node or an input node to a conjunction node specializes a rule.

The final step is to translate the trained neural network into rules. The algorithm developed for extracting rules from a revised KBNN by Fu [1993] is referred to as the KT algorithm. In brief, the algorithm heuristically searches through the rule space, distinguishing between positive attributes and negative attributes. Positive (negative) attributes refer to attributes that are linked to the concept with positive (negative) weights, assuming that the activation level of a neural node ranges between 0 and 1. To form confirming rules, the algorithm first explores combinations of positive attributes and then uses negated negative attributes in conjunction to further consolidate the positive combinations. Similarly, to form disconfirming rules, the algorithm first explores combinations of negative attributes and then uses negated positive attributes in conjunction. The distinction between these two kinds of attributes reduces the size of the search space considerably. Furthermore, through layer-by-layer search the overall search width is exponential with the depth of the network. This rule extraction algorithm consists of the following steps:

1. For each hidden and output node, search for a set S_p of positive attributes whose summed weights exceed the threshold at the node.
2. For each element p of the S_p set:
   a. Search for a set S_N of negative attributes so that the summed weights of p plus the summed weights of $(N - n)$ (where N is the set of all negative attributes and n is an element in S_N) exceed the threshold of the node.
   b. With each element n of the S_N set, form a rule: "IF p AND NOT n, THEN the concept designated by the node."

This completes our discussion of the use of KBNN for rule base refinement.

Neural production systems.   A production system is a rule-based architecture for high-level reasoning. This architecture typically consists of a *working memory* that serves as a global database of facts—a *rule base* where a set of rules is stored and an *inference engine* that selects and executes the rules that are most relevant to the current contents of the working memory. In traditional production systems, human expertise in the problem domain is captured by symbolic expressions that describe the state of the systems and the IF-THEN rules that relate these expressions and actions. In the *neural production system* proposed by Meng [1993], the rule preconditions and rule consequents are allowed to be neural networks. For example, suppose we want to encode the following rule in a vision-guided autonomous mobile robot navigation system:

IF near junction, THEN slow down and follow junction to the right

Then we can represent the entire precondition of the rule by a neural network that is trained by showing features extracted from many images containing junctions and feeding these into a neural system which then sets up its own criteria (which never have to be made explicit) for deciding when a junction is approaching. Similarly, we can present part of the consequent (e.g., "follow junction to the right") with a neural network trained to produce steering output corresponding to the approximate orientations of the hallway floor edges in the camera image.

Figure 16.22 shows the architecture of a neural production system. The working memory in the figure contains a list of facts and goals reflecting the current states of the system. The facts and goals are expressed as symbolic strings. For example, while navigating in the hallway, the working memory in the neural production system of a mobile robot navigation system may contain the following facts:

> in (corridor_C_2),
> facing (North),
> curr_location (near, junction_J_2),
> curr_goal (follow_corridor),
> next_goal (turn_right, junction_J_2).

The preprocessor in Fig. 16.22 processes and, when necessary, extracts features from the input to the production system. The processed information is then channeled to either the neural processor or directly into the working memory depending on whether a proper neural network needs to be issued to translate a given goal.

The neural networks trained to represent the symbolic terms in the working memory and the rule base reside in the database of neural networks in Fig. 16.22. Each network is represented by its symbolic name, network structure parameters, weight matrices, and recall algorithms. The neural processor fetches the relevant neural networks from the database of neural networks and then feeds the processed sensory data into these networks using the associated recall algorithms. The outputs of these neural networks are subsequently translated into symbolic terms and inserted into the working memory.

The rule base in Fig. 16.22 contains hybrid rules of mixed expressions which are embedded in neural networks and symbolic expressions. An example rule is

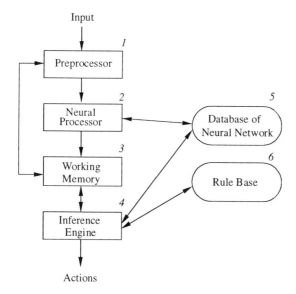

Figure 16.22 Architecture of a neural production system.

Rule1:	IF	next_goal (turn_left, junction)	AND
		facing (junction)	AND
		curr-location (near, junction)	
	THEN	*follow_corridor (slow)*.	

In the rule, the strings of italic symbols are internally represented by neural networks.

The neural production system has been applied to a vision-guided mobile robot navigation system [Meng and Kak, 1992; Meng 1993]. With the neural production system as a key component, this robot navigation system is able to exhibit some primitive navigation behavior such as hallway following using visual feedback, and also to perform high-level reasoning about its navigational environment.

16.5 CONCLUDING REMARKS

The use of dynamical back-propagation methods for system identification and control applications is discussed in this chapter. Narendra and Parthasarathy [1992] applied these methods to more-complex systems including nonlinear systems of higher order as well as multivariable systems. In [Narendra and Mukhopadhyay, 1992], a two-level hierarchical neural network controller was proposed to deal with control of a system when structural failures occur. Other related work can be found in [Narendra and Mukhopadhyay, 1991; Iiguni et al., 1991; Yabuta and Yamada, 1992; Wu et al., 1992; Mukhopadhyay and Narendra, 1993]. For CMAC and BMAC, some improved versions have been suggested. In [Lane et al., 1992], hierarchical and multilayer BMAC network architectures called *spline nets* were further proposed. In [Wong and Sideris, 1992], it was proved that CMAC learning always converges with arbitrary accuracy on any set of training data. In [Kraft and Campagna, 1990ab], the CMAC was compared to conventional adaptive controllers. In [Lin and Kim, 1991], a CMAC was combined with reinforcement learning techniques into a CMAC-based adaptive critic self-learning controller. In [Cotter and Mian, 1992], a pulsed network version of the CMAC, called PCMAC, was proposed. In neural networks for robotics applications, Bekey [1993; Yeung and Bekey, 1989, 1993] proposed a *context-sensitive* network to solve the inverse Jacobian problem in robotics. Martinetz et al. [1990] and Walter and Schulten [1993] applied neural networks to the *visuomotor coordination* of a robot. Another promising application of neural networks in robotics is in learning to accurately move and position a link carrying an unforeseen payload [Kuperstein and Wang, 1990; Leahy et al., 1991].

References on the application of neural networks in speech recognition can be found in [Lippmann, 1989a; Morgan and Scofield, 1991; Unnikrishnan et al., 1991]. A promising approach in this area is to combine neural networks with some traditional statistical speech recognition techniques such as dynamical time warping (DTW) and hidden Markov models (HMM). Bengio et al. [1992, 1993] proposed the integration of multilayer and recurrent neural networks (NNs) with HMMs for speech recognition and obtained a higher recognition rate. Bregler et al. [1993] improved the performance of speech recognition by introducing additional lipreading, so-called speech reading. Two TDNNs were used in this application, one for speech recognition and the other for lipreading. In communications, the call admission control using neural networks has been simulated in more complex situations in [Hiramatsu, 1990]. Related work includes [Rauch and Winarske, 1988], where

Hopfield networks were used for routing communication traffic, and [Mittler and Tran-Gia, 1993], where a Hopfield network was used as a scheduler for packet-switching interconnection networks.

16.6 PROBLEMS

16.1 Assume that the function of the plant shown in Fig. 16.1(b) is to convert Cartesian coordinates (x, y, z) into spherical coordinates (r, ϕ, θ), That is, the plant performs the following function:

$$x = r \sin \theta \cos \phi, \qquad y = r \sin \theta \sin \phi, \qquad z = r \cos \theta,$$

where (x, y, z) is the input and (r, ϕ, θ) is the output of the plant. The plant outputs are in the range of $0 < r < 1$, $0 < \phi < \pi/2$, and $0 < \theta < \pi/2$. Design and train a multilayer feedforward network that performs the forward identification to model the plant in the forward mode as shown in Fig. 16.1(b). Study the mapping accuracy produced by the trained network by computing the differences between the network response and the desired response value from the actual function.

16.2 Assume that the function of the plant shown in Fig. 16.1(c) is exactly the same as that indicated in Problem 16.1. Design and train a multilayer feedforward network that performs the inverse identification to model the inverse of the plant as shown in Fig. 16.1(c). Study the mapping accuracy produced by the network by computing the differences between the network response and the desired response value from the actual function.

16.3 **(a)** Assume that the function of the plant shown in Fig. 16.1(d) is exactly the same as that indicated in Problem 16.1. Based on the network learned in Problem 16.1, design and train a multilayer feedforward network that can control the plant such that plant outputs are equal to controller inputs as shown in Fig. 16.1(d). Study the plant output accuracy produced by the network by computing the differences between the plant output and the controller input values.

(b) Compare the network learned in part (a) to the network learned in Problem 16.2. Are they equivalent?

(c) Consider Fig. 16.1(c) and (d). Assume that the plant's inverse model is not well-defined, that is, more than one plant input produces the same output. (i) Is it possible to train a multilayer feedforward network as a controller by modeling the inverse of the plant directly as shown in Fig. 16.1(c)? Justify your answer. (ii) Is it possible to train a multilayer feedforward network as a controller by error back propagation through a forward model of the plant as shown in Fig. 16.1(d)? Justify your answer.

16.4 Write a program for redoing Example 16.1 and verify the results shown in Fig. 16.3.

16.5 This problem involves identifying a dynamical system using neural networks. The plant to be identified is described by model III and has the form

$$y_p(k+1) = \frac{y_p(k)}{1 + y_p^2(k)} + u^3(k),$$

where the input $u(k)$ is a random input in the interval $[-2, 2]$.

(a) What is the output range of the plant?

(b) Rewrite the above plant transfer function in the form of Eq. (16.10) [i.e., specify the corresponding $f(\cdot)$ and $g(\cdot)$ functions in Eq. (16.10)].

(c) Use the series-parallel model in the form of Eq. (16.13) to identify this plant. This model can be described by the difference equation

$$\hat{y}_p(k+1) = N^f[y_p(k)] + N^g[u(k)],$$

where each network (N^f or N^g) has a single input-output node, 20 first-hidden-layer nodes, and 10 second-hidden-layer nodes. Train both networks such that N^f and N^g approximate f and g functions, respectively. Train the network for 100,000 time steps using a random input signal uniformly distributed in the interval [-2, 2] and a learning rate of 0.1. Plot the desired and approximated f and g functions over their respective domains.

(d) Plot the outputs of the plant as well as the identification model for an input $u(k) = \sin(2\pi k/25) + \sin(2\pi k/10)$.

16.6 Repeat Problem 16.5 for identifying the plant described by model IV that has the form of

$$y_p(k+1) = f[y_p(k), y_p(k-1), y_p(k-2), u(k), u(k-1)],$$

where

$$f[x_1, x_2, x_3, x_4, x_5] = \frac{x_1 x_2 x_3 x_5 (x_3 - 1) + x_4}{1 + x_3^2 + x_2^2}.$$

(a) Let the input $u(k)$ be a random input in the interval [-1, 1]. What is the output range of the plant?

(b) Use the series-parallel model to identify the plant; that is, use a neural network N to approximate the function f, where the network N has 5 input nodes, 1 output node, 20 first-hidden-layer nodes, and 10 second-hidden-layer nodes. Train the network for 100,000 time steps using a random input signal uniformly distributed in the interval [-1, 1] and a learning rate of 0.25.

(c) Plot the outputs of the plant as well as the identification model for an input $u(k) = \sin(2\pi k/250)$ for $k \le 500$ and $u(k) = 0.8 \sin(2\pi k/250) + 0.2 \sin(2\pi k/25)$ for $k > 500$.

16.7 Consider a discrete-time plant described by the difference equation

$$x(k+1) = 2x(k) - 0.5 + [u(k)]^3,$$

where $x(k)$ is the state (output) of the plant and $u(k)$ is the input of the plant at the kth time step. Assume that the characteristic surface $(x(k), x(k+1); u(k))$ needs to be learned by a CMAC.

(a) Plot the three-dimensional characteristic surface of the above nonlinear system (refer to Fig. 16.8), where $x(k) \in [-1, 1]$.

(b) If the desired output sequence of the plant is

$$x(k) = 0.8 \sin\left(\frac{2\pi k}{5}\right) + 0.2 \sin\left(\frac{2\pi k}{9}\right),$$

what is the initial sequence of plant control input values $u(0), u(1), \ldots, u(15)$ located on the characteristic surface in part (a)?

16.8 (a) Draw the multidimensional linear B-spline receptive field functions for $s = 2, G = 4$ (see Fig. 16.13) corresponding to the following **L** matrix

$$\mathbf{L} = \begin{bmatrix} 2 & 4 \\ 3 & 5 \\ 4 & 6 \\ 5 & 7 \end{bmatrix}.$$

(b) Mark the input region that activates these receptive field functions.

16.9 Draw a fourth-order network with five input nodes and one output node. Derive a perceptron-like weight update rule for this network. What good properties might this network have aside from those owned by a third-order network?

16.10 Write a program for realizing the third-order network in Example 16.4. Train and test this program as described in the example.

16.11 In Sec. 10.2.3, we discussed the use of time-delayed neural networks for phoneme recognition. We also considered the recurrent networks introduced in Chap. 13 that are especially good at speech recognition. Compare the advantages and disadvantages of these two approaches.

16.12 What and how can other neural network models except the back-propagation network be applied to the ATM communication network introduced in Sec. 16.3?

16.13 Draw the knowledge-based neural network corresponding to the following rule base:

IF A and B, THEN X (0.8),
IF A and C, THEN Y (0.2),
IF D and E, THEN P (0.5),
IF P and B, THEN Q (0.9),
IF E and Y, THEN Z (0.1),
IF X and Q, THEN T (0.8),
IF A and T, THEN R (0.3),
IF R and Z, THEN S (0.5).

16.14 Which neural network models are suitable for use in airline seating allocation? Justify your answer.

16.15 Which neural network models are suitable for use in text-to-speech translation? Justify your answer.

17

Integrating Fuzzy Systems and Neural Networks

This chapter focuses on the basic concepts and rationale of integrating fuzzy logic and neural networks into a working functional system. This happy marriage of the techniques of fuzzy logic systems and neural networks suggests the novel idea of transforming the burden of designing fuzzy logic control and decision systems to the training and learning of connectionist neural networks. This neuro-fuzzy and/or fuzzy-neural synergistic integration reaps the benefits of both neural networks and fuzzy logic systems. That is, the neural networks provide connectionist structure (fault tolerance and distributed representation properties) and learning abilities to the fuzzy logic systems, and the fuzzy logic systems provide the neural networks with a structural framework with high-level fuzzy IF-THEN rule thinking and reasoning. These benefits can be witnessed in three major integrated systems: neural fuzzy systems, fuzzy neural networks, and fuzzy neural hybrid systems. These three integrated systems, along with their applications, will be discussed and explored in the next five chapters.

17.1 BASIC CONCEPT OF INTEGRATING FUZZY SYSTEMS AND NEURAL NETWORKS

17.1.1 General Comparisons of Fuzzy Systems and Neural Networks

Fuzzy systems and neural networks are both *numerical model–free* estimators and dynamical systems. They share the ability to improve the intelligence of systems working in uncertain, imprecise, and noisy environments. Fuzzy systems and neural networks estimate sampled functions and behave as associative memories. Both have an advantage over traditional statistical estimation and adaptive control approaches to function estimation. They estimate a function without requiring a mathematical description of how the output functionally depends on the input; that is, they learn from numerical examples. Both fuzzy and neural approaches are numerical in nature, can be processed using mathematical tools, can be partially described with theorems, and admit an algorithmic characterization that favors silicon and optical implementation. These properties distinguish fuzzy and neural approaches from the symbolic processing approaches of artificial intelligence (AI). To a certain extent, both systems and their techniques have been successfully applied to a variety of real-world systems and devices.

Although fuzzy systems and neural networks are formally similar, there are also significant differences between them. They differ in the way in which they estimate sampled functions, represent and store these samples, represent and encode structure knowledge, and associatively inference or map inputs to outputs.

Neural networks have a large number of highly interconnected processing elements (nodes) which demonstrate the ability to learn and generalize from training patterns or data. Fuzzy systems, on the other hand, base their decisions on inputs in the form of linguistic variables derived from membership functions which are formulas used to determine the fuzzy set to which a value belongs and the degree of membership in that set. The variables are then matched with the preconditions of linguistics IF-THEN rules (fuzzy logic rules), and the response of each rule is obtained through fuzzy implication. In following the compositional rule of inference, the response of each rule is weighted according to the confidence or degree of membership of its inputs, and usually the centroid of the responses is calculated to generate the appropriate output.

Basically, fuzzy systems estimate functions with *fuzzy set* samples (A_i, B_i), while neural networks use *numerical-point* samples $(\mathbf{x}_i, \mathbf{y}_i)$. For example, in a neural network $\mathbf{x}_i$ might represent the pixels that make up an image, while $\mathbf{y}_i$ might represent a classification of that vector. Given a training set consisting of pairs of $\mathbf{x}_i$ and $\mathbf{y}_i$, the neural network can learn the input-output mapping by adjusting its weights so as to perform well on the training set. In another example, if A_i is a fuzzy set characterizing the state of a factory and B_i represents the possibilities of the presence or absence of various breakdowns in the factory, then fuzzy rules and fuzzy inference may be used to determine the likelihood that one of these breakdowns may be present as a function of A_i.

Neural networks are *trainable dynamical systems* whose learning, noise-tolerance, and generalization abilities grow organically out of their connectionist structures, their dynamics, and their distributed data representation. Neural networks exploit their numerical framework with theorems, efficient numerical algorithms, and analog and digital VLSI implementations. However, they cannot directly encode *structured knowledge*. The neural network approach generally requires the specification of a nonlinear dynamical system, usually feedforward, the acquisition of a sufficiently representative set of numerical training samples, and the encoding of these training samples in the dynamical system by repeated learning cycles. They superimpose several input-output samples $(\mathbf{x}_1, \mathbf{y}_1)$, $(\mathbf{x}_2, \mathbf{y}_2)$,..., $(\mathbf{x}_m, \mathbf{y}_m)$ on a black-box web of synapses. Unless we check all the input-output cases, we do not know what the neural network has learned, and we also do not know what it will forget when it superimposes new samples $(\mathbf{x}_k, \mathbf{y}_k)$ atop the old. It is difficult for us to directly encode commonsense IF-THEN rules into the neural network; instead we must present the network with a sufficiently large set of input-output training pairs. Moreover, because the internal layers of neural networks are always opaque to the designer or user, it is difficult to determine the structure and the size of a network. In summary, neural networks are structure-free, fully distributed models. The distributivity of computations contributes to profound learning capabilities because the individual computing elements in the network are capable of adjusting their connections to carry out the best possible mapping for a given training set of objects. While the computational distributivity enhances learning, it also makes it almost impossible to come up with a reasonable interpretation of the overall structure of the network in the form of easily comprehended explicit logic constructs such as IF-THEN statements.

Fuzzy systems, on the other hand, are *structured numerical estimators.* They start from highly formalized insights about the psychology of categorization and the structure of categories found in the real world and then articulate fuzzy IF-THEN rules as a kind of expert knowledge. Fuzzy systems directly encode structured knowledge in a flexible *numerical* framework and processes it in a manner that resembles neural network processing. However, unlike the neural network approach, the fuzzy system requires only that we partially fill in a linguistic rule matrix (i.e., rows for input predicates and columns for output predicates). This task is simpler than designing and training a neural network. However, fuzzy systems encounter different difficulties such as how to determine the fuzzy logic rules and the membership functions. Although AI expert systems also exploit structured knowledge when knowledge engineers acquire it, they store and process it in a symbolic framework outside the analytical and computational numerical framework. The symbolic framework also allows us to quickly represent structured knowledge as rules but prevents us from directly applying the tools of numerical mathematics. On the contrary, the numerical framework of fuzzy systems allows us to adaptively infer and modify fuzzy systems, with neural or statistical techniques, directly from problem-domain sample data.

From the above discussion, we see that fuzzy logic and neural networks generally approach the design of intelligent systems from quite different angles. Neural networks are essentially low-level, computational algorithms that sometimes offer a good performance in dealing with sensor data used in pattern recognition and control. On the other hand, fuzzy logic provides a structure framework that utilizes and exploits these low-level capabilities of neural networks.

17.1.2 Choice of Fuzzy Systems or Neural Networks

It is understood that neural networks and fuzzy logic can be appropriately used when one or more of the state variables are continuous and when a mathematical model of the process does not exist or exists but is too difficult to encode or is too complex to be evaluated fast enough for real-time operation. Then we may need to find out which method is better to use and when it should be used. In contrast to neural network theory, fuzzy set theory and fuzzy logic as developed are an abstract system that makes no further claims regarding biological or psychological plausibility. This abstract system may sometimes be easier to use and simpler to apply to a particular problem than a neural network. The reverse may also hold. Whether to use the fuzzy system approach or the neural network approach depends on the particular application, on the availability of numerical and structured data, and on good engineering judgment. To date, engineers have applied fuzzy logic techniques largely to control problems. These problems often permit comparison with standard control-theoretic and expert-system approaches. Neural networks so far seem best applied to ill-defined pattern-recognition problems.

For some applications, there are some general guidelines for choosing a fuzzy system or a neural network. A general guideline regarding this choice is that fuzzy systems work well when experience or introspection can be used to articulate the fuzzy IF-THEN rules underlying the system behavior and/or the fuzzy sets representing the characteristics of each variable. When this is impossible, we can resort to the use of neural networks or we can apply neural network techniques to generate the fuzzy rules that constitute *adaptive fuzzy systems.*

For some control applications, when the control system owes a lot to interfacing with human operators, fuzzy control, because of its intrinsic linguistic nature, may be more appropriate. A linguistic-based control facilitates operator elicitation, understanding, and debugging; that is, it intensifies human involvement during the conception of the system. The fuzzy controller can even be exploited in the training phase of novice operators. On the other hand, neural networks, which need to be coupled with a learning method, would be more appropriate for applications where only numerical data are available as clues for the control system to set up. Based on these data, a neural network can adjust itself to reproduce the desired output in the learning phase. Also, there are many tasks where it is difficult to ask people what they do and what rules they follow in completing a task. For example, if we design a fuzzy controller to ride a bicycle by encoding your verbal instructions into rules, the controller would probably fail frequently. The problem is that your knowledge of how to ride a bicycle is stored in your wrists, in your cerebellum, and in other parts of your brain in a way that cannot be interpreted directly into words. In such cases, it may be better to use neural networks, or adaptive fuzzy systems, to imitate what you do and thereby achieve a more mature, complete, stable level of performance.

17.1.3 Reasons for Integrating Fuzzy Systems and Neural Networks

Fuzzy logic and neural networks are complementary technologies. Neural networks extract information from systems to be learned or controlled, while fuzzy logic techniques most often use verbal and linguistic information from experts. A promising approach to obtaining the benefits of both fuzzy systems and neural networks and solving their respective problems is to combine them into an integrated system. For example, one can learn rules in a hybrid fashion and then calibrate them for better whole-system performance. The common features and characteristics of fuzzy systems and neural networks warrant their integration.

The integrated system will possess the advantages of both neural networks (e.g., learning abilities, optimization abilities, and connectionist structures) and fuzzy systems (e.g., humanlike IF-THEN rules thinking and ease of incorporating expert knowledge). In this way, we can bring the low-level learning and computational power of neural networks into fuzzy systems and also high-level, humanlike IF-THEN rule thinking and reasoning of fuzzy systems into neural networks. Thus, on the neural side, more and more transparency is pursued and obtained either by prestructuring a neural network to improve its performances or by a possible interpretation of the weight matrix following the learning stage. On the fuzzy side, the development of methods allowing automatic tuning of the parameters that characterize the fuzzy system can largely draw inspiration from similar methods used in the connectionist community. Thus, neural networks can improve their transparency, making them closer to fuzzy systems, while fuzzy systems can self-adapt, making them closer to neural networks.

Integrated systems can *learn* and *adapt*. They learn new associations, new patterns, and new functional dependencies. They sample the flux of experience and encode new information. They compress or quantize the sampled flux into a small but statistically representative set of prototypes or exemplars. Broadly speaking, we may characterize the efforts at merging these two technologies in three categories:

1. *Neural fuzzy systems*: the use of neural networks as tools in fuzzy models.
2. *Fuzzy neural networks*: fuzzification of conventional neural network models.
3. *Fuzzy-neural hybrid systems*: incorporating fuzzy technologies and neural networks into hybrid systems.

In the first approach, *neural fuzzy systems* aim at providing fuzzy systems with the kind of automatic tuning methods typical of neural networks but without altering their functionality (e.g., fuzzification, defuzzification, inference engine, and fuzzy logic base). In neural fuzzy systems, neural networks are used in augmenting numerical processing of fuzzy sets, such as membership function elicitation and realization of mappings between fuzzy sets that is utilized as fuzzy rules. Since neural fuzzy systems are inherently fuzzy logic systems, they are mostly used in control applications.

In the second approach, *fuzzy neural networks* retain the basic properties and architectures of neural networks and simply "fuzzify" some of their elements. In fuzzy neural networks, a crisp neuron can become fuzzy and the response of the neuron to its lower-layer activation signal can be of a fuzzy relation type rather than a sigmoid type. One can find examples of this approach where domain knowledge becomes formalized in terms of fuzzy sets and afterward can be applied to enhance the learning algorithms of the neural networks or augment their interpretation capabilities. Since the neural architecture is conserved, what still varies is some kind of synaptic weights connecting low-level to high-level neurons. Since fuzzy neural networks are inherently neural networks, they are mostly used in pattern recognition applications.

Finally, in the third approach, both fuzzy techniques and neural networks play a key role in hybrid systems. They do their own jobs in serving different functions in the system. Making use of their individual strengths, they incorporate and complement each other to achieve a common goal. The architectures of fuzzy-neural hybrid systems are quite application-oriented, and they are suitable for both control and pattern-recognition applications.

17.2 THE EQUIVALENCE OF FUZZY INFERENCE SYSTEMS AND NEURAL NETWORKS

In the last section, we discussed the relationship between fuzzy systems and neural networks from a global point of view. We have observed their close similarities qualitatively. Next we present a more precise quantitative study of the equivalence of the functionality in fuzzy systems and neural networks in some specific cases, focusing on fuzzy inference (control) systems and multilayer feedforward neural networks. First, we demonstrate that a fuzzy inference system is capable of approximating any real, continuous function in a Borel set to any desired degree of accuracy, provided that sufficiently many fuzzy logic rules are available. On a similar note, we pointed out in Theorem 10.2 that multilayer neural networks with an arbitrarily large number of nodes in the hidden layer can approximate any real continuous function. Hence, both fuzzy inference systems and multilayer neural networks are universal approximators. This implies that we can approximate a multilayer neural network to any degree of accuracy using a fuzzy inference system and, conversely, we can approximate a fuzzy inference system to any degree of accuracy with a multilayer neural network.

We shall next consider two specific models of neural networks and fuzzy systems: the radial basis function network (RBFN) and the fuzzy inference system utilizing product inference, Gaussian membership functions, and fuzzy logic rules with singleton consequents. We shall show that these two specific models are equivalent not only in function but also in structure. Based on such equivalency, we can apply what is known about one model to the other, and vice versa; in particular, we can apply the learning rules of RBFNs to fuzzy inference systems, and the fuzzy logic rules and membership functions of fuzzy inference systems can also be utilized to find and interpret the structure [i.e., the number of radial basis functions (hidden nodes)] and parameters of RBFNs. This discussion also points out one major objective of the fusion of fuzzy systems and neural networks: automating the design of fuzzy systems utilizing the learning power of neural networks.

17.2.1 Fuzzy Inference Systems as Universal Approximators

Fuzzy inference (control) systems have been successfully used in a wide variety of practical problems, especially for industrial applications. A fundamental theoretical question about fuzzy inference systems remains unanswered, namely, why does a fuzzy inference system display such an excellent performance for such a wide variety of applications? Existing explanations are qualitative, for example, "Fuzzy inference systems can utilize linguistic information from human experts," "Fuzzy inference systems can simulate human thinking procedure," and "Fuzzy inference systems capture the approximate, inexact nature of the real world." In this section, we treat this fundamental question mathematically and systematically. We consider the class of fuzzy inference systems whose output fuzzy set of every fuzzy logic rule is a singleton. This class of fuzzy inference systems has been proved to be a universal approximator [Jou, 1992c; Wang, 1992; Kosko, 1992c]; that is, it is capable of approximating any real continuous function on a compact set to an arbitrary accuracy, provided sufficient fuzzy logic rules are available. The proof of this fundamental result by Jou [1992c], which is based on the famous Stone-Weierstrass theorem [Rudin, 1976], is discussed next.

A fuzzy inference scheme, which is based on the generalized modus ponens, can be described schematically in the following form. Here we consider multi-input–single-output (MISO) fuzzy systems, $f: \Re^n \to \Re$, because a multi-output system can always be decomposed into a collection of single-output systems.

Fact:	x_1 IS A'_1 AND x_2 is A'_2 AND $\cdots$ AND x_n is A'_n
Rule 1:	IF x_1 IS A^1_1 AND x_2 is A^1_2 AND $\cdots$ AND x_n is A^1_n, THEN y is B^1 ELSE
Rule 2:	IF x_1 IS A^2_1 AND x_2 is A^2_2 AND $\cdots$ AND x_n is A^2_n, THEN y is B^2 ELSE
	$\vdots$
Rule m:	IF x_1 IS A^m_1 AND x_2 is A^m_2 AND $\cdots$ AND x_n is A^m_n, THEN y is B^m

Conclusion: y is B' (17.1)

The n-ary variable $\mathbf{x} = (x_1, x_2, \ldots, x_n)^T$ denotes the input, and the single variable y denotes the output. For each linguistic variable x_i, U_i is the universe of discourse or collection of possible patterns; $x_i \in U_i$, $i = 1, 2,..., n$. Let U be a Cartesian product of universes $U = U_1 \times U_2 \times \cdots \times U_n$. In the consequent, let V be the universe of discourse of y. There are m membership functions for each x_i, $i = 1, 2,..., n$, and y, producing membership measurements of each variable with respect to fuzzy sets A_i^j and B^j, respectively, and $\mu_{A_i^j}(x_i)$: $U_i \rightarrow [0, 1]$ and $\mu_{B^j}(y): V \rightarrow [0, 1]$, $j = 1, 2,..., m$. Note that there are no restrictions on the form of the membership functions; they can be linear or nonlinear.

As discussed in Chap. 7, each of the fuzzy logic rules or fuzzy implications associating n input fuzzy sets with an output fuzzy set can be represented by a fuzzy relation $R^j = (A_1^j \text{ AND } A_2^j \text{ AND } \cdots \text{ AND } A_n^j) \rightarrow B^j$ defined on $U_1 \times \cdots \times U_n \times V$. Here, we consider the product operator for the fuzzy relation; that is,

$$\mu_{R^j}(x_1,..., x_n, y) = \mu_{A_1^j}(x_1) \cdots \mu_{A_n^j}(x_n) \cdot \mu_{B^j}(y). \tag{17.2}$$

The fuzzy relations R^j, $j = 1, 2,...m$, encoding the fuzzy logic rules can be aggregated to form the overall relation R by interpreting ELSE as fuzzy union; that is,

$$\mu_R(x_1,..., x_n, y) = \bigvee_{j=1}^{m} \mu_{R^j}(x_1,..., x_n, y), \tag{17.3}$$

where $\bigvee$ denotes the pairwise max operator. If the input x_i takes the fuzzy sets A_i', $i = 1, 2,..., n$, then the output fuzzy set or consequent B' can be deduced using the operation of fuzzy composition as follows:

$$B' = (A_1' \text{ AND } A_2' \text{ AND } \cdots \text{ AND } A_n') \circ R, \tag{17.4}$$

where $\circ$ denotes the max product compositional rule of inference. Explicitly, the membership function of the consequent B' is

$$\mu_{B'}(y) = \bigvee_{x_1,..., x_n} \left[\left(\prod_{i=1}^{n} \mu_{A_i'}(x_i) \right) \cdot \left(\bigvee_{j=1}^{m} \left(\prod_{i=1}^{n} \mu_{A_i^j}(x_i) \right) \cdot \mu_{B^j}(y) \right) \right]. \tag{17.5}$$

Since the above equation maps fuzzy sets to fuzzy sets, it defines a fuzzy mapping $F(A_1', A_2',..., A_n') = B'$. In practice, especially in control applications, the input fuzzy set A_i' equals numerical data a_i'. In this case, the fuzzification process can be realized by a fuzzy singleton; that is, $\mu_{A_i'}(x_i) = 1$ if $x_i = a_i'$, and $\mu_{A_i'(x_i)} = 0$ if $x_i \neq a_i'$. In this case the consequent B' in Eq. (17.5) becomes

$$\mu_{B'}(y) = \bigvee_{j=1}^{m} \left(\Pi_{i=1}^{n} \mu_{A_i^j}(x_i) \right) \cdot \mu_{B^j}(y). \tag{17.6}$$

The information in the resultant fuzzy set B' obtained from Eq. (17.5) or (17.6) resides largely in the relative values of the membership grades. We may *defuzzify* the output fuzzy set B' to produce a single numerical output which is a representative point of B'. Using the centroid defuzzification method, the final numerical output y^* inferred from the fuzzy logic rules can be uniquely determined from the output fuzzy set B' as follows:

$$y^* = \frac{\int_V \mu_{B'}(y) y \, dy}{\int_V \mu_{B'}(y) \, dy}. \tag{17.7}$$

By introducing the processes of singleton fuzzification and centroid defuzzification into the inference system, we have transformed the fuzzy mapping in Eq. (17.5) into Eq. (17.7).

Indeed Eq. (17.7) simply maps n numerical inputs x_i, $i = 1, 2,..., n$, into a single output value y. This class of fuzzy inference systems has been used widely in the area of fuzzy control.

We have just reviewed the inference process of a typical fuzzy system. Next, we discuss a simplified model in which the proof of a universal approximator will be obtained. We consider that the output fuzzy set B^j in Eq. (17.1) are singletons β^j, that is, $\mu_{B^j}(y) = 1$ if $y = \beta^j$, and $\mu_{B^j}(y) = 0$ otherwise, $j = 1, 2,..., m$. Moreover, we view the fuzzy rules with the same output singletons (e.g., $\beta^\ell = \beta^k$ for $\ell \neq k$) as distinct fuzzy rules, and they all contribute to the final inferred conclusion equally. In other words, the max operator $\bigvee$ in Eq. (17.6) is removed. With this simplification, Eq. (17.6) becomes

$$\mu_B'(y) = \begin{cases} \prod_{i=1}^{n}\mu_{A_i^j}(x_i) & \text{if } y = \beta^j \\ 0 & \text{otherwise,} \end{cases} \tag{17.8}$$

where x_i, $i = 1, 2,..., n$, are fuzzy singletons. Since the resultant fuzzy set B' is discrete, we can replace the ratio of integrals in Eq. (17.7) with a ratio of simple discrete sums and obtain the representative point of B' as follows:

$$y^* = \frac{\sum_{j=1}^{m}\beta^j\left(\prod_{i=1}^{n}\mu_{A_i^j}(x_i)\right)}{\sum_{j=1}^{m}\prod_{i=1}^{n}\mu_{A_i^j}(x_i)}. \tag{17.9}$$

We shall next show that the above simplified fuzzy inference system can be used to approximate any arbitrary function in $\mathscr{C}(\mathfrak{R}^n)$ to any desired degree of accuracy, where $\mathscr{C}(\mathfrak{R}^n)$ denotes the set of all continuous functions in $\mathfrak{R}^n$. In order to be precise about the class of simplified fuzzy inference systems under consideration, the following notations and definitions are necessary. The *support* of a real-valued function f on $\mathfrak{R}^n$ is the closure of the set of all points $\mathbf{x}$ in $\mathfrak{R}^n$ at which $f(\mathbf{x}) \neq 0$. A collection $\{V_\alpha\}$ of open subsets of $\mathfrak{R}^n$ is an *open cover* of a set E of $\mathfrak{R}^n$ if $E \subset \bigcup_\alpha V_\alpha$. Suppose U is a compact subset of $\mathfrak{R}^n$ and $\{V_\alpha\}$ is an open cover of U, then for functions $\psi_1, \psi_2,..., \psi_m$ in $\mathscr{C}(\mathfrak{R}^n)$, $\{\psi_j\}$ is called a *partition of unity* if (i) $\psi_j \in [0, 1]$ for $j = 1, 2,..., m$; (ii) each ψ_j has support in some V_α; and (iii) $\sum_{j=1}^{m}\psi_j(\mathbf{u}) = 1$ for every $\mathbf{u}$ in U [Rudin, 1976]. Using the notion of partition of unity, we can rewrite the simplified fuzzy inference system in Eq. (17.9) as follows. Let $\psi_j(\mathbf{x})$ be functions of input $\mathbf{x} = (x_1, x_2,..., x_n)$:

$$\psi_j(\mathbf{x}) = \frac{\prod_{i=1}^{n}\mu_{A_i^j}(x_i)}{\sum_{k=1}^{m}\prod_{i=1}^{n}\mu_{A_i^k}(x_i)}, \qquad j = 1, 2,..., m. \tag{17.10}$$

Assuming that the denominator $\sum_{k=1}^{m}\prod_{i=1}^{n}\mu_{A_i^k}(x_i) \neq 0$ for every $\mathbf{x}$ [i.e., for every $\mathbf{x}$, $\prod_{i=1}^{n}\mu_{A_i^k}(x_i) \neq 0$ for some $k \in \{1, 2,..., m\}$ or, equivalently, each ψ_j has support in some V_α], then $\sum_{j=1}^{m}\psi_j(\mathbf{x}) = 1$ for every $\mathbf{x}$, and thus the functions ψ_j, $j = 1, 2,..., m$, form a partition of unity. We can then define the class of fuzzy inference systems as a family of functions $f: \mathfrak{R}^n \rightarrow \mathfrak{R}$ in the form of

$$f(\mathbf{x}) = \sum_{j=1}^{m}\beta^j\psi_j(\mathbf{x}) \tag{17.11}$$

for $\mathbf{x} \in \mathfrak{R}^n$ and $\beta^j \in \mathfrak{R}$, and m is a finite number of fuzzy rules. Let us denote the family of functions f in Eq. (17.11) as $\mathscr{F}^n$. Note that Eq. (17.11) has exactly the same form as Eq. (17.9), where $\mathbf{x}$ corresponds to the input, function ψ_j corresponds to the activation of the jth fuzzy logic rule, and scalar β^j corresponds to the jth output singleton. Hence $\mathcal{F}^n$ is in fact the class of simplified fuzzy inference systems under consideration. In the representation of Eq. (17.11), we refer to ψ_j as a set of *basis functions*. This model makes use of input fuzzy sets each having a local receptive field with a sensitivity curve that changes as a function of the distance from a particular point in the input space. The use of membership functions of input fuzzy sets with overlapping receptive fields clearly provides a kind of interpolation and extrapolation.

The class of fuzzy inference systems $\mathcal{F}^n$ can be shown to approximate any real, continuous function on a compact set using the Stone-Weierstrass theorem.

Theorem 17.1

Stone-Weierstrass Theorem [Rudin, 1976]. Let $\mathcal{A}$ be a set of real, continuous functions on a compact set U. If (a) $\mathcal{A}$ is an *algebra,* (b) $\mathcal{A}$ *separates points on U,* and (c) $\mathcal{A}$ *vanishes at no point of U,* then the uniform closure of $\mathcal{A}$ consists of all real, continuous functions on U.

Detailed proof of this theorem can be found in [Rudin, 1976]. We say that a family $\mathcal{A}$ of real-valued functions defined on a set U is an *algebra* if $\mathcal{A}$ is closed under addition, multiplication, and scalar multiplication. For example, the set of all polynomials is an algebra. A family $\mathcal{A}$ is *uniformly closed* if $\mathcal{A}$ has the property that $f \in \mathcal{A}$ whenever $f_n \in \mathcal{A}$, $n = 1, 2,...$, and $f_n \rightarrow f$ uniformly on U. The *uniform closure* of $\mathcal{A}$, denoted $\mathcal{B}$, is the set of all functions that are limits of uniformly convergent sequences of members of $\mathcal{A}$. By Weierstrass's theorem, it is known that the set of continuous functions on $[a, b]$ is the uniform closure of the set of polynomials on $[a, b]$. $\mathcal{A}$ *separates points* on a set U if for every x,y in U, $x \neq y$, there exists a function f in $\mathcal{A}$ such that $f(x) \neq f(y)$. $\mathcal{A}$ *vanishes at no point of U* if for each x in U there exists an f in $\mathcal{A}$ such that $f(x) \neq 0$. Clearly, the algebra of all polynomials in one variable has these properties on $[a, b]$.

In order to use the Stone-Weierstrass theorem, we need to show that $\mathcal{F}^n$ is an algebra, $\mathcal{F}^n$ separates points on a compact set, and $\mathcal{F}^n$ vanishes at no point on the compact set. These notions are verified in the proof of the following theorem.

Theorem 17.2

The uniform closure of $\mathcal{F}^n$ consists of all real, continuous functions on a compact subset U of $\aleph^n$. In other words, for any given real, continuous function g on the compact set $U \subset \aleph^n$ and arbitrary $\epsilon > 0$, there exists an $f \in \mathcal{F}^n$ such that

$$\sup_{x \in U} |g(\mathbf{x}) - f(\mathbf{x})| < \epsilon. \tag{17.12}$$

Proof: The proof consists of three parts. The first part shows that $\mathcal{F}^n$ is an algebra. It is clear that $\mathcal{F}^n$ is closed under scalar multiplication. Let $f, g \in \mathcal{F}^n$ and $f = \sum_{i=1}^{s} \alpha_i \phi_i$ and $g = \sum_{j=1}^{t} \beta_j \psi_j$. Then, $f + g = \sum_{k=1}^{s+t} \gamma_k \theta_k$, where $\gamma_k = 2\alpha_k$ if $k \leq s$, $\gamma_k = 2\beta_{k-s}$ if $k > s$, $\theta_k = \frac{1}{2}\phi_k$ if $k \leq s$, and $\theta_k = \frac{1}{2}\psi_{k-s}$ if $k > s$. Since $\sum_{k=1}^{s+t} \theta_k = \sum_{i=1}^{s} \frac{1}{2}\phi_i + \sum_{j=1}^{t} \frac{1}{2}\psi_j = 1$, $\{\theta_k\}$ is a partition of unity. This proves that $\mathcal{F}^n$ is closed under addition. Also, $fg = \sum_{k=1}^{st} \delta_k \varphi_k$, where $\delta_k = \alpha_i \beta_j$ and $\varphi_k = \phi_i \psi_j$, and $i = \lfloor (k-1)/t \rfloor + 1$, $j = (k-1) \bmod t + 1$. Since $\sum_{k=1}^{st} \varphi_k = \sum_{i=1}^{s} \sum_{j=1}^{t} \phi_i \psi_j = \left(\sum_{i=1}^{s} \phi_i\right) \left(\sum_{j=1}^{t} \psi_j\right) = 1$, $\{\varphi_k\}$ is a partition of unity. This proves that $\mathcal{F}^n$ is closed under multiplication. Hence, we have shown that $\mathcal{F}^n$ is an algebra.

The second part shows that $\mathcal{F}^n$ separates points on the compact set U. It is clear that we can construct a partition of unity $\{\psi_j\}$ such that $\psi_j(\mathbf{x}) \neq \psi_j(\mathbf{y})$ for any $\mathbf{x}, \mathbf{y} \in U$, $\mathbf{x} \neq \mathbf{y}$. This ensures that $f(\mathbf{x}) \neq f(\mathbf{y})$. Thus, $\mathcal{F}^n$ separates points on U. The exact way to construct the required partition of unity depends on the membership functions $\mu_{A_i^j}$ used in ψ_j [see Eq. (17.10)]. We shall demonstrate this in the next section. Finally, the third part shows that $\mathcal{F}^n$ vanishes at no point on U. This, in fact, is the direct result of our assumption that the denominator of Eq. (17.10) is nonzero for every $\mathbf{x} \in U$ if we simply choose all $\beta^j > 0$, $j = 1, 2, \ldots, m$. That is, any $f \in \mathcal{F}^n$ with $\beta^j > 0$ [see Eq. (17.11)] serves as the required f and ensures that $\mathcal{F}^n$ vanishes at no point of U. Thus, Theorem 17.2 is a direct consequence of Theorem 17.1, the Stone-Weierstrass theorem.

The compact set requirement $\mathbf{x} \in U$ is satisfied whenever the possible values of $\mathbf{x}$ are bounded. Note that the only constraint on the input fuzzy sets of a fuzzy inference system in class $\mathcal{F}^n$ is that the normalized membership functions form a partition of unity; that is, the denominator in Eq. (17.10) is nonzero for every $\mathbf{x} \in U$. This is true if Gaussian membership functions are used; that is, $\mu_{A_i^j}(x_i) = \exp[-(x_i - m_i^j)^2 / 2(\sigma_i^j)^2]$, where m_i^j is the point in the ith input subspace at which the fuzzy set A_i^j achieves its maximum membership value and $\sigma_i^j \in (0, \infty)$ characterizes the shape of the Gaussian membership function. Since the Gaussian membership functions are nonzero, the denominator in Eq. (17.10) is nonzero and the corresponding ψ_j form a partition of unity. We see that if we use triangular membership functions, then the resulting ψ_j may not form a partition of unity because for an arbitrary ψ_j we cannot guarantee that the denominator of ψ_j is nonzero for every $\mathbf{x} \in U$. In this case, we need stronger conditions to guarantee that φ_j with triangular membership functions form a partition of unity.

The conclusion of the above theorem indicates that any real, continuous function over a compact set can be approximated to any degree of accuracy by the fuzzy inference system defined in Eq. (17.11). This implies that fuzzy inference systems with even the simplified form as in Eq. (17.11) are adequate for the purpose of function approximation. However, no specific form of a partition of unity $\{\psi_j\}$ is known. The theorem demonstrates that such a fuzzy inference system must exist, but it does not tell us how to find it. To find it, we need to obtain a proper partition of unity $\{\varphi_j\}$ (i.e., to find a set of proper input membership functions $\mu_{A_i^j}$) as well as proper output singletons β^j. This is indeed the problem of designing a desired fuzzy controller. Since the fuzzy inference models specified by Eq. (17.11) correspond to multilayer neural networks, it is feasible to automate the design of a simplified fuzzy inference system with the aid of the learning power of neural networks, as further discussed in the next section.

17.2.2 Equivalence of Simplified Fuzzy Inference Systems and Radial Basis Function Networks

In the previous section, we learned that the basis functions φ_j in Eq. (17.10) with Gaussian membership functions form a partition of unity and can be applied to Theorem 17.2. We thus focus on this specific type of simplified fuzzy inference system. For clarity, we single out the specific version of Theorem 17.2 for this type of fuzzy inference system in the following theorem.

Theorem 17.3

Fuzzy inference systems with product inference, centroid defuzzification, singleton consequents, and Gaussian membership functions are capable of approximating any real, continuous function on a compact set to an arbitrary accuracy.

Proof: Since the basis functions φ_j in Eq. (17.10) with Gaussian membership functions form a partition of unity, the first and third parts of the proof of Theorem 17.2 can be applied here directly. Hence, it is true that the $\mathscr{F}^n$ corresponding to the basis function φ_j is an algebra and that the $\mathscr{F}^n$ vanishes at no point on U. We shall then show that $\mathscr{F}^n$ separates points on the compact set U. This is proved by constructing a required f in the form of Eq. (17.11) having the property that $f(\mathbf{x}^1) \neq f(\mathbf{x}^2)$ for arbitrarily given $\mathbf{x}^1, \mathbf{x}^2 \in U$ with $\mathbf{x}^1 \neq \mathbf{x}^2$. Let $\mathbf{x}^1 = (x_1^1, x_2^1, \ldots, x_n^1)^T$ and $\mathbf{x}^2 = (x_1^2, x_2^2, \ldots, x_n^2)^T$. If $x_i^1 \neq x_i^2$, we define two fuzzy sets A_i^1 and A_i^2 in the ith subspace of U with

$$\mu_{A_i^1}(x_i) = \exp\left[-\frac{(x_i - x_i^1)^2}{2}\right], \qquad \text{and} \qquad \mu_{A_i^2}(x_i) = \exp\left[-\frac{(x_i - x_i^2)^2}{2}\right]. \tag{17.13}$$

If $x_i^1 = x_i^2$, then $A_i^1 = A_i^2$; that is, only one fuzzy set is defined in the ith subspace of U. Up to now, we have constructed a function f that is in the form of Eq. (17.11) with $m = 2$, where the singleton outputs β^1 and β^2 will be specified later. With this f, we have

$$f(\mathbf{x}^1) = \frac{\beta^1 + \beta^2 \prod_{i=1}^n \exp[-(x_i^1 - x_i^2)^2/2]}{1 + \prod_{i=1}^n \exp[-(x_i^1 - x_i^2)^2/2]} = \alpha\beta^1 + (1-\alpha)\beta^2, \tag{17.14}$$

$$f(\mathbf{x}^2) = \frac{\beta^2 + \beta^1 \prod_{i=1}^n \exp[-(x_i^1 - x_i^2)^2/2]}{1 + \prod_{i=1}^n \exp[-(x_i^1 - x_i^2)^2/2]} = \alpha\beta^2 + (1-\alpha)\beta^1, \tag{17.15}$$

where

$$\alpha = \frac{1}{1 + \prod_{i=1}^n \exp[-(x_i^1 - x_i^2)^2/2]}. \tag{17.16}$$

Since $\mathbf{x}^1 \neq \mathbf{x}^2$, there must be some i such that $x_i^1 \neq x_i^2$; hence, we have $\prod_{i=1}^n \exp[-(x_i^1 - x_i^2)^2/2] \neq 1$, or $\alpha \neq 1 - \alpha$. If we choose $\beta^1 = 0$ and $\beta^2 = 1$, then $f(\mathbf{x}^1) = 1 - \alpha \neq \alpha = f(\mathbf{x}^2)$. This completes the second part of the proof.

The simplified fuzzy inference system in Theorem 17.3 is, in fact, equivalent to the radial basis function network (RBFN) (see Sec. 12.6) which has one layer of hidden nodes and uses the *normalized Gaussian activation function* for hidden nodes:

$$\mu_j(\mathbf{m}^j, \sigma^j, \mathbf{x}) = \frac{\exp[-|\mathbf{x} - \mathbf{m}^j|^2/2(\sigma^j)^2]}{\sum_{k=1}^m \exp[-|\mathbf{x} - \mathbf{m}^k|^2/2(\sigma^k)^2]}, \qquad j = 1, 2, \ldots, m. \tag{17.17}$$

Each hidden node has its own receptive field in the input space, a region centered on $\mathbf{m}^j$ with a size proportional to σ^j. There are connections w_{jk} from the hidden nodes to the output nodes. For the case of one output node, we simply denote the weights to be w_j. Assuming a linear output unit, the output of a radial basis network, denoted y, is given by

$$y = \sum_{j=1}^m w_j \mu_j(\mathbf{m}^j, \sigma^j, \mathbf{x}). \tag{17.18}$$

Comparing Eq. (17.18) to Eq. (17.11) [or Eq. (17.9)], we find that the RBFNs are exactly the fuzzy inference systems with product inference, centroid defuzzification, singleton consequents, and Gaussian membership functions, provided that $\sigma_1^j = \sigma_2^j = \cdots = \sigma_n^j = \sigma^j$ since $\prod_{i=1}^n \exp[-(x_i - m_i^j)^2/2(\sigma^j)^2] = \exp[-|\mathbf{x} - \mathbf{m}^j|^2/2(\sigma^j)^2]$, where $\mathbf{m}^j = (m_1^j, m_2^j, \ldots, m_n^j)^T$. It is noted that in the equivalence of the simplified fuzzy inference system [Eq. (17.11)] and the RBFN [Eq. (17.18)], the singleton consequents β^j in the former play the role of the hidden-output connection weights w_j in the latter, and vice versa.

It is clear that the design of a simplified fuzzy inference system with Gaussian membership functions involves finding proper parameters of membership functions (i.e., m_i^j and σ_i^j). and proper singleton consequents β^j. By considering these parameters $m_i^j, \sigma_i^j(\sigma^j)$, and β^j as parameters for tuning, the learning schemes developed for the RBFN (see Sec. 12.6) can be applied to the simplified fuzzy inference system directly to automate its design owing to their equivalency. For example, we can use unsupervised learning to determine the receptive field centers $\mathbf{m}^j$ and widths σ^j, and supervised learning to determine the weight $w_j (\beta^j)$. The issues of neural learning in fuzzy inference systems will be covered in greater detail in Chap. 19.

17.2.3 Stability Analysis of Neural Networks Using Stability Conditions of Fuzzy Systems

One of the most important concepts concerning the properties of dynamical systems is stability. It is, however, difficult to analyze the stability of nonlinear systems like fuzzy systems and neural networks. In Sec. 7.3, we introduced a stability theorem for fuzzy systems that provides a sufficient condition that guarantees stability of fuzzy systems in accordance with the definition of stability in the sense of Lyapunov. In this section, we shall discuss stability of neural networks using this theorem. In fact, the stability analysis discussed here can be applied not only to neural networks but also to other nonlinear systems if the nonlinear systems can be approximated by fuzzy systems [Tanaka and Sano, 1993].

The neural network model used for stability analysis is shown in Fig. 17.1, where $x(k), x(k-1),\ldots, x(k-n+1)$ are state variables and $u(k), u(k-1),\ldots, u(k-m+1)$ are input variables. Assume that all output (activation) functions $f(v)$ of nodes in the neural networks are differentiable, $f(0) = 0$ and $f(v) \in [-1, 1]$ for all v. Moreover, assume that $u(k) = u(k-1) = \cdots = u(k-m+1) = 0$ because we are analyzing the stability of the equilibrium of neural networks.

With the background concerning the stability analysis of fuzzy systems given in Sec. 7.3, we now consider the stability analysis of neural networks using stability conditions of fuzzy systems. In order to analyze the stability of neural networks using Tanaka-Sugeno theorems (Theorems 7.6–7.8), it is necessary to express the dynamics of a neural network by a fuzzy system. The basic idea here is to represent each output function $f(v)$ in each node by a fuzzy system. Consider a simple neural network which consists of a single layer, that is,

$$v = w_1 x(k) + w_2 x(k-1),$$
$$x(k+1) = f(v), \tag{17.19}$$

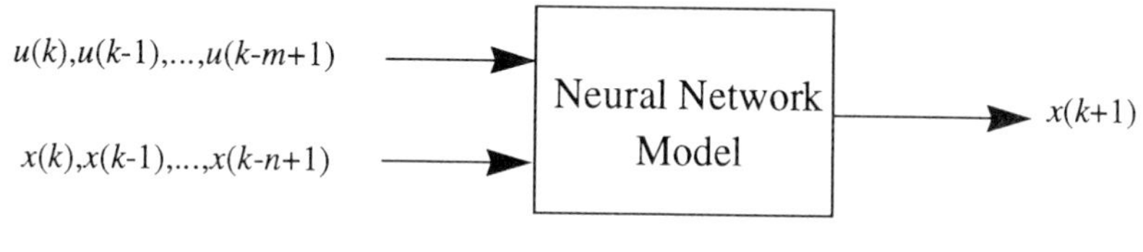

Figure 17.1   The neural network model used for stability analysis.

where w_1 and w_2 are connection weights and the output function $f(v)$ is assumed to be a sigmoid function,

$$f(v) = \frac{2}{1 + e^{-v/q}} - 1, \qquad (17.20)$$

where q is a constant that determines the slope of the function. It is noted that the output $f(v)$ satisfies the inequality

$$g_1 v \le f(v) \le g_2 v, \qquad (17.21)$$

where g_1 and g_2 are the minimum and the maximum values of $f'(v)$, that is,

$$g_1 = \min_v f'(v) = 0,$$
$$g_2 = \max_v f'(v) = 0.5/q. \qquad (17.22)$$

Therefore, this neural network can be represented by the following fuzzy system:

$$x(k+1) = f(v) = \frac{[\alpha_1(k)\,g_1 + \alpha_2(k)\,g_2]\,v}{\alpha_1(k) + \alpha_2(k)}, \qquad (17.23)$$

$$= \frac{\sum_{i=1}^2 \alpha_i(k)\,g_i\,[w_1 x(k) + w_2 x(k-1)]}{\sum_{i=1}^2 \alpha_i(k)}, \qquad (17.24)$$

where $\alpha_1(k)$, $\alpha_2(k) \in [0, 1]$ for all k. Notice that $\alpha_1(k)$ and $\alpha_2(k)$ in the suggested neural network are regarded as membership values of a fuzzy system. The corresponding edge matrices can thus be obtained as follows:

$$\mathbf{A}_1 = \begin{bmatrix} g_1 w_1 & g_1 w_2 \\ 1 & 0 \end{bmatrix}, \qquad \mathbf{A}_2 = \begin{bmatrix} g_2 w_1 & g_2 w_2 \\ 1 & 0 \end{bmatrix}. \qquad (17.25)$$

In this case, the parameter region (PR) becomes a straight line. The stability of the simple neural network can thus be analyzed using the *edge matrices* and Theorem 7.6. If we can find a common positive-definite matrix $\mathbf{P}$ such that

$$\mathbf{A}_i^T \mathbf{P} \mathbf{A}_i - \mathbf{P} < 0 \qquad i = 1, 2, \qquad (17.26)$$

then this neural network is asymptotically stable in the large. Let us illustrate this stability analysis with some examples.

Example 17.1

[Tanaka and Sano, 1993]. Consider the stability of the neural network shown in Fig. 17.2. From this figure we obtain

$$v_{11} = w_{111} x(k) + w_{121} x(k-1),$$
$$v_{12} = w_{112} x(k) + w_{122} x(k-1),$$
$$v_{21} = w_{211} f_{11}(v_{11}) + w_{212} f_{12}(v_{12}), \qquad (17.27)$$
$$x(k+1) = f_{21}(v_{21}).$$

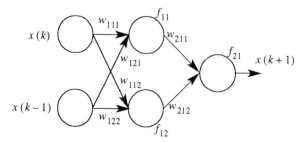

x(k)

x(k-1)

w_{111}
f_{11}
w_{211}
w_{121}
w_{112}
f_{21}
x(k+1)
w_{212}
w_{122}
f_{12}

Figure 17.2 Three-layer neural network
with two inputs used in Example 17.1.

Next, we define

$$f_{11}(v_{11}) = \frac{2}{1 + \exp(-v_{11}/q_{11})} - 1,$$

$$f_{12}(v_{12}) = \frac{2}{1 + \exp(-v_{12}/q_{12})} - 1, \qquad (17.28)$$

$$f_{21}(v_{21}) = \frac{2}{1 + \exp(-v_{21}/q_{21})} - 1,$$

as output functions of the nodes, where q are parameters of the output functions. Then, Eq. (17.28) can be represented by the following fuzzy systems, respectively,

$$f_{11}(v_{11}) = \frac{(\alpha_{111}(k)g_{111} + \alpha_{112}(k)g_{112})v_{11}}{\alpha_{111}(k) + \alpha_{112}(k)},$$

$$f_{12}(v_{12}) = \frac{(\alpha_{121}(k)g_{121} + \alpha_{122}(k)g_{122})v_{12}}{\alpha_{121}(k) + \alpha_{122}(k)}, \qquad (17.29)$$

$$f_{21}(v_{21}) = \frac{(\alpha_{211}(k)g_{211} + \alpha_{212}(k)g_{212})v_{21}}{\alpha_{211}(k) + \alpha_{212}(k)},$$

where $g_{111} = \min_v f'_{11}(v) = 0$, $g_{121} = \min_v f'_{12}(v) = 0$, $g_{212} = \min_v f'_{21}(v) = 0$, $g_{112} = \max_v f'_{11}(v) = 0.5/q_{11}$, $g_{122} = \max_v f'_{12}(v) = 0.5/q_{12}$, $g_{212} = \max_v f'_{21}(v) = 0.5/q_{21}$.
In the first case, we set $w_{111} = 1$, $w_{121} = -0.5$, $w_{112} = -1$, $w_{122} = -0.5$, $w_{211} = 1$, $w_{212} = 1$, and $q_{11} = q_{12} = q_{21} = 0.25$ ($g_{112} = g_{122} = g_{212} \equiv g_2 = 2.0$, $g_{111} = g_{121} = g_{211} \equiv g_1 = 0$). Then from Eqs. (17.27) and (17.29), we have

$$x(k+1) = \frac{1}{\sum_{i,j,k=1}^{2}\alpha_{11i}(k)\alpha_{12j}(k)\alpha_{21k}(k)} \sum_{i,j,k=1}^{2}\alpha_{11i}(k)\alpha_{12j}(k)\alpha_{21k}(k) \cdot \qquad (17.30)$$

$$\{g_k(g_iw_{211}w_{111} + g_jw_{212}w_{112})x(k) + g_k(g_iw_{211}w_{121} + g_jw_{212}w_{122})x(k-1)\}.$$

From Eq. (17.30), *edge matrices* are obtained as follows:

$$\mathbf{A}_1 = \begin{bmatrix} 0 & 0 \\ 1.0 & 0 \end{bmatrix}, \quad \mathbf{A}_2 = \begin{bmatrix} -2.0 & -1.0 \\ 1.0 & 0 \end{bmatrix}, \quad \mathbf{A}_3 = \begin{bmatrix} 2.0 & -1.0 \\ 1.0 & 0 \end{bmatrix}, \quad \mathbf{A}_4 = \begin{bmatrix} 0 & -2.0 \\ 1.0 & 0 \end{bmatrix}.$$

Figure 17.3 shows the PR for this network. There is no common positive-definite matrix **P** because $\mathbf{A}_2$, $\mathbf{A}_3$, and $\mathbf{A}_4$ are not stable matrices. Figure 17.4 shows the behavior of this neural network. As indicated in Fig. 17.4, this system is not asymptotically stable in the large. In the case of unstable neural systems, the behavior of neural networks becomes a limit cycle as a result of saturation of the output of units; that is, $f(v) \in [-1, 1]$ for all v.

Sec. 17.2   The Equivalence of Fuzzy Inference Systems and Neural Networks   **491**

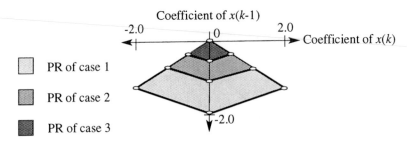

Figure 17.3 PR representations in Example 17.1.

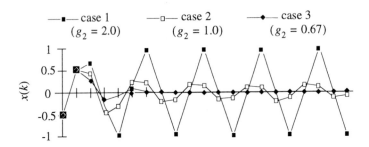

Figure 17.4 Performance of neural networks in Example 17.1.

In the second case, we assume that $q_{11} = q_{12} = q_{21} = 0.5$ ($g_{112} = g_{122} = g_{212} \triangleq g_2 = 1.0$, $g_{111} = g_{121} = g_{211} \triangleq g_1 = 0$). Then we can obtain the following edge matrices:

$$A_1 = \begin{bmatrix} 0 & 0 \\ 1.0 & 0 \end{bmatrix}, \quad A_2 = \begin{bmatrix} -1.0 & -0.5 \\ 1.0 & 0 \end{bmatrix}, \quad A_3 = \begin{bmatrix} 1.0 & -0.5 \\ 1.0 & 0 \end{bmatrix}, \quad A_4 = \begin{bmatrix} 0 & -1.0 \\ 1.0 & 0 \end{bmatrix}.$$

Figure 17.3 shows the PR of this network. It is found from Theorem 7.8 that there is no common positive-definite matrix **P** because $A_1 A_2$ is not a stable matrix. Figure 17.4 shows the behavior of this network.

In the third case, we let $q_{11} = q_{12} = q_{21} = 0.75$ ($g_{112} = g_{122} = g_{212} \equiv g_2 = 0.67$, $g_{111} = g_{121} = g_{211} \equiv g_1 = 0$). Then we can obtain the following edge matrices:

$$A_1 = \begin{bmatrix} 0 & 0 \\ 1.0 & 0 \end{bmatrix}, \quad A_2 = \begin{bmatrix} -0.44 & -0.22 \\ 1.0 & 0 \end{bmatrix},$$

$$A_3 = \begin{bmatrix} 0.44 & -0.22 \\ 1.0 & 0 \end{bmatrix}, \quad A_4 = \begin{bmatrix} 0 & -0.44 \\ 1.0 & 0 \end{bmatrix}.$$

Figure 17.3 shows the PR of this network. If we select

$$P = \begin{bmatrix} 2.42 & -0.19 \\ -0.19 & 1.12 \end{bmatrix}$$

as a common positive-definite matrix $\mathbf{P}$, then $\mathbf{A}_i^T\mathbf{PA}_i - \mathbf{P} < 0$ for $i = 1, 2, 3$, and 4. Hence, this neural network is stable. Figure 17.4 shows the behavior of this network.

The above example reveals some characteristics of the stability of neural networks. First, this stability is strongly related to the connection weights and the maximal gradient values g_2 of sigmoid functions. The eigenvalues of *edge matrices* are closer to the origin of the z plane when the connection weights or g_2 is closer to 0. As shown in Fig. 17.4, the behavior of neural networks becomes stable if g_2 is closer to 0. Second, the situation where the connection weights or g_2 is closer to 0 means that the area of the PR becomes smaller, as shown in Fig. 17.3. The PR area is related to nonlinearity represented by neural networks. Of course, nonlinearity represented by neural networks is stronger when the PR area becomes larger. Generally speaking, there is a contrary relation between the guarantee of stability and the degree of nonlinearity (i.e., the PR area).

Example 17.2

Consider the stability of the neural network shown in Fig. 17.5. Assume that $w_{111} = w_{112} = w_{121} = 0.3$, $w_{122} = -0.3$, $w_{131} = 0.2$, $w_{132} = -0.2$, $w_{211} = w_{212} = 1$, and $q_{11} = q_{12} = q_{21} = 0.5$ $(g_{112} = g_{122} = g_{212} \equiv g_2 = 1.0, g_{111} = g_{121} = g_{211} \equiv g_1 = 0)$. From this figure, we have

$$x(k+1) = \frac{1}{\sum_{i,j,k=1}^{2}\alpha_{11i}(k)\,\alpha_{12j}(k)\,\alpha_{21k}(k)}\sum_{i,j,k=1}^{2}\alpha_{11i}(k)\,\alpha_{12j}(k)\,\alpha_{21k}(k)\cdot$$

$$\{g_k\,(g_iw_{211}w_{111} + g_jw_{212}w_{112})\,x(k) + \qquad (17.31)$$

$$g_k\,(g_iw_{211}w_{121} + g_jw_{212}w_{122})\,x(k-1) + g_k\,(g_iw_{211}w_{131} + g_jw_{212}w_{132})\,x(k-2)\},$$

which is in the same manner as Eq. (17.30). From Eq. (17.31), edge matrices are obtained as follows:

$$\mathbf{A}_1 = \begin{bmatrix} 0 & 0 & 0 \\ 1 & 0 & 0 \\ 0 & 1 & 0 \end{bmatrix}, \qquad \mathbf{A}_2 = \begin{bmatrix} 0.3 & -0.3 & -0.2 \\ 1.0 & 0 & 0 \\ 0 & 1.0 & 0 \end{bmatrix},$$

$$\mathbf{A}_3 = \begin{bmatrix} 0.3 & 0.3 & 0.3 \\ 1 & 0 & 0 \\ 0 & 1.0 & 0 \end{bmatrix}, \qquad \mathbf{A}_4 = \begin{bmatrix} 0.6 & 0 & 0 \\ 1 & 0 & 0 \\ 0 & 1 & 0 \end{bmatrix}.$$

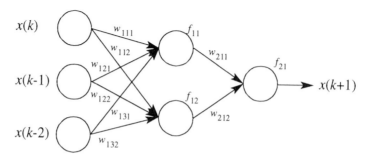

Figure 17.5 Three-layer neural network with three inputs in Example 17.2.

In this case, PR can be represented as a polyhedron because the number of state variables is 3. If we select

$$\mathbf{P} = \begin{bmatrix} 4.20 & -0.24 & -0.29 \\ -0.24 & 2.72 & 0.31 \\ -0.29 & 0.31 & 1.17 \end{bmatrix}$$

as a common **P**, then

$$\mathbf{A}_i^T \mathbf{PA}_i - \mathbf{P} < \mathbf{0}, \qquad i = 1, 2, \dots, 4.$$

Therefore, this neural network system is stable.

The above example reveals the following characteristic of the stability of neural networks. When the number of nodes in the hidden layer or the number of layers does not change, the number of consequent matrices does not increase even if the number of state variables (i.e., inputs of neural networks) increases. However, it increases exponentially if the number of nodes in the hidden layer or the number of layers increases.

17.3 CONCLUDING REMARKS

This chapter presents compelling reasons for integrating fuzzy logic and neural networks into a working functional system. Integrated neural-fuzzy or fuzzy-neural systems are more flexible and robust and have a broader application domain.

In addition to the basic concepts of integration covered in this chapter, Bersini et al. [1993] categorized the ways that neural networks can participate in the automatic adjustment of fuzzy systems into three configurations. Bezdek and Pal [1992] suggested several important ideas concerning their fuzzy neural networks. Werbos [1992] presented a general guideline for choosing and designing a fuzzy-neural hybrid system. The use of fuzzy-neural hybrid systems for fuzzy modeling is described in [Pedrycz, 1993]. The performance comparisons of fuzzy systems and neural networks in terms of approximation accuracy, memory capacity, execution speed, learning speed, and time of learning can be found in [Kajitani et al., 1991; Lou, 1993].

17.4 PROBLEMS

17.1 Fuzzy systems and neural networks are both model-free estimators. However, if a model of the controlled object (plant) were available, which system would benefit more from the known model? Justify your answer.

17.2 Describe how neural networks represent (encode) structured knowledge (e.g., IF-THEN rules) and how fuzzy systems store numerical data (e.g., numerical input-output mapping).

17.3 Neural networks perform point-to-point mapping, whereas fuzzy systems perform set-to-set mapping. A fuzzy logic rule represents one set-to-set mapping, where "set" means "fuzzy set." Using these concepts, figure out the possible ways that the learning schemes of neural networks can be used to find proper fuzzy logic rules in fuzzy systems. [*Hint:* Point-to-point mapping is a special case of set-to-set mapping with a set containing a single element (point). On the contrary, a set-to-set mapping can be considered a group of "similar" point-to-point mappings.]

17.4 Consider the following application problems to be solved by using purely fuzzy systems or purely neural networks.

(a) Printed and handwritten character recognition,
(b) Expert systems for medical diagnosis,
(c) Altitude control of satellites,
(d) Speech recognition in a noisy environment,
(e) Obstacle avoidance control of mobile robots,
(f) Stable position control of crane systems,
(g) Learning the skills of an experienced operator in a chemical plant.

For each problem, choose the proper method (fuzzy system or neural network) and explain the reason for your choice.

17.5 Which applications in Problem 17.4 can be solved by (a) neural fuzzy systems and (b) fuzzy neural networks?

17.6 In Sec.17.2.1, we considered a simplified fuzzy inference model in which the consequent of each rule was a singleton. We have shown that such simplified fuzzy inference models are universal approximators. From this proof, can we infer that normal fuzzy inference models with consequents being nonsingleton fuzzy sets are also universal approximators?

17.7 Verify the correctness of the following statement: Fuzzy inference models with trapezoidal membership functions are not necessary universal approximators.

17.8 The equivalence of simplified fuzzy inference systems and radial basis function networks was proved in Sec. 17.2.2. Hence, they can be applied to solve the same problem. Describe the different characteristics (advantages) of these two models such that we can decide which one to use in solving an assigned problem.

17.9 Consider the following fuzzy system:

$$\text{Rule 1: IF } x(k) \text{ is } A_1, \text{ THEN } x_1(k+1) = 0.1x(k) + 0.5x(k-1).$$
$$\text{Rule 2: IF } x(k) \text{ is } A_2, \text{ THEN } x_2(k+1) = 0.4x(k) + 0.2x(k-1).$$
$$\text{Rule 3: IF } x(k) \text{ is } A_3, \text{ THEN } x_3(k+1) = 0.5x(k) + 0.2x(k-1).$$
$$\text{Rule 4: IF } x(k) \text{ is } A_4, \text{ THEN } x_4(k+1) = 0.3x(k) + 0.3x(k-1).$$
$$\text{Rule 5: IF } x(k) \text{ is } A_5, \text{ THEN } x_5(k+1) = 0.35x(k) + 0.45x(k-1).$$
$$\text{Rule 6: IF } x(k) \text{ is } A_6, \text{ THEN } x_6(k+1) = 0.15x(k) + 0.5x(k-1).$$

(a) Write down the consequent matrices and show the PR of this fuzzy system.
(b) What are the edge rules of this fuzzy system?
(c) Is this fuzzy system a minimum representation? If not, find the minimum representation.
(d) Can you determine if this fuzzy system is stable?

17.10 Consider the neural network in Fig. 17.5. Find a set of weight values such that the resulting neural network is unstable. Analyze the stability of the resulting neural network using stability conditions of fuzzy systems. Write a program for simulating the behavior of this network and show that it is unstable.

18

Neural Network–Based Fuzzy Systems

The learning ability of neural networks will be utilized in this chapter to realize the key components of a general fuzzy logic inference system, including fuzzy membership functions, basic fuzzy logic operators, fuzzy inference, fuzzy reasoning, and fuzzy modeling. The neural learning techniques used are mainly multilayer feedforward networks with the back-propagation algorithm.

18.1 NEURAL REALIZATION OF BASIC FUZZY LOGIC OPERATIONS

In this section, we consider the use of neural networks in realizing fuzzy membership functions and some basic fuzzy logic operators such as fuzzy AND, fuzzy OR, and so on. This gives us the fundamentals for setting up a complete neural network–based fuzzy system.

In Part II of this book, we saw that a neural network can synthesize a network representation of a continuous function given a reasonable number of isolated instances of that function. This implies that a neural network can utilize a finite number of instances to build a membership function that might represent the (fuzzy) concept in question in a valid manner over a wide range of possibilities. Hence, a neural network, say a single-hidden-layer standard back-propagation network, can be trained to represent a membership function with an arbitrary shape.

In many applications of fuzzy logic, the membership functions have regular shapes, such as a triangular shape or a bell shape. Such a simple membership function can be realized by a single neuron, and this can be easily achieved by setting its activation function to a desired membership function. For example, to represent a bell-shaped membership function, we can use a neuron whose activation function is

496

$$a(\text{net}) = \exp\left(\frac{-(\text{net} - m)^2}{\sigma^2}\right), \tag{18.1}$$

where "net" is the net input to the neuron, m is the center (mean) of the membership function, and σ represents the width (variance) of the membership function.

We can also use normal sigmoidal neurons to represent useful membership functions. For example, to represent the three terms (fuzzy sets) "Small (S)," "Medium (M)," and "Large (L)," of a linguistic variable x in $\Re$, we can use the network shown in Fig. 18.1(a), where the outputs y_1, y_2, and y_3 indicate the grade of the membership functions $\mu_S(x)$, $\mu_M(x)$, and $\mu_L(x)$, respectively. The outputs of the nodes with the symbol + are the sums of their inputs, and the nodes with the symbol a have sigmoid functions as their activation functions. According to this figure we have, for example,

$$y_1 = \mu_S(x) = \frac{1}{1 + \exp\left[-w_g\left(x + w_c\right)\right]}. \tag{18.2}$$

Thus, the weights w_c and w_g determine the central position and the gradient of the sigmoid function, respectively. By appropriately initializing the weights, the membership functions of the fuzzy sets S, M, and L can be allocated on the universe of discourse as shown in Fig. 18.1(b). The pseudotrapezoidal membership function $\mu_M(x)$ is composed of two sigmoid functions as illustrated in Fig. 18.1(c). The sigmoid functions are shown by dotted lines, and the two functions have opposite signs.

We next consider neural network realization of basic fuzzy logic operations such as fuzzy AND, fuzzy OR, and fuzzy NOT. A straightforward means of neural realization of fuzzy logic operations is to let a neuron function as a desired fuzzy logic operation. For example, we can set the activation function of a neuron to be the min operator for a fuzzy AND operation and set the activation function of another neuron to be the max operator for a fuzzy OR operation. Similarly, we can let a neuron perform a fuzzy NOT operation. However, in some situations, especially for learning purposes, we need the *differentiability* of the neurons' activation functions. Then, we can define some differentiable functions to replace or approximate a desired but nondifferentiable fuzzy logic operation. For example, the following *softmin* operator can be used to replace the original min operator:

$$(a \wedge b) \triangleq \text{softmin}(a, b) = \frac{ae^{-ka} + be^{-kb}}{e^{-ka} + e^{-kb}}, \tag{18.3}$$

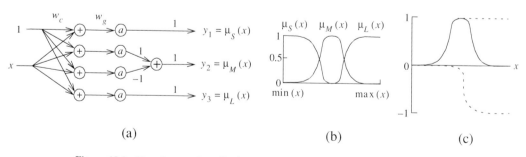

Figure 18.1 Neural network realization of simple membership functions. (a) Network structure. (b) Membership function represented in (a). (c) Composition of membership function $\mu_M(x)$ in (b).

which produces the same result in the limit but in general is not as specific as the *minimum* operator, where the parameter k controls the hardness of the softmin operation, and as $k \to \infty$, we recover the usual min operator. For k finite, we obtain a differentiable function of the inputs, which makes it convenient for calculating gradients during the learning process.

Another approach to realizing basic fuzzy logic operations with neural networks is to use the *ordered weighted averaging (OWA) neuron* proposed by Yager [1992d]. This neuron performs the OWA operation defined as follows. A mapping $f: I^n \to I$, where I is the unit interval, is called an OWA operator of dimension n if associated with f as a weighting vector $\mathbf{v} = (v_1, v_2, \dots, v_n)^T$, where $v_i \in [0, 1]$ and $\sum_i v_i = 1$ such that

$$f(a_1, a_2, \dots, a_n) = v_1 b_1 + v_2 b_2 + \cdots + v_n b_n, \tag{18.4}$$

with b_i the ith largest element in the collection $a_1, a_2, \dots, a_n$. For example, assume f is an OWA operator of size $n = 4$. Let $\mathbf{v} = (0.2, 0.3, 0.1, 0.4)^T$. Then, $f(0.6, 1, 0.3, 0.5) = (0.2)(1) + (0.3)(0.6) + (0.1)(0.5) + (0.4)(0.3) = 0.55$. The key feature of the OWA operator is the fact that the weights are not specifically assigned to a given argument but the association is determined by the ordering of the arguments.

OWA operators provide a behavior moving from one extreme of fuzzy OR (max) operation of the arguments $f(a_1, a_2, \dots, a_n) = \max_i(a_i)$, in which case $\mathbf{v} = \mathbf{v}^* = (1, 0, 0, \dots, 0)^T$, to the other extreme of fuzzy AND (min) operation of the arguments $f(a_1, a_2, \dots, a_n) = \min_i(a_i)$, in which case $\mathbf{v} = \mathbf{v}^* = (0, 0, \dots, 0, 1)^T$. Another special case of the OWA operation is $\mathbf{v} = \mathbf{v}_n = (1/n, 1/n, \dots, 1/n)^T$, which corresponds to a simple averaging of the arguments.

18.2 NEURAL NETWORK–BASED FUZZY LOGIC INFERENCE

Following our discussion of neural network realization of membership functions and basic fuzzy logic operations, we consider in this section neural network realization of fuzzy logic inference which is the kernel of a fuzzy inference system. Fuzzy inference systems can be used to learn and extrapolate complex relationships between possibility distributions for the preconditions and consequents in the rules. The nonadaptive behavior of original fuzzy inference systems can be significantly improved by using neural networks. Moreover, since different rules with the same variables can be encoded in a single network, the use of neural networks for realizing fuzzy logic inference can provide a natural mechanism for *rule conflict resolution*. The combination of fuzzy logic and neural networks can lead to the development of new algorithms and structures that provide adaptive behavior while maintaining the strong knowledge representation characteristic of fuzzy inference systems. In this section, we shall introduce some approaches to the neural network realization of fuzzy logic inference.

18.2.1 Fuzzy Inference Networks

The use of fuzzy logic to model and manage uncertainty in a rule-based system places high computational demands on an inference engine. Artificial neural networks offer the potential of parallel computation with high flexibility. We shall introduce the structured feedforward neural network proposed by Keller et al. [1992b] for fuzzy inference called a *fuzzy inference network* (see Fig. 18.2). Each basic network structure implements a single rule in the rule base of the form

$$\text{IF } X_1 \text{ is } A_1 \text{ AND } X_2 \text{ is } A_2 \text{ AND } \dots \text{ AND } X_n \text{ is } A_n, \text{ THEN } Y \text{ is } B. \qquad (18.5)$$

The fuzzy sets that characterize the possibility distribution of the facts, X_1 is $A'_1, \dots, X_n$ is A'_n, are presented to the input layer of the network. The fuzzy set A'_i is denoted by

$$A'_i = \{a'_{i1}, a'_{i2}, \dots, a'_{im_i}\}, \qquad (18.6)$$

where $a'_{i1}, a'_{i2}, \dots, a'_{im_i}$ are the membership grades of the fuzzy set A'_i at sampled points over its domain of discourse.

There are two variations of the activities in the precondition clause–checking layer (the first hidden layer). In both cases, each precondition clause of the rule determines the weights. For variation 1, the weights w_{ij} are the fuzzy complement of the precondition clause; that is, for the ith clause,

$$w_{ij} = \bar{a}_{ij} = 1 - a_{ij}, \qquad (18.7)$$

where the clause "π_{Xi} is A_i" is translated into the possibility distribution

$$\pi_{Xi} = A_i = \{a_{i1}, a_{i2}, \dots, a_{im_i}\}. \qquad (18.8)$$

Choosing weights in this way, the first layer of the fuzzy inference network generates a measure of *disagreement* between the input possibility distribution and the precondition clause distribution if each node calculates the similarity (e.g., intersections) between the input and the complement of the precondition (i.e., the weights w_{ij}). Hence, as the input moves away from the precondition, the amount of disagreement rises to 1. This evidence is then combined at the precondition clause–checking node. The purpose of the node is to determine the amount of disagreement between the precondition clause and the corresponding input data. Let the combination at the kth node be denoted by d_k; then

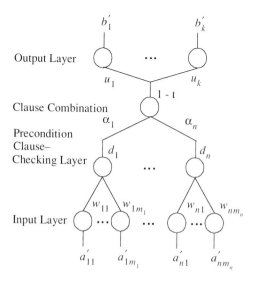

Figure 18.2 Fuzzy inference network—a structured neural network configuration for fuzzy logic inference.

$$d_k = \max_j \{w_{kj} * a'_{kj}\} = \max_j \{(1 - a_{kj}) * a'_{kj}\}, \tag{18.9}$$

where $*$ corresponds to the operation of multiplication or minimum. Hence, we have

$$d_k^1 = \max_j \{(1 - a_{kj}) \cdot a'_{kj}\}, \tag{18.10}$$

$$d_k^2 = \max_j \{\min \{(1 - a_{kj}), a'_{kj}\}\}, \tag{18.11}$$

where operators d_k^1 and d_k^2 provide a measure of the intersection of the fuzzy sets $\bar{A}_i$ and A'_i and both can be thought of as a generalization of the dot product of the weight vector and the input vector.

The second form for the precondition clause–checking layer uses the fuzzy sets A_i themselves as the weights; that is, in this case

$$\{w_{i1}, w_{i2}, \ldots, w_{im_i}\} = \pi_{Xi} = A_i = \{a_{i1}, a_{i2}, \ldots, a_{im_i}\}. \tag{18.12}$$

The combination at the kth node in the precondition clause–checking layer then becomes

$$d_k^3 = \max_j \{|a_{kj} - a'_{kj}|\}, \tag{18.13}$$

which is the max norm difference between the two functions μ_{A_k} and $\mu_{A'_k}$. Note that d_k^3 is of the same form as d_k^1 and d_k^2 but with a different set of weights. Hence, it also gives an indication of the level of disagreement.

The disagreement values for each node are combined at the next layer to produce an overall level of disagreement between the precondition clauses and the input data. The disagreement values provide inhibiting signals for the firing of the rule. The weights α_i on these links correspond to the importance of the various precondition clauses. They can either be supplied subjectively or learned through some learning scheme. The combination node then computes

$$1 - t = 1 - \max_i \{\alpha_i \cdot d_i\}. \tag{18.14}$$

The weights u_i on the output nodes carry the information from the consequent of rule as specified in the following discussion. If the proposition "Y is B" is characterized by the possibility distribution function $\pi_Y(y_i) = b_i$ for all y_i in the domain of B, then the weights are defined by

$$u_i = \bar{b}_i = 1 - b_i. \tag{18.15}$$

Each output node then computes the value

$$b'_i = 1 - \bar{b}_i(1 - t) = 1 - (1 - b_i)(1 - t) = b_i + t - b_i t. \tag{18.16}$$

From Eq. (18.16), it is observed that if $t = 0$, then the rule fires with the conclusion "Y is B" exactly. On the other hand, if the total disagreement is 1, then the conclusion of firing the rule is a possibility distribution composed entirely of 1s, hence the conclusion is "Y is UNKNOWN." The following example illustrates the above formulation.

Example 18.1
   In this example, we build up a fuzzy inference network for the rule "IF X is Low, THEN Y is High" using the disagreement measure d^1 in Eq. (18.10) for clause checking. To realize this

rule, we use the network shown in Fig. 18.2 with $n = 1$, $m_1 = k = 11$, and $\alpha_1 = 1$. The membership functions of related fuzzy sets are

$$A = \text{"Low"} = \{1, 0.67, 0.33, 0, 0, 0, 0, 0, 0, 0, 0\},$$
$$B = \text{"High"} = \{0, 0, 0, 0, 0, 0, 0.2, 0.4, 0.6, 0.8, 1\}.$$

Then, from Eq. (18.7) we have (see Fig. 18.2)

$$(w_{1,1}, w_{1,2}, w_{1,3}, w_{1,4}, w_{1,5}, \ldots, w_{1,11}) = (0, 0.33, 0.67, 1, 1, \ldots, 1).$$

Similarly, from Eq. (18.15), we have

$$(u_{1,1}, \ldots, u_{1,6}, u_{1,7}, u_{1,8}, u_{1,9}, u_{1,10}, u_{1,11}) = (1, \ldots, 1, 0.8, 0.6, 0.4, 0.2, 0).$$

Next, we test this network with the input "X is Low," that is, $A' = A = $ "Low." From Eq. (18.10), we derive $d_1^1 = 0.22$. Then from Eq. (18.14), we have $t = 0.22$. Finally, from Eq. (18.16), we obtain the induced output:

$$(b_1', b_2', \ldots, b_{11}') = (0.22, 0.22, 0.22, 0.22, 0.22, 0.22, 0.38, 0.53, 0.69, 0.84, 1).$$

Similarly, the reader can check that for the input $A' = $ "VERY Low" [see Eq. (6.4)], we have $t = 0.15$ and $(b_1', b_2', \ldots, b_{11}') = (0.15, 0.15, 0.15, 0.15, 0.15, 0.15, 0.32, 0.49, 0.66, 0.83, 1)$. It is observed that even if $A' = A = $ "Low," $B' \neq B$, and if $A' = $ "VERY Low" $\subset A = $ "Low," we have $B \subset B'$.

The following theorems characterize the properties of the fuzzy inference network [Keller et al., 1992b]. In each case, a single precondition clause rule of the form "IF X is A, THEN Y is B," is considered. The corollaries extend the results to multiple-precondition clause rules of the form "IF X_1 is A_1 AND X_2 is A_2 AND $\cdots$ AND X_n is A_n, THEN Y is B." We leave the proof of the following corollaries to the reader as exercises.

Theorem 18.1

In a single precondition clause rule, suppose that A is a crisp subset of its domain of discourse; then the fuzzy inference network produces the standard modus ponens result; that is, if the input "X is A'" is such that $A' = A$, then the network result is "Y is B," whether B is crisp or fuzzy.

Proof: Suppose A is a crisp subset of its domain of discourse and that $A' = A$. Then,

$$d^1 = \max_j \{(1 - a_j) \cdot a_j'\} = \max_j \{(1 - a_j) \cdot a_j\} = 0$$

since A is crisp, and thus $a_j = 1$ or 0. Similarly,

$$d^2 = \max_j \{(1 - a_j) \wedge a_j'\} = 0.$$

Finally, for d^3 we have

$$d^3 = \max_j \{|a_j - a_j'|\} = \max_j \{|a_j - a_j|\} = 0.$$

Hence, at the combination node, $t = 0$, and so the output layer produces

$$b_i' = 1 - (1 - b_i)(1 - t) = b_i, \qquad i = 1, 2, \ldots, k.$$

Thus, $B' = B$, and this completes the proof.

Corollary 18.1

For a multiple-clause fuzzy inference network, suppose $A_1, A_2, \ldots, A_n$ are crisp subsets of their domains of discourse. Suppose also that the inputs "X_1 is A_1', X_2 is $A_2', \ldots, X_n$ is A_n'" are such that $A_i' = A_i$ for $i = 1, 2, \ldots, n$. Then the inferred result is "Y is B."

The next theorem examines the behavior of the first variation of the network in the case where it is presented with a crisp input that is different from A and with inputs that are more specific than the restrictions imposed by the clause "X is A."

Theorem 18.2

Consider a single-clause fuzzy inference network with $\alpha = 1$, using d^1 or d^2 for clause checking. Suppose that A and A' are proper crisp subsets of their domains of discourse.

(i) If $\overline{A} \cap A' \neq \varnothing$, then the network produces the result "Y is UNKNOWN," that is, a possibility distribution for Y that is identically equal to 1.

(ii) If $A' \subset A$ (i.e., A' is more specific than A), then the result is "Y is B."

Proof

(i) Since $\overline{A} \cap A' \neq \varnothing$, there is a point v_i in the domain such that $\mu_{\overline{A}}(v_i) = \mu_{A'}(v_i) = 1$. In other words, the weight $w_i = 1 - a_i = 1 - \mu_A(v_i) = \mu_{\overline{A}}(v_i) = 1$ and $a_i' = \mu_{A'}(v_i) = 1$. Hence

$$d^i = \max_j \{ w_j * a_j' \} = 1 \qquad \text{for } i = 1, 2,$$

where "$*$" corresponds to the operation of multiplication or minimum. Since $\alpha = 1$, we have $t = 1$ at the clause combination node, and so

$$b_i' = 1 - (1 - b_i)(1 - t) = 1 \qquad \text{for all } i = 1, 2, \ldots, k.$$

(ii) Now suppose that $A' \subset A$. Then $A' \cap \overline{A} = \varnothing$, and so $d^1 = d^2 = 0$, producing the result "Y is B."

Corollary 18.2

Consider a multiple-clause fuzzy inference network with $\alpha_1 = \alpha_2 = \cdots = \alpha_n = 1$, using d^1 or d^2 for clause checking. Suppose that $A_1, A_2, \ldots, A_n$ and $A_1', A_2', \ldots, A_n'$ are proper crisp subsets of their domains of discourse.

(i) If for some $k = 1, 2, \ldots, n$, $\overline{A}_k \cap A_k' \neq \varnothing$, then the network will produce the result "Y is UNKNOWN."

(ii) If $A_k' \subset A_k$ for all $k = 1, 2, \ldots, n$, then the result will be "Y is B."

Part (ii) of the above theorem and corollary indicate that, for example, if we have the rule "IF a tomato is red, THEN it is ripe" and the fact "A tomato is very red," then the network will infer that the tomato is ripe. This is a nice property for an inference engine. The following theorem indicates that the d^3 version of the inference network produces "UNKNOWN" anytime a crisp clause does not exactly match the crisp precondition, the same as in classical modus ponens.

Theorem 18.3

Consider a single-clause fuzzy inference network with $\alpha = 1$ and d^3 for clause checking. If A and A' are crisp subsets of their domain of discourse such that $A' \neq A$, then the network inference result is "Y is UNKNOWN."

Proof: Since $A' \neq A$, there is a point v_i such that $a_i = \mu_A(v_i) \neq \mu_{A'}(v_i) = a_i'$. Then $d^3 = \max_i \{ |a_i - a_i'| \} = 1$. As before, this ensures that the result is "Y is UNKNOWN."

Corollary 18.3

Consider a multiple-clause fuzzy inference network with $\alpha_1 = \alpha_2 = \cdots = \alpha_n = 1$ that uses d^3 for clause checking. Suppose that $A_1, A_2, \ldots, A_n$ and $A'_1, A'_2, \ldots, A'_n$ are crisp subsets of their domains of discourse. If for some $k = 1, 2, \ldots, n$, $A_k \ne A'_k$, then the network answer is "Y is UNKNOWN."

In the above discussion, we focused on the case in which the preconditions consist of crisp subsets. If the clauses and the inputs are modeled by possibility distributions determined by fuzzy subsets, the behavior of the two variations of the inference network differs. First, it is noticed that the d^3 version of the fuzzy inference network satisfies Theorem 18.1 even when A is a fuzzy subset. The d^1 and d^2 versions will not produce the exact response "Y is B" when the input is "X is A," as illustrated in Example 18.1. In fact, for both d^1 and d^2, the result is a superset of B (i.e., the conclusions are less specific than B). However, there is a monotonicity inherent in these network inferences as shown in the following theorem.

Theorem 18.4

Consider a single-clause fuzzy inference network using d^1 and d^2 for clause checking. Suppose that A, A', and A'' are three fuzzy subsets such that $A'' \subset A' \subset A$. Let the results of inference with inputs "X is A'" and "X is A''" be "Y is B'" and "Y is B''," respectively. Then, $B \subset B'' \subset B'$, that is, B'' is closer to B than B'.

Proof: For each v_i in the domain of discourse of A,

$$0 \le a''_i = \mu_{A''}(v_i) \le a'_i = \mu_{A'}(v_i) \le a_i = \mu_A(v_i).$$

Hence, at the clause-checking node,

$$(d^i)'' = \max_j\{(1 - a_j) * a''_j\} \le \max_j\{(1 - a_j) * a'_j\} = (d^i)' \qquad \text{for} > e = 1, 2,$$

where $*$ corresponds to the operation of multiplication or minimum. Hence, $t'' = \alpha (d^i)'' \le t' = \alpha (d^i)'$. Finally,

$$b''_i = b_i + t'' - b_i t'' \le b'_i = b_i + t' - b_i t' \qquad \text{for } i = 1, 2, \ldots, k.$$

Clearly, from the above equations, both b''_i and b'_i are larger than b_i. This completes the proof.

Intuitively, the above theorem states that as the input becomes more specific, the output converges to the consequent. This can be observed in Example 18.1. The d^3 version of the fuzzy inference network behaves in just the opposite manner; as the input becomes more specific, the output diverges away from B. In summary, the d^1 and d^2 clause-checking rules do not produce exact results when the input matches the precondition clause precisely. When a noisy version of the input clause is presented to the network, the output deviates further. However, more-specific inputs give results closer to the desired output. On the other hand, rule d^3 works well for an exact and noisy input but does not provide better answers as the input becomes more specific. Clearly, the choice of clause-checking rule should be dictated by the type of output desired when the input does not exactly match the precondition clause.

The discussion above was based on setting the α weight values for the clause combination nodes to 1. By lowering these values for the d^1 and d^2 checking functions, a closer fit to the consequent can be achieved when the input is exactly the precondition clause. The maximum deviation occurs when the value of b_i is 0 since $b'_i = b_i + \alpha d - b_i \alpha d = \alpha d$.

Thus, when $\alpha < 1$, b_i' will be smaller, resulting in a better fit with the consequent. However, for a nonmatch ($d = 1$) when $\alpha < 1$, the output is $b_i' = 1 - (1 - b_i)(1 - \alpha d) \neq 1$ if $b_i \neq 0$, but the result should be a possibility distribution of all 1s indicating "UNKNOWN." Thus, a tradeoff between these two extremes can be determined to give a close match to "Y is B" when "X is A" and something close to "Y is UNKNOWN" when the input deviates significantly from the precondition.

18.2.2 Fuzzy Aggregation Networks

The fuzzy inference network introduced in the last section uses fixed fuzzy logic operators. They have no, or very little, trainability. We shall now introduce more-flexible neural network structures for fuzzy inference generalized from the fuzzy inference network. Since they allow more flexible and versatile fuzzy logic operators for aggregating membership functions, they are referred to as *fuzzy aggregation networks*. The node function of a fuzzy aggregation network can be any (parameterized) fuzzy aggregation operator that can be a union operator, intersection operator, or averaging operator (see Sec. 2.2.2). Because of the generalization to a parametrically defined family of aggregation operators, a learning algorithm can be implemented that allows the fuzzy aggregation networks to outdo the theoretically predicted performance.

Figure 18.3 shows the basic structure of the fuzzy aggregation network, proposed by Keller et al. [1992a], for the rule "IF X is A, THEN Y is B" and the input "X is A'." In the figure, the u in a node represents a union operator, the i is an intersection operator, and the p_i are the adjustable parameters in these operators. Assume that the possibility distributions for A and A' are sampled at n points in their domain, and that for B at m points. The nodes at the bottommost layer compute a measure of dissimilarity between A and A' (i.e., the similarity between $\overline{A}$ and A'). Each node implements an intersection operation on corresponding sampled values from A' and $\overline{A}$. Although they are shown at two input nodes, the values of $\overline{A}$ are considered weights since they are independent of the input applied to the network. The center collection node is a union operator which has the effect of focusing on the highest position of disagreement between A and A'. Finally, the result "Y is B'" is generated as the pointwise union of each element of B with the disagreement index.

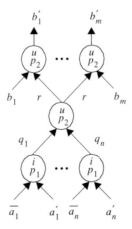

Figure 18.3 Fuzzy aggregation network.

The fuzzy aggregation network in Fig. 18.3 has the same structure as the fuzzy inference network in Fig. 18.2. However, they use different node functions and link weights. In fact, fuzzy aggregation networks also have the properties stated in Theorems 18.1, 18.2, and 18.4 no matter what types of union and intersection operators are utilized [Keller et al., 1992a].

Theorem 18.5

Consider the rule "IF X is A, THEN Y is B" and the input "X is A'." Suppose that A and A' are crisp subsets of their domain and that $A = A'$. Then the output of the fuzzy aggregation network is precisely B, whether B is crisp or fuzzy.

Proof: Let A be a crisp subset of its domain U. Then

$$a_i = \mu_A(u_i) = \begin{cases} 0 & \text{if } u_i \notin A \\ 1 & \text{if } u_i \in A. \end{cases}$$

Thus,

$$\bar{a}_i = \mu_{\bar{A}}(u_i) = \begin{cases} 1 & \text{if } u_i \notin A \\ 0 & \text{if } u_i \in A. \end{cases}$$

Using the notation from Fig. 18.3, we have

$$q_j = i(\bar{a}_j, a_j') = \begin{cases} 1 & \text{if } a_j = 0 \text{ and } a_j' = 1 \\ 0 & \text{else,} \end{cases}$$

and

$$r = u(q_1, \ldots, q_n) = \begin{cases} 1 & \text{if some } q_j = 1 \\ 0 & \text{if all } q_j = 0. \end{cases}$$

These two equalities follow from the basic properties of fuzzy intersection and union operators. Now, if $A' = A$, then each q_j will be equal to 0, and so $r = 0$. Now, $b_j' = u(r, b_j) = b_j$ since for all fuzzy union operators, $u(0, x) = x$. Hence, the output is "Y is B."

Theorem 18.6

Suppose that A and A' are nonempty crisp subsets of their domain U.

1. If $\bar{A} \cap A' \neq \emptyset$, then the result of the fuzzy aggregation network is "Y is UNKNOWN," that is, a possibility distribution consisting entirely of 1s.
2. If A' is more specific than A, that is, $A' \subseteq A$, then the output of the network is "Y is B."

Proof

1. Suppose that A and A' are proper crisp subsets of U and that $\bar{A} \cap A' \neq \emptyset$. Let $u_i \in \bar{A} \cap A'$. Then, $1 = \bar{a}_i = \mu_{\bar{A}}(u_i) = u_{A'}(u_i) = a_i'$. Thus, $q_i = i(\bar{a}_i, a_i') = 1$, and so $r = u(q_1, q_2, \ldots, q_n) = 1$. Finally, $b_j' = u(r, b_j) = u(1, b_j) = 1$ for all j. Hence, the output of the network is "Y is UNKNOWN."
2. Now suppose that A' is more specific than A. For crisp or fuzzy sets, this implies that $A' \subseteq A$ or $\mu_{A'}(u_i) \leq \mu_A(u_i)$ for all $u_i \in U$. Since $A' \subseteq A$, $\mu_{A'}(u_i) = 1$ implies $\mu_A(u_i) = 1$, and so $\mu_{\bar{A}}(u_i) = 0$. The existence of such a u_i is guaranteed since both A and A' are assumed to be nonempty. Thus, $q_i = i(\bar{a}_i, a_i') = 0$. Clearly, if $\mu_{A'}(u_j) = 0$, then $q_j = 0$. Therefore, $r = u(q_1, q_2, \ldots, q_n) = 0$ and $b_j' = u(r, b_j) = u(0, b_j) = b_j$. Hence, the network output is "Y is B."

Theorem 18.7

Suppose A, A', A'' are fuzzy subsets of U and that $A'' \subseteq A' \subseteq A$. Suppose also that the network outputs for inputs A' and A'' are B' and B'', respectively. Then $B \subseteq B'' \subseteq B'$; that is, as the inputs become more specific, so do the outputs (with the consequent distribution as a lower bound).

Proof: Suppose $A'' \subseteq A' \subseteq A$. Then we have $a_j'' = \mu_{A''}(u_j) \leq \mu_{A'}(u_j) = a_j' \leq \mu_A(u_j) = a_j$. Since all intersection operators are nondecreasing functions of each argument, $q_j'' = i(\bar{a}_j, a_j'') \leq q_j' = i(\bar{a}_j, a_j')$. Union operators are also nondecreasing, and so $r'' = u(q_1'', q_2'', \dots, q_n'') \leq r' = u(q_1', q_2', \dots, q_n')$, and finally, $b_i \leq b_i'' = u(r'', b_i) \leq u(r', b_i) = b_i'$.

The following theorems concern Yager union and Yager intersection operators specifically [see Eqs. (2.68) and (2.60)].

Theorem 18.8

Suppose that two fuzzy aggregation networks have identical union nodes. Suppose also that the first network (called the p_g net) has Yager intersection nodes with parameter p_g, that the second network (p_h net) has Yager intersection nodes with parameter p_h, and that $p_g \leq p_h$. Then, given a common input "X is A'," the outputs "Y is B'_{p_g}" and "Y is B'_{p_h}" satisfy $B'_{p_g} \subseteq B'_{p_h}$; that is, the p_g net produces a more specific output.

Proof: For the input distribution A', we have $\left(q_{p_g}\right)_j = i_{p_g}(\bar{a}_j, a_j')$ and $\left(q_{p_h}\right)_j = i_{p_h}(\bar{a}_j, a_j')$ for all j. According to the properties of Yager intersection operators, we have $\left(q_{p_g}\right)_j \leq \left(q_{p_h}\right)_j$. Since the union operators are identical and nondecreasing, we have $\left(b'_{p_g}\right)_i \leq \left(b'_{p_h}\right)_i$ for all i. Hence, $B'_{p_g} \subseteq B'_{p_h}$.

Theorem 18.9

Suppose that two fuzzy aggregation networks have identical intersection nodes and that the first network (called the p_g net) has Yager union nodes with parameter p_g, that the second network (p_h net) has Yager union nodes with parameter p_h, and that $p_g \leq p_h$. Then, given a common input, "X is A'," the outputs "Y is B'_{p_g}" and "Y is B'_{p_h}" satisfy $B'_{p_g} \subseteq B'_{p_h}$; that is, the p_g net is less specific than the p_h net.

Proof: In the current situation, both networks produce the same outputs $q_1, q_2, \dots, q_n$ at the first layer. Since $p_g \leq p_h$ according to the properties of Yager union operators, it follows that $u_{p_g}(q_1, q_2, \dots, q_n) \geq u_{p_h}(q_1, q_2, \dots, q_n)$; hence $\left(b'_{p_g}\right)_i \geq \left(b'_{p_h}\right)_i$ for all i. Therefore, $B'_{p_g} \supseteq B'_{p_h}$.

The above two theorems indicate that if the most specific output is desired, then the intersection nodes should be chosen with a small parameter value and the union nodes with a large value. However, producing the most specific output may not provide the appropriate response for inputs that are not proper subsets of the precondition.

We shall next introduce a method for training a Yager operator–based fuzzy aggregation network. Note that we can replace union and intersection nodes with averaging operators such as the generalized means operator [see Eq. (2.74)]. While they do not have as nice a theoretical basis, they possess a greater training capability since they have more defining parameters. Thus, less rigid network structures are necessary, and the resulting networks have the potential to learn complex precondition or consequent relationships. The training method described later can handle either of these situations. The goal of training the network in Fig. 18.3 is to obtain the parameter values p at each layer (i.e., parameter p_1 for each node at layer 1, parameter p_2 for the single node at layer 2 and for each node at layer 3) that minimize the following performance index J:

$$J = \sum_{i=1}^{m} w_i (b_i' - t_i)^2, \qquad (18.17)$$

where b_i' is the ith sample of the output possibility distribution, t_i is the ith sample of the target possibility distribution, and w_i is the weight of importance for t_i. The weights w_i are different when $t_i = 0$ and $t_i \neq 0$. The intuitive idea here is that those areas where the membership function is nonzero should be more important for determining network parameters than the larger region of the domain of discourse which does not belong to the support of the consequent distribution. For exponential variations of trapezoidal preconditions and consequents, for example, "MORE-OR-LESS," the region where the distributions differ is quite small. Therefore, different weights are used for the training algorithm in these areas. Many learning algorithms of neural networks can be used to train fuzzy aggregation networks based on the performance index J in Eq. (18.17). Among these, the back-propagation learning algorithm is the most representative learning rule.

18.2.3 Neural Network–Driven Fuzzy Reasoning

In this section, we shall consider neural network realization of the Takagi-Sugeno-Kang fuzzy inference model (TSK model) [Sugeno and Kang, 1988] introduced in Sec. 7.1.4. The basic idea of using neural networks to realize or generalize the TSK model is to implement the membership functions in the preconditions as well as the inference function in the consequents by proper neural networks. This approach can solve two main problems in fuzzy reasoning: the lack of a definite method for determining the membership functions and the lack of a learning function for self-tuning inference rules. The neural networks in the precondition part can learn proper membership functions, and those in the consequent part can learn the proper "action" of a rule.

One scheme for generalization of the TSK model using neural networks is the *neural network–driven fuzzy reasoning* (NDF) proposed by Takagi and Hayashi [1991]. The NDF algorithm constructs the fuzzy sets of the precondition part in a partial space of input using the back-propagation network. The inference function corresponding to the consequent is also constructed by a back-propagation network. Hence, the fuzzy inference rules in NDF have the following format:

$$R^s: \text{IF } \mathbf{x} = (x_i, \dots, x_n) \text{ is } A_s, \text{ THEN } y_s = \text{NN}_s (x_1, \dots, x_m), \qquad s = 1, 2, \dots, r, \qquad (18.18)$$

where r is the number of inference rules, A_s represents a fuzzy set of the precondition part of each inference rule, and $\text{NN}_s (\cdot)$ denotes a structure of model function characterized by a back-propagation network with input $(x_1, x_2, \dots, x_m)$ and output y_s. The number of variables m $(m \leq n)$ employed in $\text{NN}_s (\cdot)$ is determined by a method for selecting the optimum model described later. For the precondition part, a back-propagation network NN_{mem} is used for an overall expression of the preconditions. The way to determine membership functions in the precondition part using the neural network NN_{mem} is explained in Fig. 18.4. The network is trained on the input data (x_{i1}, x_{i2}), $i = 1, 2, \dots, N$, and the corresponding data attribution to the rule expressed by (R^1, R^2, R^3). The estimated values of the learned NN_{mem} are consid-

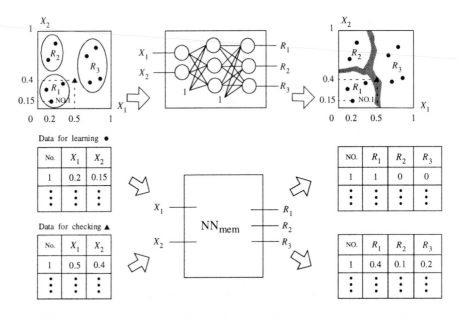

Figure 18.4 Decision on membership function in the precondition parts of rules. (Reprinted by permission of the publisher from "Construction of Fuzzy Interface Rules by NDF and NDFL," by I. Hayashi, H. Nomura, H. Yamasaki, and N. Wakami, *International Journal of Approximate Reasoning*, Vol. 6, No. 2, pages 241–266. Copyright © 1992 Elsevier Science Inc.)

ered to be the membership values of fuzzy sets in the precondition part because the estimated value represents the attribution of data to each rule.

Assume that in an NDF system, there are m inputs $x_1, x_2, \ldots, x_m$ and a single output y. The architecture of an NDF system is shown in Fig. 18.5, where NN_{mem} is the neural net-

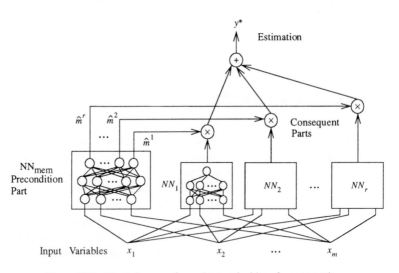

Figure 18.5 Block diagram of neural network–driven fuzzy reasoning.

work that determines the membership values of the precondition part of all rules, NN_s are the neural networks that determine control values and output y_s for the sth rule, y^* is the final control value, x_j is the input variable, and m^s is the membership value of the precondition part (i.e., the firing strength) of the sth rule. The design procedure for the NDF system is described in the following steps.

Step 1: *Selecting input-output variables and training data.* Define the output variable as y and the candidate input variables as x_j, $j = 1, 2,..., n$. In this step, the variables x_j, $j = 1, 2,..., m$, related to the observed values y_i, $i = 1, 2,..., N$, are selected by back-propagation networks. This is done by the backward elimination method described later using the sum of squared errors as a cost function. This eliminates the input variables attributed to noise and selects only those input variables that have significant correlations with the observed output values. Let $\mathbf{x}_i = (x_1,..., x_j,..., x_m)^T$ be the ith set of input values corresponding to the observed output value y_i, where $i = 1, 2,..., N$. The input-output data $(\mathbf{x}_i, y_i)$ are then divided into N_t training data (TRD) and N_c checking data (CHD), where $N_t + N_c = N$, the total number of input-output data.

Step 2: *Clustering the training data.* Divide the TRD into r classes of R^s by a clustering method, where $s = 1, 2,..., r$. The TRD for each R^s are expressed by $(\mathbf{x}_i^s, y_i^s)$, where $i = 1, 2,..., N_s$, provided that N_s is the number of TRD for R^s. The division of n-dimensional space into r here means that the number of inference rules is set to r.

Step 3: *Training NN_{mem} corresponding to the IF parts of fuzzy inference rules.* For each input vector of TRD, $\mathbf{x}_i \in R^s$, define a vector $\mathbf{m}_i = (m_i^1, m_i^2,..., m_i^r)^T$ such that $m_i^s = 1$ and $m_i^k = 0$ for $k \neq s$. An NN_{mem} with m input nodes and r output nodes is then trained on the input-output pairs $(\mathbf{x}_i, \mathbf{m}_i)$ for $i = 1, 2,..., N_t$. Hence, the NN_{mem} becomes capable of inferring the degree of attribution $\hat{m}_i^3$ of each checking data item $\mathbf{x}_i$ to R^s. The membership function of the IF part is thus defined as the inferred value $\hat{m}_i^3$ that is the output of the learned NN_{mem}, that is,

$$\mu_{A_s}(\mathbf{x}_i) = \hat{m}_i^s, \qquad i = 1, 2,..., N; s = 1, 2,..., r, \qquad (18.19)$$

where A_s represents the fuzzy set of the precondition part of the sth rule as defined in Eq. (18.18).

Step 4: *Training NN_s corresponding to the THEN part of the sth fuzzy inference rule.* The TRD input $x_{i1}^s, x_{i2}^s, ..., x_{im}^s$ and the output value y_i^s, $i = 1, 2,..., N_s$, are assigned to the input and output of the NN_s. This NN_s is the neural network of the THEN part in R^s. The training of NN_s is conducted so that the control value can be inferred. The CHD input values $x_{i1}, x_{i2},..., x_{im}$, $i = 1, 2,..., N_c$, are substituted into the obtained NN_s to obtain the sum E_m^s of the squared error:

$$E_m^s = \sum_{i=1}^{N_c} \{y_i - \mu_s(\mathbf{x}_i) \mu_{A_s}(\mathbf{x}_i)\}^2, \qquad (18.20)$$

where the estimated value $\mu_s(\mathbf{x}_i)$ is obtained as the output of NN_s. We can also calculate the error with weights by defining

$$E_m^s = \sum_{i=1}^{N_c} \mu_{A_s}(\mathbf{x}_i)\{y_i - \mu_s(\mathbf{x}_i)\,\mu_{A_s}(\mathbf{x}_i)\}^2 . \tag{18.21}$$

Step 5: *Simplifying the THEN parts by a backward elimination method.* Among the m input variables of an NN_s, one input variable x_p is arbitrarily eliminated, and the NN_s is trained again by using the TRD as in step 4. Equation (18.20) gives the squared error E_{m-1}^{sp} of the control value of the sth rule in the case of eliminating x_p. This E_{m-1}^{sp} can be estimated using the CHD:

$$E_{m-1}^{sp} = \sum_{i=1}^{N_c} \{y_i - \mu_s(\hat{\mathbf{x}}_i)\,\mu_{A_s}(\hat{\mathbf{x}}_i)\}^2 , \qquad p = 1, 2, \dots, m, \tag{18.22}$$

where $\hat{\mathbf{x}}_i = (x_{i,1}, \dots, x_{i,p-1}, x_{i,p+1}, \dots, x_{im})^T$. Comparing Eqs. (18.20) and (18.22), if

$$E_m^s > E_{m-1}^{sp}, \tag{18.23}$$

then the significance of the eliminated input variables x_p can be considered minimal and x_p can be discarded. The same operations are carried out for the remaining $(m-1)$ input variables. This elimination process is repeated until Eq. (18.23) will not hold for any remaining input variables. The model that gives the minimum E^s value is the best NN_s.

Step 6: *Decision on final output.* The following equation can derive the final control value y_i^*:

$$y_i^* = \frac{\sum_{s=1}^{r} \mu_{A_s}(\mathbf{x}_i)\,\mu_s(\mathbf{x}_i)}{\sum_{s=1}^{r} \mu_{A_s}(\mathbf{x}_i)} , \qquad i = 1, 2, \dots, N. \tag{18.24}$$

The following example illustrates the above procedure. Here, the term k layer $[u_1 \times u_2 \times \cdots u_k]$ represents the back-propagation network size, where u_i is the number of neurons in the input layer, hidden layer(s), and output layer, and k is the number of layers.

Example 18.2

[Takagi and Hayashi, 1991]. In this example, an NDF is trained on the data from $y = (1.0 + x_1^{0.5} + x_2^{-1} + x_3^{-1.5})^2$ and random noise x_4 using the following steps:

Step 1: A total of 40 input-output patterns $(x_1, x_2, x_3, x_4; y)$ are randomly chosen from the data generated by setting $x_1 = 1$ or 5, $x_2 = 1, 3,$ or 5, $x_3 = 1, 2, 3, 4,$ or 5, and $x_4 = 1$ or 5. These patterns are divided into two parts: 20 patterns for the training data and 20 patterns for the checking data; thus, $N_t = N_c = 20$, $N = 40$, and $k = 4$. Table 18.1 shows the result of the training for 15,000 iterations with a four-layer $(4 \times 3 \times 3 \times 1)$ network that uses all variables and a four-layer $(3 \times 3 \times 3 \times 1)$ network for the selection of input variables. Both training and checking data are used for these learning models. Since the estimation performance of the model that eliminates x_4 is similar

TABLE 18.1 Results of Backward Elimination
Using a Neural Network in Example 18.2

	Sum of Squared Errors
When all variables are used	0.0007
When x_1 is eliminated	0.3936
When x_2 is eliminated	0.1482
When x_3 is eliminated	0.0872
When x_4 is eliminated	0.0019

to that of the model that uses all variables relatively, input variable x_4 is negligible and can be ignored.

Step 2: The TRD are partitioned into two classes by using a conventional clustering method.

Step 3: A four-layer $(4 \times 3 \times 3 \times 2)$ network is trained for 5000 times to infer $m_i^s \in \{0, 1\}$, the degree of attribution of training data, $\mathbf{x}_i$, $i = 1, 2,..., 20$. By this training, the fuzzy number A_s in the IF parts is derived.

Step 4: The inference formula for determining the control value for the THEN parts of various control rules is identified. The first row in Table 18.2 shows the output errors E_3^s derived after 20,000 iterations of training of a four-layer $(3 \times 8 \times 8 \times 1)$ network.

Step 5: The sum of the squared error E_2^{sp} when one of the arbitrary input variables is removed from the IF parts with control rule R^s is derived. This sum, shown in Table 18.2, is obtained for control rules R^1 and R^2 after the learning of the four-layer $(2 \times 8 \times 8 \times 1)$ network for 10,000 to 20,000 iterations. Observe that all of $E_2^{1p} > E_3^1$ and $E_2^{2p} > E_3^2$ except $E_2^{21} < E_3^2$. Therefore, the obtained fuzzy model is expressed by

$$R^1: \text{ IF } \mathbf{x} = (x_1, x_2, x_3) \text{ is } A_1 \text{ , THEN } y_1 = \text{NN}_1 (x_1, x_2, x_3),$$

$$R^2: \text{ IF } \mathbf{x} = (x_1, x_2, x_3) \text{ is } A_2 \text{ , THEN } y_2 = \text{NN}_2 (x_2, x_3).$$

TABLE 18.2 Output Errors After Elimination
of Variables in Example 18.2

	Rule 1	Rule 2
When all variables are used	$E_3^1 = 27.86$	$E_3^2 = 1.93$
When x_1 is eliminated	$E_2^{11} = 42.84$	$E_2^{21} = 0.93$
When x_2 is eliminated	$E_2^{12} = 74.71$	$E_2^{22} = 119.61$
When x_3 is eliminated	$E_2^{13} = 55.27$	$E_2^{23} = 73.28$

18.3 NEURAL NETWORK–BASED FUZZY MODELING

18.3.1 Rule-Based Neural Fuzzy Modeling

Fuzzy modeling concerns the methods of describing the characteristics of a system using fuzzy inference rules. Fuzzy modeling methods have a distinguishing feature in that they can express complex nonlinear systems linguistically. However, it is not easy to identify the fuzzy rules and tune the membership functions of the fuzzy model of a nonlinear system. In this section, we shall introduce a fuzzy modeling method using neural fuzzy models with back-propagation learning [Horikawa et al. 1992]. This method can identify the fuzzy model of a nonlinear system automatically.

Three types of neural fuzzy models that realize three different types of fuzzy reasoning were proposed for fuzzy modeling [Horikawa et al., 1992]. We call these networks *fuzzy modeling networks* (FMNs). The three types of FMNs correspond to the three types of fuzzy reasoning introduced in Sec. 7.1.4. As in the networks introduced in the last section, the basic idea of the composition method of FMNs is to realize the process of fuzzy reasoning by the structure of a neural network and express the parameters of fuzzy reasoning by the connection weights of a neural network. FMNs can automatically identify the fuzzy rules and tune the membership functions by modifying the connection weights of the networks using the back-propagation learning algorithm.

The configurations of the three types of FMNs (types I, II, and III) are shown in Fig. 18.6, which also shows that the FMNs have two inputs (x_1, x_2), one output (y^*), and three membership functions in each precondition. It is observed that the membership functions in FMNs are realized by the network structures shown in Fig. 18.1. The circles and the squares in the figures represent the nodes of the networks. The notations w_c, w_g, w_f, w_s, w_a, w_r,

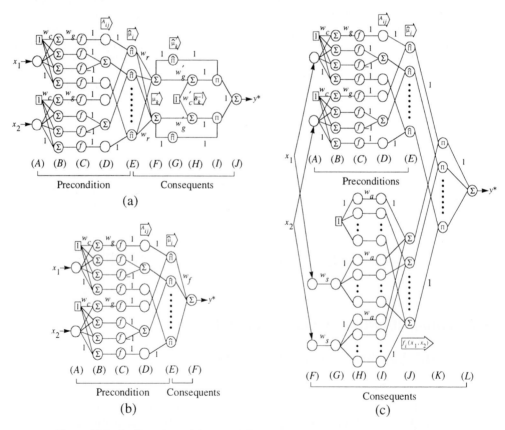

Figure 18.6 Configurations of fuzzy modeling networks. (a) Type I. (b) Type II. (c) Type III. (Adapted from Horikawa et al. [1992], © 1992 IEEE.)

w'_c, w'_g, and 1, -1 between the nodes indicate connection weights. The nodes with a symbol of 1 are the bias units with outputs of unity. The input-output relationships of the nodes with symbols f, $\sum$, $\prod$, and $\hat{\prod}$ are defined as

$$I_j^{(n)} = \sum_k w_{jk}^{(n,\,n-1)} O_k^{n-1},$$

(18.25)

$$f\colon\ O_j^{(n)} = \frac{1}{1 + \exp(I_j^{(n)})},$$

(18.26)

$$\sum\colon\ O_j^{(n)} = I_j^{(n)},$$

(18.27)

$$I_j^{(n)} = \prod_k w_{jk}^{(n,n-1)} O_k^{(n-1)},$$

(18.28)

$$\Pi\colon\ O_j^{(n)} = I_j^{(n)},$$

(18.29)

$$\hat{\Pi}\colon\ O_j^{(n)} = \frac{I_j^{(n)}}{\sum_k I_k^{(n)}},$$

(18.30)

where $I_j^{(n)}$ and $O_j^{(n)}$ are the input and output of the jth node in the nth layer, respectively, and $w_{jk}^{(n,\,n-1)}$ is the connection weight between the kth node in the $(n-1)$th layer and the jth node in the nth layer. The nodes without a symbol just deliver their inputs to succeeding layers.

According to the process of fuzzy reasoning, FMNs can be divided into precondition parts and consequent parts. The precondition part consists of layers A through E (see Fig. 18.6) and is common to all three types of FMNs. The membership functions $\mu_{A_{ij}}(\cdot)$ in the precondition are realized by layers A through D using the network structures in Fig. 18.1. As mentioned in Sec. 18.1 [see Eq. (18.2)], the weights w_c and w_g are the parameters that determine the central position and the gradient, respectively, of the sigmoid function in the nodes in layer C. The membership functions divide the input space into fuzzy subspaces, each of which corresponds to one fuzzy rule. The truth value (i.e., firing strength) of the fuzzy rule in each subspace is given by the product of the grades of the membership functions in the nodes in layer E as

$$\text{Inputs:}\ \ \mu_i = \prod_j \mu_{A_{ij}}(x_j),$$

(18.31)

$$\text{Outputs:}\ \ \hat{\mu}_i = \frac{\mu_i}{\sum_k \mu_k},$$

(18.32)

where μ_i is the truth value of the ith fuzzy rule and $\hat{\mu}_i$ is the normalized value of μ_i.

FMNs are categorized into types I, II, and III by the type of fuzzy reasoning realized in the networks in the *consequents* as follows:

Type I (*Consequent is a fuzzy variable*):

$$R_k^i\colon\ (\text{IF } x_1 \text{ is } A_{i1} \text{ AND } x_2 \text{ is } A_{i2}, \text{ THEN } y \text{ is } B_k) \text{ is } \tau_{R_k^i},$$

$$i = 1,\ldots, n;\ k = 1, 2,$$

(18.33)

$$\mu'_k = \sum_{i=1}^{n} \hat{\mu}_i \tau_{R_k^i}, \tag{18.34}$$

$$y^* = \frac{\sum_{k=1}^{2} \mu'_k \mu_{B_k}^{-1}(\mu'_k)}{\sum_{k=1}^{2} \mu'_k} = \sum_{k=1}^{2} \hat{\mu}'_k \mu_{B_k}^{-1}(\mu'_k), \tag{18.35}$$

where B_k are fuzzy sets in the consequents whose membership functions are defined in Fig. 18.7, $\tau_{R_k^i}$ is the linguistic truth value of the fuzzy rule R_k^i expressed by a single-ton in $[0, 1]$, μ'_k is the truth value of the consequent, and $\mu_{B_k}^{-1}(\cdot)$ is the inverse function of the membership function in the consequent $\mu_{B_k}(y)$. This consequent part consists of layers E through J in Fig. 18.6(a). The weights w_r in the figure represent $\tau_{R_k^i}$ in Eq. (18.33). The weights w'_c determine the positions where the grades of the membership functions in the consequents are zero, and the weights w'_g give the gradients of the membership functions. The outputs of the nodes in layers F and H give the values μ'_k and $\mu_{B_k}^{-1}(\mu'_k)$, respectively. Since $\tau_{R_k^i} \in [0, 1]$ and $\sum \hat{\mu}_i = 1$, the values of μ'_k are in the range of $[0, 1]$. This allows use of the linear activation functions realized in layers F through H for $\mu_{B_k}^{-1}(\mu'_k)$ instead of sigmoid functions. The normalized truth value in the consequent $\hat{\mu}'_k$ is calculated in layer G. The inferred value is obtained as the sum of the product of $\hat{\mu}'_k$ and $\mu_{B_k}^{-1}(\mu'_k)$ in layers I through J. This type of FMN uses the fuzzy reasoning of the first type discussed in Sec. 7.1.4 (see Figs. 7.5 and 7.6) together with the COA defuzzification method in Eq. (7.30).

Type II *(Consequent is a fuzzy singleton):*

$$R^i: \text{IF } x_1 \text{ is } A_{i1} \text{ AND } x_2 \text{ is } A_{i2}, \text{ THEN } y = f_i, \qquad i = 1, 2, \ldots, n, \tag{18.36}$$

$$y^* = \frac{\sum_{i=1}^{n} \mu_i f_i}{\sum_{i=1}^{n} \mu_i} = \sum_{i=1}^{n} \hat{\mu}_i f_i, \tag{18.37}$$

where R^i is the ith fuzzy rule, A_{i1} and A_{i2} are fuzzy sets in the preconditions, f_i is a constant, n is the number of fuzzy rules, and y^* is the inferred value. The consequent part consists of layers E through F in Fig. 18.6(b), and the weights w_f represent f_i in Eq. (18.36). The inferred value is given as the output of the node in layer F, which is the sum of the product of $\hat{\mu}_i$ and w_f. This type of FMN uses fuzzy reasoning of the second type as discussed in Sec. 7.1.4 (see Fig. 7.7), where the threshold membership function is used in the consequents.

Type III *(Consequent is a first-order linear equation):*

$$R^i: \text{IF } x_1 \text{ is } A_{i1} \text{ AND } x_{i2} \text{ is } A_{i2}, \text{ THEN } y = f_i(x_1, x_2), \qquad i = 1, 2, \ldots, n, \tag{18.38}$$

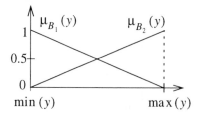

Figure 18.7 Membership functions in the consequent of a type I FMN.

$$y^* = \frac{\sum_{i=1}^{n} \mu_i f_i (x_1, x_2)}{\sum_{i=1}^{n} u_i} = \sum_{i=1}^{n} \hat{\mu}_i f_i (x_1, x_2),$$ (18.39)

where

$$f_i (x_1, x_2) = a_{i0} + a_{i1} x_1 + a_{i2} x_2, \qquad a_{ij}, j = 0, 1, 2 \text{ are constants.}$$ (18.40)

Layers F through L in Fig. 18.6(c) constitute this consequent. The weights w_s are the scaling factors of the input variables in the consequents and are fixed through the learning. In Eq. (18.40), a_{ij} ($j \neq 0$) are equal to the product of w_s and w_a. The inferred value of each fuzzy rule $f_i (x_1, x_2)$ is calculated as the output of a node in layer J. The products of $\hat{\mu}_i$ and $f_i (x_1, x_2)$ in Eq. (18.39) are calculated in layer K. Finally, the sum of the products in layer L is the inferred value of the fuzzy reasoning. This type of FMN uses fuzzy reasoning of the third type as discussed in Sec. 7.1.4.

All three types of FMNs are structured multilayer feedforward networks with differentiable activation functions. Hence, the back-propagation algorithm can be applied to these networks to identify the fuzzy rules by modifying the connection weights w_f, w_a, and w_r and tune the membership functions by updating w_c, w_g, and w'_c, w'_g.

We now consider the use of FMNs for fuzzy modeling. The process of identifying a fuzzy model is generally divided into identification of the preconditions and of the consequents. Also, each of the identifying processes is divided into identification of the structures and the parameters. The structures of a fuzzy model indicate a combination of input variables and the number of membership functions in the preconditions and in the consequents. Empirical studies show that the characteristics of a fuzzy model depend heavily on the structures rather than on the parameters of the membership functions. Selection of the structures is first performed once during the process, and the selection of structures of types I and II is made only in the preconditions since the structures of these types in the consequents are automatically determined with those in the preconditions. After the structures are selected, the FMNs identify the parameters of fuzzy models automatically. The following example illustrates the fuzzy modeling process using a type III FMN.

Example 18.3

[Horikawa et al., 1992]. In this example, the type III FMN is used to identify the same nonlinear system in Example 18.2 for comparison. Two sets of input-output patterns, TRD and CHD, are distinguished. The best structure of the fuzzy models is the first to be found using TRD and CHD. Table 18.3 lists the processes of identifying the structure in the preconditions using a type III FMN. In the table, $x_j [k]$ means that there are k membership functions in the preconditions for the input variable x_j. The input variables in the preconditions are increased step by step. In each case, the type III FMN learns either TRD or CHD until the output errors converge to a preset level. At the time of learning, only w_a is modified, and the membership functions are not tuned. The models identified with TRD and CHD are denoted as models T and C, respectively.

To compare the performance of the fuzzy models, an error index E is defined by

$$E = \sqrt{E_t^2 + E_c^2} + \text{UC},$$ (18.41)

where

$$E_t = \sqrt{\sum_{i=1}^{N_t} (y_i^T - y_i^{TT})^2},$$ (18.42)

TABLE 18.3 Identification of Structures of Fuzzy Models in Example 18.3

Steps in Identification		Structure		Criteria			
		Preconditions	Consequents	E_t	E_c	UC	E
1		$x_1[2]$	x_2, x_3, x_4	6.72	4.97	9.89	18.26
	○	$x_2[2]$	x_1, x_2, x_3, x_4	5.48	2.69	6.74	12.85
		$x_3[2]$	x_1, x_2, x_3, x_4	5.77	5.27	8.44	16.25
		$x_4[2]$	x_1, x_2, x_3	6.82	4.98	8.87	17.31
2		$x_1[2], x_2[2]$	x_1, x_2, x_3	4.46	3.31	10.73	16.29
		$x_2[3]$	x_1, x_3, x_4	4.37	2.71	9.06	14.20
	●	$x_2[2], x_3[2]$	x_1, x_2, x_3	2.46	1.75	6.66	9.68
		$x_2[2], x_4[2]$	x_1, x_2, x_3	3.34	2.06	14.25	18.18
3		$x_1[2], x_2[2], x_3[2]$	x_1, x_2, x_3	1.08	1.23	13.92	15.55
		$x_2[3], x_3[2]$	x_1, x_2, x_3	1.58	1.08	10.70	12.61
	○	$x_2[2] x_3[3]$	x_1, x_2, x_3, x_4	0.13	0.24	11.40	11.68
		$x_2[2], x_3[2], x_4[2]$	x_1, x_2, x_3	0.52	1.09	19.87	21.08

Adapted from Horikawa et al. [1992], © 1992 IEEE.

$$E_c = \sqrt{\sum_{i=1}^{N_c} (y_i^C - y_i^{CC})^2}, \qquad (18.43)$$

$$\text{UC} = \sqrt{\sum_{i=1}^{N_t} (y_i^{TC} - y_i^{TT})^2 + \sum_{i=1}^{N_c} (y_i^{CT} - y_i^{CC})^2}, \qquad (18.44)$$

where N_t and N_c are the numbers of TRD and CHD, respectively, y_i^T and y_i^C are the desired outputs in TRD and CHD, respectively, y_i^{TT} and y_i^{CT} are the values inferred by model T with the inputs from TRD and CHD, respectively, and y_i^{TC} and y_i^{CC} are the values inferred by model C with those from TRD and CHD, respectively. E_t and E_c indicate the errors of models T and C, respectively, and UC is the unbiasedness criterion. E defined in Eq. (18.41) is a criterion for evaluation of the structures of fuzzy models. The first term in Eq. (18.41) evaluates the accuracy of the models, and the second term evaluates their generality. According to this criterion in Table 18.3, the structure marked ○ is selected in each step and the structure marked ● is finally chosen as the best one. The table shows that the best structure has $x_2[2]$ and $x_3[2]$ in the preconditions and x_1, x_2 and x_3 in the consequents.

With the structure of the type III FMN identified, the next step is to train the parameters. In this learning process, the TRD is used for the identification of fuzzy models and the CHD is used for their evaluation. The type III FMN tunes membership functions by modifying the weights w_c, w_g, and w_c', w_g' and also identifies the fuzzy rules with w_r using TRD. The two membership functions in each precondition are labeled "Small (S)" and "Big (B)." Figure 18.8 shows the membership functions before and after the learning of the type III FMN. The dotted and solid lines in the figure are the membership functions before and after the learning, respectively. The identified fuzzy rules are listed in Table 18.4.

In addition to being used for fuzzy modeling, FMNs can also be applied to fuzzy control. This is done by viewing a fuzzy controller as the fuzzy model of an existing controller or an experienced operator. We shall focus on this topic of neural fuzzy control in the next chapter.

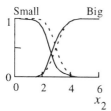 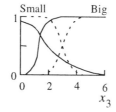

Figure 18.8 Membership functions of the identified model in Example 18.3.

TABLE 18.4 Fuzzy Rules of the Identified Model in Example 18.3

Preconditions		Consequents
x_2	x_3	$f_i(x_1, x_2, x_3)$
Small	Small	$15.6 + 2.59x_1 + 0.34x_2 - 0.15x_3$
Small	Big	$2.8 + 2.30x_1 + 0.01x_2 + 0.88x_3$
Big	Small	$6.3 + 2.31x_1 + 0.64x_2 - 0.37x_3$
Big	Big	$0.3 + 1.76x_1 + 0.14x_2 + 0.48x_3$

Adapted from Horikawa et al. [1992], © 1992 IEEE.

18.3.2 Neural Fuzzy Regression Models

In this section, we introduce methods for fuzzy regression analysis using neural networks. Let the given input-output patterns be $(\mathbf{x}_k, d_k)$, $k = 1, 2, \ldots, p$, where $\mathbf{x}_k = (x_{k1}, x_{k2}, \ldots, x_{kn})^T$ is the input vector of the kth pattern and d_k is the corresponding output. A fuzzy regression model for the given kth pattern can be represented as

$$Y(\mathbf{x}_k) = A_0 + A_1 x_{k1} + \cdots + A_n x_{kn}, \tag{18.45}$$

where parameters A_i are fuzzy numbers. Therefore, the estimated output value $Y(\mathbf{x}_k)$ is also a fuzzy number. Fuzzy regression analysis can be simplified to interval regression analysis, where interval regression models are employed. These models are also represented by Eq. (18.45), but parameters A_i are intervals. In this case, the estimated output value $Y(\mathbf{x}_k)$ is also an interval. In the following, we shall first introduce nonlinear interval regression methods using neural networks and then discuss the methods for deriving nonlinear fuzzy regression models based on interval regression models.

Interval regression models. A concept of interval regression analysis based on back-propagation networks has been proposed by Ishibuchi and Tanaka [1992ab]. This model uses two back-propagation networks. One network identifies the upper side of data intervals, and the other the lower side of data intervals. These two networks are trained independently. The aim of this method is to obtain a nonlinear interval regression model, and its learning algorithm is described as follows.

Let $g^+(\mathbf{x}_k)$ and $g^-(\mathbf{x}_k)$ be the outputs from two back-propagation networks (BPN$^+$ and BPN$^-$, respectively) corresponding to the input vector $\mathbf{x}_k$, where each network has n input nodes and a single output node. Two learning algorithms are required for the two networks BPN$^+$ and BPN$^-$ so that the outputs $g^+(\mathbf{x}_k)$ and $g^-(\mathbf{x}_k)$ approximately satisfy the following condition:

$$g^-(\mathbf{x}_k) \leq d_k \leq g^+(\mathbf{x}_k), \qquad k = 1, 2, ..., p. \tag{18.46}$$

In order to train BPN$^+$, the following cost function is defined:

$$E = \sum_{k=1}^{p} E_k = \frac{1}{2} \sum_{k=1}^{p} \alpha_k [d_k - g^+(\mathbf{x}_k)]^2, \tag{18.47}$$

where α_k is specified according to the following weighting scheme:

$$\alpha_k = \begin{cases} 1 & \text{if } d_k > g^+(\mathbf{x}_k) \\ \alpha & \text{if } d_k \leq g^+(\mathbf{x}_k), \end{cases} \tag{18.48}$$

where α is a small positive value in the open interval $(0, 1)$. Empirical study shows that a smaller value of α (e.g., $\alpha = 0.01$) leads to better satisfaction of the condition $d_k \leq g^+(\mathbf{x}_k)$. An extremely small value of α, however, makes the learning too slow. In order to accelerate learning speed and to make the approximation of Eq. (18.46) more accurate, a decreasing function instead of a constant α can be used in the weighting scheme in Eq. (18.48). One decreasing function is

$$\alpha(t) = \frac{1}{[1 + (t/2000)]^3}, \tag{18.49}$$

where t is the iteration number. Here learning is accelerated by relatively large values of $\alpha(t)$ in the early stage. Very small values of $\alpha(t)$ in the late stage of learning lead to good satisfaction of the constraint condition.

Using the back-propagation rule, a learning algorithm can be derived from the cost function in Eq. (18.47). Suppose that BPN$^+$ and BPN$^-$ are both three-layer feedforward networks with sigmoidal activation functions. Each network has n input nodes and a single output node. For the input-output pattern $(\mathbf{x}_k, d_k)$, the weights w_j (on the link from hidden node j to the output node) and w_{ji} (on the link from input node i to hidden node j) of the network BPN$^+$ are changed according to the following rules with learning constant η:

$$\Delta w_j = \eta \left(-\frac{\partial E_k}{\partial w_j} \right) = \eta \delta_k y_{kj}, \tag{18.50}$$

$$\Delta w_{ji} = \eta \left(-\frac{\partial E_k}{\partial w_{ji}} \right) = \eta \delta_{kj} x_{ki}, \tag{18.51}$$

where

$$\delta_k = \alpha_k (d_k - y_k) y_k (1 - y_k),$$
$$\delta_{kj} = y_{kj} (1 - y_{kj}) \delta_k w_j, \tag{18.52}$$

$y_k = g^+(\mathbf{x}_k)$ is the network output, and y_{kj} is the output of hidden node j when the input is $\mathbf{x}_k$. The output node bias θ and the hidden node j bias θ_j are updated in the same way. Notice that momentum terms can be added to Eqs. (18.50) and (18.51).

The use of the cost function in Eq. (18.47) for training the network BPN$^+$ can be explained as follows. Let us consider the case where α is a very small positive value in the weighting scheme [Eq. (18.48)]. In this case, if d_k is less than or equal to $g^+(\mathbf{x}_k)$, the weights w_j, w_{ji} and the biases θ, θ_j are slightly changed. On the other hand, if d_k is greater than $g^+(\mathbf{x}_k)$, the weights and the biases are changed substantially. Therefore, it can be expected that d_k is approximately less than or equal to $g^+(\mathbf{x}_k)$ after enough presentations of the pattern $\mathbf{x}_k$. This means that the constraint condition in Eq. (18.46) is approximately satisfied.

Similarly, to train the BPN$^-$ for determining $g^-(\mathbf{x}_k)$, we use the cost function in Eq. (18.47) with the following weighting scheme instead of Eq. (18.48):

$$\alpha_k = \begin{cases} \alpha & \text{if } d_k \geq g^-(\mathbf{x}_k) \\ 1 & \text{if } d_k < g^-(\mathbf{x}_k), \end{cases} \tag{18.53}$$

where α is a small positive value in $(0, 1)$. It is noted that the weighting scheme in Eq. (18.53) for $g^-(\mathbf{x})$ is the reverse of Eq. (18.48) for $g^+(\mathbf{x})$. In Eq. (18.53), we can also introduce the decreasing function $\alpha(t)$ in Eq. (18.49). A learning algorithm can also be derived from the cost function in Eq. (18.47). For the input-output pattern $(\mathbf{x}_k, d_k)$, the weights w_j and w_{ji} of the network BPN$^-$ are changed according to the learning rules [Eqs. (18.50)–(18.52)] with the weighting scheme in Eq. (18.53). This means that the two learning algorithms for determining $g^+(\mathbf{x})$ and $g^-(\mathbf{x})$ are the same except for the weighting schemes.

Using these two learning algorithms, we can determine the two functions $g^+(\mathbf{x})$ and $g^-(\mathbf{x})$ that approximately satisfy the condition $g^-(\mathbf{x}_k) \leq d_k \leq g^+(\mathbf{x}_k)$, $k = 1, 2,..., p$. A nonlinear interval model can be derived from these two functions as follows:

$$G(\mathbf{x}) = [g^+(\mathbf{x}), g^-(\mathbf{x})]. \tag{18.54}$$

Since the two function $g^+(\mathbf{x})$ and $g^-(\mathbf{x})$ are independently determined by the learning algorithms, there may be a case where $g^-(\mathbf{x}) \leq g^+(\mathbf{x})$ does not hold for all $\mathbf{x}$. If $g^-(\mathbf{x})$ is greater than $g^+(\mathbf{x})$ for some $\mathbf{x}$, then the interval model $G(\mathbf{x})$ is meaningless at that $\mathbf{x}$. To cope with such situations, the two functions $h^-(\mathbf{x})$ and $h^+(\mathbf{x})$ are introduced for modifying the interval model $G(\mathbf{x})$ as follows.

$$h^-(\mathbf{x}) = \begin{cases} g^-(\mathbf{x}) & \text{if } g^-(\mathbf{x}) \leq g^+(\mathbf{x}) \\ \frac{1}{2}(g^-(\mathbf{x}) + g^+(\mathbf{x})) & \text{if } g^-(\mathbf{x}) > g^+(\mathbf{x}), \end{cases} \tag{18.55}$$

$$h^+(\mathbf{x}) = \begin{cases} g^+(\mathbf{x}) & \text{if } g^-(\mathbf{x}) \leq g^+(\mathbf{x}) \\ \frac{1}{2}(g^-(\mathbf{x}) + g^+(\mathbf{x})) & \text{if } g^-(\mathbf{x}) > g^+(\mathbf{x}). \end{cases} \tag{18.56}$$

For these two functions, $h^-(\mathbf{x}) \leq h^+(\mathbf{x})$ holds for all $\mathbf{x}$. Hence, the following nonlinear models are always meaningful

$$G(\mathbf{x}) = [h^-(\mathbf{x}), h^+(\mathbf{x})]. \tag{18.57}$$

Example 18.4

[Ishibuchi and Tanaka, 1992a]. In order to illustrate the method for building a nonlinear interval model using the above learning algorithms, let us consider a numerical example whose input-output patterns are generated by the following mechanism:

$$x_k = 0.02 (k - 1), \qquad k = 1, 2,..., 51,$$

$$d_k = 0.2 \sin (2\pi x_k) + 0.2x_k^2 + 0.3 + (0.1x_k^2 + 0.05) \text{ rnd } [-1, 1], \tag{18.58}$$

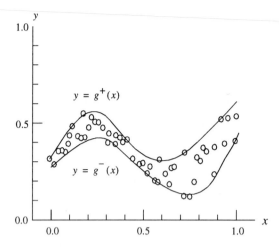

$y = g^+(x)$

$y = g^-(x)$

Figure 18.9 Simulation results from deriving the nonlinear interval model in Example 18.4. (Adapted from Ishibuchi and Tanaka [1992a]. Copyright © 1992 IOS Press. Reprinted by permission of IOS Press.)

where rnd $[-1, 1]$ represents a real number randomly generated in the interval $[-1, 1]$. We then apply the above learning algorithm with the decreasing function $\alpha(t)$ in Eq. (18.49) to determine $g^-(x)$ and $g^+(x)$ from these data using two three-layer back-propagation networks with five hidden nodes. The learning rate and momentum constant are set as 0.25 and 0.9, respectively. The simulation results after 10,000 iterations of each of the above learning algorithms are shown in Fig. 18.9. We can see from the figure that the condition $g^-(x_k) \leq d_k \leq g^+(x_k)$, $k = 1, 2, \ldots, 51$, is approximately satisfied.

Since normal back-propagation networks are used in the above approach, the learned networks are like "black boxes" and analysis of the interval representation is very difficult. Furthermore, it is difficult to find out which input mainly influences the output since the parameters are distributed in the networks. To cope with this problem, fuzzy modeling networks can be applied. Figure 18.10 shows a modified configuration of the type III FMN for identifying the interval regression model [Hashiyama et al., 1992]. The modified FMN has one precondition part and two consequent parts for identifying the upper and lower sides of the interval model. The input space is divided into fuzzy subspaces in the precondition part. In each fuzzy subspace, the upper- and lower-side models are obtained with the weighted linear equations. It is easy to apply the learning algorithm of interval regression analysis to the modified FMN. To identify the upper side [layers (F^+) to (J^+)], Eqs. (18.48)–(18.52) are used. To identify the lower side [layers (F^-) to (J^-)], Eqs. (18.50)–(18.53) are used.

Fuzzy regression models. From the interval model $G(\mathbf{x}) = [h^-(\mathbf{x}), h^+(\mathbf{x})]$ in Eqs. (18.55)–(18.56), we can derive a nonlinear fuzzy model [Ishibuchi and Tanaka, 1992ab]. We first introduce a method for doing this using symmetric triangular membership functions. Let us denote the nonlinear fuzzy model with the symmetric triangular membership function as $Y(\mathbf{x}) = (y_c(\mathbf{x}), y_w(\mathbf{x}))_L$ defined by

$$\mu_{Y(\mathbf{x})}(y) = \max\left\{1, 1 - \frac{|y - y_c(\mathbf{x})|}{y_w(\mathbf{x})}\right\}, \tag{18.59}$$

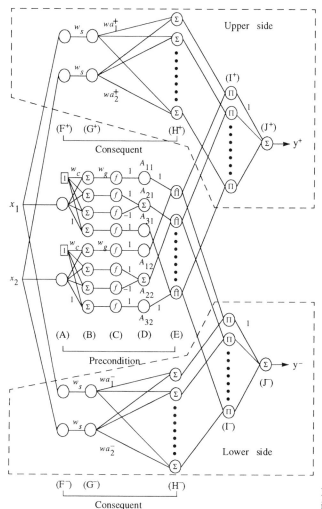

Figure 18.10 Modified type III FMN for interval regression modeling.

where $y_c(\mathbf{x})$ and $y_w(\mathbf{x})$ are the center and the spread of $Y(\mathbf{x})$, respectively. The problem now is to derive the fuzzy model $Y(\mathbf{x})$ such that for a given $\alpha \in (0, 1]$ it satisfies the following condition:

$$[Y(\mathbf{x})]_\alpha = [h^-(\mathbf{x}), h^+(\mathbf{x})] \qquad \text{for all } \mathbf{x}, \tag{18.60}$$

where $[Y(\mathbf{x})]_\alpha$ is the α-level set of the fuzzy model $Y(\mathbf{x})$. This problem can be easily solved as follows. From Eq. (18.59), we have

$$[Y(\mathbf{x})]_\alpha = [y_c(\mathbf{x}) - \alpha y_w(\mathbf{x}), y_c(\mathbf{x}) + \alpha y_w(\mathbf{x})]. \tag{18.61}$$

Hence, from Eqs. (18.60) and (18.61), we have the following relations for any α in $(0, 1)$:

$$y_c(\mathbf{x}) = \tfrac{1}{2}[h^+(\mathbf{x}) + h^-(\mathbf{x})],$$

$$y_w(\mathbf{x}) = \frac{1}{2\alpha}[h^+(\mathbf{x}) - h^-(\mathbf{x})]. \tag{18.62}$$

Using Eq. (18.62), we can derive the nonlinear fuzzy model $Y(\mathbf{x})$ that satisfies Eq. (18.60). This means that the α-level set of the derived fuzzy model $Y(\mathbf{x})$ approximately includes all the given patterns; that is, $d_k \in [Y(\mathbf{x}_k)]_\alpha$, $k = 1, 2, \ldots, p$.

We can also derive a nonlinear fuzzy model based on the trapezoid membership function. Let us define such a model, denoted by $Y(\mathbf{x}) = (y_1(\mathbf{x}), y_2(\mathbf{x}), y_3(\mathbf{x}), y_4(\mathbf{x}))$, as follows:

$$\mu_{Y(\mathbf{x})}(y) = \begin{cases} 0 & \text{if } y \le y_1(\mathbf{x}) \\ (y - y_1(\mathbf{x}))/(y_2(\mathbf{x}) - y_1(\mathbf{x})) & \text{if } y_1(\mathbf{x}) < y \le y_2(\mathbf{x}) \\ 1 & \text{if } y_2(\mathbf{x}) < y \le y_3(\mathbf{x}) \\ (y_4(\mathbf{x}) - y)/y_4(\mathbf{x}) - y_3(\mathbf{x})) & \text{if } y_3(\mathbf{x}) < y \le y_4(\mathbf{x}) \\ 0 & \text{if } y_4(\mathbf{x}) < y, \end{cases} \qquad (18.63)$$

where $y_1(\mathbf{x})$, $y_2(\mathbf{x})$, $y_3(\mathbf{x})$, and $y_4(\mathbf{x})$ correspond to four vertices of a trapezoid. Consider the case where the output values d_k in the given patterns inherently have some uncertainty. Assume that each output value d_k has uncertainty d_e. Hence, we only know that the true value of d_k is in the interval $[d_k - d_e, d_k + d_e]$. Then, by adding the uncertainty d_e to the given outputs d_k and to the interval model $G(\mathbf{x}) = [h^-(\mathbf{x}), h^+(\mathbf{x})]$, we derive the fuzzy model $Y(\mathbf{x})$ as follows:

$$\begin{aligned} y_1(\mathbf{x}) &= h^-(\mathbf{x}) - d_e, \\ y_2(\mathbf{x}) &= h^-(\mathbf{x}), \\ y_3(\mathbf{x}) &= h^+(\mathbf{x}), \\ y_4(\mathbf{x}) &= h^+(\mathbf{x}) + d_e. \end{aligned} \qquad (18.64)$$

From Eq. (18.64), we know that the kernel of the fuzzy model $Y(\mathbf{x})$ coincides with the interval model $G(\mathbf{x})$, that is $[Y(\mathbf{x})]_{\alpha=1} = [h^-(\mathbf{x}), h^+(\mathbf{x})]$. This means that all the given patterns are approximately included in the kernel of $Y(\mathbf{x})$. Equation (18.64) also indicates that the interval $[d_k - d_e, d_k + d_e]$ is approximately included in the support of the fuzzy model $Y(\mathbf{x}_k)$. The following example illustrates an application of the above techniques.

Example 18.5

[Ishibuchi and Tanaka, 1992a]. In this example, the techniques of neural fuzzy modeling are applied to a quality evaluation problem involving injection moldings. The quality of 15 injection moldings is evaluated by experts. Each expert assigns a rank of 5, 4, 3, 2, or 1 to each of the 15 injection moldings by observing the weld line of the surface, where 5 and 1 represent the highest and lowest evaluations, respectively. The problem here is to model the relation between the observation ranks given by experts and the gap depths of the weld lines as measured by a surface roughness tester.

Using the data given by the experts, we first determine the interval model $G(\mathbf{x}) = [h^-(\mathbf{x}), h^+(\mathbf{x})]$ in the same manner as in Fig. 18.9. The output functions of the neural networks are modified so that the values of $h^-(\mathbf{x})$ and $h^+(\mathbf{x})$ are in the closed interval $[1, 5]$. The simulation results are shown in Fig. 18.11(a) together with the given data denoted by closed circles. It is observed that the fuzziness involved in subjective judgments of experts is well

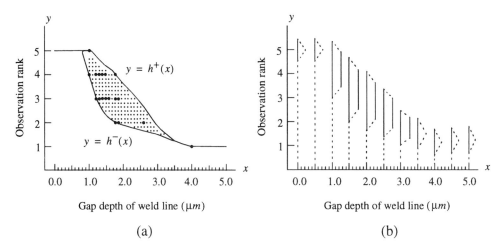

Figure 18.11 Quality evaluation problem in Example 18.5. (a) Derived interval model. (b) Estimated fuzzy numbers using the fuzzy regression model derived from the interval model in (a). (Adapted from Ishibuchi and Tanaka [1992a]. Copyright © 1992 IOS Press. Reprinted by permission of IOS Press.)

described in the interval model in Fig. 18.11(a). Since the ranks are restricted to integers, let us assume that each rank has an uncertainty of 0.5. Then we can construct the fuzzy model $Y(\mathbf{x})$ with the trapezoid membership function by setting $d_e = 0.5$ in Eq. (18.64). Estimated fuzzy numbers using the derived fuzzy model are shown in Fig. 18.11(b). From these figures, we can see that the fuzziness of the estimated fuzzy numbers is small at extremely large or small values of x. This means that the observation ranks have little uncertainty when the quality of the injection moldings is extremely high or low. On the other hand, we can also see that the fuzziness of the estimated fuzzy numbers is large at intermediate values of x. This means that the observation ranks have great uncertainty when the quality of the injection moldings is intermediate.

18.3.3 Neural Fuzzy Relational Systems

In this section, we focus on solving fuzzy relation equations through neural network training. Let X and Y be fuzzy sets in U and V, respectively, and let R be a fuzzy relation in $U \times V$. Consider the fuzzy relation equation

$$Y = X * R, \tag{18.65}$$

where $*$ is the compositional operator (e.g., max-min or max product). In Sec. 3.4, we introduced some analytical approaches to solving fuzzy relation equations. Here we shall consider some iterative approaches using neural learning. The problem here is to determine R when X and Y are given; that is, we consider problem P1 of the fuzzy relation equations described in Sec. 3.4. In other words, we want to model the relation between X (input) and Y (output) by a fuzzy relation R.

Let $U = \{x_1, x_2, \ldots, x_n\} \in \mathfrak{R}^n$ denote a finite set of input nodes and let $V = \{y_1, y_2, \ldots, y_m\} \in \mathfrak{R}^m$ be a finite set of output nodes. For the fuzzy relation equation $Y = X * R$, let us consider the max-min composition, that is,

$$\mu_Y(y_j) = \max_{x_i} \left(\min \left(\mu_x(x_i), \mu_R(x_i, y_j) \right) \right)$$

$$= \bigvee_{x_i \in U} \left[\mu_x(x_i) \wedge \mu_R(x_i, y_j) \right], \tag{18.66}$$

where X is a fuzzy set on U, Y is a fuzzy set on V, and R is a fuzzy relation $R: U \times V \rightarrow [0, 1]$ describing all relationships (connections) between input and output nodes. Using the usual vector and matrix notation, Eq. (18.66) can be written as

$$\mathbf{x} \circ \mathbf{R} \triangleq [\mu_X(x_1), \mu_X(x_2), \ldots, \mu_X(x_n)] \circ \begin{bmatrix} \mu_R(x_1, y_1) & \cdots & \mu_R(x_1, y_j) & \cdots & \mu_R(x_1, y_m) \\ \mu_R(x_2, y_1) & \cdots & \mu_R(x_2, y_j) & \cdots & \mu_R(x_2, y_m) \\ \vdots & & \vdots & & \vdots \\ \mu_R(x_n, y_1) & \cdots & \mu_R(x_n, y_j) & \cdots & \mu_R(x_n, y_m) \end{bmatrix}. \tag{18.67}$$

This equation indicates that the value $\mu_Y(y_j)$ comes from the composition of the vector $\mathbf{x}$ and the jth column of $\mathbf{R}$. This relationship can be realized by the neural network structure shown in Fig. 18.12 [Pedrycz, 1991a]. We call this network a *neural fuzzy relational network*. In this network, the output node is supposed to perform the min-max composition instead of the ordinary summation-product operation. However, following Eq. (18.66), we can deduce that to obtain the value at the output node, the input nodes should be activated to a certain degree, otherwise because of the lack of summation, the aggregation effect might be too low to activate the output; that is, the output node will never produce a significant output value. To overcome this shortcoming and obtain the entire unit interval of admissible values at the output node, a bias $\theta \in [0, 1]$ is added to each output node as follows:

$$\mu_Y(y) = \max \left[\max_{x_i} \left(\min \left(\mu_x(x_i), \mu_R(x_i, y) \right) \right), \theta(y) \right]. \tag{18.68}$$

Like an ordinary neuron, the bias can be treated as an extra input node constantly driven by the input value to 1.0. Equation (18.68) is thus the activation function used in the output node of the neural fuzzy relational network (the input nodes just pass input data forward). From this equation, it is noted that all possible values reported at this output node are not lower than this bias.

We shall now introduce the learning algorithm proposed by Pedrycz [1991a] for the neural fuzzy relational network. First, we need to define a proper performance index to be optimized within the learning process. Although it is quite common to use the Euclidean distance between the target value and the actual network output, a new performance index

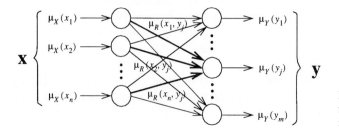

Figure 18.12 Neural fuzzy relational network for solving problem P1 of the fuzzy relation equations in Sec. 3.4.

called the *equality index* is proposed, which is strongly tied in with set-theoretic and logic-based techniques and is defined as

$$E\left(\mu_T(y), \mu_Y(y)\right) = \tfrac{1}{2}\left[\left(\mu_T(y) \to \mu_Y(y)\right) \wedge \left(\mu_Y(y) \to \mu_T(y)\right)\right.$$
$$\left. + \left(\mu_{\overline{T}}(y) \to \left(\mu_{\overline{Y}}(y)\right) \wedge \left(\left(\mu_{\overline{Y}}(y) \to \left(\mu_{\overline{T}}(y)\right)\right)\right], \right. \tag{18.69}$$

where $\mu_T(y)$ denotes a target (membership) value at the output node y and $\mu_Y(y)$ is the corresponding actual output of the network. The $\to$ denotes *implication* specified between two grades of membership. The first component in Eq. (18.69) describes a degree of equality between $\mu_T(y)$ and $\mu_Y(y)$; that is, it is viewed as the minimum degree to which $\mu_T(y)$ implies $\mu_Y(y)$, and vice versa. The second component preserves the same structure as the first one with the only difference that it applies to components of the values observed at T and Y, where $\mu_{\overline{T}}(y) = 1 - \mu_T(y)$. Since there is more than one way to express the implications, the implications are directly induced by *t*-norms (see Sec. 2.2.2) and defined by

$$\mu_T(y) \to \mu_Y(y) = \sup\{z \in [0, 1] \mid \mu_T(y)\, t z \le \mu_Y(y)\}, \tag{18.70}$$

where t is some *t*-norm. We shall use the *t*-norm given by

$$a\, t\, b = \max(0, a + b - 1), \qquad a, b \in [0, 1], \tag{18.71}$$

which is known as the *Lukasiewicz AND conjunction*. The implication induced by this *t*-norm is the well-known *Lukasiewicz implication* defined by

$$\mu_T(y) \to \mu_Y(y) = \begin{cases} \mu_Y(y) - \mu_T(y) + 1 & \text{if } \mu_T(y) > \mu_Y(y) \\ 1 & \text{otherwise.} \end{cases} \tag{18.72}$$

Inserting Eq. (18.72) into Eq. (18.69), we obtain the following expression for the equality index:

$$E\left(\mu_T(y), \mu_Y(y)\right) = \begin{cases} 1 + \mu_T(y) - \mu_Y(y) & \text{if } \mu_Y(y) > \mu_T(y) \\ 1 + \mu_Y(y) - \mu_T(y) & \text{if } \mu_Y(y) < \mu_T(y) \\ 1 & \text{if } \mu_Y(y) = \mu_T(y). \end{cases} \tag{18.73}$$

A graphical illustration of the equality index for $\mu_T(y)$ and $\mu_Y(y)$ taking all values in their domain is given in Fig. 18.13. From this figure, one learns that it is highly regular around its maximal value. This fact along with a piecewise linear form of the dependency makes

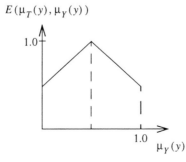

Figure 18.13 Equality index $E(\mu_T(y), \mu_Y(y))$ viewed as a function of one argument, $\mu_T(y)$ fixed.

this index especially useful for learning purposes as a good candidate for the performance index. Because of its nature, the goal in learning processes will be to maximize its value.

With the performance index chosen, we shall next derive the learning algorithm. For notational simplicity, we use x, y or x_i, y_i to denote inputs and outputs of the neural fuzzy relational network and t_i for target outputs in the following. In practice, they represent membership degrees $\mu_X(x)$, $\mu_Y(y)$, $\mu_X(x_i)$, $\mu_Y(y_i)$, and $\mu_T(t_i)$, respectively.

First, consider a single-intput–single-output network of the following form:

$$ y = f(x; a, \theta) = (x \wedge a) \vee \theta, \tag{18.74} $$

where x is an input, a and θ are the parameters that need to be determined, and a is equivalent to the fuzzy relational grade $\mu_R(x, y)$ in Eq. (18.68). For estimation purposes, we are given a set of input-output pairs (x_i, t_i), $i = 1, 2, \ldots, N$, where t_i is the target value the network is going to achieve when activated by x_i. An overall performance index is formed as a sum of equality indexes $E(t_i, y_i)$, $i = 1, 2, \ldots, N$, with y_i the network output, where the input value equals x_i:

$$ Q = \sum_{i=1}^{N} E(t_i, y_i). \tag{18.75} $$

Since our goal is to maximize the performance index, the problem now is to find the derivatives $\Delta a = \partial Q / \partial a$ and $\Delta \theta = \partial Q / \partial \theta$ such that the parameters a and θ are updated by the following gradient-descent rules:

$$ a(k+1) = a(k) + \alpha_1(k)\,\Delta a, $$
$$ \theta(k+1) = \theta(k) + \alpha_2(k)\,\Delta\theta, \tag{18.76} $$

where $\alpha_1(k)$ and $\alpha_2(k)$ are nonincreasing functions of k which underline the decreasing influence of increments Δa and $\Delta\theta$ on the values of the parameters already being accumulated. In the limit, $\alpha_1(k)$ and $\alpha_2(k)$ usually approach 0. For example, we can set $\alpha_1(k) = \alpha_2(k) = 1/(\sqrt{k}+1)$ or $1/(5\sqrt[4]{k}+10)$. A way of determining the derivatives Δa and $\Delta\theta$ is presented in the following discussion.

The sum of equality indexes in Eq. (18.75) can be split into three groups, depending upon the relationship between y_i and t_i:

$$ Q = \sum_{i:\, y_i > t_i} E(t_i, y_i) + \sum_{i:\, y_i = t_i} E(t_i, y_i) + \sum_{i:\, y_i < t_i} E(t_i, y_i), \tag{18.77} $$

where $i: y_i > t_i$ denotes index i such that $y_i > t_i$ and other summation indexes can be similarly interpreted. From Eq. (18.73) we have

$$ Q = \sum_{i:\, y_i > t_i} (1 + t_i - f(x_i; a, \theta)) + \sum_{i:\, y_i = t_i} 1 + \sum_{i:\, y_i < t_i} (1 + f(x_i; a, \theta) - t_i). \tag{18.78} $$

Then the derivatives become

$$ \Delta a = \frac{\partial Q}{\partial a} = -\sum_{i:\, y_i > t_i} \frac{\partial f(x_i; a, \theta)}{\partial a} + \sum_{i:\, y_i < t_i} \frac{\partial f(x_i; a, \theta)}{\partial a}, $$

$$ \Delta \theta = \frac{\partial Q}{\partial \theta} = -\sum_{i:\, y_i > t_i} \frac{\partial f(x_i; a, \theta)}{\partial \theta} + \sum_{i:\, y_i < t_i} \frac{\partial f(x_i; a, \theta)}{\partial \theta}. \tag{18.79} $$

For derivatives of minimum and maximum, we have the following expression [see Eq. (18.74)]:

$$\frac{\partial f(x_i; a, \theta)}{\partial a} = \frac{\partial}{\partial a} \left[(a \wedge x_i) \vee \theta \right] = \begin{cases} \partial a/\partial a & \text{if } (a \wedge x_i) \geq \theta \text{ and } a \leq x_i \\ \partial \tau/\partial a & \text{otherwise,} \end{cases} \tag{18.80}$$

where τ stands for the expression that does not include the variable a. Then we have the following result:

$$\frac{\partial}{\partial a} \left[(a \wedge x_i) \vee \theta \right] = \begin{cases} 1 & \text{if } \Phi(x_i; a, \theta), \\ 0 & \text{otherwise,} \end{cases} \tag{18.81}$$

where Φ stands for the conjunction of two predicates; that is,

$$\Phi(x_i; a, \theta) : \text{(i) } a \wedge x_i \geq \theta \quad \text{and} \quad \text{(ii) } a \leq x_i. \tag{18.82}$$

In other words, $\Phi(x_i; a, \theta) = 1$ if both conditions (i) and (ii) hold and $\Phi(x_i; a, \theta) = 0$, otherwise. The same applies for the second parameter of the function, where its derivative is controlled by a single predicate $\Psi(x_i; a, \theta)$,

$$\Psi(x_i; a, \theta) : \quad \theta \geq a \wedge x_i. \tag{18.83}$$

Overall, the increments Δa and $\Delta \theta$ are described as

$$\Delta a = - \sum_{i:\, y_i > t_i} \Phi(x_i; a, \theta) + \sum_{i:\, y_i < t_i} \Phi(x_i; a, \theta),$$

$$\Delta \theta = - \sum_{i:\, y_i > t_i} \Psi(x_i; a, \theta) + \sum_{i:\, y_i < t_i} \Psi(x_i; a, \theta). \tag{18.84}$$

Because of the Boolean character of these predicates, the increments Δa and $\Delta \theta$ are bounded by having values between $-N$ and N.

By including momentum terms in Eq. (18.76), the learning algorithm can be concisely summarized as follows:

Step 1: Initiate the parameters a and θ; that is, assign the values of $a(1), \theta(1)$.

Step 2: Cyclically process the data $(x_i; t_i)$, $i = 1, 2,..., N$, $k = 1, 2,...$, and update the values of a and θ accordingly (on-line variant of learning):

$$a(k+1) = a(k) + \alpha_1(k) \left[\frac{\Delta a(k+1)}{N} + \eta \frac{\Delta a(k)}{N} \right],$$

$$\theta(k+1) = \theta(k) + \alpha_2(k) \left[\frac{\Delta \theta(k+1)}{N} + \eta \frac{\Delta \theta(k)}{N} \right], \tag{18.85}$$

where η is a momentum constant and $\Delta a(\cdot)$ and $\Delta \theta(\cdot)$ are given by Eq. (18.84).

In visualizing the convergence properties, the following theorem provides a straightforward illustration of the performance of the learning method.

Theorem 18.10

[Pedrycz, 1991a]. For the performance index $\hat{Q} = E(c, x)$, the updating process of x,

$$x(k+1) = x(k) + \alpha(k)\frac{\partial\hat{Q}}{\partial x}, \qquad (18.86)$$

with the derivative computed as Eqs. (18.77)–(18.84), converges to c in a single step.

Proof: From Eq. (18.73), the derivative $\partial\hat{Q}/\partial x$ is expressed as

$$\frac{\partial\hat{Q}}{\partial x} = \begin{cases} 1 & \text{if } x < c \\ 0 & \text{if } x = c \\ -1 & \text{if } x > c. \end{cases} \qquad (18.87)$$

Furthermore, let the initial starting value of $x(1)$ be set to zero and let $\alpha(k)$ be considered a harmonic sequence, namely, $\alpha(k) = |c|/k$. Then

$$x(2) = x(1) + \alpha(1)\frac{\partial\hat{Q}}{\partial x} = c.$$

Next, consider the learning scheme for the neural fuzzy relational network with n inputs and a single output. For clarity, all weight parameters are collected in a single vector $\mathbf{a} = (a_1, a_2, \ldots, a_n)^T$, where a_i is equivalent to the fuzzy relational grade $\mu_R(x_i, y)$ in Eq. (18.68). The vectors $\mathbf{x}_1, \mathbf{x}_2, \ldots, \mathbf{x}_N$ and numbers $y_1, y_2, \ldots, y_N$ denote the learning or training set, where each $\mathbf{x}_i$ is a vector of values observed at the input nodes,

$$\mathbf{x}_i = (x_{i1}, x_{i2}, \ldots, x_{in})^T. \qquad (18.88)$$

Using this vector notation, the network output is given by

$$y_i = f(\mathbf{x}_i; \mathbf{a}, \theta) = \left(\bigvee_{j=1}^{n} (a_j \wedge x_{ij}) \right) \vee \theta, \qquad i = 1, 2, \ldots, N. \qquad (18.89)$$

To derive the learning algorithm, the first step is to calculate the derivative of the performance index Q with respect to the lth coordinate of $\mathbf{a}$, $l = 1, 2, \ldots, n$:

$$\Delta\mathbf{a} = \frac{\partial Q}{\partial \mathbf{a}} = \left[\frac{\partial Q}{\partial a_1}, \frac{\partial Q}{\partial a_2}, \ldots, \frac{\partial Q}{\partial a_n} \right],$$

$$\Delta\theta = \frac{\partial Q}{\partial \theta}. \qquad (18.90)$$

Similar to Eqs. (18.80)–(18.84), we have

$$\frac{\partial f(\mathbf{x}_i; \mathbf{a}, \theta)}{\partial a_s} = \frac{\partial}{\partial a_s}\left[\left(\bigvee_{j=1}^{n} (a_j \wedge x_{ij}) \right) \vee \theta \right]$$

$$= \begin{cases} \partial a_s/\partial a_s & \text{if } \bigvee_{j=1}^{n} (a_j \wedge x_{ij}) \geq \theta, \; \bigvee_{j=1, j\neq s}^{n} (a_j \wedge x_{ij}) \leq a_s \wedge x_{is}, \text{ and } a_s \leq x_{is} \\ \partial \tau/\partial a_s & \text{otherwise,} \end{cases} \qquad (18.91)$$

where τ does not depend on the parameter a_s. Hence, the predicate $\Phi\,(\mathbf{x}_i; \mathbf{a}, \theta)$ reads like a conjunction of three components:

$$\Phi: \text{(i)} \bigvee_{j=1}^{n} (a_j \wedge x_{ij}) \ge \theta, \quad \text{(ii)} \bigvee_{j=1, j\neq s}^{n} (a_j \wedge x_{ij}) \le a_s \wedge x_{is}, \quad \text{(iii)} \; a_s \le x_{is}. \tag{18.92}$$

The predicate for the increment of θ is the same as in the previous network:

$$\Psi: \bigvee_{j=1}^{n} (a_j \wedge x_{ij}) \le \theta \tag{18.93}$$

With $\Delta\mathbf{a}$ and $\Delta\theta$ derived, the vector $\mathbf{a}$ and parameter θ can be updated according to the formulas in Eq. (18.85) with scalar $a\,(\cdot)$ being replaced by vector $\mathbf{a}\,(\cdot)$. For the case of multiple output nodes, the above learning process is performed separately for each output node.

Example 18.6

[Pedrycz, 1991a]. The data set used for learning in the neural fuzzy relational network with $n = 4$ input nodes and $m = 3$ output nodes consists of four pairs $(\mathbf{x}_i, \mathbf{y}_i)$: $([0.3, 1.0, 0.5, 0.2]$, $[0.7, 0.5, 0.6])$, $([0.1, 1.0, 1.0, 0.5]$, $[0.7, 1.0, 0.6])$, $([0.5, 0.7, 0.2, 1.0]$, $[0.7, 0.7, 0.6])$, and $([1.0, 0.7, 0.5, 0.3]$, $[1.0, 0.5, 0.6])$. As mentioned before, the process of learning is completed separately for each output node. All the weights are summarized in a (4×3)-dimensional matrix. The values of the biases are collected as the entries of a three-dimensional vector Θ.

In the simulations, we set $\alpha_1\,(k) = \alpha_2\,(k) = 1/(\sqrt{k} + 1)$ and $\eta = 0.2$. Three different initial conditions are used.

1. $\mathbf{R} = 1$ and $\Theta = 0$ ($\mathbf{R}$ and Θ consisting of all 1s and 0s, respectively.). The values of the obtained weights are equal to

$$\mathbf{R} = \begin{bmatrix} 1.00 & 0.48 & 0.60 \\ 0.70 & 0.48 & 0.58 \\ 0.69 & 1.00 & 0.60 \\ 0.70 & 0.70 & 0.60 \end{bmatrix}, \quad \Theta = [0, 0, 0].$$

The values of the performance index for y_1, y_2, and y_3 are equal to 3.99, 3.99, and 3.98, respectively.

2. $\mathbf{R} = 1$ and $\Theta = 1$ ($\mathbf{R}$ and Θ consisting of all 1s). The trained weights and biases are

$$\mathbf{R} = \begin{bmatrix} 1.00 & 0.48 & 0.53 \\ 0.49 & 0.49 & 0.49 \\ 0.53 & 1.00 & 0.53 \\ 0.53 & 0.70 & 0.53 \end{bmatrix}, \quad \Theta = [0.70, 0.50, 0.60].$$

As before, the performance index attains maximal values. Observe that the values of the weights are lower in comparison to the first case. This is primarily caused by nonzero initial conditions of the biases. Additionally, the biases are equal to the minimal values observed at the output nodes of the network, compared to the learning set of data.

3. $\mathbf{R} = 0.5$ and $\Theta = 0.5$ ($\mathbf{R}$ and Θ consisting of all 0.5s.). The process of learning becomes much faster in comparison to the previous simulations. Nevertheless, for the first output node, the performance index attains a lower value equal to $Q = 3.69$. For the remaining

output nodes, we obtain maximal possible values of Q. The weights and biases derived in this way are

$$\mathbf{R} = \begin{bmatrix} 0.59 & 0.49 & 0.56 \\ 0.70 & 0.47 & 0.59 \\ 0.63 & 1.00 & 0.57 \\ 0.59 & 0.70 & 0.56 \end{bmatrix}, \quad \Theta = [0.5, 0.5, 0.5].$$

The above learning process may potentially suffer from the shortcoming of deterioration of its convergence properties. Referring to Eqs. (18.88)–(18.93), one can observe that the increments causing all the changes in the weights a_j, $j = 1, 2,..., n$, or the biases θ_i, $i = 1, 2,..., n$, have a strict Boolean character, being equal to either 0 or 1. It might happen, however, that with a certain configuration of weights and data presented at the inputs of the network, all the increments are identically equal to zero. This may subsequently lead to a slow convergence. To alleviate this problem, we can consider a relaxed version of a strict Boolean predicate "being equal" by using a multivalued fuzzy version of a crisp predicate "being included." This predicate will describe a degree of containment. More details can be found in [Pedrycz, 1991a].

18.4 CONCLUDING REMARKS

We have described several neural realizations of fuzzy membership function, fuzzy logic operators, fuzzy inference, fuzzy reasoning, and fuzzy modeling. Other approaches for realizing fuzzy logic operations, syllogisms, and extension principles using neural networks can be found in [Pao, 1989; Hsu et al., 1992]. For using neural networks for the task of fuzzy inference, Keller and Tahani [1992ab] proposed a three-layer feedforward neural network for fuzzy logic inference of conjunctive clause rules. Nie and Linkens [1992] realized fuzzy logic inference by normal (back-propagation) neural networks in which any two consecutive layers are fully connected. Keller, Hayashi, and Chen [1993] suggested an *additive hybrid fuzzy aggregation network* by adopting compensative hybrid operators. Hayashi et al. [1992] proposed a structure called *neural network–driven fuzzy reasoning with a learning function* (NDFL) for realizing the TSK inference model. This structure can obtain the optimal coefficients of linear equations in consequent parts by using a pattern search method. Takagi et al. [1992] proposed a neural network model called *neural networks designed on approximate reasoning architecture* (NARA). NARA allows easier analysis of a neural network for the purpose of performance improvement by incorporating knowledge structure into the neural network.

For rule-based neural fuzzy modeling, Horikawa et al. [1993] proposed a way to identify a fuzzy model with a minimal number of membership functions in the preconditions. Nakayama et al. [1992] applied FMNs to steer a large ship smoothly through multiple gates in demonstrating the acquisition of control strategy using FMNs. Furuhashi et al. [1993] used one FMN to obtain a fuzzy model of the controlled object (plant) and another FMN to acquire a fuzzy model for the controller. Then the stability of this fuzzy control system was analyzed based on linguistic rules.

Another approach to solving fuzzy relation equations using neural networks can be found in [Wang, 1993a]. Other interesting and related topics involving neural fuzzy relation equations include the *neural fuzzy decision systems* considered in [Francelin and Gomide, 1993] and the *neural fuzzy logic programming* discussed in [Eklund and Klawonn, 1992].

Another important topic related to neural fuzzy systems is the *evolutive neural fuzzy system* (ENFS) described by Machado and Rocha [1992]. The ENFS introduces evolutive learning techniques to neural fuzzy systems. It has been applied in disclosing the existing knowledge in natural language databases such as medical files, sets of interviews, and reports on engineering operations [Rocha et al., 1992].

18.5 PROBLEMS

18.1 Derive the exact formula of the pseudotrapezoidal membership function composed of two sigmoid functions as illustrated in Fig. 18.1(c). Check the similarities of this function with the trapezoidal membership function and the Gaussian membership function.

18.2 Design a MINNET that is similar to the MAXNET except that the former can identify and pass the minimum value of all its inputs. Explain the characteristics and function of the designed MINNET.

18.3 Check the difference between the softmin operator in Eq. (18.3) and the standard minimum operator. Find the derivative of the softmin operator with respect to a. Compare this derivative to the function $f(a, b)$, where $f(a, b) = 1$ if $a \leq b$, and $f(a, b) = 0$ if $a > b$.

18.4 **(a)** Assume f is an OWA operator of size $n = 6$. Let the weighting vector be $\mathbf{v} = (0.05, 0.25, 0.2, 0.1, 0.05, 0.35)^T$. What are $f(0.8, 1.2, 0.3, 0.9, 1.5, 2.6)$ and $f(2.1, 3.5, 0.5, 1.4, 2.2, 1.6)$?

    (b) Figure 2.6 shows the full scope of fuzzy aggregation operations. In this figure, indicate the range of fuzzy aggregation operations that the OWA operator can realize.

18.5 Rework Example 18.1 using the disagreement measure d_k^2 in Eq. (18.11) and the disagreement measure d_k^3 in Eq. (18.13).

18.6 Prove Corollaries 18.1, 18.2, and 18.3 in Sec. 18.2.1.

18.7 **(a)** Constructed a fuzzy aggregation network for the rule "IF X is Low, THEN Y is High" using the Yager union and Yager intersection operators, where

$$A = \text{``Low''} = \{1, 0.67, 0.33, 0, 0, 0, 0, 0, 0, 0, 0\}$$

$$B = \text{``High''} = \{0, 0, 0, 0, 0, 0, 0.2, 0.4, 0.6, 0.8, 1\}.$$

    (b) Given two fuzzy sets $A' = \{1, 0.45, 0.11, 0, 0, 0, 0, 0, 0, 0, 0\}$ and $A'' = \{1, 0.3, 0.04, 0, 0, 0, 0, 0, 0, 0, 0\}$ verify Theorems 18.7–18.9.

18.8 Describe the differences between partitioning the input space used by the conventional TSK fuzzy inference rules and by the NDF algorithm. Discuss the advantages and disadvantages of these differences.

18.9 Redo Example 18.2 to train an NDF network but use the training data set obtained from $y = \left(2.0 + x_1^{-0.5} + x_2^{1.5} + x_3^{-2.5} + x_4^{0.5}\right)^{2.5}$.

18.10 Draw the type III FMN that represents the following TSK fuzzy rules:

IF x_1 is A_1 AND x_2 is A_2, THEN $y = 0.1x_1 + 0.5x_2$.

IF x_1 is A_1 AND x_2 is A_3, THEN $y = 0.2x_1 + 0.7x_2$.

IF x_1 is A_2 AND x_2 is A_3, THEN $y = 0.3x_1 + 0.9x_2$.

where A_1, A_2, and A_3 represent the fuzzy sets "S," "M," and "L," respectively, as shown in Fig. 18.1(b).

18.11 Redo Example 18.3 using the type II FMN. Which type of FMN provides a better representation of the problem in the example? Justify your answer.

18.12 **(a)** Write a program for simulating the interval regression modeling problem in Example 18.4 and compare the simulation results with that shown in Fig. 18.9.
   (b) Repeat part (a) using the type III FMN shown in Fig. 18.10.

18.13 Derive the equations for setting up a fuzzy regression model based on the bell-shaped membership function.

18.14 **(a)** Solve the problem of the fuzzy relation equation described in Example 3.22 using the neural fuzzy relational network introduced in Sec. 18.3.3 and compare the results with those obtained in Example 3.22.
   (b) Use an α operator and α composition to solve the problem of the fuzzy relation equation described in Example 18.6 and compare the results with those obtained in Example 18.6.

19

Neural Fuzzy Controllers

This chapter is concerned with neural network–based fuzzy logic controllers or *neuro-fuzzy controllers* (NFCs). Since fuzzy logic control is one of the major and most successful applications of fuzzy inference, this chapter can be considered a continuation of the last chapter but focuses on neural fuzzy control rather than neural fuzzy inference. NFCs, based on a fusion of ideas from fuzzy control and neural networks, possess the advantages of both neural networks (e.g., learning abilities, optimization abilities, and connectionist structures) and fuzzy control systems (e.g., humanlike IF-THEN rule thinking and ease of incorporating expert knowledge). In this way, we can bring the low-level learning and computational power of neural networks to fuzzy control systems and also provide the high-level, humanlike IF-THEN rule thinking and reasoning of fuzzy control systems to neural networks. In brief, neural networks can improve their transparency, making them closer to fuzzy control systems, while fuzzy control systems can self-adapt, making them closer to neural networks.

In this chapter, we shall focus on structure learning and parameter learning in NFCs. We shall examine cases when they can take place sequentially and separately in two phases (Sec. 19.2), when only parameter learning (Sec. 19.3) or only structure learning is necessary (Sec. 19.4), when they can occur simultaneously in a single phase (Sec. 19.5), and when they can be performed with reinforcement signals (Sec. 19.6). All these variations of structure and parameter learning of NFCs are discussed with simulation examples.

Based on the three different types of fuzzy reasoning introduced in Sec. 7.1.4, three types of neural fuzzy controllers can be distinguished:

- **Type 1:** This type is the most formal one, with fuzzy rules in the form of Eq. (7.4). The output membership function is usually bell shaped, triangular in shape, or trapezoidal in shape. It performs fuzzy reasoning of the first type (see Sec. 7.1.4) and is illustrated in Figs. 7.5 and 7.6. The (fuzzy) response of each rule is its output membership function weighted (cut) by its firing strength, and the centroid of the responses is calculated to generate the appropriate output. When the output membership function is reduced to an impulse function, the consequent of each rule is a fuzzy singleton. A common simplified defuzzification procedure called *singleton defuzzifier* involves taking the output value with the maximum membership degree as the (crisp) response of each rule and then aggregating these responses to produce the appropriate output using Eq. (7.28).

- **Type 2:** In this type, the output membership function is a monotonic increasing function (S-type function) such as a sigmoid function. It performs fuzzy reasoning of the second type and is illustrated in Fig. 7.7. The response of a fuzzy rule is determined by its firing strength according to its output membership function. The aggregated output value of the whole NFC is a linear combination of the responses and firing strengths of fuzzy rules as indicated in Eq. (7.28). Note that the consequent of each rule becomes a fuzzy singleton when the output membership function is reduced to a threshold function.

- **Type 3:** This type uses the TSK fuzzy rules in Eq. (7.5) and performs fuzzy reasoning of the third type. The response of each rule is a linear combination of the values of input variables. The responses are then weighted and summed according to the firing strengths to obtain the final output [see Eq. (7.29)]. The consequent of each rule becomes a fuzzy singleton when all the coefficients in the consequent part become zero (i.e., only the constant term of the linear equation is left).

The main purpose of a neural fuzzy control system is to apply neural learning techniques to find and tune the parameters and/or structure of neuro-fuzzy control systems (NFCS). Fuzzy logic controllers require two major types of tuning: structural tuning and parametric tuning. Structural tuning involves tuning of the structure of fuzzy logic rules such as the number of variables to account for, and for each input or output variable the partition of the universe of discourse; the number of rules and the conjunctions that constitute them; and so on. Once a satisfactory structure of the rules is obtained, the NFCS needs to perform parametric tuning. In this parameter-learning phase, the possible parameters to be tuned include those associated with membership functions such as centers, widths, and slopes; the parameters of the parameterized fuzzy connectives; and the weights of the fuzzy logic rules.

Among the three categories of neural network learning schemes, unsupervised learning, which constructs internal models that capture regularities in their input vectors without receiving any additional information, is suitable for structure learning in order to find clusters of data indicating the presence of fuzzy logic rules. Supervised learning, which requires a teacher to specify the desired output vector, and reinforcement learning, which requires only a single scalar evaluation of the output, are suitable for parameter learning to adjust the parameters of fuzzy logic rules and/or membership functions for the desired output in neuro-fuzzy control systems. In cases where the membership functions are differentiable, we can easily derive gradient-descent-based learning methods (e.g., the back-propagation algorithm) for parameter learning. Furthermore, genetic algorithms as discussed in Chap. 14 can be utilized for structure learning by searching the space of all possible fuzzy decision tables.

There are several ways that structure learning and parameter learning can be combined in a NFC. First, they can be performed sequentially and separately in two phases: Structure learning is used first in phase one to find the proper structure of a NFC (e.g., connectivity of fuzzy logic rules), and then parameter learning is used in phase two to fine-tune the parameters (e.g., membership functions). This procedure involves *hybrid structure–parameter learning algorithms* which are suitable for the structure-parameter learning of type-1 NFCs. In some situations, only parameter learning or only structure learning is necessary when structure (such as fuzzy rules) or parameters (such as membership functions) are provided by experts. Obviously, available expert knowledge can be used to set up the initial structure and parameters of a NFC and then structure learning and/or parameter learning takes place for fine-tuning. The fundamental techniques for parameter learning and structure learning are introduced separately in Secs. 19.3 and 19.4, respectively. The techniques in Sec. 19.3.1 are suitable for type-2 NFCs, while those in Sec. 19.3.2 are suitable for type-3 NFCs. Structure learning and parameter learning can also be combined into a single phase such that the structure and parameters of a NFC can be tuned simultaneously. This results in the *on-line structure adaptive learning algorithms* discussed in Sec. 19.5. Furthermore, structure learning and parameter learning can occur with reinforcement signals (i.e., reinforcement learning) as discussed in Sec. 19.6.

19.2 NEURAL FUZZY CONTROLLERS WITH HYBRID STRUCTURE-PARAMETER LEARNING

In this section, we shall introduce some neural fuzzy control models that have both structure learning and parameter learning capabilities. A basic concept of these neural fuzzy control models is first to use structure learning algorithms to find appropriate fuzzy logic rules and then use parameter learning algorithms to fine-tune the membership functions and other parameters.

19.2.1 Fuzzy Adaptive Learning Control Network

In this section, we shall introduce a general connectionist model, the fuzzy adaptive learning control network (FALCON) proposed by Lin and Lee [1991b] to study hybrid structure-parameter learning strategies. The FALCON is a feedforward multilayer network which integrates the basic elements and functions of a traditional fuzzy logic controller into a connectionist structure that has distributed learning abilities. In this connectionist structure, the input and output nodes represent the input states and output control or decision signals, respectively, and in the hidden layers, there are nodes functioning as membership functions and fuzzy logic rules. The FALCON can be contrasted with a traditional fuzzy logic control and decision system in terms of its network structure and learning abilities. Such fuzzy control and decision networks can be constructed from training examples by neural learning techniques, and the connectionist structure can be trained to develop fuzzy logic rules and determine proper input-output membership functions. This connectionist model also provides human-understandable meaning to the normal feedforward multilayer neural network in which the internal units are always opaque to users. So, if necessary, expert knowledge can be easily incorporated into the FALCON. The connectionist structure also avoids the rule-matching time of the inference engine in the traditional fuzzy control system. We shall first introduce the structure and function of the FALCON and then consider its learning scheme.

Figure 19.1 shows the structure of the FALCON. The system has a total of five layers. The nodes in layer 1 are input nodes (*linguistic nodes*) that represent input linguistic variables, and layer 5 is the output layer. There are two linguistic nodes for each output variable. One is for training data (desired output) to feed into the network, and the other is for decision signals (actual output) to be pumped out of the network. Nodes in layers 2 and 4 are *term nodes* which act as membership functions representing the terms of the respective linguistic variables. Actually, a layer-2 node can either be a single node that performs a simple membership function (e.g., a triangle-shaped or bell-shaped function) or composed of multilayer nodes (a subneural network) that performs a complex membership function. So the total number of layers in this connectionist model can be more than 5. Each node in layer 3 is a rule node that represents one fuzzy logic rule. Thus, all the layer-3 nodes form a fuzzy rule base. Links in layers 3 and 4 function as a *connectionist inference engine*, which avoids the rule-matching process. Layer-3 links define the preconditions of the rule nodes, and layer-4 links define the consequents of the rule nodes. Therefore, for each rule node, there is at most one link (maybe none) from some term node of a linguistic node. This is true for both precondition links (links in layer 3) and consequent links (links in layer 4).

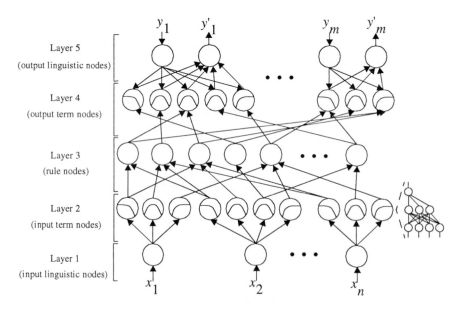

Figure 19.1 Structure of the FALCON.

The links in layers 2 and 5 are fully connected between linguistic nodes and their corresponding term nodes. The arrow on the link indicates the normal signal flow direction when the network is in use after it has been built and trained. We shall later indicate the signal propagation, layer by layer, according to the arrow direction. Signals flow only in the reverse direction in the learning or training process.

With this five-layered structure of the FALCON, we shall define the basic functions of a node. The FALCON consists of nodes that have some finite fan-in of connections represented by weight values from other nodes and a fan-out of connections to other nodes. Associated with the fan-in of a node is an integration function f which serves to combine information, activation, or evidence from other nodes. This function provides the net input to this node

$$\text{net}_i = f\!\left(u_1^{(k)}, u_2^{(k)}, \dots, u_p^{(k)}; w_1^{(k)}, w_2^{(k)}, \dots, w_p^{(k)}\right), \tag{19.1}$$

where $u_1^{(k)}, u_2^{(k)}, \dots, u_p^{(k)}$ are inputs to this node and $w_1^{(k)}, w_2^{(k)}, \dots, w_p^{(k)}$ are the associated link weights. The superscript k in the above equation indicates the layer number. A second action of each node is to output an activation value as a function of its net input:

$$\text{output} = o_i^{(k)} = a\,(\text{net}_i) = a\,(f). \tag{19.2}$$

where $a\,(\cdot)$ denotes the activation function. We shall next describe the functions of the nodes in each of the five layers of the FALCON.

- **Layer 1:** The nodes in this layer only transmit input values to the next layer directly. That is,

$$f = u_i^{(1)} \qquad \text{and} \qquad a = f. \tag{19.3}$$

  From this equation, the link weight at layer 1 $\left(w_i^{(1)}\right)$ is unity.

- **Layer 2:** If we use a single node to perform a simple membership function, then the output function of this node should be this membership function. For example, for a bell-shaped function, we have

$$f = M_{x_i}^{j}(m_{ij}, \sigma_{ij}) = -\frac{\left(u_i^{(2)} - m_{ij}\right)^2}{\sigma_{ij}^2} \qquad \text{and} \qquad a = e^f, \tag{19.4}$$

  where m_{ij} and σ_{ij} are, respectively, the center (or mean) and the width (or variance) of the bell-shaped function of the jth term of the ith input linguistic variable x_i. Hence, the link weight at layer 2 $\left(w_{ij}^{(2)}\right)$ can be interpreted as m_{ij}. If we use a set of nodes to perform a membership function, then the function of each node can be in the standard form (e.g., the sigmoid function) and the whole subnetwork is trained off-line to perform the desired membership function by a standard learning algorithm (e.g., the back-propagation algorithm).

- **Layer 3:** The links in this layer are used to perform precondition matching of fuzzy logic rules. Hence, the rule nodes perform the fuzzy AND operation,

$$f = \min\!\left(u_1^{(3)}, u_2^{(3)}, \dots, u_p^{(3)}\right) \qquad \text{and} \qquad a = f. \tag{19.5}$$

  The link weight in layer 3 $\left(w_i^{(3)}\right)$ is then unity.

- **Layer 4:** The nodes in this layer have two operation modes: *down-up* transmission and *up-down* transmission modes. In the down-up transmission mode, the links in layer 4 perform the fuzzy OR operation to integrate the fired rules which have the same consequent:

$$f = \sum_i u_i^{(4)} \qquad \text{and} \qquad a = \min(1, f). \qquad (19.6)$$

Hence, the link weight $w_i^{(4)} = 1$. In the up-down transmission mode, the nodes in this layer and the links in layer 5 function exactly the same as those in layer 2 except that only a single node is used to perform a membership function for output linguistic variables.

- **Layer 5:** There are two kinds of nodes in this layer also. The first kind of node performs up-down transmission for training data being fed into the network. For this kind of node,

$$f = y_i \qquad \text{and} \qquad a = f. \qquad (19.7)$$

The second kind of node performs down-up transmission for the decision signal output. These nodes and the layer-5 links attached to them act as the defuzzifier. If m_{ij} and σ_{ij} are, respectively, the center and the width of the membership function of the jth term of the ith output linguistic variable, then the following functions can be used to simulate the *center of area* defuzzification method in Eq. (7.30):

$$f = \sum_j w_{ij}^{(5)} u_{ij}^{(5)} = \sum_j (m_{ij}\sigma_{ij}) u_{ij}^{(5)} \qquad \text{and} \qquad a = \frac{f}{\sum_j \sigma_{ij} u_{ij}^{(5)}}. \qquad (19.8)$$

Here the link weight in layer 5 $\left(w_{ij}^{(5)}\right)$ is $m_{ij}\sigma_{ij}$.

Based on this connectionist structure, a two-phase hybrid learning algorithm is developed to determine the proper centers (m_{ij}) and widths (σ_{ij}) of the term nodes in layers 2 and 4. Also, it will learn fuzzy logic rules by determining the existence and connection types of the links at layers 3 and 4, that is, the precondition links and consequent links of the rule nodes.

We shall now present a hybrid learning algorithm to set up the FALCON from a set of supervised training data. We call the FALCON with hybrid learning FALCON-H for short. The hybrid learning algorithm consists of two separate stages of a learning strategy which combines unsupervised learning and supervised gradient-descent learning procedures to build the rule nodes and train the membership functions. This hybrid learning algorithm performs better than the purely supervised learning algorithm (e.g., the back-propagation algorithm) because of the a priori classification of training data through an overlapping receptive field before the supervised learning. The learning rate of the traditional back-propagation learning algorithm is limited by the fact that all layers of weights in the network are determined by the minimization of an error signal which is specified only as a function of the output, and a substantial fraction of the learning time is spent on the discovery of internal representation.

In phase 1 of the hybrid learning algorithm, a self-organized learning scheme (i.e., unsupervised learning) is used to locate initial membership functions and to detect the presence of fuzzy logic rules. In phase 2, a supervised learning scheme is used to optimally adjust the parameters of the membership functions for desired outputs. To initiate the learning scheme, training data and the desired or guessed coarse of fuzzy partition (i.e., the size of the term set of each input-output linguistic variable) must be provided from the outside world (or from an expert).

Before this network is trained, an initial structure of the network is first constructed. Then, during the learning process, some nodes and links in this initial network are deleted or combined to form the final structure. In its initial form (see Fig. 19.1), there are $\prod_i |T(x_i)|$ rule nodes with the inputs of each rule node coming from one possible combination of the terms of input linguistic variables under the constraint that only one term in a term set can be a rule node's input. Here $|T(x_i)|$ denotes the number of x_i terms (i.e., the number of fuzzy partitions of the input state linguistic variable x_i). So the input state space is initially divided into $|T(x_1)| \times |T(x_2)| \times \cdots \times |T(x_n)|$ linguistically defined nodes (or fuzzy cells) which represent the preconditions of fuzzy logic rules. Also, the links between the rule nodes and the output term nodes are initially fully connected, meaning that the consequents of the rule nodes are not yet decided. Only a suitable term in each output linguistic variable's term set will be chosen after the learning process.

- *Self-Organized Learning Phase*
  The problem for self-organized learning can be stated as: Given the training input data $x_i(t)$, $i = 1, 2, \ldots, n$, the corresponding desired output value $y_i^d(t)$, $i = 1, 2, \ldots, m$, the fuzzy partitions $|T(x_i)|$ and $|T(y_i)|$, and the desired shapes of membership functions, we want to locate the membership functions and find the fuzzy logic rules. In this phase, the network works in a two-sided manner; that is, the nodes and links in layer 4 are in the up-down transmission mode so that the training input and output data can be fed into the FALCON from both sides.

  First, the centers (or means) and the widths (or variances) of the membership functions are determined by self-organized learning techniques analogous to statistical clustering technique. This serves to allocate network resources efficiently by placing the domains of membership functions covering only those regions of the input-output space where data are present. Kohonen's learning rule algorithm (see Sec. 12.1.2) is adopted here to find the center m_i of the ith membership function of x, where x represents any one of the input or output linguistic variables $x_1, \ldots, x_n$, $y_1, \ldots, y_m$:

$$\| x(t) - m_{\text{closest}}(t) \| = \min_{1 \leq i \leq k} \{ \| x(t) - m_i(t) \| \}, \tag{19.9}$$

$$m_{\text{closest}}(t + 1) = m_{\text{closest}}(t) + \alpha(t) [x(t) - m_{\text{closest}}(t)], \tag{19.10}$$

$$m_i(t + 1) = m_i(t), \qquad \text{for } m_i \neq m_{\text{closest}}, \tag{19.11}$$

where $\alpha(t)$ is a monotonically decreasing scalar learning rate and $k = |T(x)|$. This adaptive formulation runs independently for each input and output linguistic variable. The determination of which of the m_i is m_{closest} can be accomplished in constant time via a winner-take-all circuit. Once the centers of the membership functions are found, their widths can be determined using the *N-nearest-neighbor* heuristic by minimizing the following objective function with respect to the widths σ_i:

$$E = \frac{1}{2}\sum_{i=1}^{N}\left[\sum_{j\in N_{\text{nearest}}}\left(\frac{m_i - m_j}{\sigma_i}\right)^2 - r\right]^2, \tag{19.12}$$

where r is an overlap parameter. Since the second learning phase will optimally adjust the centers and the widths of the membership functions, the widths can be simply determined by the first-nearest-neighbor heuristic at this stage as

$$\sigma_i = \frac{|m_i - m_{\text{closest}}|}{r}, \tag{19.13}$$

where the user initially sets r to an appropriate value.

After the parameters of the membership functions have been found, the signals from both external sides can reach the output points of term nodes in layers 2 and 4 (see Fig. 19.1). Furthermore, the outputs of term nodes in layer 2 can be transmitted to rule nodes through the initial connection of layer-3 links. So we can obtain the firing strength of each rule node. Based on these rule firing strengths [denoted as $o_i^{(3)}(t)$] and the outputs of term nodes in layer 4 [denoted as $o_j^{(4)}(t)$], we want to determine the correct consequent links (layer-4 links) of each rule node to find the existing fuzzy logic rule by *competitive learning* algorithms. As stated before, the links in layer 4 are initially fully connected. We denote the weight of the link between the ith rule node and the jth output term node as w_{ji}. The following competitive learning law is used to update these weights for each training data set [see Eq. (12.7)],

$$\dot{w}_{ji}(t) = o_j^{(4)}\left(-w_{ji} + o_i^{(3)}\right), \tag{19.14}$$

where $o_j^{(4)}$ serves as a win-loss index of the jth term node in layer 4. The essence of this law is *learn if win*. In the extreme case, if $o_j^{(4)}$ is a 0/1 threshold function, then this law indicates *learn only if win*.

After competitive learning involving the whole training data set, the link weights in layer 4 represent the strength of the existence of the corresponding rule consequent. From the links connecting a rule node and the term nodes of an output linguistic node, at most one link with maximum weight is chosen and the others are deleted. Hence, only one term in an output linguistic variable's term set can become one of the consequents of a fuzzy logic rule. If all the link weights between a rule node and the term nodes of an output linguistic node are very small, then all the corresponding links are deleted, meaning that this rule node has little or no relation to this output linguistic variable. If all the links between a rule node and the layer-4 nodes are deleted, then this rule node can be eliminated since it does not affect the outputs.

After the consequents of rule nodes are determined, a rule combination is used to reduce the number of rules. The criteria for combining a set of rule nodes into a single rule node are: (1) They have exactly the same consequents, (2) some preconditions are common to all the rule nodes in the set, and (3) the union of other preconditions of these rule nodes comprises the whole term set of some input linguistic variables. If a set of nodes meets these criteria, a new rule node with only the common preconditions can replace this set of rule nodes. An example is shown in Fig. 19.2.

Neural Fuzzy Controllers   Chap. 19

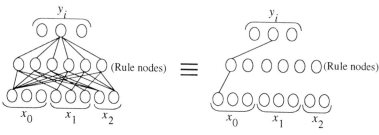

Figure 19.2 Example of combination of rule nodes in the hybrid learning algorithm for the FALCON.

- *Supervised Learning Phase*

  After the fuzzy logic rules have been determined, the whole network structure is established. The network then enters the second learning phase to adjust the parameters of the (input and output) membership functions optimally. The problem for supervised learning can be stated as: Given the training input data $x_i(t)$, $i = 1, 2,..., n$, the corresponding desired output value $y_i^d(t)$, $i = 1, 2,..., m$, the fuzzy partitions $|T(x_i)|$ and $|T(y_i)|$, and the fuzzy logic rules, adjust the parameters of the input and output membership functions optimally. The fuzzy logic rules of this network were determined in the first-phase learning or, in some application domains, they can be provided by experts. In the second-phase learning, the network works in the feedforward manner; that is, the nodes and the links in layers 4 and 5 are in the down-up transmission mode. The back-propagation algorithm is used for this supervised learning. Considering a single-output case for clarity, the goal is to minimize the error function

$$E = \tfrac{1}{2}(y^d(t) - y(t))^2, \tag{19.15}$$

  where $y^d(t)$ is the desired output and $y(t)$ is the current output. For each training data set, starting at the input nodes, a forward pass is used to compute the activity levels of all the nodes in the network to obtain the current output $y(t)$. Then, starting at the output nodes, a backward pass is used to compute $\partial E/\partial w$ for all the hidden nodes. Assuming that w is the adjustable parameter in a node (e.g., m_{ij} and σ_{ij} in our case), the general learning rule used is

$$\Delta w \propto -\frac{\partial E}{\partial w}, \tag{19.16}$$

$$w(t+1) = w(t) + \eta\left(-\frac{\partial E}{\partial w}\right), \tag{19.17}$$

  where η is the learning rate and

$$\frac{\partial E}{\partial w} = \frac{\partial E}{\partial(\text{activation function})}\frac{\partial(\text{activation function})}{\partial w} = \frac{\partial E}{\partial a}\frac{\partial a}{\partial w}. \tag{19.18}$$

  To illustrate the learning rule for each parameter, we shall show the computations of $\partial E/\partial w$, layer by layer, starting at the output nodes, and we will use bell-shaped membership functions with centers m_i and widths σ_i (single-output case) as the adjustable parameters for these computations.

- **Layer 5:** Using Eqs. (19.18) and (19.8), the adaptive rule of the center m_i is derived as

$$\frac{\partial E}{\partial m_i} = \frac{\partial E}{\partial a^{(5)}} \frac{\partial a^{(5)}}{\partial m_i} = -[y^d(t) - y(t)] \frac{\sigma_i u_i^{(5)}}{\sum_i \sigma_i u_i^{(5)}}, \tag{19.19}$$

where $a^{(5)}$ is the network output $y(t)$. Hence, the center parameter is updated by

$$m_i(t+1) = m_i(t) + \eta [y^d(t) - y(t)] \frac{\sigma_i u_i^{(5)}}{\sum_i \sigma_i u_i^{(5)}}. \tag{19.20}$$

Similarly, using Eqs. (19.18) and (19.8), the adaptive rule of the width σ_i is derived as

$$\frac{\partial E}{\partial \sigma_i} = \frac{\partial E}{\partial a^{(5)}} \frac{\partial a^{(5)}}{\partial \sigma_i}$$

$$= -[y^d(t) - y(t)] \frac{m_i u_i^{(5)}(\sum_i \sigma_i u_i^{(5)}) - (\sum_i m_i \sigma_i u_i^{(5)})u_i^{(5)}}{(\sum_i \sigma_i u_i^{(5)})^2}. \tag{19.21}$$

Hence, the width parameter is updated by

$$\sigma_i(t+1) =$$

$$\sigma_i(t) + \eta [y^d(t) - y(t)] \frac{m_i u_i^{(5)}(\sum_i \sigma_i u_i^{(5)}) - (\sum_i m_i \sigma_i u_i^{(5)})u_i^{(5)}}{(\sum_i \sigma_i u_i^{(5)})^2}. \tag{19.22}$$

The error to be propagated to the preceding layer is

$$\delta^{(5)} = -\frac{\partial E}{\partial a^{(5)}} = -\frac{\partial E}{\partial y} = y^d(t) - y(t). \tag{19.23}$$

- **Layer 4:** In the down-up transmission mode, there is no parameter to be adjusted in this layer. Only the error signals $(\delta_i^{(4)})$ need to be computed and propagated. The error signal $\delta_i^{(4)}$ is derived as

$$\delta_i^{(4)} = -\frac{\partial E}{\partial a_i^{(4)}} = -\frac{\partial E}{\partial u_i^{(5)}} = -\frac{\partial E}{\partial a^{(5)}} \frac{\partial a^{(5)}}{\partial u_i^{(5)}}, \tag{19.24}$$

where [from Eq. (19.8)]

$$\frac{\partial a^{(5)}}{\partial u_i^{(5)}} = \frac{m_i \sigma_i (\sum_i \sigma_i u_i^{(5)}) - (\sum_i m_i \sigma_i u_i^{(5)})\sigma_i}{(\sum_i \sigma_i u_i^{(5)})^2}, \tag{19.25}$$

and from Eq. (19.23),

$$-\frac{\partial E}{\partial a^{(5)}} = \delta^{(5)} = y^d(t) - y(t). \tag{19.26}$$

Hence, the error signal is

$$\delta_i^{(4)}(t) = [y^d(t) - y(t)] \frac{m_i \sigma_i (\sum_i \sigma_i u_i^{(5)}) - (\sum_i m_i \sigma_i u_i^{(5)})\sigma_i}{(\sum_i \sigma_i u_i^{(5)})^2}. \tag{19.27}$$

In the multiple-output case, the computations in layers 4 and 5 are exactly the same as the above and proceed independently for each output linguistic variable.

Layer 3: As in layer 4, only the error signals need to be computed. According to Eq. (19.6), this error signal can be derived as

$$\delta_i^{(3)} = -\frac{\partial E}{\partial a_i^{(3)}} = -\frac{\partial E}{\partial u_i^{(4)}} = -\frac{\partial E}{\partial a_i^{(4)}}\frac{\partial a_i^{(4)}}{\partial u_i^{(4)}} = -\frac{\partial E}{\partial a_i^{(4)}} = \delta_i^{(4)}. \qquad (19.28)$$

Hence, the error signal is $\delta_i^{(3)} = \delta_i^{(4)}$. If there are multiple outputs, then the error signal becomes $\delta_i^{(3)} = \sum_k \delta_k^{(4)}$, where the summation is performed over the consequents of a rule node; that is, the error of a rule node is the summation of the errors of its consequents.

Layer 2: Using Eqs. (19.18) and (19.4), the adaptive rule of m_{ij} (multi-input case) is derived as

$$\frac{\partial E}{\partial m_{ij}} = \frac{\partial E}{\partial a_i^{(2)}}\frac{\partial a_i^{(2)}}{\partial m_{ij}} = \frac{\partial E}{\partial a_i^{(2)}}e^{fi}\frac{2(u_i^{(2)}-m_{ij})}{\sigma_{ij}^2}, \qquad (19.29)$$

where

$$\frac{\partial E}{\partial a_i^{(2)}} = \frac{\partial E}{\partial u_i^{(3)}} = \frac{\partial E}{\partial a_i^{(3)}}\frac{\partial a_i^{(3)}}{\partial u_i^{(3)}}, \qquad (19.30)$$

where [from Eq. (19.28)]

$$\frac{\partial E}{\partial a_i^{(3)}} = -\delta_i^{(3)} \qquad (19.31)$$

and from Eq. (19.5),

$$\frac{\partial a_i^{(3)}}{\partial u_i^{(3)}} = \begin{cases} 1 & \text{if } u_i^{(3)} = \min(\text{inputs of rule node } i) \\ 0 & \text{otherwise.} \end{cases} \qquad (19.32)$$

Hence,

$$\frac{\partial E}{\partial a_i^{(2)}} \triangleq -\delta_i^{(2)} = \sum_k q_k, \qquad (19.33)$$

where the summation is performed over the rules nodes that $a_i^{(2)}$ feeds into and

$$q_k = \begin{cases} -\delta_k^{(3)} & \text{if } a_i^{(2)} \text{ is minimum in } k\text{th rule node's inputs} \\ 0 & \text{otherwise.} \end{cases} \qquad (19.34)$$

So the update rule of m_{ij} is

$$m_{ij}(t+1) = m_{ij}(t) + \eta\delta_i^{(2)}e^{fi}\frac{2(u_i^{(2)}-m_{ij})}{\sigma_{ij}^2}. \qquad (19.35)$$

Similarly, using Eqs. (19.18), (19.4), and (19.30)–(19.34), the update rule of σ_{ij} is derived as

$$\frac{\partial E}{\partial \sigma_{ij}} = \frac{\partial E}{\partial a_i^{(2)}}\frac{\partial a_i^{(2)}}{\partial \sigma_{ij}} = \frac{\partial E}{\partial a_i^{(2)}}e^{fi}\frac{2(u_i^{(2)}-m_{ij})^2}{\sigma_{ij}^3}. \qquad (19.36)$$

Hence, the update rule of σ_{ij} becomes

$$\sigma_{ij}(t+1) = \sigma_{ij}(t) + \eta\delta_i^{(2)}e^{fi}\frac{2(u_i^{(2)} - m_{ij})^2}{\sigma_{ij}^3}. \qquad (19.37)$$

The convergence speed of the above algorithm is found to be superior to that of the normal back-propagation scheme since the self-organized learning process in phase 1 does much of the learning work in advance. Finally, it should be noted that this back-propagation algorithm can be easily extended to train the membership function which is implemented by a subneural network instead of a single term node in layer 2 since from the above analysis the error signal can be propagated to the output node of the subneural network. Then, by using a similar back-propagation rule, the parameters in this subneural network can be adjusted.

Example 19.1

[Lin and Lee, 1991b]. In this example, the FALCON is used to simulate the control of a fuzzy car as discussed by Sugeno and Nishida [1985]. The car has the ability to learn from example to move automatically along a track with rectangular turns. The input linguistic variables are $x_0, x_1,$ and $x_2,$ which represent the distances of the car from the boundaries of the track at a corner and the current steering angle (see Fig. 19.3). The output linguistic variable y is the next steering angle. The training data are obtained when an operator guides the fuzzy car along the track. The overlap parameter r is set to 2.0, the learning rate is 0.15, and the error tolerance is 0.01. After learning, 30 fuzzy logic rules are obtained. Figure 19.4 shows the learned membership functions of x_1 and y. After the whole connectionist fuzzy logic controller is established, it is used to control the car. We keep the speed of the car constant and assume that there are sensors in the car to measure the state variables $x_0, x_1,$ and x_2 which are fed into the controller to derive the next steering angle. The simulation results show that the car can run under the control of the learned FALCON in the same way that it would be driven by a skilled driver on an S-shape or Π-shape road. This example was simulated several times with different initial steering angles, and the results obtained were nearly the same.

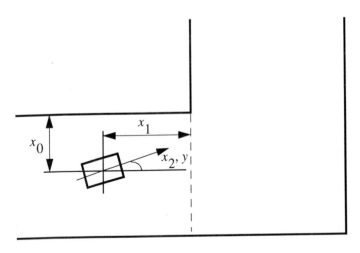

Figure 19.3 Definition of the state variables of the fuzzy car in Example 19.1.

Neural Fuzzy Controllers   Chap. 19

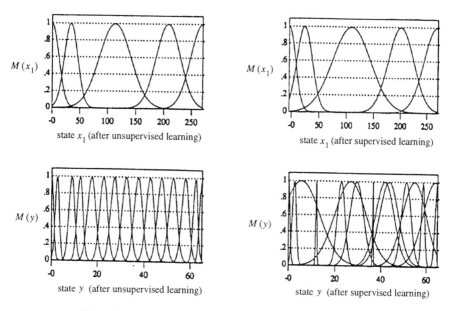

Figure 19.4 Learned membership functions for x_1 and y in Example 19.1.

19.2.2 Fuzzy Basis Function Network with Orthogonal Least Squares Learning

Another NFC is the *fuzzy basis function network* (FBFN) proposed by Wang and Mendel [1992a]. In the FBFN, a fuzzy system is represented as a series expansion of fuzzy basis functions (FBFs) which are algebraic superpositions of membership functions. Each FBF corresponds to one fuzzy logic rule. Based on the FBF representation, an orthogonal least squares (OLS) learning algorithm can be utilized to determine the significant FBFs [i.e., fuzzy logic rules (structure learning) and associated parameters (parameter learning)] from input-output training pairs. Since a linguistic fuzzy IF-THEN rule from human experts can be directly interpreted by an FBF, the FBFN provides a framework for combining both numerical and linguistic information in a uniform manner.

Consider a multi-input–single-output fuzzy control system: $X \subset \mathcal{R}^n \to Y \subset \mathcal{R}$. A multioutput system can always be separated into a group of multi-input–single-output systems (see Sec. 7.1.4). Suppose that we have M fuzzy logic rules in the following form:

$$R^j: \text{IF } x_1 \text{ is } A_1^j \text{ AND } x_2 \text{ is } A_2^j \text{ AND } \cdots \text{ AND } x_n \text{ is } A_n^j, \text{ THEN } y \text{ is } B^j, \quad (19.38)$$

where x_i, $i = 1, 2, \ldots, n$, are the input variables of the fuzzy system, y is the output variable of the fuzzy system, A_i^j and B^j are linguistic terms characterized by fuzzy membership functions $\mu_{A_i^j}(x_i)$ and $\mu_{B^j}(y)$, respectively, and $j = 1, 2, \ldots, M$. We also assume *a singleton fuzzifier, product inference, a centroid defuzzifier,* and *Gaussian membership functions* are used. Then for a given input (crisp) vector $\mathbf{x} = (x_1, x_2, \ldots, x_n)^T \in X$ we have the following defuzzified inferenced output:

$$y = f(\mathbf{x}) = \frac{\sum_{j=1}^{M} \bar{y}^j \left(\prod_{i=1}^{n} \mu_{A_i^j}(x_i) \right)}{\sum_{j=1}^{M} \left(\prod_{i=1}^{n} \mu_{A_i^j}(x_i) \right)}, \tag{19.39}$$

where $f: X \subset \mathcal{R}^n \to \mathcal{R}$, $\bar{y}^j$ is the point in the output space Y at which $\mu_{B^j}(\bar{y}^j)$ achieves its maximum value and $\mu_{A_i^j}(x_i)$ is the *Gaussian membership function* defined by

$$\mu_{A_i^j}(x_i) = a_i^j \exp \left[-\frac{1}{2} \left(\frac{x_i - m_i^j}{\sigma_i^j} \right)^2 \right], \tag{19.40}$$

where a_i^j, m_i^j, and σ_i^j are real-valued parameters with $0 < a_i^j \leq 1$.

According to Eq. (19.39), we can define *fuzzy basis functions* (FBFs) as

$$p_j(\mathbf{x}) = \frac{\prod_{i=1}^{n} \mu_{A_i^j}(x_i)}{\sum_{j=1}^{m} \prod_{i=1}^{n} \mu_{A_i^j}(x_i)}, \qquad j = 1, 2, \ldots, M, \tag{19.41}$$

where $\mu_{A_i^j}(x_i)$ are the Gaussian membership functions defined in Eq. (19.40). Then, the fuzzy control system described by Eq. (19.39) is equivalent to a *FBF expansion* or a *FBF network* (FBFN):

$$f(\mathbf{x}) = \sum_{j=1}^{M} p_j(\mathbf{x}) \theta^j, \tag{19.42}$$

where $\theta^j = \bar{y}^j \in \mathcal{R}$ are constants. In other words, the fuzzy control system described by Eq. (19.39) can be viewed as a linear combination of FBFs.

There are two points of view in training FBFNs. First, if we view all the parameters a_i^j, m_i^j, and σ_i^j in $p_j(\mathbf{x})$ as free design parameters, then the FBFN is nonlinear in the parameters. In this case, we need nonlinear optimization techniques such as the back-propagation algorithm to train the FBFN. This is similar to what was used for the FALCON in the last section. On the other hand, if all the parameters in $p_j(\mathbf{x})$ are fixed at the very beginning of the FBFN design procedure, then the only free design parameters are θ^j. In this case, $f(\mathbf{x})$ in Eq. (19.42) is linear in the parameter and some very efficient linear parameter estimation methods can be used to train or "design" the FBFN. We shall focus on utilization of the *Gram-Schmidt orthogonal least squares* (OLS) algorithm [Chen et al., 1991] to design the FBFN. This OLS learning strategy can determine the proper number of significant FBFs automatically. It is a kind of hybrid structure-parameter learning method; that is, it can find the number of significant FBFs and their associated θ^j for the FBFN.

Suppose we are given N input-output training pairs: $(\mathbf{x}(t), d(t)), t = 1, 2, \ldots, N$. The task is to design a FBFN $f(\mathbf{x})$ such that

$$d(t) = f(\mathbf{x}(t)) + e(t) = \sum_{j=1}^{M} p_j(\mathbf{x}(t)) \theta^j + e(t), \tag{19.43}$$

where the approximation error function $e(t)$ between $f(\mathbf{x}(t))$ and $d(t)$ is minimized. In order to present the OLS algorithm, Eq. (19.43) is arranged from $t = 1$ to N in a matrix form:

$$\mathbf{d} = \mathbf{P}\boldsymbol{\theta} + \mathbf{e}, \tag{19.44}$$

where $\mathbf{d} = [d(1),...,d(N)]^T$, $\mathbf{P} = [\mathbf{p}_1,...,\mathbf{p}_M]$ with $\mathbf{p}_i = [p_i(1),...,p_i(N)]^T$, $\boldsymbol{\theta} = [\theta_1,...,\theta_M]^T$, and $\mathbf{e} = [e(1),...,e(N)]^T$. To determine $\boldsymbol{\theta}$ in Eq. (19.44), the OLS algorithm is utilized. The purpose of the original Gram-Schmidt OLS algorithm is to perform an orthogonal decomposition for $\mathbf{P}$ such that $\mathbf{P} = \mathbf{WA}$, where $\mathbf{W}$ is an orthogonal matrix and $\mathbf{A}$ is an upper-triangular matrix with unity diagonal elements. Substituting $\mathbf{P} = \mathbf{WA}$ into Eq. (19.44), we have

$$\mathbf{d} = \mathbf{P}\boldsymbol{\theta} + \mathbf{e} = \mathbf{WA}\boldsymbol{\theta} + \mathbf{e} = \mathbf{Wg} + \mathbf{e}, \tag{19.45}$$

where

$$\mathbf{g} = \mathbf{A}\boldsymbol{\theta}. \tag{19.46}$$

Using the OLS algorithm, we can select some domain columns from $\mathbf{P}$ (i.e., some significant FBFs) and find the associated θ^j values to form the final FBFN. In other words, the OLS algorithm transforms the set of $\mathbf{p}_i$ into a set of orthogonal basis vectors and uses only the FBFs that correspond to the significant orthogonal basis vectors to form the final FBFN.

Since matrix $\mathbf{A}$ in Eq. (19.46) is known from the OLS algorithm, if we can find an estimate of $\mathbf{g}$, $\hat{\mathbf{g}}$, then $\mathbf{A}\boldsymbol{\theta} = \hat{\mathbf{g}}$ can be solved for $\hat{\boldsymbol{\theta}} = \mathbf{A}^{-1}\hat{\mathbf{g}}$, which is a solution for $\boldsymbol{\theta}$. To find $\hat{\mathbf{g}}$, from Eq. (19.44) we have

$$\mathbf{e} = \mathbf{d} - \mathbf{P}\boldsymbol{\theta} = \mathbf{d} - \mathbf{Wg}. \tag{19.47}$$

Taking the derivative of $\mathbf{e}^T\mathbf{e}$ with respect to $\mathbf{g}$ to determine $\hat{\mathbf{g}}$, we have

$$\hat{\mathbf{g}} = [\mathbf{W}^T\mathbf{W}]^{-1}\mathbf{W}^T\mathbf{d}, \tag{19.48}$$

or each element of $\hat{\mathbf{g}}$ can be expressed as

$$\hat{g}_i = \frac{\mathbf{w}_i^T\mathbf{d}}{\mathbf{w}_i^T\mathbf{w}_i}, \qquad i = 1, 2,..., M. \tag{19.49}$$

Once $\hat{\mathbf{g}}$ is found, we solve Eq. (19.46) for $\boldsymbol{\theta}$, $\hat{\boldsymbol{\theta}} = \mathbf{A}^{-1}\hat{\mathbf{g}}$. Then the final FBFN using all M FBFs is

$$f(\mathbf{x}) = \sum_{j=1}^{M} p_j(\mathbf{x})\,\hat{\theta}^j. \tag{19.50}$$

Now if M is huge, then it is advantageous to use fewer FBFs, say, $M_s \ll M$. That is, we want to select M_s *significant* FBFs out of the M FBFs such that the approximation error $\mathbf{e} = \mathbf{d} - \mathbf{P}\boldsymbol{\theta}$ is minimized. This can be accomplished by using the OLS algorithm and choosing each significant FBF from 1 to M_s such that the approximation error is *maximally* reduced in each selection. To understand how this can be accomplished, let us take a look at the error function in Eq. (19.47) again; we have

$$\mathbf{e}^T\mathbf{e} = \mathbf{d}^T\mathbf{d} - 2(\mathbf{d} - \mathbf{Wg})^T\mathbf{Wg} - \mathbf{g}^T\mathbf{W}^T\mathbf{Wg}. \tag{19.51}$$

Since $(\mathbf{d} - \mathbf{Wg})^T\mathbf{Wg} = 0$, we have

$$\begin{aligned} \mathbf{e}^T\mathbf{e} &= \mathbf{d}^T\mathbf{d} - \mathbf{g}^T\mathbf{W}^T\mathbf{Wg} \\ &= \mathbf{d}^T\mathbf{d} - \sum_{i=1}^{M} g_i^2\mathbf{w}_i^T\mathbf{w}_i \end{aligned} \tag{19.52}$$

or

$$\frac{\mathbf{e}^T\mathbf{e}}{\mathbf{d}^T\mathbf{d}} = 1 - \sum_{i=1}^{M} \frac{g_i^2 \mathbf{w}_i^T \mathbf{w}_i}{\mathbf{d}^T\mathbf{d}}. \qquad (19.53)$$

Thus, from the OLS algorithm, we can select the orthogonal basis vector $\mathbf{w}_i$, $i = 1, 2,..., M_s$, such that the term $g_i^2 \mathbf{w}_i^T \mathbf{w}_i / \mathbf{d}^T\mathbf{d}$ is maximized to maximally reduce the error function in Eq. (19.53). This error reduction term is the same as $[\text{err}]_k^{(i)}$ in Eqs. (19.57) and (19.63), which represents the error reduction ratio caused by $\mathbf{w}_k^{(i)}$ as discussed in the following OLS algorithm.

Algorithm OLS: Orthogonal Least-Squares (OLS) Method for FBFN.
This algorithm selects M_s ($M_s \ll N$) significant FBFs from the N input-output training pairs $(\mathbf{x}(t), d(t))$, $t = 1, 2,..., N$, where $\mathbf{x}(t) = (x_1(t),...,x_n(t))^T$.

Input: N input-output training pairs $(\mathbf{x}(t), d(t))$, $t = 1, 2,..., N$, and an integer $M_s \ll N$, which is the desired number of significant FBFs to be selected.

Output: M_s significant FBFs will be selected from the N FBFs formed from the N input-output training pairs $(\mathbf{x}(t), d(t))$, $t = 1, 2,..., N$.

Step 0 (Initial FBF determination): Form N initial FBFs, $p_j(\mathbf{x})$, in the form of Eq. (19.41) from the training data [the M in Eq. (19.41) equals N], with the parameters determined as follows:

$$a_i^j = 1, \qquad m_i^j = x_i(j),$$

$$\sigma_i^j = [\max_{j=1,...,N} x_i(j) - \min_{j=1,...,N} x_i(j)]/M_s, \qquad (19.54)$$

where $i = 1, 2,..., n$, and $j = 1, 2,..., N$.

Step 1 (Initial step): For $1 \le i \le N$, compute

$$\mathbf{w}_1^{(i)} = \mathbf{p}_i, \qquad (19.55)$$

$$g_1^{(i)} = \frac{(\mathbf{w}_1^{(i)})^T \mathbf{d}}{(\mathbf{w}_1^{(i)})^T \mathbf{w}_1^{(i)}} = \frac{\mathbf{p}_i^T \mathbf{d}}{\mathbf{p}_i^T \mathbf{p}_i}, \qquad (19.56)$$

$$[\text{err}]_1^{(i)} = \frac{(g_1^{(i)})^2 (\mathbf{w}_1^{(i)})^T \mathbf{w}_1^{(i)}}{\mathbf{d}^T\mathbf{d}} = \frac{(g_1^{(i)})^2 \mathbf{p}_i^T \mathbf{p}_i}{\mathbf{d}^T\mathbf{d}}, \qquad (19.57)$$

where $\mathbf{p}_i = [p_i(\mathbf{x}(1)),..., p_i(\mathbf{x}(N))]^T$ and $p_i(\mathbf{x}(t))$ are obtained in step 0. Then find $i_1 \in \{1, 2,..., N\}$ such that

$$[\text{err}]_1^{(i_1)} = \max_{i=1,...,N} [\text{err}]_1^{(i)} \qquad (19.58)$$

and set

$$\mathbf{w}_1 = \mathbf{w}_1^{(i_1)} = \mathbf{p}_{i_1}, \qquad g_1 = g_1^{(i_1)}. \qquad (19.59)$$

The vector $\mathbf{w}_1$ and the value g_1 in Eq. (19.59) are, respectively, the selected first column of $\mathbf{W}$ and the first element of $\mathbf{g}$ in Eq. (19.45).

Step k $(k = 2, 3,..., M_s)$: For $1 \le i \le N, i \ne i_1,..., i \ne i_{k-1}$, compute the following equations:

$$\alpha_{jk}^{(i)} = \frac{\mathbf{w}_j^T \mathbf{p}_i}{\mathbf{w}_j^T \mathbf{w}_j}, \qquad 1 \le j < k, \qquad (19.60)$$

$$w_k^i = \mathbf{p}_i - \sum_{j=1}^{k-1} \alpha_{jk}^{(i)} \mathbf{w}_j, \tag{19.61}$$

$$g_k^{(i)} = \frac{(\mathbf{w}_k^{(i)})^T \mathbf{d}}{(\mathbf{w}_k^{(i)})^T \mathbf{w}_k^{(i)}}, \tag{19.62}$$

$$[\text{err}]_k^{(i)} = \frac{(g_k^{(i)})^2 (\mathbf{w}_k^{(i)})^T \mathbf{w}_k^{(i)}}{\mathbf{d}^T \mathbf{d}}. \tag{19.63}$$

Then find $i_k \in \{1, 2, \ldots, N\}$ such that

$$[\text{err}]_k^{(i_k)} = \max_{\substack{i=1,\ldots,N \\ i \neq i_1, \ldots, i \neq i_{k-1}}} \left([\text{err}]_k^{(i)}\right), \tag{19.64}$$

and select

$$\mathbf{w}_k = \mathbf{w}_k^{(i_k)}, \qquad g_k = g_k^{(i_k)} \tag{19.65}$$

as the kth column of $\mathbf{W}$ and the kth element of $\mathbf{g}$ in Eq. (19.45).

Step ($M_s + 1$) (Final step): Solve the following triangular system for the coefficient vector for $\mathbf{\theta}^{(M_s)}$:

$$\mathbf{A}^{(M_s)} \mathbf{\theta}^{(M_s)} = \mathbf{g}^{(M_s)}, \tag{19.66}$$

where

$$\mathbf{A}^{(M_s)} = \begin{bmatrix} 1 & \alpha_{12}^{(i_2)} & \alpha_{13}^{(i_3)} & \cdots & \alpha_{1M_s}^{(i_{M_s})} \\ 0 & 1 & \alpha_{23}^{(i_3)} & \cdots & \alpha_{2M_s}^{(i_{M_s})} \\ \cdots & \cdots & \cdots & \cdots & \cdots \\ 0 & 0 & \cdots & 1 & \alpha_{M_s-1,M_s}^{(i_{M_s})} \\ 0 & 0 & 0 & \cdots & 1 \end{bmatrix}, \tag{19.67}$$

$$\mathbf{g}^{(M_s)} = \begin{bmatrix} g_1, \ldots, g_{M_s} \end{bmatrix}^T, \qquad \mathbf{\theta}^{(M_s)} = \begin{bmatrix} \theta_1^{(M_s)}, \ldots, \theta_{M_s}^{(M_s)} \end{bmatrix}^T. \tag{19.68}$$

Then the final FBFN is

$$f(\mathbf{x}) = \sum_{j=1}^{M_s} p_{i_j}(\mathbf{x}) \theta_j^{(M_s)}, \tag{19.69}$$

where $p_{i_j}(\mathbf{x})$ make up the subset of the FBFs determined in step 0 with i_j determined in the preceding steps.

END OLS

The $[\text{err}]_k^{(i)}$ in Eqs. (19.57) and (19.63) represents the error reduction ratio caused by $\mathbf{w}_k^{(i)}$ [Chen et al., 1991]. Hence, the OLS algorithm selects significant FBFs based on their error reduction ratio; that is, the FBFs with the largest error reduction ratios are retained in the final FBFN. According to the error reduction ratios, we can set a threshold value to decide how many FBFs or, equivalently, how many fuzzy logic rules M_s are to be used. The guideline is that only those FBFs whose error reduction ratios are greater than the threshold value are chosen. The following example illustrates the use of FBFNs for the control of a nonlinear ball-and-beam system.

Example 19.2

[Wang and Mendel, 1992a]. Consider the ball-and-beam system shown in Fig. 19.5. The beam is made to rotate in a vertical plane by applying a torque at the center of rotation, and the ball is free to roll along the beam. The ball is required to remain in contact with the beam. Let $\mathbf{x} = (x_1, x_2, x_3, x_4)^T \equiv (r, \dot{r}, \theta, \dot{\theta})^T$ be the state of the system and $y = r$ be the output of the system. The system can be represented by the state-space model

$$
\begin{bmatrix} \dot{x}_1 \\ \dot{x}_2 \\ \dot{x}_3 \\ \dot{x}_4 \end{bmatrix} = \begin{bmatrix} x_2 \\ B(x_1 x_4^2 - G\sin x_3) \\ x_4 \\ 0 \end{bmatrix} + \begin{bmatrix} 0 \\ 0 \\ 0 \\ 1 \end{bmatrix} u,
\tag{19.70}
$$

$$
y = x_1,
\tag{19.71}
$$

where the control u is the acceleration of θ and B and G are constant parameters. The purpose of the control is to determine $u(\mathbf{x})$ such that the closed-loop system output y will converge to zero from certain initial conditions.

Suppose that we are given N input-output training pairs $(\mathbf{x}, u)$ with $\mathbf{x}$ randomly sampled in the region $X = [-5, 5] \times [-2, 2] \times [-\pi/4, \pi/4] \times [-0.8, 0.8]$. In the simulation, $N = 200$, $M_s = 20$, and the final FBFN $f(\mathbf{x})$ of Eq. (19.69) is used as the control u in Eq. (19.70). This case is simulated for four initial conditions: $\mathbf{x}(0) = [2.4, -0.1, 0.6, 0.1]^T$, $[1.6, 0.05, -0.6, -0.05]^T$, $[-1.6, -0.05, 0.6, 0.05]^T$, and $[-2.4, 0.1, -0.6, -0.1]^T$. The ball position $y = x_1 = r$ of the closed-loop system is depicted in Fig. (19.6). It is observed that the learned FBFN can control the ball-and-beam system quite well.

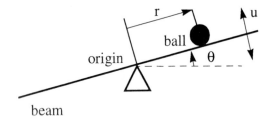

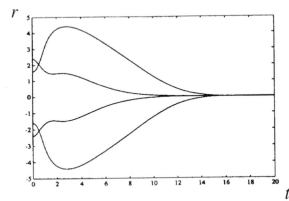

Figure 19.5 Ball-and-beam system in Example 19.2.

Figure 19.6 Simulation results for Example 19.2. (Adapted from Wang and Mendel [1992a], © 1992 IEEE.)

Neural Fuzzy Controllers   Chap. 19

19.3 PARAMETER LEARNING FOR NEURAL FUZZY CONTROLLERS

In the last section, we discussed some models of neural fuzzy controllers that can be built from a set of input-output training data pairs through hybrid structure-parameter learning. We shall next focus mainly on the techniques of parameter learning in this section, and the techniques of structure learning in the next section. Here, by "parameter learning" we mean the tuning of membership functions and other parameters in a neural fuzzy control network whose network architecture has been fixed or determined previously by expert knowledge or some structure learning techniques. The parameter learning problems considered in this section are considered supervised learning problems; that is, we are given a set of input-output training data pairs and a neural fuzzy network architecture (i.e., fuzzy logic rules) from which proper network parameters are to be determined. In this section, we shall introduce various parameter learning techniques based on different types of fuzzy logic rules. They are *fuzzy logic rules with a singleton consequent (fuzzy singleton rules)* and *TSK fuzzy rules.* The case of a fuzzy logic rule with fuzzy consequents was introduced in the last section. We shall also discuss the tuning of parameterized fuzzy operators (connectives) at the end of this section.

19.3.1 Neural Fuzzy Controllers with Fuzzy Singleton Rules

Consider the parameter learning of NFCs with fuzzy logic rules whose consequents are fuzzy singletons. Such fuzzy logic rules, called *fuzzy singleton rules,* are in the following form:

$$R^j: \text{IF } x_1 \text{ is } A_1^j \text{ AND } x_2 \text{ is } A_2^j \text{ AND } \cdots \text{ AND } x_n \text{ is } A_n^j, \text{ THEN } y \text{ is } w_j, \qquad (19.72)$$

where x_i is an input variable, y is the output variable, A_i^j are linguistic terms of the precondition part with membership functions $\mu_{A_i^j}(x_i)$, w_j is a real number of the consequent part, $j = 1, 2, \ldots, M$ and $i = 1, 2, \ldots, n$. Such a neural fuzzy system has a network structure as shown in Fig. 19.7, which is similar to the structure of the FALCON except for the output part (see Fig. 19.1). Also, this network is quite similar to the radial basis function network introduced in Sec. 12.6, especially when Gaussian membership functions are used. If product inference and a centroid defuzzifier are used, then the final output y^* of such a neural fuzzy system is calculated by

$$y^* = \frac{\sum_{j=1}^{M} \mu_j w_j}{\sum_{j=1}^{M} \mu_j}, \qquad (19.73)$$

where

$$\mu_j = \mu_{A_1^j}(x_1) \, \mu_{A_2^j}(x_2) \cdots \mu_{A_n^j}(x_n). \qquad (19.74)$$

A simplified version of Eq. (19.73) is

$$y^* = \sum_{j=1}^{M} \mu_j w_j, \qquad (19.75)$$

which does not use any division as opposed to the conventional centroid defuzzification in Eq. (19.73). Equation (19.75) is closer to the type of signal aggregation in neural networks and results in simpler learning rules than Eq. (19.73) does.

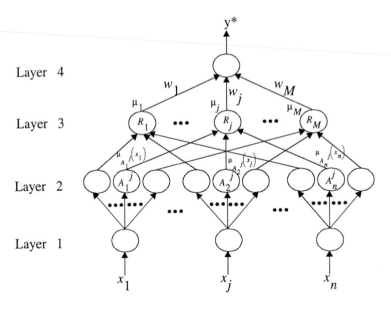

Layer 4

Layer 3

Layer 2

Layer 1

Figure 19.7 Structure of a NFC with fuzzy singleton rules.

Parameter learning of NFC with fuzzy singleton rules is the tuning of input membership functions $\mu_{A_i^j}$ and the real numbers w_j. The membership functions commonly used are bell-shaped (Gaussian) functions, triangular functions, and trapezoidal functions. More-complex parameterized functions such as B-spline functions or even the functions implemented by neural networks can also be used as input membership functions and tuned in much the same way. In this section, we shall derive the parameter learning rules for NFCs with fuzzy singleton rules using triangular membership functions.

Consider the fuzzy logic rules in Eq. (19.72), where the membership function $\mu_{A_i^j}(\cdot)$ of the precondition part is expressed by an isosceles triangle as shown in Fig. 19.8. The parameters determining the triangle are the center value a_i^j and the width b_i^j as follows:

$$\mu_{A_i^j}(x_i) = 1 - \frac{2\left|x_i - a_i^j\right|}{b_i^j}, \qquad i = 1, 2, \ldots, n; j = 1, 2, \ldots, M. \qquad (19.76)$$

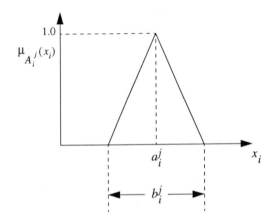

Figure 19.8 Isosceles triangular membership function.

Neural Fuzzy Controllers   Chap. 19

The output of fuzzy reasoning y can be calculated by Eqs. (19.73) and (19.74). Let us now derive the parameter learning algorithm for the above fuzzy logic rules. Assume that y^d is the desired output for some input vector $\mathbf{x} = (x_1, x_2, \ldots, x_n)^T$. The objective function to be minimized is defined by

$$E = \tfrac{1}{2}(y - y^d)^2 . \tag{19.77}$$

By substituting Eqs. (19.73) and (19.74) into Eq. (19.77), we have

$$E = \frac{1}{2}\left[\frac{\sum_{j=1}^{M}\mu_j(\mathbf{x})\,w_j}{\sum_{j=1}^{M}\mu_j(\mathbf{x})} - y^d\right]^2 = \frac{1}{2}\left[\frac{\sum_{j=1}^{M}\left(\prod_{i=1}^{n}\mu_{A_i^j}(x_i)\right)w_j}{\sum_{j=1}^{M}\left(\prod_{i=1}^{n}\mu_{A_i^j}(x_i)\right)} - y^d\right]^2 . \tag{19.78}$$

Since the shape of the membership function $\mu_{A_i^j}(\cdot)$ is defined by the center value a_i^j and the width b_i^j, the objective function E consists of the tuning parameters a_i^j, b_i^j, and w_j for $i = 1, \ldots, n$ and $j = 1, \ldots, M$. Hence, the learning rules can be derived as follows:

$$a_i^j(t+1) = a_i^j(t) - \eta_a\,\frac{\partial E}{\partial a_i^j}\,, \tag{19.79}$$

$$b_i^j(t+1) = b_i^j(t) - \eta_b\,\frac{\partial E}{\partial b_i^j}\,, \tag{19.80}$$

$$w_j(t+1) = w_j(t) - \eta_w\,\frac{\partial E}{\partial w_j}\,, \tag{19.81}$$

where the derivatives can be found from Eqs. (19.76) and (19.78) as

$$\frac{\partial E}{\partial a_i^j} = \frac{\mu_j(\mathbf{x})}{\sum_{j=1}^{M}\mu_j(\mathbf{x})}\,(y - y^d)\,(w_j - y)\,\mathrm{sgn}(x_i - a_i^j)\,\frac{2}{b_i^j\mu_{A_i^j}(x_i)}\,, \tag{19.82}$$

$$\frac{\partial E}{\partial b_i^j} = \frac{\mu_j(\mathbf{x})}{\sum_{j=1}^{M}\mu_j(\mathbf{x})}\,(y - y^d)\,(w_j - y)\,\frac{1 - \mu_{A_i^j}(x_i)}{\mu_{A_i^j}(x_i)}\,\frac{1}{b_i^j}\,, \tag{19.83}$$

$$\frac{\partial E}{\partial w_j} = \frac{\mu_j(\mathbf{x})}{\sum_{j=1}^{M}\mu_j(\mathbf{x})}\,(y - y^d). \tag{19.84}$$

Equations (19.79)–(19.84) are the update rules for tuning fuzzy singleton rules with isosceles triangular membership functions. Based on these update rules, the following steps are suggested for tuning the three sets of parameters a_i^j, b_i^j, and w_j [Nomura et al., 1992]:

Step 1: An initial setting of fuzzy logic rules is done first. The initial value of a_i^j is set so that the domain of input x_i is divided equally. The initial value of width b_i^j is set to allow overlapping of membership functions.

Step 2: The input-output training data $(x_1, \ldots, x_n, y^d)$ are input.

Step 3: Fuzzy reasoning is performed for the input data $(x_1, \ldots, x_n)$ by using Eqs. (19.73), (19.74), and (19.76). The membership value of μ_j of each inference rule and the output of fuzzy reasoning y are then calculated.

Step 4: Tuning of the real number w_j of the consequent part is performed by using Eq. (19.84).

Step 5: The fuzzy reasoning conducted in step 3 is repeated.

Step 6: Tuning of the center value a_i^j and the width b_i^j of the membership functions of the precondition part is done by substituting the tuned real number w_j obtained in step 4, the output y, the membership value μ_i, and output data y^d into Eqs. (19.82) and (19.83).

Step 7: The objective function (or the inference error) $E(t) = \frac{1}{2}[y(t) - y^d]^2$ is calculated, and steps 3 through 6 are repeated until its change $\Delta E(t) = E(t) - E(t-1)$ is less than a desired threshold value.

From Eq. (19.73), it is observed that for fuzzy singleton rules, the final inferred output y^* is a linear function of the consequent parameters w_j. Hence, given the values of the membership parameters (centers and widths) and p training data $(\mathbf{x}^{(k)}, d^{(k)}), k = 1, 2, \ldots, p$, we can form p linear equations in terms of the consequent parameters as follows:

$$
\begin{bmatrix} d^{(1)} \\ d^{(2)} \\ \vdots \\ d^{(p)} \end{bmatrix} =
\begin{bmatrix}
\overline{\mu}_1^{(1)} w_1 + \overline{\mu}_2^{(1)} w_2 + \cdots + \overline{\mu}_M^{(1)} w_M \\
\overline{\mu}_1^{(2)} w_1 + \overline{\mu}_2^{(2)} w_2 + \cdots + \overline{\mu}_M^{(2)} w_M \\
\vdots \\
\overline{\mu}_1^{(p)} w_1 + \overline{\mu}_2^{(p)} w_2 + \cdots + \overline{\mu}_M^{(p)} w_M
\end{bmatrix}
$$

$$
=
\begin{bmatrix}
\overline{\mu}_1^{(1)} & \overline{\mu}_2^{(1)} & \cdots & \overline{\mu}_M^{(1)} \\
\overline{\mu}_1^{(2)} & \overline{\mu}_2^{(2)} & \cdots & \overline{\mu}_M^{(2)} \\
\vdots & \vdots & & \vdots \\
\overline{\mu}_1^{(p)} & \overline{\mu}_2^{(p)} & \cdots & \overline{\mu}_M^{(p)}
\end{bmatrix}
\begin{bmatrix} w_1 \\ w_2 \\ \vdots \\ w_M \end{bmatrix},
$$

(19.85)

where $\overline{\mu}_j^{(k)} = \mu_j^{(k)}/\sum_{j=1}^M \mu_j^{(k)}$ and $\mu_j^{(k)}$ is the μ_j value calculated from Eq. (19.74) when the input is $\mathbf{x}^{(k)}$. For notational simplicity, Eq. (19.85) can be expressed in a matrix-vector form:

$$\mathbf{Ax} = \mathbf{d},$$

(19.86)

where $\mathbf{x} = [w_1, w_2, \ldots, w_M]^T$, $\mathbf{d} = [d^{(1)}, d^{(2)}, \ldots, d^{(p)}]^T$, and $\mathbf{A}$ is the matrix formed by the elements $\overline{\mu}_j^{(k)}$. Several approaches have been developed to solve this kind of overconstrained simultaneous linear equations and can be adopted here to find the consequent parameters w_j in a more efficient way than using Eqs. (19.81) and (19.84). One of the most concise ways to solve Eq. (19.86) is using the pseudoinverse technique,

$$\mathbf{x}^* = (\mathbf{A}^T\mathbf{A})^{-1}\mathbf{A}^T\mathbf{d},$$

(19.87)

where $(\mathbf{A}^T\mathbf{A})^{-1}\mathbf{A}^T$ is the *pseudoinverse* of $\mathbf{A}$ if $\mathbf{A}^T\mathbf{A}$ is nonsingular.

In many cases, the row vectors of matrix $\mathbf{A}$ (and the corresponding elements in $\mathbf{d}$) are obtained sequentially; hence it is desirable to compute the least squares estimate of $\mathbf{x}$ in Eq.

(19.86) recursively. Let the ith row vector of matrix $\mathbf{A}$ defined in Eq. (19.86) be $\mathbf{a}_i$ and the ith element of $\mathbf{d}$ be $d^{(i)}$; then $\mathbf{x}^*$ can be calculated recursively using the following formula:

$$\mathbf{x}_{i+1} = \mathbf{x}_i + \mathbf{S}_{i+1}\mathbf{a}_{i+1}^T \left(d^{(i+1)} - \mathbf{a}_{i+1}\mathbf{x}_i \right), \tag{19.88}$$

$$\mathbf{S}_{i+1} = \mathbf{S}_i - \frac{\mathbf{S}_i \mathbf{a}_{i+1}^T \mathbf{a}_{i+1} \mathbf{S}_i}{1 + \mathbf{a}_{i+1}\mathbf{S}_i\mathbf{a}_{i+1}^T}, \qquad i = 0, 1, \dots, p - 1, \tag{19.89}$$

$$\mathbf{x}^* = \mathbf{x}_p, \tag{19.90}$$

with initial conditions of

$$\mathbf{x}_0 = \mathbf{0} \qquad \text{and} \qquad \mathbf{S}_0 = \gamma\mathbf{I}, \tag{19.91}$$

where γ is a positive large number and $\mathbf{I}$ is the identity matrix of dimension $M \times M$.

The least squares estimate of $\mathbf{x}$ in Eq. (19.90) can also be interpreted as a Kalman filter [Kalman, 1960] for the process

$$\mathbf{x}(k + 1) = \mathbf{x}(k), \tag{19.92}$$

$$\mathbf{y}(k) = \mathbf{A}(k)\mathbf{x}(k) + \text{noise}, \tag{19.93}$$

where $\mathbf{x}(k) \equiv \mathbf{x}_k$, $\mathbf{y}(k) \equiv d^{(k)}$ and $\mathbf{A}(k) \equiv \mathbf{a}_k$. Therefore, the formula in Eqs. (19.88)–(19.90) is usually referred to as a *Kalman filter algorithm*.

Equations (19.88)–(19.90) can be derived as follows. Let

$$\mathbf{T}_i = \mathbf{A}_i^T\mathbf{A}_i, \qquad \mathbf{S}_i = \mathbf{T}_i^{-1}, \tag{19.94}$$

where $\mathbf{A}_i$ is a submatrix of $\mathbf{A}$ composed by the first ith rows of $\mathbf{A}$. Then, we have

$$\mathbf{T}_{i+1} = \mathbf{A}_i^T\mathbf{A}_i + \mathbf{a}_{i+1}^T\mathbf{a}_{i+1} = \mathbf{T}_i + \mathbf{a}_{i+1}^T\mathbf{a}_{i+1}, \tag{19.95}$$

and

$$\mathbf{S}_{i+1} = \mathbf{T}_{i+1}^{-1} = \mathbf{T}_i^{-1} - \frac{\mathbf{T}_i^{-1}\mathbf{a}_{i+1}^T\mathbf{a}_{i+1}\mathbf{T}_i^{-1}}{1 + \mathbf{a}_{i+1}\mathbf{T}_i^{-1}\mathbf{a}_{i+1}^T} = \mathbf{S}_i - \frac{\mathbf{S}_i\mathbf{a}_{i+1}^T\mathbf{a}_{i+1}\mathbf{S}_i}{1 + \mathbf{a}_{i+1}\mathbf{S}_i\mathbf{a}_{i+1}^T}, \tag{19.96}$$

which is the formula in Eq. (19.89). To derive the formula for $\mathbf{x}_{i+1}$, let us start from the relationship

$$\mathbf{A}_i\mathbf{x}_i = \mathbf{d}^i, \tag{19.97}$$

where $\mathbf{d}^i = [d^{(1)}, d^{(2)}, \dots, d^{(i)}]^T$. Then we have

$$\begin{bmatrix} \mathbf{A}_i \\ \mathbf{a}_{i+1} \end{bmatrix} \mathbf{x}_{i+1} = \begin{bmatrix} \mathbf{d}^i \\ d^{(i+1)} \end{bmatrix}, \tag{19.98}$$

and

$$\begin{bmatrix} \mathbf{A}_i \\ \mathbf{a}_{i+1} \end{bmatrix}^T \begin{bmatrix} \mathbf{A}_i \\ \mathbf{a}_{i+1} \end{bmatrix} \mathbf{x}_{i+1} = \begin{bmatrix} \mathbf{A}_i \\ \mathbf{a}_{i+1} \end{bmatrix}^T \begin{bmatrix} \mathbf{d}^i \\ d^{(i+1)} \end{bmatrix}. \tag{19.99}$$

Hence,

$$\mathbf{x}_{i+1} = \mathbf{S}_{i+1}\left[\mathbf{A}_i^T \mathbf{d}^i + d^{(i+1)}\mathbf{a}_{i+1}^T\right]$$

$$= \mathbf{x}_i - \frac{\mathbf{S}_i \mathbf{a}_{i+1}^T \mathbf{a}_{i+1}}{1 + \mathbf{a}_{i+1}\mathbf{S}_i \mathbf{a}_{i+1}^T}\,\mathbf{x}_i + d^{(i+1)}\mathbf{S}_{i+1}\mathbf{a}_{i+1}^T$$

$$= \mathbf{x}_i - \frac{\mathbf{S}_i \mathbf{a}_{i+1}^T}{1 + \mathbf{a}_{i+1}\mathbf{S}_i \mathbf{a}_{i+1}^T}\,\mathbf{a}_{i+1} + \mathbf{x}_i + d^{(i+1)}\mathbf{S}_{i+1}\mathbf{a}_{i+1}^T$$

$$= \mathbf{x}_i - \left[\mathbf{S}_i \mathbf{a}_{i+1}^T - \frac{\mathbf{S}_i \mathbf{a}_{i+1}^T \mathbf{a}_{i+1}\mathbf{S}_i \mathbf{a}_{i+1}^T}{1 + \mathbf{a}_{i+1}\mathbf{S}_i \mathbf{a}_{i+1}^T}\right]\mathbf{a}_{i+1}\mathbf{x}_i + d^{(i+1)}\mathbf{S}_{i+1}\mathbf{a}_{i+1}^T$$

$$= \mathbf{x}_i - \left[\mathbf{S}_i - \frac{\mathbf{S}_i \mathbf{a}_{i+1}^T \mathbf{a}_{i+1}\mathbf{S}_i}{1 + \mathbf{a}_{i+1}\mathbf{S}_i \mathbf{a}_{i+1}^T}\right]\mathbf{a}_i^T + \mathbf{a}_{i+1}\mathbf{x}_i + d^{(i+1)}\mathbf{S}_{i+1}\mathbf{a}_{i+1}^T$$

$$= \mathbf{x}_i - \mathbf{S}_{i+1}\mathbf{a}_{i+1}^T \mathbf{a}_{i+1}\mathbf{x}_i + d^{(i+1)}\mathbf{S}_{i+1}\mathbf{a}_{i+1}^T$$

$$= \mathbf{x}_i + \mathbf{S}_{i+1}\mathbf{a}_{i+1}^T\left[d^{(i+1)} - \mathbf{a}_{i+1}\mathbf{x}_i\right],$$

which is the formula in Eq. (19.88).

19.3.2 Neural Fuzzy Controllers with TSK Fuzzy Rules

In this section, we consider the neural fuzzy control systems with TSK fuzzy rules whose consequents are linear combinations of their preconditions. The TSK fuzzy rules are in the following forms:

$$R^j: \text{ IF } x_i \text{ is } A_i^j \text{ AND } x_2 \text{ is } A_2^j \text{ AND } \cdots \text{ AND } x_n \text{ is } A_n^j, \qquad (19.100)$$

$$\text{THEN } y = f_j = a_0^j + a_1^j x_1 + a_2^j x_2 + \cdots + a_n^j x_n,$$

where x_i is an input variable, y is the output variable, A_i^j are linguistic terms of the precondition part with membership functions $\mu_{A_i^j}(x_i)$, $a_i^j \in \mathbb{R}$ are coefficients of linear equations $f_j(x_1, x_2, \ldots, x_n)$, and $j = 1, 2, \ldots, M$, $i = 1, 2, \ldots, n$. To simplify our discussion, we shall focus on a specific NFC of this type called an *adaptive network–based fuzzy inference system* (ANFIS) [Jang, 1992].

For simplicity, assume that the fuzzy control system under consideration has two inputs x_1 and x_2 and one output y and that the rule base contains two TSK fuzzy rules as follows:

$$R^1: \text{ IF } x_1 \text{ is } A_1^1 \text{ AND } x_2 \text{ is } A_2^1, \text{ THEN } y = f_1 = a_0^1 + a_1^1 x_1 + a_2^1 x_2, \qquad (19.101)$$

$$R^2: \text{ IF } x_1 \text{ is } A_1^2 \text{ AND } x_2 \text{ is } A_2^2, \text{ THEN } y = f_2 = a_0^2 + a_1^2 x_1 + a_2^2 x_2. \qquad (19.102)$$

For given input values x_1 and x_2, the inferred output y^* is calculated by [see Eq. (7.29)]

$$y^* = \frac{\mu_1 f_1 + \mu_2 f_2}{\mu_1 + \mu_2}, \qquad (19.103)$$

where μ_j are firing strengths of R^j, $j = 1, 2$, and are given by

$$\mu_j = \mu_{A_1^j}(x_1) \cdot \mu_{A_2^j}(x_2), \qquad j = 1, 2, \tag{19.104}$$

if product inference is used. The corresponding ANFIS architecture is shown in Fig. 19.9, where node functions in the same layers are of the type described below.

- **Layer 1:** Every node in this layer is an input node that just passes external signals to the next layer.
- **Layer 2:** Every node in this layer acts as a membership function $\mu_{A_i^j}(x_i)$, and its output specifies the degree to which the given x_i satisfies the quantifier A_i^j. Usually, we choose $\mu_{A_i^j}(x_i)$ to be bell-shaped with a maximum equal to 1 and a minimum equal to 0, such as

$$\mu_{A_i^j}(x_i) = \frac{1}{1 + \{[(x_i - m_i^j)/\sigma_i^j]^2\}^{b_i^j}}, \tag{19.105}$$

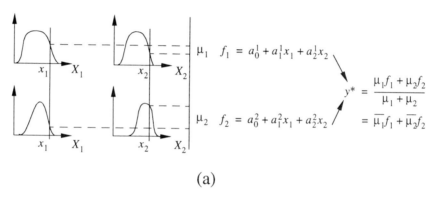

(a)

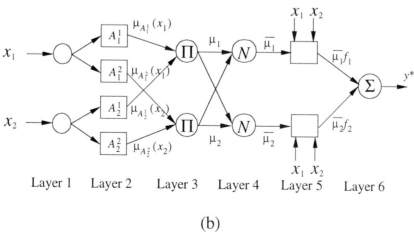

(b)

Figure 19.9 Structure of an ANFIS. (a) A fuzzy inference system. (b) Equivalent ANFIS.

$$\mu_{A_i^j}(x_i) = \exp\left\{-\left[\left(\frac{x_i - m_i^j}{\sigma_i^j}\right)^2\right]^{b_i^j}\right\},$$ (19.106)

where $\{m_i^j, \sigma_i^j, b_i^j\}$ is the parameter set to be tuned. In fact, any continuous and piece-wise-differentiable functions, such as commonly used trapezoidal or triangular membership functions, are also qualified candidates for node functions in this layer. Parameters in this layer are referred to as *precondition parameters*.

- **Layer 3:** Every node in this layer is labeled $\prod$ and multiplies the incoming signals $\mu_j = \mu_{A_1^j}(x_i) \cdot \mu_{A_2^j}(x_2)$ and sends the product out. Each node output represents the firing strength of a rule. In fact, other *t*-norm operators can be used as the node function for the generalized AND function.

- **Layer 4:** Every node in this layer is labeled N and calculates the *normalized firing strength* of a rule. That is, the *j*th node calculates the ratio of the *j*th rule's firing strength to the sum of all the rules' firing strengths, $\overline{\mu}_j = \mu_j/(\mu_{A_1^j}(x_1) + \mu_{A_2^j}(x_2))$.

- **Layer 5:** Every node *j* in this layer calculates the weighted consequent value $\overline{\mu}_j(a_0^j + a_1^j x_1 + a_2^j x_2)$, where $\overline{\mu}_j$ is the output of layer 4 and $\{a_0^j, a_1^j, a_2^j\}$ is the parameter set to be tuned. Parameters in this layer are referred to as *consequent parameters*.

- **Layer 6:** The only node in this layer is labeled $\sum$, and it sums all incoming signals to obtain the final inferred result for the whole system.

Thus, we have constructed an ANFIS that is functionally equivalent to a fuzzy control system with TSK rules. This ANFIS architecture can then update its parameters according to the back-propagation algorithm. We can derive the update rule for each parameter in the ANFIS as we did for the FALCON in Sec. 19.2.1. Moreover, the Kalman filter algorithm introduced in the last section can also be used to find the consequent parameters of an ANFIS. This is achieved by arranging all the consequent parameters in one vector $(a_0^1, a_1^1, a_2^1, a_0^2, a_1^2, a_2^2)^T$ and using the Kalman filter algorithm to solve the following over-constrained simultaneous linear equations:

$$
\begin{bmatrix}
\overline{\mu}_1^{(1)} & \overline{\mu}_1^{(1)}x_1^{(1)} & \overline{\mu}_1^{(1)}x_2^{(1)} & \overline{\mu}_2^{(1)} & \overline{\mu}_2^{(1)}x_1^{(1)} & \overline{\mu}_2^{(1)}x_2^{(1)} \\
\overline{\mu}_1^{(2)} & \overline{\mu}_1^{(2)}x_1^{(2)} & \overline{\mu}_1^{(2)}x_2^{(2)} & \overline{\mu}_2^{(2)} & \overline{\mu}_2^{(2)}x_1^{(2)} & \overline{\mu}_2^{(2)}x_2^{(2)} \\
\vdots & \vdots & \vdots & \vdots & \vdots & \vdots \\
\overline{\mu}_1^{(p)} & \overline{\mu}_1^{(p)}x_1^{(p)} & \overline{\mu}_1^{(p)}x_2^{(p)} & \overline{\mu}_2^{(p)} & \overline{\mu}_2^{(p)}x_1^{(p)} & \overline{\mu}_2^{(p)}x_2^{(p)}
\end{bmatrix}
\begin{bmatrix}
a_0^1 \\ a_1^1 \\ a_2^1 \\ a_0^2 \\ a_1^2 \\ a_2^2
\end{bmatrix}
=
\begin{bmatrix}
d^{(1)} \\ d^{(2)} \\ \vdots \\ d^{(p)}
\end{bmatrix},
$$ (19.107)

where $[(x_1^{(k)}, x_2^{(k)}), d^{(k)}]$ are the *k*th training pair, $k = 1, 2, \ldots, p$, and $\overline{\mu}_1^{(k)}$ and $\overline{\mu}_2^{(k)}$ are the third-layer outputs associated with the input $(x_1^{(k)}, x_2^{(k)})$.

19.3.3 Fuzzy Operator Tuning

In fuzzy logic rules, the total matching degree of the precondition part is calculated from the matching degree of each precondition by aggregation operators. By choosing proper aggregation operators, we can adjust the matching degree to match human intuition. Also, implication functions express the relationship between a precondition part and an action part. Thus, we can adjust the matching degree to match human intuition by choosing proper implication functions. Moreover, combination functions express the relationship between rules that are candidates for firing. By choosing proper combination functions, we can adjust a conclusion to match human intuition. Thus, it is extremely important to tune aggregation, implication, and combination functions as well as membership functions, especially for the fuzzy production rules in fuzzy expert systems. In the previous sections, we focused on the tuning of membership functions by keeping the fuzzy operators (e.g., min, max, and product operators) fixed. However, if a complex relationship exists between the conditions, we might not be able to achieve minimum errors just by tuning the membership functions. If similar characteristics exist in the relationships in some rule blocks, we must be able to efficiently tune the rule blocks by tuning the aggregation operators. Using typical *t*-norms and *t*-conorms, Gupta and Qi [1991] have shown that the performance of the fuzzy controller for a given plant depends on the choice of the *t*-norms and *t*-conorms. In this section, we shall consider automatic fuzzy operator tuning for the parametric *t*-norms and *t*-conorms whose characteristics can be modified by parameters [Miyoshi et al., 1993].

Consider a NFC with fuzzy singleton rules as shown in Fig. 19.7 and a NFC with TSK rules like the ANFIS shown in Fig. 19.9(b). Each node in layer 3 of these networks generates a signal corresponding to the aggregation of individual degrees of matching. This output signal indicates the firing strength of a fuzzy rule. The aggregation operator (i.e., the node function of layer 3) used was the product operator. In fact, other *t*-norms can be used as aggregation operators. These operators are called *conjunctive operators*. In most control, pattern classification, and query-retrieval systems, conjunctive operators play an important role and their interpretation changes across contexts. Since no single operator is suitable for all applications, we can use *parametric t-norms* as aggregation operators. For example, we can use the Dombi *t*-norm T_D, which covers a wide range of strengths, or the Hamachar *t*-norm T_H, which requires less computer power. They are defined as follows (see Table 2.3):

$$T_D(\gamma, x_1, x_2) = \frac{1}{1 + \sqrt[\gamma]{[(1 - x_1)/x_1]^\gamma + [(1 - x_2)/x_2]^\gamma}}, \qquad (19.108)$$

$$T_H(\gamma, x_1, x_2) = \frac{x_1 x_2}{\gamma + (1 - \gamma)(x_1 + x_2 - x_1 x_2)}, \qquad (19.109)$$

where the x_i are the operands and γ is a nonnegative parameter.

In some other applications, features are combined in a compensatory way. For these situations, *mean operators* are more appropriate than conjunctive operators. To find a good mean operator for a certain system, we can also implement a parametric mean operator and use training data to calibrate it. For example, we can use the one proposed by Dyckhoff and Pedrycz:

$$M_{DP}(\gamma, x_1, x_2) = \frac{(x_1^\gamma + x_2^\gamma)^{1/\gamma}}{2}, \qquad (19.110)$$

where $\gamma \geq 1$. For a given input-output training data set, the parameter γ in these parametric operators can be tuned in the same way as the other parameters in the networks. The update rules for γ can be easily derived as $\gamma(t+1) = \gamma(t) - \eta \partial E / \partial \gamma$ by using the back-propagation algorithm, where E is a proper cost (error) function and $\partial E / \partial \gamma$ is derived by the chain rule based on the derivative $\partial T_D / \partial \gamma$, $\partial T_H / \partial \gamma$, or $\partial M_{DP} / \partial \gamma$.

Next, consider a more general NFC such as the FALCON whose fuzzy logic rules have fuzzy consequents. In this case, we need implication functions to relate a precondition part and a consequent part, and combination functions to relate different rules. Assume a fuzzy controller has M fuzzy rules, each of which is of the following form:

$$R^j: \text{IF } x_1 \text{ is } A_j \text{ AND } x_2 \text{ is } B_j, \text{ THEN } y \text{ is } C_j, \qquad j = 1, 2, \dots, M. \qquad (19.111)$$

The jth rule can be represented as the fuzzy relation R^j, and its membership function is given by

$$\mu_{R^j}(x_1, x_2, y) = f\left(\mu_{A_j}(x_1), \mu_{B_j}(x_2), \mu_{C_j}(y)\right), \qquad (19.112)$$

where $f(\cdot)$ is a general representation of the implication function. Any t-norm can be used as the implication function $f(\cdot)$ in Eq. (19.112). Then the overall fuzzy relation R can be written as

$$\mu_R(x_1, x_2, y) = \overset{M}{\underset{j=1}{T^*}}\left[\mu_{R^j}(x_1, x_2, y)\right] = \overset{M}{\underset{j=1}{T^*}}\left[T\left(\mu_{A_j}(x_1), \mu_{B_j}(x_2), \mu_{C_j}(y)\right)\right], \qquad (19.113)$$

where $T[\cdot]$ represents a t-norm and $T^*[\cdot]$ represents a t-conorm. For example, we can use the Dombi t-conorm T_D^* and the Mamachar t-conorm T_H^* defined by

$$T_D^*(\gamma, x_1, x_2) = \frac{1}{1 + \sqrt[\gamma]{[x_1/(1-x_1)]^\gamma + [x_2/(1-x_2)]^\gamma}}, \qquad (19.114)$$

$$T_H^*(\gamma, x_1, x_2) = \frac{x_1 + x_2 - x_1 x_2 - (1-\gamma)x_1 x_2}{1 - (1-\gamma)x_1 x_2}, \qquad (19.115)$$

where $\gamma \geq 0$. Let us take a look at the following example to see how the learning rule of γ can be derived.

Example 19.3

[Miyoshi et al., 1993]. Consider the following set of fuzzy logic rules for a fuzzy controller:

IF x_1 is negative (N1) AND x_2 is negative (N2), THEN y is negative (N3),
IF x_1 is negative (N1) AND x_2 is positive (P2), THEN y is zero (Z3),
IF x_1 is positive (P1) AND x_2 is negative (N2), THEN y is zero (Z3),
IF x_1 is positive (P1) AND x_2 is positive (P2), THEN y is positive (P3).

Then the fuzzy inferred result can be obtained by Eq. (19.113) as follows:

$$\mu_Y(y) = T^*[\, T[\mu_{N_1}(x_1), \mu_{N_2}(x_2), \mu_{N_3}(y)],$$
$$T[\mu_{N_1}(x_1), \mu_{P_2}(x_2), \mu_{Z_3}(y)],$$
$$T[\mu_{P_1}(x_1), \mu_{N_2}(x_2), \mu_{Z_3}(y)],$$
$$T[\mu_{P_1}(x_1), \mu_{P_2}(x_2), \mu_{P_3}(y)]\,].$$

The final crisp output y^* of the controller can be calculated by the center of gravity method from $\mu_Y(y)$.

The network realizing the fuzzy controller is shown in Fig. 19.10, where external inputs x_1 and x_2 are the states of the controlled plant and y on the input side indicates the values in the output domain Y which is discretized as $Y = [y_1, y_2, ..., y_N]$. Based on the notations in the figure, we shall show how to tune T and T^* in the network using the back-propagation algorithm. The values of y^1 through y^4 and y^* in Fig. 19.10 are given as

$$y^* = \frac{y^1}{y^2}, \qquad y^1 = \sum_y yy^3, \qquad y^2 = \sum_y y^3, \qquad y^3 = T^* [\gamma_{T^*}, y^4, ...], \qquad y^4 = T [\gamma_T, y^5, ...],$$

where γ_{T^*} and γ_T are the parameters of parametric t-conorms and t-norms, respectively. Note that the equations for y^1 through y^4 and y^* are differentiable. Hence, for a defined cost function E [e.g., $E = \sum_k [y^*(k) - y^d(k)]^2/2$, where $y^*(k)$ and $y^d(k)$ are, respectively, the actual output and desired output of the controller for the kth input], we can obtain the following derivatives:

$$\frac{\partial E}{\partial \gamma_{T^*}} = \frac{dE}{dy^*} \left(\frac{dy^*}{dy^1} \frac{dy^1}{dy^3} + \frac{dy^*}{dy^2} \frac{dy^2}{dy^3} \right) \frac{dy^3}{d\gamma_{T^*}},$$

$$\frac{\partial E}{\partial \gamma_T} = \frac{dE}{dy^*} \left(\frac{\partial y^*}{dy^1} \frac{dy^1}{dy^3} + \frac{dy^*}{dy^2} \frac{dy^2}{dy^3} \right) \frac{dy^3}{dy^4} \frac{dy^4}{d\gamma_T}.$$

Based on these derivatives, the update rules for γ_{T^*} and γ_T can be written as $\gamma_{T^*}(k+1) = \gamma_{T^*}(k) - \eta \, \partial E / \partial \gamma_{T^*}$ and $\gamma_T(k+1) = \gamma_T(k) - \eta \, \partial E / \partial \gamma_T$, respectively.

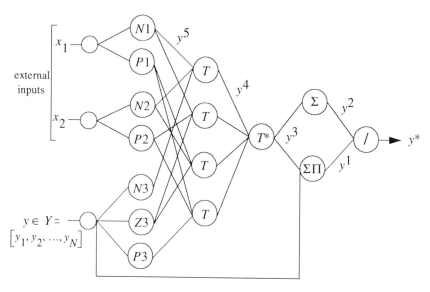

Figure 19.10 Neural fuzzy control network with operator learning used in Example 19.3.

19.4 STRUCTURE LEARNING FOR NEURAL FUZZY CONTROLLERS

In this section, we are concerned with the structure learning of neural fuzzy control systems. By *structure learning,* we mean the extraction of fuzzy logic rules from numerical training data and the tuning of fuzzy partitions of the input and output spaces. In the following sections, we shall first introduce some methods of rule extraction and then focus on the issues of fuzzy partitioning of the input (pattern) space. The tuning of the fuzzy partition of the output space will be discussed in Sec. 19.5.

19.4.1 Fuzzy Logic Rule Extraction from Numerical Training Data

Construction of fuzzy logic rules from numerical data for control and pattern classification problems consists of two phases: fuzzy partitioning of the input (pattern) space and identification of a fuzzy logic rule for each fuzzy subspace. If the fuzzy logic rules to be found consist of fuzzy consequent parts, we further need to consider the fuzzy partitioning of the output space. In this section, we assume that proper fuzzy partitions of input and/or output spaces and the associated membership functions are given beforehand. Then from a set of numerical training data, we must extract proper fuzzy logic rules.

Fuzzy logic rule extraction based on product space clustering. Let us consider a geometric fuzzy logic rule extraction procedure proposed by Kosko [1992c]. This procedure adaptively clusters training samples in the input-output product space of a fuzzy system. Each cluster formed in the input-output product space corresponds to one potential fuzzy logic rule. For illustration, assume that the fuzzy rules to be extracted are in the form of "IF x is A_i, THEN y is B_i" or (A_i, B_i), where $x \in X$ and $y \in Y$. The input-output product space is thus $X \times Y$. Suppose the r fuzzy sets $A_1, A_2, \ldots, A_r$ quantize the input universe of discourse X and the s fuzzy sets $B_1, B_2, \ldots, B_s$ quantize the output universe of discourse Y. In other words, the linguistic variable x assumes fuzzy values A_i, and linguistic variable y assumes fuzzy values B_j. Here we assume that r and s and the membership functions of the fuzzy sets A_i and B_i have been specified by the user. The fuzzy sets $\{A_i\}$ and $\{B_j\}$ define rs *fuzzy grids* F_{ij} in the input-output product space $X \times Y$. Each fuzzy grid defines one possible fuzzy logic rule.

The basic concept of automatic generation of fuzzy rules from numerical training data (x_i, y_i), $i = 1, 2, \ldots$, is to use the vector quantization algorithms to find and allocate quantization vectors of the training data to fuzzy grids on the (fuzzy) partitioned input-output product space and then determine the weight of each fuzzy grid according to the number of quantization vectors falling into it. The vector quantization algorithms include the Kohonen learning rule, the differential competitive learning (DCL) rule, and others. Let $\mathbf{t}_1, \mathbf{t}_2, \ldots, \mathbf{t}_m$ denote the m (two-dimensional) quantization vectors to be learned in the input-output product space $X \times Y$. One guideline is to choose the value of m such that $m \geq rs$ since in principle the m quantization vectors could describe a uniform distribution of product-space trajectory data. In that case, the rs fuzzy grids would each contain at least one quantization vector. The quantization vectors $\mathbf{t}_j$ naturally weigh an estimated fuzzy logic rule; the more quantization vectors clustered about a fuzzy rule (i.e., a fuzzy grid), the greater its possibility (weight) of existence. Suppose k_i quantization vectors cluster around the ith fuzzy grid. Then $k \triangleq k_1 + k_2 + \cdots + k_{rs} = m$, and the weight of the ith fuzzy rule is

$$w_i = \frac{k_i}{k}. \tag{19.116}$$

In practice we may want only a fixed number of most-frequent fuzzy rules or only the fuzzy rules with at least some minimum w_{min} since most fuzzy grids contain zero or few quantization vectors.

The above discussion extends to compound fuzzy rules and product spaces. For example, consider the fuzzy rule "IF x is A AND y is B, THEN z is C" or $(A, B; C)$. Assume the t fuzzy sets $C_1, C_2, ..., C_t$ quantize the output space Z. Hence, there are rst fuzzy grids F_{ijk}. Then Eq. (19.116) can be similarly extended. The following example illustrates the rule generation process.

Example 19.4

[Kosko, 1992c]. Let X and Y each equal the real line. Suppose the overlapping fuzzy sets NL, NM, NS, ZE, PS, PM, PL quantize the input space X. Suppose seven similar fuzzy sets quantize the output space Y. The fuzzy sets can be defined arbitrarily. In practice they are symmetric trapezoids or triangles. The boundary fuzzy sets NL and PL are usually ramp functions or clipped trapezoids. A typical fuzzy rule is "IF x is NL, THEN y is PS" or $(NL; PS)$.

Suppose that Fig. 19.11(a) represents the input-output training data $(x_1, y_1), (x_2, y_2), ...,$ in the planar product space $X \times Y$ and that these sample data are fed to a DCL algorithm. The learned 49 two-dimensional quantization vectors $\mathbf{t}_1, \mathbf{t}_2, ..., \mathbf{t}_{49}$ are distributed in the product space as shown in Fig. 19.11(b). For convenience, fuzzy grids do not overlap in Fig. 19.11(a) and (b). Figure 19.11(b) reveals 19 sample-data clusters. The weight of each cluster can be defined according to Eq. (19.116). For example, the rule $(NS; PS)$ has weight $8/49 = 0.16$, the rule $(NL; PL)$ has weight $2/49 = 0.04$, and the rule $(PL; NL)$ has weight $1/49 = 0.02$. Most fuzzy grids have zero weight and do not generate fuzzy rules. If we set a threshold of two quantization vectors per fuzzy grid (e.g., $w_{min} = 0.03$), then the product space clustering will yield 10 fuzzy rules.

Note that if this procedure is used to find fuzzy control rules, then it will map every domain fuzzy set A to a unique range fuzzy set B. Fuzzy set A cannot map to multiple fuzzy

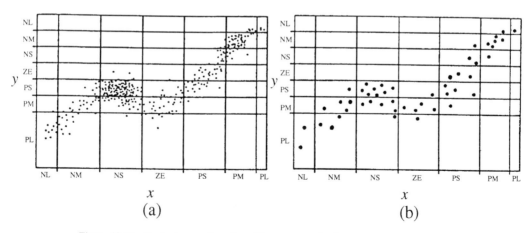

Figure 19.11 Product space clustering with vector quantization. (a) Small dots showing the distribution of observed sample data. (b) Larger dots showing the distribution of quantization vectors. The weight w_{ij} of fuzzy rule (A_i, B_j) increases as the $A_i \times B_j$ grid's count of quantization vectors increases. (Adapted from Kosko [1992c], © 1992 IEEE.)

sets B, B', B'', and so on. In this case, we estimate at most one rule per fuzzy grid column in Fig. 19.11(b). The simplest strategy is to pick only the highest-weight fuzzy grid per column. If two fuzzy grids in a column have equally high weights, we can arbitrarily pick either fuzzy rule. For example, in Fig. 19.11(b), the seven fuzzy control rules are *(NL; PL)*, *(NM; PM)*, *(NS; PS)*, *(ZE; PM)*, *(PS; PS)*, *(PM; NM)*, and *(PL; NL)*.

Fuzzy logic rule extraction based on ellipsoidal covariance learning. The key concept of the product-space clustering procedure is that through competitive learning, each quantization vector can estimate a local cluster and converge to the cluster's centroid. Here, this concept is further extended such that unsupervised competitive learning is used to estimate not only the local centroids but also the *covariances* of pattern classes [Dickerson and Kosko, 1993]. The covariance matrix of each random quantization vector defines an ellipsoid around the centroid of the pattern class. The ellipsoids define *fuzzy clusters* or rules that cover the graph of the function. Regions of sparse data give rise to large ellipsoids or less certain rules. Such a learning algorithm is thus called the *ellipsoidal covariance learning* algorithm. This learning algorithm uses first- and second-order statistics to estimate fuzzy logic rules and fuzzy sets from input-output data.

In ellipsoidal covariance learning, a neural network with the same topology as that in Fig. 12.3 is used for vector quantization. The competitive learning rule is used here [see Eq. (12.8)]:

$$\mathbf{t}_j(t+1) = \begin{cases} \mathbf{t}_j(t) + c_t[\mathbf{x}(t) - \mathbf{t}_j(t)] & \text{if the } j\text{th neuron wins} \\ \mathbf{t}_j(t) & \text{if the } j\text{th neuron loses,} \end{cases} \quad (19.117)$$

where $\mathbf{t}_j$ is the jth quantization vector to be learned and $\mathbf{x}(t)$ is the input training vector at time t. This update rule will make the quantization vectors converge exponentially to the local centroids of pattern classes. Centroids provide a first-order estimate of how the unknown probability density function $p(\mathbf{x})$ behaves in the regions $\mathbf{D}_j$. Estimators have covariances, and local covariances give a second-order estimate. Competitive learning rule can also be used to asymptotically estimate the local conditional covariance matrices $\mathbf{K}_j$:

$$\mathbf{K}_j = E\left[(\mathbf{x} - \hat{\mathbf{x}}_j)(\mathbf{x} - \hat{\mathbf{x}}_j)^T \mid \mathbf{D}_j\right]. \quad (19.118)$$

At each iteration, we estimate the unknown centroid $\hat{\mathbf{x}}_j$ as the current quantization vector $\mathbf{t}_j$. In this sense $\mathbf{K}_j$ becomes an error conditional covariance matrix. This leads to the following update rule for $\mathbf{K}_j$:

$$\mathbf{K}_j(t+1) = \begin{cases} \mathbf{K}_j(t) + d_t\left[(\mathbf{x}(t) - \mathbf{t}_j(t))(\mathbf{x}(t) - \mathbf{t}_j(t))^T - \mathbf{K}_j(t)\right] \\ \quad \text{if the } j\text{th neuron wins,} \\ \mathbf{K}_j(t) \\ \quad \text{if the } j\text{th neuron loses.} \end{cases} \quad (19.119)$$

According to this rule, $\mathbf{K}_j(t+1)$ converges to the local conditional covariance matrix.

Ellipsoidal covariance learning finds the fuzzy logic rules and fuzzy sets from the input-output training data. The covariance estimates define ellipsoids in the q-dimensional input-output product space (Fig. 19.12), where $q = n + p$ for n inputs to the fuzzy system

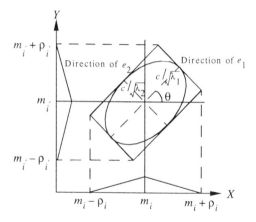

Figure 19.12 Positive-definite matrix $\mathbf{K}_j^{-1}$ defines an ellipsoid around the center $\mathbf{m}$ of the ellipsoid. The eigenvectors of $\mathbf{K}_j^{-1}$ define the axes, and the eigenvalues define the length of the axes. The ellipsoid projects onto the axes to define the input and output fuzzy sets. (Adapted from Dickerson and Kosko [1993], © 1993 IEEE.)

and p outputs of the fuzzy system. The covariance ellipsoid is the locus of all $\mathbf{x}$ in q-space that satisfy

$$c^2 = (\mathbf{x} - \mathbf{t}_j)^T \mathbf{K}_j^{-1} (\mathbf{x} - \mathbf{t}_j), \tag{19.120}$$

where c is the ellipsoid scaling constant. Assuming that $\mathbf{K}_j$ is positive-definite and the eigenvalues of $\mathbf{K}_j^{-1}$ are $\lambda_1, \lambda_2, \dots, \lambda_q$, the eigenvalues and eigenvectors of the positive-definite matrix $\mathbf{K}_j^{-1}$ define an ellipsoid in q space. The eigenvectors orient the ellipsoid. The Euclidean half-lengths of the axes equal $c/\sqrt{\lambda_1}, c/\sqrt{\lambda_2}, \dots, c/\sqrt{\lambda_q}$.

The covariance ellipsoids relate local changes in the input-output product space. The projections of the ellipsoid onto the input and output axes bound the fuzzy sets. This is illustrated in Fig. 19.13, where symmetric triangular sets are centered at the centroid. The ellipsoid itself defines a fuzzy rule between the inputs and the outputs. A quantization vector "hops" more in regions where data are sparse and so gives rise to larger ellipsoids or less certain rules. Tightly clustered data give rise to smaller ellipsoids or more certain rules. Moreover, different values of the ellipsoid scaling constant c change the size of the projections on the axis. Larger values of c smooth the data, and small values of c provide more resolution in areas where there are many quantization vectors. Ellipsoidal covariance

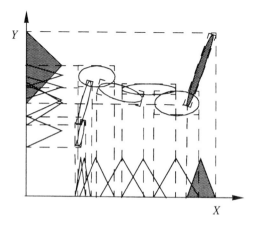

Figure 19.13 Projection of each ellipsoid onto the axes of the input-output state space defines a fuzzy rule between the inputs and the outputs. (Adapted from Dickerson and Kosko [1993], © 1993 IEEE.)

learning has been used to estimate the control surface for car velocity control [Dickerson and Kosko, 1993].

Fuzzy rule extraction based on direct matching.   We shall now introduce a simple, straightforward method proposed by Wang and Mendel [1992b] for generating fuzzy rules from numerical input-output training data. This is a one-pass build-up procedure that avoids time-consuming training. To illustrate this method, suppose we are given a set of desired input-output data pairs: $(x_1^{(1)}, x_2^{(1)}; y^{(1)})$, $(x_1^{(2)}, x_2^{(2)}, y^{(2)}), \ldots$, where x_1 and x_2 are inputs and y is the output. It is straightforward to extend this method to general multi-input–multi-output cases. The task here is to generate a set of fuzzy rules from the desired input-output pairs and use these fuzzy rules to determine a mapping $f: (x_1, x_2) \rightarrow y$. This approach consists of the following three steps:

Step 1: *Divide the input and output spaces into fuzzy regions.* Assume that the domain intervals of x_1, x_2, and y are $[x_1^-, x_1^+]$, $[x_2^-, x_2^+]$, and $[y^-, y^+]$, respectively. Divide each domain interval into N regions and assign each region a fuzzy membership function. Figure 19.14 shows an example where the domain interval of x_1 is divided into five regions, the domain interval of x_2 is divided into seven regions, and the domain interval of y is divided into five regions. The shape of each membership function is triangular; one vertex lies at the center of the region and has a membership value of unity; the other two vertices lie at the centers of the two neighboring regions and have membership values equal to zero. Of course, other divisions of the domain regions and other shapes of membership functions are possible.

Step 2: *Generate fuzzy rules from given data pairs.* First, determine the degrees of given data $x_1^{(i)}$, $x_2^{(i)}$, and $y^{(i)}$ in different regions. For example, $x_1^{(1)}$ in Fig. 19.14 has degree 0.8 in $B1$, degree 0.2 in $B2$, and zero degrees in all the other

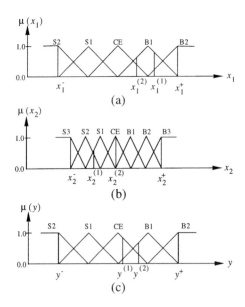

(a)

(b)

(c)

Figure 19.14   Division of input and output spaces into fuzzy regions and the corresponding membership functions. (a) $\mu(x_1)$. (b) $\mu(x_2)$. (c) $\mu(y)$. (Adapted from Wang and Mendel [1992b], © 1992 IEEE.)

regions. Similarly, $x_2^{(2)}$ in Fig. 19.14 has degree 1 in CE and zero degrees in all other regions.

Second, assign $x_1^{(i)}$, $x_2^{(i)}$, and $y^{(i)}$ to a region with maximum degree. For example, $x_1^{(1)}$ in Fig. 19.14 is assigned to $B1$ and $x_2^{(2)}$ in Fig. 19.14 is assigned to CE.

Finally, obtain one rule from one pair of desired input-output data, for example,

$$\left(x_1^{(1)}, x_2^{(1)}; y^{(1)}\right) \Rightarrow \left[x_1^{(1)} (0.8 \text{ in } B1), x_2^{(1)} (0.7 \text{ in } S1),\right.$$

$$\left. y^{(1)} (0.9 \text{ in } CE)\right] \Rightarrow \text{rule } 1;$$

R^1: IF x_1 is $B1$ AND x_2 is $S1$, THEN y is CE;

$$\left(x_1^{(2)}, x_2^{(2)}; y^{(2)}\right) \Rightarrow \left[x_1^{(2)} (0.6 \text{ in } B1), x_2^{(2)} (1 \text{ in } CE),\right.$$

$$\left. y^{(2)} (0.7 \text{ in } B1)\right] \Rightarrow \text{rule } 2;$$

R^2: IF x_1 is $B1$ AND x_2 is CE, THEN y is $B1$.

Step 3: *Assign a degree to each rule.* To resolve the possible conflict problem (i.e., rules having the same IF part but a different THEN part) and to reduce the number of rules, we assign a degree to each rule generated from data pairs and accept only the rule from a conflict group that has a maximum degree.

The following product strategy is used to assign a degree to each rule: The degree of the rule "IF x_1 is A and x_2 is B, THEN y is C," denoted by $D(\text{rule})$, is defined as

$$D(\text{rule}) = \mu_A(x_1)\, \mu_B(x_2)\, \mu_C(y). \tag{19.121}$$

For example, rule 1 has a degree of

$$D(\text{rule } 1) = \mu_{B1}(x_1)\, \mu_{S1}(x_2)\, \mu_{CE}(y)$$

$$= 0.8 \times 0.7 \times 0.9 = 0.504,$$

and rule 2 has a degree of

$$D(\text{rule } 2) = \mu_{B1}(x_1)\, \mu_{CE}(x_2)\, \mu_{B1}(y)$$

$$= 0.6 \times 1 \times 0.7 = 0.42.$$

Note that if two or more generated fuzzy rules have the same preconditions and consequents, use the rule that has maximum degree. It has been shown that this approach to building up fuzzy systems is capable of approximating any real, continuous function on a compact set to arbitrary accuracy [Wang and Mendel, 1992b].

19.4.2 Genetic Algorithms for Fuzzy Partition of Input Space

In this section, we shall introduce a flexible fuzzy partitioning method based on genetic algorithms (GAs). As we have noticed, the precondition part of a fuzzy rule can be considered a *fuzzy hyperrectangle* in the multidimensional input space, and proper fuzzy partitioning of the input (pattern) space plays an important role in the structure learning of neural fuzzy control (classification) systems. Standard fuzzy partitioning is based on (adaptive) *fuzzy grids* which we have used previously. Figure 19.15(a) illustrates the adaptive fuzzy grids for a two-dimensional input space. In this adaptive fuzzy grid scheme, a uniformly partitioned grid is taken as the initial state at the beginning of learning. As the parameters in the precondition membership functions are adjusted, the grids evolve. The location and size of the fuzzy regions, as well as the degree of overlapping among them, are optimized by, for example, the gradient-descent method. There are two problems with this scheme. First, the number of linguistic terms for each input variable is predetermined and is highly heuristic. Second, the learning complexity undergoes an exponential explosion as the number of inputs increases.

To cope with these problems, a flexible partitioning, the *fuzzy k-d trees* illustrated in Fig. 19.15(b), can be adopted. A *k-d* tree results from a series of *guillotine cuts*. By a guillotine cut, we mean a cut that is made entirely across the subspace to be partitioned; each of the regions so produced can then be subjected to independent guillotine cutting. At the beginning of the *i*th iteration step, the input space is partitioned into i regions. Then another guillotine cut is applied to one of the regions to further partition the entire space into $(i + 1)$ regions. There are various strategies for deciding which dimension to cut and where to cut it at each step. In the following, we shall employ genetic algorithms to do this.

To apply GAs to identify proper fuzzy *k-d* tree in the input space, it is crucial to define context-sensitive crossover and mutation operators so that new fuzzy partitions produced are all legal points in the solution space. For input space partitioning, the following format of a chromosome is defined:

$$[C_1 C_2 ... C_{n-1}], \tag{19.122}$$

where each C_i encodes the information for a guillotine cut in the input space and n is the total number of rules. Each C_i contains two pieces of information: the dimension on which a subspace should be cut and the point at which it should be cut. Given a chromosome, we can decode it to obtain a partition and then evaluate it by the performance of that partition. Under this definition of a chromosome, all new fuzzy partitions resulting from crossover are legal partitions. The crossover operation is demonstrated in Fig. 19.16. Assume Fig. 19.16(a) is partitioned by the chromosome $[C_1^a C_2^a C_3^a C_4^a]$ and Fig. 19.16(b) by $[C_1^b C_2^b C_3^b C_4^b]$. After a crossover operation at the middle point, we obtain two new chromosomes, $[C_1^a C_2^a C_3^b C_4^b]$ and $[C_1^b C_2^b C_3^a C_4^a]$, which correspond to Fig. 19.16(c) and (d), respectively.

The mutation operator, which varies a single guillotine cut randomly, results in a fuzzy partition slightly different from the parent fuzzy partition. Two application-dependent

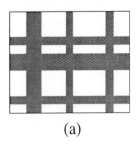

(a)

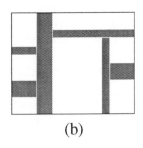

(b)

Figure 19.15 Fuzzy partitions of two-dimensional input space. (a) Adaptive fuzzy grid. (b) Fuzzy *k-d* tree.

Neural Fuzzy Controllers   Chap. 19

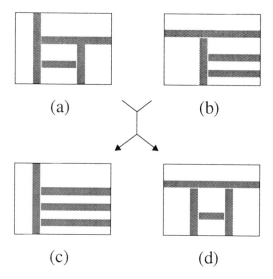

(a)   (b)

(c)   (d)

Figure 19.16 Crossover operator for input space partitioning.

mutation operators used for exploring new fuzzy partitions are defined. The first one is to switch two cuts in the partition sequence, with the switch position determined by a random number, as shown in Fig. 19.17(a), where the chromosome $[C_1C_2C_3C_4]$ is changed to $[C_1C_3C_2C_4]$. The second is to rotate the cuts, with the shift length determined randomly, as shown in Fig. 19.17(b), where the chromosome $[C_1C_2C_3C_4]$ is changed to $[C_2C_3C_4C_1]$.

The following example illustrates the use of GAs for structure learning, together with the use of the back-propagation algorithm for parameter learning, to construct a neural fuzzy classifier.

Example 19.5

In this example, we consider the use of the ANFIS introduced in Sec. 19.3.2 as a neural fuzzy classifier [Sun and Jang, 1993]. In this application of ANFIS [see Fig. 19.9(b)], the connections between layers 2 and 3 implement some fuzzy partition defined by guillotine cuts. Each network output indicates the degree to which the input vector belongs to a certain class.

Using GAs and the gradient-descent method, the neural fuzzy classifier (ANFIS) can be trained on, for example, the *Iris* categorization problem (see Example 8.4). In doing so, we first decide the number of rules, say 30, used in the simulation, that is, with 29 guillotine cuts encoded by chromosomes in the input space. In each generation, we keep a constant, say 100,

(a)

(b)

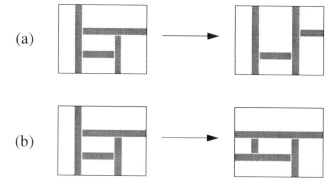

Figure 19.17 Mutation operator for input space partitioning. (a) Mutation operator 1: switching two chromosome units. In this example, cut C_2 and cut C_3 are exchanged, i.e., $[C_1C_2C_3C_4] \rightarrow [C_1C_3C_2C_4]$. (b) Mutation operator 2: rotating chromosome units. In this example, the cut sequence shifts up one position, i.e., $[C_1C_2C_3C_4] \rightarrow [C_2C_3C_4C_1]$.

chromosomes; in other words, the population size is 100. Each member of the population corresponds to an input space partition. We then construct a neural fuzzy classifier (ANFIS) based on the partition and start the gradient-descent learning process. At the end of some (say the fifth) training epoch, we take the number of misclassified patterns as the performance indicator. Based on the evaluation, the GA selects the partitions that fit better and proceeds to the next generation. Simulation results have indicated that this method requires fewer rules than general adaptive fuzzy-grid schemes.

Besides being used for the learning of fuzzy partitioning of the input space, GAs can also be employed to determine proper input and output membership functions [Karr and Gentry, 1993]. In this scheme, each chromosome (string) represents one particular set of all of the fuzzy membership functions employed by the fuzzy logic controller. Through genetic operations, proper combination of input-output membership functions can be obtained. It is also possible to determine membership functions, the number of fuzzy rules, and the rule consequent parameters simultaneously using GAs. The following example illustrates such an automatic design method for a fuzzy system with TSK rules.

Example 19.6

[Lee and Takagi, 1993]. In this example, a genetic algorithm is used to design a fuzzy controller with TSK rules for the cart-pole balancing problem. As shown in Fig. 19.18, the cart-pole balancing problem is the problem of learning how to balance an upright pole. The bottom of the pole is hinged to a cart that travels along a finite-length track to its right or its left. Both the cart and pole can move only in the vertical plane; that is, each has only one degree of freedom. There are four input state variables in this system: θ, the angle of the pole from an upright position (in degrees); $\dot{\theta}$, the angular velocity of the pole (in degrees per second); x, the horizontal position of the cart's center (in meters); and $\dot{x}$, the velocity of the cart (in meters per second). The only control action is f, which is the amount of force N applied to the cart to move it toward its left or right. The control goal is to balance the pole starting from nonzero conditions by supplying appropriate force to the cart. The behavior of these four state variables is governed by the following two second-order differential equations:

$$\ddot{\theta} = \frac{g \sin \theta + \cos \theta \left(\dfrac{-f - ml\dot{\theta}^2 \sin \theta}{m_c + m} \right)}{l \left(\dfrac{4}{3} - \dfrac{m \cos^2 \theta}{m_c + m} \right)}, \tag{19.123}$$

$$\ddot{x} = \frac{f + ml (\dot{\theta}^2 \sin \theta - \ddot{\theta} \cos \theta)}{m_c + m}, \tag{19.124}$$

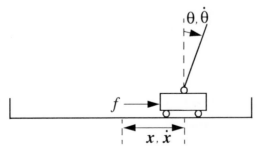

Figure 19.18   The cart-pole balancing system.

where g (acceleration due to gravity) is 9.8 meters per second squared, m_c (mass of cart) is 1.0 kilogram, m (mass of pole) is 0.1 kilogram, l (half-length of pole) is 0.5 meter, and f is the applied force in newtons.

Here, we consider only the pole angle θ and its derivative $\dot{\theta}$ as the state variables. The TSK rules considered here are of the form

$$R^i: \text{IF } \theta \text{ is } A_i \text{ AND } \dot{\theta} \text{ is } B_i, \text{ THEN } f = w_{1i}\theta + w_{2i}\dot{\theta} + w_{3i}, \qquad (19.125)$$

where f is the force imposed on the cart and $w_{ji}, j = 1, 2, 3$, are rule consequent parameters. Each membership function in the precondition part is triangular and is parameterized by a left base, a right base, and distance from the previous center point [see Fig. 19.19(a)]. By encoding the centers as a distance from the previous center (the first center was given as an absolute position) and the base values as the distance from the corresponding center point, we can use the boundary conditions of the application to eliminate unnecessary membership functions, which has the direct effect of eliminating rules. For example, all θ membership functions with center positions greater than $90°$ can be eliminated.

To use GAs, we first need to address the coding problem, that is, to define a chromosome as a set of parameters that represent an input membership function or a rule-consequent parameters set. This is illustrated in Fig. 19.19(b). By linking these chromosomes together, we can form the entire fuzzy system representation as shown in Fig. 19.19(c). The maximum number of fuzzy sets per input variable is set to 10. Note that if the input dimension is partitioned

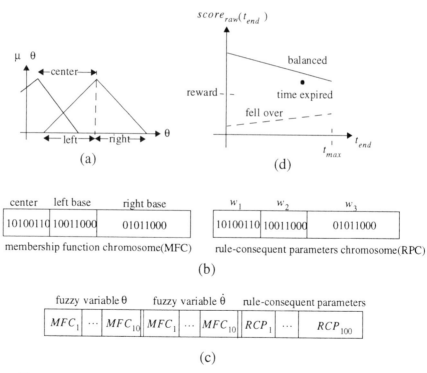

Figure 19.19   The cart-pole balancing problem in Example 19.6. (a) Representation of precondition membership functions. (b) Composite chromosomes. (c) Gene map of the whole fuzzy system. (d) Raw scoring functions. (Adapted from Lee and Takagi [1993], © 1993 IEEE.)

into $m \times n$, then the number of membership functions is $m + n$, the number of rules is mn, and the total number of system parameters is $3(m + n) + 3mn$.

The next step is to define a proper evaluation (or scoring) function. The objective of controlling an inverted pendulum here is to balance it in the shortest amount of time with as few rules as possible. To evaluate the fuzzy controller, we try it on the inverted pendulum starting with eight different initial conditions. Each trial terminates under one of the following three conditions: (1) the pole falls over, (2) the time expires, or (3) the system balances the pole ($|\theta| < \epsilon$ for some ϵ). Depending on the termination condition, we score a trial by the following rule [see Fig. 19.19(d)]:

$$
\text{score}(t_{end}) = \begin{cases} a_1(t_{max} - t_{end}) + a_2 \text{ reward} & (1) \\ \text{reward} & (2) \\ bt_{end} & (3) \end{cases}
$$

where a_1, a_2, b, and "reward" are constants, and (1) is when the pole balances, (2) is when $t_{max} = t_{end}$, and (3) is when the pole falls over ($|\theta| \geq 90°$). The general idea is that if the system balances the pole, a shorter time is better than a longer time. If the pole falls over, we recognize potential success and credit the system according to the time it kept it from falling. We then add additional terms to consider the steady-state error and to penalize the system according to the number of rules. The resulting fitness score for one trial is computed as follows:

$$
\text{score}(t_{end}) = \frac{\text{score}_{raw}(t_{end}) + c\sum_0^{t_{end}} |\theta_t|}{\text{number of rules} + \text{offset}_{rules}} \tag{19.126}
$$

The steady-state error is a simple summation of the pole angle derivation weighted with constant c. The offset$_{rules}$ parameter controls the degree of penalty for the number of rules. The scores from the trials are accumulated to form a composite score, which is used as the controller's overall fitness.

In the experiments, a GA with two-point crossover and mutation operators are used. Population size is set to 10, and crossover and mutation probabilities are 0.6 and 0.0333, respectively. An elitist strategy in which the member with the highest fitness value automatically advances to the next generation is also used. All members are initialized with random values in most experiments. In some experiments a priori knowledge is used to initialize one member of the population with seven uniformly spaced fuzzy sets for both θ and $\dot{\theta}$. Each of its 49 rules is initialized with $w_1 = w_2 = 0$ and w_3 equal to a value computed using the center points of the precondition membership functions and the control law:

$$
\text{Force} = c_1 \sin(\theta) + c_2 \dot{\theta}. \tag{19.127}
$$

The automatic design process is initiated by first setting the offset$_{rules}$ parameter and then letting the genetic algorithm produce 5000 generations of solutions. The best solution is kept, and the rest are discarded. In one experiment with the offset$_{rules}$ parameter set to 100, the method produces a symmetric system with only four rules. The obtained parameters in four consequent parts are $(w_{1i}, w_{2i}, w_{3i}) = (0.44, 1.02, -31.65), (1.54, -0.61, -30.14), (1.54, -0.61, 30.14)$, and $(0.44, 1.02, 31.65)$. The obtained triangular membership functions A_i and B_i are [in the form (center position, left base, right base)] $A_1 = A_3 = (-62.12, 57.53, 66.71), A_2 = A_4 = (62.12, 66.71, 57.53), B_1 = B_3 = (-1.99, 217.65, 240.55)$, and $B_2 = B_4 = (1.99, 240.55, 217.65)$.

Thus far, we have focused on adaptive fuzzy partitioning of the input space. This is enough if we want to set up fuzzy rules with crisp consequents. However, if the fuzzy rules to be extracted have fuzzy consequents, we may also need to have flexible schemes for adaptive fuzzy partitioning of the output space. This issue is discussed in the next section.

19.5 ON-LINE STRUCTURE-ADAPTIVE NEURAL FUZZY CONTROLLERS

In Sec. 19.2, we introduced NFCs with hybrid structure-parameter learning. We further discussed parameter learning techniques and structure learning techniques individually for NFCs in Secs. 19.3 and 19.4, respectively. In these sections, the structure and parameter learning are performed individually in two phases. In the first phase, structure learning techniques are used to find proper fuzzy partitions and fuzzy logic rules, and then in the second phase, parameter learning techniques are applied to tune membership functions and/or parametric operators. Such hybrid learning algorithms for NFCs perform well if sets of training data are available off-line. However, the two-phase learning schemes make their application inconvenient in real-time environments where training data are generated on-line. In this section, we are interested in learning schemes that combine structure and parameter learning into a single phase such that fuzzy rules and membership functions can be learned simultaneously for each on-line incoming training data pair. We shall introduce two NFCs that have such on-line structure and parameter learning capabilities. They are both generalized from the FALCON introduced in Sec. 19.2.1. Another important feature of these systems is that they can tune the fuzzy partitions of the output (action) space dynamically. This is in contrast to the schemes discussed in the last section, where only the adaptive fuzzy partitions of input (pattern) space were considered.

19.5.1 The FALCON with On-Line Supervised Structure and Parameter Learning

In Sec. 19.2.1, we introduced the FALCON along with a hybrid learning algorithm (FALCON-H). Because of its two-phase learning method, the FALCON-H is suitable for off-line learning. In this section, we shall introduce an on-line supervised structure-parameter learning algorithm proposed by Lin and Lee [1992; Lin et al., 1995] for constructing the FALCON automatically and dynamically. The resulting system is called the FALCON-O for short. This algorithm combines the back-propagation learning scheme for parameter learning and the similarity measure in Eq. (2.30) for structure learning. The similarity measure is a tool for determining the degree to which two fuzzy sets are equal. This measure will be used to find the two most similar output membership functions (output term nodes) in the FALCON. According to this measure, a new output membership function may be added, and the rule node connections (the consequent links of rule nodes) are changed properly. This on-line structure-parameter learning algorithm can find proper fuzzy logic rules, membership functions, and the size of output fuzzy partitions simultaneously. Since the FALCON-O is a single-phase learning algorithm, it is more suitable for applications in a real-time changing environment than the FALCON-H is.

Before going into the details of this on-line learning algorithm, let us consider the similarity measure that will be used for structure learning. Since bell-shaped membership functions will be used in the FALCON-O, we need to derive the exact formula of the similarity measure of two fuzzy sets with bell-shaped membership functions. However, since this formula will be incorporated into the on-line learning algorithm later, its computation time is important. To reduce the computational complexity of the exact formula (which includes the *error function* [Lin, 1994]), an approximate approach is used as follows. Since the area of the bell-shaped function $\exp\{-(x-m)^2/\sigma^2\}$ is $\sigma\sqrt{\pi}$ and its height is always 1, it can be approximated by an isosceles triangle with unity height and the length of bottom edge $2\sigma\sqrt{\pi}$. We can then compute the approximate similarity measure of two fuzzy sets A and B with membership function $\mu_A(x) = \exp\{-(x-m_1)^2/\sigma_1^2\}$ and $\mu_B(x) = \exp\{-(x-m_2)^2/\sigma_2^2\}$ with these kinds of triangular membership functions. Assume $m_1 \geq m_2$. First, we can find $|A \cap B|$:

$$
\begin{aligned}
|A \cap B| = & \frac{1}{2} \frac{h^2(m_2 - m_1 + \sqrt{\pi}(\sigma_1 + \sigma_2))}{\sqrt{\pi}(\sigma_1 + \sigma_2)} \\
& + \frac{1}{2} \frac{h^2(m_2 - m_1 + \sqrt{\pi}(\sigma_1 - \sigma_2))}{\sqrt{\pi}(\sigma_2 - \sigma_1)} + \frac{1}{2} \frac{h^2(m_2 - m_1 - \sqrt{\pi}(\sigma_1 - \sigma_2))}{\sqrt{\pi}(\sigma_1 - \sigma_2)},
\end{aligned}
\tag{19.128}
$$

where $h(x) = \max\{0, x\}$. So the approximate similarity measure [see Eq. (2.30)] is

$$
E(A, B) = \frac{|A \cap B|}{|A \cup B|} = \frac{|A \cap B|}{\sigma_1\sqrt{\pi} + \sigma_2\sqrt{\pi} - |A \cap B|},
\tag{19.129}
$$

where we use the fact that $|A| + |B| = |A \cap B| + |A \cup B|$.

The derived similarity measure will be used here for developing an on-line supervised learning algorithm for the FALCON-O with the structure shown in Fig. 19.1. One important characteristic of this learning algorithm is that it can learn the network structure and network parameters simultaneously. The learning of network structure includes determining the proper number of output term nodes in layer 4 and the proper connections between the nodes in layers 3 and 4 (see Fig. 19.1). This structure learning thus determines the coarse of the output fuzzy partitions and the finding of correct fuzzy logic rules. The learning of network parameters includes adjustment of the node parameters in layers 2 and 4, which corresponds to the learning of input and output membership functions.

Given the supervised training data, the on-line learning algorithm first determines whether or not to perform the structure learning based on the similarity measures of the output membership functions. If the structure learning is necessary, then it will further decide whether or not to add a new output term node (a new membership function), and it will also change the consequents of some fuzzy logic rules properly. After structure learning occurs, parameter learning will take place to adjust the current membership functions. This structure-parameter learning will be repeated for each on-line incoming training input-output data pair.

To initiate the learning scheme, the desired coarse of input fuzzy partitions (i.e., the size of the term set of each input linguistic variable) and the initial guessed coarse of output fuzzy partitions must be provided from the outside world. Before this network is trained, an initial structure of the network is first constructed. Then, during the learning process, new nodes may be added and some connections may be changed. The initial structure of the FALCON-O is like that of the FALCON-H. That is, at first there is only one link between a rule node and an output linguistic variable. This link is connected to some term node of the output linguistic variable. The initial candidate (term node) of the consequent of a rule node can be assigned by an expert (if possible) or chosen randomly. A suitable term in each output linguistic variable's term set is chosen for each rule node after the learning process. To determine the initial membership functions of input-output linguistic variables, an efficient method is to use identical membership functions such that their domains can cover the region of corresponding input and output spaces *evenly* according to given initial coarses of fuzzy partitions.

After the initialization process for both the structure and parameters of the network, the learning algorithm enters the training loop where each loop corresponds to a set of training input data $x_i(t)$, $i = 1,\ldots, n$, and the desired output value $y_i^d(t)$, $i = 1,\ldots, m$, at a specific time t. Basically, the idea of back propagation is used to find the errors of node outputs in each layer. Then, these errors are analyzed by the similarity measure to perform structure adjustments or parameter adjustments. As in the FALCON-H, the goal is to minimize the error function in Eq. (19.15) using the general learning rules in Eqs. (19.16)–(19.18). As in the hybrid learning algorithm in Eqs. (19.19)–(19.37), we shall show the computation of $\partial E/\partial w$, layer by layer, in describing the on-line learning rules. The same notations used in the hybrid learning algorithm are adopted here.

- **Layer 5:** This step is similar to the parameter learning phase of the FALCON-H [Eqs. (19.19)–(19.23)]. The difference is that we do not change the m_i and σ_i values immediately [i.e., we do not perform Eqs. (19.20) and (19.22) immediately] but first view them as *expected* update amounts:

$$\Delta m_i(t) = -\eta \frac{\partial E}{\partial m_i} \qquad \text{and} \qquad \Delta \sigma_i(t) = -\eta \frac{\partial E}{\partial \sigma_i}, \qquad (19.130)$$

where $\partial E/\partial m_i$ and $\partial E/\partial \sigma_i$ come from Eqs. (19.19) and (19.21), respectively. Then the following similarity measure is performed.

Similarity Measure: In this step, the system determines if the current structure should be changed or not according to the expected updated amount of the center and width parameters [Eq. (19.130)]. To do this, the expected center and width are, respectively, computed as

$$m_{i\text{-new}} = m_i(t) + \Delta m_i(t), \qquad (19.131)$$

$$\sigma_{i\text{-new}} = \sigma_i(t) + \Delta \sigma_i(t). \qquad (19.132)$$

From the current membership functions of output linguistic variables, we want to find the one that is the most similar to the expected membership function by measuring their similarity. Let $\mu(m_i, \sigma_i)$ represent the bell-shaped membership function with center m_i and width σ_i. Let

$$
\begin{aligned}
\text{degree}(i, t) &= E\big[\mu(m_{i\text{-new}}, \sigma_{i\text{-new}}), \, \mu(m_{i\text{-closest}}, \sigma_{i\text{-closest}})\big] \\
&= \max_{1 \le j \le k} E\big[\mu(m_{i\text{-new}}, \sigma_{i\text{-new}}), \, \mu(m_j, \sigma_j)\big],
\end{aligned}
\qquad (19.133)
$$

where $k = |T(y)|$ is the size of the fuzzy partition of the output linguistic variable $y(t)$ and $E(\cdot,\cdot)$ is the similarity measure as defined in Eqs. (19.128) and (19.129). After the membership μ ($m_{i\text{-closest}}$, $\sigma_{i\text{-closest}}$) most similar to the expected membership function μ ($m_{i\text{-new}}$, $\sigma_{i\text{-new}}$) has been found, the following adjustment is made:

```
IF degree (i, t) < α(t),
    THEN
        create a new node  μ(m_{i-new}, σ_{i-new}) in layer 4
            and denote this new node as the i-closest node,
        do the structure learning process,
    ELSE IF μ(m_{i-closest}, σ_{i-closest}) ≠ μ(m_i, σ_i)
            THEN
                do the structure learning process,
            ELSE
                do the following parameter adjustments in layer 5:
                    m_i(t + 1) = m_{i-new}
                    σ_i(t + 1) = σ_{i-new}
                skip the structure learning process.
```

Here, $\alpha(t)$ is a monotonically increasing scalar similarity criterion such that *lower similarity* is allowed in the initial stages of learning. According to the above judgement, degree (i, t) is first compared to the similarity criterion. If the similarity is too low, then a new term node (a new membership function) with the expected parameters is added since in this case all the current membership functions are too different from the expected one. A new node with the expected membership function is necessary, and the output connections of those just-fired rule nodes should be changed to point to this new term node through the structure learning process. If no new term node is necessary, then it will then check whether the ith term node is the i-closest node. If this is false, it means that those just-fired fuzzy logic rules should have the i-closest (term) node instead of the original ith term node as their consequent. In this case, the structure learning process should be performed to change the link connection of the current structure properly. If the ith term node is the i-closest node, then no structural change is necessary and only the parameter learning should be performed by the standard back-propagation algorithm. The structure learning process is as follows:

- **Structure Learning:** When this process is started, it means that the ith term node in layer 4 is improperly assigned as the consequent of those fuzzy logic rules that just fired *strongly*. The more proper consequent for these fuzzy logic rules should be the i-closest node. To find the rules whose consequents should be changed, we set a *firing strength threshold* β. Only those fired rules whose firing strengths are higher than this threshold are treated as *really fired* rules. Only the really fired rules need to change their consequents, since only these rules are fired strongly enough to contribute to the above results of judgment. Assuming that the term node μ (m_i, σ_i) in layer 4 has inputs from rule nodes 1, 2,..., l, in layer 3, whose corresponding firing strengths are $a_i^{(3)}$, $i = 1, 2,..., l$, then

```
IF a_i^{(3)}(t) ≥ β THEN change the consequent of the ith rule node
    from μ(m_i, σ_i) to μ(m_{i-closest}, σ_{i-closest}).
```

- **Layers 4 through 2:** Learning rules in these layers are exactly the same as those of the FALCON-H in Eqs. (19.24)–(19.37).

After the consequents of the rule nodes are determined, the *rule combination* scheme in the FALCON-H is performed to reduce the number of rules. The on-line learning algorithm provides a novel scheme combining structure learning and parameter learning such that the whole network structure can be set up on-line with proper parameters. The following example illustrates the application of this on-line learning algorithm.

Example 19.7

This example continues with the simulation performed in Example 19.1 but using the on-line learning algorithm. The input variables x_0, x_1, x_2 and the output variable y are shown in Fig. 19.3. In the simulation, we set the size of fuzzy partitions of x_0, x_1, and x_2 to 3, 5, and 5, respectively. An initial guess of the size of the fuzzy partitions of the output linguistic variable is set to 3. The initial connections between the nodes in layers 3 and 4 are set randomly. Also, in the beginning, we use identical membership functions such that their domains can cover the region of corresponding input and output spaces evenly.

After the learning process, the final number of output fuzzy partitions is 10. That is, the learning algorithm adds seven extra term nodes to layer 4 of the FALCON-O. The solid curve in Fig. 19.20 is the learning curve of the mean error with respect to the number of epochs. A large learning error can be seen at the beginning of the learning process because of our random choice of initial structure and parameters. For purposes of comparison, we superimpose the learning curves of the two-phase hybrid learning algorithm in the FALCON-H; these are the two dashed curves in Fig. 19.20. In the two-phase hybrid learning process, the number of output fuzzy partitions was set by the user. Here, two different values are used, 10 and 15. The upper dashed curve in Fig. 19.20 is the learning curve when the number of output fuzzy partitions is set to 10, which is the final number we obtained in this on-line learning. The lower dashed curve in Fig. 19.20 is the learning curve when the number of output fuzzy partitions is set to 15, which is used in Example 19.1 and produces a more satisfactory result. The dotted curve in Fig. 19.20 is the learning curve when the second phase of the two-phase hybrid learning algorithm is replaced by the on-line structure-parameter learning algorithm discussed here. In phase 1, the Kohonen learning rule and the competitive learning law are still used to determine the proper initial fuzzy logic rules and membership functions for phase-2 learning. Provided with this kind of a priori knowledge, the on-line structure-parameter learning algorithm produces fewer errors as shown by the dotted curve in Fig. 19.20.

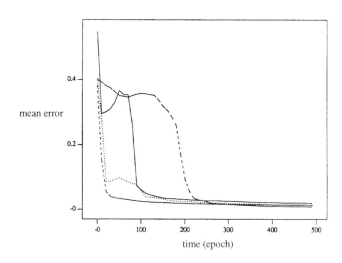

Figure 19.20 Learning curves: mean error versus time (epochs) in various fuzzy car simulations in Example 19.7.

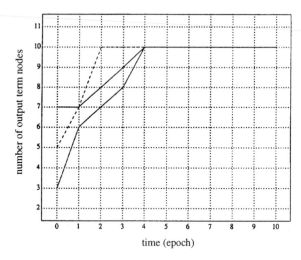

Figure 19.21   Learning curves: growing number of output term nodes versus time (epochs) in the structure-parameter learning in Example 19.7.

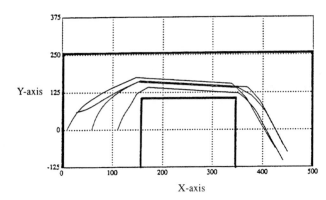

Figure 19.22   Simulation results for the fuzzy car running under control of the learned FALCON-O in Example 19.7.

To demonstrate the dynamical increase in output term nodes, three different initial guesses of the number of output fuzzy partitions are used. Figure 19.21 shows the curves of the growing number of output term nodes with respect to the number of epochs, and we can see that they all reach the final number of 10. After the whole connectionist fuzzy logic controller is established, it is used to control the fuzzy car. We keep the speed of the car constant and assume there are sensors on the car to measure the state variables x_0, x_1, and x_2 which are fed into the controller to derive the next steering angle. The simulated results are shown in Fig. 19.22 where different paths, different starting points, and different starting angles are used.

The on-line learning algorithm and the two-phase hybrid learning algorithm are two complementary schemes used to set up FALCONs. The former is good in a real-time environment, and the latter is superior when sets of training data are available off-line. The on-line learning algorithm also makes the incorporation of reinforcement learning techniques into the FALCON system feasible. We shall address the issue of using the FALCON for reinforcement learning in Sec. 19.6.

19.5.2 The FALCON with ART Neural Learning

For structure learning in neural fuzzy control systems, we examined adaptive fuzzy partitioning of the input space in Sec. 19.4.2 and adaptive fuzzy partitioning of the output space in Sec. 19.5.1. In this section, we shall introduce a FALCON that can perform more flexible fuzzy partitioning in both the input and the output spaces. This FALCON is trained by the fuzzy ART-like learning algorithm (see Sec. 20.2.4), resulting in *FALCON-ART* [Lin and Lin, 1994].

The FALCON-ART is a highly autonomous system. Initially, there are no hidden nodes (i.e., no membership functions or fuzzy rules). They are created and begin to grow as learning proceeds. The FALCON-ART can also dynamically partition the input-output spaces, tune activation (membership) functions, and find proper network connection types (fuzzy rules). The problem of space partitioning from numerical training data is basically a clustering problem. The FALCON-ART applies the fuzzy adaptive resonance theory (fuzzy ART) to perform fuzzy clustering in the input-output spaces using fuzzy hyperboxes and to find proper fuzzy logic rules dynamically by associating input clusters (hyperboxes) with output clusters (hyperboxes). The back-propagation learning scheme is then used for tuning input-output membership functions. Hence, the FALCON-ART combines the back-propagation algorithm for parameter learning and the fuzzy ART for structure learning.

The structure of the FALCON-ART model. The FALCON-ART has the same structure as the FALCON as shown in Fig. 19.1. However, the node functions in each layer are somewhat different to comply with the new on-line learning algorithm. Also, there are some restrictions on the connection types. Figure 19.23 shows the structure of the FALCON-ART. Before we describe the functions of the nodes in each of the five layers of the FALCON-ART model, we first describe the preprocessing performed in this model. In the FALCON-ART, the technique of *complement coding* used in the fuzzy ART (see Sec. 20.2.4) is adopted to normalize the input-output training vectors. Complement coding is a normalization process that rescales an n-dimensional vector in $\Re^n$, $\mathbf{x} = (x_1, x_2, \cdots, x_n)^T$, to its $2n$-dimensional complement-coding form in $[0, 1]^{2n}$, $\mathbf{x}'$ such that

$$
\begin{aligned}
\mathbf{x}' &\triangleq \left(\bar{x}_1, \bar{x}_1^{\,c}, \bar{x}_2, \bar{x}_2^{\,c}, \ldots, \bar{x}_n, \bar{x}_n^{\,c}\right)^T \\
&= \left(\bar{x}_1, 1 - \bar{x}_1, \bar{x}_2, 1 - \bar{x}_2, \ldots, \bar{x}_n, 1 - \bar{x}_n\right)^T,
\end{aligned}
\tag{19.134}
$$

where $\bar{\mathbf{x}} = (\bar{x}_1, \bar{x}_2, \cdots, \bar{x}_n)^T = \mathbf{x}/\|\mathbf{x}\|$ and $\bar{x}_1^{\,c}$ is the complement of $\bar{x}_1$, that is, $\bar{x}_1^{\,c} = 1 - \bar{x}_1$. As mentioned in Sec. 20.2.4, complement coding helps to avoid the problem of category proliferation when using fuzzy ART for fuzzy clustering. It also preserves training vector amplitude information. In applying the complement-coding technique to the FALCON, all training vectors (either input state vectors or desired output vectors) are transformed to their complement-coded forms in the preprocessing, and the transformed vectors are then used for training.

Based on the five-layered structure of the FALCON-ART shown in Fig. 19.23, we shall define the basic functions of nodes in each of the five layers of the FALCON-ART model. We employ the same notations as in Eqs. (19.1)–(19.8) except that we use $z_i^{(k)}$ instead of $u_i^{(k)}$ to represent the inputs to a node at layer k. Assume that the dimension of the input space is n, and that the dimension of the output space is m.

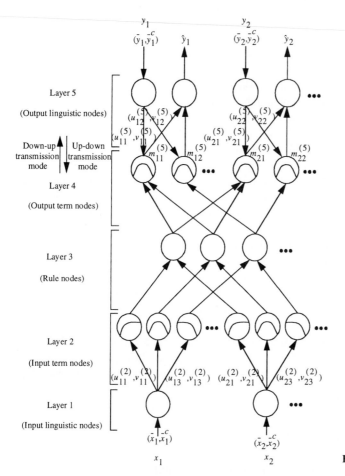

Layer 5
(Output linguistic nodes)

Down-up
transmission
mode

Up-down
transmission
mode

Layer 4
(Output term nodes)

Layer 3
(Rule nodes)

Layer 2
(Input term nodes)

Layer 1
(Input linguistic nodes)

Figure 19.23 Structure of FALCON-ART.

- **Layer 1:** Layer-1 nodes are input linguistic nodes and just transmit input signals to the next layer directly. That is,

$$f(\bar{x}_i, \bar{x}_i^c) = (\bar{x}_i, \bar{x}_i^c) = (\bar{x}_i, 1 - \bar{x}_i) \qquad \text{and} \qquad a(f) = f. \qquad (19.135)$$

From the above equation, the link weight in layer 1 $(w_i^{(1)})$ is unity. Note that because of the complement-coding process, for each input node i there are two output values $\bar{x}_i$ and $\bar{x}_i^c = 1 - \bar{x}_i$.

- **Layer 2:** Nodes in this layer are input term nodes, and each represents a term of an input linguistic variable and acts as a one-dimensional membership function. The following trapezoidal membership function is used:

$$f(z_{ij}^{(2)}) = \frac{1}{n}[1 - g(z_{ij}^{(2)} - v_{ij}^{(2)}, \gamma) - g(u_{ij}^{(2)} - z_{ij}^{(2)}, \gamma)] \qquad (19.136)$$

$$\text{and} \qquad a(f) = f,$$

where $u_{ij}^{(2)}$ and $v_{ij}^{(2)}$ are, respectively, the left-flat and right-flat points of the trapezoidal membership function of the jth input term node of the ith input linguistic node [see

Fig. 19.24(a)], $z_{ij}^{(2)}$ is the input to the jth input term node from the ith input linguistic node (i.e., $z_{ij}^{(2)} = \bar{x}_i$), and

$$g(s, \gamma) = \begin{cases} 1 & \text{if } s\gamma > 1 \\ s\gamma & \text{if } 0 \le s\gamma \le 1 \\ 0 & \text{if } s\gamma < 0. \end{cases} \qquad (19.137)$$

The parameter γ is the sensitivity parameter that regulates the fuzziness of the trapezoidal membership function. A large γ means a more crisp fuzzy set, and a smaller γ makes the fuzzy set less crisp. A set of n input term nodes (one for each input linguistic node) is connected to a rule node in layer 3 where its outputs are combined. This defines an n-dimensional membership function in the input space, with each dimension specified by one input term node in the set. Hence, each input linguistic node has the same number of term nodes in the FALCON-ART. This is also true for output linguistic nodes. A layer-2 link connects an input linguistic node to one of its term nodes. There are two weights on each layer-2 link. We denote the two weights on the link from input node i (corresponding to the input linguistic variable x_i) to its jth term node as $u_{ij}^{(2)}$ and $v_{ij}^{(2)}$ (see Fig. 19.23). These two weights define the membership function in Eq. (19.136). The two weights $u_{ij}^{(2)}$ and $v_{ij}^{(2)}$ correspond, respectively, to the two inputs $\bar{x}_i$ and $\bar{x}_i^c$ from the input linguistic node i. The two inputs to the input term node j, $\bar{x}_i$ and $\bar{x}_i^c$, will be used during the fuzzy-ART clustering process in the structure learning step to determine $u_{ij}^{(2)}$ and $v_{ij}^{(2)}$, respectively. In the parameter learning step and in normal operation, only $\bar{x}_i$ is used in the forward reasoning process [i.e., $z_{ij}^{(2)} = \bar{x}_i$ in Eq. (19.136)].

Layer 3: Nodes in this layer are rule nodes, and each represents one fuzzy logic rule. Each layer-3 node has n input term nodes fed into it, one from each input linguistic node. Hence, there are as many rule nodes in the FALCON-ART as there are term nodes of an input linguistic node (i.e., the number of rules equals the number of terms of an input linguistic variable). Note that each input linguistic variable has the same number of terms in the FALCON-ART. The links in layer 3 are used to perform pre-

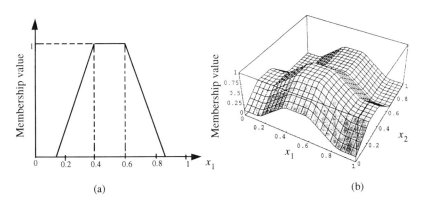

(a)　　　　　　　　　　　(b)

Figure 19.24 (a) One-dimensional trapezoidal membership function. (b) Two-dimensional trapezoidal membership function.

condition matching of fuzzy logic rules. Hence, the rule nodes perform the following operation:

$$f(z_i^{(3)}) = \sum_{i=1}^{n} z_i^{(3)} \qquad \text{and} \qquad a(f) = f, \qquad (19.138)$$

where $z_i^{(3)}$ is the ith input to a node in layer 3 and the summation is over the inputs of this node. The link weight in layer 3 $(w_i^{(3)})$ is then unity. Note that the summation in the above equation is equivalent to defining a multidimensional (n-dimensional) membership function, which is the summation of the trapezoidal functions in Eq. (19.136) over i. This forms a multidimensional trapezoidal membership function called the *hyperbox membership function* since it is defined on a hyperbox in the input space. The corners of the hyperbox are decided by the layer-2 weights $u_{ij}^{(2)}$ and $v_{ij}^{(2)}$ for all i. That is, the interval $[u_{ij}^{(2)}, v_{ij}^{(2)}]$ defines the edge of the hyperbox in the ith dimension. Hence, the weight vector $[(u_{1j}^{(2)}, v_{1j}^{(2)}),...,(u_{ij}^{(2)}, v_{ij}^{(2)}),...,(u_{nj}^{(2)}, v_{nj}^{(2)})]$ defines a hyperbox in the input space. An illustration of a two-dimensional hyperbox membership function is shown in Fig. 19.24(b). The outputs of the rule nodes are connected to sets of m output term nodes in layer 4, one for each output linguistic variable. This set of output term nodes defines an m-dimensional trapezoidal (hyperbox) membership function in the output space that specifies the consequent of the rule node. Note that different rule nodes may be connected to the same output hyperbox (i.e., they may have the same consequent) as shown in Fig. 19.23.

Layer 4: Nodes in this layer are output term nodes; each has two operating modes: *down-up* transmission and *up-down* transmission (see Fig. 19.23). In the down-up transmission mode, the links in layer 4 perform the fuzzy OR operation on fired (activated) rule nodes that have the same consequent,

$$f(z_i^{(4)}) = \max(z_1^{(4)}, z_2^{(4)}, ..., z_p^{(4)}) \qquad \text{and} \qquad a(f) = f, \qquad (19.139)$$

where $z_i^{(4)}$ is the ith input to a node in layer 4 and p is the number of inputs to this node from the rule nodes in layer 3. Hence, the link weight $w_i^{(4)} = 1$. In the up-down transmission mode, the nodes in this layer and the up-down transmission links in layer 5 function exactly like those in layer 2; each layer-4 node represents a term of an output linguistic variable and acts as a one-dimensional membership function. A set of m output term nodes, one for each output linguistic node, defines an m-dimensional hyperbox (membership function) in the output space, and there are also two weights $u_{ij}^{(5)}$ and $v_{ij}^{(5)}$ in each of the up-down transmission links in layer 5 (see Fig. 19.23). The weights define hyperboxes (and thus the associated hyperbox membership functions) in the output space. That is, the weight vector $[(u_{1j}^{(5)}, v_{1j}^{(5)}),...,(u_{ij}^{(5)}, v_{ij}^{(5)}),...,(u_{mj}^{(5)}, v_{mj}^{(5)})]$ defines a hyperbox in the output space.

- **Layer 5:** Each node in this layer is an output linguistic node and corresponds to one output linguistic variable. There are two kinds of nodes in layer 5. The first kind performs up-down transmission for training data (desired outputs) to feed into the network, acting exactly like the input linguistic nodes. For this kind of node, we have

$$f(\bar{y}_i, \bar{y}_i^c) = (\bar{y}_i, \bar{y}_i^c) = (\bar{y}_i, 1 - \bar{y}_i) \qquad \text{and} \qquad a(f) = f, \qquad (19.140)$$

where $\bar{y}_i$ is the ith element of the normalized desired output vector. Note that complement coding is also performed on the desired output vectors. Thus, there are two

Neural Fuzzy Controllers   Chap. 19

weights in each of the up-down transmission links in layer 5 (i.e., $u_{ij}^{(5)}$ and $v_{ij}^{(5)}$ as shown in Fig. 19.23). The weights define hyperboxes and the associated hyperbox membership functions in the output space. The second kind of node performs down-up transmission for decision signal output. These nodes and the layer-5 down-up transmission links attached to them act as a defuzzifier. If $u_{ij}^{(5)}$ and $v_{ij}^{(5)}$ are the corners of the hyperbox of the jth term of the ith output linguistic variable y_i, then the following functions can be used to simulate the *center of area* defuzzification method:

$$f\left(z_j^{(5)}\right) = \sum_j w_{ij}^{(5)} z_j^{(5)} = \sum_j m_{ij}^{(5)} z_j^{(5)} \qquad \text{and} \qquad a\,(f) = \frac{f}{\sum_j z_j^{(5)}}, \qquad (19.141)$$

where $z_j^{(5)}$ is the input to the ith output linguistic node from its jth term node and $m_{ij}^{(5)} = \left(u_{ij}^{(5)} + v_{ij}^{(5)}\right)/2$ denotes the center value of the output membership function of the jth term of the ith output linguistic variable. The center of a fuzzy region is defined as the point with the smallest absolute value among all the other points in the region at which the membership value is equal to 1. Here the weight $w_{ij}^{(5)}$ in a down-up transmission link in layer 5 is defined by $w_{ij}^{(5)} \triangleq m_{ij}^{(5)} = \left(u_{ij}^{(5)} + v_{ij}^{(5)}\right)/2$, where $u_{ij}^{(5)}$ and $v_{ij}^{(5)}$ are the weights in the corresponding up-down transmission link in layer 5.

The fuzzy reasoning process in the FALCON is illustrated in Fig. 19.25, which shows a graphical interpretation of the center-of-area defuzzification method. Here, we consider a two-input–two-output case. As shown in the figure, three hyperboxes (IH_1, IH_2, and IH_3) are formed in the input space, and two hyperboxes (OH_1, OH_2) are formed in the output space. These hyperboxes are defined by the weights u_{ij}, v_{ij}, u_{ij}', and v_{ij}'. The three fuzzy rules indicated in the figure are "IF $\mathbf{x}$ is IH_1, THEN $\mathbf{y}$ is OH_1 (rule 1)," "IF $\mathbf{x}$ is IH_2, THEN $\mathbf{y}$ is OH_1 (rule 2)," and "IF $\mathbf{x}$ is IH_3, THEN $\mathbf{y}$ is OH_2 (rule 3)," where $\mathbf{x} = (x_1, x_2)^T$ and $\mathbf{y} = (y_1, y_2)^T$. If an input pattern is located inside a hyperbox, the membership value is equal to 1 [see Eq. (19.137)]. In this figure, according to Eq. (19.139), z_1 is obtained by performing a fuzzy OR (max) operation on the inferred results of rules 1 and 2, which have the same consequent, OH_1. Also according to Eq. (19.139), z_2 is directly the inferred result of rule 3. Then z_1 and z_2 are defuzzified to obtain the final output according to Eq. (19.141).

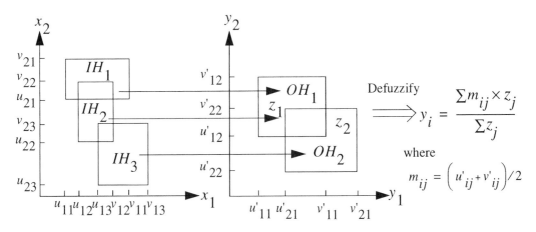

Figure 19.25 The fuzzy reasoning process in the FALCON-ART model.

The ART-based learning algorithm. Based on the above structure, an on-line, two-step learning scheme for the FALCON-ART model is outlined in the flowchart shown in Fig. 19.26. This on-line learning algorithm will determine the proper corners of the hyperbox (u_{ij} and v_{ij}) for each term node in layers 2 and 4, and will learn fuzzy logic rules and connection types of the links at layers 3 and 4 (i.e., the precondition links and consequent links of the rule nodes). For an on-line incoming training pattern, the following two steps are performed in this learning scheme. First, a structure learning scheme is used to determine proper fuzzy partitions and to detect the presence of rules. Second, a supervised learning scheme is used to optimally adjust the membership functions for the desired outputs. This learning scheme uses the *fast-learn* fuzzy ART to perform structure learning and the back-propagation algorithm to perform parameter learning. This structure-parameter learning cycle is repeated for each on-line incoming training pattern. In this learning method, only the training data need to be supplied from the outside world. The user doesn't have to provide the initial fuzzy partitions, membership functions, and fuzzy logic rules. Hence, there are no input-output term nodes and no rule nodes in the beginning of learning. They are created dynamically as learning proceeds upon receiving on-line incoming training data. In other words, the initial form of the network has only input and output linguistic nodes before it is trained. Then, during the learning process, new input and output term nodes and rule nodes are added dynamically.

The Structure Learning Step. The problem for the structure learning can be stated as: Given the training input data at time t, $x_i(t)$, $i = 1, \cdots, n$, and the desired output value $y_i^d(t)$, $i = 1, ..., m$, we want to determine proper fuzzy partitions as well as membership functions and find the fuzzy logic rules. In this step, the network works in a two-sided manner; that is, the nodes and links at layer 4 are in the up-down transmission mode so that the training input and output data can be fed into this network from both sides.

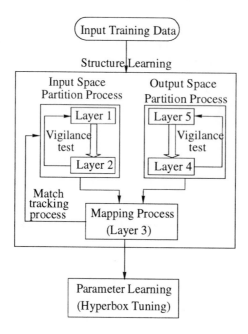

Figure 19.26 Flowchart of the on-line supervised structure-parameter learning algorithm of the FALCON-ART.

The structure learning step consists of three learning processes: the input fuzzy clustering process, the output fuzzy clustering process, and the mapping process. The first two processes are performed simultaneously on both sides of the network.

Input Fuzzy Clustering Process. We use the fuzzy ART fast-learn algorithm to find the input membership function parameters $u_{ij}^{(2)}$ and $v_{ij}^{(2)}$. This is equivalent to finding proper input space fuzzy clustering or, more precisely, to forming proper fuzzy hyperboxes in the input space. Initially, for each complement-coded input vector $\mathbf{x}'$, the values of choice functions T_j are computed by

$$T_j(\mathbf{x}') = \frac{|\mathbf{x}' \wedge \mathbf{w}_j|}{\alpha + |\mathbf{w}_j|}, \qquad j = 1, 2, \cdots, N, \qquad (19.142)$$

where $\wedge$ is the min operator acting on the pairwise elements of two vectors, $\alpha \geq 0$ is a constant, N is the current number of rule nodes, and $\mathbf{w}_j$ is the *complement weight vector,* which is defined by $\mathbf{w}_j \triangleq [(u_{1j}^{(2)}, 1 - v_{1j}^{(2)}),\ldots, (u_{ij}^{(2)}, 1 - v_{ij}^{(2)}),\ldots, (u_{nj}^{(2)}, 1 - v_{nj}^{(2)})]$. Note that $[(u_{1j}^{(2)}, v_{1j}^{(2)}),\ldots, (u_{ij}^{(2)}, v_{ij}^{(2)}),\ldots, (u_{nj}^{(2)}, v_{nj}^{(2)})]$ is the weight vector of layer-2 links associated with rule node j. The choice function value indicates the similarity between the input vector $\mathbf{x}'$ and the complement weight vector $\mathbf{w}_j$. We need to find the complement weight vector closest to $\mathbf{x}'$. This is equivalent to finding a hyperbox (category) that $\mathbf{x}'$ could belong to. The chosen category is indexed by J, where

$$T_J = \max_{j=1}^{N} T_j. \qquad (19.143)$$

Resonance occurs when the match value of the chosen category meets the vigilance criterion:

$$\frac{|\mathbf{x}' \wedge \mathbf{w}_J|}{|\mathbf{x}'|} \geq \rho, \qquad (19.144)$$

where $\rho \in [0, 1]$ is a vigilance parameter. If the vigilance criterion is not met, then a *mismatch reset* occurs. In this case, the choice function value T_J is set to 0 for the duration of the input presentation to prevent persistent selection of the same category during the search (we call this action "disabling J"). A new index J is then chosen using Eq. (19.143). The search process continues until the chosen J satisfies Eq. (19.144). This search process is indicated by the feedback arrow marked "Vigilance test" in Fig. 19.26. If no such J is found, then a new input hyperbox is created by adding a set of n new input term nodes, one for each input linguistic variable, and setting up links between the newly added input term nodes and the input linguistic nodes. The complement weight vectors on these new layer-2 links are simply given as the current input vector $\mathbf{x}'$. These newly added input term nodes and links define a new hyperbox, and thus a new category, in the input space. This newly added hyperbox is denoted as J.

Output Fuzzy Clustering Process. The output fuzzy clustering process is exactly the same as the input fuzzy clustering process except that it is performed between layers 4 and 5 which are working in the up-down transmission mode. The training pattern used now is the desired output vector after complement coding, $\mathbf{y}'$. We denote the chosen or newly added output hyperbox as K. This hyperbox is defined by the complement weight vector in layer 5, $\mathbf{w}_K = [(u_{1k}^{(5)}, 1 - v_{1k}^{(5)}),\ldots, (u_{ik}^{(5)}, 1 - v_{ik}^{(5)}),\ldots, (u_{mk}^{(5)}, 1 - v_{mk}^{(5)})]$.

These two fuzzy clustering processes produce a chosen input hyperbox indexed as J and a chosen output hyperbox indexed as K, where the input hyperbox J is defined by $\mathbf{w}_J$ and the output hyperbox K by $\mathbf{w}_K$. If the chosen input hyperbox J is not newly added, then there is a rule node J that corresponds to it. If the input hyperbox J is a newly added one, then a new rule node (indexed as J) in layer 3 is added and connected to the input term nodes that constitute it.

Mapping Process.   After the two hyperboxes in the input and output spaces are chosen in the input and output fuzzy clustering processes, the next step is to perform the mapping process that determines the connections between layer-3 and layer-4 nodes. This is equivalent to finding the consequents of fuzzy logic rules. This mapping process is described by the following algorithm, in which connecting rule node J to output hyperbox K means connecting the rule node J to the output term nodes that constitute the hyperbox K in the output space.

Step 1:   IF rule node J is a newly added node,
THEN connect rule node J to output hyperbox K.

Step 2:   ELSE IF rule node J is not connected to output hyperbox K originally, THEN disable J and perform input fuzzy clustering process to find the next qualified J [i.e., the next rule node that satisfies Eqs. (19.143) and (19.144)]. Go to step 1.

Step 3:   ELSE no structure change is necessary.

In the mapping process, hyperboxes J and K are resized according to the *fast-learn rule* of fuzzy ART by updating weights $\mathbf{w}_J$ and $\mathbf{w}_K$ as follows:

$$\mathbf{w}_J^{(\text{new})} = \mathbf{x}' \wedge \mathbf{w}_J^{(\text{old})}, \qquad \mathbf{w}_K^{(\text{new})} = \mathbf{y}' \wedge \mathbf{w}_K^{(\text{old})}. \qquad (19.145)$$

Note that once the consequent of a rule node has been determined in the mapping process, it will not be changed thereafter. We now use Fig. 19.25 to illustrate the structure learning step as follows. For a given training datum, the input fuzzy clustering process and the output fuzzy clustering process find or form proper clusters (hyperboxes) in the input and output spaces. Assume that the input and output hyperbox pair found are (J, K). The mapping process then tries to relate these two hyperboxes by setting up links between them. This is equivalent to finding a fuzzy logic rule that defines the association between an input hyperbox and an output hyperbox. If this association already exists [e.g., $(J, K) =$ (IH_1, OH_1), (IH_2, OH_1), or (IH_3, OH_2) in Fig. 19.25], then no structural change is necessary. If input hyperbox J is newly formed and thus not connected to any output hyperbox, it is connected to output hyperbox K directly. Otherwise, if input hyperbox J is associated with an output hyperbox different from K originally [e.g., $(J, K) = (\text{IH}_2, \text{OH}_2)$], then a new input hyperbox close to J will be found or formed by performing the input fuzzy clustering process again. This search, called "match tracking" (see Fig. 19.26), continues until an input hyperbox J' that can be associated with output hyperbox K is found [e.g., $(J', K) =$ (IH_3, OH_2)].

The vigilance parameter ρ is an important structure learning parameter that determines learning cluster density. High ρ values (approaching 1) tend to produce finer learning clusters; with $\rho = 1$, each training datum is assigned to its own cluster in the input (output) space. Low ρ values (approaching 0) tend to produce coarser learning clusters; with $\rho = 0$, all training data are assigned to a single cluster in the input (output) space. Clearly, a constantly high or low ρ value will result in the formation of excessively high numbers of clusters on the one hand, or very low output accuracy (and thus, low network representation power) on the other hand. For these reasons, we choose an adaptive vigilance strategy in which the ρ parameter is initially set high to allow fast FALCON-ART structure growth and then monotonically decreased to slow down cluster formation and stabilize learning. Empirical studies have shown this approach to be efficient and stable in the learning speeds and number of clusters it produces.

The Parameter Learning Step. After the network structure has been adjusted according to the current training pattern, the network then enters the second learning step to adjust the parameters of the membership functions optimally with the same training pattern. Note that the following parameter learning is performed on the whole network after structure learning, no matter whether the nodes (links) are newly added or existed originally. The problem for parameter learning can be stated as: Given the training input data $x_i(t)$, $i = 1, 2, \cdots, n$, the desired output value $y_i^d(t)$, $i = 1, 2, \cdots, m$, the input and output hyperboxes, and the fuzzy logic rules, we want to adjust the parameters of the membership functions optimally. These hyperboxes and fuzzy logic rules are learned in the previous structure learning step. In parameter learning, the network works in the feedforward manner; that is, the nodes and links at layer 4 are in the down-up transmission mode. As in the supervised learning phase of the FALCON-H [Eqs. (19.15)–(19.37)], back propagation is again used for parameter learning to find the errors of node outputs in each layer. According to the error function in Eq. (19.15) and the general update rules in Eqs. (19.16)–(19.18), we derive the learning rules layer by layer using the hyperbox membership functions with corners u_{ij} and v_{ij} as the adjustable parameters for these computations. For clarity, we consider a single-output case. Hence, the adjustable parameters in layer 5 are denoted by $u_j^{(5)}$, $v_j^{(5)}$, and $m_j^{(5)} = (u_j^{(5)} + v_j^{(5)})/2$ for the jth term node. Note that in parameter learning we use only normalized training vectors $\bar{\mathbf{x}}$ and $\bar{\mathbf{y}}$ rather than the complement-coded vectors $\mathbf{x}'$ and $\mathbf{y}'$.

- **Layer 5:** Using Eqs. (19.141) and (19.18), the update rule for the corners of the hyperbox membership function $v_j^{(5)}$ is

$$\frac{\partial E}{\partial v_j^{(5)}} = \frac{\partial E}{\partial a^{(5)}} \frac{\partial a^{(5)}}{\partial v_j^{(5)}} = -[y^d(t) - y(t)] \frac{z_j^{(5)}}{2 \sum_j z_j^{(5)}}. \tag{19.146}$$

Hence, the corner parameter is updated by

$$v_j^{(5)}(t+1) = v_j^{(5)}(t) + \eta [y^d(t) - y(t)] \frac{z_j^{(5)}}{2 \sum_j z_j^{(5)}}. \tag{19.147}$$

Similarly, using Eqs. (19.141) and (19.18), the update rule for the other corner parameter $u_j^{(5)}$ is

$$\frac{\partial E}{\partial u_j^{(5)}} = \frac{\partial E}{\partial a^{(5)}} \frac{\partial a^{(5)}}{\partial u_j^{(5)}} = -[y^d(t) - y(t)] \frac{z_j^{(5)}}{2 \sum_j z_j^{(5)}}. \tag{19.148}$$

Hence, the other corner parameter is updated by

$$u_j^{(5)}(t+1) = u_j^{(5)}(t) + \eta \, [y^d(t) - y(t)] \, \frac{z_j^{(5)}}{2\sum_j z_j^{(5)}}. \tag{19.149}$$

The error to be propagated to the preceding layer is

$$\delta^{(5)} = -\frac{\partial E}{\partial a^{(5)}} = -\frac{\partial E}{\partial y} = y^d(t) - y(t). \tag{19.150}$$

Layer 4: In the down-up transmission mode, there is no parameter to be adjusted in this layer. Only the error signal $(\delta_i^{(4)})$ needs to be computed and propagated. According to Eq. (19.141), the error signal $\delta_i^{(4)}$ is derived by

$$\delta_i^{(4)} = -\frac{\partial E}{\partial a^{(4)}} = -\frac{\partial E}{\partial a^{(5)}} \frac{\partial a^{(5)}}{\partial a^{(4)}} = \delta^{(5)} \frac{m_i^{(5)} \sum_i z_i^{(5)} - \sum_i m_i^{(5)} z_i^{(5)}}{(\sum_i z_i^{(5)})^2}. \tag{19.151}$$

In the multiple-output case, the computations in layers 5 and 4 are exactly the same as the above and proceed independently for each output linguistic variable.

- **Layer 3:** As in layer 4, only the error signals need to be computed in this layer. According to Eq. (19.139), this error signal can be derived by

$$\delta_i^{(3)} = -\frac{\partial E}{\partial a^{(3)}} = -\frac{\partial E}{\partial a^{(4)}} \frac{\partial a^{(4)}}{\partial f^{(4)}} \frac{\partial f^{(4)}}{\partial a^{(3)}} = \delta_i^{(4)} \frac{z_i^{(4)}}{z_{max}^{(4)}}, \tag{19.152}$$

where $z_{max}^{(4)} = \max(\text{inputs of the output term node } j)$. The term $z_i^{(4)}/z_{max}^{(4)}$ normalizes the error to be propagated for the fired rules with the same consequent. If there are multiple outputs, then the error signal becomes $\delta_i^{(3)} = \sum_k \delta_k^{(4)} z_k^{(4)}/z_{max}^{(4)}$, where the summation is performed over the consequents of a rule node; that is, the error of a rule node is the summation of the errors of its consequents.

- **Layer 2:** Using Eqs. (19.136) and (19.18), the update rule of $v_{ij}^{(2)}$ is derived as follows:

$$-\frac{\partial E}{\partial v_{ij}^{(2)}} = -\frac{\partial E}{\partial a^{(3)}} \frac{\partial a^{(3)}}{\partial a^{(2)}} \frac{\partial a^{(2)}}{\partial v_{ij}^{(2)}}, \tag{19.153}$$

where

$$\frac{\partial a^{(3)}}{\partial a^{(2)}} = 1 \tag{19.154}$$

$$\frac{\partial a^{(2)}}{\partial v_{ij}^{(2)}} = \begin{cases} \gamma/n & \text{if } 0 \le (\bar{x}_i - v_{ij}^{(2)})\gamma \le 1 \\ 0 & \text{otherwise.} \end{cases} \tag{19.155}$$

So the update rule of $v_{ij}^{(2)}$ is

$$v_{ij}^{(2)}(t+1) = v_{ij}^{(2)}(t) + \eta \delta_i^{(3)} \frac{\partial a^{(2)}}{\partial v_{ij}^{(2)}}. \tag{19.156}$$

Similarly, using Eqs. (19.136) and (19.18), the update rule of $u_{ij}^{(2)}$ is derived as

Neural Fuzzy Controllers Chap. 19

$$-\frac{\partial E}{\partial u_{ij}^{(2)}} = -\frac{\partial E}{\partial a^{(3)}} \frac{\partial a^{(3)}}{\partial a^{(2)}} \frac{\partial a^{(2)}}{\partial u_{ij}^{(2)}},$$ (19.157)

where

$$\frac{\partial a^{(3)}}{\partial a^{(2)}} = 1$$ (19.158)

$$\frac{\partial a^{(2)}}{\partial u_{ij}^{(2)}} = \begin{cases} -\gamma/n & \text{if } 0 \le (u_{ij}^{(2)} - \bar{x}_i)\gamma \le 1 \\ 0 & \text{otherwise.} \end{cases}$$ (19.159)

Hence, the update rule of $u_{ij}^{(2)}$ becomes

$$u_{ij}^{(2)}(t+1) = u_{ij}^{(2)}(t) + \eta \delta_i^{(3)} \frac{\partial a^{(2)}}{\partial u_{ij}^{(2)}}.$$ (19.160)

Example 19.8

In this example, the FALCON-ART is used to identify a dynamical system. The identification model has the form

$$y(k+1) = f[u(k), u(k-1), ..., u(k-p+1);$$
$$y(k), y(k-1), ..., y(k-q+1)].$$ (19.161)

Since both the unknown plant and the FALCON-ART are driven by the same input, FALCON-ART adjusts itself with the goal of causing the output of the identification model to match that of the unknown plant. Upon convergence, the input-output response relationship should match. The plant to be identified is guided by the difference equation

$$y(k+1) = \frac{y(k)}{1+y^2(k)} + u^3(k).$$ (19.162)

The output of the plant depends nonlinearly on both its past value and the input, but the effects of the input and output values are additive. In applying the FALCON-ART for this identification problem, the learning rate $\eta = 0.005$, the sensitivity parameter $\gamma = 4$, and the vigilance parameters $\rho_{input} = 0.6$ and $\rho_{output} = 0.5$ are chosen, where ρ_{input} and ρ_{output} are the vigilance parameters used in the input and the output fuzzy clustering processes, respectively. The training input patterns are generated with $u(k) = \sin(2\pi k/100)$, and the training process is continued for 60,000 time steps. Each cluster corresponds to a hyperbox in the input or the output space. Starting from zero, the number of clusters grows dynamically for incoming training data. In this example, the case of a two-input–one-output system is considered. Figure 19.27(a) illustrates the distribution of the training patterns and the final assignment of the rules (i.e., distribution of the membership functions) in the $[u(k), y(k)]$ plane. There are six hyperboxes ($IH_1, IH_2, IH_3, IH_4, IH_5, IH_6$) formed in the input space. Figure 19.27(b) shows the distribution of the output membership functions in the $y(k+1)$ domain. Three trapezoidal membership functions (OH_1, OH_2, OH_3) are generated in the output space. After the hyperboxes in the input and the output spaces are tuned or created in the fuzzy clustering process, the mapping process then determines the proper mapping between the input clusters and the output clusters. As a result, six fuzzy logic rules are formed from these hyperboxes:

Rule 1: IF **x** is IH_1, THEN y is OH_3.
Rule 2: IF **x** is IH_2, THEN y is OH_1.
Rule 3: IF **x** is IH_3, THEN y is OH_3.

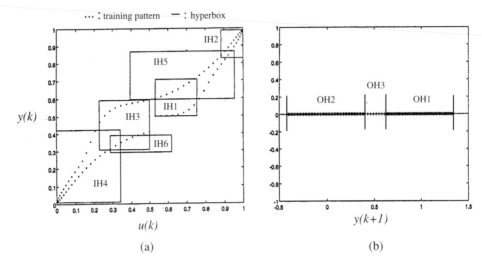

IH2

IH5

IH1

IH3

IH6

IH4

$y(k)$

$u(k)$

(a)

OH3

OH2

OH1

$y(k+1)$

(b)

Figure 19.27 Simulation results for the FALCON-ART model in Example 19.8. (a) The input training patterns and the final assignment of rules. (b) The distribution of output membership functions.

Rule 4: IF **x** is IH_4, THEN y is OH_2.
Rule 5: IF **x** is IH_5, THEN y is OH_1.
Rule 6: IF **x** is IH_6, THEN y is OH_2.

Here $\mathbf{x} = (u(k), y(k))^T$ and $y = y(k+1)$. From these fuzzy logic rules, we know rules 1 and 3 have the same consequent. Also, rules 2 and 5 and rules 4 and 6 map to the same consequent. These rules reflect the natural property that if two input data are close (similar) in the input space, the two mapped outputs are also close in the output space. The learned FALCON-ART has shown perfect identification capability.

Example 19.9

The inverted-wedge balancing control is an interesting control problem. It integrates the mechanical and electrical parts and offers a good example of a control experiment involving an unstable system. Hsu [1992] used a linear quadratic regulator to balance the inverted wedge. The controller used requires the mathematical model of the inverted wedge. In this example, the FALCON-ART is trained to keep the wedge in an upright position without using the mathematical model.

The inverted wedge is an inherently unstable nonlinear system as shown in Fig. 19.28. The sliding weights are led by a dc motor via a sprocket-and-chain mechanism. The sliding

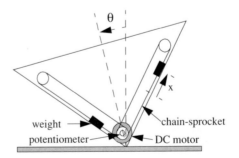

θ

x

weight
potentiometer
chain-sprocket
DC motor

Figure 19.28 Inverted wedge in Example 19.9.

Neural Fuzzy Controllers   Chap. 19

weights are in fact rechargeable batteries that supply power to all the on-board electronics. A linear power amplifier module is used for driving the motor, and a multiturn potentiometer is coupled to the motor shaft for sensing the position of the sliding weights. One type of sensor is used for sensing an absolute angle. A vertical gyro is a free gyro with a gravity-sensitive erection mechanism that keeps the gyro spin axis in the direction of gravity. A vertical gyro provides virtually unlimited bandwidth.

Let $\mathbf{q} = [\theta, x, \dot{\theta}, \dot{x}]^T$ be the state of the system and $y = \theta$ be the output of the system. θ is the wedge angle from its upright position and x is the weight displacement from the wedge center line. From [Hsu, 1992], the inverted-wedge system can be represented by a state-space model:

$$
\begin{bmatrix} \dot{q}_1 \\ \dot{q}_2 \\ \dot{q}_3 \\ \dot{q}_4 \end{bmatrix} = \begin{bmatrix} 0 & 0 & 1 & 0 \\ 0 & 0 & 0 & 1 \\ a_{31} & a_{32} & 0 & 0 \\ a_{41} & 0 & 0 & a_{44} \end{bmatrix} \begin{bmatrix} q_1 \\ q_2 \\ q_3 \\ q_4 \end{bmatrix} + \begin{bmatrix} 0 \\ 0 \\ 0 \\ b_4 \end{bmatrix} u, \tag{19.163}
$$

where $a_{31} = 15.5443$, $a_{32} = -10.9272$, $a_{41} = -5.307$, $a_{44} = -16.248$, $b_4 = 0.2297$, and u is the control signal.

In gathering the training data, the inverted wedge is controlled by the controller designed by Hsu [1992] for eight different initial states. Then the resulting eight training paths are used for training the FALCON-ART. The learning rate $\eta = 0.005$, sensitivity parameter $\gamma = 4$, and initial vigilance parameters $\rho_{input} = 0.8$ and $\rho_{output} = 0.8$ are chosen. After the learning, 33 fuzzy logic rules are generated in the simulation. The learned FALCON-ART controller is then tested at different initial conditions. Figure 19.29 shows the angular deviation (θ) of the inverted wedge at several different initial conditions under the control of the learned FALCON-ART. The results show the perfect control capability of the trained FALCON-ART model.

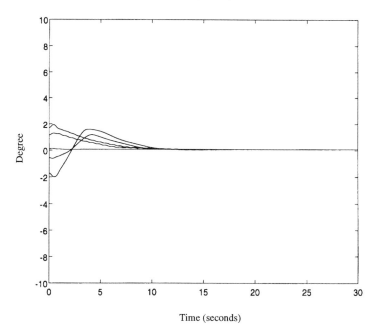

Figure 19.29 Responses θ for some initial conditions of the inverted-wedge system under the control of the learned FALCON-ART controller in Example 19.9.

19.6 NEURAL FUZZY CONTROLLERS
WITH REINFORCEMENT LEARNING

Thus far, we have focused on the supervised learning problems of neural fuzzy control systems. In other words, the learning schemes have required precise training data to indicate the exact desired output and then use the precise training data to compute the output errors for training the whole network. Unfortunately, such detailed and precise training data may be very expensive or even impossible to obtain in some real-world applications where the controlled system may be able to provide only a right-wrong binary decision of the current controller. This kind of feedback is called a *reinforcement signal*; it is very rough and coarse and is only "evaluative" as compared with the "instructive" feedback in the supervised learning problem. Training a NFC with this kind of evaluative feedback is the *reinforcement learning problem* discussed in Sec. 13.3. In this section, we shall explore two NFCs with reinforcement learning capabilities.

19.6.1 The FALCON with Reinforcement Learning

Previously, we have discussed supervised learning models of the FALCON, including the FALCON-H, FALCON-O, and FALCON-ART. In this section, we shall consider reinforcement learning of the FALCON, called FALCON-R [Lin, 1994, 1995; Lin and Lee, 1994; Lin and Lin, 1995]. The FALCON-R is a learning system that can construct a fuzzy control and decision system automatically and dynamically through a reward-penalty signal (i.e., good-bad signal) or through very simple fuzzy feedback information such as "High," "Too High," "Low," and "Too Low." Moreover, there is a possibility of a long delay between an action and the resulting reinforcement feedback information.

Unlike the supervised learning problem in which the correct "target" output values are given for each input pattern to instruct the network's learning, the reinforcement learning problem has only very simple "evaluative" or "critic" information instead of "instructive" information available for learning. In the extreme case, there is only a single bit of information to indicate whether the output is right or wrong. Figure 19.30 shows how the FALCON-R and its training environment interact in a reinforcement learning problem. The environment supplies a time-varying vector of input to the network, receives its time-varying vector of output or action and then provides a time-varying scalar reinforcement signal. Here, the reinforcement signal $r(t)$ can be in one of the following forms: (1) a two-valued number $r(t) \in \{-1, 1\}$ or $\{-1, 0\}$ such that $r(t) = 1\ (0)$ means "success" and $r(t) = -1$ means "failure"; (2) a multivalued discrete number in the range $[-1, 1]$ or $[-1, 0]$, for example, $r(t) \in \{-1, -0.5, 0, 0.5, 1\}$, which corresponds to different discrete degrees of failure or success; or (3) a real number $r(t) \in [-1, 1]$ or $[-1, 0]$, which represents a more detailed and continuous degree of failure or success. We also assume that $r(t)$ is the reinforcement signal available at time step t and is caused by the inputs and actions at time step $(t-1)$ or even affected by earlier inputs and actions. The learning is to maximize a function of this reinforcement signal, such as the expectation of its value on the upcoming time step or the expectation of some integral of its values over all future time.

There are three different classes of reinforcement learning problems (see Sec. 13.3). They are characterized by *deterministic reinforcement feedback, stochastic reinforcement feedback,* and *reinforcement feedback with long time delay.* The FALCON-R is designed to

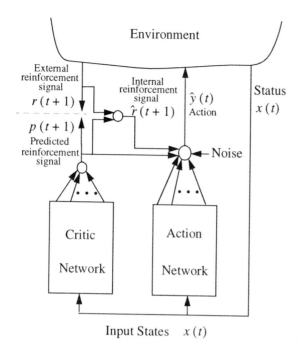

External
reinforcement
signal

$r(t+1)$

Internal
reinforcement
signal

$\hat{r}(t+1)$

$\hat{y}(t)$

Action

Environment

Status

$x(t)$

$p(t+1)$

Predicted
reinforcement
signal

Noise

Critic

Network

Action

Network

Input States $x(t)$

Figure 19.30   Structure of the FALCON-R.

resolve these three classes of reinforcement learning problems. It is a kind of reinforcement learning network with a critic as introduced in Sec. 13.3.3. The FALCON-R, shown in Fig. 19.30, integrates two FALCON-ARTs into a functional unit: one FALCON-ART, the *action network*, is used as a fuzzy controller, and the other FALCON-ART, the *critic network*, is used as a fuzzy predictor. They receive the same state input from the environment and go through different inference processes. The action network decides the best action to impose on the environment in the next time step according to the current environment status and predicted reinforcement signals. The critic network models the environment such that it can make a single- or multi-step prediction of the reinforcement signal that will eventually be obtained from the environment for the current action chosen by the action network. The predicted reinforcement signal can also provide the action network with beforehand and more detailed reward or penalty information (called *internal reinforcement signals*) about the candidate action for the action network to learn. The internal reinforcement signal can minimize the uncertainty that the action network faces to speed up its learning. Moreover, learning can proceed even in the period without any external reinforcement feedback.

Associated with the FALCON-R structure is a reinforcement structure-parameter learning algorithm basically composed of the techniques of *temporal difference, stochastic exploration,* and the on-line supervised structure-parameter learning algorithm of FALCON-ART. The flowchart of this learning algorithm is shown in Fig. 19.31, where the bottom block represents the block diagram shown in Fig. 19.26. For each input vector from the environment, starting at the input nodes, a forward pass computes the activity levels of all the nodes in the network. At the end, stochastic exploration takes place at the output node of the action network to predict its output error, and temporal difference prediction

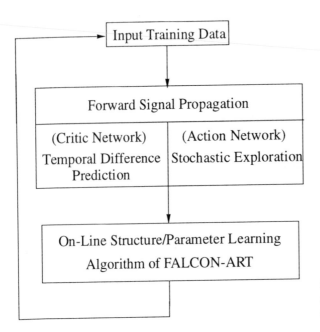

Figure 19.31 Flowchart of the reinforcement structure-parameter learning algorithm of the FALCON-R.

takes place at the output node of the critic network to predict its output error. With the output error information available, the reinforcement learning problem has been transformed to the supervised learning problem, and then the on-line supervised learning algorithm of the FALCON-ART developed in Sec. 19.5.2 can be applied directly.

The first and second classes of reinforcement learning problems can be solved using the FALCON-R with a single-step critic network. The third class of reinforcement learning problems is more difficult, and thus a more powerful multistep critic network is necessary. Since reinforcement learning with a single-step critic network is a special case of that with a multistep critic network, we shall focus on the reinforcement learning algorithms of the FALCON-R with a multistep critic network in the following.

The multistep critic network. When both the reinforcement signal and input patterns from the environment depend arbitrarily on the past history of the network output and the network receives only a reinforcement signal after a long sequence of network outputs, the credit assignment problem becomes severe. The *temporal credit assignment* problem results because we need to assign credit or blame, for an eventual success or failure, to each step individually in this long sequence. Hence, for this class of reinforcement learning problem, we must solve the temporal credit assignment problem together with the original *structure credit assignment* problem of attributing network errors to different connections or weights. The solution to the temporal credit assignment problem in the FALCON-R is to design a multistep critic network that can predict the reinforcement signal at each time step within two successive external reinforcement signals that may be separated by many time steps. This multistep critic network can ensure that both the critic network and the action network do not have to wait until the actual outcome becomes known, and they can update their parameters and structures within the period without any critic feedback from the environment.

To solve the temporal credit assignment problem, the technique based on the *temporal difference* methods introduced in Sec. 13.3.3 is used. Summarizing the important temporal difference equations for three different cases in Eqs. (13.99)–(13.101), we can use the following general temporal difference learning rule here:

$$\Delta w_t = \eta \left(r_t + \gamma p_t - p_{t-1} \right) \Delta_w p_{t-1}, \tag{19.164}$$

where γ, $0 \leq \gamma < 1$, is a discount-rate parameter, and η is the learning rate.

We shall next derive the learning rule for the multistep critic network according to Eq. (19.164). Here, $p_t \triangleq p(t)$ is the single output of the critic network for the network's current parameter $w(t)$ and current given input state vector $x(t)$ at time step t. According to Eq. (19.164), let

$$\hat{r}(t) = r(t) + \gamma p(t) - p(t-1), \qquad 0 \leq \gamma < 1. \tag{19.165}$$

Then $\hat{r}(t)$ is the multistep critic network's output node error signal. With the (predicted) desired output $p(t)$ and the output error signal $\hat{r}(t)$ available, we can use supervised learning techniques to train the critic network. Note that if the environment provides a reinforcement signal at each time step, the critic network can "single-step," or calculate the actual learning output error at each time step. Thus, the critic network can operate as either a multistep or a singlestep predictor.

Thus far, we have formulated the multistep prediction problem as a supervised learning problem, and so the on-line learning algorithm developed in Sec. 19.5.2 can be adopted directly here as follows. For structure learning, the *structure learning step* in Sec. 19.5.2 [Eqs. (19.142)–(19.145)] is performed by setting the desired output of the critic network as $p(t-1) + \hat{r}(t) = r(t) + \gamma p(t)$ or simply as $r(t)$. For parameter learning, we can derive the weight update rules based on the general temporal difference learning rule given in Eq. (19.164). The derivation is carried out in exactly the same way as that for Eqs. (19.146)–(19.160). The results listed below are thus very similar to these equations.

- **Layer 5:** As in Eq. (19.147), the update rule for the corners of the hyperbox membership function $v_j^{(5)}$ is

$$v_j^{(5)}(t+1) = v_j^{(5)}(t) + \eta \hat{r}(t) \left[\frac{z_j^{(5)}}{2\sum_j z_j^{(5)}} \right]_{t-1}, \tag{19.166}$$

where the subscript $(t-1)$ represents time displacement. Similar to Eq. (19.149), the update rule of the other corner parameter $u_j^{(5)}$ is

$$u_j^{(5)}(t+1) = u_j^{(5)}(t) + \eta \hat{r}(t) \left[\frac{z_j^{(5)}}{2\sum_j z_j^{(5)}} \right]_{t-1}. \tag{19.167}$$

As in Eq. (19.150), the error to be propagated to the preceding layer is

$$\delta^{(5)} = -\frac{\partial E}{\partial a^{(5)}} = \hat{r}(t). \tag{19.168}$$

- **Layer 4:** As in Eq. (19.151), the error to be propagated to the preceding layer is

$$\delta_i^{(4)} = -\frac{\partial E}{\partial a^{(4)}} = -\frac{\partial E}{\partial a^{(5)}}\frac{\partial a^{(5)}}{\partial a^{(4)}} = \delta^{(5)}\left[\frac{m_i^{(5)}\sum_i z_i^{(5)} - \sum_i m_i^{(5)} z_i^{(5)}}{(\sum_i z_i^{(5)})^2}\right]_{t-1}. \qquad (19.169)$$

In the multiple-output case, the computations in layers 5 and 4 are exactly the same as the above and proceed independently for each output linguistic variable.

- **Layer 3:** As in Eq. (19.152), the error to be propagated to the preceding layer is

$$\delta_i^{(3)} = -\frac{\partial E}{\partial a^{(3)}} = -\frac{\partial E}{\partial a^{(4)}}\frac{\partial a^{(4)}}{\partial f^{(4)}}\frac{\partial f^{(4)}}{\partial a^{(3)}} = \delta_i^{(4)}\left[\frac{z_i^{(4)}}{z_{\max}^{(4)}}\right]_{t-1}, \qquad (19.170)$$

where $z_{\max}^{(4)} = \max$ (inputs of output term node j). The term $z_i^{(4)}/z_{\max}^{(4)}$ normalizes the error to be propagated for the fired rules with the same consequent. If there are multiple outputs, then the error signal becomes $\delta_i^{(3)} = \sum_k \delta_k^{(4)}[z_k^{(4)}/z_{\max}^{(4)}]_{t-1}$, where the summation is over the consequents of a rule node; that is, the error of a rule node is the summation of the errors of its consequents.

- **Layer 2:** As in Eq. (19.156), the update rule of $v_{ij}^{(2)}$ is

$$v_{ij}^{(2)}(t+1) = v_{ij}^{(2)}(t) + \eta\delta_i^{(3)}\left[\frac{\partial a^{(2)}}{\partial v_{ij}^{(2)}}\right]_{t-1}, \qquad (19.171)$$

where $\partial a^{(2)}/\partial v_{ij}^{(2)}$ is given by Eq. (19.155). As in Eq. (19.160), the update rule of $u_{ij}^{(2)}$ is

$$u_{ij}^{(2)}(t+1) = u_{ij}^{(2)}(t) + \eta\delta_i^{(3)}\left[\frac{\partial a^{(2)}}{\partial u_{ij}^{(2)}}\right]_{t-1}, \qquad (19.172)$$

where $\partial a^{(2)}/\partial u_{ij}^{(2)}$ is given by Eq. (19.159).

In summary, the temporal difference technique is used to find the output error of the critic network, and the error is then used to train the critic network by the preceding two-step learning algorithm (structure learning step and parameter learning step).

The action network. We now introduce the reinforcement learning algorithm for the action network. The goal of this reinforcement structure-parameter learning algorithm is to adjust the parameters (e.g., w) of the action network to change the connection types or to add new nodes such that the reinforcement signal is a maximum; that is,

$$\Delta w \propto \frac{\partial r}{\partial w}. \qquad (19.173)$$

To determine $\partial r/\partial w$, we need to know $\partial r/\partial y$, where y is the output of the action network. (For clarity, we discuss the single-output case first.) Since the reinforcement signal does not provide any hint as to what the right answer should be in terms of a cost function, there is no gradient information and the gradient $\partial r/\partial y$ can only be estimated. If we can estimate $\partial r/\partial y$, then the on-line supervised structure-parameter learning algorithm developed in Sec. 19.5.2 can be directly applied to the action network to solve the reinforcement learning problem. To estimate the gradient information in a reinforcement learning network, there needs to be some randomness in how output actions are chosen by the action network so that the range of possible outputs can be explored to find a correct value. Thus, the output nodes (layer 5) of the action network are now designed to be stochastic units that compute their output as a stochastic function of their input.

In this learning algorithm, the gradient information $\partial r / \partial y$ is also estimated by the stochastic exploration method. In particular, the intuitive idea behind multiparameter distributions suggested by Williams [1987, 1988] is used for the stochastic search of network output units. In estimating the gradient information, the output y of the action network does not directly act on the environment. Instead, it is treated as a mean (expected) action. The actual action $\hat{y}$ is chosen by exploring a range around this mean point. This range of exploration corresponds to the variance of a probability function which is the normal distribution here. The amount of exploration $\sigma(t)$ is some nonnegative monotonically decreasing function of the predicted reinforcement signal. For example, we can use

$$\sigma(t) = \frac{k}{2}[1 - \tanh(p(t))] = \frac{k}{1 + e^{2p(t)}},\qquad (19.174)$$

where k is a search-range scaling constant which can be simply set to 1. Equation (19.174) is a monotonic decreasing function between k and 0. The $\sigma(t)$ can be interpreted as the extent to which the output node searches for a better action. Since $p(t+1)$ is the predicted reward signal, if $p(t+1)$ is small, the exploratory range $\sigma(t)$ will be large. On the contrary, if $p(t+1)$ is large, $\sigma(t)$ will be small. This amounts to narrowing the search about the mean $y(t)$ if the predicted reinforcement signal is large. This can provide a higher probability of choosing an actual action $\hat{y}(t)$, which is very close to $y(t)$, since it is expected that the mean action $y(t)$ is very close to the best action possible for the current given input vector. On the other hand, the search range about the mean $y(t)$ is broadened if the predicted reinforcement signal is small such that the actual action has a higher probability of being quite different from the mean action $y(t)$. Thus, if an expected action has a smaller predicted reinforcement signal, we can have more novel trials. In terms of searching, the use of multiparameter distributions in the stochastic nodes (the output nodes of the action network) could allow independent control of the location being searched and the breadth of the search around that location. Note that if we set the search range $\sigma(t)$ as a constant, the multiparameter probability distribution approach reduces to the single-parameter approach.

In the above two-parameter distribution approach, a predicted reinforcement signal $p(t)$ is necessary to determine the search range $\sigma(t)$. This predicted reinforcement signal can be obtained from the critic network. Once the variance has been decided, the actual output of the stochastic node can be set as

$$\hat{y}(t) = N(y(t), \sigma(t)).\qquad (19.175)$$

That is, $\hat{y}(t)$ is a normal or Gaussian random variable with a density function

$$\text{Prob}(\hat{y}) = \frac{1}{\sigma\sqrt{2\pi}}\exp\left\{\frac{-(\hat{y}-y)^2}{2\sigma^2}\right\}.\qquad (19.176)$$

For a real-world application, $\hat{y}(t)$ should be properly scaled to the final output to fit the input specifications of the controlled plant.

From the above discussion, the gradient information is estimated as

$$\frac{\partial r}{\partial y} \approx \hat{r}(t)\left[\frac{\hat{y}(t-1) - y(t-1)}{\sigma(t-1)}\right] \triangleq \hat{r}(t)\left[\frac{\hat{y} - y}{\sigma}\right]_{t-1}. \qquad (19.177)$$

We can observe that if $\hat{r}(t) > 0$, the actual action $\hat{y}(t-1)$ is better than the expected action $y(t-1)$, and so $y(t-1)$ should be moved closer to $\hat{y}(t-1)$. On the other hand, if $\hat{r}(t) < 0$, then the actual action $\hat{y}(t-1)$ is worse than the expected action $y(t-1)$, and so $y(t-1)$ should be moved further away from $\hat{y}(t-1)$.

Basically, the training of an action network is not a supervised learning problem. There are no correct target output values for each input pattern. However, in action network structure learning, we need the desired output values to determine proper output fuzzy partitions as well as membership functions and to find fuzzy logic rules. The desired output values can be estimated as

$$y_d(t) \approx y(t) + \kappa \frac{\partial r}{\partial y}, \qquad (19.178)$$

where κ is a real number in the range [0, 1] and $\partial r / \partial y$ can be replaced by $\hat{r}(t)[(\hat{y} - y)/\sigma]_{t-1}$ in Eq. (19.177). According to the input state values and the estimated desired output values, the structure learning step described in Sec. 19.5.2 can be performed on the action network directly.

The goal of action network parameter learning is to maximize the external reinforcement signal $r(t)$. Thus, we need to estimate the gradient information $\partial r / \partial y$ as we did previously. With the predicted reinforcement signal $p(t)$ and the internal reinforcement signal $\hat{r}(t)$ provided from the critic network, the action network can undertake stochastic exploration and learning. The prediction signal $p(t)$ is used to determine the variance of the normal distribution function during stochastic exploration. Then the actual output $\hat{y}(t)$ can be determined according to Eq. (19.175), and the gradient information can be obtained by Eq. (19.177). With this gradient information, action network parameter learning can be performed in exactly the same way as the critic network described previously. The exact action network parameter learning equations are the same as Eqs. (19.166)–(19.172) except that $\hat{r}(t)$ is replaced by the new error term $\hat{r}(t)[(\hat{y} - y)/\sigma]_{t-1}$.

As a summary, the flowchart of the reinforcement learning algorithm for the action network is shown in Fig. 19.31. Basically, we use the stochastic exploration method to find the output error of the action network. This error is then used for training the action network by the two-step learning algorithm (structure learning step and parameter learning step).

Example 19.10

In this example, the FALCON-R with a multistep critic network is simulated for the cart-pole balancing problem (refer to Example 19.6). This system and state variables are defined in Fig. 19.18. To formulate this problem as a reinforcement learning problem, we say that the system fails and receives a penalty signal of -1 when the pole falls past a certain angle ($\pm 12°$ is used here) or the cart runs into the boundaries of its track (the distance is 2.4 meters from the center to both boundaries of the track). The goal of this control problem is to train the FALCON-R such that it can determine a sequence of forces with proper magnitudes to apply to the cart to balance the pole for as long as possible without failure. The dynamical behavior of the system is described by Eqs. (19.123) and (19.124), where the constraints on the variables are $-12° \leq \theta \leq 12°$, $-2.4\,\text{m} \leq x \leq 2.4\,\text{m}$, and $-10\,\text{N} \leq f \leq 10\,\text{N}$.

In designing the controller, the equations of motion of the cart-pole balancing system are assumed to be *unknown* to the controller. A more challenging aspect of this problem is that the only available feedback is a failure signal that notifies the controller only when a failure occurs, that is, either $|\theta| > 12°$ or $|x| > 2.4$ m. Since no exact teaching information is available, this is a typical reinformation learning problem and the feedback failure signal serves as the reinforcement signal. Since a reinforcement signal may be available only after a long sequence of time steps in this failure avoidance task, this cart-pole balancing problem belongs to the third class of reinforcement learning problems. Thus, a multistep critic network is required for the FALCON-R. Moreover, since the goal is to avoid failure for as long as possible, there is no exact success in a finite amount of time. Also, we hope that the FALCON-R can balance the pole for as long as possible for infinite trials, not just for one particular trial, where a "trial" is defined as the time steps from an initial state to a failure. Hence, this cart-pole balancing problem is further categorized as being the third case in the third-class multistep prediction problem discussed in Sec. 13.3.3. Equation (19.164) must thus be used for the temporal difference prediction method.

From the above discussion, the reinforcement signal is defined as

$$r(t) = \begin{cases} -1 & \text{if } |\theta(t)| > 12° \text{ or } |x(t)| > 2.4\,\text{m} \\ 0 & \text{otherwise,} \end{cases} \tag{19.179}$$

and the goal is to maximize the sum $\sum_{k=0}^{\infty} \gamma^k r(t+k)$, where γ is the discount rate. In the simulations, the learning system was tested for five runs, each run starting at a different initial state. Each run consisted of a sequence of trials; each trial began with the same initial condition and ended with a failure signal indicating that either $|\theta| > 12°$ or $|x| > 2.4$ m. A run consisted of at most 60 trials unless the duration of each run exceeded 50,000 time steps. In the latter case, we considered the run "successful." The following learning parameters were used for each trial. For the action network, learning rate $\eta = 0.001$, sensitivity parameter $\gamma = 4$, and initial vigilance parameters $\rho_{\text{input}} = 0.5$ and $\rho_{\text{output}} = 0.8$. For the critic network, learning rate $\eta = 0.002$, sensitivity parameter $\gamma = 4$, and initial vigilance parameters $\rho_{\text{input}} = 0.4$ and $\rho_{\text{output}} = 0.7$, where ρ_{input} and ρ_{output} were the vigilance parameters used in the input and output fuzzy clustering processes, respectively. The simulation results in Fig. 19.32 show that the

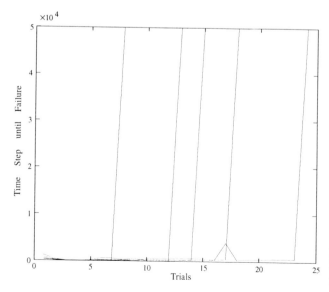

Figure 19.32 Performance of the FALCON-R on the cart-pole balancing problem in Example 19.10.

Falcon-R learned to balance the pole at the fifteenth trial on average. The average angular deviation was 0.5°. On average, there were 10 fuzzy logic rules generated in the action network and 6 fuzzy logic rules generated in the critic network after learning.

The FALCON-R has also been successfully applied to the ball-and-beam system described in Example 19.2 by formulating the problems as reinforcement learning problems. For example, the ball-and-beam system in Example 19.2 can be reformulated as follows. The system fails and receives a penalty signal of -1 when the beam falls past a certain angle (e.g., ±14°) or the ball runs to the end of the beam (e.g., the distance is 4 meters from the origin to both ends of the beam). Then it becomes a typical reinforcement learning problem and can be used to test the performance of the FALCON-R.

19.6.2 Generalized Approximate Reasoning–Based Intelligent Controller

Another neural fuzzy control system with reinforcement learning capability, called the *generalized approximate reasoning–based intelligent controller* (GARIC), has been proposed by Berenji and Khedkar [1992]. Structurally, the GARIC is very similar to the FALCON-R. Figure 19.33 shows the architecture of GARIC. It consists of two networks: an action selection network (ASN) that maps a state vector into a recommended action y using fuzzy inference and then produces an actual action $\hat{y}$ stochastically, and an action evaluation network (AEN) that maps a state vector and a failure signal into a scalar score that indicates the goodness of the state. The ASN and the AEN are parallel to the action network (fuzzy controller) and the critic network (fuzzy predictor), respectively, of the FALCON-R. The ensuing state is fed back into the GARIC along with a two-valued failure signal (reinforcement signal). Learning occurs by fine-tuning the free parameters in the two networks: The weights are adjusted in the AEN, and the parameters describing the fuzzy membership functions are changed in the ASN.

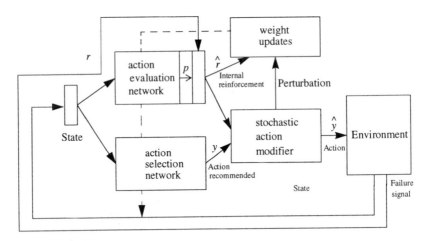

Figure 19.33 Architecture of GARIC. (Adapted from Berenji and Khedkar [1992], © 1992 IEEE.)

Neural Fuzzy Controllers   Chap. 19

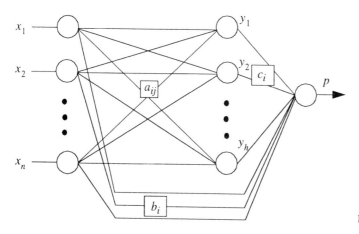

Figure 19.34 Action evaluation network.

The action evaluation network. The AEN constantly predicts reinforcements associated with different input states. It is a standard two-layer feedforward network with a sigmoidal activation function as shown in Fig. 19.34. Note that there are direct interconnections from input nodes to output nodes. The input to the AEN is the state of the plant, and the output is an evaluation of the state (or, equivalently, a prediction of the external reinforcement signal) denoted by $p(t)$. The output of each node in the AEN is calculated by the following equations:

$$y_i(t) = a\left(\sum_{j=1}^{n} a_{ij}(t) x_j(t)\right), \tag{19.180}$$

$$p(t) = \sum_{i=1}^{n} b_i(t) x_i(t) + \sum_{i=1}^{h} c_i(t) y_i(t), \tag{19.181}$$

where $a(\cdot)$ is the sigmoid function, p is the prediction of the reinforcement signal, and a_{ij}, b_i, and c_i are the corresponding link weights shown in Fig. 19.34.

The learning of the AEN is the same as that for the multistep critic network of the FALCON-R. It is based on the output error signal $\hat{r}(t)$ in Eq. (19.165), and the update rules can be derived according to Eq. (19.164) through back propagation as follows:

$$\Delta b_i(t) = \eta \hat{r}(t) x_i(t-1), \tag{19.182}$$

$$\Delta c_i(t) = \eta \hat{r}(t) y_i(t-1), \tag{19.183}$$

$$\Delta a_{ij}(t) = \eta \hat{r}(t)\left[y_i(1-y_i) \operatorname{sgn}(c_i) x_j\right]_{t-1}. \tag{19.184}$$

Note that in Eq. (19.184) the sign of a hidden node's output weight rather than its value is used. This variation is based on empirical results indicating that the algorithm is more robust if the sign of the weight is used rather than its value.

The action selection network. As shown in Fig. 19.35, the ASN is a five-layer network with each layer performing one stage of the fuzzy inference process. This structure is similar to that of the FALCON in Fig. 19.1. The functions of each layer are briefly described here.

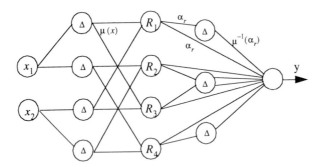

Match   Softmin   Local Mean-of-Max Weighted Sum   **Figure 19.35**   Action selection network.

- **Layer 1:** An input layer that just passes input data to the next layer.
- **Layer 2:** Each node in this layer functions as an input membership function. Here triangular membership functions are used:

$$\mu_A(x) = \begin{cases} 1 - |x - m|/r & x \in [m, m + r] \\ 1 - |x - m|/l & x \in [m - l, m] \\ 0 & \text{otherwise,} \end{cases} \qquad (19.185)$$

where $A \triangleq (m, l, r)$ indicates an input linguistic value and m, l, and r correspond to the center position, left base, and right base of the triangular membership function μ_A, respectively.

- **Layer 3:** Each node in this layer represents a fuzzy rule and implements the conjunction of all the preconditions in the rule. Its output α_r, indicating the firing strength of this rule, is calculated by

$$\alpha_r = \frac{\sum_i \mu_i e^{-k\mu_i}}{\sum_i e^{-k\mu_i}}, \qquad (19.186)$$

where μ_i is the output of a layer-2 node, which is the degree of matching between a fuzzy label occurring as one of the preconditions of rule r and the corresponding input variable. Note that Eq. (19.186) implements the softmin operation defined in Eq. (18.3).

- **Layer 4:** Each node in this layer corresponds to a consequent label, for example, B_j with membership function $\mu_{B_j}(y)$ on the output domain of a rule r. For each of the α_r supplied to it, this node computes the corresponding output action as suggested by rule r. This mapping is written as $\mu_{B_j}^{-1}(\alpha_r)$, where the inverse is taken to mean a suitable defuzzification procedure applicable to an individual rule. If $\mu_{B_j}(\cdot)$ is strictly monotonic, then the inverse exists and can be computed directly. One such function is Tsukamoto's monotonic membership function μ_T, which is characterized by two points a and b with $\mu_T(a) = 0$ and $\mu_T(b) = 1$ and is defined by

$$\mu_T(x) = \begin{cases} (-x + a)/(a - b) & x \in [a, b], a \le b, \text{ or } x \in [b, a], a > b, \\ 0 & \text{otherwise.} \end{cases} \quad (19.187)$$

Then, its inverse function can be easily derived as

$$x = \mu_T^{-1}(y) = -y(a - b) + a, \qquad y \in [0, 1]. \quad (19.188)$$

In general, the mathematical inverse of μ_{B_j} may not exist if the function is not strictly monotonic. In this case, a simple procedure for determining this inverse is as follows: If α_r is the degree to which rule r is satisfied, then $\mu_{B_j}^{-1}(\alpha_r)$ is the Y coordinate of the centroid of the set $\{y: \mu_{B_j}(y) \ge \alpha_r\}$. For a triangular fuzzy set $B_j = (m_j, l_j, r_j)$, we have

$$\mu_{B_j}^{-1}(\alpha_r) = m_j + \tfrac{1}{2}(r_j - l_j)(1 - \alpha_r). \quad (19.189)$$

This is similar to the mean-of-maximum defuzzification scheme, but the latter is applied after all rule consequents have been combined, whereas Eq. (19.189) is applied locally to each rule before the consequents are combined. This is referred to as the local mean-of-maximum (LMOM) method. It results in an unusual feature of a node in layer 4, allowing it to have multiple outputs carrying different values since sharing of consequent labels is allowed. For each rule node in layer 3 feeding it a degree, it should produce a corresponding output action that is fed to the next layer.

• **Layer 5:** Each node in this layer is an output node that combines the recommendations from all the fuzzy control rules using the following weighted sum:

$$y = \frac{\sum_r \alpha_r \mu_{B_j}^{-1}(\alpha_r)}{\sum_r \alpha_r}, \quad (19.190)$$

where μ_{B_j} is the consequent membership function of rule r. As in the output node of the action network of the FALCON-R, the expected output y is not applied to the environment directly. Stochastic exploration is performed to obtain an actual action $\hat{y}$ applied to the environment using, for example, Eqs. (19.174) and (19.175).

In the ASN, adjustable weights are present only on the input links of layers 2 and 4. The other weights are fixed at unity. Hence, the gradient-descent procedure works on only two layers of weights. As in the action network of the FALCON-R, the objective of learning of the ASN is to maximize the external reinforcement signal r. Hence, the learning rules can be derived by a back-propagation algorithm based on the estimated gradient information in Eq. (19.177). For a consequent label B_j with a generic parameter w representing m_j, l_j, or r_j, we have

$$w(t + 1) = w(t) + \eta \frac{\partial r}{\partial w}, \quad (19.191)$$

$$\frac{\partial r}{\partial w} = \frac{\partial r}{\partial y} \frac{\partial y}{\partial w} = \hat{r}(t) \left[\frac{\hat{y} - y}{\sigma} \right]_{t-1} \frac{\partial y}{\partial w}, \quad (19.192)$$

where [from Eq. (19.190)]

$$\frac{\partial y}{\partial w} = \frac{\sum_{B_j = \text{con}(R^r)} \alpha_r \left[\partial \mu_{B_j}^{-1}(\alpha_j) / \partial w \right]}{\sum_r \alpha_r},$$

(19.193)

where the summation in the numerator is taken for all the rules that have the same consequent B_j [con (R^r) is the consequent of the rule R^r]. Then from Eq. (19.189), we have

$$\frac{\partial \mu_{B_j}^{-1}(\alpha_j)}{\partial m_j} = 1, \qquad \frac{\partial \mu_{B_j}^{-1}(\alpha_j)}{\partial r_j} = \tfrac{1}{2}(1 - \alpha_j),$$

$$\frac{\partial \mu_{B_j}^{-1}(\alpha_j)}{\partial l_j} = -\tfrac{1}{2}(1 - \alpha_j).$$

(19.194)

For precondition labels, the calculations proceed similarly. The actions depend on the firing strengths α_r, which in turn depend on the membership degrees μ_i generated in layer 2 as follows:

$$\frac{\partial r}{\partial \mu_i} = \frac{\partial r}{\partial y} \frac{\partial y}{\partial \mu_i} = \hat{r}(t) \left[\frac{\hat{y} - y}{\sigma} \right]_{t-1} \frac{\partial y}{\partial \mu_i},$$

(19.195)

where

$$\frac{\partial y}{\partial \mu_i} = \sum_{\substack{r: \text{ the rules } R^r \text{ that} \\ \mu_i \text{ is fed into}}} \frac{\partial y}{\partial \alpha_r} \frac{\partial \alpha_r}{\partial \mu_i},$$

(19.196)

where from Eqs. (19.190) and (19.186),

$$\frac{\partial y}{\partial \alpha_r} = \frac{\alpha_r \mu_{B_j}^{-1}(\alpha_r) + (\mu_{B_j}^{-1})'(\alpha_r) - y}{\sum_r \alpha_r},$$

(19.197)

$$\frac{\partial \alpha_r}{\partial \mu_i} = \frac{e^{-k\mu_i}(1 + k(\alpha_r - \mu_i))}{\sum_i e^{-k\mu_i}},$$

(19.198)

where $(\mu_{B_j}^{-1})'(\cdot)$ is the derivative with respect to α_r. With the derivative $\partial r / \partial \mu_i$ available, the parameter w in the precondition part can be tuned according to the derivative $\partial r / \partial w = (\partial r / \partial \mu_i)(\partial \mu_i / \partial w)$, which can be easily derived from Eq. (19.185).

The GARIC has also been applied to the cart-pole balancing problem in Example 19.10 [Berenji and Khedkar, 1992]. With 13 predefined fuzzy logic rules and fixed input membership functions chosen properly, the GARIC learned to control the cart-pole system faster than the FALCON-R did.

19.7 CONCLUDING REMARKS

In this chapter, various neural learning techniques for determining the structure and fine-tuning the parameters of neuro-fuzzy control systems (NFCSs) are explored. As a result, various learning algorithms are developed to construct different NFCSs from input-output training data as well as from reinforcement signals. The learned NFCSs were used for various real-world application with satisfactory results.

Two-phase hybrid structure-parameter learning algorithms are found to be most useful when input-output training data are available for off-line training. Details of the FALCON-H system can be found in [Lin and Lee, 1991b; Lin, 1994, 1995]. The *fuzzy Hebbian learning law* proposed by Wang and Vachtsevanos [1992] can also be used to find fuzzy rules in the structure learning phase of the FALCON-H. Another NFCS with hybrid learning, called the FUN (fuzzy net), was proposed by Sulzberger et al. [1993]. The FUN has the same five-layer network structure as the FALCON. Wang and Mendel [1992a] have shown that the FBFN is able to uniformly approximate any real, continuous function on a compact set to arbitrary accuracy. This result is based on the Stone-Weierstrass theorem. They have also derived a back propagation–based learning strategy for FBFNs in addition to the OLS algorithm described in [Chen et al., 1991].

For the NFCS with parameter learning, Yager [1992b] proposed a set of neural network modules for realizing fuzzy controllers with fuzzy reasoning of the first type. Each fuzzy rule has a weight (*rule weight*) to indicate its importance. Training of such neural fuzzy controllers mainly involves finding proper rule weights. Nomura et al. [1992] applied the NFCS with fuzzy singleton rules to mobile robot navigation using triangular membership functions. NFCSs with fuzzy singleton rules using Gaussian membership functions were described in [Ichihashi and Tokunaga, 1993; Khan and Venkatapuram, 1993]. Based on the ANFIS, Jang [1992] proposed a generalized control scheme that can construct a fuzzy controller through *temporal back propagation* such that the state variables can follow a given desired trajectory as closely as possible.

For the NFCS with structure learning, a competitive AVQ algorithm for fuzzy rule extraction based on product-space clustering and its application can be found in [Kong and Kosko, 1992]. Other fuzzy rule extraction methods are available. Enbutsu et al. [1991] proposed a fuzzy rule extraction method for a multilayer neural network called a *rule extraction network* (REN). The REN includes input and output layers that convert input signals to membership values. Higgins and Goodman [1992] proposed a method for learning fuzzy rules from example data based on information theory. In fuzzy partitioning of input space, Ishibuchi et al. [1992] proposed a distributed representation of fuzzy rules. This approach simultaneously utilizes fuzzy rules corresponding to coarse fuzzy partitions in addition to those corresponding to fine fuzzy partitions.

For the on-line structure-adaptive NFCS, the derivation and physical meaning of fuzzy similarity measures for the FALCON-O and applications of the FALCON-O can be found in [Lin, 1994]. And for the FALCON-ART, Lin and Lin [1994] proposed a rule annihilation process for deleting unnecessary or redundant rules dynamically. Lin and Lee [1994] also proposed another type of fuzzy reinforcement learning scheme based on the FALCON-O. Reinforcement learning for NFCSs is still an on-going research topic.

19.8 PROBLEMS

19.1 Summarize the components in various types of fuzzy systems that could be learned or tuned by neural learning (including structure, parameters, operators, etc.).

19.2 Consider the following problems concerning the FALCON with hybrid and on-line learning algorithms.

(a) Explain how Eq. (19.8) approximates the *center-of-area defuzzification* method.

(b) Draw one possible structure of a fully connected FALCON with three input variables x_1, x_2, and x_3 and two output variables y_1 and y_2, where $|T(x_1)| = 2$, $|T(x_2)| = 3$, $|T(x_3)| = 2$, $|T(y_1)| = 5$, and $|T(y_2)| = 3$.

(c) Consider a FALCON with isosceles triangular input and output membership functions. Derive (i) the second phase of a hybrid (off-line) learning algorithm, and (ii) an on-line supervised learning algorithm.

(d) Perform the technique of rule combination on the following rule set and show the final rule set if $|T(x_1)| = 3$, $|T(x_2)| = 2$, $|T(x_3)| = 2$, and $|T(y)| = 3$.

$$\text{IF } x_1 \text{ is } A_1 \text{ AND } x_2 \text{ is } B_1 \text{ AND } x_3 \text{ is } C_1, \text{ THEN } y \text{ is } D_1,$$
$$\text{IF } x_1 \text{ is } A_2 \text{ AND } x_2 \text{ is } B_1 \text{ AND } x_3 \text{ is } C_1, \text{ THEN } y \text{ is } D_3,$$
$$\text{IF } x_1 \text{ is } A_3 \text{ AND } x_2 \text{ is } B_1 \text{ AND } x_3 \text{ is } C_1, \text{ THEN } y \text{ is } D_1,$$
$$\text{IF } x_1 \text{ is } A_1 \text{ AND } x_2 \text{ is } B_2 \text{ AND } x_3 \text{ is } C_1, \text{ THEN } y \text{ is } D_1,$$
$$\text{IF } x_1 \text{ is } A_2 \text{ AND } x_2 \text{ is } B_2 \text{ AND } x_3 \text{ is } C_1, \text{ THEN } y \text{ is } D_3,$$
$$\text{IF } x_1 \text{ is } A_3 \text{ AND } x_2 \text{ is } B_2 \text{ AND } x_3 \text{ is } C_1, \text{ THEN } y \text{ is } D_2,$$
$$\text{IF } x_1 \text{ is } A_1 \text{ AND } x_2 \text{ is } B_1 \text{ AND } x_3 \text{ is } C_2, \text{ THEN } y \text{ is } D_1,$$
$$\text{IF } x_1 \text{ is } A_2 \text{ AND } x_2 \text{ is } B_1 \text{ AND } x_3 \text{ is } C_2, \text{ THEN } y \text{ is } D_2,$$
$$\text{IF } x_1 \text{ is } A_3 \text{ AND } x_2 \text{ is } B_1 \text{ AND } x_3 \text{ is } C_2, \text{ THEN } y \text{ is } D_2,$$
$$\text{IF } x_1 \text{ is } A_1 \text{ AND } x_2 \text{ is } B_2 \text{ AND } x_3 \text{ is } C_2, \text{ THEN } y \text{ is } D_1,$$
$$\text{IF } x_1 \text{ is } A_2 \text{ AND } x_2 \text{ is } B_2 \text{ AND } x_3 \text{ is } C_2, \text{ THEN } y \text{ is } D_3,$$
$$\text{IF } x_1 \text{ is } A_3 \text{ AND } x_2 \text{ is } B_2 \text{ AND } x_3 \text{ is } C_2, \text{ THEN } y \text{ is } D_2.$$

19.3 Given three input-output training pairs $(x(t), d(t))$, $t = 1, 2, 3$, for a fuzzy basis function network $f(x)$ with three fuzzy basis functions to approximate a real, continuous function $d(t)$. The data are given in matrix form as

$$\mathbf{d} = \mathbf{P\theta} + \mathbf{e},$$

$$\begin{bmatrix} 1 \\ 2 \\ 3 \end{bmatrix} = \begin{bmatrix} 2 & 3 & 1 \\ 3 & 2 & 4 \\ 2 & 1 & 5 \end{bmatrix} \begin{bmatrix} \theta^1 \\ \theta^2 \\ \theta^3 \end{bmatrix} + \begin{bmatrix} e(1) \\ e(2) \\ e(3) \end{bmatrix}.$$

(a) Select two significant FBFs from these three FBFs so that the error is minimized.

(b) Obtain and express the final FBFN from the solution to part (a).

19.4 Derive a back-propagation parameter learning algorithm for the FBFN by viewing all the parameters a_i^j, m_i^j, and σ_i^j in $p_j(\mathbf{x})$ [see Eqs. (19.39) and (19.40)] as design parameters.

19.5 (a) State the similarities and differences (both in structure and function) between the fuzzy basis function network and the radial basis function network (see Sec. 12.6).

(b) Can the FBFN as a universal approximator infer that the RBFN is also a universal approximator, and vice versa?

(c) Based on the orthogonal least squares learning algorithm of the FBFN, derive an orthogonal least squares learning algorithm for the RBFN (see [Chen et al., 1991]).

19.6 Identify the following nonlinear system using various neural fuzzy systems with fuzzy singleton rules:

$$y = 4\sin(\pi x_1) + 2\cos(\pi x_2).$$

The input-output data for training the neural fuzzy systems are prepared by changing the input variables (x_1, x_2) within $[-1, 1]$ using random numbers. The desired output y^d is normalized within $[0, 1]$. Twenty input-output data pairs are employed for identification and evaluation of the nonlinear system. The learned fuzzy logic rules will express the input-output relation of the training data. In this problem, 20 fuzzy logic rules are used. Learning stops when the inference error E for the identification data is less than 0.02, where $E = \sum_{k=1}^{20}(y_k - y_k^d)^2$. Perform the identification using the following structure and learning schemes:

(a) Fuzzy singleton rules with triangular membership functions using (i) the purely gradient-descent learning algorithm and (ii) the gradient-descent and the Kalman filter learning algorithms.

(b) Fuzzy singleton rules with bell-shaped (Gaussian) membership functions using (i) the purely gradient-descent learning algorithm and (ii) the gradient-descent and the Kalman filter learning algorithms.

(c) Fuzzy singleton rules with trapezoidal membership functions using (i) the purely gradient-descent learning algorithm and (ii) the gradient-descent and the Kalman filter learning algorithms.

19.7 Derive learning algorithms in detail for neural fuzzy controllers with TSK fuzzy rules based on (i) the purely gradient-descent method and (ii) the gradient-descent and the Kalman filter methods. Write programs for implementing the derived learning algorithms and test them on the system identification as described in Problem 19.6.

19.8 Rework Example 19.3 with the following set of fuzzy rules for a fuzzy controller:

IF x_1 is $N1$ AND x_2 is $N2$ AND x_3 is $N3$, THEN y is $N4$,

IF x_1 is $N1$ AND x_2 is $N2$ AND x_3 is $P3$, THEN y is $N4$,

IF x_1 is $N1$ AND x_2 is $P2$ AND x_3 is $N3$, THEN y is $N4$,

IF x_1 is $N1$ AND x_2 is $P2$ AND x_3 is $P3$, THEN y is $Z4$,

IF x_1 is $P1$ AND x_2 is $N2$ AND x_3 is $N3$, THEN y is $Z4$,

IF x_1 is $P1$ AND x_2 is $N2$ AND x_3 is $P3$, THEN y is $P4$,

IF x_1 is $P1$ AND x_2 is $P2$ AND x_3 is $N3$, THEN y is $P4$,

IF x_1 is $P1$ AND x_2 is $P2$ AND x_3 is $P3$, THEN y is $P4$.

19.9 Extract fuzzy logic rules from the numerical input-output training data specified in Problem 19.6 using the three approaches introduced in Sec. 19.4.1. Define proper input-output membership functions for these extraction procedures. Compare the fuzzy logic rules obtained with these approaches.

19.10 Consider the use of a product-space clustering technique for fuzzy rule extraction. The fuzzy rules to be learned are in the form of: "IF x is A AND y is B, THEN z is C" or $(A, B; C)$, where $x \in X, y \in Y$, and $z \in Z$ and the input spaces X and Y are both $[-5, 5]$, and the output space Z is $[-5, 30]$. Define five triangular fuzzy sets evenly covering X, Y, and Z. Randomly generate 300 data points, (x, y, z), as observed sample data according to the relation $z = x^2 - y$. Find at least 10 fuzzy logic rules from the clustered sample data using the product-space clustering technique. Evaluate the accuracy of the derived fuzzy system as compared to the underlying system of $z = x^2 - y$.

19.11 Consider Fig. 19.12. In order to simplify the calculations, the ellipsoid can be inscribed in a hyperrectangle that has 2^q vertices at $(\pm c/\sqrt{\lambda_1}, \pm c/\sqrt{\lambda_2}, \ldots, \pm c/\sqrt{\lambda_q})$ in the rotated coordinate plane. The unit eigenvectors define *direction cosines* for each axis of the ellipse. The direction cosine γ_{ik} is the angle between the kth eigenvector and the ith axis [Hildebrand, 1976]. Show that the projection of the jth hyperrectangle onto the ith axis is the interval $\mathcal{I}_i$:

$$\mathcal{I}_i = [m_i - \rho_i, m_i + \rho_i] = \left[m_i - c \left(\frac{|\cos \gamma_{i1}|}{\sqrt{\lambda_1}} + \cdots + \frac{|\cos \gamma_{iq}|}{\sqrt{\lambda_q}} \right), \right.$$

$$\left. m_i + c \left(\frac{|\cos \gamma_{i1}|}{\sqrt{\lambda_1}} + \cdots + \frac{|\cos \gamma_{iq}|}{\sqrt{\lambda_q}} \right) \right],$$

where m_i is the center of the projection, that is, the projection of the center of the ellipsoid onto the ith axis.

19.12 (a) Prove that the formula for $|A \cap B|$ in Eq. (19.128) holds when $m_1 = m_2$.

 (b) Derive the exact formula for the similarity measure of two fuzzy sets with bell-shaped membership functions.

 (c) Consider two fuzzy sets A and B with the following bell-shaped membership functions:

$$m_A(x) = e^{-x^2} \qquad \text{and} \qquad m_B(x) = e^{-(x-0.5)^2/2}.$$

Compute their similarity measure using (i) the exact formula derived in part (a) and (ii) the approximate formula in Eq. (19.128). Compare the results in (i) and (ii) to find the error of approximation.

19.13 Based on the on-line supervised structure-parameter learning algorithm for the FALCON, derive a structure-parameter learning algorithm for the radial basis function network that can determine on-line the proper number of radial basis functions as well as network weights (parameters) for a task.

19.14 The vigilance value is important to the performance of the FALCON with ART-type neural learning (FALCON-ART).

 (a) Discuss the dependence of the stability (convergence) of the FALCON-ART on the (changing) vigilance values.

 (b) In Sec. 20.3.3, we introduced a fuzzy control scheme for tuning the vigilance values of the ART network. Find a similar fuzzy controller that can determine the vigilance values of the FALCON-ART properly in the learning process. Explain the reasons for your design in detail.

19.15 Consider the FALCON with reinforcement learning (FALCON-R).

 (a) What are the advantages and disadvantages of using a FALCON-ART instead of a normal neural network (like GARIC) to predict the external reinforcement signal?

 (b) Find a way to determine the amount of exploration $\sigma(t)$ for the action network of the FALCON-R other than that specified in Eq. (19.174).

 (c) Explain why Eq. (19.177) can estimate the gradient information of the output of the action network in the FALCON-R.

 (d) Recall the temporal difference methods discussed in Sec. 13.3.3 and derive Eq. (19.164).

19.16 Assume that we want to solve a reinforcement learning problem using either the FALCON-R or GARIC. In what situation(s) is it better to use FALCON-R than to use GARIC? (*Hint*: Consider the amount of a priori knowledge that is available.)

20

Fuzzy Logic–Based Neural Network Models

In this chapter, we shall discuss the techniques of incorporating fuzzy logic into neural network models. Systems formed in this way are called *fuzzy logic–based neural network models* or *fuzzy neural networks*. Neural networks have demonstrated their ability to classify, store, recall, and associate information. By incorporating fuzzy principles into a neural network, more user flexibility is attained and the system becomes more robust. Fuzziness in this case means more flexibility in the definition of the system; that is, the boundaries of the system may be described more vaguely, and the system may be able to reconfigure itself for best performance. In fuzzy neural networks, the numerical control parameters in the neuron and the connection weights may be replaced by fuzzy parameters. Fuzzy neural networks have greater representation power, higher training speed, and are more robust than conventional neural systems. Fuzzy neural networks are in fact fuzzified neural networks and thus are inherently neural networks. Each part of a neural network (such as activation functions, aggregation functions, weights, input-output data, etc.), each neural network model, and each neural learning algorithm can possibly be fuzzified. Based on this concept, three categories of fuzzy neural networks are identified and will be discussed in this chapter. They are fuzzy neurons, fuzzified neural models, and neural networks with fuzzy training.

20.1 FUZZY NEURONS

In this section, we shall introduce some basic models of fuzzy neurons from which fuzzy neural networks can be built. A fuzzy neuron is designed to function in much the same way as the nonfuzzy or the classical McCulloch-Pitts neuron except that it reflects the fuzzy nature of a neuron and has the ability to cope with fuzzy information. Basically, two kinds of fuzzy neuron models can be recognized [Gupta and Qi, 1991]. One comes from the *fuzzification* of nonfuzzy neuron models, and the other is a model whose input-output relations of neurons are described by fuzzy IF-THEN rules. Three types of fuzzy neural models will be discussed in this section [Hayashi et al., 1992b]: (a) a fuzzy neuron with crisp signals used to evaluate fuzzy weights, (b) a fuzzy neuron with fuzzy signals which is combined with fuzzy weights, and (c) a fuzzy neuron described by fuzzy logic equations.

20.1.1 Fuzzy Neuron of Type I

This type of fuzzy neuron, denoted by N, is shown in Fig. 20.1 and has n nonfuzzy inputs $x_1, x_2, \ldots, x_n$. The weights for N are fuzzy sets A_i, $1 \leq i \leq n$; that is, the weighting operations are replaced by membership functions. The result of each weighting operation is the membership value $\mu_{A_i}(x_i)$ of the corresponding input x_i in the fuzzy set (weight) A_i. All these membership values are aggregated together to give a single output in the interval $[0, 1]$, which may be considered the "level of confidence." The aggregation operation represented by $\otimes$ may use any aggregation operator such as min or max and any other t-norms and t-conorms (see Sec. 2.2.2). A mathematical representation of such a fuzzy neuron N is written as

$$\mu_N(x_1, x_2, \ldots, x_n) = \mu_{A_1}(x_1) \otimes \mu_{A_2}(x_2) \otimes \cdots \otimes \mu_{A_i}(x_i) \otimes \cdots \otimes \mu_{A_n}(x_n), \qquad (20.1)$$

where x_i is the ith (nonfuzzy) input to the neuron, $\mu_{A_i}(\cdot)$ is the membership function of the ith (fuzzy) weight, $\mu_N(\cdot)$ is the output membership function of the neuron, and $\otimes$ is an aggregation operator. The following example illustrates the use of type I fuzzy neurons in constructing a fuzzy neural network as a fuzzy controller.

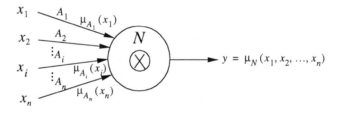

Figure 20.1   Fuzzy neuron of type I.

Example 20.1

[Hayashi et al., 1992b]. Consider the fuzzy controller specified by the rules given in Table 20.1 and the definitions of the fuzzy numbers presented in Fig. 20.2. This fuzzy controller accepts singleton inputs e = error and Δe = change in error. Given the values for e and Δe, the nine fuzzy rules are evaluated as follows:

$$\Delta_1 = \min(\mu_{F_1}(e), \mu_{G_2}(\Delta e)),$$

$$\Delta_2 = \min(\mu_{F_2}(e), \mu_{G_2}(\Delta e)),$$

$$\vdots \qquad\qquad \vdots$$

$$\Delta_9 = \min(\mu_{F_5}(e), \mu_{G_4}(\Delta e)).$$

Since some rules have the same control actions, we maximize the Δ_i corresponding to the same action A_k as follows: $\epsilon_1 = \max(\Delta_1, \Delta_2)$, $\epsilon_2 = \max(\Delta_3, \Delta_4)$, $\epsilon_3 = \Delta_5$, $\epsilon_4 = \max(\Delta_6, \Delta_7)$,

TABLE 20.1 Fuzzy Control Rules Used in Example 20.1*

Δe = Change in error

		G_1	G_2	G_3	G_4	G_5
	F_1		1 A_1			
	F_2		2 A_1		3 A_2	
e = error	F_3	4 A_2		5 A_3		6 A_4
	F_4		7 A_4		8 A_5	
	F_5				9 A_5	

*The rule number is given in the upper right-hand corner.

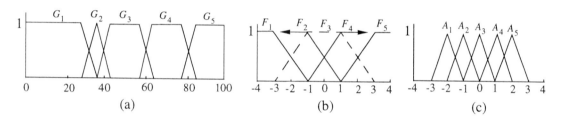

Figure 20.2 Fuzzy numbers used in Example 20.1. (a) Fuzzy numbers for error. (b) Fuzzy numbers for change in error. (c) Fuzzy numbers for output.

and $\epsilon_5 = \max(\Delta_8, \Delta_9)$. Then each ϵ_k is assigned to its A_k, $1 \le k \le 5$. To defuzzify the result, we first compute $A = \bigcup (\epsilon_k A_k)$ (where the union is taken as maximum) and then find y which is equal to the center of gravity of A; y is the defuzzified output from the controller.

This fuzzy controller, modeled as a fuzzy neural network, is displayed in Fig. 20.3. In this network, nodes 1 through 9 denote the rules, nodes 10 through 14 have no input weights,

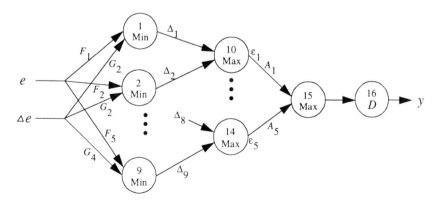

Figure 20.3 Fuzzy neural network as a fuzzy controller.

and node 16, with no weight, is the defuzzifier. Obviously, nodes 1 through 9 are fuzzy neurons of type I, but node 15 is more like a fuzzy neuron of type II, which will be introduced in the next section. The reason is that the inputs to node 15 are $\epsilon_i A_i$, $1 \le i \le 5$, which are fuzzy sets, while the inputs to node 1 are $\mu_{F_1}(e)$ and $\mu_{G_2}(\Delta e)$, which are scalars. The constructed fuzzy neural network can be expected to learn the proper fuzzy numbers F_i, G_j, and A_p given some training data $(e_k, \Delta e_k)$ for inputs and y_k^d for desired defuzzified outputs, $k = 1, 2, \ldots$. To achieve this, we need a learning algorithm so that the network will learn its weights (the fuzzy sets in the rules) from the training data. We shall cover the details of this learning issue in Sec. 20.3.

20.1.2 Fuzzy Neuron of Type II

This type of neuron, denoted by N and shown in Fig. 20.4, is similar to the type I fuzzy neurons shown in Fig. 20.1 except that all the inputs and outputs are fuzzy sets rather than crisp values. Each fuzzy input X_i undergoes a weighting operation which results in another fuzzy set $X_i' = A_i * X_i$, $1 \le i \le n$, for some operator $*$, where A_i is the ith fuzzy weight. All the modified inputs are aggregated to produce an n-dimensional fuzzy set Y. The weighting operation here is not a membership function, unlike the situation with type I fuzzy neurons; instead it is a modifier to each fuzzy input. This fuzzy neuron is mathematically described as

$$X_i' = A_i * X_i, \qquad i = 1, 2, \ldots, n,$$
$$Y = X_1' \otimes X_2' \otimes \cdots \otimes X_i' \otimes \cdots \otimes X_n',$$

$$(20.2)$$

where Y is the fuzzy set representing the output of the fuzzy neuron, X_i and X_i' are the ith inputs before and after the weighting operation, respectively, A_i is the weight on the ith synaptic connection, $\otimes$ is the aggregation operator mentioned for the type I fuzzy neuron, and $*$ is the weighting operator, such as the *multiplication of two fuzzy sets* (Sec. 5.2.2). Let us consider the following example where a fuzzy neural network consists of a number of type II fuzzy neurons for fuzzy system identification.

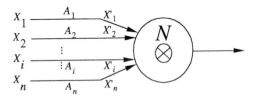

Figure 20.4   Fuzzy neuron of type II.

Example 20.2

[Hayashi et al., 1992b]. Consider a system identification problem in which we wish to find the function f that transforms the fuzzy inputs X and Y into fuzzy output Z. Here, we assume a quadratic relationship,

$$AX^2 + BXY + CY^2 = Z,$$

$$(20.3)$$

for fuzzy numbers A, B, and C. The relationship in Eq. (20.3) is implemented by the fuzzy neural network shown in Fig. 20.5, where fuzzy neurons of type II are used. The network is expected to learn A, B, and C from some training data (X_k, Y_k) for inputs and the corresponding desired output Z_k^d, $k = 1, 2, \ldots$. Such learning schemes will be discussed in Sec. 20.3.

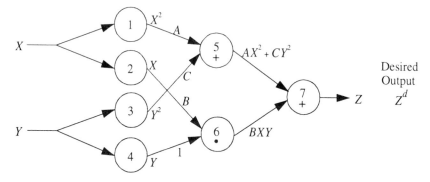

Figure 20.5 Fuzzy neural network for fitting a quadratic.

20.1.3 Fuzzy Neuron of Type III

A type III fuzzy neuron with n fuzzy inputs and one fuzzy output is shown in Fig. 20.6. The input-output relation of the fuzzy neuron is represented by one fuzzy IF-THEN rule:

$$\text{IF } X_1 \text{ AND } X_2 \text{ AND } \cdots \text{ AND } X_n, \text{ THEN } Y, \qquad (20.4)$$

where $X_1, X_2, \ldots, X_n$ are the current inputs and Y is the current output. A type III fuzzy neuron can be described by a fuzzy relation R, for example,

$$R = X_1 \times X_2 \times \cdots \times X_n \times Y, \qquad (20.5)$$

or, in the general case,

$$R = f(X_1, X_2, \ldots, X_n, Y), \qquad (20.6)$$

where $f(\cdot)$ represents an implication function. Hence, a type III fuzzy neuron is described by a fuzzy transfer relation R. Given the current inputs (fuzzy or nonfuzzy) $x_1, x_2, \ldots, x_n$, according to the compositional rule of inference, the fuzzy neuron yields output as

$$Y_i' = x_1 \circ (x_2 \circ (\cdots \circ (x_n \circ R_i) \cdots)), \qquad (20.7)$$

where $\circ$ represents any type of compositional rule of inference operator such as max t-norm. It is noted that inputs to the neuron can be either fuzzy or nonfuzzy; crisp values are a special case of fuzzy values.

A fuzzy neural network constructed from type III fuzzy neurons appears to be ideal for rule extraction from training data in fuzzy expert systems. The following example illustrates this application.

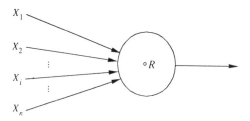

Figure 20.6 Fuzzy neuron of type III.

Example 20.3

[Hayashi et al., 1992b]. Assume we have the following rules:

$$R_r: \text{IF } X \text{ is } A_i \text{ AND } Y \text{ is } B_j, \text{THEN } Z \text{ is } C_p, \qquad \text{for } 1 \le r \le n,$$

where A_i, B_j, and C_p are fuzzy subsets of R. For simplicity, all these fuzzy sets are assumed to be symmetric triangular fuzzy numbers with fixed widths, and so they are all completely specified by their central values. Let the central values be a_i, b_j, and c_p, respectively.

Given new data $X = A'$ and $Y = B'$, some method of approximate reasoning from Chap. 6 is adopted to evaluate the rules. We first decide on an implication operator M that will produce a fuzzy relation R_r for each rule. Let $R_r(a_i, b_j, c_p) = M(A_i, B_j, C_p)$, which is a fuzzy relation in R^3 for rule r, $1 \le r \le n$. Then, given $X = A'$ and $Y = B'$, each rule computes $C'_r = (A', B') \circ R_r(a_i, b_j, c_p)$, $1 \le r \le n$. The fuzzy expert system then combines these results C'_r into one final conclusion C'. This fuzzy expert system can be modeled by a fuzzy neural network containing type III fuzzy neurons as shown in Fig. 20.7. The fuzzy relation R_r is at the node r such that each node has three parameters a_i, b_j, c_p. For example, it is assumed that A_1, B_2, C_5 appear in rule R_1, and so the parameter in this node is the central values a_1, b_2, c_5. Node $(n + 1)$ combines the inputs using the operation $*$ to obtain output Z. Hence, neurons 1 through n are type III fuzzy neurons, but neuron $(n + 1)$ is more like a type II fuzzy neuron.

Given some training data (A'_k, B'_k) for inputs with desired output Y'_k, $k = 1, 2,...$, a learning algorithm is expected to learn the correct rules (the A_i, B_j, and C_p). Such a learning algorithm will of course depend on the implication function M and the compositional rule of the inference operator $\circ$ (see Sec. 20.3 and Chap. 19).

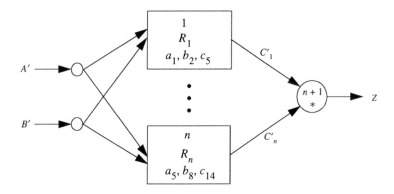

Figure 20.7   Fuzzy neural network for a fuzzy expert system.

20.2 FUZZIFICATION OF NEURAL NETWORK MODELS

In this section, we shall explore several fuzzy neural networks resulting from the direct fuzzification of existing nonfuzzy neural network models. Fuzzy neural models of this kind constitute the mainstream of existing fuzzy neural networks.

20.2.1 Fuzzy Perceptron

In Chap. 10, we discussed the single-node perceptron which, when given two classes of patterns, attempts to determine a linear decision boundary separating the two classes. The single node computes a weighted sum of the input elements, subtracts a threshold, and passes the result through a band-limiting nonlinearity such that the output y is either $+1$ or -1, indicating class 1 or class 2, respectively. As Theorem 10.1 indicates, if two sets of patterns are linearly separable, the perceptron algorithm is guaranteed to find a separating hyperplane in a finite number of steps. However, if two sets of patterns are not linearly separable, not only will the perceptron algorithm be unable to find a separating hyperplane (since one does not exist), but there will be no known method for terminating the algorithm to obtain an optimal or even a good decision boundary. Depending on the values of the sample patterns, the behavior of the perceptron algorithm can be very erratic in the nonseparable case. To solve this problem, Keller and Hunt [1985] proposed the *fuzzy perceptron* by introducing fuzzy set theory into the perceptron algorithm. We shall discuss the fuzzy perceptron and related generalizations in this section.

In the crisp perceptron learning algorithm, each training pattern (vector) has the same "importance" in adjusting the weights. However, in the nonseparable case, the classes overlap, and the patterns that cause them to overlap are primarily responsible for the erratic behavior of the crisp perceptron algorithm. In many cases, these uncertain patterns are also relatively uncharacteristic of any classes. This is where fuzzy class membership functions can improve the algorithm. The basic idea of the fuzzy perceptron is that by basing the amount of correction to the weight vector on the fuzzy memberships, vectors (patterns) whose class is less certain (membership values close to 0.5) will have less influence in determining the weight vector. Thus, for a set of sample vectors $\{x_1, x_2,..., x_p\}$, let $\mu_i(x_k)$, $i = 1, 2, k = 1, 2,..., p$, form a *fuzzy two-class partition* of these vectors specifying the degree of membership of each vector in each of two classes. This implies the following properties:

$$\sum_{i=1}^{2} \mu_i(x_k) = 1, \qquad 0 < \sum_{k=1}^{p} \mu_i(x_k) < p, \qquad \mu_i(x_k) \in [0, 1]. \qquad (20.8)$$

Then the *degrees of influence* of the pattern x_k on weight updating can be determined by $|\mu_1(x_k) - \mu_2(x_k)|^m$, where m is a constant. Accordingly, in the fuzzy perceptron algorithm, the original weight update rule in Eq. (10.7) is modified to

$$w_j(t + 1) = w_j(t) + \eta \left| \mu_1(x_k(t)) - \mu_2(x_k(t)) \right|^m [y_k^d - y(t)] x_j^{(k)},$$
$$1 \leq j \leq n + 1. \qquad (20.9)$$

Clearly, the above equation accomplishes the objective of reducing the influence of uncertainty vectors in determining the weight vector. Moreover, like the crisp perceptron, the fuzzy perceptron can find a separating hyperplane in a finite number of iterations in the linearly separable case (a proof of this can be found in [Keller and Hunt, 1985]). Note that since $|\mu_1(x_k) - \mu_2(x_k)|^m = 1$ when $\mu_1(x_k), \mu_2(x_k) \in \{0, 1\}$, the fuzzy perceptron reduces to the crisp perceptron when the membership function values are crisp.

The choice of the constant m in Eq. (20.9) plays an important part in the convergence of the fuzzy perceptron. To best utilize the fuzzy membership values, the learning algorithm makes major adjustments during early iterations when it misclassifies "typical" vectors and then in later iterations makes only minor adjustments to the weight vector. Therefore, choices of m less than 1 should be avoided since they exaggerate the fractional membership differences. The value of m chosen to obtain good results also depends on the method of assigning fuzzy memberships to the sample sets. The general rule is that if vectors in the overlap regions are assigned membership values near 0.5, then almost any value of m greater than 1 will produce good results. Conversely, if these atypical vectors have higher memberships, then larger exponents will be necessary to dampen the oscillations of the decision boundaries. This relationship will be explored further.

With the weight update rule in Eq. (20.9) for a fuzzy perceptron, we need to formulate a method for assigning fuzzy membership values to a given set of labeled sample vectors. As indicated in Eq. (20.8), the approach is to transform the crisp partition of the vectors into a fuzzy partition. The guidelines for determining the membership value of a vector for the class to which it belongs are as follows: (a) It should be 1.0 if the vector is equal to the mean of its class; (b) it should be 0.5 if the vector is equal to the mean of the other class; (c) it should be near 0.5 if the vector is equidistant from the two means; (d) it should never be less than 0.5; (e) as a vector gets closer to its mean and farther from the other mean, the membership value should approach 1.0 exponentially; (f) it should depend on relative distances from the means of the classes rather than absolute distances.

The following method of assigning fuzzy membership values, suggested by Keller and Hunt [1985], satisfies the above conditions.

For $\mathbf{x}_k$ in class 1,

$$\mu_1(\mathbf{x}_k) = 0.5 + \frac{e^{f(d_2 - d_1)/d} - e^{-f}}{2(e^f - e^{-f})}, \tag{20.10}$$

$$\mu_2(\mathbf{x}_k) = 1 - \mu_1(\mathbf{x}_k). \tag{20.11}$$

For $\mathbf{x}_k$ in class 2,

$$\mu_2(\mathbf{x}_k) = 0.5 + \frac{e^{f(d_1 - d_2)/d} - e^{-f}}{2(e^f - e^{-f})}, \tag{20.12}$$

$$\mu_1(\mathbf{x}_k) = 1 - \mu_2(\mathbf{x}_k). \tag{20.13}$$

In the above equations, d_1 is the distance from the vector to the mean of class 1, d_2 is the distance from the vector to the mean of class 2, and d is the distance between the two means. The constant f must be positive, and it controls the rate at which memberships decrease toward 0.5. It is observed that the value chosen for f is related to that of m in Eq. (20.9) in an inverse fashion; that is, as f decreases, m must increase to counteract the higher memberships for vectors in the overlap regions. It is found that any combination of m and f, where each number is greater than 2, gives excellent results in simulations.

The next question concerning the fuzzy perceptron algorithm is, What is the stopping criterion of the algorithm? Since the new fuzzy partition may be nonseparable, we need a stopping criterion for the fuzzy perceptron. The reason for setting a stopping criterion is that vectors that are uncertain (i.e., membership values in both classes are near 0.5) should not, by themselves, cause the algorithm to perform another iteration. Thus, when the algorithm performs a complete iteration through all the sample vectors, if all the corrections are due to fuzzy vectors, then the algorithm should terminate. That is, the stopping criterion can be implemented by checking the following condition when a misclassification occurs:

$$\mu_1(\mathbf{x}_k) > 0.5 + \text{BETA} \qquad \text{or} \qquad \mu_1(\mathbf{x}_k) < 0.5 - \text{BETA}, \tag{20.14}$$

where BETA defines the range around 0.5 in which a vector is considered to be uncertain. If the above condition holds, the corresponding misclassification should not cause another iteration. Note that the condition $\mu_1(\mathbf{x}_k) < 0.5 - \text{BETA}$ in Eq. (20.14) is equal to the condition $\mu_2(\mathbf{x}_k) > 0.5 + \text{BETA}$ because of the assumption in Eq. (20.8) that $\mu_1(\mathbf{x}_k) + \mu_2(\mathbf{x}_k) = 1$.

Let us discuss how to determine BETA in Eq. (20.14). A necessary condition for this stopping criterion to work is that the vectors outside the $[0.5 - \text{BETA}, 0.5 + \text{BETA}]$ range must be linearly separable. As an illustration, consider Fig. 20.8. Assume the decision line in the figure has been determined by the fuzzy perceptron algorithm. Then the dark areas are those data that do not satisfy the stopping condition. To meet this necessary condition, BETA must be chosen such that $0.5 + \text{BETA}$ is greater than or equal to the membership value of vectors that are equidistant from the means of the two classes. Hence, by setting $d_1 = d_2$ in Eqs. (20.10)–(20.13), we have

$$\text{BETA} = \frac{1 - e^{-f}}{2(e^f - e^{-f})} + \epsilon, \qquad \text{where} \quad \epsilon \geq 0. \tag{20.15}$$

The value of ϵ in this equation is important. If ϵ is too small, then the area in which a hyperplane can lie and satisfy the stopping criterion will be too constrained. The result will be that the algorithm may take a long time to terminate or may not even terminate. On the other hand, if ϵ is too large, then the algorithm may terminate too quickly, producing a nonoptimal decision boundary. From empirical studies, a value of $\epsilon = 0.02$ was found to produce very good results.

Summarizing the preceding discussion, the complete fuzzy perceptron learning algorithm is presented here.

Algorithm FPLA: Fuzzy Perceptron Learning Algorithm

Step 1 **(Initialization):** Set $w_j(0)$, $1 \leq j \leq n + 1$, to small random numbers, where $w_j(0)$, $1 \leq j \leq n$, is the initial weight associated with the jth input and $w_{n+1}(0)$ is the initial threshold value. Also, set the value of BETA according to Eq. (20.15).

Step 2: Calculate the membership degrees of all training patterns in each class using Eqs. (20.10)–(20.13).

Step 3: Set the UPDATE flag to "FALSE."

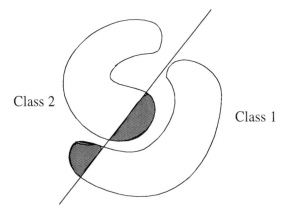

Class 2

Class 1

Figure 20.8 Fuzzy perceptron algorithm.

Step 4: Present an augmented new input pattern $\mathbf{x}_k = [x_1^{(k)}, x_2^{(k)}, \ldots, x_n^{(k)}, -1]$ (where we let $x_{n+1}^{(k)} = -1$), along with the desired output $y_k^d \in \{1, -1\}$, and calculate the actual output:

$$y(t) = \text{sgn}\left(\sum_{j=1}^{n+1} w_i(t) x_j^{(k)}\right). \tag{20.16}$$

If $y(t) = y_k^d$, then go to step 7.

Step 5: Adapt weights according to the rule

$$w_j(t+1) = w_j(t) + \eta \left| \mu_1(\mathbf{x}_k) - \mu_2(\mathbf{x}_k) \right|^m [y_k^d - y(t)] x_j^{(k)}, \tag{20.17}$$

$$1 \leq j \leq n+1.$$

Step 6: If $(\mu_1(\mathbf{x}_k) > 0.5 + \text{BETA})$ or $(\mu_1(\mathbf{x}_k) < 0.5 - \text{BETA})$, then set the UPDATE flag to "TRUE."

Step 7: If each input pattern has been presented, go to the next step; otherwise, go to step 4.

Step 8: If the UPDATE flag is "TRUE," then go to step 3; otherwise, stop and output the weights that determine the learned decision boundary.

END FPLA

The performance of the fuzzy perceptron has been compared to that of the crisp perceptron using Anderson's *Iris* data (see Fig. 8.5) [Keller and Hunt, 1985]. The fuzzy perceptron learning algorithm produced a better decision boundary and terminated in fewer iterations than its crisp counterpart. It was observed that even when used with data that were "just barely separable," the fuzzy perceptron converged in fewer iterations than its crisp counterpart, further supporting the claim that the fuzzy perceptron can make efficient use of the degree to which each vector is typical of its class.

Although we introduced membership functions into the perceptron algorithm, this technique can be used with any of the gradient-descent algorithms to produce linear (or nonlinear under appropriate transformation) decision boundaries. For example, we can derive a fuzzy functional-link network (see Sec. 10.3.1) in the same way as above. In particular, the concept of reducing the influence of uncertain data in determining the decision boundary can be applied to classification problems whose boundaries are determined by the back-propagation algorithm. One such system is introduced in the next section.

20.2.2 Fuzzy Classification with the Back-Propagation Network

In the conventional back-propagation network used for pattern classification, the number of output nodes corresponds to the number of pattern classes present. During training, the output node corresponding to the class of a pattern vector is kept clamped at state 1 while the others are clamped at state 0. Hence, the components of the desired output vector take on *crisp* two-state values. During testing, a *winner-take-all* mechanism causes the test pattern to be classified as belonging to the class corresponding to the output node with the highest activation. However, in real-world problems, the data are generally ill-defined, with overlapping or fuzzy class boundaries. Each pattern used in training may possess nonzero belongingness to more than one class. Consider, for example, a point lying in a region of overlapping classes in the feature space. In such cases it may have equal membership in each of these classes. Then there is no reason why we should follow the crisp approach of classifying this pattern as belonging to the class corresponding to the output neuron with a slightly higher activation and thereby neglect the smaller yet significant responses obtained for the other overlapping classes. In this connection, it is desirable to incorporate fuzzy concepts into back-propagation networks for fuzzy pattern classification. We shall describe one such model proposed by Pal and Mitra [1992] in this section.

To allow modeling of fuzzy data when the feature space involves overlapping pattern classes such that a pattern point may belong to more than one class with nonzero membership, we can clamp the desired membership values at the output nodes during learning instead of choosing the single class (node) with the highest activation. Then the network back-propagates the errors with respect to the desired membership values at the outputs. Hence, the error (which is back-propagated for weight updating) has inherently more significance in the case of nodes with higher membership values. The contribution of ambiguous or uncertain vectors to the weight correction is automatically reduced. This is natural since vectors that are more *typical* of their class should have more influence in determining the position and shape of the decision surface. In such a learning process, the network may become able to detect regularities in the input-output membership relation of the training set. Then when a separate set of test patterns is presented at the input layer, the output nodes generate the class membership values of the patterns in the corresponding classes. This procedure of assigning fuzzy output membership values, instead of the more conventional binary output values, enables the network to more efficiently classify fuzzy data with overlapping class boundaries.

Consider an l-class problem in which we have l nodes in the output layer. Let the n-dimensional vectors $\mathbf{m}_k$ and $\mathbf{v}_k$ denote the mean and standard deviations, respectively, of the numerical training data for the kth class C_k. We first define the weighted distance of the training pattern $\mathbf{x}_i$ from the kth class as

$$z_{ik} = \sqrt{\sum_{j=1}^{n} \left[\frac{x_{ij} - m_{kj}}{v_{kj}} \right]^2}, \qquad k = 1, 2, \ldots, l, \qquad (20.18)$$

where x_{ij} is the value of the jth component (feature) of the ith pattern point and m_{kj} and v_{kj} are the jth components of $\mathbf{m}_k$ and $\mathbf{v}_k$, respectively. The factor $1/v_{kj}$ takes care of the variance of the classes so that a feature with higher variance has less weight (significance) in characterizing a class. Then the degree of membership of the ith pattern in class C_k is defined as follows:

$$\mu_k(\mathbf{x}_i) = \frac{1}{1 + (z_{ik}/f_d)^{f_e}}, \qquad k = 1, 2, \ldots, l, \qquad (20.19)$$

where z_{ik} is the weighted distance from Eq. (20.18) and the positive constants f_d and f_e are the denominational and exponential fuzzy generators controlling the amount of fuzziness in this class membership set. According to Eq. (20.19), the greater the distance between a pattern and a class, the lower its membership value in that class. Note that the l-dimensional membership vector $[\mu_1(\mathbf{x}_i), \mu_2(\mathbf{x}_i), \ldots, \mu_l(\mathbf{x}_i)]$ has l nonzero components in the *fuzziest* case and only one nonzero component in the hard (or crisp) case. In the fuzziest case, we use the fuzzy modifier INT to enhance contrast in class membership, that is, to decrease the ambiguity in making a decision. We have

$$\mu_{\text{INT}(k)}(\mathbf{x}_i) = \begin{cases} 2\,[\mu_k(\mathbf{x}_i)\,]^2 & \text{for } 0 \le \mu_k(\mathbf{x}_i) \le 0.5 \\ 1 - 2\,[1 - \mu_k(\mathbf{x}_i)\,]^2 & \text{otherwise.} \end{cases} \tag{20.20}$$

Summarizing the above discussion, for the ith input pattern $\mathbf{x}_i$, we define the desired output of the kth output node as

$$d_k = \begin{cases} \mu_{\text{INT}(k)}(\mathbf{x}_i) & \text{in the fuzziest case} \\ \mu_k(\mathbf{x}_i) & \text{otherwise,} \end{cases} \tag{20.21}$$

where $0 \le d_k \le 1$ for all k. With the input and fuzzified desired output as paired training data, the back-propagation network is trained in a normal way (see Sec. 10.2).

20.2.3 Fuzzy Associative Memories

The *fuzzy associative memory* (FAM) proposed by Kosko [1992c] is a fuzzy system that maps fuzzy sets to fuzzy sets. It is a fuzzified version of the bidirectional associative memory (BAM) introduced in Sec. 11.2.2. FAMs behave like associative memories that map close inputs to close outputs. The simplest FAM encodes the *FAM rule* or association (A_i, B_i), which associates fuzzy set B_i with fuzzy set A_i. For example, structural knowledge of the form "If traffic is heavy in this direction, then keep the stop light green longer," represented by the association (Heavy, Longer), can be encoded directly into a FAM by setting a Hebbian-type FAM correlation matrix introduced later. In general, a FAM system consists of a bank of different FAM associations $(A_1, B_1), \ldots, (A_m, B_m)$. Each association corresponds to a different numerical FAM matrix or a different entry in a linguistic FAM bank matrix. Instead of combining these matrices as we combine neural associative memory (outer-product) matrices, we store the matrices separately and access them in parallel to avoid cross-talk.

We shall now begin with single-association FAMs to see how a numerical FAM matrix can be built to encode the fuzzy set pair (A, B), where A and B are fuzzy subsets of X and Y, respectively. We quantize the domain X to the n numerical variables $x_1, x_2, \ldots, x_n$ $(X = \{x_1, x_2, \ldots, x_n\})$ and the domain Y to the p numerical variables $y_1, y_2, \ldots, y_p$ $(Y = \{y_1, y_2, \ldots, y_p\})$. For example, let the fuzzy set pair (A, B) encode the traffic control association (Heavy, Longer). Then X might represent the traffic density and Y the green light duration. Thus, x_1 might represent zero traffic density and y_p might represent 30 seconds. A and B define the membership functions μ_A and μ_B that map the element x_i of X and y_j of Y to degrees of membership in $[0, 1]$. The membership values indicate how much x_i belongs to A and how much y_j belongs to B. Let $a_i = \mu_A(x_i)$ and $b_j = \mu_B(y_j)$; that is, $A = a_1/x_1 + a_2/x_2 + \cdots + a_n/x_n$ and $B = b_1/y_1 + b_2/y_2 + \cdots + b_p/y_p$. Then we represent A and B by the numerical membership vectors $A = (a_1, a_2, \ldots, a_n)$ and $B = (b_1, b_2, \ldots, b_p)$, respectively.

To encode the fuzzy association $(A, B) = ((a_1, \ldots, a_n), (b_1, \ldots, b_p))$ to a numerical FAM matrix, we use a fuzzified Hebbian learning rule [see Eq. (12.1) for comparison] as follows:

$$m_{ij} = \min(a_i, b_j), \tag{20.22}$$

where m_{ij} is the weight on the link from input node i to output node j of a BAM. This encoding scheme, called *correlation-minimum encoding*, gives the *fuzzy outer-product* Hebbian

FAM correlation matrix (here we misuse the notation slightly, using A as a fuzzy set as well as a vector for computation.)

$$M = A^T \circ B. \tag{20.23}$$

If $B = A$ in Eq. (20.23), we have an *autoassociative* fuzzy Hebbian FAM matrix. As an example, assume $A = (0.2, 0.5, 0.9, 1)$ and $B = (0.9, 0.5, 0.6)$; then we have

$$M = A^T \circ B = \begin{bmatrix} 0.2 \\ 0.5 \\ 0.9 \\ 1 \end{bmatrix} [0.9 \quad 0.5 \quad 0.6] = \begin{bmatrix} 0.2 & 0.2 & 0.2 \\ 0.5 & 0.5 & 0.5 \\ 0.9 & 0.5 & 0.6 \\ 0.9 & 0.5 & 0.6 \end{bmatrix}.$$

It is natural to ask whether B can be recalled using the *max-min* composition [Eq. (3.17)] $A \circ M$:

$$A \circ M = [0.9 \quad 0.5 \quad 0.6] = B,$$

$$B \circ M^T = [0.2 \quad 0.5 \quad 0.9 \quad 0.9] = A' \subset A.$$

Thus, we get perfect recall in the forward direction, $A \circ M = B$, but not in the backward direction, $B \circ M^T \neq A$. The following theorem characterizes these properties. Let the height of fuzzy sets A and B be represented as $H(A)$ and $H(B)$, respectively. Assume that A and B are normal.

Theorem 20.1

Correlation-Minimum Bidirectional FAM Theorem [Kosko, 1992a]. If $M = A^T \circ B$, then

(i) $A \circ M = B$ if and only if $H(A) \geq H(B)$,

(ii) $B \circ M^T = A$ if and only if $H(B) \geq H(A)$,

(iii) $A' \circ M \subset B$ for any A',   (20.24)

(iv) $B' \circ M^T \subset A$ for any B'.

Proof: Observe that the height $H(A)$ equals the *fuzzy norm* of A:

$$A \circ A^T = \max_i a_i \wedge a_i = \max_i a_i = H(A).$$

Then $A \circ M = A \circ (A^T \circ B) = (A \circ A^T) \circ B = H(A) \circ B = H(A) \wedge B$. And so $H(A) \wedge B = B$ if and only if $H(A) \geq H(B)$. This proves (i). Now suppose A' is an arbitrary membership vector in I^n. Then $A' \circ M = (A' \circ A^T) \circ B = (A' \circ A^T) \wedge B$, which proves (iii) since $A' \circ A^T \leq H(A)$. A similar argument using $M^T = B^T \circ A$ proves (ii) and (iv).

An alternative fuzzy Hebbian encoding scheme is called *correlation-product encoding*. In this encoding scheme, the standard mathematical outer product of the membership vectors A and B forms the FAM matrix M:

$$M = A^T B, \tag{20.25}$$

where

$$m_{ij} = a_i b_j. \tag{20.26}$$

Again consider the case where $A = (0.2, 0.5, 0.9, 1)$ and $B = (0.9, 0.5, 0.6)$. Then we encode the FAM rule (A, B) with a correlation product in the following FAM matrix M:

$$M = A^T B = \begin{bmatrix} 0.18 & 0.1 & 0.12 \\ 0.45 & 0.25 & 0.3 \\ 0.81 & 0.45 & 0.54 \\ 0.9 & 0.5 & 0.6 \end{bmatrix}.$$

Note that if $A' = (0, 0, 0, 1)$, then $A' \circ M = B$. The FAM recalls output B to the maximal degree. If $A' = (1, 0, 0, 0)$, then $A' \circ M = (0.18, 0.1, 0.12)$. The FAM recalls output B only to a degree of 0.2. It is observed that correlation-product encoding produces a matrix of scaled fuzzy set B, while correlation-minimum encoding produces a matrix of clipped fuzzy set B. The membership functions of the scaled fuzzy sets $a_i B$ all have the same shape as B. The membership functions of the clipped fuzzy sets $a_i \wedge B$ are flat at or above the a_i value. In this sense, correlation-product encoding preserves more information than correlation-minimum encoding.

Similar to Theorem 20.1, we have the following correlation-product version of the bidirectional FAM theorem.

Theorem 20.2

Correlation-Product Bidirectional FAM Theorem [Kosko, 1992a]. If $M = A^T B$ and A and B are nonzero membership vectors, then

(i) $A \circ M = B$ if and only if $H(A) = 1$,

(ii) $B \circ M^T = A$ if and only if $H(B) = 1$,

(iii) $A' \circ M \subset B$ for any A',

(iv) $B' \circ M^T \subset A$ for any B'. $\qquad\qquad$ (20.27)

Proof

$$A \circ M = A \circ (A^T B) = (A \circ A^T) B = H(A) B.$$

Since B is not an empty set, $H(A) B = B$ if and only if $H(A) = 1$. This proves (i). ($A \circ M = B$ holds trivially if B is an empty set.) For an arbitrary membership vector A' in I^n,

$$A' \circ M = (A' \circ A^T) B \subset H(A) B \subset B,$$

and since $A' \circ A \le H(A)$, (iii) is established. Similarly, (ii) and (iv) can be proved using $M^T = B^T A$.

Let us now consider a FAM system consisting of a bank of different FAM associations $(A_1, B_1), \dots, (A_m, B_m)$. The fuzzy Hebbian encoding scheme [Eq. (20.23) or (20.25)] leads to m FAM matrices $M_1, M_2, \dots, M_m$ for encoding the associations. Instead of superimposing the m matrices pointwise to distributively encode the m associations in a single matrix as usually done in neural networks, we store the m associations (A_k, B_k) separately in the FAM bank and additively superimpose the m recalled vectors B'_k:

$$B'_k = A \circ M_k = A \circ (A_k^T \circ B_k), \qquad k = 1, 2, \dots, m, \qquad (20.28)$$

where A is any membership-vector input applied in parallel to the bank of FAM rules (A_k, B_k). The recalled membership-vector output B equals a weighted sum of the individual recalled vectors B'_k:

$$B = \sum_{k=1}^{m} w_k B'_k, \tag{20.29}$$

where the nonnegative weight w_k summarizes the credibility or strength of the kth FAM rule (A_k, B_k). If we need a single numerical output in the output universe of discourse $Y = \{y_1, y_2, \ldots, y_p\}$, then we need a defuzzification process. Using the centroid defuzzification scheme, for example, the fuzzy centroid $\overline{B}$ of membership-vector B with respect to the output space Y is

$$\overline{B} = \frac{\sum_{j=1}^{p} y_j \mu_B(y_j)}{\sum_{j=1}^{p} \mu_B(y_j)}. \tag{20.30}$$

The architecture of the whole (nonlinear) FAM system F is shown in Fig. 20.9 in which F maps fuzzy sets to fuzzy sets, $F(A) = B$. Hence, F defines a fuzzy system transformation $F: I^n \rightarrow I^p$. In the extreme case, A represents the occurrence of the crisp measurement datum x_i, for example, a traffic density value of 30. In such a case, A equals a bit vector with a unity value, $a_i = 1$, and all other membership values zero, $a_j = 0$. That is, A is a fuzzy singleton. Also, if defuzzification is performed with the centroid technique, the fuzzy output B produces an exact element y_j in the output universe of discourse Y. In effect, defuzzification produces an output binary vector, again with one element equal to 1 and the other elements equal to 0. It has been shown that the FAM system can approximate any continuous function on a compact (closed and bounded) domain to any degree of accuracy [Kosko, 1992c]. In other words, FAMs are universal approximators. The following example illustrates the application of FAM systems.

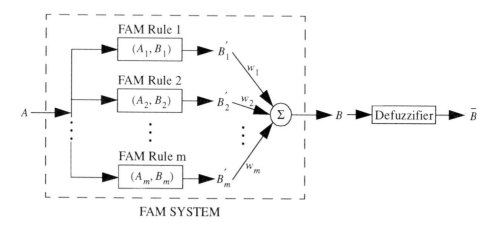

FAM SYSTEM

Figure 20.9 FAM system architecture. The FAM system F maps fuzzy sets in the unit cube I^n to fuzzy sets in the unit cube I^p. Binary input sets model exact input data. (Adapted from Kosko [1992c], © 1992 IEEE.)

Example 20.4

This example illustrates the use of FAMs in conceptual design. Design is a knowledge-intensive activity. The more knowledge and experience designers have, the better their chances of generating creative design. Design involves continuous interplay between what we want to achieve and how we want to achieve it. A designer usually associates sets of fuzzy functional requirements with sets of physical structures, and then during the design process, design solutions are retrieved from memory to solve the design problem. Thus, the design problem can be formulated as follows: Given sets of fuzzy functional requirements (*FRs*) and design constraints (*Cs*), generate the design solution(s) that can satisfy the input requirements. For example, if we want to design a very comfortable chair that can be used more or less in public, then the input requirements and constraints are

$$FR = \text{The chair must be very comfortable,}$$

$$C = \text{Use more or less in public.}$$

Design constraints have been differentiated from functional requirements since they are basically concerned with the boundaries of the design such as size, weight, and cost (the input constraints), or capacity, geometric shape, and usage (the system constraints). Having defined *FR* and *C*, the problem concerns the generation of design solution(s). Based on the work of Bahrami et al. [1991], the utilization of FAM in conceptual design is illustrated here by applying it to the idea generation phase of chair design.

To experiment with the concept, 6 generic functional requirements and 11 design constraints have been generated for designing various classes of chairs. Functional requirements are defined as *ability to adjust the chair* (*FR1*), *ability to move the chair* (*FR2*), *ability to fold the chair* (*FR3*), *stability* (*FR4*), *ability to stack the chair* (*FR5*), and *comfort* (*FR6*). Design constraints are defined as *cost* (*C1*), *size* (*C2*), *weight* (*C3*), *use for dining* (*C4*), *use for office* (*C5*), *use for relaxation* (*C6*), *use for home* (*C7*), *use for classroom* (*C8*), *use for public* (*C9*), *use for typing* (*C10*), *aesthetic look* (*C11*). The crisp universal sets **FR** of the functional requirements and **C** of the design constraints are defined as follows:

$$\mathbf{FR} = \{FR1, FR2, FR3, FR4, FR5, FR6\},$$

$$\mathbf{C} = \{C1, C2, C3, C4, C5, C6, C7, C8, C9, C10, C11\}. \tag{20.31}$$

A database of 11 different design solutions has been created (see Fig. 20.10). Each design solution (chair) satisfies a certain set of functional requirements and design constraints. For instance, an executive chair may be defined as follows:

$$FR(\text{CHAIR2}) = \{1.0/FR1, 1.0/FR2, 1.0/FR6\},$$

$$C(\text{CHAIR2}) = \{1.0/C5, 0.7/C6, 0.3/C7, 1.0/C11\},$$

which is interpreted as follows: *An executive chair is a chair that is very comfortable with a high degree of adjustability and movability. Furthermore, it is used more in the office than at home; it can also be used for relaxation; and its appearance is very important.* The fuzzy sets labeled CHAIRn, $n = 1$ to 11, are the power sets containing all possible fuzzy subsets of *FR* and *C*:

$$\mu_{FR}: \mathcal{P}(\mathbf{FR}) \rightarrow [0, 1], \qquad FR = \{\mu(x)/x \mid x \in \mathbf{FR}\},$$

$$\mu_C: \mathcal{P}(\mathbf{C}) \rightarrow [0, 1], \qquad C = \{\mu(y)/y \mid y \in \mathbf{C}\}, \tag{20.32}$$

where the sets *FR* and *C* are of level-1 fuzzy sets with a nesting of depth 1. As a possible extension, *FR* and *C* can be modified to level 2. This extension can be achieved by defining the linguistic variables such as adjustability (*FR1*), movability (*FR2*), foldability (*FR3*), stabil-

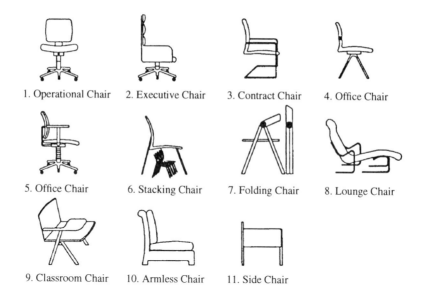

1. Operational Chair   2. Executive Chair   3. Contract Chair   4. Office Chair

5. Office Chair   6. Stacking Chair   7. Folding Chair   8. Lounge Chair

9. Classroom Chair   10. Armless Chair   11. Side Chair

Figure 20.10   Various chair design solutions. (Adapted from Bahrami et al. [1991], © 1991 IEEE.)

ity (*FR4*), stackability (*FR5*), and comfort (*FR6*) as fuzzy sets, with a similar extension for constraints.

The input as discussed above consists of two fuzzy sets, *FR* and *C*. For simplicity, these two sets have been represented as a list. Furthermore, the symbolic representation has been replaced by the positional importance of the degree of membership on the list. For example, the functional requirements and design constraints for an executive chair (CHAIR2) are represented as follows:

$$A_2 = (1.0, 1.0, 0, 0, 0, 1.0, 0, 0, 0, 1.0, 0.7, 0.3, 0, 0, 0, 0, 1.0) .$$

The first value corresponds to *FR1* (*ability to adjust the chair*), the second value corresponds to *FR2* (*ability to move the chair*), and so on. Each degree of membership is assigned to a separate input node of the FAM.

The output (second) layer of the FAM is designed to have 11 neurons, one for every class of chair. For instance, CHAIR2 is represented as follows:

$$B_2 = (0, 1.0, 0, 0, 0, 0, 0, 0, 0, 0, 0) .$$

Thus, we have a total of 11 training pattern pairs (A_i, B_i), $i = 1, 2,\dots, 11$, one pattern pair for each class of chair. Then according to Eq. (20.23), we can set up 11 fuzzy Hebbian FAM matrices, one for each pattern pair, as follows:

$$M_1 = A_1^T \circ B_1, \qquad M_2 = A_2^T \circ B_2, \qquad \dots, \qquad M_{11} = A_{11}^T \circ B_{11}. \qquad (20.33)$$

With the 11 FAM rules available, the whole FAM system is set up as shown in Fig. 20.9 (the credibility weights w_k are set to unity). Then for a given new incoming pattern *A,* which specifies new design requirements, Eqs. (20.28) and (20.29) are applied to obtain the solution *B.* Note that the defuzzification process [Eq. (20.30)] is unnecessary here.

The trained FAM system has been tested on 16 design scenarios with known solutions. The system was capable of successfully generating 14 correct solutions. For example, with the input requirements $\{1/FR1\}, \{1/C6, 1/C11\}$, the system correctly suggested an executive chair as desired despite the fact that the new input requirements were quite different from what it was trained on. Overall the system's error rate was less than 10%.

20.2.4 Fuzzy ART Models

Adaptive resonance theory (ART), as introduced in Sec. 12.4.2, has led to an evolving series of real-time neural network models for unsupervised category learning and pattern recognition. These models, including ART1, ART2, and ART3, are capable of learning stable recognition categories in response to arbitrary input sequences. In this section, we shall consider the fuzzification of ART models and discuss two fuzzified models: *fuzzy ART* and *fuzzy ARTMAP* proposed by Carpenter et al. [1991a,b, 1992]. In response to arbitrary sequences of analog or binary input vectors which may represent fuzzy or crisp sets of a feature, fuzzy ART is capable of rapid unsupervised learning of recognition categories and fuzzy ARTMAP is capable of incremental supervised learning of recognition categories and multidimensional maps.

Fuzzy ART.   Fuzzy ART incorporates computations from fuzzy set theory into the ART1 neural network which only learns to categorize binary input patterns. By incorporating computations from fuzzy set theory into ART1, Fuzzy ART can learn and categorize analog patterns. The generalization to learning both analog and binary input patterns is achieved by replacing appearances of the logical AND intersection operator ($\cap$) in ART1 by the min operator ($\wedge$) of fuzzy set theory. The min operator reduces to the intersection operator in the binary case. Let us explore the Fuzzy ART algorithm and contrast it with the ART1 algorithm in Eqs. (12.45)–(12.48). Assume each input $\mathbf{I}$ is an m-dimensional vector $(I_1, I_2, \ldots, I_m)$, where each component I_i is in the interval $[0, 1]$. Let each category (j) correspond to a vector $\mathbf{w}_j = (w_{j1}, w_{j2}, \ldots, w_{jm})^T$ of adaptive weights. The number of potential categories n ($j = 1, 2, \ldots, n$) is arbitrary. The Fuzzy ART weight vector $\mathbf{w}_j$ subsumes both the bottom-up and top-down weight vectors of ART1. The fuzzy ART algorithm is as follows:

Algorithm FART: Fuzzy ART Algorithm

  Step 1   (*Initialization*): Initially, each category is said to be *uncommitted* and is set as

$$w_{ji}(0) = 1, \qquad i = 1, 2, \ldots, m; \; 0 < \rho \le 1. \tag{20.34}$$

  Step 2   (*Category choice*): For each input $\mathbf{I}$ and category j, the choice function T_j is defined by

$$T_j(\mathbf{I}) = \frac{\left| \mathbf{I} \wedge \mathbf{w}_j \right|}{\epsilon + \left| \mathbf{w}_j \right|}, \tag{20.35}$$

where $\epsilon > 0$ is a constant, the fuzzy AND operator $\wedge$ is defined by

$$(\mathbf{x} \wedge \mathbf{y})_i \triangleq \min_i (x_i, y_i) \tag{20.36}$$

and the norm $|\cdot|$ is defined by $|\mathbf{x}| = \sum_{i=1}^{m} |x_i|$. For notational simplicity, $T_j(\mathbf{I})$ in Eq. (20.36) is written as T_j when the input $\mathbf{I}$ is fixed. T_j represents the net input to node j in F_2. For comparison, Eqs. (20.35)–(20.36) correspond to Eqs. (12.45)–(12.46). The chosen category is indexed by J, where

$$T_J = \max\{T_1, T_2, \ldots, T_n\}. \tag{20.37}$$

If more than one T_j is maximal, the category j with the smallest index is chosen. In particular, nodes become committed in the order $j = 1, 2, 3, \ldots, n$.

Step 3 (*Resonance or reset*): Resonance occurs if the match function of the chosen category meets the vigilance criterion, that is, if [see Eq. (12.47) for comparison]

$$\frac{|\mathbf{I} \wedge \mathbf{w}_J|}{|\mathbf{I}|} \geq \rho. \qquad (20.38)$$

Learning then ensues according to the equation

$$\mathbf{w}_J(t+1) = \beta \left(\mathbf{I} \wedge \mathbf{w}_J(t)\right) + (1 - \beta)\mathbf{w}_J(t). \qquad (20.39)$$

Fast learning corresponds to setting $\beta = 1$, which is the learning rule in Eq. (12.48). A *mismatch reset* occurs if

$$\frac{|\mathbf{I} \wedge \mathbf{w}_J|}{|\mathbf{I}|} < \rho. \qquad (20.40)$$

Then the value of the choice function T_J is reset to -1 for the duration of the input presentations to prevent its persistent selection during the search. A new index J is chosen by Eq. (20.37). The search process continues until the chosen J satisfies Eq. (20.38).
END FART

There are two options for the fuzzy ART algorithm: the *fast-commit–slow-recode option* and the *input normalization option*. Many applications of ART1 use fast learning [i.e., setting $\beta = 1$ in Eq. (20.39)], whereby adaptive weights fully converge to new equilibrium values in response to each input pattern. Fast learning enables a system to adapt quickly to inputs that may occur only rarely and may require immediate accurate performance. In contrast, error-based learning models like back propagation tend to average rare events with similar frequent events that may have different consequences. For efficient coding of noisy input sets in some applications, it is useful to combine fast initial learning with a slow rate of forgetting. This is called the fast-commit–slow-recode option. With this option, we set $\beta = 1$ when J is an uncommitted node and then set $\beta < 1$ after the category is committed. Then $\mathbf{w}_J(0) = \mathbf{I}$ the first time category J becomes active. This combination retains the benefit of fast learning, namely, an adequate response to inputs that may occur only rarely and in response to which accurate performance may be quickly demanded. The slow-recode operation also prevents features that have already been incorporated into a category's prototype from being erroneously deleted in response to noisy or partial inputs.

The other option of the fuzzy ART algorithm concerns normalization of input patterns; that is, for some $\gamma > 0, |\mathbf{I}| = \gamma$ for all inputs $\mathbf{I}$. Input normalization can prevent a problem of category proliferation that could otherwise occur in some analog ART systems when a large number of inputs erode the norm of weight vectors. The normalization procedure used is called *complement coding* and employs both on cells and off cells to represent an input pattern and achieves normalization while preserving amplitude information. The on-cell portion of the prototype encodes features that are critically present in category exemplars, while the off-cell portion encodes features that are critically absent. To define the complement-coding operation in its simplest form, let an input pattern $\mathbf{a}$ represent the on cell and the complement of $\mathbf{a}$, denoted by $\mathbf{a}^c$, represent the off cell, where

$$a_i^c = 1 - a_i, \qquad i = 1, 2, \ldots, m. \qquad (20.41)$$

The complement-coded input $\mathbf{I}$ to fuzzy ART is thus the $2m$-dimensional vector

$$\mathbf{I} = (\mathbf{a}, \mathbf{a}^c) = \left(a_1, \ldots, a_m, a_1^c, \ldots, a_m^c\right). \qquad (20.42)$$

Note that $|\mathbf{I}| = |(\mathbf{a}, \mathbf{a}^c)| = \sum_i a_i + (m - \sum_i a_i) = m$, and so inputs preprocessed into complement-coding form are automatically normalized. When complement coding is used, the initial condition Eq. (20.34) is replaced by $w_{ji}(0) = 1$, $i = 1, 2, \ldots, 2m$.

Consider the limit case that $\epsilon \to 0$ in Eq. (20.35). Then the choice function T_j in Eq. (20.35) becomes a fuzzy subsethood measure [see Eq. (2.32)] reflecting the degree to which the weight vector $\mathbf{w}_j$ is a fuzzy subset of the input vector $\mathbf{I}$. If

$$\frac{|\mathbf{I} \wedge \mathbf{w}_J|}{|\mathbf{w}_j|} = 1, \tag{20.43}$$

then $\mathbf{w}_j$ is a fuzzy subset of $\mathbf{I}$ and category j is said to be a *fuzzy subset choice* for input $\mathbf{I}$. In this case, according to Eq. (20.39), no recoding occurs if j is selected since $\mathbf{I} \wedge \mathbf{w}_j = \mathbf{w}_j$. Hence, the limit $\epsilon \to 0$ is called the *conservative limit* since small values of ϵ tend to minimize recoding during learning. If category j is a fuzzy subset choice, then the match function value in Eq. (20.38) becomes $|\mathbf{I} \wedge \mathbf{w}_j|/|\mathbf{I}| = |\mathbf{w}_j|/|\mathbf{I}|$. This implies that choosing J to maximize $|\mathbf{w}_j|$ among fuzzy subset choices also maximizes the opportunity for resonance in Eq. (20.38). If reset occurs for the node that maximizes $|\mathbf{w}_j|$, reset will also occur for all other subset choices. We are now ready to examine the following theorem which is of interest.

Theorem 20.3

Consider a fuzzy ART system in the conservation limit with fast learning and normalized inputs; that is, $\epsilon \cong 0$ in Eq. (20.35), $\beta = 1$ in Eq. (20.39), and $|\mathbf{I}| = \gamma$ for all inputs $\mathbf{I}$. Under these conditions, one-shot stable learning occurs; that is, no weight change or search occurs after each item of an input set is presented *just once*, although some inputs may select different categories on future trials.

Proof: According to Eqs. (20.38) and (20.39), if $\mathbf{I}$ is presented for the first time, $\mathbf{w}_j(t + 1) = \mathbf{I} \wedge \mathbf{w}_j(t)$ for some category code $J = j$ such that $|\mathbf{I} \wedge \mathbf{w}_j(t)| \geq \rho|\mathbf{I}| = \rho\gamma$. Thereafter, category j is a fuzzy subset choice of $\mathbf{I}$ by Eq. (20.43). If $\mathbf{I}$ is presented again, it will either choose $J = j$ or make another fuzzy subset choice, maximizing $|\mathbf{w}_j|$, since fuzzy subset choices in Eq. (20.43) maximize the category choice function [Eq. (20.35)] in the conservative limit. In either case, $\mathbf{w}_J(t + 1) = \mathbf{I} \wedge \mathbf{w}_J(t) = \mathbf{w}_J(t)$, which implies that neither reset nor additional learning occurs.

We shall now consider a geometric interpretation of fuzzy ART with complement coding. For simplicity and clarity, let the input set consist of two-dimensional vectors $\mathbf{a}$ preprocessed into a four-dimensional complement-coding form, that is,

$$\mathbf{I} = (\mathbf{a}, \mathbf{a}^c) = (a_1, a_2, 1 - a_1, 1 - a_2). \tag{20.44}$$

In this case, each category j has a geometric representation as a rectangle R_j as follows. Following Eq. (20.44), the weight vector $\mathbf{w}_j$ can be written in complement-coding form:

$$\mathbf{w}_j = (\mathbf{u}_j, \mathbf{v}_j^c), \tag{20.45}$$

where $\mathbf{u}_j$ and $\mathbf{v}_j$ are two-dimensional vectors. Let vector $\mathbf{u}_j$ define one corner of a rectangle R_j and let $\mathbf{v}_j$ define another corner of R_j as illustrated in Fig. 20.11(a). The size of R_j is defined to be

$$|R_j| \triangleq |\mathbf{v}_j - \mathbf{u}_j|, \tag{20.46}$$

which is equal to the height plus the width of R_j in the figure.

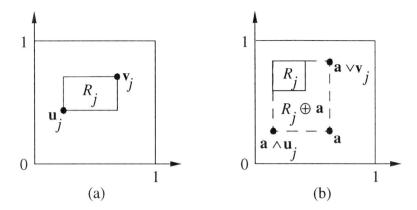

Figure 20.11 (a) In complement-coding form with $m = 2$, each weight vector $\mathbf{w}_j$ has a geometric interpretation as a rectangle R_j with corners $(\mathbf{u}_j, \mathbf{v}_j)$. (b) During fast learning, R_j expands to $R_j \oplus \mathbf{a}$, the smallest rectangle that includes R_j and $\mathbf{a}$, provided that $|R_j \oplus \mathbf{a}| \leq 2(1 - \rho)$.

In a fuzzy ART system with fast learning [i.e., $\beta = 1$ in Eq. (20.39)], $\mathbf{w}_j(0) = \mathbf{I} = (\mathbf{a}, \mathbf{a}^c)$ when J is an uncommitted node. The corners of $R_J(0)$ are then given by $\mathbf{a}$ and $(\mathbf{a}^c)^c = \mathbf{a}$. Hence, $R_J(0)$ is just the point $\mathbf{a}$. As learning proceeds, the size of $\mathbf{w}_j$ increases. In fact, the size of R_j grows as the size of $\mathbf{w}_j$ shrinks during learning, and the maximum size of R_j is determined by the vigilance parameter ρ.

Theorem 20.4

With fast learning [i.e., $\mathbf{w}_J(t + 1) = \mathbf{I} \wedge \mathbf{w}_j(t)$], each R_j equals the smallest rectangle that encloses all vectors $\mathbf{a}$ that have chosen category j, under the constraint that $|R_j| \leq 2(1 - \rho)$. In other words, during each fast-learning trial, R_J expands to $R_J \oplus \mathbf{a}$, the minimum rectangle containing R_J and $\mathbf{a}$, assuming $\mathbf{a}$ chooses category J. The corners of $R_J \oplus \mathbf{a}$ are given by $\mathbf{a} \wedge \mathbf{u}_J$ and $\mathbf{a} \vee \mathbf{v}_J$ [see Fig. 20.11(b)], where

$$(\mathbf{x} \wedge \mathbf{y})_i = \min_i(x_i, y_i) \qquad \text{and} \qquad (\mathbf{x} \vee \mathbf{y})_i = \max_i(x_i, y_i). \qquad (20.47)$$

Proof: Suppose that $\mathbf{I} = (\mathbf{a}, \mathbf{a}^c)$ chooses category J by Eq. (20.37). Because of complement coding, $|\mathbf{I}| = m$. Thus, when $m = 2$, the matching criterion in Eq. (20.38) becomes

$$|\mathbf{I} \wedge \mathbf{w}_J| \geq 2\rho. \qquad (20.48)$$

However, by Eq. (20.46),

$$
\begin{aligned}
|\mathbf{I} \wedge \mathbf{w}_j| &= |(\mathbf{a}, \mathbf{a}^c) \wedge (\mathbf{u}_j, \mathbf{v}_j^c)| = |(\mathbf{a} \wedge \mathbf{u}_j), (\mathbf{a}^c \wedge \mathbf{v}_j^c)| \\
&= |(\mathbf{a} \wedge \mathbf{u}_j), (\mathbf{a} \vee \mathbf{v}_j)^c| \\
&= |\mathbf{a} \wedge \mathbf{u}_j| + 2 - |\mathbf{a} \vee \mathbf{v}_j| \\
&= 2 - |R_j \oplus \mathbf{a}|.
\end{aligned}
\qquad (20.49)
$$

Then the matching criterion is met if and only if the expanded rectangle $R_J \oplus \mathbf{a}$ satisfies

$$|R_J \oplus \mathbf{a}| \leq 2(1 - \rho). \qquad (20.50)$$

Suppose now that the matching criterion is satisfied; then

$$\mathbf{w}_J(t+1) = \mathbf{I} \wedge \mathbf{w}_J(t) = (\mathbf{a}, \mathbf{a}^c) \wedge (\mathbf{u}_J(t), \mathbf{v}_J^c(t))$$

$$= (\mathbf{a} \wedge \mathbf{u}_J(t), \mathbf{a}^c \wedge \mathbf{v}_J^c(t)) = (\mathbf{a} \wedge \mathbf{u}_J(t), \mathbf{a} \vee \mathbf{v}_J^c(t)) \qquad (20.51)$$

$$= (\mathbf{u}_J(t), \mathbf{v}_J^c(t)).$$

Thus,

$$R_J(t+1) = R_J(t) \oplus \mathbf{a}. \qquad (20.52)$$

In particular, no weight changes occur if $\mathbf{a} \in R_J(t)$.

By the above theorem [Eq. (20.50)], if the vigilance parameter ρ is close to 1, then all R_j are small. If ρ is close 0, then some R_j may grow to fill most of the unit square $[0, 1] \times [0, 1]$. The above discussion can be easily extended to higher-dimensional input space. In response to an arbitrary sequence of analog or binary input vectors with dimension m, a fuzzy ART system with complement coding and fast learning forms stable hyperrectangular categories R_j, which include the two vertices $\wedge_j \mathbf{a}$ and $\vee_j \mathbf{a}$, where the ith component of each vector is

$$(\wedge_j \mathbf{a})_i = \min_i \{a_i: \mathbf{a} \text{ has been coded by category } j\}, \qquad (20.53)$$

$$(\vee_j \mathbf{a})_i = \max_i \{a_i: \mathbf{a} \text{ has been coded by category } j\}. \qquad (20.54)$$

From Eq. (20.51) in Theorem 20.4, we have

$$\mathbf{w}_j = (\wedge_j \mathbf{a}, (\vee_j \mathbf{a})^c). \qquad (20.55)$$

In the computer simulation given in [Carpenter et al., 1991b] which is summarized in Fig. 20.12, $m = 2$ and vectors $\mathbf{a}^{(1)}, \mathbf{a}^{(2)}, \ldots$, are selected at random from the unit square. Each frame shows the vectors $\mathbf{a}^{(t)}$ and the set of rectangles R_j present after learning occurs. The system is run in the fast-learn, conservative limit, and $\rho = 0.4$. When the first category is established, R_1 is just the point $\mathbf{a}^{(1)}$. If $\mathbf{a}^{(t)}$ lies within one or more established R_j, the rectangle chosen is the one that has the smallest size $|R_j|$. In this case, neither reset nor weight change occurs. Each new input that activates category j, but does not lie within its previously established boundaries, expands R_j unless [as in Fig. 20.12(d)] such an expansion would cause the size of R_j to exceed $2(1 - \rho) = 1.2$. As more and more inputs sample the square, all points of the square are eventually covered by a set of eight rectangles R_j, as illustrated by Fig. 20.12(g)–(i).

Fuzzy ARTMAP. ARTMAP is a class of neural network architectures that perform incremental supervised learning of recognition categories and multidimensional maps in response to input vectors presented in arbitrary order [Carpenter et al., 1991a, 1992]. Figure 20.13 shows the fuzzy ARTMAP architecture with complement coding. Each ARTMAP system includes a pair of ART modules, ART_a and ART_b that self-organize categories for arbitrary sequences of input patterns. During supervised learning, ART_a receives a stream $\{\mathbf{a}^{(p)}\}$ of input patterns and ART_b receives a stream $\{\mathbf{b}^{(p)}\}$ of input patterns, where $\{\mathbf{b}^{(p)}\}$ is the correct prediction (desired output) given $\{\mathbf{a}^{(p)}\}$.

Normally, ART_a and ART_b are fast-learn ART1 modules with coding binary input vectors. ART_a and ART_b are connected by a *map field* that resembles ART1. The name ARTMAP comes from the fact that its transformation from vectors in R^n to vectors in R^m defines a *map* that is learned by example from the correlated pairs $\{\mathbf{a}^{(p)}, \mathbf{b}^{(p)}\}$ of sequentially

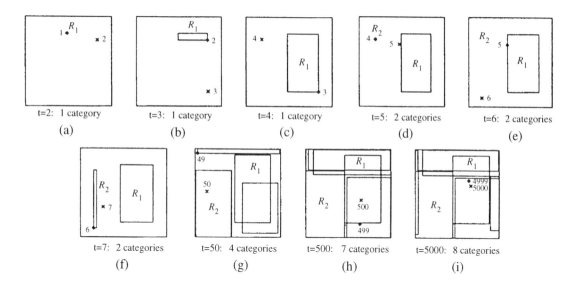

Figure 20.12 Fuzzy ART complement-coding simulation with $\alpha \cong 0$, $\beta = 1$, $\rho = 0.4$, and input vectors $\mathbf{a}^{(t)}$ selected at random from the unit square. Rectangles R_j grow during learning, and new categories are established until the entire square is covered by eight rectangles. Categories do not proliferate. A new point rectangle R_2 is established at $t = 4$ since $R_1 \oplus \mathbf{a}^{(4)}$ is too large to satisfy the match criterion in Eq. (20.38). (Reprinted from *NEURAL*, Vol. 4, G. A. Carpenter, S. Grossberg, and D. B. Rosen, "Fuzzy ART: Fast Stable Learning and Categorization of Analog Patterns by an Adaptive Resonance System," pages 759–771, Copyright 1991, with kind permission from Elsevier Science Ltd, The Boulevard, Langford Lane, Kidlington 0X5 1GB, UK.)

presented vectors, $p = 1, 2, \ldots$. This map field controls the learning of an associative map from ART_a recognition categories to ART_b recognition categories. This map does not directly associate exemplars $\mathbf{a}$ and $\mathbf{b}$ but rather associates the compressed and symbolic representations of families of exemplars $\mathbf{a}$ and $\mathbf{b}$. The map field also controls match tracking of the ART_a vigilance parameter. A mismatch at the map field between the ART_a category activated by an input $\mathbf{a}$ and the ART_b category activated by the input $\mathbf{b}$ increases ART_a vigilance by the minimum amount needed for the system to search for and, if necessary, learn a new ART_a category whose prediction matches the ART_b category. This achieves an important property of ARTMAP—*cojointly maximizing generalization and minimizing predictive error*, meaning that the system can learn to create the minimal number of ART_a recognition categories or "hidden nodes" needed to meet the accuracy criterion (least prediction error). It is noted that lower values of ART_a vigilance ρ_a enable larger categories (a smaller number of categories) to form and thus lead to broader generalization and higher code compression.

Whereas binary ARTMAP employs ART1 systems for the ART_a and ART_b modules, *fuzzy ARTMAP* substitutes fuzzy ART systems for these modules [Carpenter et al., 1992]. Since ARTMAP is a special case of fuzzy ARTMAP, we shall focus on fuzzy ARTMAP hereafter. The ART_a complement-coding preprocessor transforms the m_a-dimensional vector $\mathbf{a}$ into the $2m_a$-dimensional vector $\mathbf{A} = (\mathbf{a}, \mathbf{a}^c)$ at the ART_a layer F_0^a (see Fig. 20.13). $\mathbf{A}$ is the input vector to the ART_a layer F_1^a. Similarly, the input to F_1^b is the $2m_b$-dimensional vector $\mathbf{B} = (\mathbf{b}, \mathbf{b}^c)$. When a prediction by ART_a is disconfirmed at ART_b, inhibition of map field

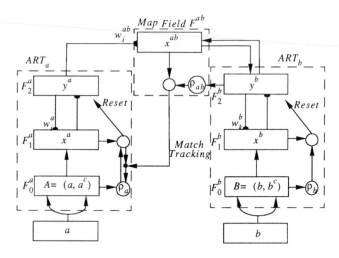

Figure 20.13 Fuzzy ARTMAP architecture (Adapted from Carpenter et al. [1992], © 1992 IEEE.)

activation induces the *match tracking* process. Match tracking raises the ART_a vigilance ρ_a to just above the F_1^a-to-F_0^a match ratio $|\mathbf{x}^a|/|\mathbf{A}|$, where $\mathbf{x}^a$ is the activity (output) vector of the ART_a layer F_1^a (see Fig. 20.13). This triggers an ART_a search which leads to activation of either an ART_a category that correctly predicts $\mathbf{b}$ or to a previously uncommitted ART_a category node. Match tracking reorganizes category structure so that predictive error is not repeated on subsequent presentations of the input. The detailed architecture of the map field is shown in Fig. 20.14. The map field is connected to F_2^b with one-to-one nonadaptive pathways in both directions. Each F_2^a node is connected to all map field nodes via adaptive pathways. A mismatch between the category predicted by $\mathbf{a}$ and the actual category of $\mathbf{b}$

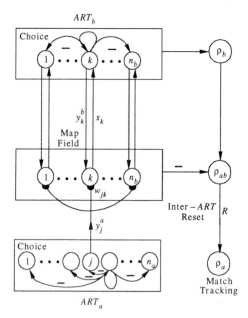

Figure 20.14 The main components of the map field.

leads to F_2^a resetting and increasing vigilance ρ_a via match tracking. The following algorithm characterizes a fuzzy ARTMAP.

Algorithm FARTMAP: Fuzzy ARTMAP Algorithm

Step 1 (ART_a and ART_b activation): Inputs to ART_a and ART_b are in the complement-coding form: For ART_a, $\mathbf{I} = \mathbf{A} = (\mathbf{a}, \mathbf{a}^c)$, and for ART_b, $\mathbf{I} = \mathbf{B} = (\mathbf{b}, \mathbf{b}^c)$. Then ART_a and ART_b process independently as a fuzzy ART network; that is, they follow Eqs. (20.34)–(20.40). Variables in ART_a or ART_b (see Figs. 20.13 and 20.14) are designated by subscripts or superscripts a and b. For ART_a, let $\mathbf{x}^a = (x_1^a, x_2^a, \ldots, x_{2m_a}^a)$ denote the F_1^a output vector, $\mathbf{y}^a = (y_1^a, y_2^a, \ldots, y_{n_a}^a)$ denote the F_2^a output vector, and $\mathbf{w}_j^a = (w_{j1}^a, w_{j2}^a, \ldots, w_{j,2m_a}^a)$ denote the jth ART_a weight vector. For ART_b, let $\mathbf{x}^b = (x_1^b, x_2^b, \ldots, x_{2m_b}^b)$ denote the F_1^b output vector, $\mathbf{y}^b = (y_1^b, y_2^b, \ldots, y_{n_b}^b)$ denote the F_2^b output vector, and $\mathbf{w}_k^b = (w_{k1}^b, w_{k2}^b, \ldots, w_{k,2m_b}^b)$ denote the kth ART_b weight vector. For the map field, let $\mathbf{x}^{ab} = (x_1^{ab}, x_2^{ab}, \ldots, x_{n_b}^{ab})$ denote the F_{ab} output vector and $\mathbf{w}_j^{ab} = (w_{j1}^{ab}, w_{j2}^{ab}, \ldots, w_{jn_b}^{ab})$ denote the weight vector from the jth F_2^a node to F^{ab}. Vectors $\mathbf{x}^a$, $\mathbf{y}^a$, $\mathbf{x}^b$, $\mathbf{y}^b$, and $\mathbf{x}^{ab}$ are set to $\mathbf{0}$ between input presentations.

Step 2 (**Map field activation**): The map field F^{ab} is activated whenever one of the ART_a or ART_b categories is active. If node J of F_2^a is chosen, then its weights $\mathbf{w}_J^{ab}$ activate F^{ab}. If node K in F_2^b is active, then node K in F^{ab} is activated by the one-to-one pathways between F_2^b and F^{ab}. If both ART_a and ART_b are active, then F^{ab} becomes active only if ART_a predicts the same category as ART_b via the weights $\mathbf{w}_J^{ab}$. That is, the F^{ab} output vector $\mathbf{x}^{ab}$ obeys

$$\mathbf{x}^{ab} = \begin{cases} \mathbf{y}^b \wedge \mathbf{w}_J^{ab} & \text{if the } J\text{th } F_2^a \text{ node is active and } F_2^b \text{ is active} \\ \mathbf{w}_J^{ab} & \text{if the } J\text{th } F_2^a \text{ node is active and } F_2^b \text{ is inactive} \\ \mathbf{y}^b & \text{if } F_2^a \text{ is inactive and } F_2^b \text{ is active} \\ 0 & \text{if } F_2^a \text{ is inactive and } F_2^b \text{ is inactive.} \end{cases} \tag{20.56}$$

According to Eq. (20.56), $\mathbf{x}^{ab} = \mathbf{0}$ if the prediction $\mathbf{w}_j^{ab}$ is disconfirmed by $\mathbf{y}^b$ (i.e., $\mathbf{y}^b \wedge \mathbf{w}_J^{ab} = \mathbf{0}$). This mismatch will trigger an ART_a search for a better category in the following match-tracking process.

Step 3 (**Match tracking**): At the start of each input presentation, the ART_a vigilance parameter ρ_a equals a baseline vigilance $\bar{\rho}_a$. Let the map field vigilance parameter be ρ_{ab}. If

$$\left| \mathbf{x}^{ab} \right| < \rho_{ab} |\mathbf{y}^b|, \tag{20.57}$$

then ρ_a is increased until it is slightly larger than $|\mathbf{A} \wedge \mathbf{w}_J^a| |\mathbf{A}|^{-1}$, where $\mathbf{A}$ is the input to F_1^a in complement-coding form. Then

$$|\mathbf{x}^a| = |\mathbf{A} \wedge \mathbf{w}_J^a| < \rho_a |\mathbf{A}|, \tag{20.58}$$

where J is the index of the active F_2^a node. When this occurs, according to Eq. (20.40), an ART_a search leads either to activation of another F_2^a node J' with

$$|\mathbf{x}^a| = |\mathbf{A} \wedge \mathbf{w}_{J'}^a| \geq \rho_a |\mathbf{A}| \tag{20.59}$$

and

$$\left| \mathbf{x}^{ab} \right| = \left| \mathbf{y}^b \wedge \mathbf{w}_{J'}^{ab} \right| \geq \rho_{ab} |\mathbf{y}^b|, \tag{20.60}$$

or, if no such F_2^a node exists (e.g., $\rho_a > 1$), to the shutdown of F_2^a for the remainder of the input presentation. In the latter situation, the association $(\mathbf{a}, \mathbf{b})$ is rejected (not learned) by the fuzzy ARTMAP unless it is re-presented to the fuzzy ARTMAP later.

Step 4 (Map field learning): Weights w_{jk}^{ab} in $F_2^a \rightarrow F^{ab}$ paths initially satisfy

$$w_{jk}^{ab}(0) = 1. \tag{20.61}$$

Then they obey the outstar learning law [see Eq. (12.44)]:

$$w_{jk}^{ab}(t+1) = w_{jk}^{ab}(t) + y_j^a(x_k - w_{jk}^{ab}), \tag{20.62}$$

which implies that during resonance with the ART_a category J active, $\mathbf{w}_J^{ab}$ approaches the map field vector $\mathbf{x}^{ab}$. With fast learning, once J learns to predict the ART_b category K, that association is permanent; that is, $w_{JK}^{ab} = 1$ for all time.

END FARTMAP

The crisp *ARTMAP algorithm* [Carpenter et al., 1991a] is identical to the above fuzzy ARTMAP algorithm except that the fuzzy AND operator ($\wedge$) in the above is replaced by a crisp intersection operator ($\cap$) and that inputs to ART_a and ART_b are either in the complement-coding form or not. The following two examples illustrate, respectively, the match-tracking and complement-coding processes in the (crisp) ARTMAP.

Example 20.5

(Carpenter et al., 1991a). This example illustrates the match-tracking process in ARTMAP fast learning without complement coding. The input pairs shown in Table 20.2 are presented in the order $(\mathbf{a}^{(1)}, \mathbf{b}^{(1)})$, $(\mathbf{a}^{(2)}, \mathbf{b}^{(2)})$, $(\mathbf{a}^{(3)}, \mathbf{b}^{(3)})$. It is observed that $\mathbf{a}^{(1)} \subset \mathbf{a}^{(2)} \subset \mathbf{a}^{(3)}$, and $\mathbf{a}^{(1)}$ and $\mathbf{a}^{(3)}$ are mapped to the same ART_b vector. We choose $\bar{\rho}_a \leq 0.6$ and $\rho_b > 0$. First, at $t = 1$, vectors $\mathbf{a}^{(1)}$ and $\mathbf{b}^{(1)}$ are presented. ART_a and ART_b are activated with categories $J = 1$ and $K = 1$, and the category $J = 1$ learns to predict category $K = 1$, thus associating $\mathbf{a}^{(1)}$ with $\mathbf{b}^{(1)}$. After this step, $\mathbf{w}_1^a(1) = \mathbf{a}^{(1)}$ and $\mathbf{w}_2^b(1) = \mathbf{b}^{(1)}$ by Eq. (20.39) with $\beta = 1$.

At $t = 2$, $\mathbf{a}^{(2)}$ and $\mathbf{b}^{(2)}$ are presented. Vector $\mathbf{a}^{(2)}$ first activates $J = 1$ without reset, since

$$\frac{\left| \mathbf{a}^{(2)} \cap \mathbf{w}_1^a \right|}{\left| \mathbf{a}^{(2)} \right|} = \frac{3}{4} \geq \rho_a = \bar{\rho}_a.$$

As in the last time step, node $J = 1$ predicts node $K = 1$. However, since

$$\frac{\left| \mathbf{b}^{(2)} \cap \mathbf{w}_1^b \right|}{\left| \mathbf{b}^{(2)} \right|} = 0 < \rho_b,$$

the ART_b search leads to activation of a different F_2^b node, $K = 2$. Because of the conflict between the prediction ($K = 1$) made by the active F_2^a node and the currently active F_2^b node ($K = 2$), the map field causes ρ_a to increase to a value slightly greater than $\left| \mathbf{a}^{(2)} \cap \mathbf{w}_1^a \right| \left| \mathbf{a}^{(2)} \right|^{-1} = \frac{3}{4} = 0.75$ while node $J = 1$ is active. This causes node $J = 1$ to be reset. Thereafter, a new F_2^a node ($J = 2$) learns to predict the current F_2^b node ($K = 2$), associating $\mathbf{a}^{(2)}$ with $\mathbf{b}^{(2)}$. After this step, $\mathbf{w}_2^a = \mathbf{a}^{(2)}$ and $\mathbf{w}_2^b = \mathbf{b}^{(2)}$.

At $t = 3$, $\mathbf{a}^{(3)}$ and $\mathbf{b}^{(3)}$ are presented. Vector $\mathbf{a}^{(3)}$ first activates $J = 2$ without ART_a reset since

$$\frac{\left| \mathbf{a}^{(3)} \cap \mathbf{w}_2^a \right|}{\left| \mathbf{a}^{(3)} \right|} = \frac{4}{5} \geq \rho_a = \bar{\rho}_a,$$

thus predicting $K = 2$ with $\mathbf{w}_2^b = \mathbf{b}^{(2)}$. However, $\mathbf{b}^{(3)}$ mismatches $\mathbf{w}_2^b$, leading to an activation of the F_2^b node $K = 1$ since $\mathbf{b}^{(3)} = \mathbf{b}^{(1)}$. Because the predicted node $(K = 2)$ then differs from the active node $(K = 1)$, the map field again causes ρ_a to increase to a value slightly greater than $|\mathbf{a}^{(3)} \cap \mathbf{w}_2^a||\mathbf{a}^{(3)}|^{-1} = 0.8$ while node $J = 2$ is active. Then node $J = 2$ as well as node $J = 1$ are reset since

$$\frac{\left|\mathbf{a}^{(3)} \cap \mathbf{w}_1^a\right|}{\left|\mathbf{a}^{(3)}\right|} = 0.6 < 0.8 < \rho_a.$$

Then $\mathbf{a}^{(3)}$ is permitted to choose an uncommitted F_2^a node $(J = 3)$ that is then associated with the active F_2^b node $(K = 1)$. Thereafter, each ART_a input predicts the correct ART_b output without search or error.

TABLE 20.2 Nested ART_a Inputs and Their Associated ART_b Inputs in Example 20.5

ART_a inputs	ART_b inputs
$\mathbf{a}^{(1)}(111000)$	$\mathbf{b}^{(1)}(1010)$
$\mathbf{a}^{(2)}(111100)$	$\mathbf{b}^{(2)}(0101)$
$\mathbf{a}^{(3)}(111110)$	$\mathbf{b}^{(3)}(1010)$

Example 20.6

[Carpenter et al., 1991a]. This example illustrates the use of ART_a complement coding. Assume that the nested input pairs in Table 20.2 are presented to an ARTMAP system in the order $(\mathbf{a}^{(3)}, \mathbf{b}^{(3)}), (\mathbf{a}^{(2)}, \mathbf{b}^{(2)}), (\mathbf{a}^{(1)}, \mathbf{b}^{(1)})$ with match tracking. Choose $\bar{\rho}_a < 0.5$ and $\rho_b > 0$. We first consider the case without complement coding.

Vectors $\mathbf{a}^{(3)}$ and $\mathbf{b}^{(3)}$ are first presented, and they activate ART_a and ART_b categories $J = 1$ and $K = 1$. The system learns to predict $\mathbf{b}^{(3)}$ given $\mathbf{a}^{(3)}$ by associating the F_2^a node $J = 1$ with the F_2^b node $K = 1$. After this step, $\mathbf{w}_1^a = \mathbf{a}^{(3)}$ and $\mathbf{w}_1^b = \mathbf{b}^{(3)}$.

Next $\mathbf{a}^{(2)}$ and $\mathbf{b}^{(2)}$ are presented. Vector $\mathbf{a}^{(2)}$ first activates $J = 1$ without reset since $|\mathbf{a}^{(2)} \cap \mathbf{w}_1^a|/|\mathbf{a}^{(2)}| = 1 \geq \rho_a = \bar{\rho}_a$. However, node $J = 1$ predicts node $K = 1$. As in the previous example, after $\mathbf{b}^{(2)}$ is presented, the F_2^b node $K = 2$ becomes active and leads to an inter-ART reset. Match tracking makes $\rho_a > 1$, and so F_2^a shuts down until the input pair $(\mathbf{a}^{(2)}, \mathbf{b}^{(2)})$ shuts off. Pattern $\mathbf{b}^{(2)}$ is coded in ART_b as $\mathbf{w}_2^b$, but no learning occurs in the ART_a and F^{ab} modules.

Next $\mathbf{a}^{(1)}$ activates $J = 1$ without reset, since $|\mathbf{a}^{(1)} \cap \mathbf{w}_1^a|/|\mathbf{a}^{(1)}| = 1 \geq \rho_a = \bar{\rho}_a$. Since $J = 1$ predicts the correct pattern $\mathbf{b}^{(1)} = \mathbf{w}_1^b$, no reset ensues. Learning does occur, however, since $\mathbf{w}_1^a$ shrinks to $\mathbf{a}^{(1)}$ according to Eq. (20.39) with $\beta = 1$. If each input can be presented only once, $\mathbf{a}^{(2)}$ does not learn to predict $\mathbf{b}^{(2)}$. However, if the input pairs are presented repeatedly, match tracking allows ART_a to establish three category nodes and an accurate mapping.

With complement coding, the correct map can be learned on-line for any $\bar{\rho}_a > 0$. The critical difference is due to the fact that $|\mathbf{a}^{(2)} \cap \mathbf{w}_1^a|/|\mathbf{a}^{(2)}|$ is now equal to $\frac{5}{6}$ when $\mathbf{a}^{(2)}$ is first presented rather than equal to 1 as before. Thus, either ART_a resets (if $\bar{\rho}_a > \frac{5}{6}$) or match tracking establishes a new ART_a node rather than shutting down on that trial (if $\bar{\rho}_a \leq \frac{5}{6}$). On the next trial, $\mathbf{a}^{(1)}$ also establishes a new ART_a category that maps to $\mathbf{b}^{(1)}$.

20.2.5 Fuzzy Kohonen Clustering Network

In Sec. 12.3, we introduced Kohonen's self-organizing feature map, called the *Kohonen clustering network* (KCN), for cluster analysis. KCNs are unsupervised networks that find the "best" set of weights for hard clusters in an iterative, sequential manner. The structure of a KCN consists of two layers, an input fan-out layer and an output (competitive) layer as shown in Fig. 12.6. Given an input vector, the nodes in the output layer compete among themselves and the winner (whose weight has the minimum distance from the input) updates its weights and those of some set of predefined neighbors according to Eq. (12.28). The process is continued until the weight vector stabilizes. In this scheme, a learning rate must be defined that decreases with time in order to force termination. Moreover, an update neighborhood function must be defined and is also reduced with time. KCNs suffer from some problems. First, they are heuristic procedures, and so *termination* is not based on optimizing any model of the process or its data. Second, the final weight vectors usually depend on the input sequence. Third, different initial conditions usually yield different results. Fourth, several parameters of KCN algorithms, such as the learning rate, the size of the update neighborhood function, and the strategy for altering these two parameters during learning, must be varied from one data set to another to achieve desirable results.

In this section, we shall introduce the *fuzzy Kohonen clustering networks* (*FKCNs*) that integrate the fuzzy c-means (FCM) model into the learning rate and updating strategies of the KCN. Since FCM algorithms are optimization procedures (see Sec. 8.1.2), whereas KCNs are not, integration of FCMs and KCNs is one way to address several problems of KCNs. In addition, such integration enables the KCNs to generate continuous-valued outputs for fuzzy clustering instead of hard clustering. On the other hand, the FCM algorithm for fuzzy membership value u_{ij} assignment is quadratic in u_{ij} for a weighting exponent of 2 [see Eq. (8.23)]. The integration of FCMs with KCNs gains in computational efficiency over the FCM algorithm because of the use of a linear weight update rule in a KCN. This integration was first considered by Huntsberger and Ajjimarangsee [1990] and then extended by Bezdek et al. [1992]. They combined the ideas of fuzzy membership values for learning rates, the parallelism of FCMs, and the structure and update rules of KCNs.

The scheme proposed by Huntsberger and Ajjimarangsee is a partial integration of KCNs and FCMs called a *partial FKCN*. Figure 20.15 shows the structure of the partial FKCN where one extra layer, a *membership layer*, is added to the output layer (called the *distance layer*) of the original Kohonen network. For a given input pattern $\mathbf{x}_j$, the node i, $i = 1, 2, \ldots, c$, in the distance layer calculates the distance d_{ij} between $\mathbf{x}_j$ and the ith prototype vector $\mathbf{v}_i$; that is,

$$d_{ij} = \| \mathbf{x}_j - \mathbf{v}_i \|^2 = (\mathbf{x}_j - \mathbf{v}_i)^T (\mathbf{x}_j - \mathbf{v}_i), \tag{20.63}$$

where c is the number of clusters and $\mathbf{v}_i$ is the input weight vector of distance-layer node i representing the prototype vector of the ith cluster. Then the membership layer maps the distances d_{ij} into membership values u_{ij} according to the equation

$$u_{ij} = \left(\sum_{k=1}^{c} \frac{d_{ij}}{d_{kj}} \right)^{-1}, \tag{20.64}$$

where $u_{ij} = 1$ if $d_{ij} = 0$ and $u_{ij} = 0$ if $d_{kj} = 0$, $k \neq i$. This form of membership value determination is based on Eq. (8.23) of the FCM algorithm. For a well-trained partial FKCN, the output u_{ij} represents the degree to which the input pattern $\mathbf{x}_j$ belongs to cluster i. However, in the learning process, these outputs need to be fed back to update the cluster centers through a feedback path between the nodes in the new third layer and the input nodes as shown in Fig. 20.15.

The learning algorithm for the partial FKCN includes the membership values in both the determination of d_{ij} as well as in the weight update rule. Moreover, the size-decreasing neighborhood is adopted in the algorithm. The partial FKCN learning algorithm is described by the following steps.

Algorithm PFKCN: Partial Fuzzy Kohonen Clustering Network Learning

Step 1: Randomly initialize weights $\mathbf{v}_i$, $i = 1, 2, ..., c$, and set the neighborhood size (NE) to be $c/2$, where c is the number of clusters.

Step 2: For each input $\mathbf{x}_j$, select the output node i^*, $1 \leq i^* \leq c$, such that d_{i^*j} is a minimum, where d_{ij} is defined by Eq. (20.63). Update $\mathbf{v}_i$ using the rule

$$\mathbf{v}_i(t + 1) = \mathbf{v}_i(t) + u_{ij}(t)[\mathbf{x}_j - \mathbf{v}_i(t)], \qquad (20.65)$$

where i includes output node i^* and each of the NE neighbors around it. Repeat step 2 until there is no change in the weights.

Step 3: Check whether NE $= 0$. If this is the case, the algorithm is finished; otherwise, NE will be reduced by 1 and the execution returns to step 2.

END PFKCN

The above algorithm automatically includes the factor u_{ij}^2 in the definition of d_{ij} with the modification of $\mathbf{v}_i(t)$ in step 2. The computational complexity is the same as that of the FCM algorithm as far as the number of update calculations is concerned, but this algorithm still has a computational advantage in the linear update rule. An even greater computational advantage is gained as a result of including the decreasing-size neighborhood in the algorithm. The neighborhood reduces the total number of update calculations since all the nodes are not included each time step 2 is executed.

The partial FKCN is a partial integration of the KCN and the FCM. This hybrid scheme falls short of being a mathematical model to be realized for KCN clustering, and no

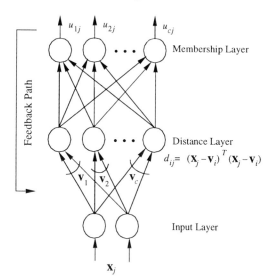

Figure 20.15 Fuzzy Kohonen clustering network (FKCN).

properties regarding termination of convergence are established. Note that termination is forced on the partial FKCN learning by ultimately shrinking the update neighborhood to the empty set. Bezdek et al. [1992] realized the complete integration of the FCM with the KCN by defining the learning rate α_{ij} for Kohonen updating as

$$\alpha_{ij}(t) = (u_{ij}(t))^{m_t}; \qquad m_t = m_0 - t\,\Delta m, \qquad \Delta m = \frac{m_0 - 1}{t_{max}}, \qquad (20.66)$$

where $u_{ij}(t)$ is calculated by Eq. (8.23) in which m is set as $m = m_t$, m_0 is a positive constant greater than 1, and t_{max} is the iteration limit. The computation of u_{ij} can be performed in the forward pass of the fuzzy Kohonen clustering network shown in Fig. 20.15. Defining the learning rate with Eq. (20.66) for α_{ij} yields the following FKCN learning algorithm.

Algorithm FKCN: Fuzzy Kohonen Clustering Network Learning

Step 1: Randomly initialize the weights v_i, $i = 1, 2,..., c$. Choose $m_0 > 1$, $t_{max} =$ iteration limit, and $\epsilon > 0$ as some small, positive constant.

Step 2: For $t = 1, 2,..., t_{max}$,

   a. Compute all cn learning rates $\{\alpha_{ij}(t), i = 1, 2,..., c, j = 1, 2,..., n\}$ with Eqs. (20.66) and (8.23);

   b. Update all c weight vectors $\{v_i(t), i = 1, 2,..., c\}$ with

$$v_i(t+1) = v_i(t) + \frac{\sum_{j=1}^{n} \alpha_{ij}(t)\,[x_j - v_i(t)]}{\sum_{j=1}^{n} \alpha_{ij}(t)}; \qquad (20.67)$$

   c. Compute $E_{t+1} = \|v(t+1) - v(t)\|^2$;

   d. If $E_{t+1} \leq \epsilon$, then stop; otherwise repeat step 2 for the next t.
   End_For

END FKCN

We observe that FKCN is not sequential since updates are done to all c weight vectors after each pass through $\{x_j, j = 1, 2,..., n\}$. Note that the learning rates $\{\alpha_{ij}\} = \{(u_{ij})^{m_t}\}$ have the following properties:

1. In the extreme case where $m_t \to \infty$, we have

$$\lim_{m_t \to \infty} \{u_{ij}(t)\} = \frac{1}{c} \qquad \text{for all } i \text{ and } j. \qquad (20.68)$$

2. In another extreme case where $m_t \to 1$, we have

$$\lim_{m_t \to 1} \{u_{ij}(t)\} = 1 \text{ or } 0 \qquad \text{for all } i \text{ and } j. \qquad (20.69)$$

3. The learning rates $\{(u_{ij}(t))^{m_t}\}$ calculated with Eq. (8.23), which for fixed c, $\{v_i(t)\}$, and m_t, have the following form for each x_j:

$$[u_{ij}(t)]^{m_t} = \left[\frac{a}{d_{ij}(t)}\right]^{m_t/(m_t-1)}, \qquad (20.70)$$

where a is a positive constant.

The effect of Eq. (20.70) is to distribute the contribution of each $\mathbf{x}_j$ to the next weight update inversely proportional to the weight's distance from $\mathbf{x}_j$. The *winner* in Eq. (20.67) is thus the $\mathbf{v}_i(t)$ closest to $\mathbf{x}_j$, and it will be moved further along the line connecting $\mathbf{v}_i(t)$ to $\mathbf{x}_j$ than any of the other weight vectors. In the limit, $m_t = 1$, the update rule reverts to hard c-means (winner take all)—but nonsequentially. Hence, although the FKCN algorithm does not manipulate the neighborhood N_t explicitly, as the KCN and partial FKCN do, the *effective* neighborhood does vary with t in the FKCN. For large values of m_t (near m_0), all c weight vectors are updated with lower individual learning rates, and as $m_t \rightarrow 1$, more and more of the unit sum is given to the winner node. In other words, the lateral distribution of learning rates is a function of t, which *sharpens* at the winner node for each $\mathbf{x}_j$ as $m_t \rightarrow 1$. Thus, the FKCN is nonsequential unsupervised learning and uses fuzzy membership values from the FCM as learning rates. This yields automatic control of both the learning rate distribution and update neighborhood. The KCN neighborhood constraint has been dropped but is embedded in the learning rate which is manipulated by reducing m_t from a large value to 1. The relationship between the FKCN and the FCM is characterized by the following theorem.

Theorem 20.5

For fixed $m_t > 1$ [i.e., $\Delta m = 0$ in Eq. (20.66)], the FKCN is a FCM.

Proof: Since Eq. (8.23) is used to compute $\{\alpha_{ij}\}$, we have only to show that the update rule [Eq. (20.67)] in the FKCN is equivalent to Eq. (8.22) in the FCM. Since

$$\frac{\sum_{j=1}^{n} \alpha_{ij}(t)\,[\mathbf{x}_j - \mathbf{v}_i(t)]}{\sum_{j=1}^{n} \alpha_{ij}(t)} = \frac{\sum_{j=1}^{n} \alpha_{ij}(t)\,\mathbf{x}_j}{\sum_{j=1}^{n} \alpha_{ij}(t)} - \mathbf{v}_i(t)\frac{\sum_{j=1}^{n} \alpha_{ij}(t)}{\sum_{j=1}^{n} \alpha_{ij}(t)},$$

the update rule in Eq. (20.67) in the FKCN becomes

$$\mathbf{v}_i(t+1) = [\mathbf{v}_i(t) - \mathbf{v}_i(t)] + \frac{\sum_{j=1}^{n} \alpha_{ij}(t)\,\mathbf{x}_j}{\sum_{j=1}^{n} \alpha_{ij}(t)} = \frac{\sum_{j=1}^{n} [u_{ij}(t)]^{m_t}\,\mathbf{x}_j}{\sum_{j=1}^{n} [u_{ij}(t)]^{m_t}},$$

which is Eq. (8.22) for $m_t = m$. This shows that with $\Delta m = 0$ the FKCN is the same as the FCM with $m = m_0$.

The FKCN has been used on Anderson's *Iris* data set (Fig. 8.5) [Bezdek et al., 1992]. In the simulation, the FKCN as well as the KCN was initialized randomly, and $\epsilon = 0.0001$ and $t_{\max} = 50,000$ were used. Figure 20.16 shows error rates obtained by various algorithms as a function of time. We found that the KCN always ran to its iteration limit ($t_{\max} = 50,000$) unless $\alpha_{ij}(t)$ was forced to zero. On the other hand, the FKCN always satisfied the termination criterion in 14 to 40 ($t = 17$ in the figure) iterations. In general, the FKCN always terminates independently of the sequence of feeding data in fewer iterations than the KCN does. Note also that the FCM ($m = 4$) and the FKCN ($m_0 = 4$, $\Delta m_0 = 0$) generate exactly the same curve as required by Theorem 20.5. Thus, the FKCN can be considered a *Kohonen network implementation of the FCM*.

20.2.6 Fuzzy RCE Neural Network

In Sec. 15.3.2, we introduced a structured adaptive network called a restricted Coulomb energy (RCE) neural network. A RCE network can be used as a pattern classifier in form-

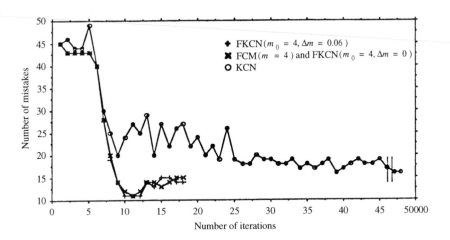

Figure 20.16 Error rates with t for a KCN and FKCN ($m_0 = 4$ and $\Delta m = 0.06$), a FKCN ($m_0 = 4$ and $\Delta m = 0$), and a FCM ($m = 4$). Note the break in the horizontal axis between 45 and 50,000. (Adapted from Bezdek et al. [1992], © 1992 IEEE.)

ing nonlinear boundaries of pattern classes. It has three layers: input layer, prototype layer, and output layer. Each input node presents one feature of the input vector, and each output node represents one category. Each hidden node in the RCE network represents one proto-type and is called a *prototype node*. In this section, we shall learn how to introduce fuzziness into this RCE neural network. One way to introduce fuzziness is to replace crisp prototypes by fuzzy (linguistic) prototypes. In such *fuzzy RCE networks,* each prototype node must define its fuzzy sets together with their corresponding membership functions for fuzzy properties.

In the fuzzy RCE network proposed by Roan et al. [1993], the triangular membership functions defined below are used for each prototype node.

$$\mu\,(x) = \begin{cases} (1/b)(-\,|\,x - a\,| + b) & \text{if } (a - b) < x < (a + b) \\ 0 & \text{otherwise,} \end{cases} \tag{20.71}$$

where a is the center and b is the width of the triangular membership function. Given that the dimension of input feature vectors is n, then n fuzzy membership functions $\{\mu_{ij}\,(x_j)$, $j = 1, 2,\ldots, n\}$ should be defined for prototype node i (denoted by p_i). For simplicity, only one common width b_i is used in prototype node p_i. Then each prototype node p_i has $(n + 1)$ parameters: $a_{i1}, a_{i2},\ldots, a_{in}$, and b_i as shown in Fig. 20.17. The learning algorithm for the fuzzy RCE network is then described as follows:

Algorithm FRCE: Fuzzy RCE (Fuzzy Restricted Coulomb Energy Network)
For each training input vector $\mathbf{x} = (x_1, x_2,\ldots, x_n)$ belonging to the kth class, perform the follow-ing steps.

Step 1: Calculate the output of all prototype nodes p_i by

$$\mathrm{OUT}_{p_i} = \Phi\left(\frac{1}{n}\sum_{j=1}^{n} \mu_{ij}\,(x_j)\right), \tag{20.72}$$

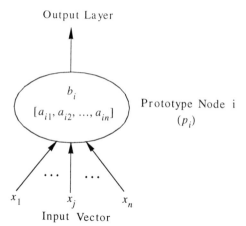

Output Layer

Prototype Node i
(p_i)

b_i
$[a_{i1}, a_{i2}, ..., a_{in}]$

x_1 x_j x_n

Input Vector

Figure 20.17 Structure of one prototype
neuron in the fuzzy RCE network.

where $\mu_{ij}(\cdot)$ is defined by Eq. (20.71) and

$$\Phi(x) = \begin{cases} x & \text{if } x > \theta \\ 0 & \text{if } x \leq \theta, \end{cases} \tag{20.73}$$

where θ is a prespecified threshold. If $\text{OUT}_{p_i} > 0$, then prototype node p_i is said to be "fired."

Step 2: If none of the prototype nodes in the kth class (i.e., the prototype nodes connected to the kth output node) is fired, then create a new prototype node p_l which connects to the kth output node and set $\mathbf{a}_l = (a_{l1}, a_{l2}, ..., a_{ln}) = \mathbf{x}$, $b_l = b_0$, where b_0 is a prespecified initial value for all membership functions.

Step 3: If any prototype node p_i that does not connect to the kth output node is fired, then reduce b_i to b_i' such that p_i cannot be fired. The value of b_i' is derived by setting $\text{OUT}_{p_i} = \theta$. Thus,

$$b_i' = \frac{\sum_{j=1}^{n} f(x_j)}{(n-k) - n\theta}, \tag{20.74}$$

where

$$f(x_j) = \begin{cases} |x_j - a_{ij}| & \text{if } (a_{ij} - b_i) < x_j < (a_{ij} + b_i) \\ 0 & \text{otherwise,} \end{cases} \tag{20.75}$$

and k is the number of nonzero $f(x_j)$.

END FRCE

In retrieving the fuzzy RCE network, we first calculate the output of all prototype nodes using Eqs. (20.72) and (20.73) and then find the prototype node with the maximum output value. If this node is connected to the kth output node, we assign the testing input vector to category k. If no prototype node is found, we reject the testing input vector.

20.2.7 Fuzzy Cerebellar Model Articulation Controller

In this section, we generalize the cerebellar model articulation controller (CMAC) introduced in Sec. 16.1.2 to the fuzzy CMAC (FCMAC) by introducing fuzziness into it. The structure of the FCMAC proposed by Jou [1992a] is shown in Fig. 20.18. It is a four-layer structure for mapping input vectors in space X to output vectors in space Y. The membership grades generated by the fuzzy sensors layer S are combined in the association layer A. Each node in layer A is considered a fuzzy unit, and it outputs a membership grade indicating its activity. Each fuzzy unit of layer A operates as the fuzzy AND function (e.g., min operator). The mapping from layer S to layer A has a structure similar to that of a CMAC; that is, a sparse and regular interconnection is built so that for any input $\mathbf{x}$ there are exactly c nodes in layer A receiving nonzero membership grades. This is used to produce generalization between nearby input vectors and no generalization between distant input vectors.

As in CMACs, to avoid the problem of requiring an unreasonably large memory for storing weights, the output of each fuzzy unit of layer A maps randomly to the postassociation layer P, containing a small number of fuzzy units. Every fuzzy unit of layer P operates like the fuzzy OR function (e.g., max operator). Let P^* denote the set of fuzzy units of layer P with nonzero membership grades for input $\mathbf{x}$. Because of the possible mapping collisions, we should have $|P^*| \le c$. Outputs of all fuzzy units of layer P are connected to the final response unit R through changeable fuzzy weights W_j, which are fuzzy numbers defined on the output range Y. In practice, fuzzy weights are usually symmetric triangles or trapezoids centered about respective values. The fuzzy units p_j of layer P and the corresponding fuzzy weights W_j can be considered in terms of the fuzzy rule association $\mu_{p_j}(\mathbf{x}) \to \mu_{W_j}(y)$. The fuzzy set of the response unit ranging over all values of the output, determined by the activities of the nodes of layer P, has the membership function

$$\mu_R(y) = \bigvee_{1 \le j \le N_p} \mu_{p_j}(\mathbf{x}) \wedge \mu_{W_j}(y) = \bigvee_{p_j \in P^*} \mu_{p_j}(\mathbf{x}) \wedge \mu_{W_j}(y), \qquad (20.76)$$

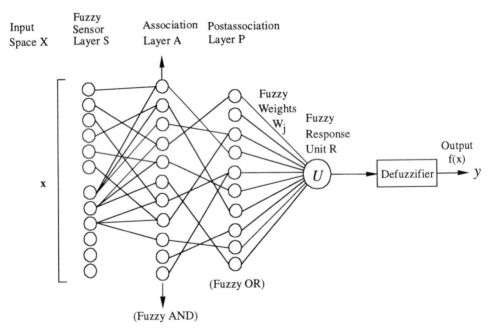

Figure 20.18 System structure of the FCMAC.

where N_p is the number of nodes in layer P. If a crisp output $f(\mathbf{x})$ is necessary, the centroid defuzzification method can be applied as follows:

$$f(\mathbf{x}) = \bar{y} = \frac{\int_Y \mu_R(y) \, y \, dy}{\int_Y \mu_R(y) \, dy}. \qquad (20.77)$$

The learning problem in the FCMAC is to determine appropriate membership functions for fuzzy weights W_j in order to represent the desired function f over the regions of interest. Suppose an element of training data is available in the form of $(\mathbf{x}, y^d)$, where y^d is the desired output of $\mathbf{x}$. Then the correction factor δ is first computed as

$$\delta = \beta(y^d - f(\mathbf{x})), \qquad (20.78)$$

where the learning rate β is between 0 and 1. Suppose all associated fuzzy weights W_j are shifted δ with respect to the universe of discourse Y. Then the new fuzzy weights W_j' have membership functions $\mu_{W_j'}(y + \delta) = \mu_{W_j}(y)$. Thus, the new fuzzy response node R' has membership function $\mu_{R'}(y + \delta) = \mu_R(y)$, and the fuzzy centroid becomes $\bar{y}' = \bar{y} + \delta$. This indicates that shifting all associated fuzzy weights with respect to the universe of discourse will deduce the same amount of shifting of the resulting response. Based on this observation, the learning rule for the FCMAC can be stated as follows. For each training pattern $(\mathbf{x}, y^d)$, δ is computed by Eq. (20.78) and the associated fuzzy weights W_j are shifted by δ:

$$\mu_{W_j(t+1)}(y + \delta) = \mu_{W_j(t)}(y). \qquad (20.79)$$

The FCMAC extends the CMAC by including fuzziness in the system architecture and the mathematical data. In fact, it can be easily shown that a FCMAC module is reduced to a CMAC module if all sensors of layer S are crisp and all weights are nonfuzzy singletons. Another similar type of FCMAC can be found in Nie and Linkens [1993], where the FCMAC has been successfully applied to a problem of multivariable blood pressure control.

20.3 NEURAL NETWORKS WITH FUZZY TRAINING

In this section, we shall discuss some ways to introduce fuzzy logic into the learning process of neural networks. These include the use of fuzzy teaching signals for training neural networks, where the networks may have either crisp parameters or fuzzy parameters, and the use of fuzzy controllers for dynamically adapting the learning parameters (e.g., the learning rate) of neural networks.

20.3.1 Neural Networks with Fuzzy Teaching Input

In most of the training in neural networks, we assume that all the training data are numerical. However, in some situations, such as in learning expert knowledge, we might have only qualitative fuzzy training data like "IF x_1 is Small AND x_2 is Large, THEN y is Small." In this section, we shall discuss the learning methods of neural networks in utilizing expert knowledge represented by fuzzy IF-THEN rules. In particular, we shall consider the multilayer feedforward network with input vectors of fuzzy numbers proposed by Ishibuchi et al. [1993a]. This is also viewed by many as a fuzzy generalization of the back-propagation algorithm.

Assume that the following S fuzzy IF-THEN rules are given by human experts:

$$\text{IF } x_1 \text{ is } A_{p1} \text{ AND } \cdots \text{ AND } x_n \text{ is } A_{pn}, \text{ THEN } y \text{ is } T_p, \qquad (20.80)$$

where $p = 1, 2, \ldots, S$, and A_{pi} and T_p are fuzzy numbers. These fuzzy rules can be viewed as the fuzzy input-output pairs

$$(\mathbf{A}_p, T_p), \qquad p = 1, 2, \ldots, S, \qquad (20.81)$$

where $\mathbf{A}_p = (A_{p1}, A_{p2}, \ldots, A_{pn})$ is a fuzzy vector. Our problem now is to approximate a nonlinear fuzzy mapping using the S fuzzy input-output pairs in Eq. (20.81). It is noted that a numerical value $x_{p'i}$ can be considered a fuzzy singleton. That is, the numerical input-output pairs $(\mathbf{x}_{p'}, y_{p'})$ are considered special cases of Eq. (20.81). Hence, Eq. (20.81) represents a general form of a training data set which can be fuzzy or numerical or even a mixture of both. In this way, we can integrate linguistic data and numerical data into a single information processing system.

We shall first introduce a neural network architecture that can handle fuzzy input vectors such that a fuzzy input vector is mapped to a fuzzy output number (vector). Before doing so, let us review some equations of *interval arithmetic* (see Sec. 5.2) that will be used here. Let $X = [x^L, x^U]$ and $Y = [y^L, y^U]$ be intervals. The superscripts L and U represent the lower limit and upper limit, respectively. Then we have

$$X + Y = [x^L, x^U] + [y^L, y^U] = [x^L + y^L, x^U + y^U] \qquad (20.82)$$

and

$$k \cdot X = k \cdot [x^L, x^U] = \begin{cases} \begin{bmatrix} kx^L, & kx^U \end{bmatrix}, & \text{if } k \geq 0 \\ \begin{bmatrix} kx^U, & kx^L \end{bmatrix}, & \text{if } k < 0, \end{cases} \qquad (20.83)$$

where k is a real number. The activation function of neural networks can also be extended to an interval input-output relation as

$$f(\text{Net}) = f([\text{net}^L, \text{net}^U]) = [f(\text{net}^L), f(\text{net}^U)], \qquad (20.84)$$

where $\text{Net} = [\text{net}^L, \text{net}^U]$ is an interval input and $f(\cdot)$ is a sigmoid function. The interval activation function defined by Eq. (20.84) is illustrated in Fig. 20.19.

The preceding discussion concerns operations on intervals. On the other hand, operations on fuzzy numbers can be defined using the concept of level sets (see Sec. 2.1) as follows:

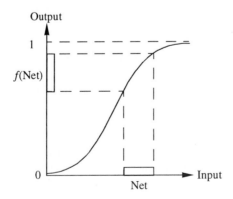

Figure 20.19 Interval activation function of each unit of a neural network. Net and $f(\text{Net})$ are an interval input and an interval output, respectively.

$$[A + B]_h = [A]_h + [B]_h \tag{20.85}$$

$$[kA]_h = k[A]_h \tag{20.86}$$

$$[f(A)]_h = f([A]_h), \tag{20.87}$$

where A and B are fuzzy numbers defined by $\mu_A(x)$ and $\mu_B(x)$, respectively, and $[\cdot]_h$ is an h-level set of a fuzzy number [see Eq. (2.11)]. Since the h-level sets of fuzzy numbers are intervals, operations on level sets coincide with operations on intervals.

We shall now use the h-level set [Eqs. (20.85)–(20.87)] to describe the process of neural networks that can handle fuzzy input vectors. Since the level sets of fuzzy numbers are intervals, the calculation of fuzzy number output requires only interval arithmetic. We shall derive the input-output relation of the neural network for an interval input vector here. Consider a multilayer feedforward network that has n input nodes, m hidden nodes, and a single output node. If the interval vector $\mathbf{X}_p = (X_{p1}, X_{p2}, ..., X_{pn})$ is presented to the input layer of the neural network, the input-output relation of each unit is explicitly calculated as follows:

Input nodes:

$$Y_{pi} = [y_{pi}^L, y_{pi}^U] = X_{pi} = [x_{pi}^L, x_{pi}^U], \qquad i = 1, 2, ..., n, \tag{20.88}$$

Hidden nodes:

$$Y_{pj} = [y_{pj}^L, y_{pj}^U] = [f(\mathrm{net}_{pj}^L), f(\mathrm{net}_{pj}^U)], \qquad j = 1, 2, ..., m, \tag{20.89}$$

$$\mathrm{net}_{pj}^L = \sum_{\substack{i=1 \\ w_{ji} \geq 0}}^{n} w_{ji} y_{pi}^L + \sum_{\substack{i=1 \\ w_{ji} < 0}}^{n} w_{ji} y_{pi}^U + \theta_j, \tag{20.90}$$

$$\mathrm{net}_{pj}^U = \sum_{\substack{i=1 \\ w_{ji} \geq 0}}^{n} w_{ji} y_{pi}^U + \sum_{\substack{i=1 \\ w_{ji} < 0}}^{n} w_{ji} y_{pi}^L + \theta_j, \tag{20.91}$$

Output node:

$$Y_p = [y_p^L, y_p^U] = [f(\mathrm{net}_p^L), f(\mathrm{net}_p^U)], \tag{20.92}$$

$$\mathrm{net}_p^L = \sum_{\substack{j=1 \\ w_j \geq 0}}^{m} w_j y_{pj}^L + \sum_{\substack{j=1 \\ w_j < 0}}^{m} w_j y_{pj}^U + \theta, \tag{20.93}$$

$$\mathrm{net}_p^U = \sum_{\substack{j=1 \\ w_j \geq 0}}^{m} w_j y_{pj}^U + \sum_{\substack{j=1 \\ w_j < 0}}^{m} w_j y_{pj}^L + \theta, \tag{20.94}$$

where the weights w_{ji}, w_j and the biases θ_j, θ are real parameters and the outputs Y_{pi}, Y_{pj}, and Y_p are intervals.

Example 20.7

[Ishibuchi et al., 1993a]. Consider the neural network in Fig. 20.20 where weights and biases are shown beside the connections and inside the nodes, respectively. The fuzzy input vector in

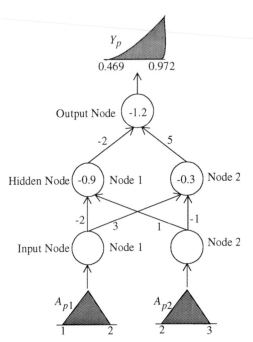

Figure 20.20   Example of fuzzy input-output relations of the neural networks in Example 20.7.

the figure is $\mathbf{A}_p = (A_{p1}, A_{p2}) = ((1.5, 0.5)_L, (2.5, 0.5)_L)$, where $A = (a, b)_L$ denotes a symmetric triangular fuzzy number with the center a and the spread b defined by the membership function

$$\mu_A(x) = \max\left\{1 - \frac{(x - a)}{b}, 0\right\}. \tag{20.95}$$

The output fuzzy number Y_p is shown in Fig. 20.20, which was drawn using Eqs. (20.88)–(20.94) on 100 level sets corresponding to $h = 0.01, 0.02, \ldots, 1.00$.

We shall now derive the learning algorithm for the aforementioned network. Using the fuzzy output Y_p and the corresponding fuzzy target output T_p, a cost function for the h-level sets of Y_p and T_p can be defined as

$$E_{ph} = \frac{([T_p]_h^L - [Y_p]_h^L)^2}{2} + \frac{([T_p]_h^U - [Y_p]_h^U)^2}{2}, \tag{20.96}$$

where $[Y_p]_h = [[Y_p]_h^L, [Y_p]_h^U]$ and $[T_p]_h = [[T_p]_h^L, [T_p]_h^U]$. This cost function is defined as the sum of the squared errors for the lower limits and for the upper limits. It is noted that the above cost function is reduced to the squared error employed in the back-propagation algorithm in the case of a nonfuzzy input vector and a nonfuzzy target output.

The learning of neural networks involves minimizing the cost function in Eq. (20.96). As in the back-propagation algorithm, the weights w_j and w_{ji} are updated according to the following rule:

$$\Delta w_j(t + 1) = -\eta \frac{\partial E_{ph}}{\partial w_j} + \alpha \Delta w_j(t), \tag{20.97}$$

$$\Delta w_{ji}(t+1) = -\eta \frac{\partial E_{ph}}{\partial w_{ji}} + \alpha\, \Delta w_{ji}(t),\qquad (20.98)$$

where $\partial E_{ph}/\partial w_j$ and $\partial E_{ph}/\partial w_{ji}$ can be calculated by the chain rule as follows [Ishibuchi et al., 1993a]:

For $\partial E_{ph}/\partial w_j$:

1. If $w_j \geq 0$, then

$$
\begin{aligned}
\frac{\partial E_{ph}}{\partial w_j} &= \frac{\partial}{\partial w_j}\left\{ \frac{(t_p^L - y_p^L)^2}{2}\right\} + \frac{\partial}{\partial w_j}\left\{ \frac{(t_p^U - y_p^U)^2}{2}\right\} \\
&= \frac{\partial}{\partial y_p^L}\left\{ \frac{(t_p^L - y_p^L)^2}{2}\right\} \frac{\partial y_p^L}{\partial net_p^L}\frac{\partial net_p^L}{\partial w_j} + \\
&\quad \frac{\partial}{\partial y_p^U}\left\{ \frac{(t_p^L - y_p^U)^2}{2}\right\} \frac{\partial y_p^L}{\partial net_p^U}\frac{\partial net_p^U}{\partial w_j} \\
&= -(t_p^L - y_p^L)y_p^L(1 - y_p^L)y_{pj}^L - (t_p^U - y_p^U)y_p^U(1 - y_p^U)y_{pj}^U \\
&\triangleq -\delta_p^L y_{pj}^L - \delta_p^U y_{pj}^U .
\end{aligned}
\qquad (20.99)
$$

2. If $w_j < 0$, then

$$
\begin{aligned}
\frac{\partial E_{ph}}{\partial w_j} &= -(t_p^L - y_p^L)y_p^L(1 - y_p^L)y_{pj}^U - (t_p^U - y_p^U)y_p^U(1 - y_p^U)y_{pj}^L \\
&\triangleq -\delta_p^L y_{pj}^U - \delta_p^U y_{pj}^L .
\end{aligned}
\qquad (20.100)
$$

For $\partial E_{ph}/\partial w_{ji}$:

1. If $w_j \geq 0$ and $w_{ji} \geq 0$, then

$$
\begin{aligned}
\frac{\partial E_{ph}}{\partial w_{ji}} &= \frac{\partial}{\partial w_{ji}}\left\{ \frac{(t_p^L - y_p^L)^2}{2}\right\} + \frac{\partial}{\partial w_{ji}}\left\{ \frac{(t_p^U - y_p^U)^2}{2}\right\} \\
&= \frac{\partial}{\partial y_p^L}\left\{ \frac{(t_p^L - y_p^L)^2}{2}\right\} \frac{\partial y_p^L}{\partial net_p^L}\frac{\partial net_p^L}{\partial y_{pj}^L}\frac{\partial y_{pj}^L}{\partial net_{pj}^L}\frac{\partial net_{pj}^L}{\partial w_{ji}} + \\
&\quad \frac{\partial}{\partial y_p^U}\left\{ \frac{(t_p^U - y_p^U)^2}{2}\right\} \frac{\partial y_p^U}{\partial net_p^U}\frac{\partial net_p^U}{\partial y_{pj}^U}\frac{\partial y_{pj}^U}{\partial net_{pj}^U}\frac{\partial net_{pj}^U}{\partial w_{ji}} \\
&= -\delta_p^L w_j y_{pj}^L(1 - y_{pj}^L)y_{pi}^L - \delta_p^U w_j y_{pj}^U(1 - y_{pj}^U)y_{pi}^U .
\end{aligned}
\qquad (20.101)
$$

2. If $w_j \geq 0$ and $w_{ji} < 0$, then

$$\frac{\partial E_{ph}}{\partial w_{ji}} = -\delta_p^L w_j y_{pj}^L (1 - y_{pj}^L) y_{pi}^U - \delta_p^U w_j y_{pj}^U (1 - y_{pj}^U) y_{pi}^L. \qquad (20.102)$$

3. If $w_j < 0$ and $w_{ji} \geq 0$, then

$$\frac{\partial E_{ph}}{\partial w_{ji}} = -\delta_p^L w_j y_{pj}^U (1 - y_{pj}^U) y_{pi}^U - \delta_p^U w_j y_{pj}^L (1 - y_{pj}^L) y_{pi}^L. \qquad (20.103)$$

4. If $w_j < 0$ and $w_{ji} < 0$, then

$$\frac{\partial E_{ph}}{\partial w_{ji}} = -\delta_p^L w_j y_{pj}^U (1 - y_{pj}^U) y_{pi}^L - \delta_p^U w_j y_{pj}^L (1 - y_{pj}^L) y_{pi}^U. \qquad (20.104)$$

In the previous discussion, the notations $t_p^L \triangleq [T_p]_h^L$, $t_p^U \triangleq [T_p]_h^U$, $y_p^L \triangleq [Y_p]_h^L$, and $y_p^U \triangleq [Y_p]_h^U$ were adopted, and δ_p^L and δ_p^U are defined as $\delta_p^L = (t_p^L - y_p^L) y_p^L (1 - y_p^L)$ and $\delta_p^U = (t_p^U - y_p^U) y_p^U (1 - y_p^U)$. We can also train the network with several values of h using the following cost function:

$$E_p = \sum_h h \cdot E_{ph} = \sum_h h \{ \tfrac{1}{2} ([T_p]_h^L - [Y_p]_h^L)^2 + (\tfrac{1}{2} [T_p]_h^U - [Y_p]_h^U)^2 \}. \qquad (20.105)$$

The following example illustrates the above procedure.

Example 20.8

[Ishibuchi et al., 1993a]. Let the input space and the output space be the unit interval $[0, 1]$. Assume that the following two fuzzy IF-THEN rules are given:

IF x is Small, THEN y is Small,

IF x is Large, THEN y is Large,

where the fuzzy numbers "Small (S)" and "Large (L)" are shown in Fig. 20.21(a). From these two rules, we obtain the two fuzzy input-output pairs (S, S) and (L, L), which are used to train a neural network with five hidden nodes. The fuzzy outputs from the trained network is shown in Fig. 20.21(b), which presents the simulation results after 10,000 epochs with $\eta = 0.5$ and $\alpha = 0.9$ using the cost function in Eq. (20.105) with $h = 0.2, 0.4, 0.6, 0.8,$ and 1.0.

To test the generalization ability of the trained neural network, three new fuzzy numbers "VERY Small (VS)," "VERY Large (VL)," and "Medium (M)" [see Fig. 20.21(c)] are presented to the input of the trained network. The corresponding fuzzy outputs Y_{VS}, Y_{VL}, and Y_M are shown in Fig. 20.21(d), which suggests good interpolations for test patterns.

20.3.2 Neural Networks with Fuzzy Parameters

In the last section, we introduced neural networks with crisp (numerical) weights and biases that can handle fuzzy input data. We shall now consider multilayer feedforward neural networks whose weights and biases are given as fuzzy numbers. Such neural networks can map an input vector of real numbers to a fuzzy output. Naturally, such networks can also map a fuzzy input vector to a fuzzy output. We shall consider only fuzzy target outputs here since crisp target output can be viewed as a special case of fuzzy target output. Two models are discussed here, one with a crisp cost function and the other with a fuzzy cost function.

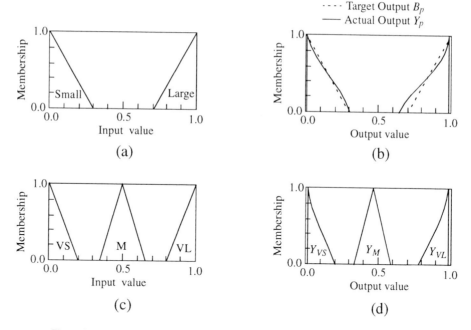

Figure 20.21 Membership functions and outputs for the neural network in Example 20.8. (a) The membership functions of the linguistic values "Small" and "Large." (b) The fuzzy actual outputs Y_p from the trained neural network and the corresponding fuzzy target outputs B_p. (c) The membership functions of the linguistic values "VERY Small," "VERY Large," and "Medium." (d) The fuzzy actual outputs Y_p from the trained neural network corresponding to the fuzzy input vectors in (c). (Adapted from Ishibuchi et al. [1993a], © 1993 IEEE.)

Crisp cost function. We first introduce the fuzzy neural model with fuzzy weights and fuzzy biases proposed by Ishibuchi et al. [1993d]. The proposed architecture is shown in Fig. 20.22, in which symmetric triangular fuzzy numbers are used for fuzzy weights and fuzzy biases:

$$W_j = (w_j^L, w_j^C, w_j^U), \qquad W_{ji} = (w_{ji}^L, w_{ji}^C, w_{ji}^U), \qquad (20.106)$$

$$\Theta = (\theta^L, \theta^C, \theta^U), \qquad \Theta_j = (\theta_j^L, \theta_j^C, \theta_j^U), \qquad (20.107)$$

where a triangular fuzzy number A is denoted as $A = (a^L, a^C, a^U)$ and a^L, a^C, and a^U are the lower limit, the center, and the upper limit of A. Since symmetric triangular fuzzy numbers are used, the following relations hold:

$$w_j^C = \frac{w_j^L + w_j^U}{2}, \qquad w_{ji}^C = \frac{w_{ji}^L + w_{ji}^U}{2}, \qquad (20.108)$$

$$\theta^C = \frac{\theta^L + \theta^U}{2}, \qquad \theta_j^C = \frac{\theta_j^L + \theta_j^U}{2}, \qquad (20.109)$$

and the h-level sets of fuzzy weights (and biases) can be calculated as

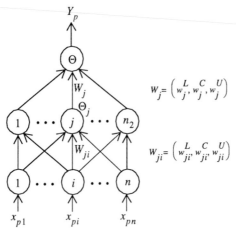

$$W_j = \left(\overset{L}{w_j}, \overset{C}{w_j}, \overset{U}{w_j} \right)$$

$$W_{ji} = \left(\overset{L}{w_{ji}}, \overset{C}{w_{ji}}, \overset{U}{w_{ji}} \right)$$

Figure 20.22 Architecture of neural networks with fuzzy weights and fuzzy biases.

$$[W_j]_h^L = w_j^L \left(1 - \frac{h}{2} \right) + \frac{w_j^U h}{2}, \qquad [W_j]_h^U = \frac{w_j^L h}{2} + w_j^U \left(1 - \frac{h}{2} \right), \qquad (20.110)$$

$$[W_{ji}]_h^L = w_{ji}^L \left(1 - \frac{h}{2} \right) + \frac{w_{ji}^U h}{2}, \qquad [W_{ji}]_h^U = \frac{w_{ji}^L h}{2} + w_{ji}^U \left(1 - \frac{h}{2} \right). \qquad (20.111)$$

When an n-dimensional real input vector $\mathbf{x}_p = (x_{p1}, x_{p2}, \ldots, x_{pn})^T$ is presented to the input nodes of the network in Fig. 20.22, the input-output relation of each node can be written in the form of an h-level set as follows:

Input nodes:

$$y_{pi} = x_{pi}, \quad i = 1, 2, \ldots, n. \qquad (20.112)$$

Hidden nodes:

$$[Y_{pj}]_h = [f(\text{Net}_{pj})]_h = f([\text{Net}_{pj}]_h), \qquad j = 1, 2, \ldots, n_2, \qquad (20.113)$$

$$[\text{Net}_{pj}]_h = \sum_{i=1}^{n} [W_{ji}]_h y_{pi} + [\Theta_j]_h, \qquad j = 1, 2, \ldots, n_2. \qquad (20.114)$$

Output nodes:

$$[Y_p]_h = [f(\text{Net}_p)]_h = f([\text{Net}_p]_h), \qquad (20.115)$$

$$[\text{Net}_p]_h = \sum_{j=1}^{n_2} [W_j]_h [Y_{pj}]_h + [\Theta]_h. \qquad (20.116)$$

The interval calculations in the above equations were derived in the last section.

We shall next consider the learning algorithm of the above network. Assume that S crisp-input–fuzzy-output pairs $(\mathbf{x}_p, T_p)$, $p = 1, 2, \ldots, S$, are given. The target output T_p is assumed to be a symmetric or nonsymmetric triangular fuzzy number $T_p = (t_p^L, t_p^C, t_p^U)$. The cost functions E_{ph} and E_p are defined exactly the same as those in Eqs. (20.96) and (20.105), respectively. Then the learning rules for the fuzzy weights (and fuzzy biases) W_j and W_{ji} can be written as

$$\Delta w_j^L (t + 1) = -\eta h \left(\frac{\partial E_{ph}}{\partial w_j^L} \right) + \alpha \, \Delta w_j^L (t) , \tag{20.117}$$

$$\Delta w_j^U (t + 1) = -\eta h \left(\frac{\partial E_{ph}}{\partial w_j^U} \right) + \alpha \, \Delta w_j^U (t) , \tag{20.118}$$

$$\Delta w_{ji}^L (t + 1) = -\eta h \left(\frac{\partial E_{ph}}{\partial w_{ji}^L} \right) + \alpha \, \Delta w_{ji}^L (t) , \tag{20.119}$$

$$\Delta w_{ji}^U (t + 1) = -\eta h \left(\frac{\partial E_{ph}}{\partial w_{ji}^U} \right) + \alpha \, \Delta w_{ji}^U (t) , \tag{20.120}$$

where the derivatives $\partial E_{ph}/\partial w_j^L$, $\partial E_{ph}/\partial w_j^U$, $\partial E_{ph}/\partial w_{ji}^L$, and $\partial E_{ph}/\partial w_{ji}^U$ can be derived from the cost function in Eq. (20.96) using Eqs. (20.110)–(20.116). For example, $\partial E_{ph}/\partial w_j^L$ is derived as follows:

1. If $0 \le [W_j]_h^L \le [W_j]_h^U$, then

$$\frac{\partial E_{ph}}{\partial w_j^L} = \frac{\partial E_{ph}^L}{\partial w_j^L} + \frac{\partial E_{ph}^U}{\partial w_j^L}$$

$$= \frac{\partial}{\partial [Y_p]_h^L} \left\{ \frac{([T_p]_h^L - [Y_p]_h^L)^2}{2} \right\} \frac{\partial [Y_p]_h^L}{\partial [\text{Net}_p]_h^L} \frac{\partial [\text{Net}_p]_h^L}{\partial [W_j]_h^L} \frac{\partial [W_j]_h^L}{\partial w_j^L} +$$

$$\frac{\partial}{\partial [Y_p]_h^U} \left\{ \frac{([T_p]_h^U - [Y_p]_h^U)^2}{2} \right\} \frac{\partial [Y_p]_h^U}{\partial [\text{Net}_p]_h^U} \frac{\partial [\text{Net}_p]_h^U}{\partial [W_j]_h^U} \frac{\partial [W_j]_h^U}{\partial w_j^L}$$

$$= -([T_p]_h^L - [Y_p]_h^L)[Y_p]_h^L(1 - [Y_p]_h^L)[Y_{pj}]_h^L \left(1 - \frac{h}{2} \right) - \tag{20.121}$$

$$([T_p]_h^U - [Y_p]_h^U)[Y_p]_h^U \frac{(1 - [Y_p]_h^U)[Y_{pj}]_h^U h}{2}$$

$$\triangleq -\delta_{ph}^L [Y_{pj}]_h^L \left(1 - \frac{h}{2} \right) - \frac{\delta_{ph}^U [Y_{pj}]_h^U h}{2} .$$

where $\delta_{ph}^L = ([T_p]_h^L - [Y_p]_h^L)[Y_p]_h^L(1 - [Y_p]_h^L)$ and $\delta_{ph}^U = ([T_p]_h^U - [Y_p]_h^U)[Y_p]_h^U (1 - [Y_p]_h^U)$.

2. If $[W_j]_h^L \le [W_j]_h^U < 0$, then

$$\frac{\partial E_{ph}}{\partial w_j^L} = -\delta_{ph}^L [Y_{pj}]_h^U \left(1 - \frac{h}{2}\right) - \frac{\delta_{ph}^U [Y_{pj}]_h^L h}{2}. \tag{20.122}$$

3. If $[W_j]_h^L < 0 \le [W_j]_h^U$, then

$$\frac{\partial E_{ph}}{\partial w_j^L} = -\delta_{ph}^L [Y_{pj}]_h^U \left(1 - \frac{h}{2}\right) - \frac{\delta_{ph}^U [Y_{pj}]_h^U h}{2}. \tag{20.123}$$

Notice that after the adjustments of the fuzzy weights using Eqs. (20.117)–(20.120), it might happen that the lower limits of fuzzy weights exceed the upper limits. To cope with this undesired situation, new fuzzy weights after the adjustments are defined as

$$w_j^L = \min \{w_j^L(t+1), w_j^U(t+1)\}, \qquad w_{ji}^L = \min \{w_{ji}^L(t+1), w_{ji}^U(t+1)\}, \tag{20.124}$$

$$w_j^U = \max \{w_j^L(t+1), w_j^U(t+1)\}, \qquad w_{ji}^U = \max \{w_{ji}^L(t+1), w_{ji}^U(t+1)\}. \tag{20.125}$$

The centers w_j^c and w_{ji}^c are then determined by Eq. (20.108). The fuzzy biases are updated in the same way as the fuzzy weights.

Example 20.9

[Ishibuchi et al., 1993d]. Consider the training data shown in Fig. 20.23(a), in which fuzzy target outputs corresponding to six input values, $x = 0.0, 0.2, ..., 1.0$, are given as triangular fuzzy numbers. Using the derived learning rules with $\eta = 0.5$, $\alpha = 0.9$, and $h = 0.2, 0.4, 0.6, 0.8$, and 1.0, a feedforward neural network with a single input node, five hidden nodes and a single output node is trained for 10,000 epochs. The actual fuzzy output from the trained neural network corresponding to 11 input values, $x = 0.0, 0.1, ..., 1.0$, are shown in Fig. 20.23(b). The results

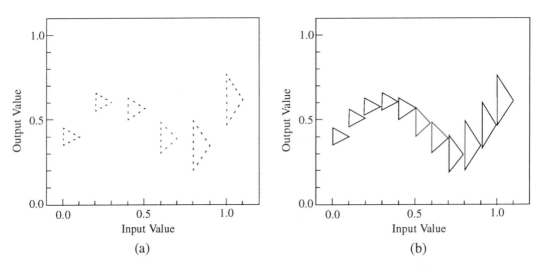

Figure 20.23 Training data and outputs for the neural network in Example 20.9. (a) Training data for the learning of the neural network. (b) Fuzzy actual outputs from the trained neural network. (Adapted from Ishibuchi et al. [1993d], © 1993 IEEE.)

indicate that good fitting to the six fuzzy target outputs and good interpolation for the five new inputs are achieved.

Fuzzy cost function. In the above discussion the learning algorithm was derived from a nonfuzzy cost function [Eq. (20.96) or Eq. (20.105)] for feedforward neural networks with fuzzy parameters. We shall consider another approach proposed by Hayashi et al. [1992c] in which the back-propagation algorithm is directly fuzzified based on a fuzzy-valued cost function. Consider the simple two-layer network shown in Fig. 20.24, where all the fuzzy inputs X_{pi} and the fuzzy output Y_p are fuzzy numbers in [0, 1] but the weights W_i may be any fuzzy subsets of the real numbers. The input-output relation of the network is described by

$$Y_p = f(\text{Net}_p),\qquad(20.126)$$

$$\text{Net}_p = \sum_{i=1}^{n} W_i X_{pi} + \Theta,\qquad(20.127)$$

where f is a sigmoid function and Θ is a fuzzy bias. Standard fuzzy arithmetic is used to compute Net_p in Eq. (20.127), and the extension principle is used to compute Y_p in Eq. (20.126) [i.e., $\mu_{Y_p}(z) = \max\{\mu_{\text{Net}_p}(x) \mid z = f(x)\}$]. For simplicity, we shall derive a learning algorithm based on a fuzzy cost function for this simple neural network. Naturally, such learning algorithm can be easily generalized to multilayer neural networks with fuzzy weights and biases that can be arbitrary fuzzy numbers.

First, given fuzzy input-output pairs $(\mathbf{X}_p, T_p)$, $p = 1, 2, \ldots, S$, the fuzzification of the usual cost function used is

$$E = \tfrac{1}{2} \sum_{p=1}^{S} (Y_p - T_p)^2,\qquad(20.128)$$

where fuzzy arithmetic is used to obtain E, which is a fuzzy number. We wish to derive a learning algorithm that will drive E to zero. However, E will not be zero because of fuzzy subtraction even when $Y_p = T_p$ for all p. Hence, a stopping condition must be defined. Suppose the support of T_p is the interval $[t_{p1}, t_{p2}]$, $1 \le p \le S$. Then if $Y_p = T_p$ for all p, the support of E is the interval $[-\lambda, \lambda]$ where

$$\lambda = \tfrac{1}{2} \sum_{p=1}^{S} (t_{p2} - t_{p1})^2.\qquad(20.129)$$

Now let $\epsilon > 0$ denote some acceptable deviation from the value of E when $Y_p = T_p$ for all p. Then the stopping condition to end the weight-updating iteration can be defined as

$$E \subset \Omega = [-\lambda - \epsilon, \lambda + \epsilon] \times [0, 1],\qquad(20.130)$$

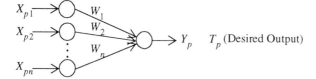

Figure 20.24 Neural network with fuzzy inputs, fuzzy output, and fuzzy weights.

which is illustrated in Fig. 20.25. With the stopping condition being defined, the following learning algorithm is performed until this stopping condition is met:

$$W_i(t+1) = W_i(t) - \eta \frac{\partial E}{\partial W_i}, \qquad i = 1, 2,\ldots, n, \qquad (20.131)$$

where η is a real-number learning rate. To evaluate the derivative in Eq. (20.131), we just differentiate as if E and W were real numbers and then replace the real numbers by fuzzy sets E, W_i, Y_p, T_p, and X_{pi},

$$\frac{\partial E}{\partial W_i} = \sum_{p=1}^{S} (Y_p - T_p)(Y_p)(1 - Y_p) X_{pi}. \qquad (20.132)$$

Equations (20.131) and (20.132) give us the fuzzified delta rule. This is a purely formal derivation because the fuzzy derivative indicated in Eq. (20.131) is not really performed.

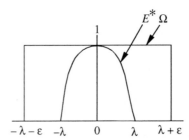

Figure 20.25 Stopping condition in Eq. (20.130), that is, stop when error E is in rectangle Ω, where E^* is the value of E when $Y_p = T_p$ for all p.

20.3.3 Fuzzy Control for Learning Parameter Adaptation

In this section, we use fuzzy control concepts and techniques to adaptively determine learning parameters in neural networks such that the performance of the neural networks will be improved. A general architecture for such systems proposed by Choi et al. [1992a] is shown in Fig. 20.26. The on-line fuzzy controller is used to adapt the value of a learning parameter according to certain heuristics. This in turn results in a change in the network performance attribute. By adaptively updating the value of the learning parameter, we arrive at the

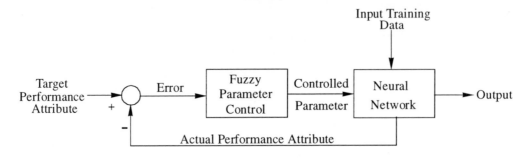

Figure 20.26 System using a fuzzy controller for the adaptation of neural learning parameters.

desired value of the performance attribute. There is usually an attribute of the neural network that we wish to control. For example, in the ART1 neural network, it is the number of classes; in the back-propagation network, it is the training error. The difference between the target and the actual attributes is fed into the fuzzy parameter controller which then determines on-line a proper value for the learning parameter(s) of a neural network. The learning parameter, for example, for ART1 is the vigilance, and for the back-propagation network they are the step size and the momentum parameter. We shall specifically discuss the use of fuzzy control for determining the learning parameters in ART1 and back-propagation networks to illustrate this scheme.

Fuzzy control of back-propagation networks. A general weight update rule in the back-propagation algorithm is

$$\Delta \mathbf{w} (t + 1) = -\alpha \nabla E (\mathbf{w} (t)) + \eta \Delta \mathbf{w} (t), \qquad (20.133)$$

where E is the cost function, α is the learning rate, and η is the momentum gain. The objective here is to design a fuzzy controller for automatic tuning of the learning parameters based on the shape of the error surface in order to achieve faster convergence. For instance, several fuzzy IF-THEN rules in such a fuzzy controller are listed below, where the change in error, CE, is an approximation of the gradient and the change in CE, CCE, is the second-order gradient information which is related to the acceleration of convergence.

- IF CE is small with no sign changes in several consecutive time steps, THEN the value of the learning parameter should be increased.
- IF sign changes occur in CE for several consecutive time steps, THEN the value of the learning parameter should be reduced with no regard to the value of CCE.
- If CE is very small AND CCE is very small, with no sign change for several consecutive time steps, THEN the value of the learning parameter as well as the momentum gain should be increased.

To quantify the sign changes in the above heuristic rules, the following *sign change parameter* is defined:

$$\text{SC} (t) = 1 - \left\| \tfrac{1}{2} \left[\text{sgn} (\text{CE} (t - 1)) + \text{sgn} (E (t)) \right] \right\|, \qquad (20.134)$$

where $\text{sgn}(\cdot)$ is the sign function and the factor $\tfrac{1}{2}$ is to ensure SC to be either 0 (no sign change) or 1 (one sign change). The cumulative sum of SC, denoted by CSC, thus can reflect the history of sign change; that is,

$$\text{CSC} (t) = \text{SC} (t) + \text{SC} (t - 1) + \text{SC} (t - 2) + \cdots. \qquad (20.135)$$

The bigger the CSC, the more frequently the sign changes have occurred. Since a five-step tracking of the sign changes is used, we define

$$\text{CSC} (t) = \sum_{m=t-4}^{t} \text{SC} (m). \qquad (20.136)$$

The complete fuzzy rules for control of the back-propagation algorithm are shown in Table 20.3.

TABLE 20.3 Decision Tables for Fuzzy Control of the Back-propagation Algorithm*

CCE \ CE	NB	NS	ZE	PS	PB
NB	NS	NS	NS	NS	NS
NS	NS	ZE	PS	ZE	NS
ZE	ZE	PS	PS	PS	ZE
PS	NS	ZE	PS	ZE	NS
PB	NS	NS	NS	NS	NS

(a)

CCE \ CE	NL	NL	ZE	PS	PL
NL	-0.01	-0.01	—	—	—
NS	-0.01	—	—	—	—
ZE	—	0.01	0.01	0.01	—
PS	—	—	—	—	-0.01
PL	—	—	—	-0.01	-0.01·

(b)

*(a) Decision table for the fuzzy control of learning rate α. Table contents represent the value of the fuzzy variable $\Delta\alpha$ for a given choice of values for CE and CCE, for $CSC(t) \leq 2$. (b) Decision table for the fuzzy control of momentum gain η. Table contents represent the value of the fuzzy variable $\Delta\eta$ for a given choice of values for CE and CCE, where — denotes no adaptation. The maximum value that η can take on is set to 1.

NB, Negative Big; NS, Negative Small; ZE, Zero; PS, Positive Small; PB, Positive Big.

The fuzzy values that CE and CCE can take on are defined in Fig. 20.27. From the tables, for instance, one can read the following rule:

IF CE is Negative Small and CCE is Zero, THEN $\Delta\alpha$ is Positive Small.

Simulation results have shown that fuzzy control back propagation results in dramatically faster convergence than regular back propagation.

Fuzzy control of ART1. In the ART1 network, as discussed in Sec. 12.4, the number of clusters formed directly depends on the value of the vigilance parameter ρ. The higher the value of ρ, the greater the number of clusters required to represent the input data. In applications where the number of desired clusters is known in advance, the value of ρ can be incrementally changed such that complete classification into the fixed number of clusters can be finally achieved. Choi et al. [1992a] designed a fuzzy controller to control the incremental updating of the value of ρ when the number of clusters is known.

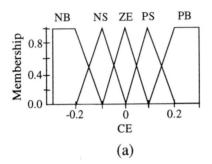

(a)

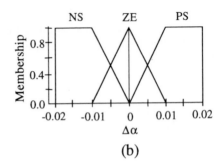

(b)

Figure 20.27 Membership functions defined for fuzzy control of the back-propagation algorithm. (a) Membership functions for CE. The same membership functions are used for CCE. NB, Negative Big; NS, Negative Small; ZE, Zero; PS, Positive Small; PB, Positive Big. (b) Membership functions for $\Delta\alpha$.

Assume that the desired number of clusters is N_d, which is known a priori. The fuzzy control process of ART1 is outlined here. First, the set of all input vectors is presented to the ART1 and classified accordingly into N_a (actual) classes. If $N_a \neq N_d$, then some adjustment of the vigilance parameter followed by another presentation of the input data is required. For example, if $N_a < N_d$, then ρ should be increased, and if $N_a > N_d$, then ρ should be decreased. The job of the fuzzy vigilance controller is to determine the magnitude of the change in ρ, $\Delta\rho$, that will let N_a approach N_d. The controller will seek to regulate the value of the vigilance parameter based on how far we are from achieving N_d classes, having started out with N_a clusters. The fuzzy rules for this application are shown in Table 20.4. The fuzzy values of E and CE are defined in Fig. 20.28. Here $E = N_d - N_a$ and CE is the change in E. Following the controller's updating of the value of ρ by $\delta\rho$, the ART1 network performs a second classification with the new value of ρ. This process continues until N_a equals N_d, at which point the classification process is over.

TABLE 20.4 Decision Table for Fuzzy Control of the ART1*

E \\ CE	NB	NS	ZE	PS	PB
NB	—	NS	ZE	PS	—
NS	NB	NS	ZE	PS	PB
ZE	NB	NS	ZE	PS	PB
PS	NB	NS	ZE	PS	PB
PB	—	NS	ZE	PS	—

*Table contents represent the value of the fuzzy variable $\delta\rho$ for given values of $E = N_d - N_a$ and CE.

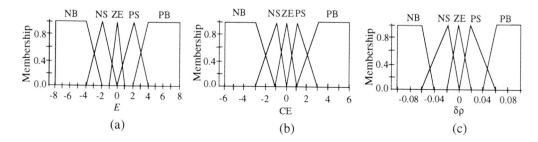

(a) (b) (c)

Figure 20.28 Membership functions defined for fuzzy control of the ART1. (a) Membership functions for E. (b) Membership functions for CE. (c) Membership functions for $\delta\rho$.

20.4 CONCLUDING REMARKS

In addition to the three types of fuzzy neurons discussed in this chapter, Yager [1992b] proposed a special class of fuzzy neurons of type I, called *OWA fuzzy neurons*. This fuzzy neuron is based on OWA aggregation operators. Lee and Lee [1975] proposed special type II fuzzy neurons that constitute the first fuzzy neural network described in the literature. Lee's fuzzy neuron is a generalization of the McCulloch-Pitts model. It can be shown that Lee's fuzzy neural network is a finite fuzzy automaton (FFA). For fuzzy neurons of type III, Kocha and Yager [1992] introduced a fuzzy weight for each precondition term such that different pieces of information can have different importance.

Considering the fuzzification of existing neural networks, we can obtain the fuzzy pocket algorithm by fuzzifying the original pocket algorithm [Gallant, 1990] in the same way as we did for the fuzzy perceptron. Kosko [1986, 1992] proposed *fuzzy cognitive maps* (FCMs) that are fuzzy signed-directed graphs with feedback used to represent causal reasoning by using numerical processing. FCMs led to the development of FAMs. Modified FCMs can be found in [Hagiwara, 1992]. Bahrami et al. [1991] proposed a strategy, called *triggering and conflict resolution strategy,* for choosing the most appropriate FAM rule for performing inference to obtain the final result for a given input pattern. Lee and Lai [1993] proposed a generalized fuzzy ART that can handle supervised learning and unsupervised learning simultaneously such that the training instances may or may not have desired outputs at any time. Linkens and Nie [1993] developed *fuzzy radial basis function networks* (FRBFNs) for representing the rule-based fuzzy knowledge and performing the associated fuzzy reasoning. Kuo et al. [1993] created a fuzzified probabilistic neural network (FPNN) by replacing the statistical function in the original network by a fuzzy measure function in the FPNN.

Extending the concept of neural networks with fuzzy teaching input in Sec. 20.3.1, Lin and Lu [1995, 1996] proposed neural fuzzy system learning with linguistic teaching signals. This system is able to process and learn numerical information as well as linguistic information by performing fuzzy supervised learning or fuzzy reinforcement learning. It can be used either as an *adaptive fuzzy expert system* or as an *adaptive fuzzy controller.* In applying fuzzy logic to assist in the learning of neural networks, Xu et al. [1992] used FAMs to implement the two crucial components in back-propagation networks, the self-adjusting learning rate and activation functions.

20.5 PROBLEMS

20.1 Consider the following problems involving type I fuzzy neurons.
  (a) What are the advantages and disadvantages of using a fuzzy neural network like the one in Fig. 20.3 to realize a fuzzy logic controller?
  (b) Use a fuzzy neural network like the one in Fig. 20.3 to realize a fuzzy logic controller that has 2 input variables, 1 output variable, and 20 fuzzy rules with 11 different consequents. Draw the structure of this network. What is the total number of nodes in this network?

20.2 This problem is to use type II fuzzy neurons for system identification. Assume that the system to be identified has the following quadratic input-output relationship:

$$AX^2 + BXY + CY^2 = Z,$$

where X, Y are inputs and Z is the output of the system, and A, B, C are triangular fuzzy numbers described by $A = [a_1, a_2, a_3]$, $B = [b_1, b_2, b_3]$, $C = [c_1, c_2, c_3]$. We are given training pairs $((X_k, Y_k), Z_k^d)$, $k = 1, 2,...,p$, where $X_k = [x_{k1}, x_{k2}, x_{k3}]$, $Y_k = [y_{k1}, y_{k2}, y_{k3}]$, and $Z_k^d = [z_{k1}^d, z_{k2}^d, z_{k3}^d]$ are triangular fuzzy numbers, where $x_{k1} \geq 0$ and $y_{k1} \geq 0$. Assume that A is negative (i.e., $a_3 < 0$) and B and C are positive (i.e., $b_1 > 0$, $c_1 > 0$). Define the cost function as $E = \frac{1}{2} \sum_{k=1}^{p} \sum_{i=1}^{3} (z_{ki} - z_{ki}^d)^2$. The problem is to tune a_i, b_i, and c_i ($1 \leq i \leq 3$) to minimize E.

(a) Show that the network outputs $Z_k = [z_{k1}, z_{k2}, z_{k3}]$ are with triangular shape involving polynomial functions for the given training input data.

(b) Derive the equations for computing z_{k1}, z_{k2}, and z_{k3} at the α-cuts of $\alpha = 0$ and $\alpha = 1$, respectively.

(c) Derive the learning rules for tuning a_i, b_i, and c_i.

(d) Perform simulations on a simple example to verify the derived learning rules.

20.3 In Theorem 10.1 we showed that if two sets of vectors are linearly separable, the perceptron learning algorithm is guaranteed to find a separating hyperplane in a finite number of steps. Does this theorem hold for the fuzzy perceptron learning algorithm? Prove or justify your answer.

20.4 Consider the following patterns from two classes in a two-dimensional pattern space:

$$\{[-3, -2]^T, [0.5, -3]^T, [-4, -2]^T, [2, 1.5]^T, [-2, -1]^T, [-0.5, 4]^T\}: \text{class 1},$$

$$\{[4, 2.5]^T, [3.5, -3]^T, [0.5, 2.5]^T, [3, -1.5]^T, [-1, 2.5]^T, [2.5, 3]^T\}: \text{class 2}.$$

Classify these patterns using (a) the perceptron learning algorithm and (b) the fuzzy perceptron learning algorithm. Compare the classification rates and the learning speed of these algorithms.

20.5 What are the advantages of the fuzzy back-propagation network over the traditional back-propagation network? Under what situations should we use fuzzy back-propagation networks rather than traditional back-propagation networks, and vice versa?

20.6 Consider the butterfly data in Fig. 8.3. Let the patterns $\{x_1, x_2, x_3, x_4, x_5, x_6, x_8\}$ belong to class 1 and the patterns $\{x_7, x_9, x_{10}, x_{11}, x_{12}, x_{13}, x_{14}, x_{15}\}$ belong to class 2. Perform fuzzy classification on these patterns with a back-propagation network by writing a program to realize the algorithms introduced in Sec. 20.2.2.

20.7 Assume fuzzy sets $A = (0.3, 0.8, 0.1, 0.1, 0.6)$ and $B = (0.9, 0.3, 0.5, 0.2)$.

(a) Find the fuzzy outer-product Hebbian FAM correlation matrix $M = A^T \circ B$ using correlation-minimum encoding.

(b) Verify that $A \circ M = B$ and $B \circ M^T = A$.

(c) Pass $A' = (0.4, 1, 0.3, 0.2, 0.6)$ through M and $B' = (0.7, 0.4, 0.6, 0.4)$ through M^T. Compare the recalled fuzzy sets to B and A, respectively.

(d) Repeat parts (a)–(c) using correlation-product encoding.

20.8 **(a)** Complete the proofs of Theorems 20.1 and 20.2.

(b) Let $M = A^T \circ B$. Show that if $B \circ M^T = A$ and $B \subset B'$, then $B' \circ M^T = A$. Show that this is also true for correlation-product encoding.

20.9 **(a)** ART2 can classify "analog" input patterns, while fuzzy ART can classify input patterns with values between 0 and 1. State the differences between and advantages of ART2 and fuzzy ART.

(b) Explain in detail the advantages of the two options of fuzzy ART: *fast-commit–slow-recode* and *input normalization*. In particular, why can the input normalization prevent the problem of category proliferation that may occur in ART2?

20.10 Write a program for implementing the fuzzy ART algorithm and run the fuzzy ART complement-coding simulation with $a \cong 0$, $\beta = 1$, $\rho = 0.4$, and input vectors $\mathbf{a}^{(t)}$ selected at random from the unit square. Compare the results to those shown in Fig. 20.12.

20.11 **(a)** Show that the learning rates $\{\alpha_{ij}\} = \{(u_{ij})^{m_t}\}$ in the FKCN learning algorithm have the properties indicated in Eqs. (20.68)–(20.70).

(b) Which is more similar to the KCN algorithm, the partial FKCN learning algorithm or the FKCN learning algorithm? Which is more similar to the FCM algorithm, the partial FKCN learning algorithm or the FKCN learning algorithm? Justify your answers.

20.12 Derive the learning algorithm for the fuzzy RCE neural network if bell-shaped membership functions, instead of the triangular membership functions in Eq. (20.71), are used for each prototype node.

20.13 CMACs as well as FCMAC are usually used as controllers. Compare the functionalities of the FCMAC with those of the standard fuzzy controller and specify the advantages and disadvantages of the FCMAC over the standard fuzzy controller.

20.14 Write a program for implementing the back-propagation learning algorithm specified in Sec. 20.3.1 for feedforward neural networks with fuzzy teaching input. Use the developed program to redo Example 20.8.

20.15 Develop a fuzzy control scheme for learning parameter adaptation of the Kohonen feature map network. The learning parameters include learning constant and neighborhood size.

21

Fuzzy Neural Systems for Pattern Recognition

We discussed some techniques for fuzzy pattern recognition in Sec. 8.1 and examined several neural network models suitable for pattern recognition in Part II of this book. In this chapter, we shall focus on fuzzy-neural integrated models for pattern recognition. In fact, we have studied several fuzzy neural models for pattern recognition in Chap. 20. For fuzzy neural classification, we have considered fuzzy perceptrons, back-propagation networks for fuzzy classifiers, fuzzy RCE neural networks, and back-propagation networks with fuzzy teaching input. For fuzzy neural clustering, we have discussed fuzzy ART, the fuzzy Kohonen clustering network, and fuzzy competitive learning rules. We shall explore more fuzzy neural models for pattern recognition in this chapter, including fuzzy neural classifiers, fuzzy neural clustering networks, and fuzzy neural models for data acquisition and feature selection. Unlike the fuzzy neural models discussed in Chap. 20, most of the fuzzy-neural integrated models considered here are not based on the fuzzification of existing neural network models.

21.1 FUZZY NEURAL CLASSIFICATION

21.1.1 Uncertainties with Two-Class Fuzzy Neural Classification Boundaries

In fuzzy classification, we usually replace the original sharp decision boundaries by fuzzy decision boundaries described by proper membership functions called *fuzzy boundary membership functions*. Consider a two-class classification problem. Suppose we have a membership function $\mu_{C_1}(\mathbf{x})$ that represents the membership of $\mathbf{x}$ in class 1, where $\mathbf{x}$ is a

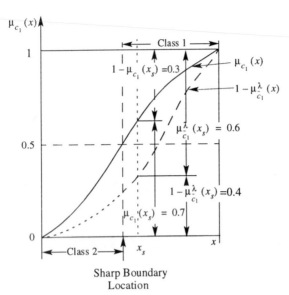

Figure 21.1 Fuzzy boundary membership function in two-class classification problems. (Adapted from Archer and Wang [1991], © 1991 IEEE.)

point with n attribute dimensions. For illustration, the membership function $\mu_{C_1}(x)$ in the case of $n = 1$ is depicted as the solid curve in Fig. 21.1. Note that when n is greater than 1, $\mu_{C_1}(\mathbf{x})$ is a surface or hypersurface. To accommodate the fuzzy boundary membership function to a sharp classification boundary, let

$$\begin{cases} \mathbf{x} \in C_1 & \text{when } \mu_{C_1}(\mathbf{x}) \geq 0.5 \\ \mathbf{x} \in C_2 & \text{otherwise.} \end{cases} \tag{21.1}$$

Hence, the values of x that satisfy $\mu_{C_1}(x) = 0.5$ define the sharp classification boundary (see Fig. 21.1). These points are the crossover points. To make Eq. (21.1) meaningful, we must ensure that the membership function $\mu_{C_1}(\mathbf{x})$ is monotonic. Hence, we assume that all the membership functions considered in this section are monotonic.

The value of a fuzzy boundary membership function emphasizes the extent to which a point in the space deviates from the sharp boundary. However, it does not provide information about the overlapping of the data sets in addition to misclassification. To see the importance of this information, let us consider the two-class classification problem in Fig. 21.2 where a sharp linear boundary separates the pattern space into two regions. Clearly, the sharp boundary itself reveals nothing about the statistical behavior of the sample data distributions. For example, the two very different sample populations in Fig. 21.2 can theoretically result in the same classification boundary. In sample population 1, observations are widely distributed over the pattern space and there is a large overlapping between the two data set classes, but in sample population 2 there is very little overlapping. Note that this problem exists for any sharp boundary functions, including those implemented by neural networks as simple feature vector extractors. Hence, information reflecting the overlapping of data classes must be provided.

In order to provide information about uncertainty based on both factors of potential misclassification (e.g., distance to the sharp boundary) and existing misclassification (e.g., degree of overlapping of the two classes in the training sample data), two membership func-

Fuzzy Neural Systems for Pattern Recognition   Chap. 21

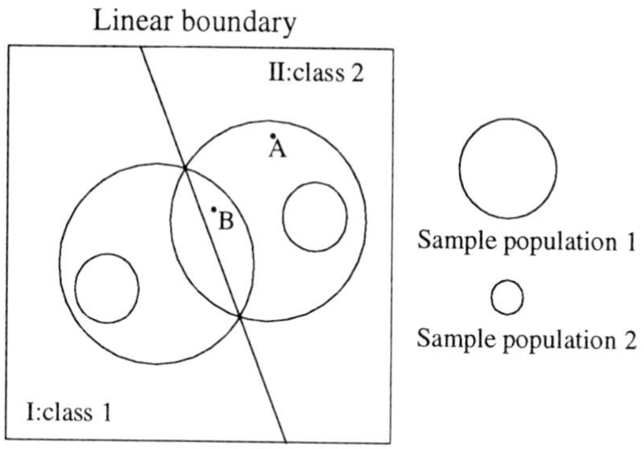

Figure 21.2 Sharp decision boundary in the two-class classification problems.

tions are needed in order to provide more complete information for classification of a new observation. One of these functions evaluates how far the new observation is from the sharp boundary and emphasizes its "possible" membership. A second fuzzy membership function specifies the overlap degree of the two data sets, revealing information about "necessity." For example, we expect to get information like this: "The sample point $\mathbf{x}_s$ is *possible* to be in class 1 with a membership grade of 0.7, and it is *necessary* to be in class 1 with a membership grade of 0.4."

Since we are concerned with the possibility and necessity that a sample point $\mathbf{x}_s$ belongs to class C_i $(i = 1, 2)$, let us view the two classes C_1 and C_2 as crisp subsets and recall the properties of possibility measures $\Pi(C_i)$ and necessity measures $N(C_i)$, discussed in Sec. 4.1.3. Since possibility and necessity measures are special types of plausibility and belief measures, respectively, we have [from Eq. (4.10)]

$$N(C_i) + N(\overline{C}_i) \leq 1, \qquad i = 1, 2, \tag{21.2}$$

which means that a lack of necessity (belief) in $\mathbf{x}_s \in C_i$ (e.g., C_1) does not imply a strong necessity (belief) in $\mathbf{x}_s \in \overline{C}_i$ (e.g., $\overline{C}_1 = C_2$). On the other hand, from Eq. (4.16) we have

$$\Pi(C_i) + \Pi(\overline{C}_i) \geq 1, \qquad i = 1, 2, \tag{21.3}$$

meaning that "$\mathbf{x}_s \in C_i$ is possible" does not necessary imply "$\mathbf{x}_s \in \overline{C}_i$ is impossible." In addition, from Eq. (4.43) we have

$$\Pi(C_i) \geq N(C_i), \qquad i = 1, 2, \tag{21.4}$$

meaning that the membership degree (grade) with "$\mathbf{x}_s \in C_i$ is possible" is always greater than that with "$\mathbf{x}_s \in \overline{C}_i$ is necessary." This complies with our intuitive thinking. Finally and most importantly, Eq. (4.40) indicates that

$$N(C_i) = 1 - \Pi(\overline{C}_i), \qquad i = 1, 2, \tag{21.5}$$

which indicates how to determine the necessity measure from the possibility measure.

From Eq. (21.5), we know that the membership grade "$\mathbf{x}_s \in C_i$ is necessary" is equal to 1 minus the grade "$\mathbf{x}_s \in \overline{C}_i$ is possible." To do this computation, we need to find the membership function of $\overline{C}_i$, $\mu_{\overline{C}_i}(\mathbf{x})$. Here we shall adopt a more general expression of fuzzy complementation, the λ complement [see Eq. (2.52)] proposed by Sugeno, that is,

$$\mu_{\overline{C}_i}^{\lambda}(\mathbf{x}) = \frac{1 - \mu_{C_i}(\mathbf{x})}{1 + \lambda \mu_{C_i}(\mathbf{x})}, \qquad \lambda > -1, \tag{21.6}$$

where λ is a parameter. Based on existing misclassifications, we can then supplement a fuzzy boundary membership function $\mu_{C_i}(\mathbf{x})$ with another membership function $\mu_{\overline{C}_i}^{\lambda}(\mathbf{x})$, which is a λ complement of $\mu_{C_i}(\mathbf{x})$. This provides more information about the uncertainty caused by misclassification. The function $[1 - \mu_{\overline{C}_i}^{\lambda}(\mathbf{x})]$ is depicted in Fig. 21.1 by the dotted line. From Eq. (21.5), we know that the value of the function $[1 - \mu_{\overline{C}_i}^{\lambda}(\mathbf{x})]$ indicates the grade that a pattern $\mathbf{x}$ is *necessary* (*believed*) to be in class C_i. As an illustration, consider the pattern x_s in the figure. Since $\mu_{C_1}(x_s) = 0.7 > \mu_{C_2}(x_s) = 1 - \mu_{C_1}(x_s) = 0.3$, we thus say that the pattern x_s is possible to be in class 1 with grade $\mu_{C_1}(x_s) = 0.7$ and is necessary to be in class 1 with grade $1 - \mu_{\overline{C}_1}^{\lambda}(x_s) = 0.4$. Similarly, when a pattern $x_{s'}$ is determined to be in C_2 based on the sharp boundary [i.e., $\mu_{C_2}(x_{s'}) = 1 - \mu_{C_1}(x_{s'}) > \mu_{C_1}(x_{s'})$], then we interpret that $x_{s'}$ is possible to be in class 2 with grade $\mu_{C_2}(x_{s'})$ and $x_{s'}$ is necessary to be in class 2 with grade $[1 - \mu_{\overline{C}_2}^{\lambda}(x_{s'})]$. The four functions, $\mu_{C_1}(x)$, $\mu_{C_2}(x)$, $[1 - \mu_{\overline{C}_1}^{\lambda}(x)]$, and $[1 - \mu_{\overline{C}_2}^{\lambda}(x)]$ are depicted in Fig. 21.3. For convenience, the two functions $\mu_{C_1}(x)$ and $[1 - \mu_{\overline{C}_1}^{\lambda}(x)]$ are depicted based on the $[x - \mu_{C_1}(x)]$ coordinate (i.e., the left y axis), and the other two functions, $\mu_{C_2}(x)$ and $[1 - \mu_{\overline{C}_2}^{\lambda}(x)]$, are drawn based on the $[x - \mu_{C_2}(x)]$ coordinate (i.e., the right y axis). This is why the curves of $\mu_{C_1}(x)$ and $\mu_{C_2}(x)$ coincide in Fig. 21.3.

To perform the above computations, we need to find the λ value in Eq. (21.6). Generally, the value λ differs from one person to another depending on the individual's subjectivity. However, one possible guideline is as follows. The initial selection of λ may be based on the ratio of the numbers of misclassifications needed to correct classifications. We may define extreme cases, where $\lambda = -1$ when the numbers of misclassifications and correct classifications are equal [in this case, the two data sets totally overlap and $\mu_{\overline{C}}^{\lambda}(\mathbf{x}) = 1$, which means that we never believe that an observation belongs to either class], and $\lambda = 0$ when no

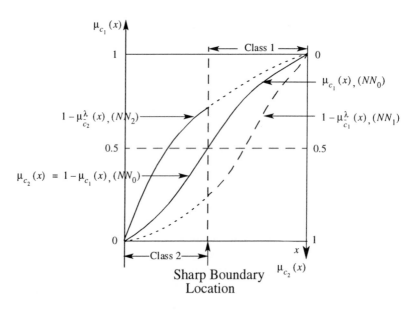

Figure 21.3 Fuzzy boundary membership functions implemented in conjunction with neural network classification. (Adapted from Archer and Wang [1991], © 1991 IEEE.)

Fuzzy Neural Systems for Pattern Recognition   Chap. 21

when no misclassification is observed [in this case, $\mu_{\bar{C}}^{\lambda}(\mathbf{x}) = 1 - \mu_C(\mathbf{x})$, which means that we should accept the sharp boundary]. Thus, λ is normally in the range of $-1 < \lambda < 0$.

According to the above analysis, two fuzzy boundary membership functions [i.e., $\mu_C(\mathbf{x})$ and $\mu_{\bar{C}}^{\lambda}(\mathbf{x})$] provide better uncertainty information than a single fuzzy boundary membership function in the two-class classification problem when both factors of potential misclassification and existing misclassification are taken into account. Since a backpropagation network (BP net) can learn to function as a membership function, a neural network model would be able to provide more complete information about uncertainty in terms of membership functions. Such a neural network model, called the *neural fuzzy membership model* (NFMM), has been proposed by Archer and Wang [1991]. The NFMM consists of three individual BP nets, each of which corresponds to one of the membership functions shown in Fig. 21.3. An algorithm for implementing the NFMM is stated below.

Algorithm NFMM: Neural Fuzzy Membership Model [Archer and Wang, 1991]

Step 1: Based on given training samples, train a BP net to find a monotonic membership function that determines a sharp classification boundary according to Eq. (21.1) and denote this BP net as NN_0. This can be done by first finding the sharp boundary using a BP net and then determining the proper fuzzy boundary membership function according to the distance of each pattern point from this sharp boundary. Note that the points on the sharp boundary should form the crossover points of this fuzzy boundary membership function.

Step 2: Find misclassification sets M_{C_1} and M_{C_2} such that $\mathbf{x}_m \in M_{C_1}$ if misclassified point $\mathbf{x}_m$ is in the C_1 region (i.e., $\mathbf{x}_m \in C_2$ but is misclassified to be in C_1) and $\mathbf{x}_m \in M_{C_2}$ if misclassified point $\mathbf{x}_m$ is in the C_2 region. If M_{C_1} and M_{C_2} are empty, this means that there is no information available regarding the fuzzy nature of the given problem and the sharp boundary must be accepted; else go to the next step to develop the fuzzy boundary.

Step 3: Based on the ratio of the number of misclassifications needed to correct classification, determine λ subjectively so that $-1 < \lambda < 0$.

Step 4: For each $\mathbf{x}_m \in M_{C_1}$ or M_{C_2}, compute the corresponding outputs of the neural network NN_0, denoted by $y(\mathbf{x}_m)$.

Step 5: Normalize the membership value for these misclassified points so that the λ complement [Eq. (21.6)] is applicable:

$$y'(\mathbf{x}_m) = \frac{y(\mathbf{x}_m) - y_{\min}}{y_{\max} - y_{\min}}, \tag{21.7}$$

where $y_{\max}$ and $y_{\min}$ are the extreme output values of NN_0.

Step 6: For each misclassified point $\mathbf{x}_m$ assign

$$\begin{cases} y'_{C_1}(\mathbf{x}_m) = y'(\mathbf{x}_m) & \text{if } \mathbf{x}_m \in M_{C_1} \\ y'_{C_2}(\mathbf{x}_m) = 1 - y'(\mathbf{x}_m) & \text{if } \mathbf{x}_m \in M_{C_2}. \end{cases} \tag{21.8}$$

Step 7: Calculate λ-complement values for the misclassified points

$$y_{\bar{C_1}}^{\lambda'}(\mathbf{x}_m) = 1 - \frac{1 - y'_{C_1}(\mathbf{x}_m)}{1 + \lambda y'_{C_1}(\mathbf{x}_m)}, \tag{21.9}$$

$$y_{\overline{C_2}}^{\lambda'}(\mathbf{x}_m) = \frac{1 - y_{C_2}'(\mathbf{x}_m)}{1 + \lambda y_{C_2}'(\mathbf{x}_m)} . \tag{21.10}$$

Step 8: Denormalize $y_{\overline{C_1}}^{\lambda'}(\mathbf{x}_m)$ and $y_{\overline{C_2}}^{\lambda'}(\mathbf{x}_m)$ for neural network learning purposes:

$$y_{\overline{C_i}}^{\lambda}(\mathbf{x}_m) = y_{\overline{C_i}}^{\lambda'}(\mathbf{x}_m)\,[y_{\max} - y_{\min}] + y_{\min}. \tag{21.11}$$

Step 9: Train the BP net NN_1 (with the same topology as NN_0 and the same extreme output values $y_{\max}$ and $y_{\min}$) with the sample set M_{C_1} such that each sample point has the λ-complement value $y_{\overline{C_i}}^{\lambda}(\mathbf{x}_m)$.

Step 10: Repeat step 9 for the BP net NN_2, and it is trained with the sample set M_{C_2}.

END NFMM

The NFMM implemented by algorithm NFMM consisting of NN_0, NN_1, and NN_2 will provide more information about fuzzy uncertainty in pattern classification. The following example illustrates the NFMM.

Example 21.1

[Archer and Wang, 1991]. Figure 21.4 shows an experimental result using simulated data. Since the pattern vector $\mathbf{x}$ has two dimensions, the fuzzy boundary membership functions represented by the y surface of the BP nets are three-dimensional in this case. Hence, contour lines are used to represent the two complement membership functions in the figure. A value of λ is subjectively selected as -0.3 for this application.

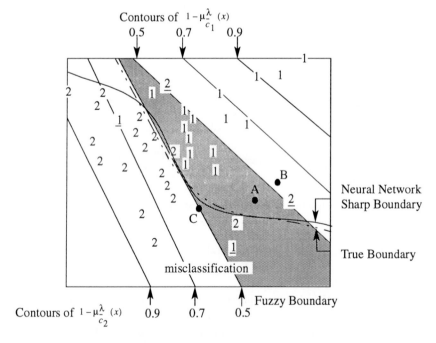

Figure 21.4 Fuzzy boundary membership functions in Example 21.1.

Figure 21.4 shows three groups of lines. The first one is the sharp boundary (shown to be close to the true boundary) representing the BP net NN_0. Any new observation in the pattern space is assigned a possibility value (classification score) by the network NN_0. This classification score indicates the possibility of the new observation belonging to one of the two classes. For example, according to NN_0, point A (0.8, 0.3) is classified as class 1 with a classification score of 0.55, which means that A possibly belongs to class 1 with a grade of 0.55. On the other side of the sharp boundary, point C (0.5, 0.3) is assigned by NN_0 with a classification score of 0.45, which only means that C possibly belongs to class 2 with a grade of 0.55. (Note that we do not discuss the issue of C belonging to class 1 here). The second group of lines are contours of $[1 - \mu_{\overline{C}_1}^\lambda(\mathbf{x})]$ generated by NN_1. They represent the necessity (belief) that a new observation belongs to class 1, given that the new observation is classified as class 1 according to the sharp boundary. For example, according to the complement fuzzy boundary membership function as shown in the contours of $[1 - \mu_{\overline{C}_1}^\lambda(\mathbf{x})(\mathbf{x})]$, A is believed to belong to class 1 with a grade of 0.4, which indicates the high uncertainty of A belonging to class 1 caused by the influence of misclassifications. On the other hand, point B (0.85, 0.4) is classified as class 1 with more certainty. The neural network NN_0 represented by the sharp boundary assigns B with a possibility grade of 0.65, and the contours of $[1 - \mu_{\overline{C}_1}^\lambda(\mathbf{x})(\mathbf{x})]$ representing NN_1 assign B with a belief of 0.55. Both are greater than 0.5. The third group of lines are contours of $[1 - \mu_{\overline{C}_2}^\lambda(\mathbf{x})(\mathbf{x})]$ generated by NN_2. They represent the belief that a new observation belongs to class 2, given that the new observation is classified as class 2 according to the sharp boundary. For example, though C possibly belongs to class 2 with a grade of 0.55, it is believed to belong to class 2 with a grade of 0.5 as shown in the contours of $[1 - \mu_{\overline{C}_2}^\lambda(\mathbf{x})(\mathbf{x})]$, which means that C is in a critical status because of the influence of miscalculations. From Fig. 21.4 one may see that, in the unshaded regions, the membership of a new observation is more certain than observations in the shaded region that might be considered a "fuzzy boundary" for a particular λ value. Within the shaded region, the necessity functions for both classes 1 and 2 are less than 0.5.

21.1.2 Multilayer Fuzzy Neural Classification Networks

A general concept of using multilayer fuzzy neural networks as pattern classifiers is to create fuzzy subsets of the pattern space in the hidden layer and then aggregate the subsets to form a final decision in the output layer. In this section, we shall introduce a fuzzy neural network classifier that creates classes by aggregating several smaller fuzzy sets into a single fuzzy set class. This classifier is called the *fuzzy min-max classification neural network* and was proposed by Simpson [1992b]. It is constructed using *hyperbox fuzzy sets,* each of which is an n-dimensional box defined by a min point and a max point with a corresponding membership function. The hyperbox fuzzy sets are aggregated to form a single fuzzy set class. Learning in this network is performed by determining proper min-max points or, equivalently, by properly placing and adjusting hyperboxes in the pattern space. This concept is quite similar to that of the fuzzy ART network introduced in Sec. 20.2.4 and to that of the FALCON-ART introduced in Sec. 19.5.2. The fuzzy ART network, the FALCON-ART, and the fuzzy min-max classification neural network all utilize hyperbox fuzzy sets as the fundamental computing element.

A diagram of a min-max hyperbox B_j in $\Re^3$ is shown in Fig. 21.5, where the min point $\mathbf{v}_j$ and the max point $\mathbf{w}_j$ are all that is required to define the hyperbox. We assume that the range along each dimension of a hyperbox is normalized from 0 to 1; hence the pattern space is the n-dimensional unit cube I^n. A membership function is associated with the hyperbox that determines the degree to which any point $\mathbf{x} \in \Re^3$ is contained within the box.

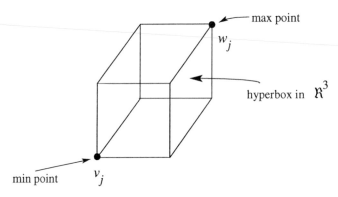

Figure 21.5   Min-max hyperbox $B_j = \{\mathbf{v}_j, \mathbf{w}_j\}$ in $\mathfrak{R}^3$.

A collection of these boxes forms a pattern class. As an example, the aggregation of several hyperboxes in I^2 is illustrated for a two-class problem in Fig. 21.6. It is noted that the hyperboxes between the classes are nonoverlapping. Let each hyperbox fuzzy set B_j be defined by the ordered set

$$B_j = \{\mathbf{x}, \mathbf{v}_j, \mathbf{w}_j, \mu_{B_j}(\mathbf{x}, \mathbf{v}_j, \mathbf{w}_j)\} \qquad \text{for all } \mathbf{x} \in I^n, \tag{21.12}$$

where $\mathbf{x}$ is an input pattern, $\mathbf{v}_j$ is the min point for B_j, $\mathbf{w}_j$ is the max point for B_j, and $\mu_{B_j}(\cdot)$ is the membership function of B_j. Then the aggregated fuzzy set that defines the kth pattern class C_k can be defined as

$$C_k = \bigcup_{j \in K} B_j \qquad \text{or} \qquad \mu_{C_k}(\mathbf{x}) = \max_{j \in K} \mu_{B_j}(\mathbf{x}), \tag{21.13}$$

where K is the index set of the hyperboxes associated with class C_k.

As for the membership function of the jth hyperbox $\mu_{B_j}(\mathbf{x})$, it must measure the degree to which the input pattern $\mathbf{x}$ falls outside the hyperbox B_j. This can be considered a measurement of how far each component is greater (less) than the max (min) point value along each dimension that falls outside the min-max bounds of the hyperbox. Also, as $\mu_{B_j}(\mathbf{x})$ approaches 1, the point should be more contained by the hyperbox, with the value 1 representing complete hyperbox containment. The function that meets these criteria is the sum of two complements—the average amount of max point violations and the average amount of min point violations. Such as membership function is defined as

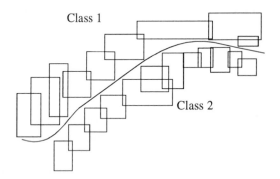

Figure 21.6   Example of fuzzy min-max hyperboxes places along the boundary of a two-class problem.

Fuzzy Neural Systems for Pattern Recognition   Chap. 21

$$\mu_{B_j}(\mathbf{x}) = \frac{1}{n}\sum_{i=1}^{n}[1 - f(x_i - w_{ji}, r) - f(v_{ji} - x_i, r)], \tag{21.14}$$

where $f(\cdot)$ is the two-parameter ramp threshold function

$$f(z, r) = \begin{cases} 1 & \text{if } zr > 1 \\ zr & \text{if } 0 \le zr \le 1 \\ 0 & \text{if } zr < 0, \end{cases} \tag{21.15}$$

where $\mathbf{x} = [x_1, x_2, \dots, x_n]^T \in I^n$ is the input pattern, $\mathbf{v}_j = [v_{j1}, v_{j2}, \dots, v_{jn}]^T$ is the min point for B_j, $\mathbf{w}_j = [w_{j1}, w_{j2}, \dots, w_{jn}]^T$ is the max point for B_j, and r is the sensitivity parameter that regulates how fast the membership values decrease as the distance between $\mathbf{x}$ and B_j increases. This membership function is also used in the FALCON-ART [see Eqs. (19.136) and (19.137)]. Illustrations of this function appear in Fig. 19.24.

The membership function given by Eq. (21.14) indicates that if an input pattern $\mathbf{x}$ falls in a hyperbox B_j, it gets full membership about B_j, that is, $\mu_{B_j}(\mathbf{x}) = 1$. The membership value decreases as it moves further away from B_j. Hence, although the learning algorithm described below allows overlapping hyperboxes from the same class and eliminates the overlapping between hyperboxes from separate classes as shown in Fig. 21.6, this does not mean that the fuzzy sets do not overlap, only that the portions of the fuzzy set representing full membership are nonoverlapping. Using this configuration, it is possible to define crisp class boundaries as a special case. These class boundaries are defined as the points where the membership values are equal.

With the understanding of fuzzy hyperboxes introduced above, we are now ready to study a fuzzy min-max classification neural network. This network has a three-layer structure as shown in Fig. 21.7(a). The input layer has n nodes, one for each of the n dimensions of the input pattern $\mathbf{x}$. The input node just passes input data to the hidden layer. Each hid-

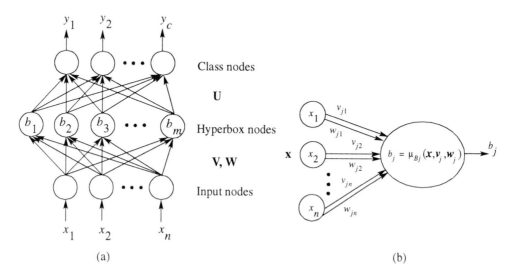

Figure 21.7 Structure of the fuzzy min-max classification neural network. (a) The three-layer neural network that implements the fuzzy min-max classifier. (b) The hyperbox node b_j for hyperbox B_j.

den node, called a *hyperbox node,* represents a hyperbox fuzzy set where the hyperbox node transfer function is the hyperbox membership function defined by Eq. (21.14). There are two sets of connections between each input node and each of the m hyperbox nodes [see Fig. 21.7(b)]; one connection weight represents the min value for that dimension, and the other connection weight represents the max value for that dimension. The dual weights between the ith input node and the jth hyperbox node are v_{ji} and w_{ji}. The min point for the jth hyperbox node is $\mathbf{v}_j = [v_{j1}, v_{j2}, \ldots, v_{jn}]^T$, and the max point is $\mathbf{w}_j = [w_{j1}, w_{j2}, \ldots, w_{jn}]^T$. In this way, the min points are stored in the matrix $\mathbf{V}$ and the max points are stored in the matrix $\mathbf{W}$ as indicated in Fig. 21.7(a). The connection weights between the hyperbox and output nodes are binary-valued and stored in the matrix $\mathbf{U}$. These weights are assigned by the formula

$$u_{\ell j} = \begin{cases} 1 & \text{if } b_j \text{ is a hyperbox for class } \ell, \\ 0 & \text{otherwise,} \end{cases} \tag{21.16}$$

where b_j is the jth hyperbox node and $u_{\ell j}$ is the weight on the link from hyperbox node j to output node ℓ. Each output node, called a class node, represents a class. Its output value y_ℓ represents the degree to which the input pattern $\mathbf{x}$ fits within the class ℓ and is defined by

$$y_\ell = \max_{j=1}^{m} u_{\ell j} b_j, \tag{21.17}$$

for each of the c class nodes. If a hard decision is required, the output node with the highest output value will be located. This can be achieved by a winner-take-all structure.

The dual weights between input nodes and hyperbox nodes are adjusted using the fuzzy min-max classification learning algorithm. Fuzzy min-max learning is an expansion-contraction process. Assume we are given a set of N training pairs $\{\mathbf{x}_k, d_k\}$, where $d_k \in \{1, 2, \ldots, c\}$ is the index of the class that the kth input pattern $\mathbf{x}_k$ belongs to. For each training pair, the learning algorithm finds a hyperbox for the same class that can expand (if necessary) to include the input. If a hyperbox cannot be found that meets the expansion criterion, then a new hyperbox is formed and added to the network. This growth process allows classes to be formed that are nonlinearly separable, existing classes to be refined over time, and new classes to be added without retraining. One of the residuals of hyperbox expansion is overlapping hyperboxes. Hyperbox overlapping is not a problem when the overlapping occurs between hyperboxes representing the same class. But when it occurs between hyperboxes that represent different classes, it is eliminated using a contraction process. Note that the contraction process eliminates the overlapping only between those portions of the fuzzy set hyperboxes from separate classes that have full membership. There is still a possibility of overlapping between nonunity-valued members of each of the fuzzy set hyperboxes.

In summary, the fuzzy min-max classification learning algorithm is a three-step process:

Step 1 (*Expansion*): Identify the hyperbox that can expand and expand it. If an expandable hyperbox cannot be found, add a new hyperbox for that class.

Step 2 (*Overlapping Test*): Determine if any overlapping exists between hyperboxes from different classes.

Step 3 (*Contraction*): If overlapping between hyperboxes that represent different classes exists, eliminate it by minimally adjusting each of the hyperboxes.

These three steps are further discussed in the following.

Fuzzy Neural Systems for Pattern Recognition   Chap. 21

Hyperbox Expansion. For a training pair $\{\mathbf{x}_k, d_k\}$, find the hyperbox B_j that meets these three conditions: (a) It provides the highest degree of membership computed from Eq. (21.14); (b) it represents the same class as d_k; and (c) it allows expansion. For the third condition, the hyperbox B_j is allowed to expand to include $\mathbf{x}_k$ if it meets the following constraint:

$$n\theta \geq \sum_{i=1}^{n} [\max(w_{ji}, x_{ki}) - \min(v_{ji}, x_{ki})], \qquad (21.18)$$

where $\theta \in [0, 1]$ is a given parameter for bounding the maximum size of a hyperbox. If such a hyperbox B_j is found, its min and max points are adjusted by the equations

$$v_{ji}^{\text{new}} = \min(v_{ji}^{\text{old}}, x_{ki}) \quad \text{and} \quad w_{ji}^{\text{new}} = \max(w_{ji}^{\text{old}}, x_{ki}), \qquad i = 1, 2, \ldots, n. \qquad (21.19)$$

Otherwise, if such a hyperbox is not found, a new hyperbox node $b_{j'}$ is added to the network and the weights vectors are set as

$$\mathbf{v}_{j'} = \mathbf{w}_{j'} = \mathbf{x}_k, \qquad (21.20)$$

indicating that the hyperbox $B_{j'}$ is a point initially. The newly added hidden node $b_{j'}$ is then assigned to class d_k by setting the weights $u_{d_k j'} = 1$ and $u_{\ell j'} = 0$ for all $\ell \neq d_k$.

Hyperbox Overlapping Test. It is necessary to eliminate any overlapping between hyperboxes that represent different classes. To determine if the expansion created any overlapping, a dimension-by-dimension comparison between hyperboxes is performed. If, for each dimension at least one of the following four cases is satisfied, then an overlapping exists between the hyperboxes. Assume that hyperbox B_j was expanded in the previous step and that hyperbox B_k represents another class and is being tested for possible overlapping. Each of the four cases is illustrated in Fig. 21.8 with the corresponding overlapping measurement shown. While testing for overlapping, the smallest overlapping along any dimension and the index of that dimension are saved for use during the contraction portion of the learning process for the purpose of eliminating the overlapping by *minimally* adjusting each of the hyperboxes. To find the smallest overlapping in all dimensions, two dummy variables s^{old} and s^{new} are used. Assuming $\delta^{\text{old}} = 1$ initially, the four test cases and their corresponding overlapping values for the ith dimension are as follows:

Case 1: For $v_{ji} < v_{ki} < w_{ji} < w_{ki}$,

$$\delta^{\text{new}} = \min(w_{ji} - v_{ki}, \delta^{\text{old}}). \qquad (21.21)$$

Case 2: For $v_{ki} < v_{ji} < w_{ki} < w_{ji}$,

$$\delta^{\text{new}} = \min(w_{ki} - v_{ji}, \delta^{\text{old}}). \qquad (21.22)$$

Case 3: For $v_{ji} < v_{ki} < w_{ki} < w_{ji}$,

$$\delta^{\text{new}} = \min(\min(w_{ki} - v_{ji}, w_{ji} - v_{ki}), \delta^{\text{old}}). \qquad (21.23)$$

Case 4: For $v_{ki} < v_{ji} < w_{ji} < w_{ki}$,

$$\delta^{\text{new}} = \min(\min(w_{ji} - v_{ki}, w_{ki} - v_{ji}), \delta^{\text{old}}). \qquad (21.24)$$

If $\delta^{\text{old}} - \delta^{\text{new}} > 0$, then $\Delta = i$ and $\Delta^{\text{old}} = \delta^{\text{new}}$, signifying that there was an overlapping for the Δth dimension and that overlap testing will proceed with the next dimension. If not, the

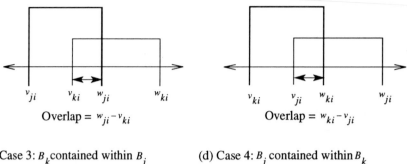

(a) Case 1: Max of B_j overlaps Min of B_k (b) Case 2: Min of B_j overlaps Max of B_k

Overlap $= w_{ji} - v_{ki}$ Overlap $= w_{ki} - v_{ji}$

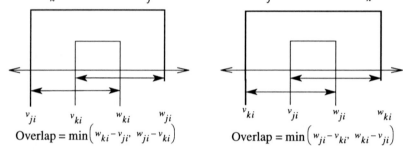

(c) Case 3: B_k contained within B_j (d) Case 4: B_j contained within B_k

Overlap $= \min\left(w_{ki} - v_{ji}, \; w_{ji} - v_{ki} \right)$ Overlap $= \min\left(w_{ji} - v_{ki}, \; w_{ki} - v_{ji} \right)$

Figure 21.8 Four cases that occur during the overlap testing. Each graph shows the relative values of two hyperboxes along one dimension.

testing stops and the overlap index variable is set to indicate that the next contraction step is not necessary, that is, $\Delta = -1$.

Hyperbox Contraction.   If $\Delta > 0$, then the Δth dimensions of the two hyperboxes are adjusted. Only one of the n dimensions is adjusted in each of the hyperboxes to keep the hyperbox size as large as possible and minimally impact the shape of the hyperboxes being formed. This minimal disturbance principle provides more robust pattern classification. To determine the proper adjustment to make, the same four cases are examined.

Case 1:   For $v_{j\Delta} < v_{k\Delta} < w_{j\Delta} < w_{k\Delta}$,

$$w_{j\Delta}^{new} = v_{k\Delta}^{new} = \frac{w_{j\Delta}^{old} + v_{k\Delta}^{old}}{2}. \tag{21.25}$$

Case 2:   For $v_{k\Delta} < v_{j\Delta} < w_{k\Delta} < w_{j\Delta}$,

$$w_{k\Delta}^{new} = v_{j\Delta}^{new} = \frac{w_{k\Delta}^{old} + v_{j\Delta}^{old}}{2}. \tag{21.26}$$

Case 3a: For $v_{j\Delta} < v_{k\Delta} < w_{k\Delta} < w_{j\Delta}$ and $(w_{k\Delta} - v_{j\Delta}) < (w_{j\Delta} - v_{k\Delta})$,

$$v_{j\Delta}^{new} = w_{k\Delta}^{old}. \tag{21.27}$$

Case 3b: For $v_{j\Delta} < v_{k\Delta} < w_{k\Delta} < w_{j\Delta}$ and $(w_{k\Delta} - v_{j\Delta}) > (w_{j\Delta} - v_{k\Delta})$,

$$w_{j\Delta}^{\text{new}} = v_{k\Delta}^{\text{old}}. \tag{21.28}$$

Case 4a: For $v_{k\Delta} < v_{j\Delta} < w_{j\Delta} < w_{k\Delta}$ and $(w_{k\Delta} - v_{j\Delta}) < (w_{j\Delta} - v_{k\Delta})$,

$$w_{k\Delta}^{\text{new}} = v_{j\Delta}^{\text{old}}. \tag{21.29}$$

Case 4b: $v_{k\Delta} < v_{j\Delta} < w_{j\Delta} < w_{k\Delta}$ and $(w_{k\Delta} - v_{j\Delta}) > (w_{j\Delta} - v_{k\Delta})$,

$$v_{k\Delta}^{\text{new}} = w_{j\Delta}^{\text{old}}. \tag{21.30}$$

Example 21.2

[Simpson, 1992b]. This example illustrates how the four two-dimensional patterns shown in Fig. 21.9(a) are used to construct a two-hyperbox classifier with a maximum hyperbox size of $\theta = 0.3$. The storage sequence is as follows.

1. Initially there is no hyperbox, and so the first input pattern $\mathbf{x}_1 = (0.2, 0.2) \in d_1$ creates a set of min and max connections of $\mathbf{v}_1 = \mathbf{w}_1 = (0.2, 0.2)$ for the hyperbox node b_1 and a class node y_1 with a unit-valued connection from b_1 to y_1.
2. The second input pattern $\mathbf{x}_2 = (0.6, 0.6) \in d_2$ creates a second hyperbox node b_2 with min and max connection values of $\mathbf{v}_2 = \mathbf{w}_2 = (0.6, 0.6)$ and a second-class node y_2 with a unit-valued connection from b_2 to y_2.

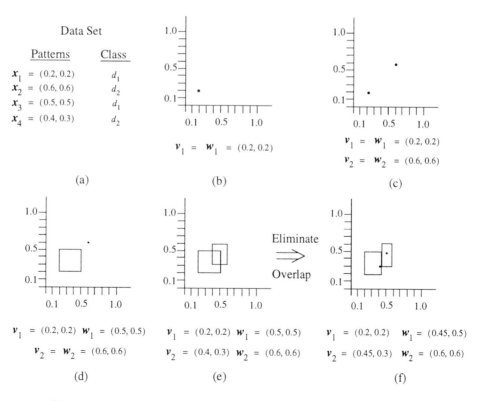

Figure 21.9 Construction of the two-hyperbox classifier in Example 21.2. (Adapted from Simpson [1992b], © 1992 IEEE.)

3. The third input pattern $\mathbf{x}_3 = (0.5, 0.5) \in d_1$ is tested for inclusion in hyperbox b_1 and found to be acceptable, and the hyperbox is expanded to include this input pattern, resulting in a set of b_1 min connections of $\mathbf{v}_1 = (0.2, 0.2)$ and max connections of $\mathbf{w}_1 = (0.5, 0.5)$.
4. The fourth input pattern $\mathbf{x}_4 = (0.4, 0.3) \in d_2$ is tested for inclusion in hyperbox b_2 and found to be acceptable to be expanded to include this input pattern, resulting in a set of b_2 min connections of $\mathbf{v}_2 = (0.4, 0.3)$ and max connections of $\mathbf{w}_2 = (0.6, 0.6)$.
5. This last expansion created an overlapping between hyperboxes b_1 and b_2, and since they are representing different classes, this overlapping must be eliminated. Because the b_2 min point overlapped the b_1 max point, these two points are manipulated to remove the overlapping, resulting in new min and max points of $\mathbf{v}_2 = (0.45, 0.3)$ and $\mathbf{w}_1 = (0.45, 0.5)$.

21.1.3 Genetic Algorithms for Fuzzy Classification Using Fuzzy Rules

This section introduces a genetic algorithm–based (GA-based) method for choosing an appropriate set of fuzzy IF-THEN rules for classification problems [Ishibuchi et al., 1993b]. The aim is to find a minimum set of fuzzy IF-THEN rules that can correctly classify all training patterns. To achieve this, we first formulate a combinatorial optimization problem that has two objectives: to maximize the number of correctly classified patterns and to minimize the number of fuzzy IF-THEN rules.

The fuzzy classifier considered here is based on the technique of *distributed* fuzzy IF-THEN rules, where grid-type fuzzy partitions on the pattern space are used. This approach simultaneously utilizes the fuzzy rules corresponding to coarse fuzzy partitions as well as those corresponding to fine fuzzy partitions. Assume that a pattern space is the unit square $[0, 1] \times [0, 1]$. Suppose that m patterns $\mathbf{x}_p = (x_{1p}, x_{2p})$, $p = 1, 2, \ldots, m$, are given as training patterns from M classes $C_1, C_2, \ldots, C_M$. That is, the classification of each $\mathbf{x}_p$ is known as one of M classes. The classification problem is to generate fuzzy IF-THEN rules that divide the pattern space into M disjoint decision areas. For this problem, the following fuzzy rule is employed:

$$R_{ij}^K: \text{ IF } x_{1p} \text{ is } A_i^K \text{ AND } x_{2p} \text{ is } A_j^K,$$
$$\text{THEN } \mathbf{x}_p \text{ belongs to } G_{ij}^K \text{ with CF } = \text{CF}_{ij}^K, \tag{21.31}$$

where K is the number of fuzzy subspaces (intervals) in each axis, R_{ij}^K is the label of the fuzzy rule, G_{ij}^K is the consequent (i.e., one of M classes), $\text{CF} \in (0, 1]$ is the grade of certainty of the fuzzy IF-THEN rule, and A_i^K and A_j^K are fuzzy sets with triangular membership functions $\mu_i^K (x_{1p})$ and $\mu_j^K (x_{2p})$ defined by

$$\mu_i^K (x) = \mu_{A_i^K} (x) = \max \left\{ 1 - \frac{|x - a_i^K|}{b^K}, 0 \right\}, \qquad i = 1, 2, \ldots, K, \tag{21.32}$$

where

$$a_i^K = \frac{i - 1}{K - 1} \text{ and } \quad b^K = \frac{1}{K - 1}, \qquad i = 1, 2, \ldots, K. \tag{21.33}$$

In the membership function of Eq. (21.32), a_i^K is the center where the grade of membership is equal to 1 and b^K is the spread of the membership function. The fuzzy partitions for $K = 2$ and $K = 3$ are shown in Fig. 21.10, where the labels of fuzzy rules are indicated in the corresponding fuzzy subspaces.

Fuzzy Neural Systems for Pattern Recognition   Chap. 21

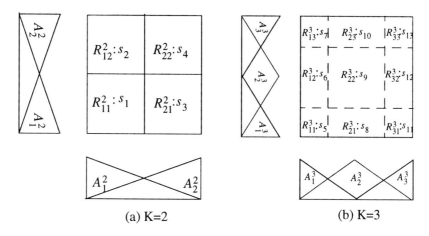

Figure 21.10   Labels of distributed fuzzy IF-THEN rules for $K = 2$ and $K = 3$.

The following procedure is used to determine the consequent G_{ij}^K and the grade of certainty CF_{ij}^K of the fuzzy IF-THEN rule in Eq. (21.31).

Derivation of Fuzzy Rules

1. Calculate β_{C_t}, $t = 1, 2, \ldots, M$, for fuzzy subspace $A_i^K \times A_j^K$ as

$$\beta_{C_t} = \sum_{x_p \in C_t} \mu_i^K(x_{1p}) \mu_j^K(x_{2p}). \tag{21.34}$$

2. Find class $y\,(C_y)$ such that

$$\beta_{C_y} = \max\{\beta_{C_1}, \beta_{C_2}, \ldots, \beta_{C_M}\}. \tag{21.35}$$

If two or more classes have the maximum value in Eq. (21.35), the consequent G_{ij}^K of the fuzzy rule corresponding to the fuzzy subspace $A_i^K \times A_j^K$ cannot be determined uniquely. In this case, let G_{ij}^K be $\varnothing$, and the corresponding rule is a dummy rule. If a single class takes the maximum value in Eq. (21.35), G_{ij}^K is determined as C_y in Eq. (21.35).

3. If a single class takes the maximum value in Eq. (21.35), the certainty factor CF_{ij}^K is determined as

$$CF_{ij}^K = \frac{\left| \beta_{C_y} - \beta \right|}{\sum_{t=1}^M \beta_{C_t}}, \tag{21.36}$$

where

$$\beta = \frac{\sum_{C_t \neq C_y} \beta_{C_t}}{M - 1}. \tag{21.37}$$

It is noted that if there is no pattern in the fuzzy subspace $A_i^K \times A_j^K$, a dummy rule is generated by the above procedure as the fuzzy rule R_{ij}^K. An example of applying this procedure to a two-class classification problem using various values of K (i.e., $K = 5, 6$) is illustrated in Fig. 21.11. The generated fuzzy IF-THEN rules are shown in the left half of Fig.

Sec. 21.1   Fuzzy Neural Classification   **675**

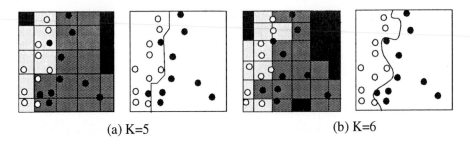

(a) K=5   (b) K=6

Figure 21.11 Generated fuzzy IF-THEN rules and classification boundaries. (Adapted from Ishibuchi et al. [1993b], © 1993 IEEE.)

21.11. In each figure in the left half, hatched area, dotted area, and solid area represent the following: hatched area—the consequent of generated fuzzy rules in the area is class 1 (closed circles); dotted area—the consequent of generated fuzzy rules in this area is class 2 (open circles); and solid area—the consequent of generated fuzzy rules in this area is $\varnothing$; that is, dummy rules are generated.

By the above procedure, K^2 rules are generated for each K. Let us denote the set of all fuzzy rules corresponding to $K = 2, 3,..., L$ by S_{ALL} as

$$S_{ALL} = \{ R_{ij}^K \mid i, j = 1, 2,..., K; K = 2, 3,..., L \}. \tag{21.38}$$

When the set S_{ALL} is derived, a new incoming pattern can be classified in the classification phase using the rules in S_{ALL} by the following procedure.

Classification of a New Pattern x_p

1. Calculate α_{C_t} for $t = 1, 2,..., M$ as

$$\alpha_{C_t} = \max\{ \mu_i^K(x_{1p}) \cdot \mu_j^K(x_{2p}) \cdot CF_{ij}^K \mid G_{ij}^K = C_t; R_{ij}^K \in S_{ALL} \}. \tag{21.39}$$

2. Find class $y (C_y)$ such that

$$\alpha_{C_y} = \max\{ \alpha_{C_1}, \alpha_{C_2},..., \alpha_{C_M} \}. \tag{21.40}$$

If two or more classes take the maximum value, then $\mathbf{x}_p$ cannot be classified (i.e., $\mathbf{x}_p$ is left as an unclassifiable pattern); else assign $\mathbf{x}_p$ to class $y (C_y)$ determined by Eq. (21.40).

Note that if there are no fuzzy rules such that $\mu_i^K(x_{1p}) \cdot \mu_j^K(x_{2p}) > 0$ and $CF_{ij}^K > 0$, the new pattern $\mathbf{x}_p$ cannot be classified. Continuing with the previous example, classification results with the fuzzy rules corresponding to $K = 5, 6$ are shown on the right in Fig. 21.11. That is, each figure in the right half was obtained by the fuzzy rules in the corresponding figure in the left half. The solid areas in the right-hand figures indicate that new patterns cannot be classified in these areas.

According to Eq. (21.38), the rule set S_{ALL} contains $2^2 + 3^2 + \cdots + L^2$ rules. It is appealing if we can select appropriate fuzzy rules from S_{ALL} to form a smaller rule set $S \subset S_{ALL}$ that keeps the classification error acceptable. We now apply GAs to this fuzzy rule selection problem which is formulated as an optimization problem:

$$\text{Maximize } f(S) = w_{\text{NCP}} \cdot \text{NCP}(S) - w_s \cdot |S|, \tag{21.41}$$
$$\text{subject to } S \subseteq S_{\text{ALL}},$$

where $\text{NCP}(S)$ is the number of patterns correctly classified by S, $|S|$ is the number of fuzzy rules in S, and w_{NCP} and w_S are corresponding weighting constants, where $0 < w_S \ll w_{\text{NCP}}$.

To apply GAs to this optimization problem, we first need to define proper coding. Let us denote the rule set S by the string $s_1 s_2 \cdots s_N$ as $S = s_1 s_2 \cdots s_N$, where $N = 2^2 + 3^2 + \cdots + L^2$ and

$$s_r = \begin{cases} 1 & \text{if the } r\text{th rule belongs to the rule set } S \\ -1 & \text{if the } r\text{th rule does not belong to the rule set } S \\ 0 & \text{if the } r\text{th rule is a dummy rule.} \end{cases} \tag{21.42}$$

Since dummy rules have no effect on fuzzy reasoning in the classification phase, they are detected and presented as $s_r = 0$ in this coding in order to remove them from the rule set S. The index r of the fuzzy rule R_{ij}^K, as indicated in Fig. 21.10, can be calculated as

$$r = 2^2 + 3^2 + \cdots + (k-1)^2 + k \cdot (i-1) + j. \tag{21.43}$$

Another essential element associated with string S is its fitness value $g(S)$ defined by the objective function $f(S)$ in Eq. (21.41) as

$$g(S) = \max\{f(S), 0\}. \tag{21.44}$$

The following genetic operations are applied to a set of individuals (i.e., population in a generation) in order to generate a new population in the next generation:

1. *Reproduction*: Each individual is selected as a parent for the new generation based on its selection probability. The selection probability of the individual S is proportional to its fitness value $g(S)$.
2. *Crossover*: One point crossover is applied to the pair of selected individuals (i.e., parents).
3. *Mutation*: The following mutation operation is applied to each bit of the generated individuals by the crossover operation: $s_r \rightarrow s_r \times (-1)$. Each bit of each individual undergoes this mutation operation with the mutation probability P_m.
4. *Elite*: The best individual (i.e., an individual with the largest fitness value) in each generation always survives and exists in the next generation.

Example 21.3

[Ishibuchi et al., 1993b]. In this example, GA is applied to the classification problem in Fig. 21.11. The related parameters are set as follows: mutation probability $P_m = 0.01$, population size in each generation is 10 individuals, stopping condition is 1000 generations, and the values of weights are $w_{\text{NCP}} = 10$ and $w_s = 1$.

At first, the fuzzy rules corresponding to $K = 2, 3, 4, 5, 6$ are generated to form the set S_{ALL} using the procedure for deriving fuzzy rules [Eqs. (21.34)–(21.37)]. There are a total of $2^2 + 3^2 + 4^2 + 5^2 + 6^2 = 90$ fuzzy rules. Therefore, the length of each individual (i.e., each string) is 90. For the population in the first generation, 10 individuals are randomly generated. The genetic operations mentioned above are applied to each generation. The fuzzy rules selected after 1000 generations and the corresponding classification results are shown in Fig. 21.12. As compared to Fig. 21.11, we can see that all the training patterns are correctly classified in Fig. 21.12 by many fewer fuzzy rules than in Fig. 21.11.

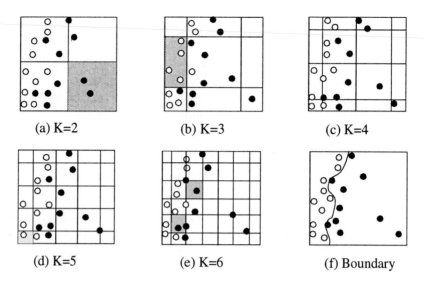

(a) K=2   (b) K=3   (c) K=4

(d) K=5   (e) K=6   (f) Boundary

Figure 21.12   Five fuzzy rules selected by GA and the classification results in Example 21.3. (Adapted from Ishibuchi et al. [1993b], © 1993 IEEE.)

21.2 FUZZY NEURAL CLUSTERING

21.2.1 Fuzzy Competitive Learning for Fuzzy Clustering

Competitive learning is one of the major clustering techniques in neural networks. By generalizing the conventional competitive learning rules, a fuzzy competitive learning rule based on the fuzzy c-means (FCM) formula has been proposed by Jou [1992b]. Since competitive learning is designed for crisp clustering, it is conceivable that fuzzy competitive learning is suitable for fuzzy clustering. The fuzzy competitive learning rule is derived by minimizing the objective function J in Eq. (8.18) and applying the FCM formulas in Eqs. (8.22) and (8.23). The problem then is to find fuzzy clusters in the input patterns and determine the cluster centers $\mathbf{v}_i$ accordingly. Applying a gradient-descent method to the objective function in Eq. (8.18) yields

$$\Delta v_{ih} = 2\eta \, (u_{ij})^m \, [x_{jh} - v_{ih}] - \eta m \, (u_{ij})^{m-1} \frac{\partial u_{ij}}{\partial v_{ih}} \, \|\mathbf{x}_j - \mathbf{v}_i\|^2, \qquad (21.45)$$

where $\mathbf{v}_i = [v_{i1}, \ldots, v_{ih}, \ldots, v_{iq}]^T$ and $\mathbf{x}_j = [x_{j1}, \ldots, x_{jh}, \ldots, x_{jq}]^T$. By differentiating Eq. (8.23) with respect to v_{ih} and using the chain rule, we obtain

$$\frac{\partial u_{ij}}{\partial v_{ih}} = 2u_{ij} \, (1 - u_{ij}) \, (m - 1)^{-1} \frac{x_{jh} - v_{ih}}{\|\mathbf{x}_j - \mathbf{v}_i\|^2}. \qquad (21.46)$$

The fuzzy competitive learning rule, which moves the weight vectors toward their respective fuzzy cluster centers, is to use Eq. (21.45) with Eq. (21.46):

$$\Delta v_{ih} = \eta \gamma_m \, [x_{jh} - v_{ih}], \qquad (21.47)$$

where

$$\gamma_m \triangleq (u_{ij})^m \left[1 - m(m-1)^{-1}(1-u_{ij}) \right],\qquad(21.48)$$

with $m \in (1, \infty)$. Thus, the objective function is minimized by the above update rule.

Clearly, the fuzzy competitive rule in Eq. (21.47) reduces to the conventional competitive learning rule in Eq. (12.7) if $u_{ij} \in \{0, 1\}$. Note that if we use the update rule in Eq. (21.47) in batch mode (i.e., we accumulate the changes Δv_{ih} for each pattern $\mathbf{x}_j$ before we actually update the weights), then the learning algorithm will correspond to the fuzzy c-means algorithm.

For a specified weighting exponent m, the term γ_m, which is determined by the membership grade u_{ij}, controls the amount of the weight v_{ih} to be updated. Figure 21.13 depicts the function $\gamma_m(u_{ik})$ given by Eq. (21.48) for several values of m. As we see in Fig. 21.13, the boundary conditions $\gamma_m(0) = 0$ and $\gamma_m(1) = 1$ are satisfied. For large m values, $\gamma_m(u_{ij})$ goes smoothly from 0 to 1 as u_{ij} goes from 0 to 1. At small m values, it makes a rather sudden rise from near $-\infty$ to 1 over a narrow range of u_{ij} near 1. In the limit $m \to \infty$, $\gamma_m(u_{ij})$ just reduces to a step function rising at 1. In the other limit $m \to 1^+$, $\gamma_m(u_{ij})$ is negative infinite except at the two end points. Note also that $\gamma_m(u_{ij}) > 0$ if $u_{ij} > 1/m$ and $\gamma_m(u_{ij}) < 0$ if $0 < u_{ij} < 1/m$. This indicates that if membership grade u_{ij} is relatively large, then we move its corresponding weight vector toward the current input vector; otherwise, we move the weight vector away from the input vector. This is analogous to *Kohonen's learning vector quantization* (LVQ) in which the weight vector is moved away from the input vector when the current cluster of the winner is incorrect.

The fuzzy competitive learning rule [Eqs. (21.47) and (21.48)] has been applied to the butterfly example described in Example 8.3. The initial weights are set according to Eq. (8.22) with randomly specified membership grades. The parameters are set as $c = 2$, $\eta = 0.01$, and $m = 1.2$ and 2. The algorithm converges within 50 iterations. In each iteration, all patterns are presented to the algorithm in random order. The simulation results show that the fuzzy competitive learning rule gives a performance compatible with that of the FCM algorithm. Moreover, the resulting membership grades for $m = 2$ are fuzzier than those for $m = 1.2$ as expected, but the cluster centers are somewhat unchanged.

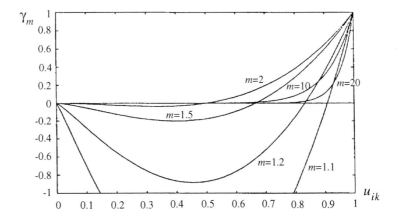

Figure 21.13 The function $\gamma_m(u_{ik})$ for several values of m.

21.2.2 Adaptive Fuzzy Leader Clustering

In addition to the competitive learning rules, the ART network is another major clustering technique in neural networks. In this section, we shall introduce an ART-like fuzzy neural classifier called the *adaptive fuzzy leader classifier.* There are many similarities between ART and the classical leader clustering algorithm. The leader clustering algorithm works as follows:

Step 1: The leader clustering system begins with a cluster centered at the location of the first input pattern x_1. This cluster is called the leader.

Step 2: For each of the remaining patterns x_k, $k = 1, 2,..., N$, the following is performed.

  a. Find the cluster closest to x_k (usually using Euclidean distance measures).

  b. If the ratio of the distance between the cluster center and x_k is less than a prespecified tolerance value, the cluster center is updated to include x_k in its cluster by averaging the location x_k with the cluster center.

  c. If the closest cluster ratio is too large, then this cluster is eliminated from the set of candidate clusters and the control returns to step 2a.

  d. If the clusters are exhausted, add a new cluster with x_k as the cluster center.

Based on these steps, a fuzzy neural realization of the leader cluster algorithm has been proposed by Newton et al. [1992]. This system is called the adaptive fuzzy leader clustering (AFLC) system. The AFLC system has an unsupervised neural network architecture developed from the concept of ART1 and includes a relocation of the cluster centers from FCM system equations for the centroid and the membership values. It can thus be considered another fuzzy modification of an ART1 neural network or, more precisely, an integration of ART1 and FCM.

Adaptive fuzzy leader clustering is a hybrid fuzzy-neural system that can be used to learn cluster structure embedded in complex data sets in a self-organizing and stable manner. Let $x_k = \{x_{k1}, x_{k2},..., x_{kn}\}$ be the kth discrete or analog-valued input vector for $k = 1, 2,..., N$, where N is the total number of samples. Figure 21.14 shows the structure and operation characteristics of an AFLC system, where x_k is an n-dimensional discrete or analog-valued input vector to the system. The AFLC system is made up of the comparison layer, the recognition layer, and the surrounding control logic. As in ART1, the initialization and update procedures in AFLC involve similarity measures between the bottom-up weights ($b_i = [b_{i1},..., b_{ij},..., b_{in}]^T$, $i = 1,..., c$) and the input vector x_k, and a verification of x_k belonging to the ith cluster by a matching of the top-down weights ($v_i = [v_{i1},..., v_{ij},... v_{in}]^T$, $i = 1,..., c$) with x_k, where c is the (current) number of clusters and $b_i = v_i / \| v_i \|$. The AFLC algorithm initially starts with the number of clusters c set to zero. The system is initialized with the input of the first input vector x_1. As in leader clustering, this first input is said to be the prototype for the first cluster. The normalized input vector $\bar{x}_k = x_k / \| x_k \| = [\bar{x}_{k1} \ \bar{x}_{k2},..., \bar{x}_{kn}]^T$ is then applied to the bottom-up weights by dot product. The node that receives the largest input activation is chosen as the expected cluster:

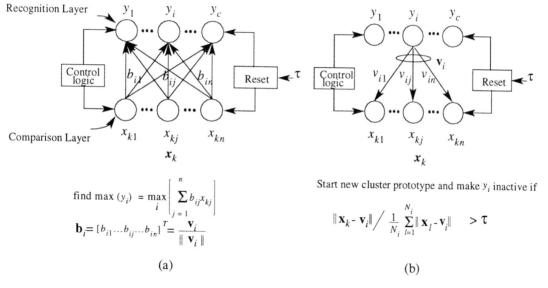

find max (y_i) = $\max\limits_{i} \left| \sum\limits_{j=1}^{n} b_{ij} x_{kj} \right|$

$\mathbf{b}_i = [b_{i1} \dots b_{ij} \dots b_{in}]^T = \dfrac{\mathbf{v}_i}{\| \mathbf{v}_i \|}$

(a)

Start new cluster prototype and make y_i inactive if

$\| \mathbf{x}_k - \mathbf{v}_i \| \Big/ \dfrac{1}{N_i} \sum\limits_{l=1}^{N_i} \| \mathbf{x}_l - \mathbf{v}_i \|$ $> \tau$

(b)

Figure 21.14 Operation characteristics of an AFLC architecture. (a) Initial stage of identifying a cluster prototype. (b) The comparison stage using the criterion of Euclidean distance ratio $D > \tau$ to reject new data samples to the cluster prototype. The reset control implies deactivation of the original prototype and activation of a new cluster prototype.

$$y_{i*} = \max_{i}\{y_i\} = \max_{i} \left\{ \sum_{j=1}^{n} b_{ij} \bar{x}_{kj} \right\}, \qquad k = 1, 2, \dots, N, \qquad (21.49)$$

and the top-down weight vector corresponding to the winning node $\mathbf{v}_{i*}$ is chosen as the expected prototype vector (winning vector). We shall use $\mathbf{v}_i$ to denote the winning vector for notation simplicity.

The recognition layer serves to initially classify an input. This first stage classification activates the prototype or top-down expectation $\mathbf{v}_i$ for a cluster, which is forwarded to the comparison layer. The comparison layer serves both as a fan-out site for the inputs and as a location for the comparison between the top-down expectation and the input. The control logic with an input-enable command allows the comparison layer to accept a new input as long as a comparison operation is not currently being processed. The control logic with a comparison-imperative command disables the acceptance of new input and initiates a comparison between the cluster prototype associated with y_i (i.e., $\mathbf{v}_i$) and the current input vector. This is the so-called *vigilance test* in ART. The reset signal is activated when a mismatch between the prototype and the input vectors occurs according to the criterion of a distance ratio threshold expressed by

$$D = \frac{\| \mathbf{x}_k - \mathbf{v}_i \|}{(1/N_i)\sum_{\ell=1}^{N_i} \| \mathbf{x}_\ell - \mathbf{v}_i \|} < \tau, \qquad (21.50)$$

where N_i is the number of samples in class i. If the ratio D is less than a user-specified threshold (vigilance parameter) τ, then the input vector is found to belong to the winning cluster y_i, and thus the index i is the final network output; otherwise, if the criterion in Eq. (21.50) is not met, then the current winner y_i in the recognition layer is disabled and a new winner is found by repeating the above process. If no y_i satisfies the distance ratio criterion (i.e., all the nodes in the recognition layer are disabled), then a new cluster is created, its prototype vector is made equal to $\mathbf{x}_k$, and the index of the new cluster is the final network output. Note that a low threshold value will result in the formation of more clusters because it will be more difficult for an input to meet the clasification criterion. A high value of τ will result in fewer, less dense clusters.

When an input is classified as belonging to an existing cluster, it is necessary to update the expectation (prototype) and the bottom-up weights associated with that cluster. First, the degree of membership $\mathbf{x}_k$ in the winning cluster is calculated. This degree of membership gives an indication, based on the current state of the system, of how heavily $\mathbf{x}_k$ should be weighted in recalculation of the class expectation. The cluster prototype is then recalculated as a weighted average of all the elements within the cluster. The weights are updated according to the FCM algorithm in Eqs. (8.22) and (8.23) with index k replaced by ℓ, index j replaced by k, and n replaced by N_i, where N_i is the number of samples in cluster i. The update rules for an AFLC are as follows: The membership value u_{ik} of the current input sample $\mathbf{x}_k$ in the winning class i is calculated using Eq. (8.23), and then the new cluster centroid for cluster i is generated using Eq. (8.22). As with the FCM, m is a parameter that defines the fuzziness of the results and is normally set between 1.5 and 30.

The AFLC algorithm can be summarized by the following steps:

Step 1: Start with no cluster; $c = 0$.

Step 2: Let $\mathbf{x}_k$ be the next input vector.

Step 3: Find the first-stage winner y_i as the cluster prototype with the maximum dot product.

Step 4: If no y_i satisfies the distance ratio criterion, create a new cluster and make its prototype vector equal to $\mathbf{x}_k$. Output the index of the new cluster.

Step 5: Otherwise, update the winner cluster prototype associated with y_i by calculating the new centroid and membership values using Eqs. (8.22) and (8.23). Output the index of y_i. Go to step 2.

AFLC, like ART, is a type of match-based learning in which a new input is learned only after being classified as belonging to a particular class. This process ensures stable and consistent learning of new inputs by updating parameters only for the winning cluster and only after classification has occurred. Because of its ART-like control structure, AFLC is capable of implementing a parallel search when the distance ratio does not satisfy the thresholding criterion. The search is arbitrated by appropriate control logic surrounding the comparison and recognition layers in Fig. 21.14. This type of search is necessary owing to the incompleteness of the classification at the first stage. For illustration, consider the two vectors (1,1) and (6,6). Both possess the same unit vector. Since the competition in the bottom-up direction consists of measuring how well the normalized input matches the weight vector for each class i, these inputs excite the same activation pattern in the recognition layer. In operation, the comparison layer serves to test the hypothesis returned by the competition performed at the recognition layer. If the hypothesis is disconfirmed by the comparison layer, that is, $D > \tau$, then the search phase continues until the correct cluster is found or a new cluster is created. Normalization of the input vectors (features) is done only in the recognition layer for finding the winning node. This normalization is essential to avoid large values of the dot product of the input features and the bottom-up weights and also to avoid initial misclassification arising from large variations in the magnitudes of the cluster prototypes. The search process, however, renormalizes only the centroid and not the input vectors again.

As we know, ART networks allow learning of even rare events. Use of the FCM learning rule in the form of Eqs. (8.22) and (8.23) allows AFLC to maintain this characteristic. Moreover, in AFLC, the amount of change in the prototype is a function of the input and its membership value. Hence, noisy features that would normally degrade the validity of the class prototype are assigned low weights to reduce the undesired effect. This makes AFLC more noise-insensitive than ART1.

Example 21.4

[Newton et al., 1992]. In this example, AFLC is applied to the clustering of the Anderson *Iris* data set mentioned in Example 8.4 (see Fig. 8.5). It consists of 150 four-dimensional feature vectors. Each pattern corresponds to characteristics of one flower from one of the species of *Iris*. Three varieties of *Iris* are represented by 50 of the feature vectors. A total of 52 runs of the AFLC algorithm for the *Iris* data for 13 different values of τ is performed, with four runs for each τ. Figure 21.15(a) shows the τ-c graph. With the Euclidean distance ratio and τ ranging between 4.5 and 5.5, the sample data are classified into three clusters with only seven misclassifications. From Fig. 21.15(a) it can be observed that the optimal number of clusters can be determined from the τ-c graph as the value of c that has $dc/d\tau = 0$, $c \neq 1$, for the maximum possible range of τ. The computed centroids of the three clusters based on all four features are shown in Fig. 21.15(b).

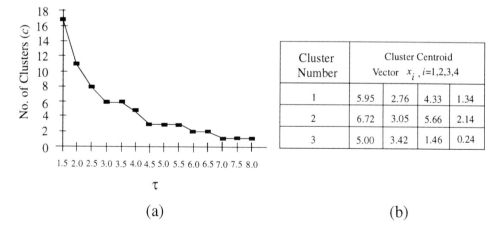

Cluster Number	Cluster Centroid Vector x_i, $i=1,2,3,4$			
1	5.95	2.76	4.33	1.34
2	6.72	3.05	5.66	2.14
3	5.00	3.42	1.46	0.24

(a)   (b)

Figure 21.15 Simulation results of applying AFLC to the *Iris* data. (a) The τ-c graph for choosing τ for unlabeled data sets. (b) Computed centroids of three *Iris* clusters based on all four feature vectors.

21.3 FUZZY NEURAL MODELS FOR IMAGE PROCESSING

21.3.1 Fuzzy Self-Supervised Multilayer Network for Object Extraction

A multilayer feedforward network with back-propagation learning has been used for image segmentation with limited success (e.g., see [Blanz and Gish, 1990; Babaguchi et al., 1990; Manjunath et al., 1990]). Since the use of multilayer feedback networks requires a set of labeled input-output data, we need a set of known images for supervised learning and then use the trained network for processing other images. The problem with this approach is that it is valid only when the images to be processed are of similar nature. Also, the training images may not always be available in real-life situations. To attack these problems, a self-organizing (or *self-supervised*) multilayer neural network architecture suitable for image processing has been proposed by Ghosh et al. [1993]. This network can be used for segmentation of images when only one image is available, and it does not require any a priori target output value for supervised learning. Instead, the network output is described as a fuzzy set, and a fuzziness measure of this fuzzy set is used as a measure of error in the system (instability of the network). This measure of error is then back-propagated to adjust the weights in each layer. Thus, the measures of fuzziness play an important role in the self-supervised back-propagation network. We shall review the measures of fuzziness (see Sec. 4.3) that are useful for the self-supervised back-propagation network.

The measure of fuzziness is to evaluate the degree of fuzziness of a fuzzy set. Such a measure of a fuzzy set A, $f(A)$, should satisfy axioms f_1 to f_3 stated in Sec. 4.3. A few measures that are useful here are described below.

1. *Index of fuzziness*: The index of fuzziness of a fuzzy set A having n supporting points, $X = \{x_1, x_2, \ldots, x_n\}$, is defined as [see Eqs. (4.73) and (4.74)]:

$$f(A) = \frac{2}{n^k} d(A, C),$$
(21.51)

where $d(A, C)$ denotes a metric distance (e.g., Hamming or Euclidean distance) of A from any of the nearest crisp set C for which

$$\mu_C(x) = \begin{cases} 0 & \text{if } \mu_A(x) \leq 0.5 \\ 1 & \text{if } \mu_A(x) > 0.5. \end{cases}$$
(21.52)

The value of k in Eq. (21.51) depends on the type of distance used. For example, $k = 1$ is used for a Hamming distance and $k = 0.5$ for a Euclidean distance. The corresponding indices of fuzziness are called the *linear index of fuzziness* $f_\ell(A)$ and the *quadratic index of fuzziness* $f_q(A)$. Thus, we have

$$f_\ell(A) = \frac{2}{n} \sum_{i=1}^{n} |\mu_A(x_i) - \mu_C(x_i)|$$

$$= \frac{2}{n} \sum_{i=1}^{n} \min\{\mu_A(x_i), (1 - \mu_A(x_i))\},$$
(21.53)

$$f_q(A) = \frac{2}{\sqrt{n}} \left[\sum_{i=1}^{n} \{\mu_A(x_i) - \mu_C(x_i)\}^2 \right]^{1/2}$$

$$= \frac{2}{\sqrt{n}} \left[\sum_{i=1}^{n} \{\min[\mu_A(x_i), (1 - \mu_A(x_i))]\}^2 \right]^{1/2}. \tag{21.54}$$

2. *Entropy:* From Eqs. (4.70) and (4.71), the entropy of a fuzzy set defined by De Luca and Termini [1972] (the *logarithmic entropy*) is

$$H_\ell(A) = \frac{1}{n \ln 2} \sum_{i=1}^{n} \{-\mu_A(x_i) \ln [\mu_A(x_i)] - [1 - \mu_A(x_i)] \ln [1 - \mu_A(x_i)]\}. \tag{21.55}$$

Another definition of entropy, the *exponential entropy,* given by Pal and Pal [1989] is

$$H_e(A) = \frac{1}{n(\sqrt{e} - 1)} \sum_{i=1}^{n} \{\mu_A(x_i) e^{1 - \mu_A(x_i)} + [1 - \mu_A(x_i)] e^{\mu_A(x_i)} - 1\}. \tag{21.56}$$

These measures will be used to compute the *error* or *measure of instability* of a multilayer self-organizing neural network.

Consider a self-supervised multilayer neural network for image segmentation or object extraction. Before describing the architecture of the network, we need to define a neighborhood system. For an $M \times N$ image lattice L the dth order neighbor N_{ij}^d of an element (i, j) is defined as

$$N_{ij}^d = \{(i, j) \in L\} \tag{21.57}$$

such that

$$(i, j) \notin N_{ij}^d, \qquad \text{and if} \qquad (k, \ell) \in N_{ij}^d, \text{then } (i, j) \in N_{k\ell}^d. \tag{21.58}$$

Different ordered neighborhood systems can be defined considering different sets of neighboring pixels of (i, j). $N^1 = \{N_{ij}^1\}$ can be obtained by taking the four nearest-neighbor pixels. Similarly, $N^2 = \{N_{ij}^2\}$ consists of the eight-pixel neighborhood (i, j), and so on (as shown in Fig. 21.16).

The three-layer version of a self-supervised multilayer network is shown in Fig. 21.17. In each layer, there are $M \times N$ sigmoidal nodes (for an $M \times N$ image), and each node corresponds to a single pixel. Besides the input and output layers, there can be a number of hidden layers (more than zero). Nodes in the same layer do not have any connections among themselves. Each node in a layer is connected to the corresponding node in the previous layer and to its neighbors (over N^d); thus each node in layer i ($i > 1$) has $|N^d| + 1$ (where $|N^d|$ is the number of pixels in N^d) links to the $(i - 1)$th layer. For N^1, a node has five links, whereas for N^2, nine links are associated with every node. However, for boundary nodes (pixels), the number of links may be less than $(|N^d| + 1)$. Every node in the output layer is also connected to the corresponding node in the input layer.

The input to an input node is given as a real number in [0, 1] which is proportional to the gray value of the corresponding pixel. Starting from the input layer, the input pattern is passed on to the output layer, and the corresponding outputs are calculated in the same way

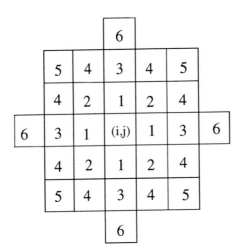

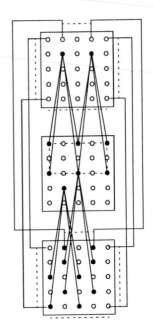

Figure 21.16 Neighborhood system N^d.

Figure 21.17 Schematic representation of self-supervised multilayer neural network. (Adapted from Ghosh et al. [1993], © 1993 IEEE.)

as in a normal back-propagation network. Note that the output value of each node in the network lies in $[0, 1]$. Since we are trying to eliminate noise and extract spatially compact regions, all initial weights are set to 1. As a result, the total input (initially) to any node lies in $[0, n_\ell]$ (where n_ℓ is the number of links a neuron has); hence, the most unbiased choice for the threshold value θ for the unipolar sigmoidal activation function is $n_\ell/2$, which is the middle of most values of the total input range.

After the network output has been obtained for a given input pattern (image) through forward propagation, the next step is to perform error back propagation for weight learning like a normal back-propagation network does. However, we do not have target output to supervise the learning now. Here our intention is to extract spatially compact regions through the process of self-organization using only one noisy image. Under ideal conditions when the image is not noisy, the network is organized such that the output status of most of the nodes in the output layer are either 0 or 1. But owing to the effect of noise, the output status of the nodes in the output layer is usually in $[0, 1]$; thus the status value represents the degree of brightness (darkness) of the corresponding pixel in the image. Therefore, the output status in the output layer may be viewed to represent a fuzzy set "BRIGHT (DARK) pixels." The number of supports of this fuzzy set is equal to the number of nodes in the output layer. The measure of fuzziness of this set, on a global level, may be considered the *error* or *instability of the whole system* as this reflects the deviation from the desired state of the network. Thus, without any a priori target output value, the fuzziness value is taken as a measure of system error and is back-propagated to adjust the weights so that the system error is reduced with the passage of time and in the limiting case becomes zero. The error measure E can also be taken as a suitable function of a fuzziness measure; that is,

$$E = g(I), \tag{21.59}$$

where I is a measure of fuzziness [Eqs. (21.53)–(21.56)] of the fuzzy set.

After the weights have been adjusted properly, the output of the nodes in the output layer is fed back to the corresponding nodes in the input layer. The second pass is then continued with this as input. The iteration (updating of weights) is continued as in the previous case until the network stabilizes, that is, until the error value (measure of fuzziness) becomes negligible. When the network stabilizes, the output status of the nodes in the output layer becomes either 0 or 1. Nodes with an output value of 0 constitute one group, and those having an output value of 1 constitute the other. Note that the scene can have any number of compact regions.

We shall next derive the weight update rules for different fuzziness measures. According to the back-propagation algorithm, the general learning rule is

$$\Delta w_{ij} = \eta \left(-\frac{\partial E}{\partial w_{ij}} \right) = \eta \left(-\frac{\partial E}{\partial y_i} \right) \left(\frac{\partial y_i}{\partial \text{net}_i} \right) \left(\frac{\partial \text{net}_i}{\partial w_{ij}} \right) = \eta \left(-\frac{\partial E}{\partial y_i} \right) a'(\text{net}_i) x_j, \tag{21.60}$$

where w_{ij} is the weight on the link from node j to node i, η is the learning constant, E is the error measure defined in Eq. (21.59), $a(\cdot)$ is the activation function, x_j is the output of node j, net_i is the net input to node i (i.e., $\text{net}_i = \sum_j w_{ij} x_j$), and y_i is the output of node i [i.e., $y_i = a(\text{net}_i)$]. Hence, if we can derive $\partial E / \partial y_i$ in Eq. (21.60) for node i, we can obtain the learning rule of the corresponding weight. We shall derive weight update rules using different fuzziness measures for the output layer in the following discussion. For the weights in the hidden layers, an update rule can then be derived by the chain rule in the same way that the normal back-propagation algorithm is derived.

1. *Learning rule for linear index of fuzziness*: Let the error measure be

$$E = g(f_\ell) = f_\ell, \tag{21.61}$$

where, from Eq. (21.53), the linear index of fuzziness is

$$f_\ell = \frac{2}{n} \sum_{i=1}^{n} \min(y_j, 1 - y_j), \tag{21.62}$$

where n is the number of output nodes. Then we have

$$-\frac{\partial E}{\partial y_i} = \begin{cases} -2/n, & 0 \le y_i \le 0.5 \\ 2/n, & 0.5 < y_i \le 1. \end{cases} \tag{21.63}$$

Thus, from Eq. (21.60), we obtain the following learning rule:

$$\Delta w_{ij} = \begin{cases} \eta\,(-2/n)\,a'(\text{net}_i)\,x_j & 0 \le y_i \le 0.5 \\ \eta\,(2/n)\,a'(\text{net}_i)\,x_j & 0.5 < y_i \le 1. \end{cases} \tag{21.64}$$

2. *Learning rule for quadratic index of fuzziness*: Let the error measure be chosen as

$$E = g(f_q) = f_q^2, \qquad (21.65)$$

where, from Eq. (21.54), the square of the quadratic index of fuzziness is

$$f_q^2 = \frac{4}{n} \left\{ \sum_{i=1}^{n} [\min(y_i, 1 - y_i)]^2 \right\}. \qquad (21.66)$$

Then we have

$$-\frac{\partial E}{\partial y_i} = \begin{cases} (4/n)(-2y_i) & 0 \le y_i \le 0.5 \\ (4/n)[2(1 - y_i)] & 0.5 < y_i \le 1. \end{cases} \qquad (21.67)$$

Thus, from Eq. (21.60), we obtain the learning rule:

$$\Delta w_{ij} = \begin{cases} -\eta\,(8y_i/n)\,a'\,(\text{net}_i)\,x_j & 0 \le y_i \le 0.5 \\ \eta\,(8/n)(1 - y_i)\,a'\,(\text{net}_i)\,x_j & 0.5 < y_i \le 1. \end{cases} \qquad (21.68)$$

3. *Learning rule for logarithmic entropy*: Consider the error measure

$$E = g(H_\ell) = H_\ell, \qquad (21.69)$$

where, from Eq. (21.55), the entropy of fuzzy set is

$$H_\ell = \frac{1}{n \ln 2} \sum_{i=1}^{n} \{ y_i \ln y_i + (1 - y_i) \ln (1 - y_i) \}. \qquad (21.70)$$

Thus

$$-\frac{\partial E}{\partial y_i} = \frac{1}{n \ln 2} \ln \frac{y_i}{1 - y_i}. \qquad (21.71)$$

Note that as $y_i \to 0$ or 1, $|\ln [y_i/(1 - y_i)]| \to \infty$, whereas, as $y_i \to 0.5$, $|\ln [y_i/(1 - y_i)]| \to 0$. This means that if we use the gradient-descent search, the rate of learning is minimum at the most unstable state (i.e., $y_i \to 0.5$). Hence, to expedite the learning, it is desirable to make a large weight correction when the network is most unstable (i.e., when all the output values are 0.5). In other words, for a neuron, the weight correction for its links should be maximum when its output status is very close to 0.5, and minimum when its output status is close to 0 or 1. This can be achieved by taking [see Eq. (21.60)]

$$\Delta w_{ij} \propto - \frac{\partial E / \partial y_i}{|\partial E / \partial y_i|^q}, \qquad q > 1, \qquad (21.72)$$

that is,

$$\Delta w_{ij} = \eta \left(- \frac{\partial E / \partial y_i}{|\partial E / \partial y_i|^q} \right) a'\,(\text{net}_i)\,x_j, \qquad q > 1, \qquad (21.73)$$

where $|\partial E / \partial y_i|$ represents the magnitude of the gradient. According to Eq. (21.73), when $q = 2$, we have

$$\Delta w_{ij} = -\eta \, \frac{1}{\partial E/\partial y_i} \, a'(net_i) \, x_j = \eta(n \ln 2) \, \frac{1}{\ln \left[y_i/(1-y_i) \right]} \, a'(net_i) \, x_j. \qquad (21.74)$$

4. *Learning rule for exponential entropy*: Consider the error measure

$$E = g \, (H_e) = H_e, \qquad (21.75)$$

where the exponential entropy as defined in Eq. (21.56) is

$$H_e = \frac{1}{n(\sqrt{e}-1)} \sum_{i=1}^{n} \{ y_i e^{1-y_i} + (1-y_i) e^{y_i} - 1 \}. \qquad (21.76)$$

Then

$$-\frac{\partial E}{\partial y_i} = -\frac{1}{n(\sqrt{e}-1)} \{ (1-y_i) e^{1-y_i} - y_i e^{y_i} \}. \qquad (21.77)$$

According to an argument similar to that for logarithmic entropy [see Eq. (21.73)], we have the following learning rule for exponential entropy:

$$\begin{aligned}
\Delta w_{ij} &= -\eta \, \frac{1}{\partial E/\partial y_i} \, a'(net_i) \, x_j \\
&= -\eta n(\sqrt{e}-1) \, \frac{1}{(1-y_i) e^{1-y_i} - y_i e^{y_i}} \, a'(net_i) \, x_j.
\end{aligned} \qquad (21.78)$$

From the above four learning rules in Eqs. (21.64), (21.68), (21.74), and (21.78), it is observed that in each case, the expression for Δw_{ij} has a common factor $\eta a'(net_i) x_j$, which can be ignored in comparing different learning rates. The remaining part of the expression for Δw_{ij} will be referred to as the *learning rate* because only that factor is different for different measures of fuzziness. It can be easily verified that in each of the four cases the learning rate is negative for $y_i \leq 0.5$ and positive for $y_i \geq 0.5$. The fuzzy self-supervised multilayer neural network has been applied to the object extraction problem which can be stated: Given a noisy realization of a scene, the objective is to estimate the original scene that has resulted in the observation. The following example shows such a simulation result.

Example 21.5

[Ghosh et al., 1993]. In this example, a three-layer fuzzy self-supervised multilayer neural network is applied to a synthetic bitonic image corrupted by noise [Fig. 21.18(a)]. The corrupted version is obtained by adding noise from a normal distribution $N(0, \sigma^2)$ with zero mean and $\sigma = 32$. The images are of dimension 128×128 and have 32 gray-scale levels. For this problem, a network with an N^2 neighborhood is used. A neuron thus receives input from nine nodes in the previous layer. The threshold value θ in this case is $\frac{9}{2} = 4.5$. The input gray levels are mapped in $[0,1]$ by a linear transformation and are given as input to the network. The network is then allowed to settle. After the network has stabilized, the output nodes having a status value of 0 constitute one region, and the output nodes with output status 1 constitute another region. The simulation results for different error measures (i.e., different measures of fuzziness) are shown in Fig. 21.18(b)–(e). The results show that the index of fuzziness is better than entropy measures for maintaining the compactness of the extracted objects. But shapes of objects are better preserved by entropy measures. This is because a high learning rate makes a neuron

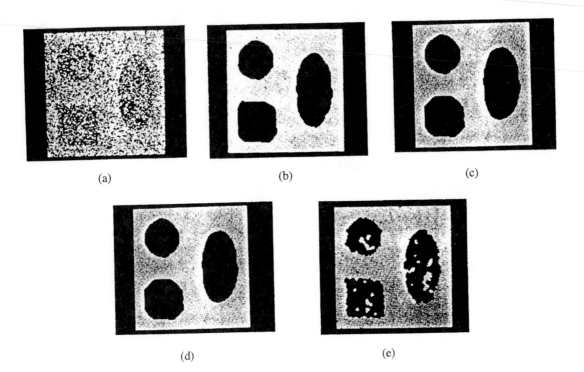

(a)   (b)   (c)

(d)   (e)

Figure 21.18 Simulation results of using the fuzzy self-supervised multilayer neural network for object extraction in Example 21.5. (Adapted from Ghosh et al. [1993], © 1993 IEEE.)

influence its neighbors to a greater extent; thus the noisy elements strongly affect the results. The system thus fails to remove all the noise. On the other hand, entropy measures enable the network to preserve object boundaries, as the learning rate is very high near the most ambiguous region ($y_i \approx 0.5$), that is, the boundaries. This indicates that a lower learning rate (i.e., indices of fuzziness) is suitable when the noise level is very high; otherwise, a higher learning rate (i.e., entropy measures) is preferred.

21.3.2 Genetic Algorithms with Fuzzy Fitness Function for Image Enhancement

The purpose of image enhancement is to improve the picture quality for visual judgment and machine understanding. One of the most popular approaches is contrast enhancement by gray-level modification. Usually, a suitable nonlinear functional mapping is used to perform this task. The simplest form of the functional mapping may be expressed as

$$x'_{mn} = x_{max} f(x_{mn}),\qquad(21.79)$$

where x_{mn} is the gray value of the (m, n)th pixel in the input image, x'_{mn} is the transformed (enhanced) value of the (m, n)th pixel, $f(x)$ is a prescribed transformation function, and x_{max} (x_{min}) is the maximum (minimum) value of the gray-level dynamical range. The most commonly used transformation functions are as follows (see Fig. 21.19):

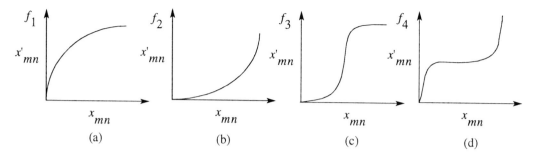

Figure 21.19 Mapping functions commonly used for contrast enhancement.

1.
$$f_1(x) = \frac{x^2}{a_1 + x^2} \quad \text{or} \quad a_1 \log(x), \quad a_1 > 0, \tag{21.80}$$

2.
$$f_2(x) = a_2 [g(x)]^2 + a_3 x + a_4, \quad 0 < a_2, a_3, a_4 < 1, \tag{21.81}$$

where

$$g(x) = \begin{cases} x - a_5 & \text{for } x > a_5 \in (x_{\min}, x_{\max}) \\ 0 & \text{otherwise,} \end{cases} \tag{21.82}$$

3.
$$f_3(x) = \left[1 + \left(\frac{x_{\max} - x_{\min}}{a_6} \right)^{a_7} \right]^{-1}, \tag{21.83}$$

4.
$$f_4(x) = \frac{1}{x_{\max}} \left[x_{\max} - a_6 \left\{ \left(\frac{x_{\max}}{x} + a_8 \right) - 1 \right\}^{-a_7} \right], \tag{21.84}$$

where $a_6, a_7 > 0$, and a_8 is the value of $f(x)$ at $x = 0$.

In the above four mapping functions, the function f_1 depicted in Fig. 21.19(a) increases the contrast within the darker area of the image, while application of the function f_2 shown in Fig. 21.19(b) produces effects exactly opposite those of f_1. The function f_3 shown in Fig. 21.19(c) results in stretching the middle-range gray levels. The function f_4 shown in Fig. 21.19(d) compresses drastically the middle-range values and at the same time stretches the gray levels of the upper and lower ends.

It is noted that although all these transformation functions result in contrast enhancement of an image, not all of them produce the desired (meaningful) enhanced version of a particular image. Since we do not know the exact function that will be suitable for a given image, it seems reasonable to use one general functional form that yields the aforesaid four functions as special cases and others, if necessary. One such function is a convex combination of these four functions:

$$f(x) = a_9 f_1(x) + a_{10} f_2(x) + a_{11} f_3(x) + a_{12} f_4(x), \tag{21.85}$$

with the constraint that

$$a_9 + a_{10} + a_{11} + a_{12} = 1. \tag{21.86}$$

Here, the multipliers (a_9 to a_{12}) are chosen according to the importance (suitability) of a function for a given image. On the other hand, the parameters (a_1 to a_8) of the respective functions are defined according to the quality of enhancement desired. It is noted that this combination enables one to stretch or compress any region of an image that one may desire. Therefore, the problem boils down to determining an optimum set of values of these 12 parameters in order to achieve the desired enhancement.

One possible way to use genetic algorithms (GAs) to determine an optimal parameter set for Eq. (12.85) [Bhandari et al., 1993]. In this scheme, a binary string of length $12q$ can be considered a chromosomal representation of the parameter set $\{a_1, a_2,..., a_{12}\}$. Here each substring of length q is assumed to be representative of each parameter. For example, if $q = 10$, then a chromosome for 12 parameters will be of length 120 such as

$$\underset{a_1}{0\,1\,1\,0\,1\,1\,0\,0\,0\,1} \quad \underset{a_2}{1\,1\,0\,1\,0\,1\,1\,1\,0\,0} \quad ... \quad \underset{a_{12}}{0\,0\,1\,1\,0\,1\,1\,0\,0\,1}. \tag{21.87}$$

After applying the genetic operators, the resulting substrings of length q are decoded into a real number in [0,1]. These parameter values are then multiplied by an appropriate factor to make them lie in their respective domains so that they can be used to compute the enhanced version. The domains of these parameters are as follows: a_1 to a_4 and a_8 to $a_{12} \in [0, 1]$; a_5 and $a_6 \in (x_{min}, x_{max})$; and $a_7 \in [0, 3]$.

In applying GAs, we need a fitness function to quantify the desired enhanced output. In this connection, the measures of fuzziness adopted in the previous section are candidates for the fitness function. Other suitable measures, including compactness [Kundu and Pal, 1990] and index of area coverage [Pal and Ghosh, 1992], can be used as fitness functions. Understandably, the combination of these measures may be a better quantitative index for evaluating image quality.

One final point of importance is that since the size of the parameter set for this problem is not small, it is intuitive that the single-point crossover operation may not be useful for fast convergence. Therefore, the multiple-point crossover operation introduced in Chap. 14 can be applied here.

21.4 FUZZY NEURAL NETWORKS FOR SPEECH RECOGNITION

Since the back-propagation learning algorithm was developed, many neural network applications for speech recognition have been proposed [Rabiner and Juang, 1993]. In particular, time-delay neural networks (TDNNs) and recurrent neural networks (RNNs) have shown a very high phoneme identification performance. Through use of a back-propagation training method, a neural network can delineate an arbitrarily complicated pattern space that conventional methods of pattern classification may fail to partition. However, there are occasions when the ability to construct substantial complexity in the decision surface is a disadvantage. Consider the circumstance when the patterns to be classified occupy overlapping regions in the pattern space; for example, speech feature vectors are typically these kinds of patterns. It is possible to build a neural network that constructs a decision surface that complete "threads" through the *implied* boundary represented by the training patterns. However, this "tightly tuned" fitting to the training patterns may not be an optimal choice for later pattern classification because some training patterns may represent outliers of the pattern ensemble. In this case, the robustness (i.e., the generalization capability) of neural networks is not as adequate as expected. This problem is essentially an overlearning of the training set, which causes a drastic performance reduction when a slight difference arises in the testing set (e.g., speaking rate differences).

Another problem arises when combining neural networks with a language model in which top-N candidate performance is required. This problem derives from simply using discrete phoneme class information as a target value in the conventional method. Thus, the neural network is trained to produce the top phoneme candidate but not the top-N candidates. However, the top-N phoneme candidate information is very important when combined with a language model in continuous speech recognition. Once the lack of phoneme candidate information occurs, it may lead to a fatal error in recognizing continuous speech.

One way to overcome these problems is to take the fuzzy neural approach, which considers the collection of patterns a fuzzy set where each pattern identifies itself with a continuous membership value. With these membership values, it is possible to modify the back-propagation algorithm (such as the fuzzy back-propagation algorithm introduced in Sec. 20.2.2) so that training patterns with large membership values play a more crucial role than those with small membership values in modifying the weights of the network. As a result, the network will unlikely be degraded by a few possible outliers in the training set. Thus, the fuzzy neural training method and the conventional neural training method for speech recognition are both based on the back-propagation algorithm. However, they differ in how they give the target values to the neural network. In the conventional method, target values are given as discrete phoneme class information, that is, 1 for the belonging class and 0s for the others. In the fuzzy neural training method, the target values are given as fuzzy phoneme class information whose values are given in between 0 and 1. This fuzzy phoneme class informs the neural network about the likelihood of the input sample to each phoneme class, in other words, the possibility of belonging to a phoneme class.

Fuzzy phoneme class information can be modeled by considering the distance, for instance, the Euclidean distance measure between the input sample and the nearest sample of each phoneme class in the training set [Komori, 1992]. The assumption that when the distance of two samples is small, these two samples are considered to be alike indicates that each sample has a possibility of belonging to the class of the other sample. However, when the distance of two samples is great, these two samples are considered to be very different, which indicates that each sample has no possibility of belonging to the class of the other sample. To model this fuzzy phoneme class information using the distance d, a likelihood transformation function $f(d)$, which can be considered a membership function, is adopted. By using a monotonous decreasing function such as

$$f(d) = e^{-\alpha d^2},\tag{21.88}$$

where $\alpha \geq 0$, as shown in Fig. 21.20, it can easily model the idea that the larger the distance is, the lower the likelihood is, and the smaller the distance is, the larger the likelihood is. Using this function, fuzzy phoneme class information can be computed according to the distance between the input sample and the nearest sample of each phoneme class in the training set.

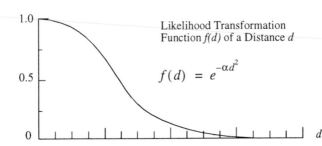

Likelihood Transformation
Function $f(d)$ of a Distance d

$$f(d) = e^{-\alpha d^2}$$

Figure 21.20 Likelihood transformation function.

The basic concept of the above-mentioned fuzzy neural training (FNT) method as well as the conventional training (CT) method is depicted in Fig. 21.21. The target values in the CT method are given as discrete phoneme class information; that is, the target value of sample $B\,(\bullet)$ is given as $\{0,1,0\}$. The target values in the FNT method are given as fuzzy phoneme class information; that is, the target value of sample $B\,(\bullet)$ is given as $\{f(d_{AB}),\, f(d_{BB}),\, f(d_{CB})\}$, where $f(d)$ is a likelihood transformation function of distance d.

Example 21.6

[Komori, 1992]. In this example, the FNT method is used for an 18-consonant identification problem. The 18 consonants are b, g, d, p, t, k, ch, ts, s, sh, h, z, m, n, N, r, w, and y. Samples for neural network training are culled from half of an isolated word database (5.7 mora per second). There are a total of 3638 training samples selected, up to 250 samples for each phoneme class. Samples for neural network testing are culled from the other half of the same database, additionally from the phrase database (7.1 mora per second) and from the sentence database (9.6 mora per second) in order to evaluate the robustness of the speaking rate. A TDNN for an 18-consonant identification is shown in Fig. 21.22. The structure of the TDNN is a feedforward neural network of four layers. The inputs for the TDNNs are 16 mel-scaled spectral power of seven frames (70 milliseconds). For training and testing, end labels of all phoneme samples are adjusted so as to be at the center of the input layer.

Two CT methods and the FNT method are compared. The two CT methods differ in the error function in the back-propagation algorithm. They are (a) the mean squared error function (MSE) and (b) the McClelland error function $\ln(1 - e^2)$. The MSE function is adopted in the

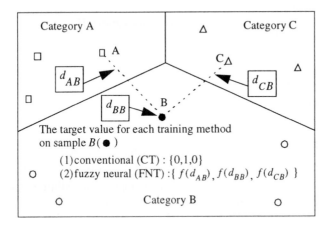

Figure 21.21 Basic concept of the fuzzy neural training method. (Adapted from Komori [1992], © 1992 IEEE.)

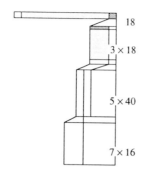

Figure 21.22   TDNN for 18-consonant identification in Example 21.6.

FNT method. The McClelland error function is well known as a fast training method when the number of classes to be identified is large since it back-propagates only the emphasized error. The Euclidean distance measure d of the seven-frame input sample is adopted. A likelihood transformation function is modeled as $f(d) = \exp(-0.005d^2)$. The value 0.005 is chosen by experience so that the target values of the second and third candidates may have certain values. In the experiment, final weights are obtained after 100 training iterations. These weights yield the highest performance on the testing data from the isolated word database.

The phoneme identification results of the 18-consonant identification are shown in Fig. 21.23. It shows the performance of the first candidate and the top-N candidates on the training and testing data (phonemes in isolated words, phrases, and sentences). The vertical axis indicates the identification rate (%) and the horizontal axis the top-N candidates. Comparing the two CT and the FNT methods, there were no big differences in identification performance on phonemes from the isolated word database, either in training or testing. However, the identification performance trained with the FNT method improved on the phoneme culled phrase data (7.1 mora per second) and the sentence database (9.6 mora per second) whose speaking rate differs from the training data (5.7 mora per second). The figures indicate that not only has the first candidate result improved but that the top-N results have also improved. Par-

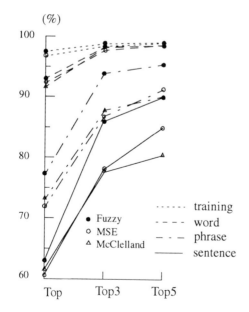

Figure 21.23   Results of identification on 18 consonants. (Adapted from Komori [1992], © 1992 IEEE.)

ticularly on the sentence data, the top-N results improved drastically. For continuous speech recognition, the top-N phoneme candidate information is very important when combined with a language model. Thus, from the improvement shown in this figure, we can expect that the FNT method will be effective in phrase and sentence recognition.

21.5 FUZZY-NEURAL HYBRID SYSTEMS FOR SYSTEM DIAGNOSIS

Previously, we focused either on bringing neural network techniques into fuzzy systems to form *neural fuzzy systems* or on introducing fuzzy logic into neural networks to form *fuzzy neural networks*. In fact, a more advanced, straightforward approach is to put them together to form a fuzzy logic and neural network incorporated system called a *fuzzy-neural hybrid system*. In such systems, fuzzy logic techniques and neural networks can be viewed as two individual subsystems. They do their own jobs by serving different purposes in a system. By making use of their individual strengths, they incorporate and complement each other to accomplish a desired task. A typical architecture of a fuzzy-neural hybrid system is shown in Fig. 21.24, where the neural network is used for input signal processing and the fuzzy logic subsystem is used for output action decisions. This system makes use of the strength of a neural network in its processing speed and the strength of fuzzy logic in its flexible reasoning capability for decision making and control. Of course, this is not the only structure for fuzzy-neural hybrid systems; we can also use fuzzy inference for input state evaluation and neural networks for control. Moreover, we can also include fuzzy neural networks or neural fuzzy systems in a fuzzy-neural hybrid system. In this section, we introduce a fuzzy-neural hybrid system for system diagnosis as a case study.

Real-time diagnosability of a system behavior has a significant importance in industry. Some applications have had a mathematical model available, and the use of explicitly rule-based algorithms has been a dominant force. However, hard logical decisions and exhaustive constraints often cause inflexible implementation of such systems in addition to the fast processing time requirement of real-time applications. In this regard, neural networks and fuzzy logic have been proven a viable alternative. A combination of these two paradigms can provide high speed, flexibility, and humanlike soft, logical decisions.

In this section, we shall introduce the fuzzy-neural hybrid system proposed by Choi et al. [1992b] for real-time nonlinear system diagnosis. This system performs real-time processing, prediction, and data fusion for general real-world system diagnosis which is usually complex, and a final decision should be based on multiple subsystem (channel)

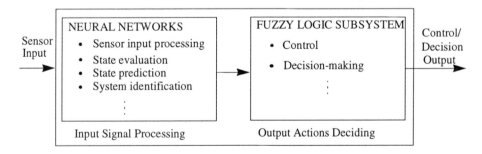

Figure 21.24 A typical architecture of fuzzy-neural hybrid systems.

diagnosis. The architecture of the fuzzy-neural diagnosis system is shown in (channels) that could be contaminated with environmental noise. Each network is trained to predict the future behavior of one time series. The prediction error and its rate of change from each channel are computed and sent to a fuzzy logic decision output stage which contains $(n + 1)$ modules. The $(n + 1)$st final-output module performs data fusion by combining n individual fuzzy decisions that are tuned to match the domain expert's needs. Thus, the basic idea is that the neural network's output predicts the normal system response and this output and the actual system response can be compared to evaluate the presence of the noise. In the case of a noticeable difference between the two responses, we can conclude "unstable" with the use of fuzzy logic.

The neural networks are trained in such a way that each one models a channel transfer function. In case of a system abnormality, the trained neural network is expected to indicate the abnormality in advance. The predicted network's output is compared to actual system output. According to the comparison results, humanlike decisions can then be implemented through fuzzy inference. The error signal (i.e., the deviation from the normal state) and the history of this error signal (i.e., the change in the error) can be part of the fuzzy input components. In a diagnostic task, one might also make use of the previous diagnostic results to arrive at the current diagnosis. For example, if the previous diagnostic result was "unsafe," and both the error and the change in the error are increasing, then one sees that the performance of the system is getting worse. The individual fuzzy decisions $D_1(t)$, $D_2(t), \ldots, D_n(t)$, resulting from each sensor signal, are then gathered in the fuzzy logic output unit for the final decision making. A feedback of the previous decision $D(t - 1)$ can also be applied with the same philosophy as explained before. We shall describe the functions of the neural network and fuzzy logic units in more detail in the following.

Predicting the behavior of a complex system can be viewed as a nonlinear mapping from past states to future states. In the fuzzy-neural diagnosis system shown in Fig. 21.25, this is done by using neural networks. In other words, the job here is to predict the time series p time steps in the future from k samples of previous inputs,

$$\bar{x}(t + p) = f_N(x(t), x(t - 1), x(t - 2), \ldots, x(t - k - 1)), \qquad (21.89)$$

where f_N represents the map learned by the neural network. Once the network extracts the underlying nonlinear map, it is then able to predict normal behavior of the system equation. We have seen several neural networks that can serve this purpose, such as back-propagation networks, radial basis function networks, and so on.

Next, consider the fuzzy logic module found in each processing channel and the output stage in Fig. 21.25. Each of them has the same basic architecture but may have different membership functions and fuzzy logic rules, thus giving each processing channel its own unique identity and behavior. Each accepts an error and a change-in-error signal (i.e., an e and $\dot{e}$ signal per channel) as well as a feedback signal $D_i(t - 1)$ (for the ith channel) and then outputs $D_i(t)$ through fuzzy reasoning based on fuzzy logic rules. Some example rules are:

IF (e is Low) AND ($\dot{e}$ is NOT High) AND ($D_1(t - 1)$ is Stable)
   THEN ($D_1(t)$ = Stable;
ELSE IF ($\dot{e}$ is High) AND (($D_1(t - 1)$ is Stable)OR ($D_1(t - 1)$ is RELATIVELY
   Stable))
   THEN ($D_1(t)$ = RELATIVELY Unstable;
ELSE IF ......

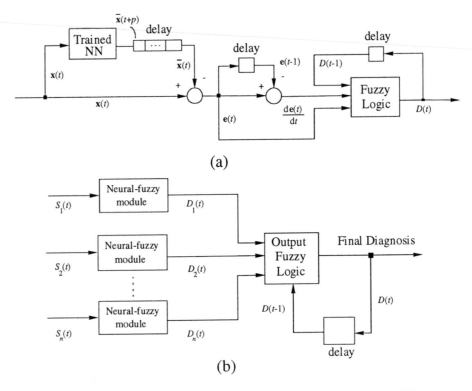

(a)

(b)

Figure 21.25 Architecture of the fuzzy-neural diagnosis system. (a) Single module. (b) Multiple modules illustrating data fusion.

A typical rule table for the fuzzy logic module in each channel is given in Table 21.1(a), where three fuzzy terms, "Low," "Med," and "High," are used for the error signals e and $\dot{e}$ and these rules have a common precondition, "$D_i(t-1)$ is Relatively Unstable (RU)." Similarly, there are fuzzy rules in the output fuzzy logic module that combines n individual fuzzy decisions for the final diagnosis. Table 21.1(b) is a typical rule table in this module for $n=2$ (two channels), where four input fuzzy terms S (Stable), RS (Relatively Stable), RU (Relatively Unstable), and U (Unstable) are used for fuzzy inference of $D_i(t)$

TABLE 21.1 Example of a Fuzzy Control Rule Table for the Fuzzy Logic Modules in the Fuzzy-Neural Diagnosis System

		$\dot{e}$						$D_1(t)$			
		Low	Med	High			S	RS	RU	U	
e	Low	RS	RU	U	$D_i(t-1)=\text{RU}$	$D_2(t)$	S	S	RS	RS	RU
	Med	RU	U	U			RS	RS	RS	RU	RU	$D(t-1)=\text{RU}$
	High	U	U	U			RU	RS	RU	RU	U
							U	RU	RU	U	U

(a)	(b)

Fuzzy Neural Systems for Pattern Recognition   Chap. 21

and $D_i(t-1)$. The rules in Table 21.1(b) have one common precondition: $D(t-1) = $ RU, where $D(t-1)$ denotes the final inferred output of the output fuzzy logic module. The exact fuzzy rules used in a fuzzy-neural diagnosis system can be provided by experts or obtained through learning processes. Also, the membership functions used can be determined heuristically or tuned by a learning procedure from trial e and $\dot{e}$ [or $D_i(t)$, $i = 1, 2, \ldots, n$]. We shall examine a heuristic approach to constructing the membership functions in the following example.

Example 21.7

[Choi et al., 1992b]. In this example, we use a two-channel fuzzy-neural diagnosis system for noise detection in a Mackey-Glass chaotic time series (see Sec. 10.2.3), which is described by the delay differential equation in Eq. (10.63), where $a = 0.2$, $b = 0.1$, and the time-delay parameter τ governs the degree of chaos. Without loss of generality, $p = 6$ and $k = 6$ in Eq. (21.89) are used in the simulation. A back-propagation network with 6 input nodes, 10 hidden nodes and 1 output node is used for each channel. In each of the two channels of the fuzzy-neural diagnosis system, 17 commonsense fuzzy rules are used to implement the required control. The associated membership functions are constructed after analyzing statistics to exploit the properties of experimental data taken from trials e and $\dot{e}$. The mean values (m_e and $m_{\dot{e}}$) and the standard deviations (σ_e and $\sigma_{\dot{e}}$) are used as a guide for membership function generation. Heuristically, a high membership value should be assigned to the events that are most likely. To obtain the statistics, 2000 samples are collected, and the means and the standard deviations are calculated as $m_e = 0.046$, $m_{\dot{e}} = 0.028$, $\sigma_e = 0.066$, and $\sigma_{\dot{e}} = 0.048$. According to these values, the way to construct the membership functions of the fuzzy terms of the linguistic variable $e(t)$ is as follows [see Fig. 21.26(a)]. The mean value is the threshold of the fuzzy set "Low." The peak of the "Med" fuzzy set is equal to $m_e + |m_e - \sigma_e|$. The transition threshold value 0.086 is chosen from $m_e + 2|m_e - \sigma_e|$. In this way, we can construct the membership functions as depicted in Fig. 21.26(a). Similarly, the membership functions of the fuzzy terms of the other linguistic variables $\dot{e}(t)$ and $D(t)$ can be constructed as shown in Figs. 21.26(b) and (c).

In computer simulations, two Mackey-Glass chaotic time series with time delays of $\tau = 17$ and $\tau = 30$ are chosen as shown in Fig. 21.27(a) and (d), respectively. The two signals are the inputs to the two channels of the fuzzy-neural diagnosis systems individually. The back-propagation network in each channel is trained to predict the associated input time series, where the learning gain and momentum gain for the back-propagation algorithm are arbitrarily chosen at 0.25 and 0.5, respectively. Once two neural networks are trained, a Gaussian random noise with zero mean and 0.1 variance is added to the original two time series. The overlapping between the corrupted true time signal and the predicted signal generated by neural networks is shown in Fig. 21.27(a) and (d). The system's task is to detect the presence

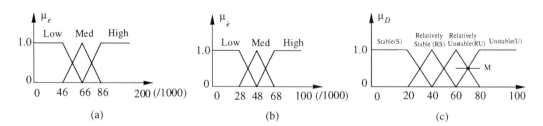

Figure 21.26 Membership functions constructed in Example 21.7. (a) Membership function for $e(t)$. (b) Membership function for $de(t)/dt$. (c) Membership function for $D(t)$.

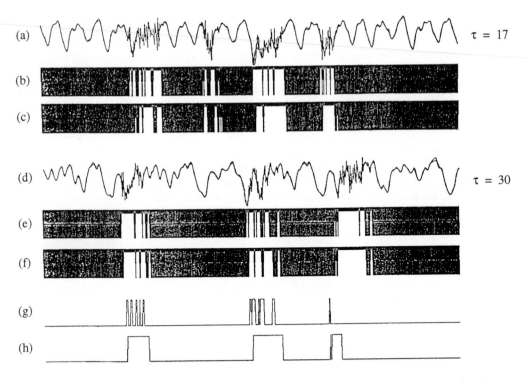

Figure 21.27 Simulation results in Example 21.7. Two channel fuzzy-neural system output used for noise detection on a Mackey-Glass chaotic time series. (Adapted from Choi et al. [1992b], © 1992 IEEE.)

of random noise. If both channels are corrupted by noise, a correct final diagnosis should be obtained by generation of a positive pulse for the duration of the noise.

For comparison, two different decision-making strategies are used, one for the neural network–based approach and the other for the original fuzzy logic–based approach. Figure 21.27(b) and (c) shows the resultant pulses for the all-neural (fuzzy logic is replaced by a neural net in Fig. 21.25) and fuzzy-neural systems, respectively, for $\tau = 17$. Analogously, Fig. 21.27(e) and (f) are for $\tau = 30$. The final fuzzy-neural diagnosis is shown in Fig. 21.27(h), which is a result of the fuzzy logic reasoning on the signals in Fig. 21.27(c) and (f). The final all-neural diagnosis is shown in Fig. 21.27(g), which is the logic AND operation of Fig. 21.27(b) and (e). By comparing Fig. 21.27(g) and (h), we see that the all-neural diagnostic shows sporadic output in the presence of noise, while fuzzy-neural diagnosis improves the overall performance so that final human decision making is less difficult.

21.6 CONCLUDING REMARKS

Various fuzzy-neural integrated models for pattern recognition are discussed in this chapter. A good review of statistical pattern recognition (PR), fuzzy PR, neural PR, and their relationships can be found in papers written by Bezdek [1992b] and Simpson [1992b, 1993] and in [Bezdek and Pal, 1992]. A good introduction to clustering algorithms can be found in Duda and Hart [1973] and Titterington et al. [1985]. An excellent book on statistical PR is [Fukunaga, 1972]. Ruck et al. [1990] have described several connections between the feedforward neural classifier net and statistical pattern recognition.

A widely used supervised technique for pattern classification is the *k-nearest neighbor* (*k*-NN) rule and its fuzzified version [Bezdek et al., 1983]. Further discussion of the fuzzy *k*-NN rule can be found in [Jozwik, 1983; Keller et al., 1985]. Some milestone papers on the *k*-NN rule and its derivatives are compiled in [Dasarathy, 1990].

For fuzzy neural classifiers, Pedrycz [1992] proposed a three-layer fuzzy neural network model for solving the pattern classification problem where the patterns belonging to the same class are distributed in certain clusters. That is, the model performs the mapping of disjoint clusters of data residing within a multidimensional unit hypercube. The comparison of fuzzy min-max classification neural networks with other neural network classifiers is discussed by Simpson [1992b].

For fuzzy neural clustering, some modifications of AFLC are possible. Kim and Mitra [1993] used a vigilance criterion different from Eq. (21.50) and a learning rule different from Eqs. 8.22) and (8.23). The new vigilance criterion incorporates a membership value into the Euclidean distance. Another modified AFLC is aimed at the identification of noise outliers in clustering [Pemmaraju and Mitra, 1993]. Simpson [1993] proposed a *fuzzy min-max clustering neural network* similar to fuzzy min-max classification neural networks, which is an ART-like fuzzy neural clustering network. Simpson and Jahns [1993] extended fuzzy min-max clustering networks to perform function approximation. Fogel and Simpson [1993] applied the techniques of evolutionary programming and information criteria to determine placement of the hyperbox cores used for fuzzy min-max clustering neural networks.

For fuzzy neural models for image processing, Blanz and Gish [1990] used a three-layer back-propagation network trained with a set of similar images for pixel classification, and Babaguchi et al. [1990] used a similar concept for histogram thresholding.

For fuzzy neural hybrid systems, Fukuda et al. [1992a,b,c] proposed a *neural-fuzzy sensor fusion system.* The system can estimate the measurement error of each sensor's measurement value using fuzzy inference. The estimated measurement errors, along with the sensor measurement values, are then put into a neural network that provides the integrated value of multiple sensors. Fukuda and Shibata [1992] proposed an architecture of a hierarchical intelligent control system. This system is an integrated approach of neuromorphic and symbolic control of a robot manipulator, including a neural network for the *servo control,* an expert system for the *symbolic control,* and a neural fuzzy module for the *skill-based control.*

Various applications of fuzzy neural integrated systems can be witnessed. For fuzzy connectionist expert systems, there are fuzzy expert system tools (FEST) proposed in [Kandel et al., 1992; Posey et al., 1992] and the combinatorial neural model (CNM) proposed by Machado and da Rocha [1992a, 1993]. FEST allows fuzziness in both data and knowledge descriptions and thus permits knowledge and/or data to be described in fuzzy terms. The CNM aims at solving classification tasks. It can provide the functions of *inquiry* and *explanation* in addition to the function of inference in expert systems. Sanchez [1992] applied a fuzzy connectionist expert system to medical diagnosis. The system allows a graded assignment of diagnosis to patients. In process control, Yamaguchi et al. [1992ab] proposed a system called the fuzzy associative memory organizing units system (FAMOUS). In FAMOUS, a set of fuzzy IF-THEN rules is used for controlling variable parameter processes. FAMOUS was constructed from the bidirectional associative memory-based neural fuzzy system (BAM-NFS) proposed by Yamaguchi et al. [1992ab]. Imasaki et al. [1993] developed a modified BAM-NFS and applied it as a command spelling corrector. In data analysis, Ichihashi and Türksen [1993] used a neural fuzzy model with singleton conse-quents and Gaussian membership functions for data analysis of pairwise comparisons for deriving the associated weights of different objects. This model was applied to evaluation of the psychological responses of human beings to vibrations based on pairwise compar-isons. In speech recognition, a good reference is [Rabiner and Juang, 1993]. To solve the problem of the long computation time of FNT discussed in this chapter, Qi et al. [1993] constructed a membership function based on geometric properties of the pattern space. Since the minimization of the mean squared error criterion function in neural networks does not necessarily lead to minimum classification error, Juang and Katagiri [1992] and Taur and Kung [1993] proposed the techniques of *minimum error (probability) classification* for speech recognition.

21.7 PROBLEMS

21.1 The basic scheme of pattern recognition includes three steps: (1) data acquisition, (2) feature selection, and (3) clustering or classification process. For each step, state one fuzzy logic scheme or neural network technique introduced in Parts I and II of this book that can perform the task specified by the step.

21.2 Two popular clustering techniques can be recognized: hierarchical clustering and partitioning clustering. A hierarchical clustering technique imposes a hierarchical structure on the data which consist of a sequence of clusters. A partitioning clustering technique organizes patterns into a small number of clusters by labeling each pattern in some way. From the fuzzy logic and neural network clustering techniques, state two clustering techniques that belong to hierarchi-cal clustering and two that belong to partitioning clustering.

21.3 Name three neural network models that can be used for both clustering and classification.

21.4 **(a)** Randomly generate 40 two-dimensional pattern vectors for each of the two classes with the following Gaussian distributions:

$$p_1(\mathbf{x}) = \frac{1}{\sigma_1\sqrt{2\pi}} \exp \frac{-\left|\mathbf{x} - \mathbf{m}_1\right|^2}{2\sigma_1^2}, \qquad p_2(\mathbf{x}) = \frac{1}{\sigma_2\sqrt{2\pi}} \exp \frac{-\left|\mathbf{x} - \mathbf{m}_2\right|^2}{2\sigma_2^2},$$

where $\mathbf{m}_1 = [1, 1]^T$, $\mathbf{m}_2 = [-1, -1]^T$, and $\sigma_1 = \sigma_2 = 1.5$. Classify these patterns using the algorithm for the "neural fuzzy membership model" (see Example 21.1).

(b) Redo part (a) but set the variances of the Gaussian distributions as $\sigma_1 = \sigma_2 = 3$.

21.5 Generalize the algorithm of the neural fuzzy membership model that solves two-class classifi-cation problems to solving multiclass classification problems. How many BP nets are neces-sary for this algorithm to solve a three-class classification problem?

21.6 **(a)** Compare the structure and functionalities of the fuzzy min-max classification neural net-work to those of the FALCON-ART.

(b) As in Fig. 21.9 (Example 21.2), illustrate the fuzzy min-max classification learning algo-rithm on the data set: $\mathbf{x}_1 = (0.7, 0.2)$ in class d_1, $\mathbf{x}_2 = (0.3, 0.5)$ in class d_2, $\mathbf{x}_3 = (0.5, 0.4)$ in class d_1, and $\mathbf{x}_4 = (0.6, 0.3)$ in class d_2.

21.7 How should one modify the functions and learning algorithm of the fuzzy min-max classifica-tion neural network if it is being used as a control network or a function approximator? (*Hint:*

Fuzzy Neural Systems for Pattern Recognition   Chap. 21

For purposes of control and function approximation, we can allow any overlapping between hyperboxes.)

21.8 How should one modify the functions and learning algorithm of the fuzzy min-max classification neural network if it is being used for pattern clustering? (*Hint*: Refer to [Simpson, 1993]).

21.9 Develop a GA-based method for fuzzy partitioning of the input space for fuzzy classification using fuzzy rules; that is, replace the grid-type fuzzy partitions on the pattern space by $(k - d)$ tree-type fuzzy partitions (see Fig. 19.15).

21.10 Write a program for implementing the fuzzy competitive learning rule in Eqs. (21.47) and (21.48) and apply this program to the butterfly example described in Example 8.3. The initial weights are set according to Eq. (8.22) with randomly specified membership grades. The parameters are set as $c = 2$, $\eta = 0.01$, and $m = 1.2$ and 2. In each iteration, all patterns are presented to the algorithm in random order. Compare the results to those for the FCM algorithm (see Sec. 8.1.2).

21.11 Discuss the advantages and disadvantages of the AFLC compared to the fuzzy ART algorithm. Can the fuzzy ART algorithm overcome background noise or outlier problems?

21.12 From the results obtained in Example 21.5 (Fig. 21.18), summarize the respective characteristics of the different measures of fuzziness used in the fuzzy self-supervised multilayer network. State some guidelines suggesting suitable measures of fuzziness to be used for some desired result (expected property of the extracted image).

21.13 Design a general functional form, other than that in Eq. (21.85), that also yields the four basic transformation functions in Eqs. (21.80)–(21.84) as special cases. What are the desirable properties of your function? Describe how GAs can be applied to find the proper parameter values of your function.

21.14 Discuss the advantages of using fuzzy neural networks for speech recognition over purely neural or fuzzy speech recognition techniques.

21.15 In contrast to the typical architecture of a fuzzy-neural hybrid system shown in Fig. 21.24, sketch and explain an architecture of a fuzzy-neural hybrid system that uses fuzzy inference for input state evaluation and neural networks for control. Use a practical application example to illustrate the use of such hybrid systems.

Appendix A

MATLAB* Fuzzy Logic Toolbox

MATLAB® (an abbreviation for MATrix LABoratory) is a technical computing environment for high-performance numerical computation and visualization. MATLAB integrates numerical analysis, matrix computation, signal processing, and graphics in an easy-to-use environment where problems and solutions are expressed just as they are written mathematically without traditional programming. Among the several toolboxes associated with MATLAB, the Fuzzy Logic Toolbox and the Neural Network Toolbox provide many predefined functions that can be called by the user to simulate various types of fuzzy logic systems and neural network models, respectively.

The Fuzzy Logic Toolbox is a collection of functions built on the MATLAB numerical computing environment. It provides a useful tool for users to create and edit fuzzy inference systems (FISs) within the framework of MATLAB, or they can build stand-alone C programs that call on fuzzy systems built with the Fuzzy Logic Toolbox. Although users can work entirely from the command line if they prefer, this toolbox relies heavily on graphical user interface (GUI) tools to help users accomplish their work. Table A.1 lists the commands provided by the MATLAB Fuzzy Logic Toolbox. These commands are divided into three groups related to membership functions, fuzzy inference, and some advanced techniques. The advanced techniques include fuzzy clustering, neural fuzzy systems, and fuzzy rule extraction from numerical training data.

This appendix is written to familiarize the reader with the use of the Fuzzy Logic Toolbox for designing and simulating *fuzzy inference systems* and *neural fuzzy systems* and

*Matlab and the Fuzzy Logic Toolbox and the Neural Network Toolbox are developed by The MathWorks, Inc. The MathWorks, Inc., 24 Prime Park Way, Natick, MA, 01760. Telephone: (508) 647-7000, Fax: (508) 647-7001, E-mail: info@mathworks. com, FTP: ftp. mathworks.com, WWW: http://www.mathworks. com.

TABLE A.1 Instruction Table for MATLAB Fuzzy Logic Toolbox

Type	Command	Function Explanation
Membership functions	dsigmf	Difference of two sigmoid membership functions
	qauss2mf	Two-sided Gaussian membership function
	gaussmf	Gaussian membership function
	gbellmf	Generalized bell-shaped membership function
	pimf	Pi-shaped membership function
	psigmf	Product of two sigmoid membership functions
	smf	S-shaped membership function
	sigmf	Sigmoid membership function
	trapmf	Trapezoidal membership function
	trimf	Triangular membership function
	zmf	Z-shaped membership function
FIS data structure management	addmf	Add membership function to FIS
	addrule	Add rule to FIS
	addvar	Add variable to FIS
	defuzz	Defuzzify membership function
	evalfis	Perform fuzzy inference calculation
	evelmf	Generic membership function evaluation
	gensurf	Generic FIS output surface
	getfis	Get fuzzy system properties
	mf2mf	Translate parameters between functions
	newfis	Create new FIS
	parsrule	Parse fuzzy rules
	plotfis	Display FIS input-output diagram
	plotmf	Display all membership functions for one variable
	readfis	Load FIS from disk
	rmmf	Remove membership function from FIS
	rmvar	Remove variable from FIS
	setfis	Set fuzzy system properties
	showfis	Display annotates FIS
	showrule	Display FIS rules
	writefis	Save FIS to disk
Advanced techniques	anfis	Training routine for TSK-type FIS
	fcm	Find clusters with fuzzy c-means clustering
	genfis1	Generate FIS matrix using generic method
	subclust	Find cluster centers with subtractive clustering

to aid the reader in the study of the Fuzzy Logic Toolbox for use in applications of fuzzy control and fuzzy pattern recognition. In the following sections, we shall first demonstrate the use of the Fuzzy Logic Toolbox to design manually the conventional fuzzy logic controller introduced in Chap. 7. We shall then describe the use of the Fuzzy Logic Toolbox to implement the fuzzy c-means (FCM) algorithm introduced in Sec. 8.1.2 for fuzzy clustering. We shall also illustrate the use of a neural fuzzy system, called ANFIS (see Sec. 19.3.2), supported in the Fuzzy Logic Toolbox. Finally, we shall demonstrate the use of the Fuzzy Logic Toolbox in applications involving water bath temperature control using fuzzy control as well as neural fuzzy control.

This appendix focuses on use of the Fuzzy Logic Toolbox via the command-line input method. Basic usage and many important and useful features of the MATLAB and

Fuzzy Logic Toolbox are not discussed here. For this information, the reader is referred to the *MATLAB User's Guide* and *Fuzzy Logic Toolbox User's Guide* published by Math-Works, Inc.

A.1 DEMONSTRATION CASES

A.1.1 A Simple Fuzzy Logic Controller

(a) Demonstration subject: Manually designed fuzzy logic controllers.

(b) Problem statement: This demonstration uses the Fuzzy Logic Toolbox to realize the fuzzy logic controller specified in Example 7.3 in Sec. 7.1.

(c) MATLAB commands for fuzzy inference:

newfis   Create new FIS.

addvar   Add variable to FIS.

addmf   Add membership function to FIS.

addrule Add rule to FIS.

plotfis Plot FIS I/O diagram.

evelfis Perform fuzzy inference calculation.

setfis   Set fuzzy system properties.

(d) Program listing:

```
a=newfis('fydemol');   % Create new FIS with filename "fydemol.fis."
% Add input variables x, y and output variable z to FIS.
a=addvar(a, 'input', 'x', [2 9]);
a=addmf(a, 'input', 1, 'A1', 'trimf', [2 5 8]);
a=addmf(a, 'input', 1, 'A2', 'trimf', [3 6 9]);
a=addvar(a, 'input', 'y', [4 11]);
a=addmf(a, 'input', 2, 'B1', 'trimf', [5 8 11]);
a=addmf(a, 'input', 2, 'B2', 'trimf', [4 7 10]);
a=addvar(a, 'output', 'z', [1 9]);
a=addmf(a, 'output', 1, 'C1', 'trimf', [1 4 7]);
a=addmf(a, 'output', 1, 'C2', 'trimf', [3 6 9]);
% Add rules to FIS.
rule=[1 1 1 1 1; 2 2 2 1 1]; a=addrule(a, rule);
% Use COA defuzzification method to find output z.
z=evalfis([4 8], a)     % Set x=4 and y=8.
% Use MOM defuzzification method to find output z.
aa=setfis(a, 'DefuzzMethod', 'mom');   % Set MOM defuzzification
    method.
z=evalfis([4 8], aa)    % Set x=4 and y=8.
```

(e) Result: The reader can see the assigned membership functions graphically using the command "plotfis(a)." In this demonstration, the final inferred value for the inputs, $x = 4$ and $y = 8$, is 4.7 for the COA defuzzification method and 4.0 for the MOM defuzzification method. These two values are the same as the z^*_{COA} value and the z^*_{MOM} value, respectively, obtained in Example 7.3.

A.1.2 A Neural Fuzzy System—ANFIS

(a) Demonstration subject: neural fuzzy systems.

(b) Problem statement: This demonstration uses a neural fuzzy system, the ANFIS introduced in Sec. 19.3.2, to predict a chaotic signal. The classical time series prediction problem is a one-step-ahead prediction of the following logistic function:

$$x(k+1) = ax(k)(1 - x(k)).$$

The behavior of the time series generated by this equation depends critically upon the value of the parameter a. If $a < 1$, the system has a single fixed point at the origin, and from a random initial value in the closed interval [0 1] the time series collapses to a constant value. For $a > 3$, the system generates a periodic attractor. Beyond the value $a = 3.6$, the system becomes chaotic. In this demonstration, we shall use the ANFIS to predict a chaotic time series with $a = 3.8$ and initial value $x(1) = 0.001$.

(c) MATLAB commands for the ANFIS:

    anfis   Training routine for TSK-type fuzzy inference system.
    genfis1   Generate FIS matrix using generic method.

(d) Program listing:

```
% Generate the training data.
x(1)=0.001;    % Initial value.
for k = 1 : 60
    x(k + 1)=3.8*x(k)*(1-x(k));
end;
trndata=[x(1:59); x(2:60)]';
% Define the rules and initial parameters of the FIS.
nummfs=5; mftype='gbellmf';
infismat=genfis1(trndata, nummfs, mftype);
% Start ANFIS training for 30 epochs.
[outfismat, error, stepsize]=anfis(trndata, infismat, 30);
pause;    % Hit any key to test the trained ANFIS.
% Set the initial condition as x(1)=0.9 and do 100 time-step
    prediction.
x(1)=0.9;
for k = 1 : 100
    x(k + 1)=3.8*x(k)*(1-x(k));
end;
hold on; plot(x(2:101), 'yo'); plot(x(2:101), 'y');
plot(evalfis(x(1:100)', outfismat)', 'r*'); plot(evalfis(x(1:100)',
    outfismat)', 'r');
xlabel('Time Step'); ylabel('Chaotic Signal " o " ANFIS Output
    " x ");
```

(e) Result: As shown in Fig. A.1, the ANFIS has a good prediction capability for the chaotic signal starting at the initial value $x(1) = 0.9$, which is different from that used in the training. It should be pointed out that the ANFIS learns to predict the chaotic signal in quite a short time.

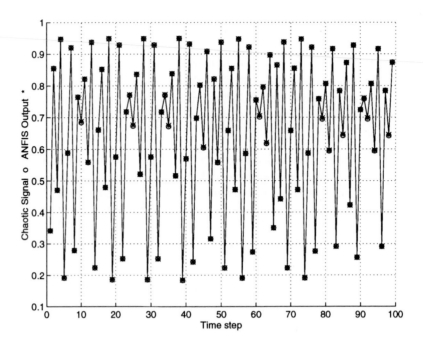

Figure A.1 Simulation result of predicting a chaotic signal using the ANFIS.

A.1.3 Fuzzy *c*-means Clustering

(a) Demonstration subject: Fuzzy clustering.

(b) Problem statement: This demonstration uses the Fuzzy Logic Toolbox to solve the butterfly clustering problem stated in Example 8.3 in Sec. 8.1.2 using the fuzzy *c*-means clustering algorithm [Eqs. (8.22) and (8.23)]. Here, the starting partition matrix $U^{(0)}$ is different from that used in Example 8.3.

(c) MATLAB commands for fuzzy *c*-means clustering:

  fcm   Find clusters with fuzzy *c*-means clustering algorithm.

(d) Program listing:

```
% Define the butterfly data.
data=[0.2 0.2 0.2 0.3 0.3 0.3 0.4 0.5 0.6 0.7 0.7 0.7 0.8 0.8 0.8
    0.1 0.4 0.7 0.2 0.4 0.6 0.4 0.4 0.4 0.2 0.4 0.6 0.1 0.4 0.7]';
% Apply fuzzy 2-means algorithm for m = 1.25 on the above data.
[center, U, obj_fcn]=fcm(data, 2, [1.25 100 0.01 1]);
hold on;    % Plot the final membership values.
plot(U(2, :), 'yo'); plot(U(2, :), 'y'); plot(U(1, :), 'ro');
    plot(U(1, :), 'r');
xlabel('Input Data Sequence'); ylabel('Membership Values');
U    % Show the final partition matrix.
```

(e) Result: The final membership values calculated by the preceding program are shown in Fig. A.2. It is observed that this figure is very similar to the one in Fig. 8.4. The *U* variable in the program indicates the partition matrix, whose final entry values are the same as those shown in Fig. 8.4.

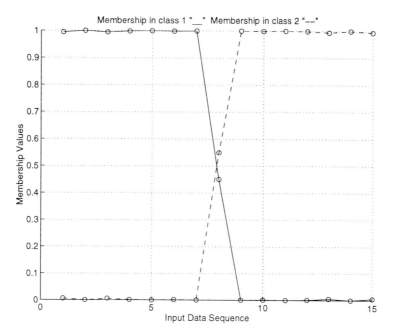

Figure A.2   Simulation result of fuzzy *c*-means clustering.

A.2 DEMONSTRATION OF FUZZY LOGIC APPLICATIONS

A.2.1 A Fuzzy Controller for Water Bath Temperature Control

(a) Problem statement: In this demonstration, we shall design a fuzzy controller for the temperature control of a water bath. The plant to be controlled is described by

$$y(k+1) = a(T_s)\, y(k) + \frac{b(T_s)}{1 + \exp^{0.5y(k)-\gamma}}\, u(k) + [1 - a(T_s)]\, Y_0,$$

where $a(T_s) = \exp^{-\alpha T_s}$ and $b(T_s) = (\beta/\alpha)(1 - \exp^{-\alpha T_s})$. The parameters of the plant are set as $\alpha = 1.00151\, \exp^{-4}$, $\beta = 8.67973\, \exp^{-3}$, $\gamma = 40$, and $Y_0 = 25°C$. The plant input $u(k)$ is limited to between 0 and 5 volts. The sampling period T_s is set as 25 seconds. The goal is to design a fuzzy controller that will control the water temperature to follow a reference profile as closely as possible. This reference profile (signal) is 35°C for $0 \le t \le 40$ minutes, 50°C for $40 \le t \le 80$ minutes, 65°C for $80 \le t \le 120$ minutes, and 80°C for $120 \le t \le 180$ minutes.

The input variables for the fuzzy controller are chosen as $e(t)$ and $c(t)$, where $e(t)$ is the performance error indicating the error between the desired water temperature and the actual measured temperature and $c(t)$ is the rate of change in the performance error $e(t)$. The output or the controlled linguistic variable is the voltage signal $u(t)$ to the heater, where the range of the output voltage is between 0 and 5 volts.

Seven fuzzy terms are defined for each linguistic variable. These fuzzy terms are from negative large (NL) to positive large (PL). Each fuzzy term is specified by a

Gaussian membership function. The reader can use the command "plotmf" to see all the membership functions of a linguistic variable graphically. As for the fuzzy rules, common sense and engineering judgment determine the entries in the fuzzy rule matrix, where a total of 25 rules are formulated. These fuzzy rules are shown in Table A.2.

Like other controllers, a fuzzy controller has some scaling parameters to be specified by the designer. In this demonstration, three gain constants need to be specified. They are GE, GC, and GU, corresponding to the process error, the change in error, and the controller's output, respectively. Finally, the discrete fuzzy centroid defuzzification strategy is used to defuzzify the fuzzy control output.

(b) Program listing:

1. Rule program listing:

```
a=newfis('fyappr1');    % Create a new FIS with filename
    "fyappr1.fis."
% Build the I/O membership functions and fuzzy rules.
% Define membership functions for the input variable "ERROR."
a=addvar(a, 'input', 'ERROR', [-1 1]);
a=addmf(a, 'input', 1, 'NL', 'gaussmf', [0.1 -1]);
a=addmf(a, 'input', 1, 'NM', 'gaussmf', [0.1 -0.6]);
a=addmf(a, 'input', 1, 'NS', 'gaussmf', [0.1 -0.3]);
a=addmf(a, 'input', 1, 'ZE', 'gaussmf', [0.1 0]);
a=addmf(a, 'input', 1, 'PS', 'gaussmf', [0.1 0.3]);
a=addmf(a, 'input', 1, 'PM', 'gaussmf', [0.1 0.6]);
a=addmf(a, 'input', 1, 'PL', 'gaussmf', [0.1 1]);
% Define membership functions for the input variable "CERROR."
a=addvar(a, 'input', 'CERROR', [-1 1]);
a=addmf(a, 'input', 2, 'NL', 'gaussmf', [0.1 -1]);
a=addmf(a, 'input', 2, 'NM', 'gaussmf', [0.1 -0.6]);
a=addmf(a, 'input', 2, 'NS', 'gaussmf', [0.1 -0.3]);
a=addmf(a, 'input', 2, 'ZE', 'gaussmf', [0.1 0]);
a=addmf(a, 'input', 2, 'PS', 'gaussmf', [0.1 0.3]);
a=addmf(a, 'input', 2, 'PM', 'gaussmf', [0.1 0.6]);
```

TABLE A.2 Fuzzy Rule Table Formulated for the Water Bath Temperature Control System*

		Error, $e(t)$						
		NL	NM	NS	ZE	PS	PM	PL
Change error, $c(t)$	PL					PL	PL	PL	PL
	PM					PM	PM	PM	PL
	PS			PS	PS	PS	PM	PL
	ZE	NL	NM	NS	ZE	PS	PM	PL
	NS			NS	NS	NS	NS	
	NM				NM			
	NL				NL			

*The preconditions are the error and the change in error, and the consequent of each rule is given inside the box.

```
a=addmf(a, 'input', 2, 'PL', 'gaussmf', [0.1 1]);
% Define membership functions for the output variable "MENU."
a=addvar(a, 'output', 'MENU', [-1 1]);
a=addmf(a, 'output', 1, 'NL', 'gaussmf', [0.1 -1]);
a=addmf(a, 'output', 1, 'NM', 'gaussmf', [0.1 -0.6]);
a=addmf(a, 'output', 1, 'NS', 'gaussmf', [0.1 -0.3]);
a=addmf(a, 'output', 1, 'ZE', 'gaussmf', [0.1 0]);
a=addmf(a, 'output', 1, 'PS', 'gaussmf', [0.1 0.3]);
a=addmf(a, 'output', 1, 'PM', 'gaussmf', [0.1 0.6]);
a=addmf(a, 'output', 1, 'PL', 'gaussmf', [0.1 1]);
% Define fuzzy rules.
rule=[...
1 2 3 3 3 4 4 4 4 4 4 5 5 5 5 5 6 6 6 6 7 7 7 7
4 4 5 4 3 7 6 5 4 3 2 1 7 6 5 4 3 7 6 5 4 7 6 5 4
1 2 5 3 3 7 6 5 4 3 2 1 7 6 5 5 3 7 6 6 6 7 7 7 7
1 1 1 1 1 1 1 1 1 1 1 1 1 1 1 1 1 1 1 1 1 1 1 1 1
1 1 1 1 1 1 1 1 1 1 1 1 1 1 1 1 1 1 1 1 1 1 1 1 1];
a=addrule(a, rule');
writefis(a, 'fyappr1');      % Save FIS to disk.
```

2. Test program listing:

```
fis=readfis('fyappr1');      % Read the file "fyappr1.fis."
% Define plant parameters.
Ts=25; p=1.00151*10^(-4); q=8.67973*10^(-3);
r=40.0; yo=25; y(1)=yo; a=exp(-p*Ts); b=(q/p)*(1-exp(-p*Ts));
% Define the reference output.
for k = 1 : 180
    if (k ≤ 40)  ref(k)=35;
    elseif (k > 40 & k ≤ 80)  ref(k)=50;
    elseif (k > 80 & k ≤ 120)  ref(k)=65;
    elseif (k > 120)  ref(k)=80; end;
end;
GE=1/15; GC=1/15; GU=450;   % Define gain constants.
pause   % Hit any key to test this fuzzy controller.
for k = 1 : 179
    e(k)=(ref(k)-y(k)); ee(k)=e(k)*GE;
    if k == 1  ce(k)=0;
    else  ce(k)=e(k)-e(k - 1); end;
    cee(k)=ce(k)*GC;
    mu(k)=evalfis([ee(k) cee(k)], fis); u(k)=mu(k)*GU;
    if (u(k)≥5)  u(k)=5;
    elseif (u(k)≤0)  u(k)=0;
    else     u(k)=u(k); end;
    y(k + 1)=a*y(k)+b/(1+exp(0.5*y(k)-r))*u(k)+(1-a)*yo;
end;
hold on; grid;   % Plot plant input/output and reference output.
plot(y(1:180), '.y'); plot(ref(1:180),'- -r'); plot(u(1:179),'g');
xlabel('Sampling Time Step kT T = 30 seconds');
ylabel('Temperature(degree)');
title('Reference Signal "_ _" Actual Output "." Control Signal
     "___" ');
```

```
pause      % Hit any key to calculate the performance index AES.
AES=sum(abs(ref-y))
```

(c) Simulation results: The test result is shown in Fig. A.3. We find that the designed fuzzy controller has a good temperature-tracking capability, but that the control signal $u(k)$ has a big change rate in the region of high temperature. This shows that the designed fuzzy controller does not perform well. In order to quantify the tracking capability for comparison in the following section, we define a performance index $\text{AES} = \sum_{k=1} |\text{ref}(k) - y(k)|$, where ref (k) is the reference signal and $y(k)$ is the actual output. In this demonstration, the performance index is $\text{AES} = 426.80$.

A.2.2 A Neural Fuzzy Controller for Water Bath Temperature Control

(a) Problem statement: In this application, we shall use the ANFIS to control the temperature of a water bath system, which is described in the preceding application demonstration. We shall implement the ANFIS controller using the direct inverse control strategy shown in Fig. 16.1(c). We first obtain the training data by imposing random input voltages to the water bath system and recording the corresponding temperatures. The ANFIS is then trained to identify the inverse model of the water bath system using the gathered training data. To start the ANFIS training, we need an FIS matrix that specifies the structure and initial parameters of the FIS for learning. The user can use the command "genfis1" to generate a FIS matrix from training

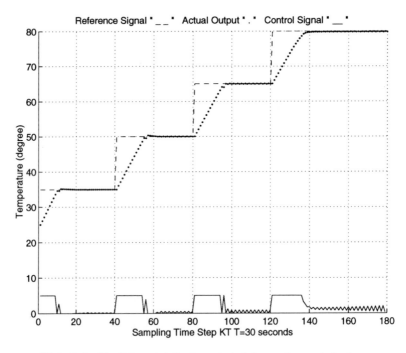

Figure A.3 Simulation result for the water bath temperature control using a manually designed fuzzy controller.

MATLAB Fuzzy Logic Toolbox   Appendix A

data using a grid-type partition according to the given number and types of membership functions. In this demonstration, we use five "gbellmf"-type membership functions. The user can also use a more powerful command, "genfis2", which can extract a set of fuzzy rules from a given set of input and output training data. This rule extraction technique is similar to those discussed in Sec. 19.4.1.

(b) Program listing:

1. Training program listing:

```
% Define plant parameters.
Ts=25; p=1.00151*10^(-4); q=8.67973*10^(-3);
r=40.0; yo=25; y(1)=yo; a=exp(-p*Ts); b=(q/p)*(1-exp(-p*Ts));
% Define training data.
for k = 1 : 120
    u(k)=rand(1, 1)*5;
    y(k + 1)=a*y(k)+b/(1+exp(0.5*y(k)-r))*u(k)+(1-a)*yo;
end;
trndata=[y(2:101); y(1:100); u(1:100)]';
% Define the rules and initial parameters of the FIS.
nummfs=5; mftype='gbellmf';
infismat=genfis1(trndata, nummfs, mftype);
pause;    % Strike any key to start ANFIS training.
[outfismat, error, stepsize]=anfis(trndata, infismat, 5);
pause;    % Strike any key to save parameters to disk.
save fyappr2.mat outfismat
```

2. Test program listing:

```
load fyappr2.mat    %Load the file "fyappr2.mat."
% Define plant parameters.
Ts=25; p=1.00151*10^(-4); q=8.67973*10^(-3);
r=40.0; yo=25; y(1)=yo; a=exp(-p*Ts); b=(q/p)*(1-exp(-p*Ts));
% Define the reference output.
for k = 1 : 180
    if (k <= 40)   ref(k)=35;
    elseif (k > 40 & k <= 80)   ref(k)=50;
    elseif (k > 80 & k <= 120)   ref(k)=65;
    elseif (k > 120)   ref(k)=80; end;
end;
% Test the learned ANFIS for 180 time steps.
for k = 1 : 179
    u(k)=evalfis([ref(k + 1) y(k)], outfismat);
    if (u(k)>=5)   u(k)=5;
    elseif (u(k)<=0)   u(k)=0;
    else    u(k)=u(k); end;
    y(k + 1)=a*y(k)+b/(1+exp(0.5*y(k)-r))*u(k)+(1-a)*yo;
end;
clg; hold on; grid;    % Plot plant input/output and reference
    output.
plot(y(1:180), '.y'); plot(ref(1:180), '- -r'); plot(u(1:179),
    'g');
xlabel('Sampling Time Step kT T=30 (seconds)');
ylabel('Temperature(degree)');
```

```
title('Reference Signal "_ _" Actual Output "." Control Signal
    "__"');
pause;    % Strike any key to calculate the performance index AES.
AES=sum(abs(ref-y))
```

(c) Simulation results: From Fig. A.4, we observe that the ANFIS has a perfect temperature-tracking capability. Furthermore, it produces a stable control signal $u(k)$ to the plant. The performance index AES = 374.0 is smaller than that of the fuzzy controller designed in the last section.

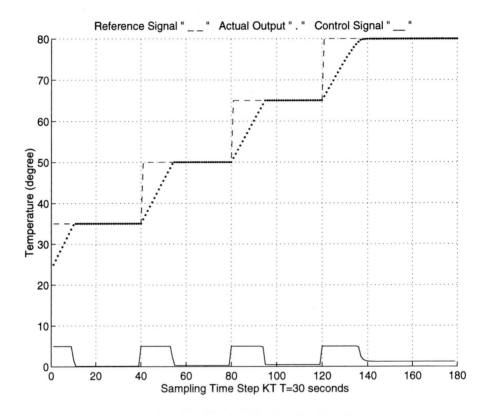

Figure A.4 Simulation result of the water bath temperature control using the ANFIS.

Appendix B

MATLAB Neural Network Toolbox

The Neural Network Toolbox is another MATLAB toolbox related to the topics in this book. The Neural Network Toolbox is a collection of predefined functions built on the MATLAB numerical computing environment. These predefined functions can be called by the user to simulate various types of neural network models. The Neural Network Toolbox is a useful tool for industry, education, and research; it helps the user to find out what works and what doesn't and helps to develop and extend the field of neural networks. Table B.1 lists all the current predefined functions in the MATLAB Neural Network Toolbox.

This appendix is written to familiarize the reader with the use of the Neural Network Toolbox for simulating various neural network models and solving some homework problems in this book. It also aims to aid the reader in studying the Neural Network Toolbox for use in neural network applications. In the following sections, we shall first demonstrate the use of the Neural Network Toolbox to simulate some of the popular neural network models introduced in this book. These include the Hebbian learning rule in Chap. 9; the perceptron, Adaline, and back-propagation networks in Chap. 10; the Hopfield network in Chap. 11; the competitive learning, the learning vector quantization, the instar-outstar network, the self-organizing feature map, and the radial basis function network in Chap. 12; and the Elman network in Chap. 13. Then, we shall describe the use of the Neural Network Toolbox for some applications introduced in Chaps. 10 and 16.

Basic usage and many important and useful features of MATLAB and the Neural Network Toolbox are not discussed here because there are other good references for this purpose. For this information, the reader is referred to the *MATLAB User's Guide* and the *Neural Network Toolbox User's Guide* published by MathWorks, Inc.

TABLE B.1 Instruction Table for MATLAB Neural Network Toolbox

Neural Network Model	Commands	Function Explanation
Transfer functions	hardlim	Hard limit transfer function
	hardlims	Symmetric hard limit transfer function
	purelin	Linear transfer function
	logsig	Log sigmoid transfer function
	tansig	Hyperbolic tangent sigmoid transfer function
	satlin	Saturating linear transfer function
	satlins	Symmetric saturating linear transfer function
Hebbian learning	learnh	Hebbian learning rule
	learnhd	Hebbian learning rule with decay
Perceptron	initp	Initialize a perceptron layer
	trainp	Train a perceptron layer with the perceptron rule
	simup	Simulate a perceptron layer
Adaline	initlin	Initialize a linear layer
	adaptwh	Adapt a linear layer with Widrow-Hoff rule
Back propagation	initff	Initialize a feedforward network up to three layers
	trainbp	Train a feedforward network with back propagation
	trainbpx	Train a network with fast back propagation
	trainlm	Train a network with Levenberg-Marquardt
	simuff	Simulate a feedforward network
	tbp1	Train a one-layer feedforward back-propagation network
Hopfield network	solvehop	Design a Hopfield network
	simuhop	Simulate a Hopfield network
Instar learning	learnis	Instar learning rule
Competitive learning	initc	Initialize a competitive layer
	trainc	Train a competitive layer
	simuc	Simulate a competitive layer
	nngenc	Generate clusters of data points
Learning vector quantization	initlvq	Initialize an LVQ network
	trainlvq	Design an LVQ network
	simulvq	Simulate an LVQ network
Self-organizing map	initsm	Initialize a self-organizing map
	trainsm	Train a self-organizing map
	simusm	Simulate a self-organizing map
Radial basis function network	solverb	Design a radial basis function network
	simurb	Simulate a radial basis function network
Elman network	initelm	Initialize an Elman recurrent network
	trainelm	Train an Elman recurrent network
	simuelm	Simulate an Elman recurrent network

B.1 DEMONSTRATION OF VARIOUS NEURAL NETWORK MODELS

B.1.1 Hebbian Learning Rule

(a) Neural network type: Hebbian learning rule [see Sec. 9.2.3, Eq. (9.20)].

(b) Problem statement: Given 200 input vectors denoted by "p" (see the program), use the Hebbian learning rule to train a five-node, single-layer network with a hard limit transfer function to act as a simple associative memory such that the output vector is the same as the input vector.

(c) MATLAB commands for the Hebbian learning rule:

learnh   Hebbian learning rule [Eq. (9.20)].

learnhd   Hebbian learning rule with decay.

(d) Program listing:

```
% Define 200 5-element input vectors.
t=[1 0 0 0; 0 1 0 0; 0 0 1 1; 0 0 1 1; 0 1 0 0];
index=floor (rand (1, 200)*4)+1; p=t(:, index);
% Define initial weights and biases.
w=eye(5); b=-0.5*ones(5, 1);
% Train the network using the Hebbian learning rule.
for i=1:200
    input=p(:, i);
    output=input;    % Set the target output to be the same as the
        input.
    dw=learnh(input, output, 1);    % Set the learning rate as 1.
    w=w+dw;
end;
% Test the trained network.
% Test to see if all the output vectors are correct (i.e., if
    N=200?).
N=0;
for i=1:200
    input=p(:, i);
    output=hardlim(w*input, b);    % output=hardlim(w*input+b).
    if input==output
        N=N+1;
    end;
end;
N
w
```

(e) Result: When all the 200 training vectors are presented to the input of the trained network, the outputs of the network are all correct. However, the Hebbian learning rule may result in arbitrarily large weights (see the variable "w"). A way to solve this problem is to use the Hebbian learning rule with decay to decrease the weights according to a decay rate. The reader can replace the command "learnh" in the preceding program by "learnhd" to see the difference between the Hebbian learning rules with and without decay rate.

B.1.2 Perception Learning Rule

(a) Neural network type: Perceptron learning rule [see Sec. 10.1.1, Eq. (10.7)].

(b) Problem statement: This demonstration uses the Neural Network Toolbox to solve the classification problem stated in Example 10.1 of Sec. 10.1.1.

(c) MATLAB commands for the perceptron:

initp   Initialize a perceptron layer.

```
trainp      Train a perceptron layer with a perceptron rule [Eq. (10.7)].
simup       Simulate a perceptron layer.
```

(d) Program listing:

```
% P defines six 2-element input vectors.
P=[-1.0 -1.5 -1.0 2.0 2.5 1.0; 0.0 -1.0 -2.0 0.0 -1.0 -2.0];
% T defines the target vectors.
T=[1 1 1 0 0 0];    % "1" represents class 1 and "0" class 2.
[w, b]=initp(P, T);    % Define an initial perceptron layer.
% Train the network using the perceptron learning rule.
[w, b, epochs, errors]=trainp (w, b, P, T, -1);    % w: weight,
    b: bias.
% Test whether [-1.0; 0.0] is correctly classified as class 1.
a=simup ([-1.0; 0.0], w, b)
```

(e) Result: As shown in Fig. B.1, a decision line is found to divide the six two-dimensional input vectors into two classes. Hence, it is a linearly separable problem and can be solved by the perceptron learning rule successfully. In the test, the input vector $[-1, 0]^T$ is correctly classified as class 1.

B.1.3 Adaline

(a) Neural network type: Linear network (see Sec. 10.1.2).

(b) Problem statement: Given the input signal $u = 0.6 \sin (2\pi k/T) + 1.2 \cos (2\pi k/T)$ and the target output signal $y = 2.5u + 2$, where $T = 10$ is the period and $k \in \{1, 2, \dots, 100\}$ is the sampling time step, we want to memorize the input-output relationship using a neural network. Because the relationship between input and output signals is linear, we shall use the adaptive linear network with the Adaline learning

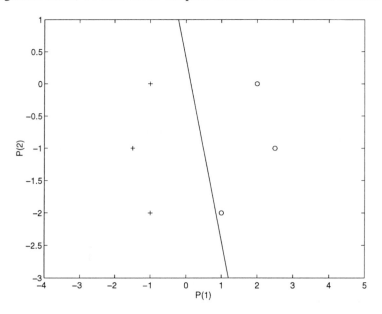

Figure B.1   Simulation result of the perceptron learning rule.

rule (Widrow-Hoff learning rule) in Eq. (10.17) to predict the target output signal in this demonstration.

(c) MATLAB commands for the Adaline:

initlin   Initialize a linear layer.

adaptwh   Adapt a linear layer with the Widrow-Hoff rule [Eq. (10.17)].

(d) Program listing:

```
% Define the input/output training signals.
for k=1:100
    u(k)=0.6*sin(2*pi*k/10)+1.2*cos(2*pi*k/10);
    y(k)=2.5*u(k)+2;
end;
% Define the initial Adaline network.
[w, b]=initlin (u, y);
% Train the network using the Adaline learning rule.
[o, e, w, b]=adaptwh(w, b, u, y, 1.0);    % Set the learning rate as 1.
% Plot the output error signal (target output - network output).
clg; grid; plot(y-o, 'y'); xlabel('Time Step'); ylabel('Error');
```

(e) Result: The error signal shown in Fig. B.2 indicates that the network output correctly tracks the target signal after the tenth time step. This demonstration shows that the linear network can learn to predict a linear signal very quickly.

B.1.4 Back Propagation

(a) Neural network type: Multilayer feedforward network (see Sec. 10.2)

(b) Problem statement: In this demonstration, we shall study the effects of learning rate, initial weight, and bias on the local minimum problems of a single-input–single-output (SISO) feedforward network with back-propagation learning. Assume

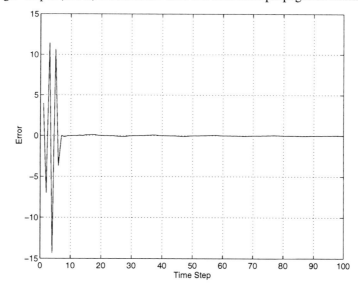

Figure B.2   Error signal from simulation result of the Adaline learning rule.

the input-output training data pairs are $(-6, 0)$, $(-6.1, 0)$, $(-4.1, 0.97)$, $(-4, 0.99)$, $(4, 0.01)$, $(4.1, 0.03)$, $(6, 1)$, $(6.1, 1)$. Use the back-propagation learning rule to train a single-node network and observe the local minimum problem under different learning rate, initial weight, and bias.

(c) MATLAB commands for back propagation:

initff   Initialize a feedforward network up to three layers.

tbp1   Train a single-layer feedforward network with back-propagation learning rule [Eqs. (10.39)–(10.44)].

simuff   Simulate a feedforward network.

(d) Program listing:

```
% Define P as input vectors and T as target vectors.
P=[-6.0 -6.1 -4.1 -4.0 +4.0 +4.1 +6.0 +6.1];
T=[+0.0 +0.0 +.97 +.99 +.01 +.03 +1.0 +1.0];
% Plot error surface graph and contour.
w_range=-1:0.1:1, b_range=-2.5:0.25:2.5;
ES=errsurf(P, T, w_range, b_range,'logsig');
plotes(w_range, b_range, ES, [60 30]);
pause;   % Choose initial weight, bias and learning rate.
w=input(' Please input initial weight:');
b=input(' Please input initial bias:');
lr=input(' Please input learning rate:');
% Train the BP network using "tbp1."
tp=[10 200 0.1 lr];
[w, b, epochs, error]=tbp1(w, b, 'logsig', P, T, tp, w_range,
    b_range, ES, [60 30]);
```

(e) Result: When we choose the initial weight, bias, and learning rate as 1, -2, and 0.1, respectively, we observe from the error surface in Fig. B.3(a) that the "weight-state ball" rolls into a very shallow valley slowly and then stays in the valley bottom. Even after we continue to train the network for 1000 epochs, the ball cannot get out

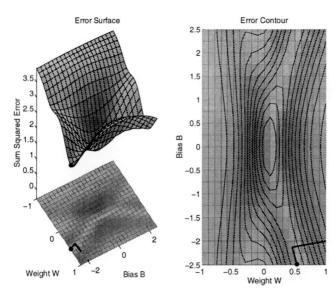

Figure B.3(a) Simulation result of the back-propagation learning rule with initial weight 1, bias -2, and learning rate 0.1.

    MATLAB Neural Network Toolbox   Appendix B

of the shallow valley and the network is obviously stuck at a local minimum. If the initial weight, bias, and learning rates are set as -1, 2, 0.1, respectively, the ball moves along the error gradient until it falls into the global minimum [see Fig. B.3(b)]. When we change the learning rate to 1, it is observed from Fig. B.3(c) that although the weight state moves toward the global minimum, it is unable to stay there stably since the movement of each time step is too large. If we reduce the learning rate to 0.01, the network moves slowly toward the global minimum. However, it moves only a short distance even after 200 epochs. Although it can finally move into the global minimum, it will take a long time [see Fig. B.3(d)]. Hence, it is important to choose a proper learning rate for stable, fast learning and choose good

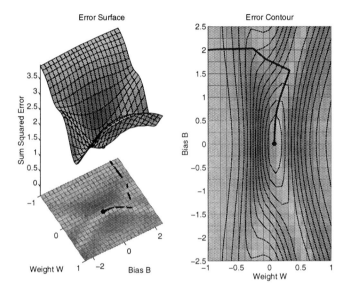

Figure B.3(b) Simulation result for the back-propagation learning rule with initial weight -1, bias 2, and learning rate 0.1.

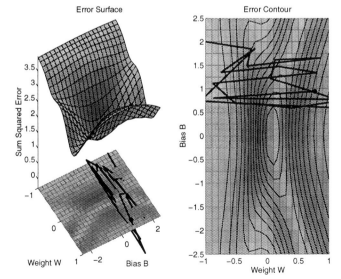

Figure B.3(c) Simulation result for the back-propagation learning rule with initial weight -1, bias 2, and learning rate 1.

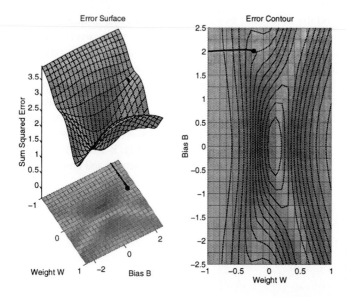

Error Surface

Error Contour

Figure B.3(d) Simulation result for the back-propagation learning rule with initial weight -1, bias 2, and learning rate 0.01.

initial weights and biases to avoid local minima. We can use the command "trainbpx," which adopts a momentum term and an adaptive learning rate, to solve real problems. In the next section, we shall use the command "trainbpx" to identify nonlinear systems.

B.1.5 Hopfield Network

(a) Neural network type: Discrete Hopfield network (see Sec. 11.1.1).

(b) Problem statement: In this demonstration, we shall use a discrete Hopfield network to store four equilibrium points, (1, 1), (1, -1), (-1, 1), and (-1, -1), and study its properties.

(c) MATLAB commands for the Hopfield network:
```
solvehop    Design (train) a Hopfield network [Eq. (11.22)].
simuhop     Simulate a Hopfield network.
```

(d) Program listing:
```
% Define 4 equilibrium points (1, 1), (1, -1), (-1, 1) and (-1, -1).
t=[1 1 -1 -1; 1 -1 1 -1];
% Build a Hopfield network to store the 4 equilibrium points.
[w, b]=solvehop(t)
pause;    % Test the network.
color='rgbmy';
for i=1:40
    a=rands(2, 1)*2;
    [a, p]=simuhop(a, w, b, 30);    %Evolve for 30 time steps.
    plot(p(1, 1), p(2, 1), 'wo', p(1, :), p(2, :),
        color(rem(i, 5)+1));
    drawnow;
end;
```

(e) Result: After the Hopfield network is designed (trained), random input vectors are presented to it to see if it can restore the stored equilibrium points. The results shown in Fig. B.4 indicate that the Hopfield network always converges to one of the four equilibrium states in 40 evolving steps.

B.1.6 Instar Learning Rule

(a) Neural network type: Instar network (see Sec. 12.1.1).

(b) Problem statement: In this demonstration, we use an instar network to recognize a vector $V = [0.2673, 0.5345, -0.8018]^T$ which is corrupted by noise. In other words, we want to recognize the vector V from the vector $P = V +$ noise.

(c) MATLAB commands for the instar learning rule:
learnis   Instar learning rule [Eq. (12.4)].

(d) Program listing:

```
% Define a normalized prototype vector.
V=[0.2673; 0.5345; -0.8018];
% Add noise to the prototype vector.
P=rands(3, 200)*0.1 + V*ones(1, 200); P=normc(P);
% Plot the normalized input vector on a sphere surface.
hold on; [x, y, z]=sphere(10);
h=surf(x*0.9, y*0.9, z*0.9, x.^2.*y.^2.*z.^2);
set(h, 'face', 'interp');
plot3(P(1, :)*0.99, P(2, :)*0.99, P(3, :)*0.99, '.k',
    'markersize',10);
view([160 -20]); colormap(cool); title('Normalized vector space');
% Set the initial weight vector of the instar network.
w=[-0.8133 0.1474 -0.5628];
```

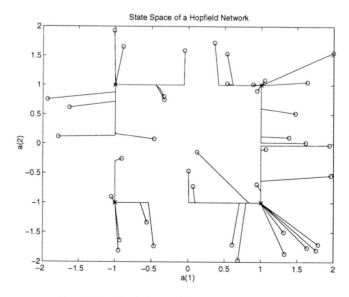

Figure B.4   Simulation result for the Hopfield network.

```
% Show the initial weight vector on the graph with marker '+'.
plot3(w(1), w(2), w(3), 'w+', 'markersize', 10, 'erasemode', 'none');
pause;     % Train the network using the instar learning rule.
lr=0.05;   % Set the learning rate.
for q=1:200
    p=P(:, q);      % Pick the qth input vector.
    a=satlin(w*p);    % Calculate network output.
    dw=learnis(w, p, a, lr);    % Apply learning rule.
    w=w+dw;    % Update weights.
    plot3(w(1),w(2),w(3),'r.','markersize',10,'erasemode','none');
end
plot3(w(1),w(2),w(3),'w+','markersize',10,'erasemode','none');
% Renormalize the weights and compare them with V.
w = normr(w)
V
```

(e) Result: Figure B.5 shows the moving path of the network's weight vector during the instar learning. After the learning, the weight vector, $\mathbf{w} = [0.2614, 0.5426, -0.7983]^T$, is approximately equal to the prototype vector V.

B.1.7 Competitive Learning Rule

(a) Neural network type: Kohonen learning rule (see Sec. 12.1.2).

(b) Problem statement: In this demonstration, we shall illustrate how to use the Kohonen learning rule to classify a set of points into six natural classes.

(c) MATLAB commands for the competitive learning:
    initc   Initialize a competitive layer.

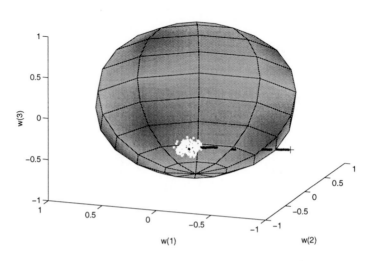

Figure B.5   Simulation result for the instar learning rule.

trainc	Train a competitive layer [Kohonen learning rule in Eq. (12.8)].
simuc	Simulate a competitive layer.
nngenc	Generate clusters of data points.

(d) Program listing:

```
% Use "nngenc" to create 80 training data points from 6 clusters.
p=nngenc([2 -2; 2 -2; 2 -2], 6, 80, 0.15);
w=initc(p, 6);    % Initialize a competitive layer with 6 nodes.
% Plot the training data points and initial weights and biases.
clg; grid; xlabel('p(1)'); ylabel('p(2)'); zlabel('p(3)');
plot3(p(1, :), p(2, :), p(3, :), 'r.'); hold on; plot3(w(:, 1),
    w(:, 2), w(:, 3), 'y+');
pause;    % Train the competitive layer.
w=trainc(w, p, [100, 1000, 0.1]);    % Learning rate=0.1, epochs=1000.
% Plot the training data points and final weights and biases.
clg; grid; xlabel('p(1), w(1)'); ylabel('p(2), w(2)'); zlabel('p(3),
    w(3)');
plot3(p(1, :), p(2, :), p(3, :), 'r.'); hold on; plot3(w(:, 1),
    w(:, 2), w(:, 3), 'w+');
pause    % Use the trained network to classify an input vector p.
p=[1; 2; 2]; a=simuc(p, w)
```

(e) Result: The + marks in Fig. B.6 indicate the weights after learning. As expected, the six final weight vectors properly represent the centers of the six clusters of the training data. In the test, we use the learned competitive layer to classify the input vector $[1, 2, 2]^T$. The result, $a = (x, 1)$, 1, indicates that the neuron x wins the competition and outputs as 1. Therefore the vector, $[1, 2, 2]^T$, belongs to class x, where $x \in \{1, 2, \ldots, 6\}$.

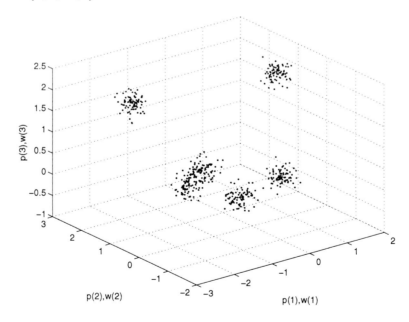

Figure B.6 Simulation result for the competitive learning rule.

B.1.8 LVQ Learning Rule (Supervised Competitive Learning Rule)

(a) Neural network type: LVQ network (see Sec. 12.1.2).

(b) Problem statement: In this demonstration, we shall use a LVQ network to classify the input vectors according to the given target classes as follows:

$$[-3, 0], [-2, 1], [-2, -1], [2, 1], [2, -1], [3, 0]: \text{class 1},$$
$$[0, 4], [0, 3], [0, 2], [0, 1], [0, -1], [0, -2], [0, -3], [0, -4]: \text{class 2}.$$

(c) MATLAB commands for the LVQ:

initlvq   Initialize an LVQ network.
trainlvq   Train an LVQ network [Eq. (12.13)].
simulvq   Simulate an LVQ network.

(d) Program listing:

```
% Define 14 2-element input vectors.
p=[-3 -2 -2 +0 +0 +0 +0 +0 +0 +0 +0 +2 +2 +3;
   +0 +1 -1 +4 +3 +2 +1 -1 -2 -3 -4 +1 -1 +0];
% Define the classes these vectors fall into.
c=[1 1 1 2 2 2 2 2 2 2 2 1 1 1];
% Use "ind2vec" to obtain the network target output vectors.
t=ind2vec(c);
% Plot these training data points.
colormap(hsv); plotvec(p, c); alabel('P(1)', 'P(2)', 'Input
   Vectors');
% Initialize a 4-node LVQ layer.
% w1: competitive-layer weights, w2: linear-layer weights.
[w1, w2]=initlvq(p, 4, t);
% Train a competitive layer using the instar learning rule.
tp=[20, 500, 0.05]; [w1, w2]=trainlvq(w1, w2, p, t, tp);
pause   % Test whether [0; 1] is correctly classified as class 2.
a=simulvq([0; 1], w1, w2)
```

(e) Result: Figure B.7 shows the input vectors and the final weight vectors of the competitive layer. In the figure, the light + are the class-1 input patterns, and the dark + are the class-2 input patterns. The light o represent weight vectors of the class-1 neurons, and the dark o represent those of the class-2 neurons. The light and dark patterns can be clearly distinguished on the screen when the reader runs the program. When we tested the learned competitive layer with the input vector $[0, 1]^T$, we obtained the result $a = (2, 1)$, 1, indicating that this vector is correctly in class 2.

B.1.9 Self-Organizing Feature Map

(a) Neural network type: Kohonen feature map network (see Sec. 12.3).

(b) Problem statement: This demonstration shows how a two-dimensional self-organizing feature map can be trained. We first create some random input data in the input space with the command "rands," and then calculate the distance of neurons according to the Manhattan distance neighborhood function "nbman." The neurons are arranged on a two-dimensional map with size of 9×9. Finally, the map is trained using the command "trainsm."

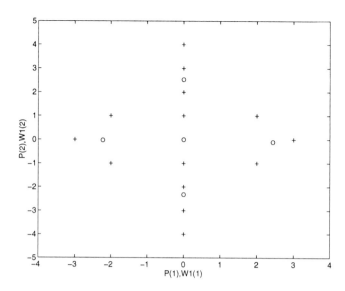

Figure B.7 Simulation result for the LVQ learning rule.

(c) MATLAB commands for the self-organizing feature map:

initsm   Initialize a self-organizing feature map.
trainsm   Train a self-organizing feature map [Eq. (12.28)].
simusm   Simulate a self-organizing feature map.

(d) Program listing:

```
% 1000 data points are created and plotted in a square input space.
p=rand(2, 500)*0.25; plot(p(1, :), p(2, :), '+r');
% Define the 81 × 81 neighborhood matrix for a layer with 9 × 9 nodes
% arranged in 2 dimensions.
m=nbman(9, 9);
% Initialize a self-organizing feature map with size of 9 × 9.
w=initsm(p, 9*9);   % w: initial weight.
clg;   % Train a self-organizing feature map.
w=trainsm(w, m, p, [1000, 5000]);
pause   % Classify input vector p=[0.2; 0.3].
p=[0.2; 0.3]; a=simusm(p, w, m)
```

(e) Result: After 5000 training cycles (see Fig. B.8), the map spreads across the input space quite evenly, reflecting the even distribution of input vectors. When the input vector [0.2, 0.3] is presented to the network, the neuron representing class 5 outputs 1.0 and all the other neurons output 0.5. This indicates that the test vector is closest to class 5.

B.1.10 Radial Basis Function Network

(a) Neural network type: Radial basis function network (see Sec. 12.6).

(b) Problem statement: Assume the relationship between the input (t) and output (y) of a system is specified by $y = \sin(t)$. In this demonstration, we shall use the RBFN to identify this system and compare the training speed of the RBFN with that of the back-propagation (BP) network with a single 10-node hidden layer for this problem.

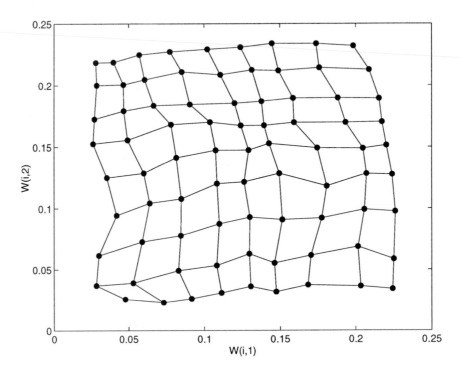

Figure B.8 Simulation result for the self-organizing feature map learning rule.

(c) MATLAB commands for the RBFN:

    solverb   Train a RBFN (see Section 12.6).
    simurb   Simulate a RBFN.

(d) Program listing:

```
% Define input vector t and target vector y.
t=0:0.3:6; y=sin(t);
% Initialize a BP network with 10 hidden nodes and one output node.
[w1, b1, w2, b2]=initff(t, 10, 'tansig', y, 'purelin');
df=100;   % Frequency of progress displays (just once).
me=5000;   % Maximum number of epochs/neurons (as many as it takes).
sse=0.01;   % Desired sum-squared error.
lr=0.01;   % Learning rate.
sc=1;   % Spread constant for radial basis functions.
pause   % Train the BP network.
tp=[df me sse lr]; flops(0), tic
[x, x, x, x, bp_ep]=trainbp(w1, b1, 'tansig', w2, b2, 'purelin', t,
    y, tp);
bp_flops=flops   % Number of floating point operations using BP.
bp_time=toc   % Training time of BP.
pause   % Train the RBFN.
tp=[df me sse sc]; flops(0), tic
[x, x, x, x, rb_n]=solverb(t, y, tp);
rb_flops=flops   % Number of floating point operations using RBFN.
rb_time=toc   % Training time of RBFN.
```

(e) Result: The learning time for the RBFN and the BP network on a personal computer is as follows.

Function	Technique	Time(s)	Flops
trainbp	BP	115.73	17806719
solverb	RBFN	2.5300	45734

Note that the learning time may vary for different initial weights and computers. From the preceding data, it is clear that the RBFN can learn much faster than the back-propagation network with fewer neurons. In fact, the command "trainbp" is included in the Neural Network Toolbox only to demonstrate how normal back-propagation learning works and is not often used to solve real-world problems. We can use the command "trainbpx," which adopts a momentum term and an adaptive learning rate, to solve real-world problems. In the next section, we shall use this command to identify nonlinear systems.

B.1.11 Elman Network

(a) Neural network type: Simple recurrent network (SRN) (see Sec. 13.1.2).

(b) Problem statement: The Elman network is a two-layer network with feedback in the first layer. This recurrent connection allows this network to both detect and generate time-varying patterns. Hence, we can use the Elman network to recognize and produce both spatial and temporal patterns. An example problem where temporal patterns are recognized and classified with a spatial pattern is the amplitude detection problem. In this demonstration, we shall illustrate the use of the Elman network on this problem. Assume three sine waves with different amplitudes are combined into a sequence which is fed into an Elman network. The target output is another sequence indicating the peak positions of the input sequence. We shall use the input and target sequences to train an Elman network and then test the amplitude detection ability of the learned Elman network.

(c) MATLAB commands for the Elman network:

initelm   Initialize an Elman recurrent network (see Sec. 13.1.2).
trainelm   Train an Elman recurrent network.
simuelm   Simulate an Elman recurrent network.

(d) Program listing:

```
% If input is a waveform with amplitude of 1, then output should
   be 1.
p1=sin(1:10); t1=ones(1, 10);
% If input is a waveform with amplitude of 2, then output should
   be 2.
p2=sin(1:10)*2; t2=ones(1, 10)*2;
% If input is a waveform with amplitude of 3, then output should
   be 3.
p3=sin(1:10)*3; t3=ones(1, 10)*3;
% The training signal is formed by repeating each waveform twice.
p=[p1 p2 p3 p1 p2 p3]; t=[t1 t2 t3 t1 t2 t3];
```

```
% Initialize an Elman network with 10 hidden nodes.
[w1, b1, w2, b2]=initelm(p, 10, t);
pause    % Train the Elman network.
[w1, b1, w2, b2]=trainelm(w1, b1, w2, b2, p, t);
% Test the Elman network using the original input sequence.
a=simuelm(p, w1, b1, w2, b2);
% Plot the network outputs and target outputs.
plot(a); hold on; plot(t, '- -r'); title('Result of Amplitude
    Detection');
xlabel('Time Step'); ylabel('Target _ _ Output __');
```

(e) Result: In the test, the original input sequence is presented to the learned Elman network and the results are shown in Fig. B.9. From the figure, we observe that the network has successfully learned to detect the amplitudes of incoming sequences. The reader can test the generalization capability of the network using other sine waves with different amplitudes.

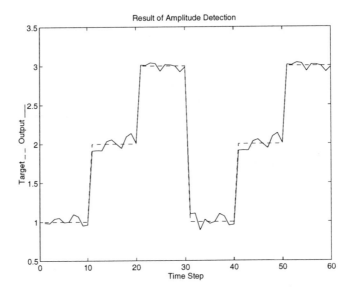

Figure B.9 Simulation result for the Elman network.

B.2 DEMONSTRATION OF NEURAL NETWORK APPLICATIONS

B.2.1 Adaptive Noise Cancelation Using the Adaline Network

(a) Problem statement: One of the most interesting applications of adaptive networks is noise cancelation (see Problem 10.6). Using an adaptive network, it is possible to subtract interference from an output signal if the signal that is correlated with the interference can be measured. In addition, because noise cancelation works by substrating, not filtering, it can remove interference even if the interference occurs at

MATLAB Neural Network Toolbox   Appendix B

the same frequencies as the desired signal. A typical noise cancelation problem occurs in the cockpit of an aircraft. While flying the aircraft, the pilot speaks into a microphone to let the passengers know that "If it were less cloudy you would all be able to see . . . ." When the pilot's voice message is sent back to all the passengers, it is corrupted by an interference signal created by the plane's engines. A function of this signal, the sum of the pilot's voice and the distorted engine noise, is also picked up by the microphone. One solution to this problem is to train a neural network to predict the combined signal from the engine signal. Since the network receives only the engine noise as its input, it can predict only the distorted engine noise in the combined signal. Hence, the network's prediction error will be the pilot's voice. In this demonstration, we assume the combined signal is "*pilot* + 3 × *engine*," where "*pilot*" represents the pilot's voice and "*engine*" the engine noise. We shall use an Adaline network (the command "adaptwh") for the noise cancelation.

(b) Program listing:

```
% Define pilot voice, engine noise and combined signal.
time=0:0.01:12; pilot=randn(1, length(time));
engine=randn(1, length(time)); pick=pilot+3*engine;
pause    % Initialize the Adaline network.
[w, b]=initlin(engine, pick);
pause    % Train the Adaline network.
[y, nerror, w, b]=adaptwh(w, b, engine, pick, 0.01);
pause    % Plot the error signal.
clg; plot((nerror-pilot)); grid; xlabel('Time Step');
    ylabel('Difference');
title('Difference between Network Error and Actual Pilot Voice');
```

(c) Simulation results: The difference between the network error and the actual pilot voice signal is shown in Fig. B.10, which indicates that the Adaline network can reproduce the pilot's voice signal quite well after only a few seconds.

B.2.2 Nonlinear System Identification

(a) Problem statement: This demonstration uses a back-propagation network to identify a nonlinear system. The nonlinear system to be identified is expressed by

$$yp(k+1) = \frac{yp(k)[yp(k-1)+2][yp(k)+2.5]}{8.5+[yp(k)]^2+[yp(k-1)]^2} + u(k),$$

where $yp(k)$ is the output of the system at the kth time step and $u(k)$ is the plant input which is a uniformly bounded function of time. The plant is stable at $u(k) \in [-2\ 2]$. Let the identification model be in the form of

$$ypi(k+1) = N(yp(k), yp(k-1)) + u(k),$$

where $N(yp(k), yp(k-1))$ represents the back-propagation network with inputs $yp(k)$ and $yp(k-1)$ and output $ypi(k+1)$ for system identification. The identification model is in fact the series-parallel model in Eq. (16.13). The goal here is to train the back-propagation network such that when an input $u(k)$ is presented to the network and to the nonlinear system, the network output $ypi(k)$ and the actual system output $yp(k)$ are very close.

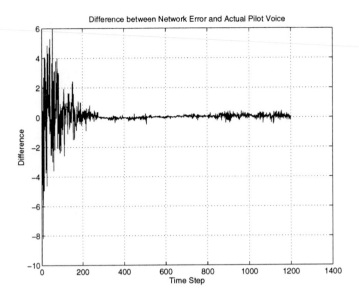

Difference between Network Error and Actual Pilot Voice

Figure B.10   Simulation result of adaptive noise cancelation using the Adaline network.

(b) Program listing:

1. Training program listing:

```
% Define initial values yp(1)=yp(2)=0.
yp(1)=0; yp(2)=0;
% Create 501 random input data from the input space [-2 2].
u=rands(1, 501)*2;
% Use 501 random input data to obtain training patterns.
for k=2:501
yp(k+1)=yp(k)*(yp(k-1)+2)*(yp(k)+2.5)/(8.5+yp(k)^2+
    yp(k-1)^2)+u(k);
out(k-1)=(yp(k+1)-u(k))/10;
in(k-1)=yp(k)/10;
end;
nno=out(1:499); nni=[in(1:499); in(2:500)];
% Build the initial BP network with 10 nodes in the first hidden
    layer,
% 20 nodes in the second layer and one output node.
[w1, b1, w2, b2, w3, b3]=initff(nni, 10, 'tansig', 20, 'tansig',
    1, 'tansig');
% Train the BP network until sse=0.05 (sum-squared error).
tp=[50, 2000, 0.05, 0.1, 1.05, 0.7, 0.35, 1.04];
for i=1:30
[w1, b1, w2, b2, w3, b3, epochs error]
=trainbpx(w1, b1, 'tansig', w2, b2, 'tansig', w3, b3, 'tansig',
    nni, nno, tp);
save a:\ bp3.mat w1 b1 w2 b2 w3 b3
end;
```

2. Recall program listing:

```
load bp3.mat;    % Load the learned weights and biases.
```

```
out_p(1)=0; out_p(2)=0; out_nn(1)=0; out_nn(2)=0;  % Define
    initial values.
pause    % Test the BP network.
for k=2:500
    if k≤200
        u(k)=2*cos(2*pi*k*0.01);
    else
        u(k)=1.2*sin(2*pi*k*0.05);
end;
out_p(k+1)=out_p(k)*(out_p(k-1)+2)
    *(out_p(k)+2.5)/(8.5+out_p(k)^2+out_p(k-1)^2)+u(k);
out_nn(k+1)=10*simuff([out_p(k)/10; out_p(k-1)/10], w1, b1,
    'tansig', w2,
b2, 'tansig', w3, b3, 'tansig')+u(k); end;
% Plot the plant output and NN output.
plot(1:501, out_p, 'y'); hold on; plot(1:501, out_nn, '- - r');
    grid;
axis ([0, 400, -4, 9]); xlabel('Time Step'); ylabel('Plant Output
    __ NN
Output _ _');
```

(c) Simulation results: After the back-propagation network is trained, its prediction power is tested for the input $u(k) = 2\cos(2\pi k/100)$, $k \leq 200$, and $u(k) = 1.2\sin(2\pi k/20)$, $200 < k \leq 500$. As shown in Fig. B.11, the learned network can predict the nonlinear system outputs quite well. In other words, the back-propagation network has been trained to identify the given nonlinear system. The reader can also use the parallel model in Eq. (16.12) as the identification model in this demonstration. The result is almost the same as that shown in Fig. B.11.

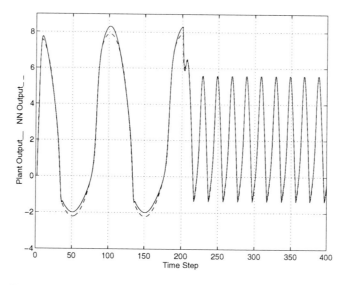

Figure B.11 Simulation result for nonlinear system identification using a back-propagation network.

Bibliography

AARTS, E., AND J. KORST [1989]. *Simulated Annealing and Boltzmann Machines.* New York: John Wiley.

ABDELNOUR, G. M., C. H. CHANG, F. H. HUANG, AND J. Y. CHEUNG [1991]. "Design of a fuzzy controller using input and output mapping factors." *IEEE Trans. Syst. Man Cybern.* 21(5):952–960.

ABE, S. [1989]. "Theories on the Hopfield neural networks." *Proc. Int. Joint Conf. Neural Networks,* vol. I, 557–564, Washington, DC.

ACKLEY, D. H., G. E. HINTON, AND T. J. SEJNOWSKI [1985]. "A learning algorithm for Boltzmann machines." *Cognitive Sci.* 9:147–169.

ACKLEY, D. H., AND M. S. LITTMAN [1990]. "Generalization and scaling in reinforcement learning." In D. S. Touretzky, ed., *Advances in Neural Information Processing Systems II,* 550–557. San Mateo, CA: Morgan Kaufmann.

ADAMO, J. M. [1980]. "L.P.L., A fuzzy programming language: 1. Syntactic aspects. 2. Semantic aspects." *Fuzzy Sets Syst.* 3:151–179, 261–289.

ADLASSNIG, K. P., G. KOLARZ, AND W. SCHEITHAUER [1985]. "Present state of the medical expert system CADIAG-2." *Med. Inf.* 24:13–20.

ADLER, D. [1993]. "Genetic algorithms and simulated annealing: A marriage proposal." *Proc. IEEE Int. Conf. Neural Networks,* vol. II, 1104–1109, San Francisco.

AIYER, S. V. B., M. NIRANJAN, AND F. FALLSIDE [1990]. "A theoretical investigation into the performance of the Hopfield model." *IEEE Trans. Neural Networks* 1(2):204–215.

AKAIKE, H. [1974]. "A new look at the statistical model identification." *IEEE Trans. Autom. Control* 19(6):716–723.

ALBERT, P. [1978]. "The algebra of fuzzy logic." *Fuzzy Sets Syst.* 1:203–230.

ALBUS, J. [1975]. "A new approach to manipulator control: The cerebellar model articulation controller (CMAC)." *Trans. ASME J. Dyn. Syst. Meas. Control* 97:220–227.

ALBUS, J. [1981]. *Brain, Behavior and Robotics.* Peterborough, NH: BYTE Books.

ALEKSANDER, I., AND H. MORTON [1990]. *An Introduction to Neural Computing.* London: Chapman and Hall.

ALLEN, R. B., AND J. ALSPECTOR [1990]. "Learning of stable states in stochastic asymmetric networks." *IEEE Trans. Neural Networks* 1(2):233–238.

ALMEIDA, L. B. [1987]. "A learning rule for asynchronous perceptrons with feedback in a combinatorial environment." *Proc. IEEE Int. Conf. Neural Networks,* vol. II, 609–618, San Diego.

ALMEIDA, L. B. [1988]. "Backpropagation in perceptrons with feedback." In E. Eckmiller and C. von der Malsburg, eds., *Neural Computers,* 199–208. New York: Springer-Verlag.

ALON, N., A. K. DEWDNEY, AND T. J. OTT [1991]. "Efficient simulation of finite automata by neural nets." *J. ACM* 38:495.

ALSINA, C. [1985]. "On a family of connectives for fuzzy sets." *Fuzzy Sets Syst.* 16:231–235.

AMANO, A., AND T. ARITSUKA [1989]. "On the use of neural network and fuzzy logic in speech recognition." *Proc. Int. Joint Conf. Neural Networks,* I301–305, Washington, DC.

AMARI, S. I. [1972]. "Learning patterns and pattern sequences by self-organizing nets of threshold elements." *IEEE Trans. Comput.* 21:1197–1206.

AMARI, S. I. [1990]. "Mathematical foundations of neurocomputing." *IEEE Proc.* 78(9):1443–1463.

AMARI, S. I. [1991]. "Dualistic geometry of the manifold of higher-order neurons." *Neural Networks* 4:443–451.

AMARI, S. I., K. KURATA, AND H. NAGAOKA [1992]. "Information geometry of Boltzmann machines." *IEEE Trans. Neural Networks* 3(2):260–271.

AMIT, D. J. [1988]. "Neural networks for counting chimes." *Proc. Nat. Acad. Sci. USA* 85:2141–2145.

AMIT, D. J., G. GUTFREUND, AND H. SOMPOLINSKY [1985]. "Spin-glass models of neural networks." *Phys. Rev. A* 32:1007–1018.

ANDERSON, B. D. O., AND J. B. MOORE [1979]. *Optimal Filtering.* Englewood Cliffs, NJ: Prentice-Hall.

ANDERSON, C. W. [1989]. "Learning to control an inverted pendulum using neural networks." *IEEE Control Syst. Mag.* April:31–36.

ANDERSON, J. A., AND E. ROSENFELD, eds. [1988]. *Neurocomputing: Foundations of Research.* Cambridge, MA: MIT Press.

ANDERSON, J. A., AND E. ROSENFELD, eds. [1990]. *Neurocomputing 2: Directions for Research.* Cambridge, MA: MIT Press.

ANDERSON, J. A., J. W. SILVERSTEIN, S. A. RITZ, AND R. S. JONES [1977]. "Distinctive features, categorical perception, and probability learning: Some applications of a neural model." *Psychol. Rev.* 84(5):413–451.

ANDERSON, S., J. W. L. MERRILL, AND R. PORT [1989]. "Dynamic speech categorization with recurrent networks." In D. S. Touretzky, G. E. Hinton, and T. J. Sejnowski, eds., *Proc. 1988 Connectionist Models Summer School,* 398–406. San Mateo, CA: Morgan Kaufmann.

ANDES, D., B. WIDROW, M. LEHR, AND E. WAN [1990]. "MRIII: A robust algorithm for training analog neural networks." *Proc. Int. Joint Conf. Neural Networks,* vol. I, 533–536, Washington, DC.

ANTOGNETTI, P., AND V. MILUTINOVIC, eds. [1991]. *Neural Networks: Concepts, Applications, and Implementations.* Englewood Cliffs, NJ: Prentice-Hall.

ANTSAKLIS, P. J. [1990]. "Special issue on neural networks for control system," *IEEE Control Syst. Mag.* 10(3):3–87.

ANTSAKLIS, P. J. [1992]. "Special issue on neural networks for control systems." *IEEE Control Syst. Mag.* 12(2):8–57.

ARABSHAHI, P., J. J. CHOI, R. J. MARKS, II, AND T. P. CAUDELL [1992]. "Fuzzy control of backpropagation." *Proc. IEEE Int. Conf. Fuzzy Syst.,* 967–972, San Diego.

ARCHER, N. P., AND S. WANG [1991]. "Fuzzy set representation of neural network classification boundaries." *IEEE Trans. Syst. Man Cybern.* 21(4):735–742.

ASAKAWA, K., AND H. TAKAGI [1994]. "Neural networks in Japan." *Commun. ACM* 37(3):106–112.

ASH, T. [1989]. "Dynamics node creation in backpropagation networks." *Connection Sci.* 1(4):365.

ATANASSOV, K. T. [1986]. "Intuitionistic fuzzy sets." *Fuzzy Sets Syst.* 20:87–96.

AUMANN, R. J. [1965]. "Integrals of set-valued functions." *J. Math. Anal. Appl.* 12:1–12.

AZIMI-SADJADI, M. R., S. SHEEDVASH, AND F. O. TRUJILLO [1993]. "Recursive dynamic node creation in multilayer neural networks." *IEEE Trans. Neural Networks* 4(2):242–256.

BAAKLINI, N., AND E. H. MAMDANI [1975]. "Prescriptive methods for deriving control policy in a fuzzy-logic controller." *Electron. Lett.* 11:625–626.

BABAGUCHI, N., K. YAMADA, K. KISE, AND Y. TEZUKU [1990]. "Connectionist model binarization." *Proc. 10th Int. Conf. Pattern Recognition,* 51–56, Atlantic City, NJ.

BAHRAMI, A., C. H. DAGLI, AND B. MODARRESS [1991]. "Fuzzy associative memory in conceptual design." *Proc. Int. Joint Conf. Neural Networks,* vol. I, 183–188, Seattle, WA.

BAHRAMI, M. [1992]. "Recognition of rules and exceptions by neural networks." *Int. J. Neural Syst.* 2:341–344.

BAKER, J. E. [1985]. "Adaptive selection methods for genetic algorithms." *Proc. Int. Conf. Genet. Algorithms Their Appl.,* 101–111, Pittsburgh.

BALAZINSKI, M., E. CZOGALA, AND T. SADOWSKI [1993]. "Control of metal-cutting using neural fuzzy controller." *Proc. IEEE Int. Conf. Fuzzy Syst.,* vol. I, 161–166, San Francisco.

BALDWIN, J. F. [1979]. "A new approach to approximate reasoning using a fuzzy logic." *Fuzzy Sets Syst.* 2:309–325.

BALDWIN, J. F. [1984]. "FRIL—A fuzzy relational inference language." *Fuzzy Sets Syst.* 14:155–174.

BALDWIN, J. F. [1986]. "Support logic programming." *Int. J. Intell. Syst.* 1:73–104.

BALDWIN, J. F. [1987]. "Evidential support logic programming." *Fuzzy Sets Syst.* 24:1–26.

BALDWIN, J. F., AND N. C. F. GUILD [1980]. "Modelling controllers using fuzzy relations." *Kybernetes* 9:223–229.

BALDWIN, J. F., AND B. W. PILSWORTH [1979]. "Fuzzy truth definition of possibility measure for decision classification." *Int. J. Man-Machine Stud.* 2:447–463.

BALDWIN, J. F., AND B. W. PILSWORTH [1982]. "Dynamic programming for fuzzy systems with fuzzy environment." *J. Math. Anal. Appl.* 85:1–23.

BANKS, S. P. [1989]. *Mathematical Theories of Nonlinear Systems.* New York: Prentice-Hall.

BARE, W. H., R. J. MULHOLLAND, AND S. S. SOFER [1990]. "Design of a self-tuning rule based controller for a gasoline refinery catalytic reformer." *IEEE Trans. Autom. Control* 35(2):156–164.

BARHEN, J., S. GULATI, AND M. ZAK [1989]. "Neural learning of constrained nonlinear transformations." *IEEE Comput.* 22(6):67–76.

BARTLETT, P. L., AND T. DOWNS [1992]. "Using random weights to train multilayer networks of hard-limiting units." *IEEE Trans. Neural Networks* 3(2):202–210.

BARTO, A. G. [1990]. "Connectionist learning for control: An overview." In W. T. Miller, III, R. S. Sutton, and P. J. Werbos, eds., *Neural Networks for Control.* Cambridge, MA: MIT Press.

BARTO, A. G., AND P. ANANDAN [1985]. "Pattern-recognizing stochastic learning automata." *IEEE Trans. Syst. Man Cybern.* 15(3):360–375.

BARTO, A. G., C. W. ANDERSON, AND R. S. SUTTON [1982]. "Synthesis of nonlinear control surfaces by a layered associative search network." *Biol. Cybern.* 43:175–185.

BARTO, A. G., AND M. I. JORDAN [1987]. "Gradient following without back-propagation in layered networks." *Proc. IEEE Int. Conf. Neural Networks,* vol. II, 629–636, San Diego.

BARTO, A. G., AND R. S. SUTTON [1981]. "Landmark learning: An illustration of associative search." *Biol. Cybern.* 42:1–8.

BARTO, A. G., R. S. SUTTON, AND C. W. ANDERSON [1983]. "Neuronlike adaptive elements that can solve difficult learning control problems." *IEEE Trans. Syst. Man Cybern.* 13(5):834–846.

BARTO, A. G., R. S. SUTTON, AND P. S. BROUWER [1981]. "Associative search network: A reinforcement learning associative memory." *Biolog. Cybern.* 40:201–211.

BARTOLINI, G., G. CASOLINO, F. DAROLI, AND M. MORTEM [1985]. "Development of performance adaptive fuzzy controllers with application to continuous casting plants." In M. Sugeno, ed., *Industrial Applications of Fuzzy Control,* 73–86. Amsterdam: North-Holland.

BATTITI, R. [1992]. "First- and second-order methods for learning: Between steepest descent and Newton's method." *Neural Comput.* 4:141–166.

BAUER, H. U., AND K. R. PAWELZIK [1992]. "Quantifying the neighborhood preservation of self-organizing feature maps." *IEEE Trans. Neural Networks* 3(4):570–579.

BECKER, S., AND Y. LeCUN [1989]. "Improving the convergence of back-propagation learning with second order methods." In D. S. Touretzky, G. E. Hinton, and T. J. Sejnowski, eds., *Proc. 1988 Connectionist Models Summer School,* 29–37. San Mateo, CA: Morgan Kaufmann.

BEKEY, G. A. [1993]. "Robotics and neural networks." In Bart Kosko, ed., *Neural Networks for Signal Processing.* Englewood Cliffs, NJ: Prentice-Hall.

BELLMAN, R., AND M. GIERTZ [1973]. "On the analytic formalism of the theory of fuzzy sets." *Inf. Sci.* 5:149–156.

BELLO, M. G. [1992]. "Enhanced training algorithms and integrated training/architecture selection for multilayer perceptron networks." *IEEE Trans. Neural Networks* 3(6):864–875.

BENGIO, Y., P. FRASCONI, AND P. SIMARD [1993]. "The problem of learning long-term dependencies in recurrent networks." *Proc. IEEE Int. Conf. Neural Networks,* vol. III, 1183–1188, San Francisco.

BENGIO, Y., R. DE MORI, G. FLAMMIA, AND R. KOMPE [1992]. "Global optimization of a neural network-hidden Markov model hybrid." *IEEE Trans. Neural Networks* 3(2):252–259.

BENSON, W. H. [1982]. "An application of fuzzy set theory to data display." In R. R. Yager, ed., *Fuzzy Sets and Possibility Theory.* New York: Pergamon Press.

BERENJI, H. R. [1992a]. Fuzzy logic controllers. In R. R. Yager and L. A. Zadeh, eds., *An Introduction to Fuzzy Logic Applications in Intelligent Systems,* 69–96. Boston: Kluwer Academic.

BERENJI, H. R. [1992b]. "A reinforcement learning-based architecture for fuzzy logic control." *Int. J. Approximate Reasoning* 6:267–292.

BERENJI, H. R., Y. Y. CHEN, C. C. LEE, J. S. JANG, AND S. MURUGESAN [1990]. "A hierarchical approach to designing approximate reasoning-based controllers for dynamic physical systems." *Proc. 6th Conf. Uncertainty Artif. Intell.,* 362–369, Cambridge, MA.

BERENJI, H. R., Y. Y. CHEN, C. C. LEE, S. MURUGESAN, AND J. S. JANG [1989]. "An experiment-based comparative study of fuzzy logic control." *Proc. Am. Control Conf.,* 2751–2753, Pittsburgh.

BERENJI, H. R., AND P. KHEDKAR [1992]. "Learning and tuning fuzzy logic controllers through reinforcements." *IEEE Trans. Neural Networks* 3(5):724–740.

BERNARD, J. A. [1988]. "Use of rule-based system for process control." *IEEE Control Syst. Mag.* 8(5):3–13.

BERSINI, H., J. P. NORDVIK, AND A. BONARINI [1993]. "A simple direct adaptive fuzzy controller derived from its neural equivalent." *Proc. IEEE Int. Conf. Fuzzy Syst.,* vol. I, 345–350, San Francisco.

BETHKE, A. D. [1981]. "Genetic algorithms as function optimizers." Doctoral dissertation, University of Michigan, Ann Arbor, MI.

Bibliography

BEZDEK, J. C. [1981]. *Pattern Recognition with Fuzzy Objective Function Algorithms.* New York: Plenum Press.

BEZDEK, J. C., ed. [1987]. *Analysis of Fuzzy Information.* Boca Raton, FL: CRC Press.

BEZDEK, J. C. [1991]. "A self-organizing and clustering algorithms." In R. Lea and J. Villereal, eds., *Proc. 2nd Joint Tech. Workshop Neural Networks Fuzzy Logic,* vol. 1, 143–158, Houston, TX.

BEZDEK, J. C. [1992a]. "Computing with uncertainty," *IEEE Commun. Mag.* 30(9):24–37.

BEZDEK, J. C. [1992b]. "On the relationship between neural networks, pattern recognition and intelligence." *Int. J. Approximate Reasoning* 6:85–107.

BEZDEK, J. C., S. CHUAH, AND D. LEEP [1983]. "Generalized *k*-nearest neighbor rules." *Fuzzy Sets Syst.* 18(3):237–256.

BEZDEK, J. C., AND S. K. PAL, eds. [1992]. *Fuzzy Models for Pattern Recognition.* New York: IEEE Press.

BEZDEK, J. C., E. C. K. TSAO, AND N. PAL [1992]. "Fuzzy Kohonen clustering networks." *Proc. IEEE Int. Conf. Fuzzy Syst.,* 1035–1046, San Diego.

BHANDARI, D., S. K. PAL, AND M. K. KUNDU [1993]. "Image enhancement incorporating fuzzy fitness function in genetic algorithms." *Proc. IEEE Int. Conf. Fuzzy Syst.,* vol. II, 1408–1413, San Francisco.

BICHSEL, M., AND P. SEITZ [1989]. "Minimum class entropy: A maximum information approach to layered networks." *Neural Networks* 2:133–141.

BILBRO, G. L., R. MANN, T. K. MILLER, W. E. SNYDER, D. E. VAN DEN BOUT, AND M. WHITE [1989]. "Optimization by mean field annealing." In D. S. Touretzky, ed., *Advances in Neural Information Processing Systems I,* 91–98. San Mateo, CA: Morgan Kaufmann.

BILBRO, G. L., W. E. SNYDER, S. J. GARNIER, AND J. W. GAULT [1992]. "Mean field annealing: A formalism for constructing GNC-Like algorithms." *IEEE Trans. Neural Networks* 3(1):131–138.

BIRX, D. L., AND S. J. PIPENBERG [1993]. "A complex mapping network for phase sensitive classification." *IEEE Trans. Neural Networks* 4(1):127–135.

BLANCO, A., AND M. DELGADO [1993]. "A direct fuzzy inference procedure by neural networks." *Fuzzy Sets Syst.* 58:133–141.

BLANZ, W. E., AND S. L. GISH [1990]. "A connectionist classifier architecture applied to image segmentation," *Proc. 10th Int. Conf. Pattern Recognition,* 272–277, Atlantic City, NJ.

BLOCKLEY, D. I. [1979]. "The role of fuzzy sets in civil engineering." *Fuzzy Sets Syst.* 2:267–278.

BODENHAUSEN, U., AND A. WAIBEL [1993]. "Application oriented automatic structuring of time-delay neural networks for high performance character and speech recognition." *Proc. IEEE Int. Conf. Neural Networks,* vol. III, 1627–1632, San Francisco.

BOENDER, C. G. E., J. G. GRAAN, AND F. A. LOOTSMA [1989]. "Multi-criteria decision analysis with fuzzy pairwise comparisons." *Fuzzy Sets Syst.* 29:133–143.

BOOKER, L. B. [1982]. "Intelligent behavior as an adaptation to the task environment." Doctoral dissertation, TR243, Logic of Computers Group, University of Michigan, Ann Arbor.

BOOKER, L. B. [1985]. "Improving the performance of genetic algorithms in classifier systems." *Proc. Int. Conf. Genet. Algorithms Their Appl.,* 80–92, Pittsburgh.

BOOSE, J. H. [1989]. "A survey of knowledge acquisition techniques and tools." *Knowl. Acquis.* 1:3–37.

BORNHOLDT, S., AND D. GRAUDENZ [1992]. "General asymmetric neural networks and structure design by genetic algorithms." *Neural Networks* 5:327–334.

BORTOLAN, G., AND R. DEGANI [1985]. "A review of some methods for ranking fuzzy subsets." *Fuzzy Sets Syst.* 15(1):1–19.

BOURLARD, H. A., AND N. MORGAN [1994]. *Connectionist Speech Recognition: A Hybrid Approach,* Boston: Kluwer Academic.

BOY, G. A., AND P. M. KUSS [1986]. "A fuzzy method for modeling of human-computer interactions in information retrieval tasks." In W. Karwowski and A. Mital, eds., *Applications of Fuzzy Set Theory in Human Factors,* 117–133. Amsterdam: Elsevier.

BRAAE, M., AND D. A. RUTHERFORD [1978]. "Fuzzy relations in a control setting." *Kybernetes* 7(3):185–188.

BRAAE, M., AND D. A. RUTHERFORD [1979a]. "Selection of parameters for a fuzzy logic controller." *Fuzzy Sets Syst.* 2(3):185–199.

BRAAE, M., AND D. A. RUTHERFORD [1979b]. "Theoretical and linguistic aspects of the fuzzy logic controller." *Automatica* 15(5):553–577.

BREGLER, C., S. MANKE, H. HILD, AND A. WAIBEL [1993]. "Bimodal sensor integration on the example of speech-reading." *Proc. IEEE Int. Conf. Neural Networks,* vol. II, 667–671, San Francisco.

BRENT, R. P. [1991]. "Fast training algorithms for multilayer neural nets." *IEEE Trans. Neural Networks* 2(3):346–354.

BRILL, F. Z., D. E. BROWN, AND W. N. MARTIN [1992]. "Fast genetic selection of features for neural network classifier." *IEEE Trans. Neural Networks* 3(2):324–328.

BRINDLE, A. [1981]. "Genetic algorithms for function optimization." Doctoral dissertation, University of Alberta, Edmonton.

BROWN, R. G. [1983]. *Introduction to Random Signal Analysis and Kalman Filtering,* New York: John Wiley.

BRYSON, A. E., AND Y. C. HO [1969]. *Applied Optimal Control.* New York: Blaisdell.

BUCKLES, B. P., F. E. PETRY, AND J. PILLAI [1990]. "Network data models for representation of uncertainty." *Fuzzy Sets Syst.* 38(2):171–190.

BUCKLEY, J. J. [1984]. "The multiple judge, multiple criteria ranking problem: A fuzzy set approach." *Fuzzy Sets Syst.* 13:25–38.

BUCKLEY, J. J. [1988]. "Possibility and necessity in optimization." *Fuzzy Sets Syst.* 25:1–13.

BUCKLEY, J. J. [1992]. "Theory of the fuzzy controller: An introduction." *Fuzzy Sets Syst.* 51:249–258.

BUCKLEY, J. J., Y. HAYASHI, AND E. CZOGALA [1992]. "On the equivalence of neural networks and fuzzy expert systems." *Proc. Int. Joint Conf. Neural Networks,* vol. II, 691–726, Baltimore, MD.

BUCKLEY, J. J., AND D. M. TUCKER [1989]. "Second generation fuzzy expert systems." *Fuzzy Sets Syst.* 31:271–284.

BUHMANN, J., AND K. SCHULTEN [1987a]. "Noise-driven temporal association in neural networks." *Europhys. Lett.* 4:1205–1209.

BUHMANN, J., AND K. SCHULTEN [1987b]. "Storing sequences of biased patterns in neural networks with stochastic dynamics." In R. Eckmiller and C. von der Malsburg, eds., *Neural Computers,* 231–242. Berlin: Springer-Verlag.

BULSARI, A. [1992]. "Training artificial neural networks for fuzzy logic." *Complex Syst.* 6:443–457.

BURR, D. J. [1981]. "Elastic matching of line drawings." *IEEE Trans. Pattern Anal. Mach. Intell.* PAMI–3(6):708–713.

BURR, D. J. [1988]. "An improved elastic net method for the travelling salesman problem." *Proc. IEEE Int. Conf. Neural Networks,* vol. I, 69–76, San Diego.

BURRASCANO, P. [1991a]. "A norm selection criterion for the generalized delta rule." *IEEE Trans. Neural Networks* 2(1):125–130.

BURRASCANO, P. [1991b]. "Learning vector quantization for the probabilistic neural network." *IEEE Trans. Neural Networks* 2(4):458–461.

BYRNE, W. [1992]. "Alternating minimization and Boltzmann machine learning." *IEEE Trans. Neural Networks* 3(4):612–620.

Bibliography

CAMPOS, L., AND J. L. VERDEGAY [1989]. "Linear programming problems and ranking of fuzzy numbers." *Fuzzy Sets Syst.* 32:1–11.

CARD, S. K., T. P. MORAN, AND A. NEWELL [1983]. *The Psychology of Human-Computer Interaction.* London: Erlbaum.

CARLSSON, C., AND P. KORHONEN [1986]. "A parametric approach to fuzzy linear programming." *Fuzzy Sets Syst.* 20:17–30.

CARPENTER, G. A., AND S. GROSSBERG [1987a]. "A massively parallel architecture for a self-organizing neural pattern recognition machine." *Comput. Vision Graphics Image Process.* 37:54–115.

CARPENTER, G. A., AND S. GROSSBERG [1987b]. "ART 2: Self-organization of stable category recognition codes for analog input patterns." *Appl. Opt.* 26:4919–4930.

CARPENTER, G. A., AND S. GROSSBERG [1988]. "The ART of adaptive pattern recognition by a self-organization neural network." *Computer* 21(3):77–88.

CARPENTER, G. A., AND S. GROSSBERG [1990]. "ART 3: Hierarchical search using chemical transmitters in self-organizing pattern recognition architectures." *Neural Networks* 3(2):129–152.

CARPENTER, G. A., AND S. GROSSBERG [1992]. "A self-organizing neural network for supervised learning, recognition, and prediction." *IEEE Commun. Mag.* 30(9):38–49.

CARPENTER, G. A., S. GROSSBERG, AND J. H. REYNOLDS [1991a]. "ARTMAP: Supervised real-time learning and classification of nonstationary data by a self-organizing neural network." *Neural Networks* 4:565–588.

CARPENTER, G. A., S. GROSSBERG, J. H. REYNOLDS, AND D. B. ROSEN [1992]. "Fuzzy ARTMAP: A neural network architecture for incremental supervised learning of analog multidimensional maps." *IEEE Trans. Neural Networks* 3(5):698–713.

CARPENTER, G. A., S. GROSSBERG, AND D. B. ROSEN [1991b]. "Fuzzy ART: Fast stable learning and categorization of analog patterns by an adaptive resonance system." *Neural Networks* 4:759–771.

CARPENTER, G. A., S. GROSSBERG, AND D. B. ROSEN [1991c]. "ART 2-A: An adaptive resonance algorithm for rapid category learning and recognition." *Neural Networks* 4:493–504.

CAUDELL, T. P. [1992]. "A hybrid optoelectronic ART-1 neural processor." *Appl. Opt.* 31:6220–6229.

CHAKRADHAL, S. T., V. D. AGRAWAL, AND M. L. BUSHNELL [1991]. *Neural Models and Algorithms for Digital Testing.* Boston: Kluwer Academic.

CHANAS, S., W. KOLODZIEJCZYK, AND A. MACHAJ [1984]. "A fuzzy approach to the transportation problem." *Fuzzy Sets Syst.* 13:211–221.

CHANG, S., AND L. A. ZADEH [1972]. "On fuzzy mapping and control." *IEEE Trans. Syst. Man Cybern.* 2:30–34.

CHAUDHARY, A. [1990]. Fuzzy logic maneuver load roll controllers for the ATW. Technical Report, Int. Rep. TFD-90-172, Rockwell International North American Aircraft Division, El Segundo, CA.

CHAUVIN, Y. [1989]. "A back-propagation algorithm with optimal use of hidden units." In D. S. Touretzky, ed., *Advances in Neural Information Processing Systems I,* 519–526. San Mateo, CA: Morgan Kaufmann.

CHEN, C. H., ed. [1991]. *Neural Networks in Pattern Recognition and Their Applications.* River Edge, NJ: World Scientific.

CHEN, D., C. L. GILES, G. Z. SUN, H. H. CHEN, Y. C. LEE, AND M. W. GOUDREAU [1993]. "Constructive learning of recurrent neural networks." *Proc. IEEE Int. Conf. Neural Networks,* vol. III, 1196–1201, San Francisco.

CHEN, S., C. F. N. COWAN, AND P. M. GRANT [1991]. "Orthogonal least squares learning algorithm for radial basis function networks." *IEEE Trans. Neural Networks* 2(2):302–309.

CHEN, Y. Y. [1989]. "The global analysis of fuzzy dynamic systems." Doctoral dissertation, University of California, Berkeley.

CHEN, Y. Y., K. Z. LIN, AND S. T. HSU [1992]. "A self-learning fuzzy controller." *Proc. IEEE Int. Conf. Fuzzy Syst.,* 189–196, San Diego.

CHESTER, M. [1993]. *Neural Networks: A Tutorial.* Englewood Cliffs, NJ: PTR Prentice-Hall.

CHIU, S., S. CHAND, D. MOORE, AND A. CHAUDHARY [1991]. "Fuzzy logic for control of roll and moment for a flexible wing aircraft." *IEEE Control Syst. Mag.* 11(4):42–48.

CHOI, J. J., P. ARABSHAHI, R. J. MARKS, II, AND T. P. CAUDELL [1992a]. "Fuzzy parameter adaptation in neural systems." *Proc. Int. Joint Conf. Neural Networks,* vol. I, 232–238, Baltimore, MD.

CHOI, J. J., H. O'KEEFE, AND P. K. BARUAH [1992b]. "Non-linear system diagnosis using neural networks and fuzzy logic." *Proc. IEEE Int. Conf. Fuzzy Syst.,* 813–820, San Diego.

CHOI, J. Y., AND C. H. CHOI [1992]. "Sensitivity analysis of multilayer perceptron with differentiable activation functions." *IEEE Trans. Neural Networks* 3(1):101–107.

CHUI, C. K. [1992]. *An Introduction to Wavelets.* New York: Academic Press.

CHUN, M. G., AND Z. BIEN [1993]. "Neurocomputational approach to solve a convexly combined fuzzy relational equation with generalized connectives." *Fuzzy Sets Syst.* 57:321–333.

CHUNG, B. M., AND J. H. OH [1993]. "Control of dynamic systems using fuzzy learning algorithm." *Fuzzy Sets Syst.* 59:1–14.

CHUNG, P. C., AND T. F. KRILE [1992]. "Characteristics of Hebbian-type associative memories having faulty interconnections." *IEEE Trans. Neural Networks* 3(6):969–980.

CILIZ, K., J. FEI, K. USLUEL, AND C. ISIK [1987]. "Practical aspects of the knowledge-based control of a mobile robot motion." *Proc. 30th Midwest Symp. Circuits Syst.* Syracuse, NY.

CIOS, K. J., AND N. LIU [1992]. "A machine learning method for generation of a neural network architecture: A continuous ID3 algorithm." *IEEE Trans. Neural Networks* 3(2):280–291.

CLEEREMANS, A., D. SERVAN-SCHREIBER, AND J. L. MCCLELLAND [1989]. "Finite state automata and simple recurrent networks." *Neural Comput.* 1:372–381.

CLYMER, J. R., P. D. COREY, AND J. A. GARDNER [1992]. "Discrete event fuzzy airport control." *IEEE Trans. Syst. Man Cybern.* 22(2):343–351.

COHEN, M. A., AND S. GROSSBERG [1983]. "Absolute stability of global pattern formation and parallel memory storage by competitive neural networks." *IEEE Trans. Syst. Man Cybern.* 13(5):815–826.

CORDES, G. A., H. B. SMARTT, J. A. JOHNSON, D. E. CLARK, AND K. L. WICKHAM [1993]. "Design and testing of a fuzzy logic/neural network hybrid controller for three-pump liquid level/temperature control." *Proc. IEEE Int. Conf. Fuzzy Syst.,* vol. I, 167–171, San Francisco.

COTTER, N. [1990]. "The Stone–Weierstrass theorem and its relationship to neural networks." *IEEE Trans. Neural Networks* 1(4):290–295.

COTTER, N. E., AND O. N. MIAN [1992]. "A pulsed neural network capable of universal approximation." *IEEE Trans. Neural Networks* 3(2):308–314.

COX, E. [1991]. "Integrating fuzzy logic into neural nets." *AI Expert* 6:43–47.

CZOGALA, E., AND K. HIROTA [1982]. "Fuzzy rule generation for fuzzy control." *Cybern. Syst.* 13(3):275–293.

CZOGALA, E., AND W. PEDRYCZ [1981]. "On identification in fuzzy systems and its applications in control problems." *Fuzzy Sets Syst.* 6(1):73–83.

CZOGALA, E., AND W. PEDRYCZ [1982]. "Control problems in fuzzy systems." *Fuzzy Sets Syst.* 7:257–273.

CZOGALA, E., AND T. RAWLIK [1989]. "Modeling of a fuzzy controller with application to the control of biological processes." *Fuzzy Sets Syst.* 31:13–22.

DA ROCHA, A. F., I. R. GUILHERME, M. THEOTO, A. M. K. MIYADAHIRA, AND M. S. KOIZUMI [1992]. "A neural net for extracting knowledge from natural language databases." *IEEE Trans. Neural Networks* 3(5):819–828.

Bibliography

DA ROCHA, A. F., AND R. YAGER [1992]. "Neural nets and fuzzy logic." In A. Kandel and G. Langholz, eds., *Hybrid Architecture for Intelligent Systems,* 3–28. Ann Arbor, MI: CRC Press.

DASARATHY, B. V. [1990]. *Nearest Neighbor (NN) Norms: NN Pattern Classification Techniques.* Los Alamitos, CA: IEEE Computer Society Press.

DAVIDOR, Y. [1990]. *Genetic Algorithms and Robotics: A Heuristic Strategy for Optimization,* Singapore: World Scientific.

DAVIS, J., T. WARMS, AND W. WINTERS [1991]. "A neural network implementation of the fuzzy *c*-means clustering algorithm." *Proc. Int. Joint Conf. Neural Networks,* vol. II, A–953, Seattle, WA.

DAVIS, L., ed. [1987]. *Genetic Algorithms and Simulated Annealing,* Pitman Series of Research Notes on Artificial Intelligence. Pitman, London.

DAVIS, L., ed. [1991]. *Handbook of Genetic Algorithms.* New York: Van Nostrand Reinhold.

DAYAN, P. [1992]. "The convergence of TD(λ) for general λ." *Mach. Learn.* 8:341–362.

DE JONG, K. A. [1975]. "An analysis of the behavior of a class of genetic adaptive systems." Doctoral dissertation, University of Michigan, Ann Arbor, MI.

DE LUCA, A., AND S. TERMINI [1972]. "A definition of a nonprobabilistic entropy in the setting of fuzzy set theory." *Inf. Control* 20:301–12.

DE OLIVEIRA, J. [1993]. "Neuron inspired learning rules for fuzzy relational structures." *Fuzzy Sets Syst.* 57:41–53.

DEFIGUEIREDO, R. J. P. [1990]. "An optimal matching-score net for pattern classification." *Proc. Int. Joint Conf. Neural Networks,* vol. 3, 909–916, San Diego.

DEFIGUEIREDO, R. J. P. [1992]. "An optimal multilayer neural interpolating (OMNI) net in a generalized Fock space setting." *Proc. Int. Joint Conf. Neural Networks,* vol. I, 111–120, Baltimore, MD.

DELGADO, M., J. L. VERDEGAY, AND M. A. VILA [1989]. "A general model for fuzzy linear programming." *Fuzzy Sets Syst.* 29:21–29.

DEMBO, A. [1989]. "On the capacity of associative memories with linear threshold functions." *IEEE Trans. Inf. Theory* 35(4):709–720.

DEMPSTER, A. P. [1967]. "Upper and lower probabilities induced by a multivalued mapping." *Ann. Math. Stat.* 38:325–339.

DENKER, J., D. SCHWARTZ, B. WITTNER, S. SOLLA, R. HOWARD, L. JACKEL, AND J. HOPFIELD [1987]. "Large automatic learning, rule extraction, and generalization." *Complex Syst.* 1:877–922.

DENKER, J. S., ed. [1986]. *Neural Networks for Computing.* New York: American Institute of Physics.

DERRIDA, B., AND R. MEIR [1988]. "Chaotic behavior of a layered neural network." *Phys. Rev. A* 38(6):3116–3119.

DESIENO, D. [1988]. "Adding a conscience to competitive learning." *Proc. IEEE Int. Conf. Neural Networks,* vol. I, 117–124, San Diego.

DEVANEY, R. L. [1987]. *An Introduction to Chaotic Dynamical Systems.* Reading, MA: Addison-Wesley.

DEYONG, M., J. POLSON, R. MOORE, C. C. WENG, AND J. LORA [1992]. "Fuzzy and adaptive control simulations for a walking machine." *IEEE Control Syst. Mag.* 12(3):43–49.

DICKERSON, J. A., AND B. KOSKO [1993]. "Fuzzy function learning with covariance ellipsoids." *Proc. IEEE Int. Conf. Neural Networks,* vol. II, 1162–1167, San Francisco.

DIEDERICH, J., ed. [1990]. *Artificial Neural Networks: Concept Learning,* Los Alamitos, CA: IEEE Computer Society Press.

DIETTERICH, T. G., H. HILD, AND G. BAKIRI [1990]. "A comparative study of ID3 and back-propagation for English text-to-speech mapping." *Proc. 7th Int. Conf. Mach. Learn.,* 24–31, Austin, TX.

DIMITRESCU, D. [1988]. "Hierarchical pattern classification." *Fuzzy Sets Syst.* 28:145–162.

DiNola, A., W. Pedrycz, S. Sessa, and E. Sanchez [1991]. "Fuzzy relation equations theory as a basis of fuzzy modelling: An overview." *Fuzzy Sets Syst.* 40:415–429.

Dombi, J. [1982]. "A general class of fuzzy operators, the DeMorgan class of fuzzy operators and fuzziness measures induced by fuzzy operators." *Fuzzy Sets Syst.* 8:149–163.

Douglas, S. C., and T. H. Y. Meng [1991]. "Linearized least-squares training of multilayer feedforward neural networks." *Proc. Int. Joint Conf. Neural Networks,* vol. I, 307–312, Seattle, WA.

Drago, G. P., and S. Ridella [1992]. "Statistically controlled activation weight initialization (SCAWI)." *IEEE Trans. Neural Networks* 3(4):627–631.

Drucker, H., and Y. LeCun [1992]. "Improving generalization performance using double backpropagation." *IEEE Trans. Neural Networks* 3(6):991–997.

Dubois, D. [1987]. "Linear programming with fuzzy data." In J. C. Bezdek, ed., *Analysis of Fuzzy Information,* Vol. 3: *Application in Engineering and Science,* Boca Raton, FL: CRC Press.

Dubois, D., and H. Prade [1980]. *Fuzzy Sets and Systems: Theory and Applications.* New York: Academic Press.

Dubois, D., and H. Prade [1982a]. "Towards fuzzy differential calculus: Part 1." *Fuzzy Sets Syst.* 8:1–17.

Dubois, D., and H. Prade [1982b]. "Integration of fuzzy mappings: Part 2." *Fuzzy Sets Syst.* 8:105–116.

Dubois, D., and H. Prade [1982c]. "Integration of fuzzy interval: Part 3." *Fuzzy Sets Syst.* 8:225–233.

Dubois, D., and H. Prade [1984]. "Fuzzy logics and the generalized modus ponens revisited." *Cybern. Syst.* 15:293–331.

Dubois, D., and H. Prade [1985a]. "Unfair coins and necessity measures: Toward a possibilistic interpretation of histograms." *Fuzzy Sets Syst.* 10(1):15–20.

Dubois, D., and H. Prade [1985b]. "A review of fuzzy set aggregation connectives." *Inf. Sci.* 36:85–121.

Dubois, D., and H. Prade [1985c]. "Fuzzy cardinality and the modeling of imprecise quantification." *Fuzzy Sets Syst.* 16:199–230.

Dubois, D., and H. Prade [1988a]. "On fuzzy syllogisms." *Comput. Intell.* 14:171–179.

Dubois, D., and H. Prade [1988b]. *Possibility Theory: An Approach to Computerized Processing of Uncertainty.* New York: Plenum Press.

Dubois, D., and H. Prade [1991]. "Fuzzy sets in approximate reasoning. Part I: Inference with possibility distributions." *Fuzzy Sets Syst.* 40:143–202.

Dubois, D., and H. Prade [1992]. "Fuzzy rules in knowledge-based systems—Modelling gradedness, uncertainty and preference." In R. R. Yager and L. A. Zadeh, eds., *An Introduction to Fuzzy Logic Applications in Intelligent Systems,* 45–68. Boston: Kluwer Academic.

Dubois, D., H. Prade, and J. Lang [1991]. "Fuzzy sets in approximate reasoning. Part II: Logic approacher." *Fuzzy Sets Syst.* 40:203–244.

Dubois, D., H. Prade, and R. R. Yager, eds. [1993]. *Fuzzy Sets for Intelligent Systems.* San Mateo, CA: Morgan Kaufmann.

Duda, R. O., and P. E. Hart [1973]. *Pattern Classification and Scene Analysis.* New York: John Wiley.

Duffy, J. J., and M. A. Franklin [1975]. "A learning identification algorithm and its application to an environmental system." *IEEE Trans. Syst. Man Cybern.* 5(2):226–240.

Dumitrescu, D. [1993]. "Fuzzy training procedures." *Fuzzy Sets Syst.* 56:155–169.

DURBIN, R., AND D. WILLSHAW [1987]. "An analogue approach to the travelling salesman problem using an elastic net method." *Nature* 326:689–691.

ECKMILLER, R., ed. [1990]. *Advanced Neural Computers.* Amsterdam: Elsevier Science.

EDWARDS, S. F., AND P. W. ANDERSON [1975]. "Theory of spin glasses." *J. Phys. F: Metal Phys.* 5:965–974.

EDWARDS, S. F., AND P. W. ANDERSON [1976]. "Theory of spin glasses: II." *J. Phys. F: Metal Phys.* 6:1927–1937.

EFSTATHIOU, J. [1987]. "Rule-based process control using fuzzy logic." In E. Sanchez and L. A. Zadeh, eds., *Approximate Reasoning in Intelligence Systems,* 145–148. New York: Pergamon Press.

EGUSA, Y., H. AKAHORI, A. MORIMURA, AND N. WAKAMI [1992]. "An electronic video camera image stabilizer operated on fuzzy theory." *Proc. IEEE Int. Conf. Fuzzy Syst.,* 851–858, San Diego.

EKLUND, P., AND F. KLAWONN [1992]. "Neural fuzzy logic programming." *IEEE Trans. Neural Networks* 3(5):815–818.

ELMAN, J. L. [1990]. "Finding structure in time." *Cognitive Sci.* 14:179–211.

ELMAN, J. L. [1991]. "Distributed representations, simple recurrent networks, and grammatical structure." *Mach. Learn.* 7:195–225.

ENBUTSU, I., K. BABA, AND N. HARA [1991]. "Fuzzy rule extraction from a multilayered neural network." *Proc. Int. Joint Conf. Neural Networks,* vol. II, 461–465, Seattle, WA.

ENGLISH, T. M., M. DEL P. GOMEZ-GIL, AND W. J. B. OLDHAM [1993]. "A comparison of neural network and nearest-neighbor classifiers of handwritten lowercase letters." *Proc. IEEE Int. Conf. Neural Networks,* vol. III, 1618–1621, San Francisco.

ERNST, E. [1982]. "Fahrplanerstellung und umlaufdisposition im container-schiffsverkehr." Doctoral dissertation, (Diss. Aachen) Frankfurt/M., Bern.

ESOGBUE, A. O., AND R. C. ELDER [1983]. "Measurement and valuation of a fuzzy mathematical model for medical diagnosis." *Fuzzy Sets Syst.* 10:223–242.

ESOGBUE, A. O., AND J. A. MURRELL [1993]. "A fuzzy adaptive controller using reinforcement learning neural networks." *Proc. IEEE Int. Conf. Fuzzy Syst.,* vol. I, 178–183, San Francisco.

ESRAGH, F., AND E. H. MAMDANI [1979]. "A general approach to linguistic approximation." *Int. J. Man-Mach. Stud.* 11:501–519.

EVANS, G. W., AND W. KARWOWSKI [1986]. A perspective on mathematical modeling in human factors. *Applications of Fuzzy Set Theory in Human Factors,* 3–27. Amsterdam: Elsevier.

EVANS, G. W., W. KARWOWSKY, AND M. R. WILHELM, eds. [1989]. *Applications of Fuzzy Set Methodologies in Industrial Engineering.* New York: Elsevier.

FAHLMAN, S. E. [1989]. "Fast-learning variations on back-propagation: An empirical study." In D. S. Touretzky, G. E. Hinton, and T. J. Sejnowski, eds., *Proc. 1988 Connectionist Models Summer School,* 38–51. San Mateo, CA: Morgan Kaufmann.

FAHLMAN, S. E. [1991]. "The recurrent cascade-correlation architecture." In R. P. Lippmann, J. E. Moody, and D. S. Touretzky, eds., *Advances in Neural Information Processing Systems III,* 190. San Mateo, CA: Morgan Kaufmann.

FAHLMAN, S. E., AND C. LEBIERE [1990]. "The cascade-correlation learning architecture." In D. S. Touretzky, ed., *Advances in Neural Information Processing Systems II,* 524–532. San Mateo, CA: Morgan Kaufmann.

FARLOW, S. J., ed. [1984]. *Self-Organizing Methods in Modeling.* New York: Dekker.

FAUSETT, L. [1994]. *Fundamentals of Neural Networks: Architectures, Algorithms, and Applications.* Englewood Cliffs, NJ: Prentice-Hall.

FELDKAMP, L. A., AND G. V. PUSKORIUS [1993]. "Trainable fuzzy and neural-fuzzy systems for idle-speed control." *Proc. IEEE Int. Conf. Fuzzy Syst.,* vol. I, 45–51, San Francisco.

FILEV, D. P., AND R. R. YAGER [1991]. "A generalized defuzzification method via BAD distributions." *Int. J. Intell. Syst.* 6(7):687–697.

FISHER, D. H., AND K. B. MCKUSICK [1989]. "An empirical comparison of ID3 and backpropagation." *Proc. 11th Int. Joint Conf. Artif. Intell.,* 788–793, Detroit.

FLORÉEN, P. [1991]. "The convergence of Hamming memory networks." *IEEE Trans. Neural Networks* 2(4):449–457.

FOGEL, D. B. [1991a]. *System Identification through Simulated Evolution: A Machine Learning Approach to Modeling.* Needham, MA: Ginn Press.

FOGEL, D. B. [1991b]. "An information criterion for optimal neural network selection." *IEEE Trans. Neural Networks* 2(5):490–497.

FOGEL, D. B. [1993]. "Using evolutionary programming to create neural networks that are capable of playing tic-tac-toe." *Proc. IEEE Int. Conf. Neural Networks,* vol. II, 875–880, San Francisco.

FOGEL, D. B., L. J. FOGEL, AND V. W. PORTO [1990]. "Evolving neural networks." *Biol. Cybern.* 63:487–493.

FOGEL, D. B., AND P. K. SIMPSON [1993]. "Evolving fuzzy clusters." *Proc. IEEE Int. Conf. Neural Networks,* vol. III, 1829–1834, San Francisco.

FOGEL, L. J., A. J. OWNERS, AND M. J. WALSH [1966]. *Artificial Intelligence through Simulated Evolution.* New York: John Wiley.

FORTUNA, L., G. MUSCATO, G. NUNNARI, AND L. OCCHIPINTI [1993]. "Neural modeling and fuzzy control: An application to control the temperature in a thermal process." *Proc. IEEE Int. Conf. Fuzzy Syst.,* vol. II, 1327–1333, San Francisco.

FRANCELIN, R. A., AND F. A. C. GOMIDE [1993]. "A neural network for fuzzy decision making problems." *Proc. IEEE Int. Conf. Fuzzy Systems,* vol. I, 655–660, San Francisco.

FRANK, M. J. [1979]. "On the simultaneous associativity of $f(x, y)$ and $x + y - f(x, y)$." *Aequationes Math.* 19:194–226.

FRANKLIN, J. A. [1989]. "Input space representation for refinement learning control." *Proc. IEEE Int. Symp. Intell. Control,* 115–122, Albany, NY.

FREAN, M. [1990]. "The upstart algorithm: A method for constructing and training feedforward neural networks." *Neural Comput.* 2:198–209.

FREEMAN, J. A., AND D. M. SKAPURA [1991]. *Neural Networks: Algorithms, Applications, and Programming Techniques.* Reading, MA: Addison-Wesley.

FREISLEBEN, B., AND T. KUNKELMANN [1993]. "Combining fuzzy logic and neural networks to control an autonomous vehicle." *Proc. IEEE Int. Conf. Fuzzy Syst.,* vol. I, 321–326, San Francisco.

FU, K. S. [1968]. *Sequential Methods in Pattern Recognition and Machine Learning.* New York: Academic Press.

FU, L. M. [1992]. "A parallel distributed approach for knowledge-based inference and learning." In A. Kandel and G. Langholz, eds., *Hybrid Architectures for Intelligent Systems,* chap. 5, 87–104. Ann Arbor, MI: CRC Press.

FU, L. M. [1993]. "Knowledge-based connectionism for revising domain theories." *IEEE Trans. Syst. Man Cybern.* 23(1):173–182.

FUJITEC, F. [1988]. Flex-8800 series elevator group control systems. Technical Report, Fujitec Co. Ltd., Osaka, Japan.

FUKUDA, T., AND T. SHIBATA [1992]. "Hierarchical intelligent control for robotic motion by using fuzzy, artificial intelligence, and neural network." *Proc. Int. Joint Conf. Neural Networks,* vol. I, 269–274, Baltimore, MD.

Bibliography

FUKUDA, T., AND T. SHIBATA [1994]. "Fuzzy-neuro-GA based intelligent robotics." In J. M. Zurada, R. J. Marks, II, and C. J. Robinson, eds., *Computational Intelligence Imitating Life,* 352–362. New York: IEEE Press.

FUKUDA, T., T. SHIBATA, M. TOKITA, AND T. MITSUOKA [1992a]. "Neuromorphic control: Adaptation and learning." *IEEE Trans. Ind. Electron.* 39(6):497–503.

FUKUDA, T., K. SHIMOJIMA, F. ARAI, AND H. MATSUURA [1992b]. "Multi-sensor integration system with fuzzy inference and neural network." *Proc. Int. Joint Conf. Neural Networks,* vol. II, 757–762, Baltimore, MD.

FUKUDA, T., K. SHIMOJIMA, F. ARAI, AND H. MATSUURA [1992c]. "Multi-sensor integration system based on fuzzy inference and neural network for industrial application." *Proc. IEEE Int. Conf. Fuzzy Syst.,* 907–914, San Diego.

FUKUNAGA, K. [1972]. *Introduction to Statistical Pattern Recognition.* New York: Academic Press.

FUKUSHIMA, K. [1988]. "Neocognitron: A hierarchical neural network capable of visual pattern recognition." *Neural Networks* 1:119–130.

FUKUSHIMA, K. [1989]. "Analysis of the process of pattern recognition by the neocognitron." *Neural Networks* 2(6):413–420.

FUKUSHIMA, K., AND S. MIYAKE [1980]. "Neocognitron: A self-organizing neural network model for a mechanism of pattern recognition unaffected by shift in position." *Biol. Cybern.* 36(4):193–202.

FUKUSHIMA, K., AND S. MIYAKE [1984]. "Neocognitron: A new algorithm for pattern recognition tolerant of deformations and shifts in position." *Pattern Recognition* 15(6):455–469.

FUKUSHIMA, K., S. MIYAKE, AND T. ITO [1983]. "Neocognitron: A neural network model for a mechanism of visual pattern recognition." *IEEE Trans. Syst. Man Cybern.* 13:826–834.

FUKUSHIMA, K., AND N. WAKE [1991]. "Handwritten alphanumeric character recognition by the neocognitron." *IEEE Trans. Neural Networks* 2(3):355–365.

FUNAHASHI, K. [1989]. "On the approximation realization of continuous mappings by neural networks." *Neural Networks* 2:183–192.

FURUHASHI, T., S. HORIKAWA, AND Y. UCHIKAWA [1993]. "An application of fuzzy neural networks to a stability analysis of fuzzy control system." *Proc. IEEE Int. Conf. Fuzzy Syst.,* vol. I, 369–374, San Francisco.

GABRIEL, M., AND J. MOORE, eds. [1990]. *Learning and Computational Neuroscience: Foundations of Adaptive Networks.* Cambridge, MA: MIT Press.

GAINES, B. R. [1976]. "Foundations of fuzzy reasoning." *Int. J. Man-Mach. Stud.* 8:623–668.

GALLAND, C. C., AND G. E. HINTON [1989]. Deterministic Boltzmann learning in networks with asymmetric connectivity. Technical Report CRG-TR-89-6, Connectionist Research Group, University of Toronto, Toronto.

GALLANT, S. I. [1986]. "Optimal linear discriminants." *Proc. Eighth Int. Conf. Pattern Recognition,* 849–852, Paris.

GALLANT, S. I. [1990]. "Perceptron-based learning algorithms." *IEEE Trans. Neural Networks* 1(2):179–191.

GELB, A., ed. [1974]. *Applied Optimal Estimation.* Cambridge, MA: MIT Press.

GEMAN, S., AND D. GEMAN [1984]. "Stochastic relaxation, Gibbs distributions, and the Bayesian restoration of images." *IEEE Trans. Pattern Anal. Mach. Intell.* PAMI–6:721–741.

GHOSH, A., N. R. PAL, AND S. K. PAL [1993]. "Self-organization for object extraction using a multilayer neural network and fuzziness measures." *IEEE Trans. Fuzzy Syst.* 1(1) 54–68.

GILES, C. L., D. CHEN, C. B. MILLER, H. H. CHEN, G. Z. SUN, AND Y. C. LEE [1991]. "Second-order recurrent neural networks for grammatical inference." *Proc. Int. Joint Conf. Neural Networks,* vol. II, 273–281, Seattle, WA.

GILES, C. L., C. B. MILLER, D. CHEN, H. H. CHEN, G. Z. SUN, AND Y. C. LEE [1992]. "Learning and extracting finite state automata with second-order recurrent neural networks." *Neural Comput.* 4:395–405.

GILES, C. L., G. Z. SUN, H. H. CHEN, Y. C. LEE, AND D. CHEN [1990]. "Higher order recurrent networks and grammatical inference." In D. S. Touretzky, ed., *Advances in Neural Information Processing Systems II.* San Mateo, CA: Morgan Kaufmann.

GILES, R. [1976]. "Lukasiewicz logic and fuzzy theory." *Int. J. Man-Mach. Stud.* 8:313–327.

GLAUBER, R. J. [1963]. "Time-dependent statistics of the Ising model." *J. Math. Phys.* 4:294–307.

GLEICK, J. [1987]. *Chaos: Making a New Science.* New York: Viking.

GODO, L., R. LÓPEX DE MÁNTARAS, C. SIERRA, AND A. VERDAGUER [1988]. "Managing linguistically expressed uncertainty in MILORD: Application to medical diagnosis." *Artif. Intell. Commun.* 1:14–31.

GOGUEN, J. A. [1967]. "L-fuzzy sets." *J. Math. Anal. Appl.* 18:145–174.

GOLDBERG, D. E. [1989]. *Genetic Algorithms in Search Optimization, and Machine Learning.* Reading, MA: Addison-Wesley.

GOLDBERG, D. E. [1994]. "Genetic and evolutionary algorithms come of age." *Commun. ACM* 37(3):113–119.

GOLDBERG, D. E., AND J. RICHARDSON [1987]. "Genetic algorithms with sharing for multimodal function optimization." *Genet. Algorithms Their Appl.: Proc. 2nd Int. Conf. Genet. Algorithms,* 41–49, Cambridge, MA.

GOLES-CHACC, E., F. FOGELMAN-SOULIE, AND D. PELLEGRIN [1985]. "Decreasing energy functions as a tool for studying threshold networks." *Discrete Appl. Math.* 12:261–277.

GOODMAN, I. R., AND H. T. NGUYEN [1985]. *Uncertainty Models for Knowledge-Based System.* Amsterdam: North-Holland.

GOODWIN, G. C., AND K. S. SIN [1984]. *Adaptive Filtering Prediction and Control.* Englewood Cliffs, NJ: Prentice-Hall.

GOTTWALD, S. [1979]. "Set theory for fuzzy sets of higher level." *Fuzzy Sets Syst.* 2:125–151.

GRABISCH, M., AND M. SUGENO [1992]. "Multi-attribute classification using fuzzy integral." *Proc. IEEE Int. Conf. Fuzzy Syst.,* 47–54, San Diego.

GRAHAM, B. P., AND R. B. NEWELL [1988]. "Fuzzy identification and control of a liquid level rig." *Fuzzy Sets Syst.* 26:255–273.

GRAHAM, B. P., AND R. B. NEWELL [1989]. "Fuzzy adaptive control of a first order process." *Fuzzy Sets Syst.* 31:47–65.

GRAHAM, I. [1991]. "Fuzzy logic in commercial expert systems—Results and prospects." *Fuzzy Sets Syst.* 40:451–472.

GRAY, D. L., AND A. N. MICHEL [1992]. "A training algorithm for binary feedforward neural networks." *IEEE Trans. Neural Networks* 3(2):176–194.

GREBOGI, C., E. OTT, AND J. A. YORKE [1987]. "Chaos, strange attractors, and fractal basin boundaries in nonlinear dynamics." *Science* 238:632–638.

GREFENSTETTE, J. J., C. L. RAMSEY, AND A. C. SCHULTZ [1990]. "Learning sequential decision rules using simulation models and competition." *Mach. Learn.* 5(4):355–381.

GROSSBERG, S. [1969a]. "Embedding fields: A theory of learning with physiological implications." *J. Math. Psychol.* 6:209–239.

GROSSBERG, S. [1969b]. "On learning and energy-entropy dependency in recurrent and nonrecurrent signed networks." *J. Stat. Phys.* 1:319–350.

GROSSBERG, S. [1969c]. "Some networks that can learn, remember, and reproduce any number of complicated space-time patterns." *J. Math. Mech.* 19:53–91.

GROSSBERG, S. [1971]. "Embedding fields: Underlying philosophy, mathematics, and applications to psychology, physiology and anatomy." *J. Cybern.* 1(1):28–50.

GROSSBERG, S. [1976a]. "Adaptive pattern classification and universal recoding: I. Parallel development and coding of neural feature detectors." *Biol. Cybern.* 23:121–134.

GROSSBERG, S. [1976b]. "Adaptive pattern classification and universal recoding: II. Feedback, expectation, olfaction, illusions." *Bio. Cybern.* 23:187–202.

GROSSBERG, S. [1976c]. "On the development of feature detectors in the visual cortex with applications to learning and reaction-diffusion systems." *Biol. Cybern.* 21:145–159.

GROSSBERG, S. [1982a]. *Studies of Mind and Brain: Neural Principles of Learning, Perception, Development, Cognition, and Motor Control.* Boston, MA: Reidel.

GROSSBERG, S. [1982b]. "Learning by neural networks." In S. Grossberg, ed., *Studies of Mind and Brain,* 65–156. Boston, MA: Reidel.

GROSSBERG, S. [1988a]. *Neural Networks and Natural Intelligence.* Cambridge, MA: MIT Press.

GROSSBERG, S. [1988b]. "Nonlinear neural networks: Principles, mechanisms, and architectures." *Neural Networks* 1:17–61.

GU, T., AND B. DUBUISSON [1990]. "Similarity of classes and fuzzy clustering." *Fuzzy Sets Syst.* 34:213–221.

GUO, H., AND S. B. GELFAND [1992]. "Classification trees with neural network feature extraction." *IEEE Trans. Neural Networks* 3(6):923–933.

GUPTA, M. M. [1990]. "Fuzzy neural network approach to control systems." *Proc. Am. Control Conf.,* vol. 3, 3019–3022, San Diego.

GUPTA, M. M., A. KANDEL, W. BANDLER, AND J. B. KISZKA, eds. [1985]. *Approximate Reasoning in Expert Systems.* Amsterdam: North-Holland.

GUPTA, M. M., AND J. QI [1991]. "On fuzzy neuron models." *Proc. Int. Joint Conf. Neural Networks,* vol. II, 431–436, Seattle, WA.

GUPTA, M. M., AND E. SANCHEZ, eds. [1982a]. *Fuzzy Information and Decision Processes.* Amsterdam: North-Holland.

GUPTA, M. M., AND E. SANCHEZ, eds. [1982b]. *Approximate Reasoning in Decision Analysis.* Amsterdam: North-Holland.

GUPTA, M. M., G. N. SARIDIS, AND B. R. GAINES, eds. [1977]. *Fuzzy Automata and Decision Processes.* Amsterdam: North-Holland.

GUPTA, M. M., AND T. YAMAKAWA, eds. [1988a]. *Fuzzy Computing: Theory, Hardware and Applications,* New York: Elsevier.

GUPTA, M. M., AND T. YAMAKAWA, eds. [1988b]. *Fuzzy Logic in Knowledge-Based Systems, Decision and Control.* Amsterdam: North-Holland.

HAGIWARA, M. [1990]. "Multidimensional associative memory." *Proc. Int. Joint Conf. Neural Networks,* vol. I, 3–6, Washington, DC.

HAGIWARA, M. [1992]. "Extended fuzzy cognitive maps." *Proc. IEEE Int. Conf. Fuzzy Syst.,* 795–800, San Diego.

HAINES, K., AND R. HECHT-NIELSEN [1988]. "A BAM with increased information storage capacity." *Proc. Int. Joint Conf. Neural Networks,* vol. 1, 181–190, San Diego.

HALL, L. O. [1991]. "Learning on fuzzy data with a backpropagation scheme." In J. Keller and R. Krishnapuram, eds., *Proc. NAFIPS 1991,* 329–332, Columbia, MO.

HALL, L. O., A. M. BENSAID, L. P. CLARKE, R. P. VELTHUIZEN, M. S. SILBIGER, AND J. C. BEZDEK [1992]. "A comparison of neural network and fuzzy clustering techniques in segmenting magnetic resonance images of the brain." *IEEE Trans. Neural Networks* 3(5):672–682.

HALL, L. O., AND A. KANDEL [1986]. *Designing Fuzzy Expert Systems.* Köln: Verlag TÜV Rheinland.

HAMACHER, H. [1978]. "Über logische verknupfungen unscharfer aussagen und deren zugehörige bewertungsfunktionen." In R. Trappl, G. J. Klir, and L. Ricciardi, eds., *Progress in Cybernetics and Systems Research,* vol. 3, 276–288, Washington DC.

HAMBLY, A. R. [1990]. *Communication Systems.* New York: Computer Science Press.

HAMPSHIRE, J. B., II, AND B. PEARLMUTTER [1990]. "Equivalence proofs for multilayer perceptron classifiers and the Bayesian discriminant function." In D. S. Touretzky, J. L. Elman, T. J. Sejnowski, and G. E. Hinton, eds., *Proc. 1990 Connectionist Models Summer School,* 159–172. San Mateo, CA: Morgan Kaufmann.

HANSON, S. J., AND D. J. BURR [1990]. "What connectionist models learn: Learning and representation in connectionist neural networks." *Brain Behav. Sci.* 13(3):471–511.

HANSON, S. J., AND L. Y. PRATT [1989]. "Comparing biases for minimal network construction with back-propagation." In D. S. Touretzky, ed., *Advances in Neural Information Processing Systems I,* 177–185. San Mateo, CA: Morgan Kaufmann.

HARP, S. A., AND T. SAMAD [1991]. "Genetic synthesis of neural network architecture." In Lawrence Davis, ed., *Handbook of Genetic Algorithms,* 202–221. New York: Van Nostrand Reinhold.

HARP, S. A., T. SAMAD, AND A. GUHA [1989]. "Towards the genetic synthesis of neural networks." In J. D. Schaffer, ed., *Proc. Third Int. Conf. Genet. Algorithms,* 360–369. San Mateo, CA: Morgan Kaufmann.

HARP, S. A., T. SAMAD, AND A. GUHA [1990]. "Designing application-specific neural networks using the genetic algorithm." In D. S. Touretzky, ed., *Advances in Neural Information Processing Systems II,* 447–454. San Mateo, CA: Morgan Kaufmann.

HARTMAN, E. J., J. D. KEELER, AND J. M. KOWALSKI [1990]. "Layered neural networks with Gaussian hidden units as universal approximations." *Neural Comput.* 2:210–215.

HASHIYAMA, T., T. FURUHASHI, AND Y. UCHIKAWA [1992]. "An interval fuzzy model using a fuzzy neural network." *Proc. Int. Joint Conf. Neural Networks,* vol. II, 745–750, Baltimore, MD.

HASSIBI, B., D. G. STORK, AND G. J. WOLFF [1993]. "Optimal brain surgeon and general network pruning." *Proc. IEEE Int. Conf. Neural Networks,* vol. 1, 293–299, San Francisco.

HASSOUN, M. H., AND J. SONG [1992]. "Adaptive Ho-Kashyap rules for perceptron training." *IEEE Trans. Neural Networks* 3(1):51–61.

HAYASHI, I., H. NOMURA, H. YAMASAKI, AND N. WAKAMI [1992a]. "Construction of fuzzy interface rules by NDF and NDFL." *Int. J. Approximate Reasoning* 6(2):241–266.

HAYASHI, I., AND H. TANAKA [1990]. "The fuzzy GMDH algorithm by possibility models and its application." *Fuzzy Sets Syst.* 36:245–258.

HAYASHI, Y. [1992]. "A neural expert system using fuzzy teaching input." *Proc. IEEE Int. Conf. Fuzzy Syst.,* 485–491, San Diego.

HAYASHI, Y., J. J. BUCKLEY, AND E. CZOGALA [1992c]. "Fuzzy neural network with fuzzy signals and weights." *Proc. Int. Joint Conf. Neural Networks,* vol. II, 696–701, Baltimore, MD.

HAYASHI, Y., E. CZOGALA, AND J. J. BUCKLEY [1992b]. "Fuzzy neural controller." *Proc. IEEE Int. Conf. Fuzzy Syst.,* 197–202, San Diego.

HAYKIN, S. [1994]. *Neural Networks: A Comprehensive Foundation.* New York: Macmillan.

HEALY, M. J., T. P. CAUDELL, AND S. D. G. SMITH [1993]. "A neural architecture for pattern sequence verification through inferencing." *IEEE Trans. Neural Networks* 4(1):9–20.

HEBB, D. O. [1949]. *The Organization of Behavior: A Neuropsychological Theory.* New York: John Wiley.

HECHT-NIELSEN, R. [1986]. Nearest matched filter classification of spatiotemporal patterns. Technical Report, Hecht-Nielsen Neurocomputer Corporation, San Diego.

Bibliography

HECHT-NIELSEN, R. [1987a]. "Counterpropagation networks." *Appl. Opt.* 26:4979–4984.

HECHT-NIELSEN, R. [1987b]. "Nearest matched filter classification of spatiotemporal patterns." *Appl. Opt.* 26(10):1892–1899.

HECHT-NIELSEN, R. [1988]. "Applications of counterpropagation networks." *Neural Networks* 1:131–139.

HECHT-NIELSEN, R. [1989]. "Theory of the backpropagation neural network." *Proc. Int. Joint Conf. Neural Networks,* vol. I, 593–611, Washington, DC.

HECHT-NIELSEN, R. [1990]. *Neurocomputing.* Reading, MA: Addison-Wesley.

HENDIN, O., D. HORN, AND M. USHER [1991]. "Chaotic behavior of a neural network with dynamical thresholds." *Int. J. Neural Syst.* 1(4):327–335.

HERTZ, J., A. KROGH, AND R. G. PALMER [1991]. *Introduction to the Theory of Neural Computation.* New York: Addison-Wesley.

HESKETH, B., R. PRYOR, M. GLEITZMAN, AND T. HESKETH [1988]. "Practical applications of psychometric evaluation of a computerized fuzzy graphic rating scale." In T. Zeteni, ed., *Fuzzy Sets in Psychology,* 425–454. Amsterdam: North-Holland.

HIGASHI, M., AND G. J. KLIR [1982]. "Measures of uncertainty and information based on possibility distributions." *Int. J. Genet. Syst.* 9:43–58.

HIGGINS, C. M., AND R. M. GOODMAN [1992]. "Learning fuzzy rule–based neural networks for function approximation." *Proc. Int. Joint Conf. Neural Networks,* vol. I, 251–256, Baltimore, MD.

HILDEBRAND, F. B. [1976]. *Advanced Calculus for Applications,* 2nd ed. Englewood Cliffs, NJ: Prentice-Hall.

HINTON, G., ed. [1990]. *Connectionist Symbol Processing.* Amsterdam: Elsevier.

HINTON, G., ed. [1991]. *Connectionist Symbol Processing, Special Issue on Artificial Intelligence.* Cambridge, MA: MIT Press.

HINTON, G. E. [1989]. "Deterministic Boltzmann learning performs steepest descent in weight space." *Neural Comput.* 1:143–150.

HINTON, G. E., J. L. MCCLELLAND, AND D. E. RUMELHART [1986]. "Distributed representation." In D. E. Rumelhart, J. L. McClelland, et al., eds., *Parallel Distributed Processing,* vol. 1, chap. 3. Cambridge, MA: MIT Press.

HINTON, G. E., AND T. J. SEJNOWSKI [1986]. "Learning and relearning in Boltzmann machines." In D. E. Rumelhart, J. L. McClelland, et al., eds., *Parallel Distributed Processing,* vol. 1, chap. 7. Cambridge, MA: MIT Press.

HIRAMATSU, A. [1990]. "ATM communications network control by neural networks." *IEEE Trans. Neural Networks* 1(1):122–130.

HIROTA, K. [1981]. "Concepts of probabilistic sets." *Fuzzy Sets Syst.* 5:31–46.

HIROTA, K. [1992]. Probabilistic sets: Probabilistic extension of fuzzy sets. In R. R. Yager and L. A. Zadeh, eds., *An Introduction to Fuzzy Logic Applications in Intelligent Systems,* 336–354. Boston: Kluwer Academic.

HIROTA, K., Y. ARAJ, AND S. HACHISU [1989]. "Fuzzy controlled robot arm playing two-dimensional ping-pong game." *Fuzzy Sets Syst.* 31:149–159.

HIROTA, K., E. CZOGALA, AND W. PEDRYCZ [1986]. "A new data-input method based on the concept of extended fuzzy expression and subjective entropy of probabilistic sets." In W. Karwowski and A. Mital, eds., *Applications of Fuzzy Set Theory in Human Factors,* 87–100. Amsterdam: Elsevier.

HIROTA, K., AND K. OZAWA [1988]. "Fuzzy flip-flop as a basis of fuzzy memory modules." In M. M. Gupta and T. Yamakawa, eds., *Fuzzy Computing,* 173–183. Amsterdam: Elsevier North-Holland.

HIROTA, K., AND K. OZAWA [1989]. "Fuzzy flip-flop and fuzzy registers." *Fuzzy Sets Syst.* 32:139–148.

HIROTA, K., AND W. PEDRYCZ [1991]. "Fuzzy logic neural networks: Design and computations." *Proc. Int. Joint Conf. Neural Networks,* 152–157, Singapore.

HIROTA, K., AND W. PEDRYCZ [1993]. "Knowledge-based networks in classification problems." *Fuzzy Sets Syst.* 59:271–279.

HIRSH, G., M. LAMOTTE, M. T. MASS, AND M. T. VIGNERON [1981]. "Phonemic classification using a fuzzy dissimilitude relation." *Fuzzy Sets Syst.* 5:267–276.

HO, Y. C., AND R. L. KASHYAP [1965]. "An algorithm for linear inequalities and its applications." *IEEE Trans. Electron. Comput.* 14:683–688.

HOLDEN, A. D. C., AND S. C. SUDDARTH [1993]. Combined neural-net/knowledge-based adaptive systems for large scale dynamic control. In C. H. Chen, ed., *Neural Networks in Pattern Recognition and Their Applications,* 1–20. Singapore: World Scientific.

HOLLAND, J. H. [1962]. "Outline for a logical theory of adaptive systems." *J. Assoc. Comput. Mach.* 3:297–314.

HOLLAND, J. H., ed. [1975]. *Adaptation in Neural and Artificial Systems,* Ann Arbor, MI: University of Michigan Press.

HOLLAND, J. H. [1987]. "Genetic algorithms and classifier systems: Foundations and future directions." *Genet. Algorithms Their Appl.: Proc. 2nd Int. Conf. Genet. Algorithms,* 82–89, Cambridge, MA.

HOLLAND, J. H., AND J. S. REITMAN [1978]. "Cognitive systems based on adaptive algorithms." In D. A. Waterman and F. Hayes-Roth, eds., *Pattern Directed Inference Systems,* 313–329. New York: Academic Press.

HOLLSTIEN, R. B. [1971]. "Artificial genetic adaptation in computer control systems." Doctoral dissertation, University of Michigan, Ann Arbor, MI.

HOLMBLAD, L. P., AND J. J. OSTERGAARD [1982]. "Control of cement kiln by fuzzy logic." In M. M. Gupta and E. Sanchez, eds. *Approximate Reasoning in Decision Analysis,* 389–400. Amsterdam: North-Holland.

HOLMSTRÖM, L., AND P. KOISTINEN [1992]. "Using additive noise in back-propagation training." *IEEE Trans. Neural Networks* 3(1):24–38.

HOPCROFT, J. E., AND J. D. ULLMAN [1979]. *Introduction to Automata Theory, Languages and Computation.* Reading, MA: Addison-Wesley.

HOPFIELD, J. J. [1982]. "Neural networks and physical systems with emergent collective computational abilities." *Proc. Nat. Acad. Sci. USA* 79:2554–2558.

HOPFIELD, J. J. [1983]. "Unlearning has a stabilizing effect in collective memories." *Nature* 304:158.

HOPFIELD, J. J. [1984]. "Neurons with graded responses have collective computational properties like those of two-state neurons." *Proc. Nat. Acad. Sci. USA* 81:3088–3092.

HOPFIELD, J. J., AND D. W. TANK [1985]. "Neural computation of decisions in optimization problems." *Biol. Cybern.* 52:141–154.

HORIKAWA, S., T. FURUHASHI, AND Y. UCHIKAWA [1992]. "On fuzzy modeling using fuzzy neural networks with the back-propagation algorithm." *IEEE Trans. Neural Networks* 3(5):801–806.

HORIKAWA, S., T. FURUHASHI, AND Y. UCHIKAWA [1993]. "On identification of structures in premises of a fuzzy model using a fuzzy neural network." *Proc. IEEE Int. Conf. Fuzzy Syst.,* vol. I, 661–666, San Francisco.

HORIKAWA, S., T. FURUHASHI, Y. UCHIKAWA, AND T. TAGAWA [1991]. "A study on fuzzy modeling using fuzzy neural networks." In T. Terano, M. Sugeno, M. Mukaidono, and K. Shigemasu, eds., *Fuzzy Engineering toward Human Friendly Systems,* 562–573. Tokyo: IOS Press.

HORNIK, K., M. STINCHCOMMBE, AND H. WHITE [1989]. "Multilayer feedforward networks are universal approximators." *Neural Networks* 2:359–366.

HOWARD, R. E., L. D. JACKEL, AND H. P. GRAF [1988]. "Electronic neural networks" *AT&T Tech. J.,* vol. 67, 58–64.

HSIAO, C. H., C. T. LIN, AND M. CASSIDY [1993]. "Application of fuzzy logic and neural networks to incident detection." *J. Transp. Eng. ASCE* 120(5):753.

HSU, L. S., H. H. TEH, P. Z. WANG, S. C. CHAN, AND K. F. LOE [1992]. "Fuzzy neural-logic systems." *Proc. Int. Joint Conf. Neural Networks,* vol. I, 245–250, Baltimore, MD.

HSU, P. [1992]. "Dynamics and control design project offers taste of real world." *IEEE Control Syst. Mag.* 12(3):31–38.

HUANG, S. C., AND Y. F. HUANG [1991]. "Bounds on the number of hidden neurons in multilayer perceptrons." *IEEE Trans. Neural Networks* 2(1):47–55.

HUANG, W. Y., AND R. P. LIPPMANN [1989]. "Neural net and traditional classifiers." In D. S. Touretzky, ed., *Advances in Neural Information Processing Systems I,* 387–396. San Mateo, CA: Morgan Kaufmann.

HUBERMAN, B. A., AND T. HOGG [1987]. "Phase transitions in artificial intelligence systems." *Artif. Intell.* 33:155–172.

HUI, S., AND S. H. ZAK [1992]. "Dynamical analysis of the brain-state-in-a-box(BSB) neural models." *IEEE Trans. Neural Networks* 3(1):86–94.

HUNG, C. C. [1993]. "Building a neuro-fuzzy learning control system." *AI Expert* November:40–50.

HUNTSBERGER, T. L., AND P. AJJIMARANGSEE [1990]. "Parallel self-organizing feature maps for unsupervised pattern recognition." *Int. J. General Syst.* 16(4):357–372.

HUSH, D. R., B. HORNE, AND J. M. SALAS [1992]. "Error surfaces for multilayer perceptrons." *IEEE Trans. Syst. Man Cybern.* 22(5):1152–1161.

HUTCHINSON, J., C. KOCH, J. LUO, AND C. MEAD [1988]. "Computing motion using analog and binary resistive networks." *IEEE Comput.* 23(3):52–63.

HWANG, C. L., AND K. YOON [1981]. *Multiple Attribute Decision Making.* Berlin: Springer-Verlag.

ICHIHASHI, H., AND M. TOKUNAGA [1993]. "Neuro-fuzzy optimal control of backing up a trailer truck." *IEEE Trans. Neural Networks* I:306–311.

ICHIHASHI, H., AND I. B. TÜRKSEN [1993]. "A neuro-fuzzy approach to data analysis of pairwise comparisons." *Int. J. Approximate Reasoning* 9:227–248.

ICHIKAWA, Y., AND Y. ISHII [1993]. "Retaining diversity of genetic algorithms for multivariable optimization and neural network learning." *Proc. IEEE Int. Conf. Neural Networks,* vol. II, 1110–1114, San Francisco.

ICHIKAWA, Y., AND T. SAWA [1992]. "Neural network application for direct feedback controllers." *IEEE Trans. Neural Networks* 3(2):224–231.

IIGUNI, Y., H. SAKAI, AND H. TOKUMARU [1991]. "A nonlinear regulator design in the presence of system uncertainties using multilayered neural networks." *IEEE Trans. Neural Networks* 2(4):410–417.

IKEDA, S., M. OCHIAI, AND Y. SAWAROGI [1976]. "Sequential GMDH algorithm and its application to river flow prediction." *IEEE Trans. Syst. Man Cybern.* 6(7):473–479.

IKONOMOPOULOS, A., L. H. TSOUKALAS, AND R. E. UHRIG [1993]. "Measurement of fuzzy values using artificial neural networks and fuzzy arithmetic." *Proc. IEEE Int. Conf. Fuzzy Syst.,* vol. I, 357–362, San Francisco.

IMASAKI, N., J. KIJI, AND T. ENDO [1992]. "A fuzzy rule structured neural network." *Jap. J. Fuzzy Theory Syst.* 4(5):625–637.

IMASAKI, N., T. YAMAGUCHI, D. MONTGOMERY, AND T. ENDO [1993]. "Fuzzy artificial network and its application to a command spelling corrector." *Proc. IEEE Int. Conf. Fuzzy Syst.,* vol. I, 635–640, San Francisco.

INGMAN, D., AND Y. MERLIS [1992]. "Maximum entropy signal reconstruction with neural networks." *IEEE Trans. Neural Networks* 3(2):195–201.

ISAKA, S. [1992]. "On neural approximation of fuzzy systems." *Proc. Int. Joint Conf. Neural Networks,* vol. I, 263–268, Baltimore, MD.

ISAKA, S., AND A. V. SEBALD [1992]. "An optimization approach for fuzzy controller design." *IEEE Trans. Syst. Man Cybern.* 22(6):1469–1473.

ISHIBUCHI, H., R. FUJIOKA, AND H. TANAKA [1993a]. "Neural networks that learn from fuzzy If-Then rules." *IEEE Trans. Fuzzy Syst.* 1(2):85–97.

ISHIBUCHI, H., K. NOZAKI, AND H. TANAKA [1992]. "Pattern classification by distributed representation of fuzzy rules." *Proc. IEEE Int. Conf. Fuzzy Syst.,* 643–650, San Diego.

ISHIBUCHI, H., K. NOZAKI, AND N. YAMAMOTO [1993b]. "Selecting fuzzy rules by genetic algorithm for classification." *Proc. IEEE Int. Conf. Fuzzy Syst.,* vol. II, 1119–1124, San Francisco.

ISHIBUCHI, H., AND H. TANAKA [1992a]. "Determination of fuzzy regression models by neural networks." In T. Terano, M. Sugeno, M. Mukaidono, and K. Shigemasu, eds., *Fuzzy Engineering toward Human Friendly Systems,* 523–534. Tokyo: IOS Press.

ISHIBUCHI, H., AND H. TANAKA [1992b]. "Fuzzy regression analysis using neural networks." *Fuzzy Sets Syst.* 50:257–265.

ISHIBUCHI, H., H. TANAKA, AND H. OKADA [1993c]. "An architecture of neural networks with interval weights and its application to fuzzy regression analysis." *Fuzzy Sets Syst.* 57:27–39.

ISHIBUCHI, H., H. TANAKA, AND H. OKADA [1993d]. "Fuzzy neural networks with fuzzy weights and fuzzy biases." *Proc. IEEE Int. Conf. Neural Networks,* vol. III, 1650–1655, San Francisco.

ISHIZUKA, M., K. S. FU, AND J. T. P. YAO [1982]. "Inference procedures with uncertainty for problem reduction method." *Inf. Sci.* 28:179–206.

ISIK, C. [1987]. "Identification and fuzzy rule-based control of a mobile robot motion." *Proc. IEEE Int. Symp. Intell. Control,* 94–99, Philadelphia.

ITOH, O., K. GOTOH, T. NAKAYAMA, AND S. TAKAMIZAWA [1987]. "Application of fuzzy control to activated sludge process." *Proc. 2nd IFSA Congr.,* 282–285. Japan: Tokyo.

IVAKHNENKO, A. G. [1968]. "The group method of data handling—A rival of stochastic approximation." *Soviet Autom. Control* 1:43–55. In Russian.

IVAKHNENKO, A. G. [1971]. "Polynomial theory of complex systems." *IEEE Trans. Syst. Man Cybern.* 1(4):364–378.

JACOBS, R. A. [1988]. "Increased rates of convergence through learning rate adaptation." *Neural Networks* 1:295–307.

JAMSHIDI, M., N. VADIEE, AND T. J. ROSS [1993]. *Fuzzy Logic and Control: Software and Hardware Applications,* vol. 2. Englewood Cliffs, NJ: Prentice-Hall.

JANG, J. S. R. [1992]. "Self-learning fuzzy controllers based on temporal back propagation." *IEEE Trans. Neural Networks* 3(5):714–723.

JANG, J. S. R., AND C. T. SUN [1993]. "Functional equivalence between radial basis function networks and fuzzy inference systems." *IEEE Trans. Neural Networks* 4(1):156–159.

JEFFRIES, C. [1991]. *Code Recognition and Set Selection with Neural Networks.* Boston: Birkhäuser.

JODOUIN, J. F. [1993]. "Putting the simple recurrent network to the test." *Proc. IEEE Int. Conf. Neural Networks,* vol. II, 1141–1146, San Francisco.

JOLLIFFE, I. T. [1986]. *Principal Component Analysis.* New York: Springer-Verlag.

JONES, A., A. KAUFMANN, AND H.-J. ZIMMERMANN, eds. [1985]. *Fuzzy Sets Theory and Applications.* Tokyo: Reidel.

JORDAN, M. I. [1986]. "Attractor dynamics and parallelism in a connectionist sequential machine." *Proc. Eighth Annual Conf. Cognitive Sci. Soc.,* 531–546, Amherst, MA.

JORDAN, M. I. [1989]. "Serial order: A parallel, distributed processing approach." In J. L. Elman and D. E. Rumelhart, eds., *Advances in Connectionist Theory: Speech.* Hillsdale, N.J.: Erlbaum.

JOU, C. C. [1992a]. "A fuzzy cerebellar model articulation controller." *Proc. IEEE Int. Conf. Fuzzy Syst.,* 1171–1178, San Diego.

JOU, C. C. [1992b]. "Fuzzy clustering using fuzzy competitive learning networks." *Proc. Int. Joint Conf. Neural Networks,* vol. II, 714–719, Baltimore, MD.

JOU, C. C. [1992c]. "On the mapping capabilities of fuzzy inference systems." *Proc. Int. Joint Conf. Neural Networks,* vol. II, 708–713, Baltimore, MD.

JOU, C. C. [1993]. "Comparing learning performance of neural networks and fuzzy systems." *Proc. IEEE Int. Conf. Neural Networks,* vol. II, 1028–1033, San Francisco.

JOZWIK, A. [1983]. "A learning scheme for a fuzzy k-nn rule." *Pattern Recognition Lett.* 1:287–289.

JUANG, B. H., AND S. KATAGIRI [1992]. "Discriminative learning for minimum error classification." *IEEE Trans. Signal Process.* 40:3043–3054.

JUDD, J. S. [1990]. *Neural Network Design and the Complexity of Learning.* Cambridge, MA: MIT Press.

KACPRZYK, J. [1983]. *Multistage Decision-Making under Fuzziness.* Köln: Verlag TÜV Rheinland.

KACPRZYK, J., AND S. A. ORLOVSKI [1987]. *Optimization Models Using Fuzzy Sets and Possibility Theory.* Boston: Dordrecht.

KAHNG, A. [1989]. "Traveling salesman heuristics and embedding dimension in the Hopfield model," *Proc. Int. Joint Conf. Neural Networks,* vol. I, 513–520, Washington, DC.

KAJITANI, Y., K. KUWATA, R. KATAYAMA, AND Y. NISHIDA [1991]. "An automatic fuzzy modeling with constraints of membership functions and a model determination for neuro and fuzzy model by plural performance indices." In T. Terano, M. Sugeno, M. Mukaidono, and K. Shigemasu, eds., *Fuzzy Engineering toward Human Friendly Systems,* 586–597. Tokyo: IOS Press.

KALMAN, R. E. [1960]. "A new approach to linear filtering and prediction problems." *J. Basic Eng.* 82:35–45.

KANDEL, A. [1982]. *Fuzzy Techniques in Pattern Recognition.* New York: John Wiley.

KANDEL, A. [1986]. *Fuzzy Mathematical Techniques with Applications.* Reading, MA: Addison-Wesley.

KANDEL, A., ed. [1992]. *Fuzzy Expert Systems.* Boca Raton, FL: CRC Press.

KANDEL, A., AND G. LANGHOLZ [1992]. *Hybrid Architectures for Intelligent Systems.* Boca Raton, FL: CRC Press.

KANDEL, A., AND S. C. LEE [1979]. *Fuzzy Switching and Automata: Theory and Applications.* New York: Crane, Russak.

KANDEL, A., M. SCHNEIDER, AND G. LANGHOLZ [1992]. "The use of fuzzy logic for the management of uncertainty in intelligent hybrid systems." In L. A. Zadeh and J. Kacprzyk, eds., *Fuzzy Logic for the Management of Uncertainty,* 569–587. New York: John Wiley.

KANG, H. [1993]. "Stability and control of fuzzy dynamic systems via cell-state transitions in fuzzy hypercubes." *IEEE Trans. Fuzzy Syst.* 1:267–279.

KANGAS, J. A., T. K. KOHONEN, AND J. T. LAAKSONEN [1990]. "Variants of self-organizing maps." *IEEE Trans. Neural Networks* 1(1):93–99.

KANIA, A. A., J. F. KISZKA, M. B. GORZALCZANY, J. R. MAJ, AND M. S. STACHOWICZ [1980]. "On stability of formal fuzziness systems." *Inf. Sci.* 22:51–68.

KARNIN, E. D. [1990]. "A simple procedure for pruning back-propagation trained neural networks." *IEEE Trans. Neural Networks* 1(2):239–241.

KARR, C. L., AND E. J. GENTRY [1993]. "Fuzzy control of pH using genetic algorithms." *IEEE Trans. Fuzzy Syst.* 1(1):46–53.

KARWOWSKI, W., E. KOSIBA, S. BENABDALLAH, AND G. SALVENDY [1989]. Fuzzy data and communication in human-computer interaction: For bad or for good. In G. Salvendy and M. J. Smith, eds., *Designing and Using Human-Computer Interfaces and Knowledge Based Systems,* 402–409. Amsterdam: Elsevier.

KARWOWSKI, W., E. KOSIBA, S. BENABDALLAH, AND G. SALVENDY [1990]. "A framework for development of fuzzy GOMS model for human-computer interaction." *Int. J. Human-Comput. Interaction* 2:287–305.

KARWOWSKI, W., AND A. MITAL, eds. [1986]. *Applications of Fuzzy Set Theory in Human Factors.* Amsterdam: Elsevier.

KARWOWSKI, W., AND G. SALVENDY [1992]. Fuzzy-set-theoretical applications in modeling of man-machine interactions. In R. R. Yager and L. A. Zadeh, eds., *An Introduction to Fuzzy Logic Applications in Intelligent Systems,* 201–220. Boston: Kluwer Academic.

KASAI, Y., AND Y. MORIMOTO [1988]. "Electronically controlled continuously variable transmission." *Proc. Int. Congr. Transport. Electron.,* 33–42, Dearborn, MI.

KASHYAP, R. L. [1980]. "Inconsistency of AIC Rule." *IEEE Trans. Autom. Control* 25(5):997–998.

KATAYAMA, R., Y. KAJITANI, K. KUWATA, AND Y. NISHIDA [1993]. "Self generating radial basis function as neuro-fuzzy model and its application of nonlinear prediction of chaotic time series." *Proc. IEEE Int. Conf. Fuzzy Syst.,* vol. I, 407–414, San Francisco.

KAUFMANN, A. [1975]. *Introduction to the Theory of Fuzzy Subsets.* New York: Academic Press.

KAUFMANN, A., AND M. M. GUPTA [1991]. *Introduction to Fuzzy Arithmetic: Theory and Applications.* New York: Van Nostrand Reinhold.

KAWAMOTO, S., K. TADA, A. ISHIGAME, AND T. TANIGUCHI [1992]. "An approach to stability analysis of second order fuzzy systems." *Proc. IEEE Int. Conf. Fuzzy Syst.,* 1427–1434, San Diego.

KAWAMURA, A., N. WATANABE, H. OKADA, AND K. ASAKAWA [1992]. "A prototype of neuro-fuzzy cooperation system." *Proc. IEEE Int. Conf. Fuzzy Syst.,* 1275–1282, San Diego.

KELLER, J. M., M. R. GRAY, AND J. A. GIVENS [1985]. "A fuzzy k-nearest neighbor algorithm." *IEEE Trans. Syst. Man Cybern.* 15(4):580–585.

KELLER, J. M., Y. HAYASHI, AND Z. CHEN [1993]. "Interpretation of nodes in networks for fuzzy logic." *Proc. IEEE Int. Conf. Fuzzy Syst.,* vol. II, 1203–1207, San Francisco.

KELLER, J. M., AND D. J. HUNT [1985]. "Incorporating fuzzy membership functions into the perceptron algorithm." *IEEE Trans. Pattern Anal. Mach. Intell.* PAMI–7(6):693–699.

KELLER, J. M., AND R. KRISHNAPURAM [1992]. "Fuzzy set methods in computer vision." In R. R. Yager and L. A. Zadeh, eds., *An Introduction to Fuzzy Logic Applications in Intelligent Systems,* 121–145. Boston: Kluwer Academic.

KELLER, J. M., R. KRISHNAPURAM, AND F. C. H. RHEE [1992a]. "Evidence aggregation networks for fuzzy logic interface." *IEEE Trans. Neural Networks* 3(5):761–769.

KELLER, J. M., AND H. TAHANI [1992a]. "Backpropagation neural networks for fuzzy logic." *Inf. Soc.* 62:205–221.

KELLER, J. M., AND H. TAHANI [1992b]. "Implementation of conjunctive and disjunctive fuzzy logic rules with neural networks." *Int. J. Approximate Reasoning* 6:221–240.

KELLER, J. M., R. R. YAGER, AND H. TAHANI [1992b]. "Neural network implementation of fuzzy logic." *Fuzzy Sets Syst.* 45:1–12.

KENNEDY, M. P., AND L. O. CHUA [1987]. "Unifying the Tank and Hopfield linear programming network and the canonical nonlinear programming network of Chua and Lin." *IEEE Trans. Circuits Syst.* CAS-34(2):210–214.

KENNEDY, M. P., AND L. O. CHUA [1988]. "Neural networks for nonlinear programming." *IEEE Trans. Circuits Syst.* CAS-35(5):554–562.

KHALID, M., AND S. OMATU [1992]. "A neural network controller for a temperature control system," *IEEE Control Syst. Mag.* 12:58–64.

KHAN, E., AND P. VENKATAPURAM [1993]. "Neufuz: Neural network based fuzzy logic design algorithms." *Proc. IEEE Int. Conf. Fuzzy Syst.,* vol. I, 647–654, San Francisco.

KHANNA, T. [1990]. *Foundations of Neural Networks.* Reading, MA: Addison-Wesley.

KICKERT, W. J. M. [1978]. *Fuzzy Theories on Decision Making.* Leiden: Nijhoff.

KICKERT, W. J. M., AND E. H. MAMDANI [1978]. "Analysis of a fuzzy logic controller." *Fuzzy Sets Syst.* 1(1):29–44.

KICKERT, W. J. M., AND H. R. VAN NAUTA LEMKE [1976]. "Application of a fuzzy logic controller in a warm water plant." *Automatica* 12(4):301–308.

KIM, Y. S., AND S. MITRA [1993]. "Integrated adaptive fuzzy clustering (IAFC) algorithm." *Proc. IEEE Int. Conf. Fuzzy Syst.,* 1264–1268, San Francisco.

KING, P. J., AND E. H. MAMDANI [1975]. "The application of fuzzy control systems to industrial processes." *Proc. IFAC World Congr.,* Boston.

KING, R. E., AND F. C. KARONIS [1988]. "Multi-level expert control of a large-scale industrial process." In M. M. Gupta and T. Yamakawa, eds., *Fuzzy Computing Theory, Hardware, and Applications,* 323–340. Amsterdam: North-Holland.

KINNEAR, K. E., JR. [1993]. "Evolving a sort: Lessons in genetic programming." *Proc. IEEE Int. Conf. Neural Networks,* vol. II, 881–888, San Francisco.

KINOSHITA, M., T. FUKUZAKI, T. SATOH, AND M. MIYAKE [1988]. "An automatic operation method for control rods in BWR plants." *Proc. Spec. Meet. In-Core Instrum. React. Core Assess.,* Cadarache, France.

KIRKPATRICK, S., C. D. GELATT, JR., AND M. P. VECCHI [1983]. "Optimization by simulated annealing." *Science* 220:671–680.

KIRKPATRICK, S., AND D. SHERRINGTON [1978]. "Infinite-ranged models of spin-glasses." *Phys. Rev.* 17:4384–4403.

KISZKA, J. B., M. M. GUPTA, AND P. N. NIKIFORUK [1985]. "Energetistic stability of fuzzy dynamic systems." *IEEE Trans. Syst. Man Cybern.* 15(6):783–792.

KLEINFELD, D. [1986]. "Sequential state generation by model neural networks." *Proc. Nat. Acad. Sci. USA* 83:9469–9473.

KLIR, G. J., AND T. A. FOLGER [1988]. *Fuzzy Sets, Uncertainty, and Information.* Englewood Cliffs, NJ: Prentice-Hall.

KLOPF, A. H. [1986]. "A drive-reinforcement model of single neuron function: An alternative to the Hebbian neuronal model." *Proc. Am. Inst. Phys.: Neural Networks Comput.,* 265–270, Snowbird, UT.

KLOPF, A. H. [1988]. "A neuronal model of classical conditioning." *Psychobiology* 16(2):85–125.

KNOPFMACHER, J. [1975]. "On measures of fuzziness." *J. Math. Anal. Appl.* 49:529–534.

KOCH, C., J. MARROQUIN, AND A. YUILLE [1986]. "Analog 'Neuronal Networks' in early vision." *Proc. Nat. Acad. Sci. USA* 83:4263–4267.

KOHONEN, T. K. [1977]. *Associative Memory: A System-Theoretical Approach.* Berlin: Springer-Verlag.

KOHONEN, T. K. [1988]. "The 'neural' phonetic typewriter." *IEEE Comput.* 27(3):11–22.

KOHONEN, T. K. [1989]. *Self-Organization and Associative Memory,* 3rd ed. New York: Springer-Verlag.

KOLMOGOROV, A. N. [1957]. "On the representation of continuous functions of many variables by superposition of continuous functions of one variable and addition." *Dokl. Akad. Nauk USSR* 114:953–956. In Russian.

KOMORI, Y. [1992]. "A neural fuzzy training approach for continue speech recognition improvement." *ICASSP,* vol. I, 405–408, San Francisco.

KONG, S. G., AND B. KOSKO [1991]. "Differential competitive learning for centroid estimation and phoneme recognition." *IEEE Trans. Neural Networks* 2(1):118–124.

KONG, S. G., AND B. KOSKO [1992]. "Adaptive fuzzy systems for backing up a truck-and-trailer." *IEEE Trans. Neural Networks* 3(2):211–223.

KOSKO, B. [1986]. "Fuzzy cognitive maps." *Int. J. Man-Mach. Stud.* 24:65–75.

KOSKO, B. [1987]. "Adaptive bidirectional associative memories." *Appl. Opt.* 26(23):4947–4959.

KOSKO, B. [1988]. "Bidirectional associative memories." *IEEE Trans. Syst. Man Cybern.* 18(1): 49–60.

KOSKO, B. [1990]. "Unsupervised learning in noise." *IEEE Trans. Neural Networks* 1(1):44–57.

KOSKO, B. [1991]. "Stochastic competitive learning." *IEEE Trans. Neural Networks* 2(5):522–529.

KOSKO, B. [1992a]. *Neural Networks and Fuzzy Systems: A Dynamical Systems Approach to Machine Intelligence.* Englewood Cliffs, NJ: Prentice-Hall.

KOSKO, B., ed. [1992b]. *Neural Networks for Signal Processing.* Englewood Cliffs, NJ: Prentice-Hall.

KOSKO, B. [1992c]. "Fuzzy systems as universal approximators." *Proc. IEEE Int. Conf. Fuzzy Syst.,* 1153–1162, San Diego.

KOZA, J. R. [1992a]. *Genetic Programming: On the Programming of Computers by Means of Natural Selection.* Cambridge, MA: MIT Press.

KOZA, J. R. [1992b]. "The genetic programming paradigm: Genetically breeding populations of computer programs to solve problems." In Branko Soucek and the IRIS Group, eds., *Dynamic, Genetic, and Chaotic Programming.* New York: John Wiley.

KOZA, J. R. [1992c]. "Hierarchical automatic function definition in genetic programming." In Darrell Whitley, ed., *Proc. Workshop Found. Genet. Algorithms Classifier Syst.,* Vail, CO.

KOZA, J. R., M. A. KEANE, AND J. P. RICE [1993]. "Performance improvement of machine learning via automatic discovery of facilitating functions as applied to a problem of symbolic system identification." *Proc. IEEE Int. Conf. Neural Networks,* vol. I, 191–198, San Francisco.

KOZA, J. R., AND J. P. RICE [1992]. *Genetic Programming: The Movie.* Cambridge, MA: MIT Press.

KRAFT, D., AND D. BUELL [1983]. "Fuzzy sets and generalized Boolean retrieval systems." *Int. J. Man-Mach. Stud.* 19:45–56.

KRAFT, L. G., III, AND D. P. CAMPAGNA [1990a]. "A comparison between CMAC neural network control and two traditional adaptive control systems." *IEEE Control Syst. Mag.* 10(3):36–43.

KRAFT, L. G., III, AND D. P. CAMPAGNA [1990b]. "A summary comparison of CMAC neural network control and traditional adaptive control systems." In T. W. Miller, III, R. S. Sutton, and P. J. Werbos, eds., *Neural Networks for Control,* 143–169. Cambridge, MA: MIT Press.

KRAMER, U., AND R. ROHR [1982]. In G. Johannsen and J. E. Rijnsdorp, eds., *Analysis, Design and Evaluations of Man-Machine Systems,* 31–35. Oxford: Pergamon Press.

KRISHNAKUMAR, K., AND D. E. GOLDBERG [1992]. "Control system optimization using genetic algorithms." *J. Guidance, Control, Dyn.* 15:735–740.

KRISHNAPURAM, R., AND L. F. CHEN [1993]. "Implementation of parallel thinning algorithms using recurrent neural networks." *IEEE Trans. Neural Networks* 4(1):142–147.

KRISHNAPURAM, R., AND J. M. KELLER [1992]. "Fuzzy set theoretic approach to computer vision: An overview." *Proc. IEEE Int. Conf. Fuzzy Syst.,* 135–142, San Diego.

KRISHNAPURAM, R., AND J. LEE [1992]. "Fuzzy-set-based hierarchical networks for information fusion in computer vision." *Neural Networks* 5:335–350.

KRISTINSSON, K., AND G. A. DUMONT [1992]. "System identification and control using genetic algorithms." *IEEE Trans. Syst. Man Cybern.* 22(5):1033–1046.

KRUSE, R., AND K. D. MEYER [1987]. *Statistics with Vague Data.* Dordrecht: Reidel.

KUNDU, M. K., AND S. K. PAL [1990]. "Automatic selection of object enhancement operator with quantitative justification based on fuzzy set theoretic measure." *Pattern Recognition Lett.* 11:811–829.

KUNG, S. Y. [1993]. *Digital Neural Networks.* Englewood Cliffs, NJ: Prentice-Hall.

KUNG, S. Y., AND J. N. HWANG [1988]. "An algebraic projection analysis for optimal hidden units size and learning rates in back-propagation learning." *Proc. IEEE Int. Conf. Neural Networks,* vol. I, 363–370, San Diego.

KUO, B. C. [1980]. *Digital Control Systems.* New York: Holt, Rinehart and Winston.

KUO, Y. H., C. I. KAO, AND J. J. CHEN [1993]. "A fuzzy neural network model and its hardware implementation." *IEEE Trans. Fuzzy Syst.* 1(3):171–183.

KUPERSTEIN, M., AND J. WANG [1990]. "Neural controller for adaptive movements with unforeseen payloads." *IEEE Trans. Neural Networks* 1(1):137–142.

KWAN, H. K., Y. CAI, AND B. ZHANG [1993]. "Membership function learning in fuzzy classification." *Int. J. Electron.* 74(6):845–850.

LACHER, R. C., S. I. HRUSKA, AND D. C. KUNCICKY [1992]. "Back-propagation learning in expert networks." *IEEE Trans. Neural Networks* 3(1):62–72.

LAKOFF, G. [1973]. "Hedges: A study in meaning criteria and the logic of fuzzy concept." *J. Phil. Logic* 2:458–508.

LANE, S. H., D. A. HANDELMAN, AND J. J. GELFAND [1992]. "Theory and development of higher-order CMAC neural networks." *IEEE Control Syst. Mag.* 12(2):23–30.

LANGARI, R., AND M. TOMIZUKA [1990a]. "Self-organizing fuzzy linguistic control systems with application to arc welding." *Proc. IEEE Workshop Intell. Robots Syst. (IROS),* 1007–1014, Tsuchiura, Japan.

LANGARI, R., AND M. TOMIZUKA [1990b]. Stability of fuzzy linguistic control systems. *Proc. IEEE Conf. Decis. Control,* 2185–2190, Hawaii.

LANGARI, R., AND M. TOMIZUKA [1991]. Analysis of stability of a class of fuzzy linguistic controllers with internal dynamics. *Proc. ASME Winter Ann. Meet.*

LARKIN, L. I. [1985]. "A fuzzy logic controller for aircraft flight control." In M. Sugeno, ed., *Industrial Applications of Fuzzy Control,* 87–104. Amsterdam: North-Holland.

LARSEN, P. M. [1980]. "Industrial applications of fuzzy logic control." *Int. J. Man-Mach. Stud.* 12(1): 3–10.

LAWLER, E. L. [1976]. *Combinatorial Optimization: Networks and Matroids.* New York: Holt, Rinehart and Winston.

LAWLER, E. L., J. K. LENSTRA, KAN RINNOOY, AND P. B. SHMOYS [1985]. *The Traveling Salesman Problem.* New York: John Wiley.

LEA, R. N., AND Y. JANI [1992]. "Fuzzy logic in autonomous orbital operations." *Int. J. Approximate Reasoning* 6(2):151–184.

LEAHY, M. B., JR., M. A. JOHNSON, AND S. K. ROGERS [1991]. "Neural network payload estimation for adaptive robot control." *IEEE Trans. Neural Networks* 2(1):93–100.

LECUN, Y. [1985]. "A learning procedure for asymmetric network." *Cognitiva* 85:599–604, Paris.

LECUN, Y., B. BOSER, J. S. DENKER, D. HENDERSON, R. E. HOWARD, W. HUBBARD, AND L. D. JACKEL [1989a]. "Backpropagation applied to handwritten zip code recognition." *Neural Comput.* 1:541–551.

LECUN, Y., J. S. DENKER, AND S. A. SOLLA [1989b]. "Optimal brain damage." In D. S. Touretzky, ed., *Neural Information Processing Systems II,* 598–605. San Mateo, CA: Morgan Kaufmann.

LEE, B. W., AND B. J. SHEU [1991]. "Modified Hopfield neural networks for retrieving the optimal solution." *IEEE Trans. Neural Networks* 2(1):137–142.

LEE, C. C. [1990]. "Fuzzy logic in control systems: Fuzzy logic controller, Parts I and II." *IEEE Trans. Syst. Man Cybern.* 20(2):404–435.

LEE, C. C. [1991a]. "A self-learning rule-based controller employing approximate reasoning and neural net concepts." *Int. J. Intell. Syst.* 6:71–93.

LEE, H. M., AND C. S. LAI [1993]. "Supervised fuzzy ART: Training of a neural network for pattern classification via combining supervised and unsupervised learning." *Proc. IEEE Int. Conf. Neural Networks,* vol. I, 323–328, San Francisco.

LEE, M. A., AND H. TAKAGI [1993]. "Integrating design stages of fuzzy systems using genetic algorithms." *Proc. IEEE Int. Conf. Fuzzy Syst.,* vol. I, 612–617, San Francisco.

LEE, S., AND R. M. KIL [1988]. "Multilayer feedforward potential function network." *Proc. Int. Joint Conf. Neural Networks,* vol. 1, 161–171, San Diego.

LEE, S. C., AND E. T. LEE [1975]. "Fuzzy neural networks." *Math. Biosci.* 23:151–177.

LEE, T. C. [1991b]. *Structure Level Adaptation for Artificial Neural Networks.* Boston: Kluwer Academic.

LEMBESSIS, E. [1984]. "Dynamical learning behavior of a rule-based self-organizing controller." Doctoral dissertation, Queen Mary College, University of London.

LEMMON, M., AND B. V. K. VIJAYA KUMAR [1992]. "Competitive learning with generalized winner-take-all activation." *IEEE Trans. Neural Networks* 3(2):167–175.

LEONARD, J. A., M. A. KRAMER, AND L. H. UNGAR [1992]. "Using radial basis functions to approximate a function and its error bounds." *IEEE Trans. Neural Networks* 3(4):624–627.

LEUNG, K. S., AND W. LAM [1988]. "Fuzzy concepts in expert systems." *Computer* 21(9):43–56.

LI, L., AND S. HAYKIN [1993]. "A cascaded recurrent neural networks for real-time nonlinear adaptive filtering." *Proc. IEEE Int. Conf. Neural Networks,* vol. II, 857–862, San Francisco.

LI, Y. F., AND C. C. LAN [1989]. "Development of fuzzy algorithms for servo systems." *IEEE Control Syst. Mag.* April:65–72.

LIN, C. J., AND C. T. LIN [1994]. "An ART-based fuzzy adaptive learning control network." *Proc. IEEE Int. Conf. Fuzzy Syst.,* vol. I, 1–6, Orlando, FL.

LIN, C. J., AND C. T. LIN [1996]. "Reinforcement learning for ART-based fuzzy adaptive learning control networks." *IEEE Trans. Neural Networks.*

LIN, C. J., AND C. T. LIN [1995]. "Adaptive fuzzy control of unstable nonlinear systems." *Int. J. Neural Syst.* 6(3):283–298.

LIN, C. S., AND H. KIM [1991]. "CMAC-based adaptive critic self-learning control." *IEEE Trans. Neural Networks* 2(5):530–533.

LIN, C. T. [1994]. *Neural Fuzzy Control Systems with Structure and Parameter Learning.* Singapore: World Scientific.

LIN, C. T. [1995]. "A neural fuzzy control system with structure and parameter learning." *Fuzzy Sets Syst.* 70:183–212.

LIN, C. T., AND C. S. G. LEE [1991a]. "A multi-valued Boltzmann machine." *Proc. Int. Joint Conf. Neural Networks,* 2546–2552, Singapore.

LIN, C. T., AND C. S. G. LEE [1991b]. "Neural-network-based fuzzy logic control and decision system." *IEEE Trans. Comput.* 40(12):1320–1336.

LIN, C. T., AND C. S. G. LEE [1992]. "Real-time supervised structure/parameter learning for fuzzy neural network." *Proc. IEEE Int. Conf. Fuzzy Syst.,* 1283–1291, San Diego.

LIN, C. T., AND C. S. G. LEE [1994]. "Reinforcement structure/parameter learning for neural-network-based fuzzy logic control systems." *IEEE Trans. Fuzzy Syst.* 2(1):46–63.

LIN, C. T., AND C. S. G. LEE [1995]. "A multi-valued Boltzmann machine." *IEEE Trans. Syst. Man Cybern.* 25(4):660–669.

LIN, C. T., C. J. LIN AND C. S. G. LEE [1995]. "Fuzzy adaptive learning control network with on-line neural learning." *Fuzzy Sets Syst.* 71:25–45.

LIN, C. T., AND Y. C. LU [1995]. "A neural fuzzy system with linguistic teaching signals." *IEEE Trans. Fuzzy Syst.* 3(2):169–189.

LIN, C. T., AND Y. C. LU [1995]. "A neural fuzzy system with fuzzy supervised learning." *IEEE Trans. Syst. Man Cybern.* 26(10).

LIN, L. J. [1992]. "Self-improving reactive agents based on reinforcement learning, planning and teaching." *Mach. Learn.* 8:293–322.

LIN, L. J. [1993]. "Hierarchical learning of robot skills by reinforcement." *Proc. IEEE Int. Conf. Neural Networks,* vol. I, 181–186, San Francisco.

LIN, W. C., F. Y. LIAO, C. K. TSAO, AND T. LINGUTLA [1991]. "A hierarchical multiple-view approach to three-dimensional object recognition." *IEEE Trans. Neural Networks* 2(1):84–92.

LINKENS, D. A., AND J. NIE [1993]. "Fuzzified RBF network-based learning control: Structure and self-construction." *Proc. IEEE Int. Conf. Neural Networks,* vol. II, 1016–1021, San Francisco.

LINSKER, R. [1988]. "Self-organization in a perceptual network." *IEEE Comput.* March:105–117.

LIPPMANN, R. P. [1987]. "An introduction to computing with neural nets," *IEEE Mag. Acoust. Signal Speech Process.* April:4–22.

LIPPMANN, R. P. [1989a]. "Review of neural networks for speech recognition." *Neural Comput.* 1:1–38.

LIPPMANN, R. P., [1989b]. "Pattern classification using neural networks." *IEEE Commun. Mag.* November:47–50, 59–64.

LIU, L. S. [1993]. "On the application of genetic algorithms for optimal control problems." Master's thesis, Department of Mechanical Engineering, Dr. Sun-Yat-Sen University, Taiwan, R.O.C.

LOGAR, A. M., E. M. CORWIN, AND W. J. B. OLDHAM [1993]. "A comparison of recurrent neural network learning algorithms." *Proc. IEEE Int. Conf. Neural Networks,* vol. II, 1129–1134, San Francisco.

LÓPEZ DE MÁNTARAS, R., J. AGUSTI, E. PLAZA, AND C. SIERRA [1992a]. "MILORD: A fuzzy expert system shell." In A. Kandel, ed., *Fuzzy Expert Systems,* 213–223. Boca Raton, FL: CRC Press.

LÓPEZ DE MÁNTARAS, R., AND J. A. MARTIN [1983]. "Classification and linguistic characterization of nondeterministic data." *Pattern Recognition Lett.* 2:33–41.

LÓPEZ DE MÁNTARAS, R., C. SIERRA, AND J. AGUSTI [1992b]. "The representation and use of uncertainty and metaknowledge in MILORD." In R. R. Yager and L. A. Zadeh, eds., *An Introduction to Fuzzy Logic Applications in Intelligent Systems,* 253–262. Boston: Kluwer Academic.

LOWEN, R. [1990]. "A fuzzy language interpolation theorem." *Fuzzy Sets Syst.* 34:33–38.

LUENBERGER, D. G. [1976]. *Linear and Nonlinear Programming.* Reading, MA: Addison-Wesley.

LUHANDJULA, M. K. [1986]. "On possibilistic linear programming." *Fuzzy Sets Syst.* 18:15–30.

LUHANDJULA, M. K. [1987]. "Multiple objective programming problems with possibilistic coefficients." *Fuzzy Sets Syst.* 21:135–145.

MAA, C. Y., AND M. A. SHANBLATT [1992a]. "Linear and quadratic programming neural network analysis." *IEEE Trans. Neural Networks* 3(4):580–594.

MAA, C. Y., AND M. A. SHANBLATT [1992b]. "A two-phase optimization neural network." *IEEE Trans. Neural Networks* 3(6):1003–1009.

MACHADO, R. J., AND A. F. DA ROCHA [1992a]. "A hybrid architecture for fuzzy connectionist expert system." In A. Kandel and G. Langholz, eds., *Hybrid Architecture for Intelligent Systems,* 135–152. Ann Arbor, MI: CRC Press.

MACHADO, R. J., AND A. F. DA ROCHA [1992b]. "Evolutive fuzzy neural networks." *Proc. IEEE Int. Conf. Fuzzy Syst.,* 493–500, San Diego.

MACHADO, R. J., AND A. F. DA ROCHA [1993]. "Inference, inquiry and explanation in expert systems by means of fuzzy neural networks." *Proc. IEEE Int. Conf. Fuzzy Syst.*, vol. I, 351–356, San Francisco.

MACKAY, H. B., AND D. J. BOZICH [1993]. "Spectral feature identification using time delay neural networks." In C. H. Dagil, S. R. T. Kumara, and Y. C. Shin, eds., *Intelligent Engineering Systems through Artificial Neural Networks*, 777–782. New York: ASME Press.

MACKEY, M. C., AND L. GLASS [1977]. "Oscillation and chaos in physiological control systems." *Science* 197:287.

MACLIN, P. S., AND J. DEMPSEY [1993]. "A neural network to diagnose liver cancer." *Proc. IEEE Int. Conf. Neural Networks*, vol. III, 1492–1497, San Francisco.

MAJANI, E., R. ERLANSON, AND Y. ABU-MOSTAFA [1989]. "On the K-winners-take-all networks." In D. S. Touretzky, ed., *Advances in Neural Information Processing Systems I*, 634–642. San Mateo, CA: Morgan Kaufmann.

MAKRAM-EBEID, S., J. A. SIRAT, AND J. R. VIALA [1989]. A rationalized back-propagation learning algorithm. *Proc. Int. Joint Conf. Neural Networks*, vol. II, 373–380, Washington, DC.

MALLOWS, C. L. [1973]. "Some comments on C_p." *Technometrics* 15:661–675.

MAMDANI, E. H. [1976]. "Advances in the linguistic synthesis of fuzzy controllers." *Int. J. Man-Machine Stud.* 8(6):669–678.

MAMDANI, E. H. [1977]. "Application of fuzzy logic to approximate reasoning using linguistic systems." *IEEE Trans. Comput.* C-26:1182–1191.

MAMDANI, E. H., AND S. ASSILIAN [1975]. "An experiment in linguistic synthesis with a fuzzy logic controller." *Int. J. Man-Mach. Stud.* 7(1):1–13.

MAMDANI, E. H., AND B. R. GAINES, eds., [1981]. *Fuzzy Reasoning and Its Applications*. London: Academic Press.

MAMMONE, R. J., AND Y. Y. ZEEVI, eds. [1991]. *Neural Networks: Theory and Applications*. Boston: Academic Press.

MANJUNATH, B. S., T. SIMCHONY, AND R. CHELAPPA [1990]. "Stochastic and deterministic networks for texture segmentation." *IEEE Trans. Acoust. Speech Signal Process.* 38(6):1039–1049.

MARCHAND, M., M. GOLEA, AND P. RUJÁN [1990]. "A convergence theorem for sequential learning in two-layer perceptrons." *Europhys. Lett.* 11:487–492.

MARKS, R. J., II, ed. [1994]. *Fuzzy Logic Technology and Applications*. New York: IEEE Press.

MARSDEN, J., AND M. MCCRACKEN [1976]. *The Hopf Bifurcation and Its Applications*. New York: Springer-Verlag.

MARTIN-CLOUAIRE, R., AND H. PRADE [1985]. "On the problems of representation and propagation of uncertainty in expert systems." *Int. J. Man-Mach. Stud.* 22:251–264.

MARTINELLI, G., F. M. MASCIOLI, AND G. BEI [1993]. "Cascade neural network for binary mapping." *IEEE Trans. Neural Networks* 4(1):148–150.

MARTINELLI, G., L. PRINA-RICOTTI, S. RAGAZZINI, AND F. M. MASCIOLI [1990]. "A pyramidal delayed perceptron." *IEEE Trans. Circuits Syst.* 37:1176–1181.

MARTINETZ, T. M., H. J. RITTER, AND K. J. SCHULTEN [1990]. "Three-dimensional neural net for learning visuomotor coordination of a robot arm." *IEEE Trans. Neural Networks* 1(1):131–136.

MATSUOKA, K. [1992]. "Noise injection into inputs in backpropagation learning." *IEEE Trans. Syst. Man Cybern.* 22(3):436–440.

MATTHEWS, M. B. [1990]. "Neural network nonlinear adaptive filtering using the extended Kalman filter algorithm." *Proc. Int. Neural Networks Conf.*, vol. I, 115–119, Paris.

MCCLELLAND, J. L. AND D. E. RUMELHART [1986]. *Parallel Distributed Processing*. Cambridge, MA: MIT Press.

McClelland, J. L., and D. E. Rumelhart [1988]. *Explorations in Parallel Distributed Procession: A Handbook of Models, Programs, and Exercises.* Cambridge, MA: MIT Press.

McCulloch, W. S., and W. Pitts [1943]. "A logical calculus of ideas immanent in nervous activity." *Bull. Math. Biophys.* 5:115–133.

McDonnell, J. R., and D. Waagen [1993]. "Evolving neural network connectivity." *Proc. IEEE Int. Conf. Neural Networks,* vol. II, 863–868, San Francisco.

McEliece, R. J., C. E. Posner, R. R. Rodemich, and S. S. Venkatesh [1987]. "The capacity of the Hopfield associative memory." *IEEE Trans. Inf. Theory* 33(4):461–482.

McInerney, M., and A. P. Dhawan [1993]. "Use of genetic algorithms with backpropagation in training of feedforward neural networks." *Proc. IEEE Int. Conf. Neural Networks,* vol. I, 203–208, San Francisco.

McNeill, D., and P. Freiberger [1993]. *Fuzzy Logic.* New York: Simon & Schuster.

Mead, C. [1989]. *Analog VLSI and Neural Systems.* Reading, MA: Addison-Wesley.

Mehrotra, K. G., C. K. Mohan, and S. Ranka [1991]. "Bounds on the number of samples needed for neural learning." *IEEE Trans. Neural Networks* 2(6):548–558.

Meng, M. [1993]. "A neural production system and its application in vision-guided mobile robot navigation." *Proc. IEEE Int. Conf. Neural Networks,* vol. II, 807–812, San Francisco.

Meng, M., and A. C. Kak [1992]. "Fast vision-guided mobile robot navigation using neural networks." *Proc. IEEE Int. Conf. Syst. Man Cybern.,* vol. 1, 111–116, Chicago.

Mézard, M. and J. P. Nadal [1989]. "Learning in feedforward layered networks: The tiling algorithm." *J. Phys.* 22:2191–2204.

Michalewicz, Z. [1992]. *Genetic Algorithms + Data Structures = Evolution Programs.* New York: Springer-Verlag.

Michalewicz, Z., and C. Z. Janikow [1991]. "Genetic algorithms for numerical optimization." *Stat. Comput.* 1:75–91.

Michalewicz, Z., and J. B. Krawezyk [1992]. "A modified genetic algorithm for optimal control problems." *Comput. Math. Appl.* 23:83–94.

Michel, A. N., J. Si, and G. Yen [1991]. "Analysis and synthesis of a class of discrete-time neural networks described on hypercubes." *IEEE Trans. Neural Networks* 2(1):32–46.

Miller, G. F., P. M. Todd, and S. U. Hegde [1989]. "Designing neural networks using genetic algorithms." In J. D. Schaffer, ed., *Proc. Third Int. Conf. Genet. Algorithms,* 379–384. San Mateo, CA: Morgan Kaufmann.

Miller, W. T., III, R. S. Sutton, and P. J. Werbos, eds., [1990]. *Neural Networks for Control.* Cambridge, MA: MIT Press.

Minsky, M. L. [1967]. *Computation: Finite and Infinite Machines.* Englewood Cliffs, NJ: Prentice-Hall.

Minsky, M. L., and S. A. Papert [1988]. *Perceptrons* (expanded ed.). Cambridge, MA: MIT Press.

Mirchandini, G., and W. Cao [1989]. "On hidden nodes in neural nets." *IEEE Trans. Circuits Syst.* 36(5):661–664.

Mittler, M., and P. Tran-Gia [1993]. "Performance of a neural net scheduler used in packet switching interconnection networks." *Proc. IEEE Int. Conf. Neural Networks,* vol. II, 695–700, San Francisco.

Miyoshi, T., S. Tano, Y. Kato, and T. Arnould [1993]. "Operator tuning in fuzzy production rules using neural networks." *Proc. IEEE Int. Conf. Fuzzy Syst.,* vol. I, 641–646, San Francisco.

Mizumoto, M. [1981]. "Fuzzy sets and their operations." *Inf. Control* 48:30–48.

Mizumoto, M. [1988]. "Fuzzy controls under various fuzzy reasoning methods." *Inf. Sci.* 45:129–151.

MIZUMOTO, M. [1989]. "Pictorial representations of fuzzy connectives. Part I: cases of t-norms, t-conorms and averaging operators." *Fuzzy Sets Syst.* 31:217–242.

MIZUMOTO, M., AND K. TANAKA [1976]. "Some properties of fuzzy sets of type 2." *Inf. Control* 31:312–340.

MONTANA, D. J., AND L. DAVIS [1989]. "Training feedforward networks using genetic algorithms." *Proc. 11th Int. Joint Conf. Artif. Intell.,* 762–767, Detroit.

MOODY, J., AND C. DARKEN [1989]. "Fast learning in networks of locally-tuned processing units." *Neural Comput.* 1:281–294.

MOORE, R. E. [1966]. *Interval Analysis.* Englewood Cliffs, NJ: Prentice-Hall.

MOORE, R. E. [1979]. *Methods and Applications of Interval Analysis.* Philadelphia, PA: SIAM.

MORGAN, D. P., AND C. L. SCOFIELD [1991]. *Neural Networks and Speech Processing.* Boston: Kluwer Academic.

MORGAN, N., ed. [1990]. *Artificial Neural Networks: Electronic Implementations.* Los Alamitos, CA: IEEE Computer Society Press.

MORI, R. D. [1983]. *Computer Models of Speech Using Fuzzy Algorithms.* New York: Plenum Press.

MOZER, M. C. [1989]. "A focused back-propagation algorithm for temporal pattern recognition." *Complex Syst.* 3:349–381.

MOZER, M. C. [1991]. *The Perception of Multiple Objects: A Connectionist Approach.* Cambridge, MA: MIT Press.

MOZER, M. C., AND P. SMOLENSKY [1989]. "Skeletonization: A technique for trimming the fat from a network via relevance assessment." In D. S. Touretzky, ed., *Advances in Neural Information Processing Systems I,* 107–115. San Mateo, CA: Morgan Kaufmann.

MUKHOPADHYAY, S., AND K. S. NARENDRA [1993]. "Disturbance rejection in nonlinear systems using neural networks." *IEEE Trans. Neural Networks* 4(1):63–72.

MUNAKATA, T. [1994]. "Commercial and industrial AI." *Commun. ACM* 37(3):23–26.

MUNAKATA, T., AND Y. JANI [1994]. "Fuzzy systems: An overview." *Commun. ACM* 37(3):69–76.

MURAKAMI, S. [1983]. "Application of fuzzy controller to automobile speed control system." *Proc. IFAC Symp. Fuzzy Inf. Knowl. Represent. Decis. Anal.,* 43–48, Marseilles, France.

MURAKAMI, S., AND M. MAEDA [1985]. "Application of fuzzy controller to automobile speed control system." In M. Sugeno, ed., *Industrial Applications of Fuzzy Control,* 105–124. Amsterdam: North-Holland.

MURAKAMI, S., F. TAKEMOTO, H. FUJIMURA, AND E. IDE [1989]. "Weld-line tracking control of arc welding robot using fuzzy logic controller." *Fuzzy Sets Syst.* 32:221–237.

MUROFUSHI, T., AND M. SUGENO [1989]. "An interpretation of fuzzy measures and the choquet integral as an integral with respect to a fuzzy measure." *Fuzzy Sets Syst.* 29:201–227.

NABET, B., AND R. B. PINTER [1991]. *Sensory Neural Networks: Lateral Inhibition.* Boston: CRC Press.

NADAL, J. [1989]. "Study of a growth algorithm for neural networks." *Int. J. Neural Syst.* 1:55–59.

NAKAYAMA, S., S. HORIKAWA, T. FURUHASHI, AND Y. UCHIKAWA [1992]. "Knowledge acquisition of strategy and tactics using fuzzy neural networks." *Proc. Int. Joint Conf. Neural Networks,* vol. II, 751–756, Baltimore, MD.

NARAZAKI, H., AND A. L. RALESCU [1992]. "A connectionist approach for rule-based inference using an improved relaxation method." *IEEE Trans. Neural Networks* 3(5):741–751.

NARAZAKI, H., AND A. L. RALESCU [1993]. "An improved synthesis method for multilayered neural networks using qualitative knowledge." *IEEE Trans. Fuzzy Syst.* 1(2):125–137.

NARENDRA, K. S. [1990]. "Adaptive control using neural networks." In W. T. Miller, III, R. S. Sutton, and P. J. Werbos, eds., *Neural Networks for Control,* 115–142. Cambridge, MA: MIT Press.

NARENDRA, K. S., AND S. MUKHOPADHYAY [1991]. "Associative learning in random environments using neural networks." *IEEE Trans. Neural Networks* 2(1):20–31.

NARENDRA, K. S., AND S. MUKHOPADHYAY [1992]. "Intelligent control using neural networks." *IEEE Control Syst. Mag.* 12(2):11–18.

NARENDRA, K. S., AND K. PARTHASARATHY [1990]. "Identification and control of dynamical systems using neural networks." *IEEE Trans. Neural Networks* 1(1):4–27.

NARENDRA, K. S., AND K. PARTHASARATHY [1991]. "Gradient methods for the optimization of dynamical systems containing neural networks." *IEEE Trans. Neural Networks* 2(2):252–262.

NARENDRA, K. S., AND K. PARTHASARATHY [1992]. "Neural networks and dynamical systems." *Int. J. Approximate Reasoning* 6:109–131.

NARENDRA, K. S., AND M. A. L. THATHACHAR [1989]. *Learning Automata: An Introduction.* Englewood Cliffs, NJ: Prentice Hall.

NAUCK, D., AND R. KRUSE [1993]. "A fuzzy neural network learning fuzzy control rules and membership functions by fuzzy error backpropagation." *Proc. IEEE Int. Conf. Neural Networks,* vol. II, 1022–1027, San Francisco.

NEGOITA, C. V. [1981]. *Fuzzy Systems.* Tunbridge Wells, England: Abacus Press.

NEGOITA, C. V. [1985]. *Expert Systems and Fuzzy Systems.* Menlo Park, CA: Benjamin/Cummings.

NEGOITA, C. V., AND H. PRADE, eds. [1986]. *Fuzzy Logic in Knowledge Engineering.* Köln: Verlag TÜV Rheinland.

NEGOITA, C. V., AND D. A. RALESCU [1987]. *Simulation, Knowledge-Based Computing and Fuzzy Statistics.* New York: Van Nostrand Reinhold.

NEGOITA, C. V., AND M. SULARIA [1976]. "On fuzzy mathematical programming and tolerances in planning." *ECECSR J.* 1:3–14.

NELSON, M. M., AND W. T. ILLINGWORTH [1991]. *A Practical Guide to Neural Nets.* Reading, MA: Addison-Wesley.

NEWTON, S. C., S. PEMMARAJU, AND S. MITRA [1992]. "Adaptive fuzzy leader clustering of complex data sets in pattern recognition." *IEEE Trans. Neural Networks* 3(5):794–800.

NGUYEN, H. T. [1978]. "On conditional possibility distributions." *Fuzzy Sets Syst.* 1:299–309.

NGUYEN, H. T. [1979]. "Some mathematical tools for linguistic probabilities." *Fuzzy Sets Syst.* 2:53–65.

NIE, J., AND D. A. LINKENS [1992]. "Neural network-based approximate reasoning: Principles and implementation." *Int. J. Control* 56(2):399–413.

NIE, J., AND D. A. LINKENS [1993]. "A fuzzified CMAC self-learning controller." *Proc. IEEE Int. Conf. Fuzzy Syst.,* vol. I, 500–505, San Francisco.

NISHIMORI, H., T. NAKAMURA, AND M. SHIINO [1990]. "Retrieval of spatiotemporal sequence in asynchronous neural network." *Phys. Rev. A* 41:3346–3354.

NOMURA, H., I. HAYASHI, AND N. WAKAMI [1992]. "A learning method of fuzzy interface rules by descent method." *Proc. IEEE Int. Conf. Fuzzy Syst.,* 203–210, San Diego.

NORTH, R. L. [1988]. "Neurocomputing: Its impact on the future of defense systems." *Defense Comput.* 1(1):

NOVÁK, V. [1989]. *Fuzzy Sets and Their Applications.* Philadelphia, PA: Hilger.

NOWLAN, S. J. [1988]. "Gain variation in recurrent error propagation networks." *Complex Syst.* 2:305–320.

OGAWA, H., K. S. FU, AND J. T. P. YAO [1985]. "SPERIL-II: An expert system for damage assessment of existing structures." In M. M. Gupta et al., eds., *Approximate Reasoning in Expert Systems,* 731–744. Amsterdam: Elsevier North-Holland.

OJA, E. [1982]. "A simplified neuron model as a principal component analyzer." *J. Math. Biol.* 15:267–273.

OJA, E. [1989]. "Neural networks, principal components, and subspaces." *Int. J. Neural Syst.* 1:61–68.

OLIKER, S., M. FURST, AND O. MAIMON [1993]. "Design architectures and training of neural networks with a distributed genetic algorithm." *Proc. IEEE Int. Conf. Neural Networks,* vol. I, 199–202, San Francisco.

OLIVER, I. M., D. J. SMITH, AND J. R. C. HOLLAND [1987]. "A study of permutation crossover operators on the traveling salesman problem." *Genet. Algorithms Their Appl.: Proc. 2nd Int. Conf. Genet. Algorithms,* 224–230, Cambridge, MA.

OLLERO, A., AND A. J. GARCIA-CEREZO [1989]. "Direct digital control, auto-tuning and supervision using fuzzy logic." *Fuzzy Sets Syst.* 30:135–153.

ONO, H., T. OHNISHI, AND Y. TERADA [1989]. "Combustion control of refuse incineration plant by fuzzy logic." *Fuzzy Sets Syst.* 32:193–206.

ORLOV, Y. V., I. G. PERSIANTSEV, AND S. P. REBRIK [1993]. "Application of neural networks to fluorescent diagnostics of organic pollution in natural waters." *Proc. IEEE Int. Conf. Neural Networks,* vol. III, 1230–1235, San Francisco.

ORLOVSKY, S. A. [1985]. "Mathematical programming problems with fuzzy parameters." In J. Kacprzyk and R. R. Yager, eds., *Management Decision Support Systems Using Fuzzy Sets and Possibility Theory,* 136–145. Köln: Verlag TÜV Rheinland.

OSTERGAARD, J. J. [1977]. "Fuzzy logic control of a heat exchange process." In M. M. Gupta, G. N. Saridis, and B. R. Gaines, eds., *Fuzzy Automata and Decision Processes,* 285–320. Amsterdam: North-Holland.

OZAWA, J., I. HAYASHI, AND N. WAKAMI [1992]. "Formulation of CMAC-fuzzy system." *Proc. IEEE Int. Conf. Fuzzy Syst.,* 1179–1186, San Diego.

PAL, N. R., AND S. K. PAL [1989]. "Object background segmentation using new definition of entropy." *Proc. Inst. Elec. Eng.,* 284–295.

PAL, S. K. [1992]. "Fuzzy sets in image processing and recognition." *Proc. IEEE Int. Conf. Fuzzy Syst.,* 119–126, San Diego.

PAL, S. K., AND D. K. DUTTA MAJUMDER [1986]. *Fuzzy Mathematical Approach to Pattern Recognition.* New York: John Wiley.

PAL, S. K., AND A. GHOSH [1992]. "Fuzzy geometry in image analysis." *Fuzzy Sets Syst.* 48:23–40.

PAL, S. K., AND S. MITRA [1992]. "Multilayer perceptron, fuzzy sets, and classification." *IEEE Trans. Neural Networks* 3(5):683–697.

PALM, R. [1989]. "Fuzzy controller for a sensor guided manipulator." *Fuzzy Sets Syst.* 31:133–149.

PAO, Y. H. [1989]. *Adaptive Pattern Recognition and Neural Networks.* Reading, MA: Addison-Wesley.

PAPPIS, C. P., AND E. H. MAMDANI [1977]. "A fuzzy logic controller for a traffic junction." *IEEE Trans. Syst. Man Cybern.* 7(10):707–717.

PARKER, D. B. [1985]. Learning logic. Technical Report TR-47, Center for Computational Research in Economics and Management Science, Massachusetts Institute of Technology, Cambridge, MA.

PATI, Y. C., AND P. S. KRISHNAPRASAD [1993]. "Analysis and synthesis of feedforward neural networks using discrete affine wavelet transformations." *IEEE Trans. Neural Networks* 4(1):73–85.

PATRICK, E. A. [1972]. *Fundamentals of Pattern Recognition.* Englewood Cliffs, NJ: Prentice-Hall.

PATRIKAR, A., AND J. PROVENCE [1993]. "Control of dynamic systems using fuzzy logic and neural networks." *Int. J. Intell. Syst.* 8:727–748.

PATYRA, M. J., AND T. M. KWON [1993]. "Processing of incomplete fuzzy data using artificial neural networks." *Proc. IEEE Int. Conf. Fuzzy Syst.,* vol. I, 429–434, San Francisco.

PAWLAK, Z. [1985]. "Rough sets." *Fuzzy Sets Syst.* 17:99–102.

PAWLAK, Z., S. K. M. WONG, AND W. ZIARKO [1988]. "Rough sets: Probabilistic versus deterministic approach." *Int. J. Man-Mach. Stud.* 29:81–95.

PEARL, J. [1988]. *Probabilistic Reasoning in Intelligent Systems.* San Mateo, CA: Morgan Kaufmann.

PEARLMUTTER, B. A. [1989]. "Learning state space trajectories in recurrent neural networks." *Neural Comput.* 1:263–269.

PECK, C. C., A. P. DHAWAN, AND C. M. MEYER [1993]. "Genetic algorithm based input selection for a neural network function approximator with applications to SSME health monitoring." *Proc. IEEE Int. Conf. Neural Networks,* vol. II, 1115–1122, San Francisco.

PEDRYCZ, W. [1981]. "An approach to the analysis of fuzzy systems." *Int. J. Control* 34(3):403–421.

PEDRYCZ, W. [1984]. "An identification of fuzzy relational systems." *Fuzzy Sets Syst.* 13:153–167.

PEDRYCZ, W. [1989]. *Fuzzy Control and Fuzzy Systems.* New York: John Wiley.

PEDRYCZ, W. [1990a]. "Fuzzy sets in pattern recognition: Methodology and methods." *Pattern Recognition* 23(1/2):121–146.

PEDRYCZ, W. [1990b]. "Inverse problem in fuzzy relational equations." *Fuzzy Sets Syst.* 36:277–291.

PEDRYCZ, W. [1991a]. "Neurocomputations in relational systems." *IEEE Trans. Pattern Anal. Mach. Intell.* PAMI–13(3):289–297.

PEDRYCZ, W. [1991b]. "A referential scheme of fuzzy decision making and its neural network structure." *IEEE Trans. Syst. Man Cybern.* 21(6):1593–1604.

PEDRYCZ, W. [1991c]. "Processing in relational structures: Fuzzy relational equations." *Fuzzy Sets Syst.* 40:77–106.

PEDRYCZ, W. [1992]. "Fuzzy neural networks with reference neurons as pattern classifiers." *IEEE Trans. Neural Networks* 3(5):770–775.

PEDRYCZ, W. [1993]. "Fuzzy neural networks and neurocomputations." *Fuzzy Sets Syst.* 56:1–28.

PEMMARAJU, S., AND S. MITRA [1993]. "Identification of noise outliers in clustering by a fuzzy neural network." *Proc. IEEE Int. Conf. Fuzzy Syst.,* 1269–1274, San Francisco.

PENG, J., AND R. J. WILLIAMS [1993]. "Efficient learning and planning within the Dyna framework." *Proc. IEEE Int. Conf. Neural Networks,* vol. I, 168–174, San Francisco.

PENG, X.-T., S. M. LIU, T. YAMAKAWA, P. WANG, AND X. LIU [1988]. "Self-regulating PID controllers and its applications to a temperature controlling process." In M. M. Gupta and T. Yamakawa, eds., *Fuzzy Computing Theory: Hardware and Applications,* 355–364. Amsterdam: Elsevier North-Holland.

PEPER, F., M. N. SHIRAZI, AND H. NODA [1993]. "A noise suppressing distance measure for competitive learning neural networks." *IEEE Trans. Neural Networks* 4(1):151–153.

PERKO, L. [1991]. *Differential Equations and Dynamical Systems.* New York: Springer-Verlag.

PERSONNZA, L., I. GUYON, AND G. DREYFUS [1985]. "Information storage and retrieval in spin-glass-like neural networks." *J. Phys. Lett.* 46:359–365.

PERSONNZA, L., I. GUYON, AND G. DREYFUS [1986]. "Collective computational properties of neural networks: New learning mechanisms." *Phys. Rev. A* 34:4217–4228.

PETERSON, C., AND J. R. ANDERSON [1987]. "A mean field theory learning algorithm for neural networks." *Complex Syst.* 1:995–1019.

PETRY, P. E., B. P. BUCKLES, A. YAZICI, AND R. GEORGE [1992]. "Fuzzy information systems." *Proc. IEEE Int. Conf. Fuzzy Syst.,* 1187–1200, San Diego.

PINEDA, F. J. [1987]. "Generalization of back-propagation to recurrent neural networks." *Phys. Rev. Lett.* 59(19):2229–2232.

PINEDA, F. J. [1988]. "Dynamics and architecture for neural computation." *J. Complexity* 4:216–245.

PINEDA, F. J. [1989]. "Recurrent back-propagation and the dynamical approach to adaptive neural computation." *Neural Comput.* 1:161–172.

PLAUT, D., S. NOWLAN, AND G. HINTON [1986]. Experiments on learning by backpropagation. Technical Report CMU-CS-86-126, Department of Computer Science, Carnegie Mellon University, Pittsburgh, PA.

POGGIO, T., AND F. GIROSI [1990]. "Networks for approximation and learning." *IEEE Proc.* 78(9):1481–1497.

POLLACK, J. B. [1987]. "Cascaded backpropagation on dynamical connectionist networks." *Proc. Ninth Conf. Cognitive Sci. Soc.,* 391–404, Seattle, WA.

POLLACK, J. B. [1989]. "Implications of recursive distributed representations." In D. S. Touretzky, ed., *Advances in Neural Information Processing Systems I,* 527. San Mateo, CA: Morgan Kaufmann.

POLLACK, J. B. [1990]. "Recursive distributed representation." *Artif. Intell.* 46:77–105.

POLLACK, J. B. [1991a]. "The induction of dynamical recognizers." *Mach. Learn.* 7:227–252.

POLLACK, J. B. [1991b]. "Recursive distributed representations." In G. Hinton, ed., *Connectionist Symbol Processing, Special Issue on Artificial Intelligence,* 77–105. Cambridge, MA: MIT Press.

POSEY, C., A. KANDEL, AND G. LANGHOLZ [1992]. "Fuzzy hybrid systems." In A. Kandel and G. Langholz, eds., *Hybrid Architecture for Intelligent Systems,* 173–197. Ann Arbor, MI: CRC Press.

POSPELOV, G. S. [1987]. "Fuzzy set theory in the USSR." *Fuzzy Sets Syst.* 22:1–24.

PRADE, H. [1985]. "A computational approach to approximate and plausible reasoning with applications to expert system." *IEEE Trans. Pattern Anal. Mach. Intell.* 7(6):747–748.

PRADE, H., AND C. V. NEGOITA, eds. [1986]. *Fuzzy Logic in Knowledge Engineering.* Köln: Verlag TÜV Rheinland.

PRADE, H., AND C. TESTEMALE [1984]. "Generalizing database relational algebra for the treatment of incomplete/uncertain information and vague queries." *Inf. Sci.* 34:115–143.

PRADE, H., AND C. TESTEMALE [1985]. "Representation of soft constraints and fuzzy attribute values by means of possibility distribution in databases." In J. Bezdek, ed., *Analysis of Fuzzy Information,* vol. 2, 213–228. Boca Raton, FL: CRC Press.

PROCYK, T. J., AND E. H. MAMDANI [1979]. "A linguistic self-organizing process controller." *Automatica* 15(1):15–30.

PUSKORIUS, G. V., AND L. A. FELDKAMP [1991]. "Decoupled extended Kalman filter training of feedforward layered networks." *Proc. Int. Joint Conf. Neural Networks,* vol. I, 771–777, Seattle, WA.

PUSKORIUS, G. V., AND L. A. FELDKAMP [1992]. "Model reference adaptive control with recurrent networks trained by the dynamic DEKF algorithm." *Proc. Int. Joint Conf. Neural Networks,* vol. II, 106–113, Baltimore, MD.

PUSKORIUS, G. V., AND L. A. FELDKAMP [1993]. "Practical considerations for Kalman filter training of recurrent neural networks." *Proc. IEEE Int. Conf. Neural Networks,* vol. III, 1189–1195, San Francisco.

QI, Y., B. R. HUNT, AND N. BI [1993]. "The use of fuzzy membership in network training for isolated word recognition." *Proc. IEEE Int. Conf. Neural Networks,* vol. III, 1823–1828, San Francisco.

QIAN, N., AND T. J. SEJNOWSKI [1989]. "Learning to solve random-dot stereograms of dense transparent surfaces with recurrent back-propagation." In D. S. Touretzky, G. E. Hinton, and T. J. Sejnowski, eds., *Proc. 1988 Connectionist Models Summer School,* 435–443. San Mateo, CA: Morgan Kaufmann.

QUINLAN, J. R. [1986]. "Induction of decision trees." *Mach. Learn.* 1:81–106.

RABINER, L., AND B. JUANG [1993]. *Fundamentals of Speech Recognition.* Englewood Cliffs, NJ: Prentice-Hall.

Bibliography

RAMACHER, R., AND U. RÜCKERT, eds. [1991]. *VLSI Design of Neural Networks.* Boston: Kluwer Academic.

RAMÍK, J., AND J. RÍMÁNEK [1985]. "Inequality relation between fuzzy numbers and its use in fuzzy optimization." *Fuzzy Sets Syst.* 16:123–138.

RAUCH, H. E., AND T. WINARSKE [1988]. "Neural networks for routing communication traffic." *IEEE Control Syst. Mag.* April:26–31.

RAY, K. S., AND D. D. MAJUMDER [1985]. "Structure of an intelligent fuzzy logic controller and its behavior." In M. M. Gupta, A. Kandel, W. Bandler, and J. B. Kiszka, eds., *Approximate Reasoning in Expert Systems,* 593–619. Amsterdam: Elsevier North-Holland.

REBER, A. S. [1967]. "Implicit learning of artificial grammars." *J. Verbal Learn. Verbal Behav.* 5:855–863.

REILLY, D. L., L. N. COOPER, AND C. ELBAUM [1982]. "A neural model for category learning." *Biol. Cybern.* 45:35–41.

REILLY, D. L., C. SCOFIELD, C. ELBAUM, AND L. N. COOPER [1987]. "Learning system architectures composed of multiple learning modules." *Proc. IEEE Int. Conf. Neural Networks,* vol. II, 495, San Diego.

RICOTTI, L. P., S. RAGAZZINI, AND G. MARTINELLI [1988]. "Learning of word stress in a sub-optimal second order back-propagation neural network." *Proc. IEEE Int. Conf. Neural Networks,* vol. I, 355–361, San Diego.

RISSANEN, J. [1978]. "Modeling by shortest data description." *Automatica* 14:465–471.

RISSANEN, J. [1980]. "Consistent order estimation of autoregression processes by shortest description of data." In O. L. R. Jacobs et al., eds., *Analysis and Optimization of Stochastic Systems.* New York: Academic Press.

RITTER, H., T. MARTINETZ, AND K. SCHULTEN [1992]. *Neural Computation and Self-Organizing Maps: An Introduction.* Reading, MA: Addison-Wesley.

ROAN, S. M., C. C. CHIANG, AND H. C. FU [1993]. "Fuzzy RCE neural network." *Proc. IEEE Int. Conf. Fuzzy Syst.,* vol. I, 629–634, San Francisco.

ROBINSON, A. J., AND F. FALLSIDE [1987]. "Static and dynamic error propagation networks with application to speech coding." In D. Z. Anderson, ed., *Neural Information Processing Systems,* 632–641. New York: American Institute of Physics.

ROHWER, R., AND B. FORREST [1987]. "Training time-dependence in neural networks." *Proc. IEEE Int. Conf. Neural Networks,* vol. II, 701–708, San Diego.

ROMANIUK, S. G., AND L. O. HALL [1990]. "FUZZNET: Towards a fuzzy connectionist expert system development tool." *Proc. Int. Joint Conf. Neural Networks,* vol. II, 483–486, Washington, DC.

ROMANIUK, S. G., AND L. O. HALL [1992]. "Learning fuzzy information in a hybrid connectionist, symbolic model." *Proc. IEEE Int. Conf. Fuzzy Syst.,* 305–312, San Diego.

ROMMELFANGER, H., R. HANUSCHECK, AND J. WOLF [1989]. "Linear programming with fuzzy objectives." *Fuzzy Sets Syst.* 29:31–48.

ROSENBLATT, F. [1958]. "The perceptron: A probabilistic model for information storage and organization in the brain." *Psychol. Rev.* 65:386–408.

ROSENFELD, A. [1992]. "Fuzzy geometry: An overview." *Proc. IEEE Int. Conf. Fuzzy Syst.,* 113–117, San Diego.

ROSENFELD, R., AND D. S. TOURETZKY [1988]. "Coarse-coded symbol memories and their properties." *Complex Syst.* 2:463–484.

ROSKA, T. [1988]. "Some qualitative aspects of neural computing circuits." *Proc. 1988 IEEE Int. Symp. Circuits Syst.,* 751–754, Helsinki.

RUBNER, J., AND K. SCHULTEN [1990]. "Development of feature detectors by self-organization." *Biol. Cybern.* 62:193–199.

RUBNER, J., AND P. TAVAN [1989]. "A self-organizing network for principal-component analysis." *Europhys. Lett.* 10:693–698.

RUCK, D. W., S. K. ROGERS, M. KABRISKY, M. E. OXLEY, AND B. W. SUTER [1990]. "The multilayer perceptron as an approximation to a Bayes optimal discriminant function." *IEEE Trans. Neural Networks* 1(4):296–298.

RUDIN, W. [1976]. *Principles of Mathematical Analysis,* 3rd ed. New York: McGraw-Hill.

RUMELHART, D. E., G. E. HINTON, AND R. J. WILLIAMS [1986a]. "Learning internal representations by error propagation." In D. E. Rumelhart, J. L. McClelland, et al., eds., *Parallel Distributed Processing,* vol. 1, chap. 8. Cambridge, MA: MIT Press.

RUMELHART, D. E., G. E. HINTON, AND R. J. WILLIAMS [1986b]. "Learning representations by back-propagation errors." *Nature* 323:533–536.

RUMELHART, D. E., AND D. ZIPSER [1986]. "Feature discovery by competitive learning." In D. E. Rumelhart, J. L. McClelland, et al., eds., *Parallel Distributed Processing,* vol. 1, chap. 5. Cambridge, MA: MIT Press.

RUSPINI, E. [1973]. "New experimental results in fuzzy clustering." *Inf. Sci.* 6:273–284.

SAATY, S. L. [1977]. "Exploring the interface between hierarchies, multiple objectives and fuzzy sets." *Fuzzy Sets Syst.* 1:57–68.

SÁNCHEZ-SINENCIO, E., AND C. LAU, eds. [1992]. *Artificial Neural Networks: Paradigms, Applications and Hardware Implementations.* New York: IEEE Press.

SAKAI, Y. [1985]. "A fuzzy controller in turning process automation." In M. Sugeno, ed., *Industrial Applications of Fuzzy Control,* 139–152. Amsterdam: North-Holland.

SAKAWA, M. [1984]. *Optimization of Linear Systems.* Tokyo: Morikita Shuppan.

SAMUEL, A. L. [1959]. "Some studies in machine learning using the game of checkers." *IBM J. Res. Develop.* 3:211–229.

SANCHEZ, E. [1976]. "Resolution of composite fuzzy relation equations." *Inf. Control* 30:38–48.

SANCHEZ, E. [1990]. "Fuzzy connectionist expert systems." In T. Yamakawa, ed., *Proc. Int. Conf. Fuzzy Logic Neural Networks,* 31–35, Iizuka, Japan.

SANCHEZ, E. [1992]. "Fuzzy logic knowledge systems and artificial neural networks in medicine and biology." In R. R. Yager and L. A. Zadeh, eds., *An Introduction to Fuzzy Logic Applications in Intelligent Systems.* Boston: Kluwer Academic.

SANCHEZ, E., AND L. A. ZADEH eds. [1987]. *Approximate Reasoning in Intelligent Systems, Decision and Control.* Oxford: Pergamon Press.

SANGER, T. D. [1989a]. "An optimality principle for unsupervised learning." In D. S. Touretzky, ed., *Advances in Neural Information Processing Systems I,* 11–19. San Mateo, CA: Morgan Kaufmann.

SANGER, T. D. [1989b]. "Optimal unsupervised learning in a single-layer linear feedforward neural network." *Neural Networks* 2:459–473.

SANKAR, A., AND R. J. MAMMONE [1991]. "Neural tree networks." In R. J. Mammone and Y. Y. Zeevi, eds., *Neural Networks: Theory and Applications,* 281–302. New York: Academic Press.

SANNER, R. M., AND J. J. E. SLOTINE [1992]. "Gaussian networks for direct adaptive control." *IEEE Trans. Neural Networks* 3(6):837–863.

SARATCHANDRAN, P. [1991]. "Dynamic programming approach to optimal weight selection in multilayer neural networks." *IEEE Trans. Neural Networks* 2(4):465–467.

SATO, M. [1990]. "A real time learning algorithm for recurrent analog neural networks." *Biol. Cybern.* 62:237–241.

SAWARAGI, T., K. SHIBATA, O. KATAI, S. IWAI, AND K. TSUKADA [1992]. "Integrated cognitive architecture for image understanding using fuzzy clustering and structured neural network." *Proc. IEEE Int. Conf. Fuzzy Syst.,* 21–28, San Diego.

SCALETTAR, R., AND A. ZEE [1988]. "Emergence of grandmother memory in feedforward networks: Learning with noise and forgetfulness." In D. Waltz and J. A. Feldman, eds., *Connectionist Models and Their Implications: Readings from Cognitive Science,* 309–332. Norwood, NJ: Ablex.

SCHAFFER, J. D. [1994]. "Combinations of genetic algorithms with neural networks and fuzzy systems." In J. M. Zurada, R. J. Marks, II, and C. J. Robinson, eds., *Computational Intelligence Imitating Life,* 371–382. New York: IEEE Press.

SCHAFFER, J. D., R. A. CARUANA, L. J. ESHELMAN, AND R. DAS [1989]. "A study of control parameters affecting online performance of genetic algorithms for function optimization." In J. D. Schaffer, ed., *Proc. Third Int. Conf. Genet. Algorithms.* San Mateo, CA: Morgan Kaufmann.

SCHARF, E. M., AND N. J. MANDIC [1985]. "The application of a fuzzy controller to the control of a multi-degree-freedom robot arm." In M. Sugeno, ed., *Industrial Applications of Fuzzy Control,* 41–62. Amsterdam: North-Holland.

SCHMIDHUBER, J. [1992a]. "A fixed size storage $O(n^3)$ time complexity learning algorithm for fully recurrent continually running networks." *Neural Comput.* 4:243–248.

SCHMIDHUBER, J. [1992b]. "Learning to control fast-weight memories: An alternative to dynamic recurrent networks." *Neural Comput.* 4:131–139.

SCHMUCKER, K. J. [1984]. *Fuzzy Sets, Natural Language Computations, and Risk Analysis.* New York: Computer Science Press.

SCHWEIZER, B., AND A. SKLAR [1961]. "Associative functions and statistical triangle inequalities." *Publ. Math. Debrecen* 8:169–186.

SERVAN-SCHREIBER, D., A. CLEEREMANS, AND J. L. MCCLELLAND [1991]. "Graded state machines: The representation of temporal contingencies in simple recurrent networks." *Mach. Learn.* 7:161–193.

SETHI, I. K., AND A. K. JAIN, eds. [1991]. *Artificial Neural Networks and Statistical Pattern Recognition.* Amsterdam: Elsevier Science.

SHAFER, G. A. [1976]. *A Mathematical Theory of Evidence.* Princeton University Press.

SHAH, S., F. PALMIERI, AND M. DATUM [1992]. "Optimal filtering algorithms for fast learning in feedforward neural networks." *Neural Networks* 5:779–787.

SHAO, S. [1988]. "Fuzzy self-organizing controller and its application for dynamic processes." *Fuzzy Sets Syst.* 26:151–164.

SHIBATA, T., AND T. FUKUDA [1993]. "Coordinative behavior in evolutionary multi-agent system by genetic algorithm." *Proc. IEEE Int. Conf. Neural Networks,* vol. I, 209–214, San Francisco.

SHIBATA, T., T. FUKUDA, K. KOSUGE, F. ARAI, M. TOKITA, AND T. MITSUOKA [1992]. "Skill based control by using fuzzy neural network for hierarchical intelligent control." *Proc. Int. Joint Conf. Neural Networks,* vol. II, 81–86, Baltimore, MD.

SHIMAMOTO, N., A. HIRAMATSU, AND K. YAMASAKI [1993]. "A dynamic routing control based on a genetic algorithm." *Proc. IEEE Int. Conf. Neural Networks,* vol. II, 1123–1128, San Francisco.

SHINGU, T., AND E. NISHIMORI [1989]. "Fuzzy based automatic focusing system for compact camera." *Proc. IFSA89,* 436–439, Seattle, WA.

SHORTLIFFE, E. H. [1976]. *Computer-Based Medical Consultation: MYCIN.* New York: Elsevier North-Holland.

SHRIVASTAVA, Y., S. DASGUPTA, AND S. M. REDDY [1992]. "Guaranteed convergence in a class of Hopfield networks." *IEEE Trans. Neural Networks* 3(6):951–961.

SHYNK, J. J. [1990]. "Performance surfaces of a single-layer perceptron." *IEEE Trans. Neural Networks* 1(3):268–274.

SHYU, H. J., J. M. LIBERT, AND S. D. MANN [1990]. "Classifying seismic signals via RCE neural network." *Proc. Int. Joint Conf. Neural Networks,* vol. 1, 101–106, Washington, DC.

SIETSMA, J., AND R. J. F. DOW [1988]. "Neural net pruning—Why and how?" *Proc. IEEE Int. Conf. Neural Networks,* vol. I, 325–333, San Diego.

SIMARD, P. Y., M. B. OTTAWAY, AND D. H. BALLARD [1989]. "Analysis of recurrent backpropagation." In D. S. Touretzky, G. E. Hinton, and T. J. Sejnowski, eds., *Proc. 1988 Connectionist Models Summer School,* 103–112. San Mateo, CA: Morgan Kaufmann.

SIMCOX, W. A. [1984]. "A method for pragmatic communication in graphic displays." *Hum. Factors* 26:483–487.

SIMPSON, P. K. [1989]. *Artificial Neural Systems: Foundations, Paradigms, Applications, and Implementations.* New York: Pergamon Press.

SIMPSON, P. K. [1990]. "Higher-ordered and intraconnected bidirectional associative memories." *IEEE Trans. Syst. Man Cybern.* 20:637–653.

SIMPSON, P. K. [1991]. "Fuzzy min-max classification with neural networks." *Heuristics J. Knowl. Eng.* 4:1–9.

SIMPSON, P. K. [1992a]. "Foundations of neural networks." In E. Sánchez-Sinencio and C. Lau, eds., *Artificial Neural Networks: Paradigms, Applications, and Hardware Implementations,* 3–24. New York: IEEE Press.

SIMPSON, P. K. [1992b]. "Fuzzy min-max neural networks—Part 1: Classification." *IEEE Trans. Neural Networks* 3(5):776–786.

SIMPSON, P. K. [1993]. "Fuzzy min-max neural networks—Part 2: Clustering." *IEEE Trans. Fuzzy Syst.* 1(1):32–45.

SIMPSON, P. K., AND G. JAHNS [1993]. "Min-max neural networks for function approximation." *Proc. IEEE Int. Conf. Neural Networks,* vol. III, 1967–1972, San Francisco.

SIN, S.-K., AND R. J. P. DEFIGUEIREDO [1992]. "An evolution-oriented learning algorithm for the optimal interpolative net." *IEEE Trans. Neural Networks* 3(2):315–323.

SIN, S.-K., AND R. J. P. DEFIGUEIREDO [1993a]. "Efficient learning procedures for optimal interpolative nets." *Neural Networks* 6(1):99–113.

SIN, S.-K., AND R. J. P. DEFIGUEIREDO [1993b]. "A method for the design of evolutionary multilayer neural networks." *Proc. IEEE Int. Conf. Neural Networks,* vol. II, 869–874, San Francisco.

SINGHAL, S., AND L. WU [1989]. "Training multilayer perceptrons with the extended Kalman algorithm." In D. S. Touretzky, ed., *Advances in Neural Information Processing Systems I,* 133–140. San Mateo, CA: Morgan Kaufmann.

SIRAT, J. A., AND J. P. NADAL [1990]. *Neural Trees: A New Tool for Classification.* Limeil-Brévannes, France: Laboratoires d'Electronique Philips.

SKALA, H. J., S. TERMINI, AND E. TRILLAS, eds. [1984]. *Aspects of Vagueness.* Dordrecht: Reidel.

SMOLENSKY, P. [1986]. "Information processing in dynamical systems: Foundations of harmony theory." In D. E. Rumelhart, J. L. McClelland, et al., eds., *Parallel Distributed Processing,* vol. 1, chap. 6. Cambridge, MA: MIT Press.

SOLLA, S. A., E. LEVIN, AND M. FLEISHER [1988]. "Accelerated learning in layered neural networks." *Complex Syst.* 2:625–639.

SOMPOLINSKY, H., AND I. KANTER [1986]. "Temporal association in asymmetric neural networks." *Phys. Rev. Lett.* 57:2861–2864.

SONTAG, E. D. [1992]. "Feedback stabilization using two-hidden-layer nets." *IEEE Trans. Neural Networks* 3(6):981–990.

SORENSON, H. W., AND D. L. ALSPACH [1971]. "Recursive Bayesian estimation using Gaussian sums." *Automatica* 7(4):465–479.

Bibliography

SPECHT, D. F. [1990a]. "Probabilistic neural networks." *Neural Networks* 3(1):281–302.

SPECHT, D. F. [1990b]. "Probabilistic neural networks and the polynomial Adaline as complementary techniques for classification." *IEEE Trans. Neural Networks* 1(1):111–121.

SPIRKOVSKA, L., AND M. B. REID [1993]. "Coarse-coded higher-order neural networks for PSRI object recognition." *IEEE Trans. Neural Networks* 4(2):276–283.

STEINBUCH, K. [1961]. "Die lernmatrix." *Kybernetik* 1(1):36–45.

STEINBUCH, K., AND U. A. W. PISKE [1963]. "Learning matrices and their applications." *IEEE Trans. Electron. Comput.* EC12:846–862.

STERZING, V., AND B. SCHÜRMANN [1993]. "Recurrent neural networks for temporal learning of time series." *Proc. IEEE Int. Conf. Neural Networks,* vol. II, 843–850, San Francisco.

STEVENSON, M., R. WINTER, AND B. WIDROW [1990]. "Sensitivity of feedforward neural networks to weight errors." *IEEE Trans. Neural Networks* 1(1):71–80.

STOEVA, S. P. [1992]. "A weight-learning algorithm for fuzzy production systems with weighting coefficients." *Fuzzy Sets Syst.* 48:87–97.

STORK, D. G. [1989]. "Self-organization, pattern recognition, and adaptive resonance networks." *J. Neural Network Comput.* Summer:26–42.

STORNETTA, W. S., T. HOGG, AND B. A. HUBERMAN [1988]. "A dynamical approach to temporal pattern processing." In D. Z. Anderson, ed., *Neural Information Processing Systems,* 750–759. New York: American Institute of Physics.

SUGENO, M., [1977]. "Fuzzy measures and fuzzy integrals—A survey." In M. M. Gupta, G. N. Saridis, and B. R. Gaines, eds. *Fuzzy Automata and Decision Processes,* 89–102. Amsterdam: North-Holland.

SUGENO, M. [1985a]. "An introductory survey of fuzzy control." *Inf. Sci.* 36:59–83.

SUGENO, M., ed. [1985b]. *Industrial Applications of Fuzzy Control.* Amsterdam: North-Holland.

SUGENO, M. [1990]. "Current projects in fuzzy control." *Proc. Workshop Fuzzy Control Syst. Space Sta. Appl.,* 65–77, Huntington Beach, CA.

SUGENO, M., AND G. T. KANG [1986]. "Fuzzy modeling and control of multilayer incinerator." *Fuzzy Sets Syst.* 18:329–346.

SUGENO, M., AND G. T. KANG [1988]. "Structure identification of fuzzy model." *Fuzzy Sets Syst.* 28(1):15–33.

SUGENO, M., AND K. MURAKAMI [1984]. "Fuzzy parking control of model car." *Proc. 23rd IEEE Conf. Decis. Control,* 902–903, Las Vegas.

SUGENO, M., AND K. MURAKAMI [1985]. "An experiment study on fuzzy parking control using a model car." In M. Sugeno, ed., *Industrial Applications of Fuzzy Control,* 125–138. Amsterdam: North-Holland.

SUGENO, M., T. MUROFUSHI, T. MORI, T. TATEMATSU, AND J. TANAKA [1989]. "Fuzzy algorithmic control of a model car by oral instructions." *Fuzzy Sets Syst.* 32:207–219.

SUGENO, M., AND M. NISHIDA [1985]. "Fuzzy control of model car." *Fuzzy Sets Syst.* 16:103–113.

SUGENO, M., AND K. TANAKA [1991]. "Successive identification of fuzzy model and its applications to prediction of complex system." *Fuzzy Sets Syst.* 42:315–344.

SUGIYAMA, K. [1986]. "Analysis and synthesis of the rule-based self-organizing controller." Doctoral dissertation, Queen Mary College, University of London.

SUGIYAMA, K. [1988]. "Rule-based self-organizing controller." In M. M. Gupta and T. Yamakawa, eds., *Fuzzy Computing Theory, Hardware and Applications,* 341–351. Amsterdam: Elsevier North-Holland.

SULZBERGER, S. M., N. N. TSHICHOLD-GÜRMAN, AND S. J. VESTLI [1993]. "FUN: Optimization of fuzzy rule based systems using neural networks." *Proc. IEEE Int. Conf. Neural Networks,* vol. I, 312–316, San Francisco.

SUN, C. T., AND J. S. JANG [1993]. "A neuro-fuzzy classifier and its applications." *Proc. IEEE Int. Conf. Fuzzy Syst.,* vol. I, 94–98, San Francisco.

SUN, G. Z., H. H. CHEN, C. L. GILES, Y. C. LEE, AND D. CHEN [1990]. "Connectionist pushdown automata that learn context-free grammars." *Proc. Int. Joint Conf. Neural Networks,* vol. I, 577, Washington, DC.

SUN, G. Z., H. H. CHEN, AND Y. C. LEE [1992]. "Green's function method for fast on-line learning algorithm of recurrent neural network." In J. E. Moody, S. J. Hanson, and R. P. Lippmann, eds., *Advances in Neural Information Processing Systems 4,* 333–340. San Mateo, CA: Morgan Kaufmann.

SUTTON, R. S. [1984]. "Temporal credit assignment in reinforcement learning." Doctoral dissertation, University of Massachusetts, Amherst.

SUTTON, R. S. [1988]. "Learning to predict by the methods of temporal differences." *Mach. Learn.* 3:9–44.

SUTTON, R. S. [1990]. "Integrated architectures for learning, planning and reacting based on approximating dynamic programming." *Proc. 7th Int. Conf. Mach. Learn.,* 216–224, Austin, TX.

SUTTON, R. S. [1991]. "Planning by incremental dynamic programming." *Proc. 8th Int. Mach. Learn. Workshop,* 353–357, Evanston, IL.

SUTTON, R. S., A. G. BARTO, AND R. J. WILLIAMS [1992]. "Reinforcement learning is direct adaptive optimal control." *IEEE Control Syst. Mag.* 12:19–22.

SYSWERDA, G. [1989]. "Uniform crossover in genetic algorithms." In J. D. Schaffer, ed., *Proc. Third Int. Conf. Genet. Algorithms,* 2–9, San Mateo, CA: Morgan Kaufmann.

SYU, M. J., AND G. T. TSAO [1993]. "Neural network approach to identify batch cell growth." *Proc. IEEE Int. Conf. Neural Networks,* vol. III, 1742–1747, San Francisco.

SZU, H. [1986]. "Fast simulated annealing." In J. S. Denker, ed., *Neural Networks for Computing,* 420–425. New York: American Institute of Physics.

TAGLIARINI, G. A., AND E. W. PAGE [1987]. "Solving constraint satisfaction problems with neural networks." *Proc. Int. Joint Conf. Neural Networks,* vol. III, 741–747, San Diego.

TAKAGI, H., AND I. HAYASHI [1991]. "NN-driven fuzzy reasoning." *Int. J. Approximate Reasoning* 5(3):191–212.

TAKAGI, H., N. SUZUKI, T. KODA, AND Y. KOJIMA [1992]. "Neural networks designed on approximate reasoning architecture and their applications." *IEEE Trans. Neural Networks* 3(5):752–760.

TAKAGI, T., AND M. SUGENO [1983]. "Derivation of fuzzy control rules from human operator's control actions." *Proc. IFAC Symp. Fuzzy Inf. Knowl. Represent. Decis. Anal.,* 55–60, Marseilles, France.

TAKAGI, T., AND M. SUGENO [1985]. "Fuzzy identification of systems and its applications to modeling and control." *IEEE Trans. Syst. Man Cybern.* 15(1):116–132.

TAKEFUJI, Y. [1992]. *Neural Network Parallel Computing.* Boston: Kluwer Academic.

TAMURA, H., AND T. KONDO [1980]. "Heuristics free group method of data handling algorithm of generating optimal partial polynomials with application to air pollution prediction." *Int. J. Syst. Sci.* 11(9):1095–1111.

TANAKA, F., AND S. F. EDWARDS [1980]. "Analytic theory of the ground state properties of a spin glass." *J. Phys. F: Metal Phys.* 10:2769–2778.

TANAKA, H., AND K. ASAI [1984]. "Fuzzy linear programming problems with fuzzy numbers." *Fuzzy Sets Syst.* 13:1–10.

TANAKA, K., AND M. SANO [1992]. "Some properties of stability of fuzzy nonlinear feedback systems." *Proc. 1992 Int. Conf. Ind. Electron. Control, Instrumen. Autom. (IECON—1992),* 1252–1257, San Diego.

TANAKA, K., AND M. SANO [1993]. "Stability analysis of neural networks using stability conditions of fuzzy systems." *Proc. IEEE Int. Conf. Fuzzy Syst.,* vol. I, 422–428, San Francisco.

TANAKA, K., AND M. SUGENO [1992]. "Stability analysis and design of fuzzy control systems." *Fuzzy Sets Syst.* 45:135–156.

TANG, K. L., AND R. J. MULHOLLAND [1987]. "Comparing fuzzy logic with classical controller designs." *IEEE Trans. Syst. Man Cybern.* SMC-17(6):1085–1087.

TANI, T., S. MURAKOSHI, T. SATO, M. UMANO, AND K. TANAKA [1993]. "Application of neuro-fuzzy hybrid control system to tank level control." *Proc. IEEE Int. Conf. Fuzzy Syst.,* vol. I, 618–623, San Francisco.

TANK, D. W., AND J. J. HOPFIELD [1986]. "Simple 'neural' optimization networks: An A/D converter, signal decision circuit and a linear programming circuit." *IEEE Trans. Circuits Syst.* 33(5):533–541.

TANSCHEIT, R., AND E. M. SCHARF [1988]. "Experiments with the use of a rule-based self-organizing controller for robotics applications." *Fuzzy Sets Syst.* 26:195–214.

TAUR, J. S., AND S. Y. KUNG [1993]. "Fuzzy-decision neural networks." *Proc. IEEE Int. Conf. Acoust. Speech Signal Process.,* vol. I, 557–580.

TENORIO, M. F., AND W. T. LEE [1990]. "Self-organizing network for optimum supervised learning." *IEEE Trans. Neural Networks* 1(1):100–110.

TERANO, T., K. ASAI, AND M. SUGENO [1992]. *Fuzzy System Theory and Its Applications.* New York: Academic Press.

TERANO, T., Y. MURAYAMA, AND N. AKIJAMA [1983]. "Human reliability and safety evaluation of man-machine systems." *Automatica* 19:719–722.

TERANO, T., AND M. SUGENO [1975]. "Conditional fuzzy measures and their applications." In L. A. Zadeh, K. S. Fu, K. Tanaka, and M. Shimura, eds., *Fuzzy Sets and Their Applications to Cognitive and Decision Processes,* 151–170. New York: Academic Press.

TESAURO, G. [1992]. "Practical issues in temporal difference learning." *Mach. Learn.* 8:257–278.

TESAURO, G., Y. HE, AND S. AHMAD [1989]. "Asymptotic convergence of back-propagation." *Neural Comput.* 1:382–391.

TESAURO, G., AND B. JANSSENS [1988]. "Scaling relationships in back-propagation learning." *Complex Syst.* 2:39–44.

TITTERINGTON, D., A. SMITH, AND U. MAKOV [1985]. *Statistical Analysis of Finite Mixture Distributions.* New York: John Wiley.

TOBI, T., T. HANAFASA, S. ITOH, AND N. KASHIWAGI [1989]. "Application of fuzzy control system to coke own gas cooling plant." *Proc. IFSA89,* 16–22, Seattle, WA.

TOGAI, M., AND S. CHIU [1987]. "A fuzzy accelerator and a programming environment for real-time fuzzy control." *Proc. 2nd IFSA Congr.,* 147–151, Tokyo, Japan.

TOGAI, M., AND P. P. WANG [1985]. "Analysis of a fuzzy dynamic system and synthesis of its controller." *Int. J. Man-Mach. Stud.* 22:355–363.

TOGAI, M., AND H. WATANABE [1986]. "Expert system on a chip: An engine for real-time approximate reasoning." *IEEE Expert Syst. Mag.* 1:55–62.

TOMITA, M. [1982]. "Dynamical construction of finite-state automata from examples using hill-climbing." *Proc. 4th Ann. Cognitive Sci. Conf.,* 105–108, Ann Arbor, MI.

TONG, R. M. [1978a]. "Synthesis of models for industrial processes–Some recent results." *Int. J. Genet. Syst.* 4:143–162.

TONG, R. M. [1978b]. "Analysis and control of fuzzy systems using finite discrete relations." *Int. J. Control* 27(3):431–440.

TONG, R. M. [1980]. "Some properties of fuzzy feedback systems." *IEEE Trans. Syst. Man Cybern.* 10(6):327–330.

TONG, R. M., M. B. BECK, AND A. LATTEN [1980]. "Fuzzy control of the activated sludge wastewater treatment process." *Automatica* 16(6):695–701.

TOOMARIAN, N., AND J. BARHEN [1992]. "Learning a trajectory using adjoint functions and teacher forcing." *Neural Networks* 5:473–484.

TOURETZKY, D. S., ed. [1989]. *Advances in Neural Information Processing Systems I.* San Mateo: CA: Morgan Kaufmann.

TOURETZKY, D. S., G. E. HINTON, AND T. J. SEJNOWSKI, eds. [1989]. *Proc. 1988 Connectionist Models Summer School.* San Mateo, CA: Morgan Kaufmann.

TSAO, E. C. K., J. C. BEZDEK, AND N. R. PAL [1992]. "Image segmentation using fuzzy clustering networks." *North Am. Fuzzy Inf. Process.,* 98–107, Piscataway, NJ.

TSUKAMOTO, Y. [1979]. "An approach to fuzzy reasoning method." In M. M. Gupta, R. K. Ragade, and R. R. Yager, eds., *Advances In Fuzzy Set Theory And Applications,* 137–149. Amsterdam: North-Holland.

TSUKAMOTO, Y., AND T. TERANO [1977]. "Failure diagnosis by using fuzzy logic." *Proc. IEEE Conf. Decis. Control,* New Orleans, LA.

TSUNG, F. S., AND G. W. COTTRELL [1993]. "Hopf bifurcation and Hopf-hopping in recurrent nets." *Proc. IEEE Int. Conf. Neural Networks,* vol. I, 39–45, San Francisco.

UMANO, M. [1982]. "FREEDOM-0: A fuzzy database system." In M. M. Gupta and E. Sanchez, eds., *Fuzzy Information and Decision Processes,* 339–347. Amsterdam: North-Holland.

UMANO, M. [1983]. "Retrieval from fuzzy database by fuzzy relational algebra." *Proc. IFAC Symp. Fuzzy Inf. Knowl. Represent. Decis. Anal.,* 1–6, Marseilles: France.

UMANO, M., M. MIZUMOTO, AND K. TANAKA [1978]. "FSTDS systems: A fuzzy set manipulation system." *Inf. Sci.* 14:115–159.

UMBERS, I. G., AND P. J. KING [1980]. "An analysis of human-decision making in cement kiln control and the implications for automation." *Int. J. Man-Mach. Stud.* 12(1):11–23.

UNNIKRISHNAN, K. P., J. J. HOPFIELD, AND D. W. TANK [1991]. "Connected-digit speaker-dependent speech recognition using a neural network with time-delayed connections." *IEEE Trans. Signal Process* 39(3):698–713.

URAGAMI, M., M. MIZUMOTO, AND K. TANANKA [1976]. "Fuzzy robot controls." *Cybernetics* 6:39–64.

VAN DEN BOUT, D. E., AND T. K. MILLER, III [1990]. "Graph partitioning using annealed networks." *IEEE Trans. Neural Networks* 1(2):192–203.

VAN DER MAAS, H., P. VERSCHURE, AND P. MOLENAAR [1990]. "A note on chaotic behavior in simple neural networks." *Neural Networks* 3:119–122.

VAN DER RHEE, F., H. R. VAN NAUTA LEMKE, AND J. G. DIJKMAN [1990]. "Knowledge based fuzzy control of systems." *IEEE Trans. Autom. Control* 35(2):148–155.

VAN HEMMEN, J. L., AND R. KÜHN [1988]. "Nonlinear neural networks." *Phys. Rev. Lett.* 57:913–916.

VEMURI, V. [1988]. *Artificial Neural Networks: Theoretical Concepts.* Los Angeles: IEEE Computer Society Press.

VENKATESH S. S., AND D. PSALTIS [1989]. "Linear and logarithmic capacities in associative neural networks." *IEEE Trans. Inf. Theory* 35(3):558–568.

VOGL, T. P., J. K. MANGIS, A. K. RIGLER, W. T. ZINK, AND D. L. ALKON [1988]. "Accelerating the convergence of the back-propagation method." *Biol. Cybern.* 59:257–263.

Bibliography 775

WAIBEL, A. [1989]. "Modular construction of time-delay neural networks for speech recognition." *Neural Comput.* 1:39–46.

WAIBEL, A., T. HANAZAWA, G. HINTON, K. SHIANO, AND K. LANG [1989]. "Phoneme recognition using time-delay neural networks." *IEEE Trans. Acoust. Speech Signal Process.* 37:328–339.

WALTER, J. A., AND K. J. SCHULTEN [1993]. "Implementation of self-organizing neural networks for visuo-motor control of an industrial robot." *IEEE Trans. Neural Networks* 4(1):86–95.

WANG, B. H., AND G. VACHTSEVANOS [1992]. "Learning fuzzy logic control: An indirect control approach." *Proc. IEEE Int. Conf. Fuzzy Syst.*, 297–304, San Diego.

WANG, L. X. [1992]. "Fuzzy systems are universal approximators." *Proc. IEEE Int. Conf. Fuzzy Syst.*, 1163–1170, San Diego.

WANG, L. X. [1993a]. "Solving fuzzy relational equations through network training." *Proc. IEEE Int. Conf. Fuzzy Syst.*, vol. II, 956–960, San Francisco.

WANG, L. X. [1993b]. "Stable adaptive fuzzy control of nonlinear systems." *IEEE Trans. Fuzzy Syst.* 1(2):146–155.

WANG, L. X. [1994]. *Adaptive Fuzzy Systems and Control.* Englewood Cliffs, NJ: Prentice-Hall.

WANG, L. X., AND J. M. MENDEL [1992a]. "Fuzzy basis functions, universal approximation, and orthogonal least-squares learning." *IEEE Trans. Neural Networks* 3(5):807–814.

WANG, L. X., AND J. M. MENDEL [1992b]. "Generating fuzzy rules by learning from examples." *IEEE Trans. Syst. Man Cybern.* 22(6):1414–1427.

WANG, P.-Z. [1982]. "Fuzzy contactability and fuzzy variables." *Fuzzy Sets Syst.* 8:81–92.

WANG, P. P., ed. [1983]. *Advances in Fuzzy Sets, Possibility Theory and Applications.* New York: Plenum Press.

WANG, P. P., AND S. K. CHANG [1980]. *Fuzzy Sets: Theory and Applications to Policy Analysis and Information Systems.* New York: Plenum Press.

WANG, T., X. ZHUANG, AND X. XING [1992]. "Weighted learning of bidirectional associative memories by global minimization." *IEEE Trans. Neural Networks* 3(6):1010–1018.

WANG, Y. F., J. B. CRUZ, AND J. H. MULLIGAN [1990]. "Two coding strategies for bidirectional associative memory." *IEEE Trans. Neural Networks* 1(1):81–92.

WANG, Y. F., J. B. CRUZ, AND J. H. MULLIGAN [1991]. "Guaranteed recall of all training pairs for bidirectional associative memory." *IEEE Trans. Neural Networks* 2(6):559–567.

WATANABE, H., AND W. DETTLOFF [1988]. "Reconfigurable fuzzy logic processor: A full custom digital VLSI." *Proc. Int. Workshop Fuzzy Syst. Appl.*, 49–50, Iizuka, Japan.

WATKINS, C. J. C. H. [1989]. "Learning with delayed rewards." Doctoral dissertation, Psychology Department, Cambridge University.

WATKINS, C. J. C. H., AND P. DAYAN [1992]. "Technical note: Q-learning." *Mach. Learn.* 8:279–292.

WATROUS, R. L. [1993]. "Speaker normalization and adaptation using second-order connectionist networks." *IEEE Trans. Neural Networks* 4(1):21–30.

WATROUS, R. L., AND G. M. KUHN [1992]. "Induction of finite-state languages using second-order recurrent networks." *Neural Comput.* 4:406–414.

WATROUS, R. L., AND L. SHASTRI [1987]. "Learning phonetic features using connectionist networks: An experiment in speech recognition." *Proc. IEEE Int. Conf. Neural Networks*, vol. IV, 381–388, San Diego.

WEIGEND, A. S., D. E. RUMELHART, AND B. A. HUBERMAN [1990]. "Back-propagation, weight elimination and time series prediction." In D. S. Touretzky, J. L. Elman, T. J. Sejnowski, and G. E. Hinton, eds., *Proc. 1990 Connectionist Models Summer School.* San Mateo, CA: Morgan Kaufmann.

WEISS, S. M., AND C. A. KULIKOWSKI [1991]. *Computer Systems That Learn: Classification and Prediction Methods from Statistics, Neural Nets, Machine Learning and Expert Systems.* San Mateo, CA: Morgan Kaufmann.

WELSTEAD, S. T. [1994]. *Neural Network and Fuzzy Logic Applications in C/C++.* New York: John Wiley.

WERBOS, P. J. [1974]. "Beyond regression: New tools for prediction and analysis in the behavioral sciences." Doctoral dissertation, Harvard University.

WERBOS, P. J. [1987]. "Building and understanding adaptive systems: A statistical/numerical approach to factory automation and brain research." *IEEE Trans. Syst. Man Cybern.* 17(1):7–20.

WERBOS, P. J. [1988]. "Generalization of backpropagation with application to a recurrent gas market model." *Neural Networks* 1:338–356.

WERBOS, P. J. [1990]. "A menu of design for reinforcement learning over time." In W. T. Miller, III, R. S. Sutton, and P. J. Werbos, eds., *Neural Networks for Control,* chap. 3. Cambridge, MA: MIT Press.

WERBOS, P. J. [1992]. "Neurocontrol and fuzzy logic: Connections and designs." *Int. J. Approximate Reasoning* 6:185–219.

WERNERS, B. [1987]. "An interactive fuzzy programming system." *Fuzzy Sets Syst.* 23:131–147.

WESSELS, L. F. A., AND E. BARNARD [1992]. "Avoiding false local minima by proper initialization of connections." *IEEE Trans. Neural Networks* 3(6):899–905.

WHITE, B. A., AND M. I. ELMASRY [1992]. "The digi-neocognitron: A digital neocognitron neural network model for VLSI." *IEEE Trans. Neural Networks* 3(1):73–86.

WHITE, H. [1989]. "Learning in artificial neural networks: A statistical perspective." *Neural Comput.* 1(4):425–469.

WHITLEY, D., AND T. HANSON [1989]. "Optimizing neural networks using fast more accurate genetic search." In J. D. Schaffer, ed., *Proc. Third Int. Conf. Genetic Algorithms.* San Mateo, CA: Morgan Kaufmann.

WIDROW, B. [1962]. "Generalization and information storage in networks of Adaline 'neurons.'" In M. C. Jovitz, G. T. Jacobi, and G. Goldstein, eds., *Self-Organizing Systems,* 435–461. Washington, DC: Spartan Books.

WIDROW, B., N. K. GUPTA, AND S. MAITRA [1973]. "Punish/reward: Learning with a critic in adaptive threshold systems." *IEEE Trans. Syst. Man Cybern.* 3:455–465.

WIDROW, B., AND M. E. HOFF, JR. [1960]. "Adaptive switching circuits." *Proc. 1960 IRE West. Elect. Show Conv. Rec.,* Part 4, 96–104, New York.

WIDROW, B., D. E. RUMELHART, AND M. A. LEHR [1994]. "Neural networks: Applications in industry, business and science." *Commun. ACM* 37(3):93–105.

WIDROW, B., AND S. D. STEARNS [1985]. *Adaptive Signal Processing.* Englewood Cliffs, NJ: Prentice-Hall.

WIDROW, B., AND R. WINTER [1988]. "Neural nets for adaptive filtering and adaptive pattern recognition." *Computer* 21(3):25–39.

WIERZCHON, S. T. [1982]. "Applications of fuzzy decision-making theory to coping with ill-defined problems." *Fuzzy Sets Syst.* 7:1–18.

WILLAEYS, D., AND N. MALVACHE [1979]. "Contribution of the fuzzy sets theory to man-machine system." In M. M. Gupta, R. K. Ragade, and R. R. Yager, eds., *Advances in Fuzzy Set Theory and Applications,* 481–497. Amsterdam: North-Holland.

WILLIAMS, R. J. [1987]. "A class of gradient-estimating algorithms for reinforcement learning in neural networks." *Proc. IEEE Int. Conf. Neural Networks,* vol. II, 601–608, San Diego.

WILLIAMS, R. J. [1988]. "On the use of backpropagation in associative reinforcement learning." *Proc. IEEE Int. Conf. Neural Networks,* vol. I, 263–270, San Diego.

WILLIAMS, R. J. [1992a]. "Simple statistical gradient-following algorithms for connectionist reinforcement learning." *Mach. Learn.* 8:229–256.

WILLIAMS, R. J. [1992b]. "Training recurrent networks using the extended Kalman filter." *Proc. Int. Joint Conf. Neural Networks,* vol. IV, 241–246, Baltimore, MD.

WILLIAMS, R. J., AND J. PENG [1990]. "An efficient gradient-based algorithm for on-line training of recurrent network trajectories." *Neural Comput.* 2:490–501.

WILLIAMS, R. J., AND D. ZIPSER [1989a]. "Experimental analysis of the real-time recurrent learning algorithm." *Connection Sci.* 1:87–111.

WILLIAMS, R. J., AND D. ZIPSER [1989b]. "A learning algorithm for continually running fully recurrent neural networks." *Neural Comput.* 1:270–280.

WILLSHAW, D. J., AND C. VON DER MALSBURG [1976]. "How patterned neural connections can be set up by self-organization." *Proc. Roy. Soc. Lond.* 194:431–445.

WILSON, V., AND G. S. PAWLEY [1988]. "On the stability of the TSP problem algorithm of Hopfield and Tank." *Biol. Cybern.* 58:63–70.

WINDHAM, M. P. [1983]. "Geometrical fuzzy clustering algorithms." *Fuzzy Sets Syst.* 10:271–279.

WINTER, R., AND B. WIDROW [1988]. "MADALINE RULE II: A training algorithm for neural networks." *Proc. IEEE Int. Conf. Neural Networks,* vol. I, 401–408, San Diego.

WOLFE, W. J., D. MATHIS, C. ANDERSON, J. ROTHMAN, M. GOTTLER, G. BRADY, R. WALKER, G. DUANE, AND G. ALAGHBAND [1991]. "K-winner networks." *IEEE Trans. Neural Networks* 2(2):310–315.

WONG, Y., AND A. SIDERIS [1992]. "Learning convergence in the cerebellar model articulation controller." *IEEE Trans. Neural Networks* 3(1):115–121.

WU, Q. H., B. H. HOGG, AND G. W. IRWIN [1992]. "A neural network regulator for turbogenerators." *IEEE Trans. Neural Networks* 3(1):95–100.

XU, C. W., AND Y. ZAILU [1987]. "Fuzzy model identification and self-learning for dynamic systems." *IEEE Trans. Syst. Man Cybern.* 17(4):683–689.

XU, H. Y., AND G. VUKOVICH [1993]. "Robotic modeling and control using a fuzzy neural network." *Proc. IEEE Int. Conf. Neural Networks,* vol. II, 1004–1009, San Francisco.

XU, H. Y., G. Z. WANG, AND C. B. BAIRD [1992]. "A fuzzy neural networks technique with fast backpropagation learning." *Proc. Int. Joint Conf. Neural Networks,* vol. I, 214–219, Baltimore, MD.

YABUTA, T., AND T. YAMADA [1992]. "Neural network controller characteristics with regard to adaptive control." *IEEE Trans. Syst. Man Cybern.* 22(1):170–176.

YAGER, R. R. [1978]. "Fuzzy decision making using unequal objectives." *Fuzzy Sets Syst.* 1:87–95.

YAGER, R. R. [1979a]. "On solving fuzzy mathematical relationships." *Inf. Control* 41:29–55.

YAGER, R. R. [1979b]. "On the measure of fuzziness and negation. Part 1: Membership in the unit interval." *Int. J. Genet. Syst.* 5:221–229.

YAGER, R. R. [1980]. "On a general class of fuzzy connectives." *Fuzzy Sets Syst.* 4:235–242.

YAGER, R. R., ed. [1982]. *Recent Advances in Fuzzy-Set and Possibility Theory.* Elmsford, NY: Pergamon Press.

YAGER, R. R. [1984a]. "Approximate reasoning as a basis for rule-based expert system." *IEEE Trans. Syst. Man Cybern.* 14(4):636–643.

YAGER, R. R. [1984b]. "A representation of the probability of fuzzy subsets." *Fuzzy Sets Syst.* 13:273–283.

YAGER, R. R. [1986]. "A characterization of the fuzzy extension principle." *Fuzzy Sets Syst.* 18:205–217.

YAGER, R. R. [1988]. "On ordered weighted averaging aggregation operations in multicriteria decision making." *IEEE Trans. Syst. Man Cybern.* 18(1):183–190.

YAGER, R. R. [1991]. "Connectives and quantifiers in fuzzy sets." *Fuzzy Sets Syst.* 40:39–76.

YAGER, R. R. [1992a]. "Expert systems using fuzzy logic." In R. R. Yager and L. A. Zadeh, eds., *An Introduction to Fuzzy Logic Applications in Intelligent Systems.* Boston: Kluwer Academic.

YAGER, R. R. [1992b]. "Implementing fuzzy logic controllers using a neural network framework." *Fuzzy Sets Syst.* 48:53–64.

YAGER, R. R. [1992c]. "Fuzzy sets and approximate reasoning in decision and control." *Proc. IEEE Int. Conf. Fuzzy Syst.,* 415–428, San Diego.

YAGER, R. R. [1992d]. "OWA neurons: A new class of fuzzy neurons." *Proc. Int. Joint Conf. Neural Networks,* vol. I, 226–231, Baltimore, MD.

YAGER, R. R., AND D. P. FILEV [1994]. *Essentials of Fuzzy Modeling and Control.* New York: John Wiley.

YAGER, R. R., S. OVCHINNIKOV, R. M. TONG, AND H. T. NGUYEN, eds. [1987]. *Fuzzy Sets and Applications: Selected Papers by L. A. Zadeh.* New York: John Wiley.

YAGER, R. R., AND L. A. ZADEH, eds. [1992]. *An Introduction to Fuzzy Logic Applications in Intelligent Systems.* Boston: Kluwer Academic.

YAGER, R. R., AND L. A. ZADEH, eds. [1994]. *Fuzzy Sets, Neural Networks and Soft Computing.* New York: Van Nostrand Reinhold.

YAGISHITA, O., O. ITOH, AND M. SUGENO [1985]. "Application of fuzzy reasoning to the water purification process." In M. Sugeno, ed., *Industrial Applications of Fuzzy Control,* 19–40. Amsterdam: North-Holland.

YAMAGUCHI, T., K. GOTO, T. TAKAGI, K. DOYA, AND T. MITA [1992a]. "Intelligent control of a flying vehicle using fuzzy associative memory system." *Proc. IEEE Int. Conf. Fuzzy Syst.,* 1139–1149, San Diego.

YAMAGUCHI, T., T. TAKAGI, AND T. MITA [1992b]. "Self-organizing control using fuzzy neural networks." *Int. J. Control* 56(2):415–439.

YAMAKAWA, T. [1987]. "A simple fuzzy computer hardware system employing min and max operations—A challenge to 6th generation computer." *Proc. 2nd IFSA Congr.,* Tokyo, Japan.

YAMAKAWA, T. [1988a]. "High-speed fuzzy controller hardware system: The MEGA-FIPs machine." *Inf. Sci.* 45(2):113–128.

YAMAKAWA, T. [1988b]. "Intrinsic fuzzy electronic circuits for 6th generation computer." In M. M. Gupta and T. Yamakawa, eds., *Fuzzy Computing,* 157–171. New York: Elsevier Science.

YAMAKAWA, T. [1989]. "Stabilization of an invented pendulum by a high-speed fuzzy logic controller hardware system." *Fuzzy Sets Syst.* 32:161–180.

YAMAKAWA, T., AND H. KABUO [1988]. "A programmable fuzzifier integrated circuit—Synthesis, design and fabrication." *Inf. Sci.* 45(2):75–112.

YAMAKAWA, T., AND T. MIKI [1986]. "The current mode fuzzy logic integrated circuits fabricated by the standard CMOS process." *IEEE Trans. Comput.* 35(2):161–167.

YAMAKAWA, T., AND K. SASAKI [1987]. "Fuzzy memory device." *Proc. 2nd IFSA Congr.,* 551–555, Tokyo, Japan.

YAMAKAWA, T., AND S. TOMODA [1989]. "A fuzzy neuron and its application to pattern recognition." In J. C. Bezdek, ed., *Proc. 3rd IFSA Congr.,* 30–38, Seattle, WA.

YAMASHITA, T. [1991]. "Stability analysis of fuzzy control system applying conventional methods." *Proc. 1991 Int. Conf. Ind. Electron. Control Instrumen. Autom. (IECON—1991),* 1579–1584, Kobe, Japan.

Bibliography

YASUNOBU, S., AND T. HASEGAWA [1986]. "Evaluation of an automatic container crane operation system based on predictive fuzzy control." *Control Theory Adv. Technol.* 2(3):419–432.

YASUNOBU, S., AND T. HASEGAWA [1987]. "Predictive fuzzy control and its application for automatic container crane operation system." *Proc. 2nd IFSA Congr.,* 349–352, Tokyo, Japan.

YASUNOBU, S., AND S. MIYAMOTO [1985]. "Automatic train operation by predictive fuzzy control." In M. Sugeno, ed., *Industrial Application of Fuzzy Control,* 1–18. Amsterdam: North-Holland.

YASUNOBU, S., S. SEKINO, AND T. HASEGAWA [1987]. "Automatic train operation and automatic crane operation systems based on predictive fuzzy control." *Proc. 2nd IFSA Congr.,* 835–838, Tokyo, Japan.

YAZICI, A., B. P. BUCKLES, AND F. E. PETRY [1990]. "A new approach for conceptual and logical design of databases." *Proc. 5th Int. Symp. Comput. Inf. Sci.*

YEN, J. [1990a]. "Generalizing the Dempster-Shafer theory to fuzzy sets." *IEEE Trans. Syst. Man Cybern.* 20(3):559–570.

YEN, J. [1990b]. "The role of fuzzy logic in the control of neural networks." In T. Yamakawa, ed., *Proc. Int. Conf. Fuzzy Logic Neural Networks,* 771–774, Iizuka, Japan.

YEN, J. [1991]. "Using fuzzy logic to integrate neural networks and knowledge-based systems." In J. Villereal and R. Lea, eds., *Proc. 2nd NASA Workshop Neural Networks Fuzzy Logic,* vol. 1, 217–233, Houston, TX.

YEUNG, D. T., AND G. A. BEKEY [1989]. "Using a context-sensitive learning network for robot arm control." *Proc. IEEE Int. Conf. Robotics Autom.,* 1441–1447, Scottsdale, AZ.

YEUNG, D. T., AND G. A. BEKEY [1993]. "On reducing learning time in context-dependent mappings." *IEEE Trans. Neural Networks* 4(1):31–42.

YOSHIDA, S., AND N. WAKABAYASHI [1992]. "Fuzzy and adaptive control simulations for a walking machine." *IEEE Control Syst. Mag.* 12(3):65–70.

YU, C., Z. CAO, AND A. KANDEL [1990]. "Application of fuzzy reasoning to the control of an activated sludge plant." *Fuzzy Sets Syst.* 38:1–14.

YUAN, F., L. A. FELDKAMP, JR., L. I. DAVIS, AND G. C. PUSKORIUS [1992]. "Training a hybrid neural-fuzzy system." *Proc. Int. Joint Conf. Neural Networks,* vol. II, 739–744, Baltimore, MD.

ZADEH, L. A. [1965]. "Fuzzy sets." *Inf. Cont.* 8:338–353.

ZADEH, L. A. [1968]. "Probability measures of fuzzy events." *J. Math. Anal. Appl.* 23:421–427.

ZADEH, L. A. [1969]. "Fuzzy algorithms." *Inf. Control* 19:94–102.

ZADEH, L. A. [1971]. "Similarity relations and fuzzy orderings." *Inf. Sci.* 3:177–206.

ZADEH, L. A. [1972]. "A fuzzy-set-theoretic interpretation of linguistic hedges." *J. Cybern.* 2(2):4–34.

ZADEH, L. A. [1973]. "Outline of a new approach to the analysis of complex systems and decision processes." *IEEE Trans. Syst. Man Cybern.* SMC-1:28–44.

ZADEH, L. A. [1975a]. "The concept of a linguistic variable and its application to approximate reasoning, Part I." *Inf. Sci.* 8:199–249.

ZADEH, L. A. [1975b]. "The concept of a linguistic variable and its application to approximate reasoning, Part II." *Inf. Sci.* 8:301–357.

ZADEH, L. A. [1976a]. "The concept of a linguistic variable and its application to approximate reasoning, Part III." *Inf. Sci.* 9:43–80.

ZADEH, L. A. [1976b]. "A fuzzy-algorithmic approach to the definition of complex or imprecise concepts." *Int. J. Man-Mach. Stud.* 8:249–291.

ZADEH, L. A. [1977]. "Fuzzy sets and their application to pattern recognition and clustering analysis." In J. V. Ryzin, ed., *Classification and Clustering,* 251–299. New York: Academic Press.

ZADEH, L. A. [1978a]. "Fuzzy sets as a basis for a theory of possibility." *Fuzzy Sets Syst.* 1(1):3–28.

ZADEH, L. A. [1978b]. "PRUF—A meaning representation language for natural languages." *Int. J. Man-Mach. Stud.* 10:395–460.

ZADEH, L. A. [1979]. "A theory of approximate reasoning." In J. Hayes, D. Michie, and L. I. Mikulich, eds. *Machine Intelligence,* vol. 9, 149–194. New York: Halstead Press.

ZADEH, L. A. [1983a]. "The role of fuzzy logic in the management of uncertainty in expert systems." *Fuzzy Sets Syst.* 11:199–227.

ZADEH, L. A. [1983b]. "A computational approach to fuzzy quantifiers in natural language." *Comp. Math Appl.* 9:149–184.

ZADEH, L. A. [1984]. "A theory of commonsense knowledge." In H. J. Skala, S. Termini, and E. Trillas, eds., *Aspects of Vagueness,* 257–296. Dordrecht: Reidel.

ZADEH, L. A. [1985]. "Syllogistic reasoning in fuzzy logic and its application to usuality and reasoning with dispositions." *IEEE Trans. Syst. Man Cybern.* 15:754–763.

ZADEH, L. A. [1986]. "Test-score semantics as a basis for a computational approach to the representation of meaning." *Lit. Linguist. Comput.* 1:24–35.

ZADEH, L. A. [1987]. "A computational theory of dispositions." *Int. J. Intell. Syst.* 2:39–63.

ZADEH, L. A. [1988]. "Fuzzy logic." *IEEE Comput.* 1:83–93.

ZADEH, L. A. [1989a]. "Knowledge representation in fuzzy logic." *IEEE Trans. Knowl. Data Eng.* 1(1):89–100.

ZADEH, L. A. [1989b]. "QSA/FL—Qualitative system analysis based on fuzzy logic." *Proc. AAAI Symp.,* Stanford University.

ZADEH, L. A. [1992]. "Knowledge representation in fuzzy logic." In R. R. Yager and L. A. Zadeh, eds., *An Introduction to Fuzzy Logic Applications in Intelligent Systems,* 1–25. Boston: Kluwer Academic.

ZADEH, L. A. [1994]. "Fuzzy logic, neural networks, and soft computing." *Commun. ACM* 37(3):77–84.

ZADEH, L. A., K. S. FU, K. TANAKA, AND M. SHIMURA, eds. [1975]. *Fuzzy Sets and Their Applications to Cognitive and Decision Processes.* New York: Academic Press.

ZEMANKOVA-LEECH, M., AND A. KANDEL [1984]. *Fuzzy Relational Data Bases–A Key to Expert Systems.* Köln: Verlag TÜV Reinland.

ZENG, Z., R. M. GOODMAN, AND P. SMYTH [1993]. "Self-clustering recurrent networks." *Proc. IEEE Int. Conf. Neural Networks,* vol. I, 33–38, San Francisco.

ZHANG, Q., AND A. BENVENISTE [1992]. "Wavelet networks." *IEEE Trans. Neural Networks* 3(6):889–898.

ZIMMERMANN, H.-J. [1976]. "Description and optimization of fuzzy systems." *Int. J. Gen. Syst.* 2:209–215.

ZIMMERMANN, H.-J. [1978]. "Fuzzy programming and linear programming with several objective functions." *Fuzzy Sets Syst.* 1:45–55.

ZIMMERMANN, H.-J. [1983]. "Fuzzy mathematical programming." *Comput. Oper. Res.* 10:291–298.

ZIMMERMANN, H.-J., [1991]. *Fuzzy Set Theory and Its Applications,* 2nd rev. ed. Boston: Kluwer Academic.

ZIMMERMANN, H.-J. [1992]. "Methods and applications of fuzzy mathematical programming." In R. R. Yager and L. A. Zadeh, eds., *An Introduction to Fuzzy Logic Applications in Intelligent Systems,* 97–120. Boston: Kluwer Academic.

ZIMMERMANN, H.-J., L. A. ZADEH, AND B. R. GAINES, eds. [1984]. *Fuzzy Sets and Decision Analysis.* New York: North-Holland.

ZIMMERMANN, H.-J., AND P. ZYSNO [1980]. "Latent connectives in human decision making." *Fuzzy Sets Syst.* 4:37–51.

ZIMMERMANN, H.-J., AND P. ZYSNO [1983]. "Decisions and evaluations by hierarchical aggregation of information." *Fuzzy Sets Syst.* 10:243–266.

ZORNETZER, S. F., J. L. DAVIS, AND C. LAU, eds. [1990]. *An Introduction to Neural and Electronic Networks.* San Diego: Academic Press.

ZURADA, J. M. [1992]. *Introduction to Artificial Neural Systems.* Singapore: Info Access & Distribution.

ZURADA, J. M., R. J. MARKS, II, AND C. J. ROBINSON, eds. [1994]. *Computational Intelligence Imitating Life.* New York: IEEE Press.

Index

Adaptive resonance theory (ART), 321, 332, 427, 433, 626, 680
   algorithm, ART1, 322
   ART1, 321, 626, 627, 630, 655, 680
   ART2, ART3, 321, 325, 337, 659
   fuzzy vigilance controller, 608, 657
   hybrid optoelectronic, 337
   real-time, 320, 325
   vigilance parameter, 321
Adaptive vector quantization (AVQ), 302, 304, 337, 605
Aggregation operator, 27, 33, 504, 531, 559, 610
Akaike's information criterion (AIC), 423, 442, 443
Algebraic product, 21, 28, 31, 45, 47, 146, 179
Algebraic sum, 21, 28, 31, 32, 60
Ambiguity, 3, 4, 63, 64, 83, 191, 619
Analog-to-digital (A/D) converter, 285, 297, 413
Approximate reasoning, 94, 121, 123, 139, 143, 145, 614
Associative reward-inaction (A_{R-I}) rule, 371
Associative reward-penalty (A_{R-P}) algorithm, 368, 371, 377, 378
   A_{R-P} learning rule, 370
Associative search element (ASE), 377, 381
Asymptotically stable, 167, 168, 170, 267, 457, 490, 491
Asynchronous transfer mode (ATM) network, 468
   call admission control, 469
   service quality control, 468
Avalanche network, 379
Averaging operator, 27, 33, 504, 506

B-spline function, 462, 476, 552
Backpropagation (BP), 236, 341
   batch-mode, 240
   convergence, 242–45, 247, 248
   delta-bar-delta, 246
   double backpropagation, 249
   dynamic BP, 448, 450, 474
   error surface, 243, 655
   focused backpropagation network, 379

function approximation, 242, 482
fuzzy control, 655
fuzzy training data, 643
   learning algorithm, 237, 239, 254, 330, 357, 515, 541, 579, 584, 653, 687
   learning factors, 244
   momentum term, 247, 252, 349, 351, 362, 426, 518, 527, 655
   network, 236, 242, 250, 330, 345, 424, 439, 469, 507, 517, 618, 665
   Newton's method, 248, 426
   self-supervised, 336, 684, 689
   size of a hidden layer, 249, 443
   temporal BP, 605
   weight initialization, 257
Backpropagation through time (BPTT), 379
Ball and beam system, 550, 600
Basic probability assignment, 67, 69, 70, 72–74, 77
Bayesian discriminant function, 242
Belief measure, 65–67, 69, 71–75, 80, 85, 131, 663
   subadditivity axiom, 65
Bidirectional associative memory (BAM), 277, 620
   adaptive (ABAM), 331, 332, 337
   additive, 316
   capacity, 280, 297
   continuous, 282, 299, 331
   discrete, 277, 297
   dummy augmentation encoding, 297
   energy function, 279, 283, 299
   multiple training encoding, 297, 299
   neural fuzzy system (BAM-NFS), 702
   outer product learning, 278
   shunting, 317
   stability, 279
   temporal associative memory, 283
   update rule, 278, 282
Bifurcation, 350
   Hopf, 353
Binary fuzzy relation, 39, 40, 43, 46, 49
   antireflexive, 47
   antisymmetric, 47, 52
   antitransitive, 47, 48
   asymmetric, 47

Fuzzy neural network, 8, 9, 482, 494, 609, 611–14, 658, 667, 696, 701
Fuzzy neuron, 609
  Lee's fuzzy neuron, 658
  OWA, 657
  type-I, 610
  type-II, 612
  type-III, 613
Fuzzy number, 17, 94, 145, 643
  comparable, 102
  fuzzy maximum, 102
  fuzzy minimum, 102
  triangular, 98, 99, 102, 109, 614, 649, 650
Fuzzy number equation, 102
Fuzzy partial ordering, 52, 53
  dominated class, 53
  dominating class, 53
  fuzzy lower bound, 54
  fuzzy upper bound, 54, 62
Fuzzy partition, 144, 159, 539, 561, 569, 573
  coarse/fine partition, 605, 674
  flexible partition, 567, 568, 579
  fuzzy hyperbox, 579, 667
  GA approach, 567
  grid-type, 568, 674
Fuzzy perceptron, 615, 616, 659
  algorithm, FPLA, 617
  stopping criterion, 616
  weight update rule, 615
Fuzzy PID control approach, 162
Fuzzy pocket algorithm, 658
Fuzzy predicate, 121, 123, 127, 146, 158
Fuzzy predicate modifier, 121
Fuzzy probabilistic neural network, 658
Fuzzy probability, 111, 121
Fuzzy qualifier, 121
  fuzzy possibility qualification, 122
  fuzzy probability qualification, 121, 122
  fuzzy truth qualification, 121
  fuzzy usuality qualification, 122
Fuzzy quantifier, 94, 121–23, 127, 129
Fuzzy radial basis function network, 658
Fuzzy RCE network, 640, 660
  algorithm, FRCE, 640
Fuzzy reasoning, control, 154
  first type, 154, 514, 534, 605

  second type, 154, 514, 534
  third type, 156, 161, 515, 534
  Tsukamoto's Method, 154
Fuzzy regression model, 517, 520
Fuzzy relation, 37, 79, 91, 92, 182, 183, 482, 484, 523, 560, 613, 614
  cylindric closure, 43
  cylindric extension, 42, 43, 92
  domain, 40
  fuzzy matrix, 39
  height, 40
  projection, 41, 43, 91, 123, 129
  range, 40
  relational joint, 46
  resolution form, 40, 50, 52
Fuzzy relation equation, 54, 55, 57, 183, 523
  α-composition, 56, 532
  α-operator, 56, 162, 184, 532
  approximate solution, 60
  largest solution, 57, 59
  solved by neural network, 523, 531
Fuzzy relational database, 194, 197, 202
  relational algebra operation, 195
  similarity-relational model, 194
  SQL, 195
Fuzzy restriction, 78, 89, 92, 115
Fuzzy rule (IF-THEN), 145
  connective, 150, 151, 159, 534, 551
  derivation, 160
  distributed fuzzy rule, 605, 674
  fuzzy singleton rule, 551, 552, 559
  lookup table, 163, 165
  MIMO, 149
  MISO, 145, 150, 483
  state/object evaluation, 175
  T-S-K rule/model, 507, 530, 534, 556, 559, 570
Fuzzy rule annihilation, 605
Fuzzy rule combination, 540, 577, 606
Fuzzy rule extraction, 562, 605, 613
  based on information theory, 605
  direct matching, 566
  ellipsoidal covariance learning, 564
  product space clustering, 562
  rule extraction network, 605

Neural-network-driven fuzzy reasoning
  (NDF), 507, 531
  backward elimination, 509, 510
  design procedure, 509
  selecting input/output variables, 509
  with learning (NDFL), 530
NeuroGENESYS, 415, 419
Neuron, artificial/biological, 205
Nonlinear dynamic system, 350
  attractor (point, periodic, strange), 350
  fractal, 250, 350
  phase transitions, 350
Normalized, fuzzy set, 13, 17, 90, 97, 148
Nullcline, 352

**Object-oriented database (OODB), 194,
  197**
  fuzzy, 197
  inheritance, 197
Optimal brain damage (OBD), 257
Optimal interpolative (OI) network, 442
Ordering of fuzzy numbers, 108, 110
  indices of comparison, 108
Orthogonal, 253, 276, 279, 302, 547
Orthogonal condition, fuzzy set, 182
Orthogonal least squares (OLS) learning, 331,
  545, 546
  algorithm, OLS, 548
  error reduction ratio, 548
  orthogonal decomposition, 547
Orthonormal, 272, 273, 298
Outlier, pattern recognition, 202, 693
Overfitting, 249, 254

**Parameter learning, 161, 212, 331, 382, 399,
  471, 534, 535, 551, 569, 587**
Parameter region (PR), fuzzy system, 171,
  490
  edge rule/matrix, 172, 490, 495
  minimum representation, 172, 495
  PR representation, 171
Partially recurrent network, 345, 346, 379
Partition of unity, 485
Pattern recognition, 181, 457, 482, 661
  deformation-invariant, 335
  PSRI, 464

Perceptron, 224, 457
  capacity, 256
  convergence theorem, 230, 615
  multilayer, 235, 427, 429
  Shynk's measure, 258
  simple, 224, 225, 256, 614
Phase space, 352, 380
Plausibility measure, 66–69, 71, 73–75, 80,
  85, 663
  subadditivity axiom, 66
Pocket algorithm, 430, 658
Pole placement approach, 162
Polynomial neural network, 442
Positive-definite matrix, 167, 168, 170, 565
Possibility measure, 75–77, 82, 92, 108, 138,
  145, 183, 200, 663
  conditional possibility distribution, 92, 93
  joint possibility distribution, 91, 93
  marginal possibility distribution, 91
  of fuzzy sets, 82
  possibility distribution, 77, 78, 89, 90, 108,
    121, 124, 139, 156, 194, 202, 498, 499,
    502, 507
  possibility distribution function, 76, 77, 79,
    89, 500
Possibility theory, 22, 78, 89
  possibility/probability consistency
    principle, 90
Principal component analysis (PCA), 302,
  336, 379
  principal component network, 303, 337
  Sanger's learning, 303, 337
Probabilistic neural network, 257
Probabilistic set, 33, 202
Probability density function, 292, 312, 327,
  330, 564
Probability measure, 72, 73, 80, 85, 111
  additivity axiom, 72
  probability distribution, 90, 157, 293, 294,
    400, 597
  probability distribution function, 73, 85
Probability of a fuzzy event, 111
Processing element (PE), 205
Production system, 472
  neural, 472
  working memory, 473

Send me a *free* directory of MATLAB based books.

The directory provides information on books that use MATLAB, MATLAB Toolboxes, and SIMULINK.

I am currently a MATLAB user: ☐ Yes ☐ No

My computer is – check all that apply:
☐ PC or Macintosh   ☐ UNIX Workstation

NAME
_____

E-MAIL
_____

TITLE
_____

COMPANY/UNIVERSITY
_____

DEPT. OR M/S
_____

ADDRESS
_____

CITY/STATE/COUNTRY/ZIP
_____

PHONE
_____

FAX
_____

GRADUATION DATE IF APPLICABLE
R-BK-LEE/364v0/KP77

For the fastest response: Fax to 508-647-7101 • E-mail to info@mathworks.com

The MATH WORKS Inc.

BUSINESS REPLY MAIL

FIRST CLASS MAIL PERMIT NO. 82 NATICK, MA

POSTAGE WILL BE PAID BY ADDRESSEE

The MathWorks, Inc.
24 Prime Park Way
Natick, MA USA 01760-9889